BYRDS

REQUIEM FOR THE TIMELESS

VOLUME 2

By the same author

Timeless Flight: The Definitive Biography Of The Byrds
Neil Young: Here We Are In The Years
Roxy Music: Style With Substance
Van Morrison: A Portrait Of The Artist
The Kinks: The Sound And The Fury
Wham ! (Confidential) The Death Of A Supergroup
Starmakers & Svengalis: The History Of British Pop Management
The Football Managers
The Guinness Encyclopaedia Of Popular Music (co-ed.)
Morrissey & Marr: The Severed Alliance
The Smiths: The Visual Documentary
The Complete Guide To The Music Of The Smiths & Morrissey/Marr
The Complete Guide To The Music Of Neil Young
Crosby, Stills, Nash & Young: The Visual Documentary
The Complete Guide To The Music Of John Lennon
The Byrds: Timeless Flight Revisited – The Sequel
The Complete Guide To The Music Of The Kinks
Neil Young: Zero To Sixty: A Critical Biography
Van Morrison: No Surrender
Morrissey: The Albums
Lennon: The Albums
Byrds: Requiem For The Timeless, Volume 1
Morrissey & Marr: The Severed Alliance: The 20th Anniversary Edition
Ray Davies: A Complicated Life

Anthology Contributions

The Bowie Companion
The Encyclopedia Of Popular Music
The Mojo Collection
Oxford Dictionary Of National Biography
Oxford Originals: An Anthology Of Writing From Lady Margaret Hall, 1879–2001

BYRDS
REQUIEM FOR THE TIMELESS

VOLUME 2

The Lives and Tragic Deaths of Gene Clark, Michael Clarke, Kevin Kelley, Gram Parsons, Clarence White and Skip Battin

Johnny Rogan

R|H

ISBN 9789529540952
Order number: JR 400202

Correspondence: r.h.bksbyrds@hotmail.com

Exclusive distributors:
Music Sales Ltd
Newmarket Road
Bury St Edmunds
Ipswich, IP33 3YB
UK

Alliance Distribution Services
9 Pioneer Avenue
Tuggerah,
NSW 2259
Australia

A catalogue record for this book is available from the British Library.

Photo credits: Page 1: Plates I–III, High school reproductions, from the Collection of Whin Oppice. Plates IV–V, courtesy of Bonnie Laible Clark. Page 2: Plate I, courtesy of Jack Godden. Plate II, courtesy of Bonnie Laible Clark. Page 3: Plates I–III, from the Collection of Whin Oppice. Page 4: courtesy of Garth Beckington. Page 5: Plate I, courtesy of Pete Long. Plate II, courtesy of Harold Sherrick. Page 6: courtesy of Harold Sherrick. Page 7: courtesy of Harry Goodwin. Page 8: Author's Collection. Page 9: Plates I–II, Author's Collection. Page 10: Plate I, courtesy of Charlie Taylor. Plate II, courtesy of Jim Carlton. Plate III, courtesy of Raffaele Galli. Plate IV, courtesy of CBS Records. Page 11: Plate I, Author's Collection. Plate II, courtesy of John Delgatto. Plate III, photo by Eve Babitz, courtesy of John Delgatto. Page 12: photo by Eve Babitz, courtesy of John Delgatto. Page 13: Plate I, courtesy of the White family archives. Plate II, courtesy of John Delgatto. Page 14: Plate I, Author's collection, originally courtesy of John Delgatto. Plate II: Author's collection. Page 15: Plate I, courtesy of Chrissie Oakes. Plates II–III, Author's Collection. Page 16: Plates I–II, Author's Collection. Every effort has been made to contact copyright holders. Any errors or omissions will be amended in subsequent editions. Any lyrics are quoted for review, study or critical purposes.

Typeset by Galleon Typesetting, Ipswich
Printed in China
Published by R/H

NOTES TO THE READER

Within the main text, albums are printed in italics, along with books, poems, radio and television programmes, plays, magazines and newspapers. Songs are in single inverted commas as are single word quotes, newspaper headlines, review titles, aphorisms and short phrases; interview quotes and citations from books are in double inverted commas. Numerical units are written up to ten and numbered thereafter, except in the use of centuries, chart positions, measurements, money, musical time and units of time.

Acronyms have full points omitted, but names of people do not. Group/band names are preceded by a lower case 'the' and only painters are 'artists'. The abbreviation of microphone is still 'mike', as it always was until tape manufacturers started printing 'mic' on their products. Decades are capitalized in order to distinguish them from ages (thus 'the Sixties' versus 'in my sixties'). English usage, not American, applies throughout so it's 'artefact' not 'artifact', 'baulk' not 'balk', 'behaviour' not 'behavior', 'cheque' not 'check', 'colour' not 'color', 'miaow' not 'meow' etc, with the exception of place names such as Pearl *Harbor* and different pronunciation from American interviewees (for example 'airplanes' instead of the English trisyllabic 'aeroplanes' and 'specialty' instead of 'speciality' – although English spelling is used for these words in the narrative). End spellings of verbs are 'ize' in accordance with *The Oxford English Dictionary* rather than computer spell checkers, with the obvious exceptions of words such as advertise, analyse, comprise, improvise, supervise, surprise, televise et al. Although some people erroneously believe that the 'ize' ending is an Americanism, this is not the case. It has been consistently used in English since the sixteenth century.

Song and album titles are displayed as they appear on the record, even if inaccurately spelt or lacking necessary commas/apostrophes. Nouns and noun compounds are usually not hyphenated except when attributive. In modern English there is a tendency to avoid such hyphenation, but exceptions apply. American English has a greater number of previously hyphenated compound words that now form a single word, whereas in British English we tend to split them into two words. Other rulings are mainly in accordance with *The New Oxford Dictionary For Writers And Editors*.

Critical reaction to Rogan's previous books on the Byrds

"This is the closest to heaven it's possible to come." **MOJO**

"This is, at least, the best biography of a group ever written . . ."
Q

"It's impossible not to admire Rogan, a man whose approach to popular music is academically exhaustive, and yet who still manages to write with an ease and generosity that puts younger gunslinger dudes to shame. Note the splendid introductory chapter where Rogan enthuses about the day when he first heard 'Mr Tambourine Man' in a flat near Dolphin Square still powered by gas. This is a book that is worth every penny and about a group that fully merits such a retrospective."
TIME OUT

"As with all the best works in rock biography, this will send you back to the music with fresh ears. In a word: definitive."
UNCUT

"Expansive enough to rival *War And Peace,* Rogan's definitive Byrds biography comes close to matching the emotional, if not geographical, range of Tolstoy's epic novel. One of the achievements is the way in which it matches its narrative flair with the incisiveness of its critical comment . . . But it's the narrative drive that makes the book so extraordinary. With its detailed research and fascinating interview material, it is a compelling portrait of collective turmoil, peopled by characters who win our sympathy at the same time as they earn our disbelief."
RECORD COLLECTOR

"Rogan's book is much more than the standard rock bio. This is music writing as social history, cultural catalogue and critical document: definitive and essential." **HOT PRESS**

"Rogan unsparingly assesses both the Byrds' music and their personal failings . . . His reporting on Crosby's near fatal cocaine addiction is at once poignant and horrifying . . . A scrupulously fair, cleanly written, and thoroughly researched take on one of the most important American groups of the Sixties."

BILLBOARD

"A detailed, gripping account of the birth and death of a dream . . . One of the best rock biographies ever written."

RECORD COLLECTOR

"A writer of real integrity." **SUNDAY TELEGRAPH**

"This is a remarkable book. Fascinating reading . . . Informative, useful and highly recommended."

COUNTRY MUSIC WORLD

"Johnny Rogan's expertise is beyond question." **Q**

"It is highly unlikely that a more committed Byrds fan than Johnny Rogan exists anywhere on this planet. He cares more passionately about the Byrds than most of the musicians who've been in the band . . . Rogan tells his convoluted tale with thoroughness and insight." **CLASSIC ROCK**

"Dense and intriguing. If you ever loved the Byrds you'll find it rewarding and, even if you didn't, it's still a fascinating slice of rock history." **MELODY MAKER**

"Invaluable . . . One of the most detailed studies available of the rise and fall of a popular group." **SOUNDS**

"Rogan is obsessive and detail hungry."

NEW MUSICAL EXPRESS

"The definitive history of one of the most volatile stories in pop history." **MANCHESTER EVENING NEWS**

"Johnny Rogan is pop's most eccentric biographer, a fanatical searcher after truth." **CITY LIFE**

"Johnny Rogan's epic biography sets a new standard . . . Lauded by the British music press, it raises the bar in rock biographies and serves notice that rock 'n' roll can be worthy of the kind of critical analysis jazz has enjoyed."

MONTREAL GAZETTE

"Rogan displays the rare ability to recall and report every minute detail of the band's career without relinquishing anything in the way of readability." **VOX**

"Rogan is a rock biographer's biographer. The guy is literally a method writer." **WHAT'S ON IN LONDON**

CONTENTS

ACKNOWLEDGEMENTS

A book of this scope would not have been possible without the contributions of a vast number of interviewees, whose memories, backed by extensive secondary source material, proved invaluable. In chapter order, I would like to thank the following:

Gene Clark chapter: several interviews with Gene by the author, plus interviews with fellow Byrds, Jim/Roger McGuinn, David Crosby, Michael Clarke and Chris Hillman. Additional author interviews with James Aderholt, Mark Andes, Matt Andes, Carlos Bernal, Garth Beckington, Hillary Beckington (formerly Kontos), Linda Loo Bopp, Sharon Brooks (née Garrett), Candie Callaway, Jack Carchio, Bonita (Bonnie) Laible Clark, David Clark, Kai Clark, Rick Clark, Jon Corneal, Michael Curtis, Saul Davis, Suzanne 'Suzy' Dick, Jim Dickson, Lizzie Donohue, Chris Ethridge, Jon Faurot, Kim Fowley, Carl Franzoni, Barry Friedman, John 'Jack' Godden, Steve Green, Charlie Greene, Bobby Hamilton, Mike Hardwick, Trace Harrill, Al Hersh, Bob Hyde, David Jackson, Peter Jamieson, Andy Kandanes, Thomas Jefferson Kaye, Dennis J. Kelley, Mary Kendall (née Pritchard), Paul Kendall, Michelle Kerr, Lenny Laks, Kenny Lynch, Larry Marks, Dewey Martin, Eamonn McCann, Patti McCormick, Jim McCummings, Michael McGibbon, Camilla McGuinn (née Spaul), Dorothy McGuinn, Barry McGuire, Terry Melcher, Joe Messina, Terri Messina, Ea Oleno, Philip Oleno, Andrew Oldham, Peter Oliva, Carla Olson, Shannon O'Neill, Gene Parsons, Michelle Phillips, Ron Rainey, Pat Robinson, Terry Rogers, Jason Ronard, Jim Seiter, Harold Sherrick, Tom Slocum, Derek Taylor, Greg Thomas, Dolores Tickner (formerly McGuinn), Eddie Tickner, Judith Tinberg (née Hogan), Cyriel Van den Hemel, John York and Dara Zimmerman.

Michael Clarke chapter: several interviews with Michael by the author, plus interviews with fellow Byrds, Jim/Roger McGuinn, Gene Clark, David Crosby and Chris Hillman. Additional interviews conducted by the author with James Aderholt, Mark Adzick, Mark Andes, Matt Andes, Carlos Bernal, Linda Loo Bopp, Jack Carchio, Jon Corneal, Muff Davis, Suzanne 'Suzy' Dick, Jim Dickson, Lizzie Donohoe, Chris Ethridge, Carl Franzoni, Steve Green, Bobby Hamilton, Mike Hardwick, Trace Harrill, Al Hersh, Bob Hyde, Bob Irwin, David Jackson, Dennis J. Kelley, Michelle Kerr, John Manikoff, Gary Marker, Dewey Martin, Patti McCormick, Camilla McGuinn (née Spaul), Terry Melcher, Terri Messina, David Muse, Scott Nienhaus, Andrew Oldham, Peter Oliva, Carla Olson, Shannon O'Neill, Gene Parsons, Michelle Phillips, Bob 'Ras' Rassmussen, Terry Rogers, Jim Seiter, Bill Siddons, Tom Slocum, Kassy Stone, Joey Stec, Derek Taylor, Greg Thomas, Dolores Tickner (formerly McGuinn) and Eddie Tickner.

Kevin Kelley chapter: author interviews with fellow Byrds, Roger McGuinn and Chris Hillman; additional interviews conducted by the author with Mark Andes, Matt Andes, Jesse Barish, Michael Barnes, Carlos Bernal, Jim Carlton, Jon Corneal, Michael Curtis, Jeff Dexter, Vicki Doney (née McClure), Geoff Gillette, Art Johnson, Jesse Lee Kincaid, Gary Marker, Marc McClure, Michael McRae, Terry Melcher, Shannon O'Neill, Gene Parsons, Bill Plummer, Jim Seiter, Charlie Taylor, Dolores Tickner (formerly McGuinn) and William 'Bill' Wolff.

Gram Parsons chapter: author interviews with the original five Byrds Jim/Roger McGuinn, Gene Clark, David Crosby, Michael Clarke and Chris Hillman; plus Skip Battin, Carlos Bernal, Jim Carlton, Jon Corneal, Chris Darrow, Saul Davis, John Delgatto, Jeff Dexter, Suzanne 'Suzy' Dick, Jim Dickson, Ian Dunlop, Chris Ethridge, Anthony 'Tony' Foutz, Gib Guilbeau, Al Hersh, Sam Hutt, Patti Johnson, Joe Kelly, Gene Leedy, Moon Martin, Terry Melcher, Shannon O'Neill, Gene Parsons, Jim Seiter,

Michelle Phillips, Tom Slocum, Joey Stec, Paul Surratt, Barry Tashian, Charlie Taylor, Dolores Tickner (formerly McGuinn) and Eddie Tickner.

Clarence White chapter: author interviews with the original five Byrds, Jim/Roger McGuinn, Gene Clark, David Crosby, Michael Clarke and Chris Hillman; latter day Byrds, John York, Gene Parsons and Skip Battin; family members Roland White, Joanne Bierbrauer (formerly Saxton, née White), Rosemarie Johnson (née White) White and Michelle White. Clarence White, unpublished taped interview courtesy of my colleague, Pete Frame. Plus additional author interviews with Carlos Bernal, June Clark, Chris Darrow, Dale Davis, John Delgatto, Jim Dickson, Chris Ethridge, Gib Guilbeau, Al Hersh, Art Johnson, Terry Melcher, Wayne Moore, Ron Rainey, Al Rosenberg (aka Al Ross), Jim Seiter, Dolores Tickner (formerly McGuinn), Eddie Tickner, Bo Wagner and Bob Warford.

Skip Battin chapter: several interviews with Skip by the author, plus interviews with fellow Byrds Roger McGuinn, David Crosby and Gene Parsons; James Aderholt, Mark Andes, Matt Andes, Patricia Battin (née Cartabiano), Carlos Bernal, Connie Cohen, Michael Curtis, Brian Cutean, Chris Darrow, Jim Dickson, Kim Fowley, Steve Green, Al Hersh, Chris Hillman, Art Johnson, Lanny Mathyssen (aka Mathijssen), Chester 'Chet' McCracken, Terry Melcher, Scott Nienhaus, Van Dyke Parks, Ron Rainey, Terry Rogers, Al Rosenberg (aka Al Ross), Jim Seiter, Peggy Taylor and Steve Young.

Additional source material, including magazines, newspapers, books, radio/television programmes, films and dates of all author's interviews over the decades, can be found in the extensive endnotes and appendices.

Thanking all the people who have contributed to my life, growing older and younger with the Byrds, is a mammoth task, but I'll try and tackle this in chronological order. Apologies in advance for any omissions.

There is a select group from the Seventies who were there when I was first writing about the Byrds. Barry Ballard always deserves special commendation for lasting the course. To this day he responds to discographical questions instantly with patience and grace. Modest, beyond measure, his generosity is inestimable. Chrissie Oakes started the Byrds Appreciation Society as a teenager and went on to produce the much missed *Full Circle*, a written archive far superior to anything online. Pete Frame, founder of *ZigZag* magazine, was another pioneer, whose research and writings were, and remain, inspirational. John Tobler, friendly as ever, was a constant presence in that decade. George Guttler, whom I met on my first Byrds excursion to America in the Seventies, remains a transatlantic pal to this day. Pete Long, a friendship forged through our mutual love of all things CSN&Y, became a world authority on Neil Young. Colin Larkin, whose publishing house, Scorpion, published *Timeless Flight*, was someone who wandered in and out of my life over the decades and, happily, continues to do so. Nick Ralph was the founder of *Dark Star* whom I lost contact with, but haven't forgotten. Two Continental correspondents whom I never met were Jean-Pierre Morisset and Raffaele Galli, the former still writes occasionally.

The Eighties introduced me to Peter Doggett, then editor of *Record Collector*, who later became an established writer. We now share the same publisher: The Bodley Head. Whenever we meet the conversation rapidly turns to the genius of Bob Dylan and David Crosby, respectively. His insightful comments are always welcome. Doug Hinman, a renowned authority on the Kinks, has invariably been available for earnest enquiries over the decades. More recently, Andy Neill has been a valuable sounding board and ally. His research skills are exemplary.

Thanks also to those involved in the book's production, notably Mark Pickard, Ken Shiplee at Galleon, Dave Blake at Hilite and designer Lisa Pettibone.

Many others, spanning decades from the Sixties to the present, have helped in various ways, directly or indirectly. Hello to: Keith Bickerton, David Blackmore, Johanne Bodde, Adrian Booth, John Brindle, Dennis Brown, Chris Charlesworth, Neal Clark, Douglas Coates, Francis Constantine, Geraint Davies, Deanna 'De De' Mollner, John Delgatto, Dennis Dragon, Simon Drew, John Einarson, Scott Erickson, Elio Espana, John Etherington, John Fallon, Ian Foster, Ray Frieders, Bill Gilroy, Bill Gore, John Graves, Sid Griffin, Jun Harada, Steve Harvey, Catherine Henry, Christopher Hjort, Barney Hoskyns, Peter Curt Holmstedt, Tom Isenhour, Ian Jones, Hans Kamermans, Siobhan Kane, Paul Kendall, Harvey Kubernik, Roger Leighton, Huw Lewis, Mark Lewisohn, Mike Masterson, Max Merry, David N. Meyer, Chris Mills, Jon Monnickendam, Akihide Nakamura, John Nork, John O'Brien, Peter O'Brien, Michael Ochs, Whin Oppice, Daragh O'Halloran, Bob Parsons, Stephen Peeples, Tom Pickles, Tony Poole, David Prockter, Viv Pyne, Geoff Reynolds, Jo Saker, Tom Sandford, Jessica Sowin, Raoul Verolleman, Teresa Walsh, John Ward, Iain Whitmore and Dave Zimmer.

From university days with sweet memories: Cathy Shea, Gill Chester, Anne MacInnes, Siobhan Dowd, Pauline Kelly and Lory Laskey. Going back further in time, I always praise schoolfriends, including Alan Culligan, Bobby Kibble, Eddie Lagan, Alan Roberts, Alan Russell, Keith Rodger, plus Anne Cesek, Deborah Novotny, George Kenyon, Wally Hammond – and the rest.

On a personal level, family members, now all long, long dead. R.I.P. My nephews (David and Michael Quinlan) and surviving cousins – good health to you all. Finally, Jackie Cuddihy for all her love, support and patience over many years, particularly during long absences.

Ending on a grim note, it is salutary to consider how many of my interviewees have since died. It is a strange experience hearing their disembodied voices taped at pubs, various meeting places or over the phone. The roll call is extensive. Listing the speakers in this book whom we will never hear again is a chilling undertaking. In addition to the six Byrds obituaries, a farewell to: James Aderholt, Patricia Battin (née Cartabiano), Garth Beckington,

Carlie Clark, Dale Davis, Suzanne 'Suzy' Dick, Jim Dickson, Chris Ethridge, Kim Fowley, Barry Friedman, John 'Jack' Godden, Charlie Greene, Gib Guilbeau, Bob Hyde, Andy Kandanes, Thomas Jefferson Kaye, Gary Marker, Larry Marks, Dewey Martin, Dorothy McGuinn, Terry Melcher, Terri Messina, Ea Oleno, Pat Robinson, Kassy Stone, Derek Taylor, Eddie Tickner and Steve Young. Sadly, there may be several names that should be on this list whom I suspect might now be long gone. Not everyone gets an obituary in a newspaper and many die unheralded.

The Byrds have been part of my life since adolescence. Symbolically, they represent something beyond my imagination. I've been writing about them for decades, always listening to their work, which never seems to date in my mind. The writing process has been an odyssey which will probably only end with mental incapacitation or a coffin lid. That word 'Timeless' comes to mind again.

Johnny Rogan
December 2016

INTRODUCTION

Requiem For The Timeless Volume 2 covers the careers of those former Byrds who are now dead. This second volume is the equivalent of several books in one. Any of these chapters could have been extended into a full-scale biography. If you consider, for example, the amount of pages featured in *Volume 1* on Gene Clark, Michael Clarke and Gram Parsons, then add those to the chapters herein, the result would be a tome of several hundred pages on each member.

From the outset I faced a structural problem with *Requiem* that was solved by splitting the work into two complementary volumes. *Volume 1* documented the exploits of the original Byrds, and the interaction of the five founding members over successive decades. This was intended to create a detailed history but also a kaleidoscope. In order to maintain the narrative flow, the solo exploits of the deceased members were held over for appraisal in these extensive obituaries.

There was no model for a work quite like this and determining the structure required considerable thought over many years. What I required was a book that was both two volumes and a single work, at one and the same time. In the end, I was inspired by memories of reading Shakespeare's *Henry IV, Parts 1 & 2*. Originally, I had read *Part 2* first and later realized that the play required no real knowledge of its predecessor in order to succeed in its own right. Indeed, it could be read as two five-act plays or even one 10-act play, with each part working completely independently of the other, while also producing a complementary whole. It was a structural trick that I have attempted to repeat in miniature for *Requiem For The Timeless*. Both volumes complement each other, yet this second volume can still be read without reference to its predecessor, or vice versa. Moreover, it is quite possible to read the volumes in reverse order and still obtain the same amount of satisfaction and understanding. Originally the chapter sequence was different. I started off writing the obituaries in order of death: Clarence White, Gram Parsons, Gene Clark, Michael Clarke, Kevin Kelley and Skip Battin. This clearly did not work as chronological cross-referencing was constantly required. The chapters became more coherent once I placed them in the timeline of each member's induction to the group.

Writing *Volume 1*, which focused on the Byrds' group activities, meant that I could develop the characters of the individual members only so far without seriously derailing the narrative. For example, the life and work of Gene Clark after the Byrds was largely restricted to those times when his career intersected with McGuinn, Crosby, Clarke and Hillman. The arc of the story could not embrace his solo work, which was clearly another book in itself. The same applied to Michael Clarke's exploits in the Flying Burrito Brothers and Firefall, Gram Parsons' days in the International Submarine Band and later with Emmylou Harris, Clarence White's bluegrass history, Skip Battin's extracurricular activities and Kevin Kelley's entire life.

Volume 2 covers all of the above while studiously avoiding the stories already detailed in the previous volume. Reading these chapters prior to submission reminds me of the importance of appreciating each and every Byrd. They were all flawed but fascinating characters whose greatness was inextricably linked to their foibles. When it came to the original five, I never wanted to choose between them or become involved in the various factional wars. That remains true to this day. Below are some observations about the six chapters.

Gene Clark. When I wrote *Timeless Flight Revisited* back in the Nineties, I included a modest, closing appraisal explaining that his story was already threatening to spill over into a separate biography. This started to take shape as early as 1997 and continues here in 2017. In the interim, two important projects emerged – John Einarson's detailed and engrossing biography, *Mr Tambourine Man* and Paul Kendall's documentary film, *The*

Byrd Who Flew Alone. There were also two symposiums curated by archivist/collector, Whin Oppice. Clark was always underestimated and and deserved such attention. I continued to research, long before and well after those commendable projects, ever eager to crystallize Clark's contribution to those epochal times. In certain respects, he resembled a lost soul whose career was constantly punctuated by setbacks. There was that wonderful run in the Byrds, from 'Mr Tambourine Man' to 'Eight Miles High', and then he was gone. From a distance of 50 years, it's difficult to express the profound sense of loss that accompanied the announcement of his departure from the Byrds. Groups of such stature weren't supposed to fracture so easily. It was akin to Lennon or McCartney leaving the Beatles. The shock was considerable, but if you're as familiar with death as I was then, you learn acceptance and carry on. Clark continued to thrive artistically, but never secured the commercial success enjoyed by the Byrds at their peak. During the singer-songwriter boom, I thought he might emerge as a Neil Young or James Taylor, but he remained the maverick outsider, doomed to cult status. And what greater cult artefact could there be than *No Other*? An album for the ages. I interviewed Clark on several occasions over the decades and at my curious best even placed advertisements in magazines asking for information. Few responded. There was always an element of mystery about the man. In person, Clark seemed vulnerable and all those wasted chances made you feel protective towards him. But I felt an obligation to remain an impartial observer. The Gene Clark chapter is a book within a book and there are hundreds more pages on his Byrds' work in *Volume 1*. I trust it does some justice to the man and his music.

Michael Clarke. Precious little has been written about Clarke, even though he was an original Byrd. Of course, he never sang with the group and was only involved in composing three of their songs. Even so, it is odd how he has escaped scrutiny in magazine articles about the Byrds, the Flying Burrito Brothers, Dillard & Clark or Firefall. In 1997, I unearthed his family background for the first time and I've been caught up in the story ever since. He was adept at avoiding interviews, but this was not due to shyness. Michael never took himself seriously enough to consider the importance of leaving an audio or visual documentary of his life and times. I joined him on the road with the sole purpose of extracting taped information, with some success. Not that it was ever easy. He was often subject to baser needs – alcohol and sex – but beneath that macho exterior was a sensitive soul. He was a talented painter and could have been a far greater drummer if he had taken the role more seriously. His entire life was a page turner, laced with humour, pathos and a beguiling innocence that he never quite lost. Looking back it's amazing how many Byrds-related bands he performed in. He was constantly underestimated, despite having played wonderfully on important songs such as 'The Bells Of Rhymney', 'Turn! Turn! Turn!' and 'Eight Miles High', to name but three. Apart from fleeting moments of anger, he rose above the serious politics that tore the original Byrds apart. Funny and self-deprecating, he retained the swagger of a superstar and the lust of a ladies' man. His was a buccaneering life but what astonished me was the lingering affection with which he was remembered by so many of his associates. Remarkable as it may sound, I believe that Michael Clarke was the most loved of all the Byrds, and not just by their female following. His contemporaries spoke with a mixture of wit and irreverence about this larger-than-life character, who embodied the free spirit of the times. Many felt he was severely underrated as a drummer and deserving of far more attention than he ever received. Even his manager, Jim Dickson, who attempted to treat each Byrd with equanimity, eventually admitted that Michael was his favourite. Like the other Byrds covered in this volume, his life ended badly and sadly but, even at the last, there was a vibrancy and defiant esprit that remained.

Kevin Kelley. The most mysterious Byrd of all. He always had a special place in my heart as he was the first non-original and a blood relation of one of the members. Symbolically, that seemed important. His stay was short, but significant. I had a lot of trouble finding him during the Seventies and after that he fell into even greater obscurity, if that was possible. Later, reading through reams of Byrds profiles, I noticed that his name was barely mentioned. Whenever I questioned McGuinn or Hillman about his role in the group, the response was the equivalent of a shrug of the shoulders, followed by a long silence. There was nothing controversial about his involvement. It was almost as if he had been erased from history. Specialist drum magazines never profiled his time in the group. Even rock journals that venerate the Sixties consistently ignored him. In the age of the internet, he remains an invisible presence, known only for having played on *Sweetheart Of The Rodeo*. Anything else was largely borrowed from some brief comments in *Volume 1* of this book or *Timeless Flight Revisited*. I spent most of 2007 conducting interviews about Kelley and writing the chapter herein. It was immensely challenging and each new nugget of information proved a revelation. Musically, Kelley worked with some great, unheralded players. He was also an accomplished songwriter. His biography had bleak moments. Reclusive and independent, he never attempted to cash in by joining any tribute outfits during the Eighties. Here was a man who spurned second chances, detached himself from Byrds' history and became lost in the end. I wanted to bring him back, partly out of curiosity, but mainly to show my appreciation. I hope this chapter enhances his reputation. At least it ensures that his career is no longer a mere question mark.

Gram Parsons. This chapter offered the opposite challenge to that of Kelley's. Here was a Byrd whose life and times have at last been well served in print. When I first wrote about the Byrds, there were no books on Parsons and precious few articles. It's strange to recall a time when many journalists could not even spell his name correctly. Back in 1968, I saw him with the Byrds at the Royal Albert Hall and the experience had a profound and lasting effect. Hearing 'Hickory Wind' before *Sweetheart Of The Rodeo* was enough to signal the arrival of an immense talent. At the time of his death, Parsons was still a fairly obscure figure, known primarily for his brief involvement with the Byrds, his pioneering work with the Flying Burrito Brothers and a promising debut album. That all changed over the decades as he became a cult figure who inspired books, films and magazine articles, many of which focused on his excesses at the expense of his art. There have been two major biographies, Ben Fong-Torres' *Hickory Wind* and David N. Meyer's *Twenty Thousand Roads.* The latter was particularly strong on his troubled family history. I have concentrated on providing as much fresh information as possible, with new interviews, backed by exclusive access to his recording contracts, notebooks and legal documents. But I end with a consideration of the Parsons mythology and why his life and death have prompted so much interest decades after his demise.

Clarence White. A musical purist and a phenomenal guitar player. He died before Gram Parsons but created no cult whatsoever. There is not a single book to his name, merely a limited number of effusive retrospectives in specialist guitar magazines and a small but dedicated presence online. Cataloguing his musical adventures during the pre-Byrds bluegrass days was a formidable task requiring many interviews and extensive endnotes. It is very much a musician's tale, but that is only part of the story. Commentators always tended to treat White with solemnity, as if imitating his in-concert, poker-faced persona. Backstage, he was happy to demonstrate guitar techniques to inquisitive fans and discuss his musical influences. Watching him socialize away from the spotlight, another character emerged – a shy, glint-eyed humorist with a mischievous streak. The Byrds liberated him in many respects, allowing access to a world stage and a lifestyle far removed from the discipline of bluegrass. Those contradictions were played out in his personal life, which nobody has ever documented – till now. Overriding everything is a tragedy that occurred just as he was blossoming into a new career that promised so much.

Skip Battin. The oldest Byrd and the only one who enjoyed chart success and a modicum of fame before joining the group. His is a panoramic tale, stretching back to the rock 'n' roll Fifties and forward to the revivalist tribute bands of the Eighties and beyond. Arguably the most approachable of the Byrds he was, at various times, an idealist and a pragmatist. Viewing his life and career with a wide lens provides a greater understanding of his motivations and achievements. His songs divided fans. 'America's Great National Pastime' sounded little more than a novelty. On the other hand, serious compositions such as 'Well Come Back Home' and 'Absolute Happiness' were a joy. He freely admitted that some of his work with Kim Fowley may not have fitted the context of the Byrds. Others would have been defensive about their contributions, but he accepted criticism with grace – no easy task for any Byrd. After a surprisingly good solo debut album, he became a journeyman once again, flitting between various offshoot bands, a working musician all his life. He served in groups under both McGuinn and Michael Clarke in different decades, which must have tested his resolve. There was always a Dorian Gray aspect to Battin. At one point, he experimented with youth serums, hoping to create his own timeless flight. He cheated time, but he could not cheat death.

Overall, these chapters, along with the contents of *Volume 1*, demonstrate that this is not simply the story of a group, but something closer to the creation of an entire subgenre of LA music. That, ultimately, is the Byrds' supreme achievement.

The chapters end with a lengthy series of Notes followed by a detailed Discography. Many anecdotes, arguments, debates and explanations are too convoluted for inclusion in the main text. This is their home. Source dates of interviews reveal much about a speaker's shifting perspective in different time periods. Discographies document the scope of an artiste's work, while also revealing what was written, held back or never heard by the public. At one point, I spent an entire year working on these.

This inevitably prompted the quite justifiable self-retort: you could have begun or even completed another book instead of tracking down serial numbers, release dates, copyright registrations, unreleased tapes and the other arcane information that makes up the appendices. Even then, it wasn't over. Everything is amplified in a book of this scope. Re-reading the text for the umpteenth time, grappling with the proofs and collating an index turns weeks into months. It is also a final reminder that the 'Requiem' theme applies equally to the author. Although I am a decade younger than the surviving Byrds, I do not expect to live long enough to complete valedictions on McGuinn, Crosby, Hillman, Parsons and York. Thankfully, I have already written vast amounts about the first three in *Volume 1*. This then, may be my final epistle, but who can say? What lies ahead is death – and thanks.

1

GENE CLARK

17 November 1944–24 May 1991

IT was part of Gene Clark's complex character that, despite the greatness of his talent, he was always one of rock music's most frustrating underachievers. For every celebrated moment of his musical life there were comparable memories of opportunities lost and projects abandoned or unrealized. At the heart of his story lies a powerful ambivalence towards the rock star life. He was capable of consuming the trappings of fame with the appetite of an excessive whilst simultaneously writing some of the most spiritually uplifting songs imaginable. He almost single-handedly kick-started the proliferation of singer-songwriter LA rock – setting an example by leaving an internationally famous group in order to pursue solo work. What seemed a daringly ambitious and innovative idea was equally symptomatic of a mercurial and fragile personality. That summed up Gene Clark's career – giant steps forward, all too often accompanied by anti-climactic retreats into culthood. He never received the commercial success that was undoubtedly his due in the late Sixties and early Seventies. This brought an enigmatic edge to his tale, as well as ensuring the undying love of his more ardent supporters.

Compared with McGuinn, Crosby or even Hillman, Clark conducted relatively few major interviews and was severely underrepresented in print. At times he could prove evasive or easily distracted. He enjoyed speaking anecdotally, but sometimes got lost in his own tale. Like many singer-songwriters, he was seldom comfortable discussing his work in depth. This was hardly surprising given the abstract nature of many of his lyrics. He was also sensitive about dissecting the characters of his fellow Byrds, always erring on the side of caution and ever wary of causing offence. My formal interviews with him over the decades were always cordial, funny, and occasionally revealing, but you always felt he was holding back. He seemed a lot freer during phone conversations or away from the tape recorder.

When relaxed, Clark was a fine raconteur, but not always a reliable narrator. Sometimes he would dispense with strict fact when telling a good story and not everyone was aware when he was simply joking. There was an elliptical quality to some of his musings and he was guarded or vague about aspects of his personal life and family history. When filling out his lifelines for the media, Clark listed his birthdate as 1941 and next to the column for 'brothers and sisters' wrote 'none'. He never explained why. Even his associates in the Byrds knew relatively little about his background, though the same could be said of each of them. In the mid-Sixties every member of the group lived in the moment. Michael Clarke's history was similarly vague at the time, simply because nobody was that interested in delving into the past. When journalists questioned Bob Dylan about his early life in Hibbing, he fabricated an adventurer's autobiography, even killing off his parents in one story. Fantasy was always a convenient refuge for an imaginative troubadour.

Jim Dickson, who shared his house with Clark for a time and worked with him over the decades, was acutely aware of his contradictions. His early life emerged in episodic asides which were not always consistent. "My first impression was that he was a farm boy who worked as a lumberjack and he was certainly strong enough for that to be believable. I didn't know how much of that was true. It turned out that his father wasn't a farmer but a designer of golf courses. I only found that out in Gene's last year. He also said his father was part-Indian. The Indians, like the Celts, have that B-deficiency. It's genetic. Many have that problem with alcohol."

Clark's asides contained a lot of truth, but often you had to read between the lines. His flippant claim in 1965 that he was an only child disguised a complicated family history. He was actually one of 13 surviving children. His mother Mary Jeanne Faherty, a descendant of Irish and German immigrants, was born on 21 June 1920, and raised in Tipton, Missouri. While working as a domestic at Milburn Golf and Country Club in Overland Park, she met and married Kelly George Clark, born 11 November 1918. Jeanne was still 23 days shy of her 21st birthday, but wasted no time in starting a large family. First-born Bonita [Bonnie] was followed by a stillborn child, Kelly Katherine, after which the father was drafted into the US Army. Jeanne conceived again during one of his spells on leave while she was staying at her grandmother Rosemary's house in Tipton. They christened their first boy Harold Eugene Clark in honour of his uncle of the same name who had been killed in action in August 1944. "He never even made it to the ground," says Bonnie of the fighter pilot.

Kelly George Clark's brief military stay provides some telling parallels with the self-defeating, topsy-turvy career path of his eldest son. The father was a robust, dynamic figure who rose to the rank of sergeant, only to be demoted to private. His downfall was precipitated by an inebriated incident and an indignant assault upon a superior officer. "That's not just a tale," Gene's sister Bonnie contends. "I have pictures of him with sergeant's stripes on his sleeve. I was told he and some guys got into a wine cellar in France. A commissioned officer then got into his face about it. When he was drunk, my dad was a little bulldog. He snapped back and was busted." Alcohol never suited Clark Snr and while under the influence his personality could change from friendly to hostile, with potentially violent consequences. In later life, Gene shared that same Jekyll and Hyde curse, which he felt was a legacy of some Native American blood on his father's side. When he was growing up, the 'Red Indian' connection was taboo, but Gene later embraced his obscure Native American roots as a badge of honour. Then again, he also claimed American outlaw connections with Jesse James. "Years later, when Gene and I were living in Northern California, we did some reading about the James Gang," his brother Rick Clark recalls. "Supposedly, we're distant relatives of Frank and Jesse James. We're kind of related to some of the families that lived around Joplin, Missouri in the 1800s. Our family's related to those people somehow." The vague qualifying words suggest that this may well have been wishful thinking on Gene's part. Having already located Native American roots, he could now turn his family history into a western odyssey. It was as if he aspired to be both a cowboy and an Indian, a victor, an outsider and a heroic rebel, all at once. During the Seventies, he even adopted a John Wayne swagger and infiltrated the actor's outer social circle, thereby adding to the western mythology.

By 1949, Gene's family had moved to Swope Park, where Kelly worked at the municipal golf course. The large urban park area included a small house in which the Clarks lived, initially without running water. This was Gene Clark's aforementioned 'farm boy' upbringing, an environment in which he experienced a rural education in South Kansas City. "Gene did live on a 'farm'," his brother Rick says, in an ambiguous reference to their rustic upbringing amid the metropolis. "We had about 20 acres when Gene was younger. We all had to go out and work before we went to school."

The Swope Park period lasted 11 years, covering Gene's childhood and early adolescence. It was a time of austerity and the simple virtues of hard work. Kelly's employment as a golf course groundskeeper was not enough to provide home comforts and the family had to be self-sufficient. They raised chickens, milked cows, churned butter, picked berries, canned vegetables, and learned many practical skills, including carpentry. Once the chores were completed the children were free to roam through the expansive woods and orchard surrounding the property. They swam, climbed cliffs, explored caves, played with canoes in Blue River, flew kites, built makeshift forts and scaled the back fence into Swope Park Zoo to see the animals. Scouting was a popular pursuit, which Gene took seriously. When his troop failed to complete an obstacle course, his competitive instincts were sufficiently inflamed to insist that everyone undertake extra exercise on a training area of his own choosing. He was very determined, even at a young age.

Not all the family's pastimes were innocent. In later years, friends marvelled and shuddered when Clark indulged in knife-throwing competitions with his musician friend, Jesse Ed Davis. They appeared to be acting like Indian braves, straight out of some Fifties western. But those games could also be traced back to Gene's childhood when the more adventurous members of his family would collect empty boxes of washing powder which were placed on trees and used for target practice. The Tide brand's bright white logo provided the perfect bull's-eye at which to aim.

Occasionally, the children's uproarious play would be interrupted by the sound of the Kansas City Southern, the train line that Clark would later immortalize in song. Memories of Swope Park also featured in his ecological ballad, 'Something's Wrong', which portrayed a pastoral idyll of joyous fields, later blighted by 'neon brambles', a bitter allusion to the demolition of his home for the modern wonder of the Interstate 435. David Clark maintains that his brother's storybook childhood had a profound effect on his songwriting and world view. More than anything, it inspired his imagination. In everyday play, he found a kind of deliverance.

Gene's fantasy schemes multiplied to include any number of adventures. With David's help, he constructed a giant catapult which fired debris to spectacular heights. He resembled a medieval monarch defending a besieged castle while also re-enacting some wartime skirmish. Gene frequently climbed a dizzyingly high elm tree, establishing a crow's nest from which he could observe the world like some sea captain on a voyage of discovery. At Halloween, he transformed his home cellar into a ghostly house of horror and took great pleasure in terrorizing one of his visiting cousins. There were also more formal activities, including an impromptu home production of Shakespeare's *Romeo And Juliet* involving all of his siblings. Inevitably, it rapidly descended into an extended sword fight, more in keeping with an Errol Flynn movie. On another occasion, he and Bonnie improvised a western, inspired by *The Lone Ranger* series. The countless cowboy and Indian black-and-white movies screened during the early Fifties provided instant stereotypes, but Native Americans were never caricatured as savage pariahs in Clark's little playlets. In a rare act of tolerance, their mother allowed the children to dress up, wear feathers plucked from a chicken, and apply lipstick 'warpaint' to their faces to add authenticity to their mock drama.

Time passed slowly in Swope Park. When he wasn't playing with his younger brothers, Gene would sometimes wander through the woods alone, away from the household bustle. There was a warm security amid the serenity, an enveloping feeling of calm in which silence itself took on a strange and powerful significance. The rural tranquillity allowed Clark to lose himself in the labyrinthine corridors of his imagination where, for brief moments, everything felt in harmony. These heightened experiences were like evanescent moments of transcendence, which he later attempted to recapture, most thrillingly in the nature imagery employed on songs such as 'For A Spanish Guitar' and 'Lady Of The North'.

Clark's schooling was traditionally Catholic. After arriving in Swope Park, he was enrolled at the recently opened Our Lady Of Lourdes on East Gregory Boulevard in Raytown, Jackson County. By the time Gene was eight years old, the building had expanded to accommodate a school and convent for the Sisters of St Joseph of Carondelet. At the entrance to the Perpetual Adoration Chapel, there were icons of Christ and Mary with exposed hearts and symbols of the chalice and the holy host. The spiritual and academic ethos of the institution appealed to the local Catholic community and enrolment trebled during Clark's childhood, soon reaching the 800 mark. Sister Agatha Irene Walsh, the principal, was a dedicated, imposing figure and an omniscient presence. Like many convent schools, Our Lady Of Lourdes provided that beguiling combination of serene patience and rigid discipline. Gene was the antithesis of the star pupil, more prone to trouble than many of his peers, but he was always encouraged to retain a firm focus. Despite a poor academic record, he was reasonably literate, with decent numerical skills and beautiful handwriting – all of which were a testament to the nuns' no-nonsense brand of teaching. "Sister Agatha Irene was responsible for that," Bonnie Clark points out. "She had outstanding handwriting herself."

The matriarch Jeanne Clark was a lifelong devout Catholic and later a member of the Altar Society. While all the family attended mass every Sunday, as required by the Catholic Church, she also took the time to attend on several weekdays, generating grace with the same dynamism with which she produced children. All the Clark clan aged over seven took Holy Communion on most Sundays, having fasted since before midnight on the Saturday evening. On the altar they could see the Tabernacle, a majestic gold box that resembled an ornate safe, attached to which was a golden key. Therein lay the Sacred Host, the literal body of Christ made whole by the miracle of transubstantiation and consumed by the supplicants in the act of communion. Nightly decades of the rosary were also recited at home, the more so when one of the family, Ada Rebecca, was afflicted with a non-malignant tumour in her skull which affected her mental development. She was later subject to sporadic fits and convulsions. The prayers of intercession did not produce a miracle cure, but she survived.

Gene's own Catholic upbringing had a significant and beneficial effect on his life and work. While preparing for Holy Communion and Confirmation, he was grounded in the Catechism and presented with complex theological concepts such as the nature of the Holy Trinity and the mysteries of faith. Catholic teaching did not shy away from the big questions, but embraced them. 'What is God?' 'What is man?' 'What are angels?' 'What is faith?' 'What is hope?' 'What is despair?' 'What is eternity?' These heady concepts were punctuated by many teasing theological conundrums: 'Has God a beginning?' 'Why did God create Hell?' 'Can anyone get out of Hell?' 'What is sanctifying grace?'

"My Catholic upbringing was important in many ways," Clark told me. "It must have influenced my songwriting too. There are questions and mysteries in there. You know those words and phrases." Indeed, Clark's best work is full of abstruse allusions, typical of a Catholic imagination. His songs include references to eternity, angels and souls, while many of his love ballads dramatize a moral complexity, with protestations of guilt, remorse and the need for forgiveness. Even an innocuously titled song such as 'So You Say You Lost Your Baby' contains some fantastical imagery and casually conceived cosmological concepts, not least the Catholic allusion to 'Tabernacle hillsides'. Many other songs, from 'Echoes' through to 'White Light', 'Strength Of Strings', 'Feelin' Higher' and 'Communications' address arcane or esoteric subject matter. The tone and diction are sometimes deceptively simple, with jaw-dropping abstractions nestling alongside everyday speech, as if unnoticed by the composer. Extracting explanation, let alone meaning, from Clark was always an impossible undertaking, as might have been expected. But the symbolism and complex imagery resonate with each fresh listening and much of it can clearly be traced back to his childhood education when the Catechism addressed profound questions of theology with the simple conviction and authority of an instruction manual.

The Catholic Church also provided an outlet for his singing. He joined the Diocese of Kansas City–St Joseph Choir and his rich, deep voice won some unexpected plaudits from the local Irish bishop. His mother must have been thrilled by the commendation as church and children brought the greatest purpose to her life. "His mother was very Christian," recalls Jack Godden, a former classmate at Our Lady Of Lourdes. "She was so devoted it was unreal. And so was Gene. I went to mass with him a bunch of times. Gene was a devout Christian then, and his family made sure of that. Maybe later he might have skipped a mass. I'd done the same, but you didn't let your parents know! The whole family loved Gene more than the world . . . and they treated me like one of their own. But, I tell you, they struggled. They had to have shifts in eating almost, as the mother had to feed up to 13 kids."

Jeanne Clark was a formidable homemaker. On Sunday mornings, before mass, she could be found outside beheading and gutting chickens and later preparing a meal suitable for an infantry. Her eldest child Bonnie assumed the role of surrogate mother for the younger siblings. "By the time we moved to Swope Park I was already a built-in babysitter. Mom loved being in the garden and I didn't so I ended up as child-carer and housekeeper. It was easier for me to do the chores than herd a bunch of younger kids into doing them. I had way too much responsibility and power for a child that age."

Raising such a large family placed demands on Jeanne who was a worrier. A child of the Depression, she had lived through the Hungry Thirties and witnessed the foreclosure of the farm where her father worked. Being forced to move home as a child made her cautious, even anxious, about her own offspring. "It was tough on her," says Bonnie. "I think she just lived for her faith and that's what kept her going." As much as anyone can remember, she seldom, if ever, ventured outside Missouri until as late as the mid-Seventies, when she visited Gene in the wake of his divorce. Living in Swope Park with a daily rota of chores left little time for socializing. "Mom did not have a lot of friends," Bonnie remarks. Maintaining discipline in her husband's absence was crucially important and Jeanne took that role very seriously. "Mother was very temperamental. Mom was the one you didn't want to cross. We all learned that early in life because she was the one who would go after us. We'd be threatened with Dad, but she was the one who inflicted corporal punishment. It was like 'Wait until your father gets home!' and then she didn't want to wait. I learned to keep a very stoic face. That's probably why I don't have wrinkles today."

The patriarch, Kelly Clark, also had his different sides. "He was a very quiet, self-effacing and tolerant man," says Bonnie. "But he had a weakness for the firewater . . . Dad was personable. He'd go into a bar and everybody wanted to buy Kelly a drink.

Then, of course, he'd have to reciprocate and buy a round for the house. That would get him into trouble with Mom because it was money that could have been spent on the family." There are several apocryphal tales of Kelly getting into a rumpus at bars, supposedly being suppressed by three policemen and vanquishing other troublemakers with his Herculean strength. Such stories mirror and pre-empt comparable exploits by Gene during his Hollywood years. The 'firewater' was the common factor.

As the eldest male child, Gene had a special place in his mother's affections, as his eldest sister well knew. "He was the favourite, and that's the truth. There was also that gender gap. The boys always got more privileges and freedom than the girls did." There was rivalry between Gene and Bonnie from an early age. "He wanted the leader role but, of course, there was me to get past. Gene used to make fun of my name, Bonita. He'd call me 'Bone Eater'. That was his sense of humour. The first conflict Gene and I had was over who was going to be Peter Pan."

This occurred back in 1953 when Gene was just nine years old. A kindly neighbour, who was widowed, liked to offer little treats to the children. "She took us under her wing and used to take us to the Starlight Theatre to see movies." One such highlight was a festive screening of the Technicolor Disney animation, *Peter Pan*. After they got home from the matinee, they ran outdoors, eager to re-enact the film in the woods. Soon there was a heated exchange. "Gene thought I should be Wendy and I thought I should be Peter Pan. I wanted the lead role." The two-year age difference usually ensured Bonnie had the edge. "I pulled some tricks on him. I remember him being pretty gullible. There were two sides to him. He was a rambunctious boy. Some things were frightening to him and he took them to heart. He had Dad's talent and more of a sociable attitude than Mom."

Outwardly, Gene Clark was strong, healthy and confident, the quintessential All American Boy, straight out of the pages of a Mark Twain adventure. He was a fearless fighter with a hunter's lack of squeamishness. When the family prepared meals, he was the one who replaced Jeanne as the beheader of chickens, unbothered by blood and guts. But, inwardly, he was nervous and highly strung, characteristics that would later leave him prone to inner demons and various neuroses. Two incidents in particular stand out from his early years.

On 25 May 1957, the Ruskin Heights Tornado struck Missouri, causing untold devastation. The stark statistics read 39 dead and 531 injured, but thousands more were traumatized. A trail of destruction over 71 miles long cut through Williamsburg, Kansas, moving inexorably through Martin City, Missouri, then onwards into Ruskin Heights and Raytown. Along the way, trees were uprooted, power lines felled and cars strewn like toys. It was as if nature itself had turned physics on its head. One car hit the top of a water tower and you could hear the sound of freight trains passing in the sky. An entire shopping centre in Ruskin Heights was levelled, along with the local high school and junior high. By the time it was all over the landscape resembled a war zone. The National Guard were brought in and martial law was declared. Families forlornly searched for children grabbed by the tornado, like Dorothy in a darker version of *The Wizard Of Oz*.

The Clark family were caught up in the drama. Jeanne had taken a couple of the children to Our Lady Of Lourdes, while David stayed at home with several of his younger siblings. Bonnie Clark, who was 15 at the time, was attending an outing organized by a local prayer group. "I had acquired a boyfriend who was Protestant, which wasn't making Mom too happy anyway. They wanted me to go on this picnic so they all showed up to see Mom. She couldn't look like the bad old witch so she let me go out that day. My boyfriend's car was an old bullet-nosed Ford, without air conditioning or ventilation. It was raining so hard that we had to have all the windows rolled up and it was packed with teenagers." Bonnie then witnessed a frightening sight. "The thunderstorm actually darkened the sky. It was pitch black. You could see a funnel cloud on the ground from where we were in Raytown. I said, 'Oh my God . . .' We bailed out of that car and into the first house that had a garage door open. We ran into the basement of some people that we didn't even know. I remember looking out the back door and watching the power lines pop and all the debris. I tried calling home but the lines were jammed. We had to take everybody else home before me – and, oh, did I get chewed. 'Why didn't you let us know where you were?' I said, 'Mom, I tried to call, I couldn't get through.'"

Gene, meanwhile, was missing. He had left that morning on a trip with his scout troop and was last seen in the Loma Vista neighbourhood of Kansas City. They had sought sanctuary from the torrential rain in a church, but falling masonry had blocked the front door, trapping them inside. As darkness descended, Gene became more agitated, overwhelmed with claustrophobic thoughts. By the time, the authorities evacuated everybody he was in a desperate state. Medics supplied him with a sedative until his father arrived to take him home. In his absence, Jeanne Clark had conducted a prayer vigil at their house, handing out rosary beads to his siblings, who were told to implore God for his safe return.

That night, Gene suffered hallucinations as he tried to sleep, re-enacting the events of the day and uttering semi-coherent sentences. His bunk bed was saturated with the perspiration of terror. Jeanne offered maternal solace, bathing his forehead with cold water and providing a change of clothes. Eventually, he fell into a deep sleep.

The terrible spectacle haunted Gene's dreams for some time. "He would wake up screaming after that," his mother recalls. Night terrors were to remain a constant throughout much of his life. While living with Jim Dickson during the early days of the Byrds, he would awake in a sweat and tell of bizarre nightmares in which he was rolled up in a carpet filled with prickling tacks and broken glass. He also acquired a lasting fear of tightly enclosed spaces. "He became extremely claustrophobic," David Clark says. "The first time I realized this was after the tornado in 1957. Before then, he'd always hung out in the cellar with the doors closed. After that he would hardly go down there for a long, long time. Then he got stuck in a scout trailer. The door closed, and I was off doing something else. When I found him, he was in total panic." Years later, Gene suffered a far more severe panic attack when he was trapped in a lift during a troubled return to the Byrds in late 1967.

The horrific tornado even blighted one of Gene's fondest childhood memories. Hereafter, the Kansas City Southern blew its distinctive horn, not merely as a welcoming sound, but to warn people that the distant rumbling it was creating was a train approaching, not a menacing tornado.

Another epochal incident occurred when Clark witnessed a plane crash in his home state, which may have been the source of his much documented fear of flying. During his time in the Byrds, he confided in McGuinn that he had been 'freaked out' by the spectacle. He seldom mentioned the tragedy or provided any accompanying details beyond saying that he was 14 years old at the time. Later, he alluded to the incident in brief conversations with his mother and his sister Bonnie. She believes it occurred at a downtown airport in Kansas City which onlookers could observe from nearby Cliff Drive, across the river. "Cliff Drive used to be a bad boy hangout, so he wasn't supposed to be there. He said that it was a plane that crashed and people were on fire, running away from it. I don't think that's something he made up."

Nevertheless, aviation records provide no information about any commercial airline crashing, let alone one involving burning passengers fleeing from the scene. Extrapolation aside, the most likely explanation, judging from press coverage, is an accident that took place in December 1958 involving a private plane. A pilot, Halton Friend, and his wife Jeannette, were flying home to Illinois, having stayed in Grand Junction, Colorado. The plane stopped off at Kansas City Municipal Airport for refuelling but, two miles north of the airport, the engine caught fire. The pilot attempted to carry out an emergency landing, but the plane was engulfed by flames. The couple were instantly killed and the wreckage scorched and damaged a house, having fallen within five feet of a property where two children were sleeping.

* * *

As he entered his teens, Clark's more macho side came to the fore, as did his sensitivity. The Clarks suffered food shortages during the worst of times. An unexpectedly brutal winter could leave their livestock poorly or under attack from coyotes or other predators. It was a constant struggle. New clothes were at a premium and the whole family had to be content with hand-me-downs. At school, several of the children were teased. The church congregation occasionally came to the rescue with second-hand items but Gene found this humiliating. When taunted, he would lose his temper and respond with his fists. Even elder kids soon thought twice about confronting him, especially after noticing his physique.

Regular workouts at home had expanded his body mass and, despite some knee problems, he excelled at sports and initially gymnastics. "He was an excellent sports person," says school-friend Jack Godden. "If he ever lost a bet, he was good about it. He wasn't a bad loser, and he was a very good winner. Gene was class action then. He worked hard with his dad and was muscle bound."

Clark's school work seemed to decline in direct proportion to his muscular growth. During his final year at Our Lady Of Lourdes, he was attracting the attention of tougher kids in gangs and was no stranger to physical aggression if seriously provoked. Jack Godden was sometimes called upon to act as his right-hand man. "We held it together in the school grounds and stuff. We watched each other's back. There were usually a few punks hanging around who liked to pick fights. I helped Gene out, and he helped me. We had local gangs then. We took on a bunch of other neighbourhood kids and had many gun fights out in the cemetery. Everybody was required to wear goggles if we were going to do that. It was a pretty mean territory that we lived in."

The nuns at Our Lady Of Lourdes took a dim view of the choir boy turned troublemaker. Corporal punishment was used for malefactors and Clark and Godden were not exempt. "They were very strict," Godden recalls. "I had welts on my hands from rulers. A stack of books almost knocked me out. I didn't do nothing. It was the person behind, but they blamed me."

Despite his tough exterior, Clark still sang in the choir and music seemed to take on greater significance in his life with each passing year. "My dad was a major influence on him," says his brother Rick Clark. "He was a good guitar picker, right up until the time he had arthritis." Among Kelly's parlour pieces were the traditional murder ballad 'Frankie And Johnny' and the Wagner marching tune 'Under The Double Eagle', later made famous by bandleader John Philip Sousa and incorporated into the repertoires of bluegrass banjoists and guitarists.

According to family legend, Gene's father was a competent, untrained musician, who could put his hand to several instruments. Before his marriage, he had played in a duo with his best friend, George Myers, occasionally appearing at local dances. David Clark believes the pair were head-hunted by the Chicago jazz drummer Gene Krupa, although whether Kelly would have been accomplished enough to play in a dance band is debatable. "David brought that up, but I have no recollection of it," Bonnie says. "I think it was George who was responsible for Dad getting to meet Mom. They were hunting buddies. We'd go over to their house and Mom and his wife Evelyn and the kids would all go out to play together. Dad and George would take a flask and go off hunting in the woods. Dad was talented. If it hadn't been for the herd that he produced he might have had a [musical] career. But he had to make a living." While Kelly's main instrument was an acoustic guitar, he could also play banjo, mandolin and mouth organ. Oddly, David has no memory of his father attempting to sing. "All of us tried to coax him into it. I never heard him try to sing at all. He refused to. Why, I don't know."

At first, Gene experimented with the mandolin, but eventually switched to guitar, occasionally accompanying his father. "He always played guitar on the front porch," Jack Godden recalls. "They were playing Woody Guthrie-type songs. Gene got real good, and his voice sounded fantastic."

Playing alongside his father was educational, but Gene's true passion was reserved for rock 'n' roll. The emergence of Elvis

Presley as a cultural icon inspired legions of teenagers, including several future members of the Byrds. The sound of rock 'n' roll was as alluring as a siren's wail and its leading characters embodied a new attitude of youthful exuberance, wilful non-conformity and confidence unbound. The self-appointed moral guardians in the media condemned this immoral pageant of deviance, decrying the vulgar gyrations of Elvis, the unspeakable antics of the epicene Little Richard and the bigamy of Jerry Lee Lewis whose cousin bride would later be exposed as a scandalous 13 years old. Clark ignored the hysteria and found salvation in the music. He loved memorable melodies and clever lyrics, identifying strongly with the Everly Brothers and Buddy Holly. The teenage drama 'Wake Up Little Susie', notable for its realistic and suggestive narrative, proved a particular favourite which he played frequently.

Between 1957–58, Clark was enrolled at Raytown High School, along with a sizeable number of adolescents from Our Lady Of Lourdes. By now, his Elvis fixation was deep. His slicked-back raven hair, a natural colour unlike Presley's black dye, made him stand out. Swanning around Swope Park, he looked like a cross between James Dean and Marlon Brando, complete with the obligatory mood swings. Clark never had to fabricate teenage angst for effect; it was already part of his personality. Briefly, he fell in with some roughnecks, seemingly a step away from being a JD, but that was most likely a pose. Never a slacker, Clark worked hard at home and continued to assist his father with manual work during the school recess.

In Raytown, Clark joined his first band after hanging out with a new friend, Joe Meyers. Gene was impressed. "He was an accomplished and quite educated player, the son of a jazz musician. I believe his father played in some famous big bands alongside the greats of that era." Meyers was the first serious musician Clark had ever encountered and he wasted no time in enlisting his assistance. "We both knew Joe and thought he was great," says Godden. "I used to think he was one of the best lead guitarists in the country! We'd go over to his house every day. He and Gene played music together till three in the morning every single night until they were good enough to gig." Godden was so impressed that he presented Clark with his first electric guitar, which he bought at a garage sale from money earned working part-time at a delicatessen. "It was only about 20 bucks, but that was quite a bit then. Luckily, I was making some money and Gene really appreciated it. It had a little amp, but it sounded good. Gene gave his dad back his other guitar."

At first, Clark and Meyers considered working as a duo and even experimented with some rudimentary songwriting. Clark later claimed he had been making up snatches of songs since he was four years old and Godden remembers him singing the lyrics to Elvis hits, then adding some of his own words to the melodies. The Clark/Meyers songwriting collaboration resulted in at least one finished song, 'Blue Ribbons', a Presley-style ballad which was captured on tape at Godden's home.

It was not long before the duo decided to form a band. Joe's brother, Mike, played bass and, after an extensive search, they settled on a high school drummer, Eddie Hitchcock. In deference to their most experienced member, they named the band Joe Meyers & The Sharks. According to Godden, who was employed as road manager and soundman, Gene switched to upright bass for a spell, in addition to singing lead. "He had a voice out of heaven, and everybody loved him." A repertoire was soon compiled consisting of the standard radio hits of the era.

The Sharks owed their start to the power of the Catholic Church. The CYO (Catholic Young Organization) arranged hops and church hall dates so welcomed the teenage musicians. Their chief supporter was Father John Giacopelli, a priest respected by old and young alike. In his pastoral capacity, he encouraged sport and music and helped Clark's friends with bookings and transport. He was even credited with inspiring divine intervention on one fateful evening. "The whole band almost got killed by Father John," Godden remembers. "We were all in the car and he was showing off. We got on to 87th Street, which is straight downhill, with hair-bend curves, and it seemed like he was going at 80 miles an hour. He lost control and the car flipped over several times. People were saying, 'Everybody's dead in that car' but nobody was killed or hurt, except for Joe, who got a scratch on the leg. It was amazing. The car looked like a smashed sardine can. Everyone said it was a miracle because a priest was driving. God was on our side."

Bonnie Clark was the only member of the Clark siblings old enough to attend his CYO gigs. "Joe Meyers was a good old boy," she says. "He had a big crush on me and was always trying to figure out a way to get a little closer." A talented dancer, Bonnie usually took the floor, but was also called upon to assist from the side of the stage. When a young girl requested 'Blue Moon', Gene gallantly dedicated the song to her. "They knew the tune, but not the lyrics," says Bonnie. "I was feeding him the words so that he could sing it to her while she was swooning."

After playing the CYO circuit, the Sharks graduated to loftier venues, relatively speaking. "They got a big engagement at the Coke Bar in Grandview where all the kids used to go," Jack Godden recalls. "It was so packed that they had to turn people away. They played there for many months. After that it was the Barn up in Lakeside and bigger places that held up to 500. The kids followed Gene, Joe and the band wherever they played."

Godden may be exaggerating the numbers, but the Sharks attracted an enviable following, largely consisting of wide-eyed Catholic girls. The one who made the strongest impression was Jody Hogsett, a pupil at the private, all girls' St Teresa's Academy, the oldest school in Kansas City, founded in 1866 by the Sisters of St Joseph of Carondelet. Jody came from an affluent family. Both her father and grandfather were attorneys, in stark contrast to the backgrounds of Clark and his circle. Although one year younger than Gene, she seemed far more sophisticated and worldly than any of them. With a keen interest in performance art she was already heading towards the University of Missouri where she would complete a degree in Theatre and Speech. Both Godden and Clark found her immensely attractive but she became Joe Meyers' girlfriend.

"It was like another lifetime," Godden rhapsodizes. "I remained friends with Gene for a long time, all my teenage years. He was like a brother to me and I loved him as a brother. I wish I could have those years back because I never had such a great time in my life as I did with Gene and Joe and the band. There were all those girls. I used to sign so many autographs it was unreal, and I didn't even play in the band! My main objective was making sure we got good acoustics in the building. They gave me money and I got free food and free beer."

Drinking was a constant temptation on the road and they could always find somebody of legal age to acquire the necessary beers. "We drank a lot and partied hard," says Godden. "It was a downfall we had. Our parents didn't know what was going on, but it was only beer." Clark was level-headed after a couple of beers but if he drank to excess he became tetchy and prone to recklessness and aggression. It was another early warning of his susceptibility to the family curse.

Girlfriends also caused problems. Clark was happy to play the field but became possessive when threatened. "He had all the girls he wanted because he was the singer in the band," says Godden. "We both did. But then he got mad at me. I thought our friendship was over because I took one of his girlfriends away. I said, 'It's not my fault, she came on to me. I'm sorry, Gene, but that's the way it is.' But he didn't like that." Such disgruntlement was disingenuous, as Clark was quite capable of bird dogging girls in similar circumstances. For a time he became romantically linked with Jody Hogsett and his band loyalties were questioned. "Joe Meyers was dating her, and her dad was the head prosecuting attorney of Kansas."

Away from the band, Godden took on the onerous task of teaching Clark to drive. Gene practised in Jack's open-hooded Studebaker, but his nervy disposition made him an unsuitable driver. "He backed into a tree, broke my tail light and wrecked my car. I didn't have a windshield and you could get busted for that, so we took the car all around the cemetery where it was all fields. We liked racing around those curves." Fast cars would continue to fascinate Clark, along with a penchant for dangerous driving.

The Sharks' strangest story centred on the mystery of their obscure single, 'Blue Ribbons'. In several interviews, including one with myself, Clark exploded with animation as he related the tale of his first shot at fame. "I recorded my first single when I was 14 years old. 'Blue Ribbons', with Joe Meyers & The Sharks. It was only for a local label but somehow somebody, I don't know how, got it to Dick Clark's *American Bandstand.* It was played on that show for a period of time as an unreleased record. I don't know whether they had a tape or an acetate, but there was a disc jockey from Kansas City who filled in for Dick Clark at one point, and he played the record on the programme." In another interview, Clark even referenced the single's B-side, a rock 'n' roll instrumental, supposedly titled 'Artesian'.

A copy of the single has never appeared on any collector's listing and neither Godden nor any member of the Clark family owns a copy, beyond the aforementioned home tape. So was this one of Clark's playful fabrications? Evidently not. He did have access to the recording process via Godden's father Bill, a radio engineer who boasted some involvement on discs by Pat Boone, Bobby Darin and Wayne Newton. Godden Snr owned Artist Recording Studio which Gene visited on several occasions. Jack Godden does not recall the Sharks completing a session there, but believes some recording was attempted. "I think my dad might have had something to do with that. He had a label too. My dad recorded songs that Gene wrote. I have all my father's tapes, but I couldn't find Gene's, so I don't know what happened to them." The most likely explanation is that the mythical single was either an acetate like the Beatles' early Quarrymen recording or a very small vinyl run comparable to Neil Young's rare Squires' single. Indeed, surviving copies of discs from Godden Snr's maroon-coloured label 'Artists' (with the place of manufacture printed as 'Kansas City Missouri') reveal that he sometimes premiered two artistes on a single disc. One pressing features Jimmy Markey and Ginny Lee, respectively –

performers as unknown to the general public as Joe Meyers & The Sharks.

After playing the local circuit for a year or more, the Sharks eventually split up, as teenage bands are prone to do, for no apparent reason. Personality conflicts, an ever present danger in such situations, may have been a factor. "We all separated and went our own way," Godden says. "Suddenly, there was no more band. Joe was one of the best friends you could have, but he and I got into a lot of squabbles. He was domineering. When Joe gets mad, he gets mad – and he could get mad over nothing, which I couldn't understand."

At the end of 1958, Kelly Clark announced that there was an opportunity to relocate to Pasadena, California. He had been short-listed for a job as superintendent at their Country Club and was considering his options. Bonnie and Gene were both excited by the prospect, even if it was a long shot. Jeanne Clark was mortified. The notion of moving from Missouri to California was almost beyond her imagination and she felt indignant that Kelly had even considered the idea without consulting her. The dream was soon forgotten, except by Gene who brooded over the lost chance. "He felt betrayed," his brother David suggests. "This was something that shaped Gene to a degree. He felt that something was taken from him that he had already been dreaming about. The trip to California." Whether Kelly would have secured the job was a moot point.

Through much of 1959, Gene was a more distant presence from his family. His time with the Sharks was also ending and a feeling of doom was in the air. Rock 'n' roll, regarded by most adults and the mainstream media as nothing more than a passing fad, suddenly appeared in terminal decline. Jerry Lee was in disgrace, Elvis was in the Army and Little Richard was an ordained minister. All this was punctuated by tragedy. On 3 February, Buddy Holly was killed in a plane crash, along with the Big Bopper (J.P. Richardson) and the teenage Latino rocker, Ritchie Valens. Clark was disheartened by the shock news, almost as if it was a personal affront. He had admired Holly's songwriting, performed Valens' 'Donna' at shows, and watched Joe Meyers imitating the Big Bopper's distinctive baritone. Now it was over. Perhaps his elders were correct. Was rock 'n' roll merely a teenage fad? In resigned moments, Clark could be heard suggesting that calypso was the new thing. For a time his countenance evinced an air of bereaved detachment, devoid of animation. His brother David was struck by this disconnection. "Gene really took it personally. It was very dramatic for him. He never talked about it and went off by himself. I went to all his favourite hiding places but I couldn't find him. He disappeared and when he reappeared it was as if it was all over and he was ready to move on." A sense of ennui lingered. "He lost interest in almost everything . . . His school work suffered to the point that his teachers contacted Mom about his behaviour. He was not aggressive or disruptive, just the opposite. He had quit going to scout meetings . . . When he played the guitar, it was like part of him had died along with those guys."

The Fifties ended on a grim note as the Clark household came to terms with changing times. Both Bonnie and Gene were considering leaving home, while their father was in search of a new job. Jeanne, stoical as ever, simply wished for constancy, but could not prevent the inevitable rifts. Her husband was determined to advance his prospects, the more so when he encountered the famous golfer Harold Lee 'Jug' McSpaden, who had racked up 17 PGA tour wins before his retirement in 1947. McSpaden was currently the owner of the Victory Hills Country Club in Wyandotte County, whose golf course had opened in 1929. He offered Kelly the post of superintendent which would mean moving from Swope Park some time in the New Year. The suggestion was irresistible, not least because of McSpaden's grand ideas. He was already planning the construction of Dub's Dread Golf Club in Kansas City, which would boast the world's longest golf course.

During the summer of 1960, the Clark family finally relocated to a more spacious house at 410 West 2nd Street in Bonner

Springs, Kansas. Kelly's job at Victory Hills Country Club brought more money into the home, but funds were still tight as they now had a monthly mortgage for the first time. The children adapted to their new surroundings relatively quickly, but occasionally missed the wild outdoors of Swope Park. Additionally, one of the brood had flown. Bonnie decided to join the Women's Army Corps and was on a train to Alabama when the family were settling in their new home. "I learned not to get into any disputes between Mom and Dad and by then there were disputes occurring." Her father saw her off with a five-word homily: "Don't forget to be yourself."

Always moving forward, Gene faced the challenge of finding a fresh group of friends while attending the local Bonner Springs High School. Seemingly, his only musical contact from the Swope Park days was the ever loyal Jack Godden, who regularly drove over. "When he moved to Bonner Springs, he really got into writing songs. Every time I went to see him, he was in his bedroom, songwriting and playing the guitar. Always. I thought it was too much, but he loved what he was doing." Godden managed to tease Clark out of his lair and take in the local sights. They still went to drive-in movies on double dates, but distance eventually took its toll on the friendship.

It took a while for Clark to establish himself with a new social circle, and he no longer put himself forward for team sports or showed much interest in studying. His saving grace was his entertainment value as a vocalist and guitar player. "He was pretty well-liked with most of the classmates," recalls fellow student Roxe Zimmerman. "He would sing and play his guitar occasionally at lunch break." There was a fair amount of revelry among Clark's friends including keg parties on the Kansas River. As always, excess alcohol brought on those disconcerting mood swings which exposed his meaner side. One evening at a Bonner Springs cafe, Clark began goading a couple of his classmates into a fight over some trivial incident. Looking on, Roxe Zimmerman became increasingly irritated by Clark's boorishness. "I went up and said, 'You want someone to fight? Fight me.' I wasn't really mad, but I was serious." Gene refused to back down and a scuffle ensued. "After that we got along fine," says Zimmerman. "I always thought he was outgoing and friendly most of the time other than that one incident."

Bonnie also witnessed a similar skirmish on one of her rare visits home on leave from the Army. Gene was angry with a football coach at school and became involved in a minor act of vandalism. There was an incident at a diner during which she felt obliged to intervene and lecture him about his excessive drinking and aggressive behaviour. She ended up escorting Gene from the premises in disgrace. This small humiliation made him furious. "It was like the snap of a finger and he was a different person. And the demon rum always brought out the demons. He didn't take well to any kind of criticism and by that time he was pretty much in rebellion against the system." Back at home, there was another drunken incident which upset his parents.

With time on their hands, Clark and his circle spent many evenings cruising around in cars all over Bonner Springs and Tonganoxie. He had recently bought a 1953 Mercury Coupe to celebrate his 16th birthday. In one of his later songs, 'Mary Sue', he looked back nostalgically to that period of innocent teenage romance. At times, it seemed like he was a character in a teen melodrama. Films and songs of the period featured misunderstood adolescents, whose exaggerated emotions were played out in small-town scenarios. Car crashes often provided the necessary catharsis, highlighting the tragedy of young death and a coming of age for the survivors. Clark was no stranger to automobile accidents, as he had demonstrated back in Raytown. Only good fortune prevented serious injury, or worse. On the final day of his school year at Bonner Springs High, he and some friends took off for a ride in a Ford Falcon. As the vehicle sped down Loring Road, it flipped over. "We took the turn way too fast," says John Papineau, one of the passengers. Everybody was shaken up, particularly Clark, who suddenly realized that his guitar-playing days could have been ended in an instant. "Through the whole thing he was worrying about his hands," Papineau concludes.

Unfortunately, this latest near escape did little to curb his recklessness. His personal speedometer remained dangerously high for the remainder of his life.

Musically, Clark's time in Bonner Springs coincided with the late blooming of the folk boom, which had been spearheaded a few years before by the massive success of the Kingston Trio's 'Tom Dooley'. Others followed, including the Brothers Four, the New Lost City Ramblers, the Limeliters, the Kingston Trio, and countless more. Gene was already singing at state music competitions and making an impression, notably with a moving rendition of the folk traditional, 'Black Is The Colour'. Judith Hogan, a schoolfriend, one year younger, also attended. "I'll never forget the afternoon that he sang a solo for the girls' glee club. He was tremendous. How I wish I had recorded him. Gene was a genuine, sincere guy. His dream was to become a recording star. He didn't have many friends at school because he was so driven towards the future." While confiding his plans, Clark did mention that he had made "a recording in some local studio and was pleased with it". This may have been a reference to the previously mentioned 'Blue Ribbons', but no other details were provided.

Hogan's family lived a few blocks away from Clark's and Gene would sometimes walk Judith home. "He'd do most of the talking as I was quiet and shy." At one point, he told her that she was his only friend. "Perhaps that was true for those few months or I was just gullible. He was kind, gentle, quiet and a loner. I don't think his classmates understood him, including me. I remember feeling a little sorry for him, and I'm not sure why." Their friendship remained casual, mainly because she was already "going steady" with her boyfriend. "One afternoon, I remember Gene and I sitting in the front yard and he found a four-leaf clover and he gave it to me and kissed me rather awkwardly. I had the feeling he'd not done too much of that."

By the summer of 1962, when Clark left school, the Urban Folk Revival had metamorphosed into a highly commercial business, underlined by the phenomenal album sales of Peter, Paul & Mary, who would enjoy singles success, most notably with a near chart-topping cover of Bob Dylan's 'Blowin' In The Wind' the following year.

Clark had come relatively late to the folk boom, but a chance encounter with some college students provided an instant conversion. Soon, he was performing regularly in the Kansas area with the Rum Runners offering the familiar folk covers of the day. It was a loose arrangement, which supplemented the income he was receiving working at the golf course with his father. One evening, which Clark vaguely estimated as "late 1962/early 1963", he encountered a rival folk group who were pulling in a larger crowd. They had a residency at Kansas City's Castaways Lounge at 4334 Main Street, a venue decorated to resemble an Hawaiian beach, complete with mock palm trees. The bar offered 'Authentic South Sea Island Enchantment' best discovered in its plentiful supply of exotic cocktails: notably the 'Scorpion', 'Miserable Bastard', 'Pagan's Delight' and 'Vicious Virgin'. Somewhat tongue in cheek, the group had named themselves the Surf Riders and dressed accordingly to fit in with the décor. "I don't think any of them had ever seen an ocean," says Gene's brother Rick. "They played 'Tom Dooley' and Peter Yarrow stuff and may even have done some Dylan songs."

Equally importantly, they had also cut an extended single, 'Hey Li Lee', for the Kansas label Mira Records. Written by their bass-fiddle and bongo player, Vic Ehly, it had been described as "a foot stomper that lends itself easily to original verses". Also on the record was a cover of 'House Of The Rising Sun'; 'Lonely Man', written by their guitarist, Mike Crumm; and the spirited 'Away With Rum', penned by lead singer, C.E. Lear. Another single, on Brass Records, featured Harry Belafonte's 'Island In The Sun' backed with the Lear, Crumm, Ehly B-side, 'Fennerio'. These were no small achievements for a local group.

Alas, the original line-up fragmented once its two founders graduated, leaving Mike Crumm (rechristened Mike Crowley) to rejuvenate the group with guitarist Jim Glover. When a vacancy arose for a third member, Clark pushed himself forward. The senior Surf Riders were amused to learn that he was working at a golf course and on his debut night at the Castaways announced: "Straight from the bulldozer in Bonner Springs, we bring you Gene Clark." The audience response was impressive. "He had a magnificent voice," Jim Glover remembers. "That voice just came from within."

Clark still worked with his father occasionally, assisting at the Victory Hills Country Club. There were tensions in the family, exacerbated by Gene's commitments with the Surf Riders. They had a date at one of the Hungry i restaurants which meant a trip to faraway Oklahoma. Kelly was annoyed with Gene for missing work and critical of his attitude. By now the youngster was more independent than ever. While appearing at the Castaways, he became romantically involved with Gay Lindsey, a sophisticated, slighter older woman, whose worldliness proved intoxicating. "Gay came from a well-to-do background," says David Clark, who sounded even more entranced with her than his brother had been. "She was well-educated, well-spoken and very modern in her dress and manner, tall and slender with a prominent physique. Her deep brown eyes mesmerised me. She was gorgeous." Unusually, Gene felt confident enough to invite her to meet his parents. Evidently, his mother did not approve of the match, fearful that she was too influential on her impressionable son. Gay was supportive of Gene's musical ambitions, even contributing towards the cost of a Gibson Hummingbird guitar. David noticed sudden changes in his attitude and look while in her presence. "Gay was all about him. She had parties and could introduce him to people. He came out of a high school jean and T-shirt style to an Ivy League, clean-cut, preppy look. It was a different presentation."

Kelly Clark was drinking more than usual in reaction to stresses at home. Jeanne was heavily pregnant with her final child, Sarah, and heading towards her 42nd birthday. That, no doubt, brought more worries. The simmering conflict between Gene and Kelly boiled over that Easter, ending in a violent confrontation. In his rage, Gene punched his father into concussion. "I witnessed it and it was a terrible thing to see," says David Clark. "They never had a close relationship, and they wanted it so badly. Many times they blew those opportunities. Both of them were stubborn men." The assault later prompted words of remorse from both parties, but it was also a turning point. Immediately after, Gene left home, moving to an apartment in Roeland Park, Johnson County, Kansas. He was now fully committed to the group and socialized with them almost exclusively. It was a time of frequent parties and musical get-togethers.

David Clark missed his brother so he was thrilled to be invited to one of the parties early that summer. Still a few months away from his 15th birthday, he was relieved when his parents allowed him to attend. It turned out to be an eventful evening. Neighbours called the police who arrived to break up the festivities and check that nobody was under age. David ended up hiding inside a window box and somehow escaped scrutiny. The visit became a treasured memory for David, representing one of the last times he would see Gene in Kansas.

Clark's stay in the Surf Riders lasted a few months more. In addition to their residency at the Castaways, they played regional dates, and taped several songs "in a garage in Kansas City". According to Gene, "There was this guy who had a studio and he recorded an album with us, which was actually a good folk record, but it was never released." The new emphasis on albums, as opposed to singles, was characteristic of the folk boom and although the Surf Riders were accomplished and extremely popular in Kansas, there was little opportunity to break out of their comfort zone.

That all changed in August 1963 when the New Christy Minstrels secured a short residency at the Starlight Theatre for a stage production of *The Unsinkable Molly Brown*. Originally formed in 1961, the ensemble was the brainchild of Randy Sparks, who had previously given his name to a Trio, including his wife Jackie Miller and vocalist Nick Woods. Sparks was a decent singer and songwriter, but even these talents were surpassed by his entrepreneurial instincts. Never afraid of overreaching, he recruited two other ensembles and musicians to form a 14-piece aggregation, who sang, played and danced like a grand performing troupe. The membership had decreased to nine by 1963, but the brand name was worth millions. They had just recorded their fourth album, *Ramblin'*, released in April, which contained a breakout hit, 'Green, Green', co-written by Sparks and the gravel-voiced Barry McGuire. By chance, there was a vacancy in the New Christy Minstrels prompted by the recent departure of the talented Dolan Ellis. His short-lived replacement, Doug Brookins, was ousted during the Minstrels' residency at the Starlight. Original member Nick Woods, also appearing in Kansas City that same week, happened to visit the Castaways, saw part of the Surf Riders' set, was impressed by their professionalism and reckoned Clark might prove a suitable candidate. He dutifully informed Randy Sparks and his management partner George Greif, who were amenable to the idea and offered the teenager a shot at instant stardom. "That was my Hollywood moment," Clark recalled. "Randy Sparks turned to George and said, 'Hire him!' What could I say? It was the chance of a lifetime, like a fairy-tale."

Ever the pragmatist, Sparks even commandeered the remaining Surf Riders, Jimmy Glover and Michael Crowley (aka Crumm), who were offered places in the Back Porch Majority, which served as a 'nursery group' for the Christies. "We stayed up all night and by breakfast the next morning we all had money to go to Los Angeles," Crowley recalls. The news came as a surprise to Clark's friends, even those who had long recognized his talent. Jack Godden was flabbergasted. "I knew Gene had a great voice, but never in my life did I imagine that would happen. I said, 'Son of a gun, Gene. This is your big chance, don't blow it!'" Joe Meyers' girlfriend Jody Hogsett remembers Gene rushing over to her family's home on Sunset Drive, giddy with excitement. She advised him to take off with the Minstrels, which came as no big surprise, but when her mother concurred, he was thrilled. David Clark believes that Gene's girlfriend, Gay Lindsey, also encouraged him to seize the opportunity, even though it spelt the end of their relationship.

Clark's family were amazed and slightly disconcerted by the speed of events. He barely had time to attend a family get-together before boarding a plane to LA. "We knew he was going to go," says his mother Jeanne. "He had already moved out of the house a couple of months before. We knew that if we put our foot down and said, 'No', that he would do it anyhow."

David Clark remembers a less resigned response at the time. "Mom was beside herself. She basically broke down and shook like a leaf. She was so afraid of all kinds of things, and some of her worst fears did eventually come true. Mom wanted Dad to go after Gene and bring him back home. He said, 'No, it's his life . . . That's his choice.' As his mother concludes with a fatalism blessed by time and distance: "So he joined the world."

The world Clark joined was head-spinningly hectic. Within days he was in CBS' Hollywood Studio contributing to a newly recorded German version of 'Green Green' ('Grun Grun'), an abridged rendition of 'The Drinkin' Gourd' and a new song, 'Natural Man'. Immediately afterwards the group flew to Hawaii and Clark phoned his parents with the enthusiasm of someone who had just landed in paradise. Within the space of a few months he travelled across America, appeared on two albums (*Today* and *Land Of Giants*), a US Top 10 single 'Saturday Night', the soundtrack to the film *Advance To The Rear* and several television shows, including the popular *Bell Telephone Hour* and *Hootenanny*. Clark struck a strange figure to some of his fellow Minstrels. "He had a different kind of countenance," says Barry McGuire. "He was very edgy and smoky and swirly. I don't know the right word. His countenance was different than most people's. I don't know if he had Indian blood in him, but there was a stoicism about him different to everybody else. He wasn't soft. He wasn't bouncy and fun and 'ho ho ho'. He wasn't that way, just very stoic and stark, but warm and inviting as a conversationalist with a couple of people."

The Christies' relentless touring schedule continued through the autumn, and they arrived in Canada on 19 October 1963. It was during a stopover in Winnipeg that Clark first heard the Beatles on the radio, an experience that prompted confusion as much as appreciation. "The sound was so different that I didn't know what to think at first. It was at once alien and familiar, a contradiction in a sense." At this stage, most Americans were oblivious to the existence of the Fab Four, but back in England their potency was tangible. Their fourth hit, 'She Loves You', was breaking sales records and, six days before Clark's Canadian visit, British newspapers were trumpeting the arrival of a new phenomenon, 'Beatlemania'.

The Christies, by contrast, were greeted with condescension by snobbish reviewers ("a rather insipid casserole of popular, folk, humorous and instrumental music") while Randy Sparks laughed all the way to the bank. Clark was still oblivious to such concerns, happy to bask in the youthful glory of national fame while gaining experience and a regular wage. He experienced the thrill of playing New York's prestigious Carnegie Hall followed by an invitation to perform at the White House in front of John F. Kennedy. While flying to a gig in Greensboro, North Carolina, the group were shocked to learn of the president's assassination in Dallas. Gene, who had always voiced support for the Catholic president, was noticeably shaken. "Everybody was very upset. I was really looking forward to playing for JFK, man. What a thrill. When it didn't happen everyone was disappointed." The week after the tragedy, the group were stationed in Uniontown, Pennsylvania for a week's residency, but nobody was in the mood for a happy singalong.

Even the death of a president did not derail the ensemble's relentless performing and recording schedule. There was a brief stopover in Kansas, during which Clark reunited with his family, but it was not an entirely happy encounter, particularly for his brother David. "He was a different person altogether, especially to me. It was like a total stranger walked into the house." David was struck by his fashionable clothes and unexpected condescension. "He was very haughty to everybody." When David got dressed to go out with him for the evening, Gene threw him a $20 bill, accompanied by the words: "Go uptown and buy yourself some clothes and then we'll go." David felt humiliated. "I said, 'What are you coming off like this for? We grew up together. We did everything. We slept in the same bed, ate off the same plate, drank from the same glass, froze in the same room . . . and you're doing this?' Then he composed himself and apologized. Things were a little better after that but it wasn't the same." This exchange was a reminder of the chasm between life in LA and Kansas. Gene was flush with success but happy to spend a night out with his brother. He had not meant to offend or act insensitively, but that was the perception. Bridging the gap between their respective lives was no longer as straightforward as it had been when he was merely a Surf Rider.

Soon, Clark was back on the road. He was looking forward to a much needed seasonal break in December but such plans were thwarted by an enforced three-week booking in Reno, Nevada, commencing on Christmas Eve. It seemed to affect Clark's emotional barometer. Travelling played on his nerves, building up tension, which was not easily relieved. "We did 300 shows a year," Barry McGuire estimates. "We flew every day, but Gene didn't like to fly. It was air flight that did it for Gene in the Christies."

Clark kept such fears to himself, but still felt under pressure. The Minstrels were a highly competitive unit, even among themselves. "Randy Sparks thought of us as a baseball team," McGuire says. "Everybody in the Christies had huge voices. Dolan Ellis, Nick Woods, myself . . . The girls were very strong too. Gene was pretty good, but he wasn't ever going to get a standing ovation after a song or curl the wallpaper at the back of the theatre when he sang."

The ever vigilant Sparks had been monitoring Clark's progress with a critical eye. Although the new boy seemed promising, he displayed little of the showbiz panache or stage presence of Dolan Ellis, the man he had replaced. "Dolan was like the mechanical man," Sparks says. "He went out every night in the third slot and was such a performer, with so much energy and with such thick skin that it didn't matter what the audience gave back. Gene Clark was not that kind of personality. He was a very good singer who played the guitar adequately, but there was no flash. You must understand, I was in a cage full of tigers when I ran the group. I had purposely formed a group of nine egos, in addition to mine . . . I came from old-fashioned showbusiness where you walked out and killed them."

There was a respite from such pressures with the exciting news that the aforementioned White House appearance was back on, courtesy of the new president, Lyndon Baines Johnson and his wife, Lady Bird. A formal dinner, with guests including baseball legend Joe Di Maggio, political commentator Walter Lippmann and composer Gian Menotti, was to be followed by a selection of operatic arias by Robert Merrill and a short set by the Minstrels.

On 14 January 1964, Clark and friends boarded a plane for their appointment with history. "It was quite a moment," says Barry McGuire. "We were playing Reno and flew from there to Washington and landed in a blizzard. Dallas was closed. The only plane that landed in Dallas that day was the one with us on it. We were supposed to have played for Kennedy but instead we were the first group in the White House after Johnson became president. It was an honour and an exciting experience. I had a presidential pass signed by President Johnson – a lifetime pass. Of course, I lost it within a month. I'd love to have it now on my office wall."

The evening's formalities required the musicians to be on their best behaviour, but McGuire and Nick Woods could not resist some juvenile antics. While being escorted through the corridors of the White House, they passed a large stairwell with a shiny brass banister in its mid-section. Giddy with bravado, they slid down, side saddle, and ended up in a heap at the bottom of the stairs, while a stone-faced guard looked on disapprovingly. Clark also had a tale to tell. Years later, he regaled those in his circle with an amusing account of how he smoked marijuana in a toilet at the White House. It sounded suspiciously reminiscent of the urban myth circulating about the Beatles smoking a joint in similar circumstances when they received their MBEs from the Queen at Buckingham Palace in 1965.

Barry McGuire believes the White House 'smoking saga' may be more than an apocryphal anecdote and reveals that Clark had recently started experimenting with marijuana. "First of all it was Art [Podell] and I, then Gene. The three of us were the only dope smokers in the group. Nobody else did. I don't know if Gene smoked in the White House toilet, but he could have done. Nobody would have known if you were smoking marijuana in those days. Nobody knew what it was. If he didn't smoke it in the White House he probably smoked it in his room at the hotel we stayed in just across the street. I know I got loaded before I went over there [to the White House]. It was a daily thing. I'd get up, roll half-a-dozen joints, smoke one, then walk out the door ready to take on the day. I had a little metal packet of throat lozenges and I kept my rolled-up joints in there so that they wouldn't get crushed. Nobody would search you. Nobody was looking. We'd walk down the street smoking a joint and nobody knew. It wasn't a big deal. Everything was so surreal in those days. It was like living in a dream. A different city, a different stage. We were all young and had no idea what we were doing or how long it was going to last. We were just enjoying each moment."

Clark's other memory of the White House visit was a more sobering one. "It was weird and sad. Both the Johnsons and the Kennedys were living in the house together because the Kennedys hadn't had time to move out yet . . . That was a trip. Hanging out with Jackie *and* Lyndon . . . a gigantic man. He was bigger than John Wayne! . . . The Johnsons' [daughters] were big fans of ours, so they followed us around the East Coast for a while. Everywhere we'd go, there'd be Secret Service guys . . . They were nice girls."

Nothing was the same for Clark after the presidential visit. The following week, the Minstrels returned to the road, but he was restive and uncertain about his future. He may have been frustrated by his subsidiary status in the group and aware that Sparks was already considering replacing him with Paul Potash from the Back Porch Majority. Temperamentally, Clark was probably too low-key onstage to fit in comfortably with the Minstrels' showbiz ethic. "The Christy Minstrels, including me, were hogs for entertainment," says McGuire. "I love to entertain. I'm not a musician. I've always gone for taking people from where they are in their troubled lives to a place of fun and excitement, to lift them out of their present situation, for a few minutes anyway, and provide a little moment of relief, like an aspirin or something. But Gene *was* a musician, and so was Art Podell." Of course, it was still possible to be both a musician and an entertainer but Clark found the dilemma more problematical as time passed. Above all, as McGuire insists, it was the constant travelling that wore down his spirit.

At the end of January, a newspaper review remarked that only eight Minstrels appeared onstage for a show in Winona, MI. The missing member was not deemed important enough to be identified; an apt comment on Clark's contribution to the revue. Gene later explained in at least two interviews that his sudden departure from the Christies came in a flash of revelation after hearing the Beatles while on the road. "They hadn't really broken wide yet. I found 'She Loves You' and 'I Want To Hold Your Hand'. I listened to them about 30 times in a row on this coffee-house jukebox. I decided they really had something more than just another hit group. There was something magical, even mystical, about this group that was really fascinating. They were truly innovative. I decided to leave the New Christy Minstrels. I quit the next morning. I remember Nick Woods saying, 'Man, what are you doing?' I said, 'I don't know, I've just got to follow my instinct.' I caught a plane out of Norfolk, Virginia, going to Los Angeles. I didn't even have a place to stay." Assuming Clark's recollection is veracious, the decision to embrace the Beatles was prophetically timed. Within a few days of his departure, 'I Want

To Hold Your Hand' had vaulted to number 1 in the US charts. On 7 February, the Beatles were mobbed upon arrival at Kennedy Airport and, two days later, an estimated 73 million viewers witnessed their legendary appearance on *The Ed Sullivan Show*. Beatlemania had taken over America.

Although he was no longer a Minstrel, Clark still took advantage of Randy Sparks' hospitality, presumably without his knowledge. In Encino, California, Sparks owned the Folkhaus, which served as a handy base for various members of the Back Porch Majority and other folk musicians in his employ. Clark stayed there for a time while plotting his next move. Years later, in a conversation with his friend Tom Slocum, Gene came up with an amusing conspiracy theory involving one of the Folkhaus' boarders. "He said John Denver had ratted him out for smoking a joint at the White House and that was the *real* reason he left the New Christy Minstrels." As so often with Clark's tall tales, this seemingly preposterous proposition may have contained some underlying half-truth.

Sparks was quick to spot the talents of John Deutschendorf, who had recently relocated from Texas and was soon singing lead with the Back Porch Majority at Randy's club Ledbetter's in Westwood. According to McGuire, Sparks told his new discovery, "Your name's too big for my marquee" and insisted he change it to John Denver. "The New Christy Minstrels had just had a big hit with the single 'Denver' and Randy had the sheet music on his wall." Deutschendorf was wary of acquiring a name that might easily be confused with that of Bob Denver, soon-to-be star of the television comedy, *Gilligan's Island*. Sparks brushed the objection aside. "Randy said, 'Listen, kid, if you play your cards right, when the name Denver is mentioned no one will even think of Bob Denver anymore.' So he changed his name on opening night and John Denver was born at Ledbetter's." Denver had good reason to be grateful to his mentor and may well have casually mentioned Clark's smoking habit but, if so, it probably resulted in Gene's removal from the Folkhaus rather than the New Christy Minstrels.

Once settled in California, Clark began writing Beatle-influenced songs, complete with Anglo inflexions as if he had just stepped off a boat from Liverpool. Famously, he encountered Jim McGuinn singing Beatles covers in the 'Folk Den' of the Troubadour and they decided to form a duo, similar to Peter And Gordon, who were about to top the US charts with 'A World Without Love'. Very soon after, David Crosby inveigled his way into the line-up, introduced them to freelance producer Jim Dickson and the Jet Set/Byrds story began.

However, there was a parallel tale underway that was largely forgotten by the participants over the years. Dickson and his business partner, Eddie Tickner, formed a music publishing company Tickson Music and taped a number of compositions outside the Byrds' orbit. Previously, Dickson had recorded several David Crosby songs with the intention of securing a solo deal. Among that short list was the startling 'Everybody's Been Burned' which Dickson never considered suitable for the Byrds, although it was successfully revived by Crosby for inclusion on *Younger Than Yesterday*. Evidently, a similar process occurred with Gene Clark.

Seven solo demos were cut at World-Pacific Studios during the spring or summer of 1964 which differ markedly from the Beatles-influenced material that Clark was pioneering with the fledgling Byrds. Clark sounds as though he is still musically and mentally attuned to the formal vocal stylings of the New Christy Minstrels. 'I'd Feel Better', with its strumming acoustic guitar and happy-go-lucky whistling, echoes the Minstrels' unthreatening commercial folk. It is an uncertain recording, with Clark even coughing nervously at one point. Thematically, the composition recalls Carole King's 'It Might As Well Rain Until September', a song of summer loss in which the adolescents can only communicate their frustrations via letter and the fantasy of reuniting in the fall. The solemn 'If There's No Love' is a further testament to Clark's romantic idealism as well as an implied criticism of the casual relationships associated with a Hollywood lifestyle. Vocally, the track is most noticeable for its striking vibrato. Roy Orbison's influence was still strong in 1964, a year in which he enjoyed massive international hits with 'It's Over' and 'Oh Pretty Woman'. Clark's stately vibrato, also detectable on parts of the archival album *Preflyte*, sounds charming but was already considered anachronistic and unsuitable for the Byrds and would soon be abandoned.

'A Worried Heart' ostensibly deals with a more adult theme inasmuch as the apotheosized lost love is now married and beyond reach. The seeming impossibility of moving on while witnessing the taunting traits of an old love in each new face are familiar 'broken heart' tropes which Clark overplays with trite imagery: "In your eyes I see the skies and ocean blue." Amusingly, he even pre-empts the lyrics of McGuinn's 'Ballad Of Easy Rider', five years before its composition, with the lines, "A river flows . . . to the sea and the wind has not a mind but still it's free." Indeed, Clark seems so impressed by this quasi-metaphysical conceit that he tells the listener, "it's with this thought I'll leave you now".

For 'The Way I Am' Clark adopts a persona more in keeping with a John Wayne western. There is polite defiance but also a chauvinistic swagger as the singer insists he could never be anybody's fool and, finally, provides a conditional offer of commitment solely on his terms. If Clark had ever been asked to write a song for a musical like *Oklahoma* or a western drama such as *High Noon*, this would have been his choice.

'Why Can't I Have Her Back Again?' is more sophisticated and looks to the future. Even the opening line "Yesterday she set me free" prepares the way for more torturous reflections such as the great 'Set You Free This Time'. While the majority of these demos should be seen as juvenilia, there is at least one that takes us into a different realm. 'That Girl', a clever arrangement framed by a subtle acoustic guitar accompaniment, includes several of the characteristics that would make Clark such an inimitable songwriter. It starts with an almost morbid fixation on an empty chair as symbolic of all that has lately been lost. Clark's love of linguistic inversion adds an archaic literary ambience while also suggesting emotional confusion as he relates his sad story. By the second verse, the empty chair has become an empty room as the mental telescope widens to take in the enormity of the narrator's loss. A haunting loneliness is evoked as we enter an inner world far bleaker than the description of the deserted house. The melancholy present in so much of his later work is captured here in a vocal that combines pain and confusion in equal measure. Apotheosis, desperation, blame, retribution and obsessive love are all examined in reflective asides. Returning for a third verse, the singer abandons external description altogether, focusing exclusively on his morbid thought processes which suddenly appear overwhelming. They 'torture' the brain, threatening insanity. Ultimately, there is no resolution as verbal expression collapses in uncertainty. In attempting the song's refrain, Clark stumbles, repeating the word 'all' then stretching syllables and words (again anticipating a later stylistic quirk) as if language can no longer convey his emotion adequately, leaving him and the listener with the simple, but unanswerable question: why did she go away and leave me alone?

It is extremely doubtful that the Byrds ever rehearsed any of these songs, let alone considered them as appropriate for their repertoire. The strongest evidence of this is the engaging 'All For Him', a love ballad self-evidently directed at a man, suggesting that it was probably written with a female vocalist in mind. Either that or Clark was being outrageously subversive in composing a gay anthem, which is extraordinarily unlikely considering the era. Had this been released by a male singer, it would surely have been banned from airplay.

Whether any of these songs were pitched to other artistes is not known but, if so, none were recorded at the time. Instead, they were filed away and left on the tape shelf as Clark busied himself writing more enduring work for the Byrds.

Clark's complete history in the Byrds has been dealt with in exhaustive detail over several hundred pages in the first volume of

Requiem For The Timeless. Taking a snapshot overview here, it is interesting to consider the constant tug of war between ambition and resistance almost from the very start of his career. After leaving the New Christy Minstrels, he was quick to prophesy pop's future, melding folk sensibilities and beat ballads. At the birth of the Byrds, it was Clark who seemed the most forceful and creative member. During those early rehearsals at World-Pacific Studios, he was the cheerleader, the dominant force, the prolific writer whose songs articulated their new direction. Rock history has often rewritten the script so that McGuinn and Crosby emerge as the creative giants and lead players, but, at the beginning, Clark was the man.

"You should have heard David when he first came in and told me about these two guys he found, McGuinn and Clark," Jim Dickson reminisces. "He said, 'They both play guitar better than me. I'm not going to play guitar. I just want to sing harmony and this guy Gene writes great songs.' The story just changes for his use. When we signed them, Gene was the most positive out of the main guys, especially up at the microphone. I just wanted 'Mr Tambourine Man' because I thought that was a career beginner. I didn't think the songs that they had themselves were developed enough. Gene to me was the one that sang the boy/girl songs. He knew what they meant, so they had feeling."

The crucial difference between Clark's early songs and those of McGuinn's was that they came from the heart. Dickson was quick to realize their aesthetic possibilities. "Just about every song he ever wrote that had anything going for it came out of relationships. Later, I'd sometimes read his songs and they didn't make sense, but I could always count on him knowing the feeling – and in my mind it's always the feeling that you invest in the song that communicates, not the clever licks. From the beginning that was a problem that I felt I had with the other Byrds. It's like they were embarrassed to show feeling or something, they wanted to be cool. Gene was different." Nobody knows how many of his songs were attempted at World-Pacific, but it is clear that quite a number were lost to posterity as the entire contents of *The Preflyte*

Sessions represent a mere sample of what was recorded over many months. Listen again to the enthralling 'For Me Again', 'The Reason Why', 'You Showed Me' and 'Tomorrow Is A Long Ways Away' and consider that these were not deemed worthy outtakes for the Byrds' first album by anyone, including Dickson, Melcher and even Gene himself.

One pivotal moment during the World-Pacific sessions that has not survived is the initial attempt at 'Mr Tambourine Man'. It is not generally known that Clark was originally allocated the role of lead singer on the track, only to miss out later when McGuinn emerged with a more convincing vocal. In a different universe, there might even be a Clark-led 'Mr Tambourine Man' and an accompanying album dominated by his songs. One person who might have appreciated hearing even more Clark originals was Bob Dylan. After the group agreed to record 'Mr Tambourine Man', he attended the sessions and complimented Clark on his songwriting. "Dylan was most interested in Gene Clark," claims Dickson. "Gene was the songwriter and Dylan understood the value of Gene Clark as a songwriter more profoundly than any of us. That, in itself, created an attitude, some of it very positive, some of it negative and jealous."

By the time of Dylan's endorsement, Gene was already in sharper competition with the other Byrds, who were carving out roles of their own. Once McGuinn assumed lead vocals on all Dylan covers and Crosby elevated himself to rhythm guitarist at Clark's expense, a new dynamic was set. For the next two years Clark would suffer an insidious loss of power and influence over the group, made worse by an increasing awareness of the importance of securing publishing rights. In the beginning, though, Clark seemed unassailable. If anyone was an innovator at this point, he was the most probable candidate. It was not merely that he wrote the majority of the songs. He was also a strong motivator and affable enough to maintain the delicate ego balance between McGuinn and Crosby. In many ways, Clark was also an important conduit between the older and younger members. He quickly bonded with Michael Clarke and, improbable as it sounds, had enough experience to assist Chris Hillman. "Chris knew nothing about bass, having played the mandolin, and I gave him his first bass lesson because I'd played upright bass with my earlier groups. It turned out he had a natural affinity for it."

During the first half of 1965, Clark fulfilled his commitments to the Byrds without encountering any problems. He was industrious, forward looking and seemed to enjoy the challenges presented to the group. There is no record of Clark ever missing a recording session, photo shoot or promotional appearance. Tellingly, no one recalls him drinking excessively, if at all. Initially, he was happy and independent in Hollywood. It was as if he had completely reinvented himself, never even bothering to send news of his good fortune to his family back in Kansas. He seemed unfazed by the coast-to-coast touring and even the plane trip to England was undertaken without complaint. Although previously afflicted by nervous tension while travelling with the Christies, Clark seemed to have adjusted to the media circus surrounding the Byrds with relative ease. In his everyday life, there was evidently no sign of the dark angst that permeated his songs of tortured romance. On the contrary, he was an upbeat character with a delightfully understated sense of humour. It was a trait that appealed to the group's ever optimistic press officer Derek Taylor, who accompanied the Byrds on their UK visit. "Gene was most amusing. He was important and I liked him as a personality. He had that laconic English feel about him. He and I loved the same situations. You could say things to Gene like, 'Have you ever noticed so and so?' And he *would* have noticed. He was very observant. He used to sing little parodies: 'Red is the colour of my true love's nose in the morning when we rise.' Although they'd yet to meet the Beatles he already had that slightly quirky Liverpool humour."

During the UK trip, Clark was introduced to the Beatles and socialized with them at fashionable haunts such as the Scotch of St James. His social skills were less impressive than Crosby's, but he still made an impression. The Byrds conducted a number of newspaper interviews that summer and reporters usually flocked towards McGuinn and Crosby for a quote. Gene tended to fade into the background on such occasions, along with Hillman and Clarke. The *NME*'s Keith Altham memorably described him as walking around in a Mountie's hat saying 'Hi', but little else. On one occasion, he was cornered by a journalist and found himself having to answer an earnest question about the origins of 'Mr Tambourine Man'. At such times, Clark borrowed a trick from the Dylan/Lennon school of put-on humour and produced a poker-faced, shaggy dog story that read like a comic script. He even claimed to have unearthed Dylan's secret source for their number 1 hit. "'Mr Tambourine Man' was written after an uncle of his [Dylan's] who kept a second-hand bookshop in Walnut Ridge, Arkansas and was never quite forgiven for it. He used to read the books back to front – the only sensible way, you know."

Alongside the Dylan covers on their first album, Clark's melodies provided the most arresting and poignant moments and underlined the crucial fact that the Byrds were no mere supplicants at the altar of Zimmerman. Songs such as 'I Knew I'd Want You', 'Here Without You' and 'You Won't Have To Cry' were so impressive that they stand alongside some of the best Lennon/McCartney material of the period as potential standards. And just to prove that he was not simply a writer of love-lorn laments, Clark provided the anti-romantic 'Feel A Whole Lot Better', a lyric that promised vicarious triumph at the moment of rejection. The song even prompted a long-standing joke in the Byrds that Gene could only write a classic when he broke up with a girlfriend. By the time of the second album, even Crosby was encouraging his partner to fall out of love as quickly as possible.

Although 'Feel A Whole Lot Better' was an undisputed pop classic, Clark could not be expected to usurp Dylan as the main provider of Byrds' A-sides. The fiasco with Cher over a rival cover of 'All I Really Want To Do' saw 'Feel A Whole Lot Better' momentarily promoted in its own right, but before too long the Byrds were back in the studio attempting 'It's All Over Now, Baby Blue' and 'The Times They Are A-Changin''. When those experiments failed, they turned to Pete Seeger's biblical adaptation

'Turn! Turn! Turn!'. By now, Clark had an expanding song catalogue, including 'The Emptiness' and 'That's What You Want' – both of which joined those earlier World-Pacific demos on the 'not required' shelf.

Clark's full flowering may have been forestalled during his time with the Byrds, but he remained streets ahead of the more sluggish McGuinn and Crosby. Indeed, the couple of songs that David submitted for inclusion were ruthlessly withheld and deemed either not strong enough or inappropriate for the Byrds. Although Crosby boasted to me that he eventually eclipsed every member of the group as a songwriter ("There isn't one of them can write as good as me and you fucking know it. And that's the truth. I'm better than them put together"), Clark never accepted that assertion. Even in the months before his death, he maintained the old view. "David was never a very strong songwriter. He comes up every once in a while with a song that people love, but he's never been consistent." He was right about Crosby's relative lack of productivity, but underestimated the quality of his greatest work. His words were also a testament to his own frustrations over the years.

As 1965 wound to a close, Gene found it increasingly difficult to find a niche for his more adventurous ideas. On the one hand he was still regarded as a purveyor of Beatleseque love ballads, a form that seemed suddenly out of vogue, while at the other extreme his more poetic excursions were deemed incoherent. "We had the feeling at the time that Gene was stretching to create the illusion of intellectual subject matter without having any substance to it," says McGuinn. "We did reject some of his songs on those grounds." For a time, passing patronage from Bob Dylan ensured that Clark continued to command attention. "Suddenly we thought we could get away with this," says Dickson of Gene's prolix lyrics. "We saw some value in Gene's stuff, Dylan saw more. Other people saw *none*. I felt we needed to select the right Gene Clark songs because a lot of them on paper didn't make literal sense. Dylan, seeing songs more as poetry, wasn't so concerned about making sense. The thing that worked for Dylan was that Gene knew what he meant, so his interpretation and feeling for the song was always perfect for the implied story. Part of the story was told in the feeling that Gene gave a song and the sureness of what he meant. The words printed on paper without Gene's phrasing made less sense . . . But Gene was accepted by poets when he wrote those songs. They sounded important and he made them sound important because they were important to him."

The combination of LSD, Hollywood girls and Dylan-watching encouraged Clark's development as a serious singer-songwriter. One of his most ambitious undertakings was 'The Emptiness' (probably the correct title of what was later inexactly referred to as 'The Day Walk'), the strangest composition Clark wrote up until this point. Its grotesque imagery evoking a "charcoal pit" of dreams in which the righteous are pictured picking pieces of their minds from the floor is a chilling phantasmagoria. Everyday objects and events are invested with grim significance and experienced with the confused rationale of an LSD devotee let loose on the streets of Hollywood. It is a place full of paranoia: the sudden scare of the inexplicable; the belief that you can't find support; and the knowledge of "the emptiness" upon realizing that everything is somewhat less significant than it was thought to be. The continual bombardment of the senses suggests a mind under great stress but a plodding 'Satisfaction'-style rhythm siphons some of the song's mystery and drama.

While 'The Emptiness' was considered too abstruse for release at the time, the enchanting 'She Don't Care About Time' was selected as the B-side for 'Turn! Turn! Turn!'. Ostensibly a love song in the earlier Clark tradition, it wanders off into metaphysical musings, conjuring a cosmology in which his own room is transposed somewhere on the "edge of time". McGuinn's beautiful Bach-inspired Rickenbacker backing enhances the lilting melody. Not wishing to include another flip-side on their next album, the group wisely followed Beatles' protocol and allowed the song to remain a treasured B-side. The massive sales of 'Turn! Turn! Turn!' ensured that 'She Don't Care About Time' was heard by more people than most of the tracks on its parent album.

It was during sessions for the Byrds' second album that Clark unveiled another new song, whose word-packed lines and tortuous dissection of another broken relationship testified to an astonishing maturity. 'Set You Free This Time' was arguably Clark's most eloquent statement to date. The song ably articulates a post-adolescent awakening to the confusing nature of sexual/emotional entanglements. There is an unusually stoical air about the composition in which the singer somehow manages to balance a sense of bitterness and longing for vengeance with a courtly love deference. At times, Clark's compression of lines, playful cadence and that strange combination of the conversational and the prolix leaves the listener almost overwhelmed. By the close of the song, the protagonist has rationalized his motives so persuasively that his nobility seems beyond question. It is as if he has had to talk his way out of a failed relationship in order to reassert his self-image as the emotional victor. The song was the most intense lyric he would compose during this era, although it would later be matched by the even more extraordinary 'Echoes'.

A promotional film of 'Set You Free This Time' was attempted but its completion was forestalled by internal bickering, culminating in the legendary fight on the beach documented in *Volume 1*. "David instigated that whole thing on the beach with 'Set You Free This Time'," Dickson says. "We wanted a close up of Gene followed by a cut from a lower angle of the rest of the heads. Because Michael was taller and the camera angle was low, he needed to be farther away for his head to be in the frame. David, not wanting to do it at all and preferring to be somewhere else, kept saying, 'This is a bunch of bullshit' and 'Wrong song'. Then he'd tell Michael, 'He's trying to make you look unimportant. You're the best looking one. How long are you going to take being put in the background?' So Michael would come down and walk through at the wrong place." When Dickson turned on Clarke, Crosby left the set pursued by his manager who was restrained by Gene Clark, which allowed David the chance to punch him in the mouth. The drama derailed the filming, thereby depriving Clark of the perfect cameo. Dickson was incensed. "I think what turned David against the song went back to when Dylan first came down to World-Pacific and thought Gene was the important one. Dylan thought he was a good songwriter – and said so. That really took the starch out of McGuinn and Crosby. Dylan liking Gene embittered Crosby for a while. That's what I felt." Whether Dickson's analysis is correct is extremely debatable. Crosby was such an instinctive, reactive character that he may simply have been caught up in the emotional moment. He always liked Clark as a person.

At least 'Set You Free This Time' secured an A-side release, an honour previously reserved for Dylan and Pete Seeger, but there was a sting in the tale. Within a week, CBS had a change of heart and relegated 'Set You Free This Time' to B-side status in favour of McGuinn/Gerst's 'It Won't Be Wrong'. It was a potentially devastating slight to Clark but the blow was soon forgotten thanks to the arrival of a new, groundbreaking composition.

Musically, the Byrds were pushing ahead in a startlingly new direction in which Crosby and McGuinn would play a more prominent role. Unveiling their new single 'Eight Miles High' b/w 'Why', the group gave the pop world a couple of new tags: 'jazz rock' and 'raga rock'. As discussed in *Volume 1*, 'Eight Miles High' had a huge impact and confirmed the Byrds' standing among rock's all-time elite. Over the years, much has been written about McGuinn's brilliant arrangement and Crosby's celebration of John Coltrane in a rock format. Rather less attention has been paid to Gene Clark, who wrote the vast majority of the lyrics and the original melody and without whose inspiration the Byrds would never have recorded this classic. 'Eight Miles High' remains a fitting tribute to all that Gene achieved in the Byrds – the perfect and unique example of Clark, Crosby and McGuinn sharing a song credit to which they each brought something special and enduring.

For a time, it seemed that Clark had everything. At the end of 1965, he had not only completed 'Eight Miles High', but considered himself the toast of Hollywood. He had been dating the beautiful Jacqui Levy, chief dancer on the television show, *Hollywood A Go-Go*. They resembled love's young dream, but some felt that she was far too sophisticated for Clark's simple tastes. A graduate of Fairfax High, she came from a privileged family and oozed a worldliness that was both intoxicating and intimidating. Crosby and Dickson predicted the relationship would most likely end in heartbreak, with Clark no doubt composing a classic composition of eternal love, lost to misfortune.

The tambourine man had recently experienced a strange epiphany during an end-of-year trip to Hawaii. Dickson witnessed what he considered Gene's greatest performance as he came bursting through the curtain singing 'Feel A Whole Lot Better'. He would never feel this confident onstage again. During the same excursion, Clark had joined several of the others in an intense LSD trip and expressed his stoned desire to remain on the island forever. Some say he was never the same after Hawaii.

Requiem For The Timeless, Volume 1 presented in expansive detail the circumstances culminating in Clark's departure from the Byrds. There was his legendary fear of flying, nervous condition, Hollywood lifestyle, intense relationship with dancer Jacqui Levy, and much more. It was a potent mix. As co-manager Ed Tickner rightly noted, there was no conspiracy against Gene from the other Byrds. At worst, he was a victim of envy over songwriting income, but still held his own as the group's chief composer right up until his leaving. In the end, a combination of all these factors meant that he was unable to fulfil the group's touring and promotional commitments. Perhaps the most remarkable aspect of his leaving was the casual disregard with which it was greeted by his fellow Byrds. No serious attempt was made to encourage him to reconsider his position and the general attitude from his fellow members was apathetic at best. Even Dickson was taken aback by the coolness of the other Byrds in what was undoubtedly the biggest crisis of their career thus far.

Publicist Derek Taylor was even more concerned and crestfallen.

Looking back over the previous two years, he notes: "Gene wasn't kindly treated by them. They'd removed his instrument and had that fucking guitar off him. I was told later it had to go. He did look good with the tambourine, and it meant he could roam free onstage. How he felt about it is another matter."

At the time, Clark accepted that decision without rancour, perhaps overwhelmed by the sheer force of Crosby's persuasive personality. Dickson later claimed that Clark's confidence was shattered by the decision and his timing was never the same thereafter. It may have had other consequences unappreciated at the time. "I did miss the guitar," Gene acknowledged, many years later. "I don't mean just musically, but also in terms of how I presented myself onstage. I was standing there with nothing but a microphone and a tambourine or a pair of maracas, which I did play, but which also served as a prop. I had to learn how to incorporate just me, without the guitar, into the stage configuration, and I learned a lot from that. Musically, I missed the guitar sometimes on those records because there were certain rhythm figures in my songs that just didn't get done unless I was there to do them."

In the original pre-censored sleevenotes for *Turn! Turn! Turn!*, Taylor had already alluded to the rivalry over songwriting credits which affected morale but even he had failed to foresee the seriousness of Gene's plight. Taylor was there on 22 February 1966, the day Clark's world came crashing down. The Byrds were already sitting aboard an aircraft ready to leave LA for New York when the unthinkable happened. Shaking with terror, Clark announced that he could not make the trip. Taylor was astonished.

"There was more fear from me when Gene got off that plane. I was sitting on his left and thinking, 'Gene, don't do it! Don't do it!' And then he got off. I remember it so well . . . I thought it was such a serious thing. I didn't like groups having rows and I don't like families having rows. It looked to me that it was deadly serious. Either that would be it or it would mean a lot of persuasion . . . I didn't like the finality of it. Whether it was trouble with the group more than fear of flying, I'm not sure. But he didn't fake it. Sometimes a walk-out is a diminished form of suicide. It's a cry for help. 'Watch me, I'm doing this, you may never see me again. I'm off.' They could have said, 'Come back, we want you, we need you.' But that wasn't the kind of people they were. 'Hey, let him go, you know . . .' I never understood why they didn't treasure him. Even now, looking at that magic carpet photograph on the front of *Fifth Dimension*, I miss him enormously. The cruel symbolism of that picture – that's it, gone, finished. I felt a great sense of loss."

If the Byrds had been entirely reliant on Gene, then he might have reverted to a Brian Wilson role, writing and recording with the group, but refusing to tour. It might have worked too. Anyone approaching Tickner/Dickson management could obtain a bundle of unreleased demos. In contemporaneous interviews the Byrds were claiming that Clark was intending to work as an independent producer. Although this sounded improbable, given his lack of studio training, an endearing story suggests that it was partly true.

One morning, Clark was sitting outside one of his favourite haunts, the Hamburger Hamlet, when he was spotted by two teenage girls from Santa Barbara High School: Candice 'Candie' Callaway and Carol Millsip. They approached him with an impudent request: "Would you write a song for us?" Clark was used to signing autographs, but this was different. To their delight, he invited them for a coffee, eager to learn more. The girls were keen fans of the Byrds and took innocent pleasure in bombarding them with bags of cookies bought from Canter's delicatessen. Michael Clarke was a favourite target. Often he was amused and perplexed to discover a white paper bag outside his apartment accompanied by a short written message: 'From your local friendly Cookie Fairies'. "We were like stalkers," Candie says. Although too young to frequent clubs, the schoolgirls enjoyed their harmless intrigue. Recently, they had even infiltrated an outdoor television shoot of Gene miming 'Set You Free This Time' for *Where The Action Is.* They were amazed to see Michael filmed on horseback, wearing a 10-gallon hat. The Byrds were in danger of falling from favour with fickle teenage fans, but Candie and Carol remained loyal.

Recently, the girls' fortunes had taken a Hollywood turn. They had taped themselves singing a couple of Beatles' songs, an unusual enough occurrence to win support from one of their friends, who was a teen reporter for the *Santa Barbara News.* A small mention in the paper eventually brought them to the attention of entrepreneur Jack Millman, who ran a production company, Music Industries, on Cahuenga Boulevard. He offered them a contract and the chance to record some material. Initially, they called themselves the Army Brats, even though neither of their families had military connections. Asking Gene Clark to write them a song was a mad idea, but their youthful optimism was boundless. They were surprised when he offered them his home phone number and even more amazed when he followed this up with a meeting. "The next thing you know he was in the office with us talking about recording a song, which hadn't been written yet."

Not long after, Clark sent them an acoustic demo titled 'Don't You Know What You Want'. It was one of the few songs he ever wrote as a commission. Candie and Carol were instructed to rehearse the number for several weeks, with special emphasis on the harmony. Gene even turned up to assist, offering suggestions for the vocal parts. "It was gruelling but fun," Candie remembers. "We worked our tail ends off to please him because he was a wonderful person, very patient, very kind and very respectful. We were only 17 and 19 years old. We could have been into something that wasn't so positive, but it turned out so wonderful." Further good news followed.

On 15 April, the girls were invited to record 'Don't You Know What You Want' as a demo at CBS. This was quite a coup and evidence enough of Clark's intent to establish a separate identity. He was responsible for hiring the studio musicians and overseeing the session. In one unguarded moment, he even told Candie and Carol that he would approach his former bandmates in the Byrds to appear on the final recording. "Gene was producing," says Candie. "He was very technical. He'd say to the drummer, 'Can you play like Michael Clarke?'" The completed demo sounded very much like the Mamas & The Papas, its pop structure disguising some acerbic lines about emotional commitment ("If you had the money and time, you would leave me"). Asked to choose a name by their backers, the duo decided upon the Cookie Fairies, in tribute to their sweet biscuit offerings to the Byrds. What happened next is unclear. The trade magazine *Record World* reported that the Cookie Fairies were preparing to record *four* Clark compositions, produced by Billy Elder. No such session was ever booked and, amid the prevarication, the prospect of a record deal foundered. It was a blow for Clark too who would have loved the prestige of writing a hit record for another artiste.

Unfortunately, there were never enough people interested in Clark as a songwriter per se to allow him the luxury of an extended retirement. Instead, he elected to strike out on his own. By this point, the contradictions in his character were self-evident. To some, he was a humble country boy from Missouri, a romantic soul, conspicuously out of place in Tinseltown. Yet, he immersed himself in the LA lifestyle with apparent glee. He was the most materialistic and spendthrift member of the group, squandering his new-found wealth on Ferraris and hanging out at glitzy clubs that even his fellow Byrds deemed crass rather than cool. The Sunset Strip girls, whom he had once regarded as impossibly sophisticated, were now part of his everyday circle. In true Hollywood tradition, he became embroiled in a clandestine affair with another star, the glamorous Michelle Phillips, ex-model, singer and pin-up fantasy of the Mamas & The Papas. This was all a long way from Kansas.

The romance with Phillips was a thrilling interlude for Clark, but not without its problems. Initially, they attempted to keep the affair a secret and avoided being seen in public together. On the other hand, they could not resist tearing around Sunset in expensive cars and also risked exposure by agreeing to a yachting trip. "I remember Gene was fooling about with Michelle when he was sailing with me in Catalina," Dickson recalls. "She was with some of the folks from the Modern Folk Quartet and they paired off over there. I don't know if there was a previous time they were together. Gene scared a lot of girls because he was not as simple as he appeared to be. He had this darker side."

Michelle Phillips was never likely to be intimidated by Clark. In common with Gene's former girlfriend Jacqui Levy, she was an urbane free spirit, familiar with Hollywood culture. Although they were equals in terms of their status as famous pop stars, Michelle was more easy-going and self-confident about their affair.

Cyrus Faryar, a mutual friend and Modern Folk Quartet alumnus, was struck by the dichotomy between their two characters and portrayed Clark as a relative innocent, swept along in the unfolding drama. "I think he was rather bemused by his relationship with Michelle. He seemed sort of taken off guard. It was as if it were a stroke of good luck that he wasn't going to question deeply or make much of. I think that he was delighted in her company and pleased to be there, but subconsciously had no expectation of its endurance. He was very reserved, and warm and friendly. Michelle was young and vivacious, and quite volatile. There was in Michelle a quite worldly quality. She looked sweet and innocent, but she wasn't really. She had grown up in Mexico, and had a childhood upbringing that was not conventional."

It was not long before Phillips became aware of her new love's neuroses. He was wracked with guilt about their liaison and it even resurrected those bad dreams that he'd suffered over the years. Michelle remembers him waking during a troubled night's sleep and insisting that she return to her own house. "What we're doing is wrong," he insisted, as if a priest was whispering in his ear. Michelle's recollection is that her estranged husband John was kept in the dark about the affair. He argued otherwise in his autobiography, claiming "I could never accuse Michelle of being devious. Just blunt and defiant. She would call me at home and interrupt herself by saying, 'What, Gene?' with her hand over the phone. 'Oh, anyway, John,' she would then continue, 'Gene and I are in bed, but before we go to sleep I wanted to ask you what time the Mamas are supposed to be at the studio tomorrow.'"

What all the parties agree on is the date and place where the affair became a public spectacle. In an unthinking moment, Michelle made the mistake of inviting Gene to a Mamas & The Papas' concert at the Melodyland Theatre in Anaheim on 4 June 1966. The show coincided with her 22nd birthday and might have passed without comment had Clark not been placed prominently in the front row. When John saw Michelle seemingly singing to her lover, in what he regarded as a blatantly provocative public act, his anger could not be contained. After the show, he chased her into the car park and told her she was fired. At first, Michelle assumed it would all blow over in a few days but she was mortified to receive some cold correspondence from her band mates declaring: "This letter is to advise you that the undersigned no longer desire to record or perform with you in the future."

"I was fired," she told me. "John virtually insisted that if Cass and Denny wanted to remain as the Mamas & The Papas they would have to agree." Clark's name was not mentioned in the letter nor reported in the press. He remained quietly in the background while bulletins from England revealed that Michelle was visiting Mexico. "That was a lie," says Michelle. Worse still, the group had already found a replacement. Lou Adler's girlfriend, Jill Gibson, quickly learned Michelle's parts and was soon singing onstage and in the studio. "Jill was already with them rehearsing in England. They didn't tell anyone. They were really sneaky about their dirty work. My marriage to John had deteriorated. We hadn't lived together for several months. He and Denny were sharing a place together. Jill had no previous experience. As far as I knew she never played professionally. But she learned the harmony parts really quickly." Gibson contributed to the group's new album but fans were alarmed by the unexplained line-up change. The Byrds had encountered some difficulties playing live immediately after Gene's departure and the Mamas & The Papas faced similar difficulties. "When Jill appeared at Forest Hills (with Simon & Garfunkel as support), people were shouting out, 'Where's Michelle?' They didn't even announce I'd left. It seemed they were always trying to pass her off as me."

For the remainder of the summer, Michelle focused on rejoining the group. "I begged them to let me back – and grovelled," she admits. John Phillips eventually relented but the rapprochement meant the end of her affair with Gene Clark. He had little stomach for the melodrama and made no attempt to win her back preferring to allow the affair to remain a treasured memory.

While Michelle went through a brief purgatory before rejoining the Mamas & The Papas, Clark was still coming to terms with the insecurity of watching the Byrds continue in his absence. While dating Michelle, he had put together a new group featuring former Leaves' guitarist Bill Rhinehart (aka Rinehart), bassist Chip Douglas and ex-Grass Roots' drummer Joel Larson. Clark's connection with Larson came via a mutual acquaintance, Michael Clarke. Larson duly recommended Douglas who was rooming with him at the time. It no doubt helped that Douglas was a former member of the Dickson-produced Modern Folk Quartet and had crossed paths with Clark during the pre-Byrds days while hanging out at the Troubadour. "They were all qualified people," Clark recalled, "but it was confusing because once again we were trying to do something and nobody could quite see what we were doing."

Clark was vague about the musical direction, initially claiming that he was pursuing a path pioneered by the Beatles on *Rubber Soul.* What that indicated was seemingly a desire to record an album of self-penned compositions with no filler and an eclectic mix of musical styles, embracing folk, pop and country. When they first started hanging out, the musicians would listen to Clark running through a selection of songs. Interestingly, Dino Valenti's 'I Don't Want To Spoil Your Party', which the Byrds had attempted in the studio in September 1965, remained a favourite warm-up number. In his leisure time, Clark continued to careen around Hollywood in his new Ferrari, a more reckless driver than he had been during his teenage years. "After every practice session we'd go down to Sunset and Gene would drive in that Ferrari," Douglas recalls. "Often I was with him and he'd scream around those turns of Sunset Plaza . . . I was scared for my life every time."

Still unwilling to tour, Clark agreed to launch his latest project with a 19-day residency at the Whisky A Go-Go from 22 June–10 July. The denizens of Sunset Strip were spoilt for choice that summer with the Whisky offering performances from challenging live acts including the Buffalo Springfield, the Doors, the Grass Roots and the Van Morrison-led Them. It was a competitive environment. Eager to promote the ex-Byrd, the club advertised his residency with an enticing announcement: 'For the first time ever, hear the new-new music of Gene Clark & The Group.'

At his best with the Byrds, Clark had been capable of wowing an audience, bursting onto the stage, singing with confidence and conviction and displaying strong stagecraft. Performing with the Group, he downplayed his Byrds history, reportedly revisiting only 'Feel A Whole Lot Better' and 'She Don't Care About Time' from the 'old days'. His stage persona was also considerably understated, more in keeping with an introspective songwriter than an entertainer. Audiences newly acquainted with the animation of Jim Morrison and the surging energy of Stephen Stills et al responded politely at best. "Nobody really went nuts," Chip Douglas admits. "How well the show went over was hard to say. We were 'medium received'. It wasn't like everyone was screaming . . . I just remember getting up, being nervous and playing our songs, and that was that. Gene was pretty nervous having his own group for the first time . . . We weren't that confident of the material and hadn't performed that much. It came off all right, but it was rough." Ending the set on a note of bravado, Clark climbed up the rafters of the venue like a demented gymnast, then disappeared into the night. It was a trick he would perform again in later years.

Despite leaving the Byrds, Clark was still contractually committed to CBS and remained under the management of Jim

Dickson and Eddie Tickner. Columbia Records agreed to back a solo album from Clark, who prepared for this opportunity by rehearsing and recording some demos with Dickson. Among the numbers they routined were 'Needing Someone', 'Keep On Pushin'' and, according to Chip Douglas, "a song called 'Madeleine' that we started to work up but never got finished". Nobody was impressed at playback time, least of all Gene. "We listened back and it was a big disappointment. It didn't sound like the Byrds, it didn't sound like the Beatles. It sounded like whatever we were doing, which was really good, but shaky . . . That was where the disappointment came in after we listened to the recording. Those sessions were a little tense, and things weren't exactly right."

Disillusioned by both the live shows and the studio run-throughs, Clark decided to dissolve the Group, unsubtly suggesting that he might still work with Rhinehart and Larson. Chip Douglas was deflated by the news. "I was like, 'OK – in other words I'm getting kicked out of the Group.' I felt rejected and weird and I thought, 'the nerve of the guy'. Apparently, I wasn't the right vibe for him. They continued for a while, but that fell apart . . . We didn't speak too much after that."

Douglas went on to join the Turtles and produce the Monkees. In an inspired moment, two years later, he approached Eddie Tickner about acquiring some Gene Clark outtakes. He was presented with a copy of some of the still unreleased *Preflyte* demos and selected 'You Showed Me', which he fondly remembered hearing McGuinn, Clark and Crosby play informally at the Troubadour in 1964. "It was one of the first songs written by Gene and McGuinn and we had passed over it long before we went to CBS," Dickson adds. "Nobody was trying to get it back or ever suggested we do it at CBS in 1965. Chip Douglas was aware that it was on tape and when he was involved in producing the Turtles, he came and got it. He wanted it specifically and had an idea for it. He changed it quite a bit. Those Turtles made it a number 1 [actually Top 10] hit." That the exiled Chip Douglas would provide Clark with his greatest chart success as a songwriter was a sweet irony. Gene would probably have called it 'karma'.

One of the problems for Dickson was his ambivalence about the prospects of Clark succeeding as a solo. "I put myself back into that time and I remember that what was really at stake was wanting to get Gene back in the Byrds and wanting to keep him occupied in the meantime because he had all these songs all the time. We needed to suck up his energy and get something going for him so that he would still be there and able to come back. To me, the Byrds always needed all five of them. They had different reasons and different values but Gene was the one that sang boy/girl songs that had feeling, even if they weren't comprehensible."

For a moment, in the autumn of 1966, it seemed that Dickson's fantasy of reuniting Clark and the Byrds might succeed. With Crosby's voice failing during the opening show of their residency at the Whisky, they urgently required assistance. Clark was happy to deputize causing a frenzy of speculation among the group's local fans. Alas, the Byrds declined to take the experiment further and Clark was still required to complete work on his forthcoming album. Dickson compromised by ensuring that a couple of Byrds guested on the recording, along with several other musicians obliquely associated with the group, including Van Dyke Parks, Clarence White and Leon Russell. "I was into the symbolism of getting Chris and Michael to play with Gene on that album to make him look like he was still in the family, so to speak. He was making publishing money and he didn't want to go on the road anymore. The other Byrds needed to go out and work. Gene had enough income from the songs and was relatively comfortable. He wasn't going to tour or help build the future of the Byrds in promotional ways. I don't think he felt insecure about that at the time. He thought he could go on and do his thing without them."

Clark continued to write regularly, sometimes committing songs to tape, several of which were mislaid, lost or remain unheard. He was still keen to exchange ideas and listen to the work of other young hopefuls. One night, while attending a party at the home of agent/promoter Dana Stevens, he was introduced to Richard 'Ritchie' Lewis, who had an interesting story to tell. Lewis, like Clark, had always loved the Beatles and the British Invasion groups since first hearing them in Dallas during the early months of 1964. He had subsequently joined the Air Force and impressed his fellow recruits with his knack for songwriting. Having recently left the services, he was keen to continue with music and started managing a high-school group, Sounds Unlimited. Their Beatle-style haircuts had caused consternation among the educational hierarchy and they were informed that they would be denied admission to school unless they trimmed their locks above the ears. This minor furore somehow prompted a case action, backed by the American Civil Liberties Union. It even made the front page of the *Dallas-Times Herald* with the headline: 'Principal Orders Haircut'. Lewis was amazed by the publicity, which even spread as far as California, attracting the attention of Dana Stevens who phoned Richard with an offer of some gigs, supposedly for fees up to $2,500 per night. Lewis, along with the group's bass player, decided to make a reconnaissance trip to Hollywood, where Stevens allowed them to stay at her house. They were taken to a local recording studio and mingled with music business people at Stevens' party. Lewis was starstruck. "I met Gene Clark, the tambourine man, that night and we just hit it off. I told him I was from Dallas. I didn't know he was from Kansas, I thought he was from California. We started talking, and he said, 'Can I hear some of your lyrics?'"

Clark was more than curious. Soon after, he turned up at Lewis' door clutching an acoustic guitar and harmonica. A fun-filled jam session followed, with Clark introducing some song ideas and kindly praising Lewis' lyrical efforts. They intended to continue the collaboration but Ritchie had to return to Dallas to earn a living. The plans for Sounds Unlimited to visit Hollywood were swiftly vetoed by the group's parents, who insisted the boys must return to school. Lewis was nevertheless surprised when Clark phoned a few days later enthusing about some new songs he was working on. Over the succeeding weeks, they enjoyed some telephone brainstorming sessions during which Gene would encourage creative feedback.

"He would actually play songs over the phone to me and say, 'What do you think about this?', 'What are we going to name this song?', and so forth. This went on for quite some time." Finally, Clark announced: "I think I've got what we need" and proceeded to sing several songs down the phone. Lewis was impressed. Soon after, a reel-to-reel tape arrived in the post featuring five songs: 'Doctor Doctor', 'On The Bright Side', 'She's Made Up Her Mind', 'That's Why (Nobody For Me)' and 'A Long Time'. The compositions were basic, with a simple acoustic guitar and harmonica backing and straightforward rhyme schemes. Both 'She's Made Up Her Mind' and 'That's Why (Nobody For Me)' mentioned trains, the latter eulogizing the Santa Fe Special, like some precursor to the celebrated 'Kansas City Southern'. Only 'A Long Time' (later covered by Rose Garden) offered lyrical sophistication. Clark copyrighted all five songs, solely in his name, between September and October 1966, but never returned to them. He also lost contact with Richard Lewis, who found a job with a television company and was often away from home. Whether Gene ever attempted to phone him during his absence is not known.

By the end of the year, Clark had shortlisted songs for his debut album. 'That's Why', his train song, had been recorded at Columbia Studios during the summer, but never made the final cut. Following up the recent rough tapes he'd sent to Lewis, Clark commandeered some session musicians for a five-song acetate, including the aforementioned 'Doctor Doctor' and 'A Long Time', plus three new compositions: 'Understand Me Too', 'On Tenth Street' and 'Big City Girl'. These were all registered for copyright on 31 October, along with 'Sometime And Again', 'She Told Me', 'While You're Here' and the haunting 'If I Hang Around', but none were earmarked for his forthcoming album.

Instead, the long player was preceded by a pilot single, the complex and fascinating 'Echoes'. Amazingly, it was pure serendipity that the song was actually recorded. As Dickson reveals: "Gene gave me a tape with another song on it and 'Echoes' was on the other end of the tape. I just found it by accident. If I hadn't found it, it would have been forgotten about. Gene never brought it forward or pressed for it. It was one of those things that he put on tape and then forgot about like hundreds of other songs of his that were lost that way."

Ostensibly, 'Echoes' is another twisted love song in the Clark tradition, but it has a deeper layer of meaning. It transports the listener to an inner world of incapacitating strangeness in which metaphor and naturalistic description combine to startling and disconcerting effect. An escape from encroaching depression becomes an odyssey in itself, a search for a trace of an opening where the familiarities of a previous time might still exist. For Clark, the composition represented a veiled chronicle of the past two years, embracing his life in the Byrds, his relationships with Jacqui Levy and Michelle Phillips, his observations of LA life and all the dreams fulfilled and lost as he passed his 21st birthday. "When he wrote 'Echoes' I was just stunned," Dickson told me. "It was about Sunset Strip and the Whisky A Go-Go. The girl that danced through the crystal panes of glass – that's the girl that danced in the glass box at the Whisky A Go-Go. The 'betrayal lies in treason' and 'teamed up to tear down each other's feelings' line is the end of the Byrds. The whole story of his experience of it is all in that song and done in such a way that I think it's a magnificent piece of writing. It was so in the moment of what was going on. Compared to some of his earlier songs – well, just listen to the difference."

Dickson contacted his old friend Leon Russell, who agreed to arrange, conduct and orchestrate the piece. Clark was astonished by the results. "I remember going over to Leon's with 'Echoes' as nothing more than a demo with my voice and coming back the next day to find him passed out next to a stack of 32 lead sheets – he'd taken the demo and written the arrangements for a 32-piece orchestra." Russell's remit was to embellish a composition which, more than anything Clark had previously recorded, betrayed the influence of Dylan in its lyrical complexity and sophistication. "That's what CBS thought," adds Dickson. "When the guy came down and heard the session he said, 'That's like Dylan with an orchestra.' He equated it with Dylan. Dylan always liked Gene and thought he was more important than the rest of them. He expressed that at that time . . . Gene was like an idiot savant in a way. He would do some incredibly stupid things, then, once in a while, he'd write something that I couldn't believe came from his head. It was so astounding to me that it had so much insight in it. Then he'd write another 100 songs that were meaningless or you couldn't figure out what to call them. We had reams and reams of stuff."

Russell's ornate arrangement transformed the song into a thrilling baroque piece, complete with a Chinese flute opening. For those listeners who had followed Clark's career from the beginning, it proved a revelation. I can still recall the thrill of listening to the single for the first time and the excited realization that the tambourine man had achieved something even greater than the sublime 'Set You Free This Time'. This was a period when the Byrds, individually and collectively, were at their exploratory best. 'Echoes' embodied that spirit of adventure. "I was very impressed," Dickson concludes. "Columbia put out 'Echoes' as a single and it bombed legitimately. The bottom was mixed out of it and it wasn't right, but I loved the lyrics. To this day I think that was one of the most powerful songs he wrote. It was a great disappointment for me because I thought that song would put Gene Clark in the right place. I took out a full page in *Billboard* and *Cash Box* with the lyrics to it."

Dickson's advertisement was a daring venture and evidence enough of his commitment to the single. In large letters, not dissimilar to a wedding invitation, it read: 'Announcing the solo debut of a first magnitude star. GENE CLARK.' Below this was an italicized print-out of the lyrics preceded by the blurb: "Former member of the New Christy Minstrels and an originator of the Byrds. Now, Gene does a single – revealing, emphatic, thought-provoking lyrics and vividly expressive music he has written himself. And a bright talent assumes even greater brilliance."

The chances of the 'first magnitude star' achieving a major hit with 'Echoes' were always remote. It was probably too esoteric for AM radio and its US release into a crowded pre-Christmas market sealed its commercial doom. If 'Echoes' had become a hit, Clark would have been a more prominent force in the rock world of the Sixties but the song passed without fanfare, thereby reducing expectation for his new album. It was terribly deflating for Clark who knew that Dickson had been betting the house on the single. There was a sense that this was Clark's 'Dylan moment', the perfect opportunity for the singer/composer to emerge as an important figure in a new world of pop sophistication. Perhaps if there had existed a serious publication or media outlet to promote this exciting departure he might have built a reputation on the song's brilliance, but this was still the age of postage stamp reviews and notices, several months away from Monterey, *Sgt Pepper's* and the novel idea of a counterculture that deserved its own forum and literature. CBS producer Larry Marks lamented Clark's lost opportunity – one among so many. "It was deflating for him, and for Jim Dickson too. Gene was proud of the song and hoped it might take him in a completely new direction. When it wasn't a hit, that shook his confidence about where to go next. How do you follow up something like 'Echoes'? It wasn't an easy question to answer."

One thing that had not changed was Clark's penchant for dating dancing girls or budding actresses. On New Year's Eve, he attended a party in the Hollywood hills hosted by Sharon Garrett, Terri Messina and Adele Yoshioka. Garrett was the most established of the three, already well known as a face about town, having appeared in the film *Beach Party*. Later, she would secure a part in the Elvis Presley movie *Speedway*. She first met Terri Jean Messina (born 17 December 1945) while searching for work on television. "I'd been a dancer and had been working in Mexico City. I met Terri on a commercial where we were riding little motorcycles followed by guys carrying a rug. We'd never done anything like this but we got paid good money for it. I remember freaking out and crying because I ran over a pigeon. We were doing this commercial for three days, and that's how we became friends." Garrett discovered that her new friend came from a respectable family based in Northridge, California and her father, Dr Joseph Messina, was an eminent physician. Seeking suitable accommodation, the girls were directed to a two-storey home in the hills which, they were reliably told, had once been occupied by silent film actor Harold Lloyd. It seemed the perfect setting and they soon settled in. "Terri and I were roommates for a long time and got on extremely well," says Garrett. "She was lovely."

By this point, Garrett was appearing on the Los Angeles-based television music show *Shivaree* taking her place among the go-go dancers who gyrated on elevated platforms behind the bandstand. The Byrds had appeared on the show several times, most notably when Gene sang 'Set You Free This Time'. His showing at the girls' New Year's Eve party was not entirely unexpected as the house had now become a scenesters' favourite. "We certainly enjoyed our time there," says Garrett. "We were all smoking pot, partying and having a good time. We were young and full of life. There were great parties up there and all sorts of people came in and out. We had a view from the hills overlooking the freeway, just across from the Hollywood Bowl. It was a stunning home."

During the festivities, Clark's fancy turned towards Terri Messina. "It transpired we had a lot of mutual friends," she says. "He'd heard about me and the girls. That's why he came to the party. Soon I went out with him, and it lasted about six months. It was pretty heavy." Sharon Garrett felt they were the perfect couple. "She was crazy about him. She was beautiful and charming and all those wonderful words that go along with it, as well as being bright and talented. Those were wonderful times and Terri was absolutely breathtaking and adorable. That's the key word. *Adorable.*"

The romance might have blossomed were it not for Clark's perennial neuroses. For a time, he and Terri frequented local clubs, but he often seemed troubled. Messina was convinced that he still carried a torch for Michelle Phillips, which proved enough to blight their brief affair. They would not meet again for another ten years.

Gene Clark With The Gosdin Brothers emerged in February 1967. In a misguided act of diplomacy, Dickson had allowed the Gosdins equal billing. The record was startling for its time and contained some of Clark's best work, but the sales returns were disappointing. "I'm still a little puzzled by the 100 per cent rejection of the public of that album," says Dickson. "It wasn't great but it was better than most people's albums that did OK. I have no explanation myself except that there was nothing on it quite right enough to have that hit single that he needed." A plausible theory, oft repeated, is that it was released in unintended competition to *Younger Than Yesterday*. Naturally, the Byrds received the lion's share of the publicity and record company commitment, supposedly to Clark's detriment. In later years, Gene used that same argument to explain the album's commercial failure. "Columbia had the Byrds who, despite their problems, were still a major act. And they had Gene Clark, who wasn't that well known. They had to decide which one had the greater potential and which one to back with promotion and exposure, and I fully understand why they chose the Byrds. My album was cut-out almost immediately but I bore the group no grudge. They let me hear *Younger Than Yesterday* after they finished it, but before it was released, and it was so beautiful that I cried."

Clark's magnanimity here sounds suspiciously like a press bite or perhaps we should read more into those tears than mere aesthetic appreciation. The Byrds were in full creative flight at this point, but even their most celebrated work would have benefited from a sprinkling of Clark's old magic. Imagine 'Echoes' as the twelfth track on the Byrds' fourth album and marvel at the prospect. Maybe Clark already had done precisely this and realized the implications. That said, it was simplistic to blame the failure of his album on the Byrds' release schedule. Would Clark have fared much better in a marketplace where the Byrds were silent? It seems doubtful. His debut album, for all its merits, was an unclassifiable record, seemingly pulling in disparate directions. *Younger Than Yesterday* was similarly eclectic but that was the work of four people, not one. In addition, they had a brand name with a history, an important consideration for any vinyl purchaser.

Clark's album introduced a multi-personality whose future direction seemed open-ended. This duality was evinced in the endearingly fustian, self-conscious rear sleeve liner notes which were clearly imitative of Dylan's expositions on *Bringing It All Back Home* and *Highway 61 Revisited.* Clark's began with the line "Within a conglomeration of projections . . ." and spoke of "Night, fog, elementations", as if multi-syllabic words alone could add gravity to his meditations. The rapture ended on a contrasting note of humility – "This is my first album." There, in essence, were the two Gene Clarks – the slightly insecure, over-expressive word poet and the simple country boy. Those same tensions played themselves out on the album with considerable success. 'Think I'm Gonna Feel Better', 'Tried So Hard' and 'Keep On Pushin'' were overly country-flavoured. The latter song, with Doug Dillard on electric banjo, even provided a secret glimpse into what Clark might have sounded like had he joined the Dillards. These songs were far more countrified than Hillman's contemporaneous compositions on *Younger Than Yesterday*, mainly because they had not been pushed through the Byrds' prism in which all styles were transmogrified. They suggested a future direction for Clark in the annals of what would become known as country rock. Confusing matters, Clark also included a couple of fairly dull rockers ('Elevator Operator' and 'Couldn't Believe Her') which sounded like filler. There were also oddities such as 'Is Yours Is Mine', another wordy composition featuring some extended meteorological metaphors. The Gosdin Brothers added crossover pop/country vocals to 'I Found You' and 'Needing Someone' which were attractive, but not riveting. Far better was 'The Same One', one of Clark's best love ballads of the period. Like 'Set You Free This Time' it is a song of loss played out like a session on a psychiatrist's couch. Its lyrical execution is eloquent without being overburdened by metaphor or oblique allusion. There is a sense of wonder and confusion about the suddenness with which a relationship can switch from devotion to abandonment in the space of a day. If this was a country song, it might well have ended with the line, "I think I'll pick myself up – and then I'll leave", but in Clark's metaphysical dimension, it becomes "I'll pick my mind up" as if the relationship has left the narrator mentally torn apart.

Clark addresses the same issue in 'So You Say You Lost Your Baby', an astonishing composition which is transformed into something greater by the expansive orchestration, courtesy of Leon Russell. The song's deceptive title, suggestive of a teen drama circa 1959, swiftly develops into a bizarre fantasy. The lyrical landscape is barely decipherable as Clark sings of 'wind stilts' and 'moon trolls' swallowed up by 'stormy dreams'. There are pilgrims making pledges and visions of an apocalypse in the image of a 'dying sun'. Then again, minus a lyric sheet to clarify the issue, this could also be a 'dying son', alluding to Christ's sacrifice, an interpretation reinforced by the preceding reference to the Tabernacle hillside, with its connotations of Mount Calvary. These were grand allusions in an otherwise deceptively straightforward composition.

The twin assaults of 'Echoes' and 'So You Say You Lost Your Baby' reveal a different path for Clark in striking contrast to 'Tried So Hard' et al. In truth, he represented both of these personae and his debut album indicated that either direction could be mined successfully. It was a dilemma which was played out at various times throughout the duration of his recording life.

There is every evidence that Clark was confident about the direction his new work was taking. Dickson's enthusiastic response to 'Echoes' appears to have inspired both men to take the experiment further. On 24 January, just before the release of

Gene Clark With The Gosdin Brothers, Clark was taken to the LA studio Sound Recorders to work on some songs, privately funded by his mentor. 'Don't Let It Fall Through' is unlike anything Clark had previously recorded, resembling nothing less than a country tune mutated into a Stax dance number. A horn arrangement by Hugh Masekela, fresh from working with the Byrds on 'So You Want To Be A Rock 'n' Roll Star', propels the song but stylistically it is bewildering. Different genres merge, offset by lyrics detached from the musical context. It was typical of Clark to mix the unmixable. Years later he would prove himself equally accepting of such mad scientist experimentation. Within a month of its recording, 'Don't Let It Fall Through' was registered for copyright but, presumably to partly finance this session, Dickson gave the rights to Leon Russell's publishing company, Skyhill Music.

A second song at that January session is of far greater significance. Arranger Leon Russell was once again enlisted to enhance an intriguing opus, mysteriously titled 'Back Street Mirror'. A basic band arrangement, overladen with flutes, trumpets and strings, results in an alluring epic remarkable for its time. This was Clark at his most Dylanesque, albeit many months after the release of *Blonde On Blonde*. There's a touch of 'Desolation Row' in the second verse when he sings of the "Duchess of Sleuth" who kept a booth selling famed quotations. Gene elongates the lyrics in a Dylan drawl, dragging out vowels and stretching multi-syllabic words for emphasis: 'inclinations', 'inspirations', 'exaggerations', 'socialized relations', 'aggravations'. The stress on pluralities adds emphasis. Yet, beneath the bombast lies a simpler love song whose chorus reprises lines familiar to any Byrds fan: "Then I felt about how hard it would be being *here without you*." It is a thrilling juxtaposition.

Clark was never a book reader nor was he known to study poetry but he had a natural ability for constructing rhyme. He also had a highly developed antennae for changes in popular culture and the skills of a first-class imitator when it came to pastiche. He had already assimilated Elvis and the Beatles, and now Dylan was his muse. Unlike Clark, Dylan was widely read and introduced a fresh new vocabulary to popular music which took in influences as diverse as Beat poetry, French symbolism, Russian formalism and the Imagist movement. Dylan could namedrop T.S. Eliot, Ezra Pound or Rimbaud in conversation with Allen Ginsberg and appeared to know what he was talking about. Clark's approach was more intuitive. In forming his poetic vision through the verbal arabesques of Bob Dylan he was connecting links with writers and poets of whom he was unaware. Clark was not attempting to engage the listener's mind in songs like 'Back Street Mirror' as much as relish in the sensory language, the wild images, peculiar rhymes and exotic symbolism that sprung unconsciously from his pen. The challenge in appreciating Clark's 'Dylanesque songs' is not to be found in some hermeneutic resolution of the words and rhythms, but rather in an engagement with a luxuriant, balletic language in which particular, often multi-syllabic, combinations coalesce, offering provocative, evanescent glimpses of meaning that can only be articulated uneasily. Much of the appeal lies in the songs' essential mystery. This was the territory that Clark was now calling his own: there was an indirect trajectory evident from 'The Day Walk' ('The Emptiness') through 'Echoes', 'Back Street Mirror' and beyond.

If Dickson was intent on CBS releasing 'Back Street Mirror', then he must have been severely deflated. There is no evidence that it was ever re-cut at Columbia or discussed as a thrilling new single. In the end, Dickson recycled the elaborate backing track for inclusion on actor David Hemmings' *Happens*, which Jim produced for MGM Records. Clark's original vocal remained in Dickson's archives and was not released until as late as 2016. It was a terrible setback at a crucial point in Clark's career robbing him of the momentum and critical acumen that such an important and ambitious song would have provided.

Clark's promotion of his debut album was half-hearted and restricted to the West Coast where he played with a short-lived backing group, featuring two future Byrds, Clarence White and

John York, plus session drummer Eddie Hoh. As early as their first meeting, York was subject to Clark's quirky sense of humour. "We were out in this parking lot. I had never spoken to Gene before except to say, 'Hi'. He said, 'John, let me give you some advice.' I thought, 'Wow. Gene Clark's going to give me some advice, I'd better pay attention.' He looked me right in the eye and said, 'Never, ever, get a blow job right before the gig.'" Whether York took the advice is not known, but he was always amused by Clark's Lennonesque wit.

Billed as the Gene Clark Group, the quartet proved short-lived. "My memory of that combination is that we just played one weekend," says York. "I just remember us at the Whisky. We practised a bunch of songs, probably for several afternoons. My main memory was that all the tables at the front were occupied by these boorish record company people. They were there to see somebody else. I don't think Gene was the headliner. They just talked through the whole show. At a certain point, Gene turned around and said, 'That's it, just jam!' And he started playing an *E* chord. We played a blues for about 20 minutes and that was the show."

The sorry spectacle was symbolic of the state of Clark's career at the time. His reluctance to tour hardly helped his prospects in the marketplace, but he continued his plan to write something substantial. "I used to lock myself in my house and just work on songs for days," he admitted. This was no idle boast. Although Clark was effectively off the radar for most of 1967, this period turned out to be one of the most productive of his entire career.

During the spring, he submitted a seven-song tape to Dickson, the contents of which were strong enough to suggest another great album was imminent. The reel comprised: 'Whatever', 'One Way Road', 'Bakersfield Train', 'Got To Get You Off My Mind', 'Back Street Mirror', 'Down On The Pier' and 'Only Colombe'. These compositions developed themes from his first album. The opening 'Whatever' addresses a love rival, pre-empting a future song with the words "it's true that she is *like no other*" and using familiar inversions ("the way I care I'll always show her"); 'One

Way Road' and 'Got To Get You Off My Mind' are similar, both alluding to losing your mind over an abandoned love; 'Bakersfield Train' imagines the narrator addressing a friend about another doomed relationship, yet "lighting another dream" when seeing each passing station along the journey. There is also a powerful, almost suicidal, threat to lay down on the tracks rather than to hear that the lost love no longer thinks of him. These relatively straightforward compositions pale alongside the final three songs which feature words worthy of 'Echoes'. 'Back Street Mirror' remains a standout and, with the Leon Russell arrangement already recorded back in January, became a key part of this showreel. Clark no doubt also had Russell in mind for the final two songs, both of which beg for a full-scale production. 'Down On The Pier', replete with melodic echoes of the Beatles' 'Norwegian Wood' via Dylan's '4th Time Around', is another abstruse lyric, with obscure allusions to Dianna and Stell in Heartbreak Hotel (note the Elvis reference) looking to free the dying thieves from shock. A pervading sense of loneliness hangs over the composition, as indeed it does in the great 'Heartbreak Hotel', with Clark's narrator trapped all day in a room while broken plaster falls on the bed where his love should be. If 'Down On The Pier' is bleak, then 'Only Colombe' is rhapsodic by comparison. The siren song of Colombe is set against some of the most lavish imagery Clark ever conjured. The original lyric, later slightly amended, speaks of the warm wind that "will not *howl* tonight", before moving into images of a sea voyage reinforced by Dylanesque pronouncements ("paralytic agencies twist their tongues into philosophies") that inflate the narrator's sentiments. The real mystery is the nature of the siren song that Colombe wails which may be for someone who brings her "her everything".

As if this wasn't enough, Clark submitted five more songs that spring, including 'Translations', 'I Just Like You' (aka 'It's Easy Now'), 'I Am Without You', 'So Much More' and 'Don't Know What You Want'. Clark now had in excess of an album's worth of original compositions ready to record for a follow-up to *Gene Clark With The Gosdin Brothers*. Unfortunately, CBS' interest was waning. President Clive Davis wrote to Eddie Tickner after hearing *Younger Than Yesterday* and congratulated the Byrds who were back in the US single charts with 'So You Want To Be A Rock 'n' Roll Star' and 'My Back Pages'. But there were no kind words for Gene Clark from the record company hierarchy or marketing men. In what seemed a premature decision, the label was already considering cutting their losses on the former Byrd. Rather than committing to an album, they were willing only to allow Clark a shot at a single, employing the orchestral trappings favoured on 'Echoes'. Unfortunately, they vetoed Dickson's recordings of 'Back Street Mirror' and 'Don't Let It Fall Through' as source material. Instead, Clark covered Canadian songwriter Ian Tyson's 'The French Girl', backed with his own lyrically complex 'Only Colombe'. It may have been a logical commercial decision to make 'The French Girl' an A-side, but it was a slight to Clark as a songwriter. Instead of hiring Leon Russell, as Clark and Dickson wished, executive director Gary Usher employed the talented Curt Boettcher, who had recently enjoyed success working with the Association. The songs were given the 'Leon Russell treatment' with harpsichord and orchestration, but there was a general sense that they weren't working as well as expected. In the end, it hardly mattered as the single was abruptly cancelled. Clark was dropped from the label with unseemly haste. Those two songs would remain in the vaults unheard for the next 24 years. CBS abandoned Clark at what seemed the height of his creative powers. He had been writing at a furious pace, worthy of Dylan, in one of rock music's most important and celebrated years. Yet, there was no longer an outlet for his prolific output. He was lost and would never fully recover his confidence after this grand fall.

Clark was the first of a new generation of songwriters to emerge from the fractured remnants of America's most successful mid-Sixties groups. Before long the list would include David Crosby, John Sebastian, Stephen Stills, Neil Young, John Phillips, Mike Nesmith, and many more. In 1967, however, solo singer-songwriters were greeted with caution. Clark was ahead of them all and, in different circumstances, his historical and cultural significance might have been cemented by the appearance of a second solo album. Despite his phenomenal catalogue, that moment passed. Although Clark was a pioneer, his track record made him appear a liability. His commercially unsuccessful debut album, on-off relationship with the Byrds, and obvious reluctance to tour all weighed against record company largesse or long-term commitment.

Worse followed when he defected from his mentors, Jim Dickson and Eddie Tickner. In reality, he would continue to remain close to them for the remainder of his life, but in the summer of 1967 changes were afoot. David Crosby had persuaded the Byrds to appoint Larry Spector as their new manager and Gene soon followed suit. No longer signed to a record company, Clark needed to attract attention. Spector jointly owned (with Hugh Masekela and Peter Fonda) a small custom record label, Chisa, which they agreed to use as a shop-window for Clark's songs. A number of promotional acetates were pressed of 'Yesterday, Am I Right', an uncopyrighted song that sounds as if it was recorded with Dickson and Russell back in January. In common with 'Don't Let It Fall Through' it features Masekela's distinctive horn arrangements and the production is strong. Those Dickson sessions were the best quality recordings available to Gene at this time, but none of the other companies seemed interested. If CBS had deemed Clark expendable after one album, who else would risk taking him on?

Remarkably, Clark had yet more material that he wished to commit to tape. Unfortunately, Spector was not in a position to finance a session as Dickson had done earlier. Instead, Clark approached Alex Del Zoppo, a keyboard player for LA band Sweetwater and a regular habitué of the Whisky. He agreed to help, assisted by some local players recruited at short notice. Under-rehearsed and lacking a producer, they completed a crude, yet revealing, eight-song acetate. Two of the songs, 'One Way Road' and 'Down On The Pier', had previously been taped in the spring. The former includes some striking chord patterns and an attractive melody. 'Down On The Pier' is newly enhanced by a steam organ, creating a circus feel, possibly inspired by the Beatles' 'Being For The Benefit Of Mr Kite'. The string-laden 'That's Alright By Me' and a denuded version of 'Yesterday, Am I Right' both sound exceptionally good. 'On Her Own' features an unnamed drummer pounding away, high in the mix, and lyrics that reveal an unfathomable depression. 'Past Tense', an observational piece on male pride, introduces Del Zoppo's electric piano. The thrilling 'Past My Door' begins in a high register, with Clark struggling to stay in key. Multi-syllabic lyrics ("blackboard explanations . . . trial examinations . . . temperature relations") again testify to Dylan's influence. Midway through, there is a sudden change of tempo, as if Clark is preparing to perform a different song or transform the composition into an elaborate suite. There is no narrative structure, just a series of disconnected images, but it is among the most intriguing compositions here. The acetate closes with the longest track, '7.30 Mode', another lyrically complex work in which plentiful adverbs intoxicate then overwhelm the listener. Clark presents a carnival of colour (shadowed blues, purple changing into blackness, grey transforming into thought) and sound (the wind's "harmonic whine", notes blown until they themselves are 'unabled'). Heavily influenced by Dylan, he introduces his own mysterious cast list à la 'Desolation Row' – the Love Man, the Flying Dutchman, Teresa and Aunt Marie. He even borrows Dylan's 'ragman' from 'Stuck Inside Of Mobile With The Memphis Blues Again' who haunts or is haunted by the same streets as the narrator in 'Echoes'. The abstruse imagery is leavened by a deceptively simple country guitar and harmonica accompaniment.

Overall, these songs were impressive, but the recording sounded inchoate in places and badly in need of an experienced producer. For reasons best known to himself, Clark provided the white label acetate with a winsome title, *Gene Clark Sings For You*, as if it was some birthday or Christmas gift. Given its questionable production quality, it seems unlikely that it was hawked around many major record labels. Tellingly, six of its eight songs were not even registered for copyright at the time. Morale must have been at a serious low.

The celebrated Summer of Love had passed Gene Clark in an instant. He had not attended the Monterey Pop Festival where the Byrds played a contentious but riveting set, assisted in part by Hugh Masekela, guesting on 'So You Want To Be A Rock 'n' Roll Star'. David Crosby had appeared onstage with the Buffalo Springfield, adding tension and political intrigue to the event. The festival closed with an anti-climactic performance from the Mamas & The Papas, still recovering from the ructions caused by Clark's brief affair with Michelle Phillips. These happenings merely underlined the extent of his fall. While the rock music aristocracy of Los Angeles and San Francisco gathered in celebration, eagerly viewed by rapacious record company executives, Gene Clark was the forgotten man, now reduced to producing desultory demo tapes that few would ever hear. His only other outside project at this point was composing the music for *Marijuana*, an educational film, narrated by Sonny Bono, that warned of the dangers of drugs. Clark's basic score was played by Spector's aspiring clients Things To Come, with Gene blowing into a harmonica on the recording. This was a long way down from his heights as a pop star in 1965–66. He desperately needed a way back.

During the autumn, David Crosby was ousted from the Byrds and, after this political coup, Clark was unexpectedly reinstated. It was a year since he had appeared onstage with the group at the Whisky in what some had vainly hoped would be a permanent reunion. Back then, Clark still had enough publishing money to feel secure, not to mention an impressive solo deal with CBS. These were leaner times and minus record company support or live work, the lure of the Byrds was irresistible.

As described in *Volume 1*, the entire debacle lasted less than a month. The group had almost completed *The Notorious Byrd Brothers* and did not require Clark's creativity in the studio. His name is not listed on any studio logs for the album, although he was interested enough to attend one late-night playback of some tracks, listening to the vocal parts from their forthcoming single, 'Goin' Back'. Additionally, McGuinn claims that Gene actually co-wrote the closing song on side one: 'Get To You'. If we are to believe McGuinn's belated account, an administrative error caused Hillman to be credited in Gene's place. Hillman has no memory of Clark contributing to the song and this story was not mentioned by anyone during the Byrds' lifetime. Tellingly, the credits were never contested by Clark and the copyright details of McGuinn/Hillman remain unchanged to this day. No doubt Clark would have been a strong songwriting presence had he persevered with the Byrds during this fractious time, but he was soon overtaken by events. Clark had convinced himself that he could undertake a short East Coast tour, but even that proved beyond his capacity. In Minneapolis he suffered a panic attack that sounded like a re-run of the nervous breakdown experienced in early 1966. Beaten and humiliated, he returned to Los Angeles. At that moment, his future resembled a closed book.

Back in Missouri, Jack Godden, one of his closest childhood friends, was preparing to visit California. Having heard that Clark was back in the Byrds, he obtained an address in Laurel Canyon and appeared at his door. There was to be no grand reunion. "For some reason, he didn't want to see me. I don't know if he was high on drugs. I was only at his door for five minutes. A woman – I don't know if she was a maid or not – told me he didn't want to see me. I couldn't believe it. I said, 'Well, if he refuses to see me, that's fine!' I was really hurt by it. And I just walked off. To this day I have no idea why he wouldn't see me. When you get to be a big shot with money and everything else, it can turn you. I guess it changed him. I heard he didn't even help his brothers or sisters or his family when he got all that money. His family were very Christian. They loved Gene more than the world. So, I don't know what happened. Maybe it was the drugs, but I'm not sure." Godden would never see his old friend again.

By early 1968, Clark was cut adrift. Larry Spector was negotiating a lucrative new contract with CBS for himself and the Byrds, his last meaningful act on behalf of the group, who had recently added another of his clients, Gram Parsons, to their depleted ranks. Clark was also terminating links with Spector meaning he was now without a publishing or record company deal.

There was a pervasive sense among the rock hierarchy that the psychedelic experimentation of 1967 had perhaps run its course. A 'back to the roots' mentality was gathering momentum. The Beatles had confined *Sgt Pepper's* to the Summer of Love and, as early as March 1968, were topping the UK charts with 'Lady Madonna', a wish-fulfilling attempt to record a genuine rock 'n' roll record, pre-empting the self-explanatory 'Get Back'. The Stones had also disavowed the psych posturing of *Their Satanic Majesties Request* in favour of the riff-driven 'Jumpin' Jack Flash' and the earthy *Beggars Banquet*. As ever, Bob Dylan was leading the charge. At the start of the year CBS released *John Wesley Harding*, a stark declaration, infused with biblical imagery, outlaw allegory and a landscape variously populated by the socially disadvantaged – the hobo, the drifter and the immigrant. After the electric maelstrom of 1966's *Blonde On Blonde*, its austere, acoustic setting was both challenging and prescriptive. If Dylan was seeking salvation in old wisdom so too were the Band with *Music From Big Pink*, which included the master's 'Tears Of Rage' and 'I Shall Be Released', both later recorded by Clark. The Byrds, meanwhile, had made their way to Nashville for *Sweetheart Of The Rodeo*.

These developments were enough for Clark to take stock and consider a similar retro route. For all their ambition, songs such as 'Back Street Mirror' and 'Only Colombe' had proven commercial dead-ends, not even achieving a release under his name. Perhaps something starker, straightforward or traditional was required. Clark pondered these questions while frequenting his favoured Hollywood haunts. He still saw himself primarily as a songwriter, but he had never been afraid to collaborate with like-minded souls. That was how he had first connected with McGuinn. His recent work with Ritchie Lewis and even the Cookie Fairies had demonstrated a willingness for teamwork with newcomers or unknowns. If current trends suggested a return to the backwoods, then Clark was more than ready to follow the examples of Dylan, the Band and the Byrds. He had some grounding in country music and a particular affection for the rockabilly stylings of his youth. He would always retain a love for the work of Roy Orbison and Elvis Presley. Within a year he would record his own version of Presley's 1956 chart-topping 'Don't Be Cruel'. Here was a direction that promised fun and satisfaction.

Nobody can confirm whether Clark ever co-wrote with H.P. 'Mac' McClanahan. If it happened, the collaboration was timely. A rockabilly revivalist of note, McClanahan was based in La Junta, Colorado, where his group Mac McClanahan & the Rhythm Busters had a residency at the Country Club. The venue's proprietor Ole Rutherford had established the short-lived Tiger Records to promote his acts. Their fourth release was 'That Nonsense Stuff' b/w 'No Sweeter Love' – both Clark/McClanahan contributions. The A-side, with prominent double bass and piano, has an air of Fifties teen machismo. The recording became a cult classic in rockabilly circles, as much for its rarity as its quality. Perhaps the teaming was nothing more than a chance encounter or an epistolary or phone connection, in common with the similarly obscure Ritchie Lewis collaborations. Or was it, as seems more likely, another Gene Clark? Who knows? Both songs are still registered at the Library of Congress under the name 'Gene Clark (aka Harold Eugene Clark)'. Confusingly, BMI credit the co-composer as Roy Eugene Clark. Years later, the publishing rights on both compositions were assigned to the Gene Clark estate, where they remain to this day.

After leaving Spector, Clark sought the counsel of Eddie Tickner. Unexpectedly, there was a new deal on the table, courtesy of A&M Records, whose titular head Jerry Moss was about to take the label into the uncharted area of what would become known as country rock. Moss appreciated Clark's songwriting and status as a former Byrd and was willing to persevere with the artiste over several albums. In the meantime, Clark had found another obscure collaborator, Laramy Smith. During preliminary sessions at A&M, Smith put together a group conveniently titled Phoenix, as if their remit was to summon a former Byrd from the flames of anonymity. Clark put the group on salary and completed work on two Smith songs: 'Los Angeles' and 'Line Down The Middle'. The first remained in the vaults for 30 years and the latter was half-heartedly issued as a single much later, without Smith's consent, under the revised title, 'Lyin' Down The Middle'. "I wrote the song in January 1968," Smith confirms, "while I was leaving Woodstock where I lived for a year. When I hit the road I wrote songs while I was driving. The song is about the dotted line that runs down the middle of the road on Highway 80 from the East to the West Coast . . . I was going to LA to join Gene Clark and form a new group with him at A&M." Two further recordings, a shorter version of the Clark rarity 'That's Alright By Me' and a reading of Dylan's 'I Pity The Poor Immigrant' from *John Wesley Harding*, completed these sessions. The experiment was discontinued due to personal and musical differences. "I wanted to do mainly country rock and Gene wanted mainly folk and bluegrass material," Smith concludes. There would be no reunion.

While this latest collaboration failed to take flight, Clark was surprised to hear that one of his protégés was about to include a couple of his compositions on their debut album. He had first encountered the members of the Rose Garden during a showcase at the Ash Grove and even offered to manage them, before thinking better of the idea. They had since found a new singer and signed with Charlie Greene and Brian Stone, managers of the Byrds' perennial rivals, Sonny & Cher and Buffalo Springfield. Now they had a deal with Atco Records. Gene had given them an acetate featuring several of his compositions, notably 'Long Time', which they included on the album, along with 'Till Today', whose melody was partly inspired by the Fortunes' 1965 hit 'You've Got Your Troubles'. In a gesture of solidarity, he attended the session and played on the recording, just as he had done with the Cookie Fairies. The album was hardly a hit but he was always pleased to boost his reputation as a songwriter.

Around the same time, there was another strange interlude with some old friends. Clark unexpectedly appeared onstage with the Gram Parsons-era Byrds at Derek Taylor's 'Farewell To Hollywood' party at Ciro's in March 1968. He resembled a soul in torment – over-eager to please, stumbling drunk and more than a little embarrassing. In the end, he fell down onstage, much to everyone's amazement, not least the Byrds' roadie, Jim Seiter, who was obliged to intervene. "He tripped over an amplifier and fell flat on his back and knocked some other stuff over. He was just lying there looking at the ceiling. I walked over and asked him if he was OK. He didn't say a word and had this terrible stare. I thought, 'Is this guy dead?' Then he got up, walked past me, jumped off the stage and was out the door and gone." So ended the briefest Byrds' reunion of Clark's career.

Musically, Gene needed to find some new ideas and a fresh collaborator to work with for his forthcoming A&M album. He discovered the perfect foil in Doug Dillard, who had recently toured with the Byrds in Europe and was now ready to connect with Clark on a work combining bluegrass, folk, pop and rock. The pair had first met in 1963 when Clark was still in the New Christy Minstrels. It soon emerged that they had much in common. Both hailed from Missouri and, after moving to Hollywood, ended up working with Jim Dickson at World-Pacific. Dickson had produced albums for the Dillards and Doug subsequently appeared on Gene's first solo long player. Unusually, both had left a successful group for an uncertain future at a time when such defections were considered career threatening. Lastly, and not insignificantly, they displayed a carefree attitude towards drink and drugs and liked to indulge for fun.

Dillard was living in a house in Beachwood Canyon, which became a jamming haven for friends and fellow musicians. The talented Bernie Leadon, an alumnus of the Scottsville Squirrel

Barkers and Hearts And Flowers, was sleeping on Doug's couch and trading banjo licks with his host when Clark came by with pages of lyrics, some of which fitted nicely with their bluegrass instrumentals. Over time, the project developed into an ad hoc group, with Clark recruiting a couple of additional players.

David Jackson had worked as house bassist at the Troubadour and backed Bob Gibson and Hoyt Axton, among others. "I'd been on *The Andy Williams Show* for three years and I'd been hanging out with the Dillards on the folk scene in LA since 1963," he says. One evening, Jackson noticed a guy with a hangdog expression shyly approaching. His eyes were lowered and he was staring tentatively like someone peering above half-rimmed, bifocal glasses. It was Gene Clark. Behind him was the more familiar face of Doug Dillard. "They said, 'We want to get together and play something.' It wasn't, 'Would you like to join a band?' Nothing was very specific. They were talking and smoking cigarettes while looking around the room. There were these long pauses between words and it was a little bit bizarre. I didn't know what to make of it. Gene's approach was very secretive and I never got a formal invitation to be in the band. We just started getting together at Doug's house on Beachwood Canyon. To my recollection, nobody ever called a rehearsal. These gatherings simply occurred. We all showed up and started making this phenomenal music. I was never privy to any of their business discussions and never heard a word about any record deal. Gene would usually come in with the basic idea of a song and by the end of the week there'd be three or four songs finalized. Gene didn't pigeonhole any of his work. He just allowed it to be free. That's the reason why he and Doug Dillard got together. It was very organic. Their attitude was 'Let's get a bass player and a guitar player' and there it was, without any effort really." The line-up was completed by mandolinist/dobro player Don Beck. This enterprise was given the provisional name: the Dillard & Clark Expedition.

Those fortunate enough to attend the musical evenings at Beachwood Canyon still speak with reverence about the quality of the performances and sense of possibility in this strange adventure. It was like hearing back porch bluegrass fused with a modern sensibility, reinforced by Clark's reflective lyrics. The words were less opaque than those heard on parts of his solo album, but no less powerful.

David Jackson's favourite memory of those get-togethers is crystallized in a lost moment of time. "We'd been playing for weeks. The sun was low and streaming in the window. Gene had the core of a song. A partial version. An idea. He was sitting on a couch playing it over and over. He'd take a break here and there, say a few things, then pick up the guitar and continue. As the day wore on, we each learned something new about this tune, as would he. Just before sundown, he had the first and second verses and two or three lines of the third. He was missing a line. The knot wasn't firm. Now he's sitting on the couch, Dillard to his right, Bernie on a chair at Gene's knee and I'm standing in the remaining quadrant with my upright bass. Gene starts the intro, which we'd played six or seven times, then he sings the verses and we go into the chorus. He comes to the third verse, then reaches that missing line and somehow ties it all together. The chorus is sung for the last time. It's gloriously beautiful. As we sing the last line and hit the last note, we lean in and our heads are very close and we're looking down. The cohesion of those voices is spectacular. I raise my head for a split second and I see a puff of smoke go up from the centre of all four heads. Everyone knew that was *the* moment. It was perfect. And the song never got played again. It never resurfaced to my knowledge. Maybe Gene sang it somewhere else, but it never reoccurred with Dillard & Clark."

Producer Larry Marks, who had also worked on *Gene Clark With The Gosdin Brothers*, recorded the group at A&M, carefully replicating the relaxed, creative atmosphere previously heard in Beachwood Canyon. "We went into the studio, sat in a circle and played the damn thing," Jackson notes. "Larry did a superb job. I always found him nothing less than supportive. He had a delightful countenance and was never derogatory to anyone in any fashion for any reason. He always allowed the players to be as musical as they possibly could be. He didn't force his ideas on anybody. He just became part of the music."

Sessions for the Dillard & Clark album continued into the autumn, interrupted momentarily by news that A&M required Clark's services on a different studio project. In their quest for modernity, the label had signed singer-songwriter John Braden, whose picturesque debut album, co-produced by the young publicist Michael Vosse, was scheduled for release shortly after Dillard & Clark's in the New Year. Already, some people in the company had expressed reservations about Braden's high-pitched vocal style, and A&M's publishing arm felt he might fare better as a songwriter. Seeking a more suitable voice to promote his demos they invited Clark to record some songs from Braden's still unreleased album. After the Dillard & Clark sessions, Clark felt free to contribute. 'Baptist Funeral' was a strong story song with a Southern edge; 'Ribbons Of Friendship', with guitarist Bruce Langhorne and Burrito Brother bassist Chris Ethridge, included a horn ensemble and string quartet; the Jacques Brel-style 'Song To Raymondo', the most intriguing of the selections, featured a pedal-steel arrangement by Sneaky Pete Kleinow, amid a circus atmosphere. Unfortunately, few ran to cover the compositions, not even Clark himself. Braden's album, which included all of these songs, was issued several months later, but sold poorly and he was dropped from the label.

Throughout this time, Doug Dillard continued picking and grinning, always ready to join anyone's party. "We ran in the same circles and he was such a delightful guy," says David Jackson. "I always considered Doug a friend, not a father figure, more of a wild uncle. He was always very supportive and very musical – still the most eclectic person I've ever met. He was amazing. He was on the match and welcomed everywhere. He definitely had a backstage pass to life at that point. Everybody wanted him around. So we found ourselves at a lot of parties and gatherings. No one would call. We would just convene."

The players were at their pioneering best during this fertile period, as evidenced by *The Fantastic Expedition Of Dillard & Clark.* It arrived in November 1968, less than three months after *Sweetheart Of The Rodeo* and three months ahead of the Flying Burrito Brothers' debut. In common with their fellow travellers' forays into what might very loosely be termed 'country rock', Dillard & Clark won favourable reviews, but sold few records. Gene would soon discover that his latest musical dream was a hard sell. "What do you do with contemporary bluegrass in 1968?", he pondered, many years later, wise after the event.

The Fantastic Expedition. . . is a groundbreaking album partly because of a lack of self-consciousness in its experimentation. The work features eight Clark originals, several written with future Eagle, Bernie Leadon. 'Train Leaves Here This Morning' would reappear on the Eagles' debut album four years later, predictably at a time when Clark was moving away from country-tinged rock. Most of the remaining tracks are of an exceptionally high standard: 'With Care From Someone' offers strong harmonies, lead banjo-playing, an enticing harmonica accompaniment and an infectious melody reminiscent of 'A Taste Of Honey'; 'The Radio Song' brings the harpsichord to country/bluegrass, an eminently suitable instrument for Clark's Elizabethan melancholia; 'She Darked The Sun' features another sprightly banjo accompaniment from Dillard, which contrasts well with Clark's icy, bitter lyrics; 'Something's Wrong', nostalgic and gently sad, anticipates the ecological protests of the Seventies; and the quasi-philosophical 'In The Plan' is surely the first 'cosmic country' outing. Clark's compositions are complemented by several bluegrass excursions, including a spirited reworking of Lester Flatt's 'Git It On Brother'. With A&M keen to promote a single as the opening cut, Dillard & Clark had returned to the studio late in the sessions for 'Out On The Side', adding organ and drums for a fuller sound, reminiscent of the Band. Clark is at his brooding best here, remorseful and reflective, like a penitent about to enter the confessional box.

One of the album's triumphs is its fearless merging of different musical genres. Clark never felt confined by tradition. Bluegrass and baroque were no more incongruous to his sensibilities than the combination of country and gospel on the later *No Other* or balladry and disco on *McGuinn, Clark & Hillman*. Faced with innovative suggestions, Clark always played the pioneer. It was instinctive.

With hindsight, the purity of *The Fantastic Expedition . . .* lies in Gene's willingness to allow the players to express themselves. He could have been more dictatorial, but regarded the record as a group effort. Dillard's contribution is exemplary. His daring use of banjo as a lead instrument is almost in defiance of rock traditions. Several songs here could have been played note for note on McGuinn's Rickenbacker and listeners would have called them minor Byrds' classics. With Dillard & Clark, the tunes exist in a different format that is even more startling because it is not folk, bluegrass or country, but an almost unclassifiable amalgam of all these influences and more.

Doug and Gene were symbiotic characters united by music, geographical location and hedonistic hijinks, but there were also key differences in their world views. "They were two sides of a coin," David Jackson says. "It seemed so logical for these two disparate people to spend so much time together. But they were different personalities. I never got the impression that Doug searched out anything. Life came to him and he accepted whatever was in front of him and rolled with the flow. Gene had a darker side. I was a bit starstruck of Gene, not because of his fame, but his talent. Then and now, my favourite art is songwriting. I've always been astonished by the great songwriters, not necessarily the famous ones, but always the great ones. If they were architects, their buildings would be skyscrapers. Even the small songs are so valuable. To pull something so insanely beautiful that speaks so deeply out of thin air, it's just an astonishing quality. So I was always agog at Gene's poetry. I liked that you used the Elizabethan word in describing Gene because it's absolutely true. There's always been a depth in his demeanour, his attitude, his melodies, his lyrics, and everything about him."

The group promoted their album with a limited number of

performances, notably an infamous residency at the Troubadour in Hollywood from 17–22 December. Michael Clarke was invited to join the group, returning from Hawaii, where he had been in relative hibernation since leaving the Byrds at the end of 1967. Evidently, he was not available or missing at the start of the residency. "There was no drummer at the opening night at the Troubadour," Jackson insists. "It was the acoustic band. I played upright bass. If there'd been a drummer I would have played electric. So there was no drums. I am adamant in my recollection of that." The band certainly needed a drummer to provide a backbeat, not least because they had failed to rehearse adequately, relying instead on the impromptu playing that had served them so well back at Beachwood Canyon. That might have proven enough were it not for the antics of Doug and Gene who went on a bender earlier that day, much to everyone's horrified amazement.

It was late afternoon, after their soundcheck, that the two compatriots elected to loosen up by visiting the nearby Italian restaurant, Dan Tana's. The rest of the band were elsewhere. "Everything was fine at the soundcheck," Jackson remembers. "I went home, took a nap, had something to eat, had a shower then drove back to the Troubadour and arrived about eight o'clock. When I walked in, somebody said, 'You need to get over to Dan Tana's. They're drinking martinis and they've dropped acid.' " Jackson was shocked by their state and knew that there was no time to undo the effects of the lethal LSD/martini combination. "I don't remember how we even got them out of Dan Tana's." The pair were still disorientated when they took the stage in front of their home crowd. Clark had evidently lost his bearings, as the audience looked on, perplexed. "He was sitting on his amp facing the back wall," says Jackson. "He should have been in the middle singing. When the lights came up, Dillard said to me, 'You know the bass player does all the talking.' That completely threw me. It had never been discussed who was to be the spokesman for the band. The stage act had never been talked about and there was Gene, still sitting on the amp. We somehow got through the first tune. Doug was supposed to play fiddle on the next number. He puts down his banjo and somehow gets Gene up to the mike. Doug has his fiddle and a big grin on his face. At the end of the tune, as we were rolling the chord, Doug puts his fiddle on the ground, jumps in the air and smashes it. Don Beck, who was on my left, a delightful little religious guy, very spiritual, looked at me with his mandolin in his hand, and said: 'Well, that's enough for me.' He grabbed his dobro and mandolin and walked off the stage. That's the end of the second song and it's my job to speak to the audience. Can you imagine? I learned a great deal from that night."

The evening was partly rescued by the presence of a pick-up drummer, Jon Corneal, a Florida native who had previously worked with Gram Parsons in the International Submarine Band and was hoping to secure a permanent spot with the Flying Burrito Brothers. "I was hanging out at the Troubadour bar," he recalls. "Gene knew who I was and he said, 'Hey, man, you got any drums with you?' They didn't have a drummer at the time. I told him I could probably scrape up a snare drum and sticks from my wagon. He said, 'Go get it and sit in with us.' So I did for that night. That was the time they dropped mescaline and did the whole set like a medley. They'd do two or three bars of each song. It wasn't supposed to be that way! They waltzed through that set so quickly. Doug and Gene were looking at each other real strange and they started walking off the stage. That's when Doug stepped right in the middle of his fiddle. He had it on the floor and forgot and broke it in half. I was just sitting there on a chair behind that snare drum with sticks and brushes. Bernie Leadon was on the bandstand too and we were saying, 'What is going on? What is this all about?'" When they reached the dressing room, they were reprimanded by the Troubadour's owner Doug Weston who told them, "You're going to be here tomorrow night and if you guys screw up on anything, it's over, and I'll never book you here again." As Corneal concludes: "After that they pretty much tried to refrain from the psychedelics."

Michael Clarke appeared on drums for the remainder of the

residency which went well enough to secure some positive comments from the local underground press. Backstage, Eddie Tickner, who had helped with the bookings and business management, seemed relieved that they had got through the week without any further hitches. "We all got paid," recalls Jackson, with retrospective relief. "Eddie had a stack of bills and he was up in the dressing room counting these off and paying everybody. A $20 bill fell off the top of the stack and I've always been impressed by the fact that it did not fall more than about three inches before he snapped it out of mid-air."

With Christmas only three days away, the payday was welcomed. While others rushed off to their homes and family, Clark was still keen to celebrate his good fortune and decided to drive to Las Vegas in his Ferrari. Jackson was invited to tag along. "I don't know why he chose me to go with him, but we went to Las Vegas. He drove 160 mph the entire way. We saw cops sitting on the side of the road. They never even turned on their lights because they knew they couldn't catch him. Gene could always just take off and do something bizarre."

A&M were keen for Dillard & Clark to tour, but Gene remained resistant, for the present. Then he came up with the concept of a 'train tour' across the States. "Years before, another large group had taken such a trip," says Jackson. "Gene talked about train companies. His idea was that we'd have a box car with a side that folded down and became a stage with a sound system and backline. So when we'd come up to a railway station people could come to the concert. Then we'd fold the damn thing up and move on to the next town." Financially, the concept didn't make much sense and was never acted upon. Coincidentally, Gram Parsons had a similar idea at the time, although his suggestion was simply to travel by train, not play dates at railway stations. In February 1969, fellow A&M act the Flying Burrito Brothers made it happen, although they were still required to fly for most of the trip. They brought along an extra passenger too. Convinced that the Burritos were a better bet and a more appropriate vehicle for his playing style, Michael Clarke defected from

Dillard & Clark, leaving them without a drummer. In came Jon Corneal, who had deputized for the missing Clarke at the Troubadour in December. Most agreed that he was more of a country drummer and better suited to their lighter style.

Meanwhile, A&M faced the dilemma of promoting the group adequately. Still hoping for a hit single, they issued 'Lyin' Down The Middle', the Clark/Laramy Smith collaboration from the previous year. With piano accompaniment from Earl Ball, it was an easy-going road song, most notable for some Everly Brothers' 'Wake Up Little Susie' guitar flourishes. The surprise B-side was 'Don't Be Cruel', sung by Clark in his best Elvis impersonator voice. It provided a secret glimpse into what he must have sounded like back in the pre-Byrds era, when he performed the song with the Sharks. The single bombed and like other Dillard & Clark singles from this period did not even receive a release in Europe, where *The Fantastic Expedition* . . . also remained an expensive import until it was belatedly issued in the summer. The same fate befell 'Why Not Your Baby', a more conscious attempt at radio friendliness with a lush string arrangement similar in style to those used on Glen Campbell's contemporaneous covers of Jimmy Webb. Clark sang beautifully, but few heard his efforts.

'Why Not Your Baby' revealed further changes in the ranks. Doug Dillard had brought in his girlfriend Donna Washburn as an additional singer. Blonde, beautiful and rumoured to be from a wealthy background, the gossip among the group was that she was the daughter of the president of the 7-Up mineral company, although nobody knew for sure. "That was the story we got," Corneal confirms. "She had a brand new pink Mustang convertible. A really nice car. Then she bought a Washburn guitar, same as her name. I guess she could afford any guitar she wanted, but we didn't see it that way. She was nice. She tried to fit in and be one of us. She was enjoying it. You didn't get any 'Big rich me, and nobody you'. She didn't put out that vibe at all."

Bernie Leadon also found her attractive and engaging, but she placed him in an awkward position after taking on the third harmony part. "That was a problem for Bernie," Corneal notes succinctly. Indeed, Leadon was so intimidated that he could no longer see a place for himself in the set-up and abruptly quit, later joining the Flying Burrito Brothers.

Despite the recent disruptions, Corneal saw no trouble ahead and enjoyed socializing with Dillard & Clark. "I liked Gene. He was what we call 'real people'. I had fun with him. We were all the same kind of alcoholics – Doug and Gene and I, and the actor Harry Dean Stanton. Harry loved to pick and sing. When we'd get together at Doug's house, we'd have these acoustic jams. I'd bring a snare drum over and we'd drink beer, play and have fun. Then we'd go places and drink Bloody Marys in the morning." A favourite spot was the Hamburger Hamlet, originally on the Sunset Strip. Chris Hillman remembers seeing them around 10.30 am one morning, imbibing martinis without a care.

A surprise visitor during this transitional period was David Clark, who had hitchhiked from Kansas in a determined attempt to reconnect with his long absent brother. It had been an arduous trek, the lowlight of which was several days spent in a jail cell in Mojave, Utah, for driving a woman's car without a proper licence. After arriving in Hollywood, David phoned Gene, only to be cross-examined by his housekeeper, who demanded proof of identity. When Gene learned that the caller had mentioned 'Big Chief Hole In The Pants', a nonsense song from the Swope Park days, he took off in his Ferrari and picked David up. It was a happy reunion with the added appeal of seeing his younger brother in the alien context of Hollywood. David stayed for several weeks during which he hung out with the musicians at the local clubs, attended some recording sessions and met several stars. He even encountered Bob Dylan. "Gene was in a booth at the Troubadour surrounded by all these crazy people and cheeky women. Bob Dylan walked in, came up and said hello to Gene. I was introduced to him and he acted like, 'So what?' I don't think he even said, 'Hi'. He just nodded. Dylan was super cool and super loaded at that point."

Recordings were underway for a second album, but the general feeling was one of progress interrupted. The first song attempted was Don Reno and Red Smiley's 'Stone Must Be The Wall' (aka 'Wall Around Your Heart'), which did not even make the final album. Clark was no longer bringing many songs to the sessions, uncertain about their direction. Dillard was eager to pursue a stronger bluegrass path and sought additional assistance. He tracked down champion fiddle player Byron Berline, who had previously worked with the Dillards on their accomplished instrumental album, *Pickin' And Fiddlin'*. It proved a lucky call. Berline was scheduled to leave the Army the next day so was free to record and tour, if necessary. "Byron had his hair high and his neck was very red," Jackson recalls. With his Army discipline, Berline avoided the excesses of Doug and Gene, but it was difficult to escape the effects of their passive smoking. "Byron didn't realize it, but he was getting high," jokes Jackson.

The new album was completed, but a schism was developing in the ranks. "There were days when we'd record and it'd be interesting," says Jackson. "People were around like Van Dyke Parks, who was my neighbour. He would show up at peripheral events. But everything got spotty after that. At this point Byron was a pretty closed individual and Doug and Gene were the opposite. The idea of a martini was fine for them, but not for Byron. Suddenly, Doug and Gene were no longer a part of my life. What happened? It just disintegrated. The first album was a high point, but it was downhill from there. There were a great many influences, Donna being one. Did Donna get on with Gene? Not well. Gene was much too secretive and Elizabethan for her. His writing wasn't as prevalent as it had been and there was a greater reliance on bluegrass. The music talent disappeared and other things interceded. It got to be far more personal, as happens in bands, and music ceased to be the primary motivator."

Berline felt much the same when analysing the changes in musical policy. "The biggest problem with that group was Doug and I wanting to pick more and I think Gene felt left out. He didn't seem to be happy most of the time but he was very difficult to read, at least for me." The fiddler's instincts proved sound.

Although a promotional tour went well and the playing was excellent, they had clearly moved far away from the reflective, experimental work evident on their previous album. Performing live allowed Dillard and Berline to show off their virtuoso instrumental abilities, leaving Clark wondering about his role in proceedings. It was similar to the detachment Leadon had felt once Donna Washburn arrived and usurped him as third vocalist. "When Byron Berline showed up on the scene, he was this super fast fiddle player," Corneal adds. "At the time he wasn't really into playing pretty Texas slow line. He could play so fast. So we found ourselves doing more and more of that incredibly speedy bluegrass. We were well lubricated at the time, a case of beer or two a piece, and it just went more in that direction. I think that was probably the reason that Gene finally walked from the group."

Clark was not ready to depart just yet. Despite his reservations, he remained on good terms with his fellow members and there were no reports of any conflicts on the road. On the contrary, the musicians enjoyed the short tour, which included some memorable moments. Chief amongst them was a family reunion. "Gene stopped off and called his folks," Corneal remembers. "We were about 50 miles out of Kansas. By the time we got there, they had a picnic fixed up for us. They were good people, salt of the earth."

Doug Dillard also took the opportunity to visit his family, after which he and Gene, evidently in riotous mood, headed for Nashville to celebrate the end of the tour. They ended up in a club nearby the Grand Ole Opry where they drank and chatted. Dillard recognized some of the locals and felt secure, but there was a strange atmosphere. Things turned ugly soon after, culminating in a bar-room brawl worthy of a John Wayne western. "Gene went to the bathroom," Dillard recalls, "and a couple of guys in there started giving him trouble, so he kicked one of them through one of the partitions in the john. He came out with a grin on his face. It wasn't about five minutes before four bouncers jumped on us. I hadn't done a thing all evening. I was sitting at the table. They picked me up, threw me against the wall, tore half the wall down." Clark was also concussed amid the melee. "They hit Gene over the head with a baseball bat. His eyes kind of rolled around a little bit, but it didn't knock him out. But they hit him hard, right on top of the head and nobody deserves that. We weren't being out of line, you know? I don't know who they thought they were."

As the dazed duo staggered out on to the street, they could hear the angry voice of the owner who was threatening to have them thrown into jail. They thought nothing of this as they stood outside the entrance to the Grand Ole Opry. Exiting the building was country star Tompall Glaser, who provided a sympathetic ear, while joking, "Don't worry about it! I've been thrown out of there too." After talking on the street for about 20 minutes, Gene and Doug decided to return to their hotel, but the drama was far from over. "Somebody hollered at us. We turned around and there were these Nashville police with guns drawn. My hands just went up in the air . . . I didn't even think about it . . . Then they took us to jail. They said, 'Are you guys singers?' I said, 'Sure'. So Gene Clark and I sang 'Amazing Grace' to them on the way to the station. We had to call our attorney in Hollywood and it cost us $350 to get out. It was like a kangaroo court. Just terrible. We tried to plead, 'Not guilty'. I hadn't done a thing, but the guy says, 'Well, you were with Gene Clark, weren't you?' I said, 'Yes'. He says, 'Throw them in jail.' I went to the bailiff and he had played with Bill Monroe at one time. He says, 'What are you guys doing here?' I ended up getting the bailiff's autograph! They finally let us go . . . We'd took a little break from our album, went back to Missouri and Nashville to visit, and that's what came of it."

In September 1969, Dillard & Clark's second album was released. *Through The Morning Through The Night* was something of an anti-climax after the exploratory nature of its predecessor. Taken as it was intended, as a bluegrass-influenced confection, the work was impressive. It included a wonderfully energetic romp through

Boudleaux-Bryant's 'Rocky Top' and a moving reading of their famous hit for the Everly Brothers, 'So Sad'. Overall, this underrated work betrayed an uncertainty of purpose, veering between country/bluegrass familiars like 'No Longer A Sweetheart Of Mine', 'Roll In My Sweet Baby's Arms' and Clark's reworking of the Beatles' 'Don't Let Me Down'. Clark aficionados understandably bemoaned the dearth of new compositions perhaps missing the point of the album, which was never intended as a singer-songwriter showcase. There were four new Clark songs, including a couple of potential standards. The title track, a powerful song of burning jealousy, was exquisitely performed. The yearning 'Polly' was even better and remains a candidate for any shortlist of greatest Clark compositions. Along with the other duets on the album, it was also a tribute to the largely unheralded Donna Washburn, whose harmonies were exhilarating throughout. Later in his life, Clark would attempt another series of duets with Carla Olson, but never managed to attain the emotional heights herein. 'Kansas City Southern' became something of a signature tune for Clark over the next few years. It evoked childhood memories of the lonesome siren sound of the train whistle and its power to inspire dreams of escaping Swope Park and Bonner Springs for a new life in the big city. Finally, there was the peculiar, vaudeville-styled 'Corner Street Bar', arguably the least representative Clark song ever recorded.

Sales returns for *Through The Morning Through The Night* were again disappointing and Clark felt creatively stifled by the stronger emphasis on bluegrass. Nevertheless, he still enjoyed carousing with Dillard and fraternizing with various hangers-on. One such person was William Winfield Creighton III, who lived in the Hollywood Hills with his girlfriend Mary, and facilitated Gene's partying. "Billy was a coke dealer," Mary says. "He ran in the rock 'n' roll neighbourhood. We used to go see Sly Stone and all these people that were in the studio. Billy was dealing to Gene. He was a drug dealer so pretty much everyone he knew, the reason was because they were using. That was his job. You can't stay up all night with Doug Dillard without doing drugs. I mean, it's not natural." Despite their rollicking late-night sessions, the shift in musical policy bothered Clark. The group were invited to play on the CBS syndicated television show *Hee Haw*, but even that could not persuade Gene to extend his stay. Before the end of 1969, he was gone.

Clark began the new decade with all the uncertainty of a performer still out of step with popular taste. His old mentor Jim Dickson once more attempted to rescue his career, utilizing the talents of the original Byrds. At the time, Dickson was producing the Flying Burrito Brothers, working with the latter-day Byrds on *(Untitled)* and had re-established his on/off friendship with David Crosby. The idea was to record a single featuring Gene assisted by his former comrades. There was no grand reunion, though. Dickson used the rhythm section of Hillman and Clarke and later overdubbed McGuinn's Rickenbacker, then brought in Crosby for the harmony part. The sumptuous 'She's The Kind Of Girl', which also features Bud Shank on flute, is a charming piece that highlights Clark's power as a balladeer. The probable B-side 'One In A Hundred' is even better, with a striking McGuinn Rickenbacker break and some breathtaking harmonies from Crosby. Clarke's drumming is restrained, yet resonant. It is almost as if the original five are constructing a Byrds' primer for Dickson's benefit, employing their individual skills to produce something magical. Alas, it was all too fleeting. The segmented nature of the recordings, involving sessions spread over the best part of a year, indicated the difficulties in organizing any kind of Byrds reunion. A&M, despite their continued involvement with the Flying Burrito Brothers and Gene Clark, failed to recognize the historic importance of these tracks and the single was never released. "They didn't have a negotiated deal to sign with the other people," Clark pointed out, although securing clearances would hardly have proven insurmountable. During the spring of 1970, Dickson also produced a novel version of 'She Darked The Sun' with Clark on lead vocal, backed by McGuinn and Hillman. This was akin to hearing Dillard & Clark through the prism of the Flying Burrito Brothers, another fascinating experiment. Equally impressive was 'Here Tonight', recorded at a session with the Burritos. It was no secret that Dickson had failed to connect with Gram Parsons and wasn't too keen on Rick Roberts either. If he harboured secret thoughts of reuniting Clark, Clarke and Hillman, that too would never be realized. Despite sterling efforts, Clark found his career at a standstill.

During the same period, there were significant changes in Gene's personal life. Just before leaving Dillard & Clark, he had encountered an attractive woman at a party and established an instant connection. She was only dimly aware of the Byrds, let alone Gene, and expressed a preference for heavier bands such as Led Zeppelin and Mountain. Her aloofness no doubt fuelled his attraction. He pursued her avidly over succeeding weeks, even turning up outside her apartment on a motorbike and offering to whisk her off to the beach to watch the sunset. Before long they became a couple. Even their consummation proved a revelation for her. "I thought that Michelangelo had popped David on my bed from the Sistine Chapel. I couldn't believe it."

Carlie Lynn McCummings, the eldest of three children, was born 12 June 1944 in Owensboro, Kentucky, and raised in Evansville, Indiana. It was a well-to-do family. Her Californian father had been in the oil business and the children, Carlie and her two younger brothers, Jimmy and Mike, had a stable upbringing. They attended private summer camps in North Carolina and occasionally visited LA where their grandmother and uncle and aunt resided. Carlie was, her brother Jimmy says, a "happy, positive, extrovert, vivacious blonde". She enjoyed ice-skating and had a passion for dancing. Jimmy, a studious teenager, suddenly enjoyed a more active social life thanks to his sister. "*American Bandstand* was a big thing. We'd come home from school and she *made* me learn to dance with her. When we were in high school or if we showed up at the same party, we'd end up dancing." Carlie attended Indiana University but dropped out in the spring of 1964 and moved to Long Beach, California. This was the start of a new adventure, leading to Hollywood. In common with Clark's previous girlfriend, Jacqui Levy, Carlie found work as a dancer, performing for a short spell at the Sunset Strip club, Gazzarri's. She also claimed to have made a couple of fleeting appearances on *Hollywood A Go-Go*. That in itself was an interesting coincidence as Levy had been the main dancer on the show at the time. After retiring her dancing shoes, McCummings secured a job as production manager at Bell Records, which had recently been bought by Columbia Pictures and was about to enter its most successful commercial phase with hits by acts such as the Partridge Family and Dawn.

Clark wooed McCummings with characteristic intensity and the couple soon moved north to the Mendocino Coast overlooking the Pacific Ocean. In the preceding months, Clark had visited the area on a brief writing retreat, staying at a local hotel and taking in the beautiful surroundings. He was enchanted by the redwood forests, the picturesque landscape and the easy-going life. It was like a grander version of his rural Missouri home and the perfect antithesis to the fast-lane lifestyle of Hollywood. At a time when many of the rock elite were embracing a back-to-roots existence, Mendocino offered an opportunity to slow down, while still enjoying the attendant luxuries provided by a healthy songwriting income. Clark was pleasantly surprised to discover that land was cheap and rents were low. Initially, the couple rented a cabin in Little River and slowly settled into the community. The local populace appeared to consist of bohemians, free spirits, craftworkers, and musicians. Even the housebuilders doing labour work were likely to be part-time poets, former beatniks or aspiring culture vultures. It was a fascinating scene with every opportunity to create, but none of the pressures so prevalent back in LA.

A mutual friend nicknamed 'English' Roger Willis introduced Gene and Carlie to Philip and Ea Oleno, who lived in nearby Albion. Philip had attended UCLA Film School, where he befriended future Doors' vocalist, Jim Morrison. Tiring of LA life, Oleno had moved to Mendocino in the summer of 1968.

Within a year, his wife Ea, a former Hollywood hairdresser, also relocated. The Olenos represented the perfect bridge between the two worlds that Clark now inhabited. "We had something in common, which was LA," says Philip. "LA had been part of our life at one time. Gene and Carlie were interesting, fascinating people. I'd sit around with Gene many nights as he composed. He'd work out his stuff on guitar and then there'd be another song. He was constantly writing."

Clark liked to visit Philip's workshop where he made metal furniture, among other pursuits. While penning a new song, 'White Light', Clark eloquently referenced the symphony of the smithy's anvil, transforming observed events into poetry, just as he had done with 'Echoes'. Gene was intrigued to learn that Mendocino had nine Indian reservations and openly discussed his own Native American ancestry, a subject that had previously been regarded as largely taboo. He was also intrigued by Oleno's book collection and interest in spiritual and new age matters. "Gene was brought up a Catholic and I was a student of the history of religions. The two of us would talk about things. I couldn't tell you what though. He was very smart, but he didn't have intellectual endeavours. He never read a book. We just talked. He was a genius poet, but intellectually . . . I couldn't say."

Another important figure in the community was Michael McGibbon, who became a close friend of the Clarks and the Olenos. McGibbon moved back and forth between Santa Barbara and Mendocino, working as a house builder and a stained-glass artist. He had met Gene briefly during the early Byrds days, but this was no time for nostalgia. "He wasn't living in the past. I never got that from him. Tales would be told, but I didn't see him reflecting. He had a very strong presence but also a humility and an ability to communicate. He was actually very tender in many respects. He wasn't a bulldozing, 'I'm famous' guy. We were all excited to be doing something and there wasn't a sense of competition, which I appreciated. If ever there was, it soon got cooled out."

Like Oleno, McGibbon noticed that Clark did not appear

well-read. "I coined this antithetical phrase 'vicarious empiricist'. I think Gene absorbed stuff from well-informed, well-educated people and was able to coalesce this into a world-view that was pretty full. It was a time of good stories. What we were doing was brainstorming. Lyrics were brought up. I didn't play an instrument but I had my own poetry and a good ear. It was like a catalyst where we'd all get excited about stuff. Part of the magic was this sense of creative fun. I was into the mystical; top-spinning and crystals, and wanted to talk esoterica. Young Philip was full of it too."

While Clark was enjoying his countercultural rural retreat, he was still the subject of gossip back in LA. A&M's Jerry Moss had kept faith in the songwriter despite the disappointing sales of Dillard & Clark. He even made a pilgrimage to Clark's rented home in Little River and encouraged him to return to the big city to record a solo album. Carlie was taken aback by the mogul's reverential approach. He seemed in awe of Gene. "It was an interesting combination. Gene was strictly an artist, strictly an aesthetic type of person, and the last thing he could figure out was taxes or books or schedules . . . and Jerry was all that."

Clark was thrilled by the prospect of a solo work and continued to compose a batch of new songs whose lyrical content promised much. In what was probably his most sustained writing spell since 1967, he completed enough material for a double album. Carlie remembers how he would discipline himself to compose once the recording sessions were approaching. "He'd just be writing and scratching it out . . . then Bam! . . . it was like a light went through him and it just came. It was amazing . . . Once he was writing and he was on a flow, he loved it . . . almost like a drug, a high. 'What do you think of this?' 'Does this sound better than this?' He'd be completely taken on another level . . . When he was trying to write and it wasn't happening . . . it was torture for him."

In an inspired moment, Clark booked time at Liberty Custom Recorders to run through a selection of demos, all of which seemed certainties for his forthcoming LP. In the end, only three –

'The Virgin', 'One In A Hundred' and '1975' – would be carried forward. The rest were never issued in his lifetime and were not even copyrighted at BMI or the Library of Congress. Given the quality of the compositions, that was in itself remarkable.

These starkly acoustic songs were predominantly written in Mendocino. 'The Lighthouse' may well have been inspired by the local coastal tower near Clark's home. The lyrics speak of "red Burgundy and memories" before moving into a deliberation about a fragmenting affair which is described in meteorological metaphors. There are also some mid-Sixties Dylan-style aphorisms: "I even gave her what she was boasting she had stolen." The final image returns to the landscape with the image of the lighthouse scanning like a beacon in search of the narrator.

'Back To The Earth Again', an ecological lament, follows a theme previously explored on Dillard & Clark's moving 'Something's Wrong'. Clark writes of concrete tombs and sarcastically enquires whether anyone has ever seen a manufactured flower in bloom. Images of pain and stark acceptance echo through several other songs. 'The Sparrow', a melodic meditation whose subject matter recalls Emily Dickinson's sparrow poems, contrasts the bird who can still fly with the troubled human condition where pain is paramount. 'Walking Through This Lifetime' also fantasizes about an existence free from pain, then ruminates on the nature of time. "The absolute must be today," the singer declares, before speculating about eternity.

Ostensibly, 'Sweet Adrienne' is a more orthodox love ballad written in honour of a woman whose complications are appealing, but subject to question. Clark's writing is typically convoluted and at times he appears to be composing the song in letter form. The conclusion is restrained in its ambiguity, subtly suggestive of promiscuity, while questioning the veracity and honour of men in a deferential tone. A hint of moral impropriety, so delicately expressed that it might easily be missed, is present in the suggestion that Adrienne's love is for *any* man.

Arguably, the greatest of these previously unreleased songs is 'The Awakening Within' which ranks alongside 'The Lighthouse' as a sinful omission from Clark's canon of work during the Seventies. He enlivens the track with some scat singing and one of his most expressive vocals. The lyrics are mesmerizing, mysterious and allusive. A chilling opening describes the reflective light of the moon which becomes a beautiful backdrop to a confusing contemplation on the imminent break-up of a relationship. But even that is not entirely clear as Clark wrestles with chronology and intent. Although he appears to be addressing another person, the *you* is equally, if not more, likely to be the narrator, caught like a weathercock in spiritual storm. The song is a wonderful example of Clark struggling with expression in order to convey a deeper meaning. Entering his amorphous time scheme is a precarious exercise. The song begins in the 'evening'. We're told that "it's the second moon since you said that you would be leaving". Most lyricists would create a solid sense of time and place, but Clark's meditations are multi-dimensional. It's not the second moon since she left but the second moon since she said she would be leaving. The neurotic exactitude adds unbearable tension to the narrative. Clark seeks patterns and designs from a comment made two moons ago that has still not come to pass. In the end, the song offers no resolution, but fades as mysteriously as it had begun. It sounds like a composition that deserved, or may well have contained, several additional verses, but we will probably never know.

If Clark ever required a coda to this series of songs then 'Only Yesterday's Gone' fits that billing. An elegy to the past, it also has a hymnal quality, offering the closing prayer: "Grace of peace come over us." Why Clark rejected these compositions is uncertain. There is no evidence that he ever attempted any in live performance nor were they considered as worthy outtakes for his next album. That he did not even bother to copy-right-register any of them is baffling. Instead, they disappeared and would not resurface until their surprise appearance 36 years later on the archival album, *Gene Clark: The Lost Studio Sessions 1964–1982.*

* * *

The producer assigned to Clark for his A&M album was the great guitarist Jesse Ed Davis, a Native American Oklahoman who was already receiving acclaim from his peers, not least Gram Parsons whose effusive comments on 'Indian Ed' enlivened several interviews with the Flying Burrito Brothers. Clark and Davis bonded immediately, although their mutual affection for alcohol would ultimately prove their undoing.

Sessions for *White Light* began in early 1971 and the pair were able to call upon some of the finest LA session players. The recordings progressed smoothly, although there was one moment early on when nature itself threatened to topple the project. Former Burrito Brother Chris Ethridge, who played bass on the album, recalls the strange events that occurred in the early hours of 9 February 1971. "My younger brother Tommy had gone to the studios, Village Recorders, with me. Bobbye Hall Porter from Motown had played percussion and I'd played bass. At three in the morning I left and drove home to Laurel Canyon as my wife was eight months' pregnant. Gene, Jesse Ed and the assistant engineer Baker [Bigsby] stayed on to mix some stuff. When I got home there was the loudest noise . . ."

What Ethridge heard were the distant rumblings of a California earthquake which hit LA at 6 am. Later that morning, he phoned Gene Clark who related a terrifying, but funny story. "Gene said that those big concrete blocks that were holding up the speakers started shaking. Then Baker jumped up and screamed 'Earthquake!' – and they took off running. They tore down the stairs and ran outside and the road was going up and down like waves. Telephone poles were just slapping from one side to the other. Then Baker ran down the street. They hollered, 'Baker, where are you going?' He said, 'I don't know!' Then he turned around and came running straight back towards them. It must have been awful."

During a break in the album's recording, Clark was called away to participate in another project. He could hardly resist an invitation from actor/director Dennis Hopper who wanted Gene to compose a couple of songs for his documentary movie, *The*

American Dreamer. In certain respects, Hopper was like an older, uber version of Gene Clark: more excessive, manic and destructive. Appropriately enough, considering his wild behaviour and lawlessness, Hopper was born in Dodge City. He not only shared with Clark the same birth state, Missouri, but evidently the same taste in women. While Clark had dated the goddess-like Michelle Phillips, Hopper had gone one step further and married her on a mountain top in Peru. The union lasted a mere eight days, a short spell even for a Hollywood marriage. Like Clark, Hopper seemed haunted by his brief relationship with the former Mama, and she would feature prominently in his notes for the forthcoming movie. "I think Michelle Phillips is probably really the only one that's really scared me badly . . . really got to my head. I find that people who play games scare the shit out of me because I'm dealing with a moment-to-moment reality and they're dealing on a level where they're planning something to happen."

Apart from this emotional connection, Clark was doubly keen to work with Hopper, having missed the chance to appear on the soundtrack of the best-selling *Easy Rider*. "Dennis had wanted me involved in *Easy Rider*," Clark claimed, "but Peter Fonda wanted McGuinn to work on that. Peter and Dennis didn't get along, and McGuinn didn't want me working on the picture if he was involved. So I never did *Easy Rider* but Dennis had me do two songs for *The American Dreamer*."

Clark faced an unusual problem when he set off to meet Hopper: a lack of new songs. Not wishing to give away anything already scheduled for recording and seemingly unwilling to contribute previously completed demos, he came up with three very fragmentary tunes, including a swiftly-penned lyric that he hoped would serve as the title track. "All I had going around in my head was the title, 'American Dreamer'. The timing could not have been worse as I was under pressure to complete *White Light* with Jesse and we were working around the clock. It was pretty intense. I managed to see a screening of the film, but it was all very rushed and I didn't really know what to make of it. They said they needed the songs that same night. I remember eating at

Chuck's Steak House near the recording studio, humming little melodies and writing down the lyrics on their cocktail napkins. Somehow, I managed to get three songs out of it, and they used two of them." The third song, a slight, elliptical composition provocatively titled 'Jimmy Christ', lay in the vaults for decades but was finally unearthed for *Here Tonight – The White Light Demos* in 2013.

Judged by his best standards, Clark's contributions to *The American Dreamer* were fairly lamentable, but it made little difference as the movie was generally regarded as an indulgence too far by Hopper and was rarely screened. Set in Taos, New Mexico, it documented a chaotic period of his life when he was editing that strange cinematic experiment, *The Last Movie.* 'Dennis Hopper is the American Dreamer' claimed the posters for his documentary. They also included the playful aphorism, 'I'd rather die fighting than die getting fat'. More than anything, *The American Dreamer* testified to Hopper's fragile mental state during this troublesome period. At times semi-coherent, he rails against the horrors of an unhappy childhood, frolics with girls in a bathtub, wanders naked in a street and fires off semi-automatic weapons. Among his rambling thoughts are words that Clark might have used when faced with interviewers who wrongly assumed he was well-read. "I don't believe in reading. By using your eyes and ears you'll find everything there is."

Carlie had accompanied Gene during his stay in LA where his wilder side was let loose. During a meal at a restaurant, he acted like some spoilt film star, flipping a table over as if he owned the place. Carlie assumed they would be ejected from the establishment for his unruly behaviour but instead the staff apologized, re-set the table and brought some fresh food. Such deference testified to his former status as a star in the Byrds. In his old Hollywood haunts, Clark could get away with such shenanigans, not least because he was still associated in people's minds with the Beatles and the Rolling Stones. He was treated like a Hollywood outlaw.

* * *

The summer of 1971 was a time of celebration. Carlie was now pregnant and the new album was recorded and awaiting release. On 12 June, Gene and Carlie were married in Mendocino. The ceremony took place at Philip and Ea Oleno's Albion home and the pair also served as witnesses. "They had a big party and lots of people from the LA music business came up," Ea remembers. "It was big. We had eight acres so people were able to camp out in the fields and stay over." Among the revellers were two Byrds, Chris Hillman and Michael Clarke. Doug Dillard and his girlfriend also stayed for a few days, wrecking a couple of rental cars along the way. Tellingly, the only family member in attendance was Gene's brother Rick who had recently relocated from Missouri and was looking after the couple's rented home in Little River while they were away in LA.

In August 1971, two months after the wedding, *White Light* was released. It proved Clark's most accomplished work to date. The songs were expertly crafted, with intriguing lyrics reminiscent of mid-period Dylan, complete with acoustic guitar and harmonica. One cover version, appropriately Dylan's 'Tears Of Rage', was in perfect keeping with the stoical mood of the work. Extraneous material, most notably a pedestrian run-through of Ben E. King's 'Stand By Me', which appeared on the final reel-to-reel, was wisely omitted. At least two more songs were left on the cutting-room floor without explanation. The impressionistic 'Opening Day', an exploration of heightened experience, presented familiar images of nature – a rising sun, murmuring breeze, pouring rain – alongside metaphysical allusions to souls and angels. 'Winter In' employed almost identical references to nature, with guitarist Jesse Ed Davis providing a prequel to his more adventurous work on the brilliant '1975'. Among the discarded demos were two quirkier compositions that were probably not in serious contention for inclusion. 'For No One', despite sharing a title with one of Paul McCartney's most celebrated works, is a slight lyric and rather featureless melody. 'Please Mr Freud', a playful dream song, is uncharacteristically light in tone, complete with wry references to Sigmund Freud and Karl Marx.

None of the above originals would be issued in Gene's lifetime.

What remains on the originally released *White Light* are seven Clark compositions, ranging from love ballads such as the Memphis-tinged 'Because Of You' and 'Where My Love Lies Asleep' to highly symbolic narratives, notably 'The Virgin', 'White Light' and 'For A Spanish Guitar'. One of the challenges facing any listener is the nature of Clark's language itself, with its sudden inversions, extended similes and otherworldly imagery. This, of course, had long been a feature of his songwriting. Since introducing 'moon trolls' into the otherwise naturalistic landscape of 'So You Say You Lost Your Baby', he had ventured into deeper abstraction on experimental lyrics such as 'Back Street Mirror' and 'Only Colombe'. The compositions on *White Light* combine the prosaic and the abstruse. Even in a seemingly uncomplicated homily on the corruption of an innocent ('The Virgin'), there is that strange, almost science-fiction allusion to 'life forms' that are deemed insane. Concretizing Clark's language into meaning proves a perilous expedition. The indeterminacies seldom surrender to easy interpretation. The title track begins with a fixed image (a silent village on a hill). This is rapidly replaced by a continuous stream of activity – the hammering of a smithy's anvil, electric lines of force that are 'ringing', clouds disturbing, flashes fleeting, and so on. Even static images appear in a state of flux. Some of the imagery is strangely familiar. 'Where My Love Lies Asleep' speculates on the 'hallways of wonder' recalling the 'hallways and staircases' of the equally mysterious 'She Don't Care About Time'.

The paradox of Clark's language is that the more adjectival information he provides, the more difficult and uncertain our response becomes. 'For A Spanish Guitar', arguably Clark's most mature work to date, begins with an image of the sea, characterized by 'dissonant bells' ringing rhymes that sing of ages asleep. The accumulation of images is almost overwhelming – and these are just the opening lines. His descriptions are so allusive and richly associative that they provoke different responses over successive plays. Ever the overreacher, Clark strives to capture the unconscious process of compositional creation. Like the life force of a beating heart, creativity is described as 'pulsating' rhythmically from soul to brain. The process by which the ethereal becomes cerebral and magically manifests itself through music anticipates later meditations, notably 'Strength Of Strings'. The heart of this mystery might have inspired Clark into metaphorical incoherence but here he uses straightforward similes (the seagull soaring in breeze) to express this effortless invention. Even the grammatically incorrect use of 'whom' sounds like an autodidact utilizing an archaism for artistic expression. Images of purity are ever present – the street beggar sitting on his throne of defeat who envisages no salvation in welfare; the innocent laughter of children, caught up in fantasies, yet unaffected by dogma. All humanity – the right, the wrong, even the insane – are part of his song.

Clark had been seduced by his own symbolism in 1966–67 when composing the ornate 'Back Street Mirror', but the songs on *White Light* are different. While the lyrics are still ambitious and ostentatious, the production is understated. The use of harmonica, in particular, grounds the songs in an earthy folksiness made more potent by Clark's earnest and precise diction. Amid the austere economy, Jesse Ed Davis adds precision and power. He excels with some expressive, cascading guitar-playing on the side-closing epics, 'One In A Hundred' and '1975'.

At a time when introspective singer-songwriters were all the rage, Gene Clark at last seemed in the perfect position to follow Crosby and McGuinn back into the big time. Unfortunately, modest promotion and a continued reluctance to tour the world ensured that Clark remained on the cult fringe. For all its merits, *White Light* appears strangely out of time, with its self-consciously cryptic song poems, subtle melodies, archaic diction, vibrato vocal and almost monophonic sound. The album's starkness is incredibly powerful and expressive but, sadly, it was ignored by the rock mainstream. There was no 'Sweet Baby James' or 'Heart Of Gold' in Clark's canon to sweeten the pill for laid-back FM listeners. Instead, they were confronted with 'maladies of meaning', 'karmic oceans', 'voices of time', cosmic riddles and odd aphorisms. This was heavy stuff and all the better for it, but no competition for the catchy melodies and easily understood lyrics of Carole King's more commercial, chart-topping *Tapestry*. Nobody rushed to cover Clark's songs from *White Light*.

Always moving forward, Clark was already working on his next project. Terry Melcher, the Byrds' original producer, had been in contact and was keen to work with him again. It was a flattering offer, not least because Melcher was willing to provide accommodation and free recording facilities. Carlie was several months' pregnant but accompanied Gene to Idlewild where they stayed in splendour for the remainder of the year. Terry was always a fine host, but this was a tense time as he was still recovering from the aftermath of the Charles Manson trial. What would have been Clark's third solo album foundered long before completion. "Terry fell away from it," recalls Jim Dickson. "He just didn't turn up enough. But there was a version of Flatt & Scruggs' 'Rough And Rocky' that Terry Melcher did that's stunning. Gene later redid it, but it didn't have the same impact." What else was recorded at Melcher's home studio is conjectural. No session logs are known to exist, although rumours persist of other songs attempted, including 'Bed Of Roses' and a lengthy version of Bruce Johnston's 'Disney Girls (1957)'.

Coincidentally, or not, Gene's former drug-dealing associate Billy Winfield appeared on the scene at this point. Given Melcher's vulnerable state and appetite for pharmaceutical relief, his presence was no doubt welcomed. "For some reason Billy rented a house in Idlewild and I moved up there too," recalls his former partner Mary Pritchard (later Kendall), who was pregnant at the time. "Idlewild was a little arts community in the mountains above Palm Springs. Gene and Carlie were already there. We used to cook and hang out together. Carlie had a jeep. So there we were these two huge pregnant women going down the mountain to the grocery store in this jeep with no top on it."

Carlie and Mary became close friends, united in pregnancy.

They enjoyed the picturesque life in Idlewild, but the arrival of another guest from Gene's past prompted some jealous reactions. "Carlie and Gene were staying in Terry's house where he had a studio. Then Michelle Phillips was there too staying with them. It was real chummy! I think Gene and Michelle were having an affair because Carlie was so preggers." Mary's suspicions were never confirmed but the presence of the former Mama & The Papas' starlet must have added a flirtatious frisson, to say the least. "I didn't spend a lot of time with Michelle," Mary says. "Carlie used to pretty much escape to my house, just to get out of there. It was a little intense for her with Michelle lurking around. Carlie would come over and we'd play solitaire. One time my mom came to visit and we were playing cards. Carlie was pretty tossed on Quaaludes and she literally fell off the chair on to the floor. We were both large women. We got pretty big when we were pregnant." Prescriptions for Quaaludes (Mandrax) specifically state that the drug should never be taken during pregnancy, so what was Carlie thinking? "Well, our rationale was that they were pure drugs, so that was that," Mary notes briskly. "Quaaludes were really big back then."

While Mary decided to have her baby in Palm Springs, Carlie insisted on returning to Los Angeles. A memorable year ended with the birth of her son, Kelly Eugene Clark, at Cedars Sinai Medical Center at 6.33 am on 20 December. Gene did not attend the birth, preferring to celebrate the event in riotous union with his LA friends.

By this stage, Clark's social circle had extended to include several film actors and directors. Back in the Sixties, he had formed a friendship with the glamorous, Missouri-born Steve McQueen, and they could frequently be seen tearing around Tinseltown on their motorcycles. McQueen later encouraged director Sam Peckinpah to include Clark's 'Through The Morning, Through The Night' in the 1972 film *The Getaway*. That lucky break brought Clark an additional revenue stream at a time when he needed money for his new family. Appearing on two movie soundtracks brought the possibility of further work and Clark was quick to connect with some of the wilder characters in the industry. He seemed to have a particular fondness for Hollywood dynasties – the Barrymores and the Carradines. Drinking buddy John Barrymore Jr was an excessive who shared Gene's carpe diem philosophy and devil-may-care recklessness. He also fulfilled Gene's cowboy fantasies on screen, having appeared in various western series, notably *Wagon Train*, *Rawhide* and *Gunsmoke*. David Carradine, star of the television series *Kung Fu*, in which he played a philosophical martial arts-trained Shaolin monk let loose in the Wild West, liked to combine an image of old style Hollywood swashbuckling mayhem with dashes of Eastern mysticism. It was a combination that appealed to Clark who affected similar contradictions. "I've many times had discussions with people who I consider to be very high people," he said. "One person, David Carradine, is very into Zen and is one of my better friends . . . I'll make one thing clear – I don't claim to be a guru or a leader or anything like that because I think that's the first point people really lose on." Gene was even beginning to sound like a Hollywood star, full of Eastern promise.

Despite the lure of Hollywood, Clark still loved the tranquillity offered by rugged Mendocino. It balanced his personality and allowed him to concentrate on making music. Having rented property all his adult life, he took the plunge and bought a two-storey home in Albion, near the Oleno's abode. A former stagecoach house from the Old West era, the property included 12 acres of land and a plentiful supply of redwood trees. The building was in a poor state of repair and had been rented to hippies when the Clarks first enquired about it. "There were orange and chartreuse walls and no plumbing," Carlie recalls. "It was really funky, but it was still magic. We found that we could get it for almost nothing because it was close to a tear-down. It was built out of virgin redwood which doesn't rot or get termites, so that's the only reason why it hadn't blown over." During the next few years, Clark would spend much time sawing timber and refurbishing the house "It was on the other ridge from us," says

Philip Oleno. "Gene put a lot of money into fixing it up. But he'd have to come and go." The renovations took longer than anticipated but, fortunately, the Clarks were able to continue renting the beach-front house on Lansing Street in Little River.

For a time, at least, Clark felt settled and happy living in Mendocino. "We wanted for nothing," says Carlie. "We didn't have a lot, but we never thought we were doing without. There would be times when we were waiting for a big royalty cheque to come and I'd make chilli for two or three nights and cornbread. The fishermen would bring these big crab pots and dump them in our kitchen. We'd have crab, and we'd go fishing. It was all just good." This idyllic life, without conflict or transgression, was always fondly remembered by Carlie, who had no idea how short-lived such happiness would be once harsher realities intervened. "I lived in a dream. We were in a dream. We had this beautiful house overlooking the ocean. We could see the ships pass in the night on the horizon. We'd wake up and have breakfast till noon, and then take a walk . . . It was a fantasy . . . I didn't have much life experience. I didn't know that that wasn't how life was . . . most people don't have that much happiness and magic in their whole lifetime . . . I don't know why I was chosen to be able to experience that for as long as I did."

Despite the paltry sales of *White Light*, Clark discovered that he was a draw in far-away Holland where the album had been voted among the year's best in leading rock magazine, *Orr*. Dutch promoters were putting together a mini-festival titled the Amsterdam Rock Circus, scheduled to take place at Holland's Olympic Stadium on 22 May 1972. They were keen to secure Clark's involvement and he was flattered enough to accept their invitation. Almost immediately, he began to backtrack and prevaricate. There had been no nationwide tour to promote *White Light* in the US and the prospect of travelling to Europe filled him with dread. He was reassured by Michael Clarke and Chris Ethridge, who had been treated like rock star royalty when they played in Holland at the end of 1970. In order to boost Clark's confidence they backed him at some college dates that spring. Five days before his intended departure, he informed an audience at California State University that he'd be appearing in Amsterdam the following Thursday. Then, he was spooked again. His wife Carlie was shocked to hear that he had contacted the promoters with the bad news that he was unable to leave America due to outstanding tax issues. The truth was he could not bear to travel and was suffering from stage fright, exacerbated by inexperience on the road since the demise of Dillard & Clark. She momentarily attempted to reason with him, but he cut the conversation short. "He just didn't want to go. He never discussed it . . . I would do everything in my power . . . Valium, drinks, anything – he just never got comfortable flying."

Clark continued his wayward career path during the early Seventies. He was effectively landlocked after *White Light* and spent the remainder of the decade shuffling back and forth between different labels. Some impetus had already been lost following his stay with Terry Melcher in Idlewild where they had failed to complete Gene's third solo album. Melcher's assistant Chris Hinshaw, who had worked as an engineer on the Byrds' albums *(Untitled)* and *Byrdmaniax*, attempted to rekindle the project in the spring of 1972. With Clark's cooperation, he enlisted a crack team of players including Clarence White (guitar), Michael Clarke (drums), Sneaky Pete Kleinow (steel guitar), Spooner Oldham (keyboards) and Byron Berline (fiddle). Any hopes that Melcher might return were extinguished during April when he was almost killed in a road accident while riding his motorcycle. He suffered two broken legs and extensive bruising requiring hospitalization and a lengthy period of convalescence. "It happened during the making of that album," says Jim Seiter. "Chris Hinshaw called me and said, 'Oh, man, Terry's had an accident and he's dying!' I said, 'What?' He ran his motorcycle head-on into a car and was in hospital. Hinshaw came back from that and he was a wreck." Working with Gene Clark hardly helped his spirits. "Hinshaw called and said, 'Can you help me do this record?'" Seiter contends. "I asked why and he said, 'because this guy's a fucking maniac' . . . It was a battle between keeping Hinshaw together and Gene sober. It was brutal, but some of the songs were pretty good." Hinshaw squandered studio time. While Clark was absent, he invited Sly Stone and his encourage over for a drink and drug-fuelled spree. A&M were upset and Clark was left out of pocket. "The record company actually was very generous," Gene acknowledged at the time. "It had more to do with a fault of mine in trusting people too much and letting them take advantage of my time in the studio."

Recording sessions continued sporadically over the next few months until A&M halted the sessions, after which the album was unceremoniously abandoned. It was a bitter blow to Clark, who had already contributed several excellent compositions to the project. "That was an album that could have been a great album but it was cut off in the making of it. It turned into an expensive project, which was not necessarily anyone's fault, but we seemed to keep getting into problems; getting the musicians, getting the right settings and so forth. We ended up with one of those half-finished products." At the time, Clark was adamant that there would be no attempt to rescue the project. "I don't want an incomplete work released on the market. I'd rather start afresh . . . I hate to go back in time. I like to keep going forward and with each song that I write I like to do better and record it better."

While Clark's latest album was foundering, his former label CBS were planning to reissue his 1967 collaboration with the Gosdin Brothers. When Jim Dickson heard about this, he contacted Clark with a view to revising the entire work. As he showed later with the Byrds' retrospective *Never Before*, Dickson had no compunction about improving an album, even if that meant adding instrumentation or overdubbing. Given a week's grace by CBS, he and Clark remixed the original 8-track recordings and re-cut several vocals, including the epochal 'Echoes'. Clark sounds more studious here, with much clearer and precise diction, as if Dickson has instructed him to pronounce his 'g's at the end of words. The album, retitled *Early LA Sessions*, and this time credited solely to Clark, is fresher in places but many felt it was a strange exercise in revisionism. They even deleted one track, 'Elevator Operator', on the grounds that it now sounded dated. Unfortunately, there were no outtakes to use in its place which meant the album's length was reduced to a pitiful 23 minutes. Clark talked up the work in the detailed liner notes: "Remixing was pretty necessary. We brought out things you couldn't even hear on the original tapes. It serves as an interesting picture of growth as it's taking place. We were just a little ahead of our time, I think. No country rock sold well until after 1969." Alas, the revamped album fared no better in 1972 than it had done in 1967 and was soon deleted.

The reunion with Dickson brought one unintended benefit to Clark. While lamenting A&M's rejection of his new album, he presented his mentor with some of the tapes and received an effusive response. Dickson was convinced that the songs had merit and felt Clark had sold himself short during discussions with his label. "Gene got more and more paranoid as it went along. He became afraid to talk to people because he thought they were playing word games with him, but he was really better at words than he knew. There's some simple things that he did on that album like 'I Remember The Railroad'. I thought that was a great piece that could be used in so many different kinds of programmes where they talked about railroads."

Seeking a sympathetic ear at A&M, Dickson contacted Dave Hubert, who was involved in foreign distribution. Back in the Sixties, Hubert had been a regular visitor to World-Pacific during the Jet Set's sojourn and had run Horizon Records which released a 12-string instrumental album by Jim McGuinn. Hubert allowed Dickson to repackage the work, which was successfully pitched to the Holland branch of A&M. They agreed to release the work-in-progress, which was bolstered by the inclusion of the two Byrds' collaborations recorded earlier: 'She's The Kind Of Girl' and 'One In A Hundred'. "The two cuts with the Byrds were done at separate times in different studios," Dickson reveals. "They didn't turn out too well, but we decided to put them together with the other old stuff." They also added 'Here

Tonight' featuring the current line-up of the Flying Burrito Brothers. With the eight songs recorded by Chris Hinshaw, there was enough material for an interim album, *Roadmaster*. Considering the work was uncompleted, it sounded surprisingly good. Among the highlights were the prescient 'Full Circle Song' and one of Clark's greatest compositions, 'In A Misty Morning', a spine-tingling observational piece with a dynamic arrangement, highlighted by Byron Berline's extraordinary fiddle work. Its depiction of an early morning drive around rain-saturated streets has an eerie quality made more chilling as a descending fog dims the city lights and the narrator's heightened thoughts recall more optimistic times. The high notes on piano from Spooner Oldham, augmented by Sneaky Pete's pedal-steel guitar, coalesce with Berline's fiddle and Clark's vocal to create a sense of foreboding. The musical accompaniment is cinematic in scope. A switch in the colour of the street lights is invested with significance, prompting the narrator into deep thoughts and an inner monologue whose tone is disconcerting. There's even a touch of David Crosby-style paranoia straight out of 'Almost Cut My Hair' in the fearful reaction to a passing police cruiser. The work closes with some extended ensemble playing, with Clark's soaring vocal almost serving as an additional instrument locked between the fiddle, piano and pedal steel to create a shimmering, reverberating effect.

Revisiting old memories, Clark re-recorded 'She Don't Care About Time', slowing the tempo and entirely altering the feel. The work concluded with 'Shooting Star', another cosmic adventure featuring the familiar elemental imagery previously heard on 'White Light' and 'Because Of You'. *Roadmaster* became a collector's item and was only available on import via Holland until it was belatedly issued in the UK on CD in 1986.

Back in Mendocino, Clark spent time fraternizing with several musicians in the community, including recent arrival Andy Kandanes. The New Jersey-born drummer had enjoyed some R&B success with the Hamilton Face Band, notably opening for Joe Cocker's Mad Dogs & Englishmen extravaganza. After a spell in San Francisco, Kandanes decided to relocate to Mendocino and was pleased to find a wealth of musical talent at his fingertips. "The Mendocino scene was great," he says. "It was like living in Woodstock in the Sixties – all kinds of stuff was going on. It was an art and music renaissance, a real close-knit community. We'd have outdoor shows and Taj Mahal might come up to play. It was a great time to be there." With each passing month, there seemed to be more new arrivals. "Johnny Barbata was there, Chris Ethridge and Booker T. Gene Parsons is still up there. A lot of people we knew from New York too: Cat Mother & The All Night Newsboys, Arlo Guthrie, Jack Elliott. It was quite the place. A cook had opened a little restaurant called the Pyewacket and there was a beautiful Victorian tavern overlooking the ocean. We settled in and started a band there, the Mendocino All Stars, an R&B outfit. They were very different. We had a lot of well-known players that came through there, like Joe Satriani. It was a pretty big band so we'd change personnel periodically. People would come and go but it was a great launching pad for players. We worked a lot on the road, touring Canada and the Western states. We were one of the first crossovers between the jazz and rock scenes. We had a big cult following. We could do an after-show in Mendocino and draw 200 people." Gene often attended such shows at the local pub, but kept a respectful distance at first, as if he was still waiting to establish his presence in this new community.

Kandanes was already aware of the Janus element in Clark's character. Rumours were rife of his wild times back in Hollywood, but in Mendocino he seemed more stable. "Gene always had an appetite for the imbibement of the day, but his drinking was sporadic then. It wasn't like he was tanked all the time. In those moments where he would drink too much, it was like Dr Jekyll and Mr Hyde. But there was actually a whole other intellectual side to Gene that many people never knew. In Hollywood, people always wanted him to be Gene Clark the rock 'n' roll star. Most of the time I spent with him he was 'real' Gene. There was no music business talk between us really. He was always interested in what was going on in [outer] space. He was an astute student of current affairs and we'd have some deep conversations. But most people never really got to see that side of Gene. It came out in some of his writing, I'm sure, but the average person that he had contact with had no idea of Gene's other side."

Within the wider rock world, Clark seemed doomed to remain on the cult fringe but received a career boost when news filtered through that the Byrds were recording a reunion album for Asylum Records. This lengthy saga, previously explored at length in the pages of *Volume 1*, refocused attention on Clark's songwriting. He contributed two of the best songs to the project, 'Full Circle' and 'Changing Heart' and was allowed to sing lead on the Neil Young covers, 'Cowgirl In The Sand' and 'See The Sky About To Rain'. The festering rivalry between Crosby and McGuinn for once worked to his advantage. David's determination to diminish his colleague's contribution meant that the spotlight fell on Gene Clark. By accident rather than design, Crosby had effectively turned the clock back to the World-Pacific days when Clark was the dominant vocalist and songwriter. Regrettably, the album was excessively maligned in the rock press, which robbed Clark of the belated glory that he might otherwise have accrued. Nevertheless, the Asylum connection brought him another solo record deal, paving the way towards his most ambitious work to date.

Clark's rapprochement with the other Byrds made him more energized, always a dangerous prospect given his penchant for manic behaviour when drunk. After the Byrds' reunion, he joined his former partner on the road in the extravagantly titled 'Adventures Of Roger McGuinn'. Clark introduced a new song 'Silver Raven', which was variously interpreted as some kind of paean to his Native American heritage and a commentary on an extra-terrestrial phenomenon. It also contained some vaguely New Eden, eco-scary apocalyptic imagery in its description of an old world dying. Most agreed that it was one of Clark's best songs and a tantalizing taster for his next album.

McGuinn's generosity towards Clark at this stage was a revealing comment on their changing relationship over the years. During the *Preflyte* era they had been close friends, written songs together and shared a musical vision that helped create the Byrds. Then they drifted apart, both socially and musically. McGuinn never officially appeared on any of Clark's albums and was not asked to contribute until Dickson brought him in to overdub some Rickenbacker work on 'She's The Kind Of Girl' and 'One In A Hundred'. Recently, however, McGuinn had rekindled the relationship, which reminded him of better days. Clark even stayed at his Malibu home for a spell and there was every likelihood that they might work together again in some casual capacity. Since ending his marriage to Dolores and leaving his family, McGuinn had married the younger Linda Gilbert and assumed the mantle of a typical Seventies rock star. He drank more, consumed cocaine with a connoisseur's appetite and enjoyed hosting parties at his home. It was a lifestyle that Clark envied and aspired to at times, even though many felt it brought out his worst traits. Once he started imbibing Clark was always likely to transform from an easy-going conversationalist into the houseguest from hell. During a party at McGuinn's home, Clark stumbled upon his host's gun collection and commandeered an Uzi which he took outside, seemingly in a macho display of strength to intimidate the most prestigious guest, Bob Dylan. Thankfully, Dylan soon made himself scarce, along with most of the other guests. In his drunken state, Clark stumbled, fell over and sprayed the area with bullets, accidentally blowing the legs off several pet goats. Road manager, Al Hersh, who vividly described the scene in *Volume 1*, felt obliged to confiscate McGuinn's gun collection before everyone got into serious trouble.

Gene's tendency to hurt the ones he loved was symptomatic of his drinking. His wife Carlie already noticed his verbal aggression and cruelty when inebriated. It is interesting to note that Bob Dylan, perhaps his greatest hero as a songwriter, could suddenly be transformed into a figure of envy and malice when alcohol befuddled Clark's senses. David Carradine recalls another incident, coincidentally again at a party thrown by Linda McGuinn with Dylan in attendance, where Clark turned up uninvited and caused a scene. Carradine was sharing a bottle of Jose Cuervo with Dylan when he noticed Gene acting like "a drunken Indian . . . staggering around with a little Martin guitar, almost dropping it". After preventing Clark from falling and smashing his instrument, Carradine resumed his conversation with Dylan, only to be interrupted by his intoxicated companion. "Gene started talking to Dylan in a loud voice, saying Bob was a no-talent wimp and he'd be nobody if the Byrds hadn't recorded his song, 'Mr Tambourine Man' . . . Bob was trying to shrink into the wall. Gene cornered him there and went on insulting him. Suddenly, with a sort of it's-a-good-day-to-die, blood-curdling cry, he came at Dylan, brandishing a pool cue. Dylan jumped, almost dropping the Jose Cuervo. I leaned in between them . . . Then he walked away. I turned to Bob, but he had split." Later that night, Carradine saw Gene pushing around his teenage daughter, Calista. After leaving her in the safe hands of Linda, he escorted Clark from the party and drove him to a friend's house where Gene caused another sensation by mistaking a young girl's bedroom for a bathroom and accidentally urinating in the presence of the sleeping beauty. The family were not amused. "Finally, Gene passed out," Carradine concluded.

It was this type of reckless behaviour, exaggerated or otherwise, that would alienate Clark from key friends in the music industry later in the decade. His drunken swashbuckling exploits could easily have been dismissed as Hollywood hijinks had they been foisted upon lesser lights. Gene's problem was that he had no safety mechanism to prevent him from upsetting those he loved or who supported him the most. Whether turning against his idol Bob Dylan or berating a millionaire music business mogul willing to offer him a much needed break, Clark always took the most self-destructive path. It was probably the worst side effect of his drinking, the unleashing of a Mr Hyde who was never afraid to offend the highest. Over the next few years this would prove his undoing, both in his personal and professional relationships.

Such considerations were far from uppermost in Clark's mind as he retreated from the glamorous madness of LA and settled back in Albion. In August 1973, there was an unexpected visitor: Carlie's brother, Jimmy, a former marine who was on a road trip. She had insisted he take a Greyhound bus and stay for a couple of nights at their rented, ocean-front home on Lansing Street. That night he joined his sister, Gene and young Kelly for dinner at the Windjammer restaurant. The following morning he witnessed the Mendocino coastline for the first time and was so overwhelmed by the scenery that he told Gene, "I don't want to leave." When a friend arrived to drive him to San Francisco, he refused to go. He settled in Mendocino County permanently, sometimes looking after Gene and Carlie's home when the family visited Los Angeles.

These were still the good times for Gene and Carlie, as her brother Jimmy acknowledges. "She was happily pregnant and life was good." Income was erratic, but there were occasional celebrations when royalty cheques arrived at six-month intervals. Jimmy recalls Gene receiving a phone call from Eddie Tickner followed by a windfall of monies from European sales after which the couple briefly returned to LA. Clark was still writing constantly, seemingly undisturbed by guests or in-laws. "I walked into a room and he was sitting in a corner picking out a song and writing the music," McCummings remembers. "I said, 'Oh, I'll split', but he told me, 'No, you won't bother me if you're quiet.' So I sat reading a book, while watching him sit there picking out chords and writing. Later I asked him, 'How do you do that?' He said, 'I don't really feel like *I* do it. I feel it comes to me.'" Clark's belief in divine inspiration was reinforced by the notion of 'automatic writing'. In this he was aided by conversations with his spiritual compadres: Philip Oleno, Michael McGibbon and, most surprisingly, Carlie, who had been reading about the life and work of Madame Blavatsky, the nineteenth-century medium and co-founder of the Theosophical Society. Blavatsky claimed to have a telepathic connection with supernatural entities named the Great Masters who communicated esoteric knowledge which she dictated. Clark was fascinated.

Gene's brother-in-law, Jimmy, was impressed by the fluency of his compositions but one song above all testified to his immense talent. Remembered by theme rather than title, Clark's comment on the political situation in Northern Ireland was most uncharacteristic. "Do you know anything of his song about Belfast?" McCummings asks, still intrigued about a great lost work. "It was one of the best things he ever did and one of the most poignant songs I ever heard in my life. I watched him write it in the house on Lansing Street. I was astonished. It was a ballad but unlike a lot of the other stuff I heard him do. The song was about the Troubles. It really cut to the chase. It wasn't taking a position. It was just very poignant about Belfast and the loss of people's lives." Like others mystified by Clark's lack of reading, McCummings could not fathom where the songwriter had found his inspiration. "I didn't think he had that much knowledge or understanding of what was going on in Ireland at the time."

The Troubles in Northern Ireland belatedly reached an international audience in a series of events spread over several years. It had hardly been much different in the UK where the British media ignored Ulster as a matter of government policy. Broadcasters were encouraged to leave reporting to locals, who better knew the region and its particular difficulties. Most news features promoted reconciliation rather than exposing corruption. Investigative journalism was not welcomed. That changed in 1966 during the two-forked anniversary celebrations of the Republican Easter Rising and the Battle of the Somme, along with news that the Queen was due to visit the country. The Easter parades passed peacefully despite the power-keg atmosphere, but visiting journalists sounded shocked and appalled. *The Sunday Times* reported: "There is a part of Britain where the crude apparatus of political and religious oppression – ballot rigging, job and housing discrimination, and an omnipresent threat of violence – comfortably co-exists with intense loyalty to the Crown." The old loyalist conviction of being misunderstood, patronized and perpetually in danger of being sold out by Westminster was no doubt reinforced by such commentaries. For nationalists, it sounded like a sudden end to a conspiracy of silence.

The British media's grim diagnosis was not shared by the youth of Belfast, many of whom saw bigotry as anachronistic and counter to the spirit of the age. Optimists perceived hope beneath the depressing headlines. Civil Rights organizations emerged, including the People's Democracy, founded at Queen's University, Belfast. Among its leading lights was the vibrant, 21-year-old Bernadette Devlin. Inspired by Martin Luther King's long walk from Selma to Montgomery, Alabama, Devlin led a march from Belfast to Derry on New Year's Day, 1969. On the fourth day, the protesters reached Burntollet Bridge, seven miles from Derry, where they were ambushed and savagely beaten by the Ulster Protestant Volunteers. The socialist Eamonn McCann was among the marchers. "When the attacks started we put our heads down and ran. One of my most vivid memories was of Bernadette Devlin urging people to *go back*. I thought, 'Go back on your own, Bernadette!' . . . We regrouped as best we could, then marched towards Derry." Later that evening, a number of inebriated Royal Ulster Constabulary officers entered the Bogside district of Derry, damaging property and chanting sectarian slogans. In the early hours they assembled outside a row of houses and launched into a macabre version of '(Theme From) The Monkees': "Hey, hey, we're the Monkees and we'll monkey you around . . . till your blood is on the ground." One female resident later informed a British government enquiry: "I looked out the window and one shouted, 'Come on, you Fenian, 'til we rape you.'" The events that day reinforced the conviction among Northern Catholics that the police were nothing more than loyalists in state uniform. Many of the civil rights marchers left that blood-splattered affray at Burntollet knowing that they required something more potent than a fatalistic rendition of 'We Shall Overcome'. The pictures of bloodied marchers went around the world.

Events whizzed by – the upsurge of the Provisional IRA, the fatal decision by the UK government to invoke the Special Powers Act and introduce Internment, pogroms, rioting and police brutality, culminating in the tragic events of Bloody Sunday when British soldiers shot dead 13 unarmed civilians during an anti-internment demonstration on 30 January 1972. Violence escalated thereafter with Catholics rioting. The unrest even inflamed moderate opinion in Dublin where an angry mob burned down the British Embassy. In London's Oxford Street, 1,500 marchers turned out for a demonstration opposing British involvement in Northern Ireland. At the centre of the crowd was John Lennon carrying a placard with the words: 'For The IRA Against British Imperialism'. Lennon gave money to the civil rights movement and offered some forthright comments. "If it's a choice between the IRA and the British Army, I'm with the IRA, but if it's a choice between violence and non-violence, I'm with non-violence." After Bloody Sunday, the Provisionals stepped up their terror campaign. Resisting Unionist protests, Conservative Prime Minister Edward Heath suspended the Northern Ireland government at Stormont and introduced direct rule from London. Having determined Ulster policies for 50 years, the Unionists had finally lost their own parliament.

The events in Northern Ireland were barely understood by many Americans who were fed the tragic highlights without too much accompanying political analysis. How any of this filtered through to Gene Clark was a bit of a mystery. "Bloody Sunday was reasonably well documented on the news," Jim McCummings remembers, "but you have to understand that we didn't have any really good television. As far as I was concerned there was no television on the Mendocino coast during those years. The only news we really got was from the *San Francisco Chronicle* which was distributed up here. It wasn't like we went out and bought the *Chronicle* every day. Current events weren't ordinary table conversation at the time."

Clark had a well-tuned antennae for songwriting inspiration but that seldom, if ever, included political matters. It's eminently possible that he learned about Northern Ireland simply from chatting to people at the local bar, the more so considering his Irish roots. However, his most likely source was neither news nor discussions but the reactions and recordings of the former Beatles, whose work had always been a touchstone since he first heard them in 1963. Amazingly, both John Lennon and Paul McCartney were each responding to Bloody Sunday in song. McCartney's Wings issued the single 'Give Ireland Back To The Irish', a simple plea for independence which was banned by the BBC. Lennon responded with 'Sunday Bloody Sunday' which not only denounced the inequities of internment but viciously attacked the Unionist hegemony in the North, dismissing them as colonial 'Anglo pigs and Scotties'. In the song's final verse his indignation and anger spilt over into hysterical hyberbole. The prison Long Kesh is described as a concentration camp and, leaving himself open to accusations of sectarianism, Lennon advocates the compulsory repatriation of Protestants who ally themselves with English rule. Even the Provisional IRA never went that far. 'Sunday Bloody Sunday' was both a stirring piece of propagandist pop and a case study in the limitations of agitprop as artistry.

All this was too much for Gene Clark, who felt uncomfortable or ill-equipped to follow either Lennon's hectoring or McCartney's sardonic sloganeering. His composition was a hymn to Belfast intended to transcend the political and religious divide. "It wasn't pro-IRA or pro-British," McCummings stresses. "It wasn't partisan. This was a song about loss and remorse. It was really profound, and I'll never forget it."

Clark still enjoyed hanging out at his favourite drinking haunts in Albion, occasionally singing a handful of songs with acoustic guitar accompaniment. He was very keen on the Mendocino All Stars, whose ranks now included a couple of new members, guitarist Billy Shay and bassist Peter Oliva. One night, Clark got drunk and decided, against his better judgement, to join the group onstage. It did not go down well. "We were up there playing with the locals," Oliva remembers, "and someone says, 'Oo! There's Gene Clark of the Byrds!' He'd just come in. I was thinking, 'Well, so what? Big deal. I don't care if it's Gene Clark of the Byrds.' He came in shit-faced and said, 'I'm playing with you guys.' He sat down and started playing these random chords. They made no sense. They were going nowhere. They had no structure. Soon, everyone walked off saying, 'Oh, man, this guy's messing with us, let's get out of here.' They all split, but I just stood there. I told myself, 'I'm not going to let this guy get in my craw, just because he was a Byrd. I don't care what he plays. I'm going to stick with him.'" When it was all over, Clark disappeared into the night.

Not long after, Oliva was up on Albion Ridge cycling home when Clark pulled up alongside him in a truck. "I was sweating and huffing and puffing. Gene said, 'What are you doing man? Throw your bike in here!' Carlie and Kelly were with him. We took off and that's when he first started talking about putting a band together." Oliva was amused by Clark's anecdotes and was amazed to learn that he had a long-term friendship with guitarist Jesse Ed Davis. "Gene told me, 'Man, Jesse Ed is so cool.' I said, 'You and Jesse Ed together! Wow, man.' Two drunken Indians – and Indian and Irish! What a lethal combination. I thought, 'Geno, I'm amazed you're alive.'"

Among the musicians in the ever evolving Mendocino All Stars was Lenny Laks, who had been a vocalist in the group, prior to Clark's arrival. "We were all music friends," Laks remembers. "Gene was the celebrity, so you didn't bother him too much, and he was kind of moody. Nevertheless, a terrific guy. We wound up over at Gene's house one afternoon and we'd got a copy of Stevie Wonder's *Innervisions* that had come out that summer. We got stuck in his house for days listening to it. Nobody would leave. He kept bringing us food. I didn't know him that well, but I could tell he was spooked. Gene was transfixed. The music was transformative. I'm sure he left that experience different than how he came in. Nobody said anything. We just laughed, someone rolled a joint, and we put the music on.

We played it over and over. It was a landmark day." The artistry of *Innervisions* inflamed Clark's imagination. From the transcendence of 'Higher Ground' to the anti-drug message of 'Too High' and the epic account of urban racism dramatized in 'Living In The City', Wonder conjured a work of immense quality and imagination on which he played multiple instruments and embraced the sonic innovations of the ARP synthesizer. It was a signpost to the future.

Gene's brother-in-law Jimmy had now settled into a routine at the Lansing Street residence. In order to allow his sister some privacy, he vacated their bay-front room and resided in an adjacent building, which they sometimes used as a sauna. It contained a single room with a bunk bed, but was a handy spot for reading and sleeping. During the day, he appeared at the house for meals and was a regular babysitter when they were away on errands or socializing. Although Gene was pleasant enough, there was some evidence of excessive behaviour and drug-taking. With Carlie about to give birth again, this was not welcomed. "I remember Gene had some cocaine on a plate. I was standing there and she took the plate and knocked it to the ground." Jimmy helped to keep Gene grounded by focusing on practical matters, specifically the ever ongoing works at the house on Middle Ridge Road. "Gene and I would drive out there in his Dodge van. We'd spend the day working. Other times when he wasn't around I'd hitchhike there to do more work. It was just something to do."

Having witnessed Clark admiring a plateful of cocaine, McCummings also noticed some disconcerting facial tics. "I'm not entirely convinced that Gene Clark was always one hundred per cent sane. There were a couple of times I saw him when he had these wild looks in his eyes as if he was suffering from schizophrenia. I don't know. Maybe it had been too much drugs."

Clark's carousing took a backseat hereafter as he devoted his time and industry to a songwriting retreat during which he would compose the bulk of what became *No Other*. "Most of my writing comes from a spiritual place," he later explained. "I think that true art forms in poetry and music, or the joining together of poetry and music, come from a spiritual place. Any amount of soul searching, whether it be by a novelist or a film maker, or anyone, makes for a more profound statement."

Clark's search for the perfect writing environment meant moving away for an extended stay at an empty house overlooking the Pacific Ocean. The property belonged to his friend, Andy Kandanes. "My house in Mendocino was on a cliff. It was great, man. Whales used to come into the cove to work their barnacles off. You couldn't touch that place now for less than two or three million." With several months' grace to think and compose, Clark saw no reason to rush and allowed the songs to emerge at their own pace. "I would just sit in the living room, which had a huge bay window, and stare at the ocean for hours at a time. People would come in and say, 'How come you're not doing anything? How can you just sit there?' But I would have a pen and paper there, and a guitar or piano, and pretty soon a thought would come and I'd write it down or put it on tape. In many instances, after a day of meditation looking at something which is a very natural force, I'd come up with something."

Clark was left to marinate in the juices of his own especial genius. His inspiration was provided by an unusual soundtrack. Far from the country rock of his fellow travellers or any forays into musical esoterica, he favoured two familiar chart albums: the Rolling Stones' *Goat's Head Soup* and Stevie Wonder's aforementioned *Innervisions.* "When I was writing *No Other* I concentrated on those two albums a lot, and was very inspired by the direction of them . . . which is ironic because *Innervisions* is a very climbing spiritual thing, while *Goat's Head Soup* has connotations of the lower forces as well. But somehow the joining of the two gave me a place to go with *No Other,* and I wanted to go in a powerful direction."

Beyond these indirect influences lay an unconscious process of creation that Clark tapped into with frequent and rewarding results. "The actual writing of a song usually comes in the form of a realization. It might be a dream. The whole of 'Some Misunderstanding' was written in a dream. I got up and wrote it down . . . I woke up and I told my wife, 'Look, I've got to get up, turn on the lights for a moment and write this down.' I wrote the song in completion because the dream was still fresh in my mind. I can't contrive a song." This was not the entire truth. In completing 'Some Misunderstanding', Clark admitted that he was also expressing his feelings about the cocaine culture of the early Seventies. "In the last few years a lot of friends of mine have gone [in] different directions and stuff, and some of them have over-indulged in some of their habits and have left their souls through the ceiling. This song expresses a little bit of feelings about that. . . ."

Clark's songwriting flurry was nearing completion when he had some further good news. Fifteen days before Kelly's second birthday, Carlie gave birth to their second child, Kai Taylor Clark, on 5 December 1973. It was a time of celebration. "I remember the night he was born," says Peter Oliva. "That same week they brought him into one of the clubs and put him on a table and the whole band just wailed away."

Around the time of Kai's birth, Carlie reconnected with her friend, Mary Pritchard. Much had changed since their time together in Idlewild. Mary had a son, Justin, born the same week as Kelly Clark, after which she had moved back to Hollywood, renting a house in Laurel Canyon. Her drug-dealing boyfriend Billy had twice been jailed and they had recently split up. Suddenly, Mary found herself homeless. Carlie persuaded her to move to Mendocino and kindly provided refuge in Lansing Street. "Their farm was pretty dishevelled and so rundown that they couldn't live in it. So I moved into their rented house. We all lived together, Carlie, her brother Jimmy, and the boys." Kelly and Justin became close friends and remained so throughout their teenage years and beyond.

The New Year promised so much for Gene Clark, both personally and professionally. His domestic life was relatively settled, despite some wild lapses in behaviour, while his cachet in LA remained strong. Crucially, he believed that his career could be transformed by his association with Asylum Records. The label had a Midas quality and a reputation for discovering and nurturing songwriting talent from Jackson Browne and Judee Sill to the Eagles. President David Geffen was a brilliant negotiator whose powerplays were already legendary in the music industry. Securing the services of the original Byrds was a miraculous achievement in itself but the entrepreneur also attracted Joni Mitchell and, in what was arguably his greatest coup, not only reunited Bob Dylan and the Band for a major tour but secured the master's signature for a studio album, *Planet Waves*.

In the past, Clark had suffered a stuttering solo career with CBS and A&M, but surely Asylum would correct that with a combination of marketing skill and promotional nous. There was every possibility that they might help him overcome his fear of touring by offering specially selected support slots to introduce him to new listeners. Judee Sill, for example, had opened for Crosby & Nash in what was a dream concert line-up. The daringly ambitious Eagles were unafraid to tour with such disparate acts as the J. Geils Band, Jethro Tull and Yes and had recently been rewarded with a more suitable supporting role on Neil Young's *Tonight's The Night* tour. Clark, who had covered two of the Canadian's songs on the Byrds' reunion album, would have been the perfect aperitif for an audience of Young aficionados. If Asylum could arrange something like this, Clark hoped, then he might yet reach the mass audience that Crosby commanded. More realistically, he might at least establish himself as a concert draw on a level with McGuinn, which was good business.

This was the optimistic scenario envisaged before the recording of the new album, but there were reasons to be cautious. Much of Asylum's early success had been due to the concomitant power of Geffen/Roberts Management, which controlled the careers of its major acts. Unlike Jackson Browne, the Eagles, and most of the other stars on the label, Clark was not part of the Geffen/Roberts stable and he dearly needed direction. There was also evidence that Asylum was no longer the artiste-friendly label it had been at its inception. Geffen had sold his interests in the record company to Warner Communications chief Steve Ross for $7 million. David remained president but no longer co-managed any of its acts. This caused considerable resentment from several artistes, notably the Eagles. There was also the seldom discussed matter of Asylum failures. David Blue and Judee Sill were part of the original stable but, maverick by nature, they wilted commercially under Geffen's aegis. Additionally, Geffen was also pursuing related projects, including the opening of the Roxy, a rock venue in direct competition with the Troubadour. That, along with the ongoing fixation with Dylan, ensured that Geffen's attention and commitment were stretched.

By early 1974, a producer had been appointed to transform Clark's new compositions into something special. Thomas Jefferson Kontos was of Greek extraction and Native American ancestry. He claimed to have been brought up on an Indian reservation in North Dakota by his grandmother, White Cloud. By 1958, he had changed his surname to Kaye and soon found lucrative employment working for Scepter Records in New York. Over the next two decades, he enjoyed a remarkable run as a producer, arranger and songwriter. Among the artistes he worked with were Dee Clark, Maxine Brown, Chuck Jackson, Bobby Moore, Bob Havens, the Shirelles, Jay & The Americans, Barbara Mauritz, Loudon Wainwright III, Link Wray and the band he named after his grandmother, White Cloud. Among his songwriting co-credits were Three Dog Night's 1971 US Top 20 hit, 'One Man Band'. More recently, he had been given a recording contract by ABC, issuing an eponymous album, followed by the newly completed, *First Grade*. The latter was a fine showcase for his songwriting and production skills, highlighted by the evocative, autobiographical 'Northern California' and the choral extravaganza 'American Lovers', written by Walter Becker and Donald Fagen of Steely Dan. Both albums demonstrated Kaye's drawing power in the industry, particularly *First Grade* which featured a startling line-up of musical heavyweights and singers, including a rare appearance by England's premier soul songstress, Dusty Springfield.

Kaye's recent track record suggested that he was not a man to be constrained by record company budgets. He was in the midst of overspending on an album by the party-loving Bobby Neuwirth, a project that had got so out of hand that only gold record status was likely to recoup Asylum Records' investment. Neuwirth had been Dylan's best pal in the mid-Sixties and retained that friendship which served as a talisman now that the great one was also signed to Asylum on a short-term deal. Kaye never dreamed of producing Gene Clark, but the portents were already there during those Neuwirth sessions. As Kaye remembered: "Neuwirth and Dylan were sitting there, and we were talking about songwriters, and they both said that their three favourite songwriters in the world were Bob Dylan, Bobby Charles and Gene Clark. Then, three days later, David Geffen called me, feeling – I think – that the only way to get me to finish the Bobby Neuwirth record was to offer me another project, and he asked whether I wanted to produce Gene Clark or Jackson Browne. I said, 'Gene Clark'. They're both great artistes, but I felt I could do more with Gene because he's different."

David Geffen was an astute judge of talent and his pairing of Clark and Kaye would prove inspired. But the combination wasn't without dangers, as Geffen was well aware. Dealing with Kaye had never been easy. At the start of Geffen's entrepreneurial career, he had initially encountered the producer in a personal capacity when overseeing the career of the singer-songwriter, Laura Nyro. Hugely talented, Nyro was a mass of contradictions: image-conscious, insecure and very controlling. "She was a very strange girl," Geffen recalls. "She had hair down to her thighs. She wore purple lipstick, Christmas balls for earrings, strange clothes." Geffen's dedication to Nyro as a mentor and father confessor was already the stuff of legend in the music business. After her disastrous appearance at 1967's Monterey Pop Festival, Geffen was waiting in the wings to console her. He promoted her songs with evangelical vigour and was instrumental in getting the 5th Dimension to record 'Stoned Soul Picnic', 'Sweet Blindness' and 'Wedding Bell Blues', all major US hits. Unfortunately, Nyro had wedding bell blues of her own, which largely centred on Tommy Kaye, whose eccentric temperament was a match for her own. "David was looking after Laura Nyro and Tommy was engaged to her," says Andy Kandanes. "They arranged this big wedding at the Plaza. Tommy was living with her and it was so weird. He was telling me she'd set the alarm clock when they had sex and she'd only allow him a certain amount of time. He claimed she was dosing his coffee with LSD. One day he stopped drinking the coffee and said, 'I don't want to marry this chick!' This was at the last minute." According to Kandanes, Geffen had to deal with the psychic fallout, but there was no denying that Kaye had made a lasting impression.

In later years, Tommy sometimes joked that Geffen's Kaye/Clark matchmaking was a piece of Machiavellian revenge. It certainly seemed that way on the evening of their first meeting. There was an ugly encounter in a restaurant that threatened to end the partnership before it had even begun. "He and I had a terrible fight," Gene recalled. "We got drunk and started yelling at each other." Clark was a picture of Catholic remorse the next morning and phoned Kaye to apologize. The producer was still stinging from the memory of Clark's verbal abuse but recognized a genuine humility in his voice. Once Kaye calmed down and accepted Clark's contrition, their friendship blossomed. "We're soul brothers," Kaye later told me. "The connection is that strong."

Clark's wife Carlie concurred with the 'soul brother' hypothesis, as did others in their circle. "Tommy Kaye and Gene were a lot like Doug and Gene," she says. "They were ludicrous together, but it wasn't meaningless insanity; it was creative obsession. They would just get so excited musically . . . Gene was an instrument that he could send to these places . . . Kaye was able to take Gene to another level."

As expected, Kaye's recruitment ensured that a wealth of session players made themselves available for the project. These included members of the LA studio supercombo, the Section, plus pianist Mike Utley, who had also appeared on *White Light*. This time Utley would take a far greater role in proceedings, working alongside Kaye and Clark as an arranger. Along the way, old friends Doug Dillard and Jesse Ed Davis turned up to provide assistance. From the outset, Kaye was the great cheerleader and insisted that no expense should be spared in ensuring that the album was perfectly recorded. "Gene played me those songs and I just flipped out. It was a very expensive record to make . . . Gene is a one-take artiste in the studio but we rehearsed for a week in a hall. On the cut 'No Other', Butch Trucks' drums got lost at the airport and we had to rent some Japanese Pearl drums which had a wonderful sound. After we cut the basic track, Lee Sklar, the bass player, brought in all his gimmicks – fuzz tones, phase shifters and the like – and asked me if he could just sit around the studio and overdub four or five bass parts in harmony . . . He wrote out the harmony parts and really did a job on it. Just knocked me out. The sound was incredible."

The sessions at Village Recorders studio that March proceeded slowly but smoothly with Clark totally focused on the project. He sat in a specially constructed vocal booth and remained there for the overdubs, fascinated by the sonic panorama that Kaye was creating. The musicians responded in kind, adding parts that were inventive and innovative. It was a thrilling arabesque. Lee Sklar remembers only one moment of serious tension. While work was concluding on the title track, Joe Cocker, who had been recording in an adjoining studio, wandered into the control room for a listen. He became so carried away by the arrangement that he unleashed a high-pitched scream of appreciation. It blew the headphones off the assembled musicians, creating havoc. Clark was so incensed that he tore down the artificial booth and headed for the control room with murderous intent. Cocker's associates ushered him from the studio just in time. That particular session had to be postponed in order to allow the musicians time to recover their hearing. It was a rare setback.

During the recording of *No Other*, Carlie and the children ventured to Hollywood, along with their teenage nanny, Dara Zimmerman. Born on 4 July 1959, the precocious Zimmerman had moved from Los Angeles to Mendocino with her mother, and became a babysitter to several of the 'rock 'n' roll moms' in the vicinity. Her first encounter with Gene occurred at this time. The LA trek was a pleasant expedition. "Carlie had this big Dodge van and she'd put pillows, blankets and a cooler in the back. She made it comfy and cosy back there for me, Kelly and Kai. We'd sit in the back, play games and I'd read them stories."

After arriving in Hollywood, they unpacked at their suite in the Tropicana Motel and headed to the Troubadour, where Clark was to appear that evening. During the afternoon soundcheck Dara was introduced to Gene while Kai lay asleep underneath a table. The party returned to the Tropicana for dinner, after which Gene and Carlie set off for the club. They stayed late, partying, then bickering, as drink flowed. On the way back, Carlie stopped off at a late-night grocery to get food for the children. Gene followed, guitar case in hand. As they reached the Tropicana, Gene stumbled into his wife, who ended up in a pool, surrounded by soggy foodstuff. Dara, Kelly and Kai were awoken by the commotion. "Gene and Carlie were screaming and yelling and woke everybody in the motel. Then the cops came. It was about 2 am and they were at the front door shining their flashlights on me and the kids. Gene calmed them down and they left and everyone went back to sleep." The next morning Gene could not locate his car keys which Dara later found sequestered in a toilet paper container in the bathroom. It was an illuminating introduction to the chaotic life of Gene Clark.

During their trips to LA, Carlie and Gene partied with Ringo Starr and attended various shows, most notably the Eagles, whose debut album had included 'Train Leaves Here This Morning'. Clark always spoke highly of the country-rock band, citing Glenn Frey's songwriting as inspirational.

Dara was struck by the contrasting personalities of her employers. "The sweeter side of Gene was when he was playing and singing and when he was with his kids. When he was sober and with Carlie he was awful happy. He'd almost have a twinkle in his eyes. But he was so extreme. Everything about him was extreme.

Carlie was very flamboyant and, I don't like to say it, but very needy. She was a very large person with a huge heart who always took over the whole room. She had to be the centre [of attention]. Her personality was huge. With Gene it worked for her because he allowed that." One other aspect of Carlie that Dara noted was her love of a good yarn. Certain biographical details and anecdotes seemed fluid, depending on her mood, intention or humour. "Carlie was nuts! She changed her story the whole time. I found out only a few years ago that she was the oldest in her family. She told me she was younger than Jimmy. I never knew how old Carlie really was at that time. Nobody saw a birth certificate! She had a good imagination, you could say. That suited her personality. Everything had to be big with Carlie and her stories were always big!"

In September 1974, the produce of Clark's recent labours were issued in the US market on Asylum Records. *No Other* was Clark's indisputable masterpiece, an astonishing phantasmagoric fusion of country, chorale and gospel, breathtaking in its audacity. In contrast to the austerity of *White Light*, the production on *No Other* was dazzling in ambition. Producer Thomas Jefferson Kaye recklessly exceeded record company budgets in order to create what he later told me was "a work that I saw as my Brian Wilson extravaganza".

The most impressive aspect of *No Other* is the ethereal feel that Clark sustains over two album sides. There are few records in rock's rich history that match this one for consistency of excellence. The work opens deceptively with 'Life's Greatest Fool', a song seemingly in the familiar country-rock tradition of the early Seventies until the chorus explodes into a gospel celebration. The lyrics are something else again – full of aphorisms and homespun philosophy, with Clark issuing conundrums like a rock Confucius. Underpinning the work is a personal symbolism, at times unfathomable, and all the more intriguing as a result.

Images of silver are scattered throughout the album, with references to a silver phial, a silver shore and a silver raven. Clark even toured subsequently with a backing group dubbed the Silverados. The song 'Silver Raven' is one of his best, with a beautifully expressive vocal and a spine-tingling guitar solo by Jesse Ed Davis. It's gratifying to picture Clark, Kaye and Davis, three doomed excessives who always lived on the edge, combining their talents with such discipline and purpose.

The title track proved the longest to commit to tape and a growing sense of frustration continued until Kaye brought in Joe Lala to provide some Cuban rhythms. "Joe was crucial in unravelling that song. His percussion fills helped a lot." Sly Stone was in attendance during part of the session and his presence seems to have permeated the music in subliminal fashion. Kaye, displaying an eccentricity worthy of Brian Wilson and Phil Spector, double-tracked Clark's vocal, then channelled the results through one of the studio's telephones in order to create that eerie, cavernous sound.

The closing track on the first side, 'Strength Of Strings', once and for all proclaimed Clark as king of the cosmic cowboys. Its premise displays a degree of ambition unseen in rock since an acid-addled Lennon envisaged Tibetan monks on mountain tops and demanded music to convey "the end of the world". Clark's brief was no less simple: what he wanted was a song to express the unconscious process by which music is assimilated. It is akin to an epic search for euphonic euphoria. Lyrically, he almost falls victim to the incoherence of New Age mysticism with talk of "the cosmic range", but what a fantastic landscape his imagination conjures. Here is a place, or state of mind, in which things are seemingly both constant (note the repetition of "always") and mutable ("there is always *change*"). The cosmology is timeless and spatially infinite, just as the narrator's psychology is perpetually both elated and melancholic. These oblique ruminations climax in a powerful image of music channelling through his soul. The backing track, an epic production in itself, features arranger/ keyboardist Mike Utley doubling the piano part by introducing Craig Doerge, aided by a veritable legion of backing singers blasting out a ghostly chorale. It is as if

Clark had told them to conjure up a rock equivalent of the music of the spheres.

Amazingly, there is no drop in quality or mystery on the second side of the record. The fascinating 'From A Silver Phial' begins with the image of a cocaine burn-out, soon to be swamped in Clark's effusive alliteration ("Said she saw the sword of sorrow sunken in the sand of searching souls"). Even the narrative technique and sense of place seem shifting, with diction that successively conjures up 'once upon a time' fairy-tale morality and a master/servant relationship straight out of a Victorian melodrama. It is as if we are witnessing a dual time scheme, stretching across a century, like the latter-day movie adaptation of Fowles' *The French Lieutenant's Woman*.

The eight-minute 'Some Misunderstanding' features the old Clark vibrato on a composition that starts in conversational mode before shifting into a densely argued philosophical tract. Like a drowning man, the narrator sees his life flashing in front of his eyes and tries to make sense of the universe. "Maybe someone can explain time," Clark asks hopefully before attempting to express the difference between a genuine visionary experience and a quick fix. As the song's inner drama unfolds, a startling array of instruments are introduced, including piano, guitar and violin, heaped layer upon layer until the song reaches its uneasy conclusion.

After the exhaustive speculation of 'Some Misunderstanding', the light country rock of 'The True One' offers some relief but, beneath the jaunty arrangement, Clark spins out some homely advice in similar fashion to the opening 'Life's Greatest Fool'.

The closing track, 'Lady Of The North' imagines a transcendent flight into the heavens, as Clark presents his most impressive vocal to date, stretching syllables and straining against an increasingly enveloping musical backing. Piano, violin, wah-wah guitar and cello interfuse until you start hearing instruments that aren't even there. At the end, the music takes flight in an elongated note that resonates in the mind long after the music has stopped. It is no wonder that so many people consider this album to be among the greatest, and most underrated, ever released. Gram Parsons once expressed his dream of writing 'Cosmic American Music' and if ever that definition could be applied to a rock record then it is this one.

There is one final mystery surrounding *No Other*: its strange artwork. It included a photo and poster of Gene decked out in satins, eye makeup and permed hair. Sexual ambiguity and androgyny were familiar enough marketing devices in early Seventies' rock, but not among West Coast musicians and singer-songwriters whose work personified a male, heterosexual ideal. Breaking that tradition was a daring move, and all the more puzzling on a record whose lyrics revealed no hint of such sensibilities. It certainly provoked some contrasting comments in Clark's circle. "Wasn't the cover of *No Other* bizarre?" says Tommy Kaye's then girlfriend, and later spouse, Hillary. "His wife Carlie and the girls Ea Oleno and Judy Hadish got Gene to dress up with clothes from the Pleasure Dome which was pretty much a chick shop. They put the makeup on him and did all that wacky stuff and he just went along with it. He was so secure in his masculinity that it didn't bother him a bit. But everybody was saying, 'What's happening to Gene? He looks like some fag.' It was hilarious He was just on a lark letting these girls play with him."

Clark confirmed as much, admitting that the camp photograph "originally started out as a hoax, a joke, a thing that we were going to do just to see if we could do it". He was probably as surprised as anybody when the people at Asylum agreed to support the spoof. For his part, Clark had always been interested in the 1920s and was intrigued by the movie stars of Tinseltown's golden era. Indeed, he was still regularly hanging out with the sons and heirs of several great Hollywood dynasties, whose members no doubt appreciated the in-joke. The artwork caused considerable puzzlement among fans and commentators. The UK music press, no strangers to the charms of glam rock from T. Rex to Roxy Music, sarcastically dubbed Clark the West Coast's first poseur. It was almost a compliment. Tommy Kaye was more prosaic, pointing out that "with the visual image of *No Other*,

Gene just wanted to take a vacation from being a cowboy".

Clark had an additional agenda about the cover that he used for his own personal amusement. After signing with Asylum, he heard industry rumours that Geffen might have gay sexual tendencies. It made him wonder to what extent he had been signed for his rugged looks as well as, or as opposed to, his musical talent. Clark built an entire fantasy around this crazy notion mainly for the entertainment of his closest friends. Putting on his deep John Wayne voice, he would fabricate a story in which "Geffen was secretly in love with him" but ultimately rejected. "That was after Gene did his David Bowie thing with the *No Other* cover," adds Tom Slocum, later a mutual friend of Clark and Kaye. The fantasy was difficult to follow and full of nonsensical quips. "Gene would go into character and say, 'Hey, Sloc, do you think he might be a peanut butter guy? I wonder if David Geffen wants to get aboard the Kansas City Southern? I don't think I have enough room in the locomotive for him.' Gene would go into another character to disguise whatever emotional thing he was confronting. At other times he'd say things like 'The Ponderosa's got the little campfire girls from the West coming over later. Do you want to come and hang out?' "

Making fun of David Geffen, even in private, was not the most sensible career move. Clark felt secure as long as there was still faith in his music, but more shocks followed. Kaye claimed that when he presented the record to Geffen, the mogul slammed the album down in angry disbelief that an investment of nearly a hundred grand had netted only eight songs. Geffen may have been angry with Kaye over the combined costs of the Bobby Neuwirth and Gene Clark projects, but his supposed objection about the number of tracks seemed petty, if true. Clark's earlier albums with A&M and Columbia were shorter in length, even if they had more songs. There were other albums of the era that offered fewer tracks than *No Other* (Frank Zappa's *Hot Rats*; Traffic's *John Barleycorn Must Die* and *The Low Spark Of High-Heeled Boys*; and various albums by the Grateful Dead) but they were usually improvisory in nature. That said, there were several important albums from fellow singer-songwriters between 1969–74 (Van Morrison's *Astral Weeks* and *Saint Dominic's Preview*; Tim Buckley's *Happy Sad*; Neil Young's *Everybody Knows This Is Nowhere* and *On The Beach*) that had the same or fewer songs than Clark's latest effort. Even Geffen's great protégé Jackson Browne released the eight-song set *Late For The Sky* during the same year as *No Other*, and would repeat that number with *The Pretender* a couple of years later. Given the above, Geffen's wrath, if reported correctly, hardly seemed justified.

At one point, Clark had considered adding more compositions but was unwilling to tamper with the lengthier tracks for fear of compromising the mood. It was a wise decision. "We could have done more songs," Clark later told me. "There were others that I could have worked on, but they didn't seem right. We were never going to be allowed to do a double album anyway, that's for sure. Also, I thought the material that we had perfectly created the mood. It wouldn't have worked if we'd edited the songs on the album. That was the point. Tommy Kaye agreed with me. It wasn't even considered."

The additional songs that Clark mentions here were not recorded during the sessions for *No Other*. This became clear when work was undertaken for a UK remastered reissue of *No Other* in 2003. A thorough search of the archives revealed various outtakes and a revised version of 'Train Leaves Here This Morning', but no hidden songs. The myth of the 'missing' *No Other* tracks had been unintentionally started by Clark himself in some vaguely worded statements to the rock press. Speaking to *Dark Star*'s Steve Burgess in 1977, he said: "I explain to a lot of people that *No Other* is not the complete *No Other* album on that record. It was originally a 13-track album, but we weren't able to do a double-record and so the rest of the songs were left unfinished. Because of the length of the cuts we couldn't include them." When Clark says "because of the length of the cuts we couldn't include them", he is not referring to the five missing tracks, as might be assumed, but the eight tracks that were actually on *No Other*. All this begs the question: what happened to the unfinished tracks? Perhaps they were recorded at rehearsals or in demo form before he began the sessions for *No Other*. Or maybe they just existed in Clark's imagination and were never recorded at all. Revealingly, no unreleased songs were registered for copyright during this period.

Despite Geffen's reservations, there was still hope that *No Other* might outsell Clark's previous records. Asylum promoted the album admirably with trade ads in the music press, but to little avail. The record climbed to number 144 in the *Billboard* charts and then disappeared. Everyone felt deflated. Clark was inconsolable. "I felt it was a truly fine album and I felt very let down, very disappointed that it didn't do better than it did. Almost to the point of depression because I thought I'd finally found a niche for my own art that I could carry on into other areas."

Presumably, Geffen concluded that his earlier criticisms were vindicated so washed his hands of the project. He seemed to be employing an accountant's logic. His label had spent big money on the recording, but they still couldn't reach the Top 100. "He was furious . . ." says Tommy Kaye. "David just dropped it and wouldn't get behind it. He wouldn't give us any money to go on tour or to subsidize a band or anything. At that time he was thinking about going into movies and he sort of lost his desire."

There were other factors that might have contributed towards Geffen's apparent apathy or anger. Less than a month before the release of *No Other*, Dylan had re-signed to Columbia Records, abandoning Asylum with the realpolitik of a medieval potentate. Geffen was saddened and enraged. He later described Dylan as "so mean, so jealous, so cheap, ego-ridden and petty, such an ingrate". The devastating putdown says much about his disillusionment with the music business at the time. Clark seemed similarly incensed with Geffen.

At one point a drunken Gene Clark attempted to confront the record mogul in Dan Tana's, which merely made matters worse. What occurred is still disputed and probably distorted by repeated second-hand testimony from non-witnesses. It has become part of Clark mythology that he accosted Geffen but those that tell that tale were not actually there. Perhaps Clark was whisked away before something serious did happen. Having spent most of the previous year writing and recording, he was now in urgent need of additional income. It was clear that *No Other* would never recoup its advance, but Clark felt obliged to promote the record as best he could. "The way *No Other* was overlooked confused and discouraged me. After that I didn't want to do *anything*. It really confused me. It didn't deflate my confidence. I knew better than to think I was a fool because nobody picked up on it. But I had to sit back and reconsider what I was doing. I had to consider what would be the best way to break through that barrier."

Reluctantly, Clark decided to go back on the road. It was his only option at the time. He could not afford to employ a full band and there was no prospect of securing well-paid dates at big venues. Instead, he drifted into the twilight zone of small club and bar dates, sometimes in far-away places in the American heartland. Even the drugs were strictly old school. Over the next year, he would survive on an unhealthy diet of speed and booze.

"Gene used to be a real 'upper' guy," says Peter Oliva. "When he visited LA he had a lot Dr Feelgoods there, and could go in and get a prescription filled for a handful of Dexedrine. He really liked uppers. He was a country boy, I'm telling you. You pop those uppers and you stay up all night playing guitar. It was like Dylan [in 1965–66] zapped on speed and writing those pages of songs."

Dara Zimmerman remembers a daily ritual. "Gene would wake up in the morning, take a black beauty, go back to sleep, then wake up again and have his coffee." Carlie dabbled only occasionally. Amusingly, she put the amphetamines to practical use. "She did speed, but she'd have it stashed for months. Then she'd take a couple of black beauties and clean the whole house before Gene came home." There was a wholesomeness about Carlie then, far removed from the drug dependency already prevalent in Mendocino. "She started out very innocently. Carlie didn't do coke with Gene. She never did a lot of drugs when I was with her as a kid. She was kind of scared of them. Later, she blew all the money she had."

When Gene was focused, untroubled by concerns about recording and touring commitments, he would sit at a table in the family parlour, guitar by his side, studiously composing a melody or committing lyrics to an ever present notepad. Often, he would venture outside to their orchard, as if seeking further inspiration. A beatific calm would descend upon the house at such moments as he lost himself in his songwriting. For both Carlie and Dara these were the happiest times at Middle Ridge.

Before setting out on tour, Gene and the family relocated to Silverado Canyon, the nineteenth-century silver mining community situated in California's Santa Ana Mountains. There he rehearsed with bass player and banjoist Duke Bardwell and guitarist Roger White. Bardwell had recently come off a touring stint with Elvis Presley, an association which greatly impressed Clark who had never lost his affection for the King. Seeking a suitable name for the group, they settled on the Silverados in tribute to the canyon. The tour commenced on a prophetically bad note. On 19 October 1974, they were scheduled to play at Hollywood's Troubadour on a bill featuring Odetta and Roger McGuinn. The unfortunate Roger White damaged his ankle in a motorcycle accident on the way and could not attend. It was a calamity that spooked Clark, whose stage paranoia returned with a vengeance. Deadening his fears with booze, he struggled through his set before joining McGuinn for a grand finale of 'Eight Miles High'. By that time, Bardwell had become an embarrassed spectator surveying this train wreck with a mixture of dread and morbid fascination. It was just the start.

The contradiction between the home-loving rustic songwriter and the weary road-addled troubadour was taking its toll on Clark. Thanksgiving offered a welcome break and an opportunity to reminisce. Ten years before, he had sat around a table at Eddie Tickner's Hollywood home toasting his good fortune. The 'Jet

Set' (McGuinn, Clark and Crosby) had recently signed a contract with CBS Records but required a more appropriate name. While the turkey was passed around, various group titles were discussed but there was truly nothing that could compare with 'The Byrds'. At that moment, Clark's optimism was unlimited. He was like a knight preparing for a crusade. Since then, so much had happened – unimagined pop fame, money, a nervous breakdown, a solo career, various collaborations, Byrds reunions and, most recently, the great *No Other*. It should have been a time of great celebration, but the album's failure cast a melancholy shadow over the festivities. Carlie was determined to make the best of it. "We all cooked with wood stoves then," recalls her friend Mary Kendall (née Pritchard). "Carlie was a great cook and an earth mama. Thanksgiving was always quite a production." Gene, ever ready to play the manly host and carve the turkey, removed the bird from the stove, placed it on a platter, then lost his grip. The contents tumbled into an adjacent bundle of chopped firewood. "The turkey was so well done it fell apart. We just picked the wood chips out of it and went on eating anyway." The desiccated bird appeared to symbolize the state of Clark's life and career. A decade on from the Byrds' formation, so much had been lost as well as won, but the present was a time of uncertainty and what lay ahead seemed bleak. Were Gene and Carlie still a happy couple? "I think at the beginning they were," says Mary, "but there were so many drugs and craziness and people and all that stuff that it was pretty hard to stay focused." Gene felt bereft, lost in the voracious revel of his senses, confused and wary of the uncharted geography of the future. What stability still existed would be further undermined when he reluctantly returned to the road with the Silverados.

Touring was a tiring slog. Clark continued to consume speed to keep awake on long drives, then put himself to sleep with fantastic amounts of alcohol. "Our act was basically a trio," says Bardwell, "with Gene on acoustic guitar and harmonica." Their performances were erratic and the venues they played spoke volumes about the low-key nature of the enterprise: Sophie's

Place in Palo Alto; Mother's Blues in Dallas; Ebbets Field in Denver. A handful of shows were bootlegged and the Denver date (19 February) was belatedly released as an archive album, *Silverado '75*, in 2008. It was an interesting set, comprising a couple of Byrds' classics ('Here Without You' and 'Set You Free This Time'), two selections from *No Other* (the title track and 'Silver Raven'), a sprightly 'Home Run King' and 'The Daylight Line', a studio version of which was never issued. The Dallas show, recorded on 24 May, featured two rarities: the fatalistic 'What Is Meant Will Be' and a metaphysical country tune, 'The Wheel Of Time'.

During autumn 1975, the band added drummer Mark Singer and pianist John Guthridge to fill out the sound. In October, they returned to Ebbets Field for a memorable performance with a similar set and a few surprises. There was an engaging revival of Dillard & Clark's 'The Radio Song', with some honky-tonk piano, an admirable attempt at 'No Other' and a keyboard-led 'Silver Raven'. Clark even excavated 'I'll Be Back' the Del Shannon-inspired Lennon/McCartney composition featured on *A Hard Day's Night*. Duke Bardwell's banjo was prominent throughout.

Nobody denies that these shows were anything less than erratic. Sometimes it worked magically, but there was always the possibility of disaster. "The drinking was stronger than him," Carlie concludes. She remembers phone calls from concerned colleagues informing her, "Gene has flipped out." All she could tell them was to leave him alone until the demons had departed. "For all the gift he had, there was another side of him that was dark." His songwriting talent could not mask his insecurities. "He didn't know where it was coming from or if it would ever come again. Why him? What did he do to deserve this? There was that whole side of it and I think it took him to the peak of insanity many times."

Her brother Jimmy expressed similar concerns. "I think music was the driving force in his life. Without trying to make it sound insulting, there were times when music was more important than his family and kids. I didn't know everything that was going on between him and my sister, but for people who get wrapped up in music, it can be like a monkey on their back. Other things end up being sacrificed."

Duke Bardwell had been impressed by Clark's songwriting, but also realized that he was a tortured soul whose demons were frequently unleashed by alcohol. He looked back on that time less than charitably. "We put in two very difficult years of low-budget travelling and performing with a drunk that gave both of us some of our most embarrassing moments ever onstage. To this day I would have to say that I will never forget watching genius and insanity go hand in hand like they did with Gene Clark."

In common with other musicians returning from long stints on the road, Clark found it difficult to readjust to normal life. His behaviour became more unpredictable and eccentric. Dara remembers one morning when he awoke, hungover from the previous evening. He took their Dodge van into the apple orchard adjoining their house and maniacally tore around the soggy ground until the vehicle was covered in mud, locking him inside. "I watched. It was pretty entertaining, actually. Gene was funny. He turned these huge circles in the yard. Then he climbed out the car window and came back into the house. He was all muddy and ranting and raving about something. Maybe Carlie hadn't cooked his eggs right."

More and more, Gene was subject to irrational rage, a likely legacy of the scary combination of speed and booze still coursing through his body after the tour. His relationship with his wife was increasingly characterized by angry outbursts. His friend Philip Oleno heard stories of screaming fights, as did others in their circle. "They were going through a very rough patch," says Michael McGibbon, "and a rough patch for them is totally devastating for normal people."

"He and Carlie got into the most outrageous fights I've ever seen anyone get into in my life," adds Dara Zimmerman. "I'm amazed they lived through some of the things they did when they were together. When I was with Carlie and the kids and he was on the road or in LA recording, it was very peaceful because she didn't drink a lot or do a lot of drugs. She wasn't real good at being a mom, but she *was* a good mom, if that makes sense. The marriage really did last a long time considering how volatile it was. There was never much middle ground with them."

Peter Oliva also knew the marriage was in serious trouble. "They lived in Middle Ridge Road which was a dirt road that had all these people on it. They used to get upset because Geno and Carlie would get drunk and fight. He'd go 90 miles per hour down this road in the middle of the night, crashing his car and having knockdown drag-out fights. It was nasty. When it ended, I think it was the best thing for Gene in a way." Carlie claims that Gene somehow avoided any damaging physical violence against her, but acknowledges that his verbal abuse was frighteningly intense and, of course, he was always capable of scrapping with others.

There was a respite from domestic problems in January 1976 when Clark entered Los Angeles' Fidelity Studios to prepare material for a new album. Tommy Kaye returned as producer and all four Silverados attended, along with several of the *No Other* crew, supervised by Mike Utley. Kaye was unfamiliar with the Silverados. As Duke Bardwell recalls: "Roger and I started playing, but were removed for being too opinionated and set in our ways regarding material. We were seriously pissed [off] at the time but, looking back, I know they were right . . . I absolutely loved the songs that man wrote."

Clark always sided with Kaye, insisting, "I'm looking for something a little more country – commercial, yes, but with a strong R&B influence . . . the best of country with the best of Motown." Turning frustration to advantage, he concluded that the last couple of years in the commercial wilderness had made him stronger. "It's easier for a band to make it when you're a little older, especially if you've been in the business and experienced success before. You're able to cope better: if you're having problems you can see the reasons for it, and not get yourself uptight. I'm experiencing a little of those tensions with my own band right now: a little lack of understanding of how the business works . . . They're experienced musicians, but they haven't seen the magnitude of success that I have, come back down from it, and spent a few years sitting in the country analysing what went wrong."

Clark's expediency was understandable. He knew that Kaye had a particular sound in his head and preferred to collaborate with musicians of his choosing. Kaye was unrepentant about replacing anyone. "Gene had started to work with the Silverado band, but it's one thing to play live and another to record in the studio. I decided they weren't quite making it. They didn't have the studio technique . . . the first two songs we cut we didn't even end up using. On 'The Daylight Line' and 'The Wheel Of Time' we didn't have Jim Fielder on bass or Sammy Creason on drums and it just wasn't sounding right." The abandonment of 'The Wheel Of Time' was regrettable. Lyrically, it was similar to the abstractions heard on *White Light* and *No Other*, with Clark pondering the destiny of the cycle that surrounds a soul. If Kaye had been producing a work as extravagant as *No Other*, this would have been a prime contender, but it was not to be.

According to Clark, they were planning to invite Motown producer Joe Porter to produce some of the tracks in order to achieve the requisite R&B flavour. Unfortunately, Porter was busy working with his wife Bobbye Hall Porter (who had previously provided some percussion for *White Light*) on a solo album, which would be released the following year. The R&B/country fusion, which had been percolating in Clark's mind since jamming with the Mendocino All Stars, was modified at this point. Kaye concentrated on recording five demos, which were presented to Asylum Records "so that they could hear what he was going to do for his next album; he did 'Sister Moon', 'Home Run King', 'Hear The Wind', 'Kansas City Southern' and 'Lonely Saturday'." On one of the rough mix reels Clark recited a revealing intro to 'Kansas City Southern', conjuring nostalgic memories: "When I was five years old, [there] used to be this train line running back behind our house called the Kansas City Southern. I don't think it's still in existence today. But one day, I remember this old black bum came up to the door looking for breadcrumbs. [He] said he'd do some work in the yard. I remember mama made him sit down in the back room, gave him a piece of toast. Then I heard the rumble of this train coming up, and he says, 'Well I'll see you. I've got to catch that Kansas City Southern.'"

It was anticipated that Asylum would immediately green light the new album project and provide a recording budget, but there was a sting in the tale. Kaye was crestfallen to discover that the label no longer wanted to work with Clark. "They told Gene that they didn't hear anything. In fact they thought it was terrible, and what's when they gave him his release."

Rather than delay the album while they shopped for a new deal, Kaye suggested they push ahead. Eddie Tickner came aboard to assist with negotiations and a surprise benefactor was found: film director Gary Legon. Over the next few months, several major labels were courted including CBS, RCA and Warner Brothers, but a deal was not forthcoming. "Columbia took a month and a half," Kaye recalls. "There was interest from Warner Brothers but, again, the deal wasn't right. We wanted to make sure we weren't going to get a label which had 30 male singer-songwriters and where we'd just get put in the same category." In attempting to avoid the problems they'd encountered at Asylum, Kaye and Clark were in danger of pricing themselves out of the market. There was an increasing air of desperation as costs mounted and all the labels backed away. Kaye decided to approach Al Coury of Capitol Records, but was told that he had just left the company and moved to RSO, home of the Bee Gees and Eric Clapton. An acronym for the Robert Stigwood Organization, RSO was a relatively new label that had evolved from a management and agency company to establish a foothold in the American marketplace. Within two years, it would become one of the most successful labels of the era, largely thanks to the sales of *Saturday Night Fever* and *Grease*, but at this point it was still gathering new acts. Kaye was by now relieved to close any reasonable deal.

"A lot of companies had passed on the album but Al Coury on the first listen said, 'OK, that's it!' We only played him rough mixes, but he understood exactly what we were doing." Clark almost scuppered the entire deal when he met Coury and his wife for a celebration meal at Dan Tana's soon after. Coury was keen to engage with the songwriter and discuss the label's aims, as well as confirming their financial commitment. Drinking heavily, Clark disgraced himself at the dinner, making sexual innuendos in front of Coury's wife and acting like a boorish boozer. "He definitely dissed Coury," says Peter Oliva. "He told him he looked like Sonny Bono, got drunk and put his feet on the table. Geno had a way of doing things like that. There were powerful men running the scene back then and Coury was pretty cool with him after that." When Kaye heard about this incident the next morning, he buried his head in his hands. Later that day, he was pleasantly surprised when Coury phoned, expressing concern about Clark's psychological state, but nevertheless committing more money to the album.

Clark's erratic behaviour was compounded by events back home in Mendocino. Left alone to bring up two children, Carlie felt more isolated. Suspecting that Gene was partying on the road probably didn't help. "We could see a split," says their neighbour Philip Oleno. Gene must have known his marriage was in trouble, but failed to grasp how badly it had deteriorated. In later years, Carlie presented an idealized portrayal of Mendocino life, but it was seldom so straightforward. She had initially avoided all hard drugs, including coke, but Mendocino was no Eden of innocence. Was she ever entirely straight while living there? "No!" her friend Mary states emphatically. "In Mendo, none of us were. We were not really upstanding citizens."

"Alcohol and drugs led to their divorce," adds Dara Zimmerman. "I took care of all the rock 'n' roll mom's babies and they'd drop them off and go out and party. They'd come home totally trashed. Gene was pretty wild. Carlie was pretty wild. They were young and it was a different time. Gene was doing speed in LA and he was on the road. I know he loved her and she loved him, but they were so bad for each other. They were like oil and water."

"I'd first met Carlie when we [Hamilton Face] were signed to Bell, before she married Gene," recalls Andy Kandanes. "I thought she was a ditzy blonde then, but she was a good mom and I genuinely liked her. She liked to party and she got a little out there when Gene was on the road. It was a situation. Mendocino wasn't exactly a non-party town. I guess she got a little bored and one thing led to another and it was unmanageable. It was a shame. She was actually a good wife to him for a long time, so I'd give her kudos for sticking it out as long as she did. For years it was a great relationship, then it just started coming apart and she started messing. God knows what she was doing. Then, she was hanging out with my wife . . . It's funny because he and I ended up in exactly the same situation. I was on the road and Gene was on the road all the time. He'd call home at three in the morning and sometimes there'd be no answer. You'd get a baby-sitter on the line. What's going on? That's not cool. So things got a little crazy. But she was a good kid."

During March 1976, Carlie and the children abruptly left the family home and took off to Hawaii. She had become involved with Mark Kimberly, whose in-laws owned the Little River Inn in Mendocino where Dara worked part-time as a busgirl. "Mark moved to Hawaii and he'd paid for Carlie and then she paid for me to come over." Gene seemed stunned by the speed of events, but made no attempt to win her back and showed little mettle in attempting to secure future access to his children. "A different man might have gone over to Hawaii to get his boys back, or something," says Oleno. "He didn't go that far. He didn't know where he'd fucked up. Nobody could tell him because nobody knew."

While not mentioning her own partying while Gene was on tour, Carlie later admitted feeling ambivalent about leaving so suddenly. "In retrospect, I would have handled it completely differently. But I was mad and I just told him that I wasn't going to stay at the farm by myself. We didn't have a security system, no locks. So I took these big nails, nailed the windows shut, packed two duffel bags, got on a plane and that was it . . . After living in Hawaii for three or four months, I just couldn't feature living in that insanity any more. The drinking was out of control . . . I'm not saying I could have kept him happy, joyous and free, but I did manage to keep a balance there sometimes. I do have an incredible amount of guilt, because I just bailed. At the time, it was the easy way out. 'I'm gone.' I was living in Hawaii on the beach with these two beautiful little brown berry boys and guys all over me . . . 'Whoa, OK, this'll work.' And Gene – it destroyed him." She claims he begged her to come back, although that may have been a message relayed by Philip and Ea. "Then I found out that, prior to going down to LA, he had a girl living in the barn on our property. When I was asleep at night he would go down and be with her. So how do you deal with that? . . . I knew the girl . . . that blew my mind." Nobody else has mentioned this girl, let alone named her or confirmed Carlie's account.

During her first month in Maui, Carlie and her family stayed in a hotel, then sublet a well-decorated vacation home near the beach, surrounded by palm trees. After a few months, Carlie petitioned for divorce and subsequently returned to Mendocino to face Gene, who was still angry and uncommunicative. "I was left in Hawaii with the boys for a couple of months," Dara Zimmerman recalls. "I had a great time. I was 17, in a great house, I had a car and two wonderful kids that I loved and adored, and no adults. We just had fun. Carlie would call all the time. She was in Mendocino trying to get her divorce signed by Gene." Those negotiations were not proceeding cordially. Without restraints, Clark's combined use of cocaine and alcohol made him unstable. He was also emotionally devastated. In one call, Carlie claimed that he had attempted to throw her out of the parlour window. Given Carlie's penchant for exaggeration and Gene's extreme volatility, Dara could only guess what really occurred.

Clark's situation was far from unique. Many of his contemporaries went through divorces and lost contact with their children for years. There was a stoical finality in their attitudes. Multiple marriages among the West Coast rock fraternity made the process almost commonplace. "When it ended I thought it was the best thing for Gene in a way," says Peter Oliva. "There was no security in it." In response, Clark sought out his local pals, drowned his sorrows and pushed ahead with the formation of a new road band. Kandanes was of similar mind. "Actually, his wife and mine, who were best friends, left at the same time. That's when he asked me to start the band. He said, 'What the hell? We'll be partners in misery here.' It kept us busy and got us back on the road. It was a win-win situation for both of us." While Clark put on a brave face to the outside world, Kandanes had no doubt that he was hurting inside. "How could you be OK with it? We both had kids, so it affected us. No doubt about it. It definitely took its toll on Gene. Many nights we'd end up at the bar at the Seagull with the whole crew. We kind of owned our own bar seats down there. It seemed more like the UK or Europe than America. You'd go down the local pub, see your buds, have a few and escape for a bit. Basically that's all we did. Our whole time consisted of playing music, having a few drinks and hanging out with the boys. Gene was at a stage where he'd had some rough times in the music business and a lot of people didn't want to deal with him."

By the summer, Clark was singing lead with the renamed Mendocino Rhythm Section in a line-up that included Andy Kandanes (drums), Peter Oliva (bass), Billy Shay (drums), Colin McNaughton (keyboards) and former Cat Mother conga player, Steve Davidson. The sound was unusual and gig reports, carried by letter rather than review, suggested Clark was experimenting with what one correspondent imaginatively described as 'Cosmic Motown'. Having recently assisted with 'tidying up' some parts of the now completed *Two Sides To Every Story*, Kandanes invited Tommy Kaye down from Malibu to appear with the band as additional guitarist. Kaye was intrigued by the set-up and, after drinking heavily with Gene, staggered out the next morning to buy a guitar. Taking control, he could not resist restructuring the group, just as he had done with the Silverados. The keyboardist and conga player were removed with clinical detachment and fresh rehearsals began.

Clark continued to gather drinking buddies and musician friends, sometimes through serendipity. Record producer Ken Mansfield was on a recuperative retreat from Los Angeles, sitting in a café in Yorkville, Mendocino County, when he first encountered the garrulous Tommy Kaye. After exchanging pleasantries and music business gossip, Mansfield witnessed the new group perform and was impressed by their rough but eclectic fusion of folk, country, blues and funk. It was partly country rock, but infused with a grittier edge. Kaye introduced Mansfield to Clark and was invited back to Middle Ridge for an all-night gathering during which they consumed beer and chilli in front of an open fire. Clark was intrigued by Mansfield's stories and they became good friends, with similar sensibilities.

Born 14 October 1937, Mansfield was seven years older than Clark, with an illustrious CV. In January 1965, the same month that Gene was recording 'Mr Tambourine Man' at CBS, Mansfield had been appointed as one of the youngest executives at Capitol Records. He subsequently became US manager of Apple Records, working with the Beatles. He even witnessed their famous final live appearance playing on the rooftop of Apple Corps in London's salubrious Savile Row on 30 January 1969. On that cold afternoon, the Beatles' impromptu 42-minute set had included 'Don't Let Me Down', which Dillard & Clark later covered as the closing track on *Through The Morning Through The Night.* While Gene appreciated Mansfield's Beatles tales, he was equally impressed by the producer's involvement with the Outlaw movement and co-production work on the recent Waylon Jennings album, *Are You Ready For The Country*. Mansfield observed Clark's dualism with a psychiatrist's eye. "If Gene liked you, he hugged you to death. If he wasn't quite sure how he felt about you, he would most likely get drunk and maybe beat you up at some point in your relationship until he made up his mind." Such outlaw behaviour did not bother Mansfield. "We were crazy cowboys . . . People expected us to be wild, accepted us that way and actually needed us to feed their fantasies."

When news of Clark's marital break-up reached Kansas, there was a concerted effort to provide succour. Brother Rick, who had already been looking after the property when Gene and Carlie had been commuting between Mendocino and Hollywood, relocated permanently with a view to following his elder sibling's career. "Once you've been to the West Coast, the Midwest doesn't have that much to offer. Carlie had run to Hawaii so I moved on to Gene's farm. There was me, Gene and [local promoter] John Desko. He was handling the bookings while we were in Mendocino and we all lived at Gene's place. Boy, that was the wildest time I've had in my entire life. We'd get out of bed about one o'clock in the afternoon, rehearse and then we'd go out and hit all the bars in town, then go home and do the same thing the next day. It was party time. I played in the band. Gene was a multi-personality guy and one of the most wonderful people I've ever known. But when he got frustrated or depressed, he'd turn to the bottle, or drugs, and his personality could change completely then."

Another new arrival in Mendocino was Tommy Kaye's wife, Hillary, who was expecting a baby in the autumn. "We came along right after Carlie had left and stayed at his farmhouse," she says. "Gene had a magical farm, and Rick was living in the huge barn. He also had this shepherd's cabin, which was a hundred years old. It was an incredible gnomish place with this huge redwood stump that they used as a table. The greatest place. I always thought Gene was at his best up in the country, having come from Kansas. I loved him and can't say enough good things about him. He was really a gentleman and had a lot of class. I was fortunate to be pregnant when I met him because he had some severe issues with women. I got over that hurdle by being a madonna. We became really close, which was great because he didn't have a lot of female friends."

Gene's friendship with Hillary proved significant. In the past, he had fraternized with sexy dancers, married a record company employee and hung out with famous rock musicians and movie actors. But Kaye's wife was a different person entirely. Over the next couple of years, she would provide him with the opportunity to infiltrate an echelon of society that he had never encountered before.

Hillary Kontos (née Hudson), born 25 July 1951, had already experienced an eventful life before meeting Gene Clark. Her birth father's family owned the Hudson Car Dealership and it was on the car lot that young Hudson courted Catholic society girl, Claudia Hill (nicknamed 'Coy'), the daughter of an architect who subsequently established a thriving restaurant business, largely centred on Newport Beach. Their happy marriage ended tragically when he was killed in a flying accident in 1962. Claudia was only widowed for a short time before attracting the attentions of Clement Lang Hirsch, a rich businessman, 18 years her senior. Hirsch was an imposing figure with an illustrious history. Born in St Louis, Missouri, in 1914, he was an enterprising young man and, at the age of 22, established the Dog Town Packing Company in Vernon, California, which he renamed Kal Kan Foods, Inc. It made him a millionaire with net assets estimated at $10 million, a hefty sum during the Sixties. Hirsch's abiding passion was horse racing and, as a member of the Jockey Club, he imported several winning thoroughbreds from South America. He was also co-founder of the Oak Tree Racing Association in Santa Anita and later a director of the US National Bank. During Clement's courtship of her mother, Hillary was uneasily adjusting to a more upmarket lifestyle. "We went from being this middle-class family on Newport Beach, where I was a surfing, beach kid, to being picked up in limousines and jetted here and there. He was head of the racetrack and would land his helicopter there to watch his horses run. It was bizarre."

Hirsch's previous marriage to Edith Mack ended with divorce in 1963 and she went on to wed actor Desi Arnaz. That same year, Clement and Claudia were married. Hillary was at a boarding school in Monterey when she heard the news and was so upset about not being previously informed that she ran away. Having lost a father and gained a stepfather within the space of a year, Hillary was emotionally vulnerable and found it difficult to adjust to these rapid changes. Her mother intervened and contacted a friend who was a Mother Superior at a convent boarding school in France. Hillary, already a rebellious teenager, took to Europe with aplomb and enjoyed her Catholic education under the nuns, whose tutelage was surprisingly liberal. The girls regularly went on clothes-buying expeditions and surreptitiously sampled cocktails and Bloody Marys during their outings. There was an eventful trip to witness Maria Callas' final performance of *La Bohème* and the nuns even agreed to accompany the girls to see the Rolling Stones when they played the Olympia, Paris, on 20 October 1964. What the nuns made of the arrests of 150 rampaging fans is not recorded.

Despite testifying to these wonderful experiences, Hillary could not be confined at a convent for too long and set out on her own adventure, travelling across Europe. She fell in with some 'gypsy kids', squatted briefly in a luxury home and dropped acid. The troupe then journeyed to Italy and ended up in Greece in 1967 where Hillary appeared as an extra and wardrobe assistant on the Michael Cacoyannis film, *The Day The Fish Came Out*, starring Tom Courtney and Candice Bergen (coincidentally Terry Melcher's girlfriend). Living rough, she contracted an infection that proved strangely resistant to antibiotics, resulting in severe back pain. Already violently ill, her condition worsened and increasing shots of morphine bamboozled her senses. A musician friend phoned her mother in America who arranged a flight home. She arrived in a wheelchair, barely alive. Doctors told her that she might be crippled for life but her grandmother personally put her through an intensive course of physiotherapy and she fully recovered.

Hillary's hippie travels and near-death experience had a profound effect upon her life. Rather than slowing her down, they encouraged a more urgent, devil-may-care philosophy, which sometimes bordered on the reckless. "I was determined to live life like there was no tomorrow." It turned out that part of her old entourage in Europe had been importing hash to San Francisco. "They had these whole rooms full of people capping acid and hash, and God knows what. A large segment of the teenage population was doing it, and I was having transcendental experiences."

In 1969, Hillary married a Los Angeles attorney and gave birth to a son, Hugh, named after her brother. "I then toned my act down and became a mother," she says. The marriage lasted three years before ending in divorce. Thereafter, she went through an uncharacteristically quiet period ("I was sick of men"), amid further changes in her mother's matrimonial life. Claudia and Clement Hirsch had separated in 1971, after which 'Coy' married Morris 'Maury' Mirkin, founder of Budget Rent A Car. In early 1975, Hillary's life changed yet again when a friend invited her out for the evening. Their destination was a hotel near the Troubadour where drummer Dallas Taylor was staying. Evidently they gained access "under the guise of going to cop some opium". Hillary proved a reluctant companion who was already threatening to go home when she was introduced to Taylor's producer friend, Thomas Jefferson Kaye. "He was the funniest guy I'd ever met. I needed a laugh more than anything else in my life right then and we just hit it off splendidly. It was the beginning of a beautiful relationship."

Kaye was still recovering from his budget-breaking productions of Bobby Neuwirth and Gene Clark for Asylum Records, while touring sporadically in promotion of his second solo album, *First Grade.* Previously married to Vicki Roman, with whom he had a son, Chris, in 1970, Kaye was now a free spirit with a wild streak. He was living in hotels, renting cars and taking perverse pleasure in scamming the establishment. A favourite tale, oft-repeated by his friends, was the 'painting scam' in which Kaye redecorated his hotel room and re-sprayed his rented car. He would then complain that the vehicle's colour had been wrongly registered on insurance documents, causing enough confusion to secure a complete refund. Demented hoteliers wondering how

Kaye's room had changed colour were also tapped for refunds. Sometimes, he had to leave town in a hurry. Andy Kandanes remembers the chaos. "Once they put one of Tommy's rented cars in the car wash and all the paint came off. After repainting his room at the Sunset Marquis, he fell asleep in the bathtub and the water went down to the next floor. I tell you for years after if you stayed there they'd always come looking for Tommy Kaye."

Hillary delighted in Kaye's tall tales and eccentricities, but her family were not so impressed when she decided to marry him. "Tommy was an enigma to them. It wasn't so much that they didn't like him as much as my mom couldn't believe that I'd marry him because she thought he was the ugliest human being she'd ever met! Of course, I didn't see Tommy like that. I saw him the way he was, which was totally different. My mother thought: 'What the hell is she doing with him?' She wanted me to marry someone – one of these idiots like a friend of her parents. At the same time, she then welcomed Tommy because that's who I was with." Hillary's pregnancy silenced any remaining doubts.

Kaye's arrival in Mendocino had invigorated everybody. "Tommy was cool," Peter Oliva recalls. "A real smart New Yorker. He knew what was going on. He was a rocker too. He'd crank his guitar up and that's what gave us that crunchy sound that you heard. Tommy would crank up that guitar – crankah crankah – it sounded like that. I liked Tommy a lot. He was like Michael Clarke, who I later played with. I called them loveable rogues. You didn't know if you could quite trust them but you loved them anyway through the whole thing."

Michael McGibbon had also recently returned to Mendocino to work on a stained-glass window and ended up hiring several of the musicians as workmen. Like everyone else, he felt enlivened by the Kayes. "I totally fell in love with Hillary and her violet eyes. Tommy was this crazy, sparky guy. He could tell a story. We liked telling stories. With him and Gene, it was like Neuwirth and Dylan. And Neuwirth was no slouch."

In September 1976, Hillary gave birth to a daughter, Eloise Robin Kaye. The baby was three months premature and barely survived. "If you'd seen her footprint at birth, you'd have said, 'My God, forget it.' She was this skeletal figure. Her hairline started on her eyebrows and went back, like Eddie Munster. And this was at birth. People were looking at her and saying, 'Isn't she beautiful?' I burst out laughing because the last thing in the world she was was beautiful. But she turned out to be the neatest child and I'm so glad they saved her." Back in Hollywood, not everyone was so supportive. "A lot of people on the Strip were saying she should be dead because it's unnatural. John Barrymore Jr went on this big trip saying she should be dead. The first time I met him he had me in tears saying, 'Ellie should be dead. That's the way it's supposed to be.' But he grew to adore her and I swear that's one of the reasons he had Drew Barrymore."

The miracle child also caught the attention of Gene Clark, who agreed to become her godfather. It was unusual for him to take such responsibility, even on these limited terms. There are no reports of his serving as a godparent for any of his siblings' offspring. The timing, coming so soon after losing his own children, may have been significant. As Hillary observes: "It's like he didn't have any relationships with other children, and it was his own children that he had such difficulty with after he and Carlie broke up."

While Eloise's birth was premature, Clark's new album was delayed. It should have been issued in September, but there were reservations about pushing it into the marketplace alongside other big RSO releases, so it was postponed until the New Year. There was an additional problem with the cover artwork which was altered in order to display a shot of Clark standing forlornly outside his house in Mendocino. Not long afterwards, Tommy Kaye took me aside and explained that the cover was deeply symbolic and intensely personal. He spoke as if he was poised to reveal some great secret about Clark's work but when I enquired about the meaning of the symbolism, he bristled. "But I told you, it's *personal*!" It would be two decades later before anyone learned more. One of Clark's friends told me that the spinning top featured on the sleeve belonged to one of his children and the whole effect was meant to be an oblique comment on his recent separation and divorce. Rick Clark completed the story, as best he could. "If you look really closely you'll see bullet holes all over the table. We were doing target practice with rifles and setting stuff up on that picnic table and shooting cans and bottles off it. There happened to be one of Gene's kid's tops laying in the sandpit in the yard and we just set it up. It was Tommy that put it on the table. Part of Tommy's thing about him and Gene was that you create a mystique so that people will always wonder. It seemed to work with you. He talked like that to me too."

Ever the provocateur, Kaye decided to introduce another new face to the Mendocino scene and called an old friend, Tom Slocum. Although born in Detroit, Slocum was raised in New York, where he worked as a singer-songwriter. He subsequently married Emmylou Harris, with whom he had a daughter, Hallie, and continued working in the music industry on various projects. He was currently employed by a publishing company owned by Bob Dylan's manager, Albert Grossman. Kaye telephoned with an enticing proposition: "Come up to Mendocino and join the band!" Slocum had already met Clark and respected his work. Arriving in Mendocino, he was immediately struck by the rugged scenery and enveloping mist. "It was rocky, windy, rainy and moody, the kind of place that was great for poets. Gene had a fine piece of land there. There was quite a concoction of people – Californian loggers and rednecks, and the old hippie community." Kaye's vision of some sort of musical collective was characteristically eccentric. Clark's group already had an abundance of players but Slocum was brought in as additional guitarist, partly to add strength in numbers. "I started hanging out with Gene and Tommy Kaye, which was an experience in itself. Gene was quite a guy to play with because he never played the same thing twice. I played with the group on a few dates and I think Johnny Barbata worked a few gigs too."

Slocum hung around and became part of the inner circle. He was funny, animated and, in common with Kaye and Clark, had a non-linear, impressionistic mode of speech, laced with opaque allusions, non sequiturs, inventive similes and an imaginative cast list of music business characters whose names and histories often served as passing metaphors to emphasize a particular point or puzzling 'in-joke'. When Clark, Kaye and Slocum were together in full flow, it was like witnessing members of a secret society addressing each other in a coded language. By the time you decoded a sentence, they were already on to a new paragraph.

Slocum's persona intrigued and perplexed several others in the circle, simply because they were never entirely sure what he did. He seemed a flighty character, a jack of all trades in the music business who knew the most unlikely people from record company owners to lawyers, publishers and even putative superstars. "Slocum's M.O. was that he knew everybody in the record business," Kandanes remembers. "He'd have lunch with Clive Davis one day, Al Smith the next. He was lunch buddies with all the presidents and a great contact. A really great guy."

Even Kaye's wife Hillary, no stranger to multiple social circles, was often mystified by Slocum's perplexing range of acquaintances. "He did stuff for everybody. Joni Mitchell. Lawyer Johanan Vigoda. All of them. He made himself indispensable to people. That was his nature. And it got around, I'm sure. I heard somebody say that he was a talented masseur and great at relaxing stars. God knows what his talents were."

Although the pair would later fall out, like so many other characters and factions in this story, Hillary was initially kind to Slocum and he was intrigued by her family history. He spoke of her in his typically opaque style, but not without affection. "Hillary was a very wealthy woman, above the law. She was the heiress to Rent A Car, a really interesting woman who fancied herself as the Stevie Nicks of the West Coast aristocrats. When I met her she was very beautiful in a really great way. She gave me this beautiful sweater as a present. It was El Paso wool from Peru. That was a wonderful gesture for my birthday in December 1976."

That same month, another new character arrived in Clark's burgeoning barn. English-born actor John Dexter had hung out in New York's Greenwich Village some years back then relocated to Hollywood and changed his name to Jason Ronard. He had recently appeared in *Helter Skelter*, a televised adaptation of the Charles Manson story. Just after Christmas, Ronard was visiting friends in Mendocino and accidentally ended up at Gene Clark's raucous New Year's Eve party. "We woke up New Year's Day on a wood pile in Gene's front yard. We had gotten so drunk and screwed up that we beat the hell out of each other. I think his brother [Rick] might have been in on it too."

Ronard's explosive entrance into Clark's circle added another alcoholic element to this band of revellers. Ronard became the new raconteur and court jester, whose lacerating irreverence and caustic humour made him sound like some darkly satirical stand-up comedian. "I'll tell you a great thing about Gene Clark, John Barrymore and Tommy Kaye," he confides. "They never gossiped. They never judged anyone or talked behind anyone's back. Normally, people would say, 'Did you see that jackass the other night?' – you'd never hear anything from them like that, no matter who the person was. They would just smile and move on to the next sentence."

Perhaps they never needed to judge their peers simply because Ronard's acid commentaries were enough to silence any conversation. Ask him about the other Byrds, the history of the group, the role of Bob Dylan or Gene Clark's importance in the scheme of things and he'd have an instant opinion, guaranteed to make your jaw drop. "I didn't get along too well with McGuinn. He was just a little too pompous for me. McGuinn thinks he's the leader of the Byrds; the leader of the Byrds is Gene Clark. Gene wrote all the songs that made money. David Crosby? We used to call him fatso. He had zero talent. He was lucky to be in there and of course he thinks he's the cat's miaow, but the guy couldn't sing and couldn't play the guitar. All he could do was harmonize. Have you seen David with an acoustic guitar singing a cappella? He sucks. He doesn't deserve any of the shit he got. All you had to do was hear Gene Clark sing. Can you imagine how jealous Jimmy McGuinn was? Nobody had a voice like Gene, except for Roy Orbison, man. When Gene Clark sang, every chick in the room was staring at him. 'Now, we pass the guitar to Jimmy McGuinn and see what he can do.' Boy, he can't do shit. All he can do is strum the 12-string. That's it . . . And Dylan? The man with zero personality. Talk about a guy that puts together three words a week. He had no personality so he was no fun to hang out with. You see. That's why Geno had to have me around because I'd say it right off the cuff and he would never say things like that."

There seemed little point in telling Ronard that McGuinn *was* the leader of the Byrds and one of rock music's most respected guitarists, nor adding that Crosby was and remains a supremely talented singer-songwriter. In Ronard World, such gods had feet of crumbling clay. That said, it's no wonder Clark enjoyed having him around for drunken evenings. He could always be relied upon to say the unsayable and apparently believed every one of his put-downs.

Over Christmas 1976, there was yet another surprise. In an unprecedented expedition, Gene's parents arrived from Kansas. They had never met Carlie or seen either of their children, but felt it was appropriate to offer moral support and festive cheer in the aftermath of the divorce and her departure. They could hardly have chosen a more inappropriate time. Gene was busy partying with his ever expanding list of friends and unlikely to curb his behaviour out of respect for his mother. It must have been tough for Jeanne Clark to witness all the drinking. Her husband had been an alcoholic, prone to violence at his worst, and Gene was displaying similar traits. His younger brother Rick was also partying, while the other members of the gang were getting high. "Everybody was sniffing a little bit of coke now and then," remembers Andy Kandanes. "Everybody. It was after the split with Carlie that Gene really got crazy."

Gene's mother suffered the ultimate culture shock seeing her favourite son seemingly on the skids and not even attempting to hide his excesses from her. "He'd wanted to insulate his family from what was going on in his life," says his sister Bonnie, but that façade was exposed in Mendocino. "When Mom went out there, she cooked them a big dinner and they got so stoned they couldn't eat it. I saw pictures that they brought back and I didn't even recognize Gene. He was so bloated. Unrecognizable." Jeanne rapidly retreated, curtailing the visit and returning with her husband to Kansas.

One month later, brother David Clark made the trip, accompanied by his family. Evidently, he intended a permanent move, but would only last a few months. "I was at a crossroads myself. I sold everything, loaded up a young family in an Econoline van and drove across country. One of the reasons I went out, apart from working on the farm, was that he needed financial assistance to get this album and road tour going. They were asking guys for contributions to match what they were putting into this. I sold a bunch of equipment and invested my money in that. Lost it all. He'd gotten heavily into coke and it became a daily routine. It was not good. That's one reason I packed up and left when I did. I knew it was going no place. I'd already lost all of my operating capital and didn't have anything left."

Gene continued to careen around Hollywood in chaotic fashion. His friend Ken Mansfield, then working with a new group, Hothead, was full of news. Hothead had been offered a show at the Whisky which they hoped would lead to greater things. Clark agreed to attend but, on the night, there was a mix-up. When he appeared at the ticket office, his name was not on the guest list. Undeterred, he headed for the stage door, situated in an adjoining alley. Despite attempting to talk his way in, he was refused entry. Mansfield was already inside when he heard the commotion. "He proceeded to punch out three security guards, two roadies working for the opening band, and a few other toughs who mistakenly joined the fray." The minor fracas turned into a brawl, spilling inexorably from the stage door to the stage. Hothead's showcase ended before it had even begun and they were told never to return. Mansfield was furious. "I didn't get much madder than I did at Gene that night. A lot of hard work and a lot of people's hopes had gone down the drain." Later that evening, Clark tracked Mansfield to a friend's house. Clutching his cowboy hat to his chest, Gene apologized profusely. The vision of Clark, forlorn and dejected, left an indelible impression. "I choose to remember him that way," Mansfield reflects. "It is crazy, but I don't think I ever loved him more than I did at that moment. Gene had a lot of hurt inside, and he just had to come out swinging sometimes to make the noise and pain go away." Clark's act of contrition caused Mansfield to look at him differently in the future. "After a while it was easy to understand why he would lose it in those moments of rage – you could see the confusion written all over his face. At the same time it was easy to see what a sweetheart he was, and you could feel the tenderness inside when he brought the repentant side of his nature to your doorstep."

In February 1977, the delayed *Two Sides To Every Story* finally appeared. The album was something of a curate's egg, uneasily mingling the country roots of Dillard & Clark with light splashings of cosmic consciousness. At the time, it was seen as a compromise and severe anti-climax after the genius of *No Other*. Viewed more sympathetically three decades on, its high moments can be treasured. It begins with the sprightly 'Home Run King', a showcase for Clark's collaborative work with Doug Dillard, with assistance from guest vocalist Emmylou Harris. Tommy Kaye later told me, in a conspiratorial aside, that this was the song that sold him on the album. Strangely, he seemed to regard Clark's simple homespun philosophy as the ultimate lyrical statement, worthy of Confucius. "When Gene said, 'You're either a newspaper boy or you're . . . Babe Ruth' I just looked at him. I said, 'Gene, that just says it all!'" Dara Zimmerman was equally enthusiastic. "I was in Middle Ridge with Gene when he wrote that baseball song. I was standing in the kitchen, listening to it. I'll never forget it. It gave me such chills and made me almost cry. It's probably my favourite song that he ever wrote."

Clark's other compositions on the album were arguably even better. 'Lonely Saturday' expresses the ambivalence of broken romance in a country setting with Clark chronicling the exact moment of abandonment; 'Sister Moon', again with Emmylou Harris, and soon to be an in-concert staple, is more phlegmatic, already predicting a beloved's future with a new companion and a conviction never to return; 'Hear The Wind', another of Clark's elemental songs, has a tenderness enhanced by vocal support from the Moore brothers and one of the best melody lines on the record; 'Past Addresses', probably the most powerful statement here, is Clark at his melancholic best, seeking salvation in fractured memories, complete with some Catholic-inspired imagery in which tears become "the blood of the saints". 'Silent Crusade', overladen with the sounds of seagulls, takes us on a metaphysical voyage over the "sea of time", ending the album on a moving and mournful note.

Perhaps reacting to the commercial failure of *No Other*, Kaye and Clark felt obliged to provide a varied musical style, with a stronger emphasis on country. A funkier version of 'Kansas City Southern', redone in honour of their new band, the bluegrass 'In The Pines' and rock 'n' roll remake 'Marylou' tended to compromise the natural flow of the album. Surprisingly, there was also a plug for New Mexico singer-songwriter James Talley, who had recently toured with Clark, and introduced him to his elegiac commentary on the plight of the mining community in 'Give My Love To Marie'. Its theme mirrored the latest Clark/Kaye composition, 'Last Of The Blue Diamond Miners', a song which regrettably was not completed in time for inclusion on the album.

Two Sides To Every Story received a predictably mixed reception. Many of Clark's supporters in the UK bemoaned its lack of adventure in comparison to *No Other*, but that was nothing compared to the reception Stateside. The then influential *Rolling Stone* printed a veritable career-stopping review which pondered: "Is this the dullest album ever made?" It continued: "Lugubrious to the point of laughableness, the once-classy Clark creeps through a series of Gibranian ballads that is so Antonioni-slow the songs actually seem to stop. Dead. Like this. Bereft of either interest or ideas, this plodding work can only be described as

California-liturgidical." It was a cruel denunciation, which did not appear to see merit in any of the songs, even the superior ones.

Back in Mendocino, Clark's reprobate band continued to act like outlaws. "We'd rehearse for ten hours every day up in Gene's ranch living on nothing but beers and jalapenos," Oliva recalls. "We'd be popping these Coors beers, and maybe a little reefer. Gene liked drinking and having a good time. He was a knife-thrower. He finally took out the wall in his house and they had to build a little partition through it. It was interesting what Gene would do. We used to go into town after rehearsing. The town hated us, man. We were like a gang. A street gang. We'd walk in there, buy drinks, have a good time and make a lot of noise. People just hated us up there, but they'd show up for our gigs."

Slocum also remembers some scary moments born of the cultural clash between the different communities. "One night we were still too awake after rehearsals and Gene said, 'Let's go to Fort Bragg!' Now, in Fort Bragg there was nobody else but loggers. These were super-redneck guys, the kind that eat their own. We went to a diner at three in the morning with Gene and his big beard. Loggers were there getting ready to chop trees. There was a blonde waitress who looked like she'd just walked off a 1950s movie. She had a full beehive hairdo and mascara that ran from Cairo to London. We had a huge breakfast and then realized nobody had any money with them." At this point, Clark turned to the waitress and asked, "Don't you recognize me? Don't you know who I am?" His pitch might have worked in Canter's or Dan Tana's but neither the loggers nor the waitress were impressed and hovered menacingly. It was only the fortuitous arrival of a local cop, who knew Clark, that prevented the situation from turning very ugly.

Clark continued to dice with danger, suffering some scary scrapes along the way. His brother David remembers one night when Gene, presumably the worse for wear, made his way home through the woods. He stumbled into some barbed wire, badly lacerating his neck. It could have been much worse. After the wounds healed he was left with some visible scarring. For future promotional photos and media appearances, he often sported scarves or neckerchiefs to disguise the marks.

With the Mendocino band now refreshed and rehearsed, they undertook a short tour, including dates in Denver and Arizona, and recorded a selection of demos for Chappell Music. Kaye and Clark were now writing together frequently, a process begun at least two years before when 'Forgive Me, Girl' was registered for copyright. The new demos included the striking band favourite 'Denver Or Wherever', 'Release Me Girl' (a rewrite of 'Forgive Me, Girl') the speedfreaks' anthem 'Seventh Avenue Train' (aka 'Hula Bula Man') and the thrilling 'Taken By Surprise' (some of whose lyrics were later incorporated into 'Feelin' Higher'). Clark also sang Kaye's 'Shades Of Blue', which would be re-recorded on numerous occasions. There was also the great 'Last Of The Blue Diamond Miners', the highlight of the group's set, scheduled for inclusion on a Thomas Jefferson Kaye solo album that was never completed. Kaye's wife Hillary also received songwriting credits on 'Crazy Ladies' and 'No Wonder'. When Tom Slocum questioned Clark about her contributions, he responded with the gnomic aside, "Well, she provided the aperitif."

In celebration of the new writing partnership, the group were now relabelled the KC Southern Band, a name that echoed his song 'Kansas City Southern' but actually took its titular initials from 'Kaye' and 'Clark'. During the spring, they played the Troubadour alongside the Alpha Band, the talented ensemble formed from the ashes of Dylan's Rolling Thunder Revue. Despite a much touted eponymous album for Arista in 1976 and a recently recorded sequel, *Spark In The Dark*, the Alpha Band's sales never matched their reputation. The KCSB's first set went well, with Oliva arrogantly claiming: "We blew them down the pipe, man!" An exaggeration perhaps, but they were in trouble later that evening when Clark nervously hit the bottle. "I loved playing with Gene when he *wasn't* drunk," Oliva says. "Gene would get crazy. Anybody when they're drunk is hard to deal with because they don't follow the script. This was one of those gigs where the first set was great and the second was hell. He disappeared from the stage. We were up there for 15 minutes saying, 'Where's Gene?' Tommy Kaye was looking around for him then, all of a sudden, we saw him up in the balcony. Somehow he got up there and started swinging from the rafters over the people's heads. I'd seen him do this more than once where he could empty a place. The Alpha Band were Dylan's protégés and all the Hollywood elite were there . . . He was a crazy guy. He's from Missouri. If you've been there you'll understand what I'm talking about."

Clark's drunken antics were not without reason. Earlier that day, he had been involved in a violent confrontation with the Troubadour's owner, Doug Weston. "It was backstage during the afternoon," says Tom Slocum, who witnessed the incident. "Gene came out of nowhere and just cold-cocked him. I'll never forget it. It was 'Boom!' I remember catching Doug. I said, 'Holy fuck, Gene, what have you done? You've just knocked out the owner of the club.' Gene wasn't drunk, he just decked him. I think it had something to do with a payment for some gig six or seven years before where Gene didn't get what he was supposed to. They had a few choice words and the next thing you know Weston, who was about 6′ 6″, is lying there flat on his ass. Gene was looking down at him, laughing. He called him a big old Texan faggot or something. It was a pretty crazy scene. Gene then grabbed a pitcher of water and threw it over him. Talk about never working in this town again. He still did the gig, but that kind of thing would come back at him in weird ways."

Coincidentally, it was also at the Troubadour that Clark met a former girlfriend who was about to transform his life. Since leaving our narrative in 1966, Terri Messina had moved to France and was engaged to be married to a wealthy, bon vivant Olympic skier. The relationship lasted several years but foundered before reaching the altar. Returning to LA, Terri secured work as a film editor. One afternoon, her roommate called with news that Gene Clark was playing at the Troubadour. Messina sounded blasé about the matter, but was persuaded to attend. "She talked me into it and immediately got us together."

Peter Oliva ended up double-dating the roommate following another meeting at the Whisky. "I hung out with the girlfriend for about a month. We went up to Mammoth [where Messina's parents owned a holiday home] and did some things together. Then I got out of that, but Terri and Gene just went on. She was cute and OK at the beginning. I think she was playing him though, man."

Who was playing whom was a debatable matter. Messina was taken aback by Clark's slightly dishevelled state and listened attentively while he related the ups and downs of the past decade, including the story of his marriage, divorce and children. He still owned the home in Albion, but it was a world away from Hollywood and held little attraction for Messina. Within a few months, it would be vacated and later ceded to Carlie and the children.

Clark's vulnerability and availability proved an attractive mix and the relationship deepened, along with his needs. "Gene wasn't in the greatest shape when I found him again," Terri remembers. "He was very depressed, alcoholic, overweight, and he had a big, full beard. I'd known Gene from years before and I wanted him to straighten himself out a little bit, get out of that old hippie bag and get off the alcohol."

Towards the end of April, the KC Southern Band set out on a memorable trip to Europe on a package tour featuring McGuinn's Thunderbyrd and the Chris Hillman Band. It was Gene's first appearance in Britain since 1965 and he clearly enjoyed the experience. He was accompanied by Terri Messina, whose importance at this point should not be underestimated. Her organizational skills, empathy and intuitive ability to keep Clark focused prompted several accolades at the time. Even some of her later critics acknowledged that she was totally together throughout the tour. Unusually for that time, she managed to avoid the stereotypical image of the 'chick' on the road by which women were either deemed too clingy and suffocating or alternatively too bossy and demanding. Loving, yet confident and independent, she seemed happy for Clark to spend time with the boys without feeling neglected. It was a trait she shared with Hillary Kontos, whose wealth and breeding meant she was never reliant on rock star largesse. "Gene had a lot of boys' nights out," she says. "He loved his space and Terri respected that. Lots of girls want to go to every gig and can't stay away. It's really the music you're competing against. Those guys lived for their music. I would see these girls worrying about their men and I'd say, 'They're hanging with the other guys playing music somewhere. That's it. There's no mystery there.' Terri always understood that."

Clark's other chief sidekick on the tour was Tommy Kaye, who played a multiple role as spiritual adviser, drinking companion, public relations adjunct, musical consultant, personal mythologizer, and much else. "Wasn't he a riot?" Hillary remarks. "Tommy loved to talk and was probably in his element there." When Messina wasn't boosting Clark's confidence, Kaye took on a similarly solicitous role. He attended several interviews, some of which might not have happened at all without his benign presence. He was constantly praising Clark's work, particularly *No Other*, and testifying to his artistic godhead. Clark spoke of him with equal awe. "Tommy and I write almost exclusively together now because our communication is excellent and we're able to exchange thoughts well, both musically and lyrically. I would even venture that Tommy and I have probably been partners for many lifetimes, and you could say that we are cosmically and psychically connected. We know and feel what we're doing instinctively, and to say how that comes about, my best thought of it is that the universe being a function of rotations from the atom or molecule right on to wherever the end of the universe is, so everything runs in cycles . . . and to say that we only live one lifetime, or that the only civilization is right here on this earth is ludicrous."

This was Gene Clark settling into his new role as rock's premier 'cosmic cowboy', an image that he felt freer to reveal in Europe where journalists, blissed out on *No Other*, loved hearing his cosmological ramblings. It was not the type of discourse you'd hear from McGuinn or Hillman. They would probably have smiled at his pretensions, but Clark, possibly for the first time ever in print and seldom hereafter, was speaking like a character from one of his more abstruse songs. "I feel that any pure force is based on the rhythm of universal motion, and anything operated on that natural force is much more spiritual. It isn't contrived . . . or if it is, we don't know about it, and it was done by a much higher mind than we know about. So I feel that tuning into a more natural force, or higher element, can maybe inspire you to come up with a more factual statement, or a more spiritual statement. Going back to that thing about cycles in lifetimes . . . somehow I knew of these things even as a small child, but I didn't know how to express them or sort them out. Through my experience of meeting people who I felt were higher minds and influences, and observing their way of expressing feelings, I've found that I've grown in my self-expression, although I don't claim to have the cat by the tail. I'm still a novice."

One thing Clark had to suffer during the visit to England was the presence of earnest journalists or writers, myself included, eager to unlock the secrets of *No Other*. At first, this was flattering and Clark was pleased to learn that the album had been re-promoted by Asylum. Unfortunately, there was a general feeling that the more recent *Two Sides To Every Story* was a regressive step and Clark was frequently called upon to defend the work which some saw as an artistic compromise. "I purposely did the album that way," he responded, "because I wanted to give a little commercial value to it, so that more people might pay attention. Not everyone in the public has the references or the consciousness to be able to understand a very profound and artistic statement. It's like saying that everyone should have a Picasso on their wall . . . not everyone can look at a Picasso and get anything out of it, but put them in a situation where he's sketched something more commercial as well as very artistic, and people are bound to see it better, and it leads them into the higher forms of the man's art too. I feel that holds true of the Byrds' electric folk-rock version of 'Mr Tambourine Man', which brought a lot more people into a Bob Dylan consciousness, whereas before they had thought of

Dylan as the guy with the weird voice, and never really gotten into the depths of what he was delivering."

You could almost hear the frustration in his voice as he spoke of the need to find an alternative way forward, a near impossibility after *No Other*. "I'd put out these albums and I was convinced of their worth, but it's definitely frustrating to think that nobody out there's even listening . . . Too many people become content with their position, they become content with the formula by which they live. They don't care to learn or know any more about life. I can't live like that . . . For my own creativity, I rely on change. Creatively a person dies when he's put in a category and told that's where he belongs and that's where he must stay. The pursuit of knowledge is the impulse behind my work."

The money/art dilemma that Clark was articulating was real enough, as was the importance of artistic progression, but the 'backwards step forwards' approach he was advocating had its limitations. Rock critics in search of 'authenticity' had little truck with commercial compromise, no matter how eloquently expressed. That said, it was easy to appreciate Clark's dilemma. He claimed that some critics or fans back in America had casually damned *No Other* with the curt epithet, 'overproduced'. It was rather like telling Dylan that 'Like A Rolling Stone' was too long or complaining to Brian Wilson that 'Good Vibrations' had too many sonic effects or suggesting that the Beatles lacked a decent tune or were too obscure with 'Strawberry Fields Forever'. No wonder Clark was frustrated. Some critics had complained that *White Light* was too stark and underproduced, then *No Other* was taken to task on the opposite charges. Was it any wonder he settled for something midway between the two?

Reviewers were uncomplimentary about the less pioneering *Two Sides To Every Story*, partly because it did not seem to follow Clark's dictum about the 'pursuit of knowledge'. *Zigzag* editor, Paul Kendall, summarized the feelings of many when arguing that Clark's subtle compromises were ultimately self-defeating and, possibly, unnecessary. "It looks like we can stand and whistle for something comparable to *No Other* until Gene's got the gold albums he seems to be after. Personally, I think he's making a big mistake. He's most unlikely ever to emulate the Eagles or Fleetwood Mac in terms of sales, no matter what he does, but at least work of the quality of *White Light* and *No Other* would guarantee him a devoted and increasingly large following, whereas the direction of *Two Sides* . . . looks likely to end up falling awkwardly between two stools. But no doubt time will show the wiser, and with the news that the album appears to be crossing over into the country charts in the States, it could be that he and Tommy will be proved right in their judgement . . . commercial acceptability still seems a pretty bogus priority when you're making music, though."

Ultimately, *Two Sides To Every Story* suffered the same critical fate as the underrated *Through The Morning Through The Night.* It was never going to be easy following up a classic album like *No Other*. Cult audiences are as unforgiving as mainstream ones, probably more so because their expectations are higher. If *Two Sides To Every Story* had come out a decade later, when Clark's career was at rock bottom, it would no doubt have been hailed as a major comeback. Other lesser releases produced later in his lifetime undeservedly received better notices, as if to underline that point. But, by then, the stakes were lower. Outside of his later excursions with McGuinn and Hillman, *Two Sides To Every Story* was the last record he would ever record for a major label. Few, if any, could have predicted such a downturn for the singer-songwriter back in 1977.

At the time, there was genuine hope that Clark might infiltrate the country market and he even spoke of the possibility of reforming Dillard & Clark for a tour, but it was all hot air. As Kendall had predicted, the album was not a commercial success. It did not even enter *Billboard*'s Top 200, a step down from *No Other* in sales. Clark and Kaye spoke passionately about the next album for RSO which would offer yet another change of direction, using the KC Southern Band on new songs like 'Denver Or Wherever' and others they were currently performing. Alas, rather than a renaissance, the European tour turned out to be something of a last hurrah.

As referenced in Chapter Thirty-Nine of *Requiem For The Timeless, Volume 1*, there were personality differences on the tour and financial wrangling, culminating in the departure of Hillman. The three ex-Byrds did reunite onstage at London's Hammersmith Odeon for an encore set, but not thereafter. As the opening act, the KC Southern Band offered a spontaneous, hard-edged sound, in striking contrast to Hillman's highly professional country rock and McGuinn's accomplished set. Clark took full advantage of RSO's hospitality, but alternated his alcohol intake with lashings of coffee and morphine-tinted cough medicine. Although he fulfilled his PR and performing commitments, he often looked nervous. On the tour bus, he appeared relaxed in the protective company of Tommy Kaye and Terri Messina, but elsewhere there were glimpses of tension.

Backstage in his dressing-room Clark stared into a mirror surrounded by light bulbs, as if he were some Hollywood idol in waiting. There were still hints of the old rock star vanity as he inspected his hair and shirt with assiduous care. The UK music press had called him a 'mountain man' with good reason. His shaggy beard and lined face testified to some recent high living. The coat, which he wore constantly, was the same one seen on the cover of *Two Sides To Every Story*. He treated it like some protective uniform, as if it was a latter-day version of Crosby's talismanic green cape. The coat was emblematic of Mendocino and further evidence of his rural persona. Whereas McGuinn and Hillman were cocaine confident, Gene appeared fragile and slightly dishevelled, a ghostly presence with an air of mystery. His eyes occasionally betrayed a disconcerting blankness, as if the man reflected in the mirror was a puzzle or a stranger. He frequently turned to Terri, who sat nearby. Few words were spoken but her demeanour was enough to assuage his troubled mood. Like a teenager preparing for a date, he reinspected his reflection for a moment, then hesitated. His short sentences were punctuated by long silences which became longer as showtime approached. Perhaps it was advanced stage fright, but there was no way of knowing. He seemed in constant need of reassurance like someone who wanted it all back but wasn't sure if he deserved it. He was, of course, bottom of the bill. After the shows, he was still slightly edgy but found comfort among his musician friends. Kaye was ever present post-performance, regaling onlookers with tales of Gene's exploits and offering in-joke allusions that only they fully understood. Tommy spoke of his friend with respect and showed awe for his artistry, but they also shared earthy appetites. Gene looked far less tense once a bottle or glass was in his hand. A shy grin returned to his face. More than anything, he resembled a man that needed a drink. After a few beers he became merry but less coherent, mumbling to himself, but seemingly in good spirits. It was only at the final date in Scotland that he was completely undone, joining McGuinn onstage in shambolic glory, while twirling the microphone in parodic imitation of the Who's Roger Daltrey.

Although the remainder of the European tour was cancelled, some of the entourage journeyed to France, where Hillary had studied as a youth. As she had demonstrated in London, Terri was deeply in love with Gene, and he seemed equally smitten. "Terri and Gene were really sweet together," says Hillary. "When those two were 'on', it was just great. It was like they were on honeymoon. We went to Paris afterwards and we just had a ball. They had so much fun. Even though the tour had folded, we just had to get over there for a couple of days. Then they went home and moved in together. That was it."

Despite the deals with Asylum and RSO, Clark was in poor financial health. His brother David ruefully recalls having to provide assistance so that Gene could pay his band's wages and fares. He stayed in Mendocino for a short time while Terri, who had no love for Gene and Carlie's dream home, remained in LA.

On 4 July 1977, Dara Zimmerman was back in Mendocino and turned up at Clark's home to celebrate her 18th birthday. A number of musicians were staying in the barn and Dara decided to join the crew, sleeping in the back bedroom next to Gene's in the house. Whether it was wise for a young girl to place herself in such an all-male environment did not bother her unduly. She was mature for her age, resolutely independent and confident in the company of older people. For a short period, she had been dating Michael Equine, drummer in Cat Mother & The All Night Newsboys. "Michael was a month younger than my mother." For several years, Cathy Zimmerman had been involved with Gene's bass player, Peter Oliva. "Peter was ten years younger than my mom and ten years older than me, so it was pretty funny."

As a babysitter, Dara had witnessed Clark at his best and worst, but since Carlie's departure his darker side was more prevalent. "He could be really mean when he was drinking. I watched him break everything in our house once. It took a long time to clean that mess up. He was drunk. He wasn't making a lot of sense most of the time. When he got out of control he was always drunk. He had Indian in him and he should never have drank whisky. It changed his personality. It destroyed him."

The familiar twinkle in his eye when he was happy could suddenly disappear, replaced by a cold, expressionless stare. "That's exactly the look," says Dara. "His pupils would turn black and he would turn into another person. It was almost like he was schizophrenic. *Possessed* is the perfect word. It would scare the crap out of me. I can still see that look. If I shut my eyes and imagine Gene at his worst that would be it."

One evening, Dara was hitching a ride to Middle Ridge when Gene appeared, offering a lift. He was on his way back from a party, clearly drunk. Although she initially refused to get in the car, he was insistent. What happened when they returned to his house was horrific. "I remember that day and it wasn't pleasant. I always felt that Gene would never hurt me." On this occasion, the chilling look in his eyes suggested he was completely out of control. "He started to attack me. I knew Gene well enough to know that there was no fighting him. So I didn't. He was really strong and when he got some crazy idea into his head, no matter what it was, you just didn't argue. I learned at a very early age to agree with Gene. Whatever he said, you just agreed and then you went as far away from him as fast as you possibly could." What made things worse was his tendency to create fantasies that made no sense. "He was delusional. In the hallway, he was saying, 'We would make the most beautiful babies. Imagine Kelly and Kai having a baby brother and sister' and talking about all this crazy shit. He was drunk on his ass and I was sick of the dog. I was crying hysterically and he's saying how we're going to be a couple and I'm like, 'Yeah, whatever, Gene!'" He then demanded to return to the party, which turned out to be another bad idea. "He got into a fight with Tommy Kaye and they started throwing things around the kitchen. Everybody was trying to pull them apart. That was my chance to bolt. I ran down the road and hitchhiked into town."

Zimmerman was so frightened by the appalling incident that she moved out of Gene's house and returned to Los Angeles. She did not complain about him attempting to force himself on her, but kept a distance thereafter. They remained friends. "I grew up with musicians and hippies in Berkeley. I was a little more astute than most. I felt grown up, so I looked at everything different than most people. I still do. There's still one side of Gene that I will *always* love. I did see something hugely good in him and a lot of it was in his music. It's hard to explain to a lot of people that I know now. While he was sitting there writing you could see his mind clicking. Gene was really a good old boy. When he was clear-headed he just wanted a good meal and to sit by a fire writing music."

These were the last of the wild times in Mendocino for Clark, who needed another fresh start. Although some of the group hoped to continue touring and recording, they went their separate ways. It was like a mass walk-out from Mendocino in favour of Los Angeles. Dara Zimmerman went to Hollywood, Tom Slocum relocated to Beachwood Drive, Tommy and Hillary Kaye settled in Laurel Canyon and Gene and Terri moved to nearby Stanley Hills Drive. Jason Ronard secured a part on the police drama series *Starsky & Hutch* and found free accommodation courtesy of the owner of the Charlie Chaplin estate, who allowed him and fellow actor John Barrymore Jr to reside in two of its cottages. A new cycle commenced.

Terri Messina faced a challenging task sorting out Gene's life after he moved back to LA. Still reeling from his divorce settlement, besieged by financial paperwork that he studiously ignored, drinking heavily and uncertain about his career, he was a mess. Among other things, she served as his style counsellor, urging him to lose weight, cut down his drinking, shave his beard, cut his hair and lose the Mendocino mountain-man image in favour of a sleeker, urban cool. Still caught up in romantic intensity, they considered marriage, but decided instead to see how living together worked out before proceeding further. "Gene and I were engaged soon after that British tour," Terri says. "I wanted to give it a little time to see what happened. He straightened himself out. He got more on top of his life and work. He'd been four years behind paying his taxes, the IRS were after him and he was broke. That's another one of the reasons he lived at my house. I paid all the bills for almost a year until he got on his feet with money coming in. He was in bad shape. But then we started to plan this marriage thing."

Clark adapted to LA life as though he had never been away. Everything was intensified in Hollywood, but he seemed capable of reinventing himself once more. Having lost his band, Clark received an unexpected boost that summer when he reconnected with McGuinn. Despite the UK/Irish package tour fiasco, the musicians had seen enough to consider their respective futures. Both were now out of contract with their record companies and decided to embark on a short tour of clubs and colleges as a duo. It was to prove one of the more rewarding episodes in Clark's career, a tension-free escapade that promised something bigger later down the line. He had seldom been so close to McGuinn and they would never be as friendly again. Already, the foundations for what would become McGuinn, Clark & Hillman were in place, but that was still some months away.

Terri Messina's rehabilitation of Clark was working. He cut down his drinking and appeared healthy and well. Even onstage, there was little or no sign of the recent tensions. Yet, over the next year, there would be slippages. Ultimately, there was no safe haven for Clark. Hollywood had its own temptations as he would soon rediscover.

Clark's public persona was still pure at this point. Looking back at his exploits in Mendocino, it is interesting to observe the contrast between the man and the myth. Clark was unknowable as far as the wider public was concerned. He did not feature regularly in the rock press and huge chunks of his life and recording career were nothing more than a blank slate. The suggestion that he might be a desperate drinker subject to boorish behaviour was anathema in those innocent times. There had never been any report of public transgressions or hints of a crazy, rock 'n' roll lifestyle. Clark's art presented the opposite image. For music fans, he was considered an introspective singer-songwriter and a deep thinker. Mystical was a word that came to mind when contemplating his work. That was the image that endured for the remainder of his life.

The coming together of McGuinn, Clark & Hillman was plotted with admirable caution. McGuinn's agent Ron Rainey, who represented the various parties, approached several record companies over a period of months before a deal was settled in early 1978. The slow pace of negotiations suited Clark, who was free from pressure, optimistic about the future and able to enjoy himself.

Some of those left behind were unimpressed by this latest turn of events. There were always warring factions in the Gene Clark story who felt he was being led astray, even if he was doing well. Peter Oliva missed the bearded, bar-loving musician who had been one of the boys back in Mendocino, but was now seeking bigger things. "Well, it was LA," he sneers. "All these guys had big houses and millions of dollars. We were living in these funky little shacks up in Mendocino. It's like he got into places where it wasn't necessarily good for him to be. You know how that stuff goes when you get into the rich scene. Tommy Kaye was married to Hillary and it was, 'Come on down to Newport Beach, and float around on yachts . . .' That kind of thing. I thought what Geno really needed was to be grounded."

While it may be tempting to contrast honest, rural Mendocino with unholy sinful LA, the dichotomy was always a false one. Mendocino, a pot dealer's paradise, was a party town where, as Kandanes and others confirm, booze and lines of coke were in plentiful supply. As Tom Slocum stresses: "After *Two Sides To Every Story* everybody broke from Mendocino because of the insanity there." Dara Zimmerman concurs. "I don't think the insanity of Mendocino ever really leaves you."

It is easy to transform Gene Clark's life into some modern day moral fable. Several of his musician friends and associates, now blessed with blurred hindsight, cannot resist the urge. Some, including Chris Hillman, maintain that he was corrupted by LA and would have been better off if he'd never made it as a rock star. They may be right, but that applies to many lives whose directions might otherwise have been very different. Clark's problems were not necessarily determined by fame or geography. Alcoholism, divorce and penury are as real in Kansas as anywhere else. Considering his psychology, ambitions and frustrations, Clark might have cut a far sadder and depressing figure had he never broken free from his home state. Indeed, he might have ended up in an even darker place in a world where there was no Byrds, no 'Eight Miles High' and no records to signify his self-validation. Like many of his generation, Clark was driven by a new version of the American Dream that pointed inexorably towards Hollywood. That was where he felt a sense of belonging, no matter how artificial the emotional terrain. "Gene never wanted to leave Hollywood during our time together," says Jim Dickson. "It was like Disneyland. He enjoyed the girls, the parties, the social life.

Jacqui Levy introduced him to the nightclub scene and he loved it. He was far more into it than the other guys, including Crosby. Gene was even into the old Hollywood haunts where an elder generation hung out. He liked the attention, and the girls were always beautiful."

Dickson still associated Clark with beauties like Jacqui Levy and Michelle Phillips, fiercely independent women who were more likely to mould him than vice versa. While in Hawaii, Dickson met Clark's former wife for the first and only time and was perplexed by her personality. "I was in Lahaina, Maui, in the late Seventies. They were separated, but it was like she still expected to be treated like a princess because she was once married to Gene Clark. You'd almost believe she *was* Gene Clark. She seemed one of those people that took over somebody else's personality, and that's who they were. It was really weird to me. I couldn't figure out how Gene was ever attracted to her." Dickson's comments, based entirely on first impressions, may sound cutting, but indicate how much the tambourine man had become associated with a certain type of Hollywood woman in his former manager's mind. It may also indicate the extent to which Carlie had changed after those idyllic early years with Gene in Mendocino which she always regarded as their happiest times.

Clark enjoyed moving in different circles. That in itself created rival factions, each of which instinctively felt they knew the *real* Gene Clark. Without wishing to contradict any one of them, it hardly needs stating that he seemed at home in the company of many different people, some of whom ended up despising each other. During the interim between the end of the KC Southern Band and the international success of McGuinn, Clark & Hillman, Gene found a new set of contacts in a previously unscaled social echelon. Since hitting Hollywood and establishing his reputation in the Byrds, Clark had enjoyed the company of glamorous dancers, aspiring actors and chart-topping pop stars. He was part of the new Hollywood and could list among his friends thespian anti-heroes such as Dennis Hopper, Steve McQueen and David Carradine. Clark was always intrigued by the former Hollywood elite, but they were as far removed from the Byrds as presidents and world leaders.

It was Tommy Kaye's wife Hillary who provided access to an older generation. As the godfather of their daughter, Eloise, Gene was invited to meet Hillary's rich, widowed mother, Claudia ('Coy'). The uncrowned Queen of Orange County, Claudia was a socialite supreme who moved in circles seemingly beyond Clark's imagination. Hillary saw no incongruity in introducing him to this new world, having convinced herself that he was already pretty urbane. "I'd always thought of him as sort of sophisticated because of his whole life. I thought he was more sophisticated than me and my gang. Let's face it, when Gene was a young kid he was driving Ferraris and racing Steve McQueen and the gang up on the hill."

Thanks to his closeness to Kaye, Tom Slocum was also allowed into Claudia's presence. "Hillary's mother was a very beautiful, raven-haired dark-eyed woman. Her maiden stock was Irish, I believe. She controlled the estate. There was Budget Rent A Car and this tremendous financial flow. People would go to Newport Beach to visit her. On the boat they'd have guests, and it would be John Wayne and his [third] wife, Pilar. I was there a couple of times and witnessed these great events. The Pilars coming over for brunch was an everyday occurrence for them."

This was no exaggeration. Pilar Wayne, who married John in 1954, owned the Fernleaf Café on Newport Beach. She was memorably described as Claudia's 'bosom friend' in the society pages of the *Los Angeles Times*. "John Wayne was my brother Casey's godfather," adds Hillary. Years later, when the Waynes' youngest daughter Marisa was engaged to marry Olympic skier Jace Romnick, Claudia opened her bayfront home on Harbor Island to introduce the bridegroom to the area's most privileged people. For Gene Clark, the chance to meet and socialize with John Wayne was akin to a once in a lifetime experience. "When Gene found out that Pilar was one of my mother's best friends and that John was a friend of the family, it tripped him out completely," says Hillary. "John was such a regular guy, so natural and cool." Several of Gene's friends testify to the actor's influence on Clark's public persona. It was there in the swagger, the stare and the laconic style of speech. "I think Gene thought he *was* John Wayne," says Andy Kandanes.

If Claudia was exotic, then her mother was no less colourful. "The grandmother was like a matriarch," says Slocum. Actor Jason Ronard agrees. "Granny Hill was about 90 years old and took a tab of speed every day to make sure she wasn't going to die. She was the greatest." One might have expected Clark to have been slightly intimidated by high-society people but a combination of Missouri manners and polite deference ensured that he was well received. "He knew my grandmother and they had a great relationship," Hillary recalls. "She was a wonderful character and loved having kids in her house on Newport Beach. We were always hanging around there when we could get to see her. I had girlfriends who'd come over to talk to my grandmother when I wasn't there. She'd be their friend and advise them really well. She was that kind of person. She loved to help people. She'd been through so much herself during the Depression, pulling herself out of that, that she loved to see people striving and liked to give them a boost, if she could. My mother and grandmother were really special people and unusual. They put up with a lot from me and my friends. I realized later that others weren't like that. They were both in the entertainment business because of the way they ran their restaurant. They hired local and touring musicians and created a place where people could hang out and have fun. This was when Newport was a sleepy place. They created events, and they dug Gene. When he was with them, he was just Gene. They were very natural together."

For a time, Clark seemed in control of his demons and determined to ensure that MC&H were successful. Summer 1978 found the group in Australia, paving the way for a world tour and the recording of a much anticipated album. According to Terri Messina, Clark was drinking moderately by his excessive standards and fulfilling his professional obligations with confidence. Nevertheless, he was still plagued by worries and insecurities and his interaction with McGuinn and Hillman was less than ideal. The underlying conflicts between the parties were documented assiduously in the lengthy McGuinn, Clark & Hillman chapters in *Requiem For The Timeless, Volume 1*. It was part of Clark's peculiar psychology that whenever fame beckoned he would revert to the bad behaviour, toxic excesses and manic spendthriftiness familiar from earlier days. Typically, when the group's advance arrived from Capitol, he immediately went out and bought a Porsche, just as he had purchased a Ferrari with his first big songwriting royalty from the Byrds.

In LA, cocaine was the ubiquitous drug of choice not only among rock stars and actors, but nightclub habitués, party lovers, professionals, and even blue collar workers. Pharmaceutically, the gap between audience and star had diminished like never before. Most of Clark's musician friends partook of cocaine, as did McGuinn, whose consumption was prodigious up until 1978. As a film editor, Terri Messina also dabbled in coke – it would have been surprising had she not – but she resented being ripped off. Her business acumen extended to her recreational pursuits to such an extent that, in the end, she elected to cut out the middle men and find the source of supply. Others encouraged this, happy to benefit from her efforts. In later years, some detractors, with axes to grind, liked to imply that she was some sort of drug baroness to the stars. "She was nothing of the sort," laughs Hillary. "She just did a teeny bit of this and that. It was just somebody doing a favour for somebody. Things were really great between Gene and Terri. There may have been some drug doing, but they had a pretty cosy relationship between themselves in spite of that. Later, though, it was something that Terri couldn't seem to shake. You know how it is. You get into something like that and you can't shake it. But all that was later."

Coincidentally, Clark's ex-wife Carlie was also spiralling towards her own drug nightmare in the aftermath of her marriage to Gene. Evidently, she was also accident prone. Michael McGibbon remembers her almost killing herself in a freak fall. "Carlie was on the headlands. It was boxed-in with fog and she couldn't see where she was going and she walked off the cliff and fell into the ocean. It's rough there and there aren't many people that would have survived that. She was a good swimmer and held on to something. There was a big rescue scene and the Mendocino crew finally got her out. She had 17 broken bones. That kid was a survivor." She needed to be. Her relationship in Hawaii had ended and she began an affair with another man in San Rafael. Her drug abuse became as bad, if not worse, than that of Clark and Messina. Dara Zimmerman recalls Carlie first taking coke recreationally during those dark, final days of her marriage in Mendocino. Once she moved to Hawaii, she became a more regular user and by the time she was in San Rafael, her intake was out of hand. Increasingly, her social circle was dominated by other users. Dara recalls visiting her and discovering "opium in the freezer, a big ball of black tar, tons of coke". The contents were not Carlie's, but she was sampling some of the drugs left by others. Given her earlier wariness of coke, this was a surprisingly sudden decline. Carlie's elder son Kelly claims that he was only seven when she started freebasing cocaine. Others assume it was considerably later. He maintains his mother was also felled by hepatitis at this time. The drug dependency continued for many years, as it did with so many characters in this story. It was telling that the two major women in Gene's life suffered similar fates at a point when he was about to hit the big time once more.

By late 1978, Clark's own coke intake was increasing, made worse by the decision to record in Miami, the new drug capital of America. McGuinn, Clark & Hillman were living together in a house, but staying in separate quarters. It was only in the studio that they communicated with any real rapport. Outside the Record Plant, a battle for supremacy between the drug cartels of Colombia and Cuba was threatening to turn Miami into a war zone. Cocaine literally rained from the heavens. In one infamous incident a preacher was denouncing the drug from the pulpit of a nearby church when a plane accidentally deposited a large stash which crashed through the church roof covering the congregation in powder. Coke was so plentiful that it was now reaching every stratum of society. In Miami musical circles, it wasn't so much a question of who was doing cocaine, as who wasn't. Seemingly every roadie and hanger-on had a sizeable supply and dealers were ten a penny. Inevitably, Clark succumbed, as did his girlfriend Terri Messina, whose addiction became ever stronger.

Despite such problems, *McGuinn, Clark & Hillman* was completed on time and released in the final week of January 1979. The ultra 'contemporary' production by the Albert Brothers divided fans and the determination to resist the Byrds' signature sound meant McGuinn's Rickenbacker was muted. As expected, Clark dominated the songwriting credits with four compositions, but his efforts were also compromised by the added effects. The beautiful 'Release Me Girl' was somewhat spoiled by an intrusive disco beat; 'Little Mama', a slight lyric and derivative melody, was vocally strong but far from great; 'Backstage Pass', an intriguing narrative with a darker aspect, was transformed into an upbeat anthem with a theatrical hey-ho chorus. Only 'Feelin' Higher', arguably the best song on the record, benefited from the Alberts' production tricks. Inspired by the sighting of a flying saucer, this Clark/Messina composition, part love song, part extra-terrestrial rumination, was given greater momentum by the inclusion of a fascinating musical coda featuring an extended piano and percussion fade out. As Ron Albert rightly says: "Part of the magic of this track is the 'Cuban Army' (Joe Lala and friends Ghia Farcia and Falco Falcore) on percussion. The whole track fell together because we had them set up live in the studio during the embryonic stages of the album. Lala's friends were just hanging around and he called them in for this and it worked beautifully. Everyone just got to the end of the song and there was no ending, so Howard [Albert] motioned Paul [Harris] to keep playing and Lala and the Army just kept percussing. The whole outro was about ten minutes long . . . we edited out everything but the key piano lines and phrases and it was done." The song stands large among Clark's metaphysical meditations and its theme of alien visitation anticipates the great 'Communications'.

It should be stressed that Clark fully supported the Albert

Brothers' production. At the time of the record's release, he told me that he 'loved' what they had done to 'Release Me Girl' and had no reservations or complaints whatsoever. After applauding the album's contemporary sound, Clark boasted about its hit potential. This was a new Gene Clark – market orientated, trendily dressed, and seemingly fixated with commercial success. Two years before, he had spoken about his work reverentially and portentously with a countenance worthy of a spiritual adviser. To paraphrase 'Release Me Girl' – "everywhere I go I find that there is *No Other*". But Clark was no longer interested in discussing *No Other*, nor referencing the seemingly passé image of the hippie troubadour. He now spoke about his work glibly at best, as if its commercial success was all. Perhaps it was understandable. Still pushing old buttons, I asked him about an aspect of his imagery that had always intrigued me.

Q. . . . I can't help notice the number of references to silver: 'Silver Raven', 'Silver Phial', 'silver on the ocean shore', even your backing band was called the Silverados. Is there any significance to all this or is it just a series of remarkable coincidences?
A. Aha! God, I have no idea. It's a word. I used it. It's a hard thing to decide. Maybe next time I'll use golden.

In an attempt to shake Clark out of auto-pilot PR mode, I presented him with the longest question I've ever asked anybody. The intention was to remind him of all that he had been through and what might await him. His response, which was evasive to the point of dismissive, indicated that he preferred to focus on the pleasures of the moment rather than making some sense of his past.

Q. Before you go Gene, I've one last question. Last night I was thinking over the events of your career and it's a remarkable story. I made a mental list of some of the things that have happened to you, well, for example . . .

At the beginning of 1966, your finest song of the early period, 'Set You Free This Time', was released as an A-side in Britain. Then, the following week, by some accident or arbitrary decision, it became a B-side.

'Eight Miles High' seemed set for number 1 [or the Top 10] in the US when it was suddenly banned in spite of your insistence that it was written about a plane flight.

For several reasons, you were forced to leave the Byrds when they were still at the peak of their career.

Your first album, Gene Clark With The Gosdin Brothers, *was accidentally released at the same time as the Byrds'* Younger Than Yesterday *and your work was ignored once more.*

You began experimenting with country rock about 18 months before it became fashionable to do so, and then you saw your co-writer go on to fame and fortune with the Eagles.

A&M accidentally released copies of your White Light *album in mono, complete with a 'stereo' sticker on the back cover.*

Roadmaster *was never released outside Holland.*

The Byrds' reunion backfired when it seemed certain to project you into superstardom.

You signed to the most successful label of the early Seventies, Asylum, released perhaps the finest album of the decade, No Other, *and it flopped.*

You then signed to the most successful label of recent times, RSO, but in spite of their Midas touch they failed to make you a million.

Now, you're with Capitol and . . . well, I can't help wondering. Looking back, do you think your career has been jinxed?

A. Wow! I don't know because now it's all coming back to me, you know, with *this* record. So far I've heard this record is a definite hit everywhere. I think this new album is great. I love it – and it's a hit already – that's for sure.

This was the answer of a star in waiting. A slicker version of the old Gene Clark: flippant, cool, cocky, evasive and anti-intellectual. He had assumed a new identity, more akin to a contemporary rock god. It was almost as if he was fashioning an image to complement the music produced by the Albert Brothers.

* * *

McGuinn, Clark & Hillman embarked on a world tour (documented in *Volume 1*) and at one point the itinerary took them to Kansas. While passing through, Gene invited his family to a surprise outing. It did not go well. Bonnie remembers everyone waiting patiently before Gene appeared at the top of a staircase wearing sunglasses. "That was the first sign," she says. He was strutting like a rock star, as if it was the mid-Sixties again. Everyone had dinner, but he and Terri kept making their excuses and disappearing to the bathroom. It was pretty obvious what they were up to.

Nothing much went right for Clark after the release of *McGuinn, Clark & Hillman*. He became even more detached from his fellows and by the summer he was missing gigs. There were various excuses and health problems, but drink and drugs were the main issues, exacerbated by a combination of nervous tension, complacency and disillusionment. It was a troublesome time and Capitol were still keen for the trio to return to Florida and complete a second album.

Miami was still synonymous with drug-taking, a view reinforced by buzz words heard in everyday conversation. If someone spoke of 'tar' they were probably not thinking of roadworks and if they mentioned 'downtown' it was unlikely that they were referring to Petula Clark's exuberant mid-Sixties chart hit. Heroin was the new chic, providing the necessary comedown after taking copious amounts of coke. Many favoured the 'speedball', a mixture of heroin and cocaine. Inevitably, Clark joined the party, although his dalliances were not made public until many years later when McGuinn casually mentioned that his ex-partner had gotten heavily into the drug.

The extent of Clark's heroin use is still hotly debated by friends and associates. "I never saw Gene do heroin in my life," says his friend, Tom Slocum. "A lot of people will say these things but I never saw any of this stuff. Gene wasn't the easiest guy in the world to know or form any kind of trustworthy relationship with. He trusted very few people about anything. I don't think it was heroin that was his problem so much as drink. Gene had that alcohol thing. He could take a drink and hold it for a while, then he'd have another one and another and the next thing you know, you've got a different person. But I never knew him to lose it in public while he was working. It was more if he was downtown in a bar. Then he could get wild. He had that side of him when he drank. Anything was possible."

Whereas other users, including his girlfriend Terri Messina, stuck to smack, Clark preferred to lubricate himself with booze, which made him voluble, self-destructive and potentially violent. Messina's attempts to sort out Clark's life was now backfiring as she slipped further into an adjoining abyss. "Terri was very sweet," says Slocum. "Come on – she's Terri! She was the instigator in getting a lot of things together in his life." Hillary Kontos concurs. "Terri was a great girl. Some people tried to paint her very black, but she always tried to do the best things for Gene. She straightened out his taxes and really got him on the right track."

"She was like the dragon lady too," cautions Andy Kandanes. "Let me tell you. I think Terri got him doing heroin to be honest. She got hooked herself. Before that she was into the coke thing, hot and heavy, doing a little bit on the side, making money, so it was always available. That's why Gene was exposed to it to the extent that he was. During the earlier years he never did heroin the whole time I was with him. I was never into it anyway. It was the one thing I wouldn't tolerate. McGuinn, Clark & Hillman were playing some place and he invited me over to his hotel room. I saw this stuff and said, 'What the hell's this?' He said, 'Oh, I've got to do this to go to sleep.' I said, 'Don't mess with it, you're not going to control it – it's going to control you.' He said, 'No, no, I've got it under control.' Well, obviously, time revealed all, and he didn't have it under control." Gene and Carlie's interdependency, both emotional and pharmaceutical, would define their relationship hereafter, but it was seldom straightforward.

Blaming Messina for Clark's using was naïve given the amount of drugs available all around them. "It's such horseshit," says Hillary. "You have to look at the big picture. Terri's whole life shifted and changed then. Before that she was a single girl. Very single. When Gene moved in, I'm surprised she didn't have a nervous breakdown. She changed her whole lifestyle and definitely tried to clean up Gene's life and did so many good things for him."

More pertinently, Messina was far from the only person in Clark's circle who shared his dependencies. There were many others hovering in the background. Gene had connections going back as far as the Byrds' era. In truth, he was merely the latest in a long line of musicians caught up in the drug trade. Back in Laurel Canyon, he was working on some songs with the Band's Rick Danko, another recreational user. There were always camp followers and hangers-on who enjoyed Clark's hospitality. Gene's brother, David, recalls a later visit when he stumbled upon a dishevelled scene whose cast list included the well-known drug dealer, Cathy Smith. A familiar figure in such circles, Smith had first met Levon Helm and Rick Danko during the Sixties and became part of the Band's encourage. Subsequently, she appeared as a backing vocalist with folk singer Hoyt Axton, another cocaine connoisseur, whom McGuinn had accompanied on the album *The Folksinger* back in the pre-Byrd days. In 1976, the Band had appeared on the television show *Saturday Night Live*, where Cathy Smith met actor John Belushi, a manic personality with a penchant for injecting speedballs, the drug of the moment. The point needs stressing that any number of people from movie stars to musicians might have been supplying Clark with drugs. He certainly did not have to go looking for them, nor did he require Messina to act as some intermediary.

"Gene just did what he wanted to," says Hillary. "The truth of the matter is that a lot of people were trying to get Gene to do drugs, if he had the money. One thing I've got to say is that I've never pushed drugs on anybody. They might have seen some around my house. Especially when I was with Tommy Kaye, there were always dealers around my house. Half the time I was taking care of my children and was pregnant or something and I wasn't even doing drugs. I'll never forget the argument I had with

Cathy Smith who was later accused of killing John Belushi. She found out that I liked opium and she was giving me all this tar and one day she told me that I owed her all this money for it. I said, 'Do you think I've been taking that stuff? I'm nursing my baby! You've got to be kidding?' And I gave it all back to her. I hadn't taken any of it. I was often not doing the drugs they were doing, at times. That's not to say I didn't do them when we could do them or when I felt like doing them."

While Hillary was about to give birth to her second daughter, Jesse Jane, Gene continued to stray. His dalliances with heroin were worrying enough, but his lifelong battle with booze was arguably causing more damage. Combining the two was the equivalent of conjuring monsters more powerful than any he had previously fought.

Clark still retained business links with former mentors Dickson and Tickner, although communication between the parties was intermittent. In the late Seventies, Dickson had found a house in North Hollywood, part of which was rented to Linda Bopp and her daughter, Gwen. When they moved out, Tickner took over the room as his office. "Gene would come by to get money," Dickson recalls. "He was all strung out and fucked up. He walked into my house completely bombed. He was saying nasty things about me to Eddie and I was sitting there in a chair in the living room, and he didn't even see me. When he saw I was there, he was all shook up and started to flee. I got mad and chased after him. He had a cab out front with the motor running. I grabbed him by the shirt front and I was going to hit him. Then I realized he was in terrible physical shape. Here's a guy that could have ripped me apart when he was younger and here I am ready to attack him, and I was already crippled by then. I couldn't do it because he was so pathetic. He must have weighed about 90 lb. He was just awful."

In November 1979, MC&H returned to Miami to record their second album, *City*. Alas, Clark was little more than a spectral presence. "Well, you know what happened," says Kandanes. "A lot of guys in Miami were getting into the downtown. They'd do coke and then want to do heroin to sleep and it was just a combination of everything that was making them crazy." Clark was incapable most of the time, unhappy and ultimately relieved to leave the city. When the record was released the following year, it bore the revealing credit, 'Roger McGuinn & Chris Hillman (Featuring Gene Clark)'. His involvement had been limited to a handful of hours and he contributed only two new songs. 'Painted Fire' was a Fifties-inspired romp with Jerry Lee Lewis-style piano. A strange aberration in the Clark canon, it seems almost as uncharacteristic of his style as the perplexing Dillard & Clark oddity, 'Corner Street Bar'. By contrast, 'Won't Let You Down' was among his best contributions to McGuinn, Clark & Hillman. More than anything, it displayed how wonderful Clark's earnest love songs sounded when complemented by McGuinn's Rickenbacker accompaniment. Sadly, that wonderful combination would never be heard on record again.

The return to Miami spelt the end of Clark's involvement with McGuinn and Hillman. Although his partners insist that he was incapable of recording, he could easily have produced more than the meagre two songs completed at the sessions. Only a month before, McGuinn, Clark & Hillman were still touring and Clark was premiering new material in concert. In addition to 'Won't Let You Down', he sang the harmonica-led '(Living In) Hard Times' and 'I Saw A Dream Come True', a ballad about mutually obsessive love which, lyrically and vocally, recalled Roy Orbison. Either of these could have been added to the album project with minimal effort.

Evidently, Clark was unconcerned or simply ready to move on. His co-dependent relationship with Messina made her an easy target for detractors. It had not always been so, as road manager Al Hersh acknowledges. "Terri had been together on the 1977 UK tour, as you well knew. She was really keeping Gene alive at that time. She later did a 180-degree turn and turned into the Yoko Ono of the McGuinn, Clark & Hillman experience because everything bad that happened got blamed on her. And in some instances, rightly. But she still made it possible for Gene even to be there. I had no idea how he was going to get there and she made it happen. I really relied on her. Just to get Gene to those sessions in Florida was a huge thing. Terri had also hooked him up with his estranged kids and I was amazed she had the wherewithal to do that. That was actually a very good experience for him for a short period of time, and made a big impact . . . but then she was copping drugs. The last image I have is of her grabbing Gene's strongbox, which was full of drugs. She ran down the street and Gene was chasing her. They were both naked and the cops came and I think they took her away, and maybe the drugs too. She probably took a fall for him. It was very complex. You know, man, he was pretty helpless. He was dependent on so many levels, even aside from the drugs. And you'd be right to say that you can't really point a finger at anybody, especially during that time period."

Encouraged by Messina, Clark did reconnect with his two sons, who turned up for visits during the spring or summer holidays. The timing was seldom ideal as both Gene and Terri were still indulging. Occasionally, Gene would rally sufficiently to play the doting parent, showering the kids with presents. In May 1980, he took them to see the newly-released movie *The Empire Strikes Back* which left a lasting impression. Such treats were welcomed, but they were a poor substitute for genuine parenting. Gene was frequently absent, either working or playing. After a late-night session, he might sleep late, so quality time with his children was limited. Sometimes, Terri was forced to play the 'stepmother' role, seldom successfully. "Gene wasn't a great father. I was the one that was getting up in the morning, feeding them, taking them out, or entertaining them. Gene was passed out on the couch, while I was doing these 'motherly' chores. It was hard on me. By the time they had to go back to their mother, I'd be going, 'Thank God!' I wasn't used to having that kind of responsibility on top of the other things I was doing. They weren't my kids and they weren't brought up the way I'd bring up my kids. My father was a respected doctor in LA, so I was brought up in a house where you didn't even walk into the living room [without permission]. Those kids had no such discipline."

"Terri didn't like us," Kelly says. "It didn't feel like she wanted us around that much . . . He wasn't sure how to handle it. He'd buy toys and we'd play around for a while . . . We weren't really around a lot, to tell you the truth." On various occasions, the boys were shunted across the neighbourhood, spending time with their uncle Rick and his girlfriend, or with Tommy and Hillary Kaye. It was hardly happy families.

"The kids showed a lot of animosity towards Terri," Hillary recalls, "but she reached out to them as much as she could, not being a woman with children herself. When they came down to visit, Gene would drop them off at our house because I had a little boy about Kelly's age, just a little older, by my first marriage. They would play with Hugh and they'd have more fun there. That suggestion was more Gene's doing than Terri's. He didn't know how to be a dad. He lost track of being a dad when Carlie took them away from him. It's like your life changes and it becomes difficult to reconnect. I understand that for men, especially when families break up. But he adored those boys."

Visiting their father was always a disorientating experience for Kelly and Kai who were never sure what awaited them in Laurel Canyon. At first, they were amazed by the opulence of LA life. Terri and Gene's home had modern facilities including cable television with movie channels, a luxury unheard of in Mendocino. Kelly even remembers a gun range out the back. On a subsequent visit, Gene appeared to be struggling. At one point, he could not even feed the children properly. "We called that the brown rice summer," Kai recalls. "Here's Dad in Laurel Canyon with a hot tub and all this stuff. He was still trying to live that life, but he was really low. Esteem-wise, it took a toll on him. If you're down on yourself it's easy to slip into a downward spiral, as we know with many artistes."

Prior to the release of *City*, Clark re-established contact with his old friends from the KC Southern Band. Andy Kandanes and Peter Oliva attempted to co-write with Gene "mainly for publishing and possibly to put another band together and tour".

Unfortunately, it was painfully clear that any such plans were unworkable. Clark invited them to Mammoth, the popular resort where Terri's parents owned a second property. It was the perfect spot to chill out, but Clark was still combating his personal demons. "His relationship with Terri definitely went down in flames because of the drugs," recalls Kandanes. "Peter and I were recording with him in Mammoth and they were just getting so crazy. I ended up grabbing everything and flushed it down the toilet. I told both of them, 'This shit's got to stop right now. It's getting too crazy. Somebody's got to stop this.' I cared about both of them and it was horrible for me to see this go on. I just couldn't deal with it anymore. They were OK for a while so I hung out with them for a few days. Once they got a clearer head, they were back to normal again, but this stuff was making them crazy, man. There's a point where you've got to know when to walk away from all of that."

Messina had already attempted to distance herself from her co-dependency with Clark, albeit with limited success. "When he got back into alcohol and drugs and into abusive behaviour, I called off getting married." Despite this, they still found it difficult to separate permanently. As Hillary recalls: "They lived together very solidly, then, all of a sudden, Gene got his own house on the same street. I always thought that was really queer. This was in Laurel Canyon. He just moved to a little house up the street. I don't know what brought it on."

The main reason for Clark's exile was his drunken temper, culminating in one episode where he struck Terri in anger. Her brother Joe was obliged to intervene and warn him off. Gene was left with a black eye. Joe later joked that his father was disappointed he hadn't gone further. He remembers Gene spent the rest of the day drunk while "getting the nerve to fight me again, but he didn't".

Clark found it difficult to stay away from Terri. Incensed by intoxication, made worse by fears of losing her, he turned up banging on her door like a drunken Fred Flintstone. Realizing a man was inside, he became angrier and smashed the door-frame.

Inside he was confronted by Bill Reid, a leading Hells Angel, who had dated Terri when she was a teenager and remained friendly with her brother, Joe. When Gene started verbally threatening Terri, Reid rushed to her defence. A fight ensued, but Clark was no longer the Byrd with super strength, his physique having been weakened by drink and drugs. Fearing the worst, Terri phoned the police, while begging Reid to restrain himself. Gene was left with a broken nose and advised never to return.

Away from Terri, Clark spent more time at Tommy Kaye's house, where a number of musician friends regularly congregated. Several acoustic ballads survive from this period, including two strongly melodic meditations: 'Once In A Lifetime' and 'If You Knew'. The former speaks of two lovers' first meeting from the view of the woman. It's a song of high romance based on a dream that ends up coming true in an enchanted night filled with desire. The accompanying 'If You Knew', whose structure recalls a 1964 Beatles composition, appears to have been inspired by the recent rift with Terri. It laments the difficulty of making a new start, while also pleading for a second chance ("Tell me why we should say goodbye"). A sense of mystery combines with a belief in an eventual reunion.

Another song, frustratingly undated but possibly from the same period, is the six-minute acoustic ballad, 'Strange And Different Way'. A veritable compendium of Clark lyrical and melodic tropes, it has echoes of 'Why Not Your Baby' and a theme that is the antithesis of 'Feel A Whole Lot Better' with Clark fantasizing about a romantic reunion. His voice has a desperate, yearning quality as he obsessively focuses on a reconciliation that his repeatedly mournful tone suggests may be nothing more than delusory. In an odd twist he takes us back in time to the final track on *Mr Tambourine Man*, imagining "we'll meet again on some bright sunny day". The effect is oddly chilling.

This latest writing spree led to discussions about forming a band. Kaye was working with Virginian guitarist Garth Beckington, who had first been introduced to Clark by John

Desko at the Hollywood Canteen in the summer of 1977. Another new entrant to the scene was Indiana-born bassist, Jon Faurot. "It was pretty nutty," he recalls. "Tommy had diabetes, drank a lot of vodka and did too much blow. But he was a great arranger and producer and we learned a lot of stuff about vocals and harmonies from him. He was always in the forefront." The quartet – Clark, Kaye, Beckington and Faurot – rehearsed for six weeks in preparation for a show at McCabe's guitar store, supporting Ramblin' Jack Elliott.

Evidently, the gig went sufficiently well to continue the experiment. Garth Beckington was aware that Clark was in a vulnerable state and still recovering from the MC&H implosion. "I don't know if any one time was more difficult than another," he cautions. "Gene had a complicated life with his children and everything, especially then. His good spirits never lasted. I mean from minute to minute. He was a physical specimen, wiry and resilient but emotionally the guy was explosive and volatile. In retrospect, I can see he was adjusting to not riding in limousines and stuff. He told me once: 'You've got to give it all up.' And he did give it all up – his wife and his children – in exchange for all his success."

Jon Faurot was impressed by Clark, but also noted an overt sensitivity. "He was a very intelligent man, way past rock 'n' roll consciousness, but I don't know if he read at all. Maybe he was automatically gifted. One time when we were playing I said, 'Why don't you try this?' He didn't get mad at me, but I learned not to mess with his flow. He didn't want to hear it. He had his own roadmap. You had to trust that he knew what he was doing. I just learned to keep my mouth shut more. Drink made him scary. One time we were funning around and he got a little edgy. Garth just grabbed me, and said: 'Don't fuck with him.'"

Clark had recently seen the future and it looked pretty bleak. On a whim, he had attended a McGuinn/Hillman show at the Roxy, fully expecting to see a full house. The results were beyond disappointing. "The bottom just dropped out of the industry," he concluded. "I joined them onstage for the last couple of songs.

Up to that point every time we played the Roxy we had filled the place. I walked through the audience and there were just a couple of hundred people there, maybe less. The vibe was bad everywhere and nothing was happening. I couldn't get work and even the big stars could not sell records. Everything went dead."

Clark's grim diagnosis was correct. During the spring of 1980, David Crosby had been touring as an acoustic solo, playing a five-night stint at London's Venue. I questioned him about Clark's current low profile and he said: "Gene can't sell. It'll probably happen to me someday." Crosby's humiliation was closer than he expected. He was proudly promoting some songs intended to grace his forthcoming solo record for Capitol, the label that was still trying to publicize McGuinn & Hillman, following the loss of Clark. Not long after, Capitol turned down Crosby's record on the grounds that it was not modern enough. He was devastated. If Crosby, with all his superstar connections and artistic rhetoric, could not retain the interest of a major record label, what hope was there for Clark?

Garth Beckington appreciated Clark's quandary and the negative implications for their future working relationship. "He was post-superstar. A reconstructed talent. Like Crosby, he couldn't believe he'd been turned down. Those guys, the Byrds, were the American Beatles. Gene told me over and over again, 'Man, you couldn't believe it. I cannot even begin to describe to you what it was like in the Byrds.' For them not to be able to get arrested was unthinkable."

While working with Kaye and company, Clark reconnected with another old friend, Jesse Ed Davis. It was symptomatic of the times that their drawing power did not extend beyond a showcase gig at McCabe's in the spring. "Jesse was something else," says Faurot. "He and Garth hung together and were tight. We later opened for him, just bar gigs. His energy level was unbelievable. Even talking with him. He was intelligent and smart enough to hang with John Lennon, who didn't suffer fools gladly. Garth would get a guitar from Fender and Jesse Ed would hock it.

There'd be some horrendous story about this guitar catching fire. He was always getting guitars off these guys. With Gene he was out of control."

Even Kaye's wife Hillary recognized that Davis was a dangerous role model for Clark. "As sweet as he was, Jesse Ed could be a bad influence. A naughty boy! One time I thought I'd talked him into saving his royalties. He'd got a cheque and wanted to score some tar. I told him: 'Jesse, you don't want to do that. Keep your money.' He convinced me that he'd bought my line. The next thing I knew he was with a bunch of guys doing drugs and taking them to dinner because he wanted to have fun. That was more important to him than saving money. He was another magical character who was always fun, until he got a stroke, which really afflicted him."

Both Clark and Davis continued to ride recklessly around Hollywood, often hanging out with actor buddies David Carradine, John Barrymore Jr and Jason Ronard. Occasionally, they stopped off at the Chaplin estate, where drink was plentiful. "Man, Jesse Ed would pass out," says Ronard. "He'd want to go into my bedroom and sleep. I had to get three guys to help. I'd say, 'Get that sweaty bastard Indian out of my bed!' He was a terrific friend. Jesse just did too much downtown. You could see his thing coming through. Those guys worked hard at dying. You've got to remember that. They didn't just accidentally die. They were working hard at it. Jesse and Gene were close because of their Indian blood. Gene was always concerned about finding his Indian roots."

Ronard, another heavy drinker, had recently finished filming the Don Siegel-directed *Escape From Alcatraz*, starring Clint Eastwood. He was in party mood, but could not help observing a fatal flaw in the characters of two of his close friends. "The saddest thing about Gene Clark is that he had the same disease as John Barrymore Jr. It's called 'fear of success'. Look at Gene's life. Every time he had a great car, a hit song or a million bucks, he'd screw it up somehow. He screwed up the Byrds, he screwed up the Mamas & The Papas. Every time it was getting towards something happening, he would sabotage it. Barrymore had the same thing. It's just the way it is. It's like you're scared to death you're going to make it again. And Gene made it three times in his career – the New Christy Minstrels, the Byrds, and then McGuinn, Clark & Hillman." In addition, of course, he was with several major labels – CBS, A&M, Asylum, RSO and Capitol. "He wouldn't stay with any of them. They'd take him out to dinner and he'd call them a bunch of Jews or a bunch of assholes."

Clark's self-destructive tendencies were matched by his lofty ambitions and immense capacity for remorse. He never lost the hunger for fame and self-validation nor fully forgave himself for squandering opportunities or blighting important relationships. In his more maudlin moments, he would cry about the loss of his children and his continued neglect of them. He spent half a lifetime trying to win back Terri Messina, only to lose her again. He even apologized to me for messing up McGuinn, Clark & Hillman. "He did that every day," Ronard agrees. "No matter what we did the night before, he'd call up and say, 'Do I have anything to apologize for?' And you'd laugh. Even if he did, you wouldn't tell him. When this guy wasn't high or drunk he was the nicest human being you ever met. The dark side, you didn't want to see. It was always his fault. But at the back of that he was going to sabotage it anyway. His subconscious kept saying, 'Screw it up, this is going to kill you if it works.' "

Clark and Kaye were still optimistic about cutting some new songs and found an ideal place to tape some preliminary recordings. Actor David Carradine owned a burned-out Victorian mansion in Laurel Canyon that he had purchased for $18,000 in the early Seventies. Over the years he had rebuilt the place, spending over $200,000 on improvements. Situated on two acres, with 40 trees, the building was an architect's dream. The ceilings were 30 foot high and finished with tempered glass surrounded by walls made of rare wood. The top floor was a magnificent open-plan room whose floor consisted of a teak deck salvaged from the *USS Los Angeles.* Kitchen and bathroom fixtures from the ship were also included. Most striking of all were the one hundred imposing windows that made the house seem invisible when viewed from some areas across the canyon. This stunning edifice was christened 'The Glass House'.

Carradine was conspicuously absent from the property, still living the "pure, holy existence of a Shaolin monk", albeit in Malibu. Various people were using the house, including his brother Christopher and, more recently, his daughter Calista, who was briefly dating Garth Beckington. "Garth stayed up there," Jon Faurot remembers. "He had a fling-a-ling with Calista here and there at that time, while I lived down in Hollywood." Faurot remembers the musicians "going up there a lot". There was a memorable Thanksgiving celebration when Gene was "kind of crazy" and drinking heavily with actor John Drew Barrymore Jr, who had just been released from an overnight stay in jail. David Carradine had a precarious relationship with Barrymore but allowed him to stay at the Glass House whenever he was passing through. "He was pushing the hippie/beatnik thing long before anybody else had even thought up those terms. He was variously rumoured to be a shaman, a sorcerer, bad news, and the inheritor of a noble theatrical heritage . . . I believed at the time that if one rejected John, one was out of the game. I knew he was an extremely dangerous man."

December 1980 proved one of the more eventful months in Clark's recent life. Eager to work, he arranged an impromptu session at the Glass House, bringing along a portable Nakamichi tape recorder. With Tommy Kaye installed as producer and arranger, Garth Beckington and Jon Faurot provided guitar and bass, respectively, and offered some rudimentary backing vocals. Rick Clark was also present and, in order to add a touch of verisimilitude, they all lined up as if they were playing a live show. The glass-panelled upper room enhanced the feel of the acoustic recording. Several years later, Beckington sent me a copy of the tape, accompanied by an epistolary account of the proceedings.

"Gene sang, played and engineered. He had a great ear and was a better engineer than most, frankly. Everything on the tape was live, standing around two microphones . . . We had been very pro, showing up at 4 o'clock, in tune and on time. We were listening back, making a couple of cassettes when a bottle of beer perched on top of the machine fell, soaking the master." Beckington remembers everyone being annoyed with Clark, whose beer bottle had caused the damage, but they wisely kept their counsel.

The surviving tape begins with 'Shades Of Blue', a Kaye composition that Tommy insisted Clark sing. The harmonies are strong here, suggesting that it had been worked on extensively prior to the Glass House session. 'Crazy Ladies' co-written by Clark, Kaye and 'Willy' Kontos (a pseudonym for Hillary), was already familiar from concert appearances. This acoustic version features a heartfelt lead vocal, superior to any live tape, although the backing chant of "you make me so crazy" doesn't work so well. The third song, 'Midnight Mare', is the only one to feature Rick Clark as co-vocalist. A spookier answer to McGuinn's 'Chestnut Mare', it includes some playful neighing and an elongated ending. 'I Don't Have You', a Beckington favourite, is a lilting ballad in which Clark projects a world of darkness. Lastly, 'I'll Change Your Life' is obviously inspired by the Beatles' 'All I've Got To Do' from *With The Beatles.* Even Clark's refrain "all you gotta do is call on me" echoes Lennon/McCartney's "you just gotta call on me". The song instantly takes us back to late 1963 when Clark first heard the Beatles and subsequently started writing songs in the same vein.

While Clark was recording 'I'll Change Your Life', Lennon was busily promoting his 'comeback' album with Yoko Ono, *Double Fantasy*. Many of the dreams of a generation ended on 8 December when he was shot dead outside the Dakota building in New York. Clark was shocked by news of the murder and deadened his despondency by embarking on a drunken binge. He ended up slumped in a hotel hallway. "Gene could drink a couple of beers," Faurot euphemistically adds. At the time, Clark was obsessing over a new song that Faurot remembers as being "about a mountain". The composition was surely 'Over The Mountain', a cascading, high-register vocal performance, the chorus of which Clark committed to tape. The track resembles the closing music of a western anthem. "He sang that goddamn song all night long," Faurot recalls. "He was just obsessed. He'd get into a vibe and just stay there and write. Gene was like that. He'd been up all night writing that song and the next day some newspaper girl came to interview him. We didn't know she was coming. She showed up and here's Gene Clark, passed out completely."

Despite his condition, Clark felt ready to perform, much to Faurot's surprise. "He could get drunk before a show. He would have you rehearse everything and have it all together and when he'd get onstage it would be completely different. We ended up doing a gig together at some hotel in Santa Barbara. It was real showy. We rode there in a limo. He did this radio interview and then we did the gig. It was the week after John Lennon was murdered and Yoko had asked for a ten-minute silent vigil on the Sunday [14 December]. So we did that. He conducted a sermon and said 'The Lord's Prayer' ['Our Father']. He messed up some of the words. The whole thing was a nightmare, but really funny."

Garth Beckington was also taken aback by Clark's religious rendition. "It was amazing to see the depth of Gene's Catholicism. But in a weird way. He never went to church, as far as I know, but there were some deep roots there. It was one of those things you'd see when he was drunk or in one of those moods. He would give us a benediction. At that Santa Barbara show, his vocal rendition of 'The Lord's Prayer' was clearly spontaneous and he forgot some words halfway through, but his sincerity was evident. I don't know if he thought he was a priest . . ."

The Catholic angle was hardly new. As previously mentioned, Clark's Catholicism had a beneficial effect on his songwriting. It was not only there in his cosmological musings and more abstruse work, but equally present in those songs of unfathomable remorse. Few articulated 'Catholic guilt' so forcibly or movingly as Clark at his best. "We used to call them Gene's Catholic songs," says Peter Oliva. "They were like Gregorian chants. His songs have this real Gregorian aspect to them. It's like you expect to smell Catholic incense in the air. He talked about that to me. He sang in the church choir. I come from a Catholic family too and I remember going to church and doing those minor scales. Like you, I always loved that 'Tabernacle hillside' line. Where did he come up with that stuff? He had his toe in the river of the muse, man. If you talked to him and didn't know he was a songwriter, you'd never guess that stuff came out of him."

During this period, one of Clark's more obscure television appearances occurred when Jason Ronard and John Barrymore Jr produced a video which was shown on local television in the Los Angeles area. "It had Bobby Neuwirth in a rare appearance," Hillary recalls. "Tommy Kaye played with the band and Gene and Garth played together on one song." Still in existence, the footage has not been seen since.

1981 was a grim, fruitless year for Clark and a troubled one for several of his friends in Laurel Canyon. Terri Messina became increasingly distant and wary of letting Clark back into her home. "We knew she was around," says Faurot. "I'm certain they were together at the time and she was a lot more understanding of the world than Carlie. But I very rarely saw Terri. She didn't really come around us." Terri's absence encouraged Gene to find alternative accommodation. Nobody was entirely sure where he was staying at certain points or what he was planning. The same could be said of others in his circle.

David Carradine had been absent from the Glass House, spending much of his time in Malibu. He had not seen his wildly independent, free-spirited teenage daughter since she had relocated to New York during her pregnancy the previous year. Her frequent disappearances added layers of mystery to her history. "Calista is more or less a mystic person," her father concluded. "All her life she's believed in magic. She doesn't take anything literally. Everything has psychic or mystic meaning. She was never able to knuckle down in school for something as prosaic as what they wanted to teach her."

When David learned that the 18-year-old was heading home, he could not resist a visit. "Calista had made it back to LA with her baby [Mariah] and was living at the Glass House again. I went over to see her and, low and behold, she was living with Gene Clark, who had tried to 'beat her up' over a pool game at Linda's party so long ago. He was very kind and loving to her now, and didn't seem to be drinking much anymore. The songs he was writing were just beautiful: some of the best rock 'n' roll around. He was a strikingly handsome man. Who could blame her?" Clark did not stay long at the Glass House, but Carradine was thankful when he intervened in a dispute. A disgruntled rival had allegedly fired a weapon at one of the windows of the Glass House which Carradine had to replace with stained glass. "Gene caught him in his lair and made him lie on the floor with a .22 rifle pressed to the small of his brain." He then "threatened to remove him from the planet if he ever bothered them again". Carradine made it sound like just another day in Clark's chaotic life.

In a supreme act of self-destructive dalliance, Gene next elected to move in with Jesse Ed Davis, whose excesses were the stuff of legend. When the pair hit town, it was usually a question of the devil take the hindmost. Tom Slocum, Clark's closest friend for many years, witnessed some of the wildcat scenes in Dan Tana's and other haunts. Clark's binges released a Pandora's Box of demons. When he was in the maelstrom of alcohol abuse, nobody could reach him. "I was pretty upset about all that stuff," Slocum reflects. "I said to him, 'You're putting your life on the line. You're putting everyone's life on the line. What if you get in your car and you kill someone?' He said, 'Ah, I'm a drunk, I'm a rock star!' – and all this shit. Later, I remember one night down in Mexico, Terri cornered him and said, 'Listen Mr Rock Star!' and really let him have it. It was all an effort to say, 'The drink!' The drink got to Gene more than any drug."

In the midst of this worst phase of excess, Gene's brother David unexpectedly appeared, bearing gifts. Their parents had just celebrated their 40th wedding anniversary and Jeanne missed Gene, who had not been in contact. David was despatched to track him down in Hollywood. Their mother had baked a heart-shaped cake with Gene's name on it. She hoped it might remind him of the family he had left behind in Missouri. When David finally found his brother, he was shocked by his dissolute state. "He was in terrible shape. He was just moving from place to place wherever he could find a flop. When I caught up with him he was in West Hollywood in an apartment complex. He was hanging out with some people with strange nicknames – Figgy and Slim. And Cathy Smith." Gene looked even worse than he had done back in Mendocino after the break-up of his marriage. David noticed his yellowing, jaundiced skin, a tell-tale sign of approaching liver disease. Even his image testified to hard times. "He had an old mountain hat with an eagle feather. He was unshaven and looked like shit. When I first saw him I didn't recognize him. I walked right by him. He said, 'Hey, where are you going?'" Psychologically, he was very shaky. After opening the present from his mother and seeing the cake, he dissolved into tears and asked: "Do I still have a family?" Before leaving, David provided a grim warning: "I told him, 'If you continue the way you are, you're not going to have a family at all because you are going to be dead. Until you clean yourself up, so far as I'm concerned, you don't have a family. You need to do something about yourself, and you need to do it now.'" Gene fell into silence, but David believes his comments had a positive effect. "That was maybe a life changer at the time. It really hit him hard."

When Gene's mother heard the latest rumours of his state, she felt dejected. Bonnie remembers her anger and disappointment, summed up in a sentence. "She said, 'I can forgive you for what you've done to the family, but I cannot forgive you for what you're doing to yourself because you're hurting my child.'" The tough love provided by his family no doubt caused him to reassess his lifestyle, but it was no easy road back.

In the realm of Gene and Jesse Ed, reality and rock mythology were blurred. "Heroin divorces you from the collective conscious," says Hillary. "You're in your own little cocoon and it's just strange." At times, the pair thought of themselves as invulnerable shamen infused with the spirits of old warriors. "You've never been around anything as frightening in your life as seeing Gene Clark doing knife-throwing contests where he'd make like he was Jim Bowie," Slocum shudders. "This was the kind of stuff he was doing with Jesse Ed. The capper for me was when Gene was throwing left hooks and right crosses in Dan Tana's. I said, 'OK, no more!' Everybody had gone to the wall to save Gene from Gene."

Not for the last time, Gene Clark was forced to find his own salvation. In what became known in his self-mythology as "the great abandonment", he fled Hollywood for the sobering environs of Hawaii and attempted to detox. It was part of Clark's psychology that he could consistently abuse his body, then turn away from the abyss through a belated exercise of strong will.

Clark and Davis were not the only victims of the harder drug scene insidiously infiltrating Hollywood and Laurel Canyon. Some of the dealers that had hung around Gene still had Tommy Kaye in their clutches. "People were coming around because of his drug debts," says Hillary. "I said to them, 'I'm supposed to pay for his drug debts? I don't think so! First of all I wasn't there, I didn't do them, I don't want them, he doesn't need them, and he doesn't need you!' That was my attitude."

Hillary's indignation was not enough to restrain these hell hounds. In the end, she had to turn to Clark, whose music business connections smoothed matters. "Gene went to a Mafia guy that owned some of the clubs in Hollywood. He got him to call the dealers and say, 'Hey, don't go after the women and children.' That got them off my back."

While Tommy Kaye was hitting his wildest phase, Hillary became pregnant again, this time suffering a miscarriage. She was referred to UCLA with a perforated uterus, and almost died. "Blood was pouring out of me faster than they could put it in. It was a miracle they saved my life. I'd had such bad luck with inter-uterine devices. Birth control – forget it. They talk about women's rights – people have no idea."

In a scenario reminiscent of the Clark/Messina saga, the relationship between the Kayes was fracturing under the combined threat of drink, drugs and abusive behaviour. "Tommy and I had been on the rocks," Hillary admits, "and after I got out of hospital I almost stabbed him to death. He was out of his mind. I realized later that a lot of this was due to his diabetes but at the time I just thought he was crazy. The way he was acting with me, breaking my things – he was a monster. They say that's what happens when some people get diabetes – they'll act really weird. It's insanity of some kind that takes over their mind from lack of sugar or too much of it. Of course Tommy wouldn't give up anything – drinking or drugs, if they were there. If I'd connected his insanity with his illness I'd probably have been more patient with him. But he was so crazy, and I didn't understand it. It was sad in the end because he was such a great guy, so funny and really quite a character."

Complicating matters was the strange development of Gene's goddaughter, Eloise. The miracle baby had become a mystery child and a source of bafflement to onlookers who marvelled at her independence. Hillary insists that she was not autistic, but it seemed as if she lived in her own world. Like Tommy and Gene, she loved music more than anything. Jon Faurot claims that she was blessed with the ability of perfect time. "She was like a little one man band," says Hillary, "clicking her tongue, stamping her foot and playing the guitar." When she started school, Hillary received worrying reports. "You'd see Eloise on occasions and think, 'Oh my God, she's retarded!' At other times she would test off the charts. She was very special and magical. The authorities and the school people weren't fond of her because they thought she was a pest and caused a lot of problems due to her high spirits." At times, she became withdrawn in a fashion that seemed almost wilful. There were periods when she stopped talking entirely. "She was just mute. It was like she had no desire to communicate with people at all. She decided that they weren't worth it or something." Like her godfather, Eloise also began acting in character. Clark sometimes took on the role of a

Mafia gangster, rejoicing in his nickname Geno and adding Italian inflexions to his speech. It often happened when he was drunk or half asleep. Eloise had a similar trick and when challenged about her lack of communication would say, "I no speaka the English."

"It made it very easy for her not to do stuff," Hillary points out. "It's hard to give somebody orders when they act like they don't know what you're talking about. It was a really good scam. But she was a great kid."

As all this was happening, Hillary and Tommy's relationship ended and he moved out of their home on Lookout Mountain Avenue and left the Canyon. In the meantime, Hillary started a relationship with Garth Beckington, whom she would marry three years later. Kaye continued his downward spiral, drinking more vodka than ever and bemoaning his fate to fellow revellers such as Jason Ronard. "Tommy would come over to my house and he'd be snorting and drinking. He'd say, 'My guitar player stole my old lady!' He didn't really care. In rock 'n' roll nobody really cares who gets what chick."

Ronard's cynicism was symptomatic of those times. Laurel Canyon had once been seen as a haven for singer-songwriter solidarity and hippie utopianism, but now it was closer to the decadent Rome of classical times. The most respected of the songwriting elite – Joni Mitchell, Neil Young, Jackson Browne et al – had long moved on. Hymns to the Canyon were in short supply by 1981. There was an increasing supply of cocaine and heroin available in the community which, in turn, froze and ossified many of the close relationships between paramours and neighbours. Peace and love were at a premium in this new age. Drug dealers plied their trade, like snakes in Eden. The rotting moral undercurrent was exposed in brutal fashion on 1 July 1981 with the infamous Wonderland Murders. A fantastic tale of drug dealing, robbery and gruesome reprisal, including a guest appearance by porn star 'Big' John Holmes, the infamous slayings at 8763 Wonderland Avenue brought back memories of the Manson killings. Four corpses were discovered, brutally bludgeoned into lifelessness by a steel pipe. The house was sprayed with blood.

Symbolically, the Wonderland Murders tolled the death knell for what remained of the Canyon's once familiar good vibes. Before the end of the year, Frank Zappa's house, another much loved haunt for Canyon freaks, was burned to the ground. Many more long-term residents had moved out by then, including Hillary who was concerned about her daughters, Eloise and Jesse Jane. "We decided to get out then," she recalls. "Eloise at that point was really having problems. She was running around naked in the street and the police were bringing her home and stuff so we decided that we had to get out of there or she'd end up a ward of the court." Fortunately, Hillary's mother Claudia had an extensive property portfolio, including a beautiful house with substantial land in Mendocino. "Garth and I decided to raise the children there," Hillary adds. "A fabulous place on ten acres of land, it had been in my family forever. It was much easier to keep track of Ellie. She would go out picking berries and have a fine old time."

When Clark learned that his goddaughter had moved to Mendocino, it reminded him of his own responsibilities as a father. His sons were also living in the area in an environment that was less than ideal. By now, Carlie had fallen further into drug hell. "I was stupid," she admits. "I messed up our children . . . our boys' lives. But that's all in retrospect . . . I just didn't have the maturity or the wherewithal to know how to deal with life on life's terms. I was told that Gene was with another girl . . . that's it, I'm out of here. It took me years to realize that I'd just blown my own happiness. And his too."

Having achieved sufficient sobriety in Hawaii to ponder his own inadequacies, Clark decided to reunite the family for Christmas. The holiday season also coincided with Kelly's tenth birthday, so some additional presents would be required. Since moving out of Terri Messina's house, Clark had squandered most of his money and was obliged to seek help from old friends. "Gene must have gone through millions of dollars," marvels

Andy Kandanes. "Believe me. I was constantly lending him money at that time. I even had to loan him enough to buy his kids presents and fly him back from Hawaii for Christmas."

Still shaky after his spell on the island of Oahu, Clark was impressed to discover that Kandanes was helping Thomas Jefferson Kaye record a privately funded solo album. "Why don't you do something with me?" he asked. Kandanes consulted Kaye who was magnanimous enough to cancel his own project in order to work on a possible follow-up to *Two Sides To Every Story*. Kaye was always a Clark evangelist, but realized that there would be problems. "You know what we're getting into, don't you?' he warned Kandanes, who replied, "Yeah, but I think he's still got it."

Initially, there were two priorities: a clean and sober Clark and a decent record deal. Neither would prove easy to secure. Clark had burned his bridges with most of the major labels and the final fiasco with McGuinn and Hillman ensured that big buck advances would not be forthcoming. With the singer-songwriter school newly deemed passé, Kandanes could barely muster a flicker of interest from anybody. "The executive staff changed at all the big companies and there were all these new kids. They weren't buying songwriters anymore. They wanted young bodies that could dance."

Seeking a sympathetic ear, Kandanes contacted Warner Brothers' vice president and head of talent acquisition, Bob Krasnow. He passed with barely a second thought. "Nobody would touch Gene with a barge pole," Kandanes says. "Nobody wanted anything to do with him because he was a live wire. He was like a time bomb and they were afraid to touch him." Kandanes next turned to the irrepressible Tom Slocum, whom he hoped might sweet talk one of his dinner buddies into fronting some money. Again the response was negative.

Eventually, Kandanes decided to finance the project independently, gambling on the hope that a deal might be secured later down the line. The segmented recordings commenced in San Francisco and continued over many months. There were constant interruptions as adjustments were made to the budget. "Working with Gene was like being in a movie," says Kandanes. "Sometimes it was business, sometimes it was absolutely nuts." The presence of Tommy Kaye ensured that alcohol temptations were always a factor. "Tommy was a little eccentric. You should have tried living with him. He and Gene were both in my house in Santa Rosa for eight months and that was something else. Tommy had split with Hillary and Gene had split with Terri and he wasn't doing good. We lived together, wrote tunes, stayed up for two or three days at a time and went to the studio, also for two or three days at a time. We got a lot of songwriting done, no doubt about that. But, oh boy, it was crazy. Tommy used to get up and drink a six pack of beer in the morning for breakfast. I'd say, 'Tommy, come on, you've got to slow down with this.' Of course, he'd got diabetes."

Clark was still fragile and susceptible to temptation. "We got him dried out," says Kandanes, "but one night I got back from the studio after doing some mixes with Tommy, and he'd drunk this superb case of a 1969 Cabernet. There was a note which said: 'Hey, I owe you a case of wine.' There was an empty box on top of the note. After that I ended up putting a lock on my wine cellar."

Despite Kandanes' optimism, the new songs that emerged were far from Clark's best and his alcohol dependency continued to pose problems. Peter Oliva visited his old friend during this period and detected signs of creative fatigue. "Geno wasn't on the same level he'd been when I knew him in the early Seventies. Back then, he was writing *all* the time. By this point, everyone was giving him a bad rep. I remember hitching to LA because I didn't have a car and I got a ride from this woman who turned out to be Frank Sinatra's secretary. She asked me, 'Do you play music?' and I told her I'd played with Gene Clark. 'Gene Clark?' she said. 'Is he still a drunk?' He obviously had a reputation in the business which stretched to Frank Sinatra's secretary and that's about as far from Gene Clark as I can imagine. Even they knew about his drink problems. That may have been another reason why the album wasn't happening. It took a lot of convincing for Gene to do it."

Considering the number of unreleased compositions Clark had in his archives, it would have been easy to excavate older songs, still unheard by his audience. Evidently, this was not considered. As Clark acknowledged: "When you're the artiste, the writer too, and you're that familiar with your product, if material sits around for too long, it sort of stagnates . . . Unless a producer comes along and hears it and asks you to go back and pay attention to it, you lose the incentive to want to work with it anymore."

Having reached an impasse, Clark decided to seek help from his former mentor, Jim Dickson. "There was a loose and human agreement between himself and Dickson that Gene would get himself together," Slocum recalls. "Gene stayed at his house for eight months at least, and the rule was 'No alcohol'. At that point Dickson read him the Riot Act. Dickson loved him like a son and loved the talent he had. He gave him shelter and took care of him. The rules were laid down. He had to cut out the drinking and shenanigans and finish the record."

Despite their evident commitment to Clark, neither Kandanes nor Dickson were familiar with his greatest work. Kandanes described *No Other* somewhat misleadingly as "a good country record" but seemed unaware of its importance or the need to produce work of similar quality. Dickson was even more detached from Clark's recent recording history. "Whatever happened in between our working together, Gene never told me. I didn't know that much about his other stuff. I'd heard somewhere that there was an album called *No Other*, but I've never heard it." When Tommy Kaye was forced to retreat from the project due to his diabetes, Kandanes gamely carried on, even co-writing several songs with Clark. "I came from a more professional background than Gene and may have been a bit more sophisticated musically, but he was a great poet. I learned a tremendous amount from him. The stuff was simple, but there was a definite art form involved. Once you got into his genre, it was amazing. He and I developed a method of working together. We'd run stuff by each other, just me, him and a guitar. He'd ask me about chord changes and there were a lot of tunes I helped him out on."

The Clark/Kandanes partnership produced two indisputably strong compositions: the affecting 'Rain Song' and country-tinged 'Rodeo Rider'. The latter was their personal tribute to Sandy Pinkard, a drinking pal from the Mendocino days. Pinkard was a talented songwriter, who had originally worked with Ramblin' Jack Elliott. After a spell in Vietnam, he moved to Nashville where he found employment as a rodeo rider. His cowboy tales had enlivened many an evening in Mendocino and he had subsequently achieved songwriting success composing 'Pecos Promenade' for Tanya Tucker, 'Beers To You' for Ray Charles and Clint Eastwood, and the country chart topper 'Coca Cola Cowboy' for Mel Tillis. Clark learned that he was about to form a duo with Richard Bowden, specializing in satirical song parodies, influenced by Homer & Jethro and Shel Silverstein. 'Rodeo Rider' was a personal tribute but was also geared towards the Nashville market. Eddie Tickner touted the song on Clark's behalf, but nobody was interested.

"Gene could have gone to Nashville closed his eyes, put on a stupid cowboy hat and made a million dollars, but he wouldn't do it," Slocum claims. "He didn't want to do it. Whenever he went to Nashville everybody wanted to hang with him and I felt even the business people wanted him around. But he said, 'Nah. Forget this. I'm going to try and stay as true as I am.' Every day there seemed to be a different Gene Clark. He was sensitive and had his dark moods, but he wasn't nearly as outrageous as some stories suggested."

Although Clark may have had hopes of achieving crossover potential at different stages of his career, he resembled a lost soul at this point. "Gene and Terri had got into a lot of trouble and needed to separate in order to clean up," Dickson remembers. "That's partly why he stayed at my house in North Hollywood. He was at a low ebb. That he would come back to me says as much. Nobody likes to go back to somebody that was previously an authority figure that they've broken loose from."

Clark agreed to accept Dickson's rules about no drugs or alcohol, knowing that he now needed his assistance to complete the album. "Tommy Kaye, Andy and Gene had tried to cut it," says Slocum, "but certain things were too loose. The bass parts needed fixing and the production had to be upgraded from a technological point of view. Plus there was a lot of political networking that still needed to be done. Dickson was ready to remix it and bring in new players."

The last time Gene had lived with Dickson was in the early days of the Byrds when he boasted an athletic body with an appetite to match. Back then, he'd complained about those weird dreams of being trapped in a roll of carpet filled with lacerating shards of glass. Now, he seemed to be living the same nightmare. "He was pacing the floor most of the time," Dickson says. "He'd take a pound can of coffee and pour a third of it in, then make coffee that you could stand a spoon up in, and drink it. He was very fidgety and extremely nervous. He was like a caged tiger, but he was bearing up under it all just to get this project done. When we went into the studio he was great. So long as there was something going on to get the job done, he was positive, helpful and very pleasant. The rest of the time he was like a wounded animal, just waiting, which depended upon Andy Kandanes getting enough money to do some more recording."

Clark's neurotic tendencies were reinforced by his absence from Terri Messina. The relationship was dominating his thoughts to such an extent that he could barely think of anything else. Dickson felt like a priest trapped in a confessional box. "I got tired of listening to him. He talked and talked and talked about Terri who I didn't know. It was nothing that really meant anything to me, but he talked to the point of exhaustion. She did come by once and he went out to the kerbside and spoke with her briefly. I never had a real conversation with Terri, so I didn't know much about her except second-hand from Gene, and I didn't think that was an objective view. After that, he *still* talked about her all the time. He was obsessed with her."

Dickson took control of the album in its final stages, bringing in Herb Pedersen and Chris Hillman as musical reinforcements. Some of Kandanes' ideas were overruled along the way. A new song, 'Blue Raven' featured Ossie Ahlers on synthesizer, in what Kandanes felt was a 'contemporary production'. He'd also brought in David Sanbourn on saxophone which was "like having Michael McDonald playing with Gene Clark". Dickson had other ideas and mixed out Sanbourn's sax in favour of a flute part from Bud Shank. The flautist, who had worked with Dickson and David Crosby during the pre-Byrds days, had subsequently played the classic solo on the Mamas & The Papas' 'California Dreamin', and appeared on Clark's 'She's The Kind Of Girl'. His credentials were outstanding and although Kandanes felt that the flute "emaciated the track" Clark supported Dickson's decision. Shortly after completing the song, Clark spoke to me on the phone, offering a teasing revelation. "Hey, Johnny Silver!" he said. "I've written a song and must have had you in mind. It says, 'this time, it's *not* silver, it's blue.' See? No silver imagery!"

Clark also recorded a song guaranteed to please Dickson: 'Mr Tambourine Man'. He had already experimented with an elongated version, trading verses with McGuinn and Hillman during the MC&H days, but they had never attempted the new adaptation in the studio. Re-recording the song was almost a therapeutic act for Clark. In the pre-Byrds era, he had provisionally been slated to sing lead until McGuinn made the vocal his own. Now he was symbolically reclaiming the composition. Tellingly, there was no Rickenbacker on the track. Instead, Ossie Ahlers was brought in as pianist, a subtle reminder of Leon Russell's lost piano work on the familiar hit version. Dickson also made some key changes. "I replaced all the harmony on 'Tambourine Man' using Herb Pedersen and that made a lot of difference." According to Clark, the new arrangement was partly inspired by some schoolchildren he had heard singing while recovering from a drug-induced haze in Hawaii. "These little children used to walk to school in front of my house every day and they would chant as they walked. Somehow, I thought it was like a pied piper or a tambourine . . . They walked in a row . . . and did their little dance. I took that rhythm and the verses to 'Mr Tambourine Man' and re-recorded it that way with the feeling of those children. That's how it happened."

The erratic nature of the recordings tested Clark's patience, but he persevered. "He really wanted that album out," Dickson says. "Once we started reworking it and I put Herb Pedersen on harmony, some of it started to sound good. He sang pretty well on most of it. Gene thought that the album might take off if he could just get it done, but you think that about every album you're working on."

With Clark's songwriting muse still to recover, they were reduced to including covers, courtesy of Tommy Kaye's 'Vanessa' and Gordon Lightfoot's familiar 'If You Could Read My Mind'. "I liked 'Vanessa'," Kandanes stresses, "but you always had to watch Tommy with the publishing. He wanted his songs on there, but that was just a hangover from the Sixties music business." The Lightfoot tune was evidently a joint decision. Dickson had already recorded the song with Hamilton Camp in 1964 and Kandanes knew Lightfoot socially. The Canadian had even included a photograph (in silhouette) of Kandanes' Mendocino house on one of his albums. "Gene's and Gordon's careers paralleled each other. They were both great songwriters and poets who had alcohol problems. Their personalities were similar too."

After a year, the album was still not finished and momentum was waning. "We wanted to do more," Kandanes says, "but I was out of pocket. We were limited because there was no financing from outside. I just did what I could. Dickson had another agenda."

Having commandeered Chris Hillman and Herb Pedersen, Dickson decided to start a parallel production project with Gene, assisted by Michael Clarke and Al Perkins. With three ex-Byrds in the mix, the experiment, variously titled Flyte and Nyte Flyte, resulted in five songs: a country rock version of Clark's 'Feel A Whole Lot Better'; Gram Parsons' 'One Hundred Years From Now' and 'Still Feeling Blue'; the Box Tops' hit 'The Letter'; and Rodney Crowell's 'No More Memories Hangin' Round'. Dickson was thrilled by the Crowell cover and applauded Clark's vocal and Clarke's drumming. "Gene was really into the song. I think it was how he felt at the time. He'd been through so many women." Slocum was also impressed by the tapes and employed the two ex-Byrds on several of his own songs, including 'Listen To Your Heart', 'So Many Nights', 'Games' and 'Come On Home'. Tickner, who represented Crowell, attempted to hustle the demos in Nashville, but the response was tepid.

Dickson was disappointed. "We cut those five songs as Nyte Flyte, then Gene said, 'I've got to finish this other album.' That involved me for several months more. The day we finished, Gene just went off his rocker. He went out and got drunk with Michael [Clarke] and tore up my house and broke a chandelier. Then he moved out. He was only cooperating with me so I'd help Andy finish the album. I wanted to do more with Nyte Flyte but once he got drunk, it was over. All I was left with were those five tracks."

As a desultory footnote to the Nyte Flyte saga, the participants (minus Michael Clarke who'd already backed out) played a two-night set at the Troubadour, but they soon drifted into other projects.

Gene and Michael reunited in early 1983, establishing the Firebyrds, a touring troupe initially featuring Mark and Matt Andes. The lengthy saga of the Firebyrds, whose exploits covered the period 1983–85, are dealt with in the succeeding chapter on Michael Clarke. Suffice to say, they undertook several strenuous tours, experienced various personnel changes and suffered all the indignities and occasional joys of a struggling road band. Given his past distaste for touring, it was a small miracle that Clark persevered without jumping ship. In truth, he had few good reasons to go back to LA in the wake of his break with Terri Messina. He still harboured hopes of winning her back and it helped to keep busy. Live work offered a distraction at a time when there was little or no hope of undertaking any studio work. The album he had recorded with Kandanes and Dickson was still doing the rounds without success, but even if all the major companies were uninterested, there were still some independent outlets to scour.

Paradoxically, the Firebyrds' low-key dates made touring easier for Clark. He never had to face large audiences, publicity demands or record company expectation. The presence of Michael Clarke, and subsequently Mendocino pal Peter Oliva, ensured that Gene could relax among familiars who were all too aware of his foibles. "Gene was just a guy," says Oliva, playing down the ex-Byrd's star status. "He wasn't famous like Bob Dylan, but people still came up and gushed over him. It was a bit like talking to fabulously wealthy people who have to scrutinize why you're talking to them in the first place. He must have felt sometimes, 'Crap, here they come again and I'm only Gene Clark from Tipton and I just want to have a drink.' I think in the end all of them, including Dylan, just want to be hanging out with the boys and playing music in a rock 'n' roll band. Gene had that with us in the Firebyrds. He loved having a band of guys and we were like pirates and there wasn't any big-time bad stuff out there. We were just travelling to the next gig, setting up and playing and having a great time. Gene loved that."

There is some truth in Oliva's rose-tinted reflections, but the touring exigencies also took their toll on everyone's health and well-being. As the later Michael Clarke chapter shows, there were also fistfights, flare-ups, money problems, hardship and insidious disillusionment. Between tours, Clark rested in LA, settling in a two-bedroom apartment in Sherman Oaks. The place served as a crash pad for musician friends, a handful of whom became short-term house guests. One such was Trace Harrill, an Alabama-born guitarist, to whom Clark had been introduced by Tom Slocum. Harrill had worked at Muscle Shoals and played with several stars while doing studio sessions for Chris Blackwell's Island Records. He joined the Firebyrds for one ill-fated tour before falling out with Michael Clarke, but his major contribution was a series of collaborations with Gene Clark captured on tape in the songwriter's kitchen. "Trace had a romantic quality," says Matt Andes, "and I found him quite fascinating. A real talent."

Clark and Slocum evidently felt the same. At a time when Gene was road weary and rusty as a songwriter, Harrill provided a necessary injection of inspiration. On 20 June 1983, they set up Clark's tape recorder and commenced a series of songs which still sound intriguing. Among the work tapes are the Roy Orbison-influenced 'I Wondered Why' with its cast of female characters – Maria, Bonita and Caroline. 'Hillbilly Child' is reminiscent of Sun-period Elvis, a 'Mystery Train' for the Eighties. 'She Cares More' (aka 'I Get Along'), boasts an enticing melody and lyrics that convey the pain and jubilation of a replacement love. There's a desperate quality to Clark's singing as he comes to grips with the ambivalence of his own passion. 'Love Opus In Time', listed on the tape box, but seemingly deleted, is followed by the acoustic 'My Favorite Things', a love song thematically similar to Bacharach & David's 'I Say A Little Prayer'. Clark develops the song via a series of urgent entreaties and with each new line it becomes more emotional, percolating from a moody ballad into an intense declaration. Harrill switches from acoustic to electric guitar along the way, occasionally adding handclaps and almost screaming what sounds like his own contribution: "You must have done something that was right, or otherwise I wouldn't think of you this way tonight."

One song of particular importance to Clark was 'Little Sister', a composition that he honed in multiple versions, as if intent on capturing its essence. At times it sounds like a philosophical Everly Brothers. Clark adopts his John Wayne persona, earnestly pledging: "My words mean more to me than life itself." Another strong melody, it includes some memorable lines: "I miss your face like the rain would miss the wind." Midway through one of the versions, Clark steps out of the song, extemporizing like a sage. He offers a stately soliloquy: ". . . and the smoke I remember from the mouths of the older men that left the bars in winter nights. I can see their words in the actual smoke – in the steam that came from their mouths. They'd be talking about how they'd take care of their children and their wives. Meanwhile, they'd also be talking about the next machine they'd invent . . ." He then returns to the song, which is suddenly altered. New verses mention the inner life and the inner soul. He might well be prophesying the fate of his own songwriting catalogue when he notes: ". . . the best things that I ever saw were miserably not sung."

Finally, there is the extraordinary 'Have You Seen The Faces Of The Dreamers In The Rain?', a chilling work in progress. Unquestionably, this is the best example extant of a Clark composition worked through from conception to near completion. After strumming on acoustic guitar, he starts to frame the words.

At first, he considers introducing steel workers and farmers into the narrative, as if he is composing a ballad for the working man. It's possible his mind is commuting back to Kansas. "They think about their small worlds," he says of the workers or dreamers. Suddenly, he shifts to the personal. "My father taught me how to love – the most important thing." He stops.

"Yes," Gene purrs with evident satisfaction. "I'll write that out!"

Further inspiration follows. "Our fathers came across the sea so many years ago/They left us here . . ." Frustratingly, he cannot find the right word to fill in the next line, so he stops again.

"Yeah," he considers. "Our fathers were all immigrants so many years ago. They left us here to carry on, their spirit . . ."

"Ah no," he chides himself. "Wait a minute. I'm getting there!"

"From many years . . ." He stops once more, then tries again. "From light years . . ." Clearly, it's still not right.

"From years and light . . ." Worse!

"From more than earthly years . . ." Now, he's almost there. "Or something like," he says to himself, "because we're immigrants from other solar systems. Let's put it in."

Suddenly, the song has gone from workers and dreamers to space explorers. "From where we *really* came!"

Pausing again, he continues composing the song as his thoughts unravel.

"Yeah, oh yes!" he says excitedly. "How about, 'If we could be the ones to know from where we really came. Our fathers wouldn't be the ones to take all the blame.' "

"If we could understand the songs and why it will fade out . . ."

By now, he seems overwhelmed by his cosmological musings. "The universal soul . . ."

Several more verses pour out of him, then he stops again.

"Anyway I lost it . . ." he concedes, but he still seems thrilled by his own ambition. "The Universal Soul. Wow!"

"How much tape do we have here?" he wonders. Finally, he attempts a near complete version, adding several new verses. Space exploration is momentarily forgotten as he returns to the nautical theme. What follows is more like a Norse saga. "All the riches, they will kill or die for . . ."

He mentions leaving behind any thoughts that might ever change the world. The lyrical scope seems grandiose. "The boats they took into the storms were only wooden toys . . ." The great odyssey is back underway. It sounds like the genesis of a Clark epic worthy of *White Light* or *No Other* in its lyrical ambition and ambience. But it will never appear. Like so many working tapes, this is a classic example of a potentially great song left on the cutting-room floor. A creative moment in time lost forever. Far inferior work would be attempted later in the decade as Clark abandoned mystery for something approaching commerciality.

While staying at Clark's home, Harrill realized that his new friend was far from well. "It was the night times that freaked me out. I discovered that he was very ill back then. He would groan all night long in his sleep, plus his teeth were always killing him. Alcohol was definitely messing with his mind." Harrill soon found himself entering Clark's strange fantasy world. "At one time he started acting like the Godfather. It was the first time I'd ever experienced this. We were talking normally, then he just went into this Godfather routine. I kind of played along a little bit, but he wouldn't let up. He just kept this up for hours." Such behaviour was all too familiar to those who had roomed with Clark when he was on tour. "He had some interesting fantasies," Peter Oliva recalls. "They involved spaceships, the mafia and samurais. He'd get drunk and start talking in his sleep. Half the time, I think he'd be talking to his demons, saying 'You gotta get out of here . . .' I'd say, 'Geno, shut up!' and then he'd turn into an Italian: 'excusa mia, please'. An amazing guy."

Gene's fantasies always had a touch of comedy. At one point, he took Harrill aside and enquired: "Would you do me the honour of marrying my sister?" The fact that Harrill had never met any of his sisters was not considered important. Nor is there any evidence of a suitably eligible sibling. It was simply another Gene Clark fantasy.

On another occasion, Clark produced a letter and a family tree, while displaying his Wild West credentials. "He showed me family pictures and stuff," says Harrill. "Now in my family there was a black sheep who'd moved to Missouri during the James Gang era. He was a pretty unsavoury character who'd married into the Clark clan. Gene said, 'Look at this family tree, man! We're related!' How true any of this was I can't say, but I always felt a kinship with him."

Harrill concludes that Clark's excesses were moderate during this phase, although a penchant for recklessness was ever present. One night, Harrill noticed that a bottle of prescription pills he'd been given had been half-emptied. "I said, 'Gene, what's mine is yours.' But what I couldn't understand was that he didn't even know what they were. He would take anything."

Harrill continued to write with Clark for a spell but, regrettably, the results were never captured in a studio session. Once he left the Firebyrds, Harrill moved out of Clark's home and they never reconnected. Their writing spree had been partly prompted by a change in Clark's business arrangements. On 30 November, he signed a three-year agreement with Daniel and Fred Bourgoise's Bug Music, who were given exclusive rights to administer and collect gross receipts from his compositions. For this service Bug were to be paid ten per cent with a provision for 25 per cent on any mechanical and performance income with respect to covers of his work by other artistes. The previous week, Clark had added a stipulation by which Slocum was provided with a ten per cent override on income earned by the publishers, Gene Clark Music. It sounded like a generous concession. Slocum had previously assisted financially with the Firebyrd album because "Gene didn't have any money for lawyers." This was his payback. "Gene was my dear friend and all, but that was quite generous." Years later, Slocum stumbled upon this document in an old briefcase and attempted to settle the issue with Bug Music.

In the absence of a revenue-spinning cover version of one of his compositions, Clark was forced back on the road. Trace Harrill was replaced by Mike Hardwick, who also ended up staying at the house as a temporary lodger. "I slept on the couch at first, then moved to the spare room. Gene was a great cook. He cooked like my mother who was also from Missouri. He'd do pasta, fried potatoes and a lot of Southern cooking."

While touring with the Firebyrds, Hardwick volunteered to room with Clark. "I was a kid more than ten years younger than Gene. I was born in 1955. Gene wanted to get to know me. He was very helpful and I was watching him and picking up everything he did musically. I learned a lot about life around those guys, Gene especially. At first, he was in good shape and things were going well. He was very amiable, gentlemanly, respectful and happy people were there, even though we were playing small clubs. The band was sounding pretty good, and the music was happening for him. He felt this was an opportunity to work and support the independent record that he had coming out. He was so hopeful that this was going to give him a chance to get back . . ."

Whatever hopes Clark harboured of returning to the big time were torpedoed by *Firebyrd*, the long overdue solo album which finally appeared in 1984 on the small, independent label, Takoma.

The work was a flawed affair, displaying the limitations of a restricted budget, worsened by a parsimonious running time, paltry promotion, unadventurous songwriting and an uncertainty of purpose. The decision to revisit 'Mr Tambourine Man', with Clark singing all the verses set against a solid piano backing, was interesting, but Clark could not resist overstating the Byrds' link by reviving 'Feel A Whole Lot Better'. The reliance on old material was distracting, particularly at a time when new product was most desirable. To those unfamiliar with Clark's song catalogue, it must have looked like he was living on past glories. Although the handful of Clark/Kandanes collaborations were pleasant enough, none were exceptional, let alone great. Overall, the package seemed strangely incomplete. If the album could have been extended to 11 or 12 tracks instead of nine, it might have sounded more cohesive. In the event, it was poorly distributed and over the years it has been licensed to more labels than I'd care to remember.

Clark's friends attempted to allay the disappointment of *Firebyrd* with kind words. According to Kandanes, Tommy Kaye phoned excitedly with news that Dylan was enthusing about Clark's cover of 'Mr Tambourine Man'. "Dylan said it was one of the best versions he'd heard. He really loved it." Given Kaye's love of fabrication, the commendation from Dylan may have been invented or exaggerated, but Clark was happy to accept the compliment. Soon after, Slocum approached studio owner Skip Saylor, who agreed to record a couple of songs. First choice was a cover of the Beatles' 'She Loves You', which the Firebyrds had incorporated into their set with some success. "'She Loves You' was basically Gene meets Sting," Slocum notes, cryptically. Clark was acutely aware of the historical importance of 'She Loves You' in his personal mythology. It was after listening to the song on a jukebox that he decided to leave the New Christy Minstrels and seek fame in Hollywood, culminating in the formation of the Byrds. Now he was in search of another beginning. Completing the session was another cover song, 'Into The Night'. "Skip was the engineer that night and it was going really well," Hardwick recalls. "Gene was happy but then it got late and he started drinking. It was only a scratch vocal and I don't think it was ever finished. Slocum paid for the session as a friend. Gene thought a lot of him. Of all the guys I met around Gene, he was the one I liked. It seemed his heart was in the right place and he was really trying to help Gene."

Slocum's good intentions came to nought. The tracks were

consigned to a tape vault, never to be released. Clark was still in the commercial wilderness, promoting an album that few people had heard at venues more befitting an obscure bar band. At a show in Dallas he revived 'I Saw A Dream Come True', last heard in concert years before. Most nights with the Firebyrds, however, allowed little opportunity for meditative reflection.

Clark was still writing, albeit far less prolifically than in the past. This might explain the odd decision to demo additional extraneous material rather than his own work. Among the perplexing selections recorded were two hits from Smokie ('Living Next Door To Alice' and their remake of 'Needles And Pins'); a couple of Badfinger songs ('Love Is Gonna Come At Last' and 'Baby Blue'); the country ballad 'The Closer You Get', originally from the Kentuckian band Exile, but made famous by both Don King and Alabama; a revival of Tab Hunter's Fifties hit, 'Young Love'; and a tepid rearrangement of 'Feel A Whole Lot Better'. "Gene just wanted to do a bunch of covers for the hell of it," says Slocum. This scant recollection provokes more questions than answers. Who chose the songs and why remains a mystery. None of these covers had been played on the road with the Firebyrds or were ever recorded by Clark elsewhere. Nor was there any evidence that he was a fan of the artistes chosen, least of all Smokie. On several of the songs, Clark's voice falters and his diction is poor, made worse by loose teeth and gum disease. This is especially noticeable on the corny reading of 'Living Next Door To Alice'. What was he thinking? Most of the songs sound like Karaoke Clark. In theory, 'Needles And Pins' might have worked. The Jackie De Shannon/Sonny Bono/Jack Nitzsche composition, a UK chart topper for the Searchers, was an obvious inspiration for Clark's 'Feel A Whole Lot Better', also included here. Unfortunately, there is no McGuinn-style Rickenbacker solo to bring either song to life. Arguably the one cover that works, in spite of itself, is 'Young Love'. On one level, it seems preposterous, if not disturbing, to hear a middle-aged man singing a teen ballad about puppy love. Clark's ravaged vocal amplifies that dramatic tension transforming the performance into a wistful, obsessive reminiscence. The result is strange but intriguing.

Whether anyone bothered to tout these tapes seems doubtful but, if so, nobody was listening. Clark was reluctantly forced back on the road. A debilitating tour of Canada took its toll on group morale and, unsurprisingly, Clark slipped back into heavy drinking to dull the pain and boredom. There were any number of comical moments along the way. At one point, Gene fired Matt Andes, who was bemused by the decision. "Gene got mad at me. I must have said something wrong. But he was drunk when he fired me. When he sobered up, it was almost embarrassing to see how remorseful he was. He didn't mean to fire me, so I was rehired immediately."

Andes has fonder memories of a residency in Toronto at the start of the tour, before they were all worn down. "We were leaving the gracious owners of this beautiful tavern. Gene arrived to say goodbye to these wonderful people. Unbeknown to us, he'd already started drinking. It was only nine in the morning. He'd snuck a glass of vodka under his flying jacket, and it was precariously balanced. We were saying our goodbyes and getting into the van and Gene decided to give this princely bow. He bowed and all this liquid spilled out on to the floor. It looked like he was throwing up at the feet of the club owner." Somehow, Clark recovered his poise and was ushered into the van before his faux pas attracted attention. "It was one of the most hilarious things I've ever seen in my life," Andes concludes. "How could you make that stuff up? We never mentioned it again."

In June 1984, the Firebyrds appeared at the LA venue, Madame Wong's West. It was to prove an auspicious night. Seated among the crowd were Textones singer Carla Olson, her manager/fiancé Saul Davis and photographer friend, Gary Nichamin. Clark's amanuensis Tom Slocum recognized Olson and, after a brief conversation, coaxed her onstage. "He dragged Carla up for the encore," Davis remembers. "Gene looked over and there's this blonde woman singing 'Feel A Whole Lot Better' with him. They'd never met before. There's actually a photo of them shaking hands literally onstage, and that's how we all met that night."

The meeting was to have important consequences for Clark's career direction. "Carla always was a sweetheart," Slocum stresses, "but if I'd ever imagined it would turn into what it turned into, I wish I'd never done it." When Davis enquired about who was representing Gene, the mischievous Missourian retorted: "Why don't you be my manager?" Although there was never a formal contract or any written agreement between them, Davis enjoyed the challenge of looking after Clark as spokesperson and manager, even taking the trouble to keep fanzines and columnists alert to the latest news. None of his predecessors had concerned themselves with such matters or sought to address or attract grass roots level support. "Saul and Gene had this loose arrangement," says Slocum. "Gene and I talked about it. I said, 'Look, if the guy can come up with something and it works, fine.' Gene was also booking gigs by himself and at one point he had an agent, Geoff Blumenauer, who represented some important clients. I thought Saul was like the rest of them."

Over the succeeding months, Davis introduced Clark to other musicians in his circle. These included the Textones and the Long Ryders. Clark guested on their records, seemingly keen to connect with a younger audience. Both Hüsker Dü and Three O'Clock had covered 'Eight Miles High' and 'Feel A Whole Lot Better', respectively, proof enough that there was still interest in his work. Perhaps it was time for a rethink.

All this proved bad news for the Firebyrds. Peter Oliva was disappointed. "All I know is that we had a band, then Saul Davis came in and it broke up." This was merely incidental. The sad truth was that the Firebyrds had run its course and Gene was ready to move on. It was his decision. In many ways, it was surprising that the group lasted this long. Reduced to a trio, following the departure of Hardwick, the Firebyrds stumbled on, playing inconsequential dates for the remainder of 1984 and into the New Year.

By early 1985, Clark was multi-tasking with a diverse number of associates. After the break-up of the Firebyrds, he continued working with Michael Clarke and found another agent, Michael

Gaiman. They came up with the grandly named '20th Anniversary Tribute To The Byrds', an enterprise that would later provoke no small resentment from McGuinn and Hillman. The adventures of the anniversarians is described at length in the succeeding chapter on Michael Clarke's career. Suffice to say, it was an eventful, if chaotic, period. Clark toured with a weird array of ex-Byrds, adding John York and even former roadie Carlos Bernal to the amorphous line-up. Several name musicians passed through the ranks, including Rick Roberts, Rick Danko, Blondie Chaplin and Greg Thomas. While the tribute shows were competent, it was Clark's intimate solo appearances before select gatherings that really caught the imagination. Here, he seemed at his best, providing stunning acoustic evocations of such classics as 'Set You Free This Time' and 'Eight Miles High'. Sometimes he offered to do requests and if you were lucky you might even hear a reading of the Beatles' 'She Loves You' or Dylan's 'Gates Of Eden'. Indeed, it was noticeable how much of his repertoire throughout this period still relied on the works of the master. Among the Dylan songs on offer were 'Mr Tambourine Man', 'Chimes Of Freedom', 'My Back Pages', 'You Ain't Going Nowhere', 'Knocking On Heaven's Door', 'It's All Over Now, Baby Blue' and even a reggae-tinged version of 'Man Gave Names To All The Animals'.

During the spring of 1985, Clark arrived in Britain for a 22-date tour, culminating in a remarkable performance at London's Dingwalls on 4 April. His set that evening covered every aspect of his recording career, embracing 'Here Without You', 'The Bells Of Rhymney, 'The World Turns All Around Her', 'American Dreamer', 'For A Spanish Guitar', 'Crazy Ladies', and much more.

Back in LA, his agent expressed astonishment upon learning about the UK visit. As Slocum reveals: "Whatever work Gene could pick up and however he could network it, he would do it. If a guy phoned from Florida and said 'Can you do these gigs?' and the price was right, he'd do them." On this occasion, Clark had dealt with the imperious Mervyn Conn, promoter of the infamous 1965 Byrds tour when they were billed as 'America's

Answer To The Beatles'. Despite this unhappy portent, the solo UK tour went well and Clark humbly appreciated the partisan cheers from hardcore fans. Apart from one night, when he drank the entire rider of his support act, Lindisfarne, he managed to restrain his customary excesses. The last time he had toured Britain was at the height of the McGuinn, Clark & Hillman enterprise, a period he now regarded as embarrassingly indulgent. "The over-pampering of artistes almost destroyed our industry. I include myself among all this. I was in a position to pursue my art the way I wanted to, without worrying about the consequences. Back then, people were just too ready to give large amounts of money to anybody. What happened was that the people who really had something to say were lost in the shuffle and indefinable from the crowd."

Clark promised to return later in the year with his band of anniversarians, but that dream would remain unrealized. John York was amazed that he had managed to fly to the UK in the first place. "Gene was several guys. Most musicians who've had a long history of drug and alcohol addiction develop multiple personalities. So, depending on who they were at that moment, that's how things went. Gene could be absolutely wonderful or he could become a monster. You never knew what was going to happen but there were certain environments that would bring out the bad and the airport was definitely one of them."

In 1985, it seemed that there was simply too much going on in Gene Clark's life. He still fretted over his seemingly doomed relationship with Terri Messina and liked to keep tabs on her movements, much to the exasperation of his friends. Jason Ronard would reassure him, but after one too many phone calls at three in the morning, he grew weary of Clark's obsession. "He called me from Europe and said, 'Jason, I want you to go up to Laurel Canyon and see who's parked in front of her house.' I said, 'OK, Gene, just give me half an hour.' I put the phone down, went into another room, watched television for half an hour then phoned back. 'Gene! Do you know whose car is outside – Jackson Browne's!' If he called me that late, I'd bust his balls."

Clark was not above being stalked himself. A girl of Caribbean origin began frequenting the house in Sherman Oaks. "She was very beautiful and voluptuous," Slocum recalls, "but I think she had a few marbles missing. One time, Gene phoned and said, 'Sloc, I slept with the stalker!' He stayed with her for a while. When Terri found out, she didn't like it much. One night, he and I were playing and we looked through the window and there was a woman with a knife. We had to call the cops. It was weird. She came back a week later in the daytime and we had to do the whole thing all over again. Call the cops. She came back twice more. One afternoon, he was in the backyard where he liked to cut grass and do his flowers. I looked over and there she was. She was very sweet and polite but Gene would get really belligerent. She'd break into this 'I love you' shit and pull out a pocket knife. Gene said to me, 'You deal with it!' and I told him, 'I don't want to, man.' Then he'd go, 'Get her out of here!' "

Clark's romantic or sexual dalliances seemed designed to deaden the memory of Terri Messina, but such thrills were short-lived. Although they had been separated, he still felt emotionally attached. Messina went through the purgatory of drug dependence, but never lost contact with Clark. "One of the reasons they weren't living together was because he would not stop," says their former friend, Hillary. "She had tried to clean up her act and wanted him to clean up his. Then she gave him an ultimatum: 'It's either my way or the highway.' "

Messina claims that Clark felt uneasy about settling in her spacious Laurel Canyon home. "It was an ego problem for him." Instead, she made the financially sound decision to rent out her own home and move into Clark's two-roomed house in Sherman Oaks. In the event of problems, she could always retreat temporarily to her parents' place in Northridge or stay with other friends. Clark was thrilled to win her back and promised to mend his ways and overcome his alcohol dependence. It was never going to be easy and, despite his good intentions, he constantly fell back into bad habits, particularly during long spells on the road. John York witnessed his inner conflict and ambivalence towards Terri, the former lover and drug buddy who was now cast in the unenviable role as counsellor and occasional muse. "It seemed to me that Terri had Gene's best interests at heart. Whatever problems they had had together with drugs, she seemed past them herself. I know that Gene really loved her. He used to tell me how much he loved her. She loved Gene and then he tried to get away from her, or vice versa, so there was a lot of emotional stuff going on."

At this point, Gene also learned about the recent adventures of his goddaughter, Eloise. The troubled child had been scrutinized by the authorities, along with her mother, Hillary. "At first they wanted her placed in the public school and not the hippie school where I sent her. Then she got diabetes that summer . . . They were trying to put her in the state hospital [saying] that she was crazy and I was crazy. They had me go for observations in San Francisco. I let them observe me and her. I think they thought I was on drugs. I was clean as a whistle. I was there for a week and they wrote up reports." Lawyers and psychologists pored over the results, which were anything but conclusive. "At school she tested borderline moron. Well, not borderline – moron. At home, she tested great." The child's schooling remained an issue. "I don't think they wanted her in public school either. She would incite the other children. I guess she was having fun."

Eloise's development had improved noticeably after the birth of her younger sister, Jesse Jane, in 1979. The aforementioned routine, where she'd played mute and ceased communicating with the outside world, ceased once she had a little sister to play with. Like her father, Tommy Kaye, Eloise had problems with diabetes, but otherwise was in reasonable health. During October 1985, she was busily preparing a costume for Halloween. She had insisted on having her hair cut short, in imitation of GI Jane. Possibly adapting to her new persona, she began enacting some strange scenes, as if she was about to be shipped abroad on some mission. "For almost a month, she was telling Garth and me that she was going to leave," says Hillary. "She was on this trip and we went along with it. 'Well, where are you going?' She'd say, 'I'm going to miss you, are you going to miss me?' We thought, 'Wow, that is too weird.' "

On 28 October 1985, Eloise Robin Kaye died. She was nine years old. "She'd just had her lunch," Hillary recalls, "and her blood sugar should have been fine. But she went into some diabetic coma while she was in the bathtub. She usually took a tub with her sister, but that night she didn't. She just slipped under the water and died. Well, she wasn't actually dead. Garth and I were in the other room watching a game and Jesse Jane was in there and she came and got us . . . The ambulance came and they thought they were going to save her but she'd already told us she was leaving. She definitely wasn't coming back into that body, no matter how much they pounded on her . . . It just wasn't going to happen."

Tommy Kaye was devastated by the news and Gene Clark was crestfallen. "Gene was very dear," Hillary recalls. "When she died he went to the church and got a priest to say masses for her. His Catholic background was coming out. He took it very seriously. He was so close to Ellie which is funny because he seemed to have such difficulties with his own children."

At the time of Eloise's death, Clark was in the middle of another arduous tour which ended with the melodramatic exit of Michael Clarke, who threw his bloodied drums at his fellow musicians and stormed off, never to return. It might have been an opportune moment for Clark to lower the curtain on the Byrds' tribute shows but financial obligations persuaded him to continue with a revamped line-up.

Despite the constant touring, Clark still needed an outlet for his songwriting. Saul Davis had already attempted to attract record company interest via a demo of six songs that Clark cut with the Textones: 'Gypsy Rider', 'Lovers Turnaround', 'Why Did You Leave Me Today', 'Winning Hand', 'Back In Time' and 'Jokers Are Wild'. "We tried to get Gene a record deal, but maybe it sounded too rock," Davis reflects, "but it had 'Gypsy Rider' on it. That could have been a number 1 record by Willie Nelson." An exaggeration perhaps, but there were definitely problems finding a niche for Clark in the Eighties. "Nobody understood at the time," says Carla Olson. "They were still knee deep in Vegas meets country."

Davis' next move was to connect Clark with Pat Robinson, a commercial, journeyman songwriter whose compositions had appeared on albums by artistes as diverse as Johnny Rivers, Joe Cocker and Laura Branigan. As with Andy Kandanes on *Firebyrd*, Clark seemed more than willing to suppress his stream of consciousness songwriting in favour of something far less challenging or adventurous. It was an uneasy compromise, but repeated a familiar pattern. He had retreated from the muse after *No Other* in the vain hope of achieving public acceptance. There was still evidence of potentially great work among his private home tapes where he was free to follow abstract thoughts and create strange narratives that were always enthralling. With Robinson, the emphasis was on traditional song structures, with a cold eye firmly focused on the marketplace. They were even pitching songs for movies, like optimistic entrants in a lottery.

Over the next few years, Clark and Robinson collaborated on dozens of songs. Their aesthetic quality was questionable, to say the least, but the productivity was impressive. Robinson knew how important it was to keep the work flowing. "It was tricky working with Geno. I had everything in the same room, everything monitored, a little bit of leakage. Mostly, we'd just slam these things down. I'd always be a stickler for writing everything down and I'd always have a tape recorder there so that we'd have a copy of this stuff. Then we'd go in and cut it right away because I had my own studio. That's how our songs came to fruition, more than a lot of other stuff that he didn't lay down. I was always the lead guitar player and he'd throw some percussion down or a rhythm part. We could knock out a song pretty quickly, and put real drums on later."

The songwriting duo were recording so much material that they decided to branch out and form a studio group. John York was invited to partake in the experiment, which went under the acronym CRY (Clark, Robinson & York). The CRY writing/recording team, abetted by the redoubtable Nicky Hopkins and occasional visitor Rick Clark, swiftly completed a catalogue of new songs including 'Carry On', 'I Need To Fly', 'Mary Sue', 'Christine', 'Sleep Will Return' and 'Somewhere After Midnight'. "We were starting to get a sound going that Gene liked," Robinson adds, "and that was kind of cool during that little period there." In brighter moments, Clark and Robinson still hoped to crack the movie market. 'With You I Can't Lose' was submitted for *Karate Kid* and 'Carry On' for *Karate Kid II*, although neither were included in the films.

The CRY recordings followed the trusted pattern of catching Clark before he lost inspiration. "You had to get him early in the evening, otherwise it got incredibly bizarre," Robinson remembers. "He was trying to break new ground and he would really get out there and go into Sherwood Forest or something. If he drank a lot, he was like an Indian. He would go back into the seventeenth century and start talking a little bit like that. He'd get really out there, which was awesome. We would capture Gene in a pretty good light and mostly the trick was to let him get on with it. Don't have him sitting around and don't split hairs with him. Do several tracks and take the best. He wasn't the kind of guy that could go in and repair things very quickly. He did it better spontaneously and in one take. So we would just throw this stuff down and fix it later. If you laboured on it or waited too long in the evening you wouldn't get the quality product."

In addition to the CRY material, Robinson continued to work independently with Clark on compositions like 'Dangerous Games', 'The Panther', 'Immigrant Girl', a song inspired by a woman that worked in the market near Gene's house, and 'Washington Square', a lyric recalling the glory days of Andy Warhol. "Gene sang those songs so well," Robinson enthuses. "But sometimes he would change the lyrics. He wouldn't want the lyric sheet and if I didn't get it and he had too many beers, he would say, 'Just let me do a pass at this', and make up new words. It used to drive me nuts! He was a really great poet. That was his forte. And his melodic sense too. He had really good ears, but you had to catch him quick."

Clark's songwriting was inconsistent. For 'Rest Of Your Life', he appeared to be channelling Elvis Presley's soliloquy on 'Are You Lonesome Tonight?' On 'Dragon's Eye', he presented a touch of Catholic mystery with references to St Christopher. Occasionally, he came up with something extraordinary. 'My Marie' stood out as one of his better melodic songs with some expressive lyrics. It also underlined the genius gap between himself and Robinson whose contributions were terribly prosaic. "Gene's lines are '. . . with your knight in tarnished armour' and mine are 'you looked a little harder' . . . Geno was such a great visual lyricist that his lines have more impact than mine most of the time. He was a hard lyricist to keep up with, so quick and bright. I like picturesque lyrics as well but they don't come naturally to me."

Clark's penchant for "too many beers" inevitably unleashed the wilder side of his personality. Recalling youthful escapades and past adventures with Jesse Ed Davis, he started throwing knives or axes at the studio walls. On at least one occasion, his outlaw games became a public spectacle, straight out of a gangster movie.

"Gene held up a liquor store one night, for fun," Robinson remembers. "He was drinking pretty heavily that night. He wanted to pick up some tequila and do some writing. So while I was looking for some Conmemorativo tequila in the store, I looked over and Gene had his hands in his pockets and had the checker put his hands up. I grabbed the bottle and threw a $20 bill on the counter and grabbed Gene before we both got shot in the back by some co-worker in the store."

If Gene was living dangerously, then the same could be said of his long-term girlfriend Terri Messina, whose on/off drug use had finally fallen foul of the law. Her brother Joe recalls picking her up after she was incarcerated overnight. A judge insisted that she must spend nine months in a treatment facility in lieu of a jail sentence. It was a tough call, especially considering Gene's continued penchant for excess which had ensured they were forced apart. Wisely, she chose to stay with her parents in Northridge from mid-November. On 15 December 1985, two days before her 40th birthday, Terri entered Cri-Help, a drug treatment centre in North Hollywood. Gene sent her a birthday card, which she treasured, but he could only support her from a distance with encouraging letters. Visits were not allowed, except for family members on Christmas Day.

Having enjoyed a life of relative privilege, Messina had to adapt quickly to the regime at Cri-Help, sleeping beside seasoned addicts on a bunk bed in a dorm with uncarpeted floors. When she first entered the facility and mingled with the other female 'inmates' her impressions were surreal. She felt as if she had stumbled into an amateur production of an Arthur Conan-Doyle murder mystery. Every one of the women referred to their comrades as 'Holmes'. It took some time for her to realize that this was not some tribute to the investigative skills of the fictional detective Sherlock Holmes, but an abbreviation of 'home girl', actually pronounced 'Homes'. The week before Christmas was a lesson in humility as she undertook various tasks, sweeping the dormitories, laundering clothes, mopping bathrooms and cleaning toilet bowls. The emphasis on physical work and regimented behaviour was designed to busy troubled minds with basic chores. Rising at 5am every morning ensured that you were genuinely weary at the close of day. Messina admitted that she usually felt too tired to become depressed. She also swore off drugs telling anyone who would listen: "I have learned my lesson. You can test me from now until doomsday!"

On 23 December, she participated in the Cri-Help Christmas party and dance, an event partly financed by former clients and associates. Terri found, to her surprise, that she greatly enjoyed the evening, especially the dancing. She also joined several of the women in a Christmas carol choir, singing to members of the public outside the facility. Observing fellow drug addicts trying to harmonize like angels appealed to her wry humour. Over the festive holidays, she socialized a bit more, struck up conversations, and was accepted by her peers. It did not escape her notice that she was one of the oldest people there. Most were young offenders from poor backgrounds. Terri found herself playing the wise owl, often telling them that it was better to get treatment early, rather than in middle age when long-term addictions can become overwhelming. Her moods wavered between optimism and fatalism. She was still consulting lawyers and planning to sell a property to finance an appeal. Although a judge was due to consider a written plea, it seemed almost certain that she would be away for the best part of a year. Gene, meanwhile, was still challenging his own demons.

While Clark hoped for an upswing in his commercial fortunes, work continued sporadically with Pat Robinson, sometimes interrupted by the unexpected arrival of distracting influences such as the irrepressible Jesse Ed Davis. "I was more like the worker bee in those days," Robinson reflects. "When I would party with Gene they'd go in the back-room and do whatever they'd want. I didn't do drugs with them. I'd never done heroin and didn't need to be taking that on. Pot was one of my favourite things and doing some coke. I was the one who had to stay a little more sober, a little more together, because I was running the board and usually playing everything too, putting down a second bass track real quickly . . . I saw these guys go through some pretty rough stuff. I could never have maintained it like they could. Then, at about six in the morning, it'd be 'Let's go and make some Billy the Kid chilli' and everyone's out making chilli. Just wildness."

By January 1986, Clark was back on the road with a new set of Byrds' tribute players. Guitarist Billy Darnell replaced Blondie Chaplin, and Greg Thomas took over from Michael Clarke. Since his time in Thunderbyrd and McGuinn, Clark & Hillman, the party-loving Thomas had gone through the familiar rehab route and was now clean and training as a drugs and alcohol counsellor. "After I got sober it took me a couple of years to get back in the scene because I was just too screwed up." A decade before he had been one of Clark's major drug buddies, but now he was seen as an angelic influence. Clark wanted to reform his ways but it was to prove a long process fraught with continual setbacks. He received regular letters from Terri, urging him to stay sober and attend AA meetings, always with the prospect of a happy-ever-after ending. At this stage, though, he still seemed in denial about the extent of his alcoholism. "He should have gone into rehab," says Thomas. "He'd cleaned up his act a little bit, but then he would binge drink. He'd clean up for two or three days and you'd think he was doing good then, all of a sudden, he'd be smashed. Sometimes you had to help him on and off the stage. At times he'd forget the lyrics. I have tapes of a lot of those live shows and we really enjoyed them. When Gene wasn't too drunk, he was really good, and that was amazing for all of us."

Terri Messina's treatment was proceeding better than expected. Amusingly, one of the main concerns among the women was not relapsing into drug abuse but putting on weight. Messina found the food too starchy for her tastes and feared the prospect of what her fellow inmates called the 'Cri-Help spread'. She vowed that once she secured limited release privileges she would take up dance classes and bike exercises.

On 8 January Messina was nervously back in court, awaiting her fate. It was good news. Reviewing her appeal, the judge decreed that, instead of nine months' incarceration, she was only required to remain at Cri-Help for 90 days. This was conditional upon her therapist agreeing that she had responded successfully to treatment and could be trusted on the outside. So began her road to sobriety which would soon impact on Gene's life.

Despite all the studio work Clark was doing with Robinson, he still had no firm recording deal or new material available in the marketplace. There were song scraps, some of which were never developed. 'Trail Of Tears', a promising acoustic sketch, was rehearsed, then abandoned. With no major record companies showing interest, Clark was willing to risk working with another small label and agreed to complete an album with Carla Olson. The idea had been germinating for some time. "I used to go over when Saul was first doing business with Gene and just hang around the house while Gene would be singing. Or we'd be playing tapes around the house of Gene's songs and I would be singing harmony. Then, one time, Sneaky Pete, Gene, me and Michael Clarke were at Gene's house and they started playing 'I'm Your Toy' ['Hot Burrito # 1'], and I started singing harmony, just sitting on the sofa. Gene turned around to me and said, 'Why don't we make a record like this with just you and the guitars?' I said, 'Yeah, what a concept for the Eighties.' "

Clark's casual comment took on concrete form when the duo entered a Los Angeles recording studio. From the outset, they determined not to follow the current trend of lavish productions and studiously avoided elaborate instrumentation or effects. "We just thought it would be great *not* to have electric instruments or drums," Olson recalls. "We didn't even use a snare, we just had a 2-inch tape box with brushes. We wanted to play behind the voices instead of having the music dominate." There was always a laid-back quality to the Clark and Olson teaming, reflecting the easy-going relationship between the parties. "Considering what we went through to make it, we were amazed how it turned out," she enthuses. "I was working at the time, so Gene was going in during the day and doing his vocals and I was coming at 9 pm after my job and doing my vocals. If we hadn't done all that singing together unintentionally before making the record, the harmonies wouldn't have been as close as they were."

One serious complicating factor during the recording was the state of Clark's health. He made an admirable attempt at abstinence, but inflammation of the abdominal cavities left him in constant pain. In order to stay straight, he over-compensated with bottles of aspirin and countless pots of coffee, both of which exacerbated his condition. Diagnosed with peritonitis, he also had advanced gum disease which affected his diction. "His teeth were loose," Olson recalls, "and he had trouble singing. When he did the vocal on 'Don't It Make You Wanta Go Home', I was thinking, 'Oh, God, we've got to get through this song because he's really in pain.' We managed to and I thought it was a beautiful vocal."

* * *

Terri Messina completed her 90 days' programme and, following her release, became an AA advocate. Keeping Gene Clark straight would test her resolve and there would be many lapses over the succeeding years. The same applied to his finances. Since the break-up with Carlie, he had never invested in property and remained in rented accommodation at 14747 Otsego, Sherman Oaks. He had vague plans to buy a place in Desert Hot Springs in California's Riverside County, but the fantasy was never realized. Terri was more practical and suggested they invest in some buy-to-let apartments in central Los Angeles and live off the rental income. Her parents had done this after retirement and it had proven profitable. As ever with Clark's finances, sensible options were ill considered and he drifted into stasis, postponing decisions until they became untenable.

After completing the sessions for the album with Carla Olson, Clark returned to the road. A major European tour was scheduled to take place between October and November 1986 featuring the Byrds' tribute band. The UK leg had been booked by Lancashire-based promoter, Brian Gannon. Five days before the band were due to arrive, Gannon received a telex informing him that Clark had fractured his shoulder. The entire tour had to be cancelled at considerable expense. Whether the injury was real or merely an excuse was never ascertained, but it did nothing to help Clark's credibility among promoters.

In December, he joined 'the California Dreamin' Caravan tour', featuring modern-day versions of the Mamas & The Papas and the Turtles. Loosely based on Dick Clark's 'Caravan Of Stars' revues from decades before, this was squarely aimed at the Sixties' nostalgia market, then in vogue. It was a strange experience for Clark, not least because David Crosby, recently released from Huntsville Prison, was backstage socializing with John Phillips. For all his indulgences, Clark had never descended as far into the abyss of self-destruction as they had done at the heights of their respective notoriety. Now they were newsworthy ex-outlaws with AA credentials, the perfect subjects for daytime television confessionals and earnest documentaries on the perils of rock star intemperance. Clark, by contrast, was still struggling with his demons, a forgotten figure whose story held no interest for mainstream media.

Encountering Crosby backstage may have been distracting, but confronting Phillips was akin to a trip into the unknown. Viewing Phillips from a distance, Clark noticed that his hair was now blond, but he still looked svelte and imposing. Turning to Tom Slocum, Clark quipped: "My God, John Phillips has turned into Errol Flynn!" Standing between them, Slocum feared an outbreak of old hostilities as if the two stars had each been transported back into 1966. "They had both tasted the fruits of intense success, but there was still this thing between them. They could hardly look into each other's eyes, let alone have a conversation. Here's Gene the catalyst for the break-up of the Mamas & The Papas, the guy who busted John Phillips' heart . . . It was like two weird prize-fighters fighting in the psychic heavyweight championship of the world."

Clark's romance with Michelle Phillips always had a fantasy element which connected in his mind to that time when he was living the Hollywood dream, playing the role of the newly liberated Byrd, a man of infinite possibilities. When his imagination was in full flow, especially under intoxication, Clark could create imaginary vistas and scenarios for his own entertainment. He could transform himself into cowboy John Wayne, Godfather Marlon Brando or some Native American chief and maintain the fantasy for an entire evening. "We used to call him Arapaho," says Carlos Bernal, who was still in the tribute band at this time. "He'd become that American Indian or Italian gangster. He was speaking in tongues when he got too drunk. It wasn't that often, but for two or three songs he'd have an episode. It wasn't pretty. Other than that he was just a tremendous guy." Tommy Kaye remembers Clark weaving an entire fantasy about an imaginary relationship with actress Sally Ann Field. After obsessively watching her films on rewind, he would speak as if they were a couple destined to be together. They had not met before and, as far as anyone knows, never did meet.

In April 1987, the Clark/Olson album *So Rebellious A Lover* was released on Rhino (US) and Demon (UK) to pretty favourable reviews. Clark fans, starved of product since *Firebyrd*, were grateful, while critics welcomed the return of a still underrated talent. For many, the duets seemed reminiscent of the celebrated Gram Parsons/Emmylou Harris partnership, although Clark had even pre-empted that as early as 1969 by singing alongside Donna Washburn on the second Dillard & Clark album. With Carla Olson, he showed how well his voice could combine with a female singer. For all that, the album was terribly tantalizing for those in search of new Clark songs. The shared credits with Olson and apparent desire to cover songs like 'Deportee' and 'Hot Burrito #1' meant that classic Clark material was in short supply. There was one truly exceptional moment in 'Del Gato', a ten-year-old composition about the West that Gene had written with his brother Rick. It had a yearning, desolate vocal and epic quality that recalled the best of Clark.

The positive response to the album encouraged Gene to consider a sequel but, like many schemes in his life, it was continually postponed until it was too late. He always felt ambivalent about the record and was never very comfortable with the limited opportunities associated with small label status. "Gene felt, 'Let's move up a step,'" Saul Davis recalls, "whereas we thought, 'Let's make a record and not worry about all that.' The record company didn't really know what to do with it. It was in that transition era before CDs, so it came out on album and cassette and the American label, for some unknown reason, didn't put it out on CD [at the time]. Then Gene had other commitments."

"We had the tunes," Olson attests, "we'd done this record and it had got all these critical accolades and Gene felt short-changed. I come from the school where just making records is a treat. He'd come from the school where you're able to make records in a way that you're comfortable with and everything's there and if you need something you call out and get it. With me, if it's there it is, and if it's not, you *still* make the record. He wanted a step up from that."

"Gene did that album with Carla and he wasn't all that pleased with it," Slocum adds, "but for what it was and the amount of money, it kept the continuity out there and showed that he was still around."

There was no major tour to promote *So Rebellious A Lover*, so Clark returned to the familiar grind of the tribute circuit. Still sensitive about the reactions of his fellow ex-Byrds, he tinkered with the idea of changing the group's name to the Silver Ravens, but promoters for shows at theme parks and casinos required the magical monicker to draw crowds. At least, a stable line-up was now established with Michael Curtis joining York, Darnell and Thomas. Curtis was pleasantly surprised to discover that Clark was stable, upbeat and seemingly alcohol free. "He'd quit drinking and Greg Thomas was helping him get cleaned up. Gene was brilliant, man. When he got healthy we did a couple of little tours and had the greatest time. He was laughing. He had a kind of cackle. He wasn't sullen, like everybody talks about him being. I loved working with him. But then, he started having a lot of stomach problems again. There'd be times when he'd have stomach cramps before we went out. He'd be doubled over. It was pretty painful."

Saul Davis was still hoping to find a record company willing to invest in Clark and, in common with Eddie Tickner, followed the trail to Nashville. "I got rejection letters from some pretty reputable Nashville A&R people. They were sick and tired of people coming from LA and Hollywood when they thought their careers were over, trying to be country artistes. I think they resented that, especially during the mid-Eighties."

There was no joy back in LA where Clark, in common with many other singer-songwriters, was still deemed passé. He never stopped writing and continued the project with Pat Robinson, but they were losing momentum. Interviewed in the late spring of 1987, he was asked about a possible solo album, and put on a brave face.

"We've got a few demos but we're going to cut a few more before we decide how we want to get started," he prevaricated, before changing the subject. "I'm glad this resurgence of popularity of music of the Sixties came about – there is so much in the lyrics and content of the music that applies today. I went through several years of real depression and it seemed like everything went wrong. Now I feel great."

Evidently, his current ambition was simply to remain healthy and survive. "In the Sixties we were victims of an experimental generation where it wasn't hip to be healthy – it was hip to be messed up and the more you were the further out you were. Everybody tried to out-do one another and kill themselves sooner. Now the consciousness is into health and exercise. It's so much more conducive to having a good life. That doesn't mean you have to be square either. I would just like to spend a few more years on this planet. We're already in enough trouble on this planet as it is, why get off too soon?"

Clark continued working with the 'Byrds', as the tribute band were frequently billed by cash-hungry promoters. The casino circuit provided steady income, but Clark was still affected by the travelling. His sobriety meant that he could no longer deaden his fears with booze, although such temptations remained ever present. "He didn't like to fly," says Curtis, stating the obvious. "I did a couple of flights back from Reno with him and he couldn't smoke on the flight anymore so he would just sit there and grab the edge of the seat. There was turbulence getting out of Reno every time, so the plane would shake around and you could see that he was not comfortable at all. I'd just talk to him and say, 'It's OK, it'll be fine. They fly this plane all the time.'"

Clark remained perpetually hopeful that a Byrds' reunion might be forthcoming, but McGuinn, Crosby and Hillman resisted lucrative entreaties, at least for the present. Although Clark had a steady income stream from his songwriting royalties, he still spent freely and continuing health problems resulted in more medical and dental bills. The touring treadmill offered a solution of sorts and Clark could not resist the temptation to continue using variants of the Byrds' name. He successfully applied to trademark the title 'Byrds', a move guaranteed to cause friction with the other founding members. McGuinn had made a gentlemen's agreement with Crosby that, following the dissolution of the latter-day CBS Byrds in early 1973, the only version of the group to use the name would be the original five. That promise had held firm for more than a decade but now Clark was challenging what the other originals considered an absolute.

When promoter David Fishof offered the 'Byrds' a place on his 'Classic SuperFest Tour', Clark lined up alongside other reconstructed Sixties acts, including the Turtles, Herman's Hermits, the Grass Roots and Paul Revere & The Raiders. The revue format meant that there was no pressure to compile a lengthy set. "We did something like five songs," Curtis recalls. "A couple of big hits and 'Knockin' On Heaven's Door'. The Turtles did the longest show, and a comedy bit. They were hilarious."

Although Clark was in no fit state to fulfil his touring obligations, he gamely carried on into 1988. Terri Messina already feared the worst. "Gene had finally got himself sober, but he was now paying dues over it. He was very ill with all these stomach problems. I kept saying to him, 'I think you've got an ulcer, you've got to get it checked.' It took forever to get him to see a doctor." Clark still insisted he was well enough to complete the lengthy itinerary. "It was a really hard tour," Messina remembers. "I said to him before he went, 'You're already sick, this will kill you.' He was in real physical trouble."

By now, Clark resembled an invalid rather than a rock star, and the shows were like scenes from a hospital drama. "We actually had oxygen offstage so that if he needed it he could walk off the stage and inhale some," says John York. "When he was a wreck, he could feel no pain, and there was a lot of pain that he was trying to mask – not just emotional pain, but physical pain. During the period when he was clean he was dealing with a lot of that. You know how it is when you have a bad toothache and what that can do to your personality. Well, he had tremendous pain in his stomach. It was an intense situation for all of us. When we realized how sick he was we said, 'You'd better go to the hospital now,' but he said, 'No, we've got two weeks to finish here.' I think we were in Reno. We went home and the next day he was in hospital and the doctors told him that if he'd waited a few more days he'd have been dead."

Terri persuaded Gene to convalesce at her parents' house in Northridge, where he was examined by her father, Dr Joseph Messina. "My dad took one look at him and said, 'He's going to die. We need to take him to UCLA.'" Clark's medical insurance was in a mess and he almost waited too long for an operation. Arguably, it was only the intervention of Terri's father that saved his life. Dr Messina referred him to a specialist in the UCLA medical school just in time. Most of Clark's stomach was removed during the operation, but he made a swift recovery that many regarded as near miraculous. His friend Tom Slocum visited him and virtually Gene's first words were "Have you got a cigarette?" Terri was trying to act the stern and benevolent disciplinarian, but Gene still managed to sneak cigarettes into the bathroom. "The doctors told Gene he had to stop smoking," she says. "I'd stayed at the hospital the first night during the operation and was going down there every day. They kept telling me, 'You've got to stop him smoking.' When Gene came out of the haze of his operation he was saying, 'Leave me some money so I can get some cigarettes.' I said, 'You can't smoke here in the hospital.' He said, 'Oh, I'll sneak one.' He was still on medication and I kept tricking him by not leaving money for smokes. I thought, 'Well, it's rough, but maybe he'll beat his habit after three weeks in the hospital.' Well, forget when he gets out of hospital. He'd been smoking *in* the hospital. When I found out Slocum had been giving him cigarettes, I blew my top. I called him 'Helpful Harry!' I didn't think it was a smart thing for him to do."

Slocum shrugged sheepishly, knowing that Clark was still a law unto himself. Incredibly, he was even conducting business deals from his bedside. Slocum was astonished. "The next thing his phone was beginning to ring off the hook. Agents were wanting to book him in Vegas. He was doing everything while he had all these tubes coming out of him. I said, 'Gene, you've just lost three-quarters of your stomach, how can you do this?' Then he had morphine. That was Gene. It was one of the most unusual recoveries I've ever seen. He went through a stomach and there was virtually nothing there. When he went home, Terri took care of him. His skin was all pink and he looked great."

The operation had a salutary effect on Clark, which lasted for some time. He quit drinking, modified his former excesses and paid closer attention to his diet. Pat Robinson even turned him on to a concoction of cayenne pepper and lemon, a familiar recipe for health freaks attempting to rid their body of unwanted toxins. "After the stomach operation, he got healthy and started working out," Michael Curtis adds. "All of a sudden his arms were muscular. He wasn't in pain anymore, he was smiling and really happy."

A couple of months after Clark's operation, two of his old friends, Garth Beckington and Hillary Kontos, were married in Reno on 9 June. It was not all good news. Thirteen days later, Jesse Ed Davis was found dead in a laundromat in Venice, California. "He'd already had a stroke and that really affected him," Hillary recalls. "He was walking with a cane and looked a shadow of his former self. He was incredibly diminished by it." Clark accepted the news of Davis' death in his usual stoic fashion, but it must have cut deeply. "When Jesse Ed died, Gene changed," York says. "They'd been like heroin brothers. I always wondered how Gene must have felt about it and how the heroin mentality might have affected him. I guess we'll never know, but there was a point when he was really clean and working."

Clark's new health kick could not have been better timed as suddenly there was news of a possible Byrds' reunion. McGuinn, Crosby and Hillman had agreed to appear together as the Byrds to celebrate the reopening of the Ash Grove. The event took place at the Wiltern Theatre in June 1988. Clark was in the auditorium that evening, but did not appear onstage. Crosby explained to the audience that this was due to his recent stomach operation, but many people were left wondering why he did not even grace the stage for a single song, or participate in the encore.

Clark made no comment, but his silence could not disguise what seemed a clear slight from his colleagues who were still indignant or upset about his use of the Byrds' name. McGuinn admits he felt aggrieved over the trademark issue, but disguised his feelings with an air of indifference. Saul Davis and Carla Olson, recently married, bumped into McGuinn one evening after a show and greeted him with a polite "Gene says 'Hi'." The reaction was quizzical. "He said, 'Gene who?'" Davis recalls. "That was the end of the conversation." Olson was not entirely surprised. "Roger and Camilla were in their little world and they just didn't want Gene. But I'll tell you, Gene definitely wanted Roger's recognition and approval because he really respected him. He told me that he thought Roger's songs were 'a little silly', but then again Gene was the antithesis of that. His songs were the darkest."

While McGuinn was inscrutably cool and Crosby diplomatically evasive, Hillman found it difficult to contain his anger. Clark made the mistake of inviting his agent Geoff Blumenauer backstage. Hillman knew Blumenauer was responsible for organizing bookings for the ersatz Byrds. A verbal confrontation followed that threatened to turn into something very nasty. Hillman warned the agent in menacing adjectives never to allow his client to appear under the Byrds' name again.

"Gene wanted to put aside all the old hostilities and let bygones be bygones," says Tom Slocum, "and if anything developed it should be the original five Byrds, or none at all." By the autumn Clark was appearing under his own name and also performing at the Palomino with his band under the less provocative title, Firebyrds. An East Coast tour followed during which Clark decided to wind down the Byrds' tribute band and try something new. The mood in the camp remained exuberant. "We were doing impressions," Curtis remembers. "Billy Darnell did a great Richard Nixon, Gene did John Wayne and I was Jack Kennedy. When we were driving we were talking like those guys. Sometimes, it would go on for half an hour at a time. Gene was up and it was fun." Curtis was allowed a cameo in the set where he sang

'Southern Cross', the classic composition that he and his brother Rick had written with Stephen Stills for inclusion on Crosby, Stills & Nash's *Daylight Again*. "Gene always gave me a great introduction, talking about Stephen Stills and what a fine song it was." Midway through Clark's rap, they noticed an audience member in a cast on crutches. As the song started, he jumped to his feet and started dancing on one leg. Without missing a beat, Clark leaned into the microphone and announced: "We even heal the lame!" Curtis was in stitches. "We started laughing so hard I couldn't finish the song. We had to stop and start all over again. It was such fun. That was the part of Gene that I really loved."

Over the next year, Clark publicly attempted to make peace with the original Byrds, playing the diplomat on any occasion when he was asked about a reunion. Like a recovering addict, he was contrite about his past and hoped to win back McGuinn's approval. "There's still a lot of healing that needs to be done there," he told me, with pained humility.

"It hurt him a lot when they wouldn't get back together to do a Byrds tour," Messina remembers. "There was a lot of money on offer and Gene needed more than anybody. And he'd been doing the right thing all that time. He'd been clean and sober, not out of control. He was showing up on time and doing his job and seemed on top of it. So they had nothing to complain about. I was surprised that David Crosby didn't stand up for him and say, 'He's not screwed up, he's back on his feet.' David probably saw us [at AA meetings] every week."

When I confronted Crosby about this, back in 1989, he was a little defensive, but clearly had no axe to grind against Clark. As a former addict, he was cautious but happy about the prospect of performing with the Byrds again. Wary of resurrecting past conflicts, he was reluctant to impose his opinions on McGuinn or Hillman too forcibly, let alone act as Clark's advocate. Crosby knew how badly the McGuinn, Clark & Hillman saga had ended, so left the decision about Clark's involvement entirely in their hands. "I'm happy to work with Roger and Christopher," he said, diplomatically avoiding the key issue.

Throughout this period, Clark clung to sobriety, attending AA functions with Terri Messina, who continued to act as his psychic protector. As a former abuser, she was hawkish about any likely transgression and not above lecturing Gene's friends about the dangers he faced. Not everyone was convinced. It was difficult to monitor Clark outside of Sherman Oaks, particularly when he was fraternizing with other musicians or recording. Often, he would become restive. "Once in a while, maybe once a month, he'd say, 'I'm going to work with Patrick for a while. We're getting together to try and work on some songs.' I'd say, 'Great, go ahead and have a good time.' He came home and he was high, so I'd phone Patrick and get on his case about it. The next day when Gene was straight I'd have a talk with him and say, 'How did this happen?'"

Like a recalcitrant schoolboy, Clark was full of apologies. "He'd say, 'We had a couple of beers and later I had a couple of lines.'" When challenged, Robinson felt indignant about Messina's paternalistic tone, knowing full well that he was one of the more responsible characters in Clark's circle and generally a regular guy. "I admit I would get upset," Messina considers. "Of course, I knew it was Gene's responsibility, number one. I would say, 'Patrick, I don't think you quite understand about AA, drug addition and alcoholism because you're a recreational drinker, but Gene has a major problem, and a person like that cannot drink or use, *at all*. This is not good.' I'd try and explain this to him but it would go in one ear and out the other. I never got the point across."

Despite periodic lapses, Clark remained straight most of the time and there was not yet any evidence of renewed addiction. Seemingly, he was still in control. David Jackson, Clark's former colleague from the Dillard & Clark days, bumped into Gene in 1989 and was pleased to catch up with the latest news and witness his recovery. "I saw Gene out here in the Valley and he said Terri was taking care of him. I'd known Terri since about 1966 and would see her often because she was always such a delight. I'd heard that she'd had a problem with heroin and separated from him, but now she was back and had cleaned up. She was nothing like a groupie girl. Terri was very effervescent, smart and funny. There was a small degree of sadness there, but nothing like the scale of Gene's melancholy. She was never on the periphery, either emotionally or intellectually. Terri was always a neatball. A wonderful woman."

Gene still seemed bewitched by Terri and happy to have won her back. They lived modestly at his sparse, rented home in Sherman Oaks, but there was still no legal commitment between them, despite Clark's periodic proposals. Unlike the other original Byrds, Clark did not rack up three or four marriages by his early forties, and Messina was in no hurry to whisk him to the altar. "There was part of me that was afraid to be married because I never wanted to go through a divorce. And I never knew what was going to happen next with him. I wanted to be fully satisfied that it was going to be on an even keel or I didn't want to be married. Yet, I didn't want to be with anyone else. I just wanted to be with him, so that's how it went."

There were spasmodic signs that Clark was attempting to re-organize his life at this point by changing some business agreements. According to Slocum, he had become disillusioned with Bug Music, having hoped that they'd achieve greater success exploiting his compositions. Their three-year arrangement had expired back in 1986, but continued on an annual basis as Clark had never exercised his option of providing a written termination by certified mail. Following a meeting with his lawyer, Martin Cohen of Cohen & Luckenbacher, Clark now decided to act. On 14 June 1989, a termination letter was drafted and sent to Clark's home for signature. Whether it was ever executed remains uncertain, but it was indicative of his intent.

Domestically, there were also changes afoot when Gene's sons Kelly and Kai came to stay for an extended period. Back in Mendocino, their mother, Carlie, was suffering her own drug torments and finding it difficult to cope. Like Terri, she would eventually overcome her addictions and, years later, became a drugs counsellor. At this point, though, she was in trouble. It must have been disorientating for the children when they moved suddenly from spacious, rural Mendocino to Clark's two-bedroomed suburban home. "It was a teeny house that was barely big enough for the two of us," Terri stresses, "much less two teenage boys who'd come to live with us. So it was tough. It would be for the best of people, believe me."

Clark was also feeling the pressures of fatherhood. "Gene had to be a dad for a year and I think it just made a nervous wreck out of him," laughs Carla Olson. "He just could not deal with it. He tried so hard to set a good example, when all he wanted to be was Gene Clark, so it was difficult to do." Clark's long-term plan was to create a situation whereby he could earn enough money to settle down, modify his excesses and somehow bring together Terri and his children in a fantasy happy family. Fulfilling that dream was to prove more difficult than he could imagine.

Re-enacting old family patterns, Messina found herself cast in the role of disciplinarian, overseeing two troubled teenagers whom she barely knew. They had few, if any, happy memories of the summers they had spent with her and Gene back in Laurel Canyon. It had always been a fraught relationship and, as rebellious teens, it was all too easy for the boys to stereotype Messina as the evil stepmother, if they chose. "I went through great lengths to help those boys," she insists. "The older son had dropped out of high school a year before he even came to us, so we put it to him that either you go back to school or get a job. One or the other. You can't do nothing. We gave him that choice and he didn't want to go back to school so he went to work. He got a couple of jobs where he was getting minimal wage and he hated it, so that didn't last."

By his own admission, Kelly Clark was something of a wild child at this stage of his life. "I wasn't getting along with my mom and I was in some trouble at school. My dad had quit drinking and I was just starting to experiment. He tried to get me together, do sober stuff and I just wasn't ready." Kelly enjoyed driving cars, drinking beer and unintentionally causing minor mayhem. In many ways, his actions mirrored the teenage exploits of his father back in Kansas. He was never likely to knuckle down to Messina's domestic regime without a struggle, but relations looked like thawing when she found him a decent job. "I was remodelling a house in Malibu working with my brother [Joe] who was the head contractor and I was doing the design work. He gave the eldest boy a job for about three months and it was a good salary for a 17-year-old. He was able to buy a car."

During a break on the project, Kelly decided to return to Mendocino to "show off his new car and hang out with his friends". Before he left, Messina lectured him about the dangers of drink driving. "We said, 'We're not even going to tell you not to drink because we know you'll do whatever you want anyway. If you're staying the night with a friend, you can drink beer, but don't drive.' That was the deal we made. He went up there and, I swear to God, if it wasn't three days later that we got a phone call. He was in jail for drink driving and in real trouble. He wanted Gene to just fly up there and bail him out. I told Gene, 'We've got to get him into rehab – that's all there is to it. This kid has a problem. You can't bail him and let him come back here to work like nothing's happened. He made a deal with us.' We pulled all kinds of strings making phone calls and found a juvenile rehab up North that he could go into. It was a six-month programme. We told him, 'We just want you to go in there for 30 days and learn about the problems you have.' It was hereditary. Gene's father was an alcoholic, Gene's an alcoholic and now his kid's drinking and the mother had her problems too. That's all we wanted him to do, but he absolutely refused."

Messina declined to allow him back in the house while she was there. Their relationship had never been good, now it was effectively non-existent. Years later, he conceded that "she was probably right . . . because we were expensive", adding "my mom was constantly nagging him [Gene] for money." Such nuances were seldom considered as resentment festered. His abiding memory was of Terri admonishing his father about the need to discipline his children. "He would get uptight about these little things, but you could tell it was lots of other stuff weighing down on him. Sometimes we'd sit around the table and drink coffee together. He'd just crack jokes and we'd be normal. But he was completely stressed out, all the time. Music, money, trying to get back to where he once was. How's that got to be? To be on top of the world for ten years and then scraping by, waiting for your next royalty cheque." As for his own behaviour, Kelly put it down to the family curse. "I was rowdy. My dad was rowdy. Put firewater in us, we're going to get a little nuts and get in trouble." After returning to Mendocino, Kelly had an epiphany during a brief spell in the county jail. It was Christmas and the end of the decade, a time for reflection and self-examination, particularly for a young adult, now just turned 18, facing an uncertain future. Not too long after, he took the AA route and elected to stay sober and turn his life around. Ironically, his father and mother were both heading down the opposite road.

Carlie Clark's descent into drug addiction had accelerated during the Eighties. Even the recent birth of a daughter, Indiana, was not enough for her to address her problems. That would come later. Former nanny Dara Zimmerman was recruited once more. "I went back to Mendocino and looked after Indiana. Carlie somehow talked me into growing pot with her along Big River. Everybody I ever knew in Mendocino grew pot or smoked it. I stopped smoking pot when I was 16 because it made me stupid and fat, and I didn't want to be stupid or fat. We were driving these dirt bikes on these deer trails down to the river. It was crazy." Carlie's pot-growing escapades ended in an almost comic reversal of fortune. The law enforcement task force CAMP (Campaign Against Marijuana Planting), which specialized in reducing the supply of marijuana by destroying crop sites, stumbled upon Carlie's secret garden and razed her mini-empire. "One day we went down there," Dara remembers, "and CAMP had pulled up all the plants which were about four feet high. They were all gone. They left cards saying, 'Thank you very much for your pot. CAMP.' They didn't bust her; they just took her plants."

Far more disconcerting was her involvement in the coke trade. "I used to babysit Indiana while Carlie was selling coke," Dara says. "When she was selling coke, she would bury it in the woods. Then she'd go back to the woods and get the money. She was freebasing and that's when I started to freak out about Carlie. I didn't like that. She kept saying, 'Do some, do some' and I didn't really want to because I was watching all these insane people coming in and out of her house. Kai was living out the back and Kelly had pretty much taken off. I went with her on one trip to San Francisco in another Dodge van. She had this special compartment built to hide the coke and she came back to Mendocino with a kilo. I didn't know what we were doing. She neglected to mention little things like that. The reason I never got into freebasing, thank God, was because I *did* try it. Carlie wouldn't make it in a little vial like most people. She'd make it in a saucepan. She gave me this big old hit. All it did was give me this huge rush, make me want to throw up so bad, then make me want more. A really bad combination. Awful. . . . I got into drugs too, but never quite to the extreme of some of them." This was the nadir of Carlie's drug odyssey. Even old friends like Mary Pritchard Kendall stayed away at the peak of the freebasing. It was a grim period, which would continue for several more years.

For a time, Kai remained in Sherman Oaks. "My mom was using at the time and we'd had a tumultuous upbringing. Kelly moved out. I hadn't lived with my father growing up but he was still my dad. I'd have liked to stay close to him but, in reality, I didn't know him that well. He and my mother wouldn't talk. They didn't get along too well. Messages were relayed through other people." Kai found some stability during this latter stay with his father. "It was really cool because I got to go to school there and live with my dad. Then I got to know him better. I remember him recording in the house in Otsego Street with wires strung across the place. A couple of times I tripped over them. He'd say, 'Ah, no! I've been working on that all night!' It was funny. He was so dedicated when he was recording and put a hundred per cent into it. Everything around him was blacked out when he was working on his music."

By the late Eighties, Gene Clark was at another crossroads. For several years, he had been intermittently working with Pat Robinson, recording demos for a solo album, collaborating on the CRY concept and touring with a tribute band, but there was still no record deal. The 'commercial' songs that he hoped might sell remained unheard by the general public, along with his more ambitious work. Reviewing the Robinson tapes provided little solace. What had seemed enterprising several years before now sounded staid and dated, a telling comment on the processed music of the period. "Gene wouldn't have released this stuff if it had been done by the Beatles," says Slocum. "He would have done something different to it musically. Gene asked me, 'What do you think of it?' It had Linn drums and synths. I said, 'It doesn't do anything for the songs. It's cheesy, man.'"

Rather than rework the old recordings, Clark felt that a new approach was preferable. Messina recalls seeing a documentary in which an ageing singer had explained how he'd won a record contract by submitting some high-quality demos which showed off his potential. The idea was to select a small number of songs and invest enough money to ensure that they were perfectly produced in a top class studio. They found an interested party in John Arrias, an accomplished engineer who ran one of Barbra Streisand's vocal studios. He negotiated a tentative tripartite arrangement with Terri and Gene, which gave them access to Hollywood's B&J's Studio. Jeff 'Skunk' Baxter was also involved in the recordings. With Messina throwing in some money and Gene's friends ready to help, progress seemed likely. "We all played for free and chipped in on getting that thing done, just trying to get some product," remembers Pat Robinson. Clark and Messina were reluctant to allow Arrias to take on the producer's role, feeling that a more empathetic voice was required. "He was demanding all sorts of things about wanting to be producer," Messina claims. "Now, Arrias, in all honesty, is a very good engineer and always has been, but we didn't think he was a great producer. He doesn't have the heart; he's too technical. So we got Tommy Kaye. Gene and I put that together. I said, 'Let's get Tommy up here because, whatever else Tommy Kaye is screwed up about, he's a damned good producer.' Tommy has heart. He's another person with total soul and that's what was lacking. I thought it would be an interesting combination because Arrias had all the high technical stuff that we needed and then Tommy could come in and put some heart and soul into it as producer. Well, Tommy came out and we'd told him we were both in AA and had been sober for a long time and we didn't want any screwing up going on with this deal at all. If he was going to be involved, he'd have to stay off everything because we wouldn't put up with it. He promised us that he'd been going to AA himself back in New York and that he was clean. But then he got out here and it wasn't true. He was drinking and screwing up, so we took him off it. It was a really difficult thing to do, but we sent him back home."

After several delays, work recommenced on the project. "The hidden motive behind it was that there was still talk of the original five Byrds coming back together," Slocum says. "Gene said, 'Look, I'll put in the time and we can do the album and take it slow' but they were still thinking maybe we can get the Byrds back together again. That was the candy in the mix." In the end, a handful of songs were completed: 'Mary Sue', I Don't Want To See You Anymore' (written by Marty Coopersmith), 'Shades Of Blue' (a Tommy Kaye composition), 'On The Run (With A Loaded Gun)' (melodically reminiscent of Bruce Springsteen's 'Dancing In The Dark') and 'Look Who's Missing Who'. The results were not as inspiring as everyone had hoped and, although reasonable, the songs still sounded clinical. Not even rumours of a Byrds' reunion could persuade any major label to invest in a Gene Clark album. The disappointing feedback eroded expectations, particularly for Arrias whose expenses were mounting. According to Messina, he got cold feet about investing a third of the income and once he backed out, the project ground to a halt. "That really bugged Gene," Slocum recalls. "He was very pissed off about it but bit his lip."

Clark's other big hope – a Byrds' reunion – also remained tantalizingly out of reach. He had long ceased touring under the Byrds' name, which had since passed into the less discriminating hands of Michael Clarke. Gene remained locked on the sidelines while three of his former colleagues started legal action against Clarke and attempted to assert their own claim to the name. In January 1989, McGuinn, Crosby and Hillman played several California dates but pointedly neglected to invite Clark. He was initially deflated and upset, but soon perked up following an unexpected turn of events. Byrds fan Tom Petty had attended their Ventura Theatre concert at which the trio had performed a rousing version of 'Feel A Whole Lot Better'. He came away inspired. "We don't know if he was a little ticked off because Gene had been excluded," Saul Davis muses, "but he went home and decided he was going to record 'Feel A Whole Lot Better'. It was the only cover song on his record [*Full Moon Fever*]. That delighted Gene, not just for the money's sake but that there was a little bittersweet instant karma revenge."

By the spring of 1989, Gene seemed stronger than ever. He told me that he hadn't had a drink in nearly two years and, even assuming this was an exaggeration, it indicated a desire to cut down on his old excesses. Inspired by Crosby's best-selling autobiography, he contacted Jim Dickson, whom he wanted to write his life story. The lack of a publisher and the fact that Dickson wasn't a writer were matters that had not apparently occurred to him. Dickson passed him over to me to discuss the writing project. He was wildly optimistic. Tom Petty's cover of 'Feel A Whole Lot Better' promised a much-needed injection of funds that Clark intended to put to good use. Although he still seemed ostracized from the battling Byrds trio, there were hints and signs that their negative feelings might be thawing. Virtually all their wrath was now directed at Michael Clarke whose defence of their lawsuit was proving more vigorous than anticipated. In advance of the expected court appearance, Clarke's side had collected several explosive affidavits, including one from Larry Spector, supposedly so damning that it threatened to rewrite the group's late 1967 tribulations from a far more cynical perspective. When the judge threw out the case and signalled a final victory for Michael Clarke, Gene had good reason to be hopeful about a settlement resulting in a possible five-way reunion, album or tour. He was now essentially managing himself, although various people would claim to represent his interests over the next year. Biding his time, he continued playing small solo gigs and occasionally appearing with Carla Olson. They even took the time to record a version of Phil Ochs' 'Changes', which was later included on the compilation *True Voices*. Olson sometimes visited Clark's home in Sherman Oaks, along with her husband, Saul Davis. They were surprised to see that he had decked out the apartment like a ranch house, complete with western furniture, a wagon wheel mounted on the wall and Indian rugs. The bedroom was full of gadgetry and fancy swivel lights. "Gene used to grind his own coffee," Olson remembers, "and he had these magical cinnamon cloves in it. He was a really methodical person and the house was immaculate. Everything was clean, at all times. You never saw it in a mess. For a guy who seemed a bit emotionally dishevelled, he was really very obsessive about having things orderly. He had a crease in his jeans and his boots were always shining. He would shake your hand and take it to his heart."

When publishing money came in, he would act the rock star, but Olson believes that was his Mr Hyde self. "It was a part of his personality that he disliked. I don't think he was a happy person living like that. He loved being able to sing about pain and suffering. That was his life. If you look back at his history, the happiest moments of Gene Clark's life probably were when he was at his absolutely lowest financial ebb. What a character, a man out of time."

With no product to promote, Clark's international reputation inevitably waned over the years, but he retained a cult following in Europe. Despite previous tour cancellations and other setbacks, promoters were still willing to take a chance and in

October 1989 a two-week series of dates was set to commence, concluding with a couple of nights at Dublin's Olympia Theatre. Coincidentally, Michael Clarke's changeling Byrds were scheduled to tour the UK at the same time. This made for an interesting story in which the parties were pitted against each other. *Time Out* magazine left its readers in no doubt where its sympathies lay. "In a few days' time some ex-compadres of Gene do their stuff under the sinfully false monicker of the Byrds. Gene (who refused to join them and good on him for that) was the first original Byrd to leave in 1966 . . . A great songwriter and artiste, a talent that is being rediscovered by the likes of Tom Petty, Richard Thompson and even Dinosaur Jr, here is a rare and very welcome chance to witness a real American music legend in action. Take it." Alas, the 'legend' lived up to his reputation as an unreliable traveller. Although advance deposits and airline tickets had been sent, word came back at the eleventh hour that Clark had cancelled due to 'illness'. He would never visit Europe again.

Clark began 1990 on a sanguine note. The healthy sales of Tom Petty's *Full Moon Fever* meant that he could look forward to a substantial stream of income from the cover of 'Feel A Whole Lot Better'. There was still strong interest in a Byrds' reunion and some lingering hope of pulling off a small label deal for a solo record. But there was always the danger of complacency. Clark had worked hard to return his body to full strength, working out and strenuously avoiding the temptations of alcohol and drugs. Suddenly, without explanation, there were worrying lapses.

On 3 February, he joined Carla Olson for a show at McCabe's, which was posthumously released under the title *Silhouetted In Light.* When he arrived at the venue, he was obviously inebriated. "Gene was a little bit like my father," Olson reflects. "When he was sober he was the nicest guy you'd want to meet, and when he wasn't he was a bastard. Not to me, personally, but to himself and the situation you were in if you were trying to do something. But 90 per cent of the time I knew Gene he was as courteous and gracious to me and Saul as anybody I've ever worked with or met." Clark was far from his best at this show, but there were always magic moments to savour. "Even the nights when he was difficult, I was as thrilled as anyone to sing with Gene. You'd start a song and he'd change the key on you. On *Silhouetted In Light*, there's a couple of mistakes that we can all laugh about now because they're bittersweet memories. Yet, even on his worst night, just to hear that voice sailing out there and to be able to sing in tandem was something to cherish. There's nobody that I could get up and sing with quite like that. We did 'Set You Free This Time' and he slowed it right down. You'd think it was too slow but when you started getting into the rhythm, you'd realize its sadness. He always said that song was too fast for him. It was a dodgy business playing with Gene Clark, not as bad as Dylan, but definitely difficult."

On 24 February 1990, exactly three weeks later, the 'Byrds' triumvirate reunited again for the Roy Orbison tribute. Clark's hopes of joining them remained the stuff of dreams. There was no invitation, merely an insouciant frostiness. Lingering ill will about his past use of the name probably played a part in their decision.

By this stage, Clark was slipping back into old habits with more frequent on/off bouts of drinking. Although he seemed to have his life back in control, he was about to lose his way once more. Inevitably, everybody has their pet theory about what may have caused Clark to fall off the wagon, but unravelling the complex psychology of addiction is a fruitless task. Terri Messina believes that it was a combination of factors, any one of which might have triggered him: a few drinks, a relieving Valium tablet, a line of coke in a weak moment. Others point out that he was frustrated with the current state of his solo career or upset by the Byrds' continued coldness. He may also have been haunted by his failings as a father, for he still spoke of the need to establish a closer relationship with his children. In contrast to his darker moments, there was also the dangerous high produced by the lucrative Tom Petty cover. Clark's instinctive reaction was to celebrate his good fortune through excess. Like any recovering addict, he faced temptations from every quarter and needed no excuse, positive or negative, to lapse into self-destructive ways. His perennial tendency to pull back from the brink encouraged the feeling that he could always seek last-minute abstinence, few realizing that a more dangerous spiral was already underway.

The fantasy life of Gene Clark was also reactivated during this period. The man who had strange daydreams about Sally Ann Field now had a fresh object of fixation. It may have been part of his imaginary rivalry with John Phillips, but Clark took pleasure in projecting preposterous illusions after encountering Chynna Phillips, then in the ascendant as part of the female trio, Wilson Phillips (alongside Brian Wilson's daughters, Carnie and Wendy). Chynna had been born to John and Michelle Phillips in 1967, long after the latter's brief affair with Gene Clark. Such chronological niceties were no impediment to Clark's florid imagination. One night, he visited a Hollywood club in the company of Slocum, where he was introduced to Chynna. It sparked one of his more bizarre flights of fancy. "Hey, Sloc," he said. "Isn't she just like me? She sounds like me." By the end of the evening he had turned her into the daughter he never had. "He had a fantasy about it," Slocum recalls. "I'd say, 'Gene, she ain't your daughter' and he'd have a hard time with that. He'd say, 'Sloc, I was there.' I said, 'Yeah, I know you were there, but I don't think so, Gene.'" In an inebriated aside, he retorted, "That's my daughter and I'm gonna write her a number 1 record." Slocum was amazed. "He made the whole thing up. It was one of Gene's complete fantasies, like the Traveling Wilburys." Around this time, Clark did indeed claim that he was a candidate to become a member of the supergroup in the aftermath of Roy Orbison's death. It was nothing more than wishful thinking. At that same time, he announced that he had written a new song, 'From Darkness' (probably 'Your Fire Burning') which he was offering to Wilson Phillips for their album. This sounded suspiciously like another of his private jokes, but he was careful to keep such reveries to himself whenever John Phillips was in the vicinity.

Once the royalties from the Tom Petty album arrived, Clark

ceased touring and distanced himself from several old friends. Instead, he partied, staying up half the night, taping ideas. Michael Curtis remembers receiving drunken phone calls at three in the morning. "He'd say, 'Curtis, come over here right now!' I'd say, 'Man, I'm sleeping, I'll see you at 10 am.' He'd say, 'No, I'll be asleep by then.' I realized there were other extracurricular activities going on. I wouldn't crawl out of bed at 3 am to join the party, but other people did."

One such was Shannon O'Neill, who also remembers receiving calls in the early hours during which Clark would play a fragment of a new song and enthuse, "You've got to hear this." Unlike Curtis, O'Neill would leave his bed, much to the chagrin of his disgruntled wife. "She'd say, 'Why the hell is he calling so late? Tell him to get off the phone and go to bed!' The next thing I'm saying, 'I'm going over to Gene's!' My wife's says, 'Are you mad?' Gene would drive other people crazy, but I totally understood it. You get excited about something you're writing and you're drinking. He had a tiny cassette recorder and that's what he was recording into sometimes. But I thought he was writing some of his best songs. I wish that somebody had recorded that stuff properly because he was a consummate writer. I think Gene was one of those guys who would have just got better. If he'd got to 60 he'd probably have been writing great songs like a Picasso of music."

Clark was so impressed by O'Neill's enthusiasm that he suggested they work together, assisted by the loyal but fallible Pat Robinson. "Gene had been working with John Arrias and he didn't like that. He just wanted to work with his friends. I think he liked partying with Pat. He'd go up there, have a drink or get high and cut these demos. That happened a lot with Gene. But I never thought the songs were as good as they could have been. It was just an excuse. That was the relief. Gene needed to get away from Terri every once in a while and that was his solace. It was like a little retreat for him."

Clark enjoyed entertaining visiting musicians, including Levon Helm, the former Band drummer, who was making decent money working with Ringo Starr & His All Starr Band. "Every time Levon came into town he would always look Gene up," says John York. "All of a sudden Gene would be staying up all night and they'd be hanging out for days at a time. As much as we loved him, Levon wasn't a good influence on Gene. Levon always had a handle on what he was doing and seemed never to lose control, but Gene liked to get really high. He was starting to feel, 'I'm happening again! I'm going to release records, do soundtracks and be Gene Clark again!' "

Evidently, being Gene Clark again required a radical re-evaluation of his career. Having already lost his recent band, he elected to seek greater autonomy by changing agents and management representatives. Saul Davis suddenly found his services were no longer needed. "I'd been cut out of the management because of Gene or Gene's girlfriend, Terri," he admits. In one of her more cutting asides, Messina referred to Davis as a "nickel and dime guy" compared to some of America's multi-billionaire moguls, while cynically suggesting that "the main thing he got together was for Gene to make an album with his old lady, Carla". The decision was Gene's. Of course, Messina had been around during the Seventies when Clark was playing stadiums and recording for major labels. Those days were long over and no one seemed any more capable of transforming him into a big star. Davis had clearly done his best in difficult circumstances. "We might not have been as successful as we should have been when I was trying to be his manager or in charge, or whatever," he acknowledges. "But things weren't as confusing as they got thereafter . . . What Gene did was, instead of having me, one person you could direct everything to, he had a lawyer, and then a publicist and about seven people instead of one. Things were so diffused. At least, Gene and Carla made that record and it *exists.*"

Clark started working with agent David Bendett, along with a new attorney. Slocum remembers the comings and goings with a jaundiced eye. "If somebody called up Saul and asked for a Gene Clark date, he would do it. Or Geoffrey Blumenauer would do it. It wasn't a formalized agreement where papers were sent. It was very loose and for anybody to go around proclaiming they were Gene Clark's manager, I thought, 'Well, no.' "

"Gene was totally turned off Saul," Messina adds. "But he retained the friendship with him. He would talk to him and kept it on an even ground, but he just didn't want to do business with him any more. The irony of the whole thing is that I never bad rapped Saul to Gene, ever. Gene bad rapped him to me. I'd always say, 'Well, I know he's not *that* big a deal but . . .' There's no question in my mind that I would have liked to have seen Gene involved with a more influential manager. Who wouldn't? But it's not like something I was putting into Gene's head all the time. A lot of the time Gene was with Saul he was sick. There wasn't all that much you could do until he got healthy anyway. So I wasn't influencing Gene to run away from him."

There is a tendency among some of Clark's friends and associates to speak about him as though he was a helpless child or perennial victim. Members of different friendship groups criticize others in the story, but often display a lack of empathy. Andy Kandanes remembers once phoning Saul Davis about Gene only to be rebuffed by the quip, "What are you, his mother?" Kandanes then threatened to send Slocum over to Gene's place, put him in a car, take him to the airport and transport him to Andy's home in Cobb, California. "I told Gene this, but he said, 'Well, he's the only guy who's got something going for me right now. So I've just got to do what I've got to do.' But he had no love for Saul."

Clark seemed to produce such extreme reactions from his friends and, as the years passed, his compartmentalized relationships saw the emergence of warring factions, who grew increasingly critical of each other. Kandanes' negative and disproportionate response to an innocuous comment from Davis, who was probably oblivious to all this negativity, underlines the sensitivities at work in the different inner circles Clark inhabited. There were a lot of similar resentments voiced for no sound or convincing reason even before his death.

"Gene used a lot of people too," says Shannon O'Neill. It's a point worth remembering when considering the frustrations of managers, friends, lovers and even family members at different times. "I liked Gene and he was a great friend," O'Neill reflects, "but I could never have done what someone like Tom Slocum did. If there was one male figure that went out to help him, it was Tommy. He was always in contact with him." But even Slocum would find his loyalty tested, particularly when Clark went off the rails. Nor was he entirely exempt from the occasional bitchy barbs from others in the inner circle.

Despite the best efforts of well-meaning managers and agents, including Davis, Blumenauer and Bendett, Clark's ambivalence towards fame and success meant that he was often a frustrating client. He enjoyed the image of being a troubadour, but craved rock godhead, while also fearing its power and effect on his psyche. It was similar to his relationship with alcohol. His capacity for self-sabotage was never far away. In another eccentric decision, he allowed Shannon O'Neill to take on a quasi-managerial role and instructed him to approach various major labels with some demos. "I couldn't get a record deal for him," O'Neill says. "It was impossible. Nobody would take a chance because he'd burnt so many bridges. I called a lot of people from different labels and as soon as I'd start talking they'd say, 'You know he's got a drinking problem or a drug problem' or 'He's known to be obstinate and we hear he gets belligerent if he's drunk.' Those stories just permeated the business and it was like fighting an uphill battle. I'd say, 'Yeah, but the guy was a member of the Byrds for Christ's sake. Forget all that. Listen to what he's got. The guy has some brilliant stuff.' "

After a few months of trying, O'Neill returned to Clark empty-handed. It seemed to vindicate the comments of previous agents and representatives, who had suffered the same stonewalling. Other well-known rabble rousers were allowed a certain licence, but Gene was seemingly regarded as a liability, at least in LA.

Clark reluctantly allowed O'Neill to check out some indie labels, although he was never entirely happy going down this route. Among the songs O'Neill was keen to promote was 'All I Want', a Clark/O'Neill/Slocum composition with a catchy chorus. There were countless acoustic demos of the song and others featuring various guest players. Slocum had been heavily involved in the writing, most notably with the jarring line, 'I know a million bitches too'. "It was a complete accident," Slocum recalls. "Gene said, 'I wouldn't say that!' and I said, 'But John Lennon would!' And I thought 'blow your cover' was a lame line from him which softened the track. I still call the beginning of that song 'Dear Prudence'. Geno liked it for what it was. What did we expect from it? Well, we didn't expect that it was going to be a number 1 song. It was more, let's see where it goes and see what happens. But I never saw somebody go through so many rewrites in my life. There were pages and pages of lyrics but in the end it stayed as it was originally."

Clark's reservations about the sexist 'bitches' lyric proved well-founded. When O'Neill later approached Shiloh Records' Dale Davis and played the song, he was so offended by the word that he refused to have anything to do with Clark. "Maybe he'd met him before. Gene was the perfect gentleman when he was sober and could charm anybody. But sometimes people were scared to death of him."

A veritable Janus figure throughout his life, Clark's career path was never predictable. In recent years, he had struggled to stay sober and save some money, but suddenly all that progress was reversed. Booze and coke were now high on his agenda as Messina could testify. "God knows what demons were inside of him to make the choice to revert to that behaviour. He was at a time of his life where things had gotten much better. Things had stabilized and he could have gotten what he wanted and achieved satisfaction with his career. Why he made that decision to go back to that self-destructive behaviour, even I don't know the exact answer to that. I can make suggestions. He felt the pressure was on and I know he was unhappy about some things that were happening, and the Tom Petty money played a part too. We had been working and making sacrifices for years so that when we finally got the money he could invest it and do something positive with it. But he took the money and started buying drugs. For a long time, he could never afford drugs and that probably helped him stay clean. When I think back on it, Gene had a hard time dealing with money."

Although his songwriting income was still healthy, basic record royalties were modest by comparison. A statement from CBS Records covering the period ending 30 June 1990 revealed earnings of $3,863.82. It was hardly a fortune but the albums covered were over 15 years old and the original royalty rates were parsimonious by modern standards. Tellingly, *The Byrds Greatest Hits* was still his biggest seller from that golden era.

Clark still hoped for a Byrds reunion and there was much talk about their nomination for a Rock 'n' Roll Hall of Fame award the following year. During the summer of 1990, McGuinn, Crosby and Hillman cut some tracks in Nashville but neglected to invite Clark. Even their great mentor Jim Dickson was upset by their attitude, which he saw as little less than callous. The inclusion of newly recorded material on the Byrds' lavish box set towards the end of the year was cutting enough, but additional insult lay in the track listing which pointedly diminished Clark's contribution to a mere handful of songs. Saul Davis, who was no longer representing Clark, valiantly rushed off indignant faxes after seeing the song selection. A letter was even despatched to me complaining about the writing credits to 'Eight Miles High' which had been mysteriously altered from Clark/McGuinn/Crosby to McGuinn/Crosby/Clark, as if to slight Gene's contribution. In fairness, those credits had been altered since the release of the extended jam session on *(Untitled)* and often appeared differently on various compilations over the years. Although this could be explained away as a trivial administrative error there was no denying the scandalous exclusion of such Clark classics as 'Here Without You' and 'Set You Free This Time' from the box. Many regarded these songs as among the Byrds' greatest. Aesthetically, there could be no justification for omitting them from a 90-song selection and, beyond mere disregard, the whiff of sour grapes or even publishing avarice was widely suspected. McGuinn seemed oblivious to such criticism, as if unaware that Clark's early songs were anything more than minor works in the Byrds' canon. He felt Clark was more than reasonably represented in the anthology, so what was the problem? Clark made no comment on the box, later admitting that he hadn't even bothered to peruse its contents. "It was just one last twist of the knife," Saul Davis suggests. "Gene was too much of a gentleman or too proud even to bring it up. You would if you were Chris or David, but not Gene."

Rising above the rivalries, Clark attempted another reinvention, this time looking back to an accomplice from the previous decade. Guitarist Garth Beckington was amazed to receive a call requesting his services. Clark claimed that he was on the brink of securing a solo deal and was preparing songs for soundtracks and considering a European tour. As Beckington remembers: "He told me, 'I'm not going to do *any* of these things unless you come down here.' It surprised the hell out of me. But Hillary and I were free and easy in those days, so we agreed. When I saw him he was pretty gaunt. He definitely wasn't carrying any weight, but he was a really resilient guy. One week he'd look terrible and the next he'd look a picture of health." Working as a duo, Clark and Beckington played a number of gigs, including a key date in San Diego and a slot supporting the Lost Planet Airmen.

In September 1990, the duo appeared at the Palomino and were joined onstage by Carla Olson. "It was really desperate," she recalls. "I was only going to play on three songs – 'Mary Sue', 'Del Gato' and 'Your Fire Burning' – and they were going to do the rest of the set, but we ended up doing 'Train Leaves Here This Morning' and 'Set You Free This Time'. Just me, Gene and Garth." Clark still indicated a wish to record again with Olson, if the gods permitted and, despite the belatedly negative comments from several of his associates, he retained a cordial relationship with Saul Davis, who voiced support on his behalf and was evidently keen to be more involved.

On 7 November, Clark and Olson took part in a birthday tribute to Gram Parsons at the Palomino. Gene liked to affect an ambivalent attitude towards the late, mythologized ex-Byrd. According to Tom Slocum, Clark quipped that if he ever met Parsons in the afterlife, he would know for sure that his soul had been sent to hell. Of course, Clark was well aware that Parsons' musical partner Emmylou Harris was previously Slocum's wife, so the morbid humour may have been exclusively for his benefit. Elsewhere, Gene had been flattering, acknowledging that 'Hot Burrito #1' (which he recorded with Olson on *So Rebellious A Lover*) was one of his favourite songs. He also admitted that 'Some Misunderstanding' had been partly inspired by Parsons' tragic death.

Despite everything, Clark still believed that he could win back the approval of his fellow original Byrds. Their interaction had always been unpredictable. If there was a good reason, they could put aside their differences at any given moment. Back in 1977, McGuinn, Clark and Hillman were barely talking to each other on a UK visit yet, within a few months, they were working together on a new project. Conflict seemed as likely to bring them together as would friendship, so it was not too perverse to assume that bad boy Michael Clarke and the exiled Gene might yet conjure a reconciliation with the other three. The stage for such a powwow was set when it was confirmed that the Byrds were to be inducted into the Rock 'n' Roll Hall of Fame early in the New Year.

It was at this point that Clark's battle with booze and drugs took a sinister direction. In November 1990, he was determined to purge the old demons once and for all. "I took him to my parents' house in Mammoth in mid-November and we were going to stay there, then come back for Christmas," Terri Messina remembers. "Mammoth is a real popular Californian ski resort, a beautiful place, and Gene loved it there, always did. So we went up there to get him straight. He didn't want to go into rehab and said he could do it on his own, so I suggested why not go up there for six weeks? We went to great lengths to make arrangements. The car was filled with all kinds of stuff because he wanted to bring recording equipment and guitars. We brought our bicycles so that we could go riding. We were going to ride our bikes, write his music and clean up."

The vacation began promisingly but, three weeks in, the idyll turned into a nightmare. "I woke in the middle of the night," Terri remembers, "and he was drunk out of his mind." While prowling the house, Gene had raided her parents' drinks cabinet and was consuming its contents with voracious abandon. "He got totally drunk and he was scary," confesses Terri, who was concerned for her own safety. "He'd get scary when he was like that. It was a nightmare night and the next day, it was all, 'No, I won't do it again, I'm sorry I did it.' It was the same old story we went through umpteen times. I went through another week of this back and forth and he was getting drunk, and then he wasn't. Then I threw the towel in and said, 'I can't take this any more. I have to get out of here. I'm going to LA. I'm going back to my house, you go back to your house and that's it. When you decide that you really want to give this up then I'll be back to live with you.'"

As a parting gesture, Clark accidentally left the water supply on, causing the pipes to burst and flooding the place. Messina's parents were not amused when the bill arrived. Terri was still haunted by Gene's latest outburst. "I went through the whole Christmas with him being totally fucked up to the max. That's when I really thought he was going to die."

Having retreated to her parents' house in Northridge, Terri was fearful of returning to Sherman Oaks. "I had to remove myself. It wasn't just because of his using. It was mostly because of the violence. Gene became abusive."

"Terri was scared for her life at times," says Sharon Brooks. "She was scared of getting hurt under those circumstances. It wasn't always that way, but she had that fear. I don't blame her. Terri was feisty, but she was only a little thing."

Few felt remorse with such conviction as Clark who knew that his verbal assaults might always end in something more physical.

Before leaving Mammoth, he made one final attempt to confront his problems by seeking spiritual salvation. He later told Slocum that he'd achieved a mescaline high and trudged up the snowy slopes to "have a word with the Big Man". He returned with one of the most extraordinary compositions of his career, a song for the ages, whose origin was steeped in mystery. 'Communications' is a timeless work; even its date and place of creation have been disputed. The song combines metaphysical speculations on the nature of angels with alien visitations, reflections on the prophets through the ages and other apocalyptical musings. It remains the ultimate Gene Clark 'cosmic consciousness' composition, a trail that had been left cold since the glory days of *No Other*. 'Communications' works on various levels. "Communicators need receivers" Clark asserts, indicating a symbiotic link between human and extra-terrestrial life. But the notion goes further than that. Oliver Lodge, the renowned physicist and member of the Royal Institution, wrote extensively about 'communications' which were translated by psychic 'operators'. In this new spiritual world, scientific and technological parlance employed terms such as 'frequencies', 'receivers' and 'receptions'. Clark achieves something similar here, transforming 'halos' into the ghostly auras of alien beings and Christ himself into an advanced cosmonaut or something similar, yet more powerful. The cosmological landscape resembles that of *No Other*, in which the naturalistic was replaced by visions of fiery rain and 'ruby's cooling sun', the setting evidently located on the 'cosmic range'. This was the eerie plain to which Clark was returning after years of underperforming. The extraordinary 'Communications' heralded a new beginning, but the darker side of Clark's personality threatened to blight all that might still be achieved.

After his binge at Mammoth and the fatal fall-out with Terri, Gene was momentarily shocked into sobriety. Alone in his room, he looked through a long list of telephone numbers in search of an empathetic listener. It was purely random. He could have called anyone. Who knows how many people he attempted to reach in his desperation? He remembered one person – Jon Corneal, from the Dillard & Clark days – whom he'd heard had 'found' religion. Perhaps he might listen. "We'd been out of touch for 20 years," Corneal says, "and somehow he got in contact again after so long. People knew I'd never changed my phone number, ever. It happened to be a time when he was just on the wagon. I asked him what had happened and he said he went up a mountain and looked at the top. He didn't tell me that he went up there to jump off but I kind of read between the lines that this might have been the case. When he got out there he yelled at God and said, 'God, if you're real just show me something. Do something. Just to show me you're real.' He said a wind came up and blew him back down the mountain. In other words he couldn't stay there any longer and he couldn't jump off either. He didn't speak those [exact] words to me but I read what he was saying. We even talked about doing a project together, half his songs and half my songs. He sounded good, man. He really did. He told me he loved to hear [television evangelist] Tammy Faye Bakker sing. He loved her. He said, 'Man, the way she cries is so real.' He'd watched *The PTL Club* at one point. I kind of identified with that because, when I sobered up, I watched it every night too."

It's probable Clark was telling Corneal precisely what he knew he would love to hear, but clearly he was reaching out at a time of spiritual crisis. "I'd heard he'd got a cheque for 400 grand [sic] or something for Tom Petty's cut on 'Feel A Whole Lot Better' and then he'd gone nuts. But he sounded good, man. I was so encouraged by him that I started growing my hair long again. And I haven't stopped since then. I've a long braid that goes right down to the crack of my butt. I look like a rock 'n' roller again!"

Apart from inspiring hair growth, Clark was newly determined to win back his lost love. Terri Messina had almost despaired of Gene during the festive period, but was amazed to receive a call early in the New Year confirming that he was genuinely sober. Although she was sceptical, Gene was so earnest that there was no denying his sincerity. "All of a sudden, he called me after the first of the year and said, 'That's it, I'm all over it, I'm not doing it anymore.' He went on and on and said, 'We're going to New York to the Hall of Fame.' God bless him, he cleaned himself up to go to the Hall of Fame. We went and we had a good time and he was totally clean." It was evident that Gene was employing the awards ceremony as a vehicle to effect a reconciliation between himself and Terri, not to mention with the other four Byrds. "She went with him, but only because Gene begged her to," Carla Olson claims. "He was going to take an actress [Rita Romero] he was seeing and then he called Terri and said, 'Honey, I've cleaned up. Will you come with me and be by my side?'"

The Byrds' induction to the Rock 'n' Roll Hall of Fame on 16 January 1991 proved an eventful evening. As if mocking this organized celebration of camaraderie, the fates decreed that the outbreak of the Gulf War should begin while the Byrds sat uneasily around a table. The downbeat mood of the evening did not entirely disguise the subtle bridge-building that was taking place as the five men faced each other for the first time in who knew when. Crosby played the mediator with the inebriated Michael Clarke, offering him some free advice on AA meetings, just as he had done with Gene some time before. Michael became so caught up in mea culpa magnanimity that he even promised to cease using the Byrds' name, a vow which would be forgotten after he'd sobered up. Gene seemed happy to be part of the occasion and no doubt relieved that he could still share a pleasant evening with old friends. There was, at least for the moment, a restoration of harmony in the face of a long and bitter history, and for that everyone was thankful. In his acceptance speech, Clark emphasized this feeling of concord. "I think, for myself, gratitude is the main thing," he began. "I've got to be really thankful to the people in my life who have supported me through the years, through my good and bad, and especially my brothers who are onstage with me and who I've enjoyed playing with more than anything else in the whole world. And especially to my beautiful lady, Terri, who has been the most support to me in my whole life. Thank you very much, and I'm proud to be here." The last song that the five Byrds played onstage was Clark's 'Feel A Whole Lot Better'. It was a title more ironic and inappropriate than anyone could have guessed.

In the aftermath of the Rock 'n' Roll Hall of Fame celebration, Clark was living dangerously. Increasingly reckless, he fell off his motorcycle one night, damaging several teeth in the process. The accident brought an unexpected chill to the new recordings that he was working on.

In February, Clark indicated a desire to push forward on a new project with Garth Beckington, who duly contacted Jon Faurot, the bassist whom they had worked with in Laurel Canyon during the late Seventies. The last time Faurot had seen Clark, he looked fit and athletic but, a decade later, the vision he encountered in Sherman Oaks was skeletal by comparison. "He looked really bad, like a junkie. I thought he had AIDS or something. He had sores on him. I think he'd been smoking a lot of crack or had been doing coke. He looked terrible which implied to me that he wasn't eating. I was totally shocked because he looked really different."

Once Faurot adjusted to Clark's new look, he realized that beneath the rough exterior was a still keen mind ready to work. "He actually had a battle plan. The Rock 'n' Roll Hall of Fame had inducted the Byrds and there was a window of opportunity in his mind to cash in on that and push his career forward. That was in his head somehow. There was a two-month period where Garth would get me and we'd go over to Gene's house and play. We played song after song and it was a lot of fun and I really learned a lot about songwriting that I didn't know. Sitting there at his kitchen table was the most fun Garth and I ever had. We'd cut stuff, go back and cut it again. He was writing a lot during that period."

When concentrating on his songwriting, Clark stayed sober and straight and surviving tapes suggest that he was lucid when in the grip of the muse. Sometimes the action shifted to Garth and Hillary's home, where there was a surprise collaboration with

Brendan Early, a former member of San Franciscan punk band, the Mutants. "Brendan was working on songs too," Faurot recalls. "If Gene liked your song, he'd jump on it."

Clark also worked alone, singing into a tape recorder in his kitchen, his vocals ravaged by smoking and his diction compromised by gum disease and tooth loss. What emerged were some of the most deeply personal and painful songs of his career. 'Pledge To You' is an eerie performance laced with apocalyptic warnings, similar in tone to the epic 'Communications'. Here was Clark at his rawest, speaking of the world ending without warning and using this imaginary Armageddon as a metaphor for his own sense of spiritual and emotional loss. For those who profess to love Clark's cosmic cowboy musings then this was very special. A fascinating fusion of the personal and the metaphysical, the song displays both Clark's rockabilly roots and his post-Dylan singer-songwriter persona. The vocal sounds oddly reminiscent of Roy Orbison and the melody is entrancing, with some meandering guitar work that adds depth to the composition. At once a song of loss and renewal, it unfolds like a last will and testament, the mood unexpectedly enhanced by the ghostly vocal with words seemingly filtered through a toothless mouth.

Clark's dental problems are also evident on the impressive 'Mississippi Detention Camp', in which he revisits his beloved fictional muse Mary Sue and returns to the childhood dreams of 'Kansas City Southern'. Far from presenting a problem, his gummy vocal invests the composition with a frightening poignancy and wistfulness as he relates a story of regret, imprisonment and the tragedy of lost times and dreams unrealized. A bank robbery goes fatally wrong for some youngsters who end up in a Mississippi detention camp. Forced to leave Mary Sue behind in Kansas, the narrator reflects on all that has been lost, but his nostalgia is a potent weapon. The song conjures prison imagery reminiscent of *Cool Hand Luke*, with Clark in the Paul Newman role. An uncredited guitarist, possibly Beckington, offers some strong accompaniment which neatly complements the bluesy lament.

On other tapes recorded late at night, Clark directly confronts his fracturing relationship with Terri Messina, who was still staying at her parents' house, too wary to be drawn back into this nightmarish psychodrama. "For the last few months of his life he was so totally abusing himself that I had to move out. When he had too much alcohol, he became violent. But we never broke up. I wasn't living with him but I was on the phone every day, trying to get him help, trying to work something out with him. But I couldn't stay there while he was drinking . . . Hillary and Garth came back and, believe me when I tell you, it was nothing to do with them. A lot of people only know what they've been told, and they've been misled. I was aware the whole time that they were there. God knows they were no angels and they've got their own problems and were into their own trip. But it wasn't their influence that got him going."

Jason Ronard concurs. "Gene is going to go off when he's going to go off and it's really not much to do with anything. It has very little to do with people. He would just do everything, if he wanted . . . Gene was a drinker who did drugs, he wasn't a drug addict who drank. In other words, after a few vodkas if anybody put anything in front of him, he'd do it. It was the mountain man in him. He never started out taking a snort and then drinking. He'd drink first and that would get him into it. He smoked a packet of non-filtered Camels and a pack of Marlboros every single day since I'd known him." Ronard was also concerned about his aspirin intake. "I said, 'Gene, that's no good for the stomach you have.' He just smiled at me for being concerned. Many times I tried to get him into detox but you cannot grab this man and put him in a car because he'll kick the shit out of you. He's a grown man, he's got to give his consent. You just couldn't help this guy. I couldn't help him and he couldn't help himself."

Ronard recalls one eventful evening when they set off in Gene's old Cadillac to see a show featuring Leon Russell. "Gene was already in very bad shape then. He pulled the glove department box down and poured out a mountain of heroin and cocaine and started hitting back off each mountain. I couldn't believe it."

Later, Jason told Garth Beckington: "Man, my buddy here's only got about six months to live."

Ronard's account sounds exaggerated, but Clark's lapses into drink and drug abuse had a worryingly cyclical character and Messina's continued absence spoke volumes. "When I'd go down, they were seeing each other, but they weren't living together," adds Hillary. "I really couldn't get a handle on what was going on, but Gene still wanted to live with her when she was with her parents. I thought at the end that they were going to get back together. I felt it was only a matter of time before they got married, really. Gene adored her and he wanted to marry her. He really needed that kind of stability with her, and I think he would have done what she wanted him to do. Gene was not a drugs seeker. They were either there or they were not. I've got to say quite honestly sometimes it was because people were pushing them on him. They were bringing them around or something, which happens a lot in the business."

Messina maintained her distance, but was seldom quiet about those whom she considered negative influences in Clark's life. Like so many other characters in this story, she was quick to judge associates, who fell in and out of favour. One such was Jason Ronard whose on/off drinking she now regarded as detrimental to Gene's progress. "He was one of the worse influences," she claims, no doubt with extreme prejudice. "He'd gone into AA and was clean for a long time and then he relapsed. So the two of them were getting screwed up together at times." Ronard's opinion of her antics over the years was no better, of course. It was another example of the lack of empathy between so many involved in Clark's circle. Such schisms would grow in succeeding years.

Gene's psychic pain at least worked to his artistic advantage. Transforming romantic hurt into song had always provided the perfect panacea. When he wasn't pleading remorse or offering pledges in song, Clark could turn momentarily vindictive, just as he had done on 'Feel A Whole Lot Better'. He went through an entire alphabet of emotions dealing with Terri Messina, including a grim humour that made his latest batch of songs even more powerful. 'Battle Of The Sexes' sounds like an Elvis lamentation from the Sun period with a fast strumming guitar and the hope that the crisis might be just a "false alarm".

'Adios Terri' is more oblique and seemingly impromptu. Adopting a toothless blues, he boasts, "I'm your old stray cat" then asks about her chateau before moving into some incongruous reflections on the Iraqi War and how 'the American Indian boys' encountered problems when entering the desert. There's a passing allusion to Ezekiel's Wheel, after which he concludes with the teasing rejoinder: "All I know it's going to be one hell of a divorce."

'Big Bad Mama' has a feral quality, commencing with a howl of anguish as he confronts his losses with a chilling, accusative tone. The effect is heightened by the strong rhythm guitar leading to a neat bridge, presumably the work of Garth Beckington. Throughout the song, Clark sounds like an old man. His gum disease makes the composition even spookier. There's an aggression in his repeated question, "What is this I smell on you?" as if he is an animal sniffing out infidelity. He even offers a sardonic answer, "You're gonna tell me that it's sugar and spice?" His accusations could easily be interpreted as a transference of his own transgressions. While all this appears like the songwriting equivalent of Dylan's 'divorce album' *Blood On The Tracks*, it is always questionable to place a reductive autobiographical interpretation on such confessional material. "So you gotta go score," Gene chides, a possible reference to Messina's or Carlie's past exploits. Of course, the words could equally apply to himself. Parts of the song story also invite memories of that terrible time when he broke up with Carlie, whom he believed had planned to run off with a rival. Indeed, the big bad mama is sometimes referred to as a 'blonde' or 'blind' mama' with "kids on the lawn". Perhaps acknowledging those fears that he had while away on tour, he asks, "Where you been while I'm gone?" Even the tears in her eyes prompt him to wonder what kind of love she is trying to disguise. In the end, he accuses his lover of laying down her armour and moving away. She is portrayed as having fallen under some spell, prompting the unanswerable question, "Where did we go wrong?" There is a dramatic finality in a concluding reference, which could be applied to either of the two female loves of his life: "She never came home." Such words transcend any autobiographical interpretation to hint at an existential loss. Clark's ability to turn heartache into drama has seldom been bettered, not least because this is not merely some lamentation of love lost but a song of mixed emotions, in which pain, sarcasm and dark humour are poignantly entwined.

If Clark was poised to complete a work of substance, it was all the more tragic that such work was never recorded in a professional studio. Worse was the realization that he might not live long enough to complete such a suite of songs. Fearing for Clark's well-being, Messina turned to his brother Rick, who agreed to visit Sherman Oaks. He was shocked by his brother's physical state and severe weight loss. His initial instinct was to take him to hospital, but the intervention was not welcomed by Gene and harsh words were spoken. Precisely what happened is conjectural, but it was enough to alienate Rick who, some say, did not see his brother alive again. Subsequently, Rick voiced resentment about various figures in Clark's circle. "He wanted to take a baseball bat to some people," Slocum says. Slocum was also critical, specifically targeting his old friend Garth Beckington as a negative influence. "Rick holds the same opinion I do, not to say echo it. People that were close to Gene didn't like Garth. There's still a lot of anger around. A lot of people think Garth was funding whatever bad shit was going down. Gene's family were very pissed off."

Such opinions were disputed by the Beckingtons and other less partisan observers. "It was just the opposite," argues Hillary, in sterling defence of her husband, who was understandably upset by the allegation. "Garth would play music with him but if Gene did stuff, Garth would leave because he knew it would throw Gene off [musically]. Gene would get very uptight and agitated. If you want to play music, that wasn't the place to go . . . Rick knows how far back we go. He ended up estranged from his brother and we never saw him much after that. Maybe that was part of it. I always thought Rick was a sweet character but he definitely had issues being Gene's brother. He was a musician too, but he wasn't Gene Clark." According to others, Clark's coke supply was provided by "a dealer in the Valley", evidence enough of his ability to procure drugs from multiple sources. He always had a lot of connections.

David Clark also attempted some tough love intervention from afar after receiving reports of his brother's state. "People were calling me and saying, 'He's killing himself!' I said, 'He's been through this before.' When I talked to him, I said, 'You are better than this bullshit. Get your head out of your ass and clean up.' He'd done it before half a dozen times that I knew of."

Complicating matters was the strange tale of Clark's throat problems. Plagued by a persistent cough, he visited a doctor and was told that he had a growth on his vocal cords. Unfortunately, there is no written evidence available about his condition, nor any indication whether it was benign or serious. Several people have mentioned hearing the news, which did not emerge publicly until long after his death. How many of these friends learned of it from Gene, rather than as repeated rumour, is debatable. Slocum, who recalls accompanying Clark to see his doctor, remembers him emerging from the surgery and immediately phoning Terri. Supposedly, he had been diagnosed with 'throat cancer'. Oddly, Messina never mentioned hearing *anything* about the matter, even when systematically listing all the possible reasons why he fell back into hard drinking and drug abuse. "She would have been the first to be told," says Hillary who, significantly, was also unaware of any such diagnosis. "I never heard anything about it," she insists. When questioned, several other close friends admit that they knew nothing of the 'cancer' or anything similar. It only became part of certain people's narratives when retrospectively hearing the claims years after his death. Andy Kandanes believes that the stories may have been exaggerated, a view echoed by Shannon O' Neill. "Slocum told *me*," O'Neill recalls. "But that was when Gene died. You know, I don't think it's true. I don't think it was documented and Gene never said anything about it. Slocum was the one who'd taken care of him, and would take him to the hospital. I think Gene probably said to Slocum, 'Man, I've probably got throat cancer' or something. Knowing Tom, he could have taken it out of context. 'Oh, the doctors think he has cancer' and he may have said something to Carla or someone else and the next thing it could have come back to Slocum who then thinks 'I knew it', when it might have been unintentionally of his own doing."

"I don't know if the throat cancer is real or not," adds John York, "but I do think that the influence of former drug buddies was there and that would have added a little spice."

Whether Clark had a laryngoscopy is again undocumented, but if he went to a doctor, it seems likely. Hillary believes he probably had a nodule, a common enough condition for singers or those who over-use their voices such as actors, teachers, drill instructors and public speakers. Tellingly, Hillary's ex-husband Tommy Kaye, one of Clark's closest friends, is the sole person who went on record in 1991 claiming that Gene had "throat cancer . . . a polyp on his vocal cords". A polyp is a larger growth than a nodule, but also generally non-cancerous. The symptoms are a rough voice and hoarseness, usually made worse by smoking. Clark was a prime candidate. Surgical intervention is rarely necessary in treating polyps or nodules. Usually, medical intervention to control stress and stop smoking is the preferred treatment, aided by therapy to avoid abusing the vocal cords by singing or speaking too loudly. Even in those rare cases where surgery is deemed necessary (usually because the polyp is too large) the most likely negative result would be a failure to sustain notes.

Carla Olson, for one, insists that Clark was never concerned about his mortality and claims his only fear might have been that any treatment could have affected his voice or singing style. "A singer with a voice like that?" Jason Ronard considers, "and he has throat cancer?" Such concerns were echoed by Kelly Clark, who was equally vague about his father's diagnosis. "Throat cancer or not, something was very awesome . . . I think he was just scared. I would be scared. I quit smoking because I don't want to have throat cancer. He smoked a lot. I think he was worried that he was going to survive but couldn't sing any more. And then what do you do? I don't know what kind of pain he was in; I don't know what medication they were giving him."

Revealingly, the psychological trauma resulting from the diagnosis of a polyp often has a profound effect on those whose livelihood or self-worth depend on the quality of their vocal tone. Some friends and family members maintain that the mislabelled 'throat cancer' probably exacerbated Clark's increasingly reckless behaviour. This would be consistent with the psychological effects of a diagnosis for a nodule or polyp. In other words, Clark may never have been in mortal danger, but the fear of surgery, itself very unlikely, could well have been enough to push him over the edge.

Other factors no doubt played a part. "They all wanted a piece of his ass," says Kandanes. "I'd get a call out of the blue and he'd say, 'Hey, what's going on?' He was doing some stuff [drugs]. It was a shame to see him slide down that far. He had some issues getting older. Gene was definitely a vain person. From my conversations with him, I could tell that he had a hard time with the ageing issue. He was always trying to work out how to stay young. I said, 'Hey, man, age gracefully brother, it's going to happen whether you like it or not.' I think he was just really depressed."

There was still a coterie of drinkers or users guaranteed to appeal to Clark's intemperate side. Throughout his life, part of him had enjoyed the story-book rock 'n' roll lifestyle, fraternizing with Hollywood bad boys. In addition, there were the passing strangers, hangers-on and recreational users who might infrequently appear at his door. It was not the ideal environment in which to conquer addiction and he was increasingly tempted. Terri became concerned when Gene admitted during one phone call that he was indulging in crack cocaine. Even she was shocked by that admission. But there was nothing that she could do to prevent his slide. "She knew some of those people," Slocum notes, "but she couldn't be around that thing, otherwise she'd end up like them." By this time, Slocum himself was wary of spending too much time in Sherman Oaks. "In the middle of the night, there'd be people coming and going and a few times I just bailed out and said, 'See you later' because it was getting way beyond my depth of tolerance. It got really weird."

Kelly Clark arrived unexpectedly one afternoon to retrieve some of his belongings from a previous visit. His father was asleep on a couch, clearly the worse for wear after a late-night drinking session. "He would party super hard, then realize 'I'm going to die' and he'd pull it together for a few days. Then someone would come over and it would be on again. I went down to see him while he was pretty messed up and stayed for about five hours. I took him to a liquor store; he bought enough liquor to last a family a week. He chugged a bunch of wine and threw up for about 20 minutes. Then I split."

Clark's rock 'n' roll fantasies were rekindled by an invitation to play a series of shows at the Cinegrill in the Roosevelt Hotel during April. He was excited by the prospect and had even compiled an imaginary guest list which included Bob Dylan, Jackson Browne, Roger McGuinn, Tom Petty, Don Henley, Bruce Springsteen, John David Souther, Bonnie Raitt, Madonna, Levon Helm, Rick Danko, Linda Ronstadt, David Crosby, Paul Simon, Herb Alpert, Tracy Chapman, Whoopi Goldberg, Steve Edwards, Dan Haggerty, Jack Nicholson, Dennis Hopper, Neil Young, Graham Nash, Jay Leno, Arsenio Hall and Christopher Walken. On the phone, he sounded simultaneously proud and starstruck. There was an almost childlike effusion as he reeled off the illustrious names in the above order. "I sent a special invitation to *all* those people," he said. "They're friends of mine. I'm going to do a star-studded opening."

In preparation for the shows, Clark continued working with Garth Beckington and Jon Faurot and recruited drummer Rick Shlosser, a colleague of Thomas Jefferson Kaye, who had previously worked with several major artistes, including Van Morrison and James Taylor. Shlosser suggested they complete the line-up with jazz pianist Stuart Elster. While Gene dreamed of a grand comeback, the prospect of another sudden rush of fame went to his head. More wild nights followed, culminating in a car crash on a Hollywood street in which he lost several teeth after smashing his head against the dashboard. "He'd already wrecked a motorcycle," Hillary reminds us, "and now he was losing his teeth. We tried to get him not to drive. We were following right behind him. It was amazing he didn't get arrested. Gene didn't handle liquor well. You could try and tell him he'd had enough and he wouldn't listen. 'I'm fine, I can drive.' We might have been able to avoid that but how do you take the keys away from somebody like him?"

Clark's timing could hardly have been worse. In addition to the Roosevelt date, he was scheduled to re-record 'Silver Raven' for possible use on a film soundtrack. The recording, if it was ever completed, was never used. The damage to his mouth was again affecting his vocal. "Gene was a man of many connections," Garth Beckington wryly notes. "He found a dentist over the weekend and got a quick pair of chompers. He ended up taking them out, almost right away." A combination of coke and booze eased the tension and lingering pain from the car crash and dental work, but left him feeling vulnerable. He continued working privately at his home but was puzzled when some tapes went missing. He seemed unsure whether they were mislaid, borrowed, given away or stolen. Slocum recalls him complaining on the phone, "Hey, man, I don't know where my tapes have gone." One song still missing from those sessions is 'San Francisco'. "I don't know what happened to that tape," Slocum says. "It was one of those convoluted things about remembering the Beatles and the Jefferson Airplane and the president."

Despite his parlous state, Clark was still eager to promote the Cinegrill shows at the Roosevelt. With its Hollywood history as a former haunt of movie stars, it had the same glamour as Ciro's in Clark's mind. An interview was arranged with Paul Zollo of *Song Talk*, but it proved a troubled encounter. "He didn't look good,"

Zollo observed. "Extremely gaunt, his weathered face had been badly fractured in a recent car crash, a few front teeth were missing, and his left ear was bandaged à la Van Gogh." Clark ate a steak, drank copious cups of coffee, then suffered a coughing fit which forced him to terminate the interview.

Nevertheless he was engagingly upbeat about the future. "I'm going to record a new solo album. I've got about four dozen beautiful unreleased songs. It's gonna be a great year for me." In a clever piece of political spin, he blamed his wretched state on the exigencies of art. Evidently, his muse was a harsh mistress. "That's why I'm tired today. I get this great streak going and I can't stop. I write all the time. I write constantly. I have so much material that I could never record it all. Writing is total sacrifice. People ask me what it takes to have the kind of reputation I have. I tell them total sacrifice. It's like being a ballet dancer. If you want to do it, you do it 100 per cent. If you don't do it that way you'll never get there. You have to give up a lot . . . So I start a solo album next month. I'm also going to do a tour, and probably another album with Carla."

The portents for the Cinegrill shows were not good. Clark and the band had been rehearsing at the Alley in North Hollywood when an old friend intervened at an inopportune moment. Back in 1964, when Clark and McGuinn first met at the Troubadour, only a few people appreciated their idea of forming a duo, influenced by Peter And Gordon and the Beatles. Among their keener supporters was Hoyt Axton, who had previously worked with McGuinn and whose song 'Willie Gene' was once part of David Crosby's solo repertoire. Like so many others from that time, Axton had become a serious drug addict, famously articulating his experiences in one of his most famous compositions, Steppenwolf's 'The Pusher'. Now he was about to enact the title of that very song, unintentionally setting in motion the final descending spiral of Clark's career. "Hoyt Axton was upstairs," Jon Faurot remembers, "and he had some dope with him. He gave Gene a bump of heroin – and that was it." Prior to Axton's arrival, the musicians felt that the rehearsals had been productive.

Gene was still straight and seemed "really together". After that, he started to unravel.

As ever, there were still moments of clarity and expressions of regret. Feeling conciliatory, Gene phoned his brother Rick and apologized for their recent falling out. It broke the ice, but not deeply enough for Rick to attend the forthcoming shows. He still felt Gene was hanging around with the wrong people and endangering himself. Ever remorseful and eager to impress, Gene also phoned Terri in Mammoth and invited her to his opening night. "He knew only to call me when he was sober, otherwise I'd freak out," Messina says. "I talked to him right before the Cinegrill and I was to come down, meet him and stay with him at the Roosevelt. I called the day I was leaving Mammoth, and he was all fucked up. So I said, 'No way.' Then I started calling other people and asked, 'Have you been around? What's he doing? What's going on?' I found out that he'd been drinking and he was an absolute mess. I said, 'And he's going on at the Cinegrill?! I don't even want to be there and see that.' I heard his hair wasn't washed and he looked terrible. He looked like he'd been up for days and hadn't taken a shower."

Clark's sudden physical decline was most uncharacteristic. He had always been well-groomed, kept his house in immaculate condition and, despite his excesses, usually played a great show and was not known for turning up loaded. Any madness usually followed the performance. The heroin hit, followed by a new bout of excessive drinking, was clearly taking its toll.

Just before the Cinegrill opening, Clark agreed to be interviewed for a radio show in Pasadena City College, the third largest community college in America. The location of the radio station proved a mystery to Clark, despite the presence of Faurot, who lived in the area. Gene had hired a luxurious Lincoln Town car for the occasion, which was not a good omen. Beckington, Faurot and Slocum agreed to accompany him in the vehicle on what sounded like the wildest ride of their lives. "Gene thought he was Steve McQueen," Faurot says. "He was driving, and it was like the chase scene in one of McQueen's films. Some poor old lady was flashing her lights at him and honking her horn. Slocum and I were like little kids at the back, holding on to each other's arms. We were scared. Garth was playing it cool in the front. If you let on to Gene you were scared then he'd really go for it." Having failed to find the radio station, Clark decided to rush back to Hollywood for further fun. Somehow they got back in one piece, then "went to some restaurant on Ventura Boulevard". Faurot was still recovering from the drive. "I was trying to pour a cup of coffee and I was shaking. It was pretty rough to spend a lot of time with Gene, especially in a car. It was weird." The three passengers eventually excused themselves and took a cab home.

Clark was keen to continue partying but somehow ended the night under arrest and languishing in jail. "Somebody got him out, or he got himself out," says Faurot. "He knew the cops. He had connection lines going all over the place. The next night he installed himself at the Roosevelt. Boy, those people didn't know what they were getting."

Garth Beckington was amused when Clark turned up wearing a rented "blue-tailed coat" with blue jeans. "I don't know what that was all about. It was just something he had in mind. He was determined to do that gig. He was really optimistic and thought he was knocking the dominoes over there. It wasn't that well attended because it was spread over several nights, but I thought it was a good gig and there was a projected European tour some weeks later."

Several old friends turned up for the shows, though there were few, if any, from Clark's superstar guest list. Many were embarrassed and saddened by the spectacle. "I had a gig the first night and couldn't make it," says Carla Olson. "So we went the second night and he was blotto by then. But he was so apologetic about it. At the end of one of the songs he couldn't remember the words and just started rambling." In the break between sets, Olson made a guest appearance. "When I was leaving the stage he put a sloppy arm around me. Then he gave me a big, wet kiss on the cheek and said, 'I love you, Carla.' I said, 'I love you too, Gene.'"

Watching his decline provided a lesson about the perils of seeking fame. "You can see the really talented people have no sense at all," Carla sighs. "Mediocre people, like me, have a regular job and feel responsible, but I'm not Gene Clark. Gene never held a job in his life. Never."

When Terri Messina heard reports that Clark was a mess, she was appalled. "I can't tell you how many sacrifices I made in my life to be with Gene Clark, and after having made a lot of those sacrifices and then seeing him revert to that behaviour and do it publicly. It was bad enough when I knew about it and nobody saw it. But then to do it in public!"

Following the lead of Rick Clark, Tom Slocum attempted an intervention to save Gene from himself. He chose the wrong moment – not that there was ever a good moment. This resulted in a falling out with Garth and Hillary that was never resolved. "Slocum tried to stop the show at the Roosevelt," Hillary claims. "He told the manager Gene was drunk as a skunk and couldn't go on. We had to bring the manager up to see Gene who was sitting down eating a steak and totally fine. The manager said, 'What's wrong with this guy? Why is he trying to stop the show?' And Gene said, 'Who knows?!' I think we had him barred from the gig that night. Slocum was never really the same after that."

"There's a bitter enmity now with Garth and Hillary," adds Faurot. "Slocum had a way of kidding Gene about things. Things were said and done while he was around at the Cinegrill and it seemed to us he was stirring up shit. It's a little vague, but he would say provocative things." While aware of Slocum's good intentions, Terri remained sceptical about his comments on the Beckingtons. "God bless him, I appreciated Slocum. He was the one who took us to the airport and picked us up every time we came back from a tour. Who else can you rely on to do that? But he promoted a lot of stuff about Garth and Hillary in all of this. He liked to think of himself as Gene's best friend. When they came in and started hanging out with Gene, I believe he got jealous of them. There was all kinds of stuff. We could talk for hours about it."

Slocum saw things differently. He felt protective, not jealous. He remembers one meeting when he simply advised Gene not to travel down that road of excess again, fearing, perhaps, that his body or psyche might no longer be able to handle the effects. Rick Clark evidently had similar reservations. For all his bravado, Gene was still suffering residual pain from his stomach operation. He had never taken good enough care of himself, despite doctor's orders. Slocum was offended and hurt by what he had witnessed at the Cinegrill and continued to voice concern for his friend whose decline had never been displayed so conspicuously to any audience. "He was my friend and I loved and cared about him. There was a lot of good that he did and some stuff that was negative, but the good far outweighed it."

What demons Clark had to contend with remains debatable. There was no doubt that he was still in the severe grip of alcoholism and the recent episode with Hoyt Axton, which accelerated his excesses, suggested a continued flirtation with heroin. However, Faurot maintains that such instances were occasional at worst. "I don't think heroin had any bearing. I don't think anyone was giving Gene heroin [apart from the Axton incident]. I don't think Gene was a heroin user. Certainly, I don't believe Garth was giving him it. I'm sure that's not true. I was with Garth almost all of the time I was with Gene. I know Garth and I know all about Garth. They'd been friends for a long time. There were other issues with crack but Gene got that from somebody else and we're moving through different time periods. I smoked pot. I'd given up drinking six months before and that was the first time I'd really played since then and I felt great . . . I've used cocaine but heroin was not my thing. Garth had always gone out of his way to shield me from that stuff because I'm younger than he is, and he's always been very judicious about keeping me away from that scene. Also I was not aware of any partying. If that was true I wasn't included. So I don't know anything about it . . . But Gene was a grown man; he was a big boy."

* * *

As documented in *Volume 1*, the Cinegrill shows were not without merit. Although Clark was capable of wandering offstage when the whim took him and sometimes singing in a slurred whisper, he could entrance the audience with powerfully emotive readings of 'Here Without You' or the startling 'Your Fire Burning'. Photographer Harold Sherrick, who was involved in filming one of the nights, was moved by the performance. "Gene was mildly intoxicated. He'd been drinking for three days before that. He was on that downward spiral because he was sick, and people didn't know it. Nevertheless, if you saw the film with 'Chimes Of Freedom', it was like he was crying out for help. He looked so tired and worn out and the song took on a whole new meaning. It was amazing – in a sad way. There were some touching, emotional moments."

Chief among them was the surprise appearance of Gene's younger son, Kai. Garth, in an admirable act of kindness, had phoned a mutual friend, William 'Billy' Watson, who was acting as the youth's mentor in Mendocino. "He was a friend of my mom," Kai says. "She was pretty heavily into drugs and Billy would take care of us. Kelly had moved out and I stayed on. I'd watch after Indiana, my sister, who was from a different father. It was a wild time." Watson was unable to attend the shows, but agreed that it would be a wonderful trip for Kai. "Billy threw me on a plane and there I was at the Cinegrill. It was a bittersweet experience – the first and only show I ever saw my dad play. I wasn't old enough to sit in the bar area so had to stay in the sound-booth. The first night was decent. He sounded OK. The second night was rough. I think he threw a cigarette into the crowd. I could tell people were put off a little bit. Dad was known for his antics. Some of the shows he was really on, but I heard others weren't so good."

"He would be toasted by the end of the show," adds Faurot. "People were saying, 'What's going on with Gene?' He looked bad and it didn't come off too well, but sometimes it did. Somehow it all made sense. Then he'd re-live the whole thing and people like David Carradine would hang out. Even Claudia showed up one night. It was a scene."

The presence of Hillary's mother, who was accompanied by an attorney who had connections with the Getty family, was a thrill to savour. All that was missing was the ghost of the late John Wayne. "Garth serenaded them into the night," Hillary adds. "He and Gene would jam and play songs they intended to record. They were still doing Gordon Lightfoot's 'If You Could Read My Mind' in rehearsal. They both loved that song."

Kai was thrilled when his father praised his guitar playing. "Look at him, he's learning," Gene told his entourage at the Roosevelt Hotel. "I was tuning a guitar harmonically and Dad thought that was impressive because he always tuned by ear. He could tune a guitar just by the sound of the strings whereas most people would need a tuner." The Cinegrill visit provided Kai with a memory to be treasured.

Clark's life was increasingly resembling a morality play full of ambiguous characters, actors, musicians, high-rollers, society swells, twilight junkies and would-be saviours. Despite his protestations of sobriety, Clark's addictive traits were more pronounced than ever. Wild swings of reform and relapse characterized his personality hereafter. A late entrant to this scenario was Karen Johnson, a publicist and artistes' relations officer at the label Private Music with AA credentials. Gene valued having somebody around to try and keep him straight and Johnson took that role very seriously. She boosted Clark's spirits by inviting Private Music signing Taj Mahal to the Cinegrill and overseeing a photo session with them after the show.

Initially, Terri was pleased to have a good angel visiting Sherman Oaks, but she later became wary of Johnson's motives. "Karen came on the scene in the last six weeks of Gene's life. I wasn't there but I was talking to him on the phone every day. I was desperately trying to get him to check in somewhere. I didn't think he could do it on his own any more. Gene thought he could still do that but he was too far gone. I told him, 'I think you really should get professional help this time and clean up.' Then he started saying, 'Well I know this girl who knows people in AA and she's coming over and talking to me all the time.' "

Gene felt an alcoholic's ambivalence towards Karen Johnson, depending upon his need and mood. Pat Robinson recalls him hissing, "Get rid of her!" on more than one occasion. "She was trying to keep him from drinking and he really resented that. He would joke with me about getting this girl out. It was like they were holding a watch over him."

Clark also told Pat and Terri that he suspected Johnson had romantic designs on him. He even claimed that they'd shared a bed. "She was trying to straighten him out and help him," recalls Shannon O'Neill. "He told me one night, 'I think she's a succubus!' I said, 'Well, I feel most of the women I know are! I think I wake up every night soulless with a woman I thought I knew!' " Clark enjoyed making light of his plight and may even have used Johnson's solicitous presence as a means of goading Terri into angry indignation. Evidently, it worked. "He said, 'She crashed here the other night and she was in my bed.' He was telling *me* this!" Karen subsequently admitted as much in print but insisted their relationship was not sexual. Unsurprisingly, Clark's teasing revelation turned Terri against Karen and she advised Gene, in astringent terms, to find a more neutral counsellor. Sorting out Gene Clark was never likely to be easy, but Johnson seemed convinced that she could help him. Considering his surroundings and exotic friends, her efforts were likely to be quixotic at best.

"Karen felt she could have helped Gene if she'd met him two or three months before," adds Carla Olson. "But all of us feel that way. My father died of alcoholism at 63. The whole time I was working with Gene it was like looking at my father and [seeing] how he would make the transition from human to subhuman or dual personality. I always felt Saul and I should have done something more drastic, but then you take the chance of alienating the person and having them never trust you again."

Of course, by this time, Davis was a more distant presence, reduced to looking at Clark from afar. "While a lot of people had grown out of it, he was still susceptible to thinking it was still 1965, and hanging out and being a cutting edge rock 'n' roll cat or movie star in the fast car and the whole deal."

Despite the portents of doom at the Cinegrill, Gene cleaned himself up and promised to take stock of his future. His new friend Karen Johnson encouraged his sobriety even though, as Terri previously pointed out, she may have become too emotionally involved in his life. For a time all was well. Several people who saw him in the weeks after the Cinegrill show were pleased to find him coherent and seemingly back in control of his life. Alas, this was to prove deceptive as he oscillated unpredictably between sobriety and temptation. Pat Robinson witnessed the extremes of behaviour that characterized Clark's drinking. "He did almost bring it around. I would tell him that you've got to do it gradually. All of a sudden, he'd go from not doing a lot of physical work to putting together a baseball team. He'd show up with a glove and say, 'Come on, let's play baseball!' I'd say, 'Gene, we've got to take this easy here, we're not used to this.' I would worry when I'd see him do stuff like that because mentally he would think he could do anything."

During mid-May, Robinson visited Clark at Sherman Oaks and found him out the back feverishly working out with a basketball. He was still eager to record and was busy making home demos in order to maintain momentum. Karen Johnson was still hopeful that she could conclude a deal with Private Music and Gene seemed excited about the likelihood of recording a new album. His collaboration with Garth Beckington was also progressing and there was talk of more live shows. "We'd gotten these matching Washburn guitars and that was the plan," Beckington remembers. "He wanted to do a duet." Clark spoke about a world tour, including dates in Japan and Europe. Although this sounded fanciful to some, a detailed itinerary was already in place for a return visit to England and Ireland. The duo was scheduled to appear at the Cambridge Folk Festival alongside Steve Earle, Suzanne Vega and Janis Ian. Several other shows in Dublin and across England were pencilled in for July and a projected appearance at Bath's Moles Club (22 July) was to be recorded live.

During the second week of May, Shannon O'Neill visited Clark's home to pick up some liner notes that Gene had written for a Sneaky Pete Kleinow album. Clark was exuberant and full of plans. He was trying to kick his cigarette habit – no doubt on doctor's orders – and, evidently sober, seemed to have improved markedly since the Cinegrill debacle. He spoke a lot about the future and how his career was picking up again. In one of his Delphic asides, he again talked of forming a baseball team, presumably with fellow musicians. He seldom sounded better.

Clark's period of abstinence ended abruptly less than a week later. "He was sober and really together, then he fell off the wagon again," says Faurot. There are several theories about what prompted his relapse, but Clark seldom needed a logical reason to court excess. "He got very upset about his parents who were having their 50th [wedding] anniversary and he couldn't go," recalls Hillary. "I don't know why he took that to heart, but it was suddenly making him drink a lot." Indeed, her husband Garth remembers him embarking on a drinking binge that continued for several days. Jason Ronard claims he was planning to accompany Gene and his brother Rick on the trip to the Midwest but, if so, that idea was soon forgotten. David Clark recalls phoning Gene who was still prevaricating about attending. "I said, 'If you're coming to Kansas City phone me and I'll meet you at the airport.' I bluntly told him, 'If you're not in the shape to be presentable at Mom and Dad's 50th anniversary, you won't go.' I don't know what transpired after that. He didn't sound like he was in drastic throes. I'd talked to him a few times the month before when he was absolutely incoherent."

Jon Faurot was hovering around Sherman Oaks, having been delegated to collect outstanding cheques for the musicians who had accompanied Clark at the Cinegrill. Faurot also had some good news. His friend Howie Epstein, bass player for Tom Petty, was producing a record for John Prine and wanted Clark to add some harmonies to one of the tracks. While at Sherman Oaks, Faurot says he was "hanging with Gene and playing some songs".

What happened next only Faurot witnessed. It was a Thursday evening. "He had been drinking a lot of vodka and we were the only ones in the house. I wasn't drinking. We were playing guitars and then he went over the edge with too much alcohol and curled up on the couch. He leaned over and passed out. I took his shoes off, I think, put a blanket over him and left. The next day I was there early in the morning because I had to be in the Valley for some reason. When I showed up at his house he was already up. He wanted me to go to the liquor store with him to get more vodka, which I refused to do. I wouldn't drive with him. So I waited there until he came back. He had some vodka and then I left. He wanted some pot but I didn't have any pot so he didn't have anything, just vodka."

Faurot estimates he had arrived at Clark's home just before eight o'clock that Friday morning. Approximately one hour later, Gene's landlord, Ray Berry, saw him at the back of the house, seemingly sober, although from a distance he could not really tell. At around noon, Faurot received a call from Howie Epstein complaining that Clark was late for the session he was due to attend. Faurot immediately rang Clark, but there was no answer. Either sensing something was amiss or keen to ensure Clark didn't miss the date, he decided to drive over to the house. "I walked into the kitchen and I saw his body on the living room floor. When somebody's dead, it's not like they're asleep, that's all I can tell you. He was gone. I knew he was dead when I looked at him. He'd actually puked, so I cleaned him up a little bit, turned him over and tried to see if there was a heartbeat. Then I got up and called 911 immediately. I said, 'I think this guy's dead.' The paramedics came within a couple of minutes."

While awaiting the arrival of the ambulance, Faurot had phoned his friend Jason Ronard. Initially, there was no answer but, soon after, the actor picked up the message and rang back. "Jason Ronard was the only person I knew who could help me figure out what to do because I couldn't find Gene's phone book and I knew Jason knew everybody. I'll never forget this: I walked outside and Jason was getting out of his car and I just threw my arms up and he said, 'Oh, man.'"

"I couldn't look at Gene," Ronard recalls. "I knew because of my [acting] training that I would have that image in my head and I didn't want it. I wanted to remember him as I knew him. I couldn't look at his body."

Ronard immediately phoned Terri Messina in Northridge and Carlie Clark in Mendocino. He then briefly searched the house in a vain attempt to locate some guns which he assumed were on the premises. "Gene had a couple of guns and Jason wanted to get them out of there, just to make sure the kids didn't [find them]." No weapons were discovered. Not long after, Terri, supported by her mother, and brother Joe, arrived outside, soon followed by others, including former representative Saul Davis, who then took on phone duties, calling Tom Slocum, who was in the middle of another call with Shannon O'Neill. Suddenly, time stopped. "Gene's dead . . ." Slocum said, then rang off, promising to call back. It was a confusing moment. O'Neill's wife, well aware of Slocum's penchant for metaphorical allusion, felt his words were open to multiple interpretation. Still concerned, O'Neill phoned Clark's number and learned the worst in six short words: "You'd better get over here now."

O'Neill felt conflicted. "It was one of the weirdest and worst days of my life. I only lived a couple of miles away from Gene and I was driving over and I said to myself, 'I can't do this.' So I started driving to Palmdale. I got half-way there and thought, 'I can't do this either!' So I went to the house. It was surreal. A couple of other people were there. One of my ex-girlfriends, Helen [Margaret], who used to babysit for Hillary, showed up. I thought, 'Wow, this is bizarre!' I never expected that. I'd gotten there early . . . I took my guitar. He had my 12-string that I took back because I would never have got my guitar back [otherwise]. I took all my cassettes that I was writing with Gene . . . I didn't want my stuff mixed in with his. I'm glad I did that because if I hadn't they would be in the pile of stuff and nobody would have known what was what and it would have been hard to prove."

Shannon O'Neill was the only person to keep a contemporaneous record of the events that day. He recorded many of his phone calls at the time, including several from Gene, which still survive. After returning home, he wrote his impressions of those terrible events of 24 May while his memory was still fresh. It began with his phone call to Tom Slocum:

'Hello!'

'Hey, what are you doing?'
'Getting ready to go into the studio to finish mixing the album.'

'Have you talked to our boy lately?'
'I went over and picked up Sneaky Pete's liner notes a few days ago. That was the only thing needed by the record company to release Sneaky's album. They're good!'

'I know, he read them to me. The punctuation's a little shaky.'
'Yeah, well . . .'

'I think he's drinking a little too much Dewar's [nervous laugh]*'*
'I don't know. He seemed OK when I was over there.'

'Next time he might not be so lucky [agitated voice]. *The cops will make the DUI [drinking under the influence] stick, or they'll pick him up and whack him good.'*
'Well, I'm more afraid he'll hurt himself or die . . .'

'I hear someone calling me on the other line. Hold on . . .'

[A few seconds pass and Slocum is back on the line]

'He's dead. Hold on.'

[Silence. After which Slocum can be heard picking up the phone again]

'Tommy, are you serious?'
'I'll call you right back.'

O'Neill then starts his own narration:

I call my wife at work. I tell her the story and she says maybe Tommy's just angry and really fed up with him. At least something to that effect. She tells me to call Gene's [house] myself.

'Hello?' [Clark's home phone]
'Geno?'

'Who's this?' [I tell him]
'You'd better get over here now.'

"Less than a week ago, Gene and I stood in his kitchen, both lighting up half-smoked cigarettes. We were both quitting and agreed, 'Every once in a while you just have to light up.' I was picking up the second set of liner notes for Sneaky's project. Gene was looking good, healthy. Talking about the Cinegrill gig, the Petty record, the past and future of music. 'The Raven' ['Silver Raven'], the Norton, Tri-Star, new songs, new records, his project, my project, our personal relationships, friends, new gigs, starting a baseball team, the Rock 'n' Roll Hall of Fame, and so on. Gene was really up. Something was definitely happening. You could see it, hear it, and feel it. Music was coming back to its roots. Country, folk, rock 'n' roll – but with a whole new energy. We both felt it, and it wasn't hard to see a lot of people in the business were picking up to that too.

Now what? Driving around, taking the most indirect way to Gene's house. I finally drive up and park. Everything seems perfectly normal from the outside. I walk through the kitchen. Someone who was working with Gene asks, 'You want to see him?' I can't answer. I just follow him into the living room. Gene's mostly covered up on the floor. Terri's crying. She introduces me to her mother and brother and says, 'Gene, you really did it this time.' This has got to be some bizarre nightmare that seems way too real. I remember just sitting there on the couch unable to speak to anyone. I finally asked, 'What happened?' Booze seemed to be the general consensus. Tommy [Slocum] arrives and comes through the living room entrance.

'Well, Geno, you can fly now.'

Everyone is just sitting there looking at Gene. Some pace. There's an occasional outburst. The phones keep ringing.

'Keep that line free. The priest is going to call back.'

Someone asked about the last rites. I said I thought you were supposed to receive them as soon as possible, but wasn't sure. The guys from the mortuary arrive. Somebody's got to make a decision. We all agree to stand in a circle around Gene holding hands and say a final prayer ourselves for him. As I look down at Gene, as weird as this sounds, the expression on his face is the most peaceful and relaxed I've ever seen on him. He looks happy, no more trouble or tension. I feel a little relief.

This is just the beginning. All the questions that will probably never be answered, all the confusion and after the fact solutions I have within myself. I've lost a good friend. I feel empty. I hurt. Friends have died before. This time it's different. Gene was a survivor, a brilliant writer and singer. He had just completed some of the best songs I'd heard him write. This is crazy! Why now? What next?

My wife and I decide to let the machine pick up calls, and we head out to Joshua Tree in the upper desert for the Memorial weekend. Over 20 years our circle of friends have found solace and answers out in the desert. This seemed to be the only solution for the moment.

God bless you, Geno, wherever you are."

Terri had the unenviable task of phoning Gene's parents in Kansas. They were in the midst of finalizing celebrations for their 50th wedding anniversary which were due to take place the next day. Most of Gene's relatives, including his brothers and sisters, were already there. Rick and his wife Nancy were staying at David's house when the phone rang. Nancy picked up the receiver as the brothers were outside fishing in a pond, as if they were back in Swope Park. Fearful of her husband's response, Nancy took David aside and told him his father urgently needed to talk to him. "It was a total shock when Dad told me Gene was dead. I had just talked to him on the Wednesday morning [two days before]." Rick's reaction was initially a combination of anger and denial. David remembers virtually wrestling him to the ground and screaming, "This is happening, man." While the elder brother felt obliged to act like the responsible one, he was suffering irrational pangs of guilt, wondering if he could somehow have saved Gene from himself. "I had to come to grips with it. A lot of times in my life, I thought, 'If I had done this differently or could have stayed with him . . .' You know what: it wouldn't have made a damn bit of difference."

Everyone was devastated but it was too late to cancel the anniversary celebrations. Three hundred invitations had long been despatched bearing the words: 'Mr and Mrs Kelly Clark invite you to join them on Spiritual Harvest and to bear witness to the wisdom that can only be gained by respect and understanding.' What should have been a celebration was closer to a wake for those closest to Gene. On Saturday, a service was held at the Sacred Heart Church in Bonner Springs. The reception at the adjacent Eagles Hall went well in the circumstances, but the news of Gene's demise haunted the family. "We got the word at 2 pm the day before," recalls the matriarch Jeanne Clark. "I felt we should just go ahead and do it. I feel today like I wasn't even there. We went through this church ceremony and everything. It was almost like I slammed a door so I could get through it." Gene's brother David was already making plans to fly to Los Angeles with Rick and Nancy, wary about what might be happening at Gene's house.

David Clark had good reason to be concerned. Following Terri's call on the Friday afternoon, the scene at Sherman Oaks had descended into chaos. "There was a whole scene there," says Faurot. "I left because I'd had enough and I was exhausted. After a while some other people showed up. From what I understand it was a zoo. It never occurred to me that stuff like that would happen."

Emotions were running high that afternoon as they stood over the corpse. Members of Messina's family were on hand to offer support and guidance and Saul Davis was also there to pay his respects. It was at this point that the scenario became very ugly. Slocum was absolutely appalled when Davis unilaterally decided to "start calling up the press while Gene is still dead on the floor". Predictably, Terri was even more aghast and lost emotional control when her brother stumbled upon Saul in their bedroom, rifling through Gene's possessions. Harsh words were spoken and Davis was made to feel like a criminal, although he later argued that he had not acted irresponsibly. "Gene's lying on the floor and I'm immediately thinking of the guy in the Temptations who died that week, David Ruffin. He scored somewhere on the street and they found him dead. So I'm thinking, if there's anything around here, I don't want that to be part of it. So I'm in Gene's bedroom going through his drawers and anything that I saw, like some pills of various sorts, God knows what they were, but I took them and flushed them down the toilet. I called Chris Hillman to say, 'This is what happened' and then I called the newspapers. There was nothing I could do for Gene anymore. I talked to some people at the *LA Times* and *Rolling Stone*, just to make sure that whatever came out on the wire was as clean as possible."

Neither Slocum nor Messina were remotely convinced by Saul Davis' professed good intentions. Terri accused him of trying to get his name in the papers (where he was later referred to as Clark's 'manager') and searching Gene's possessions without permission. "I abhorred Saul Davis," she later said, a stiletto-tongued reaction that sounds disproportionate, but summed up the festering ill feeling that was already spreading. As Davis left, he was obliged to open his briefcase and wallet to check that he had not taken anything from the bedroom. It was a regrettable affair and a taster of more bitterness and sadness to come. The relationship between Saul and Terri never recovered from the events of that afternoon and soon they would find themselves on opposite sides as the dispute over Clark's estate began in earnest.

This was the start of all sorts of fall-outs and backbiting that continued almost unremittingly in the years after Clark's death. There were vociferous claims and counter-claims about who wanted to take various items out of the house. At one point, Gene's landlord Ray Berry, who was well into his seventies, intervened. He threatened to throw everybody out of the house. "It got to be quite confrontational," says Slocum. "Shannon and I ended up having to play cop. Terri had been living with Gene, but they had separated. But she'd left her complete wardrobe there. She left and took some of her clothes and some tapes with her." Terri also took some other personal effects, including letters, photos, notebooks and the Rock 'n' Roll Hall of Fame award that he had dedicated to her. "I wasn't going to start packing all my stuff so I just took what I thought were very important items that I wanted to make sure I had. I was going back to my parents' place so the house was going to be left to people who I didn't have any supervision over. There were conversations going on with my mother, my brother and me, and I wasn't in the best mental state at the time. Gene had just died and his body was still on the floor."

Perhaps the one dignified moment that horrible afternoon was when the remaining people – primarily Slocum, Shannon and Messina – had gathered around Clark's body and recited the Lord's Prayer. "I was looking down at Gene and saying, 'Get up!' " Slocum says. "He didn't, but he did have a smile on his face which was very unusual. When you go over old ground like this, it still hurts."

Back in Mendocino, Carlie faced the burden of informing her children that their father was dead. Kai, who was living in a trailer on their property, was informed first. "I remember that morning like it was yesterday." He can still picture his baby stepsister, Indiana, excitedly rushing towards him. "Mom's got some news for you!" she said. She had overheard part of Carlie's phone call and assumed that Kai was about to receive some special treat. He was devastated by the grim report. The next task was locating Kelly. "He was a bit estranged from home and was off on his own, living with friends, but he was still around." Carlie found him in a woodland area where he and his teenage pals were skateboarding on ramps. "Having to tell those boys that their dad was gone was the hardest thing I've ever done in my life. Right then, I would have gone back with him in a heartbeat."

Kelly Clark suffered mixed emotions, notably an intense anger towards his father, as he and Kai prepared for the ordeal that awaited them in Los Angeles. They appeared late at the scene and decided to stay until their uncles arrived. David, Rick and Nancy flew from Kansas City to LAX where they were picked up by Terri and her mother. By the time they reached Sherman Oaks, Kelly – who had never taken Terri to heart – declined to allow the Messinas access. "I was already a little bit of an angry dude, but I just got pretty pissed off at the whole LA thing. His house was absolutely ruined. Cigarette burns everywhere. I thought to myself 'How could his friends let him get like this?'" Kai was also bemused. "I think it took a couple of days for us to get there. A crazy time. I was just 17, a bit angry and I don't think I really comprehended everything. I was in shock."

David Clark was stunned to see how sparse the property was and also wondered what had happened. "By that time, Kelly was fit to be tied and the house was ransacked. It was awful." A number of items were unaccounted for, including some of Clark's recording equipment, which had evidently been 'missing' since before his death. Of course, it is quite possible that Clark himself sold this, as everyone acknowledges that he was virtually broke at the time. Shannon O'Neill remembers Terri showing him a bank statement in Gene's name which had a zero balance, a telling document on the state of his financial affairs. "I think Kelly began to understand that his father didn't have as much money as he thought he did because royalties come and royalties go," adds Hillary. "He couldn't believe what was in the bank when Geno died. But things were just beginning to gel then. He'd just gotten a lot of contracts, he was supposed to play that day with Howie Epstein and he had a tour lined up and a record deal in the works. Things would have changed, but at the time he didn't have a lot of money and that was that."

Not everyone was part of Clark's current network of friends

and many only heard about the tragedy via the media. "I heard it on the news," recalls former Firebyrds' member Mike Hardwick. "My wife and I found a comfortable bar in our neighbourhood and sat and talked about him. We're not big drinkers and partiers and for us to do that was out of the ordinary. I lived at his house so I could picture him on the floor. It was very sad. I felt the guy was never given a chance, he was just too nice and didn't really say no to anyone. He had a lot of people that were trying to help him out and help themselves through him and it's unfortunate. A lot of his craziness had to do with his health and it's all connected. I believe deep down that if he was around today, he'd have such a wonderful life and would be giving so much to the world."

Back in England, I was awoken by a phone call on Saturday morning confirming the news, but it was difficult to take in. Unlike the death of John Lennon, there was no cathartic sense of a nation in mourning, no tributes on radio or television, not even a mention on the national news. It seemed like a bad dream. Several people I spoke to over the next week were unaware of the sad tidings, while others were alarmed to discover the cold facts buried in the small print of their Sunday newspapers. It would be several days more before the serious national and music press responded with suitably sombre and sympathetic obituaries. By that time, the eerie sense of emptiness that so often accompanies the shock of sudden death had been replaced by some sort of shared acceptance. The tambourine man had left our lives.

As the person who had discovered Gene's body, Faurot felt obliged to explain the circumstances of his death. That need became more urgent when rumours circulated about whether drugs might have been involved. "There were no drugs," he insists. "I'm absolutely certain about that. Gene didn't have any money, that's why we couldn't get paid. He was asking me for pot and he didn't even like pot. He just wanted something. The whole thing is absurd. If there were drugs in the house I would have done them! I didn't go looking through his house but I knew he didn't have any money and he didn't have any drugs. I knew that for sure. There was no way." Although cynics suspected that Clark might have died of a drugs overdose, a heart attack was the actual cause. The newspaper euphemism 'natural causes' did not disguise the fact that Gene's lifestyle played a part in his premature death. Blood pressure, hyper-tension, liver problems, smoking, stomach pains, a highly-strung personality, excitable over-exercise and drug/alcohol binges all weakened his heart and contributed to his demise. The 'throat cancer' played no part and, contrary to a rather strange story emanating from Pat Robinson, there was no evidence that Clark had an aneurysm, or anything similar.

Even in death, Gene Clark was unable to escape the excesses of Hollywood. His family arranged for the body to be viewed at the Praiswater-Meyer Mitchell Mortuary in Van Nuys, but the event threatened to turn into a circus. Gene was dressed in the checked lumber jacket that he wore on the front cover of *Two Sides To Every Story* and people were milling around paying their respects. Chief amongst them was the drunken figure of David Carradine, the actor who had married and subsequently divorced McGuinn's third wife, Linda, and was about to add a macabre footnote to the Gene Clark story. Onlookers were at first nonplussed, then horrified, as they saw him leaning over the corpse and crying, "You fucked that girl when she was only . . . Wake up! Wake up!" When the body failed to respond to Carradine's accusations, he became more distraught. "It was bizarre," Slocum recalls. "He grabbed Gene's body, picked him up by the lapels and we had to get the security guys to remove him because Carradine was over the top." David Clark was equally amazed. "He was nearly ready to drag the body out. It was a scary moment."

According to Shannon O'Neill, he and Slocum were part of the security team. "I was at the back and all I remember is someone shouting, 'Come on, Geno, let's get the fuck out of here! Get the fuck up!' The next thing I know Slocum is walking down the aisle, looking at me and panicking. So I went over, and there was David Carradine. We were saying, 'Hey, man, you've got to go!' I remember walking him out and he really smelt like he'd hit the bottle that day. I was thinking, 'This is pretty strange. This guy knows karate and he's probably going to kick my ass.'"

"It was insane," concludes Terri. "Carradine and his wife were there and he was totally drunk and causing a scene. I was offended myself. Gene was raised a Catholic and I was raised a Catholic, and I had a reverence and respect for it. Carradine was accusing Gene of having an affair with his daughter Calista and he was yelling all these things. It was weird."

"How stupid," adds Hillary. "Gene had hardly anything to do with Calista. Garth and Calista were boyfriend and girlfriend before he and I got together." Carradine bumped into several members of the Clark family a few days afterwards, but no apology was forthcoming. He seemed puzzled by everyone's reaction, pointing out that he had only been attempting to pay his respects, albeit in bizarre fashion.

In contrast to the melodrama at the viewing, Gene's subsequent funeral ceremony back in Tipton, Missouri, was a more civilized and respectful gathering, consisting mainly of family and in-laws. Gene was laid to rest at St Andrew's Catholic Cemetery on a hill overlooking his childhood town. Even here, everything was far from stress free. Terri Messina was indignant at the unexpected presence of Karen Johnson, who had barely known Gene for more than several weeks. "After he died, she's like his long lost best friend, or whatever she thinks she is. She flies to Missouri and befriends the sons, who I already have a problem with, and his family. She flies to the funeral like *she's* the old lady. Unbelievable."

After discussions with the family, Karen subsequently recommended the estate be administered by her former husband, Scott Johnson, whose law firm was based in distant Baltimore. "If that wasn't the most sad postscript to the whole thing, I don't know," Messina recoiled. "It's beyond my imagination."

Under California law, which has not recognized common-law marriage since 1895, Gene's estate automatically reverted to his sons. Terri Messina had paid an unexpectedly high price for never marrying and neglecting to encourage Gene to make a will naming her as his beneficiary. "I had no legal attachment to it at all," she laments, "except if I took it to court and fought to show that I had lived with him all those years and was his common-law wife and that I did have a claim on the estate because of all the time I spent with him and the effort I'd made. I had accompanied him on all those tours and had been his business manager and sidekick . . . So, the suit was frozen. I invested several thousand dollars of my own, then I was told that if I wanted to fight this all the way it would probably cost $100,000. At that point, it had emotionally so drained me that I had a major intervention from my family who stepped in and said, 'Look, you have your own talents, you don't have to live the rest of your life doing the Gene Clark story,' so I had to let it go."

Gene Clark would no doubt have been upset by the bitterness and lack of harmony between the two sets of people that he loved most. The Clark family were angry that Messina retained some of Gene's personal effects, including his notebooks, the Rock 'n' Roll Hall of Fame award and a cache of home recordings. She countered that these were the least that she deserved and cited his words at the induction ceremony back in January as proof of his intentions. "Gene always said Terri was the love of his life," John York stresses. "I just think she wanted recognition as to who she was." With both parties claiming the moral high ground, a civilized compromise proved impossible. The enmity between the two factions was a sad valediction and regrettable coda to Gene Clark's life story.

None of the original Byrds attended Clark's funeral service in Kansas, nor the previous public viewing of the body at Van Nuys. It was only much later, after the obituaries had been written and digested, that some comments were forthcoming. The Byrds' fanzine *Full Circle* printed tributes from Michael Clarke and John York which were respectful and moving. Chris Hillman rose above the spectre of past differences to offer a more personal and analytical memorial, which reminded us of all that Clark had lost as well as gained since his glory days in the Byrds. "We lost Gene the other day," he began. "It doesn't matter how or why. He's just gone. I think we lost Gene in 1967. I know I never did find that young, innocent kid from Bonner Springs, Kansas, again. And he so touched my life back then! At one time he was the power in the Byrds, not McGuinn, not Crosby – it was Gene who would bust through the stage curtain banging on a tambourine coming on like a young Prince Valiant. A hero, our savior. Few in the audience could take their eyes off this presence. I know, I was hiding in the back with Michael, watching, waiting . . . He *was* the songwriter. He had the 'gift' that none of the rest of us had developed yet. He had control over the demons who constantly stalk us. And then something happened to the kid from Kansas. He grew up. He lost his grip. The demons were set free! And he never regained his balance again. Oh, there were still moments of brilliance through the years, Dillard & Clark, solo albums, even the first McGuinn, Clark & Hillman album . . . What deep inner part of his soul conjured up songs like 'Set You Free . . .', 'Feel A Whole Lot Better', 'Feelin' Higher', 'Eight Miles High' – so many great songs! We learned a lot of songwriting from him and in the process learned a little about ourselves. I think the city (LA) ate him up and spit him out. He suffers no more. He left me a lot of wonderful memories and allowed me to share a small part of his life. I'm so glad we all made peace on that rainy night last Jan, our *final* moment of glory. The Byrds have flown away. I'll miss them."

Gene Clark's death was a salutary comment on the times in which he lived. His life was an enigma, full of great moments, blighted by lost opportunities and questionable career decisions. There were periods when he seemed set to emerge as one of the greatest singer-songwriters of his era, but a conjunction of bad luck and wilful self-destruction all too often banished him to the cult fringe. His ambivalence towards fame was palpable. He craved success and recognition, then recoiled in horror at the moment of consummation. All too often his neuroses and mood swings propelled him towards abandonment in alcohol. At other times, he craved the affluent rock star life that contrasted so markedly with his humble upbringing back in Missouri. It was a conflict that he never fully resolved. As Terri Messina concludes: "He was a great guy when he was straight. That's the Gene Clark I loved. I was never in love with the alcoholic, drug addict part of it, ever. Whatever Gene was guilty of, and he was guilty of abusing alcohol and drugs and he was guilty of being self-destructive, but he was never a dishonest person. Ever. He was one of the most loyal and honourable people I've ever known."

The fate of Terri Messina was a sad coda to the Gene Clark story. "I actually had to go into therapy for months after Gene died because I was so distraught over the whole thing, not only losing him, but the whole estate thing. It was my fault we never married and my fault that there wasn't a will because Gene would have written one at any time I told him to. The thing is I'm a human being too and I was suffering emotionally. I had my ups and downs. I went from being a very efficient person to being a non-efficient person for a while from everything that was going on. There were times when I would throw in the towel too, if you follow me, because it would get too much for even me to handle."

Sharon Garrett Brooks reckons the entire affair put Terri "in a tailspin". She seemed increasingly withdrawn, in marked contrast to her previously ebullient self. "After Gene died she was not a happy camper," Hillary Beckington confirms. "She did not see that coming and it just fractured her. Kelly should be thankful that Terri didn't marry Gene. I couldn't believe she didn't marry him because he adored her. But maybe it was meant to be that way. She had money, and the children had nothing, so it was good that Kelly and Kai had all of that legacy instead of her. It's really strange the way it worked out."

After surrendering her questionable claims against the estate, Messina continued to fret over her reputation and was bitter about many of the factions who had turned against her. "I've heard so many rumours of these people trying to belittle my position when I was with Gene for all those years as his old lady.

Some stepped in after his death and wanted to run the show or build up their prominence in Gene's life and cut me out of it. I think a lot of them were insecure about me and my family because they knew I came from a very strong family and they were worried that I might take over." The sad truth was that Messina had cut herself out of any rapprochement by fighting the estate. Given her poor relationship with Gene's children, it is equally doubtful she would ever have had any say in the administration of the estate even if she'd acted like a saint.

On several occasions, she came up with ideas to enhance Gene's legacy – a book of lyrics, a screenplay for a television film – but they came to nothing. Unable to reach out to any of Gene's family and few of his old friends, she felt bereft at times. Some of the terrible comments about her that later appeared in print only made matters worse and fed her depression. "She felt bad about it and the public perception," says Hillary. "I told her, 'Who cares what they write about you? It doesn't matter. People that know you know the truth.' But she took it to heart. It was almost as if she'd lost her will to live in a way, although she was taking care of her parents. I think that kept her going."

Terri always retained her fatalistic love for Gene, but sometimes she lapsed into morbidity. "It is so painful and sometimes I think that I can't stay here anymore, that I want to be with Gene wherever he is. I miss him so much, he was so much a part of me and I was so much a part of him, I don't think I will ever feel right again until I am with him . . . I have been treated disrespectfully and insensitively . . . Sometimes I think, what good is life in such a world anyway that is so unfair."

Over time, there were changes in her physical appearance. Like Gene, she suffered dental problems and had to have some teeth replaced, causing unforeseen problems. A fluctuating waistline was also evident. "She put on a lot of weight," Hillary recalls. "The last time I saw her I gave her some tips about shedding it. She was taking methadone and that stuff is notorious for putting weight on people. She tried to straighten herself out but sometimes that can be worse than what you're trying to cure. But she was still cute. I couldn't stand to see her looking heavy, she was such a doll."

On 21 August 2007 Terri took her own life. She was 61. Even in death she could not escape cruel vilification. One Clark online forum included a comment appallingly headlined: 'Ding dong the witch is dead'.

The Clark family faced mixed emotions after Gene's death. Jeanne Clark, who always regarded Gene as her favourite, was devastated. "When Mom got wind of the kind of life he was living it caused a terrible rift between them and that never got healed," claims her daughter Bonnie. "I had to get her into grief counselling so that she could handle his death. She was still so angry with him." On 29 March 2000, her husband Kelly George Clark died. They had been married for over 59 years. Six weeks later, on 11 May, Jeanne passed away at the Olathe Medical Center. She was buried in the Resurrection Cemetery in Lenexa.

Rick Clark kept a relatively low profile following his brother's demise. "I dropped out completely for about seven years and just didn't want anything to do with music," he told me in the summer of 1999. "There was a lot of bad feeling at the time of Gene's death. So much back-stabbing went on, so I just threw up my hands and said, 'Forget it!' I know all the people but I don't speak to any of them." As the millennium approached, he was full of plans and projects. He had completed a solo album and was busy organizing a tribute concert for his brother, scheduled to take place in Kansas. Time passed. Neither the album nor the concert was mentioned again. He suffered a downward curve over the next decade but was rescued from near obscurity or oblivion. He even played a tribute show in Kansas City to celebrate what would have been his brother's 70th birthday. He had survived.

Kelly Clark was still an angry young man at the time of his father's death and cynical about the music business. Over the next decade, while administering the estate, he had to learn more than he cared to about the machinations of the industry. He was never tempted to follow his father's career having witnessed one too many dark episodes during childhood visits to LA. In his more philosophic moments, he offered some positive words. "I'm proud of the things he did and the person he was. What little I know of him, he was a fun guy to be around. He wrote amazing poetry and songs, had great loves and great wars."

Kai Clark retained more innocent and idealistic memories of the father he seldom saw. As a teenager he took up guitar and, later in life, became a musician. With his interest in roots music and alternate country, he was always happy to perform Gene Clark songs. On 29 April 2011 at the Roxy in LA, the Kai Clark Band played the whole of *Two Sides To Every Story*. He was even joined onstage by members of the short-lived Group (Joel Larson, Chip Douglas and Bill Rhinehart) that had performed with Gene in Hollywood back in 1966. In September 2014, he joined Jon Faurot ("the poor guy who found Dad") onstage at a show in Mendocino following the screening of the celebrated television/DVD documentary, *The Byrd Who Flew Alone*. Happy to play the tributarian, Kai also appeared at LA's Hotel Café two months later, celebrating what would have been his father's 70th birthday. The tribute concerts continue to this day. "This younger generation respects my father," Kai concludes. "They love Dad's stuff and it's a great thing to see. He deserves this. The music's speaking for itself now. All these years later, Dad is speaking from the grave through his music. And that's really what he wanted."

Carlie Clark, the divorced mother, was also deeply affected by Gene's death. In 1991, she was still enmeshed in serious drug abuse and her prospects seemed bleak. Subsequently, she entered a rehab programme, just as Terri Messina had done a decade before, and reformed her ways. In the meantime, she had placed her own claim for some of the monies from Clark's estate. Kai confirms this. "My father was supposed to pay child support for years and years and he never did, as far as I'm aware. Once the estate was cleared obviously there was back child support that she felt was owed. I don't think she ever talked to us about it. She was given money [from the estate]. I don't even remember the amount. But she'd raised us herself, so it was something she deserved, I'm sure." Carlie spent the later part of her life with her daughter, Indiana Espinoza, in the Auburn/Sacramento area working as a drugs counsellor, often helping young women with children. "I think she was pretty proud of the last years of her life – and with good reason," says her brother, Jimmy. In 2013, she featured heavily in the documentary, *The Byrd Who Flew Alone*. The woman who had once walked off a cliff on the Mendocino headlands was still accident prone. Prior to filming, she had a fall and her face was badly bruised during the recording. In late 2013, she underwent chemotherapy for cancer, which had spread from her lungs to her liver. Her brother Jimmy believes she understated the seriousness of her illness. "Carlie was not known for burdening people with her problems. Even her daughter, Indiana, had no idea she was so close to dying. It was very much Carlie not to talk about what was bothering her." On 8 April 2014, she died in Roseville, California, another casualty on that long list of family, friends and associates of Gene Clark. A celebration of her life took place at her brother Jimmy's home in Comptche, Mendocino on 25 May.

Among the sadder aspects of the Clark story were the countless fall-outs and bitterness between the various subsidiary characters. It is difficult to think of anyone who was not affected by this. The criticisms often sound petty, excessive or over-emotional. But such is the way when death strikes so suddenly and family, former friends and business associates find themselves divided. As Tom Slocum astutely observes: "They all got into that insanity where the next thing you know the first person to point the finger is the last person to take the blame and they all end up shooting each other in the foot. If there was an observer, they'd say, 'Why are you guys killing each other? Stop this shit!' They *all* ended up getting hurt." Slocum was not immune to the toxic fall-out either as his soured relationship with the Beckingtons confirms. He also objected to some alleged comments in print from David Clark at one point. Of course, all that was nothing compared to the bigger issues between the estate and Terri Messina, not to mention the rest of the cast list. The different factions in this saga created their own landscape of heroes and villains and it is wise to be cautious about their assessments. There is little transparently black and white in Clark World. Many of the comments from the leading and minor players are extreme. The worst ones make for exciting reading but their venom is unworthy of print, or worse, misleading. It is easy to accuse various parties of being self-serving. The mischievous side of Gene Clark would probably have been amused by some of the retrospective barbs, but he would also have been saddened to observe so many of his former friends at loggerheads. There is a different, more charitable view of events that few among the various conflicting circles acknowledge. Rather than contempt, it seems nobler to credit the contributions of those involved. Clark had many good friends and supporters, and he often tested their loyalty. Looking at the history more objectively, there are no straightforward heroes or villains. Most of the cast did their best in trying circumstances. In death, Clark generated extremes of emotion among the living, and that says much in itself.

The musical legacy of Gene Clark became the key story in the years after his death, and the debate about unreleased songs and lost albums continues to this day. His estate was frozen for several years while lawyers locked horns over the respective claims of Terri Messina and Gene's sons, Kelly and Kai. Even while that was being resolved, there were other outstanding matters that required attention. "The person valuing the estate for the court isn't an expert in the music business, so that person has to learn the situation," Saul Davis reminds us. "They have to reconcile how the dozens and dozens of unreleased songs have zero value and how 'Feel A Whole Lot Better' has just earned $90–100,000 in the last 12 months. So they have to put a different weight and value on each one. And then there are all the songs in the middle. And what are the unreleased tapes worth? Well, they're worth nothing because they're earning nothing. But there was a lot of stuff like that and the American wheels of justice going forward."

Fortunately, some albums did emerge during this frustrating period. *Echoes*, a compilation issued by Legacy/Sony in September 1991, proved the perfect companion to the Byrds' box set, offering several important songs – 'I Knew I'd Want You', 'Here Without You', 'Set You Free This Time' and 'If You're Gone' – excluded from the larger work. The inclusion of virtually all of Clark's first album was also welcome, but the real excitement was reserved for the previously unheard and unreleased single from 1967, 'Only Colombe'/'The French Girl'. Due to an administrative error, the latter was credited to Clark instead of its true composer, Ian Tyson. Strangely enough, it was the closing acoustic demo remix of 'So You Say You Lost Your Baby' that proved the most astounding new find. Not only did it complement the orchestral version heard earlier on the album, but enabled the listener to eavesdrop on a session at which Clark was at his most commanding. If only they could have unearthed the pre-orchestrated 'Echoes'. It would be fascinating to hear an entire compilation of Clark's acoustic demos from this period, assuming the tapes could be found, but that seems unlikely.

One year after *Echoes*, a belated live album appeared by Clark and Carla Olson. *Silhouetted In Light* was a 73-minute audio-verité recording from a show at McCabe's, Santa Monica, on 3 February 1990. It was a very spontaneous collaboration, the recording of which was fortuitous. "At the end of that night, the sound person tapped guitarist Duane Jarvis on the shoulder and said, 'Would you like a tape?'" Davis recalls. "He gave it to Duane and we didn't even know about it. After Gene passed away, Duane called me and said, 'By the way, I have this tape from McCabe's.' I said, 'I can't believe it.' It was primitive but perfect as far as being a representation of that night and allowing us to put out something that people might want to hear."

Although obviously unintended for commercial release, the album provided a souvenir for fans starved of material. From the on-stage banter, it's clear that Gene and Carla enjoyed working together and there were several references to a promised second album which, of course, would never be recorded. The set was most notable for an early version of 'Your Fire Burning', one of Clark's most thrilling late period songs. As well as highlights from *So Rebellious A Lover*, Gene reached back to the Byrds' golden era for 'Set You Free This Time' and 'She Don't Care About Time'. Alas, none of Clark's solo live appearances from this period were deemed suitable for release and they can only be heard on bootlegs or rough tapes.

Three years later, the compilation *This Byrd Has Flown* was issued by Edsel Records. Alas, this was little more than the 1984 *Firebyrd* album, augmented by three previously unavailable tracks: 'C'est La Bonne Rue', 'Dixie Flyer' and 'All I Want'. Fans expecting to hear a serious archival work would have to wait several more years.

Terri Messina retained many of Clark's working tapes and demos, including recordings made in the final year of his life. In addition, she had material stretching back to their Laurel Canyon days in the late Seventies, which she had financed. On some tapes she could be heard offering support and advice. Of course none of this material could be issued without the permission of the estate. There was no thawing of bitterness on anyone's part, so the recordings stay buried. "I'm only willing to part with them if they're willing to make a deal with me," Messina told me in 1996. "If they're not willing to make a deal with me, then they're never going to hear it, and nobody else will either, which is too bad. He wrote a lot of brilliant stuff. I think there's some of the best material he'd done in his entire career, and it's absolutely brilliant. A lot of them were love songs to me. They're very personal and I'm not willing to hand them over for everyone else to make money and me not get *anything* out of it. Forget it. I'd rather just keep them as my love letters."

At one point, Pat Robinson, who was planning to exhume his

own archives, offered to act as an invisible intermediary between Messina and the estate. "She spent $15,000 suing the estate and pissed everybody off. No one would do business with her. Being friends with her, I said, 'I'll make the deal and cut you in. No one has to know you're involved and I'll give you half of my publishing for being involved in the deal. You won't have to go after the estate.' The estate wouldn't grant her a licence. Then she didn't do anything and we had a bit of an argument. I said, 'Listen, I don't have to be doing this with you and unless you're going to do something to earn your way I feel this is a little one-sided.'" The deal was never made.

Instead, Robinson pushed forward with his own project. After seeking legal advice he assumed he had the rights to release the recordings undertaken at his studio. By November 1996 he was starting to clean and remix the tapes. He did not foresee any problems with the estate. "Kelly and Kai are pretty good pals with me and they trust me. We've giving them $10,000 per CD. There's not a lot of money involved with this stuff, but we're doing the best we can." Robinson planned to co-produce one CD with John Arrias and another with Dennis Dragon, the drummer who had once played weekends with the final line-up of the Clarence White-era Byrds. It was hoped that Dragon might replace the dated-sounding Linn drums used on the original demos.

Weeks later, Saul Davis, who was by now working closely with the estate, sent out a private warning during our interview. "If Pat's already working on something and cleaning stuff up, then I don't know about it. And if he hasn't made a deal with the kids then it's illegal so we'll have to deal with it at that point. Any discussion of any record label is fantasy. It's totally nonsensical. A deal needs to be struck with the kids and, hopefully, I'll be involved with Scott Johnson and there'll be some quality control. Just because something's been recorded doesn't mean that it should exist in a commercial sense."

Oblivious to any such objections or problems, Robinson approached the UK-based Charly Records in 1997. At first they received two cassette tapes of 48 songs under the title, 'Gene Project With Byrds'. That piqued their interest sufficiently to open negotiations. In November, they asked me to act as consultant on the project. A typed fax was added to their letter ominously titled, 'Artist: Byrds'. Evidently, Robinson was now pitching this as a Byrds-related project. The sheet for 'Artists: Byrds' featured 47 songs, but the titles differed significantly from those on the aforementioned cassette tapes. Eleven songs from the 'Gene Project With Byrds' were excluded and the new listing included 'Mr Tambourine Man', 'Eight Miles High' and 'Chimes Of Freedom'. In addition, Robinson's 'Watchpocket Publishing' enclosed a fax listing the songwriting credits for 40 songs. Two other tapes arrived at the same time: one labelled 'Geno, Nicky and Pat' featured 22 songs; another titled 'Writing Roughs' offered 15 songs in inchoate form.

At this stage, I responded to Charly, sternly insisting that I would not be involved in any such project if the name 'Byrds' was used on any release. A conference call was arranged between myself, Charly and Robinson where these matters were discussed. Robinson claimed that Clark always referred to these tapes as 'Byrds songs' but I argued that this was misleading, pointing out that Clark had adamantly refused to use the title Byrds on any record and ceased using the name in concert. This was evident enough from interviews conducted during the closing years of his life. More pertinently, I contended that if Charly were to release these tapes under the name 'Byrds' then it would be counter-productive. Fans would feel affronted or cheated, music magazines would dismiss the work or, even worse, decline to review it. This sounded deflating, but nobody argued the opposite, and Robinson conceded the point.

There was, however, some good news. Listening to the tapes, I thought the 'Writing Roughs', which Robinson had considered far too crude for consideration, were ideal for hard-core collectors. Unlike the clinically produced songs with their Linn drums and synth accompaniment, these roughs had a certain charm as works in progress. I proposed that, instead of a double album with the Byrds name appended, they should produce a three-CD box set titled 'Gene Clark: The Lost Decade'. Robinson concurred while Charly, which specialized in bargain-priced box sets of rock 'n' roll legends, saw merit and profit in the idea. At least the Byrds' name was saved from desecration.

Thereafter, there was a long silence. Robinson sounded excited by the box set concept but hinted that he wasn't entirely sure about signing with Charly and mentioned that a German company had also been in contact recently. Another year flew by, but there was no further progress or news of any additional communication between Charly and Robinson. Presumably, the project had been abandoned, but even that was never confirmed. There was merely further silence.

Meanwhile, A&M Records trawled their archives for a formidable double CD collection, *Flying High*. Released in 1998, this eminently thorough compilation licenced several Byrds' tracks – 'Feel A Whole Lot Better', 'Set You Free This Time' and 'She Don't Care About Time' – plus key selections from *Roadmaster*, *No Other* and *Two Sides To Every Story*. Its main attraction was the previously unissued material, notably 'Los Angeles', 'That's Alright By Me', two previously unheard Dillard & Clark cover songs and, most importantly, a couple of *White Light*-period rarities: 'Opening Day' and 'Winter In'. Overall, the compilation was a fine sampler for new listeners, which also whetted the appetite of hard-core fans in search of further unreleased gems.

The CRY-era recordings (featuring Clark, Robinson and York, with Nicky Hopkins) remained unreleased, but there was an attempt to revive the moribund project in 1999. It was suggested that Carla Olson should assume the 'C' now that Clark was dead. John York was not keen and, according to Pat, vetoed the idea. Soon after, Robinson and York independently supervised *CRY*, an obscure release on the label Coyote, which featured re-recordings of a dozen of the songs. Few people, beyond hard-core collectors, ever heard the disc.

By the end of the century, arbitrary selections from Pat Robinson's tape archives began to appear on several labels on the

Continent, erroneously credited to 'The Byrds'. Even more worryingly, the Clark/Robinson compositions were sometimes packaged together with songs recorded by a 'fake Byrds'. The entire unsavoury saga is discussed extensively in the succeeding Endnotes.

While Robinson's 'Geno Project' temporarily drifted into limbo, his former mentor Saul Davis was preparing his own release, with the cooperation of the Clark estate. *Gypsy Angel*, issued in July 2001, was a tantalizing work, most notable for a series of strong compositions, several written during the final years of Clark's life. The two opening songs, 'Pledge To You' and 'Mississippi Detention Camp', both discussed earlier, are raw and spooky, one deeply personal, the other a reflective prison song. The performances testify to their creator's ongoing battle with drink, drugs and gum disease, but there is an emotional depth in the work that is impressive. Several other songs here approach these same heights. 'Dark Of My Moon' is almost a trademark Clark composition, both melodic and melancholic, with dark-night imagery redolent of a minor Elizabethan poet. Clearly from a different session to the opening two songs, this was Clark with teeth intact. 'Freedom Walk' sounds as though it was recorded at the same time as 'Mississippi Detention Camp'. It features some impressive guitar passages and a fascinating arrangement, with subtle shades of 'Eight Miles High' in places. 'Kathleen', less impressive technically, has background hiss and signs of imperfection on the surviving tape. Nevertheless, it's a strong composition with traditional roots, the theme partly echoing the tale of Odysseus and Penelope. Coincidentally, McGuinn had explored that same myth on the similarly named 'Kathleen's Song' (on *Byrdmaniax*), even taking on the female role in the song. It's also notable how Clark adds another character named Kathleen in 'Back In My Life Again'.

There is an improvement in sound quality during the latter part of *Gypsy Angel* but, with the exception of 'Your Fire Burning', the content is less impressive. 'Love Wins Again' sounds like Clark on auto-pilot, using hackneyed card imagery and an over-familiar melody borrowed from 'Feel A Whole Lot Better'. Both 'Rock Of Ages' and 'Day For Night' (which features some strained whistling) are even less arresting, having already appeared in different form elsewhere.

Gypsy Angel remains an intriguing artefact, guaranteed to divide listeners unused to hearing Clark's work in relatively primitive form. It was regrettable that the packaging was not more informative. Oddly, the liner notes consisted of a basic bio written back in 1996, apparently adapted from the internet, complete with typographical errors. There were no reflections on the merits or otherwise of the new compositions. When precisely were they recorded? What was the time gap between the various sessions – months, years? What information there was proved frustratingly sketchy. Supposedly, much of the record was originally intended for a Clark/Olson record, yet it was difficult to imagine the first two numbers, for example, fitting easily into such a work. The dentally challenged songs have a rawness and intensity that would surely have been compromised by any dilution.

Overall, *Gypsy Angel* was a fractured snapshot: primitive, wayward, erratic, emotionally gripping and often inspiring, it transcends its limited remit by the sheer quality of its compositions. It is an important release due to the greatness that lurks within. At least four, maybe five, of these songs confirm that Clark was still writing some of his best work in the period leading up to his death. Indeed, if other contemporaneous compositions such as 'Adios Terri' or 'Big Bad Mama' could have been added to this package, and someone had invested in a professional recording, then this would arguably have been one of his most notable achievements.

Two months after *Gypsy Angel* was issued, a 2-CD package was scheduled for release by the UK-based Delta Music: *Under The Silvery Moon*. Label manager Peter Jamieson had been in contact with Pat Robinson over the previous two years and, unlike Charly Records, successfully licensed the recordings, which included much of the CRY material. Robinson had sought legal advice and claims he was assured that he could conclude a deal based on the fact that he owned the tapes, had partial copyright in the recordings and had paid for the sessions, the majority of which were done at Lobo Canyon and Silvery Moon Studios. Shortly before the release date, Delta were contacted by Saul Davis. Soon after, the estate issued a cease and desist order. Robinson was now in a precarious position. He had signed an agreement with Delta confirming that he had the right to license the tapes. Delta contacted their lawyers in America and even considered contesting the issue but decided the expenses weren't worth the risk so agreed to work with the estate. Initially, Jamieson thought everything would be resolved before Christmas, but Delta would not issue a revised version until 2003. Copies of the original, which Jamieson estimated at merely a thousand, were crushed, instantly making the 2-CD set a collector's item. The 29-song package had boasted '13 original songs, two previously unreleased cover versions, 14 new recordings of others works and a 16-page deluxe booklet'. It was a fairly representative collection of CRY songs and other material recorded during the Eighties. Robinson had removed most of the intrusive overdubs, evident on the aforementioned Continental bootlegs. However, the songs were of varying quality. Among the better selections were 'My Marie', 'Mary Sue', 'Carry On', 'Washington Square', 'More Than That Now', 'Nothing But An Angel' and 'Dragon's Eye'. Often absent was a sense of mystery or emotional depth. At times, Clark appeared to be self-consciously seeking a generic sound rather than pursuing his own path. The songs were pleasant enough and testified to the commercial side of his songwriting but lacked distinction. *Under The Silvery Moon* was far superior in production to the primitively recorded *Gypsy Angel*, but the latter featured more compelling material. Combine them and a picture of two very different Gene Clarks emerge: a singer-songwriter attempting to adjust to changing times and fashions; an individual voice and song poet composing arcane and challenging work.

Arguments among the survivors in Clark World continued to fester, often without logic or reason. Saul Davis' close relationship with the estate had already provoked negative comments from Terri Messina and other antagonists were now joining that chorus, notably Jim Dickson. "Gene would rip Saul Davis' face off if he could come back and do it," he said, and that was not the worst of his taunts. Dickson was hardly a disinterested observer and his harsh opinion was coloured by Davis' previous involvement in the doomed publishing lawsuit by Polly Parsons (see pages 792–800). Dickson and Messina both argue that Gene was hostile towards Davis and no longer wished to work with him at the time of his death. Others such as Andy Kandanes or some members of the Firebyrds may have had their own reasons for resenting his involvement. Even the normally unflappable Mike Hardwick sounded defensive. "I don't like saying things about Saul . . . he means nothing to me and he can do me no harm." The presence of Davis' wife Carla Olson on various recordings was a further source of contention or envy from some quarters. Delta Music's Peter Jamieson was less than effusive, but that was hardly unexpected. Some people attract exaggerated criticism. Yet, there is no evidence to suggest that Davis did anything harmful to Clark during their time working together. And as he rightly points out, nobody who represented or worked with Clark during the Eighties benefited significantly in financial terms. Everything had been an uphill struggle.

Another musical chapter of Clark's career almost reached release stage: the Firebyrds. Mike Hardwick, the youngest member of the troupe, had collected soundboard cassette tapes of their gigs during his tenure. He subsequently had the recordings transferred to digital and archived the results. Evangeline, the UK label responsible for *Gypsy Angel*, expressed interest at one point and Hardwick had the tapes mastered at a recording studio, then précised the collection into a 'best of' compilation. He was torpedoed by a legal letter from the Clark estate. Rather than debate the issue or surrender the tapes, he simply placed them back on a shelf where they remain to this day for the entertainment of old friends. "It's too bad," he says. "I don't want to look like a guy who's trying to make a buck out of this. I just wanted to do the right thing and send some money to Michael's mother. All I'd have wanted was a producer credit and then all the funds to be divided among Gene's estate and Michael's estate and whoever else was involved."

In October 2001, another Clark project was proposed. It was already known that a handful of acetates of *Gene Clark Sings For You* were in existence, but none had yet reached the hands of the estate. Sid Griffin, who had been represented by Saul Davis while in the Long Ryders and involved in the A&M compilation, *Flying High*, had access to an acetate. He duly wrote to attorney Scott Johnson, passing on snippets of the recordings in the hope of negotiating a deal for his own custom label, Prima Records. The initial response was positive although, obviously, additional work would be required to ensure the recordings were of sufficient quality for release. The great bonus, however, was that, in addition to the *Gene Clark Sings For You* material, the package would include 'If I Hang Around' (a 1966 demo previously available on the Australian compilation, *Byrd Parts 2*) and 'That's What You Want'. The latter was a thrill, a solo acoustic recording, registered for copyright on 1 November 1965 while the Byrds were in the studio working on *Turn! Turn! Turn!*. Structurally similar to 'Set You Free This Time', the song dissected a relationship largely from the woman's point of view, with Clark playing the quizzical narrator. Jim Dickson recalls Clark's state of mind when composing both of these songs. "The Byrds had been used to these folk chicks that were laid-back, then all of a sudden they were faced with high-pressure girls who weren't prepared to just sit and adore you like a simple girl from home. They had complex desires and wishes, and places where they wanted to go and be seen with you. Gene had to ease himself into it. He came to love it all and wallow in it and hurt himself with it." 'That's What You Want' was an impressive artefact from that time and a crucial addition to *Gene Clark Sings For You*, not least because it ensured the entire package featured ten songs.

At first, Griffin was puzzled to receive a response, not from

Scott Johnson, but rather his old friend, Saul Davis. Confused, he rushed off an email to Johnson who quickly responded pointing out that the estate had a good working relationship with Davis on such projects and had supplied him with the information about the tracks as a matter of courtesy. Johnson next suggested that Griffin make a financial offer to the estate, as Evangeline and Delta had done, before proceeding any further. Griffin sought advice, made a very modest offer, but no further replies were forthcoming.

One project that did reach fruition, years after its intended release, was *Under The Silvery Moon*. Delta Music had negotiated with the estate and waited patiently for events to unfold. Following the destruction of the original double album, the package devolved into a single album of 14 songs. Delta label manager Peter Jamieson suspected that the estate might stagger the previous 29-song set across two separate releases to maximize income, but this was never the case as time proved. Who was responsible for pruning the album is not entirely clear. Kai Clark has no memory of selecting or vetoing any tracks. "I probably listened to them," he acknowledges. "We probably just said, 'Fine'. I don't think we ever said, 'You've got to have this song or that song.' I don't ever remember saying I wanted it to be a single album. It's a mystery to me."

The shortened version emerged as a much weaker release, marked by some perplexing decisions. Arguably, it made sense to delete previously issued songs such as 'Deportee', 'Del Gato', 'Gypsy Rider' et al, plus the covers of Arthur Alexander's 'You Better Move On' and John Fogerty's 'Almost Saturday Night'. Yet they chose to include two non-Clark compositions, Goffin & King's 'Will You Love Me Tomorrow?' and John York's 'You Just Love Cocaine'. Several superior Clark/Robinson songs were sacrificed without explanation. While you could see a case for ignoring the dull and derivative 'Dancing On The Moon' or even average but unspectacular compositions such as 'Liona', 'The Panther' and 'The Hurting Game', several others were surely keepers. 'Washington Square' was one of the best of the Clark/Robinson narrative songs; 'Dragon's Eye' had a spooky feel missing from most of the other collaborations; the Roy Orbison-influenced 'With You I Can't Lose' was an enticing melody, and 'That Part Of You' was vintage Clark without any distracting effects. Overall, it was an anti-climactic conclusion to a work already spoiled by pre-release bootlegs, unofficial Continental issues, disagreements and a cancelled but superior double album.

Clark's former record labels were aware of his cult status and responded with a couple of key reissues. *White Light* reappeared in July 2002, blessed with the bonus tracks, 'Opening Day' and 'Winter In', plus a cover of Ben E. King's 'Stand By Me' and the psalmodic 'Ship Of The Lord'. There was even greater expectation for the following year's *No Other*, but its additional tracks proved something of an anti-climax. They included 'Train Leaves Here This Morning' and rudimentary run-throughs of 'Silver Raven', 'No Other', 'From A Silver Phial', 'Some Misunderstanding' and 'Lady Of The North'. Two other alternate takes were listed as 'potential bonus material' but failed to make the cut: 'Strength Of Strings' and 'The True One'. Overall, the anaemic additional material emphasized the remarkable contribution that producer Tommy Kaye (who died in 1994) had made to the main body of the album.

By February 2003, Sid Griffin had lost patience. Despite further attempts to contact the estate, he still had not received a firm 'no', let alone 'yes', to his *Gene Clark Sings For You* proposal. He felt ignored. In desperation, he wrote to Rick Clark urging him to contact Kelly and Kai on his behalf. None of those parties responded. However, two days later, Saul Davis expressed his own invective opinion, informing Griffin that he now regarded him as some "self-righteous whore" and, bizarrely, "the lowest scumbag on earth". A simple 'no thanks' would have sufficed. The abuse was puzzling, the more so considering Davis' previous working relationship with the Long Ryders. Yet, it also underlined the extent to which different factions in the Clark story, including former associates and friends, could end up fostering bitter enmities for no good reason.

Sporadic releases continued in recent years. In April 2008, the label Collectors Choice issued *Silverado '75*, a radio recording of a Denver show from 19 February 1975. The same label issued the two-disc *Gene Clark With Carla Olson In Concert*, featuring six songs from Mountain Stage, West Virginia, three demos recorded in Clark's 'living room' and a rather unnecessary re-run of *Silhouetted In Light*. In March 2013, Omnivore Records issued *Here Tonight*, a selection of demos from the *White Light* period. Among the tracks were the previously discussed rarities, 'Jimmy Christ' and 'Please Mr Freud'. A month later, High Moon Records released a long overdue CD reissue of *Two Sides To Every Story*.

In November/December 2016, the eagerly-awaited *Gene Clark: The Lost Studio Sessions 1964–1982* was issued on Sierra Records. This was the most important and expansive release undertaken since Clark's death with a wealth of previously unreleased material, including the 1964 solo sessions with Jim Dickson, studio sessions from 1967, never before heard rarities from the *White Light* era and the Nyte Flyte recordings from 1982. It is hoped that this bumper bundle package might promote additional interest in Clark and pave the way for further archival excavations.

What is left? The *Gene Clark Sings For You* acetate, with 'If I Hang Around' and 'That's What You Want', is still worthy of release. Equally or more importantly, there is a demo tape from 1966 that Jim Dickson generously handed over to Len Freedman in 1989 when he purchased the Tickson Music catalogue. The songs comprise: 'One Way Road'; 'Whatever'; 'Down On The Pier'; 'Bakersfield Train'; 'Back Street Mirror'; 'Got To Get You Off My Mind'; 'Only Colombe'; 'Translations'; 'I Just Like You'; 'I Am Without You'; 'So Much More' and 'Don't [You] Know What You Want'. Another Clark composition, 'It's Easy Now', listed on the tape box, has been crossed out, presumed lost. There is also the Terri Messina reel-to-reel and cassette collection which has yet to be archived, the Glass House tapes (previously discussed), live recordings and various demos and home tapes from the Seventies and Eighties, plus those crucial recordings from the final months of his life, including 'Big Bad Mama', 'Adios Terri', and others. Taken as a whole, the formidable unreleased catalogue of Gene Clark may eventually reinforce his reputation as one of the most important and underrated singer-songwriters to emerge from the mid-Sixties.

Inevitably, Clark's wilder exploits now tend to dominate the narrative of his life. While many acknowledge his dual personality, his warmer, sensitive side tends to be swamped by tales of his excesses. This is partly because such stories are more exciting and easier to recollect. Clark's underlying goodness, that positive side of his personality, was often a passive trait, a state of mind rather than action and less easily articulated, even by his family, close friends and loved ones. Everyday life can be unbearably banal, subject to endless contradiction, exaggerated hopes and fears, digressions, pseudo-profound ruminations, prevarications, self-absorption and erratic progress. Clark experienced all these and more. For those who'd followed his work and life in the Sixties and Seventies, biographical details were scant. He was never subjected to lengthy, probing interviews which may have been a blessing. The image of Clark, at least during his lifetime, was filtered through the prism of record reviews and the subject matter of songs. This allowed him to attain a mystique in keeping with his work.

As with most cultural biography, images are set in stone, only to be cracked when conflicting information emerges that challenges the stereotype. As we now know, Clark was a more complex, rounded, vulnerable person whose flaws were inextricably linked with his genius. Human fallibility is only gradually integrated into a rock persona. It is a sometimes painful process by which the public readjusts its vision to accommodate what was previously unthinkable. The vision of the Beatles as loveable mop tops and Elvis as an all-American icon of non-pharmaceutical healthy living were once ingrained in the public's consciousness to such an extent that they seemed inviolable. Yet, over time, heresy can be assimilated and synthesized to create another image. Such is the case with Gene Clark. His hell-raising tales can now be understood in conjunction with his artistic persona without tainting his legacy. The paradox of such revelations is that the baser stories are ultimately consumed into the myth and emerge as the least important aspect of the picture. In one crucial sense, those who invested their aesthetic appreciation in *White Light* and *No Other* in search of some enduring truth were ultimately right all along. The art speaks loudest and ultimately eclipses the biography. If the mystique of Clark has been disturbed by revelations about his life, that all disappears when you immerse yourself in the purity of the work. That is his final lesson.

GENE CLARK: NOTES

page 10: "My first impression . . ." Jim Dickson, interviewed by the author. London/Maui, Hawaii: 3 August 1998.

page 11: "His flippant claim in 1965 that he was an only child . . ." Clark's contention that he was an only child almost caused a moment of embarrassment when I encountered his brother, Rick, amid a humorous exchange in the late Seventies. I had been invited to attend a McGuinn, Clark & Hillman concert at the Universal Amphitheatre but there was confusion outside the venue. "Somebody find Al Hersh!" barked Stephen Stills' manager Ken Weiss who, like me, was momentarily blocked from getting inside. An even more indignant figure was pleading, "Hey, man, let us in, I'm Gene's brother!" I smiled inwardly. Having memorized Gene's lifelines as a teenager, I *knew* that he was an only child. I was tempted to say something, but admired the chutzpah of this interloper. Looking more closely, I was surprised to see how much he resembled Gene, although he lacked that familiar raven hair. Could he be somehow telling the truth? Maybe he was a cousin . . . It was only later that I learned the 'only child' reference was one of Gene's inventions, as unreliable as his '1941' birthdate. The confusion always made me wary of taking Gene's stories literally although, in fairness, both Michael Clarke and Chris Hillman had been equally circumspect about their dates of birth. That said, Gene was prone to understatement or exaggeration in certain circumstances. At one point in the Eighties, he was pushing the story about Brian Jones supposedly co-writing 'Eight Miles High' but when challenged admitted that they were just sitting around when he first started thinking about composing the song. On another occasion in the Eighties, he played down his fear of flying insisting, against overwhelming evidence to the contrary, that he had no problem travelling by plane. The interviewer was too polite to ask why he had journeyed to the city by train. There were other examples of such contradictions over the years. Although you could argue that this suggested insecurity, it was more likely Clark's sense of mischief. He may also have been inspired by Bob Dylan, who famously mythologized his early years during interviews in the mid-Sixties.

page 11: ". . . he was actually the third of 13 surviving children . . ." The complete list of Clark's siblings comprises Bonita [Bonnie] Elizabeth (born: 13 March 1942), Kelly Katherine [stillborn] (23 March 1943), Harold Eugene [Gene] (born: 17 November 1944), Nancy Patricia (born: 7 July 1946), Mary Delores (born: 28 August 1947), David Austin (born: 18 September 1948), Daniel Oscar (born: 23 November 1949), Christine Rose (born: 8 December 1950), George Richard [Rick] (born: 18 March 1952), Kelly Randall [Randy] (born: 31 May 1953), Ada Rebecca (born: 5 August 1954), Kevin Lee (born: 12 January 1956), Brian Charles (born: 9 July 1959) and Sarah Margaret (born: 19 April 1963). The parents, Kelly and Jeanne, were married on 29 May 1941 and started a family almost immediately.

page 11: ". . . Mary Jeanne Faherty, a descendant of Irish and German immigrants . . ." Documenting the history of the Clark family is a precarious undertaking. Daughter Bonita [Bonnie] appears to have the most interest in genealogy. "My grandmother [Rosemary Sommerhauser] was German Catholic," she says. "She was born in Birk bei Siegburg on 1 April 1859 and died in Boonville, Missouri, on 13 November 1933. Her father [Joseph] emigrated to this country and she was the first American-born child in her entire family. There was still a lot of that home-country influence going on in our family for generations. My grandfather came from near Berlin." As for the Irish connection, that is less easily traceable. "Our ancestors sailed with a group of five families from Galway Bay and they landed in Baltimore, Maryland. They got out before the potato famine. They journeyed and founded a community in Illinois." See later note for information on Clark's alleged Native American history.

page 11: "He never even made it . . ." Bonita 'Bonnie' Clark Laible, interviewed by the author. London/Bonner Springs, Kansas: 8 November 2011. Bonnie confirms: "He was named after my father's younger brother who worked in the paratroopers. I have a picture of Harold Eugene Clark and I do remember his memorial service. I have memories of being three years old. A lot of things were retold so many times that I don't know if they're my memories or just pictures in my mind."

page 11: "That's not just a tale . . ." ibid.

page 11: ". . . a legacy of some Native American blood on his father's side . . ." Bonnie explains: "I don't have any family history on Grandma Clark. That's really thin. She died quite young and didn't have a whole lot of connection with her family. We can trace back Dad to his great grandfather in Iowa. His name was George Douglas Clark. As far as what the heritage is and whether there's any truth to the Indian blood is hard to say. But I have pictures of my father and grandmother and there's no doubt in my mind. We're either Native American Indians or Indian Indians!" David Clark believes that his great-great-grandfather, supposedly named 'Clarke', originally came from England. "There were two brothers that came from England and settled around Adel, Iowa. Their last name had the English 'e' on it: Clarke. The story goes that the younger brother met an Indian woman. There's been speculation as to whether she was a princess or an ordinary woman, but that doesn't matter much. In those days, you did not interact with Native Americans. That was taboo. But he wanted to marry her. According to the story, he and his brother had a falling out so he dropped the English 'e' and moved from Adel, Iowa to what is now the Buffalo Bolivar, Missouri area. I heard this mentioned in family lore from some of the older folks. The rest is a little vague." At one stage, David did some genealogical digging and claims to have found a curious detail in the Clark history, which may or may not be true. "There were some conflicting dates. It stopped where one of the Clark family was hung as a horse thief. Gene got such a kick out of that when I told him. He thought it was hilarious." Whether any written documents exist to confirm any of this is doubtful.

page 11: "Years later . . ." Rick Clark, interviewed by the author. London/ Orcutt, California: 23 June 1999.

page 12: ". . . a small house in which the Clarks lived . . ." Gene's sister Bonnie remembers: "It was very rural and very rough when we first moved out there. Electricity? Just enough to run lights and a refrigerator. No running water. That was put in maybe five years after we got established and it looked like we were going to be there for a while. When we first moved in, my mom so hated that place. I did not know that until I talked to her in later years. It was primitive. There were two stoves, one in the living room and one in the dining room and a kerosene stove out in the kitchen. The ones in the living room and dining room burned either wood or coal. We had none in the bedrooms. There was frost on the windows in the wintertime."

page 12: "Gene did live on a 'farm' . . ." Rick Clark/Rogan. London/ Orcutt, California: 23 June 1999.

page 15: "Despite a poor academic record, he was surprisingly literate, with decent numerical skills and beautiful handwriting . . ." In later years, Clark and Dickson presented me with some songwriting transcripts, accompanied by a note, 'With thanks forever'. Gene's lavish handwriting was appealing and the vocabulary and spelling looked fairly good given his limited education. There were only occasional lapses, notably the amusing "With eggsagerations [sic]" in his transcription of the song 'Back Street Mirror'. On reflection, he was probably thinking of an image of eggs being thrown at a window when he sang: "My mind got pasted to the window with eggsagerations . . ." It later struck me how much neater and error free this work was compared to the song transcripts and notebooks of Gram Parsons, who was privately educated and had attended Harvard. Of course, a number of the entries in Parsons' notebooks were written when he was not sober.

page 15: "Sister Agatha Irene . . ." Bonita 'Bonnie' Clark Laible/Rogan. Bonner Springs, Kansas/London: 8 November 2011. David Clark additionally credits his mother as a positive influence on Gene's later writing. "My mom was a stickler for using correct language and so was my grandmother."

page 16: "My Catholic upbringing . . ." Gene Clark, interviewed by the author. Hollywood, California/Waldport, Oregon: 28–29 April 1989.

page 16: "His mother was very Christian . . ." John 'Jack' Godden, interviewed by the author. London/Belton, Missouri: 11 October 2008.

page 17: "By the time we moved . . ." Bonnie Clark Laible/Rogan. London/Bonner Springs, Kansas: 8 November 2011.

page 17: "It was tough on her . . ." ibid.

page 17: "Mom did not have a lot . . ." ibid.

page 17: "Mother was very temperamental . . ." ibid.

page 17: "He was a very quiet . . ." ibid.

page 18: "He was the favourite . . ." ibid.

page 18: "He wanted the leader role . . ." ibid.

page 18: "She took us under her wing . . ." ibid.

page 18: "Gene thought I should be . . ." ibid.

page 18: "I pulled some tricks . . ." ibid.

page 19: "I had acquired . . ." ibid.

page 19: "The thunderstorm actually darkened . . ." ibid.

page 20: "He would wake up screaming . . ." Jeanne Clark, interviewed by Brian Burnes. *Kansas City Star Magazine*: 17 January 1999. Bonnie Clark has no firm recollection of Gene's night terrors, but that was not entirely surprising. "The girls and boys were in separate rooms so we didn't interact about things like that. Of course being a manly man he wouldn't tell me about his nightmares."

page 20: "He became extremely claustrophobic . . ." David Clark, interviewed by the author. London/Montrose, Colorado: 7 November 2016.

page 21: ". . . when Clark witnessed a plane crash in Kansas . . ." Rick Clark always assumed the story was apocryphal until many years later when his mother told him Gene had actually mentioned the incident to her. So Jeanne Clark, Bonnie and Rick effectively confirm the plane crash story, albeit without providing extensive details. David Clark always remained in the dark. "This is a story I heard for a long time. I did everything with Gene then and knew just about every mood and everything else. Never in his whole life did he mention that to me. He refused to get on the plane with the Byrds. I think maybe this was largely concocted to explain what they called his fear of flying." This is not so. The plane crash was not mentioned in print until long after Clark had left the Byrds, initially during an interview with McGuinn. It seems Gene just kept the details to himself, a not untypical reaction.

page 21: "Cliff Drive used to be . . ." Bonnie Clark Laible/Rogan. London/ Bonner Springs, Kansas: 8 November 2011.

page 21: "The Clarks suffered food shortages . . ." This undoubtedly tainted some of the more idyllic memories associated with growing up in Swope Park. "There were pros and cons," admits David Clark. "I think what ground on everybody was that things weren't improving. It was getting worse and disintegrating as far as our living conditions, even down to what we were eating for dinner. It became grinding and hard . . . When we first moved to Swope Park, the family had been living in Kansas City [at 4427 Mission Road] in a nice neighbourhood. Things weren't so bad. At Swope Park, Gene was relegated to doing all the hard things that Dad couldn't even get to or didn't have time to do. Even I started milking cows and taking care of stock at six years old. It was a way of life but I never had the resentment for it that Gene did. That may have been because I was born into it."

page 22: "He was an excellent sports person . . ." Godden/Rogan. London/ Belton, Missouri: 11 October 2008.

page 22: "We held it together in the school grounds . . ." Godden was still pugnacious, even at the advanced age of 65. On the day of our interview, he told me that he'd had an eventful morning. He had discovered a 17-year-old attempting to break into his car. Jack apprehended him while still in his underwear. The police told him he was lucky the kid wasn't carrying a knife or a gun. The story testifies to his and Gene's tough upbringing.

page 22: "They were very strict . . ." ibid.

page 23: "My dad was a major influence . . ." Rick Clark/Rogan. London/ Orcutt, California: 23 June 1999. Confronted by the same question, Rick's brother David told me: "My dad's influence on Gene was twofold. For one, there was the musical influence but the other advice was to do things to the best of your ability as long as the situation allowed. And not to apologize to anybody for anything if you did your best with it. This was the philosophy my dad lived under."

page 23: "David brought that up . . ." Bonnie Clark Laible/Rogan. London/ Bonner Springs, Kansas: 8 November 2011.

page 23: "All of us tried . . ." David Clark/Rogan. London/Montrose, Colorado: 7 November 2016.
page 23: "He always played guitar . . ." Godden/Rogan. London/Belton, Missouri: 11 October 2008.
page 24: "He was an accomplished . . ." Gene Clark/Rogan. Hollywood, California/Waldport, Oregon: 28–29 April 1989.
page 24: "We both knew Joe . . ." Godden/Rogan. London/Belton, Missouri: 11 October 2008.
page 25: "It was only about 20 bucks . . ." ibid.
page 25: ". . . at least one finished song, 'Blue Ribbons' . . ." Back in 1999, Gene's brother Rick Clark told me about the surviving tape. "My mom had it up until recently and she gave it to my nephew, Kelly. He was going to have it remastered and I believe it was going to be released at a later date. Gene was 14 when he recorded that." David Clark also remembers at least one novelty song that Gene wrote as a joke. It was titled 'Big Chief Hole In The Pants'.
page 25: "He had a voice out of heaven . . ." Godden/Rogan. London/Belton, Missouri: 11 October 2008.
page 25: "The whole band almost got killed . . ." ibid.
page 26: "Joe Meyers was a good . . ." Bonnie Clark Laible/Rogan. London/Bonner Springs, Kansas: 8 November 2011.
page 26: "They knew the tune . . ." ibid.
page 26: "They got a big engagement . . ." Godden/Rogan. London/Belton, Missouri: 11 October 2008.
page 27: "It was like another lifetime . . ." ibid.
page 27: "We drank a lot . . ." ibid.
page 27: "He had all the girls . . ." ibid.
page 27: "Joe Meyers was dating her . . ." ibid.
page 27: "He backed into a tree . . ." ibid.
page 28: "I recorded my first single . . ." Gene Clark, interviewed by Barry Ballard. *Omaha Rainbow* 15: December 1977. Rick Clark was vague about the recording when I spoke to him in 1999, admitting that he had not yet heard the tape. He could not recall any vinyl artefact, but conceded that his memory of that time was unreliable. He was, of course, only about six years old. "I don't think it was ever released on a label and I don't think they signed with anybody. Maybe it got local radio airplay in the late Fifties. This was way back when I was a little kid. My mom and dad would be able to give you more information about that. Gene may have appeared on a couple of local TV shows back then. I was eight years younger than Gene so I wasn't really into music. I was still playing with frogs." Rick's brother David is equally vague about the recording, but speculates long after the event. "It was an acetate that was done as a test tape. There were a couple of copies of it made at the time. One survived pretty much intact. The boys (Kelly and Kai) had it remastered onto a reel-to-reel. On one of the tapes there

was nothing left, the second tape had enough to remaster it and put it on a tape. I swear I don't know how that thing survived because it lay in a closet in the upstairs room of Mom and Dad's house from the time Gene went off with the New Christy Minstrels." David never saw an actual disc on a label and assumed there was no commercial recording, but admits, "I wasn't privy to what Gene was doing when he was in high school. Our age made a big difference on how much interaction we had. I think Jack Godden brought a small tape player to the house and played it way back then." David expressed little interest in any such recording at the time. "I felt I was being deprived of my running mate and buddy and wasn't real happy with the whole thing." The hunt for an actual disc is still on but it's likely very few were pressed, perhaps only a handful, and possibly none survived. Nevertheless the existence of other recordings on Jack Godden's father's custom label provides hope that this mysterious artefact might still be languishing in some Kansas attic.

page 28: "I think my dad . . ." Godden/Rogan. London/Belton, Missouri: 11 October 2008.

page 28: "One pressing features Jimmy Markey and Ginny Lee . . ." The A-side credited to Jimmy Markey (with accompaniment) was titled 'My Helen' (composed by Bob Doherty); the B-side was Ginny Lee's 'Go On And Fall In Love'.

page 29: "We all separated . . ." Godden/Rogan. London/Belton, Missouri: 11 October 2008.

page 29: "He felt betrayed . . ." David Clark/Rogan. London/Montrose, Colorado: 7 November 2016. David adds that the vetoed move to the West Coast affected others in the family. "It did not help Dad's confidence or perspective on life. By the time that came up even somebody as young as myself was looking for any opportunity to get out of the situation we were in. It had its really good points, but also its bad points. The destitution was one of the worst parts of it because Dad's income from the City of Kansas Missouri was not enough to support that number of children in the family at that time."

page 30: "Gene really took it personally . . ." David Clark/Rogan. London/Montrose, Colorado: 7 November 2016.

page 30: "He lost interest . . ." David Clark, *Hours Of Joy: A True American Story* (No imprint. Printed in Overland Park, Kansas, 2016), p. 200.

page 31: "I learned not to get into any disputes . . ." Bonita Clark enlisted for two years, but did not quite complete her term. "I ran up against Mother Nature and my first husband," she says. "I married a guy from Florida and stayed there for about five years. I was 19 when I got married, late in 1961." She was divorced in March 1967 on her 25th birthday.

page 31: "When he moved to Bonner Springs . . ." Godden/Rogan. London/Belton, Missouri: 11 October 2008.

page 31: "He was pretty well-liked . . ." Roxe Zimmerman, interviewed by Jesse Truesdale. *Bonner Springs Chieftain*: 17 January 2007.
page 31: "I went up . . ." ibid.
page 32: "After that we got along . . ." ibid.
page 32: "It was like the snap of a finger . . ." Bonnie Clark Laible/Rogan. London/Bonner Springs, Kansas: 8 November 2011.
page 32: "We took the turn . . ." John Papineau, interviewed by Jesse Truesdale. *Bonner Springs Chieftain*: 17 January 2007.
page 32: "Through the whole thing . . ." ibid.
page 33: "I'll never forget . . ." Judith Tinberg (née Hogan), email interview with the author: 25–26 June 2015. Additional information provided in conversation. Kansas City, Missouri: 21 November 2014.
page 33: ". . . a recording in some local studio . . ." ibid.
page 33: "He'd do most of the talking . . ." ibid.
page 33: "Perhaps that was true . . ." ibid.
page 33: "One afternoon . . ." ibid.
page 34: "late 1962 . . ." Clark/Ballard. *Omaha Rainbow* 15: December 1977.
page 34: "I don't think any of them . . ." Rick Clark/Rogan. London/Orcutt, California: 23 June 1999.
page 34: ". . . an extended single, 'Hey Li Lee' . . ." Released on Mira Records (MEP 101), the single, like most US releases, does not contain a year of release, but it was most likely issued between 1961 and 1962. It was accompanied by a promotional sheet which provides a tantalizing history of the group: "The Surf Riders, the bright young trio currently appearing at the Castaways Lounge in Kansas City, are relatively newcomers to the entertainment business. Roommates at a small mid-western university, Vic Ehly, bongo and fiddle man, and C.E. Lear, lead singer and guitar player, became a popular on-campus calypso duo. In September of 1960, Mike Crumm came to the university with his beat-up guitar. Mike had led a folk-singing quartet at his high school and it was not long until the three boys got together in a jam session. There, the Surf Riders were born. During the school year the boys made pocket money playing for civic clubs and youth groups in small towns and big cities throughout the Midwest. On one of these tours they were 'discovered' and brought to the Castaways where they have been belting out their particular brand of humor and music for enthusiastic audiences. The Surf Riders do not fall into any particular group type. 'We just like to have fun with good songs,' they say, and have fun they do. Their versatility and enthusiasm are evidenced by the songs on this their first recording effort." Whether the Surf Riders ever recorded any other singles is, at best, conjectural. The group title may have been used by other artistes across the country. One single I unearthed was 'Panel Five' issued by the Surf Riders on Festival Custom Pressing in 1963. Alas, there is no writing credit on the disc. It may well

be of Australian origin. The Surf Riders' name was also used for an instrumental single issued on Decca (US) in 1963: 'The Birds' b/w 'Blues For The Birds'. Both sides were inspired by the Alfred Hitchcock film of the same year and written by band leader, Sonny Burke. Coincidentally, the Byrds later used the promotional ads for Hitchcock's film during their 1965 UK tour, when advertisements announced: 'The Byrds Is Coming'.

page 35: "He had a magnificent voice . . ." Jim Glover, interviewed by Brian Burnes. *Kansas City Star Magazine*: 17 January 1999.

page 35: "Gay came from . . ." David Clark/Rogan. London/Montrose, Colorado: 7 November 2016. Confusingly, Gay Lindsey is referred to as Gala Chambers in Einarson's biography. David Clark admits he was responsible for that error. "When I did that interview with John, I hadn't thought about all of this in a long time. Gala Chambers was another person. I mixed the names up. I got confused with Gay and Gala. Gala Chambers was the girlfriend of my younger brother, Dan. When I read his book, I went, 'Damn!'"

page 35: "Gay was all about him . . ." ibid.

page 36: "I witnessed it . . ." ibid.

page 36: ". . . in a garage . . ." Clark/Ballard. *Omaha Rainbow* 15: December 1977.

page 36: "There was this guy . . ." ibid.

page 36: "Originally formed in 1961 . . ." The New Christy Minstrels took their name from the nineteenth-century ensemble Christy's Minstrels (founded by Edwin P. Christy) who specialized in popularizing Stephen Foster songs and Negro spirituals, usually performed in blackface. Sparks' original idea was to use the group for recording purposes only, with the individual members touring solo or with other musicians. Once they signed to CBS Records, Randy Sparks was encouraged to team up with Greif-Garris Management (George Greif and Sid Garris) leading to television exposure on *The Andy Williams Show*. They toured extensively and recorded prolifically. Sparks retired from performing duties in May 1963 to concentrate on songwriting for the group. At the time Clark was recruited, the line-up comprised Nick Woods, Art Podell, Barry McGuire, Barry Kane, Larry Ramos, Clarence Treat, Jackie Miller and Gayle Caldwell.

page 37: "That was my Hollywood moment . . ." Gene Clark/Rogan. Hollywood, California/Waldport, Oregon: 28–29 April 1989.

page 37: ". . . Sparks even commandeered the remaining Surf Riders . . ." This meant the Castaways Lounge was deprived of a major attraction. The Tiki bar found a replacement group, the Bluemont Singers, whose membership had attended Kansas State University. They went on to record an album, *The Bluemont Singers*, whose sleeve boasted "ballads, blues, bluegrass, folk songs by the Bluemont Singers . . . at the Castaways" on the local label, Brass Records.

page 37: "We stayed up all night . . ." Mike Crowley, interviewed by Brian Burnes. *Kansas City Star Magazine*: 17 January 1999.

page 37: "I knew Gene had a great voice . . ." Godden/Rogan. London/Belton, Missouri: 11 October 2008.

page 38: ". . . it spelt the end of their relationship . . ." David Clark, who was enamoured of Gay Lindsey, has no idea what happened to her. "I don't know if they ever had any more communication or interaction. Gene didn't come back to Kansas very often." Although Gene did return to the area on a subsequent stopover, his former girlfriend was absent. "I was surprised not to see her," David told me. "I even looked for her because I assumed she'd be there. Gene never mentioned her much during the rest of his life. Apparently they said their goodbyes and that was it. She knew that he was moving on to a different life. Gay had a whole life for herself. She understood that this was an opportunity that comes to so very few. I think she was a catalyst in moving him along. Keeping the secret from Mom and Dad until he was ready to go on the plane, I think she was part of that. She understood that if he had a lot of time to think about it and the pressure from family he might not do it."

David next provided oddly contradictory viewpoints on Gene's motivations. Recalling the Swope Park period, he said: "Gene had made up his mind that he just wasn't going to live that way and was going to do something about it and when the opportunities came along, he didn't hesitate in taking them." Minutes later, he suggested that there was great hesitation about leaving Kansas. "He was not sure about it. He was very apprehensive. He wasn't sure if he wouldn't be back the next week. He didn't know what the greater world out there was going to be like."

page 38: "We knew he was going to go . . ." Jeanne Clark/Burnes. *Kansas City Star Magazine*: 17 January 1999.

page 38: "Mom was beside herself . . ." David Clark. Unedited transcript for the 2013 DVD documentary, *The Byrd Who Flew Alone – The Triumph and Tragedy of Gene Clark*. Four Sun Productions: 2013.

page 38: ". . . appeared on two albums (*Today* and *Land Of Giants*) . . ." Although Clark appears on the cover of the album *Merry Christmas!* the work was completed several weeks before his arrival. New Christy Minstrels chronicler Tom Pickles, who has seen archive photos from that CBS session, confirms that *Merry Christmas!* (issued in October 1963) featured Clark's short-lived predecessor, Doug Brookins. "This despite previous testimonies by several Minstrels, including Randy Sparks." Pickles estimates that Clark arrived three weeks after the sessions for *Merry Christmas!* were completed. His first recordings with the NCM occurred on 19 August and featured 'Grun Grun' (the German version of 'Green Green'), an abridged version of 'The Drinkin' Gourd' (omitting its first verse) and "the final tracks for

'Natural Man'." After returning from Hawaii, the group recorded 'Saturday Night' in September and it was released the following month. The chronology is complicated by the delayed release of *Land Of Giants* which, although recorded in December 1963 ("a week after the Kennedy assassination", Tom Pickles reveals) did not appear until July 1964, several months after Clark's departure. In January 1964, the ensemble recorded *Today*, which was issued two months later. The chronology suggests that Gene must have appeared on this record too, but whether he attended the session cannot be confirmed. When pushed, NCM expert Tom Pickles concedes: "The truth is no one remembers, and Columbia doesn't have a roster of the members in their session records – only the hired session musicians." He suggests Gene "probably" appeared which, barring the belatedly discovery of photo evidence from the sessions, is the closest we're likely to get in determining the issue. However, Clark did definitely appear on the film soundtrack of MGM's *Advance To The Rear*, adapted by Hugo Montenegro who, of course, would later work with both the Byrds and Clark.

page 38: "So he joined . . ." Jeanne Clark, interviewed by Brian Burnes. *Kansas City Star Magazine*: 17 January 1999.

page 38: "He had a different kind of countenance . . ." Barry McGuire, interviewed by the author. Rosslare, Co. Wexford, Republic of Ireland: 1–2 August 2008.

page 39: "The sound was so different . . ." Gene Clark/Rogan. Hollywood, California/Waldport, Oregon: 28–29 April 1989.

page 39: ". . . a rather insipid casserole . . ." review of the New Christy Minstrels at the Arena, Winnipeg on 19 October 1963. *Winnipeg Free Press*: 21 October 1963.

page 39: "Everybody was very upset . . ." Gene Clark, interviewed by Paul Zollo. *Song Talk*: Spring 1991.

page 39: "He was a different person . . ." David Clark. Unedited transcript for the 2013 DVD documentary, *The Byrd Who Flew Alone – The Triumph and Tragedy of Gene Clark*. Four Sun Productions: 2013.

page 40: "He was very haughty . . ." ibid.

page 40: "Go uptown . . ." ibid.

page 40: "We did 300 shows a year . . ." McGuire/Rogan. Rosslare, Co. Wexford, Republic of Ireland: 1–2 August 2008.

page 40: "Randy Sparks thought of us . . ." ibid.

page 41: "Dolan was like the mechanical man . . ." Randy Sparks, interviewed by Brian Burnes. *Kansas City Star Magazine*: 17 January 1999.

page 41: "It was quite a moment . . ." McGuire/Rogan. Rosslare, Co. Wexford, Republic of Ireland: 1–2 August 2008.

page 42: "First of all . . ." ibid.

page 42: "It was weird and sad . . ." Clark/Zollo. *Song Talk*: Spring 1991.

page 43: ". . . Sparks was already considering replacing him with Paul Potash from the Back Porch Majority . . ." Randy Sparks would have fired Clark if he had not quit. Gene surely knew this when he decided to relocate to LA. Strangely enough, his former colleague Mike Crumm (Crowley) proved a more comfortable and accomplished performer when working in the Back Porch Majority. Years later, Sparks concluded that in recruiting Gene for the Christies, he had probably chosen the wrong Surf Rider.

page 43: "The Christy Minstrels, including me . . ." McGuire/Rogan. Rosslare, Co. Wexford, Republic of Ireland: 1–2 August 2008.

page 43: "They hadn't really broken wide yet . . ." Gene Clark, interviewed by Frank Beeson. *Bucketful Of Brains* 21: July 1987. This quote was preceded by an anecdote in which Clark outlined his increasing fascination with the group. "I had a day off and took a cab. The cab driver says, 'Hey, did you ever hear of the Beatles?' I said, 'Yeah, I heard of them, but what is all this about?' He said, 'Well, look at this book. My daughter just got back from England.' So he gave me a book called *The Beatles*. It showed pictures of girls fainting and everything. I thought, 'Wow! I haven't seen anything like this since Elvis Presley! This is pretty far out.' So I put a search out to find some of their records." While the gist of this story may well be correct, there was no book titled *The Beatles* published in the UK. It's likely that Clark was referring to *The True Story Of The Beatles* (Beat Publications) written by Billy Shepherd (a pseudonym used by *Record Mirror*'s Peter Jones) which appeared at the end of March 1964. However, by then, the Beatles were long established in the American consciousness and Gene had already relocated to California. The more famous Beatles' book *Love Me Do: The Beatles' Progress* by Michael Braun did not appear till later the same year. It seems that Clark's chronology is slightly off or perhaps the taxi driver presented him with a newspaper article or a copy of the photo book *Meet The Beatles* or the fanzine *The Beatles Book*, which had been available since August 1963.

page 44: "He said John Denver had ratted him . . ." Tom Slocum, interviewed by the author. London/Taluca Lake, California: 16 September 1998.

page 44: "Your name's too big . . ." McGuire/Rogan. Rosslare, Co. Wexford, Republic of Ireland: 1–2 August 2008.

page 44: "The New Christy Minstrels had just had a big hit . . ." ibid.

page 44: "Randy said . . ." ibid.

page 48: "You should have heard David . . ." Dickson/Rogan. London/Costa Mesa, California: 24 May 2009.

page 48: "Just about every song he ever wrote . . ." Dickson/Rogan. London/Maui, Hawaii: 3 August 1998.

page 49: "Dylan was most interested in Gene Clark . . ." Dickson/Rogan. Waldport, Oregon: 26–30 April 1989.

page 50: "Chris knew nothing . . ." Gene Clark, interviewed by Bruce Eder. *Goldmine*: 11 January 1991.

page 50: ". . . never even bothering to send news of his good fortune to his family . . ." David Clark claims that Gene "kept that pretty distant from the family". Less convincingly, he says, "It wasn't until the first album actually was printed and came out that we knew he was in a group called the Byrds, because he sent some copies of the album home." How could this be? The album was not issued until 21 June 1965 by which time 'Mr Tambourine Man' had been a number 1 hit and 'All I Really Want To Do' had been released. Moreover, the Byrds had appeared in magazine spreads and television shows, including the nationally broadcast *Hullabaloo*. It is inconceivable that the Clark family would have been unaware that Gene was a member of the Byrds, the more so considering David Clark's claim: "I knew basically what was in the Top 40." Even if he hadn't, others in the community would have conveyed the exciting news. Additionally, Bonnie Clark recalls first learning of Gene being in the Byrds when she saw a spread in a fashion magazine which she assumed was the first article on them. This was presumably the *Cosmopolitan* article, published as early as March 1965. David Clark also adds that several magazines printed that Gene was born in San Fernando Valley. "Columbia had decided he should be a California boy and not from Bonner Springs, Kansas." There are no known clippings or features where Clark was ever connected with San Fernando Valley. In the Byrds' oft-printed 'Life Lines' under the section 'Present Home', it actually says 'Bonner, Springs, Kansas'. Under the section 'Education', it states: 'Raytown, Missouri, Bonner Springs, Kansas'. There is no subterfuge here. Presumably, David Clark is confusing all this with the previously mentioned, and more hurtful, reference to 'Brothers and Sisters': 'None.'

page 50: "Gene was most amusing . . ." Derek Taylor, interviewed by the author. London: 13 February 1997.

page 51: "'Mr Tambourine Man' was written . . ." Gene Clark, interviewed by Richard Bruce. *Music Echo*: 11 September 1965.

page 52: "There isn't one of them . . ." David Crosby, interviewed by the author. London: 22–23 April 1980.

page 52: "David was never a very strong songwriter . . ." Clark/Eder. *Goldmine*: 11 January 1991.

page 52: "We had the feeling . . ." Roger McGuinn, unpublished, undated interview by Jim Prichard, *c.* spring 2003.

page 52: "Suddenly we thought we could get away with this . . ." Dickson/Rogan. Waldport, Oregon: 26–30 April 1989.

page 53: ". . . 'The Emptiness' (probably the correct title of what was later referred to as 'The Day Walk') . . ." This song has a convoluted history. It was registered for copyright as 'The Emptiness' on 1 November 1965, but was not issued on *Turn! Turn! Turn!* as might have been expected. Oddly, no such song was ever logged in CBS' vaults, or so it seemed. Decades later, a previously unknown 1965 Byrds song was found on tape which was clearly sung by Gene Clark. He could not recall much about the composition, let alone its title, so suggested that they call it 'Never Before'. He was thrilled when it became the title track of the 1987 Byrds' archive album of the same name. However, during Sony's subsequent remastering of the original albums, it was discovered that the song had actually been recorded in September 1965 without a session number and logged under the curious title, 'The Day Walk'. However, no song of that title was ever registered for copyright which is perplexing. Was 'The Day Walk' simply one of those 'best guess' titles added to a tape box in haste, as was often the case? Conversely, 'The Emptiness', conspicuous by its absence from any album, and assumed to be a completely different composition, *was* registered for copyright on the same date as four songs later included on *Turn! Turn! Turn!*. Even more tellingly, the lyrics to 'The Day Walk' include the title of 'The Emptiness' in one of its key verses: "*the emptiness* of a thing that's less than it was thought to be . . ." Alas, a lyric sheet in Clark's own handwriting with the original title 'The Emptiness' (which would provide definitive proof) is not known to have survived.

page 54: "David instigated that whole thing . . ." Dickson/Rogan. Waldport, Oregon: 26–30 April 1989.

page 55: "I think what turned David against the song . . ." Dickson/ Rogan. London/Maui, Hawaii: 3 August 1998.

page 55: "Rather less attention has been paid to Gene Clark . . ." Clark's role in writing 'Eight Miles High' was discussed and analysed in *Volume 1* of this book. Witnesses ranging from Jim Dickson to Derek Taylor point out that he was the main composer of the song and its chief lyricist. In later years there was something of a storm in a teacup controversy about the alteration of the writing credits which originally read: G. Clark, J. McGuinn, D. Crosby. In February 1991, Clark's former representative Saul Davis wrote to me complaining about the contents of the first Byrds' box set which I had criticized in print for failing to include several of Clark's major songs. Davis seized on the point that the songwriting credit for 'Eight Miles High' had been mysteriously altered in favour of 'R. McGuinn, G. Clark, D. Crosby'. In fact, this was nothing new, so I didn't even bother to comment on the matter which I felt was of minimal importance. However, the point was taken up in earnest many years later by author John Einarson in his Gene Clark biography. Although David Crosby told him that he felt the re-ordering of the credits had no significance, Einarson concluded with a rhetorical conundrum. "The question remains: would Roger McGuinn have altered the credits if Gene were still alive?"

This minor conspiracy theory is rather torpedoed by the fact that such an alteration had already been made over 20 years before Clark's death.

On the 1970 Byrds double album *(Untitled),* 'Eight Miles High' is credited to McGuinn/Crosby/Clark.

Arguably this reordering was partly justified at the time as the new elongated live version was a 16-minute jam that went way beyond the original melody. Despite the song's length, the lyrics were hardly featured at all and merely consisted of a coda featuring nothing more than the opening verse. That said, it is odd that Crosby was elevated to second position in the credits. They could hardly claim it was alphabetical. Once this alteration was made, it was always likely to be repeated in error on reissues of the original version of the song. McGuinn, of course, would have had no say in this. He was completely innocent.

The unfortunate implication that McGuinn had deliberately doctored history for purposes of self-glorification is further undermined by the credits on the accompanying *20 Essential Tracks From the Boxed Set: 1965–1990.* Here, the credits read 'G. Clark, D. Crosby, R. McGuinn'. Within the space of two years, McGuinn had dropped from first to third place in the credits, now even lower than his status had been on the original 1966 single. With the reissue of *Fifth Dimension* in 1996, the credits dramatically changed again, this time reading McGuinn, Crosby, Clark – repeating those on (*Untitled),* but now applied to the original track. This was the most severe demotion of Gene to date. These snakes and ladders reversals and anomalies underline the point that the various credits since the single's first appearance were arbitrary. It is also important to note that McGuinn had previously credited Clark for choosing the title 'Eight Miles High'. They had been discussing the height at which planes fly and McGuinn estimated that it was about six miles high. McGuinn recalls Gene changing it to eight because it "sounded more poetic". Clark repeated this story in an interview just before he died, but credited McGuinn rather than himself for changing it from six to eight. So, in the end, Clark was crediting McGuinn for something that Roger believed was suggested by Gene.

By the time of the second Byrds' box set *There Is A Season* in 2006, the credit was back to the original order of Clark, McGuinn, Crosby. The accompanying compilation, *The Very Best Of The Byrds*, also stuck with that name sequence, suggesting that everybody was back on track, at last.

Focusing on the 'Eight Miles High' credit is something of a red herring. A more profitable source of confusion is *The Notorious Byrd Brothers,* whose order of credits seems arbitrary at best. I recall Hillman telling my colleague Pete Frame that there was no significance whatsoever in whose name was placed first. It was supposedly no clue as to who might have contributed most to the composition. Of course the real oddity here was 'Get To You', which McGuinn later claimed should have been co-credited to Clark, not Hillman. McGuinn believes this was a result of some administrative mix-up. It has yet to be corrected and evidently was never challenged by Clark during his lifetime. Indeed, Clark did not once comment on the song in print. Hillman, for his part, believes the published credit is correct and has no memory whatsoever of Clark's involvement. So perhaps McGuinn's recollection of events is faulty but his suggestion that Clark wanted to create another song involving a plane flight to England has a strong resonance. Perhaps deeper research might throw further light on this.

On the matter of credits and conspiracies, there is another important instance where Clark has actually trumped McGuinn. The cover of the 1973 released Byrds reunion album reads: 'Gene Clark, Chris Hillman, David Crosby, Roger McGuinn, Michael Clarke'. It is neither alphabetical nor logical to have McGuinn relegated to fourth position but Clark should have been pleased about it – oh, and Chris Hillman too!

page 57: "Gene wasn't kindly treated . . ." Taylor/Rogan. London: 13 February 1997.

page 57: "I did miss the guitar . . ." Clark/Eder. *Goldmine*: 11 January 1991.

page 57: "There was more fear from me . . ." Taylor/Rogan. London: 13 February 1997.

page 58: "Would you write a song . . ." Candie Callaway Mullins, speaking at the Gene Clark Symposium. Kansas City, Missouri: 21 November 2014. Author's notes and follow-up questions.

page 58: "We were like stalkers . . ." ibid.

page 59: "The next thing you know . . ." ibid.

page 59: "It was gruelling . . ." ibid.

page 60: "Gene was producing . . ." ibid.

page 61: "I remember Gene was fooling about . . ." Dickson/Rogan. London/Maui, Hawaii: 3 August 1998.

page 61: "I think he was rather bemused . . ." Cyrus Faryar, quoted in Matthew Greenwald, *Go Where You Wanna Go: The Oral History Of The Mamas & The Papas* (New York: Cooper Square Press, 2002), p. 137.

page 61: "I could never accuse Michelle . . ." *Papa John An Autobiography*, John Phillips with Jim Jerome. (London: W.H. Allen, 1986), p. 158

page 62: "This letter is to advise you . . ." Letter to Mrs Michelle Gilliam Phillips dated 28 June 1966, signed by John Phillips, Dennis Doherty and Cass Elliot.

page 62: "I was fired . . ." Michelle Phillips, interviewed by the author. Beverly Hills, California: 16 July 1979.

page 62: "That was a lie . . ." ibid.

page 62: "Jill was already with them . . ." ibid.

page 62: "When Jill appeared . . ." ibid.

page 63: "I begged them . . ." ibid.

page 63: "They were all qualified people . . ." Clark/Ballard. *Omaha Rainbow* 15: December 1977.

page 63–64: "After every practice . . ." Chip Douglas, interviewed by Chris Hollow. *Tarantula: The Sand Pepples' Fanzine*: 13 May/4 June 2004.
page 64: "Nobody really went nuts . . ." ibid.
page 65: "a song called 'Madeleine' . . . ibid.
page 65: "We listened back . . ." ibid.
page 65: "I was like, 'OK' . . ." ibid.
page 65: "It was one of the first songs . . ." Dickson/Rogan. Waldport, Oregon: 26–30 April 1989.
page 66: "I put myself back . . ." Dickson/Rogan. London/Maui, Hawaii: 3 August 1998.
page 66: "I was into the symbolism . . ." Dickson/Rogan. London/Maui, Hawaii: 7 July 1997.
page 67: "I met Gene Clark . . ." Richard 'Ritchie' Lewis, addressing the Gene Clark Symposium. Kansas City, Missouri: 21 November 2014.
page 68: "He would actually . . ." ibid.
page 68: ". . . . the haunting 'If I Hang Around' . . ." This song was issued posthumously on Australia's Raven Records' compilation, *Byrd Parts 2*, in 2003, with Chip Douglas adding bass and harmony to the original demo.
page 69: "Instead, the long player was preceded by a pilot single . . ." On 11 October 1966, publicist Derek Taylor despatched a typed memo headed 'For Immediate Release'. It stated: "Gene Clark, former member of the Byrds, has been signed to an exclusive recording contract by Columbia Records. Clark, 22, former folk singer and New Christy Minstrel, will be featured as a soloist. Negotiations between Gene Clark's management and the label's A&R vice president, Bill Gallagher – when the latter was in Hollywood last week – resulted in plans to rush release Clark's first single before the end of October. An album will follow on January 1, next year. Gene Clark, who left the Byrds in the spring of this year, has spent the past six months assembling material for his solo effort and he now has 30 completed tunes and lyrics – eight of them already recorded tracks. Top-side of the first single – waxed in Columbia's Hollywood studios – is titled 'Echoes'. Words and music were penned by Gene who is backed on the song by a 16-piece orchestra, directed by Leon Russell, one of Los Angeles' leading arrangers. Flip side of the single will be a more formal upbeat rocker.

"Gene Clark, farmer's son and one of a family of 13 from Kansas City, Missouri, was – with Jim McGuinn and David Crosby – one of the founders of the Byrds in the summer of 1964. He is a prolific songwriter; his contributions to Byrds recordings include 'Eight Miles High', 'I'll Feel A Whole Lot Better', 'Set You Free' – all single chart items – and album tracks 'It's No Use', 'You Won't Have To Cry', 'Here Without You', 'I Knew I'd Want You', 'The World Turns All Around Her' and 'If You're Gone'. He is managed by James Dickson and Ed Tickner, who are also responsible for the direction of the Byrds.

Since he left the Byrds, Gene has, from time to time, performed with the Columbia group and he is still free to do so when the whim takes him. But his solo career is paramount and there's no question of him returning to the Byrds as a full-time performer."

page 69: "Gene gave me a tape . . ." Dickson/Rogan. London/Maui, Hawaii: 3 August 1998.

page 69: "When he wrote 'Echoes' . . ." Dickson/Rogan. Waldport, Oregon: 26–30 April 1989.

page 69: "I remember going over to Leon's . . ." Clark/Eder. *Goldmine*: 11 January 1991. It was actually a 16-piece, not a 32-piece orchestra.

page 70: "That's what CBS thought . . ." Dickson/Rogan. London/Maui, Hawaii: 7 July 1997.

page 70: "I was very impressed . . ." Dickson/Rogan. Waldport, Oregon: 26–30 April 1989.

page 70: "Former member . . ." Advertisement placed in *Billboard* and *Cash Box* by Tickson Management.

page 71: "It was deflating . . ." Larry Marks, interviewed by the author. London/Los Angeles, California: 9 October 2007.

page 72: "I'd been a dancer . . ." Sharon Brooks (née Garrett), interviewed by the author. London/Hollywood, California: 7–8 October 2007.

page 72: "Terri and I were roommates . . ." ibid.

page 72: "We certainly enjoyed our time . . ." ibid.

page 72: "It transpired . . ." Terri Messina, interviewed by the author. North Hollywood, California: 1–2 September 1996.

page 72: "She was crazy about him . . ." Sharon Brooks (née Garrett)/ Rogan. London/Hollywood, California: 7–8 October 2007.

page 73: "I'm still a little puzzled . . ." Dickson/Rogan. Waldport, Oregon: 26–30 April 1989.

page 73: "Columbia had the Byrds . . ." Clark/Eder. *Goldmine*: 11 January 1991.

page 74: "Within a conglomeration . . ." Extract from rear cover of *Gene Clark & The Gosdin Brothers*.

page 74: "This is my first album . . ." ibid.

page 75: "On 24 January . . ." It may seem extraordinary that Clark would record these songs as early as this. However, the information is correct. It is not clear how many songs were recorded at this session, but 8-track one-inch tape reels of the two songs survive. Copies of these were sent to me by John Delgatto (administrator of Dickson's recording archives) and they are clearly dated 1/24/66. On the tape box, 'Back Street Mirror' is incorrectly titled 'Without You'. This mistake was hardly surprising as the words 'Back Street Mirror' do not appear in the song. Clark was clearly following the example of Dylan, who had already started this trend on singles such as 'Positively 4th Street' and 'Rainy Day Women # 12 & 35'. On the original manuscript of 'Back Street Mirror', the song was actually titled 'How Hard It Would Be' but Clark studiously crossed out that title replacing it with 'Back Street Mirror' on every page.

It seems almost certain that the Masekela-arranged 'Yesterday, Am I Right' (later transferred to an acetate) was recorded at the same time as 'Don't Let It Fall Through' and 'Back Street Mirror' but the actual reel has not survived, so we cannot be entirely sure. Far less likely, though possible, is that 'That's Alright By Me' (subsequently featured on the summer acetate titled *Gene Clark Sings For You*), complete with a string accompaniment, may also emanate from this Dickson/Russell session.

page 76: "Dickson gave the rights to Leon Russell's publishing company . . ." Interestingly, Tickson Music retained the rights for the superior 'Back Street Mirror' and, excepting 'Don't Let It Fall Through', no other Gene Clark song was assigned to Skyhill. Such horse trading was not untypical of Dickson. Years before, he had been involved in a trade-off with Jac Holzman of Elektra Records over the rights to 'Please Let Me Love You'/'Don't Be Long'. The Byrds had wanted to re-record the B-side (later retitled 'It Won't Be Wrong') for CBS and Dickson suggested to Elektra that they split the rights on each song, allowing Holzman to select one. He rightly figured Holzman would choose 'Please Let Me Love You' rather than 'Don't Be Long'.

page 78: "We were out in this parking lot . . ." John York, interviewed by the author. London/Claremont, Los Angeles, California: 11 June 2007.

page 78: "My memory of that combination . . ." ibid.

page 78: "I used to lock myself in my house . . ." Unsourced quote from Gene Clark, included in J.P. Morisset's tribute article, 'Flying Forever' published in *Bucketful Of Brains.* I contacted Morisset but he could no longer remember the source and had not kept his notes about the article.

page 83: "Tellingly, six of its eight songs were not even registered for copyright . . ." Only 'One Way Road' and 'Down On The Pier' were registered (both on 21 April 1967). Of course, Tickson Music had ceased representing Clark by the end of the summer of 1967. They had always been more diligent about such registrations. Spector may not have bothered as the songs had not been released by Clark or covered by any other artiste.

page 83–84: "His name is not listed . . ." There is no documented evidence that Clark ever appeared on any song on *The Notorious Byrd Brothers.* No session listing has ever emerged confirming his presence. In contemporaneous interviews, there was no mention of him recording anything. Revealingly, Clark himself never claimed any involvement in the work. Moreover, McGuinn, Hillman and Clarke have no memories of working with him at the sessions. Producer Gary Usher doesn't mention Clark contributing to any session and road manager Jim Seiter, who was present during the recordings of 'Goin' Back', insists he was definitely not in attendance. Indeed, Seiter mentioned that session to me in detail back in the Seventies when his memory was fresher than today. In the recreated and highly questionable accounts of the recordings that Seiter belatedly wrote decades later, he still denies Gene's involvement. In 2005, writer John Einarson claimed that Clark did add a vocal part to 'Goin' Back' (even though it was first recorded prior to his reinstatement). His source was John Noreen (from the group the Rose Garden) who recalled: "They were doing some overdubs on 'Goin' Back'. None of the band was there. Gene was putting on a vocal." The veracity of this account is contentious considering the lapse in time, but it is certainly worth noting. Interestingly, fellow Rose Garden member Bill Fleming offers a totally different memory of those events, claiming that Clark was not present in the studio, but merely viewing from the control room. "The only person I saw on the other side of the glass was McGuinn. Gene and Hillman weren't in the studio. It looked to me like the song was already done." Obviously, the matter will never be resolved to everyone's satisfaction but, in the absence of any definitive documentation, I remain understandably sceptical about the retrospective claims of Clark's involvement. Any documentation on the matter would be most gratefully received.

page 84: "For some reason, he didn't want to see me . . ." Godden/Rogan. London/Belton, Missouri: 11 October 2008.

page 86: "Perhaps the teaming . . ." The first Clark song not to be published by Tickson Music was the earlier 'Don't Let It Fall Through', credited to Leon Russell's Skyhill Music. Neither 'That Nonsense Stuff' nor 'No Sweeter Love' had any publisher details on the submissions listed at the Library of Congress. This may have been intentional as Clark was no longer with Tickson Music and had yet to sign to A&M's publishing arm Irving Music so he was technically a free agent. On 11 November 1996, both these songs were registered to Gene Clark Music by Kelly and Kai Clark and, tellingly, they remain there at the time of writing over 20 years later. On the original single, the credits read 'Gene Clark/McClanahan', notably printing Clark's name first and in full. Further details about his possible involvement are not known.

page 87: ". . . a group conveniently titled Phoenix . . ." The line-up of Phoenix featured Laramy Smith (guitar/vocals), Wayne Bruns (bass) and Aaron Vandervordt (drums).

page 87: "The first remained in the vaults for 30 years . . ." Evidently, it was not considered valuable enough to reissue. In the summer of 1977 I received a copy of a reel-to-reel tape of 'Los Angeles' that I was told had been retrieved from a dumpster, along with a bunch of other stuff thrown out by A&M.

page 87: "I wrote the song . . ." Laramy Smith, uncredited online, email interview, dated 2010.

page 87: "I wanted to do . . ." ibid.

page 88: "He tripped over an amplifier . . ." Jim Seiter, interviewed by the author. London/Macao, People's Republic of China: 28 June 2007.

page 89: "I'd been on *The Andy Williams Show* . . ." David Jackson, interviewed by the author. London/Van Nuys, California: 4 October 2007.

page 89: "They said, 'We want to . . .'" ibid.

page 90: "We'd been playing for weeks . . ." ibid.

page 90: "We went into the studio . . ." ibid.

page 91: "Unfortunately, few ran to cover the compositions . . ." One exception was an Australian group, Autumn, who recorded 'Song To Raymondo' for a single.

page 91: "We ran in the same circles . . ." Jackson/Rogan. London/Van Nuys, California: 4 October 2007.

page 92: "What do you do . . ." Gene Clark, interviewed by Andy Darlington. *Full Circle* 10: September 1991.

page 92: "The work features eight Clark originals . . ." This refers to the original vinyl release. Confusingly, the album was later reissued on CD in the UK by Edsel Records, complete with the original sleeve and artwork, but with additional songs. There were no new liner notes explaining the insertion of the bonus tracks, 'Why Not Your Baby', 'Lyin' Down The Middle' and 'Don't Be Cruel', which had first been issued as singles releases. Regrettably, Edsel did not feature these as bonus tracks at the close of the CD, preceded by the traditional long pause, but incorporated the songs into the main body of the work, compromising the original album in the process.

page 93: "They were two sides . . ." Jackson/Rogan. London/Van Nuys, California: 4 October 2007.

page 94: "There was no drummer . . ." ibid.

page 94: "Everything was fine . . ." ibid.

page 94: "I don't remember . . ." ibid.

page 94: "He was sitting on his amp . . ." ibid.

page 95: "I was hanging out . . ." Jon Corneal, interviewed by the author. London/Winter Haven, Florida: 24 June 2007.

page 95: "You're going to be here . . ." ibid.

page 95: "After that they pretty much . . ." ibid. Questions remain about this remarkable evening. The acid seems to have taken its toll on some memories, while others overplay their involvement, creating confusion. Jackson provided the most expressive account, but under cross-examination rapidly changed from insisting that a drummer couldn't possibly have been present to admitting that Michael Clarke might have been there. A photo, featured in John Einarson's biography, dated December, may or may not be from the opening night at the Troubadour. Dillard & Clark were booked there from 17–22 December, but Einarson now suspects that there was a presentation night the previous month, around Thanksgiving. This may be the 'acoustic night' that Jackson insists was their debut. Then there is the accompanying testimony of Jon Corneal confirming his presence instead of Clarke. Corneal, unless he is suffering from a remarkable degree of false memory syndrome, provides too vivid and detailed an account to be dismissed. The most plausible explanation, for what it's worth, is that this was an all acoustic line-up, but Corneal guested at the last minute on snare drum. Michael Clarke was subsequently appointed as the drummer proper and much later down the line Corneal was invited to join, perhaps partly because he had already established a relationship with the Expedition at that eventful, disastrous evening. This is just my conjectural take on the events having spoken to the participants while attempting to reconcile the various contradictions into something approaching a plausible explanation. Of course, it must be stressed that plausibility and actuality are not always the same.

page 96: "We all got paid . . ." Jackson/Rogan. London/Van Nuys, California: 4 October 2007.

page 96: "I don't know why he chose me . . ." ibid.

page 96: "Years before . . ." ibid.

page 97: "That was the story we got . . ." Corneal/Rogan. London/ Winter Haven, Florida: 24 June 2007.

page 97: "That was a problem for Bernie . . ." ibid.

page 98: "I liked Gene . . ." ibid.

page 98: "Gene was in a booth . . ." David Clark/Rogan. London/ Montrose, Colorado: 7 November 2016.

page 99: "Byron had his hair high . . ." Jackson/Rogan. London/Van Nuys, California: 4 October 2007.

page 99: "Byron didn't realize it . . ." ibid.

page 99: "There were days when we'd record . . ." ibid.

page 99: "The biggest problem . . ." Byron Berline, interviewed by Luke Torn. *Uncut* 132: May 2008.

page 100: "When Byron Berlina showed up . . . " Corneal/Rogan. London/ Winter Haven, Florida: 24 June 2007.

page 100: "Gene stopped off . . ." ibid.

page 100: "Gene went to the bathroom . . ." Doug Dillard, interviewed by Peter O'Brien. *Omaha Rainbow* 10: September 1976.

page 101: "They hit Gene over the head . . ." ibid.

page 101: "Don't worry about it! . . ." ibid.

page 101: "Somebody hollered at us . . ." ibid.

page 102: " 'Kansas City Southern' became something of a signature tune for Clark . . ." Drummer Jon Corneal was effusive about this song and the album's title track. As he told me: "If you listen to 'Kansas City Southern', you're a kid laying in bed at night thinking of that train going to LA to a big world somewhere else that has interesting, exciting things going on. And once Gene got to LA he tried to adapt but the big city chewed him up and spit him out. 'Through The Morning, Through The Night', the waltz, was another beautiful song. I would love to record that. It's a hit song. A&M wasn't sure what to do with it, I guess. Just as they weren't sure what to do with the Flying Burrito Brothers." It's worth noting that the duet team of Robert Plant and Alison Krauss focused attention on two of the album's best songs when they recorded 'Polly Come Home' and 'Through The Morning, Through The Night' on their album *Raising Sand* in 2007.

page 102: "Billy was a coke dealer . . ." Mary Kendall (née Pritchard), interviewed by the author. London/San Diego, California: 30 September–1 October 2016. Mary Pritchard sometimes used her stepfather's surname, Jacobsen. In the Fifties she modelled under the pseudonym Tracy Ames. She later married musician Tom Kendall during the Seventies and retained his surname after their marriage ended.

page 103: "Before the end of 1969, he was gone . . ." David Clark now sees Gene's abandonment of projects as a defining feature of his artistic life. "The one thing about Gene and his life is that when he got into something he went after it all the way. He really pursued it to perfection. But there was something else about him: he would get to a certain point with something where either he got tired of it or it wasn't working the way he thought it should. Then, he just turned around and walked away from it. This was really hard for a lot of people and especially his music constituents in the industry at the time. That was just his nature. If he lost interest in it, he'd give it up."

page 103: "They didn't have a negotiated deal . . ." Gene Clark, interviewed by Jan Donkers. Hollywood, California: October 1972.

page 104: "I thought that Michelangelo . . ." Carlie Clark. Unedited transcript of interview for the 2013 DVD documentary, *The Byrd Who Flew Alone – The Triumph and Tragedy of Gene Clark*. Four Sun Productions: 2013.

page 104: ". . . her two younger brothers . . ." James 'Jimmy' was born in Owensboro, Kentucky, on 27 August 1945, and Michael 'Mike' was born in Evansville, Indiana, on 18 August 1949. Their Californian father, James W. McCummings, was born on 23 August 1906. Although their mother, Charlotte Heck, was raised in Owensboro, Kentucky, she and her twin sister, Elizabeth (Betty), were born in Oil City, Pennsylvania, on 18 May 1915.

page 104: ". . . happy, positive, extrovert . . ." Jim McCummings, interviewed by the author. London/Comptche, California: 30 September 2016.

page 104: "*American Bandstand* . . ." ibid.

page 104: ". . . but dropped out in the spring of 1964 . . ." Carlie's brother Jimmy confirms that she left Indiana University before completing her course. Elsewhere, Carlie claimed she *had* graduated, an apparent exaggeration. In passing, she mentioned the possibility of doing a master's degree although there is no evidence that she had sufficient qualifications as an undergraduate to register for such a course. "She moved to

Long Beach because my grandmother lived there at the time," her brother Jimmy adds. "Way down below was the Hollywood Freeway and across the Canyon we could see the Hollywood sign. It was a nice neighbourhood and you could walk right to the beach." In November 1965, Jim enlisted in the Marine Corps but was not required for active duty for 120 days. During the spring of 1966, he visited his sister in Long Beach to enjoy a long party before he left. During the autumn of 1967, he was sent to Yuma which enabled him to see Carlie in Hollywood where she was working for Bell Records. "One of her really good friends out there was Jimmy Ford. He was a composer who wrote stuff for Sly and the Family Stone and others. He was from Harland County, Kentucky. He was never her boyfriend but he was always a good friend. One time I asked my sister to get me tickets to see Iron Butterfly. I thought she and I were going but Jimmy Ford took me. A good old boy from Kentucky, he took me clubbing all night around Hollywood."

page 105: "Philip had attended UCLA Film School, where he befriended future Doors vocalist, Jim Morrison . . ." Morrison was not a popular figure with the Byrds and neither Crosby nor Clark had fond memories of the man. "I did know him," Gene told Paul Zollo in *Song Talk*, "but not well, and my encounters with Jim were not always that positive. Jim and I were not close. He had his own thing going, I had my own thing going, we were both very busy, but we did see each other and we did play together a couple of times. The Byrds and the Doors were at the Whisky at the same time and Jim wanted me to come up and play some harmonica while he sang, and I did so, and that was fun."

page 106: "We had something in common . . ." Philip Oleno, interviewed by the author. London/Mendocino, California: 26 September 2008.

page 106: "Gene was brought up a Catholic . . ." ibid.

page 106: "He wasn't living . . ." Michael McGibbon, interviewed by the author. London/Périgord, Dordoyne, France: 12 November 2011.

page 107: "I coined this antithetical phrase . . ." ibid.

page 107: "It was an interesting combination . . ." Carlie Clark. Unedited transcript of interview for the 2013 DVD documentary, *The Byrd Who Flew Alone – The Triumph and Tragedy of Gene Clark*. Four Sun Productions: 2013.

page 107: "He'd just be writing . . ." ibid.

page 110: "My younger brother Tommy . . ." Chris Ethridge, interviewed by the author. Meridian, Mississippi: 28 March 2009.

page 110: "Gene said that those big concrete blocks . . ." ibid.

page 111: "I think Michelle Phillips . . ." Dennis Hopper's liner notes to *The American Dreamer* soundtrack album.

page 111: "Dennis had wanted me involved in *Easy Rider* . . ." Clark/Eder. *Goldmine*: 11 January 1991.

page 111: "All I had going . . ." Clark/Rogan. Hollywood, California/Waldport, Oregon: 28–29 April 1989.

page 112: "I don't believe in reading . . ." Dennis Hopper, in the motion picture, *The American Dreamer*.

page 113: "On 12 June . . ." John Einarson's book dates the wedding as 12 June 1970, Carlie's birthday, but the marriage certificate confirms that it was exactly one year later: 12 June 1971. The ceremony was conducted by Barry Mitchell, an evangelical from Comptche, Mendocino.

page 113: "They had a big party . . ." Ea Oleno, interviewed by the author. London/Mendocino, California: 26 September 2008.

page 113: ". . . *White Light* was released . . ." In recent years, there has been an annoying tendency among some reviewers and commentators to refer to the album as *Gene Clark*, adding that it is 'popularly known' as *White Light*. This is not and never was the case. On the actual album, it *is* titled *White Light* in capital letters on both sides of the vinyl disc. Unfortunately, the art department neglected to include the title on the cover artwork. As Clark himself told me, this was simply a mistake. Some may say this oversight begs the question: is the correct title *Gene Clark* or *White Light*? Well, I'd argue that it is what is printed on the record rather than the sleeve artwork that determines the correct title. The Rolling Stones' debut album, for example, has no title on the cover but it is always known and referred to as *The Rolling Stones*. It should be added that the sleeve of *White Light* wrongly abbreviates 'For A Spanish Guitar' (as it is written on the vinyl record and in copyright registrations) to 'Spanish Guitar'.

page 116: "Terry fell away from it . . ." Dickson/Rogan. London/Costa Mesa, California: 10 January 2006.

page 116: "No session logs are known to exist . . ." During the mid-Nineties, I received a letter from Saul Davis enquiring about the album's contents. He mentioned, in passing, the two tracks 'Bed Of Roses' and 'Disney Girls (1957)' but whether they were ever taped is uncertain.

page 116: "For some reason . . ." Mary Kendall/Rogan. London/San Diego, California: 30 September–1 October 2016.

page 117: "Carlie and Gene were staying . . ." ibid.

page 117: "I didn't spend a lot of time . . ." ibid.

page 117: "Well, our rationale . . ." ibid.

page 118: "I've many times had discussions . . ." Gene Clark, interviewed by Steve Burgess. *Dark Star* 9: June 1977.

page 118: "There were orange . . ." Carlie Clark. Unedited transcript of interview for the 2013 DVD documentary, *The Byrd Who Flew Alone – The Triumph and Tragedy of Gene Clark*. Four Sun Productions: 2013.

page 118: "It was on the other ridge . . ." Philip Oleno/Rogan. London/Mendocino, California: 26 September 2008.

page 119: "We wanted for nothing . . ." Carlie Clark. Unedited transcript of interview for the 2013 DVD documentary, *The Byrd Who Flew Alone – The Triumph and Tragedy of Gene Clark*. Four Sun Productions: 2013.

page 119: "I lived in a dream . . ." ibid.
page 120: "He just didn't want to go . . ." ibid.
page 120: "It happened during the making of that album . . ." Jim Seiter interviewed by the author. London/Los Angeles, California: 18 October 1999.
page 120: "Hinshaw called and said . . ." ibid.
page 121: "The record company . . ." Clark/Donkers. Hollywood, California: October 1972.
page 121: "That was an album . . ." Clark/Burgess. *Dark Star* 9: June 1977.
page 121: "I don't want an incomplete work . . ." Clark/Donkers. Hollywood, California: October 1972.
page 122: "Remixing was pretty necessary . . ." Gene Clark, quoted in the liner notes for *Early LA Sessions.*
page 122: "Gene got more . . ." Dickson/Rogan. London/Maui, Hawaii: 7 July 1997.
page 122: "The two cuts with the Byrds . . ." ibid.
page 123: "*Roadmaster* remained a collector's item . . ." The sparse packaging of the original vinyl *Roadmaster* left much to be desired and did not even feature a photo of Clark on the front cover. While there are specific recording dates included on the sleeve, notably for 'She's The Kind Of Girl' and 'One In A Hundred', I cannot entirely testify to their veracity. On both the 1973 Holland A&M recording and the 1986 reissue on Edsel in the UK, the track 'Roadmaster' was erroneously credited to Clark instead of Freddy Weller and Spooner Oldham. McGuinn supposedly made an uncredited appearance on 'Rough And Rocky' (although it may not have been this particular version) and, if we are to believe Rick Clark, the younger brother also guested on vocals on this track. Chris Hinshaw's original mixes for the album were misplaced and, although they have since been rediscovered among the Dickson archives, they have not been utilized on any reissue. In explaining his own involvement in the album, Dickson recalls petitioning Dave Hubert following a trip to Europe where he noticed that there was an interest in Flying Burrito Brothers' bootlegs. This may have been the case, at least in terms of tapes. However, in another interview, Dickson made a passing reference to Gene Clark bootlegs, alongside those of the Flying Burrito Brothers. Suffice to say, there were no Clark bootlegs in circulation at this time in Europe, not even tapes. As an avid collector at the time with a pretty good list of fellow enthusiasts, I can confirm the absolute dearth of such material from personal experience. On reflection, Dickson probably saw either a Byrds or Flying Burrito Brothers bootleg during his visit.
page 124: "The Mendocino scene . . ." Andy Kandanes, interviewed by the author. London/Cobb, California: 1–2 October 2007.
page 124: "Johnny Barbata was there . . ." ibid.
page 124: "Gene always had an appetite. . ." ibid.

page 127: "a drunken Indian . . ." David Carradine, *Endless Highway* (Vermont, Journey: 1995), pp. 428–429.

page 127: "Gene started talking . . ." ibid.

page 127: "Finally, Gene passed out . . ." ibid.

page 128: "I don't want to leave . . ." Jim McCummings, email to the author: 15 September 2016. In a later interview, McCummings told me: "They had moved from Little River up to Mendo and were living in that ocean-front house. The setting was wonderful. The first night I spent there Carlie said, 'You'll only be here a night or two, so I'll make up this couch in this bay window'. I woke up in the morning, still on East Coast time whereas Gene and Carlie were on rock 'n' roll time. The bay window was 12 feet from the edge of a bluff; you looked across to this rock cliff with pine trees over it. I thought I'd died and gone to heaven. I'd never seen the North California coast. They lived on the very last house on the ocean side of the road going north outside the village of Mendocino before you got back to the highway."

page 128: "She was happily pregnant . . ." McCummings/Rogan. London/Comptche, California: 30 September 2016.

page 128: "I walked into a room . . ." ibid.

page 129: "Do you know anything . . ." ibid.

page 129: "I didn't think he had that much knowledge . . ." ibid.

page 129: "There is a part of Britain . . ." Insight. *The Sunday Times*: June 1966.

page 130: ". . . the People's Democracy, founded at Queen's University . . ." The People's Democracy spoke of social revolution, but its egalitarian, non-sectarian ideals appealed to relatively few Protestants, not least one suspects because its leftish sloganeering echoed the Marxist rhetoric of the old Official IRA. Newly radicalized students, more militant in the wake of anti-war protests in America, France and Britain had lost patience with a corrupt police force and a paternalistic government whose reforms seemed timid and half-hearted. By contrast, hard-line Unionists spoke of IRA intrusions, communist sympathizers and enemies of the state. The peace train was about to come off the rails.

page 130: "When the attacks started . . ." Eamonn McCann, interviewed by the author. Derry, Northern Ireland: 11 June 2005.

page 130: "One female resident . . ." The woman, identified as Mrs Donnelly, telephoned the police to complain about the abuse, only to discover that it was the police who were rampaging up and down the street, smashing windows and causing havoc.

page 131: "If it's a choice . . ." John Lennon, interviewed by Tariq Ali and Robin Blackburn. *Red Mole*: 21 February 1971.

page 131: "Bloody Sunday was reasonably well documented . . ." McCummings/Rogan. London/Comptche, California: 30 September 2016.

page 132: "It wasn't pro-IRA . . ." ibid.

page 132: "We were up there . . ." Peter Oliva, interviewed by the author. London/Vacaville, California: 16 July 2007.

page 133: "I was sweating . . ." ibid.

page 133: "Gene told me . . ." ibid.

page 133: "We were all music friends . . ." Lenny Laks, interviewed by the author. London/Mendocino, California: 28 November 2016.

page 134: "I remember Gene . . ." McCummings/Rogan. London/Comptche, California: 30 September 2016.

page 134: "Gene and I would drive . . ." ibid.

page 134: "I'm not entirely convinced . . ." ibid. This endnote seems as good a place as any to consider Clark's 'nervous condition'. McCummings' reference to 'schizophrenia' (also used by Dara Zimmerman later in the chapter) sounds like an extreme inflation of those 'mood swings' that many others noticed in Clark over the years. Almost everyone acknowledges that the key ingredient was alcohol. Einarson, in his authoritative biography and recent liner notes, posits the notion that Clark may have had 'bipolar disorder'. The major problem with this interesting theory is that Clark was never diagnosed with such a condition, nor did he ever see a psychologist or psychiatrist as far as anyway knows. These days bipolar, the new politer term for 'manic depression', is fairly common and, unfortunately, has become something of a catch-all term among the public for what might previously have been referred to, in less clinical terms, as extreme mood swings. At what point 'mood swings' become bipolarity is still a contentious issue. It is not made easier by the rate of misdiagnosis. A survey in 2000 by the Depressive and Manic-Depressive Association found that misdiagnosis was as high as 70 per cent. And, of course, these were from living patients, not a long dead rock star. It is a questionable undertaking, however intriguing, to attempt to impose a modern diagnosis on someone from a different time. This is rather like attempting to prove that Caesar or Napoleon were paranoid, narcissistic, or subject to a plethora of other conditions.

The one aspect about Clark of which we have real evidence is his alcoholism. He attended AA meetings, acknowledging his problem. The bizarre behaviour and chaotic episodes in his biography were almost invariably prompted by excessive drinking. Einarson believes that Clark 'self medicated' his 'bipolar tendencies' with drink. In this sense, the 'bipolar' condition is seen as the problem and the alcohol merely the medication to stave off its worst effects. That said, there's surely an equally strong argument for the drink causing the depression. Gene's brother, Rick, nevertheless supports Einarson's contention, maintaining that Gene had "a kind of a bipolar, manic-depressive personality", although the vagueness of that description underlines the degree of supposition involved. Rick concludes: "God knows what could have been had Gene gotten some treatment when he needed it . . . Hence a really great, sensitive, intuitive, intelligent songwriter ended up dead at the age of 46 rather than living a longer, more productive life. He did go to AA for three years, but they never treated him for any of his psychological problems." (Einarson, p. 16).

This moving interpretation supposes much and ignores much more. The role of alcohol in Gene's life and the nature of that addiction were complex. To suggest that Clark was employing drink as 'self-medication' underestimates the psychological power of alcohol per se. Virtually everyone interviewed testifies that Gene had a far greater problem dealing with drink then he ever did with drugs. Many of these issues may have been addressed at his AA meetings, though those details are, of course, privileged. Numerous witnesses and intimates point out that Clark was physiologically as well as psychologically disposed towards alcoholism. His father drank heavily and rumours of Native American ancestry are often used as an explanation for Clark's physical reaction to alcohol. His circumstances as a young rock star arguably made him more susceptible to inebriation, but those who suggest he might have been fine had he never left Kansas and went to Hollywood miss the point. The chances are that Clark would have been a problem drinker whether he lived in Kansas or Timbuktu. Alcoholism has little respect for place or lifestyle. There is also the possibility, if not likelihood, that Clark fatally loved drink. He certainly found it more difficult to kick than even the most additive of pharmaceutical drugs.

The suggestion that psychological treatment might have 'saved' Clark is another imponderable. For most of his life he never sought treatment for alcohol problems and, even when he did, the results were only fleetingly successful. There is no evidence that he ever took any medication to control or prohibit his drinking, let alone considered entering a rehab programme. Even later in his life his favoured strategies for tacking his alcohol intake were sporadic dry-outs and short-term abstinence. Since 'bipolar disorder' is considered a chemical imbalance of the brain, the standard treatment is a combination of anti-psychotic drugs and mood stabilizers. One of the drawbacks of these is a possibility of inhibiting creative activity by interfering with the artistic process. Several interviewees note the intensity with which Clark wrote songs, sometimes staying up till the early hours or working endlessly on a lyric or theme, crossing out lines and reworking them until he was satisfied. If psychotropic drugs might have alleviated his depression or nervous tension, the pay off would probably have been a diminishing of his artistry. If Clark had been offered a magic pill that might have cured his manic behaviour at the expense of his art, would he have accepted that treatment? I would suggest not.

Of course, all this is predicated on the unproven supposition that Clark had 'bipolar disorder' in the first place. There is strong evidence to suggest that that this was never the case. By its very nature, bipolar disorder is a debilitating and impairing condition that is not conducive to creativity. The severe swings in mood prevent the subject from focusing clearly, let alone producing the prolific body of work associated with Clark.

Unwise though it is to suggest Clark suffered any psychological disorder – we can never know – there is surely a better argument for cyclothymia, a condition which combines a milder form of depression with episodes of mania or hyper mania. That might at least explain his continued creativity in the depths of an otherwise debilitating condition. Attention might also be paid to the link between melancholia and short-term manic episodes in the context of artistic creativity, but that is a thesis in itself. Without a living patient all we are left with are the accounts of associates and intimates filtered through the inevitable biases of biography. This is further complicated by historical distance and the psychology of a rock star attempting to adjust to the exaggerated pressures and almost fantasy lifestyle associated with the music industry during that peak period of the Sixties and Seventies.

There are other telling considerations. Even within the context of the Byrds, Gene Clark was not the member most afflicted by sharp shifts of mood from melancholia to exuberance. That person was surely David Crosby, whose highs and lows were more extreme, as evidenced by countless testimony and his autobiography. Unlike Clark, Crosby was examined by psychologists and doctors. Some of their findings suggest similar symptoms to those of his former bandmate. Tested on the Rorschach Interpretation, the conclusion was that Crosby, in his drug days, was a "poorly integrated, emotionally tempestuous, intrinsically restless, and impulsive man". The test record adds, "this patient has used drugs over the years to contain his agitations and his depressions – although he, himself, may not be fully aware of this. His restlessness is very persuasive, and there are strong suggestions that even as a youngster he has not coped well with external strictures imposed upon him or with rules and regulations in general." However, there was never any suggestion in this report or elsewhere that Crosby suffered from 'bipolar disorder'. It is salutary to consider that any diagnosis of Clark might have suggested a similar form of underlying depression without the bipolar tag. In some respects, his condition is inextricably linked to his career and creativity. Mood swings are fairly common in his field as many a memoir reveals. Who knows what might have emerged from a clinical evaluation of the various Byrds. What would a medic or psychologist conclude about Clark's 'nervous condition', his fears and neuroses, highs and lows, his alcohol and drug use? What would they have made of Hillman's anger issues or McGuinn's instances of emotional coldness and detachment? And, reflecting upon the characters in this volume: consider Michael Clarke's combined use of alcohol and cocaine; Kevin Kelley's isolation and dark nights of the soul; Gram Parsons' self-destructive tendencies and Skip Battin's disturbing issues at home. Each or all of these could be slotted into some psychological category of convenience, which might explain much, but also leave so many questions unanswered. On the issue of Clark's alleged, undiagnosed 'bipolarity' (or hypomania, or cyclothymia or schizophrenia, or dysthymia, or any other label) similar caution is advised. It's an interesting, but ultimately reductive analysis. All of the Byrds were complex creatures, several of them excessive in their pharmaceutical and alcohol consumption for reasons that can produce endless debate, conjecture and contradiction. Gene was a part of this larger, puzzling cast list.

page 134: "Most of my writing . . ." Gene Clark, interviewed by Paul Kendall. *ZigZag* 73: June 1977.

page 135: "My house in Mendocino . . ." Kandanes/Rogan. London/Cobb, California: 1–2 October 2007.

page 135: "I would just sit in the living room . . ." Clark/Paul Kendall. *ZigZag* 73: June 1977.

page 135: "When I was writing . . ." ibid.

page 135: "The actual writing . . ." Clark/Burgess. *Dark Star* 9: June 1977.

page 136: "In the last few years . . ." Gene Clark, introduction to 'Some Misunderstanding' onstage at Mother Blues, Dallas, Texas: 24 May 1975.

page 136: "I remember the night . . ." Oliva/Rogan. London/Vacaville, California: 16 July 2007.

page 136: "Their farm was pretty dishevelled . . ." Mary Kendall/Rogan. London/San Diego, California: 30 September–1 October 2016.

page 139: "Neuwirth and Dylan . . ." Clark/Paul Kendall. *ZigZag* 73: June 1977.

page 139: "She was a very strange girl . . ." David Geffen, quoted in Joe Smith: *Off The Record: An Oral History Of Popular Music* (New York, Warner Brothers, 1988).

page 140: "David was looking after Laura Nyro . . ." Kandanes/Rogan. London/Cobb, California: 1–2 October 2007.

page 140: "He and I had a terrible fight . . ." Clark/Ballard. *Omaha Rainbow* 15: December 1977.

page 140: "We're soul brothers . . ." Thomas Jefferson Kaye, interviewed by the author. London: 2 May 1977.

page 140: "Tommy Kaye and Gene . . ." Carlie Clark. Unedited transcript of interview for the 2013 DVD documentary, *The Byrd Who Flew Alone – The Triumph and Tragedy of Gene Clark.* Four Sun Productions: 2013.

page 141: "Along the way, old friends Doug Dillard . . ." An oft-repeated tale in the Clark mythology is the day Gene and Doug were trapped in a Hollywood house, surrounded by police ready to arrest them. The pair had supposedly been drinking and abusing drugs for several days and became alarmed upon hearing a loudspeaker blare, "The house is surrounded, come out with your hands up!" After flushing away various illegal substances in the bathroom, they sheepishly emerged to confront the officers, only to hear the words, "It's a wrap." What they assumed was a bust had actually been a crew filming a cop show. Gene's former wife Carlie has told this tale more than once, often embellishing the details for comic effect. She says it occurred when Kelly was three and Kai was a year old, thereby placing the incident during the recording of *No Other*. By her own admission, she was back in Mendocino at the time and did not actually witness the event. Funnily enough, I have heard this exact tale, with slightly different details, from Tom Slocum. Once more, a film crew were recording a cop show and Clark and his friend ended up flushing their stash down the toilet. In this alternative version, Dillard was replaced in the narrative by Tommy Kaye. "'They were up for a couple of days working on arrangements for *No Other* and hearing LA police choppers overhead." It's unlikely that *two* such incidents could have occurred involving both Dillard and Kaye, but with Gene Clark, who can be sure?

page 141: "Gene played me those songs . . ." Thomas Jefferson Kaye, interviewed by Barry Ballard. London to Manchester: 2 May 1977. Published in *Omaha Rainbow* 14: September 1977.

page 142: "Carlie had this big Dodge van . . ." Dara Zimmerman, interviewed by the author. London/Mohave Valley, Arizona: 11 November 2016.

page 142: "Gene and Carlie were screaming . . ." ibid.

page 142: "The sweeter side . . ." ibid.

page 143: "Carlie was nuts! . . ." ibid.

page 143: ". . . a work that I saw as my Brian Wilson extravaganza . . ." Thomas Jefferson Kaye, interviewed by the author. London: 30 April 1977.

page 144: "Joe was crucial . . ." ibid.

page 146: "Wasn't the cover of *No Other* bizarre? . . ." Hillary Beckington, interviewed by the author. London/Mendocino, California: 16 October 2008.

page 146: ". . . originally started out as a hoax . . ." Clark/Burgess. *Dark Star* 9: June 1977.

page 147: "Geffen was secretly in love . . ." Slocum/Rogan. Taluca Lake, California: 19–20 November 1996.

page 147: "Gene would go into character . . ." ibid.

page 148: "We could have done more songs . . ." Clark/Rogan. Hollywood, California/Waldport, Oregon: 28–29 April 1989.

page 148: "I explain to a lot of people . . ." Clark/Burgess. *Dark Star* 9: June 1977.

page 149: "I felt it was a truly fine album . . ." Gene Clark, interviewed by Monty Smith. *Omaha Rainbow* 15: December 1977.

page 149: "He was furious . . ." Thomas Jefferson Kaye/Ballard. London to Manchester: 2 May 1977. Published in *Omaha Rainbow* 14: September 1977.

page 149: ". . . so mean, so jealous . . ." David Geffen, quoted in Tom King,

David Geffen: A Biography Of New Hollywood (London: Hutchinson, 2000), p. 252.

page 149: ". . . possibly distorted by repeated second-hand testimony from non-witnesses . . ." A particularly colourful account of the alleged incident is described by David Clark (who acknowledges that he was not there) in the documentary film, *The Byrd Who Flew Alone – The Triumph and Tragedy of Gene Clark.* Gene never mentioned the story in print and Geffen claims he has no memory of any such incident ever occurring. Kai Clark suggests, in jest: "David Geffen probably didn't want anyone to know that somebody had punched him in the mouth, I'm sure." Not that Gene ever confided in Kai either, leaving us only with a Hollywood tale based on rumour. Still, it seems likely something happened, or nearly happened.

page 150: "The way *No Other* was overlooked . . ." Gene Clark, interviewed by Allan Jones. *Melody Maker*: 14 May 1977.

page 150: "Gene used to be a real 'upper' guy . . ." Oliva/Rogan. London/ Vacaville, California: 16 July 2007.

page 150: "Gene would wake up . . ." Dara Zimmerman/Rogan. London/ Mohave Valley, Arizona: 11 November 2016.

page 150: "She did speed . . ." ibid.

page 150: "She started out very innocently . . ." ibid.

page 151: ". . . Bardwell had recently come off a touring stint with Elvis Presley . . ." Baton Rouge-born Bardwell had an interesting musical pedigree. His father Stanford had the wonderful idea of naming his children after famous American universities. In addition to Duke, there were the siblings Stanford Jr, Tulane, Harvard, Princeton, Auburn and Cornell. Alas, Duke was not bound for academe. As a teenager he appeared in various local R&B bands, including the Greek Fountains who released a single, 'Countin' The Steps', on Mercury Records. An album followed on Montel/Michelle: *The Greek Fountain River Front Band Takes Requests.* The group toured with several big groups of the mid-Sixties, including the Animals, the Dave Clark Five, Sonny & Cher and Paul Revere & The Raiders. After touring and recording with Tom Rush, Bardwell started songwriting, then worked with Jose Feliciano. In 1973, Elvis Presley's drummer Ronnie Tutt attended a Feliciano session and was impressed enough by Bardwell to suggest he audition for the King. During January 1974, Bardwell began an extensive tour with Presley which was initially interspersed alongside his club dates with Clark.

page 152: "We all cooked . . ." Mary Kendall/Rogan. London/San Diego, California: 30 September–1 October 2016.

page 152: "The turkey was so well done . . ." ibid.

page 152: "I think at the beginning . . ." Mary Kendall/Rogan. London/ San Diego, California: 30 September–1 October 2016.

page 152: "Our act was basically a trio . . ." Duke Bardwell, interviewed on the website *Flying Shoes*: 1999.

page 153: "The drinking was stronger . . ." Carlie Clark. Unedited transcript of interview for the 2013 DVD documentary, *The Byrd Who Flew Alone – The Triumph and Tragedy of Gene Clark.* Four Sun Productions: 2013.

page 153: "For all the gift . . ." ibid.

page 153: "He didn't know . . ." ibid.

page 153: "I think music . . ." McCummings/Rogan. London/Comptche, California: 30 September 2016.

page 154: "We put in two very difficult years . . ." Duke Bardwell, interviewed on the website *Flying Shoes*: 1999.

page 154: "I watched . . ." Dara Zimmerman/Rogan. London/Mohave Valley, Arizona: 11 November 2016.

page 154: "They were going through . . ." McGibbon/Rogan. London/Périgord, Dordoyne, France: 12 November 2011.

page 154: "He and Carlie . . ." Dara Zimmerman/Rogan. London/Mohave Valley, Arizona: 11 November 2016.

page 155: "They lived in Middle Ridge Road . . ." Oliva/Rogan. London/Vacaville, California: 16 July 2007.

page 155: "Roger and I started playing . . ." Duke Bardwell, interviewed on the website *Flying Shoes*: 1999.

page 155: "I'm looking for something . . ." Gene Clark, interviewed by Mick Brown. *Sounds*: 24 January 1976.

page 155: "It's easier for a band . . ." ibid.

page 156: "Gene had started to work . . ." Thomas Jefferson Kaye/Ballard. London to Manchester: 2 May 1977. Published in *Omaha Rainbow* 14: September 1977.

page 156: ". . . so that they could hear . . ." Clark/Paul Kendall. *ZigZag* 73: June 1977.

page 157: "They told Gene that . . ." ibid.

page 157: "Columbia took a month . . ." Thomas Jefferson Kaye/Ballard. London to Manchester: 2 May 1977. Published in *Omaha Rainbow* 14: September 1977.

page 158: "A lot of companies had passed . . ." Thomas Jefferson Kaye/Kendall. *ZigZag* 73: June 1977.

page 158: "He definitely dissed Coury . . ." Oliva/Rogan. London/ Vacaville, California: 16 July 2007.

page 158: "We could see a split . . ." Philip Oleno/Rogan. London/Mendocino, California: 26 September 2008.

page 158: "No! . . ." Mary Kendall/Rogan. London/San Diego, California: 30 September 1–October 2016.

page 158: "Alcohol and drugs . . ." Dara Zimmerman/Rogan. London/Mohave Valley, Arizona: 11 November 2016.

page 159: "I'd first met Carlie . . ." Kandanes/Rogan. London/Cobb, California: 1–2 October 2007.

page 159: "Mark moved to Hawaii . . ." Dara Zimmerman/Rogan. London/ Mohave Valley, Arizona: 11 November 2016.
page 159: "A different man . . ." Philip Oleno/Rogan. London/ Mendocino, California: 26 September 2008.
page 159: "In retrospect . . ." Carlie Clark. Unedited transcript of interview for the 2013 DVD documentary, *The Byrd Who Flew Alone – The Triumph and Tragedy of Gene Clark.* Four Sun Productions: 2013.
page 160: "Then I found out . . ." ibid.
page 160: "I was left in Hawaii . . ." Dara Zimmerman/Rogan. London/ Mohave Valley, Arizona: 11 November 2016.
page 161: "When it ended . . ." Oliva/Rogan. London/Vacaville, California: 16 July 2007.
page 161: "Actually, his wife . . ." Kandanes/Rogan. London/Cobb, California: 1–2 October 2007.
page 161: "How could you be OK . . ." ibid.
page 162: "If Gene liked you . . ." Ken Mansfield. *Between Wyomings* (Nashville, Thomas Nelson, 2009), p. 15.
page 162–163: "We were crazy . . ." ibid.
page 163: "Once you've been to the West Coast . . ." Rick Clark/Rogan. London/Orcutt, California: 23 June 1999.
page 163: "We came along right after Carlie . . ." Hillary Beckington/ Rogan. London/Mendocino, California: 16 October 2008.
page 164: "We went from being this middle-class family . . ." ibid.
page 166: "I was determined . . ." ibid.
page 166: "They had these whole rooms . . ." ibid.
page 166: "I then toned my act down . . ." ibid.
page 166: "I was sick of men . . ." ibid.
page 166: ". . . Morris 'Maury' Mirkin . . ." Mirkin died in June 1980, thereby making Hillary a likely heiress twice over via two multi-millionaire stepfathers.
page 166: ". . . under the guise . . ." ibid.
page 166: "He was the funniest guy . . ." ibid.
page 167: "Once they put . . ." Kandanes/Rogan. London/Cobb, California: 1–2 October 2007.
page 167: "Tommy was an enigma . . ." Hillary Beckington/Rogan. London/ Mendocino, California: 16 October 2008.
page 167: "Tommy was cool . . ." Oliva/Rogan. London/Vacaville, California: 16 July 2007.
page 167: "I totally fell in love . . ." McGibbon/Rogan. London/Périgord, Dordoyne, France: 12 November 2011.
page 168: "If you'd seen her footprint . . ." Hillary Beckington/Rogan. London/Mendocino, California: 16 October 2008.
page 168: "A lot of people . . ." ibid.
page 168: "It's like he didn't . . ." ibid.

page 168: "But I told you . . ." Thomas Jefferson Kaye/Rogan. London: 2 May 1977.

page 169: "If you look really closely . . ." Rick Clark/Rogan. London/Orcutt, California: 23 June 1999.

page 169: "Come up to Mendocino . . ." Slocum/Rogan. Taluca Lake, California: 19–20 November 1996.

page 169: "It was rocky . . ." ibid.

page 169: "I started hanging out . . ." ibid.

page 170: "Slocum's M.O. . . ." Kandanes/Rogan. London/Cobb, California: 1–2 October 2007.

page 170: "He did stuff for everybody . . ." Hillary Beckington/Rogan. London/Mendocino, California: 16 October 2008.

page 170: "Hillary was a very wealthy woman . . ." Slocum/Rogan. Taluca Lake, California: 19–20 November 1996.

page 171: "We woke up New Year's Day . . ." Jason Ronard, interviewed by the author. London/West Hollywood, California: 21 September 2008.

page 171: "I'll tell you a great thing . . ." ibid.

page 171: "I didn't get along too well . . ." ibid.

page 172: "Everybody was sniffing . . ." Kandanes/Rogan. London/Cobb, California: 1–2 October 2007.

page 172: "He'd wanted to insulate . . ." Bonnie Clark Laible/Rogan. London/Bonner Springs, Kansas: 8 November 2011.

page 173: "When Mom went out there . . ." ibid. David Clark also remembers hearing the news about his mother cooking them Christmas dinner. "That was very unpleasant. Especially for Mom. She was appalled."

page 173: "I was at a crossroads . . ." David Clark/Rogan. London/Montrose, Colorado: 7 November 2016.

page 173: "He proceeded to punch . . ." Ken Mansfield. *Between Wyomings* (Nashville, Thomas Nelson, 2009), p. 16. In a previous interview, before he committed his account to paper, Mansfield provided a marginally different version of this story. The essential details are the same, except that Hothead are not mentioned, and the act whom Gene interrupts are named Scarlet. Presumably, they were the support act Mansfield mentions here.

page 173: "I didn't get much madder . . ." ibid.

page 174: "I choose to remember . . ." ibid.

page 174: "After a while . . ." Ken Mansfield and Marshall Terrill. *Rock And A Heart Place* (Racine, Wisconsin, BroadSheet Publishing Group, 2015).

page 174: "When Gene said . . ." Kaye/Rogan. London: 2 May 1977.

page 174: "I was in Middle Ridge . . ." Dara Zimmerman/Rogan. London/Mohave Valley, Arizona: 11 November 2016.

page 175: "Is this the dullest . . ." Reviewer Paul Nelson. *Rolling Stone* 239: 1977.

page 176: "We'd rehearse for 10 hours . . ." Oliva/Rogan. London/ Vacaville, California: 16 July 2007.

page 176: "One night . . ." Slocum/Rogan. Taluca Lake, California: 19–20 November 1996.

page 177: "Well, she provided . . ." Slocum/Rogan. London/Taluca Lake, California: 27 December 1999.

page 177: "We blew them down the pipe . . ." Oliva/Rogan. London/ Vacaville, California: 16 July 2007.

page 177: "I loved playing with Gene . . ." ibid.

page 178: "It was backstage . . ." Slocum/Rogan. London/Taluca Lake, California: 27 December 1999.

page 178: "She talked me into it . . ." Terri Messina/Rogan. North Hollywood, California: 1–2 September 1996.

page 179: "I hung out with the girlfriend . . ." Oliva/Rogan. London/ Vacaville, California: 16 July 2007.

page 179: "Gene wasn't in the greatest shape . . ." Terri Messina/Rogan. North Hollywood, California: 1–2 September 1996.

page 180: "Gene had a lot of boys' nights . . ." Hillary Beckington/Rogan. London/Mendocino, California: 16 October 2008.

page 180: "Wasn't he a riot? . . ." ibid.

page 180: "Tommy and I write . . ." Clark/Paul Kendall. *ZigZag* 73: June 1977.

page 181: "I feel that any pure force . . ." ibid.

page 181: "I purposely did the album . . ." ibid.

page 182: "I'd put out these albums . . ." Clark/Allan Jones. *Melody Maker*: 14 May 1977.

page 182: "It looks like . . ." Clark/Paul Kendall. *ZigZag* 73: June 1977.

page 184: "Backstage in his dressing-room . . ." A fan who had travelled from the Continent was allowed in to wish Gene well. He handed me a camera and asked if I would take a photograph of them together. "Please, my hands are shaking," he said. I felt that Gene looked the more nervous of the two.

page 185: "Terri and Gene . . ." Hillary Beckington/Rogan. London/ Mendocino, California: 16 October 2008.

page 186: "Michael was a month younger . . ." Dara Zimmerman/Rogan. London/Mohave Valley, Arizona: 11 November 2016.

page 186: "Peter was ten years younger . . ." ibid.

page 186: "He could be really mean . . ."

page 186: "That's exactly the look . . ." ibid.

page 186: "I remember that day . . ." ibid.

page 186: "He started to attack me . . ." ibid.

page 187: "He was delusional . . ." ibid.

page 187: "He got into a fight . . ." ibid.

page 187: "I grew up . . ." ibid.

page 188: "Gene and I were engaged . . ." Terri Messina/Rogan. North Hollywood, California: 1–2 September 1996.
page 190: "Well, it was LA . . ." Oliva/Rogan. London/Vacaville, California: 16 July 2007.
page 190: "After *Two Sides To Every Story* . . ." Slocum/Rogan. London/Taluca Lake, California: 27 December 1999.
page 190: "I don't think . . ." Dara Zimmerman/Rogan. London/Mohave Valley, Arizona: 11 November 2016.
page 190: "Gene never wanted to leave Hollywood . . ." Dickson/Rogan. Waldport, Oregon: 26–30 April 1989.
page 191: "I was in Lahaina . . ." Jim Dickson, interviewed by the author. London/Costa Mesa, California: 10 January 2006.
page 192: "I'd always thought of him . . ." Hillary Beckington/Rogan. London/Mendocino, California: 16 October 2008.
page 192: "Hillary's mother . . ." Slocum/Rogan. London/Taluca Lake, California: 27 December 1999.
page 192: "John Wayne was my brother Casey's godfather . . ." Hillary Beckington/Rogan. London/Mendocino, California: 16 October 2008.
page 192: "When Gene found out . . ." ibid.
page 193: "I think Gene thought . . ." Kandanes/Rogan. London/Cobb, California: 1–2 October 2007.
page 193: "The grandmother . . ." Slocum/Rogan. London/Taluca Lake: 27 December 1999.
page 193: "Granny Hill was about 90 . . ." Ronard/Rogan. London/West Hollywood, California: 21 September 2008.
page 193: "He knew my grandmother . . ." Hillary Beckington/Rogan. London/Mendocino, California: 16 October 2008.
page 194: "She was nothing of the sort . . ." ibid.
page 194: "Carlie was on the headlands . . ." McGibbon/Rogan. London/Périgord, Dordoyne, France: 12 November 2011.

Carlie's brother Jim provides additional details about the accident. "Philip Oleno was with her the night of that fall. So was Carlie's boyfriend at the time. Carlie had been in a bar in town. They were parked on the headlands. She got out of the car to take a leak in the dark, walked back to the sound of their voices and then walked right off the bluff. They were in Philip's truck and she had the keys, so he had to run a mile from this western point on the headlands all the way to the Mendocino Volunteer Fire Department. He pulled the alarm on the outside of the building to summon the fire department. Carlie survived the fall and crawled out on the rocks. All her injuries were in her left arm. She had fallen on that left arm and had 11 breaks in her biceps and fingers and no other significant injuries. It's possible she stepped off the bluff, slid and fell and eventually landed on the rocks and managed to pull herself through the water and get in a safe place. They brought her up in a cliff rescue."

page 194: "Part of the magic . . ." Ron Albert. *McGuinn, Clark & Hillman*, Capitol press release: February 1979.
page 197: "*Q. . . . I can't help notice . . .*" Clark/Rogan. *Dark Star* 20: May 1979.
page 197: "A. Aha! . . ." ibid.
page 197: "Q. *Before you go Gene . . .*" ibid.
page 198: "A. Wow! . . ." ibid.
page 199: "That was the first sign . . ." Bonnie Laible Clark. Unedited transcript of interview for the 2013 DVD documentary, *The Byrd Who Flew Alone – The Triumph and Tragedy of Gene Clark*. Four Sun Productions: 2013.
page 199: "I never saw Gene . . ." Slocum/Rogan. Taluca Lake, California: 19–20 November 1996.
page 200: "Terri was very sweet . . ." Slocum/Rogan. London/Taluca Lake, California: 27 December 1999.
page 200: "Terri was a great girl . . ." Hillary Beckington/Rogan. London/Mendocino, California: 16 October 2008.
page 200: "She was like the dragon lady . . ." Kandanes/Rogan. London/Cobb, California: 1–2 October 2007.
page 200: "It's such horseshit . . ." Hillary Beckington/Rogan. London/Mendocino, California: 16 October 2008.
page 201: "Gene just did what he wanted to . . ." ibid.
page 202: "Gene would come by . . ." Dickson/Rogan. London/Maui, Hawaii: 7 July 1997.
page 202: "Well, you know what happened . . ." Kandanes/Rogan. London/Cobb, California: 1–2 October 2007.
page 203: ". . . he sang the harmonica-led '(Living In) Hard Times' and 'I Saw A Dream Come True' . . ." These appeared on a tape of McGuinn, Clark & Hillman's show at Mount Union College, Alliance, Ohio: 12 October 1979.
page 203: "Terri had been together . . ." Hersh/Rogan. London/Topanga Canyon, California: 12 April 2008.
page 204: "Gene wasn't a great father . . ." Terri Messina/Rogan. North Hollywood, California: 1–2 September 1996.
page 205: "Terri didn't like us . . ." Kelly Clark. Unedited transcript of interview for the 2013 DVD documentary, *The Byrd Who Flew Alone – The Triumph and Tragedy of Gene Clark*. Four Sun Productions: 2013.
page 205: "The kids showed a lot . . ." Hillary Beckington/Rogan. London/Mendocino, California: 16 October 2008.
page 205: "We called that the brown rice . . ." Kai Clark, interviewed by the author. London/Auburn, California: 25 September 2016.
page 205: ". . . mainly for publishing . . ." Kandanes/Rogan. London/Cobb, California: 1–2 October 2007.
page 206: "His relationship with Terri . . ." ibid.

page 206: "When he got back into alcohol . . ." Terri Messina/Rogan. North Hollywood, California: 1–2 September 1996.

page 206: "They lived together very solidly . . ." Hillary Beckington/ Rogan. London/Mendocino, California: 16 October 2008.

page 206: ". . . getting the nerve . . ." Joe Messina, interviewed by the author. London/Woodland Hills, Los Angeles, California: 22 April 2015.

page 207: ". . . Garth Beckington . . ." Beckington came from a military family, his father having served in the Marine Corps. Garth later attended the University of North Carolina, but did not complete his course. He subsequently moved to New York and played there until 1976. Finally, he made his way to California, working with musician friend, Brendan Early.

page 208: "It was pretty nutty . . ." Jon Faurot, interviewed by the author. London/West Hollywood, California: 20 September 2008.

page 208: "I don't know if any one time . . ." Garth Beckington, interviewed by the author. London/Mendocino, California: 17 October 2008.

page 208: "He was a very intelligent man . . ." Faurot/Rogan. London/West Hollywood, California: 20 September 2008.

page 208: "The bottom just dropped out . . ." Gene Clark, interviewed by Barry Ballard. *Omaha Rainbow* 36, Spring 1985.

page 209: "Gene can't sell . . ." Crosby/Rogan. London: 22–23 April 1980.

page 209: "He was post-superstar . . ." Garth Beckington/Rogan. London/Mendocino, California: 17 October 2008.

page 209: "Jesse was something else . . ." Faurot/Rogan. London/West Hollywood, California: 20 September 2008. Garth Beckington also spoke highly of Jesse Ed Davis. "I met Jesse Ed through Gene," he told me. "Jesse Ed was a great man, an incredibly intelligent, well-educated, well-spoken, hilarious dude. Jesse Ed's guitars were nowhere, so I just started lending him one of my guitars. At one point, I said, 'Jesse Ed, you *will* bring this back!' He promised he would, and he did. But with Gene, I don't know . . . The Native American thing was a subject between those guys that I wasn't privy to. They got along, and they were friends, for sure. But they were both prickly. They were both that way in general. Jesse Ed was very sardonic. A caustic guy, but always funny. He was an entertaining fellow and a great player."

page 210: "As sweet as he was . . ." Hillary Beckington/Rogan. London/Mendocino, California: 16 October 2008.

page 210: "Man, Jesse Ed would pass out . . ." Ronard/Rogan. London/West Hollywood, California: 21 September 2008.

page 210: "The saddest thing about Gene Clark . . ." ibid.

page 211: "He wouldn't stay . . ." ibid.

page 211: "He did that every day . . ." ibid.

page 212: ". . . pure, holy existence . . ." David Carradine, *Endless Highway* (Vermont, Journey: 1995), p. 433.

page 212: "Garth stayed up there . . ." Jon Faurot, interviewed by the author. London/Fort Bragg, California: 13 November 2016.
page 212: ". . . going up there . . ." ibid.
page 212: ". . . kind of crazy . . . " ibid.
page 212: "He was pushing . . ." David Carradine, *Endless Highway* (Vermont, Journey: 1995), p. 368.
page 212: "Gene sang . . ." Letter to author, dated 3 November 1999. Beckington's letter adds: "I don't know what happened to that reel or remember what happened after that, except that, quite unexpectedly, I found my copy a few years ago, and since then have kept better care. After you listen to it, I think you'll agree that there are some great tunes and very good performances – no overdubbing, no boxes, no echo, no reverb, no compression – just microphones and a recorder . . . Gene had one of those old TEAC 4-track reel-to-reel machines. Faurot and I were working with Tommy, so Gene asked us to do this. Of course, we did, though Tommy insisted on Gene singing 'Shades Of Blue'. Tommy produced it and did the back-up vocal arranging himself, myself and Faurot. I played guitar and sang and Jon Faurot played bass and sang. Rick [Clark] was there for that one tune ['Midnight Mare'], and Tommy played a little guitar and sang and produced . . . I just wish I had the tapes we made at his pad the week or three before he died. I do have some rehearsal tapes for the Cinegrill gig we did in April before he died, and somebody has tapes of all four of those gigs, but I don't think they come close to this tape . . . Hope you dig this . . . Check 'I Don't Have You' . . ."
page 213: "Gene could drink . . ." Faurot/Rogan. London/West Hollywood, California: 20 September 2008.
page 213–214: ". . . about a mountain . . ." ibid.
page 214: "He sang that goddamn song . . ." ibid.
page 214: "He could get drunk . . ." ibid.
page 214: "It was amazing to see . . ." Garth Beckington/Rogan. London/Mendocino, California: 17 October 2008.
page 214: "We used to call them Gene's Catholic songs . . ." Oliva/Rogan. London/Vacaville, California: 16 July 2007.
page 215: "It had Bobby Neuwirth . . ." Hillary Beckington/Rogan. London/Mendocino, California: 16 October 2008.
page 215: "We knew she was around . . ." Faurot/Rogan. London/West Hollywood, California: 20 September 2008.
page 215: "Calista is more or less . . ." David Carradine, *Endless Highway* (Vermont, Journey: 1995), p. 404.
page 216: "Calista had made it . . ." ibid.
page 216: "Gene caught him . . ." ibid.
page 216: "I was pretty upset . . ." Slocum/Rogan. Taluca Lake, California: 19–20 November 1996.
page 217: "He was in terrible shape . . ." David Clark/Rogan. London/Montrose, Colorado: 7 November 2016.

page 217: "He had an old mountain hat . . ." ibid.
page 217: "I told him, 'If you continue . . .'" David Clark. Unedited interview of transcript for the 2013 DVD documentary, *The Byrd Who Flew Alone – The Triumph and Tragedy of Gene Clark*. Four Sun Productions: 2013.
page 217: "That was maybe a life changer . . ." David Clark/Rogan. London/Montrose, Colorado: 7 November 2016.
page 217: "She said . . ." Bonnie Clark Laible/Rogan. London/Bonner Springs, Kansas: 8 November 2011.
page 217: "Heroin divorces you . . ." Hillary Beckington/Rogan. London/Mendocino, California: 16 October 2008.
page 218: "You've never been around anything . . ." Slocum/Rogan. Taluca Lake, California: 19–20 November 1996.
page 218: "People were coming around . . ." Hillary Beckington/Rogan. London/Mendocino, California: 16 October 2008.
page 218: "Gene went to a Mafia guy . . ." ibid.
page 218: "Blood was pouring out of me . . ." ibid.
page 219: "Tommy and I had been on the rocks . . ." ibid.
page 219: "She was like a little one man band . . ." ibid.
page 219: "You'd see Eloise . . ." ibid.
page 219: "She was just mute . . ." ibid.
page 220: "It made it very easy . . ." ibid.
page 220: "Tommy would come over . . ." Ronard/Rogan. London/West Hollywood, California: 21 September 2008.
page 221: "We decided to get out . . ." Hillary Beckington/Rogan. London/Mendocino, California: 16 October 2008.
page 221: "Garth and I decided . . ." ibid.
page 221: "I was stupid . . ." Carlie Clark. Unedited transcript of interview for the 2013 DVD documentary, *The Byrd Who Flew Alone – The Triumph and Tragedy of Gene Clark*. Four Sun Productions: 2013.
page 221: "Gene must have gone through millions . . ." Kandanes/Rogan. London/Cobb, California: 1–2 October 2007.
page 222: "Why don't you do something . . ." ibid.
page 222: "You know what we're getting . . ." ibid.
page 222: "The executive staff changed . . ." ibid.
page 222: "Nobody would touch Gene . . ." ibid.
page 222–223: "Working with Gene . . ." ibid.
page 223: "Tommy was a little eccentric . . ." ibid.
page 223: "We got him dried out . . ." ibid.
page 223: "Geno wasn't on the same level . . ." Oliva/Rogan. London/Vacaville, California: 16 July 2007.
page 224: "When you're the artiste . . ." Gene Clark, interviewed by Barry Ballard. *Omaha Rainbow* 36: Spring 1985.
page 224: "There was a loose and human agreement . . ." Slocum/Rogan. Taluca Lake, California: 19–20 November 1996.

page 224: "Whatever happened in between . . ." Dickson/Rogan. London/ Costa Mesa, California: 10 January 2006.
page 224: "I came from a more professional . . ." Kandanes/Rogan. London/Cobb, California: 1–2 October 2007.
page 225: "Gene could have gone . . ." Slocum/Rogan. Taluca Lake, California: 19–20 November 1996.
page 225: "Gene and Terri had got . . ." Dickson/Rogan. London/Maui, Hawaii: 7 July 1997.
page 226: "Tommy Kaye, Andy and Gene . . ." Slocum/Rogan. Taluca Lake, California: 19–20 November 1996.
page 226: "He was pacing the floor . . ." Dickson/Rogan. London/Maui, Hawaii: 3 August 1998.
page 226: "I got tired of listening . . ." ibid.
page 227: ". . . like having Michael McDonald . . ." Kandanes/Rogan. London/Cobb, California: 1–2 October 2007.
page 227: ". . . emaciated . . ." ibid.
page 227: "Hey, Johnny Silver! . . ." Gene Clark, interviewed by the author. London/Hollywood, California: 28 June 1982.
page 227: "I replaced all the harmony . . ." Dickson/Rogan. London/Costa Mesa, California: 8 November 2009.
page 227: "These little children . . ." Gene Clark, interviewed on KMET Radio, Los Angeles, California. Date unknown.
page 228: "He really wanted that album . . ." Dickson/Rogan. London/ Costa Mesa, California: 8 November 2009.
page 228: "I liked 'Vanessa' . . ." Kandanes/Rogan. London/Cobb, California: 1–2 October 2007.
page 228: "Gene's and Gordon's careers . . ." ibid.
page 228: "We wanted to do more . . ." ibid.
page 228: "Gene was really into the song . . ." Dickson/Rogan. London/ Costa Mesa, California: 8 November 2009.
page 229: "We cut those five songs . . ." Dickson/Rogan. London/Maui, Hawaii: 7 July 1997.
page 230: "Gene was just a guy . . ." Oliva/Rogan. London/Vacaville, California: 16 July 2007.
page 230: "Trace had a romantic quality . . ." Matt Andes/Rogan. London/ Johnson City, Texas: 30 September 2007.
page 233: "It was the night times . . ." Trace Harrill, interviewed by the author. London/San Rafael, California: 3 October 2008.
page 233: "At one time he started acting . . ." ibid.
page 233: "He had some interesting fantasies . . ." Oliva/Rogan. London/ Vacaville, California: 16 July 2007.
page 234: "Would you do me the honour . . ." Harrill/Rogan. London/ San Rafael, California: 3 October 2008. Clark could create a comedy of errors, even unwittingly. "He was instrumental in my divorce," jokes Harrill. "We both had phones by our bed. My wife called in the

middle of the night and I hadn't seen Gene that day even though we were living together. She said, 'Is Trace there?' and Gene said 'No'. But I was there! That was the last straw for her."

page 234: "He showed me family pictures . . ." ibid.

page 234: "I said, 'Gene . . .' " ibid.

page 234: "Harrill continued to write . . ." One composition, 'Kathleen', later emerged in revised form on a home recording included in the posthumous collection, *Gypsy Angel.*

page 235: "Gene didn't have any money . . ." Slocum/Rogan. London/Hollywood, California: June 2002.

page 235: "Gene was my dear friend . . ." ibid.

page 235: "I slept on the couch . . ." Mike Hardwick, interviewed by the author. London/Dallas, Texas: 10 September 2007.

page 235: "I was a kid . . ." ibid.

page 236: "Dylan said it was one . . ." Kandanes/Rogan. London/Cobb, California: 1–2 October 2007.

page 236: " 'She Loves You' was basically . . ." Slocum/Rogan. Taluca Lake, California: 19–20 November 1996. Slocum is probably referring to the Police-inspired guitar work on the record. This arrangement was introduced to the Firebyrds by Mark Andes during his short spell in the band.

page 236: "Skip was the engineer . . ." Hardwick/Rogan. London/Dallas, Texas: 10 September 2007.

page 238: "Gene got mad at me . . ." Matt Andes/Rogan. London/Johnson City, Texas: 30 September 2007.

page 238: "We were leaving . . ." ibid.

page 238: "It was one of the most . . ." ibid.

page 238: "He dragged Carla . . ." Saul Davis, interviewed by the author. London: 24 November 1996.

page 239: "Carla always was a sweetheart . . ." Slocum/Rogan. Taluca Lake, California: 19–20 November 1996.

page 239: "Saul and Gene . . ." ibid.

page 239: "Clark guested on their records . . ." Clark sang on the title track to the Textones' 1984 album, *Midnight Mission*; sang his own composition, 'Day For Night', on the Textones' 1989 work, *Through The Canyon*; and appeared on 1990's *Back In Time* vocalising on the Pat Robinson/Dick Holler composition, 'Jokers Are Wild'. He featured on Carla Olson's 1989 eponymous album, singing 'Broken Hearts And Broken Dreams'. He was also guest vocalist on the Long Ryders' 'Ivory Tower', from their album, *Native Sons.*

page 239: "All I know is . . ." Oliva/Rogan. London/Vacaville, California: 16 July 2007.

page 240: "Whatever work Gene could pick . . ." Slocum/Rogan. Taluca Lake, California: 19–20 November 1996.

page 241: "The over-pampering of artistes . . ." Gene Clark, interviewed by Barry Alfonso. *BAM* 15: February 1985.

page 241: "Gene was several guys . . ." John York, interviewed by the author. London/Claremont, California: 11 June 2007.
page 241: "He called me from Europe . . ." Ronard/Rogan. London/West Hollywood, California: 21 September 2008.
page 242: "She was very beautiful . . ." Slocum/Rogan. Taluca Lake, California: 19–20 November 1996.
page 242: "One of the reasons . . ." Hillary Beckington/Rogan. London/Mendocino, California: 16 October 2008.
page 242: "It was an ego problem . . ." Terri Messina/Rogan. North Hollywood, California: 1–2 September 1996.
page 243: "It seemed to me . . ." York/Rogan. London/Claremont, California: 11 June 2007.
page 243: "At first they wanted her . . ." Hillary Beckington/Rogan. London/Mendocino, California: 16 October 2008.
page 243: "At school she tested . . ." ibid.
page 243: "For almost a month . . ." ibid.
page 244: "She'd just had her lunch . . ." ibid.
page 244: "Gene was very dear . . ." ibid.
page 244: "We tried to get Gene . . ." Saul Davis/Rogan. London: 24 November 1996.
page 245: "Nobody understood . . ." Carla Olson, interviewed by the author. London: 24 November 1996.
page 245: "It was tricky . . ." Pat Robinson, interviewed by the author. London/Agoura, California: 9 November 1996.
page 246: "We were starting . . ." ibid.
page 246: "You had to get him early . . ." ibid.
page 246: "Gene sang those songs . . ." ibid. 'Dangerous Games' and 'Washington Square' were later incorporated into the CRY repertoire.
page 247: " 'My Marie' stood out . . ." Pat Robinson, interviewed by Jon Storey, included in the uncensored sleeve notes of the original 2-CD version of *Under The Silvery Moon*.
page 247: "Gene held up a liquor store . . ." ibid.
page 249: "I was more like the worker bee . . ." Robinson/Rogan London/Agoura, California: 9 November 1996.
page 249: "After I got sober . . ." Greg Thomas, interviewed by the author. London/Hollywood, California: 3–4 July 2007.
page 250: "He should have gone . . ." ibid.
page 250: "I used to go over . . ." Olson/Rogan. London: 24 November 1996.
page 251: "We just thought . . ." ibid.
page 251: "Considering what we went through . . ." ibid.
page 251: "His teeth were loose . . ." ibid.
page 253: "My God, John Phillips . . ." Slocum/Rogan. London/Taluca Lake: 20 April 1999.
page 253: "They had both tasted . . ." ibid.

page 253: "We used to call him Awopaho . . ." Carlos Bernal, interviewed by the author. London/Los Angeles, California: 10 April 2008.
page 254: "Gene felt . . ." Saul Davis/Rogan. London: 24 November 1996.
page 254: "We had the tunes . . ." Olson/Rogan. London: 24 November 1996.
page 255: "Gene did that album . . ." Slocum/Rogan. Taluca Lake, California: 19–20 November 1996.
page 255: "He'd quit drinking . . ." Michael Curtis, interviewed by the author. London/Nashville, Tennessee: 16 September 2007.
page 255: "I got rejection letters . . ." Saul Davis/Rogan. London: 24 November 1996.
page 255: "We've got a few demos . . ." Gene Clark, interviewed by Frank Beeson. *Bucketful Of Brains* 22: September 1987.
page 256: "In the Sixties . . ." ibid.
page 256: "He didn't like to fly . . ." Michael Curtis/Rogan. London/Nashville, Tennessee: 16 September 2007.
page 257: "We did something like . . ." ibid.
page 257: "Gene had finally . . ." Terri Messina/Rogan. North Hollywood, California: 1–2 September 1996.
page 257: "We actually had oxygen . . ." York/Rogan. London/Rancho Cucamonga, California: 27 October 1996.
page 258: "My dad took one look . . ." Terri Messina/Rogan. North Hollywood, California: 1–2 September 1996.
page 258: "The doctors told Gene . . ." ibid.
page 258: "The next thing . . ." Slocum/Rogan. Taluca Lake, California: 19–20 November 1996.
page 259: "After the stomach operation . . ." Michael Curtis/Rogan. London/Nashville, Tennessee: 16 September 2007.
page 259: "He'd already had a stroke . . ." Hillary Beckington/Rogan. London/Mendocino, California: 16 October 2008.
page 259: "When Jesse Ed died . . ." York/Rogan. London/Rancho Cucamonga, California: 25 May 1997.
page 260: "Gene says 'Hi' . . ." Saul Davis/Rogan. London: 24 November 1996.
page 260: "He said, 'Gene who?' . . ." ibid.
page 260: "Roger and Camilla . . ." Olson/Rogan. London: 24 November 1996.
page 260: "Gene wanted to put aside . . ." Slocum/Rogan. Taluca Lake, California: 19–20 November 1996.
page 260: ". . . to wind down the Byrds' tribute band . . ." Clark's backing band were already making plans of their own, initially under the name, the Maps Of The Stars' Homes. "That was John York, and Greg and Billy and me," says Michael Curtis. "There came a point where I had some songs and Greg had a tune that he wanted to record, so the four of us mortgaged stuff and went into a studio in Reno that we really liked.

We'd spent a lot of time in Reno at the Paris Casino through the years. We got to know these people and they gave us a half-way decent deal. So we went in and cut all these songs, including 'Gypsy Rider'. We were planning a group of our own and the Maps Of The Stars' Homes was a name that Greg came up with. We eventually settled on Django. We had some great stuff and there were people interested. But then John York left the band and wanted to do his own thing."

page 260: "We were doing impressions . . ." Michael Curtis/Rogan. London/Nashville, Tennessee: 16 September 2007.

page 261: "Gene always gave me . . ." ibid.

page 261: "We started laughing . . ." ibid.

page 261: "There's still a lot of healing . . ." Clark/Rogan. Hollywood, California/Waldport, Oregon: 28 April 1989.

page 261: "It hurt him a lot . . ." Terri Messina/Rogan. North Hollywood, California: 1–2 September 1996.

page 261: "I'm happy to work . . ." David Crosby, interviewed by the author. London: 21 February 1989.

page 262: "Once in a while . . ." Terri Messina/Rogan. North Hollywood, California: 1–2 September 1996.

page 262: "He'd say, 'We had a couple of beers . . .' " ibid.

page 262: "I admit I would . . ." ibid.

page 262: "I saw Gene out here . . ." David Jackson/Rogan. London/Van Nuys, California: 4 October 2007.

page 263: "There was part of me . . ." Terri Messina/Rogan. North Hollywood, California: 1–2 September 1996.

page 264: "It was a teeny house . . ." ibid.

page 264: "Gene had to be a dad . . ." Olson/Rogan. London: 24 November 1996.

page 264: "I went through . . ." Terri Messina/Rogan. North Hollywood, California: 1–2 September 1996.

page 264: "I wasn't getting along . . ." Kelly Clark. Unedited transcript of interview for the 2013 DVD documentary, *The Byrd Who Flew Alone – The Triumph and Tragedy of Gene Clark*. Four Sun Productions: 2013.

page 265: "I was remodelling . . ." Terri Messina/Rogan. North Hollywood, California: 1–2 September 1996.

page 265: ". . . show off his new car . . ." ibid.

page 265: "We said, 'we're not even . . .' " ibid.

page 265: ". . . probably right . . ." Kelly Clark. Unedited transcript of interview for the 2013 DVD documentary, *The Byrd Who Flew Alone – The Triumph and Tragedy of Gene Clark*. Four Sun Productions: 2013.

page 265: ". . . my mom was constantly . . ." ibid.

page 265: "He would get uptight . . ." ibid.

page 266: "I was rowdy . . ." ibid.

page 266: "I went back to Mendocino . . ." Dara Zimmerman/Rogan. London/Mohave Valley, Arizona: 11 November 2016.

page 266: "One day . . ." ibid.
page 267: "I used to babysit . . ." ibid.
page 267: "My mom was using . . ." Kai Clark/Rogan. London/Auburn, California: 25 September 2016.
page 267: "It was really cool . . ." ibid.
page 268: "Gene wouldn't have released . . ." Tom Slocum, interviewed by the author. London/Hollywood, California: June 2002. Gene's friend Shannon O'Neill was also critical of the recordings. Even the writing credits on some songs was questioned by Rick Clark. As Slocum adds: "I heard a tape of 'Washington Square' and I remember writing half of it with Gene! Pat Robinson never lived in Washington Square, but I did. I said to Gene, 'Hey, what is this?' He said, 'Oh, Pat and I changed the song.' I said, 'OK!' "
page 268: "We all played for free . . ." Robinson/Rogan. London/Agoura, California: 9 November 1996.
page 268: "He was demanding . . ." Terri Messina/Rogan. North Hollywood, California: 1–2 September 1996. Comparing the approaches of Kaye and Arrias, Tom Slocum recalls that "Terri put it all quite succinctly one day stating: 'Tommy put the sex in Gene's music.' "
page 269: "The hidden motive . . ." Slocum/Rogan. Taluca Lake, California: 19–20 November 1996.
page 269–270: "That really bugged Gene . . ." ibid.
page 270: "We don't know . . ." Saul Davis/Rogan. London: 24 November 1996.
page 271: ". . . a version of Phil Ochs' 'Changes' . . ." According to Carla Olson: "We copped the Jim and Jean arrangement for 'Changes' because it was so good. I just sang background vocals. It wasn't meant to be a duet. It was Gene's thing and we really wanted to highlight him on it. Little did we know that it was the last thing we'd do together. He sang beautifully and played guitar too. Doing anything musically with Gene was always a pleasure and he always kept you guessing. Some of his songs should have been standards by other people. There are songs that he wrote that are absolutely timeless."
page 271: "Gene used to grind . . ." Olson/Rogan. London: 24 November 1996.
page 271: "It was a part of his personality . . ." ibid.
page 272: "In a few days . . ." *Time Out*: October 1989.
page 272: "On 3 February, he joined Carla Olson for a show at McCabe's . . ." Clark and Olson also appeared for a 'Beatles Night' show at LA's Club Lingerie on 8 April. They planned to sing the Beatles' 'I Need You' but, according to Olson, they ended up performing 'Eight Days A Week'.
page 272: "Gene was a little bit . . ." Olson/Rogan. London: 24 November 1996.
page 273: "Even the nights . . ." ibid. At the McCabe's show, Clark played

a thrilling new composition, 'Your Fire Burning'. He later taped the song for Carla Olson. "I remember when Gene sat down and played it, there's this little passage where it goes to the chorus, 'Now that it's over'. He stopped in the middle while he was taping it and said, 'That's my Bee Gees' passage.' He was so proud of that."

page 273: "Lingering ill will . . ." Saul Davis also believes that old wounds and past bitterness played a part. "There was that falling out because of Michael and Gene going out as the tribute to the Byrds. But the whole thing goes back to everyone opening their royalty cheques in 1965 and Gene's getting three or ten times more [money] . . . Whether things were resolved in that regard is one thing, but although the Byrds' tribute tour and Gene and Michael was over and resolved in a business/time sense, that didn't mean that it was resolved in a 'bitter taste in the mouth' sense. Even though they'd shaken hands and said everything's cool, that didn't mean that there weren't ill feelings just because of the power of the egos."

page 274: "Hey, Sloc . . ." Slocum/Rogan. Taluca Lake, California: 19–20 November 1996.

page 274: "He had a fantasy about it . . ." ibid.

page 274: "That's my daughter . . ." ibid.

page 274: "He made the whole thing up . . ." ibid.

page 275: "He'd say, 'Curtis . . .'" Michael Curtis/Rogan. London/Nashville, Tennessee: 16 September 2007.

page 275: "You've got to hear . . ." Shannon O'Neill, interviewed by the author. London/Thousand Oaks, California: 7 October 2007.

page 275: "She'd say, 'Why the hell . . .'" ibid.

page 275: "Gene had been working . . ." ibid.

page 276: "Every time Levon . . ." York/Rogan. London/Rancho Cucamonga, California: 25 May 1997.

page 276: "I'd been cut out . . ." Saul Davis/Rogan. London: 24 November 1996.

page 276: ". . . nickel and dime . . ." Terri Messina/Rogan. North Hollywood, California: 1–2 September 1996.

page 276: ". . . for Gene to make an album with his old lady, Carla . . ." Interestingly, Olson provided a rather chauvinistic opinion about the role of the female companion in rock. "I never had a problem with Terri. But, very often, playing in a band with guys (I've got four guys in my band), they've all got girlfriends and they all have an opinion about how their husbands should be paid or how he should be billed or how many rooms he should get. And Terri always had very big opinions that Gene should get more and I think in a lot of ways that's one of the reasons why the [Byrds] reunion was sabotaged too because women get involved in things they really shouldn't get involved in."

page 276: "We might not have been . . ." Saul Davis/Rogan. London: 24 November 1996.

page 276: "If somebody called . . ." Slocum/Rogan. Taluca Lake, California: 19–20 November 1996.
page 277: "Gene was totally . . ." Terri Messina/Rogan. North Hollywood, California: 1–2 September 1996.
page 277: "What are you . . ." Kandanes/Rogan. London/Cobb, California: 1–2 October 2007.
page 277: "I told Gene this . . ." ibid.
page 277: "Gene used a lot of people . . ." Shannon O'Neill/Rogan. London/ Thousand Oaks, California: 7 October 2007.
page 278: "I liked Gene . . ." ibid.
page 278: "I couldn't get a record deal . . ." ibid.
page 279: "It was a complete accident . . ." Slocum/Rogan. Taluca Lake, California: 19–20 November 1996.
page 279: "Maybe he'd met him . . ." Shannon O'Neill/Rogan. London/ Thousand Oaks, California: 7 October 2007.
page 279: "God knows what demons . . ." Terri Messina/Rogan. North Hollywood, California: 1–2 September 1996.
page 280: "Tellingly, *The Byrds Greatest Hits* . . ." The hits compilation sold 12,072 units over the previous half-year, compared with *Mr Tambourine Man* (630 sold), *Turn! Turn! Turn!* (700 sold) and *Fifth Dimension* (1,114 sold).
page 281: "It was just one last twist . . ." Saul Davis/Rogan. London: 24 November 1996.
page 281: "He told me . . ." Garth Beckington/Rogan. London/ Mendocino, California: 17 October 2008.
page 281: "It was really desperate . . ." Olson/Rogan. London: 24 November 1996.
page 282: "I took him to my parents' house . . ." Terri Messina/Rogan. North Hollywood, California: 1–2 September 1996.
page 283: "I woke in the middle . . ." ibid.
page 283: "He got totally drunk . . ." ibid.
page 283: "I went through . . ." ibid.
page 283: "I had to remove myself . . ." ibid.
page 283: "Terri was scared . . ." Sharon Brooks (née Garrett)/Rogan. London/Hollywood, California: 7–8 October 2007.
page 284: ". . . have a word . . ." Slocum/Rogan. Taluca Lake, California: 19–20 November 1996.
page 284: " 'Communications' is a timeless work; even its date and place of creation has been disputed . . ." I first received a copy of 'Communications' in the early Nineties, not that long after Clark's death. It was clearly titled 'Communications' on the tape box and indeed the lyrics also used the plural. The succeeding songs on that tape included 'Battle Of The Sexes', 'Adios Terri' and 'Big Bad Mama', among others. It was clear, lyrically and vocally, that the songs came from Gene's post Rock 'n' Roll Hall of Fame period. Subsequently, I interviewed several people

from that time, one of whom told me the story behind these songs. The quotes are in *Timeless Flight Revisited.* Clark's close friend Tom Slocum insists the tape of 'Communications' was done at Clark's home in Sherman Oaks. After the 'Mammoth incident' in late 1990, Gene climbed the nearby mount and supposedly came back with this song about extra-terrestrial intervention, biblical prophecy (with references to Ezekiel's Wheel) and speculation about the nature of angels. It was said to be about 11 minutes long. The tape I was given was considerably shorter, fading 'Hey Jude'-like at the end with an elongated chant. So who knows how long it might have been? The other songs, straight after 'Communications', are the break-up compositions 'Adios Terri' and 'Big Bad Mama', recorded in the period leading up to his death.

On a related note, a couple of years after acquiring the tape with 'Communications', I was contacted by Garth Beckington who, out of the blue, sent a rare recording from 1980 known as 'The Glass House Tapes'. This was accompanied by a two-page letter in small writing in which he told me the story of how these tapes were recorded and provided track-by-track commentaries. The songs on the Glass House tapes comprised: 'Shades Of Blue', 'Crazy Ladies', 'Midnight Mare', 'I Don't Have You' and 'I'll Change Your Life'. This becomes significant later.

Several years after this, John Einarson wrote a revealing biography of Gene Clark. Therein, he mentioned 'Communications', or 'Communication' as he now called it, which he said was appended to those aforementioned five songs referred to as the Glass House tapes from 1980. Einarson, in an online comment, concluded that I had been misinformed about the genesis and date of the song. I duly went back to Einarson's source, Jon Faurot, and he said it was indeed on the tape he played for Einarson, which he had assumed were part of the Glass House tapes. However, he also informed Einarson that these tapes were not necessarily recorded at a single session, as might have been supposed. This begged further questions. Could 'Communications' have been added belatedly to the original Glass House tapes? Faurot thought this was unlikely and doesn't recall it. That said, he acknowledged that all things are possible and would need to listen more closely. No further reply was forthcoming at that point. Aurally, it is difficult to distinguish the time period. It should be noted that the participants on the 1980 Glass House tapes (Faurot and Beckington) were later reunited with Clark at the Cinegrill in the period just before his death when the 'Communications' I had was reportedly recorded on tape. Could it be that Clark was reviving 'Communications' from the Glass House period or was it a completely new song, as I'd previously stated, that was retrospectively added to the old 1980 tape? It's as if 'Communications' exists in two time periods simultaneously which is strangely fitting for such an 'out there' song.

Resolving this mystery at first seemed impossible. On the Glass House tape I was sent, years before Einarson's book, there was no 'Communications'. More pertinently, Beckington's letter and detailed notes make no mention of the song whatsoever. Yet, he comments in some detail on the other five, saying "Check 'I Don't Have You'" with obvious enthusiasm. Surely, he would have recalled or mentioned 'Communications' if it was part of the recording. It's such an important song and not one you're likely to forget. Plus, how come it's not on the 1980 tape that he sent to me? When later questioned, he had no memory of ever recording 'Communications' in 1980. Faurot, who hadn't heard the tape in years, remained uncertain and puzzled.

Equally interesting are the contents of the 1990–1991 tape I received in which 'Communications' was followed by 'Adios Terri' et al. On one of these, Gene, teeth missing after the car crash shortly before his death, sings a chilling song which includes a reference to Ezekiel's Wheel. Of course, 'Communications' also includes a mention of Ezekiel's Wheel. This tends to suggest that both these songs are from the same period which would date 'Communications' as post-Mammoth, as previously stated, rather than from 1980. Or is this just another 'coincidence'? How likely is it that Clark would use that same allusion in two songs separated by 10 years? Again the mystery deepens. At one point I wondered if there might be two 'Communications'. Given the musicians involved, it made sense that a song they did in 1980 might be revived a decade later. Maybe Gene's tale of climbing the mountain and composing 'Communications' was an exaggeration and what he meant was that he remembered the song and, in the circumstances, decided to revive it. Unfortunately, I then discovered that both versions of 'Communications' are identical. Could it be that the tape Einarson heard simply had 'Communications' from 1990 tagged on to the end of the 1980 Glass House tapes? Maybe the subsidiary players were going through old and new songs. That might explain why the 'Glass House' tape Einarson heard featured 'Communications' whereas the tape I received, many years earlier, did not include the song and Beckington did not even connect it with that time. Who knows?

To reiterate, 'Communications' appears to exist fully formed in two different time periods, simultaneously. Alas, there is no copyright registration for 'Communications' from either 1980 or 1990 that might resolve this issue. Until recently, my comments were: "You'll have to make up your own minds about which time period it fits given the above."

The deaths of Tommy Kaye and Garth Beckington stymied further investigation. Extended correspondence with Jon Faurot suggested that my original comments on 'Communications' were correct. "First of all," Faurot wrote, "the tape that Einarson got came from me. I gave it to him in Pasadena. I'm not sure how that song 'Communications' could end up on a Glass House tape. I don't remember cutting the song, playing it or anything about it. I don't think it was on the Glass House tape at all. I don't think I even know the song. I remember all the titles on the Glass House, 'Midnight Mare' and 'I'll Change Your Life' and the rest, but I don't remember that song at all. It sounds like something that would have happened later on." This reiterated Beckington's earlier comments to me.

Finally, in 2016, I was at last able to get a tape of 'Communications' to Jon Faurot with instructions to study the recording. He confirmed that he would know instantly if it was a 'Glass House' recording. Soon after, he replied with a near definitive ruling. "This track has only one acoustic guitar, played by Gene, who had a distinctive strumming style. There is no bass guitar. There is at least one female singer, maybe two. It was recorded on a small recorder which has some kind of built-in automatic compression. This is *not* part of our 'Glass House' sessions, Garth are I are not playing on this and the singers don't sound like Tommy, Rick, Garth and me. The chorus feels familiar but I don't remember the song. Very interesting track." I wondered whether the singer might be a male falsetto, but Faurot was sceptical. "I would bet money there is a girl singing on this track. An awfully high falsetto for a guy. I have listened to this on headphones quite a few times and I'm sure it isn't Garth and me, as we would be playing on it, not just singing and there is only Gene's guitar strumming away. There is a guy singing, maybe two. I do know that it's *not* part of the 'Glass House' tapes."

page 285: "We'd been out of touch . . ." Jon Corneal, interviewed by the author. London/Winter Haven, Florida: 24 June 2007.
page 285: "I'd heard he'd got a cheque . . ." ibid.
page 285: "All of a sudden, he called . . ." Terri Messina/Rogan. North Hollywood, California: 1–2 September 1996.
page 286: "She went with him . . ." Olson/Rogan. London: 24 November 1996.
page 286: "I think, for myself . . ." Gene Clark, speech at the Rock 'n' Roll Hall of Fame. New York: 16 January 1991.
page 287: "He looked really bad . . ." Faurot/Rogan. London/West Hollywood, California: 20 September 2008.
page 287: "He actually had . . ." ibid.
page 288: "Brendan was working . . ." ibid.
page 289: "For the last few months . . ." Terri Messina/Rogan. North Hollywood, California: 1–2 September 1996.
page 289: "Gene is going to go off . . ." Ronard/Rogan. London/West Hollywood, California: 21 September 2008.
page 289: "I said, 'Gene . . .' " ibid.
page 289: "Gene was already in very bad shape . . ." ibid.
page 290: "Man, my buddy . . ." ibid.

page 290: "When I'd go down . . ." Hillary Beckington/Rogan. London/Mendocino, California: 16 October 2008.
page 290: "He was one of the worse influences . . ." Terri Messina/Rogan. North Hollywood, California: 1–2 September 1996.
page 292: "He wanted to take . . ." Slocum/Rogan. Taluca Lake, California: 19–20 November 1996.
page 292: "Rick holds the same opinion . . ." ibid.
page 292: "It was just the opposite . . ." Hillary Beckington/Rogan. London/Mendocino, California: 16 October 2008.
page 293: ". . . a dealer in the Valley . . ." Jon Faurot, interviewed by the author. London/Fort Bragg, California: 13 November 2016.
page 293: "People were calling . . ." David Clark/Rogan. London/Montrose, Colorado: 7 November 2016.
page 293: "She would have been the first . . ." Hillary Beckington/Rogan. London/Mendocino, California: 16 October 2008.
page 293: "I never heard anything . . ." ibid.
page 293: "Slocum told me . . ." Shannon O'Neill/Rogan. London/Thousand Oaks, California: 7 October 2007.
page 294: "I don't know . . ." York/Rogan. London/Rancho Cucamonga, California: 25 May 1997.
page 294: ". . . throat cancer . . . a polyp . . ." Thomas Jefferson Kaye, unpublished interview with Ken Viola: 1991.
page 294: "A singer with a voice . . ." Ronard/Rogan. London/West Hollywood, California: 21 September 2008.
page 294–295: "Throat cancer or not . . ." Kelly Clark. Unedited transcript of interview for the 2013 DVD documentary, *The Byrd Who Flew Alone – The Triumph and Tragedy of Gene Clark*. Four Sun Productions: 2013.
page 295: "They all wanted a piece . . ." Kandanes/Rogan. London/Cobb, California: 1–2 October 2007.
page 295: "She knew some of those . . ." Slocum/Rogan. Taluca Lake, California: 19–20 November 1996.
page 296: "In the middle of the night . . ." ibid.
page 296: "He would party . . ." Kelly Clark. Unedited transcript of interview for the 2013 DVD documentary, *The Byrd Who Flew Alone – The Triumph and Tragedy of Gene Clark*. Four Sun Productions: 2013.
page 296: "I sent a special invitation . . ." Gene Clark, phone call recorded by Shannon O'Neill: April 1991.
page 297: "He'd already wrecked . . ." Hillary Beckington/Rogan. London/Mendocino, California: 16 October 2008.
page 297: "Gene was a man . . ." Garth Beckington/Rogan. London/Mendocino, California: 17 October 2008.
page 297: "Hey, man . . ." Slocum/Rogan. Taluca Lake, California: 19–20 November 1996.
page 297: "I don't know what happened . . ." ibid.

page 297: "He didn't look good . . ." Paul Zollo. *Song Talk*: Spring 1991.
page 298: "I'm going to record . . ." Clark/Zollo. *Song Talk*: Spring 1991.
page 298: "That's why I'm tired . . ." ibid.
page 298: "Among their keener supporters was Hoyt Axton . . ." McGuinn had played guitar on Axton's first album, *The Balladeer* and opened for him as support act at the Troubadour. Coincidentally, McGuinn had first been inspired to take up music after hearing Elvis Presley's 'Heartbreak Hotel'. That song had been written by Hoyt's mother, Mae Axton.
page 298: "Hoyt Axton was upstairs . . ." Faurot/Rogan. London/West Hollywood, California: 20 September 2008.
page 299: "He knew only to call me . . ." Terri Messina/Rogan. North Hollywood, California: 1–2 September 1996.
page 299: "Gene thought he was . . ." Faurot/Rogan. London/West Hollywood, California: 20 September 2008.
page 300: ". . . went to some restaurant . . ." ibid.
page 300: "I was trying . . ." ibid.
page 300: "Somebody got him out . . ." ibid.
page 300: "I don't know what that . . ." Garth Beckington/Rogan. London/Mendocino, California: 17 October 2008.
page 300: "I had a gig the first night . . ." Olson/Rogan. London: 24 November 1996.
page 300: "When I was leaving . . ." ibid.
page 301: "You can see . . ." ibid.
page 301: "I can't tell you . . ." Terri Messina/Rogan. North Hollywood, California: 1–2 September 1996.
page 301: "Slocum tried to stop . . ." Hillary Beckington/Rogan. London/Mendocino, California: 16 October 2008.
page 301: "There's a bitter enmity . . ." Faurot/Rogan. London/West Hollywood, California: 20 September 2008. The 'feud', if that's what it was, actually goes back to 1997 when Slocum made what Garth considered an unflattering comment on his wife in my book, *Timeless Flight Revisited.* This was Slocum's gnomic reference to Hillary as a "Rent A Car heiress above the law . . ." Beckington wrote me a two-page letter in November 1999 stating: "Terri Messina brought your book by recently to show to my wife, Hillary, and me. I enjoyed your chapter on Gene, although the bit about my wife was biased by Slocum, a charming raconteur in his own mind . . . Enough of that. I appreciate your appreciation of Gene, so I thought I'd send you this tape." Evidently, Hillary felt she had been slighted by Slocum. "We met each other and I took an instant dislike to the guy and his whole bullshit . . . and after that he was always putting me down as some dog food heiress or Rent A Car troll or I don't know what . . ." The quote, from my reading, sounded admiring as much as critical. Then again, Slocum's pronouncements were often laden with funny but characteristically opaque allusions, prompting

ambiguous reactions from some of his listeners, depending on their interpretation of his words.

page 301: "God bless him . . ." Terri Messina/Rogan. North Hollywood, California: 1–2 September 1996.

page 302: "He was my friend . . ." Slocum/Rogan. London/Taluca Lake, California: 19–20 November 1996.

page 302: "I don't think heroin . . ." Faurot/Rogan. London/West Hollywood, California: 20 September 2008.

page 303: "Although Clark was capable of wandering offstage . . ." Shannon O'Neill could not watch a videotape of the Cinegrill season until long after Clark's death. "It was too painful. Gene wasn't in good shape there." The video lay in a box and was only unearthed when Shannon and his wife were preparing to move to a new house. They decided to watch the show but, midway through, O'Neill realized there might be something incriminating in the footage that he had never considered. It was almost as if Gene's ghost was playing some macabre trick on his old buddy. "We put the tape on," O'Neill says. "There's Gene. He gets off the stage, sits down at a table in front of me, smokes a cigarette and drinks a beer. My wife's looking closely at the tape and saying, 'Isn't that you sitting near Gene? That is you, isn't it? Who's that girl with you?' I said, 'I don't know who that is. It can't be me with her.' Then I turn around [on the videotape] and it *is* me. I thought, 'Why didn't I watch this tape before showing it?' Finally, the girl in the film turns around and – it's my wife! I said, 'Yeah!' Gene would have really appreciated that one. If he could have sat there watching that tape with me, watching me sweat, he would've thought it was hilarious!"

page 303: "Gene was mildly intoxicated . . ." Harold Sherrick, interviewed by the author. London/Los Angeles, California: 17 September 2016. Sherrick later sold the Cinegrill footage to the producer and documentary director, Andrew Solt.

page 303: "He was a friend of my mom . . ." Kai Clark/Rogan. London/Auburn, California: 25 September 2016.

page 303: "Billy threw me on a plane . . ." ibid.

page 303: "He would be toasted . . ." Faurot/Rogan. London/West Hollywood, California: 20 September 2008.

page 304: "Garth serenaded them . . ." Hillary Beckington/Rogan. London/Mendocino, California: 16 October 2008.

page 304: "Look at him . . ." Kai Clark/Rogan. London/Auburn, California: 25 September 2016.

page 304: "I was tuning a guitar . . ." ibid.

page 304: "Karen came on the scene . . ." Terri Messina/Rogan. North Hollywood, California: 1–2 September 1996.

page 305: "Get rid of her! . . ." Robinson/Rogan. London/Agoura, California: 9 November 1996.

page 305: "She was trying to keep him . . ." ibid.

page 305: "She was trying to straighten . . ." Shannon O'Neill/Rogan. London/Thousand Oaks, California: 7 October 2007.
page 305: "He said, 'She crashed here . . .'" Terri Messina/Rogan. North Hollywood, California: 1–2 September 1996.
page 305: "Karen felt . . ." Olson/Rogan. London: 24 November 1996.
page 305: "While a lot of people . . ." Saul Davis/Rogan. London: 24 November 1996.
page 306: "He did almost . . ." London/Agoura, California: 9 November 1996.
page 306: "We'd gotten these matching . . ." Garth Beckington/Rogan. London/Mendocino, California: 17 October 2008.
page 306: "Several other shows . . ." The printed itinerary reads: 19–20th July Dublin; 21st York; 22nd Bath, Moles Club; 23rd Crewkerne, near Yeovil; 24th London, Mean Fiddler; 25th Manchester; 26th York; 27–28th Cambridge Folk Festival; 29th Brighton; 30th London, Half Moon, Putney; 31st London, Weaver's Arms.
page 307: "He was sober . . ." Faurot/Rogan. London/West Hollywood, California: 20 September 2008.
page 307: "He got very upset . . ." Hillary Beckington/Rogan. London/Mendocino, California: 16 October 2008.
page 307: "I said, 'If you're coming . . .'" David Clark/Rogan. London/Montrose, Colorado: 7 November 2016.
page 308: ". . . hanging with Gene . . ." Faurot/Rogan. London/West Hollywood, California: 20 September 2008.
page 308: "He had been drinking . . ." ibid.
page 308: "I walked into the kitchen . . ." ibid.
page 308: "Jason Ronard was . . ." ibid.
page 309: "I couldn't look . . ." Ronard/Rogan. London/West Hollywood, California: 21 September 2008.
page 309: "Gene had a couple of guns . . ." ibid.
page 309: ". . . calling Tom Slocum . . ." Slocum says he was called by Davis. O'Neill assumed it was Jon Faurot who made the call, but since the call was made to Slocum, not him, he cannot be sure.
page 309: "Gene's dead . . ." Shannon O'Neill/Rogan. London/Thousand Oaks, California: 7 October 2007.
page 309: "It was one of the weirdest . . ." ibid.
page 310: "'Hello!' . . ." Shannon O'Neill, previously unpublished notes on Clark's death: 1991.
page 311: "Less than a week . . ." ibid.
page 312: "It was a total shock . . ." David Clark/Rogan. London/ Montrose, Colorado: 7 November 2016.
page 313: "I had to come to grips . . ." ibid.
page 313: "We got the word . . ." Jeanne Clark/Burnes. *Kansas City Star Magazine*: 17 January 1999.
page 313: "There was a whole scene . . ." Faurot/Rogan. London/West

Hollywood, California: 20 September 2008. Jason Ronard also left the scene early and returned to the home of Garth and Hillary where he was living at the time. "Garth just couldn't believe it," he remembers.

page 314: ". . . start calling up . . ." Slocum/Rogan. Taluca Lake, California: 19–20 November 1996.

page 314: "Gene's lying on the floor . . ." Saul Davis/Rogan. London: 24 November 1996.

page 314: "I abhorred Saul Davis . . ." Terri Messina/Rogan. North Hollywood, California: 1–2 September 1996.

page 315: "It got to be . . ." Slocum/Rogan. Taluca Lake, California: 19–20 November 1996.

page 315: "I wasn't going to start . . ." Terri Messina/Rogan. North Hollywood, California: 1–2 September 1996.

page 315: "I was looking down . . ." Slocum/Rogan. Taluca Lake, California: 19–20 November 1996.

page 315: "I remember that morning . . ." Kai Clark/Rogan. London/Auburn, California: 25 September 2016.

page 315: "Mom's got some news . . ." ibid.

page 315: "He was a bit estranged . . ." ibid.

page 316: "Having to tell . . ." Carlie Clark. Unedited transcript of interview for the 2013 DVD documentary, *The Byrd Who Flew Alone – The Triumph and Tragedy of Gene Clark*. Four Sun Productions: 2013. Carlie spoke as if she'd told the boys the news at the same moment, but this was not the case. Kai confirms: "Mom may recall it as Kelly being there but in actuality I heard and then I know Mom went and found him or sent someone to find him."

page 316: "I was already . . ." Kelly Clark. Unedited transcript of interview for the 2013 DVD documentary, *The Byrd Who Flew Alone – The Triumph and Tragedy of Gene Clark*. Four Sun Productions: 2013.

page 316: "I think it took a couple of days . . ." Kai Clark/Rogan. London/Auburn, California: 25 September 2016.

page 316: "By that time . . ." David Clark/Rogan. London/Montrose, Colorado: 7 November 2016.

page 316: "I think Kelly began . . ." Hillary Beckington/Rogan. London/Mendocino, California: 16 October 2008.

page 317: "I heard it on the news . . ." Hardwick/Rogan. London/Dallas, Texas: 10 September 2007.

page 317: "There were no drugs . . ." Faurot/Rogan. London/West Hollywood, California: 20 September 2008. Faurot's repeated insistence on resolving the drugs question was sharpened by some comments from Carlie Clark which were later printed in John Einarson's detailed biography. When she was later interviewed for the documentary *The Byrd Who Flew Alone*, she repeated this story, although it was wisely omitted from the programme. "I was in Mendocino when Jon called from LA and said that CNN was at the house, and I'd better let the boys know that

Gene was dead. And I said 'What do you mean?' And he said, 'Hasn't anybody called you?' and I said, 'No'. And he said 'Well, Gene's dead . . . we came over to pick him up to go to rehearsal and he'd passed away.' I said, 'Did you call the police?' and he said 'No, because there's drugs here' and I remember saying, 'Well, they're not going to bust him now.'"

Faurot was so annoyed by this allegation that he telephoned Carlie, determined to put her right on the matter. So, did she ever concede that her memory was at fault? "I don't think she conceded it," he admits, "but she couldn't really get past my argument. I don't remember her saying, 'You were really right', but I was so strong and so adamant that she couldn't argue with me. I was there. She was in Mendocino. And I *didn't* call her. Jason did. I didn't even know her number. The AA has its place, but that's the way those people always are. People who get into it turn it into their lives." At the time of Gene's death, Carlie was still heavily addicted to drugs and regularly using. Who knows what she said during the phone call. By the time she was interviewed, years later, she had cleaned up and perhaps felt a need to add a moral dimension to her former husband's death as a warning to others about the dangers of substance abuse. She assumed that there must have been drugs involved and, inadvertently or otherwise, created a minor conspiracy when arguably none existed. That she was still repeating this disputed story years later without ever addressing Faurot's objections is revealing in itself.

page 318: ". . . that girl when she was only . . ." Both Messina and Slocum confirm Carradine's words virtually verbatim, adding that he was very drunk, or worse. Others agree. The less than reliable Pat Robinson, who had once incorrectly stated that Clark died from an aneurysm, wrongly claimed that Carradine had said, "You pissed on my daughter." Einarson, in a rare lapse, wrote: "Carradine was alluding to an alleged incident in the early Eighties when, following an argument with Bob Dylan at David's house, Gene unintentionally wandered into Calista Carradine's bedroom and urinated." This never occurred. In his autobiography *Endless Highway* (Vermont: Journey Editions, 1995), pp. 428–429, where the incident is sourced, Carradine makes it quite clear that his daughter remained at Linda McGuinn's home while he drove Clark to a house where the urination occurred. The girl was the daughter of the unnamed hosts. Clearly, this was a completely different person.

page 318: "It was bizarre . . ." Slocum/Rogan. Taluca Lake, California: 19–20 November 1996.

page 318: "He was nearly ready . . ." David Clark/Rogan. London/ Montrose, Colorado: 7 November 2016.

page 318: "I was at the back . . ." Shannon O'Neill/Rogan. London/ Thousand Oaks, California: 7 October 2007.

page 319: "It was insane . . ." Terri Messina/Rogan. North Hollywood, California: 1–2 September 1996. Messina claims that she was told that the viewing of the body was only going to be attended by family and friends. In deference to their wishes, she did not invite a number of people "who were very close to Gene and would have liked to have gone. There were dearly beloved friends that should have been there to support me." Seeing Carradine attend added insult to injury. "I was upset about that. We did not hang around with Carradine. Carradine was an associate of Gene's and they knew each other and spent time together over the years. But those times when I was with Gene, we never spent time with David Carradine. He was not one of his close friends, so I was very offended by that."

page 319: "How stupid . . ." Hillary Beckington/Rogan. London/Mendocino, California: 16 October 2008.

page 319: "After he died . . ." Terri Messina/Rogan. North Hollywood, California: 1–2 September 1996.

page 319: "If that wasn't . . ." ibid.

page 320: "I had no legal attachment . . ." ibid.

page 320: "Gene always said . . ." York/Rogan. London/Rancho Cucamonga, California: 25 May 1997.

page 320: "We lost Gene . . ." Chris Hillman's valedictory tribute to Gene Clark. *Full Circle* 10: 1991.

page 322: "He was a great guy . . ." Terri Messina/Rogan. North Hollywood, California: 1–2 September 1996.

page 322: "I actually had to go . . ." ibid.

page 322: ". . . in a tailspin . . ." Sharon Brooks (née Garrett)/Rogan. London/Hollywood, California: 7–8 October 2007.

page 322: "After Gene died . . ." Hillary Beckington/Rogan. London/Mendocino, California: 16 October 2008.

page 322: "I've heard so many rumours . . ." Terri Messina/Rogan. North Hollywood, California: 1–2 September 1996.

page 323: "She felt bad . . ." Hillary Beckington/Rogan. London/Mendocino, California: 16 October 2008.

page 323: "She put on . . ." ibid.

page 324: "When Mom got wind . . ." Bonnie Clark Laible/Rogan. London/Bonner Springs, Kansas: 8 November 2011.

page 324: "I dropped out . . ." Rick Clark/Rogan. London/Orcutt, California: 23 June 1999.

page 325: "I'm proud of the things . . ." Kelly Clark. Unedited transcript for the 2013 DVD documentary, *The Byrd Who Flew Alone – The Triumph and Tragedy of Gene Clark*. Four Sun Productions: 2013.

page 325: ". . . the poor guy . . ." Kai Clark/Rogan. London/Auburn, California: 25 September 2016.

page 325: "This younger generation . . ." ibid.

page 325: "My father was supposed to pay . . ." ibid.

page 326: "I think she was pretty proud . . ." McCummings/Rogan. London/Comptche, California: 30 September 2016.

page 326: "Carlie was not known . . ." ibid. Jimmy McCummings estimates that it was approximately six months from diagnosis to death. "Carlie had a spot on her lung and difficulties with her liver. They zapped the spot on the lung . . . I was told that she was getting chemotherapy for her cancer and it's like if you burn yourself you get a blister. There was excess fluid in her abdomen. They were using a large hypodermic needle withdrawing half a pint at a time. But some of the places where these fluids gathered were inaccessible or tucked behind major organs. I kept wondering what would happen to all this stuff they couldn't remove. This is something that Kai may have learned from going to a doctor's appointment with his mom that she wasn't really sharing with anyone. Her daughter didn't have a clue she was dying. She'd spent two days visiting her at the hospital, then Kai took over. On the Sunday, Indiana went home to Reno and Carlie quickly went into a coma. My brother and I got a message to get over to the hospital in Roseville. We were only there a little while on the Tuesday when she passed away. She did a pretty good job of hiding from us how ill she was."

page 326: "They all got into that insanity . . ." Tom Slocum, interviewed by the author. London/Taluca Lake, California: 20 April 1999.

page 327: "The person valuing the estate . . ." Saul Davis/Rogan. London: 24 November 1996.

page 328: "At the end of that night . . ." ibid.

page 329: "I'm only willing . . ." Terri Messina/Rogan. North Hollywood, California: 1–2 September 1996.

page 330: "She spent $15,000 . . ." Pat Robinson, interviewed by the author. London/Agoura, California: 19 January 1997.

page 330: "Kelly and Kai . . ." ibid.

page 330: "If Pat's already working . . ." Saul Davis/Rogan. London: 24 November 1996.

page 331: "'Gene Project With Byrds' . . ." The two cassette tapes consisted of the following titles, written in Robinson's hand. (Some titles were slightly amended on later releases).

Tape 1. Side 1: 'I Don't Want To See You Anymore'; 'Look Who's Missing Who'; 'Shades Of Blue'; 'When Jokers Are Wild'; 'As If We Didn't Know'; 'What Happens Then'; 'Will You Love Me Tomorrow'; 'Slip Away'; 'Love's A Loaded Word'; 'Boyfriend, Girlfriend'; 'Prisoners Of Time'.

Tape 1. Side 2: 'I Need To Fly'; 'After The Storm'; 'Sleep Will Return'; 'Somewhere After Midnight'; 'A Rose Is A Rose'; 'Cocaine'; 'Shows No Mercy'; 'Surrender'; 'Can't Say Yes, Can't Say No'; 'Dragon's Eye'; 'My Marie' (Jeff's); 'Dangerous Games'; 'My Marie' (original).

Tape 2. Side 1: 'Carry On'; 'Cocaine'; 'Mary Sue' (original); 'Dancing On The Moon'; 'You And I'; 'The Hurtin' Game'; 'The Panther'; 'Nothing But An Angel'; 'Don't You Know'; 'You Better Move On'; 'On The Run (Loaded Gun)'; 'Washington Square'.

Tape 3. Side 2: 'Carry On'; 'With You I Can't Lose'; 'That Part Of You'; 'Immigrant Girl'; 'Once In A Lifetime'; 'Boyfriend, Girlfriend; 'Falling For You'.

page 331: 'Artist: Byrds'. The sheet featured 47 songs. The track listing comprised: 'Mr Tambourine Man'; 'Eight Miles High'; 'Chimes Of Freedom'; 'I Shall Be Released'; 'You Better Move On'; 'Hang Touch' [sic]; 'Dragon's Eye'; 'Tell It Like It Is'; 'Love Deluxe'; 'Where Does Love Go?'; 'Mary Sue'; 'Nothin' But An Angel'; 'The Only Chance You Take'; 'Looking For Reasons'; 'Love's A Loaded Word'; 'Love Holds On'; 'Bulletproof Heart'; 'Never Should've Loved You'; 'It's All In Your Eyes'; 'True Blue'; 'Slip Away'; 'My Marie'; 'Liona'; 'Feel A Whole Lot Better'; 'Train Leaves Here This Morning'; 'Here Without Love'; 'Immigrant Girl'; 'The Panther'; 'When You Love Someone'; 'As If We Didn't Know'; 'Quicksand'; 'Fair Game'; 'Dancing On The Moon'; 'You Just Love Cocaine'; 'Next Time Around'; 'More Than That Now'; 'Don't You Know'; 'Prisoners Of Time'; 'Boyfriend, Girlfriend'; 'One More Two Time'; 'Muscle And Bone'; 'United And Divided'; 'Reconsider Me'; 'I Need Love'; 'Dangerous Games'; 'Washington Square'.

page 331: "Eleven songs from the 'Gene Project With Byrds' were excluded . . ." My notes list the following omissions: 'I Don't Want To See You Anymore'; 'On The Run (With A Loaded Gun)'; 'Look Who's Missing Who'; 'What Happens Then'; 'Will You Love Me Tomorrow'; 'I Need To Fly'; 'Raised On Moonlight'; 'With You I Can't Lose'; 'That Part Of You'; 'Falling For You'; 'Once In A Lifetime'.

page 331: ". . . 'Geno, Nicky and Pat' featured 22 songs . . ." The cassette tape comprised: 'Washington Square'; 'Liona'; 'Carry On'; 'With You I Can't Lose'; 'That Part Of You'; 'The Hurtin' Game'; 'The Panther'; 'At Every Rainbow's End'; 'Immigrant Girl'; 'Fallin' For You'; 'You And I'; 'You Better Move On'; 'On The Run'; 'Dangerous Games'; 'My Marie'; 'Dancing On The Moon'; 'The Rest Of Your Life'; 'Blue Raven'; 'Rodeo Rider'; 'Sleep Will Return'; 'Somewhere After Midnight'; 'I Need To Fly'; 'After The Storm'. The track listing accompanying the tape omits 'Blue Raven', but it appears on the tape sent to me. In a revealing letter, Robinson partly explained how some of the songwriting credits were negotiated: "Most of the writing was done by Geno and I – however, Geno liked a lot of songs that I had written alone, and wanted to record them as well – therefore, the 5 per cent shares of those songs where he and Nicky had minimal contributions, and no share if he was just recording them. We made an agreement not to walk all over each other's material so that we could maintain our own catalogs. But at the same time Geno wanted his name on those songs in which he had even minor input, so we agreed that 5 per cent interest was fair enough to accommodate each other's needs."

page 331: ". . . 'Writing Roughs' offered 15 songs . . ." The cassette tape comprised: 'Evangeline'; 'The Panther'; 'Have You Ever Seen A Man?'; 'You Wouldn't Be So Proud'; 'Dragon's Eye'; 'I Don't Really Want To Hear It'; 'I Wish You Knew'; 'Something About A New Romance'; 'You And I'; 'Fallen Angel'; 'Let The Winds Blow'; 'Nothin' But An Angel'; 'Never Say What's On Your Mind'; 'Liona'; 'Will To Survive'. The track listing accompanying the tape omits 'I Wish You Knew', 'Liona', 'Never Say What's On Your Mind' and 'Will To Survive', although they are clearly audible on the tape. Even more oddly, 'Evangeline', 'The Panther', 'Have You Ever Seen A Man?' and 'You Wouldn't Be So Proud' do not appear on the tape despatched to me.

page 332: 'Gene Clark: The Lost Decade'. A track selection for this project was never compiled but it would have included all the Gene Clark co-compositions and 'Writing Roughs' listed above.

page 333: "The entire unsavoury saga is discussed in the Endnotes . . ." What were euphemistically known as 'unofficial recordings' of the Pat Robinson/Gene Clark material first emerged on releases dated 2000, notably *Mr Tambourine Man* and *The Alternate Takes*, both of which featured 'Love's A Loaded Word', 'Boyfriends, Girlfriends' [pluralized], 'Quicksand', 'The Panther', 'Dragon's Eye', 'Dangerous Games', 'My Marie' and 'Washington Square', plus Robinson's 'Slip Away' and a cover of Arthur Alexander's 'You Better Move On'. A subsequent release titled *The Byrds* and later *It's All In Your Eyes* featured 'Carry On', 'Love Deluxe', 'Where Does The Love Go', 'Boyfriends, Girlfriends', 'Mary Sue', plus Robinson's 'Next Time Around' and 'It's All In Your Eyes', and John York's 'You Just Love Cocaine'. There was also a double album, *The Byrds Most Famous Hits – The Album* that included the CRY-era related songs: 'Quicksand', 'Tell It Like It Is', 'As If We Didn't Know', 'The Panther', 'Dragon's Eye', 'Slip Away', 'Dangerous Games', 'My Marie', 'Washington Square', 'Prisoners Of Time', 'You Better Move On', 'One More Two Time', 'You Just Love Cocaine', 'Love's A Loaded Word', 'Boyfriend, Girlfriend', 'Carry On', 'Reconsider Me', 'Where Does The Love Go', 'Next Time Around', 'Fair Game', 'Mary Sue', 'Love Deluxe' and 'United Or Divided' (uncredited, written by Pat Robinson and Harriet Schock). A seemingly interminable variety of these albums were issued on the Continent including *The Byrds: 30th Anniversary Album* and *Eight Miles High – The Greatest Hits Of The Byrds.*

Unsurprisingly, all these releases featured unrepresentative photos of various incarnations of the Byrds. In one remarkable case – *The 30th Anniversary Album* – the cover photo actually pictured the Sixties English mod group, the Birds, whose line-up included Ronnie Wood. The notes on several of these records claim that the material was 'licensed from Pat Robinson'. He was certainly seeking a European deal at the time, as he told me, but whether any papers were signed has never been ascertained. Some of the compositions co-written by Clark were largely the work of Robinson who also takes lead vocals on 'Boyfriend, Girlfriend', 'Fair Game', 'Love's A Loaded Word', 'Love Deluxe', 'Quicksand', 'Prisoners Of Time', 'Slip Away' and 'Where Does The Love Go'. Many of the Clark compositions included – some with slightly different titles – were eventually released on the two *Under The Silvery Moon* collections on Delta. Their initial double album of that title was, of course, famously withdrawn prior to release after falling foul of the Gene Clark Estate.

But all this was merely part of an even stranger story. Listeners to the 'unofficial recordings' will have been further baffled by the inclusion of a number of songs that had nothing whatsoever to do with Pat Robinson or Gene Clark or CRY. These included versions of 'Mr Tambourine Man', 'All I Really Want To Do', 'Turn! Turn! Turn!' and 'Eight Miles High' by a covers band using the Byrds' name. On the 2000 *Mr Tambourine Man* recording, for example, 'Eight Miles High' was erroneously co-credited to Michael Clarke instead of Gene Clark. Its inclusion was made more bizarre by a seeming inability to decipher the lyrics of the original. Instead of "Nowhere is there warmth to be found" the vocalist sings "No grey mist there want to be found" and bowdlerizes several other lines – "some just shapeless forms" emerging as "just shake their scorns". The fragrant misrepresentation was summed up in a closing medley of supposed hits: 'Mr Tambourine Man', 'Turn! Turn! Turn!', 'Time And Place' and 'It Won't Be Wrong'. Of course, the Byrds never recorded a song called 'Time And Place' and although this was credited to Roger McGuinn and Harvey Gerst on this recording, neither ever wrote a composition of that title. Similarly, 'It Won't Be Wrong' was not the familiar Byrds' hit (composed by McGuinn/Gerst and credited here as such) but a completely different song, presumably written by the musicians on the album. What had happened here? Why were these oddities mingled in with the Clark/Robinson songs and where had they come from?

The answer could be found in several earlier releases, the first of which was titled *The Best Of The Byrds* issued on K-Tel Records back in 1996. Its contents were reissued on variant titles such as *The New Byrds Play The Greatest Hits* and *The Magic Collection*. These works featured such obscure songs as 'Outa Sight', 'Do You Remember', 'Quit This', 'Home Again', 'Time And Place' and 'Sarah Jane', all credited to 'McCulloch and Chapman'. Even here, there was inconsistency. On *The New Byrds Play The Byrds*, for example, these songs were preposterously credited to McQuinn [sic]/Levy, while 'You Ain't Going Nowhere' was not the familiar Bob Dylan composition but a different song of the same title. Its chorus "You ain't going nowhere/No time, don't sit there/Don't be afraid you know we care" underlined the differences. The composing credit simply read 'Crest', whoever that was. On related releases, the wrongly credited Levy became the even more incorrect 'G. Lely' compounding the errors. And so it went.

What had kickstarted this unfortunate saga was revealed in a court hearing during March 1998. K-Tel testified that they had purchased the Byrds recordings, along with others by Mott The Hoople, the New Animals and Paper Lace, for $75,000 after an approach from an American company named McCulloch Chapman Music. According to K-Tel the deal was negotiated by Danny McCulloch (a former member of the New Animals) who claimed the recordings were by the original artistes. The court action had not resulted from anyone connected with the Byrds but a certain Phil Holbrook, who had bought the Mott The Hoople CD on mail order. "It sounded absolutely terrible," he testified. "I couldn't believe my ears. What made it worse is that the singer was trying to imitate [Ian] Hunter's distinctive style. But he was hopeless." After Holbrook brought the matter to the attention of Mott's management they alerted trading standards officials and provided a written statement from singer Ian Hunter that it was not his voice on any of the recordings. K-Tel's defence confirmed that once the matter had been brought to their attention they had withdrawn the release the previous August. Alas they were no longer in contact with McCulloch but intended to instigate proceedings if he could be found. K-Tel admitted two charges under the Trade Descriptions Act of supplying a CD with a false description and were fined £4,000 on each count. They were also ordered to pay £1,488 costs.

Nobody on behalf of the Byrds entered the proceedings but their CD was presumably withdrawn too. A trading standards representative noted: "This prosecution sends out a warning to record companies that they must be diligent in checking the accuracy and details of recordings they wish to sell, however old they may be."

What he evidently had not considered was the Continental market where these tracks reappeared on the various CDs and labels mentioned above. It was a terrible outcome that Clark's CRY material should be interspersed with these other unauthorized recordings.

page 333: "'Kathleen', less impressive technically . . ." An interesting appreciation of 'Kathleen' can be found on The Clarkophile website.

page 336: "Gene would rip . . ." Dickson/Rogan. London/Costa Mesa, California: 10 January 2006.

page 336: "I don't like saying . . ." Hardwick/Rogan. London/Dallas, Texas: 10 September 2007.

page 336: "It's too bad . . ." ibid. The Firebyrds' compilation comprised: 'For A Spanish Guitar', 'Silver Raven', 'Gypsy Rider', 'I Saw A Dream Come True', 'Rodeo Rider', 'Rest Of Your Life', 'Blue Raven', Introduction, 'Vanessa', 'Eight Miles High', 'Seventh Avenue Train', 'Something About You', 'You Showed Me', 'She Loves You' and 'No Other'. As Hardwick concludes: "To hear the talking between the songs, that was the real Gene Clark. He was very amiable, very gentlemanly, very respectful and he was so happy people were there. He was having such a great time playing his songs, even though we were playing small clubs out there with a four-piece band.

page 337: "The Byrds had been used . . ." Dickson/Rogan. Waldport, Oregon: 26–30 April 1989.

page 338: "I probably listened to them . . ." Kai Clark/Rogan. London/ Auburn, California: 25 September 2016.

page 339: "the lowest scumbag . . ." email to Sid Griffin from Saul Davis: 14 February 2003.

page 340: ". . . Len Freedman in 1989 when he purchased the Tickson Music catalogue . . ." On 31 March 1989, Dickson and Tickner transferred the Tickson Music catalogue to Len Freedman. The date of recordation was as late as 1 October 1996 and included 148 songs. The unreleased titles on the tape that Dickson gave to Freedman were not included in this listing but, then again, neither were many other songs that Clark never issued in his lifetime. The document does include 'A Worried Heart' in the listing but oddly none of the other 1964 solo recordings premiered on the 2016 Sierra box set. Ian Tyson's 'The French Girl' is erroneously included in the listing as a Clark composition, repeating the mistake on the *Echoes* compilation.

page 341: ". . . as one of the most important and underrated singer-songwriters . . ." Clark's critical reputation has fluctuated over the years, but his cult appeal remains intact. In 2007, Robert Plant and Alison Krause included 'Polly' and 'Through The Morning, Through The Night' on the best-selling *Raising Sand.* As recently as 2014, the great *No Other* inspired a collective of musicians – including members of Fleet Foxes, Beach House, Grizzly Bear and the Walkmen, plus Iain Matthews – to commemorate the album with a series of concerts.

2

MICHAEL CLARKE

3 June 1946 – 19 December 1993

THE death of Michael Clarke at the age of 47 closely followed Gene Clark's demise. Only two years before, the Byrds were one of the few major groups from the Sixties with a full line-up still alive. Suddenly, they were more decimated than either the Rolling Stones, the Beatles or the Beach Boys. Clarke was generally regarded as the most easy-going and uncomplicated member of the original Byrds. As the sole non-singer/songwriter in the group, he was never a creative threat to his fellow members, so his role in the party politics seldom extended beyond occasional flare-ups at recording sessions, which were soon forgotten.

On reflection, it seems incredible that Clarke was still only 21 years old when he *left* the group. Few people knew this at the time as he had lied about his age. Like Gene Clark and Chris Hillman, he used a fake identity card in order to hang out at clubs and bars and by the time the Byrds hit Ciro's it seemed sensible to add two years to his life. While other groups disguised their true ages to make themselves appear younger, Michael, Gene and Chris did precisely the opposite. Even at the time of Gene's and Michael's deaths, some pop encyclopaedias and reference books still printed the old statistics, oblivious to the small subterfuges of these former teenage pop stars.

Most of the myths began when they were filling in their 'Lifelines' for dissemination to the world's pop press. Under the section 'Brothers and Sisters', Gene wrote *none*, thereby giving the impression that he was some lonely kid rather than the second eldest of a large family of six brothers and six sisters. Michael was even more circumspect, suggesting that Clarke was his real name and that he had been born in Stockbridge, New York. Both were fabrications that followed him throughout his life and were even featured in several obituaries. Few knew the real story about how he had changed his surname from Dick to Clarke, inspired by the *Dick Clark Show*; few bothered to mention his parents, James and Suzanne (Suzy), or discuss his formative years in Spokane, Washington.

There were other myths too. He was once said to have travelled extensively as a child, even spending some time in Europe. Years later, he admitted to me that he'd never set foot on European soil until the Byrds arrived in England in 1965. The other enduring myth was that he had been discovered on the street outside the Troubadour and had never played drums before. These too were exaggerations, for Michael was already aware of the group's existence and was not completely unfamiliar with a drumkit, although he had never played professionally. "It was wishful thinking, most of it," his mother Suzy says of the early errors. "He was born here at the Sacred Heart Hospital in Spokane. It's true that we went to Houston, Texas, almost every year because my husband's folks were from there. But he lived all his early life here. I guess he thought it was more exciting to be born somewhere else. He told me that everything happened so fast and he was just putting people on at first, but then he got caught up in it. The [surname] Dick was a hard name to live with. My husband told me that. I'm so naïve, I didn't know. I still live with it right now. Michael was the only one of the Byrds that had no serious previous experience of playing or doing anything spectacular. But he did play congas and bongos and he had this natural talent for which he didn't have to make any excuses at all. He must have had this image of what he wanted to be. But he did a lot of things is all I can say. Michael had big expectations of himself."

Michael's expectations started early in his life. Unsettled at school, he fancied himself the class rebel and defied authority through the simple expedient of absenteeism. This was to remain a lifelong trait. If pushed too hard, he would disappear in search of something more pleasurable. "He skipped school and you've got to be there to get anywhere," his mother says. "He didn't rehearse with the school band, he didn't have any real teaching and he couldn't read music. He played in the basement here in Spokane with his small group of musicians. It was basic R&B, but he had such a great love for jazz and that era of George Shearing. Dave Brubeck's drummer Joe Morello was his hero."

Inspired by these jazz giants, Michael scoffed at the idea of settling into a straight job in Spokane, preferring to dream of travelling to exotic places and enjoying a beatnik, bohemian lifestyle. "He went to work *once*," his mother recalls, with exasperated mirth. "He worked as a labourer with his dad, who was a plumber and pipe fitter. He went in for one or two days, then said, 'No, that's not for me. I'm not going to do that.' And he didn't ever do it again. It was hard work, but it paid really good money. He had the physique. It didn't hurt him a bit. But he was like a vagabond."

At one point, around his 16th birthday, he attempted to enlist in the Navy. "They wouldn't take him mainly because he was too young," Suzy remembers, "and also because he had flat feet. He always liked the ocean, and he liked water anywhere. He would have stayed in the water until he disintegrated. It was good for him. It was soothing and he needed something to calm him down."

Michael's restless spirit ensured that he would not remain in Spokane for long. Suzy Dick, a pianist who had played in jazz bands, remembers him asking her: "How come you didn't hit the big time?" She patiently explained: "Well, I got married, had children and my husband wouldn't let me play for 20 years, so I had to take that time off." Michael considered this for a second before announcing: "Well, I'm going to make it big. I'm going to hit the big time." He wasted no time attempting to secure that goal like a kid intent on running away with the circus. Barely out of school, he began his glamorous trek to the West Coast, hanging out on beaches, painting like a beatnik and playing bongos in coffee-houses. "The beatnik word was going around at that time," he told me. "I suppose I was one. What the hell? It was wonderful. There was freedom. Everyone else I knew was having to work and be something that they hated. I absolutely refused to do that."

Michael's adventures were interrupted during 1963 when he learned that his mother had fallen ill with viral pleurisy. He returned home for a brief spell while she was convalescing. On 22 November, he was listening to the radio with some friends in his basement room when a newsreader interrupted the music to announce that President Kennedy had been assassinated. "They came up and told me," his mother remembers. "Michael was very moved by it. Everybody banded together in mourning. We watched the cortege and Michael listened to the drums."

Soon, Clarke was back in San Francisco, which is where he first met Jim McGuinn and David Crosby and changed his surname from Dick to Clarke. Subsequently, he was invited to join the fledgling Jet Set in LA, having been inducted immediately after meeting them on the street. These early exploits are documented at far greater length in the first volume of this book. After a period of rehearsing as a quartet, the group eventually added Chris Hillman, and the Byrds' story began in earnest. Hillman immediately recognized that Clarke had something the others did not possess. "Michael had a background . . . he knew blues and he knew Muddy Waters and stuff like that. He actually had more access to rock 'n' roll than any of us. . . . Having varied backgrounds musically, it created this strange band and it created that strange sound that we came up with."

Back in Spokane, Michael's parents received sporadic bulletins about his progress but were uncertain what to believe. "In one letter he mentioned Doris Day's son, and my husband said, 'Yeah, sure!' But I said, 'Well, it's *possible*. Everything's happening there.'" As it transpired, the truth was more fantastic than anything their son could have fabricated.

Michael Clarke was an instant teen idol, whose presence added immense appeal to the Byrds' image. From 1965–67, audiences paid more attention to his Rolling Stones looks than his drumming abilities. As Crosby told me: "He had Brian's hair and Mick's lips. I remember he looked so much like them that he got me into the first *TAMI Show* (in 1964) because they thought that he *was* Brian Jones. We ran up to the door and the girls were yelling at us and the guy there thought it was a couple of Stones and let us in. Michael meant very well, and he was a good guy. I liked him a lot."

Clarke became a fashion-conscious free spirit, whose carefree ways and generosity were endearing, if sometimes exasperating. He was thrilled when the group were kitted out in Beatle suits, but grew bored with the image very quickly. The group's suits were later conveniently stolen but, before that incident, Clarke had already given his away to Little Richard's drummer. Clothes swapping would remain one of his more eccentric traits thereafter. Even in later years if he liked your jacket, he'd say: "Here, you can have mine! Give me your one."

Clarke exploited his good looks like a teenage Lothario and was frequently seen in the company of several Hollywood beauties, including Toni Basil, Deana 'De De' Mollner, Peggy Lipton and Cher. Toni Basil's appreciation was evident from the moment the Byrds played their residency at Ciro's, even before the chart-topping success of 'Mr Tambourine Man'. "I remember Toni Basil there," says manager Jim Dickson. "She went after him like a barracuda. She saw him looking cute, and he was stunned by her. He was still so simple with all of that Hollywood stuff. When they first played Ciro's, she snatched him right away. It was just amazing to me. He was dumbfounded that these girls would grab hold of him and capture him. They didn't much care about who he might be or anything. They just *wanted* him. Through my time with Michael that pretty much never ended."

Clarke's status as a sex symbol always boosted the confidence of those around him, not least Gene Clark, whose shyness melted when he moved in with Michael and set Hollywood alight looking for girls. "Michael had the nerve of Dick Tracy," Dickson adds. Even producer Terry Melcher hung out with the drummer for fun. "I was going out with his girlfriend's sister," Michael recalls. "Terry was dating Claudia Martin (Dean Martin's daughter) and I was going out with Deana Martin, who was two years' younger than me. We got along quite well." There was no shortage of girls on tour, although even Clarke sometimes felt overwhelmed by their intensity. At one show, a female fan gripped him so tightly that two police officers and three National Guardsmen were required to restrain her. The story was even reported in the press.

Among the many dancers in his social circle, Clarke was most closely associated with Deanna Dail ('De De') Mollner, a long-haired blonde, who stood at 5 foot 10 inches without shoes. Sporty, confident, gregarious and fun, Deanna suited Michael's outgoing personality. Photogenically, they resembled an almost iconic pop couple. Her appearances as one of the Gazzarri club dancers on television's *Hollywood A Go-Go* made her a national teenage treasure, even among those who never knew her name. Her image belied an urbane, sophisticated upbringing, far removed from Clarke's modest background. The daughter of the gold-winning Olympic basketball player Art Mollner, she was raised as a member of the Science of Mind, a philosophy combining religion and science inspired by writer Ernest Holmes. With its emphasis on positive thinking, integration, meditation and spiritual healing, it was the type of pseudo-religion that would probably have appealed to McGuinn. Mollner went on to study archaeology at UCLA, but her love of dance and childhood friendship with Beverly Hills resident Mimi Machu saw them both become accomplished go-go dancers. Deanna hung out with the original Ciro's crew and was photographed with the Byrds, Carl Franzoni and the rest. One of her many memories of dating Michael was attending a party thrown by the Beatles during their 1965 visit to LA. The story, as documented in *Volume 1* and elsewhere, tells of Crosby and McGuinn, accompanied by Peter Fonda and Lennon and Harrison, experimenting with acid and discussing ragas. Of course, there is no mention whatsoever of Clarke who, as so often in these tales, is written out of the script. But, as Mollner confirms unprompted, he was there. "It was for the Beatles and very heavy stuff happened," she adds.

Clarke's carpe diem attitude to life and remarkable self-confidence enshrined his popularity. Nevertheless, Dickson sometimes felt called upon to play the finger-wagging paternal figure, particularly when Clarke was living in his basement apartment. But it was impossible to bridle the drummer's free spirit. On one occasion, the pair were walking through a parking lot when Michael, probably high on something, impetuously grabbed an expensive Japanese-manufactured calculator from an open car window. Dickson was appalled and gave him a stern moral lecture, which appeared to have no discernible effect. Ever the mischievous child, Clarke simply shrugged his shoulders apologetically while waiting for Dickson to exhaust his indignation. Nothing more was said on the matter but, at a later date when he was a little more affluent, Clarke appeared at his manager's door one night, visibly dejected. His car had been stolen. Dickson immediately offered to drive him to the local police department to report the matter, but Clarke demurred. "It's karma, man!" he said. Evidently, the episode with the calculator had pricked his conscience. Dickson was amazed. "In the end, he didn't even bother to report the stolen car. He just let it go."

Musically, Clarke was still a novice but at a time when session drummers dominated pop that was hardly a problem. The other Byrds innocently perpetuated the myth that the sum of his musical experience consisted of playing congas on the beach, and he never bothered to correct that impression. In fact, Clarke had played around with baby drumkits since he was a child and even appeared briefly in a neighbourhood garage group, although admittedly never before large audiences at a professional venue. Their most notable date was playing in the front window at the opening of a store in Spokane.

That Michael started working with the Byrds thumping away on cardboard boxes added to his enduring image of amateurish enthusiasm. But he was a quick learner and he always had a distinctive sound. The eccentric military-style drumming on the *Preflyte* recording of 'Mr Tambourine Man' was pure Clarke and, as Dickson duly notes, the basis of that arrangement was retained on the studio version cut at Columbia.

Although technically limited, Clarke always had his champions. When Dylan had turned up during the World-Pacific rehearsals, it wasn't Crosby or McGuinn who caught his attention, but the guy sitting behind the cardboard boxes. Dickson was amused by the memory. "Michael was playing a tambourine on top of a cardboard box when Dylan saw him and he was charmed by it. Michael looked so good. He paid such attention to what he was doing, and he had no instrument." The king of folk was entranced by the sound that Clarke captured. It was the type of feel that he would later echo when recording *The Basement Tapes.*

During the Byrds' first flush of fame, Clarke hung out with Dylan at local coffee-houses and clubs. He was liked and accepted, partly because he was so easy-going, non-intrusive and immune to the groupie-style worship that Dylan often disdained among his following. "Michael was one of those people that everyone immediately had affection for," Dickson adds. "It was the same for Dylan. He thought Michael was a nice guy, there's no other way to put it. That was Michael's natural state. He was like a Huckleberry Finn character. They got on well and that did not surprise me."

Clarke always knew his limitations as a player and was at first intimidated by the prospect of playing a Ludwig drumkit at a professional recording session. "When Michael first got his drums, the drumsticks flew out of his hands and he was ready to walk out. I told him, 'None of them has ever worked with a drummer before, you've got plenty of time to learn.'" Dickson's patience was soon rewarded. He was impressed by Clarke's chunky playing, particularly during the first residency at Ciro's in the spring of 1965. "David was the keeper of time," he jokes, recalling Crosby's frequent complaints about Gene and Michael's timing. At one performance, Dickson placed a metronome on the stage, which merely confirmed that they were all playing out of time. "Michael wasn't any worse than anyone else."

The dance troupe at Ciro's interacted with Clarke's rhythm to such an extent that he maintained a perfect beat that enabled the Byrds to soar to heights that they seldom, if ever, reached thereafter with the original line-up. Long before Clarke's death, with words unsweetened by bereavement, Dickson paid a fitting tribute to the drummer when recalling those moments. "The first wonderful thing he did was 'The Bells Of Rhymney'. It had this flow, this feel, this power. Everybody waited for that to dance to . . . It was magical in the studio too. Drums always sounded great in the CBS studio when they first recorded them. On those big floor speakers, a Ray Gerhardt drum recording sounded better than you expected. Always. No matter who was out there. How they were going to wind up in the mix, you couldn't tell. Michael had a cymbal pattern worked out which Terry Melcher mixed out of the record. You usually had to. Terry didn't know enough to say, 'This is the exception, we should really bring it up.' He lost a lot of Michael there. Terry featured the voice. He mixed the mono for AM radio play to the exception of everything else. The stereo mix was just a nuisance. 'I'll get it out of the way and I'll bring up the voices because maybe the folkies will like it.' I felt the other way. Stereo gives you a chance to bring up the music and not drown out the voices. You could put the voices nearer the centre and some of the music out on the edge. Open it up, so that you could have the power. I was more worried about the Byrds sounding wimpy like Chad & Jeremy . . ."

Clarke's power generally came through even more powerfully in those mono mixes specifically issued as singles, most notably his brilliant work on 'Turn! Turn! Turn!' and 'Eight Miles High'. His struggles and triumphs are captured on the CBS session tapes where he accepts instructions from Terry Melcher and others, patiently repeating takes. There are some wonderful moments, from the cymbal chimes of 'The Bells Of Rhymney' to his accidental creation of a dramatic stop/start delay on 'Turn! Turn!

Turn!'. He could also provide many surprises, not least his ability on harmonica. Tellingly, it was when Paul McCartney and George Harrison attended a Byrds session on 23/24 August 1965 that Clarke offered to add a harmonica break to an early take of 'The Times They Are A-Changin''. Both Clark and McGuinn had each attempted the part without success, but with a couple of Beatles in attendance, Clarke was unfazed. Michael can also be seen playing the instrument in backstage film of the Byrds on tour, cool and unflustered as ever.

Any problems that the Byrds had in the studio with Clarke were mainly due to his confusion or frustration at their lack of communication and preparation. Dickson was often exasperated. "They'd get the whole song worked up, all the harmonies worked out. McGuinn would show what he was going to play and David knew what he was going to play, so it was ready before Michael ever got a chance to work on it. And Michael, not being a trained musician, had to learn every hit of the drum from memory. He had to know what to play and memorize it all. That takes time. He was always better on every song *after* it was recorded. I tried to get them to rehearse with him. They wouldn't do it. In the Burritos I got them to rehearse a little bit more and they began to get good in rehearsal and go into the studio and make it happen. But for Michael in the Byrds, it was very frustrating."

That frustration sometimes spilled out into salty streams of invective that can still be heard on the session reels from *Mr Tambourine Man* through to *The Notorious Byrd Brothers*. Although Clarke had to bear the brunt of many criticisms in the studio, he rarely reacted with anything other than retaliatory verbal abuse. The exception was a cathartic moment in 1965 when he left his drum stool to punch David Crosby in the face. Nobody, Crosby excepted, regarded that as a sacking offence. Clarke's friendly nature and unwillingness to involve himself in the Byrds' more serious disputes ensured that he was always well-liked. When the group terminated their management contract with Eddie Tickner and Jim Dickson, Clarke was the most reluctant signatory. "Michael went where it was easiest," Dickson notes. "He said, 'I'll be out of a job if I don't go.' He came in and hung his head and felt bad about leaving us. He was the only one of them that faced up to it. The rest of them just sent a letter. When I was at Monterey [in June 1967 when the decision had been made] they never even admitted what was happening. They couldn't face it. They had no courage."

Clarke's composing credits as a Byrd were minimal. Apart from the co-writing namecheck on 'Wild Mountain Thyme', his major contribution was 'Captain Soul', an instrumental played in the hard, R&B style that he always preferred. It provided another chance to show off his harmonica playing, complete with heavy breathing. "That was my style," he says. "I played R&B whereas Gene Clark was more folk." Although the number emerged during a studio jam, Clarke argued that he deserved far more than the quarter writing credit allocated. "Those guys are absolute cruel bastards," he snarled, a little theatrically. In fairness, McGuinn agreed that "essentially, it was Mike Clarke's trip" but the jam session ensured the four-way split. Later, Clarke also co-wrote the inspiring 'Artificial Energy', providing some key lines, as well as coining its distinctive title as a euphemism for the effects of speed.

Somehow Clarke survived the troubled sessions for *The Notorious Byrd Brothers* and was still playing in the Byrds as late as December 1967 when the streamlined trio performed at various venues in California. They had even incorporated the ambitious unreleased version of 'Milestones' into their set, much to Clarke's satisfaction. Alas, there was no new dawn for this line-up. Having already threatened to quit and more than once expressed his weariness of playing in the Byrds, the drummer was deemed dispensable and was asked to leave by McGuinn and Hillman. It was hardly surprising. During the sessions for *Notorious*, he had complained that he didn't like their new songs and became embroiled in a bitter, yet hilarious, argument with David Crosby. Clarke, who always preferred to record quickly and play hard, had little affection for soft rock. Earlier he was known for playing with such intensity that he sometimes broke his drumsticks.

Up until the end, he was always capable of making mischief, sometimes innocently. Amusingly, even his horse could create problems. There it is on the cover of *The Notorious Byrd Brothers* where Crosby's figure might have stood. This symbolic image later caused terrible ructions between McGuinn and Crosby but Michael could never take these ego battles seriously.

The complete story of Clarke's tenure in the Byrds is detailed in *Volume 1* of this book, but some additional stories and questions remain. On 3 January 1968, he officially left the Byrds, having signed a letter prepared by Beverly Hills' lawyer Jay L. Cooper, headed 'Agreement For Sale of Partnership Interest'. The document stated: "Whereas the Byrds is a partnership consisting of James Roger McGuinn, Christopher Hillman and Michael Clarke. The parties have agreed that it is in the best interests of all concerned that Michael Clarke resign as a member of said partnership and transfer his one third (1/3) interest partnership to the remaining partners." Whether it was ever in Clarke's "best interests" to relinquish his partnership stake sounded like a moot question. The remainder of the letter was akin to a complete surrender. Clarke agreed to "hereby irrevocably sign, transfer, and set over to each of the remaining partners a one-half (1/2) share of all my right, title and interest as a partner in the partnership of the Byrds and its assets, goodwill and partnership affairs. I shall be responsible for and pay all income taxes on my share of the profits of the partnership for its fiscal year next ending as well as such other taxes as may be assessed against me."

It was typical of Clarke's cool that he left without a fuss. There were no bitter comments to the press, let alone any suggestions of compensation. Whether he even bothered to appoint anybody to represent his interests or negotiate terms is not known, but it does not seem likely. The termination letter outlined his rewards in stark terms: "I shall be entitled to my share of record royalty income from Columbia Records with respect to each and every recording on which I have performed to date." His only other asset was, of course, the drumkit he already owned. "The remaining partners hereby transfer, assign and convey to me whatever interest, if any, they may have in the musical instruments, amplifiers etc, customarily used by me. Said equipment shall be my sole and separate property." Tellingly, in light of events decades later, he agreed not to use the name 'Byrds' but at least he could remain in the pop business and form a new group, as if that was some kind of gracious concession. "If I so elect, I may engage, alone, or with others, in a line of business similar to that of the partnership; provided that, however, I acknowledge that I have no further rights in and to the partnership name, 'The Byrds'."

What happened next compounds the notion that Clarke was blasé in his decision making and naïve in business dealings. If he had remained in the Byrds for a couple of more months, he would have shared some of the substantial advance that McGuinn and Hillman secured upon renewing their contract with CBS in February 1968. "Michael's compensation for the entire name of the Byrds turns out to be his drums and his royalties, which he was entitled to anyway," quips Steve Green, who later represented Clarke in the bitter legal action over the Byrds' name in 1989. "Exactly 45 days later they collected $150,000 from CBS. Michael says he knew nothing of this when he signed his rights away. You know Michael. What does he know? They went to his house and he just signed the paper. He should have said, 'Hey, I'm holding on. Give me some money, *then* I'll discuss leaving.'" These days, lawyers would have demanded all sorts of termination awards or limited future percentages, but back then the music business was less litigious. In any case, Michael was too carefree to worry about such matters. He departed with a shrug of the shoulders, hanging out in Hawaii, until he was ready to return to the music scene.

Clarke settled in Maui for a time, evidently still infused by the western imagery captured on the cover of *The Notorious Byrd Brothers*. "He bought a horse and took it to Maui," Dickson reveals. "I don't know what prompted him to go, but he was out there on his own. Even I'd not brought my boat there yet." Like a latter-day cowboy, Clarke rode his steed down the crater of the 10,000 feet high Mount Haleakala, surveying his new kingdom along the way. The fate of Clarke's horse is alas not recorded, but equestrian fees likely took their toll. In one of the more remarkable and endearing decisions of his life, the once world-famous drummer applied for work at the recently opened Buzz's Wharf restaurant, above the Ma'alaea Boat Club. He was offered a job as a 'busboy', collecting plates and clearing tables. Between the hours, he enjoyed looking out at the harbour, scouring the southern coastline of Maui, watching the surfers and the passing pods of humpback whales in the distance. Unfortunately, his employment was short lived. Like other eateries on the island, Buzz's Wharf served food, accompanied by a fresh orchid for ostentatious effect. On one occasion, Michael was told by his supervisor to collect any orchid, unpolluted by gravy or left abandoned, for reuse on the next platter. "If they weren't damaged they'd use them again," says Dickson. "That offended Michael so much that he quit. He just walked right out. I would never have thought that Michael would have cared that much about an orchid."

When visiting the drummer in Maui, Dickson noted how removed he seemed from the ego-driven environs of Hollywood. "I don't think he ever mentioned the Byrds unless we were talking about some person in it. He didn't go around telling other people there that he was in the Byrds. He did play drums a couple of times with other guys over there, but it was never a case of 'this is Michael Clarke from the Byrds'. He just played." Indeed, Clarke's only connection with the current Byrds that year was when he unexpectedly turned up at the Hollywood Troubadour in April and deputized for Kevin Kelley in a one-off performance. Equally suddenly he returned to Hawaii without explanation.

Towards the end of 1968, Clarke was invited back to LA to team up with Dillard & Clark. They had just completed a stunning debut album, *The Fantastic Expedition Of Dillard & Clark,* and required a drummer for live performances. Gene Clark considered Michael the natural choice, not just as a musician but as a soul mate, whose presence promised fun and frolics. David Jackson, the Expedition's string bass player, was entranced by Clarke's personality and, like so many others, marvelled at his ability to attract women. "Michael knew at a very early age that he had this something which made women go crazy. If I knew what that was, I'd be a happy man today. I loved him deeply. He was a joyous, life-consuming pointer of pussy. If there was a girl in a room that would reciprocate an invitation, he would find her in a New York second . . . When he'd go into a bar, he'd put on his famous drummer smile and the ladies would go crazy. His job was to make sure those vulvas were quivering . . . but that guy was such a jewel. Funny, intelligent, poised, effervescent. And he would never exclude anyone from his party. Whoever was there was part of it. He would start talking to a girl and all of a sudden there'd be five girls and he'd always include me, and Gene. Michael was completely out-front, shirt open, teeth glimmering, unabashed. If somebody really wanted to know his credentials he'd say, 'OK, I'll tell you – *the Byrds*'. But that wasn't of interest to him. It was only of interest if some pretty girl with large breasts *needed* credentials . . . I never saw him depressed or worried about money. Not once. Michael was a con man with no con. He was always interested in the next moment not the previous one . . . Everybody had to work at having a good time, but not Michael. He had a great time every moment of the day."

Clarke's carefree caprice ensured that he was always happy to take whatever life offered. When Dillard & Clark decided to pursue a rootsier second album, he acknowledged that the party was over and effortlessly ingratiated himself with former Byrds, Chris Hillman and Gram Parsons. The Flying Burrito Brothers had just completed their classic debut album, *The Gilded Palace Of Sin*, and urgently needed a permanent drummer. Remarkably, they had already been through five percussionists: Eddie Hoh, Chuck Blackwell, Sam Goldstein, Popeye Phillips and Jon Corneal. Although he was way down the list, Clarke proved the perfect candidate. His departure from the Byrds had not been accompanied by any bitterness and Hillman rightly predicted that his temperament would be crucial in alleviating ego battles and easing creative tensions. Clarke would remain a Burrito for almost as long as he had been a Byrd "Chris and I were still friendly," Clarke told me, "and I was already aware of Gram. I'd first met him during *The Notorious Byrd Brothers*, before I moved to Hawaii. Chris had this house over Topanga Stables, where we used to ride. Gram appeared at the stables too."

Clarke's chief assets to the Burritos were his no-frills playing, friendliness, hospitality, unrestrained hedonism and a love of the road. These traits were sufficient to convince Parsons that he had discovered another kindred spirit. Clarke remembers auditioning for the Burritos by playing along with some tunes from their debut album. Long before he had finished, Parsons pulled him aside and said, "Drummer boy, let's just go out and have some fun."

The fun continued on the road where booze, cocaine and mescaline were part of the daily diet. Encouraging Clarke's excesses was probably not the most sensible way of integrating him into the band. From the outset, he felt that partying was at least as important as playing, while rehearsals were sometimes regarded as a chore rather than a necessity. Regrettably, the band ethos merely reinforced these notions. Complacency threatened to undo the Burritos even before they set out on their first tour. A crucially important showcase gig organized by their label, A&M, was treated with disdain by several members of the group, who turned up stoned. Their ramshackle performance in front of record company executives was a disconcerting preface to their tour which would further strain the patience and expense account of the A&M hierarchy. In a typically wilful moment of extravagance, the Burritos decided to travel by train for part of the itinerary, even filming the events on a home-movie camera. The tenure of the 'Train Tour' was set by a sending-off party during which the participants gorged themselves on dope-filled cookies. Clarke remembers awakening every day to what he dubbed 'the psychedelic breakfast' – a head-spinning combination of mescaline and psilocybin capsules. Rather than discussing their set list, the group members concentrated on consuming a formidable supply of drugs and spending as much money as possible on their record company's tab.

In order to spice up life on the road, they started a poker school, which soon challenged the music for priority. Thousands of dollars would regularly change hands with games sometimes lasting all night without a break. By the time they reached Chicago, two days later, Clarke and his comrades were wasted. "We'd gotten the flu or pneumonia from travelling. We were sick and had been playing poker all night. Gram and I and Chris got a doctor who gave us a big shot of antibiotics and this cough medicine. We had this meeting that night with all the record company promotion people. We got there and passed out in our food. Chris was lying on a bench, Gram was out on his feet and I was dribbling."

Even through sickness, the poker playing continued and would be remembered long after the live performances had been forgotten. Clarke encapsulated those moments during an animated anecdote in which he cast himself as a 'Luke The Drifter' card sharp taking on the slicker and wealthy Riverboat gambler, Gram Parsons. "Playing with Gram was tricky because he wasn't frightened to bluff, even with a dead hand. A trust fund gives you a lot of confidence in poker and he had me down to a chip and a chair. I found a few bucks in my pocket, but that just made me feel worse, so I started tearing them up in front of him. Then Chris Ethridge came over and handed me this purse. I thought, 'Great, how generous, he's slipping me $100', but it was empty! I said, 'What the hell?' Then he told me it was a lucky Indian purse. Maybe he was joking, but I've got to tell you, it worked. I called it the 'magic purse'. I turned the tables on Gram, won every hand and left the table with a couple of thousand dollars. A good night. The next morning we celebrated with a $200 breakfast from Maxim's, below the classy Astor Towers where we were staying."

Next on the itinerary was a drive to Detroit during which Clarke and company nearly managed to kill themselves while frantically taking a turn off the highway. Throughout the drama, they continued playing poker across the backseat, clutching their cards close to their chests while defying gravity. Thereafter, they doubled back to Chicago, where they were evidently coherent enough to appear on Studs Terkel's celebrated radio show without causing an incident. Live, they acquitted themselves adequately, albeit with a reliance on what Clarke termed "feel before technique". Almost every tour date produced a story, usually involving prescription medicines or illicit drugs. Seemingly, the only straight and sober person on the road was the elder steel guitarist Sneaky Pete Kleinow, who pointedly absented himself from the partying. At the Boston Tea Party (20–23 February), the Burritos shared the bill with the Byrds for the first time and ended the shows with an all-star jamming session. "It was funny seeing everybody, like watching a film," Clarke reminisced. "McGuinn had a new set of Byrds, but we had more original Byrds than he had."

After Chicago and Boston, the Burritos had an important booking in New York at Steve Paul's Scene, one of the city's hipper music venues. A&M had alerted the local music media to the event, but the Burritos missed this showcase, much to the record company's chagrin. "We got caught in a blizzard and blew the opening night," Clarke says. "But I enjoyed the other sets we did there. It was always late when we went on and we'd stay there till daybreak. Chris Ethridge was playing bass and knocked a jar of talcum powder from his amplifier. He was so drunk, he thought it was a pile of cocaine on the floor. I said, 'Ssh, don't tell everyone!'" The final night of the tour took them to Philadelphia, where they each commandeered a hotel suite and took full advantage of the record company credit card. Clarke remembers Gram Parsons opening a trunk containing a selection of bejewelled turbans and Eastern fineries. They decided to baffle their audience by conducting a bizarre cross-cultural fashion experiment, combining *Arabian Nights* turbans with Nashville-style Nudie suits. Parsons ended the evening by falling off his piano stool while Clarke laughed at the absurdity of the spectacle.

The Burritos returned to LA, still hopeful of achieving some crossover success between the country and rock markets, but they were ahead of their time. Critical acclaim could not mask the fact that *The Gilded Palace Of Sin* was merely a moderate seller by a cult band with a penchant for on-the-road extravagance beyond their station. Clarke was keen for them to play more R&B and seemed delighted when Parsons announced that Larry Williams and Johnny 'Guitar' Watson had been employed to produce a one-off single, 'The Train Song', inspired by the recent tour. The sessions degenerated in a blitz of cocaine, which pleased Clarke but did nothing to improve the quality of a questionable recording. The single flopped, but the memory of Williams lingered every time they played 'Bony Moronie' and 'Dizzy Miss Lizzy'.

Over the next few months, the group stayed on the West Coast, alternating between club and bar dates and playing low on the bill at several rock festivals. Clarke still had a tendency to speed up his drumming when he became excited or drank too much, but the other players were also inconsistent. Rather like the mid-period Byrds, the Burritos offered inspired moments in concert, sometimes spoiled by lapses in discipline. A bootleg of two of their shows in San Francisco, released officially in 2007 as *Live At The Avalon Ballroom 1969*, captures the band in all their erratic glory. The flaws are self-evident, although in fairness these recorded performances were not intended for public consumption and the group were only the support act, sandwiched between several San Franciscan favourites. Clarke had clearly settled into the band. At one point in the show, Parsons announced – "from Seattle on the drums, Michael Clarke" – adding another piece of misinformation about the drummer's geographical origins.

For Clarke, part of the appeal of the Flying Burrito Brothers was their sense of community and camaraderie on the road. Throughout this period, he proved himself a trouper, gamely turning up at shows in a cast after fracturing his left foot in a 'motorcycle accident'. Evidently, it was more a comic mishap than a daredevil dice with death. Clarke had stopped at some traffic lights on Sunset Boulevard after which his Harley accelerated too quickly, rising in the air like a wild steed and dismounting its rider. As he lay helpless on the ground, the bike landed on his ankle causing the damage. He did not ask for sympathy or time off and continued to consume drink and drugs with happy abandon. There was still a lot of ribbing from other band members about his playing, sometimes prompting flare-ups, which usually ended with Michael threatening to quit, then disappearing to hang out with cooler dudes, usually the Tulsa musicians so beloved of Parsons. "When Michael's leg was healing everybody was giving him shit because he had trouble with his foot," recalls one associate. "He wasn't the world's best drummer, but he could play a great backbeat. He'd say, 'Screw you guys,' then he'd be with someone else. Michael loved R&B and had one of the best collections of obscure records you ever saw."

During 1969, the Burritos played the same circuit as the Byrds and there were several more get-togethers and late-night jams. Even their road managers seemed interchangeable, with Jim Seiter defecting to the Burritos only to return to the Byrds later in the year. Frank Blanco would also work for both groups and the Burritos additionally acquired two more larger-than-life characters, Robert Firks, a recent inmate of San Quentin, and Phil Kaufman, who had served time at a correctional facility alongside Charles Manson. The younger Carlos Bernal wisely remained on the periphery, understandably wary of Chris Hillman in the aftermath of a heated affair with his wife, Anya. Clarke was amused by all these intrigues and loved hanging out with the roadies, who always had a regular supply of booze and drugs.

Shortly after joining the Burritos, Clarke shared accommodation with Hillman and Parsons on Beverly Glen Drive. It was a predictably chaotic household, characterized by the participants' already familiar indulgences. By the end of the summer, all three had moved out, with Clarke ultimately relocating to Lake Malibu approximately a year later, where he moved into a house with Carlos Bernal and Frank Blanco. Bernal had occasionally turned up at Burrito shows, carefully avoiding Hillman but maintaining friendly relations with Parsons and Kleinow. "They were always exciting gigs," he says. "The tour managers were Frank Blanco,

Robert Firks and the Mangler (Kaufman), who I always thought of as the pretender to the throne. Their bus driver was also a tour manager, a 300 lb black guy from Los Angeles named Jerome Starks. These were the guys." Living with Clarke enabled Bernal to indulge both his pharmaceutical and sexual appetites. "It was always a real good time. Michael was mischievous and funny. He was like a big nine-year-old that didn't grow up. I had the best of times with Michael. It was a lot of fun out there at Lake Malibu in the summer. He was easy-going and we owned horses together. We shared girlfriends too. This was before sexual diseases would kill you. You could share girlfriends and we were out in Lake Malibu having our summer of love."

In addition to the usual groupies, Clarke was surrounded by a bevy of beautiful starlets, who retained a discreet and respectable distance but were no doubt amused by tales of his erotic escapades. "Girls were always there getting suntanned," Bernal reminisces. "Linda Hager from the *Hee Haw Show* was our next door neighbour on one side and Deborah Whalley lived down the road – she was very friendly and a beautiful equestrian. Ronnie Blakely would come over to visit there and she was always a pleasure to see by the swimming pool."

Clarke felt he was in hound dog heaven in Lake Malibu. It seemed as if he had been transported into a fantasy beach movie and cast as the leading man. Years before, he had seen Deborah Whalley in such movies as *Gidget Goes Hawaiian* and *Blanket Beach Bingo*, the stuff of teenage dreams. Wandering down near the bottom of the lake one day, Clarke met an even more striking embodiment of American womanhood – Elizabeth Montgomery, star of the long-running television sitcom *Bewitched*. "She became friends with Michael," Bernal adds, "and because of that we got to visit and 'sit' at her house on the Lake. She was going out with Robert Foxworth at the time and they kept a house there."

Before Malibu, Clarke was still struggling with the Flying Burrito Brothers whose career appeared in commercial and artistic decline. They had already lost Chris Ethridge, whose contributions to *The Gilded Palace Of Sin* had been exemplary.

Weary of the exigencies of the road and in need of a better income, he sought session work. Clarke was also tempted to find other employment and his love of R&B brought him into closer contact with a coterie of players who hung around with Brandon de Wilde and Leon Russell. These included Ralph Scala, Ron Gilbert and Joey Stec (all ex-members of the Blues Magoos), Randy Naylor (ex-Poor), guitarist David Doud and the accomplished bassist Carl Radle, occasionally abetted by other Tulsa players. After enjoying many late-night jamming sessions, several of them decided to take the project further and form a group: the Dependables.

Clarke spoke of the Dependables with great relish while providing absolutely no information about their history which remains chronologically sketchy. Earl McGrath, then head of Clean Records, an associate label of Atlantic, evidently funded some recordings during this period. "Michael was hanging around with Earl and Ahmet Ertegun," Joey Stec recalls. "We recorded at Paramount in Los Angeles with Michael on drums. We did some R&B tunes and a few originals. It was hot, man. I have almost everything I recorded but I don't have this tape. I would give anything to have a copy."

The Burritos briefly continued as a quartet without Chris Ethridge before recruiting Bernie Leadon. Meanwhile, Gram Parsons was becoming frustrated by their lowly status. With each passing month, he seemed increasingly detached and apathetic, while seeking vicarious excitement in drug abuse. Morale worsened when he started hanging out with the Rolling Stones, who were completing *Let It Bleed* in Los Angeles. Parsons hoped that Keith Richards might produce the Burritos, but Hillman had already asked former mentor Jim Dickson. In an attempt to stave off a crisis, Hillman reluctantly took on bass duties for the first time since leaving the Byrds. Clarke was happy to have Dickson back and even moved into his house for a brief period, as if determined to improve his own behaviour and reliability. Parsons stayed remote from Dickson who initially recorded some rough practice tapes, which featured country standards and other favourites from their live shows. Later, Dickson returned to these tapes in a vain attempt to produce a more spirited album. The results, belatedly issued in Europe during 1973 as *Honky Tonk Heaven*, indicated the lopsided nature of the recordings, veering uneasily between exuberance and incompetence.

"I don't remember Michael ever coming to a Burritos' rehearsal drunk or anything, like Gram did," Dickson stresses. "Michael was OK, but he wasn't very enthusiastic about the Burritos because it was so fucked up. When the rest of the band wasn't any good, Michael played some sloppy drums but if the band was on top of it, then so was Michael. When they gave him time to learn the songs, he was there. In the long run, Michael was the least of their problems – for me, anyway."

While preparing for the new studio album, Clarke learned that the band had been added to the bill of a high profile concert, courtesy of the Rolling Stones. Clearly, Parsons' networking had proven fruitful. The hype surrounding this event was born of media pressure. A stinging attack in the music press about the Stones' inflated ticket prices had prompted Mick Jagger to respond with the conciliatory promise of a free concert at San Francisco's Golden Gate Park. When that idea fell through, further venues were considered, culminating in the late announcement that the event would take place at the Altamont Speedway on 6 December.

Clarke was excited at the prospect of seeing the Rolling Stones' perform, while admitting that it would be a strange experience given the death of Brian Jones, the Stone with whom he had always been compared in mid-Sixties' pop profiles. The bond between the Stones and the Burritos had been strengthened by the starstruck ambition of Gram Parsons, who had become firm friends with Keith Richards since first meeting him in May 1968 when the Byrds visited England. Unwittingly, Jagger and Richards had proven catalysts in his leaving of the Byrds two months later on the eve of a controversial tour of South Africa. Thereafter, Parsons had briefly hung out with Richards at his home, only to discover that they shared a passion for country music. Parsons had been quick to re-establish contact once the Stones landed in America, spending as much time as possible with Richards, even to the point of ignoring his Burritos commitments. The Stones were busily incorporating stronger country elements into their repertoire and Parsons was regarded as an inspirational force. Although cynics suggested that he was simply being used, his fraternization with Richards had actually proven productive. Several members of the Stones turned up at some of the Burritos' more obscure club dates. Although Clarke and Hillman were far too cool to solicit a support slot on the Stones' free concert, Parsons had no such reservations. After hearing about the booking, Clarke was pleased about the exposure the Flying Burrito Brothers would receive and looked forward to an enjoyable day.

The Altamont disaster will be examined in the succeeding chapter on Gram Parsons in this volume. Suffice to say, Clarke's memories of that December day are unique. Despite the savagery of the Hell's Angels and the terrible slaying of Meredith Hunter, the more negative aspects of the festival magically passed by the drummer, who was blissed out for the most part. In the subsequent film of the event, *Gimme Shelter*, he can be seen flailing away on the drumkit during a brief segment of 'Six Days On The Road'. The positive response to the Burritos' set, a rarity at Altamont, ensured that Clarke was confident and comfortable. With Jim Dickson backstage and Crosby on the bill with CSN&Y, the event was something of a mini-Byrds reunion, albeit a troubled one. Crosby, a self-professed friend of the Angels, witnessed the carnage out-front and announced, "Hey, crazy people, stop hurting each other, man. You don't have to. Please, man. You can always talk, man." His words were as ineffectual as Grace Slick's pleas for amity earlier in the day. The military-trained Stephen Stills prided himself on clearing the stage within 90 seconds, after which CSN&Y were whisked away by helicopter. Dickson had similar ideas and left immediately, accompanied by Hillman and Kleinow. Ever the prevaricator, Clarke decided to stay and watch the Stones' set. He seemed invigorated by the plentiful supply of beer and the attractive presence of the iridescent Michelle Phillips and her best friend, Ann Marshall. Parsons, meanwhile, was ensconced in the Stones' trailer van. Bernie Leadon, against his better judgement, also stayed.

From a safe distance, Clarke observed the terrible events unfold, but it was all a blur. At first, his mind commuted back to the spring of 1965 when the Byrds had supported the Rolling Stones. During a show at Long Beach, he had witnessed the police clubbing a crowd of over-excited teenagers that had circled the Stones' getaway car. But this was far worse. While the Rolling Stones played on, oblivious to the full extent of the horror, Clarke was still wandering around, having lost sight of Michelle Phillips whose drink had been spiked with acid. She ended up leaving the site with Parsons and the Stones in a lightning departure aboard a helicopter. Leadon was now stranded, but Clarke still seemed unfazed and figured rightly that his boyish charms would save the day. He quickly reconnected with Ann Marshall and met an old friend, the well-known choreographer, Toni Basil.

Michael had first encountered Basil when he was 'impersonating' Brian Jones and successfully getting the Byrds on to the set of the 1964 concert film, *The TAMI Show*. Clarke, in common with the other Byrds, always enjoyed the company of dancers and Basil was a glamorous part of the Hollywood scene. She was evidently pleased to reconnect with Clarke and more than happy to offer a lift in her car, with Leadon tagging along. Always the opportunist, Clarke ended up in Sausalito, commandeering the rooms that the absent Gram Parsons had booked for a now redundant post-performance party.

Nothing was quite the same after Altamont. The Burritos resumed work on their second album, but Parsons had clearly lost interest. He was still smarting from their rejection of his maudlin '$1000 Wedding'. Even Clarke had negative memories of the song, complaining that they had wasted countless hours trying to make it work. "It was a big drag and we wore out any enthusiasm we might have had." Dickson realized that Parsons was detached from the project and Hillman felt little sympathy for his former songwriting partner. When Parsons excitedly presented them with a brilliant unreleased Jagger/Richards' composition, 'Wild Horses', Hillman dared question its quality.

Released in spring 1970, *Burrito Deluxe* was a disappointing anti-climax, marked by a significant decline in songwriting quality and a seeming lack of purpose. There were a handful of strong tracks, but little of the innovation captured so effortlessly on the great *Gilded Palace Of Sin*. Clarke played pretty well throughout, but had few fond memories of the sessions. Meanwhile, the Burritos remained heavily in debt to A&M and were still playing locally for little money. They showcased the album with a week-long appearance at the Troubadour (7–14 April) during which the familiar Burritos' hedonism was publicly displayed. Upstairs in the dressing room, Clarke was already high and heading for a fall. Around him was the familiar retinue, including manager Jim Dickson and some musician friends, notably Joey Stec and Ralph Scala from the fast disintegrating Blues Magoos. "Michael was popping a handful of pills," Stec vividly recalls, "and he had a jug [of beer] in his hand. He was staggering down the stairs and I told him, 'You're crazy', but he said, 'Never mind, I got it.'" Somehow, Clarke stumbled through most of the set, but his pharmaceutical abuse finally caught up with him and he dramatically collapsed. "He fell off the drum pedestal and passed out," Stec marvels. "I was front row centre and Chris and Gram just looked at me. So I ran up and finished the set with them on drums – and I was a guitarist! Back then our chops were good, so I could do those last two songs. I played cross stick, two and four, because I'm not a drummer."

The troubled Troubadour performance was a harbinger of further woes. An important promotional tour was dramatically interrupted when Parsons broke his leg in a motorcycle accident. This merely accelerated his already prodigious drug intake and he was in poor shape when he returned to the road a month later. Somewhere amid this interregnum Clarke reconnected with his friends in the still evolving Dependables. Guitarist Joey Stec remembers a flurry of phone calls after which they booked some shows in Aspen, Colorado "at a club called the Galaxy". Former Ikette Claudia Lennear (aka Lanier) tagged along to offer vocal support and Burritos' road manager Frank Blanco was roped in to assist with transportation. On the eve of their departure, Clarke turned up in Stec's driveway with a brand new Volvo, much to everyone's surprise. The drummer was suspiciously circumspect about this new acquisition but Stec agreed to allow him to leave it in his garage for safekeeping. When they finally returned from Aspen, Clarke was acting strangely. Then he demanded an unusual favour. Stec was instructed to take the prized Volvo from his garage to a particular street and leave it outside a house. No further explanation was forthcoming. "It turned out the car belonged to Jerry Wexler's daughter, Anita," he later learned. "Michael met her in the Troubadour and gave her a good one at the back and she fell in love with him and gave him the car to use for a couple of days before he went on the road. [At first] he didn't want to give it back because he liked the car so much. He figured it was Anita Wexler, so what the hell does she need money for? He'd hidden the car in my garage. Jerry Wexler's daughter's car!"

Further problems lay ahead. Parsons' visible deterioration and unreliability jeopardized the Burritos' momentum, causing Clarke to weigh up his options. "Michael did the Dependables for a while," Stec claims. "He was in and out of the Burritos at the time. You couldn't keep track of this. Michael could disappear like the Invisible Man. Then some bullshit happened with our business deal and he went back to the Burritos. It wasn't until 1971, over a year later, that we recorded the Dependables album for United Artists without Michael." Ironically, Clarke was replaced by Chuck Blackwell, the famed Tulsa drummer who had previously played on part of *The Gilded Palace Of Sin*. Clarke's decision to stay with the Burritos ultimately proved sound as the Dependables album was cancelled and only appeared decades later as an archival release.

* * *

By the end of June 1970, Hillman finally lost patience with Parsons and, following a show at the Brass Ring on Ventura Boulevard, he informed his partner that he was now an ex-Burrito. In order to punctuate the point, he punched his fist through Parsons' Gibson guitar. Amid this psychodrama, Clarke uncharacteristically joined in the baiting, taunting Gram with the words, "You're out of the band, man." Clarke's barbs were largely braggadocio and were forgotten by the following morning. Parsons also assumed that the blow-up was nothing out of the ordinary, but he had severely underestimated Hillman's wrath. When they met again a few days later at the A&M car lot, Hillman was unrepentant and refused to allow Parsons back into the band.

The Burritos gamely carried on as a quartet, just as they had done when Chris Ethridge left, but it was obvious that new blood was required. Coincidentally, Eddie Tickner, who had been managing the group since the reappointment of Dickson, received a call from Columbia Records recommending a singer-songwriter, whom they felt needed a band to fulfill his potential. Rick Roberts may have seen himself as a soloist, but was thrilled by the opportunity to join the Burritos as a songwriting partner. During an audition at A&M, he impressed Hillman and Clarke with his David Crosby-inspired harmonies. One song stood out from his repertoire of self-penned compositions: the haunting 'Colorado', a poignant meditation thematically similar to Gram Parsons' signature tune, 'Hickory Wind'. Clarke was the first to accept Roberts as a fully integrated member. Following Rick's debut performance with the Burritos at the Whisky, the drummer could be heard telling everyone that he was their "great new lead singer".

On 27 November, two months after Roberts' arrival, the Burritos flew to the Netherlands for their first foreign tour. They almost missed the trip when Clarke was delayed by airline officials who noted that the name on his passport was 'Michael James Dick'. He never did fully surrender his family title. The visit to Holland proved a revelation. Amazingly, they were greeted by mobs of journalists at the airport and had to conduct a press conference, sat at a table with individual microphones. Nor was this merely media hype. They played to sizeable audiences at Amsterdam's famous Concertgebouw and other venues. This was everything Parsons would have dreamed of for the group but he was no longer there for the accolades. Michael Clarke took all this adulation in his stride, effortlessly reverting to the laid-back character who waltzed through legions of well-wishers during the madness of 1965.

A short UK tour followed in December, which was also a minor triumph. When the tickets went on sale, I feared for the Burritos, just as I had done when the Byrds had played the Royal Albert Hall with Parsons in 1968. Now I was worried because Parsons was absent and knew that many concertgoers were unaware of the recent key personnel change. Additionally, reports of the group's live shows emanating from the States over the years suggested that their playing was terribly inconsistent. Confounding such concerns, they played an astonishingly accomplished set at London's Lyceum Ballroom. Roberts' songs sounded exceptionally good, Clarke and Hillman offered a strong rhythm and their professionalism was self-evident. Clarke seldom sounded better. Hillman looked commanding, even playing the diplomat in interviews, insisting that Parsons had left the Burritos of his own volition and seemingly wishing him well.

The group returned to the US with a new sense of purpose and soon began work on their third album. "I was disappointed with *Burrito Deluxe* but liked the 'blue' album," Dickson says. "The album was done with a great sense of care on the one hand, but maybe not much excitement. The best thing was I was able to get Michael to rehearse with them before he went into the studio, which meant he played a lot better. There had always been a problem when he was working with the Byrds; they didn't give him enough time beforehand."

Clarke's playing on *The Flying Burrito Brothers* is noticeably solid and Roberts' songwriting impressive, ranging from the classic career highlight 'Colorado' to the Amsterdam-inspired

'Four Days Of Rain', the sprightly 'Why Are You Crying?' and love lorn 'Just Can't Be', the latter highlighted by Kleinow's eerie sounding steel guitar. The album received a modicum of critical acclaim and was proclaimed the Burritos' finest work to date in both *Billboard* and the influential UK rock magazine, *ZigZag*. Regrettably, these positive notices were not reflected in sales receipts. For all their efforts, the group remained a cult item rather than a mainstream band. Worse still, they were about to suffer further damaging line-up changes. Kleinow had felt marginalized since the first album where his bizarre steel lead breaks had proven such a crucial part of the group's sound. Shortly after completing *The Flying Burrito Brothers* he handed in his notice. In later interviews, he cited the group's excessive drug use as the primary reason for his departure, although everyone knew that the real hedonistic highs had occurred during Parsons' tenure. Jim Dickson believed that Kleinow was more disillusioned about the group's rejection of his songwriting efforts. That, combined with subtle changes in musical direction, modest financial remuneration and an emotional distance from his fellow players, probably convinced him to quit. Coincidentally, his replacement Al Perkins, nicknamed 'the Preacher' by the road crew, was an even more abstemious character, a fundamentalist Christian who neither drank nor smoked.

By contrast, Clarke's alcohol consumption was increasing and he was never likely to be tamed or converted. Some critics marvelled at his longevity. One concert reviewer that summer noted with evident surprise: "Michael Clarke is still the drummer, lasting longer than I ever thought he would. Not because of any lack of prowess, but because Michael has always seemed permanently impermanent, no matter what he's doing." There was a moment when Hillman considered replacing Clarke with Don Henley, whom Perkins had recently played alongside in Shiloh. Perkins was wide-eyed about the multi-talented Henley who not only drummed but sang with authority and wrote good songs too. Hillman was nearly swayed, but soon thought better of the idea. As ever, Clarke could charm his detractors when he sensed a crisis. As Rick Roberts explains: "If he didn't think it was important he'd go out and get stoned and drunk before we went onstage and we would really threaten to fire him. Then, always in the nick of time, he'd shape up and start to play real good. After a while everything would get rosy and he'd start to get drunk again. It was a cycle."

The next Burritos' casualty was not Clarke, but Bernie Leadon. He had been unsettled since the appointment of Rick Roberts whose promotion as the group's leading singer-songwriter seriously reduced his own standing. On *Burrito Deluxe*, Leadon had been given a cameo on the self-penned 'God's Own Singer' but that was unlikely to happen again given Roberts' prolific songwriting output. Feeling demoted and disillusioned, Leadon sought new opportunities and teamed up with Don Henley, the drummer who had almost been invited to replace Clarke. Along with Glenn Frey, they went on to form the original line-up of the Eagles, whose commercial brand of country rock would achieve sales figures about which the Burritos could only fantasize.

Following Leadon's departure in July 1971, Hillman took on a more prominent role as the group's main singer and bravely elected to expand the line-up with some bluegrass players. The Burritos had already incorporated a bluegrass segment in their live performances and this had proven popular, particularly with their Amsterdam audience. At first, Hillman approached guitarist/banjoist Kenny Wertz who, like Leadon, had once played alongside him in the Scottsville Squirrel Barkers. Wertz had recently joined Country Gazette, who were managed by Eddie Tickner and later produced by Jim Dickson. Over the summer, two other members of the Gazette became auxiliary Burritos: champion fiddle player Byron Berline and Roger Bush on upright bass. In concert, the septet proved the most accomplished musical line-up of the group to date and it made perfect sense to capture the results on a live album.

The incorporation of bluegrass into the set may have indicated a lessening in Clarke's importance, particularly considering Hillman's recent threat to replace him with Don Henley. But

Clarke was no wallflower. Unexpectedly, he began to influence the Burritos' musical policy by insisting that they play more R&B and high energy rock 'n' roll to offset the country material. In this, he was backed by Dickson, who felt the balance would work to the group's advantage when producing their live album. The result was a more eclectic set, featuring FBB classics, bluegrass standards and a final section where Clarke could enjoy reprising oldies like 'Wake Up Little Susie', the R&B mainstay '(Ain't That) A Lot Of Love' and the Byrds' old Chuck Berry standby, 'Roll Over Beethoven'.

Although the group appeared to be entering a welcome period of stability, Hillman was becoming restless and frustrated. The Burritos had reached a commercial plateau and the sales of their fine third album suggested that they would never hit the US Top 100, unless they fluked a hit single. They were still a decent concert draw and could have continued pulling in regular money for years, but that was not enough for Hillman. "It got to the point, as with the Byrds, where I was not getting any satisfaction from it," he told me. "Bernie had left three months before and he was a very important part of that group. However, I thought we had a real good stage band with Rick and Al Perkins. We'd done that European tour and were real good, but when we returned to the States A&M Records didn't go a goddamn thing. I was very frustrated. We were in the process of making a live album when I gave notice that I was quitting. I didn't really know what I was going to do."

That last paragraph requires some chronological qualification. Back in the summer, several of the Burritos had attended a show by Stephen Stills & the Memphis Horns at the Public Hall, Cleveland (20 July). The perennially sociable Michael Clarke was eager to get backstage and hang out, prompting a meeting that would prove immensely significant. At the time, Stills was in poor psychological shape, drinking heavily in the wake of an ill-fated romance and keen to try something new. He was already playing the pastoral ballad 'Jesus Gave Love Away For Free' in his set and had some new compositions that would clearly benefit from the input of seasoned country players. Coincidentally or not, Stills was envisioning an album combining rock, R&B, bluegrass and country in daring fashion. In certain respects, it was similar to the multi-instrumental work that the new Burritos were performing, only more ambitious and highlighted by Stills' superior songwriting. The concept was so momentous that it could not be contained within the confines of a single album. Not too long afterwards, Hillman received a call from Stills inviting the group to visit Miami during October to contribute to his new record. Ironically, Clarke was left behind as Stills already had a permanent drummer, Dallas Taylor. The sessions went so well that Stills offered Hillman and Perkins a full-time spot in his band.

"We went down there and it turned out he wanted to start a band," says Hillman. "At the time, having given notice to the Burritos, I thought, 'Great!' The band wasn't known as Manassas yet as we hadn't really got a title." The Burritos were still recording their live album when Hillman broke the news. Dickson was appalled by the timing which effectively meant that the concert album would be a requiem rather than a new start. Clarke was predictably blasé about the bombshell announcement, even though it meant the end of his career as a Burrito. He had no intention of remaining in the group without Hillman, even if they elected to continue. Dickson was of similar mind. Still, it cannot have escaped Clarke's memory that he was largely responsible for setting off these series of events. As Al Perkins notes: "If it hadn't been for Michael making an entrance and talking with Stephen we would never have gotten the invitation to go to Stephen's hotel room and talk about recording with them. Michael was a real talker and that's how Manassas got started."

In February 1972, Clarke's swansong with the band, *Last Of The Red Hot Burritos*, was released to critical acclaim and modest sales. With an optimism worthy of Mr Micawber in Dickens' *David Copperfield*, Clarke decided to take another extended vacation and returned to Hawaii, promising to play R&B in the future. During his sojourn in semi-retirement, Michael met the wealthy Robin King (aka McNamara, Henderson), whose background could hardly have been more different from his own. Her grandparents had bought property in Hawaii after the attack on Pearl Harbor, which established the family fortune. "Everybody was selling because they thought the Japanese were going to move in and take over the island," Michael's mother explains. "The grandmother bought up all that waterside property at Waikiki Beach and leased it to a hotel. So Robin and her mother always had a big trust fund. Robin was in various boarding schools and travelled around a lot. She was in Hawaii but had been all over the world. Robin never had to work, but she did a lot of things, like selling sharks' teeth in a boutique. She was high energy and a woman of the world and a little younger than Michael, a three-year age difference." Robin was completely entranced by Michael and, as early as their first meeting, told him that he would be a genetically ideal parent. With her trust fund, she enjoyed a privileged lifestyle that later included a heavy partying period with Michael. While living with Robin, the drummer jokingly told his colleagues that he would never have to work again.

Hawaii had always symbolized a spiritual retreat for both Michael and Gene, ever since an acid-induced visit in December 1965. As avid sailors, Crosby and Dickson both had strong connections with the islands and Jim would later retire there for many years. Although now isolated from the Hollywood high life, Clarke was never short of visitors and Robin was, by all accounts, a vivacious host and a party-loving girl. For some, it seemed her connection with the Byrds had been written in the stars. "I'd known Robin from a long time back," Dickson recalls. "My brother used to date her sister (Jeannie) when they were teenagers. He used to sneak the two of them out of their private school. He was the skipper of their stepfather's boat. Bill King was a very wealthy man and so was her mother, Barbara. At the time I was with Michael and Robin on the island, they weren't drinking much . . . Robin didn't flaunt money when she was with Michael. She bought a little house up in Makawao and they lived there and had property around it, but they weren't out spending money or buying fancy clothes or anything."

Makawao seemed a perfect resting place for Clarke. One of the state's largest paniolo towns, it had an old world western charm, but also boasted an active arts community, with a number of boutiques and galleries. Every Independence Day, there was a big parade followed by a rodeo where cowboys showed off their skills, navigating their horses around barrels and performing seemingly impossible rope tricks. Children rode calves like rodeo riders and local historians impressed tourists with stories of how the panilos were the first cowboys in America and had taught the Hawaiians how to herd cattle.

Clarke loved westerns, horses and, of course, painting. Makawao fulfilled most of his needs but, despite his hints at retirement, he was always drawn back into the music business by former friends. Having previously guested on some sessions with Gene Clark, he rejoined the original Byrds in late 1972 for their reunion album, where his playing prompted some effusive comments from the previously critical David Crosby. On the extant tapes, Crosby can be heard complimenting the drummer for his work on 'Laughing': "Michael played the perfect intro." Several years later he added with unintended condescension: "Michael really cooked. He played things I didn't even know he was capable of." Clarke would have enjoyed performing live with his old friends, but an anticipated Byrds' tour was not forthcoming.

"I wasn't satisfied with it," Clarke said of the Byrds' Asylum album. "No one contributed their best material. Chris was with Manassas and David was with CS&N. I'd just flown in from Hawaii. David always underestimated me, and I always overestimated him. I don't mean to be crude. David was brilliant during that period of time. The songs that he came up with were powerful. Gene sang 'See The Sky About To Rain' and personally I think that should have been a single, but it wasn't. Too bad."

Following the release of the Byrds' reunion album, Clarke became a father. Robin had a troubled pregnancy, but gave birth to a son on 17 July 1973. The baby's shortened name was Zak, the same as Ringo Starr's eldest boy, which was surely no coincidence. Oddly enough, Zachary shared the same birthday as both Michael's mother and great grandmother. Michael and Robin continued to live in Hawaii. Many felt he was never happier or more fulfilled. Robin was bright, effervescent and shared Michael's *joie de vivre* and carefree ways. Jim Dickson remembers that time with considerable affection and always felt warm towards the couple. "Robin was funny. She used to say, 'I always know when you're coming over – it's the only time Michael cleans the house. It's like daddy's visiting!' I would never have imagined Michael cleaning the house for me if she hadn't told me that. Evidently, Michael did it all, and she was so surprised she had to tell me about it. Michael was always friendly to me. I never really had a problem with him, except when I slapped him on the beach that time [during the doomed filming of 'Set You Free This Time'] because he was listening to David instead of me and wasting film. Michael was never mad at me, though, and I never had to persuade him into anything, unlike the others. Michael was much more a friend to me than any of them and behaved that way when I saw him in Maui. He was the most civil and the most fun to hang out with. I never had any negative feelings about him at all. *Ever.*"

Robin and Michael married during this blissful period and the family briefly stayed in Spokane before starting a new life. Always blessed with the ability to fall on his feet, Clarke was asked by Rick Roberts to join a new band based in Boulder, Colorado. Since the demise of the Burritos, Roberts had released two inspired but commercially unsuccessful solo albums for A&M and was in search of a new deal. Initially, all he wanted was a backing band, but after playing some dates as 'Rick Roberts And Firefall', he decided to promote them as equals. In May 1975, the group received an offer to tour as Chris Hillman's backing band. Roberts, lead guitarist Jock Bartley and bassist Mark Andes made the trip, but Clarke was not invited. Still smarting from memories of the Burritos' break-up, Hillman insisted it would be saner to leave the drummer behind. Clarke was unfazed by this snub and instead displayed a previously unforeseen talent by building a new house for his family. "Michael would surprise you," recalls later Firefall bandmate David Muse. "He was a great carpenter too!" Clarke's construction work was interrupted when he learned that Hillman had fallen ill with hepatitis following an opening night show at New York's Bitter End. In desperation, Roberts flew Clarke and singer Larry Burnett to the club for what was effectively Firefall's big début. Atlantic Records had already heard the band's demos and, after seeing them live, offered a lucrative recording contract. In August 1975, they were signed, after which multi-instrumentalist David Muse was added to the line-up. Clarke was about to enjoy his luckiest streak since joining the Byrds.

Having struggled through the early country rock years with Dillard & Clark and the Flying Burrito Brothers, Clarke was amused and amazed by the colossal success of Firefall, who registered six US Top 40 singles and several gold and platinum albums during the second half of the Seventies. By the close of the decade, Clarke found himself in an unprecedented position as the most commercially successful of the original Byrds, the others of whom were losing major label patronage. David Crosby was astounded by this turn of events and after hearing Clarke's work in Firefall told me: "He's pretty damn good!"

The Boulder years were among the most eventful in Clarke's action-packed life. Everyone was taken aback by the speed with which Firefall's debut album went gold and over the next few years this otherwise modest band would experience every cliché in the rock 'n' roll lexicon: massive-selling records, jet-setting tours, drug abuse, management disputes, financial waste, marriage upheavals, internecine strife and, most fundamentally, a failure to realize how quickly and matter of factly the cold hand of history can transmute miniature rock gods into almost forgotten footnotes of an unfashionable age. Clarke was subject to all of these yet somehow managed to retain a sense of self amid the chaos. "Michael was definitely an enigma," says Mark Adzick, who worked and partied with the drummer while overseeing Boulder's

Mountain Ears recording studio. "He was loveable and outrageous and had a lot of talent but, at the same time, he would piss it away. He sabotaged himself a lot and that was frustrating. Many people go through life and perhaps get one shot. Some don't even get that. Here's a guy who not only had one but two, three, maybe four chances. From cardboard boxes in the Byrds, via Dillard & Clark to the Flying Burrito Brothers, and Firefall. He even played with Etta James at one point. If you get a shot, you make it happen, but he was very much like a kid. He was obviously the stereotypical drummer, the wild crazy guy. He didn't have really fancy licks but he had a way of focusing during those sessions and live performances."

Adzick experienced all these traits first hand when he made the seemingly eccentric decision to employ Clarke to add drum parts to a money-spinning advertising jingle, financed by a Midwest corporation. "It was very difficult. There were times when he really annoyed people because he'd show up late. Normally, we'd do several takes and it would take a long time to get the drum sound. I remember this particular morning: we'd started the session when Michael showed up; he'd stayed up all night and had too much cocaine. He was still drunk, trying to drink coffee. It really pissed me off. But, don't you know it, he went in there and did it perfectly in *one* take. Then he was out of there. Lots of drummers are good in the studio but it's difficult for them to keep the beat going in an arena or stadium filled with people. That was another one of the beautiful things about Michael. If you were riding around in a car listening to music, he'd be pounding on the dashboard, totally out of time. I'd ask, 'What are you pounding too?' and he'd laugh and say, 'I'm just pounding, Marky!' Then he'd get onstage in front of thousands of people and he'd be impeccable. We used to call him the human metronome."

Adzick's memories of the human metronome were echoed in countless other testimonies from puzzled contemporaries. Muff Davis, a music entrepreneur of all shades, could never quite comprehend Clarke's contradictory nature. "We would use him in the studio occasionally when he was available. When I became aware of who he was, how long he'd been around, and what he had done, I was in awe of him. Yet he was a regular guy. You'd never have figured him for a rock star. He didn't seem to be there, but he was *always* there. Does that make sense? He was hyper, forever going at a hundred miles an hour, and yet he was focused. He seemed wasted, but he wasn't; he had a ton of energy. He was a party animal, but he always did what he was supposed to do – and I never knew how he did it. The guy was incredible. He was a great drummer – one of my favourites. No flash. Solid. Right there. He played simple, never stretched out too much. I don't ever recall him doing a drum solo now that I think about it. But he made it work. He's still one of my favourite drummers of all time. I guess he could have played with anybody he wanted to but he stuck with Rickie Roberts and those guys. Michael was incredible and somehow inspirational – but you could *never* figure that."

This may sound like overstatement but there was something strange about Clarke's inconsistency as a player. David Crosby lamented his seeming inability to keep time, but when he concentrated he could reach inexplicable heights, particularly on 'The Bells Of Rhymney', 'Turn! Turn! Turn!' and 'Eight Miles High'. Even something as wayward as the demo of 'I Know You Rider', in which Clarke speeds up and loses time, has an energy and intensity that makes for fascinating listening. "There were certain fields that he had complete mastery of," says Mark Andes. "He was limited and his time was marginal but there were moments when he would play the perfect thing. It was uncanny. Of course, he was always stylistically definitive. The take that captures Michael at his best is surely 'Turn! Turn! Turn!' which has one of the most brilliant drum parts."

During the Boulder years, Clarke liked to record locally. Upon arrival at a studio, his favourite phrase was "Have you got any drugs?" If the answer was 'yes', he would gleefully indulge. If 'no', he'd smile and retort, "Fine, we'll do mine!" Clarke's indulgences sometimes proved dangerous. Matt Andes (Mark's younger brother) occasionally visited Boulder, and chose the city as the perfect spot for his honeymoon. He enjoyed socializing with Michael but was shocked one evening to learn that the drummer had almost died. "He damn near killed himself in a horrible accident coming down to Boulder one night. There was a very treacherous mountain pass. It was a winter crash, and there was ice involved. He'd been drinking and lost control of the car. He knocked his front teeth out and had to have them fixed. He had to recuperate in hospital and he was there for quite a while recovering from that."

Given his recalcitrant behaviour, Clarke's industry was impressive. He always enjoyed working through the night. Dawn was a signal to push forward rather than to cease. "We'll wrap this up when the bars are open, *then* get some breakfast", he would announce. Later, he would talk excitedly about opening an after-hours club for musicians. Nobody was entirely sure whether he was joking or not. A procession of people – bartenders, showgirls, gamblers, drunks, fans, friends, fellow players – would pass by his table, eager to join his ever expanding circle. The circus was the same, irrespective of the venue.

"Everybody knew Michael Clarke," Adzick attests. "*Everybody.* I don't care where I went in the music business. And everybody had nice things to say about him. He was generous and had a good heart and you could tell he came from good people. I went travelling with the guys and it was amazing. At Miami Airport, you might see half-a-dozen internationally famous musicians on any given day and every single one of them would spot Michael. They'd walk over and give him a big hug. I wasn't starstruck but this really amazed me. The Stones came through once and Keith Richards was shit-faced but when he saw Michael in the airport he shouted 'Michael!' and threw his arms around him. Everybody was the same. Michael Clarke was one of the classic rock 'n' roll icons of our generation."

Of course, not everybody spoke of Clarke in such angelic terms. On tour with Firefall, he was the trickster, whose roguish behaviour could easily slip from funny to boorish, depending upon his alcohol or pharmaceutical intake. "He was an amazing character, funny and charming, but he was also a rascal," says Mark Andes. "Sometimes you'd wonder if he'd been in your room and gone through your stuff. Unfortunately, he was a major drug addict and a drinker and was high a lot of his life. Some moments that was sad to see and ultimately it was his undoing."

David Muse was aware of the demons that could be unleashed if Clarke went completely over the edge, but the effects were always temporary and seldom serious. "Michael could rub you up the wrong way. When I was in Firefall, even though I'd grown up with Rick Roberts and we'd played in some early bands together, for some reason I bonded with Michael and we became really good friends. We used to hang out and play tennis together. His personality was different from mine but when we started butting heads we got it straightened out from the start. When it got weird, he'd stay out of my way and I'd stay out of his way. I told him, 'Don't get in my face.' He knew I was serious and whenever he started pulling his crap I'd walk away, so we never had any problems at all." The other members developed similar survival strategies in dealing with one another and, for a time, all was well.

Clarke's greater challenge lay in maintaining his marriage amid the tumultuous temptations of a touring life in which drink, drugs and debauchery increasingly assumed the spectral qualities of allegorical figures in a medieval moral pageant. Robin was never likely to play the demure maiden and her indignation matched his rock star self-righteousness. Both Mark Andes and David Muse witnessed their tragi-comic battles where harsh words and hard liquor distorted civilized communication. "I saw them have a 'fistfight' and I think Michael was getting the worst end of it," Muse jokes. The saddest part of the story was the realization that the marriage was fragmenting under the combined weight of empty bottles and a fool's gallery of gold and platinum records.

"It was pretty stormy with all the drinking and stuff," Clarke's mother recalls. "They were both happy for a while but they battled a lot and they were both drinking." Although Michael and Robin remained on amicable terms much of the time, his raucous lifestyle, increasing intoxication and frequent absences ultimately resulted in separation and divorce. Robin returned to Hawaii, while he felt obliged to remain in Boulder with Firefall. Like several other ex-Byrds, he missed many years of fatherhood along the way. "Robin never kept Zachary away from us," Suzy Dick stresses. "She saw to it that we saw him as much as possible. She'd call us and kept us in touch with Zak while he was growing up. It was a real strange relationship but that was typical of the type that Michael would have because he was that way. They were in close contact all the time because of Zachary. Robin was not vindictive as far as the marriage was concerned because it was both their faults. It was a pretty chaotic marriage. It was wild. When they had moved here to Spokane they seemed to be happy, but when they drank, they fought. They fought a lot, but they never held any grudges. That was the thing I liked about them."

The dissolution of Clarke's marriage was set against the continued success of Firefall whose sales were increasing exponentially, as gold turned to platinum on albums like *Luna Sea* and *Élan*. Clarke took all this in his stride – ever willing to enjoy rock star excesses yet equally capable of acting like a regular guy. His predictable reaction to Robin's departure was to hit the bars of Boulder with renewed energy and temporarily lose himself in an alcoholic daze, surrounded by pretty women. "Michael had an incredible talent for making any woman he met develop an overwhelming desire to mother him within the first 30 minutes of making their acquaintance," Rick Roberts says. "And he didn't even do it consciously. He always played at being a bad ass, but everyone saw through that to the gentle, big-hearted guy he really was . . . If there was a party in the same zip code you could count on Michael being the first one there and the last to leave. He drank too much and he sniffed too much, but then so did a lot of us." Oddly, for such a socialite, he seemed vulnerable when alone and, unlike many rock stars, downplayed his fame, even allowing saloon bar pals to become prized friends.

One night he was drinking in the Catacombs, a local hotspot, where he enjoyed relaxing and eyeing girls. Drinking into the late hours, he befriended the bartender, a college kid named Bob Rassmussen, whom everyone called 'Ras'. Despite their age difference, they shared a mutual interest in beer and girls. "You know how Michael was," Ras remarks. "He'd try and pick up waitresses and stuff like that." Remarkably, Ras had no inkling that he was in the company of Firefall's famous drummer. Clarke was so intent on securing his female conquests that he did not think to mention his status. Soon after, they were exchanging small talk over a drink when Clarke said: "Do you want to go to Red Rocks tomorrow night?" Ras, who had seen both the Beatles and Jimi Hendrix play at the famous Boulder venue, was keen enough – but who was appearing there? Almost as an afterthought, Michael added, "Well, I'm playing there. Do you want to take a limo with me?" Ras was astonished. "I couldn't believe it. He said he was in Firefall. And we *did* take a limo. They kicked ass and played good. He befriended me and we hung around together for about ten years. We were pretty tight. He still wouldn't tell anybody who he was. If we went to some other town, or even in Boulder, if he wasn't recognized he would never say he was in a famous band. I always wanted him to because it would have been good for me to say, 'I know this guy, I'm with him', but he was very humble about that."

Nevertheless, Clarke wasn't shy about enjoying the largesse offered by club owners eager to attract anyone in Firefall and frequently hung out with local bands and visiting luminaries. Ras was sometimes embarrassed when Clarke ushered him through the back door of a club, insisting that he didn't have to pay for admission. At the end of the evening, the headlining act would socialize with Clarke, who always introduced Ras as if he was a star too. The bartender was given free tickets for all the Firefall concerts he wished to attend and even accompanied Clarke to a recording session at Criteria Studios in Miami. "I waited in the car park, but Michael was saying, 'Come on in!' The Albert Brothers were there and then Eric Clapton appeared. It seemed that he and Eric were the best of friends and the first thing Michael did was introduce me. Then he went off with the Alberts and I was left there with Eric Clapton. I didn't know what to say. We sat and talked for about half-an-hour about fly fishing. Turned out Eric was one of the best fly fishers around. Hanging around with Michael, you'd always meet musicians."

Back in downtown Boulder, the drinking duo spent a lot of time at the Blue Note club. Clarke had taken a shine to the attractive bar manager, Joy Mittelstadt. He had first seen her when she was working as a cocktail waitress at the Hungry Farmer nightclub on the east of town and they had instantly clicked. Mittelstadt, described somewhat patronisingly as a "farm girl from Wisconsin", had previously worked at a resort on Mackinac Island, Lake Huron, Michigan, where she became romantically involved with an aspiring singer-songwriter, John Manikoff. After two summers on the island, the pair packed up a car and moved to Colorado in search of new adventures. Their relationship petered out but they remained friends. Manikoff joined the ranks of local players hanging out and hoping for a break, while Mittelstadt determined to gain experience in clubland, always dreaming of one day opening her own establishment. "She was a really smart kid and had a good mind," says Manikoff. "Mathematically proficient and cute. Courageous too. I believe her father owned a bar when she was a little girl so she'd grown up in that environment and felt real comfortable with it."

Clarke soon became a permanent fixture at the Blue Note and when he was called upon to tour with Firefall, he invited Mittelstadt along. They would later marry at a chapel in Las Vegas and set up home back in Boulder. For all his high living and bachelor ways, Clarke had a strong dependency on women and craved affection, even though he was always likely to sabotage a relationship as a result of his wilfulness or reckless inebriated infidelities. That said, his marriage to Joy was applauded by his friends, who saw her as a stabilizing force in his life. "Joy was very responsible," says Mark Adzick, who had previously been known to terrorize the town with Clarke on girl-hunting expeditions. "She went to work, she managed people, made good money, had a decent home and took care of him. I don't know if it was a classic co-dependent thing – I would imagine so to a certain degree. There was a complement there. She was a driving force and the main reason he came home before the sun came up. Obviously, it later got to the point where it was too much, but she was really good for him. I know John Manikoff recognized that as well and really admired his former girlfriend for taking on that role. Michael needed somebody to take care of him. If she wasn't in the picture, it would have been one of his buddies, believe me. He didn't like to be alone. Some people tend to isolate when they're getting high, but he didn't. He was plain fun. There was never a dull moment when you were in a bar with Michael Clarke. Never."

Firefall should have spawned several multi-millionaires among its line-up, but the membership somehow conspired to squander record company advances, touring income and publishing monies in every imaginable way. Manager Milt Levy negotiated their record contract with Atlantic, but they later fell out with him in spectacular fashion. Litigation followed. It proved expensive and debilitating. Other managers came and went along the way. At one stage, Rick Roberts appointed a former IRS agent as his personal business manager. It was probably a good idea, but evidently he did not learn from the experience. Ironically, he later fell foul of the IRS over some late income tax returns from the Firefall days and discovered the frightening wonders of compound interest and penalties.

Wasting money was an art form in Firefall. Their productivity looked impressive in terms of album releases, but the small print spoke volumes. The platinum *Elan* had begun as a Tom Dowd project, only to be completely re-recorded by the Albert Brothers. Meanwhile, Firefall were treated like rock gods, albeit on deductible expenses. "We were a high maintenance act," Mark Andes notes, audibly trailing off as he mentally calculates the price of their extravagances. Adzick remembers limousine drivers acting like surrogate parents, delicately negotiating individuals from their beds, then driving them to the airport. The more sensible idea of appointing a road manager to herd them into a communal rental bus was evidently unacceptable. "They got into jets, then they got into chartered jets," Adzick recalls with a shake of the head.

Within a couple of years, Firefall effectively became a two-tiered band, with Roberts and Burnett emerging as the major beneficiaries courtesy of their songwriting income. Mark Andes cannot remember ending up with more than $500 a week as overheads eroded advances to a startling degree. Even the wealthier members of the group sometimes felt the pinch. "Rick made quite a bit on royalties but he spent his money in extravagant ways. He would rent beautiful places, drive fancy cars and he had a lot of cocaine on him all the time, smoked the best pot and drank lots of brandy. That's expensive."

By far the largest expense was reserved for recreational pursuits and the Firefall triumvirate of Roberts, Burnett and Clarke became seasoned connoisseurs. David Muse smoked pot constantly before performing onstage, wrongly believing it made him a better player. Later, when he started listening to live tapes, he realized "it sucked". As always Clarke was living well beyond his means. Unlike the songwriters Roberts and Burnett, he did not have the luxury of publishing income, but that did not stop him from matching their intake. "Michael, Larry and Rickie got a little excessive with everything," Muse understates, "they were the ones [who were] abusive with drugs and alcohol more than anybody else. Mark was always straight, and Jock. We just did light stuff."

Evidently, the word 'straight' had a flexible meaning in Firefall. Mark Andes didn't quite fit that billing, and admits snorting heroin at the time. "I wanted to know why Larry found it so wonderful. There was always heroin because of Larry. He was ecstatic the day he developed diabetes because he could get syringes legally. It was a really twisted time." Indeed, Burnett's dalliances alone were life threatening. "I carried Larry into emergency twice while we were on the road," Mark Adzick recalls. "Those guys spent hundreds of thousands of dollars on drugs. It's not the feel good story that we all like to talk about. That's the reality."

"Everybody was doing drugs, but there was a definite line that David, Jock and I didn't cross," Andes adds. "We were not making the money that those guys were, excluding Michael. We were aware when Larry wasn't answering his phone or Rick couldn't sing the next day because he was up all night doing blow."

Their pharmaceutical transgressions might have been excusable if the music had been innovative or exciting, but the opposite was the case. Their studio work increasingly sounded dead fish cold, sterile and emotionally remote. Rick Roberts no doubt enjoyed his belated and fully deserved chart success but somewhere beneath that fog of brandy and cocaine, he must have realized that his later Firefall songs paled in comparison to his compositional work with the Burritos. His songwriting had been far more impressive on his two underrated solo albums, *Windmills* and *She Is A Song*, back in the early Seventies. It was difficult to escape the conclusion that Firefall were moving backwards creatively, even while their record sales were increasing. "The whole thing kept spiralling downwards," Larry Burnett admits. "Producers got fed up with us. Nobody really wanted to work with us. We were just this unreliable six-headed monster running around . . . I had a number of hospitalizations along the way. There was all kinds of bad stuff going on. And there's consequences to all that."

Clarke was never a character to consider consequences, particularly when presented with a line of cocaine or a tray of drinks. Overindulgence brought out his John Wayne swagger and that unappealing coke-induced arrogance that blighted both empathy and artistry. Roberts and Burnett battled the same demons. Observing from a distance, Mark Adzick well understood the pitfalls. "It affected their judgement. Pretty soon whatever artistic endeavour you're in it's not as good as you think. If you're mixing something in the studio, your highs and mid-ranges are off because your head's full of cocaine. Your judgement is off, then your relationships with other people are off and the teamwork dissipates."

By the late Seventies, Adzick had relocated to New York to work for McGraw Hill Publishing but enjoyed a reunion with Firefall when they appeared at an outdoor show in Central Park. Making his way backstage at the soundcheck, he was greeted by a drum roll from Clarke who shouted out his nickname, 'Redman!' "After the gig we got together, the dealer came and we got into the limos and went around town. That night we partied with Andy Warhol. I had a ball. That was pretty much the end of my serious partying. I missed them a lot."

Clarke's partying days were far from over. Easily distracted, he was happy to socialize with other friends when relations in Firefall became too intense. With McGuinn, Clark & Hillman still riding high, there was always hope of an on-stage reunion of the original five Byrds for the first time since 1966. It came tantalizingly close at times. David Crosby twice joined the trio when they appeared at San Francisco's Boarding House and LA's Roxy, and a few months later Clarke did the same at shows in Portland and Denver. Ras was at Clarke's house when a call came through from the Rainbow club in Denver where the band was hanging out. "Gene Clark and Chris Hillman were partying and as they were playing locally they thought it would be cool to ask Michael to come down and sit in for a couple of songs. It was the neatest thing in the world to have four-fifths of the Byrds." Of course, it would have been even neater if the full quintet had played but conflicting schedules and a lack of will on the part of the participants meant that the dream remained unrealized.

Clarke's Firefall commitments never prevented him from fraternizing with other musicians. He became particularly close to the Willie Nelson Band, whose ranks at one time included former Burrito bassist Chris Ethridge. Nelson's band had toured with Firefall and Clarke established a strong rapport with the road crew. When they played in Texas, he stayed at the apartment of their road manager, James Aderholt, a party-loving Vietnam veteran whose distinctive image conjured visions of a superannuated cattle drover, complete with cowboy hat. "Michael was one of the best hellraisers I ever ran into," he growls, fully aware of the frightening connotations that such an accolade infers. Whenever Nelson played Boulder, Clarke could always rely on a call.

His friend Ras remembers him taking the stage with Nelson at Red Rocks, looking a little out of place as he played tambourine rather than drums. The other members of Firefall were happy enough for Clarke to extend his social circle, although they became exasperated when this interfered with their own schedule. "Mike disappeared to Mexico with some of the guys from Willie Nelson's band," Andes recalls. "He spent a couple of days there and then came straggling back. I thought it was funny. He was such a rogue."

There was a weariness about Firefall when they recorded their fourth album. Released in 1980, *Undertow* did not come close to emulating the US Top 30 success of its predecessors, languishing at a lowly number 68. The record industry had already turned away from country rock towards disco and new wave. Established stars were losing contracts every month. Firefall were deemed so passé in the UK that Atlantic declined to issue *Undertow* at all. The band were evidently unaware of this slight, still believing that platinum status in their homeland was secure. But musical changes in the European market would soon rebound across the Atlantic like a cultural tsunami. In a hubristic effort to re-establish their standing on an international level, Firefall toured Japan. When they returned, they faced the pressure of recording a fifth album and urgently needed a new career strategy in an increasingly uncertain marketplace.

Already, some of the members were losing interest, including Clarke, whose behaviour became more erratic. His traditional response to conflict was to take off and have fun, irrespective of the consequences. David Muse finally woke up to the realization that Firefall were in terminal decline. "There was no career development," he laments. "It just fell together. I consider the first Firefall album to be the best – we had nothing to lose then. It changed after that. We got into the whole success thing. Rickie and Larry had publishing deals and they had to have so many songs on each album to get money. We went through a bunch of managers . . . You could make a comic strip about us if you really thought about it. We had a lot of talent and made some good music and could have made a lot more if everybody would have lightened up on their lifestyles and banded together. But we were fighting each other as things went on and it got a little weird towards the end."

Mark Andes was the first to act following yet another change of management. Still slightly aggrieved about the division of income in the band and their lack of discipline, he could see only a bleak future. "It was David, Jock and I trying to get these guys on path. The band would rehearse a lot but I thought it was the musicians who were making it happen. We'd drag in the 'creative guys' and the drummer. Ultimately, it was a battle that I couldn't justify spending that much energy on." At a band meeting, Andes announced that he was leaving. "I said, 'Man, I'm out of here. This is one of the most self-destructive bands I've ever been in, and I congratulate you . . .' "

Andes' departure had a predictably negative effect on Clarke's attitude and behaviour. Increasingly, he reverted to that apathetic, prickly figure, familiar from the *Notorious*-era Byrds. Back then, he had watched with bemusement as Crosby was fired and Clark was reinstated, only to leave again. The uncertainty made him lose focus, disrupt or miss recording sessions and goad McGuinn and Hillman into firing him. Now history was repeating itself. "He started missing rehearsals and was out there with his habits and stuff," Muse remembers. In an unexpected twist, Firefall called a band meeting during which Clarke's fate was put to a vote of confidence.

"He was actually fired," Muse marvels. "They brought Michael over and it was just a terrible thing in my book. Everybody had lots of different reasons. I didn't go along with it, but I was outvoted. We were kind of a democracy where the majority won. At the meeting my argument was – 'What are you guys talking about? You've all got habits too!'" Clarke accepted the news with a stoical shrug of the shoulders, but Muse was not fooled. "To be honest, he was taken aback. Even though he'd been in the Byrds and the Flying Burrito Brothers, he didn't have much money. Yet, that didn't seem to bother him. He just flowed along and figured a way to make things work for himself. I have to give that to him. He kept on going. He didn't just sit around and go, 'Oh my gosh, I got fired!'"

Nor did Clarke allow himself to be consumed with bitterness. He was well aware of his shortcomings and remained friends with Roberts and the rest. They replaced him and recorded one more album but, within a year, it was effectively all over. Burnett went on a week-long drinking binge during which he was shooting up coke and heroin. The experience left him convinced that he was about to die. He was due to fly to Nevada with Firefall, but freaked out at the airport and booked himself on a flight to his family's home in Washington D.C. Soon after, he checked into a psychiatric hospital and began his long road back to recovery and sobriety. Meanwhile, Rick Roberts, by now severely disillusioned, quit the band he had founded for an uncertain future. He was left to rue the original decision to make Firefall a band of equals and belatedly realized that the fired drummer had been right all along. "Democracies don't work within a band framework. Michael Clarke was the only guy who had enough sense to know that you can't all be chiefs, there has to be some Indians. Michael said, 'Rick, you can have my vote in any band vote.' I thought it was . . . well considered. It *was* my band. They all got its musical direction from me, to a large extent. Michael gave me the vote for two reasons: he had faith in my musical judgement and capabilities, and also he didn't want to have to make all the band meetings. The two reasons were equally important."

Back in Boulder, Michael Clarke now had time on his hands. Much of it was spent hanging out at the Blue Note, drinking and listening to whichever band was passing through town. It also enabled him to discover some new friends. One evening, his wife Joy invited her former boyfriend John Manikoff to join them for dinner. Five years younger than Clarke, Manikoff was regarded as the new kid in town, a ball of energy, brimming with confidence and ambition, but too enamoured of Boulder's drinking culture and wild lifestyle to plot a sober and sensible career course. Locals complained about his impulsive behaviour and acerbic humour, but conceded that he had a certain charisma. In temperament, he sounded very much like a younger version of Michael Clarke, so it was hardly surprising that they became fast friends. "Michael and I hit it off right away," he remembers. "I really liked him – he was an amazing guy. These were the partying days and Michael was certainly a professional in that realm. He was very approachable for somebody who had been such a big star. That was one of the first things I liked about him. He was fun to be around, with lots of charisma. He could show up anywhere and get a lot of attention, and not just because he was a star. He had that command of a room the minute he walked in . . . Plus, he had balls. More balls than anybody I had ever met."

The entrepreneurial Muff Davis, who'd known Manikoff from the Michigan days, took on the thankless task of acting as his manager. They argued a lot about nothing in particular and it usually ended with Davis accusing his charge of not working hard enough. "He was a very talented singer-songwriter who felt the world owed him a living. He was playing the rock star when he wasn't a rock star." Davis was in full argumentative flow one evening when Clarke turned up and acted as peacemaker. "I was ready to kill Manikoff but Michael calmed me down and said, 'You probably don't want to do that.'" Later, Clarke and Manikoff hit the town, drinking themselves silly. "You could hang out with him all night long, just chill and talk and he was so funny and surprisingly interesting," says Manikoff. "Of course, his reputation preceded him but I was surprised what a gentle soul he was. He was great to me – like a brother."

Clarke enjoyed playing the big brother role which extended to teaching Manikoff the rudiments of sorting out his own laundry. He also bombarded him with the quick fire aphorisms he had picked up after two decades in the music business. Chief among them was the dictum: "Always say yes and never turn anything down." This was a lesson he had first learned while playing cardboard boxes with the Byrds. "Michael told me things that I still use in my life to this day," says Manikoff. "His attitude was 'Don't be shy and don't turn down any job offer; you can always fail later.' It was good advice."

By March 1981, Manikoff and Clarke were sufficiently in cahoots to consider forming a band. Recruiting local players Michael Reese (guitar) and Milt Muth (bass), they dubbed the quartet the Bad Boys, in mock tribute to their outlaw reputation. They certainly lived up to the billing when they launched their new enterprise on the local radio station KBCO. Manikoff became so excited during the live interview that he let slip some four-letter words, no doubt abetted by the ever mischievous Michael. After a couple of warnings, the frazzled DJ Peter Rodman pulled the plug and ejected them from the studio. They retired to the nearby Boulderado Hotel and drank the night away like prototype punk rockers. Thanks to Clarke's wife Joy, they were booked to play the Blue Note and began rehearsing at the Mountain Ears studio, with a view to recording some demos. At this point, Manikoff regarded Clarke as a hard-drinking friend and a competent, journeyman drummer. While respecting his history in various bands, he had accepted the popular notion that Clarke's talent was based on image rather than musicianship. Those who had listened closely to 'Turn! Turn! Turn!' or 'Eight Miles High' knew otherwise, but that had not stopped cynics from speculating, incorrectly, that Clarke's parts were the work of some session player. Tellingly, both Gene Clark and Chris Hillman had specifically chosen Clarke to play drums in their post-Byrds ventures, even though they had the pick of LA's finest. Manikoff had not considered these anomalies and still wondered how well his new friend would fare in a more hard-rocking outfit.

Their first rehearsal proved a revelation. "I'd walked through the door thinking this guy was a lesser musician than he was. When we got together to play I was absolutely astounded by his ability as a drummer. He was really talented. Through the years, I've always been angered whenever he's talked about as a lesser member of *any* band. Now, I believe that Michael had more to do with creating these bands than anyone gives him credit for. He may not have been a schooled musician, but the drummer is the foundation. If you think about it, the Byrds rose to stardom when Michael was with them. The same with Firefall. And the minute Michael disappears from these bands, look what happens to them. I really believe Michael had a kind of genius."

The Bad Boys made their live debut at the Blue Note, performing over the weekend of 3–4 April in front of 290 people, many of them fellow musicians. Larry Burnett, just weeks away from leaving Firefall, attended, along with Rick Roberts and several other local luminaries. "I remember Larry coming up to me after the show," says Manikoff. "He said, 'Johnny, your band's wonderful, I've never heard Michael play like that.' He was real excited about it. Michael enjoyed it. It was a hard-driving rock band and Michael was never known as being that kind of drummer. I thought we were world class. If we hadn't been so insane and if the timing had been different then we would have been big. But we imploded."

The Bad Boys played a few more gigs, some of which were taped, as were some tracks at Mountain Ears, but their volatility undermined their ambition. "It was almost a comical, stereotypical fighting band," Manikoff scoffs. "I had a fistfight with the bass player on my girlfriend's lawn and Michael and I went at it a couple of times. It was insane. The whole project lasted just a few months, half a year at the most." All that remains of the Bad Boys are some fading memories and a handful of recordings, now gathering dust, in the tape collection of Muff Davis.

Almost immediately, Clarke found new employment in the band of Texas-based country singer Jerry Jeff Walker, composer of the classic 'Mr Bojangles'. As with so many events in Michael's life, there was a touch of serendipity involved. Walker's previous drummer was also based in Boulder but he was evidently too flashy for his employer's taste. He had even committed the apparently unpardonable sin of wearing drum gloves when he played.

Coincidentally, Walker's tour manager was the uproarious James Aderholt, who had already established a strong rapport with Clarke while working with Willie Nelson. He persuaded his new boss that the former Firefall drummer would be the perfect replacement, while conveniently neglecting to add that Clarke's temperament might pose a problem to anyone averse to rebellious behaviour. Aderholt spent a long afternoon drinking with Clarke before popping the question. Obeying his immemorial dictum 'Always Say Yes', the drummer retorted, "Fly me down to rehearsals and we'll see what happens from there." If nothing else, he had blagged a free trip to Texas, his father's home state and a place he always enjoyed visiting. Once there, any lingering prevarication evaporated. "Sure enough he got high from these rehearsals," Aderholt recalls. "That's how he ended up with those guys."

Working in Walker's band was a new experience for Clarke, inasmuch as he was a hired player rather than an equal partner. The Byrds, Burritos and Firefall had all been democracies to a degree, but here the sole focus was on the titular head. Walker's birth name was Ronald Clyde Crosby, which would have amused Michael had anyone ever told him that he was working alongside another *Crosby*. Clarke was always likely to rebel but, remarkably, he stayed with Walker for the best part of two years and featured on his 1982 album, *Cow Jazz*. Walker had a rigorous touring schedule but tended to wind down somewhat during the first three months of the year which suited Clarke. The regimented work load seemed to bring a fresh stability to his life, at least for the moment. As Muff Davis quips: "Joy married a rock star. Why? She should have known better, but I think it worked because he was gone most of the time!" Unfortunately, Clarke's absences meant he was more susceptible to carnal temptations which inevitably put a strain on his marriage. Joy confided her fears to her old boyfriend John Manikoff, but he offered little sympathy. "Joy would come over crying and I'd sit with her and say, 'Look, Joy, you knew exactly who you were marrying. Come on, give me a break here. This is ridiculous.'" Against the odds, the marriage survived, at least for a time.

Meanwhile, Clarke found himself playing his customary elder brother figure while settling into Walker's band. His latest admirer was rhythm and steel guitarist Mike Hardwick, a Burritos' fan who had followed Clarke's career and was thrilled by his inclusion in the band. "Michael was a loveable character and there's not a person I know that doesn't have a warm spot in their hearts for something he did, but he was also a prankster and a clown. Up until I met him, I'd never played in a band with someone I was a huge fan of. When Jerry Jeff hired me I had to borrow records to learn his songs but I'd listened to all Michael's stuff. So you can imagine how wonderful it was to play with someone who'd been on hit records and really knew that type of music . . . It was a tremendous learning experience." The lessons seeped into everyday life. Hardwick often witnessed Clarke's familiar excesses but was invariably warned: "Don't let me catch *you* doing this!" The guitarist was always amazed by Michael's capacity to turn in a strong performance, irrespective of his alcohol or drug intake. "He took a lot of pride in his playing. He might have been a crazy man but he knew he was there to play a show. It was OK to have a couple of beers but you'd better be ready to play, that's what it was all about. His attitude was: 'Don't cause the rest of them not to be able to have a good night.' So everybody played great. Then afterwards, who knows what happened!"

Clarke's fellow musicians, by now familiar with his wild side, also appreciated meeting his polite and solicitous parents, who turned up for a show in Washington. "We always tried to go and see him," his mother says. "My husband, whether he was into the music or not, was always loyal to his son, so we went everywhere that we could to hear and support him. If I'd known he was going to live for such a short time, I would have been with him more of the time. But who knows these things?"

Jerry Jeff Walker maintained an emotional distance from Clarke, befitting an employer. As James Aderholt admits: "Jerry Jeff was a hard man to work with. He wanted things his way, pretty much, even from the musicians. So, he didn't want the drummer to take much of a spotlight." Hardwick detected some annoyance, even resentment, from Walker when fans or journalists congregated backstage to reminisce with the drummer about his time in the Byrds, the Burritos or Firefall. "He would fire him! Jerry and Michael were similar in a lot of ways. Jerry would get mad at Michael but he would do this with everyone. He'd get mad and you'd be fired and the next day you'd be hired again." Such moments aside, Clarke's time with Walker passed without major incident, which came as a relief following the cycle of psychodramas in Firefall.

In February 1983, Clarke received a phone call from John Manikoff inviting him to California to audition for a new band featuring Rick Roberts. A producer was already in place, along with other musicians, and they were hoping to secure some record company interest. Clarke predictably used his 'Always Say Yes' motto, while remembering to request free airline tickets. On this occasion, he did not impress the producer, but still enjoyed a break in LA before returning to Boulder. He felt vindicated when the enterprise foundered soon after. A more promising project occurred during the same period when Jim Dickson, always an instigator of Byrds' reunions, brought Clarke, Clark and Hillman together, along with Herb Pedersen and Al Perkins, to record some demos under the name Nyte Flyte. It was symptomatic of the times that a live reunion did not extend beyond a two-night stint at the Palomino, by which point Michael had moved on. Those studio sessions were never released in Clarke's lifetime, but Dickson retained a completed mix, different from the roughs that circulated among collectors. He was impassioned about 'No Memories Hangin' Round' not least because of Clarke's drumming. "The reason I wanted to get this to you was to prove that Michael could go into the studio and play well on a ballad, not just the chunkier stuff. Even Chris Hillman was astounded when he heard the mix. He said, 'Is that really Michael? Are you sure?' I said, 'You were there! Of course it's Michael! He's the only one that played on those sessions.'"

Seeing California again evidently made Clarke homesick for the state where he had first tasted fame. He and Joy decided to start a new life there in the autumn, leaving behind Boulder, whose lustre as a country music city was by now irrevocably tarnished. Michael Hardwick helped them load their furniture on to his Chevrolet pick-up truck and drove with Michael to their new home, a small apartment adjacent to Venice Beach. Joy was the more industrious one during this period and ran a thriving nightclub At My Place, which specialized in jazz acts. Clarke was apparently in no hurry to find work and remembers his wife ribbing him for "sitting around on my ass painting on the beach".

Clarke urgently needed a new challenge, not least to supplement his income. He found himself unexpectedly back in Byrdland as a result of Gene Clark's forlorn attempts to revitalize his solo career. Having recorded the album *Firebyrd*, Clark was willing to tour and several of his friends came to his rescue. Andy Kandanes, who had co-produced and financed the album, was approached by a Mendocino pal, Ray Chambers of TKO Management, and a touring band gradually emerged. Mark Andes, then on temporary leave from chart band Heart, remembers sitting in his kitchen jamming with his brother Matt and Clarke. "We should call ourselves the Firebyrds," Mark said. "As in Firefall and the Byrds." Kandanes spent the best part of two months readying them for the road. "Michael was the drummer, and I'd sit in with them once in a while. I went on tour just to make sure everything was OK. We had some good people. When I sent them out for the first time, they were real tight. They had a good show and a lot of continuity." The Firebyrds' tour passed without incident, largely because the contrite Clark was stone cold sober and Michael Clarke was drinking moderately, at least in comparison to his normally gargantuan intake.

"Man, they broke the mould when they made that guy," Matt

Andes says of Clarke. "It was wonderful playing with him. He became a very accomplished drummer and we had this vibe. Mike liked me because I could play bad ass slide guitar. Ry Cooder was my big influence when I was younger. Onstage, I would look at Mike while we were playing and it would just light him up. We fed off each other's enthusiasm . . . He was a big burly buffoon of a guy, but just hilarious. And he could not even help himself not to be hilarious. He was hilarious when he was trying to be serious."

Clarke's mood was heightened when Mark suggested a change in the set list, restricting the quieter folk ballads in favour of some heavier material. "I said, 'Let's make this thing rock!' Michael loved that, and so did Gene. Mike and I had forged a really good relationship musically and he was probably playing better than ever at that point. He had his act together musically and it reached out to the crowd. People were going, 'Wow!' We played places like the Coach House in San Juan Capistrano, and people had no expectations. I felt I was in the right place at the right time doing what I needed to be doing."

Unfortunately, Mark Andes' ongoing commitments to Heart meant that he couldn't continue with the Firebyrds indefinitely. Andy Kandanes, who had provided his services free, also returned home and, before long, the old familiar demons re-emerged to devour the resolve of the ex-Byrds. Gene Clark, meanwhile, approached Peter Oliva, his former bandmate from the Mendocino Rhythm Section and KC Southern Band, who agreed to take Mark Andes' spot on bass. Oliva could be as brash as Clarke when he wanted, which meant they inevitably locked horns. "Mike was a loveable rogue. He'd get up in your face and try to be the big bad dude. You'd just stand up and butt chests with him and he'd say, 'Man, I'm not going to waste time scarring my fingers on your face.' I'd reply, 'OK, Mike, you just save your fingers!' He'd always act like he was drunk but that's just the way he was. When you got down to it, he was just a lamb and we had a great time together. I have warm thoughts about those days. There aren't the same characters now. They're more neutered."

One thing Clarke could never be described as was neutered. Inveterate womanizing was a feature of his life on the road. "Michael Clarke couldn't keep his dick in his pants," Oliva adds. "Seriously. I never knew anybody that [would say] 'Do or die I'm getting laid tonight.' Somehow he always got what he was after. He was a pussy hound."

In order to bolster the sound, the group decided to add a fifth member, briefly appointing guitarist Tim Goodman, who had to leave soon after due to some album commitments. He was replaced by the charismatic Trace Harrill. A veteran of Muscle Shoals, Harrill had already gained a wealth of experience working alongside his friend Wayne Perkins as a session player for Island Records, appearing uncredited on a number of albums. Perkins was hotly tipped to join the Rolling Stones at one point and Harrill also fraternized with the group, picking up some of their bad habits along the way. Tom Slocum introduced him to the Firebyrds and he soon established a productive working relationship with Gene Clark. Unfortunately, despite his rock 'n' roll credentials, he made an unlikely enemy of Michael Clarke. "I was a bit worried about Michael," says Harrill. "There were vibrations . . . You know how dogs are. They can come together and get on fine but sometimes two of them see each other and they just battle."

Clarke's alpha male aggression was evident during Harrill's first serious rehearsal, which took place on the eve of a hastily organized trip to Canada. Later that evening, everyone had packed up their equipment and wisely returned home to get some sleep, leaving Harrill and Clarke alone. After winding down, Harrill assumed the drummer would move his equipment into the trailer outside but he seemingly took umbrage at this request. "Michael just walked away like he was some kind of star. The equipment had to be put away and there was nobody else to do it but me. It was a terrible lack of respect. He was more or less saying, 'Boy, take care of my shit!' I was about ten years younger than him."

A series of unfortunate incidents followed. The tour coordinator had taken some Valium and fallen into a deep sleep, then the phone rang and Harrill found himself negotiating with a Valley girl threatening to kill herself. The drama continued when they missed their plane flight and their equipment was delayed. Somehow they arrived at the gig on time, but there was no opportunity to soundcheck properly. Harrill, who had been up all night, was hampered by a guitar that was out of tune, made worse by some pre-gig indulgences. "I made a really big mistake," he admits. "Everybody had a little part of a reefer before we went on, but I took two and just got lost. The show went all right but I blew a few tunes. The guy who went on the road with us was furious and I was too tired to argue with him. I didn't tell him what had happened. I wished I'd stayed home and let Michael take the blame."

The next day, Clarke took control and demanded Harrill play every song, which he did with ease. Matt Andes maintains the performances went well and recalls with exuberance their opening show at Solana Beach's Belly Up Tavern where their soundcheck was so energetic that the support act sheepishly declined to come on. "They were an acoustic duo and our soundcheck was so awesome that they packed up and went home. It was electrifying to be up there with Michael Clarke and the guys." The succeeding Canadian tour passed without conflict, although Harrill felt Clarke remained frosty towards him. Matt Andes was intrigued by the dynamic and fascinated by Harrill's rock 'n' roll persona, which was redolent of Keith Richards' wayward cool. "Trace had talent," Andes says. "He had a vibe about him that was kind of mysterious. I couldn't put my finger on it, but he had almost like a James Dean thing going on. Trace could have done something, just on his vibe alone."

Although Clarke had a history of mentoring younger musicians, he was clearly out of tune with Harrill's 'vibe'. "We got home and everything seemed to be fine," Harrill recalls. "We went to the office to get our pay. Out of the blue, Michael said, 'You're out of the group. You're not a Byrd anymore.' That hurt. I looked at Matt and he appeared just as shocked, although I tried to hide my shock. Michael said it with real hostility. I knew he was out to get me. Ha! At first I thought he'd had a powwow with Gene, but then I got a call from Gene saying, 'Just because you're out of the group doesn't mean we can't work together.' So we kept writing. But they were old friends and of course they needed each other. I would say Michael seemed to be running the group as leader." This was unlikely, but there was no doubting that Clarke had a strong veto.

In January 1984, the Firebyrds were back in rehearsal with a vacant guitar spot to fill. The brilliant Jesse Ed Davis turned up one evening to socialize with Gene which caused excitement and consternation in equal measure. The notion of Davis touring with the Firebyrds was a mouth-watering prospect, tainted only by memories of his past association with Clark, which had ended in heroin hell. The musicians revered Davis but were wary of his excesses and privately wondered whether he would commit himself to an arduous tour.

Even the Firebyrds' management expressed concern that Clark might be 'led astray' by his former drug buddy and their view prevailed. "That was the big heartbreaker," recalls Matt Andes. "Jesse Ed played with us during rehearsals. He could be staggering down the street but when you put a guitar on him, he'd play brilliantly. Take the guitar off and he'd stagger back down the street. There it was in black and white: the drunk Indian. We loved everything he had done, but how could you invite him into this project? God, it would have been like a time bomb waiting to go off. Imagine Gene and Jesse Ed together – and then throw in Michael Clarke. He'd try and match them. If those three had been together on the road, drunk in hotel lobbies . . . holy mackerel, that would have reached the papers, man!"

Having arranged an extensive North American tour, TKO Management appointed the grizzled Texan James Aderholt as road manager. This raised Clarke's spirits and he was even more enthusiastic when Aderholt suggested they invite the young guitarist Mike Hardwick along. "You can't imagine how thrilled I was," Hardwick says. "I left quite a bit of money on the table leaving Jerry Jeff to go and play with Gene and Michael, but I knew what I was getting into." At their first rehearsal, Hardwick eagerly learned the new songs and felt comfortable playing alongside Clarke again. When Gene Clark insisted they play some additional Byrds hits, Hardwick impressed the crew by performing note perfect renditions at the first time of asking. "I knew all the old songs better than they did. Gene looked at me, grinned and said, 'Thank you for being here!'"

As a long-time fan of the Burritos and an advocate of the cult Clark album *No Other*, Hardwick felt he was in Byrd heaven, although that impression would be sorely tested during the weeks ahead. A punishing itinerary was arranged for the group, taking in New Mexico, Texas, Kansas, Cleveland, Boston and New York, followed by an extensive Canadian tour, ending with some dates in California. Their first performance took place at the Line Camp, just outside Santa Fe, New Mexico. "It was a famous old place that I'd played often with Jerry Jeff Walker," says Hardwick. "It was in the foothills. That night it was snowing badly and hardly anyone showed up. But the band ripped through it and it was really good . . . Not only was I in a band with the famous Michael Clarke but I was the one that, apart from the bass player, had to play the notes and really pay attention to what he was doing. It was such a wonderful time for me musically. I'll never forget it. I look back and still think that was the best band I ever played in." Further proof of acceptance occurred after the show when, unlike the unfortunate Trace Harrill, Hardwick was not required to lug the band's equipment but watched in amazement as Gene Clark carried his amplifier through the snow. "It was a heavy Fender Twin and he just grabbed it. I said, 'I can get that' and he said, 'No'. I found myself thinking, 'Wow, Gene Clark's carrying my amplifier to the parking lot.' I felt I was right where I wanted to be."

The dream start provided no indication of what lay ahead, although Clarke's rumbustious nature was always likely to provide unexpected drama. Both Peter Oliva and Matt Andes had already experienced his macho posturing and responded in kind.

Ominously, there was even a frivolous physical exchange on the night they set out on the second leg of their tour. The group had driven to Amarillo to pick up Hardwick who treated them to a sumptuous barbecue at his house, after which they freshened up with the intention of leaving at midnight. When they assembled in the van, Clarke was conspicuously absent. News reports predicted a likely blizzard en route, so the need for a punctual departure was paramount. After what seemed an eternity, Matt Andes finally lost patience and went off in search of Michael, who had just emerged from the shower and was in no hurry to join his colleagues. "I went upstairs and there was Michael, bare-chested, drying his hair in front of the mirror. I said, 'You son of a bitch, don't you realize we're all in the van waiting for you?' He gave me some lip, so I popped him right in the chest. We'd gotten into this fun habit of getting tanked up on a few beers and slugging each other. It was just macho stuff to see who could punch hardest in the shoulder. But it was getting ridiculous after a while. We were all bruised and sore. For days afterwards, Michael was complaining that his sternum hurt whenever he played the drums. I said, 'I'll do it again, you bastard!' So that was a good one. I popped him, but it was out of love. I loved Michael and didn't mean to hurt him, so we stopped the slug fest for a time. It was like kids fighting and wrestling – but then somebody lands one."

Clarke's aching chest was forgotten by the time they reached New York, where spirits were momentarily enlivened. "We had wonderful nights there at the Lone Star Café," Andes recalls. "Paul Schaeffer came to the gig, plus Rick Danko and these friends from the past. It was like a parade of celebrities and it was wonderful to meet these people." There was already some consternation about the distance travelled between bookings and fears about the organization as they drove to Toronto. As often happened when they played a big city gig, the response was positive and the working conditions and accommodation more than reasonable. However, by this time, the two original Byrds were slipping back into their immemorial excesses, with predictably raucous results.

"Oh man, we did a lovely gig and they put us up in this modern hotel in the heart of Toronto," Matt remembers. "It was a very upper crust place where you'd want to act respectable. Gene had been drinking and he and Michael were arguing about something on the way back from the gig. Then they started physically fighting in the hotel lobby. They were choking each other and wrestling in the foyer. Important clients and well-dressed people were coming in. It was very embarrassing. I hightailed it to hell but, sure enough, when I went to my room later I noticed Gene's door was open. As I scooted by, they were *still* fighting, locked in a bear hug, wrestling. I said, 'Goodnight, fellows!' The last thing I saw they were falling into Gene's closet, still locked in a bear hug."

Road manager James Aderholt knew better than to reprimand them for their behaviour. "Michael always had fights," he says. "He and Gene fought in their rooms every once in a while, but I never knew what they were about and I didn't pay any attention to it. The next day things would be fine. These were little knock-down drag outs, but no one ever had a black eye or scratched knuckles, so they couldn't have been that bad."

All this was an eye-opening experience for the younger Hardwick, but he too kept his counsel. "They were like brothers and would do things to each other that no one else could do. They fought, but let anyone get in between them or fight one of them and you'd have to take the other one on. I don't think the music would have been the same without either of them. Gene had spent a lot of time with Michael being the drummer. Those Byrds guys had a tremendous bond. They'd been through adversity and done so many things in such a short time at an early age. It was almost like they'd been in the army and experienced a war together. Anyone that wasn't there didn't have that bond. Gene could have gotten other people, but Michael was the guy. They always kept in touch and remained close."

After Toronto, the Firebyrds undertook an extensive tour of Canada. It was a stamina-sapping saga akin to a survival course. "What that band went through, no band should have to go through," states Hardwick. "It went way beyond just not making money. Hope was disappearing quickly. It was the longest time I've ever been away from home on a straight run. Eight or nine weeks from January, driving across the US and across North America in the dead of winter."

There were some disconcerting portents as they made their way through Canada. North of Edmonton, they saw some blinking lights in the distance and stumbled upon a gory scene. Two cars had collided and one lay stranded in a ditch, its occupants in a seemingly critical condition. "It was in the middle of nowhere," Hardwick recalls. "There was no reason for any accident to happen. Can you imagine two cars colliding in an intersection?" A young couple, barely conscious, were trapped inside. The impact of the collision had propelled the woman from the front seat to the back. "Michael and Gene went down, then everyone else. The woman was very hurt and couldn't move by the time we got there. Someone there had a CB radio and had called for help." While they waited for the ambulance to arrive, Michael and Gene offered sympathetic words. "Gene reached inside the car, held the woman's hand and comforted her. He stayed with her and told her to hang on, that help was on its way." The incident provided a salutary warning of the dangers they might face on this most arduous of tours.

"Everyone felt stretched and had to find their own way of dealing with it," says Hardwick. "Pay was gone and we were on the road with a tour book. A lot of the dates seemed misrepresented. It was like we were a Byrds covers band being booked into the wrong clubs. I guess bands still tour like that and things happen. But it was tough to take when you have two former Byrds in your band. I was the new kid and I was still used to planes and tour buses. We were scamming the club out of beers because there was no money. Michael and Gene weren't doing drugs then. There was no hard drug use because it was impossible. Maybe they could buy some codeine pills to share."

Even their burly Texan road manager James Aderholt was out of pocket. "I didn't make one penny. I lost 55 pounds, which didn't hurt me any because I was overweight at the time. I subsisted on whatever we had on the deli tray. There was never any money. Every dime I got, if it didn't go in the gas tank, I had to send it home to the booker. I kept enough for gas and the hotels and that was it."

Although Clarke might have been expected to rage against these sparse conditions, he displayed surprising fortitude, as if the road offered a partial sanctuary that he could never find in his domestic life. After his baser needs were met, practical problems tended to fade in the mists of alcohol-induced insouciance. "Michael just liked being out, running around," says Aderholt. "Everybody was there for the ride, apart from Matt Andes. Almost every hotel we stayed in, there were these touring strippers. A lot of the US girls worked in topless bars and they'd go to Canada. They'd tour across the country, just like us, and they'd be there at the bar. So Michael was fine. As long as there was enough money for Michael to have cocktails, that's all he cared about."

Even the cocktails were placed in jeopardy at some dates, where the audience numbered a mere handful of people. Aderholt remembers how "a couple of shows were pulled because they couldn't sell any tickets at all". At such times, Clarke would relieve his blues with female company. One morning, the group were alarmed to discover that their van was missing, along with Michael Clarke. Andes asked a few questions and unearthed a scary story. "He'd schmoozed one of the waitresses in whatever bar we were working at and had taken her out into the countryside in the hinterlands in the dead of winter. He was only wearing jeans and a sports jacket. As dawn arrived, he realized he'd driven the van into Lake Superior with this girl from God knows where, and they were stuck." Clarke dined out on the story for years afterwards. "Yeah, I was stuck in Lake Superior, covered in ice and snow," he later told me. "I could see the shore ahead and there was smoke coming from somewhere. I walked through the snow in shoes that were falling apart and stumbled upon this Indian settlement. I told those Canadian Indians, 'You've gotta haul me out, please man!' and they saved the day. They wheeled out this pick-up truck and I looked up and it was full of dead wolves with sharp teeth and carcass eyes. I thought I was a goner, but they were cool."

On the road following the incident, Clarke nearly got into more trouble by attempting to rejuvenate his cold body with copious amounts of beer. Desperate to relieve his bladder, he told Hardwick to pull up, unaware that a cop car was watching their every move. In his befuddled state, Clarke even left his beer can on the roof as they drove off, spraying the highway with the remnants of his adventure. When the police caught up, they seemed genuinely baffled by the spectacle they witnessed inside the vehicle. "Are you a hockey team or something?" the officer enquired. Clarke would probably have claimed undeserved hockey godhead had he not been semi-conscious and incoherent. Somehow, they escaped unscathed with a salutary warning about the dangers of drinking and public urination. Afterwards, Clarke fell into a deep sleep, happy as a baby.

Gene Clark was also employing alcohol as a numbing device, aided by codeine. This road medicine was not just desirable but necessary given the chill factor and claustrophobic conditions in the van. Inevitably, there were minor illnesses along the way and increased tensions, exacerbated by lack of money, insufficient food and frequent weariness. In addition to the occasional Clark/Clarke fisticuffs, there was a falling out between Oliva and Andes which would never have happened had they not been stuck in a van every day. "Matt and I were fighting all the way across the country," Oliva recalls. "It was nasty. Matt's a brilliant guitar player, but close quarters, that's what was going on."

"The only worthwhile part was that hour onstage playing with these Byrds legends," says Andes. "We were in places with names like Saskatchewan and Thunder Bay with a bunch of drunk Canucks in the audience. They didn't know or care who they were going to see and they were drinking this amazingly strong beer. They were yelling 'Can you play Def Leppard?' I thought, 'You morons don't know what you're watching here.' That happened a lot. We had hip audiences in the bigger places but on these whistle-stop dates it was back to screaming Canadian cowboys wanting Def Leppard."

In an attempt to improve the set list, Matt Andes approached Gene one evening and asked: "Can we play 'The Bells Of Rhymney'?" It was one of Andes' favourite Byrds songs and he knew the solo well enough to perform a more than competent cover version. What he did not realize was the mythology surrounding the song, which had previously been a highlight of the Byrds' set back in the Ciro's days. More pertinently, it had generally been regarded as Michael Clarke's most inspired moment in live performance. His distinctive cymbal work transfixed everybody. When they played the song in Canada, a vestige of the old magic remained and Clark and Clarke were sufficiently energized to offer an animated rendition. "We tried it at the soundcheck and it really took off," Andes recalls. "It was awesome. We had fun doing it and it would make the hair stand up on my neck every time we played it. It was one of my proudest moments and we nailed it, but it was wasted in front of those drunken Def Leppard fans." Alas, the song did not remain in the set for much longer, much to Andes' regret.

Andes' blues were such that some doubted whether he would even complete the tour. "We all wanted to finish it," says Hardwick. "But it was really bad. Matt was ready to go, but he stayed. We were saying, 'Come on, Matt, it's only another week and a half.'" Intriguingly, Gene Clark, who had a habit of blowing tours, gritted his teeth and braved the conditions, as if fearful of losing even more credibility among his peers in the business. He knew that he and Michael's former manager Eddie Tickner was watching their progress from a distance and they dearly hoped that he might later represent them. The remote possibility of a more lucrative tour or record deal proved enough to keep the ex-Byrds on the road.

Meanwhile, the troubled Andes found solace in humour, documenting their more absurd adventures in a series of drawings. "We had a lot of time on our hands, so I would sketch

Michael, and James Aderholt in his cowboy hat. I made postcards of these silly drawings of our predicaments. James was a pretty good target and usually got the brunt of my sarcasm and good-natured humour." Clarke laughed at Andes' caricatures, but also craved something more serious. He became uncharacteristically wistful after experiencing the breathtaking sights from the bus and regretted not packing an easel and paints. "He'd look at these places and say, 'Fuck the music, we should be painting this!' We'd both go off looking at these landscapes and shared some wonderful intimate moments on those spectacular stops. I've always regretted that I never painted with Michael. It would have been so easy. Later, he visited me in Venice, where I'd inherited my mother's little bungalow. He'd show up early in the morning and we should have painted together then too."

The purgatorial tour of Canada eased somewhat when they reached Calgary, where the proprietor of the Long Horn Saloon treated them with unexpected beneficence. Andes' road woes were solved when he made the unilateral decision to travel to their next destination by train. "They were travelling over the Rockies in this rented van and trailer. I thought, 'You're kidding, right?' so I made some calls and booked a Canadian Rail sleeping car and met them a day and a half later in Vancouver. I had the time of my life going over the Canadian Rockies in a beautiful old train. It was like being in a *National Geographic* magazine and was one of the most spectacular things I've ever seen in my life."

The robust Clarke claimed to be the fittest of the bunch when they ended their stint in Los Angeles, although he too had been stretched by adversities during those long weeks. Apart from nearly losing himself on Lake Superior, he had suffered a panic attack that provided his fellows with enough ammunition to pinprick his macho image. The incident occurred when they were driving to Texas during the first leg of the tour. "When we got to Dallas we were done," Aderholt remembers. "That was the last show and everybody went out and partied. I knew a ton of people and had a lot of friends who showed up. Several of the Dallas Cowboys came to the show and a couple of guys from Jerry Jeff's band. Anyway, Michael went out with some people and I don't know what he did but he became really ill. We had to take him to a hospital in a town about 80 miles from Dallas."

Clarke had met an amphetamine dealer in Austin and taken so much speed that his body was rapt by convulsions. "He'd really overdone it," Andes recalls. "As we were driving to Dallas, he was lying on the back seat saying, 'Get me to the hospital, I'm having a heart attack!' We were saying, 'Calm down, buddy, we'll get you there.' I tried talking him down because he was really fried from whatever he'd been doing. Once we got there they hooked him up to some liquid Valium and calmed him down. He was convinced he'd had a near death experience." There was a bizarre interlude when the attendant doctor asked Clarke about any history of drug or alcohol use. He coyly admitted recently partying with speed, then detailed his drinking binges, cocaine consumption and other drug experimentation over the years. Comically, he kept interrupting himself as some new past transgression entered his mind. After jotting down this litany of abuse, the physician stared at his notepad in near disbelief. "We were outside the doctor's office eavesdropping, trying to stifle our laughter," says Andes. "Poor Mike was really sheepish about copping this crap. It rattled him to have to tell the truth, but he wanted to know if he was going to live or die, so he unloaded to this doctor. It was morbidly funny. He humbled himself. It was an anxiety attack. He was scared but we got him back home, safe and sound."

Clarke's sudden concern about his health may have been partly prompted by the shock news that his father had suffered a stroke. Their relationship had been fractious since Michael's adolescence, but he was upset after hearing of his condition and turned to an unexpected source of comfort, Gene Clark. "Michael used to call the hospital and they'd both talk to my husband," says Suzy Dick. "This was right after the stroke, and they both sounded loaded, for sure. They did a lot of drinking. Michael told me that Gene would have martinis in the morning, but they would call the hospital and talk to his dad."

While Clarke was dealing with his father's stroke, the Firebyrds went through a temporary hiatus. Financial needs and a promise of better bookings convinced them to tour again. When the departure date was abruptly rearranged, Matt Andes finally lost patience and told them, "I can't put my life on hold for you guys, screw this." Electing to carry on as a four piece, they were forced to rearrange the set. Clarke seemed determined to transform them into a hard-rocking outfit, arguing that they were in danger of being blown away by more bombastic bar bands. It was a cogent argument but not one that was easy to accommodate in a set dominated by Gene Clark songs.

"It was Gene's band and material," Hardwick notes, "but Michael was a huge presence and exerted a big influence on how things should be done, and that was important. Michael wanted the band to kick ass. Gene might not have wanted everybody to get their ass kicked, but he wanted them to go home and think about the show. Michael's attitude was more 'slam it out and take no prisoners' whereas Gene wanted a little more finesse. But this was the early Eighties – the era of Loverboy. When you turned on the radio, there were big, loud guitars and drums. Michael felt we had to change with the times."

In the end, Clarke was overruled and, despite losing Andes' slide work, the band actually moved in a more pronounced country direction, with Hardwick sometimes switching to pedal steel guitar. "We were able to pull off Dillard & Clark stuff like 'Train Leaves Here This Morning' and 'Through The Morning, Through The Night'," Oliva recalls. Regrettably, the new direction did not improve bookings and after a second tour, Hardwick also left.

By late 1984, the Firebyrds had devolved into a trio, in parodic imitation of the Byrds at the end of 1967. They were reduced to fulfilling obscure dates in faraway places with limited resources. Clarke could not even justify transporting his drumkit to some shows and would use whatever equipment was available at the venue. Pick-up players were arbitrarily recruited to fill out the sound. On 14 December, the trio turned up at Woody's

Roadhouse in Burlington, Vermont, resembling nothing less than a bar band, no longer even living off past glories. The support band, Connecticut combo China Doll, were playing an unlikely blend of reggae and Grateful Dead material as the Firebyrds arrived. Their guitarist, Jack Carchio, was a big fan of the Byrds and Firefall and had hoped this gig might attract a decent audience. Instead, it served as a burning testament to how unfashionable country rock had become by the mid-Eighties. Worse than that was the realization that the old gods from the Byrds were now working on a shoestring budget. "They didn't bring any equipment and there was no road manager that I saw," says Carchio, "just Gene on acoustic and Peter Oliva with a bass. Michael came in with some sticks and used our guy's drumkit. They then approached our band leader because whoever was supposed to play guitar with them didn't show up. So they just pointed in my direction. I had about 20 minutes of prep with Peter in the dressing room. I was familiar with the stuff because when I'd first learned to play the guitar I was a Byrds fan and anything that was a Byrds tune I knew . . . I had a country rock style so I was able to play along, just watching Gene who was MC and led the whole thing."

As a result, the set wasn't the train wreck that it might have been. Clarke even took the opportunity to follow China Doll's lead by incorporating some choppy reggae-style rhythms. "We did 'You Really Got A Hold On Me' which Michael started off as a reggae spoof. Gene had already done several songs solo and Peter performed 'Mercury Blues', the only number he sang lead on." Unfortunately, all this was rendered redundant by the appalling turn-out. "Only ten people turned up and that was for the whole night. I should have made $200 but ended up losing money. But, hey, I thought, 'I've lost money but I got to play with two guys I really admired.' I was not only a big Byrds fan but really loved Firefall. Where else would I get to play with guys like that? It was serendipity."

The starstruck Carchio was so enamoured of the former Byrds that he begged the group to take him away with them. "We all went to breakfast after the show, sat around and exchanged telephone numbers. I was trying to persuade them to take me on tour. I said, 'Well, your guitar player didn't show up. Here I am, ready to go.' I wasn't happy with China Doll or Connecticut and was single and had no ties. But Gene Clark said, 'I can get Ry Cooder, I don't need anyone else.' I agreed with him, but I was also thinking, 'Well, if he can get Ry Cooder, why isn't he here?' "

The notion of Ry Cooder appearing to a handful of people at venues like Woody's Roadhouse was appealingly preposterous but ably displayed either the deluded grandeur or sardonic humour of the two former Byrds. The Firebyrds' idea had by now run its course and when Peter Oliva moved on before Christmas, Clark and Clarke were the only two left, a situation with eerie echoes of the post-*Notorious* season when McGuinn and Hillman were the sole surviving Byrds.

In January 1985, Jack Carchio was surprised to receive a call from Michael Clarke offering him the chance to play guitar at a nearby venue, the Rocking Horse Café in Hartford, Connecticut. Clarke had evidently been busy as several other local musicians were recruited, including saxophonist Paul Nigro from the band Mr Big. "It seemed thrown together," Carchio remembers. "I was the first to arrive, then other players started trickling in. It was the strangest music scene I'd ever been involved in. There was a rhythm guitar player but Gene pointed to me for all the solos he wanted played, so I did my bit, but it was a very cold atmosphere onstage. I was standing at the end of the stage and everybody had their back to me and nobody was talking, although Gene and Michael were friendly. This gig wasn't as tight as the Hartford one because the people involved were younger and weren't so familiar with the Byrds' material. There wasn't even a set list. Gene would just say, 'We're going to do a song' and tell us the key and we'd follow along." Afterwards, the musicians shared some beers, but this time Carchio made no attempt to nominate himself as a future Firebyrd. He would never hear from either Byrd again. Nor would Nigro, who died, aged 29, the following year.

* * *

Despite the disintegration of the Firebyrds, Michael and Gene were keen to carry on working together. Although the times seemed against them, there was evidence that a stronger Byrds reunion or tribute might attract more lucrative touring opportunities. They noted with interest how former Band members Levon Helm and Rick Danko had worked together as a duo, even appearing at the Lone Star Café. That duet had evolved into an almost full scale Band reunion in 1983. Although Robbie Robertson was missing from their ranks, they were reasonably well received in concert and made some decent money. At one point, they shared booking agents with the Firebyrds, establishing a connection that would soon prove of benefit to both parties.

By the beginning of 1985, Clark and Clarke were ready to turn the vogue for Sixties nostalgia to their commercial advantage. Within a few months, it would be 20 years since 'Mr Tambourine Man' had topped the charts in the US and UK. The time seemed right to remind the world of this epoch by effecting another reunion. They hoped to persuade the remaining three original Byrds to put aside old differences, but it was already obvious that David Crosby would be uninterested. That same month he had just entered New Jersey's Fair Oaks Hospital in a forlorn attempt to kick his freebasing habit. Over the next few months, his troubled odyssey would include periods banged up in the Tombs and Rikers Island, before he was finally transferred to Dallas County Jail. His off-time was spent on reunion tours as part of Crosby, Stills & Nash which, for all its limitations, provided a healthier income than any fantastical notion of a Byrds' get-together. The Clark/Clarke duo did attempt to involve McGuinn, whose presence would have provided the 'reunion' with enough credibility to attract major bookings. Still smarting from memories of McGuinn, Clark & Hillman and content to play the solo troubadour, he displayed no interest. Hillman seemed a more likely bet, but his antipathy was, if anything, even more pronounced. He voiced indignation and anger about them daring to bill themselves as the 'Firebyrds', although that was hardly a major crime (even McGuinn had recorded and toured as

Thunderbyrd). In desperation, Gene and Michael decided to look further afield and approached latter-day Byrd Gene Parsons but, wary of the road, he elected to stay home in Caspar, Mendocino. Undeterred, Clarke believed he could still construct a pseudo-Byrds. One night, he phoned his old friend Ras back in Boulder, full of inebriated excitement. "He got his little book out and told me, 'I'm going to call Tom Petty. He's got the same damn voice as Roger McGuinn and he'll do it!' But he wouldn't commit either."

In order to save money, Michael and Joy briefly stayed at Gene Clark's rented home in Sherman Oaks. It was not an ideal situation as the apartment became a late-night musicians' haven. Even while attempting to form the Byrds-related group, Clarke could not resist helping old friends and invited John Manikoff for dinner on several occasions. Jamming sessions ensued, but Manikoff was a little wary of the company. "Michael thought I was talented and he wanted me to play with Gene, who would always bring the guitar out. But it was a one-way thing. Gene preferred everybody to listen to him play. It was his show. Gene always made me nervous. He was a little hard-edged for me. I tell you that guy could drink, and that's coming from somebody that could drink. He could really hurt himself. But Michael was different. He wasn't dark. When he drank, he was fun to be around."

By now, they'd decided to concentrate on a revue-style '20th Anniversary Tribute To The Byrds' with a line-up including the Band's Rick Danko (bass) and Richard Manuel (keyboards), Burrito/Firefall alumnus Rick Roberts (guitar/vocals) and *Holland*-era Beach Boy Blondie Chaplin (lead guitar/vocals). Still searching for one more Byrd, Clarke bumped into John York at the Palomino and press-ganged him into the group as 12-string guitarist and occasional vocalist. After only two days' rehearsal, they set out on an extensive tour, including a showcase at their favourite New York venue, the Lone Star Café on 13 February. The weight of talent ensured that the performances were an entertaining mixture of songs, largely consisting of Byrds' classics and favourites from the Band and Firefall, plus Chaplin's Beach Boys' cameo, 'Sail On Sailor'. The mood was generally upbeat and there were even deluded hopes of record company interest. As ever, the Byrds' drummer retained that remarkable ability to play the regular guy, equally adept at fraternizing with rock legends or establishing unlikely friendships with fans.

One such was Las Vegas resident Dennis Kelley who attended a show at the Beverly Theatre, Beverly Hills, naively expecting to see the original Byrds. "I had high expectations. At the time, I didn't know about all the bitterness, backbiting and alcoholic haze that several members were into. I really thought McGuinn would be there, or maybe even Bob Dylan." After adjusting his expectations, Kelley struck up a conversation with Michael Clarke in the lobby and offered to buy him a drink. Improbably enough, the drummer declined. By chance, Clarke mentioned that they were soon heading to Cincinnati, where Kelley had been born and raised. On a whim, he decided to rope in a high-school friend and see their concert at Bogart's. This time, Clarke did accept a drink and even gave Kelley his address and phone number. Remarkably, they established a friendship in the succeeding years with Kelley taking on a role similar to that of 'Ras' back in the Boulder times.

The 20th Anniversary Tour rolled on through 1985 and the revue expanded to include a revamped Flying Burrito Brothers as support, with a line-up including Sneaky Pete Kleinow and Skip Battin. Thankfully, the absent Chris Hillman's opinions were not recorded, although he would have grimaced at one billing for the Burritos which referred to them as the 'original' line-up, presumably assisted by the ghost of Gram Parsons. By the summer, promoters had become more daring or careless and dropped the preambles, boldly proclaiming the rump revue as 'the Byrds'. It was a terrible affront to McGuinn and Hillman who could only utter withering comments on the entire enterprise. The anniversarians talked up the show in fanzine interviews but it was evident that the novelty was beginning to wane. Although the gigs were a step up from the Firebyrds, Michael was becoming bored and losing heart. For a time, he absented himself and Band pianist Richard Manuel deputized on drums, before leaving along with colleague Rick Danko for another Band reunion.

Danko compared the tribute Byrds to "an off-Broadway play" but for John York, it was more like being trapped aboard a pirate vessel. "It was thrown together and there was no work ethic whatsoever. Some of us thought that something worthwhile *could* be done. It started out at a certain level and then went downhill. Out of that first three-month tour, there were maybe three nights when the music was amazing, but it was purely by accident. Even now, somebody will send me a tape and the music is incredible but it's total balls to the wall full-out rock 'n' roll. I hate to say there's no artistry to it but the method of playing was [one of] total reckless abandon. The tapes have charm but if you listened too much you'd get tired of it. On tour, it was like a buddy film. It had positive and negative sides depending upon what Michael and Gene's bloodstreams were like. They both had that John Wayne swagger and I don't know where they got it from. Maybe from watching cowboy movies as a kid. It was hilarious, but it could also get violent. I watched them have fistfights and when it was all over they'd have a beer together. I saw them get onstage and they'd start duking it out in front of everybody. You'd get out of the way and afterwards they'd just laugh about it."

While York felt ambivalent about the shows, others were more positive. Carlos Bernal, who joined the ranks for a spell, was thrilled when pianist Nicky Hopkins agreed to perform at some dates. "I have to tell you, I was having the time of my life," Bernal enthuses, "and they were paying me good money. When Nicky came into the band I bought an extra long guitar cord just so I could stand over by his left hand and watch him play."

Towards the end of the year, following a series of gigs in Canada, Clarke abandoned the group in characteristically dramatic fashion. John York remembers a performance at Knott's Berry Farm, Buena Park, California, where the drummer finally snapped. "That place was like Disneyland. It was just before

Christmas and we were all waiting to get paid. Michael came back from the office and said, 'Guys, I'm taking the money!' Then he threw his drums at us. He didn't have the whole kit, just his snare drum and cymbal and I picked them both up. I kept the drum and I gave Billy Darnell [Blondie Chaplin's replacement] the cymbal. That was the last gig from that particular combination of Byrds. Michael took the cheque, then left. Gene said, 'That's it, I've had enough, I'm getting Greg Thomas.' I still have the drum which has blood on it because Michael used to bleed when he played."

Clarke offered a disingenuous parting shot and was soon rationalizing his departure. "I don't speak much on that. We tried it for a year and it didn't really ever approach 'big time'. It's not the original Byrds, it's kind of a copy band. I think the band should be put to rest, and I'm sure that Roger and Chris agree . . . We were out there trying to put the name Byrds back on the map . . . Too many personnel changes. You don't get a record company interested in you that way . . . I didn't feel it was moving forward, so I left. I think Gene should do something else."

Michael Clarke was certainly keen to try something else, but for the moment his direction remained uncertain. At one point, he rented a Malibu beach house from actor David Carradine. Recalling his pre-Byrds exploits, he seemed content to relax, enjoy his freedom and spend more time painting. John Manikoff, who later became an artist, was surprised to find that he and Michael shared another interest outside music. "That was the part of Michael that other people didn't know. He enjoyed painting and even then may have felt he had a future in it. He and Joy lived in Malibu for a time and I visited him there about ten times."

It seems safe to conclude that not much painting was completed when Manikoff arrived in town. "Michael and I would drink all night partying, snort coke, and hang out on the beach. At seven in the morning, we'd hit the one bar on the beach that opened at six. We'd drink Bloody Marys and talk for hours. It was insane." One trait that Manikoff noticed, even in quieter times, was Clarke's insomnia. "Michael never slept then. If he went to bed at four in the morning, he'd wake up at six. He wasn't one of those people that slept till noon. But he used to dream a lot. He used to say to me, 'Johnny, I had this dream . . .' This guy Jim Dickson was somebody who was in his dreams a lot, and Crosby. He'd tell me David was there and they were all sitting around playing. It was like he had this premonition about life."

It wasn't long before Clarke's other partying pals descended on Malibu, eager to have fun and lead him astray. Among them was perennial roadie and recently appointed 'Byrds' tributarian Carlos Bernal, who regarded hedonistic excess as an almost holy rite. Having previously shared a house with Clarke in Malibu during the early Burritos days, he was more than familiar with his drinking routine. The roadie's major obstacle was Clarke's hard-working wife who was vainly attempting to establish some order around his increasingly dissolute lifestyle. "Joy didn't like me coming round because she knew me and Michael would go day drinking," Bernal says. "She didn't like day drinking. So when I visited we had to be careful. He'd drink my beer and say *I* had it. I couldn't believe it."

Clarke's womanizing and alcohol abuse contributed to the unravelling of his marriage over time. While he was coming to the end of another cycle in his life, his former wife Robin was undergoing a more startling epiphany. After many years of high-living, she was admitted to hospital with pancreas trouble. There was more drama when she was involved in a car crash, during which Zak was fortunate to escape with a deep scar to the forehead. Robin heeded medical advice and, unlike her ex-husband, became a teetotaller hereafter.

After splitting with Joy, Clarke decided to quit the music business and completely reinvent himself in the surprise setting of Hilton Head, South Carolina. During his last days with the Byrds' tribute band, he had played a gig there at the Old Post Office. Among the patrons was aspiring actress Kassy Stone, who soon drew the flirtatious attentions of both Carlos Bernal and Michael. Playing Cupid, Stone introduced Clarke to her friend Joan Pound, who managed a lingerie store in the area. This no doubt appealed to Clarke's erotic imagination. There was instant chemistry between them which was sufficient to persuade him to move to Hilton Head after leaving the Tribute Byrds. Following a whirlwind romance, he moved into her house and took up painting again in earnest. During his first few weeks in town, he worked as a bartender, just like his Boulder-based pal, Ras. Unfortunately, Clarke could not resist the temptation of free drinks and was dismissed for being drunk on duty. For a time, he supplemented his income painting houses and, when pushed, undertook building work. "He went out and pounded nails and hurt his hands," Matt Andes remembers. "He had to do that to make a living for a time and I commended him. Suddenly, he was there in South Carolina with this wonderful woman, Joan."

It was a sign of Clarke's inner confidence that he chose not to use his Byrds status as a calling card, but settled into the local community with characteristic modesty. Cementing friendships, he established a close association with Kassy's partner, Terry Rogers. Born in Texas, Rogers had moved to Macon as a child and learned music under the aegis of his gospel singing family. During the Seventies, he founded Rogers, Pound & Greene, later Rogers & Pound (Joan's brother, Brian), opening shows for acts like Foghat, It's A Beautiful Day and the James Gang as well as undertaking session work at Capricorn Studios. Like several other characters in the Michael Clarke story, Rogers was also a keen artist and it was this interest, along with music, that inspired an enduring friendship. "Michael was an amazing painter," he maintains. "That's what he wanted to do when I first got to know him down in South Carolina."

Kassy Stone was already aware of Clarke's Don Juan reputation, but remained resistant to his charms. "I was probably the only girl he didn't try to screw," she laughs, "because I was involved with Terry and they became such good friends. Michael didn't have to show his personality because he was a star. All he had to say was that he was Michael Clarke. But he was an intelligent and charming person and, at that point, he wasn't anything like a drunk. I felt I got to see his real personality." Over the next year, this circle of friends grew even closer and Clarke dutifully served as best man at Terry and Kassy's wedding which took place at sea on 14 September 1987.

Clarke gave no indication that he was missing life as a surrogate Byrd. The tribute game had continued in his absence with Gene leading the band for a couple of years. Inevitably, their touring schedule eventually brought them back to Hilton Head and Clarke seemed happy to watch Greg Thomas playing in his spot. John York was intrigued by his low profile. "Michael came to the gig and we asked him if he wanted to play on a song, but he said, 'No, I haven't drummed for so long.' But we got him up and he played on 'Mr Tambourine Man'. All his friends were there and they were blown away. They had no idea he was a musician. Most of them thought he was a housepainter."

Although Clarke tried to stay sober, his hedonistic ways soon returned to wreak vengeance on all attempts to settle into a suburban lifestyle. The day drinking that Joy had so dreaded crept back as part of his routine. Dennis Kelley noticed the signs after inviting Michael and Joan to his Las Vegas home. "At that time I didn't know the extent of his drinking. One morning I came downstairs to the kitchen and Michael was standing there with a 10-inch glass full of vodka. He was putting a splash of orange juice on top so that nobody would know. This was him getting out of bed in the morning to get on an even keel. He almost walked through a sliding glass door going out to the swimming pool but bounced off of it. Still, we had a great time. I took him gambling and we played baseball on the street." Clarke injured his shin, but his alcohol consumption helped ease the pain and he was still eating reasonably well. "He really liked big barbecues," Kelley adds. "The main thing I remember about Michael was his intense love of family. He loved the rock 'n' roll lifestyle but he also hoped to someday be more normal."

Clarke's ambivalence about what he wanted was demonstrated

in his relationship with Joan. As Kassy Stone recalls: "He hung out and painted and was trying to get a divorce because Joan, being a Southern girl, wanted to get married too. But he remained married to Joy." When Stone challenged him, he made the excuse that tax issues were a factor in his non-decision. As the months dragged on, matters worsened. "There wasn't really any future there," says Stone. "Joan was eager to get him out because of his wild lifestyle, even while he lived with her. It was very miserable for Joan and she was on the phone to me all the time because I'd introduced them. I knew things about Michael I didn't need to know! It was unpleasant and she was most unhappy . . . He was fooling around and that's why she was so angry. Plus, he was drinking, then suffering health problems. He also ran up some big phone bills." As he would often do in later years, the impecunious painter left her with some art as recompense. It was a sad end to an affiliation that had lasted over two years.

In May 1988, Clarke returned to his family home in Spokane, seeking another fresh start. Initially, he was still cut up about his last relationship. "Joan was a real sweetie," his mother recalls. "She stayed in touch with him for a while, but his drinking split them up. She loved Michael. When he came here after they split up he was still in love with her and was crying. She was still calling him and he was still calling her. He was trying to get over her and he told me that he was having a rough time doing it. He told her he was quitting drinking, but he wasn't. He was here for eight months and he stayed drunk the whole time. But he was one of those functioning drunks. You're never completely drunk, but you're never sober. He just functioned that way. It had been going on for many years and that's the way he lived. That's what was killing him. His body never got a chance to get rid of the alcohol and purify itself. We tried everything we knew to help him, but he said he didn't like life without booze. He was afraid to be sober."

Suzy Dick was well qualified to empathize with Michael's

alcoholism, having overcome her own demons only a few years before. "I didn't know anything about alcohol," she recalls. "I didn't start drinking until I was 50. I had my first drink of wine at 50 and then I became a full-blown alcoholic, not drunk, just drinking all the time at a certain level. So I knew what Michael was doing when he came home because I'd already quit. My drinking lasted ten years and I quit when I was 60 [in 1984]. This was maintenance drinking, but you wouldn't believe how much I could consume."

Despite his alcohol dependency, Clarke sought a salvation of sorts by focusing on his art. It was almost as if he was taking on the mantle of his father whose stroke had forced him to quit painting in 1984. "My husband exhibited his paintings at a park here in Spokane," says Suzy. "He loved to paint, although he wasn't a professional. But he still sold a few. I was sorry to see him stop." Relations between father and son improved for a time, but that peace could be easily broken, particularly when Michael's drinking took hold. "Once they were together for a while they would get into it over something," says Suzy. Nevertheless, Clarke seemed determined to start anew, even though he was now 42. "He sat downstairs and painted and painted as much as he could. It kept him occupied. He was awful organized. Any painting you see with an '88' on it was done here."

Before long, Michael was running short of money and surviving solely on his royalties. His ex-wife Robin and son Zachary visited Spokane during the spring and she generously sent him some much-needed cash to help out during this belt-tightening period. Away from the rock star scene and freed from the shackles of the Byrds' myth, Clarke gradually adapted to a humbler lifestyle. He told his mother that he was intending to return to school and find a day job to supplement his artistic pursuits. "He was painting and trying to be an artist, but he felt he ought to get some other job. He wasn't qualified to do anything without a high-school diploma and he'd never needed one before, so he thought he'd try to get one. And then the music came back."

* * *

Clarke was astonished and elated to learn that there was an entrepreneurial coup to put back together the original Byrds for a tour and likely spin-off video and live album. It was described, seemingly with no exaggeration, as a million dollar deal. At a point when he was struggling financially and attempting to find a new direction, his abandoned past promised fresh glories and the opportunity to win everything back. Anger and frustration followed upon learning that McGuinn had declined the promoter's solicitations, while Crosby and Hillman seemed relatively uninterested. Business figures hovered in the background hoping to broker a deal, but in the end nothing was forthcoming. Having come so close to a lucrative windfall, Clarke understandably found it difficult to concentrate his attention on securing a high-school diploma and seeking a mundane job. His drinking continued and he risked damage to his liver through the indiscriminate use of prescription drugs. One evening, he raided the medicine chest of a girlfriend's father in Spokane and consumed a cocktail of pills which, mixed with booze, might easily have killed him. "He took all sorts of drugs all at once," his mother remembers. "I called the pharmacist who said, 'If I were you, I'd get him to hospital.' I said, 'I don't think he'll go.' His eyes were like pinpoints and he was just bouncing off the wall before that. Then he passed out. It really worried me that he was messing with prescription drugs." Michael was too zonked out to consider the consequence of his actions. Instead, he slept off his bad night and merely smiled at his dangerous excesses.

In January 1989, Michael left Spokane and sought the advice of Artists International manager Steve Green, who persuaded him that a Byrds' band under his own aegis could make money, irrespective of his former comrades' activities. Teaming up with Terry Rogers, who brought in guitarist Jerry Sorn, they added a tepid Byrds' flavouring by recruiting Skip Battin (keyboards) and Carlos Bernal (bass). "Michael was always busy trying to find Byrds," says Bernal. "He was saying, 'I've got to get some money, I need some Byrds, you're a Byrd, you're coming with me!'" Bernal knew better than to argue and psyched himself up for a bumpy ride. Gigging at small venues across America, Clarke found contentment of a kind and with Rogers providing stability and efficiency, more bookings were forthcoming. Inevitably, it wasn't long before Clarke's mischievous side emerged. Freed from his former role as road manager, Bernal at last enjoyed rock star hedonism first hand and revelled in this new freedom by forming an unholy alliance with Clarke. "Michael was pretty rowdy and those guys Tom [sic] and Jerry started referring to us as the Monster and his Friend. Luckily, I was the friend. Michael was always a kidder and they took him too seriously. As soon as he saw that, he gave them a run for their money. But they did the job well enough."

Rogers found Bernal fun and entertaining, but became wary of his darker side. "I'm sure that had partially to do with his drug consumption. He was a pretty bad influence on Michael who I was always trying to keep as sober as possible, at least until we got through the show. No matter where you were Carlos would always come up with the drugs, so that was always going to be a problem one way or the other."

After a show in Alabama, Bernal became involved in a contretemps with somebody and threw a few bar stools around to express his anger. "When he went over the edge, he went over hard," Rogers notes. Acting like a Seventies rock star may have provided a therapeutic release, but it was deemed unsuitable for these leaner times. Suddenly, Bernal was no longer there.

Roadie Greg Tramps sent out an urgent call to John York saying, "You've got to help us, man, we've got no bass player." York agreed to fly out but was terribly conflicted about the group, feeling that he was cheapening himself by becoming involved. "When you fall out of favour and don't have a record you fall prey to this lower-level business world of the record industry. For a while, we got out on the road and all of a sudden the gigs weren't even there." York doused his misgivings with alcohol but continued to feel bitter about the prominent role given to Rogers and Sorn at the expense of himself and Battin. "I was uncomfortable with these two other guys singing all the songs when I'd played bass with the Byrds. And I wanted to help. I thought, 'Let's see how much respect there is.' Nobody asked me to sing, so I only did two tours before it became unbearable . . . But Michael was always an interesting guy . . . You love him and you hate him. He had this bad boy image. On the one hand, I thought it was interesting that he should at last have the chance to show how he would run a band because he'd never had that chance. But his style was not one that would make you feel secure about how things were being run. I loved playing music with him because he played with such reckless abandon. He was not a guy who studied drums; he'd get on them and just hit those things. There was a certain verve that I really respected. But the non-musical aspects of being in a group were a bit difficult with Michael. He was not a guy who planned ahead. It was a bit like being on a pirate ship with a guy who'd say periodically, 'Every man for himself!' I always felt, 'No, that's not how I'd do it!'"

Clarke was perversely determined to keep his version of the Byrds on the road. "Michael was desperate at that point," says Matt Andes. "He didn't want his tool box back. He knew he wasn't going to do that anymore. When he went back out as the Byrds he made a vow to himself that he would never work construction again. I ended up with a gift from Michael – a wooden, handmade tool box and his tool belts with nail and hammer pouch. Maybe he thought I was going to work construction! It was a wonderful keepsake and whenever I need it, I just adore the fact that I have his old tool belt. It's a wonderful memory for me."

Audaciously billing his group as the Byrds eventually brought Clarke into bitter conflict with his former colleagues, culminating in a much publicized court battle, the full details of which were previously analysed in *Volume 1*. His emphatic preliminary victory over McGuinn, Crosby and Hillman proved pyrrhic at best, enabling him to make a living without any real hope of receiving the kind of money enjoyed during the Firefall days.

The acrimonious court action over the Byrds' name understandably alienated Clarke from McGuinn, Crosby and Hillman. Acting as the mediating reporter, I felt obliged to hear the arguments from every camp, still vainly hoping that the quintet might reconcile their differences and realize that their greatest strengths, aesthetically and commercially, lay in the magical five-man reunion. It seemed a tough sell until you considered that in the past each of them had been ostracized by one or more of the others. Nevertheless, this latest fall-out ranked high in their history of mutual bitterness. In an angry exchange, Hillman told me that he would never work with Michael again. Crosby and McGuinn were annoyed and indignant at the drummer's presumption and simply wanted the Byrds to end. Clarke called them 'assholes' for suing him, but I felt his words were largely macho bravado. They had all said bad things about each other at one time or another. Even in attack, Clarke, like David Crosby, had a tendency to change mood suddenly and qualify an insult with a sympathy born of nostalgia. "Screw those guys! They sued me and I don't like them anymore," he'd say. Then, leaning forward, he'd suddenly think of Chris Hillman and add, "I can't say anything derogatory about Chris. Regardless of what he's ever done, he'll always be my friend. We used to ride horses together. He's an excellent rider. Chris and I lived together for years, played poker and had the best of times."

Clarke's tendency to switch abruptly from invective to praise was a trait he shared with most of the other Byrds. In various conversations, they betrayed the same ambivalence towards his character. Despite all his critical remarks about Clarke, Crosby often showed a big brother affection for the drummer and seemed to take genuine delight in his successes after the Byrds. Even during the court case, David blamed manager Steve Green for supposedly leading Michael astray, and seemed to believe he could knock some sense into the kid if they could only get to him alone, away from lawyers and businessmen. The cooler McGuinn felt the same and, for all his anger, Hillman surely agreed. Not that it was easy to 'knock sense' into Michael. He was an experienced student of Byrds' politics and was wary of being bamboozled by the others. His default defence revealed the same tactics heard in studio debates, where he'd trade insults freely and pinprick all pretensions of artistic superiority. There was one interview where he told me: "McGuinn can't play guitar, how's that?" He had a grin on his face and probably guessed that I'd turn off the tape recorder in exasperation at his obtuse idiocy. It was a clever ruse.

Hillman grouched to me about Clarke's shortcomings as a drummer at the height of the legal dispute and Crosby was even more scathing. Other observers, like Dickson, argued the opposite. Former roadie Carlos Bernal, who had worked alongside every drummer in the Byrds, including Kevin Kelley, Gene Parsons and John Guerin, retained a special affection for Michael. "He was the best drummer ever for the Byrds' music. He was the most exciting rock 'n' roll drummer of all. He may not have been technically or fundamentally correct, or top of his class at some of the rudiments, but when he played in concert there was nobody like him."

The existence of the ersatz Byrds angered and embarrassed his former colleagues, not to mention a sizeable section of his audience, but Clarke's crew were incapable of inflicting much harm, beyond righteous indignation. It was simply pin money, playing to indiscriminate audiences content to hear showband-style pastiches of old Sixties' hits. Loyal fans felt insulted, and understandably so, but securing such a prized title brought its own problems. The great irony was that the acquisition of the Byrds' name, far from earning praise or riches, ultimately proved a heavy millstone around the necks of the winners. For many fans, the idea of playing as the Byrds was akin to passing yourself off as the Beatles or the Stones. Even Clarke's trusted friends told him as much. "You can't call yourselves the Beatles and just have Ringo in there," Ras summarized. There was an aesthetic sanctity about the Byrds' title which transcended personal, financial and judicial squabbles. The Byrds' mythos, like that of the Beatles, was a terrible burden to bear, pitifully beyond Clarke or any other newly manufactured line-up. In time, Crosby, McGuinn and Hillman appreciated this truth. They may also have realized that the various songwriting squabbles and personal disputes, which took place at the Byrds' peak, ultimately affected the group's legacy far more profoundly than the continued existence of a copycat band that few would ever see or hear. As long as Michael's Byrds didn't make records, the world was safe.

In the autumn of 1989, the 'Byrds' brigand set out on a European tour. It proved a ramshackle affair, taking in the backwaters of the beat revivalist circuit. Upon arrival in England, Clarke told me that the group was basically run by himself and Terry Rogers. At times, Michael resembled a latter-day John Wayne, old in the saddle but still in strong physical shape. He could be charming and self-effacing, but what struck you most was his confidence and powerful presence. An enervating cocktail of vodka and arrogance brought some unintentional humour to even the most anti-climactic of performances. During one show on the tour, he complained about a faulty drum stool, then walked to the front of the stage and lectured the audience on its shortcomings as a piece of furniture. He then threatened to cancel the show unless a replacement was found immediately. This was a grand gesture worthy of David Crosby and all the more amusing for having taken place in the faintly ludicrous setting of the Beck's Theatre, Hayes. After all the ups and downs of the previous two-and-a-half decades, the drummer had clearly never forgotten that time when the world was seemingly at his command. He was still Michael Clarke of the Byrds.

Although I had spoken to Clarke on numerous occasions over the years, they were usually late-night phone calls updating his whereabouts and plans while exchanging anecdotes. The price of interviewing Clarke at length involved suspending all expectations and falling into his peculiar time scheme, which meant suffering his tendency to postpone plans at a moment's notice. It was a trait he shared with Gene Clark. The only solution was to follow him around like a dog and seize the moment. Clarke insisted I join the UK tour partly, I suspect, because he enjoyed the company and wanted someone to play Bobby Neuwirth to his Bob Dylan. The only person who didn't get the joke was guitarist

Jerry Sorn who had a bizarrely inflated view of the band's importance. One late evening at a hotel bar, he took me aside and claimed I was a bad influence on Clarke and demanded I stop speaking to him about the past and concentrate entirely on the musicianship of the current line-up. At first, I assumed he had to be joking, but he was in deadly earnest. In fairness, Sorn was probably correct to point out that I had over-excited Clarke, whose volatility was always a concern, but I argued that his animation was positive, and had certainly improved his stage performance that particular evening. More importantly, his Byrds' past *was* the story – not his current band. Playing alongside a revamped Herman's Hermits was hardly newsworthy; these new 'Byrds' had never recorded or released anything; no music paper deemed them worthy of a concert review, let alone an interview . . . and so on. Amazingly, Sorn then told me I was 'off the tour' and did not wish me to speak to Clarke again. Trapped in a hotel foyer in the early hours, I was preparing to leave when Michael came staggering through the entrance, having previously disappeared to God knows where. Hearing this nugget of news, he exploded: "This ain't no goddamn democracy. He doesn't know who he's talking to. He just doesn't know who you are, man." Then, in a display worthy of Dylan in *Don't Look Back*, he frogmarched me to the concierge's desk and demanded, "Get this guy a room, *now*." Then, turning to me with a devilish grin, he added: "And I'm deducting the cost of the room from the guitarist's wages." He seemed to take immense satisfaction from that, as if he was the god of misrule. The incident indicated his generosity, albeit at someone else's expense. Largesse and mischief were inextricably linked in his personality. The following morning, I offered to buy him a drink and he said: "Thanks, get me a vodka!" Before I even reached the bar, he threw in the wallet-shrinking punchline, "Make it a treble!"

In keeping with his Lothario image, Michael was accompanied by a new girlfriend, Lee Elliot, whom he had met in Majorca on the Spanish leg of the tour. Although in her mid-twenties, she barely looked out of her teens and obviously knew little of the

Byrds' illustrious history. Her relationship with Michael was already subject to his mood swings, no doubt exacerbated by his enormous consumption of vodka. Sometimes they resembled love's young dream, then there would be a sudden falling out, with Clarke issuing brutal broadsides. The sexual chemistry between them was very strong but seemingly too explosive to last. Naively, I assumed that after the group's appearance in Manchester she would probably return home to her native Ellesmere Port.

After the tour, I learned that she had returned to America with Clarke. They stayed at Rogers' house for a time, during which Lee made increasingly urgent attempts to secure citizenship. She finally achieved that aim when Michael elected to become a husband for the third time. It seemed a most unlikely turn of events, but nothing in Clarke's life was ever predictable. "We were amazed it lasted so long," Terry Rogers admits. "It continued to be quite volatile the whole time." Meanwhile, Michael's drinking rose to worryingly high levels. "There were small periods when he was trying to quit or at least cut down drastically," Rogers recalls, "and he did for a time. But then he would go back on it."

Clarke's relationship with Lee seemed almost as dangerously addictive as his drinking. The wild mood swings that characterized their interaction continued, even when she was not physically present. When the group accepted an 11-day tour of Italy, she remained in America, but still exerted a strong influence over the transatlantic phone. "They weren't married yet, I believe," Rogers remembers. "But every day he would be on the phone to her for hours having this huge row. He rang up unbelievable phone bills and of course he was drinking twice as much as a result. It was pure hell."

Normally, Rogers' quiet diplomacy might have calmed the beast in Michael, but the guitarist was nursing a serious back injury which drained his resolve. "The day before the tour I'd been gathering building materials and threw my back out so I was in a lot of pain. I was walking with a cane and lying flat on the floor in my hotel room while Michael was being a dickhead. I had no patience left at that point because of the pain. I loved Michael very much. He was a very good friend but there were certainly many times when I could have shot him." Ignored by Rogers, who refused to leave his room or discuss the drummer's romantic problems, Clarke's frustration spilled over into adolescent violence. "Finally, he broke down the door of my room, jumped on top of me in the bed and started choking me on the floor. Skip heard the commotion and ran in and tackled him. Then I dragged my mattress into the bathroom, locked the door and put a chair underneath the doorknob. That's how I spent one night in Italy. The next day Michael was saying, 'Oh, I'm sorry, man, I love you, man.' "

At the end of the European tour, Rogers told Clarke that he could no longer tolerate his drinking and was quitting. Apart from anything else, Rogers had fallen out with Lee, whom he believed had been boosting Michael's ego by supposedly telling him, "You can't pay Terry that much, you're the guy that's the original Byrd. You don't need him." Whether such words were spoken remains uncertain.

The emphasis on Michael as 'the original Byrd' was crucially important and without his presence the final link with the name would have been lost. On the other hand, without Rogers' business acumen on the road there was nobody to hold the operation together. When Clarke attempted to form a new set of ersatz Byrds, the agency Artists International initially refused to accept bookings. Undeterred, Clarke found a Nashville bass player, then perused his phone book and plucked out the name Michael Curtis, who had been working with drummer Dewey Martin and Billy Darnell in another 'tribute band', Buffalo Springfield Again.

During the Firefall days, Clarke and Curtis had shared the same accountant, Dottie Ross, but they had never performed together. Curtis had also played bass with Gene Clark's Byrds' tribute band but was happy to become lead guitarist, along with Darnell. Curtis diligently rehearsed the repertoire for a week, reassured by Clarke's blasé rejoinder, "Curtis, it'll be OK, you know what you're doing." The drummer's only concern was that they could play the big three: 'Turn! Turn! Turn!', 'So You Want To Be A Rock 'n' Roll Star' and 'Eight Miles High'.

"We did two shows at the Saveloy, a high school theatre in Santa Barbara," Curtis remembers. "We pulled it off and got a good crowd. The funniest thing was that Michael wouldn't be there until curtain time. Suddenly, he'd be behind the drums and we'd say, 'Let's go.' As soon as we finished the last note of 'Eight Miles High' I'd turn around and he wasn't there. He always knew when to leave." Clarke scored some substances that night which made him more convinced than ever that he could run a band. But apart from a handful of dates backing Gene Clark, his promotional activities foundered. For a time, he stayed at home with Lee where, she claimed, they tried to write some songs, no doubt assisted by his vodka intake.

After an impasse lasting several months, he re-established relations with Terry Rogers and returned to the Tribute game. "Michael was never much of a businessman," says Rogers. "I was the one person he could trust to do the job and I was willing to do it, and I was good at it. We paid everybody well, but if there was a profit to be made above that, then Michael and I would split that. I felt I was very much earning it. When he couldn't get a band together, he called and said, 'Look, I'm sorry, whatever you want, just come back.'"

The Eighties had proven a tough decade for Clarke, but he was not alone. For many, the passing of the glory years had led to greater self-awareness and re-evaluation. Hollywood witnessed a new cultural revolution among the rock aristocracy that deserves a book of its own. The age of rehabilitation had arrived for a number of Clarke's old friends, who stepped back from the abyss, sought sobriety and renounced past vices. Organizations like Alcoholics Anonymous appeared to be bulging with new members, several of whom had been Clarke's former drinking partners. Others were establishing themselves as minor celebrity drug counsellors, transforming their former addictions into classic case studies that served as warnings to new initiates. The clean-up message spread far and wide, as Clarke could testify. It was as if all the old ravers had been corralled into submission. Looking through his back pages, he catalogued a long list embracing such names as David Crosby, Greg Thomas, Dallas Taylor, John Manikoff, Matt Andes – and many more. Even Gene Clark, the most prodigious of alcohol lovers, was currently on the wagon. Peer group pressure alone might have saved Clarke's troubled liver, but he shied away from such temperate trends. The newly abstemious Matt Andes was nevertheless aware of his curiosity. "Michael was fascinated by me being sober and he'd check in every once in a while and say 'Are you still doing that sober thing?' I'd say, 'Yeah, it's working. I'm still going to AA meetings.' He looked at me and said: 'Goddamn!' He was working around the perimeter of this thing. I told him, 'It's up to you. If you've had enough let me know. I'll take you to your first damn meeting if you want.'"

That was never likely to happen. During a stop-off with the 'Byrds' in Las Vegas, Clarke spent an evening with Dennis Kelley, who agreed to accompany him on a drive to their next gig in Phoenix. "He'd been drinking the night before, so he got some McDonald's to eat, along with a pint of vodka and a six-pack. The ride was about five hours, but he got through the vodka and the six-pack, then played the concert and drank more. His consumption was amazing." After the show, Clarke stumbled to his motel door, fumbled in his pockets for his key and watched helplessly as loose change spilt across the floor. Staring at this scene, he turned to Kelley and said: "Look at me, I can't help myself, I'm just like a little kid." It was a poignant moment. Kelley would never see him face to face again. "I hoped I could do something to help him but for somebody that far along there's not much you can do."

James Aderholt also met Clarke during this period when the band passed through Dallas. "It was three in the morning when he called me. He was with some lady friends of mine and said, 'Come out and party.' I said, 'No, but I'll come over to the hotel and we'll have breakfast.' Of course, all we did was drink. It went on till eight in the morning, and he rolled out of Dallas about 9.30. That was the last time I saw Michael. He said, 'I still owe you a thousand and I'm going to have my manager send you that money.'"

There was a strangely fatalistic quality about Clarke continuing with the 'Byrds'. The money was unspectacular, there was no hope of securing a record contract and every serious commentator implored him to abandon the band and seek some rapprochement with his former colleagues. Regrettably, there seemed no way forward. Even close friends were amazed that he was still on the road, punishing his body, drinking more heavily than ever and living from day to day. John Manikoff remembers phone calls that usually ended with the plea: "Michael? What the hell are you doing?" Clarke took the ribbing with a shrug of the shoulders. "He'd tell me these stories and I'd roll my eyes. He was going out with these bands that he called Byrds. It was the silliest thing. One time he called and said, 'Johnny, you've got to come and see the Byrds!' I told him, 'Michael – the Byrds? What are you talking about?' When I showed up he was thrilled to see me, but he was playing at Magic Mountain, some theme park, with kids and their families eating cotton candy. What the hell was that about? He said, 'It's a gig and I'm glad to be playing.' He reminded me of those old R&B guys that would show up anywhere with a smile on their face, even if it was the biggest dump you ever saw. And Michael was adamant that he had the right to do it. Everybody else in the Byrds was up in arms about it."

Clarke's relationship with the original Byrds remained frosty, but there was always a false but lingering hope of a reconciliation. In January 1991 the five reconvened at the Rock 'n' Roll Hall of Fame induction. He was ostracized initially, but as the evening progressed they could not resist inviting him to join their table. A peace of sorts was declared and if someone with enough influence and clout could have persuaded them to tour or record, then there's no doubt that Clarke would have agreed to relinquish his claims on the Byrds' name. After two bottles of wine, he was willing to give it away for nothing, like a genial drunk trying to keep everybody happy, at least until the next time. His apogee was appearing onstage that evening, not as the original Byrds' drummer, but front of stage, sharing a microphone with Gene Clark as they all sang 'Mr Tambourine Man'.

A few months after the Hall of Fame induction, McGuinn was touring with the Headlights and found himself booked to play a Florida date on the same night as Clarke's version of the Byrds. "I never expected it to happen," McGuinn lamented. "Michael said he was going to quit using the name once he'd made a little money. I wish it would just dry up." Ironically, Clarke's crew were playing at the oddly named Philmore, a venue originally known as Fillmore South, until the wrath of Bill Graham forced a name change. "Counterfeit club books counterfeit band," McGuinn taunted sarcastically.

While Clarke was still in moral battle with McGuinn, Crosby and Hillman, his sole remaining ally in the original Byrds died on 24 May 1991. Gene Clark's excesses mirrored those of Michael. It was not so long ago that they had been on the road together, laughing, drinking and brawling. Now the tambourine man was gone. Clarke never dealt well with death, but felt sufficiently moved to pen a loving tribute to his old friend. Prefaced by some lines from Dylan Thomas' poem *Do Not Go Gentle Into That Good Night*, Michael's valediction (printed in full in *Volume 1* of this book) was heartfelt. "Expression is man's most potent instrument of progress," Clarke wrote, in an uncharacteristically lofty style. "His success is inevitably measured or limited by his ability to communicate his thoughts to others. Gene Clark was one of the most successful and loving people I ever met. A continuous battle raged between Gene and himself, which, in the end found its way onto paper and into song, where it settled." With commendable discretion, Clarke did not address his colleague's frailties, instead focusing entirely on his artistry. Perhaps the circumstances of his death were too painful to consider, especially in light of Clarke's own decline Rather than learning from the fate of his friend, he continued drinking. Evasion and denial were easier options.

* * *

With his recent marriage to Lee entering another tempestuous stage, Clarke fortuitously met painter Susan Paul. "I was sitting on a plane in first class, miserably unhappy that I was having to leave Tampa," she recalls. "They were getting ready to close the door, when someone said, 'Hold it! We've a latecomer'. I was thinking it would be really nice if some good-looking guy got on. Then Michael walked in, and that's how we met. He was tall, thin and tanned." During the flight, Susan explained that she was organizing a fund-raising event, involving singer Amy Grant, for a drug rehabilitation programme. Eager to impress, Clarke offered the services of his Byrds, but was crestfallen when she replied: "Are they a baseball team?"

The pair continued to keep in touch but Clarke's romantic designs were immediately thwarted when Susan learned that he was still married to Lee. After agreeing to stay friends, they drifted apart for several months, a period during which Clarke continued his erratic progress on the oldies tour circuit. At one show, he surprised everybody by singing 'The Banana Boat Song', a rare vocal appearance which would seldom be repeated. On the way to another show, he missed a connecting plane and the group was forced to recruit a drummer from the audience. Increasingly, his drinking was not only affecting his playing but seriously damaging his health. Terry Rogers recalls a tentative attempt to persuade Clarke to reform his ways, but Michael never liked to be lectured and shrugged off good advice. "He really wanted to clean up," Rogers thinks, "but he was like a kid sometimes." Michael was particularly squeamish about the prospect of seeing a doctor. Again and again he put off the dreaded visit even when his legs and torso were swelling to alarming proportions. Clearly, liver disease was taking its toll. "I'm not a doctor, so I don't know how that worked," Rogers admits, "but I guess the poison had gone through his system."

In May 1992, Michael called Susan Paul from New York and asked her to meet him at the airport. It was clear that he had suffered a rift with Lee. Although Susan was reluctant to drop everything, the urgency in his voice persuaded her to attend.

When she saw Michael, she was deeply shocked. Extreme weight loss made him appear skeletal, an image exacerbated by a severe hair-cut. "He looked awful. Then he told me he and his wife had split." Immediately after, Clarke returned to the road, but kept in contact, running up more expensive phone bills, while speaking for hours through the night. Upon his return to Florida, he told Susan, "I don't really want to be alone", and she invited him to stay at her house in Tampa. Initially, their relationship was platonic but, on Independence Day, he announced to his band that he was planning to divorce Lee and marry Susan. "Do you usually marry somebody without sleeping with them?" she retorted with mock indignation. Michael looked at her and replied with cocky assurance, "You won't be disappointed, I promise you."

The couple settled in Tampa and over the next few months Clarke attempted to curb his drinking, and even took up painting again. "There was a drastic difference in his work at that time," Susan explains. "A lot of it had to do with his eyesight failing because of alcoholism. Previously, his work had been very intricate, with lots of tiny details."

Work began in earnest when Michael's agent called with the exciting news that two paintings from Clarke's portfolio had been sold and were to be displayed at a Rock 'n' Roll Art Expo in Philadelphia. Unfortunately, Clarke had already sold the paintings in question so, under pressure, he agreed to replicate the originals. At first he borrowed Susan Paul's glasses, then used a projector to magnify a slide of the original paintings which he copied from. As he was about to complete the work he discovered, to his horror, that Paul had put the slide on screen in reverse and the new painting was an inverted mirror image of the original. Turning to Susan, he exploded: "If you think that I'm going to re-do this painting, then you're out of your mind." The new paintings were still taken to Philadelphia for exhibition and the existence of two separate works, one in reverse, merely added a humorous gloss to Clarke's artistic reputation.

Clarke's ongoing battle with alcoholism continued in Tampa.

During a brief spell of sobriety, he phoned his old mentor Jim Dickson and was full of good news. "The last time I communicated with Michael he sent me a watercolour painting that was beautiful. He was so proud of it. When I spoke to him he wasn't drinking and he was kind of proud of that. He would expose me to things that he was proud about. To that extent I was another father figure. He didn't usually tell me when things were bad. I just wouldn't hear from him. When he sent the painting and told me he wasn't drinking I was very pleased but I didn't know he was doing any serious drinking at the time anyway."

Lee Elliott, meanwhile, had taken up with a formidable fellow named Shotgun, whose heavy reputation intimidated Michael sufficiently to ensure that he paid maintenance to his estranged third wife. "Michael was going through the shakes and I was there with him wiping the sweat from him," Susan Paul remembers. "After four days, he was a little better, and then the phone rang. It was Lee. Michael said, 'Do me a favour and drive me to this bar. I need to give her money.' It was ridiculous. I dropped him off at this bar in this sleazy place and he said, 'Do you want to come in and meet her boyfriend, Shotgun?' I said, 'No, I don't want to meet Shotgun! I don't want to be around people like that.' When I picked him up later, he came out drunk."

By the autumn of 1992, Clarke's alcoholism had worsened. "He kept drinking and drinking," Susan Paul recalls. "I said, 'Michael, if you don't get sober I'm not going to marry you, and you won't have to divorce Lee. Make a choice between me and the vodka.' He said, 'Do you think I'm stupid? I'm not going to lose you over a bottle of vodka.' Then, another couple of months went by and he was even worse. He was drinking two litre bottles a day. So I just said, 'That's it.' I packed his things and left a note."

Susan hoped that Michael would return to his family home in Spokane, but instead he moved back with Lee. Their sometimes stormy, interdependent relationship continued its wayward course over the next and final year of his life. Occasionally, he would phone Susan and suggest a reconciliation, but she refused to be involved until he renounced alcohol. Eventually, they met at an airport in May 1993, a point when Clarke was at his lowest ebb. "He sat down on the floor and put his arms around my legs and started crying. I took off his glasses and his eye whites were yellow. They weren't bloodshot, but yellow from jaundice. I told him he had to see a doctor. He said, 'You should have come back.'"

Clarke's condition was no doubt exacerbated by the news that his father had died that same month. "Michael took his death really badly," his mother remembers. "He stayed drunk from the time his father died and he didn't come home for the funeral. He was never able to handle the death of anybody he loved. He couldn't come to his grandmother's funeral either, poor guy."

Even in his parlous condition, Clarke continued along his reckless path. He neglected to see a doctor until a royalty cheque arrived that August. Following his visit, he was informed that he had cirrhosis of the liver and warned that the content of a single beer any time during this period could mean the difference between life and death. "In the last few months in particular, he knew he was dying," Terry Rogers points out. "But he was real slow to admit that. He wanted to pretend, even to me, that the doctor had said that he was going to be OK. It was obvious that he was not. He wasn't even going to call his mother or son, or anybody."

"He went on tour and didn't totally quit drinking," Suzy adds. "He used to call me from his shows and he'd say, 'I'm not drinking' and I'd say, 'Good'. He was puffed up to his neck with fluid and he had to wear floppy clothes but he still went ahead and played. Michael had real determination. Terry told me that they didn't all know what his condition was, but they knew he was swollen and in bad shape. They saw him drink beer. Terry said Lee was complaining all the time about Michael being a stick in the mud and not having fun. And he could hardly eat. He'd throw up. He was miserable all the time, so I guess he just gave up and went ahead and drank some beer."

While contemporaries like Dallas Taylor and David Crosby

were saved by liver transplants, Clarke was not so lucky. Since he had failed to reform his ways before falling ill, he was not deemed a suitable candidate for a donated liver. Moreover, his condition was such that it may already have been too late. "It wouldn't have done any good anyway," says David Muse. "Being an alcoholic, as Michael was, doesn't sit well if you're waiting for a healthy liver. Michael did it to himself. He was sad about it at the end when he realized what he'd done to himself. He had so much to live for and he really didn't want to go. But when you go down that road, the faster you go the sooner you get to the end." Back at Michael's house, Lee was still on the scene, coping badly with the realization that he was terminally ill. It cannot have helped knowing that she had little or no support from his friends. Seemingly, nobody took her side or empathized with the problems she was facing, which cannot have been easy. While he was in hospital, she showed up unexpectedly, prompting another of their memorable rows, while others looked on aghast. Soon after, they split for the final time.

In November 1993, Susan Paul received another of Michael's worried calls. "I really need to see you, no bullshit, it's really important," he implored. At this point, he was alone again. She tentatively agreed to pick him up on the Tuesday before Thanksgiving, but he failed to call back. Two days later she phoned his house to invite him for Thanksgiving dinner, only to be greeted by the answer phone. Assuming he was on the road performing, she fulfilled an appointment out of town but felt uneasy enough to ring again. This time Michael answered, explaining that he had just returned from hospital and urgently needed to see her. "I went to his house from the airport," she remembers. "When he opened the door, I almost passed out. If I'd gone to the hospital to see him, I would have walked right by him. His face was totally sunken, just like a skull that had skin hanging over it, but no real distinguishable features. From his mid-chest down, he was swollen. His testicles were the size of a basketball and he could barely walk. It was the most horrifying thing. I just stood there and he said, 'I guess I don't look so hot, huh.'"

In spite of his condition, Clarke attempted to convince himself that all might still be well. He looked to the future with irrational optimism, once again projecting a new cycle of divorce and remarriage as a panacea to his ills. Turning to Susan, he announced, "I want us to get married. I'll be all right. I just need to take a year off." He then started to laugh and added, "Well, maybe two years!"

"I wanted to believe that with all my heart," Susan Paul reflects, "but I just looked at him and knew there was no way he was going to pull through." As well as neglecting to take his medication, Clarke was prone to accidents. The previous night he had tried to take a bath but, after stepping into the tub, he noticed that his feet had turned bright red. Having lost all feeling in his legs due to the severe swelling, Michael was unaware that he had suffered severe burns from scalding water. He was taken back into hospital and treated. After draining fluid from his abdomen to reduce further swelling, the doctor confirmed that Michael did not have long to live. He was advised to return home to sort out his affairs.

Time stood still at that moment. "He was sitting in his wheelchair, wearing a bathrobe and nothing else because it was too uncomfortable," Susan explains. "We were there in the hospital waiting for the doctor to leave the room." Once they were alone, a deathly silence ensued, which Michael finally broke with the words, "What am I supposed to do?" There was no pat answer to the grave news and all that Susan could think of in her grief was her mother's stoical platitude, "No matter how horrible a situation always look for the humour."

"All I wanted to do was sit on the floor and cry, but I looked at him and said, 'Michael, look to the humour.' He looked at me and said, 'You know, you're sick! What could be so fucking funny about me sitting in this chair waiting to die?' I said, 'I don't know, but I'm sure if you think about it for a while, you'll come up with something.' I was standing there shaking, and I turned away from him. Then, all of a sudden, he said, 'I've got it! I get to screw the IRS.' And he started to laugh."

Michael's gallows humour continued on the drive back when

he requested that they should purchase some sweets. "He wanted to binge!" Susan explains. "He said, 'If I'm dying, I'm going to eat anything I want.' So we stopped at this drug store. He was wearing just his bathrobe and was barefoot. He walked up the aisle to the candy counter and picked up a small packet of red liquorice and peanut butter cups, then said, 'Let's go.' I was a wreck in that moment. I started picking up miniature bags of candy and filling his arms with them. He said, 'You're going nuts! What's wrong with you?' I said, 'What's wrong with *me*?! You don't even know how to binge right!' Then he said, 'All right, calm down', and we paid the cashier."

That evening David Muse of Firefall came over, while Susan and Michael ate candy and watched television. As they sat viewing a nature programme, Clarke pointed at the trees and mountains on the screen and said, "I'm going to miss that." Turning to Susan, he asked her to visit the desert after he died as it was a place where he always felt at peace.

Muse spent more time with Clarke than any other musician during these final days and did his utmost to ensure Michael was as comfortable as possible. They discussed his terminal condition and Clarke confessed that alcohol was worse than any drug he had experimented with over the years. "That was weird because Michael had probably done everything," says Muse. "I tried to get Rickie Roberts to come down because I wanted him to have closure with Michael and say goodbye to a friend. I couldn't get him to see him, but he did call a couple of times. Rickie was fighting his own demons and I wanted to say, '*This* can happen to you too.' It wasn't a pretty sight, I have to tell you. Dying of alcoholism is probably one of the worst ways to go. Towards the end, Michael looked like he was nine months pregnant but when you saw his face, the skin was hanging from the bones."

Even on his deathbed, Clarke retained the capacity to surprise. "You never knew what was going to come out of his mouth," Muse adds. "We talked about death and he said, 'What I'll miss most is never going to a baseball game again.' I never knew he'd ever been to a baseball game. Where the hell did that come from?

It was kind of funny. Of all the things he could have missed, it was baseball!"

Initially, Michael had been reluctant to inform his family about the extent of his decline. In the end, Susan Paul had the unenviable task of telling his relatives the sad news. It came at a particularly bad time for his mother, who was still recovering from the recent loss of Michael's father, James. At first, she hoped that Michael might be able to fly to Spokane but he seemed reluctant to leave and in the end was too unwell to travel. Once they realized that he would probably not survive Christmas, his family, including his mother, first wife Robin, and their son Zachary (McNamara), rushed to Florida to be by his side. The son, whom he had not seen for a few years, was also intending to pursue a career as a musician, albeit as a stand-up bass player rather than a drummer. For Michael, it was a last chance to be with his family. "I would have been there earlier but I didn't have the money to go," his mother explains. "Steve Green paid my fare. Robin got there the day before I did, so Zachary got to talk with Michael. Zachary loved his dad but he didn't get much chance to spend time with him because of the alcohol."

Despite the family reunion, there was still no escaping the chaos that characterized Michael's life. Both Robin and Suzy hoped to persuade him to make a will, so that his estate would be in order. Having led such a free and easy life, Clarke was not about to break old habits by sorting out his affairs. When asked to consider the matter he prevaricated, offering the tired response, "Let's do it tomorrow", after which he would drift into sleep.

"He thought he had longer and so did we all," his mother points out. "It was his pancreas that took him. If it had been his liver he would have hung on a bit longer, but it was the pancreas that took him so fast. He was out of it on painkillers and he didn't want to be. There was no way you could talk to him and before then I couldn't do anything over the phone to get him to make a will. He just didn't get around to it. He just wasn't facing reality at the time that it was going to be so soon. I really had intentions of persuading him to make a will but when I got there it was too late."

On the day before he died, just prior to his mother's arrival, Michael had a sudden burst of energy. After he was showered and dressed, he told Robin and Susan that he felt a little better. They offered to take him out in the wheelchair for a walk, but he refused saying, "I just want to stand in the porch with the sun on my face." As he took in the morning air, he suddenly began to sing, "I feel good", as if he were James Brown. He then came bounding back into the living room, lay down on the sofa and fell asleep. At that moment, Robin started to cry.

An egret had been perched outside Michael's house since their arrival and had just flown away. It seemed symbolic. Robin told Susan, "When an egret leaves your door, it's carrying your spirit to heaven."

Still on painkillers, Michael was barely able to eat but Susan Paul recalls him requesting a banana ice pop. "I went out and got him one and it fell through his hands. He got me to hold it, then he started coughing and the nurse said she was going to give him something to relieve the congestion and suggested we all get some rest. I drove back to my apartment and Robin and Zachary went back to the place where they were staying. When I got home the phone rang and the nurse said, 'You should come back now.' "

John York once said that Michael ran his group as if it was a pirate ship, with the drummer cast as Long John Silver. On 19 December 1993, he died in the appropriately named Treasure Island, attended by Suzy, Robin and Susan. His mother, whom he always spoke of with tremendous affection, cradled him in her arms just before he passed away. Susan Paul recalls arriving at the moment of his death, with Robin standing in the doorway, saying, "Thank God you're here, hurry up." As they entered the room, Susan watched as Michael's head nodded on to his mother's shoulder. "It had to be this way, he was in such pain," she said.

In common with Gene Clark, Michael's failure to provide a will caused major problems. If he had realized the turmoil that would follow his death, he would surely have ensured that the estate was settled. Then again, he might have appreciated the cosmic black humour that followed his demise. Although Lee seemed in no position to want to take control of his affairs, she was the main beneficiary as a matter of law. There was no love lost between the various parties and Lee was cast in the role of villain of the piece by many of Clarke's friends and relatives. "I never really got to know Lee," Michael's mother reflects, "and when I got there Robin was so against her that I didn't have any association with her at all. I didn't talk to her afterwards. I just didn't feel up to it because I knew she had left him and had gone to live with this other guy. I felt she had abandoned him and that hurt me and I wasn't able to talk to her without getting upset, so I didn't. And I should have. I should have done it and I'm sorry I didn't. She called me after I got home and tried to talk to me. I apologized for the way I was at the time, but I was in shock. I was sorry about it because I'm not one that holds a grudge. I never have and I still don't hold a grudge against her. She felt comfortable that I didn't blame her and I truthfully didn't. I couldn't put the brunt of that on her because it takes two. I knew Michael well enough to know that he contributed a lot to it."

With Clarke's estate still in confusion, nobody was entirely sure whether Lee could claim all the drummer's future royalties. Robin contested the issue and royalty cheques were withheld. The Byrds' appearance on the soundtrack of the film *Forrest Gump* produced an unexpected income stream, but the account remained in escrow. It was several years into the new millennium before the parties reached a settlement.

Prior to his death, Clarke had specifically asked Terry Rogers to carry on playing as the Byrds but, after completing a couple of shows in Michael's memory, he decided to let the name rest. Before long, Steve Green, who had financed Clarke's court action, was inundated with requests from promoters for a touring version of the Byrds. He convinced Terry Rogers that there was still a viable market for a tribute band of some kind. Rogers was not entirely happy about using the name Byrds, especially in view of the bad publicity they had received since the court case. Eventually, he came up with a compromise. "We're calling it the Byrds' Celebration," he told me. "I just want people to know who they are coming to see and not expect David Crosby or Roger McGuinn." In an attempt to add authenticity, Rogers invited Skip Battin and Gene Parsons back and also recruited a Crosby fan and Nicolette Larson sideman, Scott Nienhaus, who played 12-string Rickenbacker and could be called upon to perform songs like 'Triad'. If they'd all been 20 years younger and looked like they'd stepped off the cover of the first Byrds' album, then a touring tribute revue might have proven a hit. Unfortunately, they were still saddled with the negative feeling connected with Michael's Byrds and, worse still, their 'Celebration' suffix was invariably deleted from concert advertisements. In one flagrant misuse, they appeared on UK television's *Cue The Music* boldly billed as the Byrds, while the ignorant presenter credited them as the real thing, cataloguing the many classic hits they had supposedly recorded. It was painful viewing.

Thankfully, the musicians did lead a double life, with the existence of the Rogers/Nienhaus Band, whose privately produced CD *Empty Room* was dedicated to Michael Clarke. "The photo on the front of the CD is an old black and white photograph of a house and an empty room," Rogers points out. "In the room, I superimposed one of Michael's paintings in full colour. It came out nice. All his family were real pleased."

Clarke's paintings were saved by his family and placed in storage by Susan Paul. Several of his water-colours were included in Dick Gautier and Jim McMullan's 1994 book, *Musicians As Artists*. A number of other paintings can be found in the homes of several of his musician friends. Mark Andes, for example, currently has three on display. Their value has increased since Clarke's death but few, if any, were bought as serious investments. Occasionally, Clarke used them as a form of currency during belt-tightening times. The young Mike Hardwick secured one such painting through a circuitous route. "The last time I saw Michael, he owed me some money and offered me a painting, but I didn't want to take it. I felt it was too much a part of him. My wife always wished I had. Later, I shared this story with Mark Andes and he gave me one from his collection. Thanks to Mark's generosity, I have a piece of Michael Clarke in my home. It's worth everything to me. I treasure that painting."

While Michael's artwork, royalties and use of the Byrds' name all took time to sort out, a more pressing problem concerned the immediate fate of his remains. Clarke had requested that he be cremated and arrangements were duly made with the funeral hall. Unfortunately, Michael's mourners had split into two camps: his mother, former wife Robin, son Zachary and friend Susan Paul; and Lee, and her mother. As Michael Clarke's widow, Lee was obliged to sign the order giving permission for his body to be cremated. She did this, on the express condition that she would be the one to receive his ashes. This caused friction among his blood family, and it didn't help that neither of the parties wanted to deal with the other. "The people at the funeral hall were completely on the side of Michael's mother and Robin," Terry Rogers insists. In accordance with the law, the funeral home retained the ashes for 30 days, during which Zachary made several calls stressing that his family wanted to be involved in the disposal of his remains. When Lee arrived at the funeral home, she was made aware of the family's wishes and her mother suggested that some positive gesture should be made in their direction. Eventually, somebody came up with the idea that the ashes should be divided between the two parties. A sympathetic representative of the funeral home later told Michael's mother that she had received the majority of the ashes, the remainder of which were given to Lee.

The prospect of various parties fighting over the ownership of his ashes would have appealed to Michael's sense of humour, although he would not have liked the idea of causing his mother any upset. Prior to his death he had requested that his remains be scattered across the ocean. On 3 June 1994, on what would have been Michael's 48th birthday, Susan Paul boarded a boat and fulfilled that final wish on the family's behalf. "I went a mile off shore from where I was living in Florida and scattered the ashes through hand-made Hawaiian lace that Zachary had sent me. I scattered the ashes through the lace, through roses and carnations. Michael loved flowers."

During his final days, Clarke had expressed a wish to appear on television in the hope of alerting young people to the dangers of alcoholism. Susan Paul was supportive. "I promised him that if it was the last thing I'd do, I'd get that message across." Subsequently, she became involved in a foundation titled the Campaign for Alcohol-Free Kids. "We've written a letter from the grave from Michael. I want to put together all the footage I have of him and edit it. Then I'd like to have all the people in the industry who were his friends, and who've survived their bouts with drugs and alcohol, on film and take it to high schools around the country." The lengthy letter was a final mea culpa from Michael Clarke, written in a characteristically forthright style:

Dear Young Friends,

You don't know me, but I am in the Rock 'n Roll Hall of Fame. I was the drummer for 'The Byrds'. We were almost as popular as 'The Beatles'. Back in the 60s everyone knew who we were. Your parents will remember, I was a famous rock 'n' roll superstar. My band performed for millions all over the world. Our songs, 'Mr Tambourine Man', 'Eight Miles High' and 'Turn! Turn! Turn!' are still played constantly on the radio. Our concerts were often sold out. I made a lot of money and had everything going for me including a problem I want to share with you. I was a drunk. Alcohol killed me on December 19, 1993 when I was only 47 years old. It's embarrassing to have to share with you my stupidity that resulted in my death. But you need to know that what happened to me can happen to you. Honest to God, it can. Dying of alcoholism is not an easy death. You have a right to know the truth. Really, you need to know the whole truth.

Don't stop reading my letter yet. What I am about to tell you is real serious. It is no lie. It is time for you to be told the facts of drinking too much beer, wine or distilled spirits. You need to know the facts about the horrible death I suffered and the excruciating pain and embarrassment I went through at the end. I did not die of too many drugs like coke or pot. I died of too much alcohol which is really the most lethal drug of all. Trust me, this is no joke.

When I died I weighed only about 75 pounds. I had been a great looking teen and handsome man who was 6' 2" and my normal weight was 175 pounds. I was a real ladies' man and women loved me when I was healthy, but right before I died I was a horrible mess. My face was unrecognizable to my family and friends. You would have shuddered from the sight of me, I looked like a walking skeleton. I was so weak, I couldn't even smile.

I started drinking alcohol when I was 14 years old and until two weeks before I died, I could hardly remember ever being sober again. Sometimes when I was drunk I was mean. I am sure some of my friends could no longer stand me. I am lucky I did not kill anyone driving drunk and wind up in prison. For years, I would drink a two litre bottle of vodka almost every day and while I was performing I would drink beer onstage in between songs. When I was young I did not care about what would happen when I got older and just kept drinking, but believe me, when you grow up you want to live a full life. I know I did, but I robbed myself of about 30 years that I could have had fun with my fame and money and I cheated my son out of having his father. Please believe me when I say 'I wish I had never taken the first drink. I wish I was alive today.'

I got hooked, that's right hooked on alcohol. It is addictive just like crack cocaine and many people like myself find it impossible to stop. We are called 'alcoholics'. And for people who start and get hooked and cannot stop, it is a fatal disease and can lead to other serious problems like teenage pregnancy, child abuse, crime and premature accidental death. For a young person alcohol is an illegal drug. Alcohol is more harmful than all the other illegal drugs combined. I know you can get it easily; I did. But don't be stupid like me. Too many beers or other alcoholic beverages can ruin your life. If you get hooked you may not finish school and get a good job, you may lose your health and friends and family. I did other drugs too, but none like alcohol. Alcohol is so addictive that I warn you if you get hooked you may not be able to stop by yourself or even if you get help. It is that powerful.

Right before I died, my liver disintegrated inside my body. You could see pieces of it breaking off in my guts with a special type of X-ray picture taken called a sonogram. When I died my liver was the size of a dime. My pancreas and kidneys were also affected by my drinking. Because I destroyed my liver with alcohol, my wastes had no way to leave my body and as a result my testicles swelled up to the size of a basketball. You can't even imagine how painful they were. It was like someone took a sledge hammer and hit them about 1,000 times and wouldn't stop. My chest, stomach and legs swelled up so huge I was the size of a sumo wrestler. I could hardly move. My eyes turned yellow and my skin was discolored from the toxic wastes in my body. I had to go to the hospital so the doctors could drain the poisonous fluid from my abdomen to keep me from exploding. They inserted a catheter into my bladder through my urethra to draw off the urine into a plastic bag attached to my leg with an elastic strap. I screamed with the pain. I lost all my dignity and there was nothing more they could do to save me, so they sent me home to face death.

All of my vital organs stopped functioning and my body started to shrivel from the inside. The pain was so unbearable that even the morphine they gave me didn't help. I couldn't eat and I felt nauseated all the time. They gave me suppositories for the nausea but they did no good at all. I knew I was soon going to die. Believe me when the end comes, it is not like you think. I didn't want to go. Two weeks later I died. Before I died I made my soulmate, Susan Paul, promise me to get this message to you. Please, please I say to you with tears in my eyes, say no to alcohol the worst drug of all and if you already have a problem with it, plead with your parents, your doctor or friends to get you help.

If you are drinking at your age you are abusing alcohol. Let me warn you that you face a crisis in your life. You might live to be 47 like me and then die a nightmarish death like I did, or you could be killed or disfigured today in an alcohol related crash. And if you drink too much alcohol in one sitting, alcohol poisoning will shut down your breathing and you will die.

Alcohol is a bad drug and a bad trip. Please think about what I have told you. Look what it did to me. It could happen to you too. So if you drink, stop! If you can't stop do everything in your power to get help. If you haven't started drinking yet, don't even take the first drink. My first drink eventually killed me. I don't want to see what happened to me happen to any of you. Trust me, you don't want to suffer like I did, really, it's no joke.

God Bless you all,

With all my love,

Michael Clarke
Drummer for the Byrds

Suzy Dick was left to live with the memory of a son whose existence was cruelly curtailed by a combination of alcohol abuse and the pressures engendered by the rock 'n' roll lifestyle myth. Following his death, she was contacted by Chris Hillman who told her that he was disbanding the Desert Rose Band and curtailing touring in order to spend more time with his family. "He said Michael's death taught him that. I was glad and happy for him because I know what it can do. It can tear up families and it's not worth it when children are involved. You can't go back and re-live that, you have to do it now."

Reflecting on Michael's eventful life, she adds, "He always wanted to do things big. Later, when I looked back on it, I thought, 'Well, he did what he set out to do and lived a lifetime in those 47 years.' He played, painted and he loved. He has broken more hearts than anyone I've ever known. He was certainly a heart-throb. I can name you any number of women that still love him, regardless of what he did. There's just some people you love for special reasons and you never stop loving them."

It was especially poignant that Michael died during the festive season, a time he always loved. "Christmas was his favourite time of year," Suzy concludes. "If he was ever able to get home, he'd come for Christmas. It's ironic he died just before then. He wanted to live till Christmas, but it wasn't possible. He'd put up a Christmas tree and sat there and looked at it. The Christ of Christmas was his saviour and that's where I figure he is now, with Jesus. That's my only consolation to know that. He made his peace with God at the end. He'd been raised that way, but life has strange quirks and you get away from things you basically believe. All along though, he had a spiritual sense. I'm sure he'd never talk about that – you'd have to know him deeply. When you're dying you start thinking about where you're going, and he did. We talked about it and he told me he'd made his peace with God."

MICHAEL CLARKE: NOTES

page 409: "It was wishful thinking . . ." Suzy Dick, interviewed by the author. London/Spokane, Washington: 11 May 1997. Funnily enough, Clarke told me that he liked his family surname later in life, but he was probably teased about it in his teens. The fabrications were nothing more than idle humour.

page 410: "He skipped school . . ." ibid.

page 410: "He went to work *once* . . ." Suzy Dick, interviewed by the author. London/Spokane, Washington: 23 July 1997.

page 410: "They wouldn't take him . . ." ibid.

page 410: "How come you didn't hit . . ." ibid.

page 410: "Well, I'm going to make it big . . ." ibid.

page 411: "The beatnik word . . ." Michael Clarke, interviewed by the author. London and Manchester: 14–15 October 1989.

page 411: "They came up and told me . . ." Suzy Dick, interviewed by the author. London/Spokane, Washington: 24 June 1997.

page 411: "Michael had a background . . ." Chris Hillman, interviewed for the radio CD *In The Studio*: 1989.

page 411: "In one letter he mentioned . . ." Suzy Dick/Rogan. London/Spokane, Washington: 11 May 1997.

page 412: "He had Brian's hair . . ." David Crosby, interviewed by the author. London: 22–23 April 1980.

page 412: "Here, you can have mine! . . ." Gary Marker, interviewed by the author. London/Los Angeles, California: 28 February 2007. "Well everybody liked Michael," Marker adds. "We used to exchange jackets. I was a lot skinnier then. He said, 'That's a great jacket you've got, I really like it.' It was a leather jacket. I said, 'Here you want it, it's yours.' He said, 'You can have mine'. Then he gave him his jacket. I may still have it. Hey, this was the Sixties!" Musician Tom Slocum also remembers swapping clothes with Michael. Slocum received a jacket which Clarke claimed John Lennon had given him back in the Sixties. He thought little of giving it away. Slocum was sceptical at first but later noticed that it was the same as the one Lennon wore on the cover of *Rubber Soul.* "It was a great story," Slocum laughs. "I was out with Michael and he said, 'Listen, I'll trade you this John Lennon jacket from *Rubber Soul* for that blue peacoat you've got.' I asked him where he got the jacket and he said, 'Keith Allison from Paul Revere & The Raiders gave it to me.' I said, 'Wait, I'm trying to get this together. Keith got it from John Lennon and he gave it to *you*?' I checked it out and it turned out to be the same designer. I said, 'Jesus, Michael, John Lennon's jacket? Don't they keep that stuff in a Beatles box or something?' Michael would do stuff like that."

page 412: "I remember Toni Basil there . . ." Jim Dickson, interviewed by the author. London/Costa Mesa, California: 30–31 July 2010.

page 413: "Michael had the nerve of Dick Tracy . . ." Jim Dickson, interviewed by the author. Waldport, Oregon: 26–30 April 1989.

page 413: "I was going out with . . ." Michael Clarke, interviewed by the author. London and Manchester: 14–15 October 1989.

page 413: "The story was even reported . . ." The account of the frenzied fan appeared in the college magazine *Indian War Hoop* (April 1966) as part of a review of the Byrds' appearance at the Swing Auditorium Orange County Fairgrounds (15 April 1966), where they were supported by the Buffalo Springfield.

page 414: "It was for the Beatles . . ." Deanna 'De De' Mollner, e-mail to the author. Puerto Vallarta, Jalisco, Mexico: 24 October 2015.

page 414: "It's karma . . ." Clarke/Rogan. London and Manchester: 14–15 October 1989.

page 414: "In the end . . ." Dickson/Rogan. Waldport, Oregon: 26–30 April 1989.

page 415: "Michael was playing a tambourine . . ." Jim Dickson, interviewed by the author. London/Costa Mesa, California: 24 May 2009.

page 415: "Michael was one of those people . . ." ibid.

page 415: "When Michael first got his drums . . ." ibid.

page 415: "David was the keeper of time . . ." Dickson/Rogan. Waldport, Oregon: 26–30 April 1989.

page 416: "Michael wasn't any worse . . ." ibid.
page 416: "The first wonderful thing . . ." ibid.
page 417: ". . . Paul McCartney and George Harrison attended a Byrds session on 23/24 August 1965 . . ." CBS listed the session as 23 August, but Tony Barrow's diary in *Beatles Monthly* 27 (October 1965) suggests it was the following night. The Beatles had arrived in LA on the morning of 23 August, so it could have been either date. Presumably, the Byrds were listening to a playback or overdubbing.
page 417: "They'd get the whole song . . ." Dickson/Rogan. Waldport, Oregon: 26–30 April 1989.
page 417: "Michael went where it was easiest . . ." Jim Dickson, interviewed by the author. London/Maui, Hawaii: 7 July 1997.
page 418: "That was my style . . ." Michael Clarke, interviewed by the author. Redington Beach, Florida: 4 May 1989.
page 418: "Those guys are absolute cruel . . ." Clarke/Rogan. London and Manchester: 14–15 October 1989.
page 418: ". . . essentially, it was Mike Clarke's . . ." Roger McGuinn, interviewed by the author. Leeds: 4 May 1977.
page 419: "Whereas the Byrds is a partnership . . ." 'Agreement For Sale of Partnership Interest' letter prepared by lawyer Jay L. Cooper.
page 419: ". . . hereby irrevocably sign . . ." ibid.
page 419: "I shall be entitled to my share of record royalty . . ." ibid.
page 420: "The remaining partners . . ." ibid.
page 420: "If I so elect . . ." ibid. The remainder of the letter left little or no room for ambiguity, firmly closing the door on any retrospective action. "Appropriate announcements will be made by the partnership to the substantial effect that I have completely disposed my interest as a partner in the firm. I will execute any and all documents necessary to carry out the purpose and intent of this Agreement . . . The execution and delivery of this agreement by me and the acceptance thereof by the remaining partners shall operate as a full mutual release and discharge of all past and present claims and obligations whatsoever, whether in law or in equity, as between myself on the one part, and the firm and the remaining partners individually and jointly, on the other part."
page 420: "Michael's compensation . . ." Steve Green, interviewed by the author. New York: 3 May 1989.
page 420: "He bought a horse . . ." Dickson/Rogan. London/Costa Mesa, California: 24 May 2009.
page 421: "If they weren't damaged . . ." ibid.
page 421: "I don't think he ever mentioned . . ." ibid.
page 422: "Michael knew at a very early age . . ." David Jackson, interviewed by the author. London/Van Nuys, California: 4 October 2007.
page 423: "Chris and I were still friendly . . ." Clarke/Rogan. London and Manchester: 14–15 October 1989.
page 423: "Drummer boy . . ." ibid.

page 424: "We'd gotten the flu . . ." ibid.
page 424: "Playing with Gram was tricky . . ." ibid.
page 425: "It was funny seeing everybody . . ." ibid.
page 425: "We got caught in a blizzard . . ." ibid.
page 427: "When Michael's leg was healing . . ." Joey Stec, interviewed by the author. London/Los Angeles: 10/12 May 2009. Nobody else remembers Michael owning such an impressive collection of obscure records. His peripatetic lifestyle meant that he lived sparsely with few possessions. Then again, Clarke was known for exchanging clothes and other items of interest. People were also generous to him. It is quite possible that he picked up a cache of records over the years and could just as easily have given them away.
page 427: "They were always exciting gigs . . ." Carlos Bernal, interviewed by the author. London/Los Angeles, California: 10 April 2008. The 'Mangler' may have already ended his association with the group by this point. In the book *Hot Burritos* (Jawbone, 2008), author John Einarson reveals that Kaufman and Jim Seiter's employment "was terminated in a letter dated September 16 and signed by the four remaining band members. Hillman had never been happy with the duo's stewardship of the group." Indeed, while Hillman lavishes praise on both Frank Blanco and Robert Firks, he disparages Seiter and Kaufman with some scathing comments.
page 428: "It was always a real good time . . ." Bernal/Rogan. London/Los Angeles, California: 10 April 2008.
page 428: "Girls were always there . . ." ibid.
page 428: "Years before, he had seen Deborah Whalley . . ." According to Michael's mother, he had dated Whalley back in the Sixties.
page 428: "She became friends with Michael . . ." Bernal/Rogan. London/Los Angeles, California: 10 April 2008.
page 429: "Michael was hanging around with Earl . . ." Stec/Rogan. London/Los Angeles, California: 10/12 May 2009.
page 430: "I don't remember Michael ever coming . . ." Dickson/Rogan. London/Costa Mesa, California: 24 May 2009.
page 432: "It was a big drag . . ." Clarke/Rogan. London and Manchester: 14–15 October 1989.
page 433: "Michael was popping a handful of pills . . ." Stec/Rogan. London/Los Angeles: 10/12 May 2009.
page 434: ". . . at a club called the Galaxy . . ." Stec claims that Clarke may also have appeared with them at the Topanga Corral and Thee Experience. Stec estimates that Clarke's live performances most likely took place around this period in 1970. As he notes: "It was 1969, the concept; 1970 performing; and 1971 doing the album (without Michael)." The work was never issued and all but forgotten until Stec unearthed the tapes which were released in 2003 on Sonic Past Music as *Klatu Berradda Niktu*, credited to the Dependables.

Stec remained friendly with Clarke and their paths continued to cross with often uproarious consequences. The drummer enjoyed playing the rock 'n' roll scoundrel and, as has been demonstrated, he was always willing to crash a party when he wasn't busy entertaining on his own account. Stec remembers later meeting Clarke at the Troubadour one evening only to find himself caught up in another adventure. "The Allman Brothers were playing LA and they were staying at the Beverly Hills Hotel. Michael says, 'Come on let's see Greg.' So we went there and as we were leaving the room Michael gets this look in his eyes. I always knew it. He went to the desk and said, 'Hey we just left Greg's room. Give me a room, put it on the Allman Brothers' account – I'm Michael Clarke from the Byrds and Burrito Brothers.' We got that room and Michael's up there ordering Dom Perignon and snorting coke off hand-crafted crystal mirrors. We must have spent $13–14,000 that night. In the morning Michael's waking me up and saying, 'Come on, let's go man.' I said, 'What? Why are you dressed?' He said, 'They're checking out in a few minutes. I don't want to get stuck with this bill!'"

page 434: "It turned out . . ." Stec/Rogan. London/Los Angeles, California: 10–12 May 2009.

page 434: "Michael did the Dependables . . ." ibid.

page 436: "I was disappointed with *Burrito Deluxe* . . ." Dickson/Rogan. London/Costa Mesa, California: 10 January 2006.

page 437: "Michael Clarke is still the drummer . . ." Anonymous music paper review, dated 3 July 1971, referring to the Flying Burrito Brothers' concert at the Aquarius Theatre. The support act was Cherokee, whose eponymous album was produced by Hillman.

page 438: "If he didn't think it was important . . ." Rick Roberts, interviewed by Jerry Gilbert. *Let It Rock*: October 1972.

page 439: "It got to the point, as with the Byrds . . ." Chris Hillman, interviewed by the author. London: 28 April 1977.

page 440: "We went down there . . ." ibid. In later interviews, Hillman compressed these events, implying that Stills' Philadelphia concert (20 July 1971) happened just before he attended his recording session in Miami. In 1977, Hillman told me: "Well, I just ran into Stephen in Cleveland during his first solo tour. He called me two weeks later and asked whether Byron, Al and I might come down and do some country stuff on his new album. We went down there and, as it turned out, he wanted to start a band, so he asked Al and I to join." A few years after our encounter, Hillman was interviewed by Dave Zimmer for *Crosby, Stills & Nash: The Authorized Biography* in which he said: "I was as bored with the Burrito Brothers as David had been with the Byrds. And I was broke. So, when I saw Stills was in town, I went to his show and it was obvious he was ready to get into something else. We talked afterwards and, a week later, I got a call from Stephen. He said, 'Meet me in Miami.'" Those Miami sessions did not take place until October. This begs the crucial question: did Hillman announce he was leaving the Burritos before he was offered the opportunity to join what would become Manassas, or after? Judging from the above chronology, I believe Hillman genuinely did not know he was leaving the group at the time he met Stills in Cleveland. Evidently, in the interim, he handed in his notice and it was only after recording with Stills in Miami during October that he and Perkins were actually invited to join Manassas.

page 440: "If it hadn't been for Michael . . ." Al Perkins, quoted in John Einarson with Chris Hillman. *Hot Burritos: The True Story Of The Flying Burrito Brothers* (London: Jawbone, 2008).

page 441: "Everybody was selling . . ." Suzy Dick/Rogan. London/ Spokane, Washington: 11 May 1997. Robin had previously been married and had a daughter, Hoku, who was born with Down's Syndrome and resided at a care home in Hawaii.

page 441: "I'd known Robin from a long time back . . ." Dickson/Rogan. London/Maui, Hawaii: 7 July 1997.

page 442: "Michael really cooked . . ." David Crosby, interviewed by the author. London: 23 April 1980. The condescension was typical of Crosby when discussing Clarke, but it should be noted that the drummer already had an impressive CV. In addition to his many Byrds recordings, he had appeared on releases by Gene Clark, the Gosdin Brothers, Dillard & Clark, the Flying Burrito Brothers and Barry McGuire. Over the next year, he would also guest on albums by Roger McGuinn and Terry Melcher. The list speaks for itself.

page 442: "I wasn't satisfied with it . . ." Clarke/Rogan. London and Manchester: 14–15 October 1989.

page 443: "Robin was funny . . ." Dickson/Rogan. London/Maui, Hawaii: 7 July 1997.

page 443: "Initially, all he wanted was a backing band . . ." Roberts elaborated on this, stating: "Having been told so many times that you are a good singer and songwriter, but you need a band, I thought I'd fool them this time and have a back-up band before it started. Firefall started out as Rick Roberts And Firefall. They were to back me on a prospective album deal that was coming together, and it never did. When it fell through we had already been playing around for two or three months. That was in 1974 and we liked the way it sounded so we dropped the 'Rick Roberts' and just called it Firefall, and decided to make it a band." (Rick Roberts interviewed by Mick Skidmore. Cambridge, Massachusetts: June 1984. Printed in *Omaha Rainbow* 35: Summer 1984).

page 444: "Michael would surprise you . . ." David Muse, interviewed by the author. London/Tampa, Florida: 12 October 2007.

page 444: "He's pretty damn good . . ." Crosby/Rogan. London: 22–23 April 1980.

page 444: "Michael was definitely an enigma . . ." Mark Adzick, interviewed by the author. London/Minnesota, Minneapolis: 1–2 October 2007.

page 445: "He was loveable . . ." ibid.
page 445: "It was very difficult . . ." ibid.
page 445–446: "We used to use him in the studio . . ." Muff Davis, interviewed by the author. London/Denver, Colorado: 10 October 2007.
page 446: "There were certain fields . . ." Mark Andes, interviewed by the author. London/Austin, Texas: 30 September 2007.
page 447: "He damn near killed himself . . ." Matt Andes, interviewed by the author. London/Johnson City, Texas: 30 September 2007.
page 447: "Everybody knew Michael Clarke . . ." Adzick/Rogan. London/Minnesota, Minneapolis: 1–2 October 2007.
page 448: "He was an amazing character . . ." Mark Andes/Rogan. London/Austin, Texas: 30 September 2007.
page 448: "Michael could rub you up . . ." Muse/Rogan. London/Tampa, Florida: 12 October 2007.
page 448: "I saw them have a 'fistfight' . . ." ibid.
page 448: "It was pretty stormy . . ." Suzy Dick/Rogan. London/Spokane, Washington: 11 May 1997.
page 449: "Robin never kept Zachary away . . ." Suzy Dick/Rogan. London/Spokane, Washington: 23 July 1997.
page 449: "Michael had an incredible talent . . ." Rick Roberts, interviewed by Jason Smith. *Fantastic Expedition* 6: 2011.
page 450: "You know how Michael was . . ." Bob 'Ras' Rassmussen, interviewed by the author. London/Boulder, Colorado: 10 October 2007.
page 450: "Do you want to go to Red Rocks . . ." ibid.
page 450: "Well, I'm playing there . . ." ibid.
page 450: "I couldn't believe it . . ." ibid.
page 450–451: "I waited in the car park . . ." ibid.
page 451: ". . . farm girl from Wisconsin . . ." John Manikoff, interviewed by the author. East Lancing, Michigan: 28 September 2007.
page 451: "She was a really smart kid . . ." ibid.
page 451–452: "Joy was very responsible . . ." Adzick/Rogan. London/Minnesota, Minneapolis: 1–2 October 2007.
page 452: "She went to work . . ." ibid.
page 452: "We were a high maintenance act . . ." Mark Andes/Rogan. London/Austin, Texas: 30 September 2007.
page 453: "They got into jets . . ." Adzick/Rogan. London/Minnesota, Minneapolis: 1–2 October 2007.
page 453: "Rick made quite a bit on royalties . . ." Mark Andes/Rogan. London/Austin, Texas: 30 September 2007.
page 453: ". . . it sucked . . ." Muse/Rogan. London/Tampa, Florida: 12 October 2007.
page 453: "Michael, Larry and Rickie . . ." ibid.
page 453: "I wanted to know why Larry found it so wonderful . . ." Mark Andes/Rogan. London/Austin, Texas: 30 September 2007. "It was sick," Andes adds. "And my son was just born. I was a family guy. I was

on another plane and gradually got into doing drugs, then realizing in 1980 that Firefall were going to self-destruct." Seeing the band's demise in advance was evidently enough for Andes to quit his hedonistic dalliances. "Rick was inconsistent with his vocals and it was very hit and miss musically. We could be wonderful. We played concerts with the Allman Brothers and Heart. We opened for the Beach Boys in Europe and Japan and we played some great shows. There were some outstanding songs too. 'Sharp Shooting At The Senator' was one song that Larry wrote which was really rocking. It'll probably never see the light of day."

page 454: "I carried Larry into emergency . . ." Adzick/Rogan. London/Minnesota, Minneapolis: 1–2 October 2007.

page 454: "Everybody was doing drugs . . ." Mark Andes/Rogan. London/Austin, Texas: 30 September 2007.

page 454: "The whole thing kept spiralling downwards . . ." Larry Burnett, interviewed by Clyde Bradley for Classic Rock Revisited website.

page 454: "It affected their judgement . . ." Adzick/Rogan. London/Minnesota, Minneapolis: 1–2 October 2007.

page 455: "After the gig . . ." ibid.

page 455: "Gene Clark and Chris Hillman were partying . . ." Rassmussen/Rogan. London/Boulder, Colorado: 10 October 2007.

page 456: "Michael was one of the best hellraisers . . ." James Aderholt, interviewed by the author. London/Dallas, Texas: 8 October 2007.

page 456: "Mike disappeared to Mexico . . ." Mark Andes/Rogan. London/Austin, Texas: 30 September 2007.

page 456–457: "There was no career development . . ." Muse/Rogan. London/Tampa, Florida: 12 October 2007.

page 457: "It was David, Jock and I . . ." Mark Andes/Rogan. London/Austin, Texas: 30 September 2007.

page 457: "I said, 'Man, I'm out of here . . .'" ibid.

page 457: "He started missing rehearsals . . ." Muse/Rogan. London/Tampa, Florida: 12 October 2007.

page 457: "He was actually fired . . ." ibid.

page 458: "To be honest . . ." ibid.

page 458: "Democracies don't work . . ." Roberts/Skidmore. Cambridge, Massachusetts: June 1984. Printed in *Omaha Rainbow* 35: Summer 1984.

page 459: "Michael and I hit it off right away . . ." Manikoff/Rogan. East Lancing, Michigan: 28 September 2007.

page 459: "He was a very talented singer . . ." Muff Davis/Rogan. London/Denver, Colorado: 10 October 2007.

page 459: "I was ready to kill Manikoff . . ." ibid.

page 459: "You could hang out with him . . ." Manikoff/Rogan. East Lancing, Michigan: 28 September 2007.

page 460: "Always say yes . . ." ibid.

page 460: "Michael told me things . . ." ibid.

page 460–461: "I'd walked through the door . . ." ibid.
page 461: "I remember Larry coming up to me . . ." ibid.
page 461: "It was almost a comical, stereotypical fighting band . . ." ibid.
page 462: "Fly me down to rehearsals . . ." Aderholt/Rogan. London/Dallas, Texas: 8 October 2007.
page 462: "Sure enough he got high . . ." ibid.
page 462: "Joy married a rock star . . ." Muff Davis/Rogan. London/Denver, Colorado: 10 October 2007.
page 463: "Joy would come over crying . . ." Manikoff/Rogan. London/East Lancing, Michigan: 28 September 2007.
page 463: "Michael was a loveable character . . ." Mike Hardwick, interviewed by the author. London/Dallas, Texas: 10 September 2007.
page 463: "Don't let me catch *you* . . ." ibid.
page 463: "He took a lot of pride . . ." ibid.
page 463: "We always tried . . ." Suzy Dick/Rogan. London/Spokane, Washington: 11 May 1997.
page 464: "Jerry Jeff was a hard man . . ." Aderholt/Rogan. London/Dallas, Texas: 8 October 2007.
page 464: "He would fire him! . . ." Hardwick/Rogan. London/Dallas, Texas: 10 September 2007.
page 464: "The reason I wanted . . ." Dickson/Rogan. London/Costa Mesa, California: 30–31 July 2010.
page 465: ". . . sitting around on my ass . . ." Michael Clarke, interviewed by the author. Late night telephone call from unstated destination: May 1989.
page 465: "We should call ourselves . . ." Mark Andes/Rogan. London/Austin, Texas: 30 September 2007.
page 465: "Michael was the drummer . . ." Andy Kandanes, interviewed by the author. London/Cobb, California: 1–2 October 2007.
page 465: "Man, they broke the mould . . ." Matt Andes/Rogan. London/Johnson City, Texas: 30 September 2007.
page 466: "I said, 'Let's make this thing rock!' . . ." Mark Andes/Rogan. London/Austin, Texas: 30 September 2007.
page 466: "Mike was a loveable rogue . . ." Peter Oliva, interviewed by the author. London/Vacaville, California: 16 July 2007.
page 467: "Michael Clarke couldn't keep his dick . . ." ibid.
page 467: "I was a bit worried about Michael . . ." Trace Harrill, interviewed by the author. London/San Rafael, California: 3 October 2008.
page 467: "Michael just walked away . . ." ibid.
page 468: "I made a really big mistake . . ." ibid.
page 468: "They were an acoustic duo . . ." Matt Andes/Rogan. London/Johnson City, Texas: 30 September 2007.
page 468: "Trace had talent . . ." ibid.
page 468: "We got home . . ." Harrill/Rogan. London/San Rafael, California: 3 October 2008.

page 469: "That was the big heartbreaker . . ." Matt Andes/Rogan. London/Johnson City, Texas: 30 September 2007.
page 469: "You can't imagine how thrilled . . ." Hardwick/Rogan. London/Dallas, Texas: 10 September 2007.
page 470: "I knew all the old songs . . ." ibid.
page 470: "It was a famous old place . . ." ibid.
page 470: "It was a heavy Fender Twin . . ." ibid.
page 471: "I went upstairs . . ." Matt Andes/Rogan. London/Johnson City, Texas: 30 September 2007.
page 471: "We had wonderful nights there . . ." ibid.
page 472: "Oh man, we did a lovely gig . . ." ibid.
page 472: "Michael always had fights . . ." Aderholt/Rogan. London/Dallas, Texas: 8 October 2007.
page 472: "They were like brothers . . ." Hardwick/Rogan. London/Dallas, Texas: 10 September 2007.
page 472: "What that band went through . . ." ibid.
page 473: "It was in the middle of nowhere . . ." ibid.
page 473: "Michael and Gene went down . . ." ibid.
page 473: "Gene reached inside the car . . ." ibid.
page 473: "Everyone felt stretched . . ." ibid.
page 473: "I didn't make one penny . . ." Aderholt/Rogan. London/Dallas, Texas: 8 October 2007.
page 474: "Michael just liked being out . . ." ibid.
page 474: ". . . a couple of shows . . ." ibid.
page 474: "He'd schmoozed one of the waitresses . . ." Matt Andes/Rogan. London/Johnson City, Texas: 30 September 2007.
page 474: "Yeah, I was stuck in Lake Superior . . ." Clarke/Rogan. London and Manchester: 14–15 October 1989.
page 475: "Are you a hockey team or something? . . ." ibid.
page 475: "Matt and I were fighting . . ." Oliva/Rogan. London/Vacaville, California: 16 July 2007.
page 475: "The only worthwhile part . . ." Matt Andes/Rogan. London/Johnson City, Texas: 30 September 2007.
page 476: "Can we play 'The Bells Of Rhymney'? . . ." ibid.
page 476: "We tried it at the soundcheck . . ." ibid.
page 476: "We all wanted to finish it . . ." Hardwick/Rogan. London/Dallas, Texas: 10 September 2007.
page 476: "We had a lot of time . . ." Matt Andes/Rogan. London/Johnson City, Texas: 30 September 2007.
page 477: "He'd look at these places . . ." ibid.
page 477: "They were travelling over the Rockies . . ." ibid.
page 477: "When we got to Dallas . . ." Aderholt/Rogan. London/Dallas, Texas: 8 October 2007.
page 478: "He'd really overdone it . . ." Matt Andes/Rogan. London/Johnson City, Texas: 30 September 2007.

page 478: "We were outside the doctor's office . . ." ibid.
page 478: "Michael used to call the hospital . . ." Suzy Dick/Rogan. Spokane, Washington: 23 July 1997.
page 479: "I can't put my life on hold . . ." Matt Andes/Rogan. London/ Johnson City, Texas: 30 September 2007.
page 479: "It was Gene's band . . ." Hardwick/Rogan. London/Dallas, Texas: 10 September 2007.
page 479: "We were able to pull off . . ." Oliva/Rogan. London/Vacaville, California: 16 July 2007.
page 480: "They didn't bring any equipment . . ." Jack Carchio Jr, interviewed by the author. London/Miami, Florida: 5 July 2007. Although some internet sites claim Carchio appeared onstage with the Mike Hardwick version of the Firebyrds, this is incorrect. The only dates he played were with the truncated line-ups at Woody's Roadhouse, Burlington, Vermont on 14 December 1984 and the Rocking Horse Café, Hartford, Connecticut on 31 January 1985.
page 480: "We did 'You Really Got A Hold On Me' . . ." ibid. The song had also been an inspiration for Clark's composition, 'Little Mama'.
page 480: "Only 10 people turned up . . ." ibid.
page 480–481: "We all went to breakfast . . ." ibid.
page 481: "It seemed thrown together . . ." ibid.
page 483: "He got his little book out . . ." Rassmussen/Rogan. London/ Boulder, Colorado: 10 October 2007.
page 483: "Michael thought I was talented . . ." Manikoff/Rogan. London/ East Lancing, Michigan: 28 September 2007.
page 483: ". . . they set out on an extensive tour . . ." The line-up of the '20th Anniversary Tribute' tour fluctuated over the months. After playing for three weeks in February, there was a brief hiatus while the Band members left to fulfill other commitments. "I did 12 shows with Richie [Manuel]," Danko said at the time, then returned to the tribute Byrds to play the Midwest, East and West Coasts. Manuel was still there during May and was briefly interviewed after a show in Fairfield County, but appeared to miss a number of shows thereafter. He is also not listed on tape recordings of the first Lone Star gig.
page 484: "I had high expectations . . ." Dennis J. Kelley, interviewed by the author. London/Las Vegas, Nevada: 1 July 2007.
page 485: "It was thrown together . . ." York/Rogan. London/Claremont, California: 11 June 2007.
page 485: "I have to tell you . . ." Bernal/Rogan. London/Los Angeles, California: 10 April 2008.
page 485: "That place was like Disneyland . . ." John York, interviewed by the author. London/Rancho Cucamonga, California: 27 October 1996.
page 486: "I don't speak much on that . . ." Michael Clarke, interviewed by Paul Moratto. *Cosmic American Music News*: Fall/Winter 1986.

page 486: "That was the part of Michael . . ." Manikoff/Rogan. East Lancing, Michigan: 28 September 2007.
page 486: "Michael and I would drink . . ." ibid.
page 487: "Michael never slept . . ." ibid.
page 487: "Joy didn't like me coming round . . ." Bernal/Rogan. London/Los Angeles, California: 10 April 2008.
page 488: "He went out and pounded nails . . ." Matt Andes/Rogan. London/Johnson City, Texas: 30 September 2007.
page 488: "Michael was an amazing painter . . ." Terry Rogers, interviewed by the author. London/Nashville, Tennessee: 20 January 1997.
page 488: "I was probably the only girl he didn't try to screw . . ." Kassy Stone, interviewed by the author. London/Nashville, Tennessee: 26 May 1997.
page 489: "Michael came to the gig . . ." York/Rogan. London/Rancho Cucamonga, California: 27 October 1996.
page 489: "At that time . . ." Dennis J. Kelley/Rogan. London/Las Vegas, Nevada: 1 July 2007.
page 489: "He really liked big barbecues . . ." ibid.
page 490: "He hung out and painted . . ." Stone/Rogan. London/Nashville, Tennessee: 26 May 1997.
page 490: "There wasn't really any future there . . ." ibid.
page 490: "Joan was a real sweetie . . ." Suzy Dick/Rogan. London/Spokane, Washington: 11 May 1997.
page 491: "I didn't know anything about alcohol . . ." ibid. I relate this detailed account of Suzy Dick's battle with alcoholism from many years ago partly in order to counter Chris Hillman's gratuitous and chronologically misleading statement in the book *Hot Burritos,* where he casually informs us: ". . . he had a terrible childhood . . . she was a lounge singer and an alcoholic."
page 491: "My husband exhibited his paintings . . ." ibid.
page 491: "Once they were together . . ." ibid.
page 491: "He sat downstairs . . ." ibid.
page 491: "He was painting and trying to be an artist . . ." ibid.
page 492: "He took all sorts of drugs all at once . . ." Suzy Dick/Rogan. London/Spokane, Washington: 29 May 1997.
page 492: "Michael was always busy . . ." Bernal/Rogan. London/Los Angeles, California: 10 April 2008.
page 493: "Michael was pretty rowdy . . ." ibid.
page 493: "I'm sure that had partially to do . . ." Terry Rogers, interviewed by the author. East Alton, Illinois: 14–15 July 2007.
page 493: "When he went over the edge . . ." ibid.
page 493: "You've got to help us . . ." ibid.
page 493: "When you fall out of favour . . ." York/Rogan. London/Rancho Cucamonga, California: 27 October 1996.
page 493: "I was uncomfortable . . ." ibid.

page 494: "Michael was desperate . . ." Matt Andes/Rogan. London/Johnson City, Texas: 30 September 2007.
page 495: "Screw those guys! . . ." Clarke/Rogan. London and Manchester: 14–15 October 1989.
page 495: "I can't say anything derogatory . . ." ibid.
page 496: "McGuinn can't play guitar . . ." ibid.
page 496: "He was the best drummer ever . . ." Bernal/Rogan. London/Los Angeles, California: 10 April 2008.
page 496: "You can't call yourselves the Beatles . . ." Rassmussen/Rogan. London/Boulder, Colorado: 10 October 2007.
page 498: "This ain't no goddamn democracy . . ." Clarke/Rogan. London, early hours of 15 October 1989.
page 498: "And I'm deducting the cost . . ." ibid.
page 498: "Get this guy . . ." ibid.
page 498: "Thanks . . ." Clarke/Rogan. London: 15 October 1989.
page 498: "Make it a treble! . . ." ibid.
page 498: The account of the UK tour and Lee Elliot relationship was witnessed by the author. Although I did not formally interview Lee Elliot, I spoke and drank with her throughout the tour. While looking back at my notes and archives, I remembered writing an extensive account of Clarke's visit, which was published in *Full Circle* 5: January 1990. Headlined 'Three Days On The Road', it starts with some comments on the group's appearance at London's Dominion Theatre on 11 October 1989, then provides a revealing behind-the-scenes look at the state of the enterprise. The following was written immediately after the tour.

"The first thing that strikes you is the audience – essentially supper club in composition. Gowns, perms and perfume abound and some people are even eating chocolates. This is a Sixties revival evening, the Northern club circuit, transposed to central London, which means that the majority of the audience have as much affection for Herman's Hermits and the Merseybeats as they do for this controversial Byrds line-up. Scattered among the middle-aged couples are some younger fans and beside me are two teenage girls whose looks, dress and makeup betray an enduring debt to Cathy McGowan and Dusty Springfield, respectively. They hand jive and sway in their seats throughout the Hermits and Merseybeats section of the show and will do so again, in culturally anachronistic style, to the strains of 'Mr Tambourine Man'. In short – this is one hell of a strange evening.

When the Byrds finally take the stage, a quick head count reveals that John York is absent. It is only later that I learn the reason why. As they launch into 'Feel A Whole Lot Better', Skip Battin comes into focus – white-haired, grey-bearded and dewy-eyed. He has aged considerably since the early years and it's quite a shock to see him there onstage at 56, the Rip Van Winkle of rock 'n' roll. Battin brings a certain authenticity to the group but it does not stretch far beyond his improvised bass solo on 'Eight Miles High'. He is not given leave to sing any of his songs, which he admits are 'not appropriate and don't fit in; even you said that in *Timeless Flight*.' To some extent, he's correct, but if he is not allowed or does not wish to sing 'Citizen Kane', 'Absolute Happiness', 'Well Come Back Home' and the rest, one begins to question his actual involvement in the set-up. Ironically, Skip is allowed a couple of cameo appearances on 'Mr Spaceman' and 'You Ain't Going Nowhere' (which he previously included with the refried Burritos) but these were always McGuinn vocals during his days with the Byrds and, not surprisingly, sound totally unlike the originals – which brings us to the new 'lead singer'.

Terry Rogers, despite the Georgia drawl and silver earrings, does occasionally sound like McGuinn as a vocalist, though to what extent this is intentional is debatable. He's a good singer and judging from his two compositions, 'Pirates' and 'Tricou House' (ironically similar to McGuinn's 'Don't You Write Her Off') a fair songwriter too. Nineteen years ago, he might have been an acceptable addition to a weakened Byrds line-up but to try and step into McGuinn's shoes is nothing less then sheer folly. What emerges is not a new group at all but something closer to a showband, re-running the old hits, imitating the intonations and chord sequences yet predictably failing to conjure the magic that only authenticity brings. It's rather like witnessing a rock 'n' roll *Invasion Of The Bodysnatchers* with the songs systematically drained of real passion and emotion, even though they are generally performed with showband competence. Jerry Sorn, the guitarist who has already taken much flak for not using a 12-string Rickenbacker, cannot resist cock-rock cliches during 'Eight Miles High' which is momentarily transformed into a heavy metal excursion of embarrassingly excessive proportions.

Michael Clarke alone looks the part. Still the renowned king of 4/4, he retains a vestige of the pop star looks on which he has built a career. It is easy to imagine him playing with a group of much younger guys and maybe one day he will. There must be a more convincing route to long-term success than playing the oldies circuit and rehashing Byrds songs with only two new numbers thrown in. Even the original Byrds never had such reverence for or reliance upon their own history.

After the Dominion show I was invited back to the group's Bloomsbury hotel where we drank until the early hours. It was there that I heard that John York had been ousted. Battin, who is still friendly with his erstwhile colleague, jokes that it was the second time he'd replaced him in the group. I also learned from Skip that he is presently recording demos of 'electronic music' and seems particularly anxious to mail me the recorded results. He certainly appears to have moved a long way from 'America's Great National Pastime'. My opening question to him is: 'Hey, Skip, in 1969 it was Buddhism, 1979 it was cocaine, what's 1989?' Smiling, he explains that he was never greatly into cocaine, that was just symptomatic of the period, and 1989 was a matter of experimenting with new material and playing these 'Byrds' gigs. He still enjoys reading esoteric literature of the New Age variety and is keen to visit various London bookshops – but the late nights and gigging schedule thwart such ambitions. His future in the 'Byrds' also appears open to debate. 'As it stands at the moment, you don't know what will happen,' he confesses, with disarming frankness.

In order to learn more about the Byrds from Michael Clarke, I decided to follow the tour for a few days and that was to prove amusing and eventful. The key gig of the itinerary took place in the unlikely setting of a small theatre in Hayes, Middlesex. After a first show during which they played to 100 people, there was a long period backstage and an intriguing conversation with Michael Clarke which was to have unforeseen consequences. Having downed copious amounts of vodka (the only substance vice during the tour incidentally, which was thoroughly drug free) Clarke was in talkative mood and at his humorous best. He specifically invited me over for a chat and after reassuring the 23-year-old girl he had brought from Majorca that she was free to listen in, we spoke nostalgically about the 'old days'. This was Clarke's first trip to England since the Burritos played the Lyceum in London way back in 1970. Now that was a memorable gig, as I reminded him, though he was critical of the Lyceum as a venue. In playful mood, I told his girlfriend that several of the Ciro's girls were crazy about Michael and one girl became distraught after seeing her god with Cher. She was convinced that they were having an affair. Determined to discover the truth behind this rumour, I questioned Clarke on his love life and though he insisted that they were just good friends, he was clearly flattered by the notion. Other famous names merely brought an enigmatic smile to his face and the words, 'You're a card, man!'.

Apart from his sex symbol status in the Byrds, the other interesting aspect of Clarke's tenure was the circumstances surrounding his departure. We hit murky waters here and exchanged various conspiracy theories – or was it all innocent? That, in turn, led to questions about the possibility of a reunion of the original Byrds. He was clearly ambivalent about the idea. His public comments have been particularly acerbic and littered with swear words. In private, and away from his new colleagues, he seems less censorious and laughingly explains: 'If they gave me $1 million maybe I'd do it.' Our talk progressed to a discussion about the personalities of the original Byrds and Clarke teased me about a recent meeting with Chris Hillman. 'Did he karate chop you?' he asked while taking a martial arts stance and attacking me in mock fashion. 'No way,' I recalled. 'He was eating a banana at the time . . .'

Inevitably, the chat switched to Crosby and the many loving confrontations over the years. Michael was annoyed to learn that his drumming on the stereo version of 'Lady Friend' on *Never Before* had been replaced, though he concedes that he was not easy to contact during the time the album was mixed. In light of recent conflicts this latest affront to history obviously bites deep into Clarke's ego and with seconds to go before the Byrds are due to appear onstage, he seems more than usually psyched up.

Backstage, Clarke has already found problems with a faulty drum stool and threatens to cancel the show if a replacement is not found immediately. This is a grand, intimidating gesture worthy of Crosby and underlines that power that Clarke wields when he chooses to let loose his temper. Various minions scurry around, arguing among themselves about Michael's unreasonable, imperious attitude – but they forget his status in 1965. At the Beck Theatre, Hayes, all this big-time drama seems faintly ludicrous, but Clarke is in deadly earnest and brings the tour its finest and most spontaneous moment when he grabs the stool and walks to the front microphone to explain its shortcomings to the bewildered audience. After that, the show perks up. If you close your eyes, concentrate real hard, sing along and drink as much as Michael, then you can almost suspend disbelief that this is something akin to a poor latter day Byrds' gig. It takes an enormous amount of self-delusion and alcohol, however, and one look at the stage and the mirage will vanish. Everybody needs a degree of self-delusion during this tour, including the new guys. At every date they announce their cursory two songs to be included 'on the next Byrds album'. Of course, there is no new Byrds album to hit the racks and, indeed, the group are not signed to any label. 'There's a lot of record company interest though,' they plead. 'Well, we'll see' seems the most suitable response.

After the Hayes show I had intended to return home and resume the tour the following morning but at 2 am I find myself back at the Byrds out-of-town hotel. Stranded. Jerry Sorn buys me a drink at the bar and we exchange pleasantries until, suddenly, and totally unexpectedly, he rounds on me with a bombshell. 'I don't want you to talk to Michael about the past,' he insists. I can hardly believe my ears. "What else am I supposed to talk to him about?' I demand, incredulously. Sorn explains, rather unconvincingly to my mind, that he is protecting the interests of the other 'Byrds', who demonstrably seem in a somewhat insecure position. He concedes that the Hayes show was their best but reckons it could have been disastrous because I'd worked up Michael to a pitch beforehand by dwelling on the exploits of Hillman, not to mention various early Byrds conflicts. 'It was just conversation', I maintain, 'and anyway Michael started it off by talking to me.' The conversation continues in this vein with Sorn suggesting that I should concentrate on the 'new Byrds', not the court case or old wounds. I retort that he can hardly dismiss a 25-year history if he claims to use the Byrds name, besides which the only people that Clarke and I both know happen to be his former colleagues. What else would we naturally talk about but them? And, furthermore, why should Sorn try and inhibit my conversation with somebody else? If Michael was bored or irritated he would certainly have made it known.

By this time, the tour manager, Tony Gayle, has joined in and the discussion has switched to *Never Before*. Why did I dwell on Michael's non-drumming on 'Lady Friend'? They reckon it was a deliberate attempt to wind up their employer. 'You milked it for all you could get.'

'Oh yeah, I admit that, of course I did', I respond with ingratiating honesty. 'Wouldn't anyone who was interested in the Byrds?' They laugh uproariously at this apparent admission of guilt. Gayle then says something along the lines of 'I know what you journalists are after.' Another argument erupts as I explain that I am *not* a journalist, never have been . . . and, in any case, who the hell is interested in the *new* Byrds anyway? Nobody is likely to review any of their shows. Michael's reminiscences are hardly likely to reach the pages of the *Sun* and the current tour can hardly be described as some pop group saturnalia of Fellini proportions. So what's their problem and why are they giving me such a hard time? My argumentative indignation is apparently enough to doom me in their eyes and I am informed that they don't want me on the bus tomorrow. I'm a thoroughly bad influence and the driver insists I seek concrete permission from the tour promoter if I want to get on the bus the following morning. The fact that I do not even know the tour promoter's name seems academic in the circumstances. Although I try and continue arguing from a new rational angle, Sorn is weary, throws up his hands and storms off. So there I am stranded in Hayes and effectively exiled.

At 3.30 am, I fortuitously bump into Michael and his girlfriend and humorously explain the situation which, in shorthand, reads: I've been unceremoniously kicked off the tour! Clarke is characteristically cool and smiles wickedly before adding: 'You're on the bus. He doesn't know who he's talking to, man.' Without further ado he whisks me to reception, books me a room and threatens to deduct the cost from the lead guitarist's wages. 'This ain't no goddamn democracy!' he observes with an insightful frankness, 'those guys work for me.' He later reveals that he and Terry Rogers are effectively partners in the new venture and the power base rests with them. However, judging from the reactions during the tour, I would have thought the true power lies with Michael alone.

The following morning I find myself back on the tour but travelling to Manchester. Sorn is sitting behind me and we're not talking, probably out of embarrassment more than resentment. Clarke, who obviously saw Sorn earlier that morning, suddenly announces that, as I have already written extensively about the old Byrds, I should talk about the new line-up. I greet the announcement with an icy stare and can almost picture Sorn smiling in the background. Michael playfully strangles me to confirm my suspicions. Ignoring Clarke's instructions, we talk instead about his early coffee house days and how Crosby initially invited him to join the Byrds. Conducting an interview in such conditions is impossible and everything peters out within 25 minutes. Clarke has clearly been playing the diplomat and will continue to do so until he is alone.

Hours later, in Manchester, I offer to buy Michael a vodka. 'Make it a treble,' he enthuses, while criticizing British measures. Although he tries to defer another interview until the soundcheck I persist and we spend the afternoon discussing the key musicians in the Byrds' story. It's important for me to balance Clarke's opinions against those of the other members and generally he follows the 'traditional' storyline. In discussing the famous 'beach incident' of 1965, for example, he points the finger at Crosby for causing the disruption, a view with which Jim Dickson wholeheartedly agreed. Occasionally, Clarke shows a modest reluctance to criticize while at other times he can be damning. Chris Hillman gets a surprisingly positive overview: 'I'm not saying anything derogatory about Chris. Regardless of what he's ever done, he'll always be my friend. We used to ride horses together. He's an excellent rider. Chris and I lived together for years, played poker and had the best of times.' In many ways, these words sum up Clarke's attitude to the original Byrds far more than his other vituperative asides: 'Screw those guys, they sued me and I don't like them anymore!' Like all the other Byrds, Michael Clarke has good and bad memories of the original group and several festering resentments, yet he was always the least difficult member to deal with, mainly because his creative contribution and ambition were not those of a singer-songwriter. In view of all this, it is somewhat ironic that he should both control the name and be perceived as enemy number 1 in the old Byrds camp. Perhaps his most perceptive and revealing comment, however, came with the realization that every one of the Byrds has been the villain of the piece at different stages of the game. Derek Taylor once told me that 'the Byrds were always delightfully dangerous' but Clarke provides a more prosaic final analysis: 'None of us were easy to work with. Ever. We were all bastards. Seriously, I'm not kidding. We were very difficult. Just ask Jim Dickson.'"

page 499: "We were amazed it lasted . . ." Rogers/Rogan. London/Nashville, Tennessee: 20 January 1997.

page 499: "There were small periods . . ." ibid.

page 499: "They weren't married yet, I believe . . ." ibid.

page 499: "The day before the tour . . ." Rogers/Rogan. East Alton, Illinois: 14–15 July 2007.
page 500: "Finally, he broke down the door . . ." ibid.
page 500: "You can't pay Terry . . ." ibid.
page 500: "Curtis, it'll be OK . . ." Michael Curtis, interviewed by the author. London/Nashville, Tennessee: 16 September 2007.
page 501: "We did two shows at the Saveloy . . ." ibid.
page 501: "Michael was never much of a businessman . . ." Rogers/Rogan. East Alton, Illinois: 14–15 July 2007.
page 502: "Michael was fascinated . . ." Matt Andes/Rogan. London/Johnson City, Texas: 30 September 2007.
page 502: "He'd been drinking . . ." Dennis J. Kelley/Rogan. London/Las Vegas, Nevada: 1 July 2007.
page 502: "Look at me . . ." ibid.
page 502: "It was three in the morning . . ." Aderholt/Rogan. London/Dallas, Texas: 8 October 2007.
page 503: "Michael? . . ." Manikoff/Rogan. East Lancing, Michigan: 28 September 2007.
page 503: "He'd tell me these stories . . ." ibid.
page 504: "I never expected it to happen . . ." Roger McGuinn, uncredited interview, quoted in *Full Circle* 10: 1991.
page 504: "Counterfeit club . . ." ibid.
page 504: "Expression is man's most potent instrument . . ." Michael Clarke's valedictory tribute to Gene Clark. *Full Circle* 10: 1991.
page 505: "I was sitting on a plane . . ." Susan Paul, interviewed by the author. London/Tampa, Florida: 13 April 1997.
page 505: "Are they a baseball team? . . ." ibid.
page 505: "He really wanted to clean up . . ." Rogers/Rogan. London/Nashville, Tennessee: 20 January 1997.
page 505: "I'm not a doctor . . ." ibid.
page 506: "He looked awful . . ." Paul/Rogan.
London/Tampa, Florida: 13 April 1997.
page 506: "I don't want to be alone . . ." ibid.
page 506: "Do you usually marry . . ." ibid.
page 506: "You won't be disappointed . . ." ibid.
page 506: "There was a drastic difference . . ." ibid.
page 506: "If you think that I'm going to re-do . . ." ibid.
page 507: "The last time I communicated with Michael . . ." Dickson/Rogan. London/Costa Mesa, California: 24 May 2009.
page 507: "Michael was going through the shakes . . ." Paul/Rogan.
London/Tampa, Florida: 13 April 1997.
page 507: "He kept drinking and drinking . . ." ibid.
page 508: "He sat down on the floor . . ." ibid.
page 508: "Michael took his death really badly . . ." Suzy Dick/Rogan. London/Spokane, Washington: 29 May 1997.

page 508: "In the last few months . . ." Rogers/Rogan. London/Nashville, Tennessee: 20 January 1997.
page 508: "He went on tour . . ." Suzy Dick/Rogan. London/Spokane, Washington: 29 May 1997.
page 509: "It wouldn't have done any good . . ." Muse/Rogan. London/Tampa, Florida: 12 October 2007.
page 509: "I really need to see you . . ." Paul/Rogan. London/Tampa, Florida: 13 April 1997.
page 509: "I went to his house from the airport . . ." ibid.
page 510: "I want us to get married . . ." ibid.
page 510: "I wanted to believe that . . ." ibid.
page 510: "He was sitting in his wheelchair . . ." ibid.
page 510: "What am I supposed to do? . . ." ibid.
page 510: "No matter how horrible . . ." ibid.
page 510: "All I wanted to do . . ." ibid.
page 511: "He wanted to binge . . ." ibid.
page 511: "I'm going to miss that . . ." ibid.
page 511: "That was weird . . ." Muse/Rogan. London/Tampa, Florida: 12 October 2007. Muse still wonders whether Roberts might have changed his ways had he seen Michael on his deathbed. Instead he continued drinking for many years. "Rickie used to do coke, but it was alcohol that basically screwed him up . . . He's not drinking now. He's been sober for quite a while but he did the damage anyway." In 2006, Roberts had a fall at his house, the aftermath of which almost took him into the obituary columns. "He had swelling of the brain and didn't know it. He ended up going to hospital and almost died. If they hadn't caught it when they did, he would have died. He's started to have physical therapy but last summer, he couldn't even get out of bed. He couldn't walk and when you talked to him he couldn't really understand and had to really concentrate. But I talked to him the other day and he was very fluid. He could understand everything I was saying. He'd been through physical therapy and started walking for the first time in a year. That was good. He's had two or three chances and I think he's getting a fourth. He might even be a cat!"
page 511: "You never knew . . ." ibid. Even on his deathbed, Clarke retained his sense of humour, leaving David Muse with an unresolved mystery and another story to tell. "Michael knew how to work it. He was the teenage idol and the one who used to get the most mail. Early on, we had a tour and we were on the bus. I don't think Michael was with anybody at the time. We were partying, so everyone went up to the hotel rooms, leaving Michael on the bus with this girl. The next morning, I came down to the bus to get in my bunk and it was hot and sweaty. Basically Michael had been with this girl and had a relationship with her. Rather than go to his bunk, he went to mine. I said 'Hey, that's my bunk!' I confronted him and, of course, he denied it. He never

would admit it. The funny part of this story is that when I was with him on the afternoon/night he died, I point blank asked him again. 'Come on, Michael, tell me, was that you in my bunk?' He said, 'No, man, it wasn't me!' So he denied it all the way through to his deathbed. Michael knew the liar's code: once you lie, don't ever admit it!" Of course, it is equally, if not more likely, that Clarke – an inveterate Lothario – had forgotten the entire incident.

page 512: "I would have been there earlier . . ." Suzy Dick/Rogan. London/Spokane, Washington: 29 May 1997.

page 512: "He thought he had longer . . ." ibid.

page 513: "I just want to stand . . ." Paul/Rogan. London/Tampa, Florida: 13 April 1997.

page 513: "I feel good . . ." ibid.

page 513: "When an egret . . ." ibid.

page 513: "I went and got him one . . ." ibid.

page 513: "Thank God . . ." ibid.

page 513: "It had to be this way . . ." Suzy Dick/Rogan. London/Spokane, Washington: 29 May 1997.

page 514: "I never really got to know Lee . . ." ibid.

page 514: "We're calling it the Byrds' Celebration . . ." Rogers/Rogan. London/Nashville, Tennessee: 20 January 1997.

page 515: "The photo on the front . . ." ibid.

page 515: "The last time I saw Michael . . ." Hardwick/Rogan. London/Dallas, Texas: 10 September 2007.

page 516: "The people at the funeral hall . . ." ibid.

page 516: "I went a mile off shore . . ." Paul/Rogan. London/Tampa, Florida: 13 April 1997.

page 517: "I promised him . . ." ibid.

page 517: "We've written a letter from the grave . . ." ibid.

page 517: "*Dear Young Friends . . .* " Michael Clarke's undated letter for the Campaign for Alcohol-Free Kids. One last mystery thrown up by this letter is the contention that Clarke was drinking heavily since the age of 14. Although he may well have had his first beer at that age, it would be an exaggeration to suggest that he was drinking regularly or excessively at that point. "If he was drinking at 14, we didn't know it at the time," his mother says. "But he said he had his first drink when he was pretty young in the ninth grade. He told me he was drinking at 17, but I wouldn't say he was drinking heavily then . . . maybe he was into marijuana because we couldn't smell anything even when we thought he was drinking." During the early months of the Byrds, while staying with Jim Dickson, Clarke was not drinking at all. This too is revealing and contradicts the tone of the letter. Dickson remembers the folk crowd frowning on drinkers. Ironically, when Terry Melcher offered Clarke a shot of vodka during sessions for their first CBS album, he declined. "I doubt he drank vodka at all then," his mother adds. Chris Hillman, who played in the Byrds and Burritos with Clarke for many years only mentions his drinking heavily for the first time during his spell with the Burritos at the end of the Sixties.

page 520: "He said Michael's death taught him that . . ." Suzy Dick/Rogan. London/Spokane, Washington: 29 May 1997.

page 520: "He always wanted to do things big . . ." ibid.

page 521: "Christmas was his favourite time . . ." ibid.

3

KEVIN KELLEY

25 March 1943 – 6 April 2002

"HE was Chris Hillman's cousin." Those words might have been engraved on Kevin Daniel Kelley's tombstone as it seemed they were uttered by almost everybody that knew him in the music business. Being defined by reference to your cousin is an unenviable fate and in Kelley's case a severe injustice since he was a decent player and a formidable personality in his own right. Nevertheless, it was the Hillman/Byrds connection that emblazoned his curriculum vitae and although he appeared in several other accomplished aggregations, he never achieved a comparable level of fame. Kelley probably had the lowest profile of all the subsidiary Byrds, never once appearing in any of the 'tribute bands' or agreeing to be interviewed at length about his career. As a result, various aspects of his life, including the circumstances leading up to his death, have been shrouded in intrigue and mystery.

Kevin Kelley died in penury, but he was born into affluence. His father was a prominent Beverly Hills lawyer with links to the entertainment industry representing, among others, Rick Nelson's parents, Ozzie and Harriet. The Kelleys were wealthy enough to own property, including a holiday home on South Catalina Island. As a child, Kevin displayed an aptitude for music and first played drums in the school orchestra at grade school. He also expressed an interest in the classics. "Ever since the age of 12, I wanted to be a composer," he said. "I heard Beethoven's *Fifth* and thought, 'Hey, wow! That's what I want to do.'" Soon he became director of the Beverly Hills High School Band and joined the school choir as well as taking up guitar and piano. One of the highlights of those times was conducting the band in concert at the Hollywood Bowl. In later years, he recalled this moment with nostalgic pride.

While many of his contemporaries practised in garage groups or learned to play by ear, Kelley pursued his classical studies, enrolling for courses at both Santa Monica College and Los Angeles City College. His education ensured that he was always able to converse easily with seasoned session players and producers while also inculcating a self-confidence in his opinions and abilities as a musical arranger. If his studious background distinguished him from the average Hollywood rock drummer, then his post-college employment was even more surprising.

While most of the original Byrds agonized about how to avoid the draft, Kelley completed a three-year spell of duty in the Marines. The experience had a profound effect on his personality and bearing. His peers were puzzled by this classically trained marine, who hardly resembled a young serviceman. Now, Michael Clarke or Gene Clark you could imagine as a strapping marine, but Kelley was small and dumpy with a baby face and slightly high voice. What possessed him to join the famously tough Marine Corps?

The answer probably lay in his troubled early life. As an only child, Kelley faced a difficult adjustment when his parents separated, then divorced. He lived with his mother but his father remained a powerful, if distant, presence whose love and approval were craved, but seldom reciprocated. "After the divorce when Kevin went to live with his mom, he had a very hard time pleasing his dad," a friend remembers. "The father was a pretty cold guy. Kevin was about 5 foot 7 inches and probably weighed 135 lb, but he made it through the marines. He had to do this three-mile course with a 60 lb pack on his back. Well, he had pneumonia but he wouldn't tell anybody. Somehow he made it all the way through that course with a 105 degree fever. He was a little guy but he knew how to push himself. One time, some former linebacker started giving him a hard time so Kevin picked him up and threw him down the stairs. He was a tough little guy. And he did all that to impress his dad."

"Kevin was shattered by his parents' divorce," recalls another musician friend and confidant, Charlie Taylor. "I believe he was only six years old at the time. He was close to his mom and, of course, her sister, who was Chris Hillman's mother. Kevin's dad had been an administrative officer during World War II in General Patton's Third Army. The father remarried and I don't think he spent much time back with Kevin. He was stern. You'd think that he would have appreciated his son being in the marines enough to want to be around him. But when Kevin mentioned his father, it was always in a sad context. It was like a relationship that was never fulfilled."

Tellingly, Kelley abandoned music during his service years, declining an opportunity to play in the Marine band. Instead, he concentrated on working in communications in San Diego, then transferred to Japan for his final year. It was there that he claimed to have discovered an interest in Far Eastern religions, though nobody can recall this having much impact in his later life. The legacy of the marines was a mental and physical toughness which Kelley retained during his initial involvement in the LA music scene. In the same way that military school tended to reinforce the 'leadership' qualities of Stephen Stills in his dealings with the Buffalo Springfield, Kelley's period in the services made him appear officious or dogmatic to several of the more laid-back players he first encountered. "Boot camp is a harrowing experience," says Marc McClure, who later worked with Kelley. "You either end up in the brig for insubordination or you make it through and you're indoctrinated. How do you lose that information? Kevin was a cryptographer and this was a very powerful position. He used to say that even if a five-star general walked into his place and gave him orders, if he hadn't gone through the proper channels, Kevin could shoot him. He said, 'I had my .45 and I could pull it out and shoot him if I wanted.' I think he enjoyed that little power trip. So back in LA you suddenly have a cryptographer in the band. Are you kidding me? That's an IQ that's probably at least 20 above everybody around you. You don't get that job easily."

Kelley was still uncertain about pursuing a musical career as his classical education had instilled strong prejudices against pop and rock 'n' roll. However, like many of his generation, he was secretly thrilled by the sight and sound of the Beatles. "I wasn't supposed to like that kind of music, so I didn't want anyone to know I did, and I wasn't quite sure I did, really." For a time, Kelley backed the talented folk singer-songwriter Tim Hardin, but it was cousin Chris Hillman's elevation to celebrity in the Byrds that inspired a musical volte face. "It wasn't until I heard the Byrds that I knew I really liked rock 'n' roll. Before that I had a closed mind, closed ears and a closed heart."

During the summer of 1965 when 'Mr Tambourine Man' was topping the charts on both sides of the Atlantic, the drumming cryptographer was asked to join one of the most promising and talented outfits performing on the Hollywood circuit: the Rising Sons.

Today, they would be called a supergroup but during the mid-Sixties the impressive roll call of musicians that comprised the Rising Sons were still unknowns. Their story began not in LA but on the East Coast where blues enthusiast Henry St Clair Fredericks Jr was studying animal husbandry at the University of Massachusetts, Amherst. While there, he formed his first group, the Electras, who earned good money playing the college circuit with a repertoire of R&B covers, including material from Ray Charles, the Isley Brothers, the Contours and Chubby Checker. Early in 1961, Fredericks changed his first name to Henri before settling on the more exotic Taj Mahal. After graduation, Mahal spent time in New York's Greenwich Village, soaking up the scene and meeting many of its leading lights, including Bob Dylan, Phil Ochs and Ramblin' Jack Elliott. He also extended his blues knowledge, attending performances by Lightnin' Hopkins, Big Joe Williams and Roosevelt Sykes, among many others. By

1964, Taj Mahal had launched a career as a soloist on the folk circuit appearing at the leading clubs and coffee-houses of the era, including the famous Club 47 in Cambridge, where Joan Baez made her name. During a hootenanny he was hosting there Mahal heard a promising 12-string guitarist: Stephen Nicholas Gerlach.

Nick Gerlach was the nephew of Folkways recording artiste Fred Gerlach, a renowned teacher of folk guitar. While attending college, Nick was a regular at LA's folk haunts and spent a lot of time at the Ash Grove, meeting and befriending various musicians including the Reverend Gary Davis, whom he invited to stay at his apartment. Davis repaid this hospitality by teaching him his fingerpicking style which, combined with Uncle Fred's tutelage, ensured that Gerlach was a cut above the average player. Inflamed by adventure, the young guitarist offered to drive Davis back East in April 1964. The blind bluesman and his chauffeur spent time together at Davis' home in Long Island and attended a folk festival in Amherst. Gerlach subsequently fell in with the Cambridge crowd and after being spotted by Taj Mahal at Club 47 ended up sharing a house with the animal husbandry graduate.

In common with Taj Mahal, Gerlach understood the potency of an unusual name, so rechristened himself Jesse Lee Kincaid. Joan Baez's agent Manny Greenhill recognized the male duo's talent and booked them on the local coffee-house circuit. Kincaid soon inveigled Mahal with colourful stories of Hollywood and how it could prove a haven for aspiring folkies. In January 1965, they relocated to Los Angeles, setting their sights on such key venues as the Ash Grove, the Troubadour and the New Balladeer. That same month, the Byrds had just recorded 'Mr Tambourine Man', with Jim McGuinn providing the signature 12-string solo. Like McGuinn, Kincaid was approaching folk with a Beatle beat and even looked like a Byrd with his carefully coiffured bangs and Cuban heels. Stranger still, Kincaid had previously dated, and came close to marrying, McGuinn's new girlfriend and later wife, Dolores DeLeon.

One evening, Kincaid's colleague Ryland Cooder, who had

also been a pupil of Fred Gerlach, guested with the duo during their set at the Ash Grove. Ry, the son of folklorists William and Emma Cooder, was already a prodigious guitarist with a vast, eclectic knowledge of ragtime, blues, R&B, country, and much else. He even had some studio experience, which was a rare commodity. The Ash Grove collaboration worked so well that Cooder invited them to appear alongside him and his jazz bass guitarist friend Gary Marker at the annual Teenage Fair held at the Hollywood Palladium. Marker next recruited drummer Ed Cassidy which led to the formation of the Rising Sons, a name coined by Kincaid.

The Rising Sons' artistic remit was to reinvigorate country/ blues for a younger, modern audience. Kincaid's Beatles/Dylan interests meant that they were capable of offering some commercial folk rock in a vaguely Byrds' vein. The jazz backgrounds of Marker and Cassidy added to the complex musical mix. Initial performances were well received and, according to local legend, a stoned David Crosby once leaped upon a table at the Troubadour to lead a heartfelt chorus of "long live the Rising Sons". There was also record company interest, most notably from CBS, home of the Byrds.

At this juncture, there was a line-up change when Ed Cassidy was forced to take time off after injuring his wrist. Initially, the group considered hiring a temporary replacement, but then there was a rethink. "Ed either broke his wrist or pulled some ligaments," Gary Marker recalls. "We went to Chris Hillman and asked him whether he knew any drummers and he said, 'Well, why don't you try my cousin, Kevin? He's a pretty good drummer.' So we auditioned him and a couple of other people and said, 'OK, it's Kevin.'"

Jesse Lee Kincaid felt that Cassidy's playing may have been too jazzy for the band while Marker maintains that the bald-headed drummer's age was also causing concern. "Ry Cooder was saying things like 'He'll be too old and if we get famous he'll never cut it on the road' and Taj Mahal had the same feeling. They were both wrong of course. He was still playing occasionally in his mid-eighties." Cassidy's departure was confirmed when they discovered that he had been tinkering on another project (the Red Roosters) featuring his 14-year-old soon-to-be stepson Randy Wolfe (later Randy California) which would eventually evolve into Spirit.

So, by luck rather than design, Kevin Kelley became a Rising Son. "Kevin's mother had a house in Beverly Hills and he had a van, so we could move our gear around," Jesse Lee Kincaid remembers. "We practised from 10 am every day at his mother's place, so my first impression of him was that he was the guy who gave us a place to rehearse. He seemed very together, but a little too punctual. It wouldn't be long before his way of organizing things began to clash with those of other members of the band."

Both Marker and Kincaid confirm that Kelley joined just as they were signing to CBS Records. Their audition demos for Columbia, which had featured Ed Cassidy, were overseen by the senior head of A&R Allen Stanton, whose strict studio protocol caused the same problems that the Byrds would encounter when they worked with him on their third album. "He was just abysmal," complains Gary Marker with a typically blunt appraisal. "His big hit was Ruby & The Romantics' 'Our Day Will Come'. We spent a whole night recording stuff which was just junk because he had it all divided up. I had to stand on top of a chair to see Kevin because I couldn't hear him. I said, 'This guy has no idea how to record a live performing band' because that's what we were. It went badly." Taj Mahal was equally critical, complaining about Stanton interrupting a session and questioning Cooder's use of a bottleneck guitar.

It wasn't Stanton's technical abilities that were ever criticized but the generation gap and lack of musical empathy between the parties. Realizing this, Stanton made the eminently sensible decision to assign the group the services of Terry Melcher. As Gary Marker recalls: "When Terry walked in, we went 'Oh, boy! He's going to have us doing "ding ding ding" with 12-strings,' but he wasn't like that at all. He wanted to know what *we* wanted to do! He had a very open mind about stuff and spent a lot of time experimenting and finding out what we were comfortable with. Finally, he decided that the best thing was to record us live with vocals, maybe a scratch vocal and come back and do it again. We did a lot of acoustic stuff with him and that was his idea. He said, 'Play acoustic, I'm doing *these* songs, I'm setting up the microphones and vocals. Everything's live, let's just see what we get.' It was a good deal and he was not inflexible. He was willing to try just about anything."

Recordings commenced in September 1965 at the same time that Melcher was busily working on *Turn! Turn! Turn!*, the Byrds' second album, "We would often pass them as they were finishing their session and we were coming in to do ours," Kincaid remembers. For Kelley, it was quite a coup to be on the same label and share the same producer as the Byrds. "Columbia Studio A was a former radio station at CBS," explains Gary Marker. "It was huge. They used to call it the basketball court because it was so large and there was a big control room. We'd come in, set up, go into the booth and Terry would say, 'What do you want to do today?' Brian Wilson might wander in or Bob Dylan. You're sitting there doing basic tracks and all of these giants in the business would be watching you play or hanging around in the booth. You'd look up and think, 'Are they listening or are they just chatting? What's going on?' Everybody knew Terry and they would drop by his recording sessions. Even Dylan, for Christ sake. And he was thought of as Mr Mystery back then in his polka dot shirts. He'd walk in and say, 'Hey, Terry, what's going on, man?'"

If the musicians were a little starstruck, then they were soon brought down to earth by Melcher's darker machinations. Just as he had done with the Byrds, Terry made a powerplay for the Rising Sons' publishing, even suggesting that Columbia publicist Billy James should take on an additional management role. Jim Dickson, who co-owned both the Byrds' management and publishing interests, had successfully stood up to Melcher, but the Rising Sons had no experienced intermediary to argue their case.

The result was instant conflict. "Terry came from a wealthy background and he was used to calling the shots," says Kincaid. "He wanted to manage the band and he also wanted us to sign 100 per cent of all the publishing on our material . . . I resisted and he got very ornery and said, 'Look, sign the deal or you're *never* going to work in Hollywood again. I'll make sure you get dropped from the label.' He got mean and put a real bad vibe on us."

Melcher's threats were largely bluster, inspired and encouraged by his rapacious and greedy stepfather, Marty Melcher, who clearly understood where the real money lay in popular music. "Basically, Terry was a likeable guy," says Marker, echoing the views of many others who had personal and professional dealings with the producer. "There was all this stuff going on, but it was just the way business was done at the time. He wasn't an evil person. Terry didn't need the publishing, but he needed a sense of independence. Columbia Records had a strict policy that you didn't have anything on the side. If you did, you could be fired. So you couldn't have any independent agreements with their assigned artistes, you just worked out your producer's deal. They gave you a really big title but they really didn't pay much money. So everybody was working an angle. Essentially, Terry said, 'If you don't sign up with us, we can bury you. We just won't record you or put records out.' It was a straight up threat. Everybody got upset about it. I said, 'Well, this is what they do. This is the way the business is. I'm not that opposed to it if it gets us off the ground. Everybody can make their money and it will be fine and we can do what we want. Let's go with it and see what happens.' The others said, 'No'. Cooder didn't want to do it and Taj was just incensed about the whole thing."

The ill feeling sowed discontent in the ranks and a lingering belief that Melcher may have disowned them or even sabotaged their career. This was not the case. Melcher had failed to acquire the Byrds' publishing but worked tirelessly promoting their singles and championing them to other executives at Columbia. The unsavoury publishing incident with the Rising Sons would probably have been forgotten if they had managed to translate their potential into a hit single, but their commercial appeal was limited. "Terry tried to get in there and make some sense out of it all," Kincaid admits. "We spent a lot of time in the studio and actually recorded quite a bit looking for that elusive hit. In those days if you didn't have a hit single you didn't get an album. We were in the studio for a year or so trying to get that hit . . . Blues artistes weren't having hit singles at the time. Everyone liked us in the clubs. Live, it went down great . . . We were constantly working, mostly on Sunset Strip. We did something like ten days opening for Otis Redding at the Whisky A Go-Go. We worked all the time and we were popular, gigging a lot. When we weren't working in the clubs at night, we'd be in the studios in the daytime. There was a sudden onslaught of constant work and recording. It was very fast and intense . . . I had a little knack of being able to imitate songwriting styles and like everybody else copied the Beatles. By trying to do that I was able to generate some innocent pop ditties that were in that genre. They weren't great songs because I hadn't developed my understanding of life to say anything, but they were imitative in that mould so in clubs people responded well to our sound. We could do the Beatley stuff and the blues. We covered all of the styles and it was working really well. But I think we got lost in the mix with Columbia. They were too big a company to hang in with us."

For all their talent, the Rising Sons were not the most harmonious bunch. Personality clashes were always likely to occur in such a musically eclectic set-up. As the last member to join, Kelley might have been expected to take a subsidiary role in the decision-making, but that was not his way. Rhythm sections often produce tight musical and personal friendships, but Kelley and bassist Gary Marker were frequently at odds with each other. "Kevin was a difficult person to get along with," Marker complains. "I thought he was obnoxious. A know-it-all. A lot of drummers are like that. They think they know everything about music. There was something about his personality which was irksome and it worsened as time went on. I tried to be friends with him but it just got worse and worse. That's all I can say. I don't know how else to put it. If you had to deal with him then, you would know how difficult he was to get along with. He wanted to rearrange all the songs. He'd get real sniffy if you didn't want to do the songs his way. So it just wasn't fun. He was classic passive-aggressive. 'Well, if that's what you want to do, do whatever you want.' And he'd flay his arms. He was very juvenile in his behaviour then, but we all were for Christ's sake. You get a bunch of young guys in a room with all that testosterone flying around and they have the delusion that they're going to own the world . . . If things get out of hand they'll just turn the volume up. It can get pretty funny after a while."

Although Marker's comments were characteristically fiery, he conceded that Kelley was a strong musical asset. "Kevin was a good drummer. There wasn't anything wrong with the way he played drums. Some of his musical ideas were good but he was just so obnoxious about it that I couldn't get along with him. He had a nice, high voice, he was almost a boy soprano. We would try to get him in on choruses and stuff like that. Sometimes he could do it and sometimes he couldn't or he wanted to spontaneously rewrite his harmony part. I would try to work with him but I was struggling anyway because I was essentially a jazz bass player trying to do all this solid rock. My nature was to meander and play whatever the hell I wanted to and it didn't fit real well at the time. Finally, they let me make up my own stuff. 'They' being mainly Cooder who was musically the rock in the band. Everything was held together by him. If he stopped playing, it would start falling apart. If he'd had eight arms he would have tried to do all of it at once. He could play the bass lines and all the high ends, add-ins and foreign parts – the whole deal. He could do anything. Taj could've done it too. He didn't quite have the technique Ry had, of course, but he was very savvy."

Kincaid avoided any confrontations with his fellow players, but recognized the frosty group dynamics. "Kevin was a little too much on paying attention to details. I know Ry was particularly irritated by him. Ry was a guy who was very individualistic and he could find fault with things for his own particular reasons. He'd clash easily with people. With Kevin, there was a little bit of an edge there. He was a detail-oriented person who wouldn't just let it flow. I think that aspect of his personality dogged Kevin throughout his life. He was in the Marines and that was something foreign to us at the time. I think he wanted to have some leadership role and maybe that might have been part of the clash. Musically, he wasn't the leader but personality-wise perhaps he aspired to that."

As the most pacific member of the group, Kincaid sometimes attempted to lighten tensions by making fun of Kelley's gravitas. "Kevin had the full cartoon voice, almost like Elmer Fudd," Marker laughs. "Jesse used to write songs and sing in the background: 'Mississippi mud, don't look now, everybody here looks like Elmer Fudd.' And he was thinking about Kevin. Of course, Kevin never knew what was going on."

Kelley's lighter side was more often expressed when he was away from the group. Teenager Matt Andes, whose elder brother Mark was later a member of Spirit, was a keen follower of the Rising Sons and a slide guitar disciple of Ry Cooder. Andes admired Kelley and told him of his musical ambitions which, at that point, did not extend much further than playing informally with friends, including his elder brother Mark, at Chatsworth High School. When Kelley learned that they were entering the school's 'battle of the bands' competition, he mischievously agreed to accompany them. "We were huge Rising Sons fans and couldn't believe we were getting Kevin Kelley to play with us in this little high school band. It was like 'We're not worthy!' As a joke we came up with the name the Matt Andes Twist Combo. Someone misheard it and wrote down the *Mad* Andes Twist Combo which was an even better name!"

One of Matt Andes' friends was due to play in a rival band but after hearing Kelley limbering up felt so intimidated that he withdrew his name. Andes was giddy with excitement and laughter. "Kevin just sat in and kicked ass for us at this silly battle of the bands and we actually won the sucker. We had a blast, let me tell you. I was already playing slide and had a bright electric dobro.

The sound was like country rock or ethnic music compared to the other bands who were just playing covers. It was pretty cosmic what Kevin did for us. Kevin was such a dear person, a wonderful little guy, a great drummer, and very ahead of his time."

In February 1966, the Rising Sons issued their first and only single: 'Candy Man' b/w 'The Devil's Got My Woman'. It was a testament to Melcher's and Columbia's confusion about how to market the group. As an uneasy compromise they chose a couple of blues staples, but elected to spotlight Kincaid on both sides in preference to Mahal. "That was curious because I was not a very good singer," Kincaid confesses, "and Taj was clearly the lead singer in the band. So that was a guaranteed failure." Mahal was indignant about the decision, and with good reason. Had the recording succeeded, CBS would no doubt have continued to feature Kincaid's vocals and diluted the blues elements.

While recording sessions continued intermittently, Melcher decided to pursue the Tin Pan Alley route and unearth a new song from a name writer. Goffin & King's 'Take A Giant Step' was a canny choice and the group were much relieved when Taj Mahal was reinstated as lead vocalist. In a striking attempt at pop modernity, they completed a psychedelic arrangement, loosely based on the Yardbirds' baroque experimentation on 'Over Under Sideways Down'. Melcher was still worried that Mahal's vocals sounded too black and suggested some McGuinn-style method acting. "Imagine you're a white guy imitating Ray Charles," he told the bemused singer. Jesse Lee Kincaid was given the arduous task of tutoring his bandmate in the finer points of vanilla phrasing. "I remember conducting Taj's vocals in the studio trying to get him to sing as white as possible and keep him on track. We were trying to get him to be a pop singer on 'Take A Giant Step' instead of going with the blues. It was weird. They were coming from such a white bread approach. There wasn't a blues R&B vibe happening in the company so they didn't get it."

Although the song gained some premature airplay in San Francisco, CBS abruptly vetoed its release, supposedly fearing that it would be banned as a drug song because of the lyric's invitation to "take a giant step outside your mind". The composition later appeared on the B-side of the Monkees' debut single 'Last Train To Clarksville' without provoking any raised voices from the moral guardians of American youth.

Any hopes of an attendant album were all but dashed by the decision to cancel the single. Disillusionment quickly followed. "I think Taj began to realize that he didn't need this band to be who he was," Kincaid acknowledges. "I'm sure other people were saying, 'Look, get rid of these white guys – you're the man.' He was beginning to see that was the direction too. Subsequently, we broke up. Well we didn't break up. What happened was that Ry kind of left. He said 'I'm quitting the band.' Then Taj said, 'Well I'm quitting too unless we change our name to just Taj Mahal.' He issued that as an ultimatum. Then it just ran out of steam. We'd done all we could do together. We weren't great mates or anything like the Stones – who came from the same place and had lived together. We were going on the wrong track to nowhere fast."

The group had one last stop before oblivion beckoned. In an attempt to alleviate tensions they dismissed Kevin Kelley. Kincaid and Cooder had to scour Sunset Strip on a motor scooter before finding a replacement, Frank Lupica. "He played with us at our final gig at the Santa Monica Civic. That was the only one that Kevin didn't play since joining. Taj did stay with Columbia, but we moved on."

Kincaid subsequently recorded a couple of singles for Capitol, while Mahal and Cooder ignited the pages of blues and rock history. Marker, who later worked with Captain Beefheart, formed a new group Fusion which, as its name suggested, threatened to bridge the gap between rock and jazz. Tellingly, despite his withering comments earlier, Marker chose Kelley as his new drummer. In spite of past personality clashes, there was no doubting his qualities as a player.

The Fusion project had actually begun during the final days of the Rising Sons when Marker started jamming with saxophonist/woodwind player Harvey Lane, keyboardist Ricky Luther and guitarist William (aka Bill/Billy/David) Wolff. Kelley formed a lasting friendship with Wolff who is generally regarded as his closest ally and ultimately the administrator of his estate. "Kevin was a very energetic guy then," Wolff stresses, "a go-getter and pretty ambitious." Although Fusion would later sign to Atco Records for a one-off album, their prospects during Kelley's tenure were deflatingly dull.

Struggling for regular cash, Kevin was reduced to supplementing his income working at a men's clothing shop. It was at this point that an unexpected vacancy arose in the Byrds. All it took was a phone call from Chris Hillman to transform Kelley's career. "He said, 'Sorry guys, see you later'," Marker concludes.

The Byrds were at their lowest ebb at the end of 1967. During the final months of the year, they had undergone a purge unprecedented even by their self-destructive standards. David Crosby had been unceremoniously fired and Gene Clark uneasily reinstated before falling victim to familiar demons. In a final twist of the knife, the rebellious and unsettled Michael Clarke was excised from the line-up, leaving McGuinn and Hillman as the only survivors. The title of their new album *The Notorious Byrd Brothers,* suggested that they were renegades united in camaraderie, but this was a gang in name only. A Christmas joke among their detractors was that McGuinn and Hillman were about to reinvent themselves as the new Simon & Garfunkel. Despite the festive gloom, Kelley's sudden arrival allowed them to continue playing live, although it was no easy task replicating the complex studio experimentation that had highlighted their recent work. From a fan's point of view, the appointment of Kelley was a welcome distraction from the bewildering exodus of recent times. At least the Byrds were still alive and the myth that they were notorious brothers was given a certain credence by the presence of a genuine family member, even if it was a cousin.

As the first non-original Byrd, Kelley accepted his subsidiary role with good grace. There was no question of adding his name to the Byrds' CBS contract and, in common with every one of his successors, Kelley would remain a salaried employee for the duration of his membership. This was hardly surprising since McGuinn and Hillman were currently renegotiating their CBS deal for a substantial sum of money, which was to be shared with their much maligned manager, Larry Spector. The Byrds was no longer a democracy but a duopoly, although that did not mean that Kelley was not part of the line-up. Contractual realities notwithstanding, he was a Byrd, as every publicity hand-out and photograph would confirm.

Even in their streamlined state, the Byrds were able to make a living, though they were forced to work harder than ever and extend their gigging schedule into previously uncharted backwaters. "I intermittently hung out with Kevin during the time he was in the Byrds, but he was pretty busy," Wolff recalls. "When he joined the Byrds, suddenly he had a pretty decent pay cheque and rented a little house down in Topanga which at that time was regarded as very desirable. I recall he was making $300 a week which we all considered a lot of money then."

Performing as a trio was proving so difficult that a decision was made to add a fourth player, ostensibly to play keyboards and enhance the vocal blend. Less than two months after Kelley's recruitment, Gram Parsons joined the ranks. So began the group's headlong pursuit into country music, complete with a new image, a groundbreaking appearance at Nashville's Grand Ole Opry and a series of recording sessions culminating in the belatedly acclaimed *Sweetheart Of The Rodeo* on which Kelley excelled. His drumming is outstanding, most notably on 'Nothing Was Delivered' where he fashions one of the greatest percussive finales in the Byrds' illustrious history. Although it remained unheard in his lifetime, he was even allowed a vocal cameo on his composition, 'All I Have Are Memories'. It was a good enough performance to have won a place on the album but was regrettably omitted.

The drummer immediately bonded with Gram Parsons and would speak of him fondly in later years, recalling his Southern charm, worldly intelligence and musical passion. Although Parsons' period in the Byrds would eventually end in turmoil, Kelley enjoyed their interaction. "Kevin was a peace and love kind of guy, who looked like Howdy Doody," remembers roadie Jimmi Seiter. "Obviously, Gram and Kevin were completely different people. Gram was more outgoing than any of them at the time. Kevin stayed to himself more. All the Byrds basically stayed to themselves. If I knew that Gram was going to end up being such a cult star I would have paid more attention then."

The combination of old and new Byrds in the line-up nevertheless worked well. There was little doubt that the recent recruits re-energized the group at a time when it was close to complete collapse. Kelley was fortunate to visit Europe twice with the Byrds during the spring and summer of 1968 and initially all went well. McGuinn's former wife, Dolores, remembers Kelley as a very reserved character who seemed content to remain in the shadows of more powerful egos. When the Byrds famously visited Stonehenge in the company of Mick Jagger and Keith Richards and a small retinue of wives, girlfriends and close associates, Kelley's name was conspicuously absent from all accounts of the proceedings. Yet he was there, a quiet, humble presence. Seiter has similar memories of a somewhat introverted character who may have joined in some backstage revelries but was more likely to be spotted sitting in a corner, his face buried in a book. He seemed almost unrecognizable compared to the thrusting, argumentative figure described by Gary Marker in his account of the Rising Sons. Everyone's portrayal of Kelley as a Byrd suggests a humble, undemonstrative figure, respectful, even deferential, towards McGuinn and Hillman.

The Kelley-era Byrds' first foray to Britain was a low-key showcase at the recently launched underground venue, Middle Earth. In an era when the rock press was in its infancy, there was little likelihood of a lengthy review. However, at least one prominent music writer was in attendance: Pete Frame, founder of *ZigZag* magazine. The publication later included a feature mentioning the show and, significantly, it was Kelley's contribution that was singled out for special praise. Two months later, the Byrds were booked to play their biggest show in years, jointly headlining a charity event at London's Royal Albert Hall attended by over 4,000 people. It was to prove the biggest audience of Kevin Kelley's performing life.

Although rock history books focus on the problems that the Byrds encountered performing country music in 1968, their Albert Hall show promised much. A new single 'You Ain't Going Nowhere' was played frequently on radio and restored them to the UK Top 50 for the first time since the glorious 'Eight Miles High'. CBS' press office did a sterling job securing the group a key interview in a national newspaper, an outlet that still tended to treat pop music sparingly and often with disdain. Britain's best-selling music paper *New Musical Express* even went as far as agreeing to review the concert for a full-scale feature. The stakes were now unexpectedly high.

From a fan's perspective, it is difficult to convey the feeling of expectation, even fear, that this concert provided. Over the years, the British music press had regularly featured guest columnists from America, several of whom had commented unfavourably on the Byrds' live performances. Memories also lingered of their controversial UK tour of 1965, when they had suffered a critical mauling. Returning to play a highly publicized show at the Royal Albert Hall in front of several thousand people, including various members of the rock aristocracy, was a bold move. As reported in *Volume 1*, the show was a triumph. The rhythm section sounded particularly strong, no small achievement at the Royal Albert Hall, and the concert provided a career highlight for Kelley.

The Byrds seemed destined for great things, but their euphoria lasted less than 12 hours. When they awoke the next morning they were greeted with the scarcely believable news that Gram Parsons had quit. This was immediately followed by their nightmare tour of South Africa. While the Byrds received blanket condemnation for their poor performances, Kelley's drumming was praised for its power and precision. One local journalist even claimed: "Kevin Kelley must be among the world's best." Overall, the tour proved a debilitating experience which sapped morale and effectively signalled the death knell for this particular line-up. With McGuinn in emotional retreat and Hillman on the brink of leaving, Kelley found himself increasingly isolated. "Although he was Chris' cousin, they didn't seem very close at that time," notes McGuinn's ex-wife, Dolores. "I don't think they hung out together. Kevin's downfall was the timing of his arrival in the Byrds coinciding with South Africa. Poor guy. I guess in the family tree of the Byrds he was probably the lowest on the totem pole."

The appointment of Clarence White in place of Gram Parsons might have stabilized the Byrds but only worsened Kelley's position. White had his own agenda and was keen to bring in his former Nashville West buddy, Gene Parsons, as the next Byrds' drummer. Even Parsons was coy about replacing Kelley and could find little to justify his own appointment on musical terms, beyond the vague suggestion that the Byrds may have required a heavier, rock 'n' roll drummer. Yet, only two months before in South Africa, Kelley had reportedly broken his drumsticks while playing 'Eight Miles High' with intense abandon. Ironically, Parsons had more in common with Kelley than he did with any other Byrds' drummer. When Gene was fired four years later, the excuse offered by McGuinn was exactly that levelled against Kelley: he was too much of a country player who couldn't play 4/4 rock 'n' roll time. It was political rather than musical reasons that ended Kelley's tenure in the group after less than a year. He was a victim of history.

Kelley's contribution to the Byrds has provoked markedly contrasting comments from critics over the years. His studio work has been widely applauded, not least by his replacement in the Byrds, Gene Parsons, who insisted his drumming on *Sweetheart Of The Rodeo* was top notch. The only criticisms of his live performances concern his timing, although they appear to be over-stated. McGuinn, speaking in 1969 when he had no reason to be diplomatic, reckoned that Kevin's playing was fine, "except under pressure on stage. If you had a big crowd, he'd sort of break up a little bit – his timing would go bad." It was no doubt these fleeting moments that provoked the more acerbic comments of Jimmi Seiter printed in *Volume 1* of this book. In hindsight, he still feels that Kelley's playing was erratic, but admits that there were extenuating circumstances. "I realize I was critical because percussion and rhythm instruments were what I grew up playing. When you listen and it's not sitting in a groove then you know it's not right. You couldn't mix it then. With the sound systems today you could add more and no one would know. Those bands would never have made it in today's world, man. But the business was where it was at. The Byrds were a phenomenon for their time. It was just different and the band was different. This was country music, so Kevin played with brushes sometimes and used timbales instead of tom-toms. A weird sound. Michael Clarke had been very laid-back and had feel. Between his foot and his hi-hat hand he had a really good feel and he could hit a groove. Rushing and dragging was a problem with him, but that was OK. For me, Kevin was always rushing. It was very frantic. Clarence would raise his eyebrows at it because it was probably just blowing his mind. But that was just the way Kevin played. He always played on top of the beat and wouldn't lock down and sit in a groove. It was weird, that's all. He was a good jazz drummer and here he was playing in the Byrds when they were a country band. Go figure!"

As 1968 closed, Kelley faced a period of readjustment. Rejected by the Byrds, his world was suddenly turned upside down. Although there were any number of Byrds' offshoot bands, Kelley never played in any of them. The closest he came to the Flying Burrito Brothers was a brief stint backing songwriter Shannon O'Neill, who was also employing bassist Chris Ethridge and steel guitarist Sneaky Pete Kleinow. Kelley's relationship with his cousin Chris Hillman remained tellingly distant. They would never play together again.

As well as losing the Byrds, Kelley also suffered in love. "Lynn Naugh was Kevin's girlfriend and she was absolutely stunning," recalls Matt Andes, who dated her identical twin sister, Terri.

"They had these dancer bodies and dark reddish hair. Both of them were gorgeous." Kelley seemed besotted with Lynn, but his brief period in the Byrds had already taken its toll on their nascent relationship. Some of his friends believe that he was distracted momentarily by the allure of fame and treated Lynn cavalierly, much to his later regret. When she ended the romance, he was crestfallen. Over time, this doomed love affair began to take on immense significance in his life as neurotic introspection festered into maudlin regret resulting in endless dark nights of the soul. "Kevin seemed emotionally reserved," Jesse Lee Kincaid considers. "But he pined for her till his dying day. She separated from him and he remained broken-hearted about that for the rest of his life. He never married."

In an attempt to kickstart his career, Kelley formed a new group, the Train, teaming up with Bill Wolff, his pal from Fusion, and 'Dr' Eric Hord, the multi-talented guitarist and soul mate of the Mamas & The Papas. While some fancifully assumed that the doctor received his title by distributing prescription drugs, the truth was more mundane. He had acquired the nickname after purchasing a doctor's bag to carry his instruments. Hord was an innovative musician, equally capable of playing jazz and raga, and a welcome addition to the group. Although they practised regularly at Kelley's house, the project failed to develop and was soon abandoned. Meanwhile, session work provided some much needed income and networking contacts. Kelley accompanied several members of Spirit, including the Andes brothers, while working on John Fahey's 1969 album, *Yellow Princess*. That same year, he and Wolff contributed to Frank Kinsel's *At Home*, which also featured flautist Jesse Barish, an aspiring singer-songwriter who happily turned out to be a Rising Sons fan. "I remember going to Ciro's in Hollywood and the Rising Sons were just mind-blowing. So I was aware of Kevin, even before we met. He was a famous guy, and I wasn't!" Another attendee at the Kinsel session was keyboardist Grant Johnson. "I'd known Grant since 1963," says Wolff. "Now I don't throw this word around lightly, but he's a bona fide genius. A ballsed out jazz player, who could play virtually any style with absolute conviction. If you heard him play ragtime you'd think he was Scott Joplin. He was phenomenal." The Johnson connection enabled Kelley to team up with another talented group, in urgent need of assistance.

Fever Tree had trekked to LA from Houston, Texas, under the guidance of married journalists Scott and Vivian Holtzman, who took on their production, management and lyric writing. During 1968, they logged a minor hit with 'San Francisco Girls (Return Of The Native)'. Their promotion in LA included billboards advertising 'Fever Tree Is Coming', coincidentally echoing the Byrds 1965 UK promotional campaign with its ominous warning 'The Byrds Is Coming'. A further point of comparison was their adoption of 'Hey Joe' in their stage act and later on record. While Kelley was touring with the Byrds, Fever Tree were on their tail, appearing at several of the same venues, including the Kaleidoscope. But after a whirlwind flurry of three albums for Uni/MCA, Fever Tree were in deep trouble. Drummer John Tuttle was gone, along with keyboardist Rob Landes, and fresh blood was required in the studio to complete another album for Ampex Records.

Sadly, *For Sale* turned out to be a posthumous work, despite the best efforts of the Holtzmans who wrote three of the songs, 'You're Not The Same (Baby)', 'Hey Mister' and 'Girl (Oh Girl) Don't Push Me', and oversaw production, bringing in several members of the Wrecking Crew. On the album sleeve, Kelley is listed first in the credits which was over-flattering. Among the hotchpotch of material is an interesting take on Love's 'She Comes In Colors' and a strong Jim Morrison-like vocal from Dennis Keller on 'Come On In'. The work culminates in a side long, 13-minute version of 'Hey Joe', complete with Grant Johnson's distinctive keyboard arrangement which ingeniously incorporates the 'Needles And Pins'/'Feel A Whole Lot Better' riff, as if he were attempting to create a musical concordance of the Byrds. The Fever Tree studio sojourn with Johnson left Kelley even keener to form a new group, preferably from scratch. After returning from a tour with Phil Ochs, he fell in with a salon of musicians whom he would work with in various permutations over the next five years.

Although usually portrayed as a loner by his contemporaries and associates, Kelley retained strong links with key friends and, improbably enough, found himself surrounded by radical thinkers, steeped in the communal ideals espoused by the counterculture. Chief among these was a UCLA psychology student, Michael Barnes, an anti-war activist and hippie proselytizer who had joined acid guru Timothy Leary in the impressively titled League Of Spiritual Discovery (LSD). Barnes was essentially a love and peace protester with an endearingly straightforward and utilitarian outlook. "I didn't think that killing people was a very productive thing to do." He organized several love-ins and was a prominent figure at the LA version of the Human Be-In which took place in Elysian Park on 26 March 1967 and inspired David Crosby's evocative composition, 'Tribal Gathering'. Barnes was astounded by the number of people that turned out for the Easter Sunday love-in and, intoxicated by the potency of the counterculture, became radicalized by the movement. Barnes was living at a communal headquarters on Franklin Street in Santa Monica where he plotted against his own university using the vaguely agitprop tactics advocated by the provocatively titled Guerrilla Theater. Clad in Grim Reaper costumes and death masks, Barnes' group carried a large coffin to the campus grounds, symbolizing the fate of those non-students who had been drafted and killed in Vietnam. "We would go and attack UCLA," he recalls. "We climbed up on one of the roofs of the building and threw down 5,000 paper planes saying 'Stop The War'. We were crazy, but we had great times. Not one person living in the Franklin Street house went in the Army – not *one*." The FBI took a dim view of Barnes' 'craziness' and monitored the activities at Franklin Street with increasing vigilance, interviewing neighbours and appearing at the house regularly. On one occasion, they made three visits during a single day. What they found was an expanding commune of students and aspiring musicians, whose passing ranks now included several of Kevin Kelley's musical outer circle: Bill Wolff, Jesse Barish and occasional Crazy Horse pianist John Blanton.

By 1970, Barnes had moved to Nichols Canyon where he set up a new commune, assisted by the ubiquitous Wolff. Meanwhile, Barish and Blanton were playing in Malibu in a short-lived group Trees, who sought the patronage of John Phillips as producer and saviour. Phillips declined, but invited them to join him on an extensive summer tour, promoting the connoisseur's classic, *Wolfking Of LA*. Barish had the privilege of playing the familiar flute part during the nightly performance of the Mamas & The Papas' 'California Dreamin''. By the time he returned to the Nichols Canyon commune in the autumn, Barish was surprised to see a new occupant: Kevin Kelley.

Kelley was housed in a room adjacent to the downstairs garage and, uncommonly for a commune, retained his independence and privacy. Despite his background as a former marine, he had no problems sharing living quarters with several anti-war protestors. "We talked about it," Barnes recalls, "but it never bothered me. By that point Kevin's consciousness had been raised and he'd changed his perception about the usefulness of war. Vietnam had become a debacle and, marine or no marine, I think Kevin had seen the light. He was on board with most of the thinking in the house. No one in that house was violent. Kevin was fairly quiet, kept to himself and spent a lot of time in his room. I remember him as a very nice man. I really enjoyed talking with him. We had some wonderful debates. I saw him as a wise man and a very gentle soul. I don't think I ever saw him get angry with anyone. No one in the house was like that."

While Kelley was settling in, Jesse Barish continued to target Hollywood in an attempt to forward his songwriting career. One afternoon, he was wandering around near A&M Records when he spotted producer Denny Cordell. The young entrepreneur was already a legend in the industry thanks to his gold-star production of Procol Harum's 'A Whiter Shade Of Pale', along with various hits from Georgie Fame to Joe Cocker. Cordell was currently riding a wave of success courtesy of *Mad Dogs And Englishmen*, the celebrated double album featuring a 21-musician ensemble led by Joe Cocker and Leon Russell. Barish buttonholed Cordell long enough to win an audience with Cocker and his bandmate Chris Stainton in Laurel Canyon. Exhausted from touring, Cocker was unreceptive to Barish's entreaties and showed scant interest in his songs. Cordell, who had recently established Shelter Records with Leon Russell, was still on the lookout for new artistes and encouraged Barish, who duly recorded some demos, backed by his friend Bill Wolff on slide guitar. "Cordell really liked the vibe that Wolff and I had," says Barish, who was amazed to be offered a solo deal. The intention was to concentrate on Barish as a singer-songwriter, using Wolff as back-up. It seemed a sound idea on Cordell's part as the new decade looked set to be dominated by confessional troubadours. All four members of Crosby, Stills, Nash & Young were careering into solo endeavours, while others, ranging from James Taylor (*Sweet Baby James*) to Joni Mitchell (*Ladies Of The Canyon*), Carole King (then recording *Tapestry*) and many more, seemed destined for superstardom.

While Cordell envisaged a folk/blues recording, Barish was already considering a new direction. "I had a different vision, I thought I was Keith Richards!" It was Michael Barnes who had first voiced what sounded like scripted dialogue from a Broadway hippie musical: "Hey, man, why don't we form a band together or something?" Barnes was undeterred by the fact that the only musical instrument he played was the Jew's Harp. Once the marijuana smoke had cleared, it was agreed that he would be better placed working as Barish's manager, negotiator and spiritual adviser. Meanwhile, Kevin Kelley agreed to join the enterprise, using the downstairs garage for endless rehearsals. He even suggested a suitable bass player, Kenny Kaufmann, whom Wolff seconded.

"Kevin fitted in perfectly with the vibe of the band," Barnes recalls. "There was a whole lot of smoking going on, and Kevin really liked his smoke. Hashish was the drug of choice and there were various others in the group that also loved it so he fitted in. He never missed a rehearsal, stoned though he might have been. I mean this guy would smoke hashish from the moment he got up to the moment he went to sleep. I don't know how he could carry on like that. If I smoke hash, I'm toasted for three hours. I'm done. I can't talk. My linearity goes right to hell . . . But Kevin just carried on, man. He lived that. He was still organized. He'd go out and practise. We'd hear him beating the crap out of those drums downstairs. He'd wake everyone up. We'd say, 'What the hell are you doing, man, it's nine o clock in the morning?' 'I'm practising!' Kevin was very meticulous. This guy set up a schedule and he stuck to it. I can testify to that because he woke me up, regularly."

Wolff was also capable of getting zonked out on occasion, while Barish enjoyed adding some hallucinogenics to the mix. "The band lasted about a year and a half," he says, "but it seemed like 12 years. We would lock ourselves in Kevin's room and take LSD and that felt like a year or two right then and there in one night! We'd have some marathon [sessions]. Kevin and I had a lot of really good times. He was a sweet guy and we instantly became friends. We used to love to take long drives, talk and smoke together. He didn't smoke cigarettes, just the other. And he drank like an Irishman. He loved his Irish whiskey."

Cordell was invited over to Nichols Canyon and agreed to sign the band to Shelter, although Barish was the only artiste named on the contract. Barnes remained firm but cool throughout the negotiations and, according to Wolff, secured an advance of $15,000. "Jesse was certainly not the most talented musician there, but the best songwriter and he wrote all the tunes," Barnes explains. "You couldn't beat the back-up with Wolff, a great musician, and Kevin brought a lot to the band. He brought stability, in spite of the fact that he may have been stoned on hash. He was the heartbeat of the band and a wonderful addition. I don't think the band would have lasted as long without him."

At Cordell's suggestion, the group relocated to Skyhill, Leon Russell's home studio in the Hollywood hills, where they spent an age recording what would become their sole album. "It was kind of an insane asylum," says Wolff. "We recorded this album without any supervision whatsoever. It took us about a year. It was a lot of fun but I think it would have been better if Cordell had helped us out with the producing." Instead, it was engineer Fred Hill, who had the responsibility of seeing through the project.

As the work was nearing completion, they faced an unexpected crisis. By this stage, they had settled on the name Jesse, Wolff & Wings, an apposite comment on the history of the band which had begun as a duo, then added a couple of wing players for the rhythm section. One afternoon, Barnes was called into the offices of Shelter's distributor, Capitol Records, and told that the band must change its name. Paul McCartney was about to launch his group Wings and Capitol, his label in the USA, were keen to avoid causing any confusion in the marketplace or risk any possibly of offending the great Beatle. Barnes' protests were brushed aside. Thankfully, during a subsequent band discussion, Kelley came up with a solution, advocating the alternative spelling 'Whings'. His logic appeared to be borrowed from the Byrds whose magic 'y' had resulted in a brilliant group title.

The long overdue *Jesse, Wolff & Whings* finally emerged in the spring of 1972. Stylistically, it sounded closer to the roots rock and boogie of Little Feat or the Doobie Brothers, rather than the folk rock of the Byrds or the slicker country stylings of the Eagles. Wolff's dominant slide guitar work added an authentic edge while Barish's flute solos seemed unusual in such musical company. Kelley provided a solid backing and could also be heard clearly on backing vocals, most notably on 'Another Song For You'. Barish composed every track on the album, generally spurning the familiar love lorn lyrics of the early Seventies singer-songwriter in favour of earthier songs about the city, the highway or life on the road. Despite its promise, the work was largely ignored by critics and record buyers alike. Barish was not entirely surprised, having despaired of his vocal contribution along the way. "I look at it as an exercise in identity crisis," he now says.

"There were a few moments that were OK, but I just did my vocals so many times that I blew my voice out. I can hear the strain there. I don't sound relaxed and I don't like the sound of my voice. We were pretty loaded and pretty out there."

A promotional tour saw the group supporting Leon Russell, Spirit and Hot Tuna. Kelley's experience was a valued asset on the road. "He worked hard and was very organized," Barnes notes. "That was evident when we travelled. We had a road manager but Kevin was careful with his equipment and he always helped the roadie put his stuff away. It was never 'I was a Byrd and you're going to schlep my stuff around!' Kevin was part of everything. That spoke a lot about his character. When we were miking him, he was very conscious of how he sounded. He wasn't one of those drummers that liked to overwhelm everybody, although he certainly wanted to make sure that everything was miked properly. He was very meticulous and I really respected that."

The band continued for a time, often playing in the Bay Area of Marin County alongside such West Coast favourites as Seatrain and Copperhead. Barish then became uncertain about the group's future and disillusioned about the poor-selling album. "It was a dictatorship," joked Wolff, when asked about the group dynamics. "Jesse was the star of the band for sure. What he said went. Kevin could be outspoken but we didn't have any problem with that. I don't think we even discussed musical direction. It was just how the arrangements should be put together. In that sense it was democratic musically but it wasn't democratic on the level of who was going to be in the band or what kind of business decisions were going to be made. That was all Jesse."

Increasingly, Barish seemed haunted by Cordell's original vision of his career, as if realizing that he had taken a wrong direction. "I just wanted to be solo again and do it as Jesse, so I let everybody go, Bill, Kevin and everyone." A new musical direction followed, with Barish offering some mellow "swing, jazzy, blues tunes". After travelling to Nashville, work began on another album, for which Wolff recruited keyboardist Grant Johnson and drummer Steve Swallow. Soon after, Cordell pulled the plug on the project. "Cordell was great," Barish concludes. "He saw something in me but he eventually dropped me. He said, 'I can't afford to mentor you while you figure out who you are.' He saw potential but didn't know how long it was going to take for me to actually get somewhere. I think I disappointed him when I turned [from a singer-songwriter] into Jesse, Wolff & Whings with a rock 'n' roll record. I don't know what Kevin felt about it all, but we stayed friends afterwards. I always liked his drumming. He was unique. A great musician and a true talent. Kevin was trained in music theory and he could read and play timpani in orchestras. I've always been a hippie musician, but he was a *real* musician."

Kelley showed no visible signs of disappointment about the failure of Jesse, Wolff & Whings. Instead, he returned to life as a garage player, this time renting a capacious house at 4450 Colbath Avenue, Sherman Oaks, with a fresh set of musicians. Jim Messina's then girlfriend Kathy Patrick had first introduced him to Geoff Gillette in 1970 when the keyboardist had arrived in Laurel Canyon seeking fame for his extravagantly titled band, Captain Electric & The Flying Lapels. After slogging around the LA circuit, the band fell apart in 1973. Gillette briefly worked with the talented, hard-drinking, deep-voiced, folk troubadour Tim Rose before wisely embarking on a new career as a sound engineer. Gillette was invaluable to Kelley as a sounding board for new ideas while his engineering skills ensured that an array of musicians regularly appeared at the soundproofed studio they'd set up in the back garage. One of their roommates for a time was the intense but likeable Alex Dmochowski, a Polish bass player and songwriter whose teasing pseudonym, Erroneous, added an air of mystery to his already complex persona. Having toured with John Mayall, Dmochowski elected to extend his stay in America and was invited to appear on Frank Zappa's 1972 album *Waka /Jawaka*. When a rival ratted on him to the Immigration Services, they dramatically appeared at Kelley's house and removed Erroneous, who was subsequently deported.

Among the many visitors to the Kelley sanctum was Capitol recording artiste Marc McClure, who had recently recorded a couple of albums with Joyous Noise and was working on a solo album. His manager, Gary Downey, had heard of a new band being put together and encouraged his client to audition. Essentially a country rock outfit, Bandana was fronted by a promising singer, Patti Peyton. Working with vocalist Michael McRae, she had previously recorded demos with steel guitarist Al Perkins, then decided to put a band on the road. McClure and Kelley were eager to assist.

"Once Kevin was in, boy he was in!" says McRae. "He was a great drummer. Always right in the pocket. Always steady. If he had ideas to share, they were good. He was positive and supportive. It wasn't about money either. He just loved being part of it. He sang on a couple of tunes and we did them live. It wasn't just Patti and me upfront. Kevin sang and had some neat songs. We'd often get together, smoke a joint and play some music. He was one of the most gentle people I ever met in my life. One of those 'old soul' characters. He was pretty even keeled when we were together, and he was a gentleman." All of the band, except Kelley, relocated to a house in Woodland Hills. One of their neighbours, drummer Erik 'Deputy' Dalton of Country Gazette fame, was then working at the Sundance Saloon in Calabasas and secured Bandana a regular booking. "We played there frequently, indoors and outdoors," McRae remembers. "On the porch, we'd all be crowded around the drums playing. It was a lot of fun."

The Sundance became Kelley's favourite watering hole and he jammed there regularly alongside fellow drummer Barry Jenkins, another ex-Animal Hilton Valentine (guitar), and former New Animals/Family bassist John Weider. Others spotted onstage included Andy Summers (later of the Police) and world-champion fiddle player, Byron Berline. Even blues guitarist Luther Tucker was there. Sometimes the players would come back to the garage in Sherman Oaks and continue playing through the night. "Kevin could play any style with anybody," says singer-songwriter Charlie Taylor, then a Sundance habitué in search of glory. "He'd get up there and play five hours at a whack. People would be getting up and down from the bandstand and he'd still be playing. He loved jazz too. Kevin got me connected to a lot of people in the music business. He said my writing style reminded him of Gram. I guess that was because I came from the South. He was one of the first people that ever validated me as a songwriter. Kevin was so generous. He took me places and introduced me to all his friends. Everybody. He was proud of me and took an almost parental interest, always giving me advice. A great friend."

Geoff Gillette also spent many late nights in Kelley's company, usually discussing the meaning of life. "He was a melancholic Irishman, but he was so engaging. He was deep and philosophic and it was really fun to hang out with him." Two subjects rarely mentioned were his time in the Byrds and his feelings about Chris Hillman. "Kevin had a hard time after the Byrds, going from being a rock star to struggling in the Valley with various musical endeavours. He never lost his musical dreams though. His relationship with his cousin Chris was distant and he was too proud to ever ask for help. Kevin was very independent and wanted to be indebted to no one. He was a loner."

Kelley's excessive dope smoking continued throughout this period and there was soon evidence of stronger substances. "Kevin was a connoisseur of the pharmaceuticals," Charlie Taylor explains. "He always had the best of everything. If it was cocaine he had the best, if it was hash, it was the same . . . He always had the best reefer in town. Sometimes I could not feel my face. I remember being in his room one time and he had what must have been a quart bottle full of hash oil. I had no idea where it came from."

More alarmingly, Kelley briefly became involved in some small-time drug dealing after befriending a well-known dealer from Topanga Canyon who used an import business specializing in pottery and rugs from Central America as a front. "Obviously, there were drugs coming in with those shipments," says Taylor, "and I think that's where Kevin was getting a lot of the stuff that he did." Kevin's contact considered himself a relative innocent, caught up in the romance of the cocaine trade which offered easy money and guaranteed outlaw status among his many musician pals. Corruption, betrayal and death are the other handmaidens of serious drug dealing as the neophyte importer was to discover in April 1972. One heavy-duty supplier found himself in urgent need of substantial cash and descended upon Topanga to connect with Kelley's dealer friend.

The psychotic supplier did not take this trip lightly. Timing is often crucial in such matters and his inexperienced quarry became concerned when he was unable to produce the required money, having expected 24 hours' grace to conclude matters. What might have been considered an administrative hiccup in any other line of business rapidly turned into a bloodbath when the supplier freaked out and shot one of the dealer's partners twice in the head. The wounds were fatal. He then attempted to shoot the dealer who was carrying a gun and responded in kind, killing the supplier with a single shot. Although he had acted in self-defence, Kelley's dealer fled the scene, leaving the bodies behind, along with a substantial amount of money. The corpse-filled car was discovered the next day and the news sent shock waves across the Canyon. It was a timely reminder to the peace-loving community of the darker aspects of the hippie dream. As Mark Andes concludes, "That's when it all changed . . . that drug-related shooting changed the vibe in Topanga." For many, it was never the same again. Some residents responded in the same way as those Hollywood celebrities affected by the seismic shock of the Manson murders. Improved home security, a wariness of strangers and a decline in unrestrained partying were all part of this immediate panacea. A few, including Andes, felt so disillusioned that they vacated the Canyon. It was left to former Topanga resident Neil Young to sum up the macabre mood in his chilling but riveting song 'Tired Eyes', a bowdlerized reconstruction of the killings in which the double homicide is transformed into a confused tale about a man "who shot *four* men in a cocaine deal".

Kelley was stunned by the shootings, not least because several of his closest friends were living in Topanga. Even Charlie Taylor was affected by the incident, having previously been told by Kelley that the music-loving, gun-wielding young dealer had been intending either to finance a record or hire a producer on his behalf. "That was a wake-up call for Kevin," says Taylor, "but it wasn't enough of a wake-up call." Kelley compensated for his loss of supply lines by temporarily increasing his alcohol intake. "I guess that's why God invented whiskey so that the Irish wouldn't conquer the world," Taylor muses.

Although Kelley's drinking was not serious at this point, there was already evidence of its maudlin effects on his personality. "Kevin was a cynical person," his friend Michael Barnes agrees. "It would manifest itself when you talked to him about politics or people. Often there was a thread of distaste. A mistrust of people. We all got along well and I know we loved each other. But I believe he generally saw the human race as leaving a whole lot to be desired and that was expressed in conversation." This encroaching misanthropy was also noticed by Wolff, who concluded that "his sense of justice may have caused him to bump up against people. He felt outraged when the little guy got screwed, which happens most of the time. So, in that sense, he had a chip on his shoulder but he was a very smart and reasonable guy in some ways."

With the Byrds, Fever Tree and Jesse, Wolff & Whings now history, Kelley felt the need to extend himself once more. His perennial interest in jazz remained strong and his musical circle widened to embrace several virtuoso players/performers. Kelley always enjoyed the challenge of jamming but never expected to be asked to join a band of such technical calibre. That was about to change as he embarked on arguably the most promising and ambitious project of his career.

The trio of Art Johnson (guitar), Bill Plummer (bass) and Lynn Blessing (vibes/percussion/keyboards) were seasoned jazz musicians with an already bulging list of guest credits on countless albums and concert billings. Prior to meeting Kelley, they had found common ground on the road. "We were travelling around playing for different symphony orchestras doing modern work that involved electric guitar, electric bass and vibraphone set to a full orchestra," Johnson explains. When the orchestra tour ended, Johnson suggested that the trio should branch out from their classical/jazz environs and try something new. Art already had one foot in the rock world having taught guitar to various players, including former Byrd and fellow Topanga resident, Skip Battin. Observing lesser players become household names and sometimes millionaires, Johnson started writing his own songs which he considered "passable tunes". "I said, 'Let's just get something simple together.' I was fingerpicking a Yamaha guitar, Bill was playing upright bass and Lynn had a small set of drums and one cymbal covered in towels, just like Jim Keltner loved to do." Sensing that this was probably a final throw of the dice to reach a wider audience, they named themselves Last Chance.

Last Chance were not blessed by good fortune. One evening, following a promising recording session at Wally Heider's, Johnson and Blessing returned to their home in Silver Lake only to discover that it had been burned to the ground. Their bandmate Bill Plummer came to the rescue, providing blankets, bedding and new clothes, then finding them a temporary repose in the office and living quarters of a friendly manager/agent Gary Downey. Intrigued by their tapes and sympathetic to their current plight, Downey agreed to represent them. Another of his clients, Kelley's pal Marc McClure, visited the office one afternoon, heard the story and listened to the tapes with a keen ear. Having got nowhere with Kelley on the recent Bandana project, McClure offered his services as an additional singer, songwriter and guitarist. Now all they needed was a new name.

Plummer and Johnson took off on a road trip and, while passing through Idaho, spotted a sign which read: Gas, Food & Lodging. They both agreed that it would make a memorable band name, like a pastiche of Crosby, Stills & Nash. After returning to LA, they played their first gig with McClure at the Ash Grove and went down well. There was even a touch of showmanship during the set. Johnson remembers: "Marc and I had a trick where I would reach over and pick his guitar while he was playing and he would turn around, go under his guitar and pick my mandolin. Our left hands would still be doing the work but our right hands would be on each other's instruments. It brought the house down every time."

McClure invited the band to Kelley's garage where they rehearsed and jammed. They soon found they had much in common. Johnson expressed his admiration for Kevin's playing on *Sweetheart Of The Rodeo*, while Plummer reminisced about working with his former compatriots Ry Cooder and Terry Melcher during sessions for Pamela Polland's group, Gentle Soul. Even Lynn Blessing could offer a post-Kelley Byrds' connection having recorded 'Child Of The Universe' on his 1969 album, *Sunset Painter*. The camaraderie was so strong that Kelley was invited to complete the line-up, allowing Blessing to concentrate on keyboards and vibraphone. "Wow, think about that," Charlie Taylor exclaims. "Kevin's playing with Bill Plummer, Artie Johnson, Lynn Blessing and Marc McClure. There has to be a great deal of respect there because all those cats were wonderful jazz players and there's Kevin, holding down the foundation."

Inevitably, the group received a residency at Kelley's favourite tavern: the Sundance Saloon in Calabasas. Already, they had developed a tight vocal harmony, enhanced by some delicate arrangements from Johnson and McClure. Their musicianship ensured that they stood leagues apart from the many boogie bar bands on the circuit. "Wolff and I were jazz players and Marc had a very definite improviser's consciousness," says Johnson. "When he played solos they weren't something he made up in his room, he just closed his eyes and let rip." Audiences were thrilled by their playing but largely oblivious to their backgrounds, let alone their pedigree as session players. "It's a very simple formula," Johnson remarks. "You've got five guys who've all been there. Marc had been on Capitol Records, had the big push and was almost a star; Bill had been playing with everybody from Miles Davis to the Rolling Stones [*Exile On Main Street*]; I'd done the same with Paul Horn, Tim Weisberg, Lena Horne, Pat Boone,

O.C. Smith etc; Lynn was a sideman for Gábor Szabó, John Klemmer and Tommy Peltier. And Kevin had his professional arena with the Byrds. So you have these sidemen that nobody had really heard of who were very creative and could deliver the goods. Some nights went better than others but I cannot remember that band ever having a railroad accident or a derailment.

"Kevin was a laid-back, quiet guy but very aware of what was going on. He had a professionalism because he'd been under the spotlight. You see that's what divides everybody. You've got millions of musicians, but who has been there? Who has played in front of thousands, been in studios or backed up famous people? Those are the real musicians. The rest are really well-intentioned amateurs, no matter how well they play. That's my opinion. Kevin was a guy who'd been under the pressure of the spotlight and so he knew what to do and when to do it. Now his drumming wasn't always really precise, but it never bothered me because he always had the right pattern for the right song."

Bill Plummer provided a similar assessment: "Kevin had a lot of technique and we were able to sit down and play well together from the very beginning. A wonderful drummer. I enjoyed working as a bass player with him all the time. We had a real good lockdown time-wise and he was never one to insert. He never said: 'You should play it *this* way.' We were always very automatic in what we did with the music. He had a great concept of the things that we were doing beyond infusing jazz into that band. We were more like a country, bluegrass, jazz band with a lot of solos and improvisation."

Away from Kelley's garage, Gas, Food & Lodging also rented time at Buffalo Gap Rehearsal Studios. It was a canny arrangement by Bill Plummer who sublet the studio to other musicians. "He used to rent to Linda Ronstadt and all kinds of people to rehearse there," says Johnson "They'd pay our bills so we could rehearse all the time and do some recording." As he had always demonstrated, Kelley was also a pragmatist who contributed significantly to the band's organization, as well as offering valuable musical input. "There were constant band meetings,"

Johnson recalls, "because we were trying to figure out how to get out of the ditch and get something going. Kevin was a good observer as any good musician should be and he was a plain speaking businessman. To him it was really cut and dry. Either we do it this way and it works, or we do it that way and it doesn't work. There were no grey areas."

Interestingly, the forthright views which had caused Kelley so much resentment from certain quarters within the Rising Sons appeared to have the opposite effect in Gas, Food & Lodging. "Sure, he was opinionated," says Marc McClure, "but that didn't bother me. I had my own opinion and everybody's allowed one." Kelley's history as a marine cryptographer encouraged close friends to nickname him 'Crypto', a title no doubt partly inspired by Superman's dog, Krypto. Others noticed that beneath the drummer's quiet persona lay a wry and engaging humour. "Oh, Kevin was a wonderful, bubbly guy," says Plummer, a personality assessment that several contemporaries, more aware of his darker side, would consider wide of the mark. "He was very friendly, very musical and always had a good attitude. I can't say enough about him as a person. He was a great guy. It's true he had a dry humour. Maybe he got that from the service. Things are a lot drier there. When I found out that he had been in the Marine Corps I was very surprised because he had such an easy-going personality. I never saw him angry. *Ever.*"

One taboo subject for Kelley in most of his bands was any discussion about the Byrds. "It was the past and Kevin had a lot of stuff inside him," says Jesse Barish. Members of the Rising Sons agree. Yet, in Gas, Food & Lodging, he was comfortable enough to offer a rare laconic aside. "It's true that he didn't really reference the Byrds that much," Art Johnson admits. "He was moving on now that he was in our band. But the occasional comment would come up. Like he'd joke, 'You're not going to play 12-string are you?' That kind of a deal. Kevin was fine with me. He didn't have the vibrancy of a Skip Battin but he was a positive guy who was there to do the deed and play."

Gigging locally and recording voraciously were not sufficient to keep Gas, Food & Lodging in comfortable circumstances. Always in demand, they continued to accept session work, not only from the jazz greats but also from several cult figures seeking success in the golden age of the singer-songwriter. Art Johnson appeared on Tom Waits' debut album *Closing Time* in 1973 and the following year undertook a European tour with Tim Buckley which included the cream of Warner Brothers' new roster of artistes. Kelley also kept busy, working with Geoff Gillette, then joining the complete line-up of Gas, Food & Lodging (bar Blessing) on an important guest session that would remain in the tape vaults for over 30 years.

Judee Sill was a minor sensation among connoisseurs of the singer-songwriter school when she released her eponymous album in 1972 on David Geffen's new label, Asylum. The record was a revelation, showcasing Sill's crystal-clear diction on songs marked by a personal symbolism and laden with erotic and religious imagery. Compositions such as 'The Lamb Ran Away With The Crown' had a transcendent quality with a distinctly Blakean innocence and charm set against a graceful melody. The ethereal 'The Archetypal Man' couched its mystery with classical similes ("fleeter even than Mercury") while 'Enchanted Sky Machines' threw in some post-apocalypse, escapist science fiction elements of the Crosby/Stills/Kantner ('Wooden Ships') and Neil Young ('After The Goldrush') variety. Others like the overwrought, dramatically orchestrated 'Jesus Was A Crossmaker' presented a peculiar cosmology that somehow managed to incorporate silver angels and reflections on Jesus' working life with bitter memories of betrayal and abandonment by a rock 'n' roll bandit and heart-breaker, generally assumed to be the romantically perfidious heart-throb singer-songwriter J.D. Souther.

Sill's second album *Heart Food* bombed following a falling-out with her mentor, David Geffen. Though she may not have known at the time, Sill was already on Asylum's deportation list while recording her final record in 1974 at Michael Nesmith's Studios in Van Nuys. Nevertheless, she found the perfect session players in Gas, Food & Lodging who intuitively connected with her eclectic mix of classical baroque, country-tinged folk and subtle jazz leanings. It was not a world away from the ambitious blend of styles that they were offering to audiences at the Sundance Saloon.

Kevin Kelley established an instant rapport with the complex songstress. They shared dark troubled pasts, haunted by memories of unresolved relationships with fathers or father figures. Musically, they were a cut above most of their rock contemporaries by virtue of their classical tuition. Plus, they were both excessives. Kelley chain-smoked joints and had recently been fraternizing with drug dealers and supplying small amounts of dope to friends in defiance of the law. Sill had already done time and run up a $150-a-day heroin habit, the memory of which hovered uneasily over her career. Another striking coincidence was that Sill's middle name was Lynn, the same as Kelley's lost love and immemorial muse. The intense, neurotic romanticism that always threatened to blight Kelley's future love life was echoed in Sill's obsessive devotion to J.D. Souther who "went into the chambers of my heart and left it in disarray," as she eloquently explained. Finally, they were both animal lovers. Sill habitually imported rare reptiles while Kelley was constantly followed around by his faithful Doberman, Rufus. "He loved Rufus and when the dog died I'm sure he felt like he'd lost his best friend," Charlie Taylor reminds us.

Taylor was intrigued by the rapport between Kevin and Judee and like many others was thrilled by her arcane mystical artwork and bohemian household, which promised Bacchanalian pleasures way beyond the experience of the young Kentuckian. Whether the Kelley/Sill relationship was platonic, romantic or sexual – or all three – remains conjectural. "Kevin dated her for a bit," says Taylor. "He took me over to a party at her house one time. I was just in awe of all these people at the party but Kevin seemed to know them all. Judee was very nice to me and obviously very talented. They dated a few times."

The selling of Gas, Food & Lodging was proving harder than

expected. There were several tantalizing moments, but a major deal was forever left floating in the air. The Doors' producer Paul Rothchild turned up at the Sundance on A& R patrol one evening and stayed for their entire set. Still nothing happened. "Bill, Art and I used to drink a little bit of tequila and go to the record companies and try to shop a tape, but we really didn't get anywhere," Marc McClure laments. Manager Gary Downey was also industrious and knocked on the doors of Capitol, RCA and Warner Brothers without success. Given their jazz backgrounds, it was hoped that the group might appear on some movie soundtrack. Downey was a former Hollywood stuntman, among whose credits was taking the tumbles and falls of Captain Kirk (William Shatner) in the science fiction series, *Star Trek*. But even his connections could not transform the band's fortunes. As Art Johnson says: "There were a lot of laughs and a lot of trials and tribulations because we put so much time in and so much energy. We recorded so much and it never really went beyond level one which was a shame because it deserved to. Especially when you consider the talent of the guys."

The Sundance Saloon continued to provide sweet relief for Gas, Food & Lodging, although sometimes it must have seemed as though the audience was made up entirely of their musical peers. Among the visiting musicians were Judee Sill, Charlie Taylor, Jesse Lee Kincaid, Skip Battin, Rick Vito . . . and many more.

The Curtis Brothers, who lived around the corner from Kelley in Sherman Oaks, became Sundance regulars and were so impressed by Gas, Food & Lodging that they adapted material from their set. "What a great band," Michael Curtis exclaims. "We went to see them in Calabasas at Kevin's request and they played this song called 'Fade Away' [composed by Art Johnson]. We fell in love with it and recorded it on our first Polydor album. It was a powerful ballad. We were prolific at the time and I think that was the only song we didn't write on the record."

By the mid-Seventies, the passion and belief that everyone felt about Gas, Food & Lodging were starting to wane. Lynn Blessing was the first to leave, enticed away by an irresistible offer from Al Jarreau. The foursome soldiered on but their progress was always likely to be interrupted by extracurricular pursuits. An interregnum occurred when Art Johnson embarked on another extensive tour, this time with a second generation line-up of the Association. Kelley, meanwhile, played locally, briefly appearing with singer Valerie Ford, playing a selection of soul, reggae and R&B covers, augmented by some of her own compositions. Before long, however, he drifted away, determined to follow Judee Sill's lead and concentrate on his songwriting.

The surviving members of Gas, Food & Lodging are still puzzled about their failure. How did they miss out? It was probably a combination of factors. They seldom played outside their comfort zone of Calabasas arguing, logically enough, that there was no point in touring without an album deal. In any case, most of them needed to be free and available for regular bread and butter session work. Their image may also have been a problem. It was difficult to pretend that seasoned jazz musicians were cosmic cowboys with a commercial product to sell. Record companies were more adventurous back then but niche marketing was still a consideration and Gas, Food & Lodging's melding of jazz and country may have been perceived as a little too outré. Lastly, they may simply have been unlucky. Without a Geffen or a Rothchild to champion them, they remained locked in their familiar role as the sultans of the Sundance Saloon.

It must have been enormously frustrating for Gas, Food & Lodging to receive back-slapping praise from well-meaning peers, several of whom seemed to find securing major record deals a relative cinch. "We were all frustrated by that." Johnson admits. "I'm even more frustrated listening to the stuff 30 years later. Marc McClure has copies of the tapes and played them for me recently. I was blown away by the quality of our arrangements, our instrumental presence and our vocals. If anybody heard this today, I'm not sure they'd believe it. It should be released. It's about as good as it gets as a fusion of country, pop, jazz and baroque with classical and chorale. It's got so many elements going on. It was definitely a mirror of its time taken to the nth degree. I don't think there was any group that hip. At that time I just thought it was OK but listening back to it now it seems pretty deep. I'm quite shocked, actually. We were really the New Grass band before there was anything called New Grass. There's a tune on there with me playing mandolin and Lynn Blessing on vibes and it's faster than shit. I'd like Marty Stuart and his group of guys to hear it. We were really so far ahead of it all and perhaps that was the problem making it work. Maybe we were too far ahead."

Kelley's decision to cease playing drums and focus on his songwriting was not an entire surprise. Even in Gas, Food & Lodging, he sang some of his own compositions onstage, such as 'Dusty Road', which still survives on tape. Geoff Gillette had been well aware of Kelley's ambition since the beginning of the Seventies. "Even though Kevin was known as a drummer – he had a funky, almost sloppy New Orleans style – his true passion was writing songs on guitar. He was an especially talented lyricist and wrote many great songs." Among them was the affecting country ballad 'Look At Me', co-written with Charlie Taylor, one of many that Gillette recorded professionally during free time at the studio where he worked as a house engineer. "I think Snuff Garrett published one of our songs," Taylor recalls vaguely. "We went up to his office and met Tanya Tucker and her dad – she was about 13 or 14 years old then. When we were going down the elevator, we ran into Mark Volman and Howard Kaylan from the Turtles whom Kevin knew during his high school days. I had a different relationship with Kevin than many. I would bring ideas and if he liked them we'd sit down and write. I did not compete with him – he was kind of a mentor and we were never formal band members so he was there as a guide and a friend."

The Curtis Brothers also socialized with Kelley, often hanging out in his garage or recording demos at a nearby studio run by a mutual friend, Reggie Fisher. "There was lots of beer swilling and joint rolling," recalls Michael Curtis. "Kevin was a sweet man and we all loved him. He played with us on a song called 'Wild

Seas', which I still have somewhere. It had a really funky beat. We also cut 'Looking For Lightning' with him. As a drummer he had a light jazz approach and a great sense of time because he played the guitar, sang and wrote. He wrote some really cool songs and there was one called 'Dreamer' that he veered towards my brother Rick. I begged Kevin to give me a tape of it so that I could sing it. I still remember the first verse and the chorus. It was a cool fingerpicking number that was really neat."

With his songwriting progressing, Kelley embarked on his first serious relationship since the doomed affair with Lynn Naugh. His new partner was Marc McClure's younger sister, Vicky. They first met at a barbecue evening and somehow clicked. Although young and impressionable, Vicky already had an eventful and troubled history. Upon leaving high school she had married a surfer dude, after which she surrendered to the temptations of the early Seventies drug culture. The hedonism ended with a spell in an outpatients' rehabilitation programme during which she underwent the catharsis of psychodrama therapy. "It was very trendy at the time," she notes. Soon after, her two-year marriage foundered when her husband announced his decision to pursue a former flame from high school. Still reeling, and intensely vulnerable, she seemed swept away by Kelley and immediately left her nearby house to move into his home. "I was completely without bearings, but Kevin was there and he was willing," she says. "So I went from one bed to another which was really foolish."

Despite the speed of the romance, the relationship initially flourished. McClure was impressed by Kelley's organization and tidiness ("His room was immaculate"). He was flattered by the quiet attention of a considerably younger woman, who loved music and offered uncritical support. "We spent endless hours listening to Stevie Wonder's *Innervisions* and *Fulfillingness' First Finale*," she remembers. "We were totally enraptured with that. And I spent a tremendous amount of time listening to Aretha Franklin, who was my mentor. So we would sing every night and play. He played guitar and I would sing along. He taught me all these songs that we planned to do for these gigs he mentioned. He was very melancholy, but sweet and very sentimental."

A self-confessed "dreamy person", Vicky McClure was nevertheless sufficiently grounded to hold down a regular job working as a medical assistant in North Hollywood. Although their relationship was always close, there seemed a distinct lack of verbal communication, as if they spent their entire time singing, smoking lots of pot, drinking fine wine from Trader Joe's, staying at home and listening to records. Whereas his male colleagues generally perceived Kelley as a tough ex-marine with a dry wit and implacable persona, Vicky McClure was exposed to his more vulnerable, insecure side. "Well it's wonderful that you can get these different perspectives, but being female and being a romantic object I would certainly have a completely different take on him than a guy would. And being ten years younger than he, I was really just a little thing, you know. We had a lovely harmony when we sang together and it was great fun for him to have an in-house musician that he could just mould to do whatever he wanted. I was pretty adaptable. I sang harmony and lead on his original songs. I didn't have a piano to play there, but I did play a bit of guitar when he wasn't watching. Kevin was tender-hearted, but he seemed a very melancholy person. It was hard for him to be positive."

Even with Vicky, Kevin seemed emotionally guarded. She cannot recall him mentioning his past relationship with Lynn, nor providing much detail about his past musical exploits or complex relationship with Chris Hillman. "I was a great fan of the Byrds but he didn't mention them much. There was a definite kind of envy, which would be natural, as in 'I wish I'd been as fortunate as Chris. Why did they pay attention to Chris and not me?' – that sort of thing. A lot of musicians are apt to blow their own horn but he didn't do that really. He had a self-effacing sort of opinion. He always lifted Chris up, but wouldn't build himself up, which is unusual."

By far the most powerful insight that Vicky McClure acquired about Kelley concerned his disturbing relationship with his father. Other intimates knew about this history, but she was unfortunate enough to witness it first hand. "I did meet his father. We went there one Thanksgiving and it was a memory that remains quite marked. The house was very cold. Young and semi-conscious as I was, I could sense that, and it was really heavy. It was like walking into a tomb in his father's house. A vacuum. It was as though the life force had been sapped out of you. It was horrible. Horrible! It was such a strange and cold relationship between them. There was no warmth coming from this man and no relationship with his son. It was heartbreaking. I thought Kevin was a defeated person. Again, a lot of it I'm sure had to do with his father."

In spite of his problems, Kelley was serious about showcasing his songwriting. A series of evenings were booked at the Sundance Saloon during which he played his new compositions, backed by the bar band, with Vicky on accompanying vocals. Alas, nobody thought to tape the event.

According to Vicky McClure, Kelley's solo performances were a combination of the familiar and the new. "Musically, it sounded a little like the Byrds, Buffalo Springfield, Crosby, Stills & Nash – the stuff we all came out of. That was the background. But there was also a definite jazz element to it because of his association with Gas, Food & Lodging. I remember one of Kevin's songs, 'Let Yourself Go', which was really fun to sing. He had a sweet voice and was very sensitive. He was a decent songwriter, but I always had a sense that they weren't quite good enough and didn't have that element X. They didn't have the right hook in terms of a hit song. There was also that Stevie element . . ."

The 'Stevie element' no doubt came from their immersion in the recent work of the former boy genius. This was hardly surprising as Kelley's housemate Geoff Gillette worked as the house engineer at the studio where Stevie Wonder recorded *Songs In The Key Of Life*. While Vicky questioned the commercial viability of Kelley's songwriting, her brother Mark was intrigued by the compositions and their unusual construction. "Kevin was very serious about his writing. He wrote a lot of really good songs too.

His singing fitted well with the tunes that he wrote. There was a definite style there. 'Sail Away' was one of my favourite tunes. I did a vocal arrangement for it. We used to sit around in the living room and sing it. Some of the songs, only he could play. They were an interesting combination of rhythm & blues, and . . . well, it's hard for me to explain. They were very funny to listen to too because he did a funky black thing with them that was very cool. It wasn't like the Rising Sons or Taj Mahal but more like the Temptations! Motown! Very wild! I tried to figure it out. Those Motown lyrics sometimes take two verses to come around to the rhyme; it's more talkative and then suddenly you realize, 'Oh my God, there's a rhyme there.' And Kevin had a bunch of tunes like that which would catch you by surprise. I found it really odd. Where was he coming from? They were very well thought out. He was good."

Perhaps the most obscure artefact in post-Byrds lore is a 14-song acoustic demo tape of Kelley's work from this period. It commences with 'All I Have Are Memories', the country-tinged lament previously recorded with the Byrds. Here, Kelley treats the song with a more intense, bluesy vocal style. The remaining compositions display his strengths and limitations as a singer-songwriter. There is a strong, over-reliance on nature imagery with frequent references to sun, sea, rainbows and dreamy romanticism. 'Dreaming My Life Away' is a template of this style, complete with a slight and unexpected Van Morrison influence. Kelley clearly has a preference for blues structures although his high voice is more suited to country. 'The Drifter' chronicles a journey from Oklahoma to California to find a fantasy wife and family. The narrator ends up drinking and watching cartoons, a premonition perhaps of Kelley's later days. Drinking wine and reminiscing about the past are also the subjects of 'Dusty Road', one of Kelley's more delicate acoustic ballads. Singer-songwriter sentimentality is present on 'I Found Paradise', an extreme apotheosis, even by Kelley's standards. 'Let Yourself Go' sounds more generic of the LA school of Seventies' songwriting, with strumming guitar and more drinking references, reinforced by extravagant, overreaching lines such as "ride along rainbows across the sky". 'Looking For Freedom', with its references to "chasing ageless rainbows", sounds like more of the same but the acoustic guitar work is compelling and the lyrics better focused. 'Baby's Coming Back Today' and 'Travelin' Mood' are train songs, derivative in structure, but not unappealing. 'Rat Race' resembles a hippie complaint, made more personal by the admission, "like a gypsy I drink too much wine". The previously discussed 'Sail Away' features one of his best vocal cameos and the plaintive, romantic imagery complements the mood. 'Summertime Romance' is another attempt to write a modern-day country standard with Kelley yodelling part of the verse while referencing the late-night romantic attractions of a troubadour "playing in the Deep Blue Sea from 9 till 2". The penultimate song on the tape is arguably the most intriguing. 'The Wind (Has Always Been My Friend)' sounds as though Kelley is channelling David Crosby, with some graceful fingerpicking and a beautiful vocal performance. Indeed, its opening lines resemble a lyrical fusion of Crosby's composition 'Laughing' and Stephen Stills' 'You Don't Have To Cry': "In the morning when the sun rises I open my eyes to the sounds of children laughing in the sun . . ." The tape session ends with 'You Got To Be Free', the liveliest song on offer and a suitably rousing finale.

Kelley's chances of finding belated success as a singer-songwriter were always remote. By 1976–77, there was a persistent feeling among A&R scouts that the boom was over. Although, Kelley's unusual song stylings showed promise, the times were swiftly turning against him. "It was very difficult," Vicky McClure agrees. "He was negative and the music business was changing so much at the time. The record companies had been throwing money at people, then it suddenly dried up. Kids coming out of college were pursuing studio gigs or creating gigs for themselves – it was a different mentality. All of these musicians that came out of the Sixties were always dreaming about being rich and famous and getting that record deal. That went on for a long time, and it still goes on. I know people that are still trying to do it!"

As Kelley's prospects foundered, so did his two-year relationship with Vicky McClure. "Kevin was definitely beaten," she contends. "He was really beaten down by so many things and I'm sure I contributed a nail to it by breaking his heart. I know that I did. I broke up with him on Valentine's Day. I'll never forget it. He had presented me with a hyacinth in a pot. It was a beautiful bloom that came in springtime, one of the first blooms. He gave it to me on Valentine's Day and I broke up with him. The next morning the flower had collapsed."

The wilting flower symbolized Kelley's final defeat as far as Vicky McClure was concerned, but he disguised his pain as best he could. The next time they met, he told her: "I'll be fine. I knew you were just a stepping stone." His words seemed intended to relieve her of any guilt as much as salvaging his pride. There was talk of a new girlfriend, but nobody recalls anything serious occurring. Instead, he moved into Marc McClure's house in Tarzana. Marc had just broken up with his girlfriend and so welcomed the presence of another bachelor who was unlucky in love and happy to split the rent. The arrangement worked surprisingly well. "God, we were like the Babbling Bickersons sometimes," McClure jokes, recalling the old American radio series. "He would be the wife hitting me over the head for not picking up after myself! Kevin was not the gregarious type, he was someone quiet. But in his comfort zone he was very smart and his wit was an uncommon one. He had a very educated sense of humour. The stuff that he'd find funny would take other people three or four seconds to get because he was a bright guy. His humour was a little beyond most people. I always got the jokes though!" Bill Plummer, then living in San Diego, visited the 'odd couple' and found Kelley in a relatively upbeat mood and still as house-proud as ever. "Marc didn't want to take any money from me but Kevin insisted I wash all the dishes and keep the house clean."

Vicky McClure had seldom experienced the lighter side of Kevin's personality but was not surprised by Marc's ability to bring him out of himself. "If you just listen to my brother's voice, he's so charming and gregarious. He's really lovely and his contemporaries adore him. They love his energy. He has a wonderful sense of humour and is very entertaining."

Kelley "kept the home fires burning" through much of 1977 while Marc McClure toured with Spanky & Our Gang. Whenever McClure returned, Kelley would have completed a few more songs, although there was no obvious outlet for them. His meticulous care was evident in every aspect of his songwriting. "He wrote on guitar and piano," McClure confirms. "I wouldn't say he was a great guitar player but considering the time he would spend arranging the tune, it sounded like he knew exactly what he was doing. I'm sure if you asked him to take it up a half-step he'd go 'OK, well I'll be back in a week with the new arrangement.'" Occasionally, Kelley would still drag his drumkit out for a local gig if someone caught him at the right moment. Musician Shannon O'Neill recalls jamming with him at the Palomino, along with steel guitarist Sneaky Pete Kleinow. McClure also remembers Kelley playing with some pick-up band at a pizza joint in Chatsworth, but such outings were rare.

As the Seventies wound to a close, Kelley's hopes of a recording career had all but vanished. Session work had dried up, along with any performing opportunities. Ever practical, he took a job delivering flowers, which he continued to do for many years, utilizing the van-driving skills that had been so useful during his time in the Rising Sons. Most of his friends had by now moved away or were busy with family commitments. The rock world had long forgotten his existence and his only claim to fame was a footnote in the Byrds' story. Even scholars of West Coast music and avid Byrds fans knew nothing of his circumstances. A popular pastime among such rock connoisseurs was scouring the back sleeves of albums to ascertain the names of session musicians or guest players. It was often a way of determining the likely quality of an otherwise obscure work. This meant that a few people belatedly learned of Jesse, Wolff & Whings, although the album was long since deleted. Kelley's other credits were disputed. During Dylan's Rolling Thunder Revue, Joan Baez featured a Kevin Kelley on piano. Was this the forgotten Byrd? Alas not. The former drummer guested on a handful of albums but was never a strong enough pianist or guitarist to secure session work on either of those instruments. It was presumably the 'other' Kevin Kelley whose name graced albums by Tim Buckley, James Taylor and Eric Andersen.

As for Gas, Food & Lodging, they appear to have escaped a single reference in any of the many encyclopaedias of popular music. Remarkably, at the time of writing, no website, magazine or book has ever mentioned Kelley's involvement with a band whose work probably represented his most ambitious musical undertaking. If Kelley remains an obscurity on the internet, then it should come as no shock that his status back in 1979 came under the category of 'missing'. In magazines like *ZigZag* or *Dark Star*, which boasted the only readership remotely interested in such arcane detail, he was the forgotten Byrd. Pete Frame's detailed Byrds' family tree famously described John York as having "disappeared into thin air". By comparison, Kelley had seemingly vacated the cosmos.

While researching the Byrds' biography in 1976–77, I valiantly tracked down John York in Los Angeles to conduct his only interview of the decade, but finding Kelley proved even more difficult. He chose to remain invisible to everyone within the Byrds' community, including his cousin Chris Hillman. Two years later, I interviewed Hillman once more and asked the dreaded 'KK' question. "My cousin, Kevin?!" Hillman replied, as though I was enquiring about the whereabouts of some missing Soviet spy. "We sent him to the hospital!" he joked. "We put him in the funny farm." His slightly nervous laughter suggested some private jest that made no sense to me. Then, becoming more serious, he confided, "I don't know where Kevin is. I haven't seen him in three years and he lives in this town too." Finally, in light-hearted fashion, he concluded with another jest: "But Kevin was always one of the stranger members of our family."

Kevin Kelley wasn't the only name in his circle to disappear from the pages of rock literature. The fate of his former friend Judee Sill also provoked blank looks from most contemporaries at this time. It was only Bill Plummer's persistence in retrieving her lost tapes that allowed listeners to savour her post-*Heart Food* recordings decades later. For much of the late Seventies she was in considerable pain, the legacy of a near fatal car injury. "Well, she had that accident and broke her back," Plummer recounts, a little hazily. "When she got pushed down the stairs and broke her back again, there was a long stretch when she was bedridden and in a full cast. They developed a spinal bypass for her at UCLA and then we did the 'memorial session' for her last demos. I tried many times to get things done for her but it was difficult to work with Judee. We got a settlement for her broken back . . . then she went down to Mexico, came back with a bunch of bad shit and died. That's how it all went down on Thanksgiving Day, 1979."

The Eighties was a decade of reckoning for every one of the surviving Byrds. All were forced to readjust their lives and find meaning in a world that no longer considered them gods or even fallen princes. Some sought salvation in the Lord, others in the bottle or the freebase pipe. Few seemed destined ever to record for a major label again. It was a time when the phrase "the good old days" was no mere cliché but a brutal reality. Kelley had suffered these belt-tightening times well in advance of the others and continued his flower deliveries with a mixture of stoicism and sadness.

One of Kelley's fantasies was that he might one day inherit the idyllic home that his father owned on South Catalina. Even that dream was about to end. As Bill Wolff says: "One of the things that really scarred him was his father's death. Kevin was going over there, hanging out and helping to take care of him. Finally, when Kevin's dad died, he didn't leave him one red cent. And he was quite well-off. To the best of my knowledge he gave it all to his wife, the stepmother. Kevin was crushed by this. The two things that haunted him for the rest of his life were that incident and losing Lynn [Naugh]."

"He always had a very prickly relationship with his father," adds Jesse Barish. "When his dad passed away and he got nothing that just added to his melancholy and resentment." Another blow was his mother's emphysema-related death, an event which exacerbated his isolation during the Eighties. Charlie Taylor, by then settled in Nashville, occasionally stayed with Kelley when he was visiting Los Angeles. The ex-marine had clearly lost a lot of his former spark in the intervening years. "It was tough to watch somebody disintegrate like that. When I was in LA on business, I'd take him out to dinner. He'd meet me at the airport and I'd give him 20 bucks. Geoff Gillette used to do that too. We'd hire him to pick us up or take us to the airport because we knew he needed the money. I'd send him $50 or $100 at Christmas and he was very appreciative of it. He still delivered flowers and there's nothing wrong with that. But he was always on the verge of having a nervous breakdown. I don't know that he ever had one, but I think he felt embarrassed about his station in life. He was a musician for sure but he was conflicted. I can't say what the genesis of all that was but it was always difficult to watch. He was always holding a torch for that girl Lynn when I saw him. I never met her but he told me they talked from time to time, but then she married at some point."

In 1984, Vicky McClure received an unexpected phone call from the boyfriend she had left on St Valentine's Day seven years before. Kevin had been sitting at home watching televised commentary on the summer Olympics in Los Angeles and there was Vicky on screen singing. He was so surprised by her moment of international fame that he could not resist offering a humble congratulations. The conversation was friendly but a little guarded, which was understandable considering the passage of time. "We shared a few pleasantries," McClure remembers, "but we didn't have much to say." It was the last time they would talk. In the succeeding years, she would receive intermittent bulletins about her former beau, all of which reinforced her perennial conviction that he was a 'beaten man'. "He didn't have enough fire and life in him. He was just so beaten, that's all I can say. Maybe the better word is resigned to a minimal, very narrow, more desperate life without hope, without purpose, without reason. He was in mental anguish and wasting away really. It was like that song Paul Simon wrote, 'A Most Peculiar Man'. Sad. Alone."

The cavalcade of surrogate Byrds 'tribute' bands during the Eighties was like a clarion or carrion call to ex-members to relive former glories. Gene Clark, Michael Clarke, John York, Gene Parsons and Skip Battin all volunteered their services, while the 'original' Byrds (in the form of McGuinn, Crosby & Hillman) also briefly reconvened for legal reasons. Even roadie Carlos Bernal, infamous for masquerading as Gram Parsons during the Byrds' disastrous 1968 South African tour, was welcomed back into the spotlight. It seemed only a matter of time before the conspicuously absent Kelley would be requested to join an ersatz Byrds, but it never happened. It says much for his obscurity that nobody considered tracking him down. Nor did he ever offer his services. In May 1985, one of my perennial pen pals, Jean-Pierre Morisset, interviewed Hillman and proffered essentially the same question that I had asked a decade before. "What is Kevin Kelley doing?" Once again, Hillman sounded somewhat taken aback as he replied defensively: "He lives only six miles away from my place, but I haven't seen him in four years. The last time we met was at a funeral. When we have family reunions he is always invited but never comes." Although some cynics may disagree, Hillman's sketch of a reclusive, less sociable personality sounded convincing. By this point, Kelley was drinking more heavily and was a predictable absentee from family events. However, his old friends testify that he was always pleased and even eager to hear from his cousin.

Kelley's wariness of offending Hillman, combined with his own misgivings, would probably have made him paranoid about joining any 'Byrds tribute' venture. "I know Kevin really respected Chris," Charlie Taylor says. "I saw Gene and Michael in Atlanta and they were in pretty bad shape. I'm not sure Kevin would have joined any of those bands. He was such a proud person. In the end, he was a marine. For all his shortcomings he had a lot of character."

Mark McClure concurs. "I don't know whether Kevin would have done it. I think it would have been against his set of principles or something or he would have thought it was in some way beneath him. He had strange references to his self-worth. It might have made him some money and it would have been fun but he'd likely say, 'I'm sorry I'm not going to join a copy band.' As you say, he had higher musical values."

By the late Eighties, the once outwardly self-assured Kelley seemed a much more subdued figure to visiting friends. "Early on, he was very confident, but I think he lost that," Taylor suggests. Charlie was taken aback by the extent of his friend's humility when they both attended a performance by Taj Mahal in Orange County. Kelley was reticent yet determined to go backstage after the show and see his former bandmate from the Rising Sons. Afterwards, driving home, he seemed lost in thought but emphasized how great it was to see Mahal again. "That was probably the last time Taj ever saw him. They hadn't seen each other in years but Kevin made a point of going out there to see him. It was like closure."

Despite his increasing consumption, Kelley's drinking at this point was arguably no worse than several other of his musician friends and certainly way below the gargantuan thirsts of fellow ex-Byrds Gene Clark or Michael Clarke. Like many drinkers, Kelley had moments of intense clarity during which he could rally and even make a renewed attempt to improve his life. At such moments, his marine training served him well. Since leaving the Byrds he had attempted to reinvent himself on numerous occasions, changing musical styles, switching instruments and persevering with songwriting. Now, he suddenly took an interest in song publishing. Marc McClure, who had moved to Boulder, Colorado, would phone him occasionally and was surprised to learn that Kelley was supplementing his flower delivery routine by freelancing for a music publisher. "He was trying to get this guy's catalogue up to date and making sure his royalties were coming in. I can't remember the name, except that it was a pretty famous black artiste."

Ironically, Kelley's interest in the publishing game was about to bring him into bitter conflict with several of his ex-colleagues from the Rising Sons. At the beginning of the Nineties news filtered through that Sony Records were planning to exhume the lost recordings of the Rising Sons for an archival release. Back in 1965, the group had formed Blind Lemon Publishing to administer their song catalogue, which largely consisted of arrangements of traditional material, along with several compositions from Jesse Lee Kincaid. Since no album was ever issued by the Rising Sons, the publishing company had failed to generate any income over the years and was declared inactive.

With the impending release of the archive album, Kincaid sought to reactivate the publishing and was shocked to discover that the sole ownership of Blind Lemon had been claimed by Kevin Kelley. "There was a dispute," Kincaid confirms. "I realized that we had to activate the publishing for the songs that were going to be on the album. But Kevin creamed the entire ownership of the company which had been a five-person, democratic entity. Once that paperwork was entered into the books at BMI I had a heck of a time returning it to its original five-person operation. He didn't have to account to anybody. He claimed ownership of the entire company. Nobody was really in communication and I was the only writer in the band. I was the one that was being affected here. They were my songs. He wouldn't respond to any letters or communication I sent to him about the subject for the remainder of his life. It was a big hassle."

"It got worse," says Gary Marker, who joined the debate from the sidelines. "He had arguments with Jesse and then everybody got pissed off. Ry Cooder was saying, 'Man, he hasn't changed a bit in 20 years – he's still a prick?' I told Kevin, "But the songs aren't yours, they're Jesse's! Jesse had agreed to run the company and we were going to turn the royalties over to him so that he could also do the Rising Sons' business and deal with Sony. But Kevin wouldn't give it up. He wanted to run the publishing. He had all these airy-fairy excuses why he wanted to control the company and said he should do that because he knew more about the music business."

The dispute continued for over a decade, even surviving Kelley's death. Eventually, his executor Bill Wolff agreed to allow Kincaid to administer the publishing more than ten years after the 1992 release of the Rising Sons' archival album. Ever the sardonic humorist, Marker was heard to remark, "This is really amazing when you think about it. The guy is dead and he's still causing trouble! It's brilliant!"

Even Wolff found it impossible to defend his former friend. "I think in a perverted way Kevin felt that nobody else was taking care of it and he was the one. So, as he was doing it, he should get paid for it. That was his warped thinking. It was really a rotten thing to do. It's not like the guy wasn't without contradictions, you know."

The publishing debacle underlines some of the inconsistencies in Kelley's character, particularly in his final years. Many old friends point to his integrity as a champion of 'the little guy' and a firm believer in honesty and justice. On the other hand, his stubbornness and self-conviction were all too familiar traits. In the unfortunate Blind Lemon affair, these warring characteristics collided head-on. Kelley's recent, albeit limited, experience working in publishing evidently convinced him that he was best placed to administer the income arising from the songs. Most likely, he required the self-validation, esteem and sense of achievement missing from other areas of his life. Alcohol abuse no doubt added to his self-aggrandizing delusion, which may account for his otherwise inexplicable denial of the facts and haughty avoidance of Kincaid. As old friend and psychologist Michael Barnes kindly notes: "I really think Kevin was multi-dimensional."

The 1992 release of *The Rising Sons Featuring Ry Cooder & Taj Mahal* also proved divisive. "It was a miserable assemblage," says bassist Gary Marker, who had unsuccessfully attempted to broker a deal between Sony Records and original producer Terry Melcher. "That's why it pissed me off. I asked them, 'Why don't you get Terry back to mix it? It's his stuff!' I called him in Carmel and told him they didn't have all the tapes. He said, 'Yeah, I know, I used to cut them up and put your stuff on Paul Revere & The Raiders and vice versa and bill them off from one to the other.' Then he said he'd do it. I told Sony, 'He'll do it free on his time and fly himself there', but they said, 'No! We've got a guy . . .' I have a scratchy old mono mix that Terry did for 'Take A Giant Step' and I listened to the one on that retrospective collection and they're worlds apart. Terry recorded knowing what he wanted to do later. He had an idea in his head about how he was going to mix it and only he knew what it was going to sound like. He was a hell of a lot better and smarter than anybody gave him credit for."

Critical reaction to the album was generally positive. It was fascinating to hear these early experiments, although the problems that the group presented seemed self-evident. Eclectic to a fatal degree, the Rising Sons seemed trapped between two different styles that failed to gel. With retrospective logic, Melcher pinpointed the dilemma in a brief aside: "If I had it to do over, I would've found some Beatle-type group and put Kincaid in there, and had another group with Ry and Taj."

Despite Marker's reservations, the other members of the group responded positively to the release, none more than Kevin Kelley, who was thrilled. He called Charlie Taylor the morning the CD arrived and "was on cloud nine". Marc McClure received a copy in the post, accompanied by further effusive comments. Other old friends recall a similar reaction.

Although he was in danger of falling into a rut, Kelley was still in contact with several old friends. Jesse Barish, whose mother lived a few blocks away, always made a point of visiting Kevin after breakfast. Often, they would take off for the day or hang out at Barish's place near Venice Beach. "We'd take walks on the beach and buy T-shirts. There was a time, particularly in 1993–94, when he'd come down pretty regularly. We always had a good time. But later that didn't happen so much. He got deeper into drinking and stuff."

Jesse Lee Kincaid had been another occasional visitor, but their contact had ceased since the dispute over the Rising Sons' publishing. Kelley must have been wondering whether it had been worth antagonizing his ex-colleagues since the financial rewards turned out to be negligible. He soon learned that the group were still bound to the terms of their original contract under which they were paid a specified amount per record sold, as opposed to a percentage. It was rather like playing a gig, then discovering that your fee for the evening was based on 1965 prices.

Kelley's euphoria over the Rising Sons' album rapidly turned to disillusionment. Marc McClure, recently returned from Colorado, visited him for the first time in a decade and noticed a profound change. "He'd gone from lightly cynical to very cynical to miserable over a period of years. It was a slow spiral down. He spent a lot more time alone in his apartment. It's like you get up in the morning, look at yourself in the mirror and say, 'You know what, I'm not going to be able to do anything about this.' When you get into that headspace, that has got to totally depress you. He had plumped up and he was not very healthy. He seemed a little depressed – a lot of it had to do with not playing or being in the industry, and not having more to show for what he'd done. Plus, his girlfriend situation was few and far between to the point of nothing because he'd plumped up like a little gnome. He didn't feel like going out and socializing."

Almost every person who contacted Kelley during the Nineties mentions his continuing and increasingly obsessive fixation on his great lost love, Lynn. "He would always reminisce about her," McClure recalls. "Well, you know what a man's mind will do to the memory of a woman." Over the years she had been placed on a pedestal and apotheosized to such a degree that her importance had taken on mythic proportions. Nobody dared mention that Kelley had never spoken in such grandiloquent romantic terms about her when they were together. He knew that his cavalier treatment had precipitated their break-up, but found a perverse melancholic comfort in mentally sifting through the ashes of their relationship, even though the slightest spark had been extinguished over two decades before. Indeed, she was long since married, though even that fact fuelled rather than relieved his grief. These intense feelings were exacerbated by his drinking which allowed his mind to commute back to a non-existent golden age filled with poignant moments and conveniently stripped of pain, disagreement or mundanity. By transforming Kevin and Lynn into a cross between Romeo and Juliet, Lancelot and Guinevere and Tristan and Iseult (albeit without the illicit connotations), he found fresh justification for maintaining a sense of inertia in the present.

"There was this idealization of her, but it wasn't real," adds Michael Barnes. "At a certain point you've got to figure that it wasn't meant to be and move on. You can't hold on to what could have been. Between the weight gain and the bouts with alcoholism and depression, it was just too much. The Scottish have an expression: 'What's for you won't go by you.' Kevin just kept holding on to this fantasy of this woman. It was very sad."

Kelley's belated deification of Lynn was not entirely without reason. The maudlin remembrance, heightened by alcohol, inspired many of his songs. Although some remained in fragmentary form, others were worked on over time and captured the desolation reignited by the pain of memory. This was the closest that Kelley achieved in reaching catharsis during these years. Lynn remained the convenient muse that could be relied upon to inspire him to push the bottle aside for a spell and put pen to paper.

By the mid to late Nineties the world of Kevin Kelley had shrank alarmingly – musically, socially and geographically. As he went further into agoraphobic retreat, there were no more trips to Venice Beach, no more gigs and a dearth of old friends. Even the flower delivery job that had kept him grounded for so long was now at an end.

Charlie Taylor remembers seeing Kelley for the last time during this period. He was shocked by his physical decline, weight gain and breathlessness. "I told him, 'Kevin, you need to get on some programme and lose some weight and tackle the bad habits.'" Kelley nodded in agreement, then changed the subject. "He was disciplined but he lost that towards the end."

Jesse Barish noticed the same symptoms. "Man, he was a mess physically. He just didn't take care of his body. He was huge. You probably remember him as being a pretty skinny guy, but he just blew up. And he still had that baby face. Some people like Orson Welles could carry a lot of weight and kind of make it work. I know other people that are really big but with Kevin – it didn't look right. The bigger he became the more he wanted to just stay in and drink."

While virtually everyone blames Kelley's psychological and physical decline on alcoholism, his drinking was not merely a symptom of stress or depression. Throughout this period he was often suffering considerable physical discomfort and turned to alcohol as a means of anaesthetizing the pain. "His health started getting bad," says Wolff. "He had very high blood pressure. He had hyperglycaemia and he was overweight. He also had some pretty serious back trouble. Oh, he also had emphysema. So he was really in very poor shape physically." The emphysema, which explains the breathlessness noticed by Taylor, was particularly upsetting for Kelley as his mother had died from the condition. He had consciously avoided cigarettes since the early Seventies in the hope of avoiding the condition, although his colossal consumption of dope cannot have helped matters. The knowledge that any one of the above disorders was likely to attract the attention of the Grim Reaper played on Kelley's mind to such an extent that he became increasingly fatalistic.

Meditations on death, whether expressed on the phone or in person, can have a disconcerting effect on the listener. After hearing one of Kelley's doomed diatribes, Barish became extremely concerned for his safety. "He'd become more reclusive. He called me one time and sounded really messed up, so I called Wolff and said, 'I think Kevin's going to do something drastic, man.' Wolff went over there because Kevin was talking suicidal stuff. I was afraid that he was going to check himself out." Soon after that,

Wolff, assisted by Kelley's friends, encouraged him to enter a rehabilitation programme. Gus Duffy, who knew Kelley from their mutual friendship with Geoff Gillette years before, had connections with Alcoholics' Anonymous and offered his support. "We got him into rehab," Barish confirms, "and he got clean for a month or two. Wolff and I tried to keep an eye on him, but you can't babysit somebody. They're going to do what they want to do. Kevin went to a few AA meetings, but I don't really think that was his thing. We were all struggling with our own demons, to be honest with you. We tried to help Kevin as much as we could but we couldn't be with him 24/7 and you can't help someone like that anyway if they want to drink." Kelley started drinking moderately, believing he could control his intake, but before long his consumption increased to alarming proportions.

Marc McClure continued to visit Kelley's apartment but it gradually became a painful duty rather than a pleasure. "You don't really have that many good friends in your life anyway. The ones that can come over will at least relate to you. But I don't think he was listening to any of us. I was trying to get him to lose weight and bringing him over cases of diet shake and big boxes of vitamins. I said 'Kevin, please, try these for two weeks!' But he didn't bother. I'd check on him and bring up some food that was better than a can of beans but mostly he was living on wine and crackers or whisky. He wasn't in good shape. We'd sit down but it was hard to stay there because he was miserable all the time. I told him, 'You've got to get on some regime or you're going down. You're looking like you're dying here, laddie.' I didn't expect him to live very long. He could have done. But I don't think, in his mind, he had that much to bother living for. It was sad."

On 23 March 2001, Jesse Barish received a call from Kelley, who was in a philosophic, but positive mood. Recoiling from recent setbacks, he had started writing again and that very day had completed a new composition whose lyrics summed up his wildest hopes. It was titled 'Home Again'. Barish was thrilled by the quality of the work and hoped this might inspire Kelley towards loftier heights. "He actually wrote a lot of songs and was a great songwriter. He spoke that lyric to me on the phone and I said, 'Wow, Kevin that was really beautiful.' I never found out whether he'd put music to it before he died."

Towards the end of 2001, Kelley received an unexpected call from Jim Carlton, a former member of the Legends who had known Gram Parsons since his teenage years. Carlton still played music and supplemented his income writing for guitar magazines and record companies. Recently, he had been commissioned by Sundazed Records to assist with the packaging of an archival album *Sundazed IV*, a 180-gram LP aimed at the collectors' market featuring rarities from the *Sweetheart Of The Rodeo* sessions. McGuinn and Hillman had already provided some good soundbites and Carlton hoped that Kelley might have some fond recollections of his most famous recording. Instead, Carlton was confronted by an emotionally distraught outburst, laced with paranoia and conspiracy theories. Enquiring about the instrumental, 'All I Have Is Memories', Kelley pointed out to Carlton that the correct title was 'All I Have Are Memories'. This was the only accurate point he made during the entire conversation. Kelley was upset that he had not received recognition for his work on *Sweetheart*, maintaining that Jon Corneal had been wrongly credited in his place. He also insisted that no vocal take for 'All I Have Are Memories' was ever cut because the others did not rate him as a singer and wished to highlight the instrumental virtuosity of Clarence White and Lloyd Green at his expense.

"He broke down and cried," Carlton remembers. "He said he didn't get credit. Probably he was drinking. I had to call Sundazed and tell them that this 'interview' was virtually unusable because the guy was breaking down. I still have the recording but I just felt so terrible. I haven't listened to it since. I salvaged what I could. He was emotionally unavailable by the time the interview was over and had gone to pieces."

The saddest aspect of the story was that all of Kelley's fears and insecurities were ungrounded. When interviewed, Chris Hillman had always insisted that it was his cousin who played on *Sweetheart*

Of The Rodeo. Jon Corneal had never made any significant claim either, merely noting that "they had me play on some cuts that they weren't real happy with." Pushed further, he told me, "I know I played on 'Lazy Days' and maybe a couple more but I'm sorry I can't tell you exactly what." Revealingly, 'Lazy Days' was a former International Submarine Band song which probably explains why Corneal was brought in. More pertinently, 'Lazy Days' was not part of the original *Sweetheart Of The Rodeo*. Indeed, it is probable that Corneal's contributions were, like 'Lazy Days', mere outtakes rather than the selections on the album as originally released. Kelley's contention that Corneal had replaced him in the credits was also mistaken. As the back sleeve of *Sweetheart Of The Rodeo* reveals, a wealth of musicians are credited but the first four listed are McGuinn, Hillman, Parsons and Kelley, with Corneal placed sixth. "I think the way that whole thing went down hurt his feelings a lot," says Corneal, "and I never realized this until a couple of years ago when somebody emailed me from California. Kevin was very depressed over the years and apparently that whole thing had put him in that direction mentally. I didn't have any idea that that had happened until after he was deceased. Nobody's name was any bigger than anybody else's. It's a shame, man. I felt terrible about it because he just misunderstood."

Kelley's final misunderstanding was the enduring belief that he had been prevented from singing 'All I Have Are Memories'. In 2003, Sony issued a Legacy edition of *Sweetheart Of The Rodeo* unveiling a complete vocal version of the track, the only song Kelley ever sang lead on during his spell in the Byrds. Sadly, he would never hear or even remember this precious moment.

In his final days, Kelley's thoughts turned towards his famous cousin. Since the Byrds, there had been a distance between them which had never been resolved. "Kevin was in touch with Hillman at various points but they had a contentious relationship for sure," says Wolff.

"It really bothered him," adds Shannon O'Neill. "Their mothers were sisters and I think he really felt that Chris let him down a bit because they were close when they were kids but not when they got older. They didn't talk for a long time. I don't know what happened, but there was some friction there. It was something that Kevin was really upset and very hurt about. Kevin was just an unassuming guy who had a little apartment and didn't do a hell of a lot. I don't think Chris saw him as a valid entity in the music business . . . Kelley had told me that he was really upset with Hillman because he never called him anymore and I think Kevin was intimidated that Chris was doing fairly well and he didn't want to call Chris because he felt that might make him uncomfortable."

O'Neill's comments on the lack of communication were correct, although he was hardly an impartial witness in assessing the psychology of Hillman. As a friend and collaborator of Gene Clark, he had heard similar complaints in the past. "Chris intimidated Gene the same way. He said something about his playing and Gene was really upset about it." Hillman could certainly be forthright, but Clark was equally capable of responding in kind. As for Kelley, it is telling that he made no specific complaint about Chris beyond a lingering regret that they were not closer.

The criticisms of Kelley and Clark were still festering in the back of O'Neill's mind when he had an unexpected confrontation with Hillman. By sheer coincidence, Hillman was living in the same gated community as O'Neill's brother and one evening their paths crossed. Hillman had opened the gate using his password and Shannon followed him through without doing the same. Annoyed by this breach of gated community protocol, Hillman turned around and sneered: "Hey, man, why didn't you use your own code to get in?" Burning with indignation, O'Neill blurted out the first wounding remark that entered his head. "Shit, man, why don't *you* get in touch with Kevin!" Hillman was momentarily stunned as he always seemed to be when a stranger or journalist mentioned his cousin's name. His surprise immediately turned to defensive anger. "Chris got really pissed," O'Neill recalls. "He said, 'Hey, Kevin's got a phone, he can call me whenever he wants!' I was pissed off too. I thought I was going to be in a fistfight. It was the weirdest thing. When I got back I told Kevin I'd run into Chris and that's the last I heard of it. It wasn't much more than a few months later that Kevin died."

What O'Neill did not know was that there was contact between the cousins in the aftermath of his conflict with Hillman. A phone conversation took place which ended badly for Kevin. Chris was no doubt trying to help by administering strong advice and some necessary tough love. Over the years, Hillman had witnessed, from a distance, the demise of Gram Parsons, Gene Clark and Michael Clarke. Their deaths, wasteful and largely self-inflicted, had left him frustrated and critical of the excesses that accompanied rock star life at its most hedonistic. Kelley's decline was more low-key, but equally insidious. Kevin's reaction to Hillman's well-meaning phone call was not dissimilar to the emotional outpouring that had greeted Jim Carlton earlier. Confronting his demons was no easy task for Kelley in his parlous situation. Distraught, he phoned Charlie Taylor in Nashville and poured out his heart. Taylor listened patiently and was moved by his friend's plight. "I know Kevin loved Chris and respected him. Kevin called me in tears and said that Chris had told him to clean up his act and stuff. He was all upset that Chris had read him the riot act . . . I said, 'Well, Chris loves you, Kevin. That's why he's talking to you like that. You need to hear it.'" Kelley didn't seem entirely convinced but conceded: "Well, I know, but it's tough coming from *him*." Attempting a softer approach, Taylor suggested Kevin should leave Los Angeles and take a vacation in order to try and rid himself of his bad habits. "I'm not rich but I said, 'I'll put you up for a few weeks and maybe you can get a new perspective.' A month later he was dead."

On 6 April 2002, Kelley's body was discovered at his apartment on Whitsett Avenue in North Hollywood. He had suffered a fatal heart attack, the legacy of years of abuse. The date of death was an approximation as the body had evidently lain there for some time before a neighbour alerted the authorities. With no known next of kin to inform, police searched the apartment for other contact details. One of the first people to learn of the bereavement was Geoff Gillette whose phone number had been found on Kelley's desk. Bill Wolff also received the dreaded call and knew he would soon be besieged by the bureaucracy of death. Some time before, he had agreed to be Kelley's executor, having already contributed to rehab costs. Kelley's finances were in a dreadful state at the time of his death which came as no surprise to those who had witnessed his decline over the years. The apartment rent was overdue and Wolff realized he had only 48 hours to collect Kelley's effects and clear the place. Jesse Barish and Geoff Gillette agreed to come over and help, and Marc McClure also popped by later. What they witnessed was far from pretty. "It was a gruesome scene because he'd been vomiting blood all over the joint," says Wolff. "It was horrific."

"It was a really sad day," Barish adds. "We cleaned out his apartment. There was family stuff there but he had no heirs – no wife, no kids, no mom, no dad – and we didn't know what his relationship was with Chris Hillman. They'd always had a pretty testy relationship and I never knew what it was. So it was a bad day and we were there to take care of it. There was nobody else. Kevin was like a hermit who'd had a heart attack. It was difficult, but we all loved him."

Among the keepsakes Barish took were a smoking pipe that they shared in headier times, a bass drum head with the distinctive Jesse, Wolff & Whings logo and some framed photos. Wolff removed some Navajo rugs which he had always admired. McClure retrieved some old albums and paid Wolff for the van that Kelley had previously used to deliver flowers. "I still drive it to this day. It's good because it keeps him in my mind."

Perhaps the most poignant and unexpected memento for Barish was a typed manuscript that lay on Kelley's desk. It was the complete lyrics to 'Home Again', the song that had excited Kevin so much that he'd recited the words over the phone to Barish in a moment of pride. "I never knew if he put music to it, but I just thought it was a beautiful lyric and so touching. It was almost like a prophecy. I decided to write some music for it. Kevin and I had never really collaborated so, posthumously, I wrote a song with him. Some day I'll record it."

Sadly, many of Kelley's belongings were either lost, thrown away or remain unaccounted for. McClure remembers a manila folder which included handwritten copies of Kevin's songs, but cannot recall seeing it at the apartment. Oddly, there were no cassette tapes of his unreleased songs or any privately recorded performances documenting a creative life stretching back before the Byrds days. Most of Kelley's possessions and ephemera received the black bag treatment that is usually the lot of the impoverished elderly who die without issue. "It was such an overwhelming day and there was so much stuff there," Barish recalls. "Kevin wrote these great songs, but we didn't see any tapes there. We had to clean out this guy's entire life in a day. We tossed away tons of stuff. We didn't know what to do with it. We weren't in touch with Chris Hillman and there was no place to store this stuff. I didn't know what was what. There were old family photographs that we just tossed away, man, and it was really sad. This was like the end of the line."

Wolff was left with the onerous task of arranging the funeral, for which the drummer had made no provision. By this point, Wolff had contacted Hillman who, he claims, agreed to contribute a significant sum to offset the funeral expenses. As if proving the old adage 'No good deed goes unpunished', Wolff later damned Hillman with a mouthful of poisonous rebukes. He was even more indignant after hassling Hillman for a second cheque and still felt disgruntled by the financial outcome. "I really dislike that guy," he told me, amid a barrage of saltier insults. It seemed an excessive reaction in the circumstances. Hillman must have been left wondering why he offered to help in the first place.

Sudden death often unleashes raw emotion and suppressed bitterness, as was evident in the aforementioned obituaries of Gene Clark and Michael Clarke. At least nobody was fighting over Kelley's estate, the value of which was in any case meagre. Wolff's wrath and worries about additional funeral costs were resolved painlessly after a meeting with a counsellor from the LAPD who pointed out that Kelley's service record made him eligible for burial in an Armed Services cemetery in Riverside, California. So it was that Kevin Kelley ended his days in a quiet ceremony, honoured as an ex-marine.

One week after Kelley's death, Geoff Gillette attended a jazz festival in New Orleans. Taj Mahal was on the bill and, after the show, Gillette went backstage to pass on the sad news. He presented Mahal with a picture of the Rising Sons playing live that had been found at Kevin's apartment. Paying his own tribute, Gillette concluded: "It was a great privilege to have known Kevin and I have great memories of our journey together."

Wolff still felt the need to commemorate Kelley's passing by gathering together as many old friends as possible for an intimate tribute. It says much for Jesse Lee Kincaid that he was one of the first to accept the invitation, despite the fact that the dispute over the Rising Sons' publishing had yet to be resolved. Gary Marker was not so forgiving and declined to attend. "Jesse Lee called and wanted to know if I'd be going to the memorial service with him. Well, it was 400 miles away and I had two small kids and a lot of responsibilities, so I said, 'I don't think so'. Jesse said, 'What do you mean? He played with us! He was one of us!' I had higher priorities here."

The memorial, which took place at a Sportsmen's Lodge in Studio City, included figures from every stage of Kelley's creative life. Kincaid was there from the Rising Sons: Ricky Luther and Harvey Lane recalled his brief spell in Fusion; Chris Hillman represented the Byrds; Michael Barnes, the commune days in Nichols Canyon; Bill 'Stumak' Nugent, the many evening sessions back in Sherman Oaks; Jesse & Wolff, of course, and Mark McClure from Gas, Food & Lodging. In total, some two dozen people turned up.

Still haunted by the disturbing images he had witnessed at Kelley's apartment, Wolff suffered a sleepless night on the eve of the service. He had intended to prepare a formal reading but instead arrived with some handwritten notes and admits he "stumbled through". Recalling Kelley's spell in the marines, he stressed his indomitable personality and refusal to be cowed, adding how he'd once thrown a large-sized bully down a flight of stairs. "I relayed that little story to convey that when Kevin was younger he was a real fighter, but then, towards the end, he just gave up and that's what saddened me the most."

After finishing his tribute, Wolff invited contributions from anybody who wished to speak. Hillman stood up and offered a brief homily, the contents of which have escaped the memories of everyone present. "Chris' words were quite short," says Kincaid, who wisely chose to provide a musical tribute instead. "I just sang a song I'd composed called 'River Of Love'. The words were 'The river of love keeps flowing while time waits to take us away.' It was a song about life and death that I thought was related to the occasion. A few other people had some reminiscences which followed."

"It was a lovely evening," says Michael Barnes, who spoke fondly of his friendship with Kelley. "We all talked about him. My memories were of a gentle soul who got lost. He got lost, man. Alcohol has got to be one of the worst drugs around."

One of the most moving moments of the evening was when Marc McClure performed Kelley's composition, 'Sail Away'. "When Marc sang that, everybody realized what a great songwriter Kevin was," Jesse Barish remembers. McClure relied upon his stage professionalism to get through the performance without cracking up. "Oh God, it was sad for me," Mark says. "I had my tears. I missed him. I felt really bad for Kevin and I was sad that there was nothing in the long run that I could do to make him change his direction. The spread was nice and everybody was allowed their say. It was mellow. But it was sad for me."

Along with McClure's performance, the most poignant tribute came from Jesse Barish, who recited the song poem 'Home Again' which he felt testified to Kelley's unheralded talents as a songwriter of originality and distinction. In common with 'Sail Away', Kelley employed nautical imagery to convey a life buffeted by sea and storm, a modern day *Odyssey* in which the dream of a happy homecoming is never lost. Considering Kelley's alcoholic depression and isolation during the period of composition, the words positively articulated a belief in salvation, even amid his darkest hour.

I was sailing the sea in an open boat,
the waves almost washed me overboard,
seeking to find one true heart,
honesty unignored,
the storm is growing stronger now,
the rain is falling harder,
if I could keep holding on,
hold on a little longer.
I'll be home again, home again, home with my true friend
I'll be home again.

Will my hopes be lost at sea,
my heart could be broken forever
things can change so that you don't give up
this dream I'll never surrender.
I'll be home again, home again, home with my true friend
I'll be home again.

The sea can crush you on the rocks,
I've heard terror in lonely cries,
meeting you has changed my life,
this cannot be denied;
I was seeking safe harbour,
searching for an unselfish lover.
Fate answered my wayward call
with a place to rest and discover.
I'll be home again, home again, home with my true friend
I'll be home

Wolff estimates that Kevin Kelley wrote between 30 and 40 compositions during his lifetime. Apart from the Byrds' 'All I Have Are Memories', none have been released thus far. A number of songs, several of them recorded professionally, are buried among the personal tape archives of his former friends and collaborators. Whether these will ever be exhumed remains uncertain but it would be a fitting tribute to Kelley's memory if the world finally heard from the still silent singer-songwriter.

KEVIN KELLEY: NOTES

page 543: "Ever since I was 12 . . ." unearthed from author's archives. Undated CBS/Columbia promotional artiste biography, circa May 1968.

page 544: "After the divorce . . ." William (aka Bill/David) Wolff, interviewed by the author. London/Los Angeles, California: 11 March 2007.

page 545: "Kevin was shattered . . ." Charlie Taylor, interviewed by the author. London/Nashville, Tennessee: 16 September 2007.

page 545: "Boot camp is a harrowing experience . . ." Marc McClure, interviewed by the author. London/San Diego, California: 14 April 2007.

page 546: "I wasn't supposed to like that kind of music . . ." unearthed from author's archives. Undated CBS/Columbia promotional artiste biography, circa May 1968.

page 546: "It wasn't until . . ." ibid.

page 548: "Initial performances were well-received . . ." Over time, the Rising Sons played most of the familiar LA clubs of the period – the Ash Grove, the New Balladeer, Ciro's, the Trip and the Whisky A Go-Go. The 'multi-racial' angle provided by Taj Mahal's presence encouraged promoters to feature the group as support to several major black stars, with varying results. Mahal remembers one of their toughest gigs was supporting the Temptations at the Trip. The Motown group's slick act attracted an audience that felt no connection with the blues/pop fusion offered by the Rising Sons. Other dates involving Otis Redding and Martha & The Vandellas were more favourably received. Among the group's early fans was the teenage Matt Andes who told me: "My big musical influence when I was young was Ry Cooder. I heard him play live with the Rising Sons when I was 16 and he changed my life. I made a personal vow that I was going to really try hard to do just a fraction of what Ry could do. We went to Devonshire Downs (in Northridge) which is right down from the boulevard where my brother Mark and I grew up. The Rising Sons were opening for Martha Reeves and the Vandellas and the audience was half-black/half-white. Everybody was standing by the walls not even going close to the stage when the Rising Sons started playing. It was like a Hollywood movie. Within a minute and a half everybody rushed the stage. They won those kids over, a black/white audience within two minutes of playing."

page 548: "Ed either broke his wrist . . ." Gary Marker, interviewed by the author. London/Los Angeles, California: 28 February 2007. Ironically, Cassidy's injury came about as a result of attempting to imitate Michael Clarke's muscular style. Interviewed by John Platt, in *Comstock Lode* 3, Cassidy recalled: "The Byrds had just come out then. Mike Clarke was with them, he'd played for just a few weeks and I noticed from watching him that in rock you had to play much harder just to be heard. I was used to playing very tasty. I was considered too loud for jazz, but you couldn't hear me at all. So in the process of changing the position of my wrist whilst I was playing, it tore a ligament. The doctor said he could either put it in a cast for six weeks or I'd have something chronic for the rest of my life. So at that point I had to leave the band."

page 548: "Ry Cooder was saying things . . ." Marker/Rogan. London/Los Angeles, California: 28 February 2007.

page 549: "Cassidy's departure was confirmed . . ." In addition to Cassidy and Randy Wolfe (California), the Red Roosters featured Mark Andes (bass) and Jay Ferguson (vocals). They were subsequently joined by keyboardist John Locke, initially under the name Spirits Rebellious, before adopting the name Spirit. Their first four albums, *Spirit, The Family That Plays Together, Clear Spirit* and *Twelve Dreams Of Dr Sardonicus* were among the most musically adventurous rock albums of the period. Indeed, even their later work, most notably the double album, *Spirit Of '76,* still sounds impressive.

page 549: "Kevin's mother had a house . . ." Jesse Lee Kincaid, interviewed by the author. London/Marin County, California: 5 March 2007.

page 549: "He was just abysmal . . ." Marker/Rogan. London/Los Angeles, California: 28 February 2007. While Marker states that Kevin Kelley was the drummer on these sessions, Cassidy was present on the original demos for CBS. Cassidy recalls: "We'd been playing around and we'd done some recording and I didn't know what was going to happen to the recordings."

page 549: "When Terry walked in . . ." Marker/Rogan. London/Los Angeles, California: 28 February 2007.

page 550: "We would often pass them . . ." Kincaid/Rogan. London/Marin County, California: 5 March 2007.

page 550: "Columbia Studio A was a former radio station . . ." Marker/Rogan. London/Los Angeles, California: 28 February 2007.

page 551: "Terry came from a wealthy background . . ." Kincaid/Rogan. London/Marin County, California: 5 March 2007.

page 551: "Basically, Terry was a likeable guy . . ." Marker/Rogan. London/Los Angeles, California: 28 February 2007.

page 552: "Terry tried to get in there . . ." Kincaid/Rogan. London/Marin County, California: 5 March 2007.

page 552: "Kevin was a difficult person . . ." Marker/Rogan. London/Los Angeles, California: 28 February 2007.

page 553: "Kevin was a good drummer . . ." ibid.

page 553: "Kevin was a little much . . ." Kincaid/Rogan. London/Marin County, California: 5 March 2007.

page 554: "Kevin had the full cartoon voice . . ." Marker/Rogan. London/Los Angeles, California: 28 February 2007.

page 554: "We were huge Rising Sons fans . . ." Matt Andes, interviewed by the author. London/Johnson City, Texas: 30 September 2007. The line-up of the Matt Andes Twist Combo for this gig is not entirely certain. Apart from Kelley, it most likely comprised Matt Andes (lead/bottleneck guitar), Mark Andes (bass), Mark Fondelier (sometimes written Fondiler and Fondelear) (vocals), Jay Ferguson (vocals) and Denny Bruce (drums). The latter line-up gained more prominence in 1966 when they played regularly on Sunset Strip under the name Western Union.

page 544: "Kevin just sat in . . ." ibid.

page 555: "That was curious . . ." Kincaid/Rogan. London/Marin County, California: 5 March 2007.

page 555: "Mahal was indignant about the decision . . ." This view was shared by others in the group, most notably Gary Marker. "The first thing I was disappointed about was the single which had Jesse Lee singing lead on both songs. Even Taj was saying, 'What's going on? Aren't I the lead singer in the band?' They said, 'Well, we think this'll do OK.' Taj was ready to quit the band at that point because Jesse was not a good singer. Neil Young hadn't become popular yet. He made it OK to sing 'shitty'. Jesse would have fitted right in today; he could've been a singer-songwriter, singing out of tune with a half-octave range. Bob Dylan was the exception then. He was a guy with a weird voice but it was effective. We all knew that he was in character every time he was singing. Neil Young wasn't, and neither was Jesse. They were really singing at the far range of their abilities. So, I thought it was crazy. I said we should put out something with Taj singing lead. Then the next single was supposed to be 'Take A Giant Step' but they put the kibosh on that immediately because Columbia said it was a drug song. There was a little pseudo-rave up in there – and that was a very funny thing. Ryland kept trying to put a little guitar break in 'Take A Giant Step', a mini rave up. He said, 'Well if it's good enough for the Yardbirds it's good enough for us.' I said, 'Get Jimmy Page in, he's in town. He's down there with Jackie De Shannon. He'll come over, he knows about that stuff.' But Jimmy wouldn't come over and play on the session, so Jesse said, 'Give me the guitar, I'll go in there. Just plug it into the board and let me do this.' In two takes he had this airy-fairy psychedelic thing going on. It took no time at all. Ryland is going 'What?!' Ryland likes things very organized, very methodical, and he thinks about stuff. He's good at some spontaneous things if he's playing bottleneck, but if he's playing finger style he works it out very carefully. You'd never see Ry Cooder out in front of some Chicago blues band playing endless choruses of screaming lead guitar. That would never happen."

page 555: "I remember conducting Taj's vocals . . ." Kincaid/Rogan. London/Marin County, California: 5 March 2007.

page 556: "The composition later appeared . . ." The Monkees' version featured a slightly amended lyric – "take a try and step outside your mind".

page 556: "I think Taj began to realize . . ." ibid.

page 556: "He played with us . . ." ibid.

page 557: "Kevin was a very energetic guy . . ." Wolff/Rogan. London/Los Angeles, California: 11 March 2007.

page 557: "He said, 'Sorry guys, see you later' . . ." Marker/Rogan. London/Los Angeles, California: 28 February 2007. When discussing Kelley's career, Gary Marker noted: "He was fired from every band he'd been in . . ." However, this assertion is contradicted by Marker's own admission that Kelley walked away from Fusion to join the Byrds. Fusion went on to record an album for Atco Records after Kelley's departure.

page 558: "I intermittently hung out with Kevin . . ." Wolff/Rogan. London/Los Angeles, California: 11 March 2007.

page 558: "The drummer immediately bonded with Gram Parsons . . ." Kelley's appreciation of Gram Parsons was noted by several of his contemporaries, including his friend, Charlie Taylor. "Kevin thought a lot of Gram and said he was a great songwriter."

page 559: "Kevin was a peace and love kind of guy . . ." Jim Seiter, interviewed by the author. Macao, People's Republic Of China/London: 28 June 2007.

page 559–560: ". . . significantly, it was Kelley's contribution that was singled out . . ." See *Zigzag* 32, in which Frame enthuses, "Kevin Kelley . . . he was great – terrific player, I thought . . ."

page 560: "Kevin Kelley must be . . ." Charles Stoneman. *Rhodesia Herald*: 26 July 1968.

page 561: "Although he was Chris' cousin . . ." Dolores Tickner (formerly McGuinn), interviewed by the author. Tucson, Arizona: 13 January 2007.

page 561: ". . . except under pressure . . ." Roger McGuinn, interviewed by Vincent Flanders. De Pauw University: 9 May 1969, and Indianapolis Coliseum: 14 February 1970.

page 562: "I realize I was critical . . ." Seiter/Rogan. Macao, People's Republic Of China/London: 28 June 2007.

page 562: "Lynn Naugh was Kevin's girlfriend . . ." Matt Andes/Rogan. London/Johnson City, Texas: 30 September 2007.

page 563: "Kevin seemed emotionally reserved . . ." Kincaid/Rogan. London/Marin County, California: 5 March 2007.

page 563: "I remember going to Ciro's . . ." Jesse Barish, interviewed by the author. London/Venice Beach, California: 12–13 April 2007.

page 563: "I'd known Grant since 1963 . . ." Wolff/Rogan. London/Los Angeles, California: 11 March 2007.

page 565: "I didn't think that killing people . . ." Michael Barnes, interviewed by the author. London/Los Angeles, California: 24 April 2007.

page 565: "We would go and attack UCLA . . ." ibid.

page 566: "Barish had the privilege of playing . . ." For Barish, the collaboration with Phillips was a cross between a stoned reverie and a testament to the power of positive thinking. "It was pretty glamorous for a hippie guy like me to go to Bel Air to rehearse. When you're a hippie and you're stoned you have fantasies. Well, I always had fantasies of meeting John Phillips. I daydreamed that I was hitching down Sunset and John picked me up and we became friends. Then, here I was in his band. He really liked my playing. We went to New York and stayed at the funky hotel, the Chelsea."

page 566: "We talked about it . . ." Barnes/Rogan. London/Los Angeles, California: 24 April 2007.

page 567: "Cordell really liked the vibe . . ." Wolff/Rogan. London/Los Angeles, California: 11 March 2007.

page 567: "I had a different vision . . ." Barish/Rogan. London/Venice Beach, California: 12–13 April 2007.

page 567: "Hey, man . . ." Barnes/Rogan. London/Los Angeles, California: 24 April 2007.

page 567: "Kevin fitted in perfectly . . ." ibid.

page 568: "The band lasted . . ." Barish/Rogan. London/Venice Beach, California: 12–13 April 2007.

page 568: "Jesse was certainly not . . ." Barnes/Rogan. London/Los Angeles, California: 24 April 2007.

page 569: "It was kind of an insane asylum . . ." Wolff/Rogan. London/Los Angeles, California: 11 March 2007.

page 569: "I look at it as an exercise in identity crisis . . ." Barish/Rogan. London/Venice Beach, California: 12–13 April 2007.

page 570: "He worked hard . . ." Barnes/Rogan. London/Los Angeles, California: 24 April 2007.

page 570: "It was a dictatorship . . ." Wolff/Rogan. London/Los Angeles, California: 11 March 2007.

page 570: "I just wanted to be solo again . . ." Barish/Rogan. London/Venice Beach, California: 12–13 April 2007.

page 571: "Cordell was great . . ." ibid. After the demise of Jesse, Wolff & Whings, Barish remained in Marin County where he befriended Marty Balin of the Jefferson Starship. Balin secured him a deal with RCA in 1977 and produced two albums, *Jesse Barish* and *Mercury Shoes*. Barish returned the favour by composing the Starship's 1978 US Top 10 hit,

'Count On Me', and several album tracks. He also contributed to Balin's solo album before completing one of his own: *Cherry Road* (2003).

page 572: "Essentially a country rock outfit, Bandana . . ." The Bandana line-up featured Patti Peyton (vocals), Michael McRae (vocals), Marc McClure (guitar), Ron Iglot (bass) and Kevin Kelley (drums). Patti Peyton had previously played in a group with Van Dyke Parks. Interestingly, manager Gary Downey was then an actor on the *Ozzie And Harriet Show*. Coincidentally or otherwise, Kelley's father represented the showbiz family.

page 572: "Once Kevin was in . . ." Michael McRae, interviewed by the author. London/Nashville, Tennessee: 14 September 2008.

page 572: "We played there frequently . . ." ibid.

page 572: "Kevin could play any style . . ." Charlie Taylor/Rogan. London/Nashville, Tennessee: 16 September 2007.

page 573: "He was a melancholic Irishman . . ." Geoff Gillette, email reply to author: 21 September 2007.

page 573: "Kevin had a hard time after the Byrds . . ." ibid.

page 573: "Kevin was a connoisseur of the pharmaceuticals . . ." Charlie Taylor/Rogan. London/Nashville, Tennessee: 16 September 2007.

page 573: "Obviously, there were drugs coming in . . ." ibid.

page 574: "That's when it all changed . . ." Mark Andes, interviewed by the author. London/Austin, Texas: 29–30 September 2007.

page 575: "That was a wake-up call . . ." Charlie Taylor/Rogan. London/Nashville, Tennessee: 16 September 2007.

page 575: "I guess that's why God invented whiskey . . ." ibid.

page 575: "Kevin was a cynical person . . ." Barnes/Rogan. London/Los Angeles, California: 24 April 2007.

page 575: ". . . his sense of justice . . ." Wolff/Rogan. London/Los Angeles, California: 11 March 2007.

page 575: "We were travelling around . . ." Art Johnson, interviewed by the author. London/Nice, France: 17 June 2007.

page 576: "I said, 'Let's just get something simple together . . .' " ibid.

page 576: "Marc and I had a trick . . ." ibid.

page 577: "Wow, think about that . . ." Charlie Taylor/Rogan. London/Nashville, Tennessee: 16 September 2007.

page 577: "Wolff and I were jazz players . . ." Johnson/Rogan. London/Nice, France: 17 June 2007.

page 577: "It's a very simple formula . . ." ibid.

page 578: "Kevin was a laid-back, quiet guy . . ." ibid.

page 578: "Kevin had a lot of technique . . ." Bill Plummer, interviewed by the author. London/Laramie, Wyoming: 10 June 2007.

page 578: "He used to rent to Linda Ronstadt . . ." Johnson/Rogan. London/Nice, France: 17 June 2007.

page 578–579: "There were constant band meetings . . ." ibid.

page 579: "Sure, he was opinionated . . ." McClure/Rogan. London/San Diego, California: 14 April 2007.
page 579: 'Oh, Kevin was a wonderful, bubbly guy . . ." Plummer/Rogan. London/Laramie, Wyoming: 10 June 2007.
page 579: "It was the past . . ." Barish/Rogan. London/Venice Beach, California: 12–13 April 2007.
page 579: "It's true that he didn't really reference the Byrds . . ." Johnson/Rogan. London/Nice, France: 17 June 2007.
page 581: "He loved Rufus . . ." Charlie Taylor/Rogan. London/Nashville, Tennessee: 16 September 2007.
page 581: "Kevin dated her for a bit . . ." ibid.
page 582: "Bill, Art and I used to drink . . ." Marc McClure/Rogan. London/San Diego, California: 14 April 2007.
page 582: "There were a lot of laughs . . ." Johnson/Rogan. London/Nice, France: 17 June 2007.
page 582: "What a great band . . ." Michael Curtis, interviewed by the author. London/Nashville, Tennessee: 16 September 2007.
page 583: "Kelley, meanwhile, played locally, briefly appearing with singer Valerie Ford . . ." A tape of at least one of their performances still exists featuring half-a-dozen songs, commencing with an unlikely cover of Bob Marley's 'Stir It Up'.
page 583: "We were all frustrated by that . . ." Johnson/Rogan. London/Nice, France: 17 June 2007. The original Gas, Food & Lodging tapes are still in the possession of Bill Plummer and there is every possibility that they will be released, the more so given their publicity herein. Archival nostalgia is a strange phenomenon. It will be fascinating to hear whether the work (of which I have heard only a small portion) stands the test of time or merits the extravagant claims of Art Johnson. Either way, it should prove a fitting testament to Kelley and the others.
page 584: "Even though Kevin was known as a drummer . . ." Geoff Gillette, email reply to author: 6 July 2007.
page 584: "Among them was the affecting 'Look At Me' . . ." Produced by Geoff Gillette and Charlie Taylor, 'Look At Me' features Kelley on lead vocal backed by Alex 'Erroneous' Dmochowski (bass), Bill 'Stumak' Nugent (saxophone), Geoff Gillette (piano), Greg Leroy (guitar) and Bill Wolff (guitar). Kelley also plays on Charlie Taylor's 'No Easy Way Out' with the same backing group, augmented by Taylor (rhythm acoustic guitar) and featuring lead vocalist Patti Schauer.
page 584: "I think Snuff Garrett published one of our songs . . ." Charlie Taylor/Rogan. London/Nashville, Tennessee: 16 September 2007.
page 584: "There was lots of beer swilling . . ." Curtis/Rogan. London/Nashville, Tennessee: 16 September 2007.
page 585: "It was very trendy . . ." Vicky Doney (née McClure), interviewed by the author. London/Pen Argyl, Northampton County, Pennsylvania: 24 April 2007.

page 585: "I was completely without bearings . . ." ibid.
page 585: "His room was immaculate . . ." ibid.
page 585: "We spent endless hours listening . . ." ibid.
page 586: "Well it's wonderful that you can get these different perspectives . . ." ibid.
page 586: "I was a great fan of the Byrds . . ." ibid.
page 587: "I did meet his father . . ." ibid.
page 587: "Musically, it sounded a little like the Byrds . . ." ibid.
page 587: "Kevin was very serious about his writing . . ." Marc McClure/Rogan. London/San Diego, California: 14 April 2007.
page 589: "It was very difficult . . ." Doney (née McClure)/Rogan. London/Pen Argyl, Northampton County, Pennsylvania: 24 April 2007.
page 590: "Kevin was definitely beaten . . ." ibid.
page 590: "I'll be fine . . ." ibid.
page 590: "God, we were like the Babbling Bickersons . . ." Marc McClure/Rogan. London/San Diego, California. 14 April 2007.
page 590: "Marc didn't want to take any money . . ." Plummer/Rogan. London/Laramie, Wyoming: 10 June 2007.
page 591: "If you just listen to my brother's voice . . ." Doney (née McClure)/Rogan. London/Pen Argyl, Northampton County, Pennsylvania: 24 April 2007.
page 591: "He wrote on guitar and piano . . ." Marc McClure/Rogan. London/San Diego, California: 14 April 2007.
page 591: "Musician Shannon O'Neill recalls jamming . . ." One such performance was at a club called JR's where they played a handful of songs while the local band took their break. Later that evening, they were enjoying a meal when a disgruntled member of the billed group came over to their table and remonstrated with them. "He was a big rodeo guy," O'Neill recalls. "It was bizarre because he was blowing off and saying, 'I grew up with the Byrds and the Burritos' and he had no idea who he was talking to. It pissed me off so much but Kevin was an ex-marine and he just sat there. I got so mad that when I got home I said, 'We've got to go back there . . ." O'Neill practised like crazy over the next few days and encouraged Kelley and Kleinow to do the same. When they took the stage during the interval the following week, they played a blistering couple of songs that so intimidated their adversary that he interrupted them with the words, "That was great." Then, he politely took the instruments back. A couple of weeks later, he asked O'Neill to produce an album. What O'Neill remembered most about the incident was the contrast between his own sense of indignation and the lackadaisical attitudes of Kelley and Kleinow. "Both those men were very laid-back and neither bothered to come out and volunteer information about who they were. Kevin probably turned down a couple of things because of that . . ."
page 592: ". . . disappeared into thin air . . ." Quoted in the family tree

'Byrds Of A Feather 1', copyright dated February 1979 and featured in *Pete Frame's Rock Family Trees* (London: Omnibus Press, 1980).

page 592: "My cousin, Kevin?! . . ." Chris Hillman, interviewed by the author. New York/Miami, Florida: 26 January 1979.

page 592: "We sent him to the hospital . . ." ibid.

page 592: "But Kevin was always . . ." ibid.

page 593: "It was only Bill Plummer's persistence . . ." Plummer's odyssey began when Sill fell out with Asylum. "I had more or less taken over her management and we were trying to get Asylum to release the stuff. But after we did the demos and the recordings she had her final giant fight with them and they just said, 'That's it. You're out of here.' So I went to a lady called Carol Thompson, who was the wife of Richard Thompson, our piano player in the Brotherhood. She was Billy Sherrill's secretary and one of the main A&R people at Asylum. I told her, 'I'm handling Judee now, what are you going to do with those tapes?' I didn't know they were sitting on her desk. She just picked them up and said, 'They're yours!' After getting hold of all the mastertapes I started the remixing and mastering." The work finally appeared under the title *Dreams Come True* in 2005.

page 593: "Well, she had that accident . . ." Plummer/Rogan. London/Laramie, Wyoming: 10 June 2007.

page 593: "One of the things that really scarred him . . ." Wolff/Rogan. London/Los Angeles, California: 11 March 2007.

page 594: "He always had a very prickly relationship with his father . . ." Barish/Rogan. London/Venice Beach, California: 12–13 April 2007.

page 594: "It was tough to watch somebody disintegrate like that . . ." Charlie Taylor/Rogan. London/Nashville, Tennessee: 16 September 2007.

page 594: "We shared a few pleasantries . . ." Doney (née McClure)/Rogan. London/Pen Argyl, Northampton County, Pennsylvania: 24 April 2007.

page 594: "He didn't have enough fire . . ." ibid.

page 595: "He lives only six miles . . ." Chris Hillman, interviewed by Jean-Pierre Morisset, May 1985, printed in *Farther Along* 5: Fall/Winter 1986.

page 595: "I know Kevin really respected Chris . . ." Charlie Taylor/Rogan. London/Nashville, Tennessee: 16 September 2007.

page 596: "I don't know whether Kevin would have done it . . ." Marc McClure/Rogan. London/San Diego, California: 14 April 2007.

page 596: "Early on, he was very confident . . ." Charlie Taylor/Rogan. London/Nashville, Tennessee: 16 September 2007.

page 596: "That was probably the last time . . ." ibid.

page 596: "He was trying to get this guy's catalogue up to date . . ." Marc McClure/Rogan. London/San Diego, California: 14 April 2007.

page 597: "There was a dispute . . ." Kincaid/Rogan. London/Marin County, California: 5 March 2007.

page 597: "It got worse . . ." Marker/Rogan. London/Los Angeles, California: 28 February 2007.

page 598: "This is really amazing . . ." ibid.

page 598: "The guy is dead . . ." ibid. Gary Marker's frankness tended to irk Kelley's friend and executor William Wolff. "Jesse Lee Kincaid is a pretty sweet guy and he wouldn't air that kind of stuff, but Gary would. When he called me a couple of times he was very negative about Kevin and I got pretty defensive and said, 'Listen, he was one of my best friends for the past 30 years, I don't want to hear this shit!' He just kept ragging and ragging, then he sent me a bunch of emails and wanted me to stay in touch and I never responded. Gary would not be reluctant to cast aspirations."

page 598: "I think in a perverted way . . ." Marker/Rogan. London/Los Angeles, California: 28 February 2007.

page 598: "I really think Kevin was multi-dimensional . . ." Barnes/Rogan. London/Los Angeles, California: 24 April 2007.

page 598: "It was a miserable assemblage . . ." Marker/Rogan. London/Los Angeles, California: 28 February 2007.

page 598: "That's why it pissed me off . . ." ibid.

page 599: "If I had it to do over . . ." Terry Melcher, interviewed by Mark Kirkeby, quoted in the liner notes for the Rising Sons CD.

page 599: "Despite Marker's reservations . . ." Jesse Lee Kincaid expressed similar ambivalence about the release. "I felt good and bad. It was fantastic that it was issued 30 years later. But maybe Columbia was hip to this. Maybe they realized when they signed acts that they might not be successful now but 30 years down the road they might put out a legacy edition and make money on the deal. From a business point of view we had signed a contract that was not favourable in terms of publishing royalties and we'd agreed to not a statutory publishing rate but a penny-and-a-half per song which was statutory at the time. So [we received] only a penny-and-a-half when it came out in 1992 per song when the statutory royalty rate had gone up to about 7 cents. We didn't go up with it because we signed to a penny-and-a-half in 1965."

page 599: "We'd take walks on the beach . . ." Barish/Rogan. London/Venice Beach, California: 12–13 April 2007.

page 600: "He'd gone from lightly cynical to very cynical . . ." Marc McClure/Rogan. London/San Diego, California: 14 April 2007.

page 600: "He would always reminisce about her . . ." ibid.

page 601: "Indeed, she had long since married . . ." The details of Lynn's marriage, including the date, the place and her occupation at the time, vary from speaker to speaker. They have therefore been omitted from the main text. Gary Marker's apocryphal account – minus extraneous details – has him informing Kelley that her husband wrote the screenplay for a famous motion picture and became a millionaire. When Marker revealed this rumour – true or not – Kelley's reaction was supposedly a shocked silence. "One of the things Kevin always wanted was to be famous. He wanted to be a famous songwriter or a famous drummer and to be somebody. He was just a terribly insecure guy who wanted to be recognized. The whole thing is really sad."

page 601: "There was this idealization of her . . ." Barnes/Rogan. London/Los Angeles, California: 24 April 2007.

page 601: "I told him, 'Kevin, you need to get on some programme . . .'" Charlie Taylor/Rogan. London/Nashville, Tennessee: 16 September 2007.

page 602: "He was disciplined . . ." ibid.

page 602: "Man, he was a mess physically . . ." Barish/Rogan. London/Venice Beach, California: 12–13 April 2007.

page 602: "His health started getting bad . . ." Wolff/Rogan. London/Los Angeles, California: 11 March 2007.

page 602: "He'd become more reclusive . . ." Barish/Rogan. London/Venice Beach, California: 12–13 April 2007.

page 603: "We got him into rehab . . ." ibid.

page 603: "You don't really have that many good friends . . ." Marc McClure/Rogan. San Diego, California: 14 April 2007.

page 604: "He actually wrote a lot of songs . . ." Barish/Rogan. London/Venice Beach, California: 12–13 April 2007.

page 604: "He broke down and cried . . ." Jim Carlton, interviewed by the author. London/Mount Dora, Florida: 12 March 2007.

page 604: "When interviewed Chris Hillman had always insisted . . ." Interviewed by *Zigzag* less than three years after the album's release, when his memory was still relatively fresh, Hillman was grilled on this issue and simply said, "It was Kevin."

page 605: ". . . they had me play on some cuts . . ." Jon Corneal, interviewed by the author. London/Winter Haven, Florida: 24 June 2007.

page 605: "I know I played on 'Lazy Days' . . ." ibid.

page 605: "I think the way that whole thing went down . . ." ibid.

page 605: "Kevin was in touch with Hillman . . ." Wolff/Rogan. London/Los Angeles, California: 11 March 2007.

page 605: "It really bothered him . . ." Shannon O'Neill, interviewed by the author. London/Thousand Oaks, California: 7 October 2007.

page 606: "Chris intimidated Gene . . ." ibid.

page 606: "Hey, man, why didn't you use your own code . . ." ibid.

page 606: "Shit, man . . ." ibid.

page 606: "Chris got really pissed . . ." ibid.

page 607: "I know Kevin loved Chris . . ." Charlie Taylor/Rogan. London/Nashville, Tennessee: 16 September 2007.

page 607: "I'm not rich . . ." ibid.

page 608: "It was a gruesome scene . . ." Wolff/Rogan. London/Los Angeles, California: 11 March 2007.

page 608: "It was a really sad day . . ." Barish/Rogan. London/Venice Beach, California: 12–13 April 2007.

page 608: "I still drive it . . ." Marc McClure/Rogan. London/San Diego, California: 14 April 2007.

page 608: "I never knew if he put music to it . . ." Barish/Rogan. London/Venice Beach, California: 12–13 April 2007.

page 609: "It was such an overwhelming day . . ." ibid.

page 609: "I really dislike that guy . . ." Wolff/Rogan. London/Los Angeles, California: 11 March 2007. Gary Marker sympathized with Wolff's position, pointing out that he had already made a financial contribution to Kelley by assisting with his rehab. The same could be said of several others in Kelley's circle. Marker also contends that Kelley had run up various credit card debts prior to his death, although nobody else mentioned this to me.

page 610: "It was a great privilege . . ." Geoff Gillette, email reply to author: 21 September 2007.

page 610: "Jesse Lee called . . ." Marker/Rogan. London/Los Angeles, California: 28 February 2007.

page 611: "I relayed that little story . . ." Wolff/Rogan. London/Los Angeles, California: 11 March 2007.

page 611: "Chris' words were quite short . . ." Kincaid/Rogan. London/Marin County, California: 5 March 2007.

page 611: "It was a lovely evening . . ." Barnes/Rogan. London/Los Angeles, California: 24 April 2007.

page 611: "When Marc sang that . . ." Barish/Rogan. London/Venice Beach, California: 12–13 April 2007.

page 611: "Oh God, it was sad for me . . ." Marc McClure/Rogan. London/San Diego: California: 14 April 2007.

Gene Clark at Raytown High School (left and middle) and Bonner Springs High School (right).

Harold Eugene Clark, who was killed in action during August 1944.

The Clark family, pictured in the early 1940s. Left to right (back row): Gene's grandfather, Joel Clark; Gene's grandmother, Ada Clark; Gene's father, Kelly; Gene's aunt, Majorie Clark; Gene's uncle, Harold Eugene Clark. Front row: Gene's uncles, Clark and Lloyd Clark (brothers of Harold Eugene Clark).

Gene and schoolfriend Jack Godden.

Gene's father, Kelly, playing guitar, 1973. Looking on are Bonnie's son, Kelly Clark Howell, and Gene's youngest sister, Sarah.

Unused outdoor photos from *No Other* (*from the Collection of Whin Oppice*).

Gene, with beer and smokes, pictured in Albion, circa 1977.

Touring as part of McGuinn, Clark & Hillman, 1979.

Gene after the Cinegrill show, April 1991, snapped by Harold Sherrick.

Harold Sherrick's moving portrait. This is the last known photograph of Gene.

Michael Clarke on the August 1965 UK tour.

Michael Clarke, 1967.

Kevin Kelley on the Byrds' visit to London, 1968.

Kevin Kelley, early 1968.

Kevin Kelley on the Byrds' visit to London, 1968.

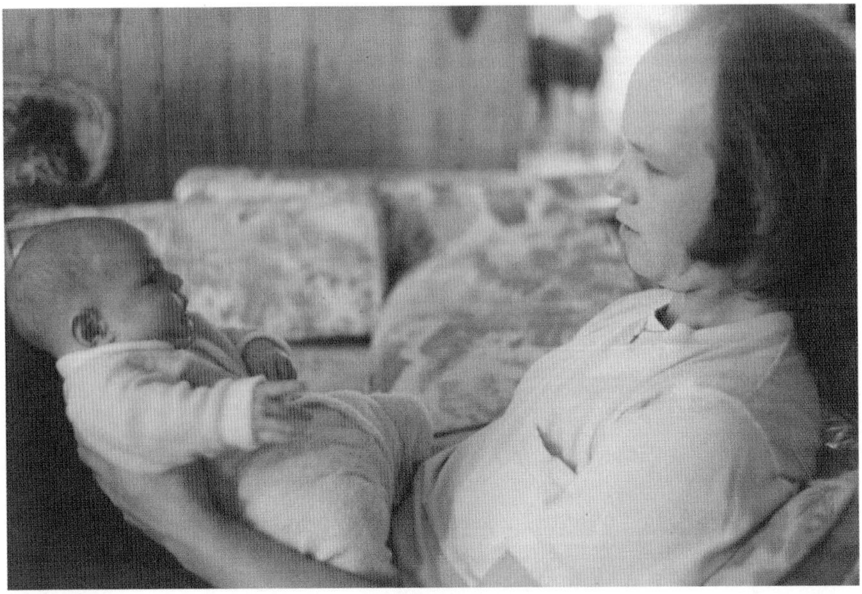

Kevin Kelley in 1973, holding Charlie Taylor's daughter, Simone.

The Legends. L. to R: Jim Stafford, Bill Waldrop, Lamar Braxton and Gram Parsons.

Onstage in Europe, May 1968.

L. to R: Gram Parsons, Kevin Kelley, Chris Hillman and Roger McGuinn.

Gram Parsons, backstage during one of the Byrds' fleeting UK appearances in 1968.

Gram Parsons, UK visit, 1968.

Gram's living quarters at the Chateau Marmont, Sunset Boulevard.

Gram Parsons on the roof of the Chateau Marmont, photographed by Eve Babibz (courtesy of John Delgatto).

The White family performing at the Riverside Rancho in 1954. L. to R. Joanne, Roland, Eric and Clarence.

The Reasons (aka Nashville West): Gib Guilbeau, Clarence White, Wayne Moore and Gene Parsons.

Clarence and Roland backstage.

Clarence and Roger onstage in London, 1971.

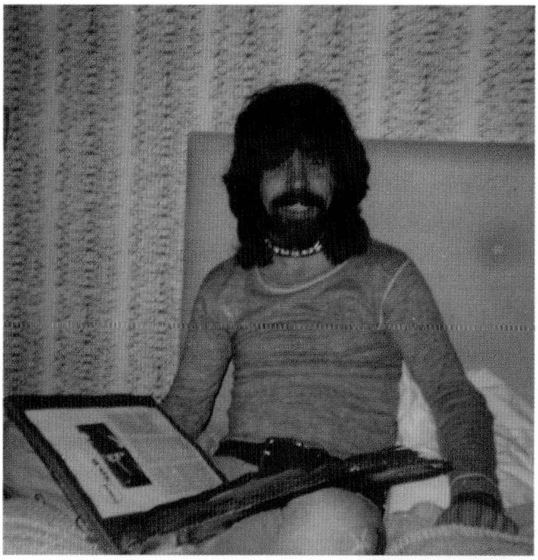
Clarence in Bristol, 4 May 1971.

Clarence on the 1971 UK tour.

Clarence, 1971.

Skip Battin, onstage with the Byrds: 1971 UK tour.

Promotional photograph for Battin's 1973 debut album, *Skip*.

4

GRAM PARSONS

5 November 1946 – 19 September 1973

"YOU must remember something – he was never a member of the Byrds," says Chris Hillman, in one of his sporadic eruptions on the subject. "He was hired as a sideman. That's very important. When people say 'ex-Byrd', he wasn't a Byrd. The Byrds were the five original guys." Hillman's casuistry is impressive, albeit misleading. Contractually, *nobody* was a Byrd except the 'five original guys' and that exclusion list includes Clarence White who appeared on eight studio albums and was a full-time member for longer than Clark, Crosby, Clarke or even Hillman. But group membership is not determined solely by the cold print of a contract. If this was so, then neither Hillman nor Clarke were Byrds at the time the group recorded 'Mr Tambourine Man' and posed for their first promotional photograph. Indeed, if manager Jim Dickson had not appended Hillman's name to the CBS contract on 12 March 1965, then he might have spent years in the limbo world of the 'non-Byrd'. Beyond de facto contractual status is the everyday reality of recording, performance and presentation. CBS Records declared Parsons a Byrd in all their biographical material and McGuinn and Hillman echoed that mantra in interviews of the period. Fans, record purchasers and concertgoers were encouraged to accept Parsons and drummer Kevin Kelley as fully fledged Byrds – and we did. Paradoxically, this was no denial of the importance of the original Byrds, but it was accepted that they were no more. Gram Parsons' contribution to the group was immense and, all myth aside, he remains a crucial part of the story – just ask anybody who attended a show at the time or bought *Sweetheart Of The Rodeo*. Parsons was part of a brave new incarnation of the Byrds that many of us hoped would continue for years. That it ended so abruptly should not detract from its importance.

Gram Parsons has long since transcended his brief stay in the Byrds to become a poster boy and spiritual godfather of Americana, a musical subgenre that owes much to his innovative blend of country, soul and rhythm & blues. At the time I wrote my first book on the Byrds, all that existed on Parsons were a small batch of clippings, a handful of albums and some first-hand memories from past associates. Over the years, everything has changed. There have been books, documentaries, a film and countless magazine retrospectives testifying to his cult appeal. Indeed, we have reached a point when arguably more has been written about Parsons than almost any other Byrd. Crosby no doubt has the edge due to his CSN&Y association, but the peculiar fascination with Parsons shows few signs of abating. For those of us who actually saw him perform with the Byrds and lived through those times, his rise to cult godhead has been a mysterious and surprising process. It seems hard to believe now that there was a time when music journalists struggled to decipher his first name, often referring to him as Graham or Grahm. Nobody does that any more.

Ingram Cecil Connor III, to give him his full title, was born in Winter Haven, Florida and raised in Waycross, Georgia. His family history was the stuff of fiction, resembling nothing less than a series of chapters from a William Faulkner novel combined with selected scenes taken from the acts of a Tennessee Williams play. Dominating the narrative was the overbearing presence of the Snively family, the beneficiaries of a citrus empire whose scarcely believable wealth made them seem like potentates in Winter Haven. Snively Groves' millions could be computed across the breakfast tables of America where fresh and concentrated orange juice were consumed with luxurious abandon.

Gram's mother, Avis, enjoyed the privileged life of a Southern belle, surrounded by servants and privy to a seemingly unlimited expense account. In keeping with her upbringing she was privately educated, attended finishing school and secured a BA in Home Economics, a subject she saw befitting her role as the perfect hostess rather than the thrifty housewife.

Gram's father was an entirely different species. Ingram Cecil Connor, born to an affluent family in Columbia, Tennessee, was an adventurer and a decorated war hero who had witnessed the horrors of Pearl Harbor first hand. He rose through the ranks to squadron commander and eventually major, flying 50 combat missions against the Japanese. His exploits as a fighter pilot ended when he was struck down by malaria and hospitalized, a nightmarish experience that he seldom spoke about in later years. After receiving a Presidential citation for bravery, he returned to America, continuing to serve in the Air Force as an intelligence officer instructor. While stationed near Winter Haven, he befriended a fellow serviceman, John Snively, who introduced him to his sister, Avis. In March 1945, Major Connor and Avis married at an evening ceremony at her parents' house. The lavish wedding was trumpeted in the local press with due reverence. Even Avis' bridal dress was described with poetic eloquence. "Her veil was held by a halo of illusions." Nineteen months later Gram was born. A second child, 'Little' Avis, would follow in 1951.

After leaving the Army Air Corps, Major Connor had considered a career as a civil or aeronautical engineer, but instead accepted an offer to join the Snively family business, albeit far away from their centre of operations in Winter Haven. Their new home was Waycross, Georgia, where the Major was installed as head of the Snively fruit-box manufacturing plant. The posting was less challenging than anticipated, leaving its president plenty of time to indulge his favourite pastimes: drinking, hunting and fishing. Since his service days, he had become universally known as 'Coon Dog' Connor in tribute to his hangdog expression, sad canine eyes, and love of the hunt. Hunting was a hobby that he willingly passed on to his son, frequently taking him into the woods on shooting and scouting expeditions. He also inculcated the boy's embryonic interest in music. 'Coon Dog' loved music all his life and had been a keen record collector. Some said music soothed his troubled soul, alleviating traumatic war memories. Encouraged by his father, Gram agreed to take piano lessons and over time became proficient, but never accomplished. "I'd have to say the biggest influence on my career was an old brown radio I used to have," he said, years later. "I listened to it constantly and I heard everything, from the *Grand Ole Opry* to rock 'n' roll." It was enough to inspire a playful romp on the piano which he christened 'The Gram Boogie'.

An event of greater significance occurred on 22 February 1956 when Gram attended an Elvis Presley concert at the City Auditorium in Waycross. Befitting an extended member of the Snively clan, Gram was ushered into the presence of the King and supposedly received his autograph, along with some encouraging words. The concert had a profound effect on the boy, not only due to Presley's charisma but the supporting cast of performers which included Justin Tubb, the Louvin Brothers, Mother Maybelle and the Carter Sisters (featuring June Carter) and Mercury recording artiste, Benny Martin. This was his first experience of hearing live country music and inspired a lifelong love of the Louvin Brothers whose influence would emerge more fully in later years.

Gram's childhood may have resembled that of a boy prince surrounded by fancy toys and perpetual treats, but such opulence came with a hidden price tag. Although his parents doted on the child, their love was not unconditional, let alone always available. Coon Dog, for all his outdoor pursuits and carefree bonhomie, was a brooding character, whose melancholia increased in direct proportion to his alcohol intake. Mother Avis was also a heavy drinker, whose alcoholism was couched in the genteel habits of her class. She floated gently on a liquid diet of afternoon cocktails, pre-dinner drinks, after-dinner beverages and an ever spiralling intake of spirits freely available at the many social events she engineered or attended. Over time, the warm rush provided by alcohol would be countered by the inexplicable aftertaste of depression, which Avis combated with the help of prescription drugs. It was a slippery slope. For all the devotion heaped upon him, Gram spent a lot of time enjoying his own company and much of his early nurturing was provided by the black servants in the Connors' employ. Like aristocratic Victorian parents, Coon Dog and Avis sometimes appeared emotionally detached from their children, even when they lavished attention on them.

If alcohol was the snake in the Connor/Snively Eden, it had yet to impinge on Gram's consciousness. He was a confident, well-behaved child who betrayed no signs of any hidden neurosis. Unlike other families in which drink is often accompanied by verbal or physical violence, Gram's parents maintained a deceptively civil and affectionate relationship, despite their voluminous intake. Whatever problems they may had in their marriage were anesthetized. If anything, drinking made them sentimental rather than surly towards each other, at least for a time. This also afforded Gram an independence which several of his friends envied. He seemed adept at organizing his own social calendar, entertaining friends, foraging toy stores at a moment's whim or instructing his chauffeur to ready the car for spontaneous shopping, sporting or hunting expeditions.

This Peter Pan utopia was rudely interrupted when Avis abruptly decided to instil some discipline into her self-governing son. Indulgent though she was, Avis realized that the boy was coasting, insufficiently challenged and in danger of becoming spoiled. In September 1957, he was despatched to Bolles School, a quasi-military institution in Jacksonville, Florida, whose boarders were groomed to think of themselves as officers and gentlemen. Although it was a painful transition, he adapted to the school's demands. Four months later, his mother wrote effusively to the principal: "We are delighted with all the school has done for Gram. He seems so happy."

Gram's supposed happiness was marred by two key deaths in the family during 1958. Dynasties create their own gods and monsters and so it was with the Snively clan. In January, the great patriarch John Snively Senior passed away, just as the family business was enjoying a post-war peak. What he left behind was an orange empire whose assets would be fought over and dissipated with wanton abandon over the next decade. One family member saved from this sorry saga was Coon Dog Connor, who was found slumped on top of his bed, having shot himself in the head with a .32 calibre revolver on 23 December. He was only 11 days away from his 42nd birthday. The certificate of death declared the cause as accidental, although it was generally assumed to be suicide. Inevitably, there was speculation about events leading up to the fatality, including suggestions of marital infidelity, alienation from the Snively family and alcoholic despair. All these reasons were plausible, none provable.

Coincidentally or otherwise, Gram's school reports noted a decline in his behaviour after his father's death. The regimentation of military training and exercise had become oppressive and the young cadet's attitude was enough to single him out as a rebel. By the close of the school year, Bolles' superintendent Major DeWitt Hooker informed Avis that they no longer wished to accept her son as a boarder. The degree of Gram's recalcitrance is underlined by the fact that even the seemingly all-powerful Snively family name could not save him from expulsion. That summer of 1959, Avis took Gram and 'Little' Avis on a train journey across America, visiting various tourist attractions, national parks and even gaining the boy entry to supper shows by Tony Bennett and Nat 'King' Cole. Concerned about Gram's failure at Bolles, his mother persevered in the belief that boarding school was best. During the autumn, she shipped him off to Graham-Eckes School in Palm Beach. Gram was as unhappy there as he had been at Bolles. His only distractions appeared to be strumming on the guitar, attempting to form a group called Red Coats Now and writing pleading, therapeutic letters, begging to be released. After completing the Michaelmas semester, his wish was granted and he returned to a new life in Winter Haven during Christmas 1959, where he was enrolled at a private Catholic school, St Joseph's, which accepted a limited number of non-Catholics among the student intake.

In the midst of this unfolding drama, Avis had been wooed by a womanizing divorcee, Robert Ellis Parsons. A financial consultant who had worked in pre-Castro Cuba, Parsons was predictably perceived as a parvenu and gold-digger by the Snively family. Many felt that description was perfectly correct. His credibility was not helped by the speed with which he married Avis and his insistence that his new stepchildren acquire fresh birth certificates, rebranding them Parsons.

Within the space of a year, Gram's life had been turned upside down. His father had blown his brains out, a new stepfather had appeared seemingly from nowhere, his schooling had been thrown into chaos and the family had left Waycross and relocated to Winter Haven. But once he entered the walls of St Joseph's, a calm descended upon his troubled spirit, apparently obliterating any outward sign of the traumas recently visited upon him. Perhaps he was suppressing his hurt. His young sister had been told by their mother, "You must be brave", and took that to mean that she should not cry over Coon Dog's death. Gram displayed a similar stoicism. Fellow students recall a confident, well-adjusted youth, who caused no problems for the nuns, some of whom evidently entrusted him to monitor or entertain their classes if they were suddenly called away on some errand.

While certain writers and interviewees have tended to portray his time back in Waycross with his biological father as a tragic, lost golden age from which he never recovered, Parsons himself betrayed more ambiguous feelings. "I was scared to death of Waycross. My father's name was Coon Dog and he was really into it . . . And I dug it as long as I was with him, but he passed on early. When I was about 13, I got my new parents. The Parsons are from New Orleans, and it's much more acceptable. But when I was a Connor from Georgia, I didn't like it too much."

Robert ('Bob') Parsons has always been portrayed as the evil stepfather in the mythological life story of his son. This negative caricature has been maintained by surviving members of the Snively family, whose judgements are hardly disinterested, having been channelled through now ancient filial resentments. Among their circle, the image of Bob Parsons as a heartless gold digger and inveterate con man is cast in stone. Only a handful of survivors from that time dispute the stereotype. "Bob Parsons was probably one of the most outstanding guys I ever met," says architect Gene Leedy. "A real handsome guy, and a fantastic gourmet cook. First class . . . The elder Snivelys were a real screwed-up family back then. They had a lot of money in those days, so everybody said he married John Snively Jr's sister for her money. Of course the Snivelys never liked him. They were the ones that said he was a con man and stuff, which was bullshit."

To some extent, Parsons Snr is a victim of inherited history, simply because he never had the chance to offer his side of the story to the numerous chroniclers of his son's early life. As a result, even examples of his emotional kindness to his step-children are easily transformed into cynical attempts to win their approval. He has been represented as a Machiavellian manipulator, an embezzler, a serial adulterer and scandalously implicated as an accomplice in Avis' alcoholism and premature death. Like a pantomime villain, he has even been defamed by people who never knew him. Chris Hillman, who only recalls meeting Parsons Snr when he turned up one afternoon to speak to Gram, nevertheless felt sufficiently qualified to offer a devastating character assessment. "Gram's stepfather was a disgusting, evil, manipulative person. I mean, he bought Gram a club to perform in when he was a teenager! How can you ever get a full, open vision or goal in your mind if those things occur in your life?" This appraisal arguably tells us more about Hillman's distaste for unearned privilege than it does about Bob Parsons' character. If a seemingly supportive gesture such as purchasing a club to assist your stepson's musical career is equated with *evil* manipulation, then Parsons Snr clearly has no hope of redemption. Whatever his shortcomings, he seems frozen like some grim fairy-tale figure or Shakespearian villain in a predestined role. If Gram has become rock's doomed, conflicted hero prince Hamlet, Avis the weak, feckless Gertrude, 'Little' Avis the tragic Ophelia, then Robert Parsons is the calculating Claudius, the embodiment of corruption who "may smile, and smile, and be a villain".

If we are to believe the many commentaries on Gram's life, he supposedly saw through his stepfather's cosy manipulation and ended up resenting or hating the man. Some writers believe he always felt that way. But the facts of the story get in the way of such a simplistic reading. It was Robert Parsons to whom Gram turned at moments of crisis, even in later life. The stepfather used his influence to assist Gram's passage to Harvard and saved him from the draft, for no apparent benefit to himself. Tellingly, when Gram married, he not only invited his stepfather to the wedding, but relied on him to organize the reception. Why would you want somebody you supposedly disliked so much at your wedding? Most revealing of all is the indisputable fact that not once in his life did Gram ever consider relinquishing the Parsons name, even after entering the music business where name changes were common currency.

At the end of 1959, Gram befriended another non-Catholic St Joseph's fee-paying pupil, Jim Carlton. They shared a keen interest in music, and Parsons was intrigued to learn that Jim's father, Ben Carlton, had been a studio guitarist on radio and television back in Chicago and had once appeared on a session with the wildcat Virginian rocker, Gene Vincent. Since moving to Florida, Carlton Snr had been working in a four-piece combo on a television and radio show, *Florida Calling*, sponsored by the Florida Citrus Commission. "They were trying to sell Gram's grandfather's oranges," Jim notes laconically. The boys later became bandmates and remained best friends throughout Gram's short life. Although this was less than a year after Coon Dog's death, Carlton saw no evidence of any dark side to Gram's character nor any indication that he was perturbed by the presence of a new father figure. "He never talked about it," says Carlton of the family tragedy. "Not to me anyway – and we were very close. Bob Parsons has gotten short shrift from the ink he's received, and it's a shame. Gram and Bob had a very good relationship. They liked each other and Bob treated Gram as an adult. They may have had spats, but I certainly never saw any. Gram and I hung out with Bob and the adults. They had booze and good stories and our peers, the football players and high-school kids, were pretty boring by contrast. So we were always hanging out with the adults. Gram was playing guitar and banjo and I'd accompany him on guitar. He had enormous magnetism. At that age kids always called themselves by their last name, as in 'Hey, Carlton . . .' But he was always Gram. At first I thought his last name was Graham! There was this tacit understanding of the respect he commanded. He was a very precocious kid with a lot of charisma. That generated considerable jealousy among the other adolescent males because the girls loved this guy. He wasn't particularly handsome and his features weren't classic, but the package was a good one."

In 1960, Parsons acquired a Fender Stratocaster guitar and was invited to join an amateur rock 'n' roll group, the Pacers, whose repertoire featured the hits of the era. Despite his lack of experience, Parsons confidently assumed lead vocals, reprising his favourite Elvis Presley numbers and subtly incorporating some of the King's daring choreography. Exploiting the Snively social circuit, Gram secured gigs at country clubs and teen dances and allowed the group to practise at his house. Carlton was unimpressed by the music, while conceding that "nobody was any good then". What he noticed was Parsons' self-belief and emerging sex appeal. "He was grooming himself to be a personality. This was the obvious avenue because he was good at it. He had a lot of talent and a magnetism onstage. It was a glamour deal, like being a football hero. I learned that early on. If you've got a big phallic symbol in your hand like a guitar, you're going to attract girls."

Even at the age of 14, Parsons was dating regularly and although the relationships were innocent, their number was surprisingly large. The roll call included such names as Judy Cox, Susan Whitehead, Donna Kirtley and Pamela Carnes. Parsons even managed to maintain an epistolary romance with an old flame from Waycross, Connie O' Connell. Considering the period, this was remarkably precocious behaviour, although Carlton insists that he too was showing a keen interest in girls at the same age. The effects on Parsons were manifested in his nascent songwriting. With a muse to flatter, he started putting pen to paper, creating sentimental ditties in the Brill Building fashion of the time. "He was forever writing songs with girls' names," Carlton recalls. "He wrote one called 'Judy' and another called 'Pam'." Neither survived beyond the time span of the respective romance, nor were they captured on tape or in performance.

The Elvis imitations with the Pacers did not last beyond a year. It had been a fun escapade, but Parsons was already on the lookout for a marginally more accomplished unit. He found the perfect candidate in ace guitarist Jimmy Stafford, a dedicated player from the other side of the tracks in nearby Eloise. Three years older than Parsons and Carlton, he became an elder brother figure whose playing they revered. "Stafford was taking lessons from my dad," says Carlton. "He said, 'This kid's got it! The dangerous thing is that he actually has enough talent to become a pro and ruin his life.'" Ben Carlton liked to play the doleful Jeremiah, warning the kids of the pitfalls of the music business, the false glamour, the vanities of stardom, and the greater likelihood that they would all end up broke and disillusioned. His litany usually concluded with the caveat, "Don't become a professional musician, play at the weekend and work to become a dentist or something." The boys were never likely to be swayed by this sensible advice, least of all Gram Parsons who knew that he would never suffer financially no matter which career direction he chose.

In 1961, Parsons, Stafford, and drummer Lamar Braxton formed the Legends who, like the Pacers, specialized in Ventures-influenced instrumentals, supplemented by rock 'n' roll familiars. Gram valiantly attempted upmarket vocal cameos on 'Blue Moon', 'Ebb Tide', 'Harbor Lights' and 'Stormy Weather'. In order to bolster their sound, the trio recruited tenor saxophonist

Buddy Canova, along with two other players, Grant Lacerte (trumpet) and Lloyd Morgan (alto sax). The brass section appeared intermittently depending on their availability and the importance of the gig. Lacking a bass player proved a serious drawback, but Parsons agreed to take a chance on Jim Carlton, who had just begun playing stand-up bass. Jim Stafford, still taking occasional guitar lessons from Carlton's father, supported the move which added a slight rockabilly edge to the Legends' sound.

"We were all beginners," admits Carlton. "It was all *C*, *A*-Minor, *F* and *G*-7 chords, very basic. Stafford was the only really good player." What they lacked in substance was compensated for with style. Carlton remembers Gram's mother purchasing a wardrobe of stage gear comprising red sports coats in various sizes, dark pants, white shirts and black string ties. Although Gram had not yet learned to drive, an expensive Volkswagen bus was purchased for the band, with the words 'The Legends' painted on its sides in bold capitals. The group played the familiar local circuit of youth clubs, school gymnasiums and teen dances, sometimes venturing as far as Tampa. "We'd hop off at the weekend at whichever gig," Carlton says. "Somebody would score a case of beer which we'd drink and then build a pyramid of beer cans on the dresser of the hotel where we were staying. It was adolescent fun – as much as you could have as a kid with your clothes on. We just had a good time playing music which we were thrilled about. We'd make 15 bucks a night and that was good folding money back then."

Robert Parsons reinforced his position as a Snively in-law when Avis gave birth to a daughter, Diane, in September 1961. Although he no longer needed to covet Gram's approval, he supported his stepson's musical ambitions unconditionally. Predictably, this earned further rebukes from the Snively family who felt the boy simply needed to fulfil his destiny among the orange groves. Jim Carlton was well aware of this culture clash between old money and modern manners. "Gram's family had so much money that there was never a question of him having to support himself. But Gram's cousins were like good old boys. They were very agricultural, citrus people who would drop by in trucks and tramp through the groves. Gram was disinclined to do that. He was very urbane and sophisticated. Gram was no shit-kicking hick or good old boy. If Gram had been reared in Wisconsin he might have become a big polka star. He wanted to be a celebrity."

In Parsons' orbit, celebrity was most closely associated with Elvis and rock 'n' roll. Straight country music was a style apart. "Gram became a great exponent of country," Carlton acknowledges, "but he didn't live it. He wasn't raised listening to country music. On the contrary. He had albums by Peter Nero and James Moody and jazz and pop. I once learned a bit of 'Steel Guitar Rag' and played it to him. He said, 'Carlton, what the hell are you doing?' Then, he mocked me on the piano, playing in a Floyd Cramer style. He wasn't a big country fan until the opportunity arose and then he exploited it brilliantly."

By now, Parsons had moved to Winter Haven High School and was enjoying a lifestyle more befitting a playboy bachelor than a teenager. After school, he could retire to his personal suite and, if the whim took him, tinker on the piano, whose sound was insulated from the rest of the house by a double door connected to his room. Unlike most teenagers, he enjoyed an adult's privacy, cocooned in his private sanctum, a veritable Graceland which Carlton extravagantly nicknamed 'the playground of the stars'. "He had a marvellous lifestyle for a kid of that era, with an entire wing of the house to himself. He had his own television, bathroom and refrigerator. It was a wonderful place to have friends around. For breakfast, we could have anything we wanted. It was usually peanut butter, Canadian bacon on bagels and Pepsi's – totally unhealthy stuff that a kid would love. So he was indulged and had a pretty good life."

In addition to his allowance and treats, Parsons received an extra five dollars a week for cleaning the family swimming pool. "That's the only work I ever heard of him doing, and I don't know if he ever did it, to tell you the truth." In keeping with his playboy image, Gram regularly availed himself of the Parsons' drinks cabinet and enjoyed clandestine late-night assignations with older girls, some of whom, according to Carlton, offered sexual gratification. His 'playground of the stars' had a separate entrance from the rest of the house, so he could come and go at all hours undetected, if necessary covering his absence with a 'gone out tonight, back soon' handwritten note to the servants. "When my family went on vacation I left him the keys to our house and that was his little lair for a while," Carlton remembers. "At a later time, I remember him calling in the middle of the night to meet me half-way between our houses. He had a date and wanted to employ the fold-down seats of our Nash Rambler. There were raging hormones back then, as you can guess."

The Legends' prospects momentarily improved when they appointed a manager from nearby Auburndale. Sam Killebrew was related to the baseball player, Harmon Killebrew. For Parsons, this was testament enough to his entrepreneurial skills. In an attempt to extend the group's appeal, they continued to use their 'secret weapon' brass section. This meant that they could function as either a four-piece garage group or a fully fledged showband, depending on the venue and importance of the booking. Even their driver, Doug Wiggins, was occasionally roped in as an extra vocalist. The enterprise remained engagingly amateur and Parsons always retained a promiscuous attitude towards the group, a trait he would carry forward to his professional career. There were several other groups on the circuit more able and accomplished than the Legends, most notably the Rumors, whose lead singer/guitarist was Kent LaVoie. In a hubristic attempt to improve his own musical prospects, Parsons suggested forming a new band combining the talents of LaVoie and Stafford. LaVoie was unimpressed by Parsons' lax attitude towards rehearsal and elected to stick with the Rumors. However, he did invite his new friends as guests on a show at the Tiger's Den in Cocoa Beach. Parsons' party piece was playing the organ accompaniment on a cover of Freddy Cannon's 'Palisades Park'.

LaVoie's reservations about Gram's punctuality and attitude

appeared to be confirmed that evening when he was unspeakably late. When he finally arrived onstage, he offered the seemingly ridiculous excuse: "We hit a cow!" It was only when LaVoie witnessed the Legends' dented bus, festooned with cow fragments, that he realized Parsons was telling the truth. After the gig, Gram discovered that he had broken several ribs during the collision and was treated at a nearby hospital. He would never appear onstage with the Rumors again.

Gram returned to Cocoa Beach to see another band from Auburndale, the Dynamics. This was no social outing, but a recruitment mission. Never the most secure unit, the Legends had already lost their manager Sam Killebrew, along with their rhythm section. Jim Carlton, despite his closeness to Parsons, sought new challenges and a change of instrument, ending up in the coincidentally named, Clark Still & the Dynamics. Faced with this crisis, Parsons persuaded the [Auburndale] Dynamics' drummer Jon Corneal and guitarist Gerald 'Jesse' Chambers to switch allegiances. "We had a job that evening at the Cocoa Beach," Corneal recalls. "He introduced himself at our rehearsal and we invited him to sit in with us. Back then, we had songwriter Bobby Braddock on piano. The one thing I remember was that Gram's guitar was gold-plated. Everything that would normally be chrome was gold. He had all kinds of ideas and plans for the future. He was pretty good. So, basically, he stole the Dynamics' rhythm section."

The reconstructed Legends established themselves as Parsons' most accomplished group to date. Even Carlton admitted that the new group, which now featured an electric bass in place of his acoustic stand-up, was superior. "The best edition of the Legends was Gram, Stafford, Corneal and Gerald Chambers. They were the hottest, tightest and most amplified. Gerald and Gram sang great harmony, like the Everly Brothers. Unfortunately, it didn't last long because everyone was reaching college age."

The elder Jim Stafford, easily the most talented of the Legends, sought better money playing for various bar and lounge groups and was replaced by Bill Waldrop. The group continued to secure gigs, including a slot on the Saturday afternoon local television programme, *Hi-Time*. Their short set included covers of Ray Charles' 'What'd I Say' and the Everly Brothers' 'Let It Be Me'. Despite the many line-up changes, there was no animosity shown towards the departing members, who remained in touch. The Legends would not survive 1963, but that was not the end of the story. Defying Ben Carlton's dire warnings about the pitfalls of the music business, several of the players established successful careers. Jim Stafford charted with 'Spiders And Snakes', hosted his own television show and established his own theatre; the Rumors' Kent LaVoie reinvented himself as Lobo and enjoyed an international hit with the single 'Me And You And A Dog Named Boo'; Jon Corneal became a country rock journeyman, with spells in the International Submarine Band, Dillard & Clark and the Flying Burrito Brothers; fellow Dynamic Bobby Braddock found fame as a songwriter, penning the Tammy Wynette standard 'D-I-V-O-R-C-E', among others; Gerald Chambers changed his first name to Jesse and toured with Ricky Skaggs; Jim Carlton wrote scripts for the Smothers Brothers, performed as a stand-up comedian, wrote music articles and continued playing as a soloist. Tragedy also played a part in the story, not only with the fate of Gram Parsons, but his bandmate Bill Waldrop who, within a couple of years of the Legends' demise, was decapitated by a helicopter blade.

Even while the Legends were still active, Parsons had been pursuing a parallel career playing folk music. Family friend, Lewis David 'Buddy' Freeman, who knew more about horses than music, was inveigled into the role of 'personal manager'. As a result, Gram played the earnest troubadour at various society soirees, barbecues and parties. The audiences were reasonably attentive, if not particularly discriminating, but the money was good, and there was always plenty to eat and drink. Tellingly, Freeman never once booked the Legends or offered to assist them. He was far too fastidious to dirty his hands working with a pop group, even one largely consisting of well-heeled kids. As would become apparent, his sole interest was in promoting Parsons alone.

Gram's extended network ensured that he was always in demand. His latest pal was Dick McNeer who, like Jon Corneal and others in his circle, came from a wealthy citrus-growing family. The duo, assisted by singing roadie Doug Wiggins and Legends' auxiliary trumpeter Grant Lacerte, played a few dates on the country club circuit. Since they were already performing several songs from the repertoire of Peter, Paul & Mary, it was no leap of the imagination to consider constructing a folk trio in similar vein. Gram already had the perfect 'Mary' in mind.

Patricia 'Patti' Johnson was a year younger than Parsons and they shared much in common. Her father was also in the citrus business and rented an office at the Snively plant. Although the Johnsons were not in the same echelon of wealth, they moved in similar circles and Patti often attended parties with Gram's female cousins. By the time she reached 17, Johnson had achieved dream girl status. As contemporaneous photographs reveal, she was strikingly beautiful, with shoulder-length blonde hair – like a cross between Mary Travers and the New Journeymen's Michelle Phillips. Although a celebrated cheerleader, she was no slave to female pin-up vacuity, but harboured fierce ambitions to succeed as a visual artist. Nor did her gifts end there. "I sang at talent shows in high school and did improvisational dance," she says. "I'd make up my own stuff and perform at clubs, parties and school dances. I was always into music." Parsons first noticed this Renaissance woman when she was performing between sets at a Legends show. He spent most of the interlude feasting his eyes on her contorting body, seemingly fascinated. "I didn't know him," she admits, "but I knew who he was and he was just staring at me through the whole thing." A couple of weeks later, Parsons struck up a conversation, complimented her dancing and casually suggested a date. "He said, 'I'm playing at this place and I'm getting a car for my birthday, so I can pick you up.'" Romance blossomed quickly. Several contemporaries testify to Parsons' intense infatuation, maintaining that Johnson was the love of his adolescent life.

Much of their time was spent driving around in Gram's car, listening to the radio, singing along to their favourite hits and perfecting the harmonic blend on Everly Brothers tunes. Back at Parsons' house on Piedmont Drive, Patti would sit attentively as he played piano and impressed her with the latest song he had learned. It was one such day when he proposed the idea of forming a Peter, Paul & Mary-influenced trio, having no doubt already discussed his plan with Dick McNeer. After rehearsing a handful of tunes, Johnson expressed an interest in playing along with the boys, but was firmly put in her place. "No, you can't do that," Parsons insisted. "You're the girl singer. Girl singers don't play the guitar. We play, you sing!" In an attempt to impress their folk credibility on the student population, they named themselves the Village Vanguards in honour of the legendary New York jazz/folk club.

While these fantasies were still formulating, Johnson learned that there was one more obstacle to overcome: an 'audition' before Gram's imperious mother. The reason for this was never explained or addressed by any of the parties involved. "I just did what I was told," says Johnson. "I assume that because we were singing at these Snively parties and social events his mother wanted to make sure she wasn't going to be embarrassed. And we were representing her son. But it was kind of weird. She was sitting in the living room and I had to go in and sing a cappella. Gram stood off to the side while I sang to her. The room was half dark and I was absolutely terrified. This was Big Avis – we're talking about a very important person here." Patti completed her party piece, but there was no applause or any flicker of appreciation. "There was nothing! I stopped singing and she was just sitting there looking at me. Gram then escorted me out of the living room. I was thinking, 'Am I in, or what?'"

As nothing further was heard on the matter, the answer was evidently 'yes'. Avis' non-reaction may been an example of aristocratic disdain, but a more likely source of her blissfully bemused detachment could be traced to an empty martini glass. Since remarrying, her already prodigious alcohol intake had scaled terrifyingly new heights. It was a family trait. Alcohol ravaged the Snively clan like a wind-driven plague. Even in her happiest moments, Avis had celebrated good fortune with a drink. After the recent birth of Diane, she seemed in the grip of post-natal depression, made worse by the realization that her new husband's wandering eye was firmly fixed on the recently appointed babysitter, Bonnie Muma, a 19-year-old Winter Haven alumna only a couple of years older than Patti Johnson.

While unsubstantiated rumours about Avis' fidelity are commonplace, Robert Parsons' adultery has never been disputed. Although there was no question of divorce or any certainty that the relationship would continue, it was enough to taint the marriage. "Avis became such a hopeless alcoholic that Bob started an affair with the babysitter who was a gorgeous little girl," Gene Leedy remembers. "One day, he said to me, 'I'm going down to Palm Beach to stay with Bonnie for the weekend; I'm going to sleep in a four-poster bed.' He asked me, 'Have you ever smelt a 19-year-old girl in the morning? She smells gorgeous.' I thought, 'What's the big deal? My wife smells good in the morning too!' But I thought about it and, with Avis getting drunk a lot of the time, she'd even throw up in bed. So Avis probably didn't smell too good in the morning . . . She'd get up, have a Bloody Mary before breakfast, then eat a little. After dinner she played bridge with lots of people and they'd have gin and tonics. They got really mad at my wife once when they realized she was drinking water instead of gin and tonic. About five o'clock, they'd start hitting the martinis. By about eight o'clock, Avis was just blind drunk and hostile as hell. So that was the typical lifestyle. Bob was just a caregiver for her towards the end."

The once sociable drinking that had brought Avis and Bob closer now had the opposite effect, sometimes producing surly, volatile outbursts that were not always hidden behind closed doors. Then again, they could just as easily revert to the familiar image of the perfect couple whose closeness and bonhomie had frequently been commented upon by friends and associates. Late one Friday evening, just as Patti and Gram were completing work on some new songs, Bob knocked on the door and announced, "We're going to Tampa for dinner at the Columbia." Patti was astonished. "Tampa was over an hour away and this was 10.30 at night. Avis was already tanked and they were getting in a Jaguar to drive to Tampa for dinner. I remember thinking, 'God, this woman has probably not eaten all day and she's going to Tampa.' It was odd."

Despite the coldness experienced during her audition, Patti recognized Avis' finer attributes. "She was really supportive of Gram and her opinions were important. They were very, very close. She was one of his biggest fans, and so was Bob Parsons. I really liked Avis, she was a wonderful person. I felt sorry for her though, because I knew how lonely she was. When you drink that much, you're really lonely. I remember going to the house in the afternoons after school and she'd be sitting there drinking. She drank gin, and that's one of the hardest things on your body. It's like slow poison. There was a saying at the parties that Avis had her 'gin and whispers'. That means you just 'whisper' some vermouth over the gin to make a martini. In other words, it was straight gin she was drinking!"

The effects of his mother's alcoholism on Gram's state of mind were well disguised from friends. Even with Patti, he would only reveal so much before clamming up or turning his attention to music. "He didn't really talk about it. He did tell me that his father had committed suicide around Christmas . . . The emotional baggage that he had to carry with him was just endless. I spent two Christmases at his house and saw the damage. I don't know how he dealt with it, I really don't. It was heavy duty and a big psychological load for him to carry. There was a lot of stuff, but he never let it get in the way of his music. He was dedicated to playing music and would have pursued that no matter what was going on in his life. That was the way he expressed his emotions and feelings."

* * *

The Peter, Paul & Mary project began with regular get-togethers at Parsons' house. A repertoire was soon established featuring solemn covers of Woody Guthrie's 'This Land Is Your Land', Bob Dylan's 'Don't Think Twice, It's All Right' and Pete Seeger's 'Where Have All The Flowers Gone?' and 'Puff The Magic Dragon' – all channelled through the harmonic prism dictated by PP&M. "We sang some English ballads too," Patti Johnson adds. "Gram had a book called *Child Ballads* and we would go through it and pick out stuff that we could harmonize on. I remember doing the Joan Baez record, 'Silver Dagger'. I was probably the first female Gram ever sang with. We had six or seven songs. It was pretty much commercial folk, but it wasn't too hokey or corny. We were more into trying to be serious. I don't know if he was writing during that period. He never came to me and said, 'I wrote this song.' We did covers." If his songwriting had yet to emerge, Parsons was not beyond fabricating authorship. In one of his more audacious moments, he attempted to convince his mother that he had written the wistful 'It Was A Very Good Year', an Ervin Drake composition he had borrowed from the Kingston Trio's *Going Places*.

The Village Vanguards' debut gig was a nervous affair played out in front of their school peers. Despite her previous solo showcases, Johnson admits she was terrified. "I swear to you my knees were literally knocking. The first time we ever sang publicly was in the high school gymnasium at some sort of rally. I still have a photo of us there. Gram was great about promotion and kept saying, 'Come on, you can do this, it's good.' He was very supportive and we were a really good combination."

They continued playing, sometimes appearing as the 'folk interlude' for garage group peers, but also enjoying headline status. On 29 March 1963, they entered the Polk County Kiwanis Show at the Nora Mayo Hall and finished third. Playing with the Village Vanguards and the Legends increasingly took up Parsons' time and he was frequently absent from school. Often, he would appear for registration in the morning, then furtively slip away for the remainder of the day. Nobody was entirely sure where he went.

Parsons was already compartmentalizing his life, which was probably inevitable considering the different bands and social circles in which he was obliged to mingle. This also explains the contrasting views on his character and motivations. If Patti Johnson was his great love and muse at this time, she was nevertheless kept in the dark about his wilder antics and shielded from his excesses. Unlike some of his more raucous male friends, she had no idea that he was raiding his parents' drinks cabinet or conducting pharmaceutical experiments with Avis' ever ready supply of prescription drugs. This was the image he promoted to the bad boys in his company who duly applauded his bravado. With Patti, he preferred to be seen as the gallant, romantic, dedicated musician whose frequent absences could be explained away as artistic temperament. Other girls would have been suspicious of such behaviour, but Johnson was an independent spirit who trusted her instincts and never wanted to be seen as clingy or emotionally oppressive. "We each had our artistic endeavours. We were both very artistic, moody and complex and needed time alone to do these things. So when he would disappear, it didn't matter. I'd be doing my thing, so there wasn't a problem. We were on the same wavelength. But Gram did disappear. There would be periods of time where I had no idea where he was. I think that became a theme throughout his life. I didn't question it or ask him where he'd been. In those days a girl would not call a boy, he'd call her. His family would go off on a yacht somewhere, so it was like he lived in a different world than me. I never bugged him about it. A lot of times he said he was taking music lessons in this little town Lakeland, which was nearby. He was also going to a psychiatrist. There was a lot of family stuff to deal with."

The revelation that Parsons was seeing a psychiatrist, while never previously printed, is far from surprising. It is not presumptuous to suggest that the entire family needed counselling, but the more traditional remedy back then was drunken oblivion. Gram's relationship with his stepfather remained ambivalent, oscillating wildly between admiration and resentment, depending on the circumstances. His interaction with his mother was equally complex – a devoted son, who spent most of his time defying her wishes by secretly absconding from school. On one such occasion, he persuaded Patti to accompany him on a mini-adventure. "Gram said, 'Let's skip school tomorrow and drive to Palm Beach.'" His mission was to buy some caviar for a party that Avis and Bob were throwing. "This was not a sloppy deal. We got all dressed up. I was wearing pearls, high heels and a suit and Gram wore his best jacket. We drove their Jaguar across state and picked up this huge can of caviar. I was invited to the party that night and they had this champagne drink, 'French 75', a fancy party concoction in a big punch bowl. After three or four of those we got drunk. Gram and I didn't drink together. We smoked some Menthol cigarettes on occasion, but we really weren't into drugs or alcohol at all. If he did the drug thing with his buddies raiding the medicine cabinet, I didn't know about it. I think I would have noticed that, but then again, he was absent so much that he could have been in a drunken stupor and I wouldn't know about it."

After the party, still tipsy from the 'French 75', they decided to head off for a romantic drive. "We drove through this little town, Eagle Lake," Johnson continues, "and this big fat cop pulled us over. Gram got out of the car and he talked this cop out of giving us a ticket for speeding and drinking. We were sent home and that was it. He could do that over and over. Gram could charm people. He had a great way of talking his way out of things, which was good and bad. He knew how to handle situations, but it was a manipulative way of doing things, which he learned from his family."

Parsons' behaviour would soon cause more problems. With the close of the school year fast approaching, he came up with his most audacious and covert plan to date. Only this time, it was not his alone. Soon after Patti's 17th birthday, when Gram himself was still 15, they made the momentous decision to elope. "We just wanted to go off and be together," says the intended bride. "We were going to Georgia because you can get married there without paternal permission when you're under age. Then we were going to go down to Miami and sing in folk clubs . . . Gram and I had planned to elope for weeks and I was putting little articles of clothing in his car. We were planning our escape. It was a typical teenage 'let's run off and get married' thing. We were in love and wanted to go off and be adults. We were tired of being dragged around by our parents. We thought of ourselves as creative people who needed freedom to do stuff without all the restrictions. We figured that if we got married we could do that. Plus, it was going to be fun – we were going to have a great time."

The getaway scheme was organized to follow a booking at the Women's Club at Lake Howard, where the Legends and the Village Vanguards shared the bill. Parsons seemed at the apotheosis of his adolescence that evening. There he was, the star of two bands, the consummate earnest folkie and the garage group rocker, teetering on the brink of a melodramatic elopement with a Winter Haven cheerleader and talented artist. It was as if all his worlds had come together in a single night of celebration. According to one apocryphal account in print, he was so excited that he even blurted out news of the nuptials to the audience. "There was no big announcement," Patti Johnson insists. "But we did get stopped by my dad. Somebody tipped him off. We still don't know who. Somebody ratted us out and he stopped us as we were leaving the dance."

While Mr Johnson played the protective father that was nothing compared to the powerplays of the aggrieved Avis. Once roused from her martini haze, she could be splendidly domineering. If there was one thing a Snively took ultra seriously, it was dynasty. Marriage was not merely an expression of love and commitment, but the key to the family fortune. Avis may have breached that rule in marrying both her husbands, but that did not mean she was happy to allow her son the same licence. Gram was not merely grounded but effectively reconditioned. Having lived the life of a playboy, he now resembled what he actually was – a 15-year-old out of his depth. Suddenly, all his deceptions and foibles were exposed – his absences from school, his willingness to abandon a college career and leave Winter Haven, his multi-musical exploits which went way beyond extracurricular activity and, worst of all, an intended elopement. Without explanation, even to the puzzled principal, Parsons was immediately removed from school, expressly forbidden from seeing his girlfriend and no longer available for concert appearances. He would never play in the Village Vanguards or the Legends again.

Avis' reaction was understandable but proved devastating for Patti Johnson, who felt abandoned, and worse. "Gram never showed up for the rest of the school year. It was a really tough and emotional time and I didn't seem to have anybody on my team. Gram kind of disappeared, which was his habit. When things got tough, he just didn't show up. So Gram and I were put in this very bad light. I don't know why people were angry with us. We weren't hurting anybody. We just wanted to get married."

Johnson was all but thrown to the rumour-mongering wolves of Winter Haven High, who took perverse pleasure in speculating upon recent events. Johnson remembers enduring 56 days of hell, fruitlessly awaiting Gram's return, while her peers teased her about having a baby. Secretly relishing the prospect of a front row seat at the school's raciest melodrama, student gossips encouraged tittle-tattle, transforming the romantic elopement into a Brill Building saga of teenage pregnancy, discovery and rejection. Parsons' mysterious absence and Johnson's reluctance to discuss the relationship merely added fuel to fiery gossip.

Over 40 years later, biographers were still speculating on this key incident, acknowledging that the rumours were exaggerated, yet still quoting apocryphal stories from anonymous school contemporaries or onlookers. So was Patti Johnson Gram's great lost love, his sexual partner and the girl he assumed might be pregnant with his child? Not according to Johnson, who provides a revealing and frank assessment of the relationship.

"There was speculation about the pregnancy, and school was very difficult. But what did they know? I was never pregnant. There was no way I could have been pregnant. It's really not true. We were sweethearts but we were *never* lovers. We were not sexually active. Don't get me wrong, we made out like crazy. Everybody made out, but we never had a sexual relationship. I know Gram would have, but I was too scared to . . . And you know what? I had no clue if Gram had had sex. This was the early Sixties in a small Southern town. I had a very Southern father who was very strict. There was not going to be any funny stuff going on. It was a different era. Back in those days, boys just wanted to have sex and brag to their friends: 'Yeah, I had her.' I was not going to allow that to happen. I wanted Gram's respect and I wanted him to love me as a person, not as a sex thing. So, I'm really glad we didn't have sex in a lot of respects. Sure, I fantasized about it, and what it would have been like, but I'm glad that it didn't ever happen . . . That would have just complicated it so much more because then I would have been like, 'well, maybe he had me and left me'. Back then, that was really possible. Guys used girls and bragged about them. I've had enough baggage with this already: if we would have been lovers and there had been rejection, I would have always been convinced that it was because we had sex, which was my greatest fear. So, the honest to God truth is that I am glad Gram and I *didn't* have sex."

Parsons' exile was compounded by the news that he had spectacularly failed his junior year. Avis was not amused and immediately sought a contingency plan. Meanwhile, the abandoned Patti Johnson was left wondering whether her beau would fulfil his promise to accompany her to the high-school prom. Despite all the melodrama, Parsons knew that staying away would represent the ultimate insult so, reluctantly, he played the Southern gentleman. Alas, his courtesy did not extend as far as actually looking after his escort. During the orchestra band's intermission, Parsons and Jim Stafford sang a couple of songs and afterwards the revellers continued partying till breakfast. There were no intimate moments, nor any attempt by Parsons to explain his absence or address the pregnancy taunts that Johnson had suffered from her class mates. Gram made it visibly clear that he was attending under emotional duress. He studiously avoided Patti for most of the evening, preferring the company of his male friends. That night Johnson was voted 'best looking girl' at the prom, but the accolade was now so meaningless that it failed to register. "I cried all night," she remembers. "He was just gone. He was there physically, but he was not with me . . . It broke my heart."

While Patti Johnson was preparing to leave Winter Haven to study art at the University of Alabama, Parsons was persuaded to repeat his junior year. His destination was Bolles School, the dreaded military institution he had attended back in 1957. Fortunately, the ethos of the academy was currently undergoing a profound change. The retirement of Major DeWitt Hooker, combined with falling rolls, had persuaded the school committee to declassify its military status in favour of a more liberal agenda. Parsons was relieved to hear that he would be treated like a student rather than a cadet. In return for his cooperation, Avis agreed to allow and support his musical activities, albeit not unconditionally. Acting *in loco parentis*, family friend 'Buddy' Freedman was encouraged to look after Gram's interests and, if necessary, assist with any solo concerts he might undertake on the Snively social circuit. Evidently, it was not anticipated that he would be working with a group again any time soon.

Parsons was appreciated as an exotic specimen by his Bolles classmates. During leisure hours, he was seldom seen without his guitar and exuded a style and confidence that was as admired as much as it was envied. In defiance of the academy's former crew-cut militarism, he wore his hair daringly long for the time and, later in the year, added some blond highlights. Both staff and students seem to have adopted him as Bolles' resident bohemian. His tutors included Robert Hubbard, a former Harvard graduate and hearty drinker, who encouraged his work in English, believing that beating beneath his folk-singer persona was the heart of a poet. He was intrigued to see that Parsons owned a copy of *The English And Scottish Popular Ballads* (edited by Francis James Child), a multi-volume set that had provided additional material for himself and Patti in the Village Vanguards.

The book was immediately added to Hubbard's esoteric curriculum, as if in tribute to his favourite pupil.

Parsons' humour, self-assurance and rebellious spirit amused and exasperated his colleagues in equal measure. Fellow student Luke Lewis was impressed, but treaded warily at times. "He was driven and stuck out from the pack, even then . . . He got me in a couple of fights. He was one of those characters that would get inside a barroom and get people riled up, then step back and watch the trouble start. He didn't mind playing with your mind and telling some lies in a while."

Within weeks of his enrolment, Parsons unexpectedly stumbled upon his next musical group. Buddy Freeman had booked Gram to appear at the Greenville Memorial Auditorium as the intermission act on a radio talent show, *The Coca-Cola Hi-Fi Club Hootenanny*. The singer was also invited to join the judging panel. While perusing the list of acts, he noticed the oddly spelt Shilos and sought them out, initially to confirm that they would not be performing 'The Hills Of Shiloh' which he was intending to sing during the intermission. Although listed as a trio, the Shilos featured only *two* members that evening: Paul Surratt (banjo) and Joe Kelly (upright bass). Their guitarist, George Wrigley, had been detained in hospital after becoming embroiled in a fight. Parsons established a rapport with the duo after learning that they were keen fans of the Journeymen. "What makes the stars go where they are?" philosophizes Paul Surratt when recalling that first meeting. "We liked the Journeymen, but hardly anybody else we knew did. We were with Gram and somehow we ended up singing 'Chase The Rising Sun'. It was the first time we sang together. All of a sudden we hit some harmony – it sounded like six people singing instead of three. 'What was *that*?' we thought. It was a magic thing that happened. The next night we did 'Chase The Rising Sun' onstage with Gram – and we won the competition. We did the song again afterwards. Gram was very polished. He was a real good-looking dude with a Florida tan. His hair was longer than ours and I think he had a purple shirt on and a gold medallion. I always tell everybody that if I could ever find a time machine I would always want to go back to the night we first met Gram. That night changed my life."

The streamlined Shilos had not expected to make much impression at the talent show without their main guitarist, let alone win the competition. Evidently, nobody saw anything untoward about Parsons voting for the group whom he had accompanied onstage. After the show, there was excited talk about continuing the 'Journeymen experiment'. The next day Parsons invited his new friends to meet Buddy Freeman. "I couldn't believe it," says Surratt. "I couldn't sleep that night because I was so excited." The cautious Freeman was sceptical about his boy working with the Shilos, not least because he had not even met the hospitalized George Wrigley. Parsons was adamant, however, and soon the quartet were busily rehearsing songs, which was no small feat given the geographical distance between them.

Freeman was careful not to infringe on Parsons' school commitments too much, but still managed to secure bookings at society luncheons, high-school functions and supermarket openings – usually for decent fees. Aware that he was regarded as Parsons' man, Freeman went out of his way to ensure that the others did not feel neglected when Gram was back at school in Florida. "We were a bunch of kids but if it hadn't been for Buddy Freeman we'd never have got as far as we did," says Surratt. "There were local television shows we did without Gram and even restaurant commercials, where we'd sing." Joe Kelly concurs. "I have to credit him because he helped us with publicity. Plus, when we did some shows that weren't in our area, he did the transportation and drove us to different places. He did a lot of things for us."

Parsons still betrayed an odd mixture of over-confidence and insecurity, telling his fellow Shilos that he was the composer of one of their most popular stage numbers, 'You Know My Name'. The song was actually borrowed from the New Christy Minstrels'

1963 album, *In Person*. Parsons was more truthful about 'Julianne', another NCM number, featured on their LP, *Tell Tall Tales*. He was equally extravagant with fabrications when confronted by local reporters and smiled sardonically when an article referred to him as 'RCA recording artist Gram Parsons of Cypress Gardens, Fla'. In his fantasy world, he now shared a record label with his idol, Elvis Presley. Even the rock 'n' roll king never conducted himself with such regal disdain or benign condescension as Parsons demonstrated when congratulating the press on their fine town and musical taste. "I like Greenville's attitude toward folk music," he began, like a dignitary addressing the proletariat. "Not only is Greenville a wonderful audience to play to, but I was astounded at the amount of fine talent in the area. As you know, I plan to do some work with one of your groups."

The Shilos enjoyed playing to high-school audiences in Greenville and Gram also invited them to perform at Bolles. Joe Kelly remembers a packed gymnasium of appreciative students. "It was a good crowd and we did a pretty long set." Photos from the period capture Parsons at his youthful zenith: clad in tight, white trousers, he sits with his legs on a stool, knees spread, smiling, his face framed by a suspiciously blond fringe. The image was sufficient to impress girls from the nearby Bartram Academy. After one show, his guitar went missing only to be returned anonymously some days later. A besotted Bartram student had been sleeping with the instrument, presumably while fantasizing about its owner. "I couldn't believe it," says Surratt. "He was incredible. Some girl left class and followed him around all day long like a puppy. Here was some snooty girl that would never look at you twice and she just skipped classes and followed him. He wasn't like a regular 16-year-old. Our mothers were even in love with him. I'd never seen anything like it in my whole life."

One Bertram student who grew close to Parsons during this period was Margaret Fisher. They shared a love of books, a sentient glamour, a rebellious streak – and alcoholic parents. Their rapport was sparky, a free trade of compliments, sometimes disguised as insults. When Parsons asked Fisher's opinion of Jack

Kerouac, she suggested that *On The Road* was not particularly well-written. "Well, Margaret Fisher," he reprimanded, "that just shows how ignorant you are."

"Well, if I'm so ignorant, what are *you* doing here?" she replied.

"I'm here because we're going to see wonderful things in our life and most people around here aren't going to see shit."

If Parsons sounded aloof and elitist that was not an impression he projected to everybody. During his second stay at Bolles, he befriended a number of students who shared or admired his musical interests. The high-spirited Luke Lewis continued to enjoy his company and was impressed by the amount of time he spent on vocal exercises to improve his delivery. Lewis recalls the evening of 22 November 1963 when a number of students congregated at the school's boathouse to mourn the assassination of President John F. Kennedy. Gram played and sang into the early hours impressing Lewis with his expressive cover of 'You Know My Name'. Another of Parsons' acolytes was Dennis Hupp, a folk enthusiast who wrote his own songs. Gram learned his arrangement of 'Mary Don't You Weep', a Negro spiritual patriotic ballad, inspired by the Battle of the Alamo. It was soon added to the Shilos' set.

Parsons returned to Winter Haven for Christmas 1963, but it was a sombre time. His mother was drinking more than ever and, according to Fisher, he seemed angry with his stepfather. The New Year brought blessed relief in the personage of the Beatles, whose single 'I Want To Hold Your Hand' rocketed to number 1. Their celebrated debut appearance on *The Ed Sullivan Show* attracted an estimated record-breaking 73 million viewers. Even Elvis Presley's epochal performance on the programme eight years before had not matched that remarkable figure. Parsons later admitted that the Beatles made a great impact on his musical outlook, although this was never reflected in his work with the Shilos. They continued to play an over-familiar folk repertoire, incorporating the songs of Peter, Paul & Mary, the Kingston Trio and the New Christy Minstrels, among others.

On 14 February, five days after the Beatles' Sullivan sensation, the Shilos were appearing at a hootenanny, accompanied by two auxiliary members: Marilyn Garrett and Kathy Fowler. Their manager, Buddy Freeman, was convinced that a larger aggregation based on the New Christy model would enhance the Shilos' commercial appeal. Not everyone agreed. Several members felt the variety-style revue, which sometimes ran to two hours and featured solo performances by Parsons and Fowler, distracted attention from the core group. "I had mixed feelings," Joe Kelly admits. "We didn't mind singing a few songs with them, but we definitely wanted to have a separate identity."

Ever the flirt, Parsons ingratiated himself with Marilyn Garrett, who was also his manager's cousin. Over dinner, he played guitar and introduced a new song, 'The Hand Within The Glove', which he claimed to have composed in her honour. Its melancholic air, earnest execution and literary qualities were evident from the opening verse: "The shadow of many years has gone, so have my dreams . . ." After returning to school, he wrote Marilyn flattering letters on Bolles-inscribed stationery expressing his appreciation of her contribution to the Shilos. Clearly, his impressions were in direct opposition to those of his bandmate Joe Kelly.

Additionally, there was mild friction between Parsons and George Wrigley who acted as though Gram was a cad for daring to take Marilyn on a date. He might have been even more envious if he knew about their epistolary relationship which continued intermittently over the next year. Parsons' letters revealed his own vulnerability and frustration that their romance had not developed into something greater. "Every night I go to sleep listening to Ian & Sylvia and fall asleep thinking about you. I have the most beautiful, vivid dreams of you singing their songs . . . I can't live by 'ifs' and 'maybes'. I've never been too adept at concealing myself. This isn't a spur of the moment decision. I've thought about you since the weekend in Charleston."

The rivalry with Wrigley continued over musical presentation. "I think George was jealous of Gram," says Surratt. "They were both really intelligent and were always arguing and trying to outdo one another. It was funny. But George's arrangements and discipline had a lot to do with the group and he always insisted that we rehearse a lot, which helped." The group dynamic was revealing, both musically and personally. "It was pretty much democratic," Kelly says. "Along with Gram, I was the one with the most formal vocal training and a lot of the harmonies were my creation, whereas I was probably the weakest instrumentalist there. Gram obviously came from a very polished background and had sophistication. He seemed more worldly and was very charming. But he could also fool around . . . George was a lot more down to earth. He was inherently a bossier type. Sometimes he'd call us a bit juvenile, which we probably were. We tended to joke around. He was a little more serious and had insecurities. If there was a girl we were interested in, we'd go up and talk. George would envisage someone and put them on a pedestal. 'That girl is so wonderful, she's my dream girl . . .' But he wouldn't talk to her! While we'd be having water fights, he'd be up at the house reading a book. He was working on an experiment. He was trying to make an artificial heart in his bedroom. He ordered an artificial heart microvalve at one time. We were only 17–18, and he was a little bit different."

The onset of spring brought good news for Parsons. On 14 March, the National Thespian Society presented him with a Certificate of Recognition for Dramatic Interpretation, with special praise for his humorous turns. At the same time, Buddy Freeman was still attempting to develop the Shilos' stage act. They remained resistant to his wish to transform them into a musical revue, and there were further signs of petulance and rebellion. Using his Snively connections, Parsons arranged a recording date at Chicago's Universal Studios, ostensibly to promote Cypress Gardens at the forthcoming World's Fair. Freeman had only the vaguest notion of these plans and was affronted by Parsons' failure to keep him informed. It was only at the last minute that he learned the band were flying to Chicago, prompting some drastic amendments to his diary. Parsons travelled ahead of the band and was already ensconced at the Palmer House Hotel, blithely running up credit on some fancy clothes. Freeman was indignant when his protégé insisted he foot the bill. He was equally disappointed by the session. The Shilos had not prepared material in advance or taken the trip seriously enough. Parsons revamped a Shilos' tune ('Raise Some Ruckus Tonight') with new lyrics for the topical 'Surfinanny', a surf meets folk novelty. The rest consisted of covers such as 'Julianne', already familiar from their New Christy Minstrels-inspired revue.

The most bizarre episode in the Shilos' history occurred shortly after the Chicago debacle. Although they did not hear of the story till considerably later, Freeman supposedly turned down the chance for them to audition for *The Ed Sullivan Show*. Or did he? No written documentation of any proposed audition exists and the claim was not made until well after the manager had parted from the group. An appearance on the Sullivan show was the acme of achievement for any aspiring band. Since the Beatles' cameos earlier in the year, every manager in the business was desperate to secure such a lucrative slot. It was a likely passport to stardom and, for an unsigned group, a fantastic opportunity to attract interest from a major record company. Freeman reportedly offered the glib, "they weren't ready" as his explanation for turning down the opportunity. Never mind that this was a once-in-a-lifetime chance. On almost every conceivable level, his logic made no sense whatsoever. The Shilos had appeared on local television on numerous occasions, played live at many big functions and worked in recording studios. *The Ed Sullivan Show* hardly demanded the finesse of a classical concerto. All they would be required to do was perform a single song for a handful of minutes. Child acts and animals had graced the show in the past. How tough could it be? More importantly, what's the worst that could have happened if they had secured a place on the show? Short of disgracing themselves, it could only have helped their career. Even if they had totally embarrassed themselves or insulted Sullivan, it might still have worked to their advantage.

"I'm with you," says Surratt reacting to the above points. "I don't believe Buddy thought we weren't ready. I think he may have had it in the works and maybe just held it over us after we left his management . . . Maybe he was just using that to control us after the event. It's a funny story and, as you say, there's no proof. I just wish it had happened."

The myth of the lost Sullivan audition is better understood in the context of what happened next. Relations between Freeman and the band deteriorated as he attempted, with limited success, to impose some discipline. During the summer of 1964, the Shilos secured a residency at a historical theme park in Myrtle Beach, South Carolina. They were obliged to play seven sets a day, a regime that improved their playing but also encouraged a greater need for post-performance relaxation. Renting a house near the beach, the band partied hard and were soon invaded by a battalion of crash pad strays and camp followers. "We had three guys from Special Forces staying there," says Joe Kelly, "and one guy named Geronimo used to sleep with a sheath knife in his teeth and a mosquito net over his head. One guy was a military dependent who had a car and could get us food at the commissary for half of what we'd pay anywhere else. We'd go to work at nine and be back around eight at night. We ate out. The only meal we had there was doughnuts every morning."

When Freeman arrived one weekend, he was appalled by their living conditions and bohemian attitude. A Free Presbyterian churchgoer, Freeman had limited patience for their vacation lifestyle while they felt he was too paternalistic and strait-laced. They also objected to his hefty management commission, fooling themselves into believing that they could book themselves with equal ease. "He wasn't even coming to the beach," says Kelly, "but he was going to take a 20 per cent cut out of what we were making when we were doing seven half-hour shows every day of the week. We told him we thought it was fair for him to get a share, but not an equal cut. He got all huffy with us." After a humiliating exchange of words, Freeman was unceremoniously fired and vowed never to work with them, or any other band, again. "It was a drag," says Surratt. "He was a wonderful guy and he really cared about us and we hurt him very badly when we left. When you break up with somebody you throw away their old letters. He had tapes of us doing stuff in major studios, which he'd kept. Buddy destroyed the tapes because he was mad at us. I always hoped that he hadn't really done that and kept the tapes in storage somewhere. We may never know. A lot of it had to do with the hurt. I loved Buddy dearly at the end. He believed in us and, in many ways, he was like a Brian Epstein: very meticulous. He cared about the act and wanted us to build a show while we cared more about being just who we were. He'd wanted those two girls [Kathy Fowler and Marilyn Garrett] to continue performing with us, but we always felt we were a group. A manager's job is hard. Now, I think how important he was in bringing Gram to us."

The summer of 1964 proved eventful for Parsons. Back in Winter Haven, he was full of wild and whirling ideas. Inspired by the television series *Route 66*, he fantasized about an epic road trip, traversing the country in his sports car like some teenage playboy. He attempted to entice Jim Carlton along, completing ignoring the fact that his friend had just applied to enlist with the National Guard as a precaution against being drafted to serve in Vietnam. "While I knew his idea was quixotic, I couldn't have gone anyway. When I mentioned my army application, he said, 'Well, can't you just tell them that they got the wrong guy?' 'Sure, Gram, why didn't I think of that?!'" Later, after basic training, the reluctant cadet presented himself before Parsons who stared thoughtfully at his new crew-cut, then uttered the priceless rejoinder, "Carlton, that haircut does nothing for you." He was rather more charitable at the time of his best friend's high-school graduation. Writing in his year book, Gram managed to sound both optimistic and nostalgic: "Perhaps someday we'll both find out what we want. If so we can't help but get it. In the meantime, we must suck knowledge, like cyanide, from an old peach pit. See you in the 'Playground of the Stars'."

Parsons seemed determined to pursue his own adventure into stardom and spent the remainder of the summer in New York, earnestly embracing the mantle of the starving folk singer. He was joined in this quest by the Shilos, who stayed at lodgings in Orchard Street while he availed himself of a loft space, courtesy of the partially blind Tennessee-born blues guitarist, Sleepy John Estes. There, Parsons met a colourful cast of characters, including a performance poet known as 'Normal', whose recitations entranced the impressionable youngsters. "Norman was his name, but they called him Normal," Joe Kelly recalls. "He'd get up and do this bizarre stuff, but the funny thing is I *still* remember his poetry. 'Jackie's in the street again/And no one gives a damn.' This wasn't South Carolina. This was New York. And it was like Noah's Ark: two of every kind." Their other great discovery was singer Zahariah Ryan, "a cute, petite Jewish girl from the Village" with "an olive complexion, big eyes and straight dark hair". Zah and Gram became very close for a time and he would later immortalize her in song. The group survived on a poor diet financed by 'pass the hat' performances at the Café Rafio and Café Wha? Fortunately, their busy schedule in Myrtle Beach had sharpened their singing and playing. "We got up at one of those hootenannies at the Bitter End," Paul Surratt remembers, "and we blew everybody off the stage. Even if the Kingston Trio had been on the stage, we wouldn't have been afraid. That's how confident we were."

One evening, guitarist George Wrigley bumped into John Phillips in Greenwich Village. As inveterate Journeymen fans, the Shilos had met Phillips backstage on numerous occasions and when he learned that Surratt and Kelly were also staying in the Village, he invited the group over to his apartment. There they met his wife, Michelle, who was modelling lingerie while working with John in the short-lived New Journeymen. She showed them her scrapbooks of modelling assignments, a visual experience not easily forgotten.

Former Journeymen banjoist Dick Weissman was also around and found time to record a few songs with Parsons at a local studio, Musicmakers. The tapes were consigned to the vaults and subsequently wiped. All that remains are six rough recordings previously captured on tape at Weissman's apartment. The self-penned compositions, accompanied by a stark acoustic guitar backing, testify to the spirit of Greenwich Village. 'The Rains Come Down' betrays the vocal influence of Fred Neil, complete with meteorological metaphors. The aforementioned 'The Hand Within The Glove' is deemed sufficiently important for Gram to provide a convoluted and incoherent explanation about its 'meaning' ("It's a series of questions and answers"). 'Rolling Stone' is a simple cowboy song, all "tumbleweeds and prairie grass". 'Darkest Years' sounds like a Civil War lament in which the narrator dies in battle. 'That Kind Of Livin'' is the sole upbeat number and singalong from the session. Saving the best for last, 'A River Is Made Out Of Raindrops' features a more expressive vocal, busier guitar work and period piece Dylan-like lyrics. Weissman was uncertain about the commercial worth of the songs but agreed that Parsons was a young talent.

Eager to offer further assistance, John Phillips directed them to the offices of Albert Grossman, the imperious manager of Bob Dylan and Peter, Paul & Mary. Surratt cannot recall actually meeting the great man, but they did impress one of his assistants, who seemed keen to book them for a show at the Bitter End. It came to nothing once he discovered they were still at high school. "We were a bunch of kids and didn't follow through on that," Surratt regrets. "Buddy was gone, so we had nobody to keep on at us."

Nevertheless, the New York trip had proven a great adventure and Parsons would re-establish contact with both John and Michelle later in his career. He also remained friendly with Zahariah Ryan for a while, but they lost contact after she moved to Canada. There were other women in the Village whom Parsons befriended or dated. Margaret Fisher remembers attending a dance at Bolles some time later where Gram's guest was a sophisticated New Yorker, sporting an elegant black, cocktail dress. Years later, Paul Surratt learned of another encounter, when he received a letter from a woman purporting to be the mother of a previously undocumented offspring. "The letter said: 'Do you remember me?' She then described exactly where we were in Greenwich Village. Then she concluded: 'I had Gram's child but I never wanted to bother him about it.'" As with several episodes in Parsons' sexual history, truth and myth are difficult to separate.

The Greenwich Village experience encouraged Parsons to expand his folk interests and soon he was proselytizing the work of Hamilton Camp and Fred Neil, among others. Back in Winter Haven, he would often drive out to Lakeland and relax at the coffee-house the Other Room, owned by entrepreneur Jay Irwin, a former jazz trombonist who also co-ran a music store, Casswin Music. Parsons persuaded Irwin to finance an acetate recording, overseen by engineer Ernie Garrison, of two recent compositions: 'Big Country' and 'Race Between Me And The Wind' (later correctly titled 'Race With The Wind'). The former was a western ballad, extolling the joys of personal freedom, complete with lines that only Gram could have written: "I've known girls with fine silk gowns . . ." 'Race With The Wind' was an assured performance that might have found a home on some cowboy movie soundtrack. Parsons' diction seldom sounded as forcibly earnest as this and although the vocal execution and portentous lyrics are stylized, there is a chilling, prophetic moment where he sings of his as yet imaginary journey "from a comfortable home to a strange land".

The absence of Buddy Freeman as manager became more noticeable after the boys returned to high school in the autumn of 1964. Their contact was more sporadic and bookings were sparse. An unlikely impresario came to their rescue in the form of Robert Parsons. In a typically extravagant gesture, he transformed an empty warehouse into a teetotal teenage nightclub named the Derry Down. For a modest one dollar you could see 'Gram Parsons & The Shilos', as they were now billed. The club's décor was based on that of an English Inn, albeit one without any beer.

Instead, they served non-alcoholic cocktails whose titles, 'Falstaff' and 'Hotspur', betrayed a passing familiarity with Shakespeare's *Henry IV, Parts 1 & 2.* Whether Parsons Snr restricted himself to the non-alcohol rule seems unlikely, but he threw himself into the project, even cooking hamburgers (christened 'derryburgers') for the kids. "He was a gourmet cook," Gene Leedy reminds us, "but he did his research and realized these kids wouldn't pay more than 50 cents for a burger. He said, 'Gene, what kind of guy spends a dollar and a half on a hamburger, cooks it, and sells it for 50 cents?' I helped him fix up this beautiful bar that served non-alcoholic drinks. He had an off-duty policeman chaperoning everything. The kids were always well-behaved because if you screwed up, you lost your card. He did so many things for Gram and always treated his friends as adults. Jim Carlton will tell you that too. I don't know of any classier guy that I ever met." Surratt also remembers Gram's stepfather with fondness and never saw them exchange a cross word during his time in Winter Haven.

"They got on well from what I saw. He had a tremendous influence on Gram, especially regarding manners and the way he dressed and held himself. Gram's stepfather *was* that image." Joe Kelly concurred. "Bob Parsons was a decent guy. He got along fairly well with Gram. I can't recall witnessing any harsh words between them. Not once. He was good, and he put up with us. He let us stay and hang around the house during the day-time."

The Derry Down performances were well attended and Jim Carlton recorded a complete show for posterity on 20 December. Back home for Christmas, Patti Johnson was intrigued to learn that her former boyfriend was playing downtown in a club bought by his stepfather. More worldly and sophisticated since starting at university, she was keen to reconnect with Gram, if for no other reason than to expunge the memory of their last meeting. "I didn't know where Gram had been since I'd graduated from high school. I was heavily into Joan Baez and Bob Dylan and in the middle of the Civil Rights Movement and Alabama. So I went to the Derry Down and he was onstage with the Shilos." After the show, Johnson asked to see Parsons, but was rebuffed. All she was told was that Gram was somewhere 'getting high' and couldn't see her. Indignant at the rejection, she did not pursue the issue and Parsons failed to contact her during the remainder of the holidays. "It was awful because I really wanted to talk to him. We had no closure whatsoever." They would not meet again until the end of 1965.

The Shilos closed 1964 with a memorable New Year's Eve performance at a private function. There, they witnessed more examples of Gram's moneyed background. "We got ready to leave at 11.30," Joe Kelly recalls. "Some person, who had more than his share of drink, said, 'You're not going to quit now, are you? I'll give you $100 to play.' I said, 'Show me the money' and, indeed, he showed me the money. I grabbed the other guys and we put the lyrics to every song we knew to a blues thing which lasted for over 20 minutes till we got to midnight. People were pretty rowdy by then." It was an eventful end to an exciting year.

Only months away from completing his senior year at high school, Parsons was taped for posterity in March 1965, both solo and with the Shilos. Jim Carlton owned a Sony reel-to-reel tape recorder that a family friend had recently brought back from Tokyo and was keen to learn some of the Greenwich Village familiars that Gram was currently playing. Four covers were completed: Journeymen Dick Weissman's mining disaster ballad 'They Still Go Down'; an overly polite rendition of Tom Paxton's 'The Last Thing On My Mind'; a rousing arrangement of Hamilton Camp's 'Pride Of Man', complete with bracing flourishes on Carlton's Gibson B-25 six-string guitar; and the sprightly 'Hey Nellie Nellie', a civil rights number, recently popularized by Judy Collins, among others. The real find, however, was a Parsons' original inspired by Zahariah Ryan, one of the loft dwellers he had shared accommodation with in the Village. 'Zah's Blues' is an extraordinarily precocious composition in which the narrator looks back wearily on life, musing "I wore my life like a crown." The lyrics are matched by an unexpectedly impressive baritone, framed in a minor chord arrangement, oozing faux jazz sophistication. What it displays most provocatively is the possibility of a completely different musical career – with a voice to match.

Several days after recording at Carlton's house, the Shilos descended upon the Bob Jones University in Greenville on 20 March and paid $33.70 to avail themselves of the college radio station's studio. There, they cut nine songs while crowding around a single microphone. The results, along with a home recording of the previously mentioned 'Surfinanny', were issued 14 years later on Sierra Records as *The Early Years.* Given the restrictions placed upon them, the Shilos sound very professional. The harmonies are well executed and the playing impressive. Parsons would never be this disciplined again as a singer, even though he is trapped within a style that seldom allows him to break free. The tape was intended for promotional purposes, so everyone is on their best behaviour, eager to make a good impression. Parsons' vocals are rich, precise and perfectly in tune. The relaxed spontaneity and fractured emotion evident in his later work are conspicuous by their absence here. There is only one moment when the mask slips. On 'Zah's Blues', Parsons momentarily sings off-key, as if caught up in the emotion of the composition. "I love that song," Surratt says. "I've always had a fantasy of going back to a studio and having somebody add soft brushes and some really nice acoustic bass playing. That would be a fun thing to do. When Gram's voice cracked there, it was so real and human." As well as reprising songs like 'Big Country' (erroneously credited to Jay Irwin on the album sleeve), 'Mary Don't You Weep' and 'They Still Go Down', Parsons includes the traditional folk ballad 'On My Journey Home' and the Negro spiritual, 'Oh Didn't They Crucify The Lord'. The Shilos also feature a spirited reading of 'The Bells Of Rhymney' based on Seeger's original. Unlike the Byrds, who were recording a folk-rock version of the song during the same period, the Shilos seldom stray from their traditional base. Nevertheless, their arrangements are impressive, particularly on the opening 'I May Be Right', based around an Earl Scruggs-style banjo solo by

George Wrigley. The influence of Dick Weissman on their song selection is telling. While they dutifully feature material from his 1964 album *Things That Trouble My Mind*, they avoid his version of Dylan's 'A Hard Rain's A-Gonna Fall'. Evidently, that was too modern and controversial for a band still locked in the more commercial folk world of the early Sixties.

The Early Years is not a definitive representation of the Shilos' folk repertoire. "We had about 30 songs," says Paul Surratt, who regrets that more material was not recorded. "Gram would sing Josh White's 'A Man Who Couldn't Walk Around' about Roosevelt and [Marty Robbins'] '3:10 To Yuma'." Surratt also has a home recording of Parsons performing another of the Child ballads, 'Great Selchie Of Shule Skerry', which had recently been made famous by Judy Collins. Other live songs evidently never captured on studio tape include the traditional 'Spanish Is The Loving Tongue', the New Christy Minstrels' 'You Know My Name' and the Journeymen's 'Soft Blow The Summer Winds'. "I would give a thousand dollars to hear Gram sing those songs again," says Surratt. "And I'd give $10,000 to have a video of the local television shows we did together. But at least we got to do them."

Whether Parsons saw any future for the Shilos is doubtful. By this point, he had applied to Harvard, an apparently overreaching gesture considering his mediocre school record. One of his tutors remembers him submitting Dylan's 'Mr Tambourine Man' as part of an assignment. Parsons' plagiarism was uncovered when the Byrds picked up airplay on the song, which would hit number 1 soon after. The deception came as no surprise to his mentor, Robert Hubbard, who had previously reprimanded Gram for claiming to have written a Lawrence Ferlinghetti poem. The news that Parsons had been accepted by Harvard was a miracle, partly conjured by a concerted campaign. Family friend Gene Leedy recalls Bob Parsons encouraging influential ex-Harvard pals in his circle to contact the university, effusively recommending his stepson. "He made a trip there unannounced and took Gram with him. He probably manufactured a few connections. You've got to realize that Bob Parsons was a hell of a salesman. Gram was a talented musician and I think Harvard was trying to get a little more diversity into the student body then."

Back at Bolles, Robert Hubbard, another Harvard graduate, prepared him for the entrance exam and persuaded other members of staff to look kindly on his foibles. Even when these avenues had been exhausted, the boy had another shot at winning acceptance. "He told me he got into Harvard on the basis of an essay," says Jim Carlton. "Then he received a letter from Harvard enquiring about his choice of bed sheets. It said: 'Do you want white, pin-stripe or Harvard crimson?' He thought that was very amusing."

Unsurprisingly, Parsons seemed more detached from the Shilos as summer approached. It is salutary to consider that the recording session at Bob Jones University was not paid for by Parsons, but by Paul Surratt's father. The tapes were sent out to promoters along with a polite PR letter, but there is little evidence that Parsons was actively involved in the campaign. It was Surratt who seemed most determined to sustain the momentum, lending Gram his Martin D-28 guitar and saying nothing when it was returned badly scratched. "I was trying to save the group," he says. "I used to take the songs we'd taped to Nashville and play them to different people. They all said, 'No. Folk music's passé." Surratt must have feared the worst as Parsons had already betrayed reservations about the Shilos' lack of ambition. "Before we went to Greenwich Village, we were riding in a car and he said: 'They're not going to make it. You and I will make it, but they won't.' I thought that was strange at the time."

On 27 May 1965, Parsons wrote to Surratt expressing his concerns about the future. "I've been thinking, if we want to make it as a group we're going to have to do some serious rearranging," he began ominously. His eminently sensible plan was that they should forget the familiar folk favourites and concentrate on his own songs. "I'm sure my music is going to be as big as Dylan's" he added, in a breathtaking flourish of egocentricity. "We are going to have to cash in on this thing Dylan's started, and like it or not we'll be associated with him. I still want very much to make it with the Shilos. I always have."

Those final words sounded more desperate than committed. With Harvard looming for Parsons, it was difficult to see how the group could continue, unless they moved to Massachusetts in the autumn. In any event, there was little sign that they were keen to follow his desire to pursue a folk-rock direction. Surratt admits that he was no Dylan disciple and preferred the material they were currently performing. He also suspects that Parsons was already thinking of adding country material to their set, although his view may be coloured by subsequent events. The one example he provides is the song 'They Gotta Quit Kickin' My Dog Around', but this was no aberration into a new country Shilos. On the contrary, the song was in their familiar commercial folk repertoire having just appeared on *The New Christy Minstrels Sing And Play Cowboys And Indians.*

Within two months of Parsons' ambiguous letter, the Shilos were no more. After performing with them at a beach party in Garden City, South Carolina, Parsons prepared to head north. Wrigley and Kelly went to college and Surratt was drafted and joined the Navy. "It all ended," he laments. "That was the last time we ever played together. I went into a deep depression for weeks. I thought my whole life had ended."

Parsons had good reason to follow Surratt into the abyss of depression, though not for musical reasons. During the preceding months, he had witnessed the deterioration of his mother's health, in tandem with her marriage. Her drinking had reached such dangerous levels that she was confined to hospital in the weeks prior to Gram's graduation. It is here that the most serious allegations against Robert Parsons are voiced. His detractors insist he hastened her demise by smuggling drink into the hospital and effectively administering cocktails on her deathbed. If true, it merely testifies to their mutual disregard for the effects of alcohol. Parsons Snr had no hesitation in dispensing similarly lethal doses to his own body only a few years later.

On 5 June 1965, Avis died, three days short of her 42nd birthday. The cause was cirrhosis of the liver exacerbated by alcohol-induced malnutrition. Gene Leedy regarded any criticisms of Bob Parsons as both unfounded and misguided. "What happened was, she didn't like the food in hospital so every evening Bob would go down to the Sundown Restaurant, best in town, and get her a plate of food. Of course, she demanded to have a drink. He'd take her a drink, but he wasn't trying to poison her. That's horseshit. Dr Dorman, who was our family doctor and Avis and Bob's doctor, was a good friend of mine. When Avis died, he demanded an autopsy. I asked, 'Why did you do that?' He said, 'Well, I didn't want Bob Parsons to get credit for killing her.' She was a hopeless alcoholic. The doctor told me, 'If you could have seen her brain, you'd never drink again.' It was totally pickled. That proved Bob didn't kill her. It had nothing to do with drinks she had in the hospital."

Gram learned of his mother's death while attending his graduation ceremony at Bolles. Immediately, he returned to Winter Haven. He conducted himself with an air of Southern stoicism, fielding sympathetic calls and personal condolences with a resigned, polite air. "I remember that day very vividly," says Jim Carlton. "I called him and said: 'Can I get you out of there?' He said: 'Oh thank you. Come get me.' I picked him up and took him to Donna Kirtley's home near Cypress Gardens. She was a girlfriend. I knew he needed to get out of there because he was taking so many calls from so many people."

After Avis' death, Gram spent the summer in New York, still pursuing his dream of establishing himself as a folk singer in the Village. "I pictured myself as a sort of male Joan Baez," he said. "I was singing protest songs and such. I think I was hip to how carried away I'd gotten by the time I graduated from high school."

Folk rock was at its apotheosis during that great summer of 1965. The Byrds had hit number 1 with 'Mr Tambourine Man', Sonny & Cher soon followed with 'I Got You Babe' and Bob Dylan almost did the same with the epic, groundbreaking 'Like A

Rolling Stone'. Even visiting British acts like the Beatles and the Rolling Stones demonstrated the influence of the protest movement in the existential lyricism of 'Help!' and '(I Can't Get No) Satisfaction', respectively. Village habitués like the Shilos' friend John Phillips had already seen enough to seek the promised land in LA, along with many others, including John Sebastian and Stephen Stills. Parsons hung out with those that remained, notably Richie Furay, whom he impressed with a promising composition, recently completed. 'Brass Buttons' was adapted from a poem, *Prereminiscence*, that Parsons had written for *Bolles' Literary Magazine* earlier in the year. In common with the best of Parsons' work, the lyrics are allusive and hint at some deeper meaning that proves evanescent. The song's imagery offers fleeting glimpses of an unspecified figure, made momentarily manifest by a handful of adjectives detailing what sounds like peculiarly archaic garb. Were the brass buttons and silver shoes the property of some Southern society gal or the ornate uniform of a privileged Bolles' military man? Was the song an oblique tribute to his mother? No more clues are provided beyond a strong sense that this was a song of memory, an interpretation reinforced by the additional verses in the original poem. As with 'Zah's Blues', its narrator sounds reflective and world-weary, a figure old before his time. Richie Furay, always a connoisseur of unusual lyrics (as he would display by memorizing Neil Young's oblique 'Nowadays, Clancy Can't Even Sing') treasured 'Brass Buttons' which he would later record with Poco.

Another music fan Parsons encountered while in the Village was Brandon de Wilde, best known as the child actor in the western *Shane*, and later for playing alongside Paul Newman in *Hud*. Having recently completed the war film *In Harm's Way*, de Wilde was attempting to reinvent himself as a singer-songwriter and encouraging his backers to hunt for a record deal. The transition from actor to singer was never easy, unless you were playing the lounge circuit and staying in character. But several Hollywood stars, including David Hemmings and Peter Fonda, were also intent on 'crossing over', using their 'Byrds connections' as an entrée. Brandon de Wilde forged a strong friendship with Parsons destined to last. On 15 August they joined over 55,000 people at New York's Shea Stadium to witness the Beatles. The hysteria underlined the new potency of pop music leaving onlookers in little doubt of what the future held.

Parsons claimed to have seen the Beatles from a closer distance while attending a party organized by the millionaire Broadway producer, David Merrick. Given de Wilde's thespian connections this was eminently possible, but never confirmed. Before heading for Harvard, Parsons and de Wilde harmonized on some Everly Brothers tunes, then promised to reconnect later in the year.

Whatever academic aspirations Gram might have entertained were blighted by the Greenwich Village interlude. From the moment he enrolled at Harvard, his primary interest was music. He spent much time scouring the local clubs in Cambridge, which still entertained folk, blues and jazz icons from another age. Bulletin boards were festooned with cards offering second-hand instruments for sale or seeking like-minded musicians to form a band. Within weeks of arriving at university, Parsons fell in with a loose grouping of jazz aficionados whom he named the Like. Once they realized his limitations as a jazz player, they swiftly moved on, although one student named Tom Snow kept the faith.

In urgent need of new musicians, Parsons bypassed student jazz enthusiasts and fell in with two Cambridge-based players. John Nuese was playing guitar in the Trolls but bonded with Gram during a late-night acoustic jam and committed himself to the revamped Like. Nuese recommended his friend Ian Dunlop for the bass spot and Tom Snow was retained as pianist. The individuals had contrasting musical tastes ranging from country to R&B and jazz, but they shared a love of experimentation and, like Parsons, came from privileged backgrounds. Nuese was the son of a judge, while Dunlop's father was a psychiatrist. After a short period rehearsing together, the Like found a soulful drummer, Mickey Gauvin, who was playing in a bar band in downtown Boston.

Back at Harvard, Parsons was busy self-mythologizing his summer visits to New York, namedropping vague connections with the Beatles and Bob Dylan. He spun these tales with such matter-of-fact insouciance that they seemed believable. Occasionally he went too far. His new roommate Larry Piro took him at his word and saw no reason to doubt his claims when presented with written 'evidence'. "He even received a telegram which he said was from Bob Dylan. Dylan spelled out a birthday wish using all of Gram's song titles, signed 'Buttons and Bows'. I think I was the only one who saw it." Another favourite fantasy that would soon transfer from gossip into print was the 'RCA deal'. Only, it wasn't a deal or even an audition, but merely an opportunity to back Brandon de Wilde on a number of songs he was pitching to the label. While in New York with de Wilde, Parsons had met Barbra Streisand's agent Marty Erlichman, whom he claimed had facilitated these recordings. On 28 October, the Like entered RCA's New York studio and cut a handful of songs including de Wilde's rendition of Buck Owens' 'Together Again'. The actor was deadly serious about pursuing his musical ambitions and spent considerable time working with Parsons' musicians. He even became an 'unofficial' member of the band. "We had a very good relationship," says Dunlop. "Our first major involvement was going to New York and working on his songs. He was seeing if he could get a deal and was interested in music but, of course, he had his own career that would come and go. Something would come up, like a role in a television series or a guest appearance, and he'd go off."

The group captured an authentic country sound while working with de Wilde, anticipating Gram's later experiments in the genre. At this point though, Parsons was more into folk rock with a distinctive Byrds' flavour. Ever charming, he was allowed to record two of his own compositions with the Like. 'I Can't Make It Any More' (aka 'Just Can't Take It Any More') sounded just like the Byrds' 'Chimes Of Freedom' and the Dylan influence was equally present on 'November Night(s)'. On the demonstration tape the ensemble was humorously named 'Gram Parsons And The Tinkers', as if they were a Gaelic ceilidh band.

Parsons cut an exotic figure among his campus contemporaries and was quick to cement his reputation with some premature and preposterous publicity. The student newspaper, the *Harvard Crimson*, accepted his boasts without question and excitedly announced: "A Harvard freshman has signed the second largest promotional contract in RCA Victor's history – exceeded only by Elvis Presley." As if that wasn't enough, they added: "Gram himself admitted that the Beatles are interested in two of his songs for their next album."

This puff piece underlined the maxim that the bigger the lie the more likely it is to be believed. Rather than being laughed off campus for such bragging, Parsons attracted the interest of the *Boston Sunday Globe* who sent their young reporter William Fripp to cover the story. He was amused to meet an over-confident student unafraid to namedrop Bach, the Beatles and 'Bobby' Dylan. Indeed, Parsons spoke as though his name might follow next on that illustrious list. "Bobby asks questions and hints at emotion. I want to answer some of the questions teenagers ask about love, to describe the gamut of feelings and how to deal with them." What followed was even funnier. In his usual disingenuous way, Parsons mythologized his recent exploits, inspiring Fripp to pen a slightly tongue-in-cheek apologia for a kid evidently too talented to concentrate on his studies. "It's not that Gram Parsons can't adjust to the freshman grind at Harvard," Fripp wrote. "It's all these other things, like calls from Ed Sullivan, frigging [frugging] with the Beatles at Arthur, wrapping up that contract with RCA Victor. Rarefied things like that, they keep a boy busy, on edge." This cocktail of half-lies and hyperbole required a surgeon's scalpel to cut through to the truth. The Ed Sullivan quip was an obvious reference to Buddy Freeman's previous boast, itself a likely exaggeration; the Beatles' allusion probably stemmed from seeing them in New York, echoing an improbable tale Gram told of being mistaken for Ringo one evening in Greenwich Village; the fanciful 'RCA contract' story had already been broadcast during the Shilos' period and could now be regurgitated thanks to Brandon de Wilde.

These were heady times for Parsons. Only days away from his 19th birthday, he could hardly fathom his luck upon learning that Ted Polumbaum, a freelance photojournalist for *Life* magazine, was heading for Harvard to profile the young musician as part of a general feature on new student arrivals at America's most prestigious Ivy League universities. Other photographers had been despatched elsewhere on similar assignments in what sounded like a quest for the 'Men of Tomorrow'. It was a brilliant idea and Parsons' involvement was solely due to his inflated profile courtesy of the *Boston Sunday Globe*.

The arrival of a photographer from *Life* caused a commotion. Fellow student David W. Johnson was amazed to see a group of long-haired musicians on the steps of the Widener Library. "The centre of attention was the group's leader, Gram Parsons. Up close, Parsons appeared remarkably self-possessed and confident. He was lean and good-looking . . . I felt awed that a contemporary could be so far along the road to the American Dream we grew up on: being Elvis." In truth, Parsons had barely started on that road, but his instinct for procuring publicity was impressive.

Ted Polumbaum did not merely snap some promotional shots for his magazine, as might have been expected, but followed Parsons around campus on numerous occasions, taking hundreds of black and white photos. This was a visual archive worthy of a presidential visit. Parsons is pictured exercising in the gym, eating in the university canteen, smoking a cigarette while chatting outside the music room and strolling across the campus grounds in a turtleneck sweater, his right eye obscured by an unruly fringe. There are also posed shots of him performing with the Like, including an appearance at the Freshman Union on his birthday. The entire back wall is covered in congratulatory graffiti, with large painted messages testifying to his popularity or ego: "Gram Parsons Is Out Of Sight", "Happy 19th Gram", "A True Friend". Someone has even included a fragmented verse: "When old friends get together that's when kindly similes . . ." underneath which is a psychedelic illustration. This was some birthday celebration.

Polumbaum continued to follow Parsons like a stalker, snapping some beautiful shots of the student in his living quarters at Pennypacker Hall. In one sequence, he is pictured writing notes at a desk on which a strategically placed copy of Dr Sidney Cohen's *The Beyond Within: The LSD Story* can be glimpsed alongside a collection of LPs and a portable record player. Arguably, the most dramatically revealing portrait of all shows his clean-cut colleague Larry Piro studying in an adjoining room, while peering in with an expression of curiosity or appreciation. Gram sits cross-legged on the floor, eyes closed, strumming an acoustic guitar while singing. All around him are the tools of the singer-songwriter: a single candle illuminates an open notebook of songs, a second acoustic guitar sits on a nearby settee and a crumpled cigarette packet lies empty on the floor.

Parsons already resembled a star in student's clothing. *Life* promised him a quick route to fame, then forestalled such godhead by spiking the grand article on America's finest freshmen, probably for logistical reasons. All that remained was that breathtaking cache of photographs, consigned to the archives for decades.

Having tasted the aphrodisiac ambrosia of minor celebrity Parsons was never likely to remain a humble undergraduate, even at an institution as august as Harvard. "His whole experience of Harvard as a student was secondary," says Larry Piro. "He wanted to play. He wanted to write songs." For all his outward bluster, Parsons admitted feeling academically out of his depth. "I was turned off by the fact that I had to study all these things I didn't understand. I lasted four or five months by playing music and having good times." This was not the entire truth. While at Harvard he forged an enduring friendship with his freshman adviser James Ellison Thomas, a postgraduate from the Divinity School universally known to students by the acronym, 'Jet'.

Thomas was a young, progressive tutor seemingly unconcerned by Parsons' academic shortcomings. He treated him almost as an equal, sometimes taking on the role of a sympathetic elder brother figure. When Gram later told a reporter that he majored in Theology, he was probably referring to the many late-night philosophical discussions with his ecclesiastical mentor. Thomas enjoyed their engaging conversations and felt that the freshman was "intellectually capable" enough to complete his degree while admitting that "his real interest was his music".

Another feature of Parsons' short stay at Harvard was his experimentation with LSD, which usually took place at the weekends when prying eyes were less attentive. He was clearly fascinated by the vivid accounts of patients who had taken part in the research trials at Veterans Administration Hospital during the Fifties, as clinically documented in Dr Cohen's *The Beyond Within: The LSD Story*. A couple of old friends from Bolles, eager to see Harvard, visited Parsons' dorm and were shocked to witness his condition. He was barely coherent. Jet Thomas also experienced the disconcerting sight of Parsons on LSD when the student turned up at his apartment one evening, tearful and mentally confused. Unusually, Gram opened up about his family problems, expressing concern about the fate of his sister Avis, whom he had left behind. 'Little Avis' had moved to New Orleans with her stepsister, Diane, and stepfather Bob Parsons, who would later marry the family's teenage babysitter, Bonnie Muma.

On 8 November, Gram wrote a touching letter to his sister, expressing his concerns for her future in a philosophical tone that clearly reflected his own fears and misgivings. "I wish there was some one thing I could tell you," he began, "some clear advice or magic spell to whisk away all the things that are bothering you right now . . . The best thing we can do is learn from the past and live our lives the right way so, in time, when we can do something to change things, we will be real people. Not haunted by what life has done to us. We have the advantage of seeing definite examples of what can happen when people permit life to tangle them so badly that there is no escape."

Parsons' determination to live life his own way and escape a troubled family legacy pushed him further towards a career in music. Although he remained on Harvard's student list until early in the New Year, he had effectively left the university by the end of 1965. Jet Thomas supported his decision but never felt he had been wasting his time. "Harvard was very good for him. His patterns were disastrous before he got there. He wanted to play music and yet he was in college. He couldn't do both things at the same time. But it was a positive experience."

That much is emphasized by the number of songs he completed during this period. Parsons was never known as a prolific writer. In later years his output was sparse in comparison with many of his contemporaries but the discipline engendered by Harvard proved advantageous. His roommate Larry Piro remembers him composing songs into the night like a student completing an overdue essay for an important tutorial. "They were complete songs," he stresses. "They were performable." Parsons' ever present notebook listed 22 self-penned compositions up to this point, at least seven of which remain lost or were never captured on tape: 'A Place To Be Going', 'Between Your Hands And Mine', 'Honda Rides', 'Night Walk', 'Small Boy's World', 'Some Blues Thing' and 'Won't Ask Me'.

Just before Christmas, Parsons visited Bob, Little Avis and Diane at their new home in New Orleans, then returned to Winter Haven for the remainder of the festive period. He enjoyed Christmas dinner with the Carlton family, impressing Jim's father Ben with his liberal sensibilities during a conversation about bigotry in the South.

On 26 December, he taped six more songs at Carlton's house, including two stunning originals, the aforementioned 'Brass Buttons' and 'Wheel Of Fortune', an affecting, ornate composition, clearly inspired by the Dylan school of folk rock. Respectful covers of Fred Neil's 'Other Side To This Life' (mistakenly retitled 'Another Side Of This Life') and Billy Edd Wheeler's 'High Flyin' Bird' fitted in well with the set. The only aberrations were two fairly uninspired covers of songs that had already been over-assimilated into the folk, pop, rock and even Merseybeat idioms: the Reverend Gary Davis' 'Candy Man' and Leiber & Stoller's 'Searchin''.

Before leaving Winter Haven again, Parsons made an unexpected visit to the home of his former girlfriend, Patti Johnson. Unbeknownst to him, she had already been through a personal odyssey since their break-up. "I had gotten away from my whole 'Gram thing' and was trying to become a good artist and have a career in it. My parents thought nobody but queers and weirdos did art. And I had the long hair. This was before hippies and after beatniks." After enrolling at the University of Alabama, she became involved with the Civil Rights Movement and fell foul of the more extreme reactionary elements in her community. "I had the Ku Klux Klan chasing me all over campus because I looked like an outside agitator. I couldn't take the pressure anymore. I was afraid I was going to get shot." Switching colleges, Johnson moved to LA and enrolled at the California Institute of the Arts (formerly Chouinard Art Institute) and seemed even more sophisticated when she came home for her Christmas vacation. Having been snubbed by Parsons at the Derry Down the previous year, the last thing she expected was a surprise visit. "It was unannounced," she says. "He just showed up. My mom was mad at me about something, the vibe was bad and all of a sudden Gram shows up. He told me his mom had died that June and he wanted me to go out and smoke pot, but I didn't want to. I don't know why. Something was bothering me. I felt, 'Wait, do I want to go out and get high with somebody that I've got these issues with?' I was fragile and I wasn't sure I wanted to deal with all that. I felt like I couldn't handle it, so I said 'No'. Then he said, 'Well why don't we just get married?' I looked at him and replied, 'Gram, you know you broke my heart and I'm not going to let you do that again.' . . . I sensed that he was just being chivalrous. He was trying to make up for what he hadn't done."

Even by Parsons' casual standards, this was extraordinary. He had already toyed with Johnson's emotions by agreeing to elope, before changing his mind, then disappearing and subsequently refusing to see her. Now, he was proposing again. Most people might have proffered an apology for past behaviour, humbly requested a date and hoped for the best, but Parsons was acting as if he could turn back the clock in an instant. His emotional reasoning was at best opaque, at worst thoughtlessly selfish. As Johnson explains, "It went from 'Let's go smoke pot' to 'Let's get married!' You're the only person I've told this to before. It was mind-boggling. If this had been years before and we were in a different situation, it would have been awesome but for him to just waltz in here unannounced and then ask me to get married! It was very strange . . . Something was telling me this was really wrong. As much as I loved him, I knew if I had said yes it would have been the most destructive event of my life. It was like: 'What is he doing?' OK, he was really in mourning for his mother. He had just lost her to alcoholism and he was at some weird juncture in his life. I think he was just grabbing for anything at that point. And maybe he was just using me . . . and then it would never happen. When I thought about it after he left, I realized that he had a bigger path. I would have just been some thing that he was dragging around. I sensed that he was going somewhere I didn't belong and that didn't have any part of me being with him. So I thought, 'No, I'm not doing that.' And that was the last time I saw him . . . I'm sure Gram never thought of me again after he left Winter Haven and went off on his journey. I was a part of a life that he left behind."

As Johnson readily admits, Parsons' proposal could hardly have been serious. That he never attempted to contact her again speaks volumes about his lack of emotional commitment. Within days, he had left Winter Haven, Patti Johnson and Harvard University to start a new adventure in New York. Soon, Parsons was joined by the members of the Like, excepting Tom Snow, who was obliged to remain at the Berklee School of Music to complete his studies. After a short spell at Brandon de Wilde's apartment, the musicians found a large house in the Bronx which they soon transformed into a bohemian enclave. Copious amounts of psychedelics and marijuana were consumed when available, with Parsons even experimenting with a horse tranquillizer in an attempt to achieve a unique high. But the Bronx was no hippie heaven and the musicians were ambitious and keen to succeed. "We were working protracted engagements at clubs," Dunlop recalls. "We weren't living on nothing. We were hard-working musicians, not getting rich, but scraping by." They also had a new name which Dunlop claims to have borrowed from a children's television programme, *Little Rascals*: the International Submarine Band.

While their new name sounded like a cross between a bubblegum cartoon group and a band of psychedelic explorers, the music they were creating bore no resemblance to either. In searching for a style, they were increasingly drawn towards both country and rhythm & blues. Attempting to date Parsons' initial forays into country music is a perilous undertaking complicated by fractured and occasionally contradictory reminiscences from former colleagues. Paul Surratt thinks Parsons was already moving towards country during the final phase of the Shilos; Reverend Jet Thomas recalls his charge singing Hank Williams ballads to ease his troubled soul while at Harvard; Jim Stafford feels he may have encouraged Parsons to switch to country at some indeterminable period in the mid-Sixties; John Nuese insists he turned Gram on to both Merle Haggard and Buck Owens; Ian Dunlop cites their shared appreciation of Ray Charles' 1962 album *Modern Sounds In Country And Western Music* as another defining moment. Probably everyone on this list deserves some credit for inspiring Parsons on his eventful expedition into the heart of country music. What is easily forgotten is evidence of his own interest in roots music from an early age. Like many of his generation, Parsons experienced country music through the prism of rockabilly and rock 'n' roll. Among his favourite performers of the Fifties were Elvis, Jerry Lee Lewis and Carl Perkins – all of whom could claim some credit for pioneering a musical form later termed 'country rock'. As Parsons explained: "On our local station I would get country music mixed with some rockabilly, and I liked some of the country music, the early Ira Louvin and Charlie Louvin stuff, early Everly Brothers . . ."

Parsons also claimed that he was touched by country even while playing the part of the earnest folkie. "I was singing protest songs [but] by the time I graduated from high school, that's when I got into bluegrass. One of my favourite records was by the Scottsville Squirrel Barkers [*Blue Grass Favorites*]. That was Chris Hillman's group, though I didn't know he was in it. And I would have given my left knee to be in it. The Dillards were another one of my favourites . . ." Unreleased tapes of the Shilos at the Derry Down confirm that last point. At one stage, Parsons repeats almost verbatim one of the Dillards' comedic routines from the recently released album *Live!!! Almost!!!* Clearly, his fellow Submarine Band members were rekindling a musical love that had always been present. "They reintroduced me to country music after I'd forgotten about it for ten years," Parsons concluded.

The International Submarine Band were beginning to mix country and R&B during rehearsals in the Bronx. Mostly, they were lurching towards an unspecified style influenced by the records they loved. Two new releases proved particularly inspiring. The album *Together Again/My Heart Skips A Beat* by Buck Owens & The Buckaroos included a cover of the Drifters' hit 'Save The Last Dance For Me' which Dunlop and Parsons regarded as a fascinating crossover. The album also featured 'Truck Drivin' Man' (composed by Terry Fell), which was immediately incorporated into the ISB's set. During the same period, Ray Charles issued the groundbreaking *Country And Western Meets Rhythm And Blues,* which expanded the ideas displayed on the two volumes of 1962's *Modern Sounds In Country And Western Music.* Charles' new album opened with Buck Owens' 'Together Again', which also became a major hit. "It was a reaffirmation," says Dunlop. "We'd started messing around with country-based songs and it was like we'd all clicked on the same idea, like a confluence of two big rivers." Brandon de Wilde was also caught up in the excitement and recorded a demo of 'Together Again', backed by the International Submarine Band.

The R&B/country elements were reinforced by the presence of two visiting musicians, Barry Tashian and Billy Briggs from the Boston-based band, the Remains. Compared to their hosts, Tashian and Briggs were minor celebrities having recorded several singles for Epic and appeared on *Ed Sullivan's Christmas Show*. It says much for Parsons' personality that he always felt comfortable with the success of Tashian, Briggs and de Wilde and there was never any hint of envy or one-upmanship. "We didn't go to the Bronx that often," says Tashian. "It was a bit of a run to get there from mid-town. The Bronx visit was a respite from Manhattan – the house was airy and light with high ceilings and big windows. I'd sit up in their attic rehearsal room and listen. Brandon was there. One night we all went to his house and sat around his kitchen table and got high. He was a fast-paced individual and very funny. A great guy. He was into the music and so wanted to be part of the band, but it never happened."

In February 1966, the ISB finally landed a recording session with a small label. Ascot Records, whose greatest successes came from licensing Manfred Mann's releases for the US market, agreed to cut a one-off International Submarine Band single, 'The Russians Are Coming! The Russians Are Coming!', written by Johnny Mandel. Inspired by the cold war comedy film of the same repeated title, it was totally unrepresentative of the group – a slight instrumental. Parsons' contribution was negligible at best. For the B-side, the band raided the aforementioned Buck Owens album for 'Truck Drivin' Man', Parsons' first recorded attempt at what might loosely be termed country rock. The track was produced by Jack Lewis and manager Monte Kay, an established entrepreneur who had recently taken on the band, adding them to a client list that included the Modern Jazz Quartet and Diahann Carroll.

While awaiting the single's release, the ISB secured a touring support slot with chart star Freddy Cannon, well known for such hits as 'Tallahassee Lassie', 'Way Down Yonder In New Orleans' and 'Palisades Park'. The tour ended with a visit to Winter Haven where Parsons spent time with his extended family and reconnected with Jim Carlton for another private recording session. The tapes, dated 18 April, display no sign of Gram's current immersion in country music, even though 'Truck Drivin' Man' had come out that same week. Instead, he offers textbook renditions of coffee-house familiars featuring Buffy Sainte-Marie's 'Codeine', Tim Hardin's 'Reputation' and Fred Neil's 'That's The Bag I'm In'. His downbeat take on the traditional 'Willie Gene' has none of the cool drama of David Crosby's demo version (recorded the previous year) and there are no self-penned songs on display. Barry Tashian cannot recall Parsons writing any songs at this point, while Dunlop felt ambivalent about what he heard. "Did I rate him as a songwriter? I was slightly perplexed by the structure of some of his songs. They weren't exactly my cup of tea but they were developed in a lyrical sense. As I remember, they were crafted. His writing was ongoing and I saw a couple of songs in that period progress but some of the musicians in the group thought that they might not be delivered [successfully] in an electric band format."

Although little recorded evidence remains of this version of the International Submarine Band, they cut a number of sessions for different labels. Evidently, unlike Gram's pal Jim Carlton, none of the band owned an expensive home tape recorder to capture works in progress. "Technology was out of everybody's reach," says Ian Dunlop. "The only place we could record was in a recording studio. It was like a screen test in the old movie days. A session would be set up where you'd go in and do a few songs in an afternoon. We did that numerous times in New York for different labels. It was a long list of songs. I've never heard them since."

During this fertile period, Parsons faced the perilous attentions of the draft board, an inevitable consequence of leaving Harvard. "Every young American male had a problem with the draft," Dunlop recalls. "They either went to Vietnam, did a runner or went through some terrific farce to get a classification that made them ineligible." Several people in Parsons' circle, including Brandon de Wilde and Florida friends Jim Carlton, Jim Stafford and Kent LaVoie, had avoided duty abroad by joining the National Guard, which meant a brief spell in boot camp. But this was not Parsons' way. He preferred the draft-dodging methods also favoured by various members of the Byrds. In Gram's case, this meant staying up for days, ingesting a modicum of LSD and acting as irrationally as possible. It was enough to convince the draft board that he was unfit for military service.

During the summer of 1966, the International Submarine Band were enjoying an artistically prosperous spell and playing regularly at radio-sponsored concerts and venues like Trudie Heller's in Greenwich Village and even the hip discotheque Ondine on East 59th Street, famously home to Andy Warhol's crowd. Arguably, the live highlight of the ISB's career was a performance in Central Park, supporting the Young Rascals. "That was the biggest gig we ever did," Dunlop confirms. "It was a free concert. New York subsidized public concerts based on socialist principles that came out of policies from the 1930s. It was a terrific gig. Headliners the Rascals were certainly bigger than the Byrds at that time, so it was very exciting. We turned up the amps as loud as they would go, although the equipment was very small back then. We played uptempo stuff along with this crossover country material. That gave us a new burst of energy and propelled us forward. The general feeling in the band was pretty good."

Unfortunately, the positivity proved short-lived. It was difficult to reconcile a love of country music with the sounds emanating from New York discotheques. "We were always trying to do hard rock or rhythm & blues or country music at the same time," Parsons said, "and nobody understood it, and we were nuts anyway." As autumn turned to winter, the band felt increasingly out of place, the more so when their friend Brandon de Wilde relocated to Los Angeles. Manager Monte Kay came to the rescue by securing another one-off single deal, this time with Columbia Records (CBS), home of the Byrds. In October 1966, the ISB entered the label's New York Studio A and rapidly recorded a couple of Parsons' compositions with producer Jack Lewis. 'Sum Up Broke' (co-written by John Nuese) sounds like a UK beat group staple and is probably the least recognizable Parsons-related recording ever issued. Its garage group appeal notwithstanding, the entire execution seems oddly out of time and about as far away from country music as could possibly be imagined. The B-side 'One Day Week', the lesser of the two songs, has a pastoral flavour, with a 'Six Days On The Road'-style riff set against a more orthodox rock backing.

Columbia rushed out the single a month before Christmas but by then Parsons had left New York to sample the attractions of Los Angeles. Brandon de Wilde had been writing encouraging notes urging his friend to visit and Parsons needed little persuading. The former child actor and aspiring rock singer was now immersed in the Hollywood counterculture, having befriended actors Peter Fonda and Jack Nicholson and added his name to Jim Dickson's CAFF protest complaining about police harassment on the Strip. Inevitably, he had also drifted into the orbit of David Crosby, who was then living in Beverly Glen with his girlfriend, Nancy Ross.

Ross was the privileged daughter of wealthy parents and had attended private school in the Santa Barbara area where she had first met Crosby during his rebellious youth. In an interview with author Ben Fong-Torres she claimed to have married one of Eleanor Roosevelt's grandsons, after which she was allegedly involved with actor Steve McQueen. Her romance with Crosby was rudely interrupted when de Wilde introduced her to Gram Parsons. They instantly became a couple. Parsons returned to the Bronx long enough to invite the other members of the ISB to follow him back to LA. That same month, he also found time to visit Jim Carlton and record two more home-taped songs that would complete the collection issued 35 years later on the archival album, *Another Side Of This Life: The Lost Recordings Of Gram Parsons*. Revealingly, both were self-penned compositions which displayed Parsons' debt to Bob Dylan. 'I Just Can't Take It

Anymore' took its melody wholesale from 'Chimes Of Freedom' while the lyrics had strong thematic echoes of 'It Ain't Me Babe'. For late 1966, it already appeared terribly dated. "It sounds so strange without a group," Parsons observes at the close of the song, as if by apology. The attendant 'November Nights' was more sophisticated and engaging with some ornate imagery and a melodic lilt reminiscent of 'Norwegian Wood'-period Beatles. Parsons described the tune as 'Bachian,' while telling his friend Carlton, "You really have to listen to the phrasing of it because it's really wild."

The arrival of the International Submarine Band on the West Coast in early 1967 invigorated Parsons who was soon enjoying the company of several Hollywood luminaries, courtesy of his friend, Brandon de Wilde. With a trust fund at his disposal, Gram was free from financial concerns and settled with Nancy in a fancy Tudor-styled apartment complex in Sweetzer Avenue, Hollywood, while the band stayed in Laurel Canyon. For a time there was a concerted effort to attract record company and media attention. The band played support on shows for the Doors, Love, Iron Butterfly and the Peanut Butter Conspiracy, while Parsons' networking proved productive. Having won over Crosby's girlfriend, he next ingratiated himself with David's inner circle of musical and acting buddies. The road led from de Wilde to former Ciro's habitués Peter Fonda and Jack Nicholson, South African émigré Hugh Masekela (trumpeter on 'So You Want To Be A Rock 'n' Roll Star') and even film producer Roger Corman, who had worked with Crosby's father Floyd on countless films during the Fifties and Sixties. Corman was directing an LSD-inspired movie *The Trip*, featuring Peter Fonda, who suggested the ISB provide a suitable song for the soundtrack. Parsons came up with the bizarrely inappropriate 'Lazy Days', a basic Chuck Berry meets Buck Owens composition, that had nothing to do with psychedelia or acid. Unsurprisingly, it was rejected by Corman, who brought in Mike Bloomfield's new band, the highly accomplished Electric Flag, whose improvisational qualities embraced jazz, rock and blues, with some innovative Moog synthesizer effects added to the mix. The ISB were briefly featured miming but their own music was not included. As if to compensate for that lost opportunity, Fonda offered to record his own performance of Parsons' 'November Nights' employing Masekela as producer. It was issued on the trumpeter's small, independent African jazz label Chisa, but limited distribution meant it fared no better than the company's previous releases by the Bwanas and Letta [Mbulu].

Parsons' failure to produce suitable music for *The Trip* was no reflection on his lack of familiarity with the counterculture. He regularly ingested LSD and also took a keen interest in the whole smorgasbord of psychic phenomena, astrology and alternative religions. His former mentor, the Reverend Jet Thomas, had recently secured a post at Pomona College, the liberal arts institution in nearby Claremont. They continued to enjoy 'theological debates' at a time when Gram seemed open to anything. He attended a meeting of the spiritual organization Subud, which was still attracting many devotees from the entertainment industry. Coincidentally, Jim McGuinn, a practitioner for over two years, was about to change his Christian name to Roger, having submitted a number of names beginning with 'R' to the organization's headquarters in Indonesia. Whether Parsons knew of this at the time is unlikely, but he was probably aware that folk singer Hamilton (formerly Bob) Camp, whose work he enjoyed and covered, had also been renamed by Subud several years before.

Unlike McGuinn, Parsons seemed uncommitted and flighty in his spiritual pursuits. At one point, he displayed a passing interest in Scientology, the system founded by the controversial science fiction writer L. Ron Hubbard in 1950. His book *Dianetics* had shot to the top of the best sellers listings during Parsons' teenage years. Other publications such as the confusingly titled *Have You Lived Before This Life?* documented reincarnation experiences revealed by LRH's subjects during the therapeutic procedure known as 'auditing'. Their testimonies were amplified by Hubbard who claimed to have lived many past lives, some on other planets. In other writings, he even asserted that he had visited Heaven 43 trillion years ago. Parsons evidently did not pursue Scientology to the point of being 'audited' and the subject soon disappeared from his conversation. Friends testify to a keener interest in a seemingly obscure psychic named Jacques Honduras. Barry Tashian, who followed the ISB to the West Coast, remembers Parsons referring to 'the Great Universal Power'. "He tried to get closer to God in whatever concept of God he had. Religion was really woven into the fabric of the culture of the South." Of course, Parsons' interests went far beyond that culture into what would later be termed 'New Age Spirituality'. Tashian remembers "Gram putting his fingers together and saying, 'This is how you complete the electrical circuit of your body.'" Parsons tried the same trick on Jim Carlton, who politely turned away and raised his eyes to the ceiling in disbelief. "We were very stoned at the time," he adds.

The International Submarine Band were not setting Hollywood alight and found to their dismay that live work was no longer forthcoming. Parsons' desire to push forward into country music also met resistance. The band were keen to record, but approaches to the big labels like Capitol invariably produced rejections. "We had quite a few meetings with record companies," says Dunlop, "but they all went sour because of this taint of country music. There was a freeze on our energy, creativity and action. Things just started to go flat."

In order to earn money and rediscover the joy of playing at this difficult time, several of the members performed in an offshoot band that Dunlop playfully named the Flying Burrito Brothers. The saga of the *original* Flying Burrito Brothers is one of the great unrevealed mysteries of late Sixties West Coast music history. Its fluctuating membership, unlisted live concerts and unknown set lists have all added to the legend. "We worked for weeks in a row with that first version of the Flying Burrito Brothers," confirms Dunlop. "Dozens of days. We appeared six nights a week at clubs in LA, then on Sunday, our day off, we'd play at a club in the

Valley, the Prelude. Towards the end of that, we started doing some higher profile gigs, maybe on Sunset Boulevard or somewhere like that."

Although keen to earn money, these prototype Burritos also saw themselves as mavericks, distancing themselves from the machinations of the music business. "That was absolutely deliberate," says Dunlop. "We had the memories of the promises that weren't kept. Some of us were very genuinely taking a stand and making a statement . . . It was an antidote to 'bands'. It was more like we *weren't* seeking record label deals. We weren't seeking anything. We were all refugees from that sometimes demoralizing experience, but we were still trying to pay the rent. The International Submarine Band had stopped paying the rent."

Parsons was initially intrigued and excited about the Flying Burrito Brothers idea, as he usually was when confronted by anything new. "He was with us at the first gig we played under that name," Barry Tashian remembers. "We just played whatever songs anybody knew. There were high school songs, rock 'n' roll numbers, whatever." Ian Dunlop confirms that Parsons was present at some of these early shows, which had a liberating effect on everyone present. "It was all quite retro in that we were playing stuff we knew from a wide background of music. We actually played a couple of things that could be called 'post bop' or 'hard bop', if you know what that is. There were some aspects of Western swing and early R&B and soul music. We had to keep it pretty danceable because it was club work. We did play some strange stuff and it went down well. People liked it."

In different circumstances, at another time period, Parsons might have been tempted to pursue the Flying Burrito Brothers' musically eclectic mix, but he was keener to concentrate on country. Recently, he had befriended Bob Buchanan, a talented songwriter/guitarist, and former member of the New Christy Minstrels. They'd first encountered each other while visiting Parsons' idol Fred Neil, who was then renting a home in LA. Having recently switched from folk label Elektra to the Hollywood-based major

Capitol, Neil was doing well. He had released the unheralded classic *Fred Neil* (featuring his signature tune 'The Dolphins' and the much covered 'Everybody's Talkin'') and was already working on the follow-up, *Sessions*. "We stayed with Denny Doherty on Appian Way at the very top of Laurel Canyon," Neil's close friend Bob Simone remembers. "It was a wild time, maybe a little too wild. When word got out that he was in town, everybody wanted to see him. Gram Parsons was around, and for a couple of days I heard them sing 'You Don't Miss Your Water' so many times I thought it would drive me insane."

The Parsons/Buchanan team modelled themselves on the Everly Brothers and worked up a repertoire of their favourite George Jones and Buck Owens songs. Every Thursday night at the Palomino in North Hollywood, they would enter the talent contest, invariably losing to some Johnny Cash soundalike. Even without Buchanan's company, Parsons continued a relentless round of visits to Californian honky tonks, eventually alighting on the notoriously boisterous Aces Club in the City Of Industry. The all-night patrons were not known for their easy acceptance of long hairs. Parsons remembers almost getting killed on a couple of occasions claiming that it was only his emotive singing that prevented a horde of rednecks from beating him senseless. Supposedly, they bought him a celebratory drink instead.

Although the members of the International Submarine Band were growing apart, the unit was still alive and suddenly there was record company interest. Alas, it came not from any major label but two new smaller outfits, neither of which could offer a substantial advance or provide any history of chart success. It was Steve Alsberg, the ISB's road manager, who provided the initial link to LHI Records, via a connection with Suzi Jane Hokom, the girlfriend of the label's owner Lee Hazlewood.

The 37-year-old Hazlewood had already served a long history in the music business as a hit writer, producer, arranger, soloist, duettist and all-round entrepreneur. He first achieved chart success with Sanford Clark's 'The Fool' in 1955, then enjoyed a sensational run of hits with guitar star Duane Eddy, following which he produced superstar offspring Dino, Desi & Billy and Nancy Sinatra. It was after Sinatra's international success with 'These Boots Are Made For Walkin'' that LHI (Lee Hazlewood Industries) was launched in 1966. The roster reflected Hazlewood's diverse taste with single releases by Amarillo-based garage group the Kitchen Cinq, actor Virgil Warner, expatriate British duo Raul Danks & Jon Taylor, Hollywood hair stylist Lynn Castle ('The Lady Barber') and the manufactured studio group, the Shacklefords. It was an odd assortment, but nobody could deny Hazlewood's pedigree. Suzi Jane Hokom's recommendation proved well-timed as LHI had just entered the albums market with two releases in 1967: the Kitchen Cinq's *Everything But . . . The Kitchen Cinq* and *Lee Hazlewood Presents The 98% American Mom & Apple Pie 1929 Crash Band* (a typically eccentric vaudevillian reworking of notable Hazlewood hits). For a label as stylistically diverse as this, the country leanings of the International Submarine Band held no fear.

Parsons was probably fortunate even to secure a meeting with Hazlewood, who seemed at the peak of his commercial powers that spring. Frank & Nancy Sinatra's 'Somethin' Stupid' was currently number 1 in both the US and UK, continuing his run of hits for the Reprise label. Although he had some experience of working with country artistes, Hazlewood had precious little time to work with an unschooled act so he left the ISB project in the hands of his industrious girlfriend, Suzi Jane Hokom. However, he did persuade Parsons to accept a less than generous deal.

When Parsons returned to the band with news of Hazlewood's offer, he was disappointed by the reception. Dunlop was unimpressed by the proposed advance and had meanwhile come up with an alternative idea. "I had an offer that was more interesting from another company." In an odd parallel to the Hazlewood introduction, Dunlop had been approached by a female intermediary, who said that her boss was searching for new talent for his record label. Dunlop was fascinated to learn that the company was Jay Ward Productions. Ward was already a legend in the world of animated cartoons with a cast list of colourful characters such as Crusader Rabbit, Captain Crunch, Rocky & Bullwinkle, Peabody & Sherman, Hoppity Hooper and George Of The Jungle. Ward had made his fortune with revenue from *The Bullwinkle Show* and had even bought an island 'Moosylvania' whose name was borrowed from his cartoon character's imaginary home. During the early Sixties, Ward had travelled across America in a circus wagon, mischievously campaigning for his fictional state to be made part of the union. He even attempted to enter the White House hoping to meet President John F. Kennedy, but was thwarted by armed guards. The hype encouraged Ward to form Jay Ward Records, a novelty label that issued *A Salute To Moosylvania!! – Recorded Live At The Moosylvania Jazz Festival.* A 7-inch record, played at 33.3 rpm, it parodied the popular jazz festivals of the period. Although there was nothing in any of this to suggest that Ward knew anything about country, jazz or pop music, Dunlop felt he was a better bet than Lee Hazlewood's LHI. Ward's headquarters on Sunset Boulevard was a thriving enterprise, which made additional money from memorabilia, merchandizing and even selling tapes of classic radio recordings via mail order. It all sounded delightfully eccentric, but the proposed tie-up probably said more about Dunlop's interest in cartoons and art than any appreciation of music business politics. Nevertheless, he remained adamant. "The way I looked at it, they were young, they were hungry, they had money to spend and it might be a really nice place to be. That was one reason. Plus, I was disenchanted with LHI – there was very little money on the table from them. The A&R woman I'd contacted seemed to recognize the basic precept that we were forwarding, the idea of mixing country and rock."

Parsons was ultimately unconvinced and elected to stick with LHI. Dunlop admits that this decision contributed to an ever expanding chasm that blighted any hope of continuing with the band. "Several things happened at once. It was a general malaise. After having some high-profile gigs in Los Angeles, then getting rejected by record companies and playing with other people – all this defused the focus on the Submarine Band." In the end, guitarist John Nuese stayed with Gram while the others returned to the twilight dimension of the Flying Burrito Brothers, playing obscure gigs with an expanding line-up of highly talented musicians. Nothing more was heard from Jay Ward.

As Parsons acknowledged: "Finally, I got an album together, but it took breaking the group up. Everybody wasn't into country so much, they were into really small clubs . . ." He went on to make the seemingly preposterous claim that he had agreed to record the album without benefit of royalties, telling Hazlewood, "OK, just let me record an album, I won't take any money for it, unless it's a Top 10 album; just give me the money to go into the studio." This bizarre comment probably says more about the fate of the record, Parsons' subsequent breach of contract, and the likely settlement that resulted. The actual terms of the LHI contract remain undocumented, but Parsons knew enough people in the music business to ensure that he was well represented.

Chief amongst his potential advisers was the astute Larry Spector, whom he had first met several months before. Spector represented Peter Fonda, Dennis Hopper, Brandon de Wilde, Hugh Masekela and, crucially, David Crosby, who successfully engineered his dramatic management takeover of the Byrds, which was formalized in June 1967. With a client list embracing some of the hippest actors and musicians in Hollywood, Spector was pleased to add Parsons to their ranks, not least because Fonda had already recorded one of his songs. When the other members of the Submarine Band first arrived in Los Angeles, it was Spector who arranged their accommodation, securing a house in Laurel Canyon. He also used his connections to find them work, employing Dunlop as a film extra when times were tough. Oddly, Spector's name has never been mentioned in connection with the LHI negotiations, although it seems inconceivable that he was not involved at some stage, particularly later when Hazlewood was threatening legal retribution.

Most likely, the LHI deal was the same offered to every other artiste on the label. Having been rejected by all the major record companies, Parsons was not complaining at the time. It was a bold move for Hazlewood to delegate the production to his girlfriend, Suzi Jane Hokom. If Hazlewood was a multi-tasking musical Renaissance man, then Hokom was evidently groomed as his female apprentice. Thus far, she had recorded two singles under her own name: the catchy 'Need All The Help I Can Get' for MGM and 'Little War'/'Goode Tyme Music' for LHI. She had also served as muse for Hazlewood who wrote and recorded 'Suzi Jane Is Back In Town' in her honour, along with several other collaborations. Echoing the successful Nancy Sinatra/Lee Hazlewood duets on hits like 'Jackson' and 'Summer Wine', she was carefully teamed with actor Virgil Warner for several singles. But, most audaciously, Hokom was allowed to produce LHI's first single and album by the Kitchen Cinq. The notion of a female producer was anathema in the Sixties (and in the Seventies for that matter) and Hokom's appointment was completely unexpected. Her youth and stunning looks could easily have counted against her in the studio at a time when musicians were not used to being directed by a woman. From a historical viewpoint, she is exceptional among her peers as possibly the sole female pop producer in Hollywood – a notable achievement.

With the LHI deal signed, Parsons was obliged to recruit new musicians to expand the ISB line-up. A visit to Winter Haven that June allowed him the opportunity to see family and friends and consider fresh candidates. The now pregnant Nancy accompanied him on this reconnaissance mission during which they stayed at his favourite hotel in Cypress Gardens. "We also spent a few days at the Snively mansion while the family was away," recalls Jim Carlton. "Gram and I did some acid there and I remember soaking up the real or imagined vibes from earlier decades and imagining antebellum scenarios, although the place wasn't really that old. We then visited Gram's grandmother, Mrs Carl Looker, who had a home on the property. She was marvellous and regaled us with the stories of old, allowing three youngsters in on her early life."

While seeking other former bandmates from the Legends,

Parsons heard that Jon Corneal was back in town. The drummer had relocated to Nashville in July 1964 where he'd played behind Hal Willis and toured or worked with the Wilburn Brothers, Kitty Wells, Roy Drusky and Connie Smith. He was amazed to discover that Parsons was suddenly an expert on country music with a collection featuring Buck Owens, Merle Haggard, George Jones and Loretta Lynn. He could barely stifle his laughter when recalling that the last time they'd met, Parsons was a committed folk enthusiast who derided Corneal's country leanings. Still, there was no doubting Parsons' enthusiasm or powers of persuasion.

Eager to expand his horizons, Corneal agreed to visit Hollywood and join the reconstituted ISB. Parsons was not so lucky with former Legends guitarist Gerald Chambers, who mistrusted his rhetoric and declined to be involved. Gram's habit of casually mentioning that he was earning $100 an hour as a session musician clearly hindered his chances of convincing anybody, beyond Corneal, that he was being truthful.

That month, the Beatles had issued the groundbreaking *Sgt Pepper's Lonely Hearts Club Band* and Parsons purchased a copy which dominated the turntable at the mansion. Oddly, it was not the orchestral kitchen-sink drama 'She's Leaving Home', the raga-influenced 'Within You, Without You' or the experimental epic 'A Day In The Life' that attracted his attention, but rather the modest Ringo vocal cameo, 'With A Little Help From My Friends'. "He played that song incessantly," recalls Carlton. "He also travelled with a reel-to-reel of Albert King and another of Don Rich on which he'd overdubbed himself on the harmony. There was a Hammond B-3 in his living room and I had a Fender bass and we'd jam on minor blues for what seemed like hours. He played good keyboards and a very respectable five-string banjo too."

Nancy returned to Los Angeles, but Gram decided to extend his stay in Winter Haven and was soon back at the Cypress Gardens Holiday Inn, accompanied by what Carlton described as "a couple of honeys". He was in generous mood that summer, buoyed by an annual trust fund estimated somewhere between

$30,000 and $100,000. "Gram came back to get his stipend," says Carlton. "He spread several thousand dollars on the bed. Then Page [Helen Page], the family secretary, would deliver matured bonds worth between $100 to $500 apiece on a daily basis." Parsons took full advantage of room service and brushed off Carlton's humble thanks for free lunches with the quip, "Ah, forget it, it's on some dead relative." Later, they both got high, then chilled out in the summer air, lying on top of a boathouse while contemplating the universe. As Carlton recalls: "There was little light pollution then and the star canopy was amazing, especially if you were under the influence of good pot. Sounds a little gay now but, I promise you, it was not!"

With his trust fund, sexually available 'honeys' and time on his hands, Parsons sashayed around Winter Haven like a prince. On one occasion, he was pursued by a young waitress after leaving his sunglasses behind at a restaurant. "Thank you so much," he drawled seductively. "You're a fine country lady." Later, he told Carlton that the shades were a prized gift from Peter Fonda who had worn them in the film, *The Wild Angels*. Parsons showed his own wild side when he intervened in a fracas, rescuing Carlton from a beating by a group of thugs following some adolescent misunderstanding. Gram had just been onstage bravely crooning a cover of Tony Bennett's evergreen, 'I Left My Heart In San Francisco'. "He sang it pretty badly, I'm sorry to say," was Carlton's curt critique.

The boys enjoyed another musical get-together at Corneal's Tudor house in Auburndale, attended by several members of the Purple Underground, a garage group Jim had recently joined. "They looked at us like a dog looks at a clock," says Carlton, who was playing along on bass with Corneal and Parsons. "The Purple Underground were very impressed with Gram, but unsure how to react to country music. We did get Corneal stoned one night for the first time in his life and it was hilarious. He couldn't remember the word 'spoon'. But he performed a drum solo – sans drums – that I have to say was impressive."

Back in LA, preparations were underway for an ISB recording

session. Parsons, Nuese and Corneal were keen to enlist some noted country players and scoured the bars and honky tonks before stumbling upon pedal steel player extraordinaire Jay Dee Maness who, in turn, recommended pianist Earl Ball. The ubiquitous session bass player Joe Osborn and guitarist Donnie Owens completed the line-up, which assembled at Hollywood's Western Recorders, Studio 3, on 12 July. According to Corneal, they attempted four songs with the intention of releasing a single, before successfully completing two Parsons' originals: 'Blue Eyes' and 'Luxury Liner'. The compositions display Parsons' love of Bakersfield country: his vocals, magically shorn of the studious folk delivery evident during his Shilos' sojourn, are confident and zestful; the lyrics are wry, cliché-free and perfectly suited to the musical arrangements.

LHI could hardly have anticipated a better start but instead of striking while the musicians were hot, the label elected to postpone any further recording for several months. The pilot single 'Blue Eyes'/'Luxury Liner' would not appear until 1968 and there were no attempts to revive the International Submarine Band's suspended career as live performers. Corneal recalls joining Parsons during a few impromptu appearances at country bars, but nothing more strenuous was considered. Instead, Gram spent languorous afternoons hanging out at Peter Fonda's house surrounded by Hollywood's rock and acting aristocracy. Corneal was invited over and underwent a seismic culture shock. "David Crosby was there and that was the first time I ever met him. They were all naked, including the women and girls. I was super overweight and I wasn't going to let anyone see what I looked like, so everybody was naked but me. Then Larry Spector showed up and all the girls put their clothes on. It was the weirdest thing because he's a fag, you know. . . I didn't see Spector socially . . . I wasn't comfortable around the guy myself."

Unlike Corneal, Gram enjoyed this cosmopolitan milieu and his wit and good manners were welcomed. With Dennis Hopper in tow, the clique encouraged irreverent humour and Corneal remembers Parsons lambasting the Doors, much to everyone's amusement. "Larry Hagman was hanging out and they were treating him like he was a has-been, but this was before J.R. and *Dallas*." Having spent so much time in Nashville, the drummer found it difficult to adapt to the free love ethos espoused by many in Parsons' circle. "Sex was free. I was brought up with this Southern Christian background and I couldn't believe that you didn't have to work for it. But the girls out there, they'd freely give. It was hard to get used to for me."

Corneal was spared any further carnal temptations by the need to work. With the International Submarine Band temporarily grounded, he returned to Nashville but agreed to come back if and when any recordings resumed. LHI's amorphous schedule was bad news for the ISB, who needed Parsons to stay focused on the project. By temperament, he was easily distracted and the notion of band loyalty was alien to his sensibility. There was the ever present danger that something more appealing might capture his imagination, particularly as his social circle extended.

A sign of things to come occurred that summer when Gram first met Chris Hillman while standing in line at a Beverly Hills bank. The pair found instant common ground in their love of country music. Sharing the same manager in Larry Spector meant that their orbits were bound to meet over the succeeding months. Ian Dunlop remembers "social events with Chris and Gram in the same place, parties and stuff, probably at Spector's house" long before Parsons was even considered as a Byrd.

With no recording or touring commitments, Parsons was free to explore clubs and bars, and fraternize with whomever he chose. During his travels, he reconnected with his old friends in the Flying Burrito Brothers, whose musical exploits continued to confound. "Occasionally, we'd get a profile gig," says Dunlop. "We did one with Clear Light who were totally psychedelic. We were playing very rootsy Americana and Fats Domino songs. It was very reactionary." At times, the Burritos were more like a revue than a band. As Tashian explains: "There was Ian Dunlop and Mickey Gauvin from the Submarine Band, and me and Bill

Briggs from the Remains and we later fell in with [saxophonist] Bobby Keyes (aka Keys) from Lubbock, Texas and Jimmy 'Junior' Markham from Tulsa, Oklahoma, and started playing seven nights a week as the Main Street Blues Band." Keyes and Markham were established players whose impressive horn parts added a funky element to the sound. "They were into blues and R&B and Junior Markham played trumpet, harmonica and sang too," says Tashian, who still has a live tape of the band. Their repertoire included Stax instrumentals and familiar soul classics such as Sam & Dave's 'Soul Man' and 'Hold On I'm Coming', Otis Redding's 'I've Been Loving You Too Long', Sam Cooke's 'Shake', along with group favourites including Fats Domino's 'Poor Me' and Roy Orbison's 'Dream Baby'.

Parsons was intrigued by this musical mix, but even more impressed by the new players that the Burritos were attracting to their shows. Markham and Keyes were friendly with Bonnie & Delaney (as they were then known), whom Parsons soon singled out as likely greats. The horn section were also closely associated with a coterie of Oklahoma musicians and session players who worked with the brilliant Leon Russell. "We hung out with some of those musicians," Dunlop remembers. "There was quite a bit of that. Different people would be available for gigs and that's how we got to know that crowd of musicians and friends of Bobby Keyes and Jimmy Markham. Jimmy Karstein, who had played drums with Taj Mahal, was with us at some gigs. A lot of people sat in because the gigs were interminable. They often continued from 10 pm to 2 am. It was such a relief after doing a six-night stint at a club. Levon Helm came in one night and sat in. Gram certainly did a couple of earlier ones, but that was more when the International Submarine Band was still a unit before we parted."

The roll call of respected musicians associated with the Flying Burrito Brothers and the Main Street Blues Band sister project has inevitably created misconceptions and myths concerning who played with whom. Some writers claim that Leon Russell and Delaney & Bonnie actually appeared onstage with the Burritos.

Did it ever happen? Not according to Dunlop or Tashian, although Ian recalls playing on the same bill as Russell who "was in a band with some of the guys we played with". Dunlop also remembers the Burritos recording some material with Native American guitarist Jesse Ed Davis at Russell's home studio in Hollywood, the tapes of which he has never heard since. Tashian was mightily impressed by Davis who "showed me some cool stuff on the guitar". Parsons did not attend that session, but was similarly enamoured of Davis, whom he was soon proclaiming as the ultimate guitar god. "Indian Ed'll lay more guitar on you than any of them blues guitar people you can name. Indian Ed is the cream of the crop; he's better than Clapton and Hendrix put together."

Probably the peak of these supersession get-togethers occurred some time afterwards when Tashian learned of a star gathering at Hollywood's Gold Star Studio. "Leon had a big thing there one night. Somehow I got wind of it. I actually called the studio myself and said, 'Leon, this is Barry Tashian here. I hear you're having a jamming session. I've got Ian and Bill Briggs . . .' Maybe Gram was there and maybe he wasn't. Leon said, 'Hurry up, come over.' So we all went and every person in that scene was there that night, including Rita Coolidge, Bobby Keyes and Jimmy Gordon. Leon played piano and everybody just jammed along with whatever he wanted to do. It seemed like an hour for each song. Jesse Ed was there. I was just trying to soak up what I could. All these people were such great players."

Parsons' extended musical circle was now so wide that the International Submarine Band was in danger of becoming an afterthought. He was still working on the side with Bob Buchanan and found another able amanuensis in former Electric Flag keyboardist Barry Goldberg with whom he wrote the heartfelt country ballad, 'Do You Know How It Feels To Be Lonesome?' In November, the long overdue International Submarine Band album project was revived. "I was flown back from Nashville to finish it," says Corneal, who was still optimistic about the future of the group. Rather than rely on the ever busy session player Joe Osborn, they appointed a new bassist, Mississippi-born Chris Ethridge, whose background was in rhythm & blues. He had already toured with Johnny Rivers and was looking for new work when Michael Bloomfield mentioned Parsons' name. With their shared Southern background, Parsons and Ethridge formed an instant friendship which was further cemented when the Mississippian revealed that he was buddies with Bonnie & Delaney and the Leon Russell set. After some intense rehearsals at Suzi Jane Hokom's Laurel Canyon home, the musicians returned to Western Recorders and completed the album in less than a month.

The brevity of the sessions disguised several underlying tensions. While Corneal felt that Hokom did a fine job, and Parsons never complained publicly about her work, she suffered a personality clash with John Nuese. Amusingly, they even disagreed about what they were supposed to be disagreeing about. Nuese criticized her "piecemeal recording" technique and use of overdubbing, insisting that the band should have been recorded live. She completely contradicted his account by pointing out that the album *was* cut live. Any pretence that the band was a democratic unit was also revealed as delusory. "It was a Gram album with the band behind him," says Bob Buchanan, who played and sang backing vocals during the November sessions. "They called it the International Submarine Band, but Gram picked the songs and the harmonies. It was all Gram. Even Suzi Jane was obligated to get along with him."

The four-month lay-off between sessions hindered the band's progress, leaving them rusty and ill-prepared. Parsons had failed to take advantage of the break and squandered the opportunity to write a batch of fresh compositions. There was nothing from his pen to equal the quality of 'Blue Eyes' or 'Luxury Liner'. The recent collaboration with Barry Goldberg had produced only one completed song and they would never write together again. Parsons' solo effort, 'Strong Boy', was pleasant enough, but hardly riveting, saved only by a powerful performance from

Maness and Ball. In fairness to Parsons, he probably never envisaged the ISB album as a pure showcase for his songwriting. Unlike the serious singer-songwriters in his orbit, he was equally interested in excavating and presenting material that had inspired his own work. Rock critics would sometimes judge this work harshly, partly because they did not respect the country tradition of covering other people's more famous tunes. That said, it could be argued that Parsons overdoes the homage to his heroes at the expense of his own development. The choice of extraneous material is oddly hit and miss, with questionable readings of Johnny Cash's 'I Still Miss Someone' and 'Folsom Prison Blues' (segueing into the Arthur Crudup-composed Elvis classic, 'That's All Right, Mama'). Documenting his personal musical journey, Parsons attempts the fatalistic, anti-materialist 'A Satisfied Mind', a lament that had already travelled from country via Porter Wagoner, through the folk repertoires of Hamilton Camp, the Byrds, Joan Baez and Ian & Sylvia. Suzi Jane Hokom realized the potential of exploiting both sides of Parsons – the composer and the interpreter. Having already chosen 'Blue Eyes'/'Luxury Liner' as a first single, she now concentrated on two covers as a likely sequel. Jack Clement's 'Miller's Cave', a 1964 hit for Bobby Bare, was a teaser – a macabre murder ballad made more funny and sinister by its jaunty tone, with Parsons adding a personal touch by switching the scene to Waycross, Georgia. The cover of Merle Haggard's 'I Must Be Somebody Else You've Known' teems with puppy enthusiasm and a vocal sincerity that justifies Parsons' decision to reinterpret country classics for a longhair, rock audience. Hokom placed particular emphasis on these two songs, specifically recruiting vocalist/guitarist Glen Campbell and pianist Bob Felts to embellish the track. She and her duet partner Virgil Warner were also on standby as backup singers.

Parsons later complained that the recordings were rushed, but recognized that it was "probably the best country album I've done because it had a lot of real quick shuffle, brilliant sounding country . . ." Its shortcomings were partly the result of the ISB's disunity – the new line-up never managed to perform a single live show. In addition, Parsons neglected to write enough new songs, thereby compromising the quality of the work, although this was not entirely due to a failure of the muse.

His personal life had already been rocked by the revelation of Nancy Lee Ross' pregnancy and he was now uncertain how to proceed. He confided his fears to manager Larry Spector and several of his closer friends. "That was the heaviest emotional scene we had seen Gram go through," says John Nuese. "It was tearing him up constantly during that period." According to Ross, Parsons had suggested terminating the pregnancy, but relented following a verbal blast from Peter Fonda. The mother, of course, never considered this as an option in any case. Seemingly accepting the situation, Parsons recommended naming the child Justin, after Fonda's son, always assuming it was male. On 1 December, Ross gave birth to a girl, who was christened Polly.

Coincidentally, the sessions for the ISB album were completed that same week, but Parsons' attention was already elsewhere. On 6 December, the Byrds also completed a troubled yet productive spell in the studio recording an album seemingly blighted by the recent departure of David Crosby. The final cut, 'Artificial Energy', co-written by Michael Clarke, signalled the end of the drummer's three-year period as a Byrd. Parsons' co-writer Barry Goldberg attended that final session, contributing keyboards to the track. It's possible Gram tagged along too as he always insisted that he witnessed some of these recordings.

With the Byrds reduced to a duo, manager Larry Spector knew they were in serious trouble. Several of Parsons' associates, including Ian Dunlop and Jon Corneal, believe that he was already being groomed as a Byrd and a call from Spector was eagerly expected. With everything uncertain, the International Submarine Band remained in limbo and Gram – as he often did in such circumstances – left town.

Parsons' latest escapade involved an extensive cross-country train journey from Los Angeles to Miami, Winter Haven, Nashville, Chicago, then back to LA again. The trip took up most of

January 1968 and proved eventful. Stopping off in Miami, Parsons visited Coconut Grove where his friend and ISB recruit Bob Buchanan was hanging out with the enigmatic troubadour Fred Neil. Musically, they were a talented triumvirate but poor role models for each other. Both Neil and Buchanan were heroin addicts at a time when Parsons was merely dabbling with the drug. And while Neil was a great musical mentor, his detachment from the industry, unreliability and refusal to tour were not the traits that Parsons needed in his dealings with the International Submarine Band.

After Coconut Grove, Parsons and Buchanan spent some time in Winter Haven where Gram was able to replenish his funds once more and enjoy his homecoming. Carlton remembers being invited to an acoustic jamming session at the Cypress Gardens Hotel, prior to which he had to drive 20 miles to Lakeland in order to borrow Gram an acoustic guitar from their friend, Jay Irwin. Having just played with Fred Neil, Parsons was keen to reprise his repertoire that evening. "Gram was always very influenced by Fred Neil," says Carlton. "He would copy his singing in that hotel room. Fred always loved to use a 7th chord in place of a major chord – that was his musical apologia. So they were singing 'The Dolphins' and other Fred Neil songs, plus Mel Tillis' 'Survival Of The Fittest'." Carlton also claims that Parsons was singing a prototype version of 'Hickory Wind', which would be completed later on the trip.

During their stay, the latest edition of *Playboy* had hit the stands. Feasting their eyes on the contents, Parsons and Buchanan excitedly realized that they had recently met the 'playmate of the month' Nancy Harwood. This somehow led to a heated discussion of the merits of Suzi Jane Hokom, although Parsons seemed more interested in complimenting her lascivious looks than analysing the intricacies of her production technique.

The fate of the International Submarine Band was brought to the forefront of Parsons' mind on the next leg of the train journey when he and Buchanan descended on Nashville. Corneal was still living there and had recently been joined by John Nuese, so this was effectively a group summit. After showing his hosts the sights, Corneal attempted to find out what plans Parsons and LHI had for the band's future. Evidently, the drummer was encouraged enough by the discussion to agree to sell his home and move back to LA permanently. At the end of their short stay, Corneal, accompanied by Nuese, drove Parsons and Buchanan to Union Station and saw them off on the train. The ever impetuous Gram saw no reason why the drummer and guitarist should even bother to sort out their affairs. "Why don't you come with us now?" he suggested. Corneal was dumbfounded by the question, which summed up Parsons' carpe diem recklessness. "I can't, man," he spluttered. "My car's outside and there's a parking meter running!"

With Corneal left scratching his head on the station platform, the train pulled away. The next phase of the journey included a stop-off in Chicago, where Buchanan took his friend on a tour of the local music clubs. Finally, they boarded the *Sante Fe Chief* to LA, a most productive ride during which Parsons coaxed Buchanan to help him complete the great 'Hickory Wind'.

Having reassured the members of the International Submarine Band that their group project was still alive, Parsons was swiftly seduced by the prospect of joining the Byrds. In the end it was Hillman who made the call, but the guiding hand of Spector was ever present. Hiring Parsons made perfect sense, not least because he was one of Spector's underachieving clients, just as Gene Clark had been when he returned to the fold a few months before. Since first meeting Gram in a bank the previous summer, Hillman had crossed paths with him occasionally and they shared several other friends, including fellow train traveller Bob Buchanan.

Parsons' five-month stay in the Byrds is documented at great length in the first volume of this book. Suffice to say, he inspired their groundbreaking Nashville album *Sweetheart Of The Rodeo*, toured extensively, twice visited the UK, met Mick Jagger and Keith Richards and, finally, abandoned the Byrds on the eve of their controversial tour of South Africa. By any standards, it was a whirlwind affair and one of the most eventful periods in the entire history of the Byrds – which is saying much. It ended in bitterness, disillusionment and a lingering suspicion that Parsons had somehow been unfairly treated. Most of the evidence for this came from Parsons himself, who later provided a critique cum conspiracy theory about *Sweetheart Of The Rodeo* which remained unchallenged for years. It was an impressive compendium of criticisms, but riddled with sophistry, misleading accusations and falsehoods.

His main objection was the oft-repeated tale of a threatened lawsuit from Lee Hazlewood, which prompted CBS to insist that his vocals should be overdubbed and erased. He claimed that by the time the issue was resolved only 'Hickory Wind' remained in its original pristine state. In addition, 'Life In Prison' and 'You're Still On My Mind' were supposedly warm-up numbers, never intended for inclusion in their primitive form. "It was a great album that might as well have never been recorded," he concluded scornfully. "So there's another *Sweetheart Of The Rodeo* – and I dig it." That last sentence was guaranteed to appeal to conspiracy theorists who maintained that a classic work had been tampered with and destroyed. If we were to believe Parsons, the released *Sweetheart* bore about as much relation to his original as the Beach Boys' *Smiley Smile* did to the legendary lost *Smile*.

As is often the case with rock mythology, the reality was not so straightforward. Parsons' assertions were ultimately torpedoed by the release of the Byrds' first box set in 1990, which proved that his vocals were still in the tape vaults and had never actually been erased. Further session details indicated that the so-called rough 'warm-up numbers' he'd complained about had been worked into the ground. For instance, there were dozens of takes of 'You're Still On My Mind' and it seemed retrospectively clear that such songs were always intended as part of the album. Worse still, some reviewers, including one of Parsons' partisan biographers, were forced to admit that McGuinn's vocals, with the exception of 'The Christian Life', often sounded more impressive. "Gram's version of 'You Don't Miss Your Water' is especially lugubrious," admits writer David Meyer. "McGuinn sings it far more convincingly. As sung by McGuinn, the song is no longer the soul shouter's anthem that Gram strives to re-create, but a folk-country lament, an updating of an Appalachian ballad . . . McGuinn sounds more connected to its essence."

A second criticism from Parsons was that the album contained "too much of that old Byrds' sound . . .", which hardly made sonic sense until you realized he was referring to the inclusion of the Dylan songs that bookended the album. For many listeners, those were two of the album's highlights and, on reflection, it is surprising that there were not more Dylan compositions on offer. The Byrds could easily have featured further selections from the unreleased *Basement Tapes* that were in their possession. Indeed, the next Byrds' album would include a belated cover of 'This Wheel's On Fire', proving that very point.

Even weirder was Parsons' complaint that "this cat, the producer of the album, decided it should go Hollywood freaky, and it wasn't the time for that". Whatever its merits or shortcomings, the last thing *Sweetheart* could reasonably be described as is "Hollywood freaky". It strove for authenticity and disdained artifice. Unlike later 'country rock' recordings there was no pressure to add a rock 'n' roll beat to make the songs sound more accessible or FM radio friendly. Producer Gary Usher, who was no stranger to psychedelic effects, showed commendable restraint in ensuring that the album reflected its Nashville origin. There was no attempt to add a gospel choir, as Bob Johnston later did with the Byrds' version of 'Lay Lady Lay', or beef up the production with a cast of Hollywood session players and extravagant overdubs in the fashion of Terry Melcher on *Byrdmaniax*.

As Usher and McGuinn rightly argue, *Sweetheart* ended up – as they intended it should – as a Byrds album, on which Parsons sang lead on some tracks. If McGuinn had truly wished to sabotage the album in his favour, he would have delved further into *The Basement Tapes* or insisted that his fine outtake of 'Pretty Polly' was featured, at the expense of one of Parsons' tunes. Moreover, the construction of *Sweetheart* is remarkably consistent with what happened to extraneous material after Parsons' departure. On the next album, *Dr Byrds & Mr Hyde*, McGuinn was the featured vocalist on every cut, even though Clarence White and Gene Parsons had brought along songs such as 'Your Gentle Ways Of Loving Me'. The same thing happened with the cover of 'Tulsa County' on the next album. Even on *(Untitled)*, it was only the intervention of co-producer Jim Dickson that enabled White's rendition of "Take A Whiff" to replace McGuinn's reading. No doubt if Gram had stayed in the Byrds, he would have secured even more lead vocal spots but, arguably, he was fortunate to receive such a prominent profile, particularly in 1968. It was only in the final years of the Byrds that McGuinn loosened his grip and allowed the subsidiary members to perform their own new songs. Ironically, this decision brought him more criticism than commendation.

By the spring of 1968, Parsons had effectively abandoned the International Submarine Band at a time when they were at their most vulnerable. Jon Corneal had just burned his bridges in Nashville and relocated to Laurel Canyon where he rented a home, with John Nuese installed as a lodger. Stranded, without any serious prospects of recovery, the band perversely soldiered on, vainly attempting to find a replacement for their charismatic front man. "I was left holding the bag trying to keep the band together and paying the rent until my money ran out," Corneal laments. "We tried to reform. I auditioned Cass Elliot's sister Leah [Kunkel]. Then, I flew a guy in from Nashville: Larry Fullam. I'd worked with him with the Grand Opry star Connie Smith and he sang real good and played bass, but he didn't fit in. We were a bunch of hippie freaks by then whereas he was straight and still had a pompadour. It was a foreign world to him so he came back to Nashville. Then we almost had Brandon de Wilde join the group. He was a good friend who'd come over and jam with us or we'd go over to his place in Topanga. He had a D-28 Martin and loved to sit around playing Buck Owens songs. He would have been a key ingredient with his name as an actor." Unfortunately, contractual problems prevented de Wilde's involvement, after which even the tenacious Corneal at last conceded defeat and moved on. Some time later, he was informed of another lost opportunity. "Suzi Jane Hokom said she and Lee Hazlewood were at a party in New York with George Harrison and they played him the album. George loved it and wanted it for Apple Records, but Lee wouldn't do it."

Often cited, somewhat extravagantly, as the 'first country rock album', the ISB's *Safe At Home* foundered in the marketplace, which was hardly a surprise given LHI's limited budget and distribution. Indeed, fleeting reviews in the rock press were only achieved as a result of Parsons' concomitant spell in the Byrds. Attempts to order the album were presumably hampered by the fact that it shared the same serial number (12001) as another LHI release: *Lee Hazlewood Presents The 98% American Mom & Apple Pie 1929 Crash Band.* Its commercial failure left most of the group feeling both disappointed and disillusioned. Corneal's only consolation was the belief that he had contributed to a pioneering work. "It was timing. The timing was good for the Byrds to have hits and it worked out for them for a while. But the Burritos didn't happen and nor did the International Submarine Band. The disc jockey B. Mitchel Reed, who was on one of the underground radio stations in LA, compared us to the Beatles because of the life in our music. He was brave enough to play the record and it got a good reaction there, but when they shipped it to country stations they looked at the cover and said: 'The International Submarine Band? This can't be country. This is a bunch of hippies!' There was nothing country about the name. But if you played it you'd have found some hot stuff. I think it's better than anything they're playing on country stations today. Gee, I don't care what anybody says, it's a benchmark album. It was even pre-*Sweetheart Of The Rodeo*. What can I say? We broke ground with that record."

By mid-July 1968, Parsons had said goodbye to both the ISB and the Byrds, but he was already plotting a new project. Meanwhile, he hung out with Keith Richards at his West Sussex home, Redlands, and accompanied him to LA later that month. Richards was fascinated to learn the difference between Nashville and Bakersfield country and Parsons showed him some tuning tricks he had picked up in Music City. "The reason Gram and I were together more than other musicians is because I really wanted to learn what Gram had to offer," says Richards. "Gram was special. If he was in a room everyone else became sweet. Anything that Gram was involved in had a touch of magic to it."

For Gram, Redlands had its own magic. While there, he met several new contacts, notably filmmaker Anthony Foutz, a Zelig figure whose circle of friends embraced several leading counter-culture giants of the Sixties. Eight years older than Parsons, Foutz was a world traveller with an illustrious history. Like Gram, he'd had a trust fund. He also co-owned 'The Door', a beatnik coffee-house on Waikiki Beach. From there, he enjoyed an adventurous period in Africa and the Congo, then moved to Italy where he spent most of the Sixties. His father had worked as an executive for Walt Disney and Foutz also joined the movie industry, assisting Italian director Marco Ferreri on a number of films, and briefly crossing paths with Gillo Pontecorvo and Orson Welles. Another of his mentors was B-movie film producer Herman Cohen, whose writing credits included the cult film, *I Was A Teenage Werewolf.* During the early Sixties, Foutz had befriended Albert Grossman, Bob Dylan's manager, and introduced him and his wife Sally to Ferreri. "Albert invited us to Bearsville, Woodstock when Dylan was living with them." Marco, in turn, introduced Foutz to Libyan-born Italian painter Mario Schifano, "the Andy Warhol of Italy", and the first serious love of the young Anita Pallenberg (later the paramour of both Brian Jones and Keith Richards). Coincidentally, Schifano subsequently had an affair with Marianne Faithfull when she was still with Mick Jagger. In the midst of all this, Foutz found his way to the Rolling Stones.

During 1968, Foutz was writing a 'psychedelic western', partly as a medium for his use of special effects. His mentor Ferreri encouraged the idea. At the same time, the movie *Barbarella* was in production which brought Foutz back into contact with Anita Pallenberg who, in turn, was about to star in Ferreri's film *Dillinger Is Dead.* "We were all interacting," Foutz says. "Keith used to visit Anita and that's how I met him." Foutz's film concept was titled *Maxagasm*, a starring vehicle for three of the Rolling Stones – Jagger, Richards and Jones – with Pallenberg and Faithfull playing the female leads. Actor James Coburn was cast as the hero, Cowboy. "It wasn't about musicians running around being cute," Foutz stresses. "They were playing mercenaries, living in the desert."

For a time, Foutz and the Stones shared the same agent – Sandy Lieberson – and he helped package the *Maxagasm* idea. Playwright Sam Shepard agreed to provide the dialogue and Richards invited the writers to stay at his Sussex home, Redlands. "It was like being in Marrakech inside this English farmhouse," Foutz recalls. "Keith said, 'I'm not having any more police visiting me.' So he expanded the moat and they were digging it while we were up all night writing."

Enter Gram Parsons. Foutz had first encountered him on the Byrds' earlier visit to London. While Tony was staying at a hotel in Hyde Park, Marianne Faithfull turned up in her Cadillac and announced, "I've found this beautiful boy!" They spent an evening at Mick Jagger's home in Chester Square where Foutz remembers Gram reclining like a feline on a creamy carpet. He appeared to have found his perfect home and social milieu. Since then, so much had changed. Gram had abruptly abandoned the Byrds on the morning after their triumphant appearance at 'Sounds '68' at the Royal Albert Hall. While they set forth on a soul-sapping tour of South Africa, he accepted Keith Richards' invitation to stay at Redlands.

Foutz found Parsons an excellent conversationalist and enjoyed hearing how he had accompanied Jagger and Richards on a visit to Stonehenge two months before. Gram had been given a copy of John Michel's *The Flying Saucer Vision: The Holy Grail Restored*, an esoteric treatise linking Arthurian legend with UFOs.

"Michel had a big influence on *Maxagasm*," Foutz enthuses. "UFOs, ley lines, all that. I'd come from California where UFOs were a phenomenon with all that anecdotal stuff. So when Gram was staying at Redlands we became good friends."

On 20 July, Parsons was back in LA accompanied by Richards, Anita Pallenberg and Stones' photographer Michael Cooper. During their stay, Foutz organized a trip to Joshua Tree National Monument in the California desert. For this memorable expedition they were joined by another larger-than-life character: Philip Kaufman. He had once been a roommate of Foutz's Hollywood High schoolfriend, Tom Prendergast. When Jagger mentioned that that he needed a driver and general dogsbody for the Stones, Tony recommended the uproarious Phil, while knowing he had no previous experience in the music business. Jagger later rechristened him the 'Executive Nanny', an accurate enough job title. Parsons liked the notion of a rock 'n' roll valet, particularly one with such a mordant sense of humour. The musicians in the party were fuelled by coke and mescaline as they climbed to the top of Cap Rock. Gram and Keith played guitars and sang as they all watched the sun rise. It was reminiscent of the previous Stonehenge visit, amid tales of UFOs and extra-terrestrial visitations. The scenery had a profound effect on everyone and became a favourite spot for meditation among friends. "We went up there two or three times," Foutz says. On their way back, photographer Michael Cooper took a revealing shot of them in their car. Anita sits in the front seat, flanked by Kaufman and Foutz. In the back, Keith lies slumped and smiling with his legs hanging out of the vehicle. Next to him is Gram clutching a briefcase, the contents of which appear tantalizing.

Parsons had already plotted his next move: the formation of his own version of the Flying Burrito Brothers. Chris Ethridge was roped in, Clarence White declined, then suddenly another candidate emerged. In mid-September, Chris Hillman quit the Byrds in melodramatic fashion. Still reeling from the aftermath of a disastrous South African tour, ongoing financial arguments with manager Larry Spector, and an impending divorce, the troubled bassist was ready to wipe the slate on his Byrds' career and start afresh. Improbably, he made his peace with the man he had felt like killing back in July. Parsons' Southern charm had proven irresistible, and his willingness to apologize assuaged Hillman's anger. They soon moved into a house in Reseda, in the San Fernando Valley, intent on composing an album's worth of songs. Remarkably, they even mastered the art of working in daylight hours to maximize their output. "Everything was really great, and it was a particularly productive period," Hillman says. "Both of us were involved in a series of romantic problems, and we'd get up every morning and write songs together . . . some of the best songs I've ever been associated with." Occasionally, an inspirational line would emerge from the subconscious, later to be hammered into completion through sheer hard work. "To give you an example," Hillman explains, "I woke up one morning and said, 'This old town's filled with sin, it'll swallow you in', and Gram finished the second part of it. As far as lyrics and melody went, Gram and I shared it all the way."

Parsons was so excited by the collaborative rush with Hillman that he could not resist telling his rock star friends in London. When Keith Richards and Anita Pallenberg were at art dealer Robert Fraser's London flat in Mount Street, Tony Foutz remembers seeing a telegram pinned to the front door featuring the line "on the 31st floor a gold-plated door . . ." from 'Sin City'. "Gram wanted to show Keith the lyrics he'd just written."

At this point, the friendship between Parsons and Hillman – both personally and professionally – was peaking. They even shared stories about their early lives. Hillman learned a little about the history of the Snivelys and the shocking revelation that Parsons' father had committed suicide when the boy was barely 12. Hillman's own father had killed himself when Chris was still a teenager and this mutual loss created a bond between them. Living together, they discovered that, despite their differing social backgrounds, they had much in common, not least a profound love of country music.

On their free nights, the songwriters would visit country bars on Lankershim Boulevard, including the Palomino. It was in an adjacent bar that they caught up with and enlisted pedal steel player, Sneaky Pete Kleinow. Born in 1934, Kleinow was a decade older than Hillman and Parsons, with a history steeped in country music. He acquired his nickname 'Sneaky' while working with Smokey Rogers, a contemporary of Western swing legends, Spade Cooley and Tex Williams. Kleinow was also a cartoon animator and produced the eerie sonic special effects on the science fiction television programme *The Outer Limits* and the 1962 Academy Award-winning movie, *The Wonderful World Of The Brothers Grimm*. Parsons had previously seen him deputizing for Red Rhodes at the Palomino and was so impressed that he had once attempted to persuade McGuinn to recruit him as a Byrd. McGuinn declined, but now Parsons was free to pursue his ambitions without deferring to a higher authority. Kleinow was an eccentric but unique steel guitarist, very different from the traditional players in Nashville. He used an early Fender model which Parsons described as "funkier and older than the funkiest, oldest Telecaster ever made". Kleinow's strange tunings created a distinctive sound, heightened by his use of fuzz tone. His remit in the Burritos recalled the advice once given to Lloyd Green about where to play on 'You Ain't Going Nowhere' from *Sweetheart Of The Rodeo*: play *everywhere*. Kleinow provided the Burritos' signature sound and, in time, would be hailed by some as the Jimi Hendrix of the steel guitar.

With Ethridge already committed, and the line-up nearly complete, the Burritos attracted attention from Warner Brothers, but eventually signed to the smaller A&M Records. Label head Jerry Moss and his partner Herb Alpert were keen to branch out from the safe confines of the Tijuana Brass into uncharted musical territories. They had already secured the services of Dillard & Clark and, over the next few years, would establish A&M as an unlikely home for some of the most innovative purveyors of 'country rock', including the Flying Burrito Brothers, Gene Clark, Steve Young and Seatrain.

Parsons wasted no time in squandering the record company advance. All the Burritos were taken to Nudie's Rodeo Tailors and kitted with distinctive fineries featuring designs of their own choosing. Parsons' garish white suit was festooned with depictions of marijuana plants and pills, an apt comment on his excessive lifestyle. A tabernacle red cross on the rear added a religious dimension.

The debut album was recorded with extraordinary rapidity, even though they were having trouble finding a drummer. First choice Eddie Hoh left after recording a couple of tracks, and several other session drummers filled in before Parsons again called on Jon Corneal. He played on five of the songs and accompanied the group at several local dates, but all was not well. "I had an alcohol problem at the time," Corneal admits. "We'd have rehearsals and they'd have beer in the coolers. It just made it easy for somebody like me." Onstage, Corneal felt out of sorts. "I never let drinking slow me down before, but that was a period of time when . . . I can't really explain it other than I had physically lost 90 lb in nine months. Between 1967–68, I went from 230 to 140 lbs and I was just feeling weak. Alcohol got to me quicker and, at the time, we were introduced to some other things that . . . people back home would not approve of, let me put it that way."

Corneal's coyness betrays his aversion to the drug scene and the same fish out of water culture shock he had previously experienced when visiting Peter Fonda's house. For Hillman, the problem lay deeper. He has always maintained that Parsons treated Corneal with disdain for reasons of snobbishness and class consciousness. "Here they were, both from Florida, but Jon was from the other side of the tracks; somebody who should be in the orange groves picking oranges. 'How dare you play in a band with me!' "

Hillman's impressions were based on false assumptions. "I heard that and it pisses me off," says Corneal. "I don't know why Hillman would think that, other than maybe Gram misrepresented me to him. You know Gram had a silver tongue and he could persuade people anyway he wanted . . . We had a two-storey British Tudor house on a lake with a terraced lawn with a landscape. It looked like Cypress Gardens. The walls were two-and-a-half feet thick, much nicer than the house Gram was brought up in, or any house he ever lived in. So [Hillman's comments are] just total bullshit." Parsons' Winter Haven colleague Jim Carlton testifies to Corneal's opulence. "His dad was the town mayor and a wealthy citrus grower. When I first met Jon he was driving a new 1963 fast-back Ford Sprint convertible, a very cool car for a teenager. They had a gorgeous home and lots of land."

Parsons' condescension towards Corneal was based on cultural rather than class distinctions. While the sophisticate Gram went to Harvard and lived in New York and Los Angeles, Corneal moved to Nashville at 17, missed out on college, and toured with country stars. They could hardly have experienced more contrasting worlds. As Corneal says: "Here [in Florida] when somebody said 'hillbilly' it was a cuss word, but in Nashville it was a good word. They called each other hillbillies with an affectionate tone. A lot of stars I worked for had barely made it through school. Some of them never graduated, but they were stars and made a lot of money. I spoke with a Midwestern accent, but I wanted to be a hillbilly so bad I rehearsed talking like a hick. By the time I was out in LA with those people, I was pushing that a little hard. That was my act. Chris probably thought I was a damn, dumb hillbilly. Basically, it's as much my fault as anybody's because I'd dumbed myself down." Corneal was finally given a ticket back to Florida. His only tangible reward from his short spell in the Burritos was a red Nudie suit, which he locked in a closet. A perennial bit player in the Byrds' story, he would return in another chapter (see previous Gene Clark obituary) after accepting a spot in the Dillard & Clark Expedition.

Between recording an album, fashioning an image and fretting over suitable drummers, Parsons found time to add further complications to his personal life. While staying with Hillman, he had enjoyed playing the happy bachelor, but suddenly that was no longer enough. Seemingly out of nowhere, Parsons had a romantic rush of blood to the head, a trait that usually brought confusion and misery to the apotheosized object of his desire. Months before, he had split up with his girlfriend Nancy Ross, but now he was ready to propose marriage. A $1,000 bridal gown was ordered from Nudie's and a wedding date set for 31 January 1969. Prevarication followed and the ceremony was never performed. No proper explanation was forthcoming. Many believed that the entire idea was predicated on Hank Williams' marriage to second wife Billie Jean Jones, a year before his death. The service was held at the Shreveport Municipal Auditorium and over 14,000 ticket purchasers attended. Was Parsons thinking of the nuptials more in terms of a career enhancing publicity stunt than a genuine commitment? The intended bride evidently thought so. "I knew already that it was a big, awful joke," she said. "The fact that he would set up this elaborate ruse – the man I loved with my immortal soul . . ." In an unexpected twist to the tale, Ross turned to former ISB drummer Mickey Gauvin. In an opaque aside, she mused, "Do you remember the sacred sexuality, the ancient temples? I wasn't getting back at Gram, I was fulfilling myself with a temple boy!" The negative portrayal of Parsons here does not address the crucial point that the marriage proposal was also a psychological volte face, either to assuage guilt or pluck an instant happy ending from a seemingly doomed relationship. Nobody then knew that, only a few years before, Gram had done precisely the same thing to girlfriend Patti Johnson in far more baffling circumstances.

In February 1969, A&M released the Burritos' debut album, *The Gilded Palace Of Sin*. In keeping with Parsons' vision, the cover was a strikingly iconic portrait of the band in their Nudie suits, posing in the freezing cold of the Pear Blossom desert in the early morning, accompanied by two vampish models, Suzanne and Bridget. Buying the album required a leap of faith as there was no pilot single to judge its likely contents and precious little radio airplay. I can still recall hesitating at the moment of purchase after perusing the ominous track listing, which appeared to include three instrumentals: 'Christine's Tune', 'Hot Burrito # 1' and 'Hot Burrito # 2'. Fortunately, these odd titles turned out to be *vocal* tracks. More surprisingly, they were by far the best songs on the record.

'Christine's Tune', the invigorating opener, is dominated by Kleinow's fuzz tone pedal steel, set against some acerbic lyrics penned by Parsons and Hillman, whose vocals are swamped with effects similar to the phased Donald Duck treatment on the Byrds' 'Artificial Energy'. "There was a girl named Christine whom Gram and I hated so much we wrote a song about her one day," Hillman told me, decades ago. "Christine was causing trouble between us and the 'wives'. She was always real sweet, but she'd be causing trouble behind our backs. The reason we [later] changed the title to 'Devil In Disguise' [on *Last Of The Red Hot Burritos*] was because the poor girl was killed six months later." Some commentators wrongly assumed that the girl in question was former GTO 'Miss' Christine Fryka (cover 'star' of Frank Zappa's *Hot Rats*), even though she was not killed, but died of a drugs overdose over three years later on 5 November 1972 (coincidentally, Gram's 26th birthday). The true Christine was actually David Crosby's great love, Christine Gail Hinton, who was tragically killed in an automobile accident on 30 September 1969, several months after the release of *The Gilded Palace Of Sin*.

Parsons' most celebrated contribution to the album was 'Hot Burrito # 1', co-written with Ethridge, who also played the haunting piano opening. "They were nice tunes," he says of the 'Hot Burrito' songs. "Way back when I was a teenager in Meridian, we had a piano at my house and I'd always go in there and mess around with chords and stuff. I'd written some melodies and also some words, which we took and used from that time. I wrote: 'You may be sweet and nice, but that won't keep you warm at night.' Then we just went from there. He got into the emotion of it. He started talking about a chick and how they were together, but now she's with somebody else. It's a very touching song. It's kind of risqué too. You could certainly take it that way." The song remains Parsons' finest vocal performance, a masterclass in phrasing in which emotional containment teeters on the precipice of neuroticism. There is a spine-tingling moment when his voice cracks while singing "I'm your toy . . ." that could never be duplicated in live performance, or even hinted at in any cover of the song. This was Gram Parsons at his purest and best, mining the emotional centre of country music, denuding its form of sentimental artifice and creating a song that transcends its time. Oddly, no commentator, biographer or journalist has discussed the song's lyrical content in any depth. Like the best of his compositions, there is a fascinating ambiguity at work here. Ostensibly, it is a song of deference and sensitivity, even while it is complaining about romantic loss. But it is also sexually charged and contains some of Parsons' most explicit and erotic lines. That they are couched in playful ambiguity makes them even more impressive. In the second verse, the narrator reveals that the object of his proprietorial affection once allowed him to "feel" her. Indeed, he sings, "you let me feel you – *deep inside*". These hints of sexual touch are heightened by the agonizing tone in which he sings the line. The additional, "nobody knew, nobody saw . . ." acknowledges that the act is private or possibly forbidden. In the next line, the girl's response is recalled as tearful, like the cry of a virgin, imagined or otherwise. What makes the song so intriguing is the emotional tone which suggests a deep hurt couched in old boy gallantry, beneath which lies a hint of something more furtive, fumbling and disturbing.

'Hot Burrito # 2', another composition originally conceived by Ethridge in his teen years, proves a perfect companion piece. "I had that opening lick, 'doo doo doo doo' and the words, 'Well you loved me and you sold all my clothes'. We took it from there and Gram helped me finish the words. That's the way it went. You can tell from the other songs he wrote that he never had any melodies like that." The second Hot Burrito opus has similar depths to its predecessor but the tenor is more urgent to the point of desperation. Session drummer Popeye Phillips adds to the tension, just as he does on 'Hot Burrito # 1'. Sneaky Pete's steel drives the song to a pitch of intensity which Parsons follows until exasperation is transformed into frantic need. "You'd better love me . . ." is almost threatening in its demand, while the profanity "Jesus Christ" can be interpreted as both a vexatious punctuation directed to his beloved and a despairing prayer to a higher power. It is as if Parsons is applying the fire and brimstone preaching of the Louvin Brothers to a domestic scene in the everyday life of an LA rock star.

'Sin City' follows the same process, albeit more revealingly. Here, Satan is actually named, and a California earthquake is invested with apocalyptic significance. As mentioned in *Volume 1* of this book, the chorus was a bitter riposte to their former manager, Larry Spector. According to McGuinn's ex-wife Dolores, Roger owned a green mohair suit in 1968, which may elucidate another of the song's lines. Hillman was happy to complete the lyrical analysis: "Larry Spector, the manager, lived on the 31st floor of a brand new condominium building. He had a gold-plated door. The song has a bit of Edgar Cayce and earthquake predictions – we beat Nostradamus to it all. It was fun. It was a tongue-in-cheek deal, but it was a really good song. Bobby Kennedy's in the song. ["a friend came to town"]. Roger and I had worked a show with him when he was running in the presidential primaries. I left and Roger stayed around. Then Bobby Kennedy came down to meet the people on the show. Like a big dope I kick myself for not staying around. A few months later he came back to LA and was assassinated. There's a little bit of everything in 'Sin City' . . . We predicted earthquakes, militarism and rampant fundamentalism."

Parsons' dream of fusing R&B, country and Southern soul is partially realized on his excursions into Memphis and Music Shoals-inspired covers of songs popularized by James Carr and Aretha Franklin: Dan Penn and Spooner Oldham's 'Dark End Of The Street' and the Penn/Chips Moman collaboration, 'Do Right Woman'. The high harmony on the latter is provided by David Crosby, whom Hillman pulled in from a nearby session. Clearly, they did not tell Crosby that they had just denounced his girlfriend, Christine, in playfully demeaning fashion.

With the International Submarine Band already forgotten, Parsons revived 'Do You Know How It Feels To Be Lonesome?' from their doomed album, *Safe At Home*. Arguably less expressive in its FBB incarnation, the song nevertheless hits home thanks to the deceptively spry melody and vocal, both of which make light of the maudlin lyrics.

Spontaneity was key in the writing and recording of the album, as evidenced by 'My Uncle'. While living with Hillman, Parsons received an inquiry from the draft board about his medical records, and this song was the result. Parsons adds some drama to the tale, reading the letter with "trembling hands", citing some pointed questions about his mother and father and, of course, immortalizing an imaginary uncle who, with Bob Parsons-style cunning, secures him a three-year contract for an unspecified job in Canada. This amusing draft-dodging saga, which contrasts starkly with the Byrds' deadly serious 'Draft Morning', had even more resonance in 1968, but it hasn't dated. Hillman, freed from years of playing bass guitar with the Byrds, produces some delightful mandolin flourishes, transforming this slice of social commentary into a country homily.

The three remaining tracks on the album deserve special attention in a future Hillman obituary (should I live to write it). 'Wheels', 'Juanita' and 'Hippie Boy' are the only collaborations on which Hillman's name is placed first in the writing credits, a possible indicator of his dominance. What is interesting is the extent to which they reflect Parsons' own circumstances. The prophetic 'Wheels' was inspired by Gram's difficulties as a budding biker; 'Juanita' is a song of redemption, as bitter as 'Christine's Tune' in its first verse about love gone bad, but as poignant as 'Hot Burrito # 1' in its final acceptance of the 17-year-old muse whose innocence restores life and love to the narrator. Hillman closes *The Gilded Palace Of Sin* with the strange 'Hippie Boy', which has echoes of Hank Williams' 'Luke The Drifter' and Tex Ritter's 'Hillbilly Heaven'. The song is also a throwback to the days when the Byrds ended their albums on a peculiar or parodic note. Parsons must have been amused by his partner's droll TV evangelist narration, complete with the familiar FBB subtext of uniting country fans and longhairs, this time in the tale of a conversation between a member of each community, which includes an allusion to the 1968 Democratic Convention and the unspecified death of a young hippie boy, whose remains are carried in a small box. The story closes with the maxim "Never carry more than you can eat", echoing Dylan's lyrical aphorisms, most recently heard at the close of 'The Ballad Of Frankie Lee And Judas Priest' in which he'd advised us not to "go mistaking paradise for that home across the road". It was not entirely surprising that Dylan later applauded the song in print. He was probably doubly amused by the tuneless Pentecostal chorus tagged on at the end.

The Gilded Palace Of Sin is now lauded by many as one of the first and greatest 'country rock' albums of its era, even though the term was still a neologism back then. The work received a glowing review in *Rolling Stone* from Stanley Booth, a fellow Georgian, who became close friends with Parsons and the Stones for a time. Booth referred to Parsons as the 'head Burrito' in his opening sentence, then spent five long paragraphs on the cultural history of Waycross, followed by a short critique of *Safe At Home*, and some passing comments on Gram's contribution to *Sweetheart Of The Rodeo*. Only then did he tackle the Burritos' debut with a brief summation. While admitting that it lacked the 'surface charm' of *Sweetheart*, he felt it was Parsons' most personal work to date and concluded: "Gram Parsons is a good old boy."

One month later, the *New York Times* namechecked Parsons in a catch-all review covering recent releases by ex-Byrds. The occasional curmudgeon Robert Christgau was obviously a big fan. "If this were a time for conceptual geniuses," he wrote, "Parsons would rank with Peter Townshend and McGuinn. He has absorbed and transmuted all the Calvinist morality, chin-up self-pity, and interpersonal warmth that grace the best country music, and found a steel guitarist (Sneaky Pete) who adds just the right musical flavour . . . A brilliant LP. And yet, for all Parsons' brilliance, you wonder whether he would have gotten it all together without working for a few months with ol' Roger McGuinn of the Byrds. If every broken group can produce as much good music as the Byrds, rock will be alive for a long time to come."

These were remarkable plugs for a still relatively unknown singer. As he'd demonstrated with the International Submarine Band, Parsons had enough clout and talent to secure some prominent reviews, but his efforts were never rewarded with decent sales. *The Gilded Palace Of Sin* became a cult classic but performed poorly in the marketplace, never achieving a chart position anywhere near that of the more celebrated *Sweetheart Of The Rodeo*.

As the album was being readied for release, the Burritos finally solved their 'drummer problem' by enlisting ex-Byrd Michael Clarke. His adventures in the Flying Burrito Brothers are documented at length in the obituary chapter elsewhere in this book. Suffice to say, it was a period when drug abuse, gambling and fun on the road rivalled the music for prominence. This was especially evident on the so-called 'Train Tour', a financially ruinous escapade that passed in a whirl of lysergic abandon. Even years later, the participants tended to reminisce about cards, girls or substances, depending upon their preference. Music was hardly mentioned. The gigs were sloppy at times but also inspired in their spontaneity. Nobody disagrees that they were terribly inconsistent.

At least Parsons was enjoying himself. He was pleased to see Tompall Glaser, Waylon Jennings and Roger Miller attending an early show at the Whisky, especially after the incident with the Byrds on the *Grand Ole Opry*. There were many other memories, enough to fill a small book of tour anecdotes. "In Philadelphia, Gram went out and bought us all turbans complete with jewels and feathers," Hillman recalls. "So we wore those onstage too. It was all very weird. Gram had an amazing sense of humour . . . very bright guy. He was great fun to be around that time." The group had planned to tour England and appear in Continental Europe, but were defeated by bad organization, a lack of proper work permits and associated problems. "The Burritos seemed to have a really bright future," adds Hillman, "but things somehow didn't fall into place and after the first few months, it was downhill all the way . . . Despite the fact that some great musicians went through the band, it never fulfilled the hopes we had for it."

The band retained its champions, whose ranks now included Barrett Hansen (aka DJ Dr Demento), who penned a surprisingly analytical appraisal in the teen zine, *Hit Parader*. "*The Gilded Palace Of Sin* has won them a fair amount of national recognition," he noted. "In terms of musicianship, the Burrito Brothers come off a good deal better than the Byrds did on *Sweetheart*. The singing is generally stronger (though still hardly in the Buck Owens' league) and Sneaky Pete does very nice things with his steel guitar . . . This is a group that can play for the hip and pseudo-hip at the Whisky A Go-Go on Sunset Strip one night, then buzz out to north Hollywood the next night and please the people at the Palomino Club – strictly C&W. They can be very country and very hip. All this is an impressive accomplishment. The only thing wrong with the Flying Burrito Brothers and their careful country-rock blend is that they work too hard at it. Instead of just doing their thing, they seem intent upon constantly reminding us that they are trying so hard at being these two unlike things, rock and country, together."

Bringing country and rock together was part of Parsons' dream but, unlike many of his successors, he chose not to take the easy route by gradually surrendering the country in favour of the rock. Although he was later critical of the Eagles for presenting a slicker, more radio-friendly adaptation of 'country rock', he still supported lesser lights. A&M had recently signed Steve Young, a talented singer-songwriter, who had relocated from Alabama to California six years before. His debut album, *Rock Salt & Nails*, was recorded in the same studio as *The Gilded Palace Of Sin*, overseen by producer Tommy LiPuma. Several leading players in the country field guested on the work, including A&M signings Gene Clark and Gram Parsons. "LiPuma played Gram some of the songs and he really liked them," Young recalls. "I was a little resistant because he wanted to play organ, and I didn't think that was such a great idea. I sometimes saw Gram around the Troubadour and he couldn't figure out why I wasn't more into trying to make it, like he was. His attitude was 'Come on, let's put this on the map!' He tried to befriend me and help and he was supportive. But he ran into that part of me that I don't exactly understand. It's almost like 'anti-career' or something." Unsurprisingly, Young fared no better commercially than Gram or Gene, but left the world with a cult 'country rock' album, even more obscure than the work of the Burritos. "A&M didn't know what to make of that album," he adds. "They sent it to Nashville, and Nashville said, 'We don't know what this is, it's not really country music.' It was the same old story. That album made an impression on a lot of musicians in LA who were into that whole country rock scene, but not on the public."

Steve Young's words applied equally to the career of the Flying Burrito Brothers, whose early promise foundered on the rocks of hedonistic excess and pervasive disillusionment. A&M persevered, despite the band running up huge bills on the road. Parsons was initially grateful to the company, although his words may have been disingenuous. "They've let us follow our concept," he remarked. "They are in it for the money like every other record company, and if people start buying our records they'll let us run with the ball. If I have to pay more dues, I'm willing to, because I dig honky tonk and rock 'n' roll – and being on the street doesn't bug me at all." The problem was that people weren't buying the record, Parsons' wasn't willing to continue 'paying dues' and his imagined street life was financed by a seemingly inexhaustible trust fund.

After a few months, cracks began to appear in the group dynamic. Their performances were still erratic, which was part of the appeal for those in search of spontaneity and shabby glory. But Hillman knew they should have been better. A document of their show at the Avalon Ballroom later appeared on bootleg and was officially released in November 2007 preposterously credited to 'Gram

Parsons and the Flying Burrito Brothers'. It was an untidy performance and the musical flaws are self-evident. In fairness, these shows were never intended for release and the group were only the support act, sandwiched between several San Franciscan acts. Regrettably, a more representative document of Parsons' live talent as a Burrito was never captured, except on bootleg tapes which make any sensible critical judgment almost impossible.

Hereafter, Parsons seemed increasingly ruled by whims and passing indulgences. He recruited R&B legends Larry Williams and Johnny 'Guitar' Watson to produce an unsuccessful single, 'The Train Song'. The session seemed more like an excuse to party with his heroes. It was a worrying indication of how far intemperance and self-indulgence had replaced musical innovation as the primary goal. The once thrilling songwriting collaboration with Hillman was already a distant memory. The duo moved to Nichols Canyon, then found another house. Hillman remembers "strange women coming in and out, a lot of powder, liquor. Gram was drunk and stupid a lot. He was a funny dude . . . We were hoodlums then, really, the outlaw band."

By the summer, the outlaws had lost a member of the gang: Chris Ethridge. Weary of playing for minimum financial reward, he elected to return to session work. Parsons hinted that the dreaded 'musical differences' may also have contributed to his decision. "He wasn't a country bass player. It should have been obvious to me because he's such a great studio musician. He realized it before anyone and said, 'Oh man, I'm sorry.' What we needed was someone who could play country shuffle." Parsons' reasoning here was a little muddled. He knew that Ethridge provided the R&B bass style that was a crucial part of the sound on *The Gilded Palace Of Sin*. While the Burritos may have needed more of a 'country shuffle' when playing clubs like the Palomino, they could ill afford to lose the R&B components that Gram had long since regarded as central to his vision. Looking back, Parsons pinpointed Ethridge's departure as the start of a long period of disenchantment and sagging morale. "I suppose about the time he split I got disillusioned. He was part of the group. He was the person who convinced me to come back from England when I had already split with the Byrds . . . I liked writing with him a whole lot, and it just blew my mind that he wasn't the right bass player. When he was missing, it seemed that the idea had been wrong, that we had picked the wrong people. I didn't know quite how to say it to Chris [Hillman] without getting in a fistfight about it. So I tried to stick it out and make it work . . ."

Evidently Parsons wasn't trying too hard. When the Burritos supported the Byrds that August at Carnegie Hall, he was singled out for some scathing criticism in *Billboard*: "Screaming pretensions and garish self-delusions reduced the potentially excellent band to a group ego-trip. Parsons' voice is matronly and his sickly Elvis fantasies are unpleasant to watch."

Such impressions were not echoed elsewhere. Generally, the Burritos did reasonably well playing at several major rock festivals, though never near the top of the bill. They also performed some dates at prisons literally playing before a captive audience. No doubt the huge success that Johnny Cash enjoyed with his recordings at Folsom Prison and San Quentin proved inspirational, but the Burritos were never captured live on these rare moments.

That summer of 1969, Joan Baez had sung 'Drug Store Truck Drivin' Man' at Woodstock and it would later be featured on the treble album film soundtrack. Baez was evidently something of a Parsons' connoisseur and also recorded 'Hickory Wind'. Carlos Bernal, who worked with the Byrds and Baez, thought it would be a great idea to bring them together. "Gram was playing 'Dark End Of The Street' on the piano," he recalls. "He was doing a good job. Joan was also in Nashville and she was recording 'Hickory Wind', so I introduced them. I remember it was awkward and I was sorry I'd done it. I think she was just glad when he left so that she could get back to work. She was the queen bee in her studio."

As time passed, Parsons became increasingly frustrated by the Burritos' lack of progress and low bill status, while they complained about his apathy, unreliability and drug use. After playing some gigs as a quartet, the band recruited guitarist Bernie Leadon, who had once played with Hillman in the Scottsville Squirrel Barkers and latterly joined Dillard & Clark. Reluctantly, Hillman took up the bass guitar for the first time since leaving the Byrds. Gram spent less time with the group having discovered new friends, including Linda Lawrence, the former girlfriend of Rolling Stone, Brian Jones.

The sense of lives no longer travelling in parallel directions was reinforced when Parsons left the house he had been sharing with Hillman. This encouraged Chris to curtail some of his wilder ways and focus on the band. By contrast, Parsons was intent on speeding his pace on the road to excess. Easily bored and constantly seduced by new opportunities, he moved to the Chateau Marmont, on Sunset Boulevard. A monument to rock star splendour, the Chateau housed a Who's Who of local celebrities, including Oscar-winning actors, artists and counterculture vultures. Parsons shared a suite with long-term resident Tony Foutz, the filmmaker he had befriended at Redlands the previous year. They had already reconnected at Brandon de Wilde's home in Topanga some time before. Away from the Burritos, Parsons and de Wilde had recorded two impressive demos, duetting on 'Hickory Wind' and 'Do Right Woman'. Their circle of friends was continually expanding.

Foutz's ongoing involvement with the Stones' UFO-linked movie *Maxagasm* was foundering, despite interest from Universal Pictures. His agent had just seen a news article about a 'Space Convention' hosted by UFO hunter George Van Tassel. It was scheduled to take place at the Giant Rock Airport near Joshua Tree. After raising $10,000, the agent suggested, "Go shoot something and we'll see if we can drum up some interest in *Maxagasm*."

Once again, Foutz rounded up a party of actors and friends including Gram, Michelle Phillips and photographer Andee Cohen, who memorably described the storyline as featuring "four cosmic kittens who were banished in outer space and came here to clean up the planet". With Kaufman providing the transportation, the troupe assembled for what was later described as "a *Wizard Of Oz* for the Sixties counterculture". A key figure in the original shooting was Ted Markland, 'the Mayor of Joshua Tree' who had checked out the first convention with Lenny Bruce back in 1955 and even boasted his own mountain top. Also present, but not acting, were Linda Lawrence and the five-year-old Julian Jones, her son by Brian.

What Foutz had anticipated as a documentary soon developed into another film, tentatively titled *Saturation 70*. Having retired to the Chateau to write a treatment, Foutz was suddenly convinced that Julian should be the key figure in the movie. The child was reconfigured into a Victorian waif who had somehow fallen through time and space. The twin mission of the unnamed characters played by Parsons, Phillips and Cohen was to save Earth and somehow return the young boy to the 1800s. With such a fluid script, Gram's complete lack of acting experience was not considered a problem. As Foutz recalls: "Gram liked the idea of being in a film and being a star. He liked creativity. He was a very smart guy and he lived very much in his own world. He had his own telescope on life. He was very impractical in many ways. He'd get these cheques for $25,000 and they'd just be sitting in a drawer. But he was very inquisitive, knowledgeable and sensitive about emotions. The Chateau was a wonderful environment for us, full of creative people. It was a sanctum more than anything. I didn't even have a car because you didn't have to go any place."

Filming continued intermittently between October 1969 and June 1970, with an expansive list of cameo parts for actor/director Christian Marquand, tailor Nudie Cohn, the Stones' aristocratic pal Prince Stanislas Klossowski de Rola, and even the enigmatic producer, Phil Spector. "Everybody hung out, everybody was accessible, everybody was spontaneous," Foutz remembers. "It was before attitudes came and people had to start bullet-proofing themselves." When Foutz was considering incidental music, Parsons recommended Roger McGuinn and his Moog synthesizer. More surprisingly, Gram suggested that he would be happy to collaborate with his former Byrds' nemesis on some songs for the proposed soundtrack. There were other coincidental connections. Christian Marquand had directed *Candy* for which the Byrds had provided the title track; Foutz had appeared in the film, playing himself. Roger invited Foutz to stay at his home for a few nights to discuss the venture. Its innovative aspects proved particularly appealing. "McGuinn's complex," Foutz notes. "Most musicians are spontaneous and live in the moment. He was very analytical." Always interested in film projects and technology, McGuinn agreed to contribute the Moog parts and had no problem working with Gram, if necessary. Foutz was most struck by a handful of sage words from Roger which appeared especially heartfelt. "He said, 'Take care of him.' He knew Gram was vulnerable and sensitive in a very fundamental way." What might have been a great collaboration was ultimately scuppered by a lack of funding made worse by the impending oil crisis and stock market reversals. The footage of *Saturation 70* was ultimately lost, feared destroyed. Only a few stills and a short promotional reel survive.

Although the film was never completed, it at least distracted Parsons from his ongoing problems with the Flying Burrito Brothers. Watching Foutz write and film even inspired some parodic imitation from Gram. Doodling in his notebook, he concocted a 'science fiction play'. "A vague two dimensional synopsis on the beginning . . ." he began earnestly, then rambled on incoherently about its contents. "From a script simply titled 'See Pearl Buck'," he concluded. Could he possibly have been referring to the American writer Pearl Sydenstricker Buck whose novel *The Good Earth* was a best seller in 1931? Who knows?

Parsons became even more distanced from the Burritos after the Rolling Stones arrived in Los Angeles on 17 October 1969 to complete work on their album, *Let It Bleed* and rehearse for their first US tour in three years. Writer Stanley Booth, who had previously penned an effusive review of *The Gilded Palace Of Sin*, first met Parsons when he turned up at the Stones' rented house a couple of days later. Although he was flanked by Jagger and Richards, he nevertheless stood out. "He was physically one of the handsomest people that you'd ever want to meet. He was just obviously someone who lived on an idealistic plane. He had such humour and such focus . . . A lot of people resented Gram because of his gifts and because he had money from home. Keith said he was the best gentleman he ever met."

Parsons spent as much time as possible with Keith Richards, organizing another trip to the Joshua Tree National Monument, where they contemplated the secrets of the universe, assisted by copious amounts of mescaline and coke. Parsons vainly hoped that his friend might find time in his busy schedule to produce the next Burritos' album. Instead, that task was assigned to Jim Dickson, whom Hillman had approached in search of stability. Dickson had attended one of the Burritos' shows at the Whisky during the summer and was aghast at the sight of Ethridge, zonked out on downers. Hillman confirmed that line-up changes were already afoot and promised, more in hope than expectation, that the band would be ready to record at the end of the year. Parsons was disturbed by this shift in the power dynamics and remained remote from Dickson who proceeded slowly, first routining the group on some practice tapes where they played a selection of country standards, intermingled with material from their live set. The following year, Dickson would return to these tapes in a desperate salvage operation. Tellingly, the material included Parsons' tired rendition of the Stones' 'Honky Tonk Women', alongside some better covers, most notably, the Bee Gees' 'To Love Somebody'.

Parsons' adoration of the Stones coincided with their increasing immersion in country blues. They had already experimented with country on 1968's *Beggars Banquet*, notably on 'Dear Doctor'. Keith Richards had since picked up some guitar tunings from Gram and learned even more from the brilliant slide player Ry Cooder, who tutored him on the finer points of *G* tuning. Jagger affected a distinctive drawl to add some Southern grit to the vocals. The return to a rootsier style was a risky venture in some respects, but the Stones knew their market well. 'Honky Tonk Women' became the biggest summer hit of 1969, topping the charts in both the US and UK for four and five weeks, respectively. The new album, *Let In Bleed*, promised to be a classic, but not everybody was happy. Ry Cooder felt his artistic lifeblood had been systematically drained away by the Stones whom he referred to as "bloodsuckers". Some claimed Parsons was also a victim of Richards' voracious creative appetite. Former road manager Jim Seiter remembers Parsons playing 'Country Honk' on piano some time before and telling him he should push Jagger/Richards for a share of the songwriting income, a fantasy in the Stones' world. Whether Parsons deserved a credit was academic. "It was a great honour bestowed on me," he retorted. Evidently, his major contribution was suggesting they bring in world champion fiddle player Byron Berline to add a touch of authentic country to the track.

While Parsons was fraternizing with the Stones, the Burritos were left in limbo. "Gram was over at Keith's house all the goddamn time and wouldn't show up for rehearsals," says Bernie Leadon. "He just wanted to be with Keith. The music, the chicks, the drugs. He was fascinated by Jagger and Jagger's appeal. He definitely saw himself as that pop idol/tragic figure . . . a merging of the Hank Williams tradition and the Mick Jagger style. He always wanted to be a Rolling Stone, really . . ."

Evidently a metamorphosis had already begun. Since befriending the Stones, Parsons gradually acquired a more effeminate image, sporting scarves and silks, in imitation of Jagger. Accoutrements like eye liner, painted nails and frosted hair would soon complete the picture. Supposedly, Parsons even took to grabbing Richards' hand and skipping across a room, like some pantomime fairy. Gram fearlessly introduced this daring androgyny to audiences at the Palomino, no doubt relishing their disquiet. "He was doing this mild cross-dressing playing these redneck country bars where people just wanted to kill us," laughs Hillman. "That, along with Nudie suits, made it quite interesting for that one-year period."

When the Burritos were booked to play a gig in El Monte, Hillman was alarmed to discover that Parsons was nowhere to be found. Eventually, he figured that Gram must be enjoying the company of the Stones. "He was almost like a lapdog to those guys. They were in LA recording and the Burritos had a local show to do. I couldn't find Gram. I had to track him down. He was hanging around with the Stones in the studio. I went in to get him and he didn't want to do the show. Jagger got into his face about it and said, 'You have a responsibility to Chris Hillman and you have a responsibility to an audience and to your band. You have to go to work *now*. We're busy.' I'll never forget that. Jagger's a professional guy – look at what he's done with his life."

Others outside the immediate Burritos' circle were also aware of Parsons' infatuation with the Stones. Roger McGuinn and his wife Dolores were on the guest list for the Stones' second show at the Los Angeles Forum on 8 November. As they approached the venue, they were met by an extraordinary sight. "It's so weird," Dolores recalls. "When we got there, we saw Gram in his top hat trying to get in backstage and banging on the door. It's such a strange image I have of him. That was so weird, and Roger was shocked to witness it." Seeing Parsons acting like a groupie convinced McGuinn that his ex-bandmate was making a fool of himself. Like several others, he took the cynical view that Gram was little more than a cipher in the Stones' inner circle. "They pulled him over and started romancing him, and they ripped him off for all he knew," was his opinion some years later.

Despite such suspicions, it was clear that Richards had a genuine brotherly affection for Parsons. Three days before the Forum concert, the Stones had thrown a surprise birthday party for him at the house they were renting from Stephen Stills. Earlier that evening, Parsons was introduced to Gretchen Lisi Burrell, the 17-year-old daughter of newscaster, Larry Burrell. She described their meeting as "love at first sight" and found him "very charming, funny, adorable and sweet". They would soon embark on a relationship as stormy and eventful as all the others in his life.

Parsons may have been starstruck by the Stones, but he was still capable of using their friendship to his own benefit. Upon arrival in the States, the group had suffered a stinging attack over concert ticket prices. Jagger mollified his critics by promising a free show at San Francisco's Golden Gate Park. He no doubt envisaged another Hyde Park, where legions of fans had gathered peacefully to enjoy music and pay a respectful farewell to the recently deceased Brian Jones. Transposed to the love capital of the world, the Stones would surely recreate that perfect vibe. Self-consciously recalling a recent festival that they had not attended, Jagger spoke of a 'winter Woodstock'. In what can now be appreciated as a painful piece of dramatic irony, he claimed it would be "a microcosm of society which sets examples for the rest of America as to how one can behave in large gatherings".

Shortly after this announcement, several members of the Stones turned up for a Burritos' show at the Topanga Corral. Keith Richards was impressed by Parsons' stage charisma which he had previously observed back in London but never experienced in such an intimate setting. It did not seem to matter whether the singer was in tune or off-key. He still connected emotionally with the audience, particularly on his most intense songs. Richards reckoned Gram was "the only guy I know who could make every chick in the audience weep – which is a rare quality". Parsons was eager to secure a support slot on the Stones' 'free concert'. He became even more interested upon learning that the event was to be filmed. In order to ensure that everyone in his orbit was happy, he offered to finance his own travel arrangements. After hearing this news, Hillman agreed that it was an excellent opportunity to improve the Burritos' painfully low profile.

Finalizing a venue for the 'winter Woodstock' was proving more difficult than anticipated. A permit to perform at Golden Gate Park was not forthcoming, prompting fears that the concert would be cancelled. Eventually, an impasse was seemingly resolved when the president of the Sears Point Raceway offered assistance. A stop press in the counterculture bible *Rolling Stone* announced: "It's on. It will be a little Woodstock, and even more exciting, it will be an *instant* Woodstock." Unfortunately, there was a last-minute hitch. While the stage was under construction, corporate owners Filmways demanded rights for any film taken at the event. The Stones resisted and after a flurry of activity, settled on an alternative venue – the Altamont Speedway, 50 miles east of San Francisco. By now it was the eve of the concert.

The Flying Burrito Brothers were about to discover that their dream date at Altamont was actually the stuff of nightmares. The Devil incarnate could hardly have conjured a darker mirror for the optimism of the age in the aftermath of Woodstock. The fateful decision to employ Hell's Angels to police Altamont was akin to an open invitation to anarchy. Their sudden arrival near the front of the stage immediately changed the entire tenor of the festival. Peace-seeking hippies, suckling mothers and stoned adolescents found themselves confronted by brutish, leather-clad man mountains brandishing bike chains and lead-weighted, sawn-off pool cues. Intoxicated by power, beer and red wine, their idea of law enforcement was akin to a Klan confederacy overseeing a black civil rights protest. Additional potency was added to this grim spectacle by the presence of a strain of bad acid which had already provoked several psychotic seizures. Backstage, medics voiced concern and were increasingly harried. The show had barely begun.

These auguries of ill fortune were also visited upon the Burritos' retinue as they approached Altamont on that fateful 6 December. While attempting to bypass miles of traffic congestion, Sneaky Pete Kleinow drove their van into a ditch. Some in the group were forced to hitch rides from passing Hell's Angels, then make their way through the festival crowd to the stage. By that time, opening act Santana had completed their set and the Angels were flexing their muscles with violent outbursts, including the beating of a young man whose only crime appeared to be daring to display his naked body. The Burritos' roadies offered him refuge in their trailer van. During the Jefferson Airplane's performance, the violence accelerated. "Why are we hurting each other?" singer Grace Slick implored, but her rhetorical question remained unanswered. Instead, the random assaults continued.

When Marty Balin intervened to help, he was beaten unconscious. Speaking into the microphone, Paul Kantner quipped: "The Hell's Angels have just smashed Marty Balin and knocked him out for a while." This laconic remark risked another bludgeoning, but this time the Angels held back. Remarkably, the Burritos were blessed with a momentary outbreak of Angelic composure and completed their set without incident, performing 'Six Days On The Road', 'High Fashion Queen', 'Cody, Cody' and 'Lazy Days'. "The simple verities of their countrified electric music soothed the warriors; there were no fights," *Rolling Stone* reported.

The ferocity of the Hell's Angels accelerated with the Stones' set, especially when Jagger started singing 'Sympathy For The Devil'. A terrifying climax occurred during 'Under My Thumb' when a lean black man in a green suit could be seen running towards the stage, only to be buried in a melee of Angels' arms. This was 18-year-old Meredith Hunter. After producing a gun, he was fatally stabbed to death while film cameras were still rolling. Reportedly, his final words were the puzzled and conciliatory rejoinder: "I wasn't going to shoot you."

While the Rolling Stones played on, oblivious to the full extent of the horror, many backstage were also unaware that an actual murder had occurred. The subsequent film, *Gimme Shelter*, shows the group leaving the concert in a helicopter, as if they are exiting a war zone. Climbing aboard at the last second is Parsons, accompanied by Michelle Phillips. Fellow passenger Stanley Booth remembers a failed attempt at amours. "Gram was kissing Michelle, trying to make out with her, and she seemed to be enduring it like a high school senior trying to make do with a sophomore boy on the way home from a church hayride." Later that evening, at the palatial Huntington Hotel in San Francisco, Parsons heard a rough mix of Jagger/Richards 'Wild Horses'. He implored them to allow him to record the song and permission was granted on condition that it would never be issued as a single. It was the only good news on that grim day.

* * *

Parsons was not on his best form during the recording of *Burrito Deluxe*. His absences with the Stones had caused frustration, friction and resentment. Early in the sessions, the band rejected one of his new compositions, '$1000 Wedding', which Hillman dismissed as a mawkish dirge. The problem lay with the singer as much as the song. "I had problems with Gram," producer Jim Dickson remembers. "He'd come in so whacked out on downers and sleeping pills that he'd seldom be any good. Gram was indulging and had been spending all his time hanging out with Mick Jagger, which was more important to him than the Flying Burrito Brothers. He did get 'Wild Horses' as a result but, beyond that, all it did was take away from the group. This frustrated Chris because he wanted to do a good job and was prevented by Gram showing up late, or not showing up at all . . . There were too many drugs and he wasn't concentrating. I couldn't get him to focus on his performances. He was so laid back that he was hardly singing most of the time. We were not unfriendly and he was generally polite, but unfocused. Chris' lack of respect for Gram probably kept me from seeing the positive side of him. So I never got close to Gram. I had no respect for him because he didn't respect what he was doing. But there are a lot of other 'Gram Parsons' in different time slots where he behaved differently . . . Chris sees things in black and white. He tends to remember that part where Gram didn't contribute."

Hillman's frustration was palpable. The once easy communication he had with Parsons was now replaced by open disdain. "Gram and I just couldn't seem to hook up again. *Burrito Deluxe* was written and recorded without any of the feeling or intensity of the first album, and it seemed that we were walking on different roads. He was getting into a lot of drugs and he just went headlong in the direction of physical abuse, and it was an area where I couldn't help him at all. There was nothing that any of us could do."

Parsons also felt alienated from the recording, largely because he no longer had the full support of Hillman, whom he felt was more likely to defer to Dickson. "The second album was a mistake. It was a mistake to get Jim Dickson involved. We should have been more careful than that. It's commercial. That's what Jim Dickson was aiming at, trying to make it commercial . . . he dictated to Chris Hillman for some reason. Chris was always listening to what Jim says. I think it's because of the *Mr Tambourine Man* album."

Having abandoned '$1000 Wedding', Parsons turned to the country songbook and suggested they record Harlan Howard's 'Image Of Me'. Dickson momentarily felt that this might energize everybody, but his hopes were dashed due to simple bad luck. "Gram did a dynamite vocal and the machine at A&M erased it. He tried like hell to do it again that well, but he couldn't." The take featured on the album emphasizes his point. Parsons' vocal is tentative and appears low in the mix, as if to disguise its shortcomings.

Reaching backwards for inspiration, Parsons revived 'Lazy Days', a composition already recorded unsuccessfully by both the International Submarine Band and the Byrds. With the false hope of an A-side single and the promise of an opening track on the album, Parsons performed by far the best version to date. Its competence initially left Dickson mystified. "All of a sudden, a couple of songs popped up and one of them was 'Lazy Days'. They all knew this song. I wondered how they'd learned it because I'd been to every rehearsal. Later, I found out 'Lazy Days' had been recorded at the *Sweetheart* sessions. Chris, of course, knew that. Parsons gave the publishing to Almo Irving [the publishing arm of A&M]. He was fulfilling his publishing obligations to them with an old song. All this chicanery was going on."

Parsons produced two other songs of note, with help from his fellow members. 'Cody, Cody' sounded like a Byrds tune augmented by mandolin and steel. A self-questioning love song with a quasi-philosophical tone, it used the old Parsons' trick of disguising lyrical vagueness with vocal conviction. 'Older Guys', inspired by sitting around Malibu Beach, sounded like a subtle dig at Bob Parsons disguised as a catchy novelty single.

Bernie Leadon was allowed a vocal cameo on his own

composition, 'God's Own Singer' and also provided the music for 'Man In The Fog', for which Parsons added some throwaway lyrics. Nevertheless, it was one of the more interesting arrangements, with a Cajun-style accordion played by roadie Frankie Blanco's uncle, Leopoldo C. Carbajal. Leon Russell, who was rehearsing in a studio nearby, popped in to add a piano part, which transformed the track.

Dickson could have done with a lot more help from Russell, whom he had always revered, even before employing his services on 'Mr Tambourine Man'. Parsons, a more recent convert, was intrigued by Russell's latest project, Mad Dogs And Englishmen, a star-studded ensemble whose roots-based sound encapsulated everything that he had hoped to achieve since forming the Flying Burrito Brothers. Dickson was also aware of the contrast between the two bands and admitted that Russell's rehearsals had the unintended effect of sucking the life out of the Burritos.

It may have been subliminal memory taking over, but Russell's presence reminded Dickson that they urgently needed a strong single to promote the album. Predictably, he turned to the Dylan songbook, selecting 'If You Gotta Go', previously a major UK success for Manfred Mann. Parsons failed to invest the song with the arch tone or suggestiveness that the lyric deserved, and it sounded terribly haphazard. "At the last minute Chris doubled the tempo on the bass and I shouldn't have let him," Dickson regrets. "It made it worse. It ended up sounding rushed. I couldn't get what I wanted out of Gram on that. It was frustrating."

Hillman was left to fill out the album, reviving 'Farther Along' from his bluegrass days and collaborating with Parsons on two more tunes. Although he later dismissed these contributions, they were not without merit. The country rocker 'High Fashion Queen' remained in the set long after Parsons left the group, while 'Down In The Churchyard' was deemed strong enough to be re-recorded by Hillman for his first solo album.

The most important track and grand finale was the six-minute 'Wild Horses', one of the most powerful Jagger/Richards songs ever leased to another artiste. That the Burritos were allowed to release their version a full year before the Stones' own was the ultimate compliment. Dickson was well aware of the song's importance and was thrilled when Leon Russell returned to provide a stately piano accompaniment that transformed the track. Parsons' deeply moving vocal ably articulates the pained vulnerability at the song's centre. Whatever else they had succeeded or failed to achieve on *Burrito Deluxe*, they must have known that this one song would be enough to rescue the album in any critic's eyes.

Amazingly, Hillman did not share this viewpoint. Having already damned '$1000 Wedding' at the start of the sessions, he was scarcely more charitable to the sweeping, epical 'Wild Horses'. "You're talking to the caustic one here," he reminds us. "I didn't like that song. I thought it was the most maudlin, depressing song I'd ever heard. I was going, 'Another ballad? Let's get some life back into this music. Let's get back into country shuffles, and country music – what we set out to do with this thing.' He brought 'Wild Horses' in, and I didn't like it. I didn't like the Stones' version either. I didn't care for the song."

Beyond simple aesthetic objections, Hillman's comments implied something deeper, which Dickson detected in a passing summation. "The thing Chris Hillman has never been able to face is that the reason Gram was important was that he expressed feeling. Chris can't. Gram, whether he was sloppy or musically poor, could get up there and girls sensed that there was a person there. With Chris – he's more like a robot."

Looking back at his time with Parsons, Dickson feels that the album sessions were probably doomed from the outset. "By the time I got involved with Gram he was so wrapped up in the Rolling Stones that he didn't pay any attention to the Burritos. He'd come in, and then he'd go, and that's when he and Chris grew apart. Chris grew real jealous of Gram's attention to the Rolling Stones. It was very destructive. It was what made the Burritos not good anymore . . . I don't think I did a good job on Gram's voice when we did 'Wild Horses' . . . I think I was resenting it. I didn't make him sound magic. I could have played more with the echo and tape delay on his voice and made him more dramatic. I guess I was a little angry with him. Gram was a nightmare then."

Away from the Burritos, Parsons brooded and drank. His chaotic lifestyle was reflected in his untidy journals. One loose-leaved stationery pad was simply titled 'My Book' as though it was compiled by a child. Another featured a photo of a smiling, short-skirted cheerleader on its cover. The majority of the entries were written during this troubled period and provide some insight into Parsons' fractured state of mind. He scribbles the lyrics to 'Wild Horses' again and again, as if he might suddenly forget them. The same occurs with '$1,000 Wedding' which is roughly committed to paper, accompanied by little sketches. Tellingly, these were the two compositions that met most resistance during the recent album sessions. There are a couple of songs transcribed in pristine hand but they are not his own: Jimmie Rodgers' 'Lookin' For A New Mama' and Merle Haggard's 'Mother, Queen Of My Heart'. The first is a fantasy about finding a more servile woman, the latter a eulogy to a deceased mother whom the angels have called away. The themes speak for themselves. In addition to the songs, there are set lists from an undated Troubadour performance. One of these reveals that the Burritos played 'Heartbreak Hotel', which Parsons had first heard live at the Elvis Presley show he attended in Waycross in February 1956.

Judging from many of the scribbled entries in his notebook, Parsons appears to have been drunk or stoned. Often, he can't even write in a straight line. Reality and artistic waywardness combine wonderfully over two pages simply titled 'Tax Time'. Here we see Parsons' pyrrhic attempt to sort out his finances. There are long division calculations, details of the interest he has received from his Midland bank account and a crude profit and loss computation covering monies related to the International Submarine Band, the Byrds, his time in London and other expenses leading up to Altamont. The three-year time frame suggests that Parsons was either late submitting his tax returns or was possibly facing some questions from the IRS.

Burrito Deluxe was released in the spring of 1970. The cover artwork featured a shot of a rhinestone-covered Burrito, while the rear displayed the band in smiling prayer, wearing unattractive anti-contamination suits, borrowed from the set of Tony Foutz's uncompleted UFO movie. The album received mixed reviews, but 'Wild Horses' was singled out by *Rolling Stone* as indisputably excellent. It was not enough to rescue sales, which were again disappointing. The album failed to register in the US charts, no doubt prompting serious questions at A&M.

Parsons later distanced himself from the recording of *Burrito Deluxe*, which he described as a "death blow" to the group. "I can't really claim to have participated in that. I did what was asked of me, and that was it. It's a pretty lousy thing to have to admit." By this stage, he was on borrowed time in the Burritos, whose prospects were less than promising. "I wanted to see if the album was going to be a freak hit. And I split. I was starting to duck out of road gigs about that time. Starting to say, 'I can't handle it. I don't want to go to Seattle for 800 bucks. No thank you.' "

Waning commitment coincided with heightened drug use, creating a damaging spiral of self-destructive behaviour. In the midst of this was a family problem, which Parsons felt ill-equipped to tackle. Over the past year, his sister Avis had suffered a troubled marriage, soon annulled, fallen pregnant and was abusing pills to such an extent that she needed medical assistance. Bob Parsons had her enrolled in a programme at De Paul Hospital in New Orleans, inevitably provoking suspicion from members of her extended family. On several occasions, she phoned her brother, begging him to engineer her discharge, but he was usually incoherent or too strung out to act. In the end, she absconded and was picked up by her paternal uncle Tom and his wife Pauline, who had been alerted by the hospital. While staying with them in Nashville, she gave birth to a daughter, also called Avis.

Parsons was back on the road by the time he learned that he was now an uncle with a niece. It did nothing to alleviate his excesses. During a tour of the Midwest in May, he was wasted much of the time. "He hated to fly, so he would take a lot of these red sleeping pills," says Hillman. "In Washington, they refused to let him board the plane. He was in a wheelchair wasted on these pills; it was getting really sad."

Michael Clarke's mother attended a show in Portland and was taken aback by Parsons' state. "I met Gram once, and if you want to meet a crazy boy – well, he was just a nut. I shouldn't judge, but I was visiting my sister, who lives in Vancouver, Washington, down by Portland, and we went to see the Burritos. He had a big stovepiped hat that he wore all the time. He and Bernie Leadon were acting up, and you couldn't get a sensible word out of Gram. He could barely talk at all. It was sad."

After returning to LA, Parsons was ready to have some fun. He spent time with the Shilos' former mentor turned rock aristocrat, John Phillips, who was still living in resplendent glory on the publishing royalties from his hits with the Mamas & The Papas. Phillips was considering a project based on the Romantic poets, an appropriate idea considering that he was already living the life of Byron. Around this time, he had befriended Elvis Presley, attending his shows at the International Hotel in Las Vegas, and joining him on nocturnal bike rides. It was surely no coincidence that Parsons also took several friends to the International and bought a Harley Davidson motorcycle, just like his hero. Given Gram's excessive escapades, it was not the most sensible purchase. "He wasn't strong enough to hold it all the time," says Hillman. "I knew he would eat it on that bike."

The incident occurred at Bel Air. John Phillips and his later wife Genevieve Waite were riding ahead on a BSA Triumph. Gram was some way behind, accompanied by Maggie Thrett, a singer actress, who had enjoyed minor chart success with 'Soupy' and a small part in *Star Trek*. Parsons' bike had not been repaired properly and the front fork detached from the wheel throwing him perilously on to the road. Phillips doubled back to find him, bloodied and semi-conscious. Threttt was shaken, but unharmed. Before drifting into insensibility, Parsons mumbled, "John, take me on that long white ride." Later, when he was reminded of his 'dying utterance', Gram was delighted and declared himself a poet. The bard suffered a broken leg and minor head injuries for which he was administered painkillers.

The injury forced the Burritos to cancel a visit to London, where they had never previously performed. Parsons' recuperation was as slow as expected, but he was back on the road the following month, assisted by pharmaceuticals. On 26 June, the group appeared at the Jam Factory in San Antonio, Texas. Gram was on good form, even teasing the audience about playing 'San Antonio Rose', which Sneaky Pete duly did on steel guitar. The set also included a revival of the Byrds' 'One Hundred Years From Now', plus Parsons' covers of Merle Haggard's 'I'm A Lonesome Fugitive' and Buck Owens' 'Don't Let Her Know'. His singing seemed fine that night and there was no indication of any friction, onstage or off.

Four days later, the Burritos appeared at the Brass Ring on Ventura Boulevard. Parsons was late turning up for the show, inebriated and stoned. Hillman's friend Joey Stec attended, but saw nothing particularly untoward. He still equated the Burritos with cocaine, so the sight of Parsons wasted came as no surprise. Even his broken leg was typically Burritonian, a reminder of Michael Clarke's similar mishap the previous year. Most of the band had over-indulged in the past and the notion that they might take the moral high ground with Parsons seemed faintly ludicrous. What Stec had not bargained on was Hillman's simmering aggression. "I love Chris, but he's an intimidating fuck. He needs his ass kicked. Even though he's 65 now, he still needs his ass kicked . . . There'd been this ongoing animosity between Chris and Gram. We were at the Brass Ring and I was talking to Michael. They went onstage and Gram was acting a bit like Elvis Presley and getting really high. In the middle of a song, he forgot the words. They walked offstage and into the kitchen.

Gram comes in the door and Chris takes the guitar out of his hands. It was a blonde Gibson Dove – and he breaks it over Gram's head. Right there in the fucking kitchen between sets." Roadie Phil Kaufman, whom Parsons invited along to watch the show, claims that "Gram was so stoned that Chris took Gram's guitar and smashed it. Just completely destroyed it, like he was Pete Townshend." Others in attendance, including Hillman himself, point out that he actually punched a large hole in the guitar, like the karate kid. The intention of smashing Parsons over the head was nevertheless an accurate projection of what was on Hillman's mind, as he told his victim immediately afterwards. "He was so out of it by then that he simply had to go," says Hillman. "That was the end of it, and it was unpleasant." Parsons bumped into Hillman at the A&M car lot a few days later and momentarily assumed he might be forgiven, but Chris was adamant. "When our ways parted in 1970 I swore that I'd never work with him again."

While these dramatic events were unfolding, Jim Dickson was working on some old rehearsal tapes from the previous year in the forlorn hope that they might have enough material to complete another record, simply to reduce their debt to A&M. "After *Burrito Deluxe,* I was so disappointed that I felt we needed to get something out that was fun and that you could dance to. That was my thinking at the time. Herb Pedersen came in and added acoustic guitar and did all the harmony parts." The idea made no aesthetic sense as the material consisted mainly of covers, dashed off in rehearsal. *Burrito Deluxe* was a masterpiece by comparison, so it was no surprise when the project was cancelled. The sessions were later released in the Netherlands, a bastion of Burritos' fandom, under the title *Honky Tonk Heaven.*

Away from the Burritos, Parsons spent most of his time at Terry Melcher's house in Benedict Canyon. At that stage, the Byrds' producer was coming to terms with the fall-out from the Manson slayings. He still lived in fear that a deranged member of the cult might attempt a revenge killing. The gun-toting Melcher had been deadening his fears with alcohol, drugs and women friends, and Parsons was quick to join the party. "Gram was either drinking to forget or to remember, or *both*," Melcher notes. "There was a touch of fatalism about him. At times, he felt like a victim of circumstance, recalling the losses he experienced in his family. There were also moments of bitterness or paranoia about his time in the Byrds and Burritos. But they were fleeting. That came across in some of his conversations, but you could never be sure if he meant it. It soon passed. You'd have to be a psychologist to unravel it all. Of course, these were heady times and we were loaded a lot. Mostly, he was good company and had a neat sense of humour. That's what I liked about him."

Back at the Chateau, Tony Foutz witnessed these latest developments. "At the time we were living together Terry Melcher came into his life. I think Terry blew him up with a lot of 'You're going to be a star at the Hollywood Bowl.' Gram did have an ego. He probably had fantasies about being another Rolling Stones. Who knows what his fantasies were? He did like to hang out. But he was very sensitive in the sense that he got hurt by a lot of that stuff. He wasn't tough like Mick or Keith. He didn't have that street savvy. They were combat veterans."

Despite his hedonistic behaviour, Parsons was sociable and confident enough to contribute to a variety of extracurricular projects throughout this period. Following his appearance on Steve Young's *Rock Salt & Nails*, he sang harmony on the Byrds' 'All The Things' on *(Untitled)*, contributed vocals to Delaney & Bonnie's *Motel Shot* and Fred Neil's *Other Side Of This Life*, and his old composition 'Apple Tree' was covered by Johnny Rivers on *Slim Slo Slider*. All of these were mere distractions from Gram's primary goal – the completion of a solo album.

With time on his hands, Melcher was convinced that their partying dalliances could be transformed into something resembling real work. He pitched a deal to A&M's titular head Jerry Moss, who agreed to finance a Parsons solo record with Melcher as producer. When Melcher's sometime adversary Jim Dickson heard the news, he was cynical about the outcome. "I had been working with Terry on *(Untitled)* and he was drinking and taking too many downers. He had a bodyguard because of Manson and he was in bad shape. I saw Jerry Moss on the A&M lot and told him, 'Don't expect too much out of Terry . . .' He got mad at me. 'How can you talk that way about him after all he's done for you?' A few weeks later, I saw him again, and he apologized. Terry had thrown up in his brand new custom-made Yamaha piano. He'd had it tuned and carefully shipped over. It was his pride and joy. Jerry said my warning was well placed."

Having lost Moss' support, Melcher continued with the sessions, still convinced that he could get something from Parsons. "They would think up great album titles for days, like 'These Blues Have Made A Nigger Out Of Me' and 'Money Honey'," says Melcher's personal assistant, Ginny Ganahl. "The way they related to each other was really like outlaws, being born to money." As he would later do with *Byrdmaniax*, Terry invited singer Merry Clayton to add a powerful gospel backing, most notably on 'White Line Fever', but Gram was swamped by the arrangement. Barry Tashian, who was visiting LA at the time, recalls a small reunion of former Parsons' musical associates at Melcher's house. "We were sitting around, singing with Gram and just having fun really. But he was working towards something then. One night, we all went over to Terry Melcher's house to sing some songs for Terry. Later, there was a recording with Gram and Terry at A&M's studios. Mickey Gauvin played drums, I sang, Chris Ethridge was on bass and Claudia Lennear was there too. The only song I remember was 'White Line Fever'. At the end of the session, I was getting fed up with how much Gram was getting into drugs. I couldn't hang out any more with him, so I stayed at Brandon de Wilde's house . . . There was a distance that hadn't been there before. I felt like I didn't know him as well any longer. I'd felt more intimacy with him back in the Submarine Band days. He was still a good, fun-loving guy, but it was almost like he was back at high school or something. Anything was possible." The sporadic sessions with Melcher continued with a revolving cast of musicians.

Parsons revived the project, recutting several of the songs with another heavy drinker, Jesse Ed Davis. "I backed Gram on some of those," recalls singer/guitarist, Moon Martin. "Jesse Ed produced four or five cuts in-between Gram's record deals with A&M and Warners. Parsons took his own money, went into the studio and had Jesse produce. I played guitar on the tracks. It fell through and subsequently Jesse took the tracks and put them out with his own voice. You can hear 'White Line Fever' on *Ululu* with my guitar work – that was one of them. I have the tapes somewhere. Gram was doing a lot of cocaine at the time and I didn't think he could sing that well."

The Melcher-produced album was later remixed at Olympic Studios in London. Its track listing featured ten songs: Oldham/Penn's 'Do Right Woman', George Jones' 'Family Bible', Harlan Howard's 'I Fall To Pieces', Parsons' 'Brass Buttons', Eddie Hinton's 'It's All Wrong', Boudleaux Bryant's 'Sleepless Nights', Wanda Jackson's 'Your Love', Roy Orbison's 'Dream Baby', the aforementioned 'White Line Fever', and Dickey Lee's 'She Thinks I Still Care'. The tapes supposedly disappeared, an appropriate coda to the disorganized and dissolute lifestyle celebrated in Benedict Canyon. Commentators always assumed that the recordings had been irrevocably lost, but this is not the case. Thankfully, the tapes still exist, perfectly preserved in a vault. They remain unissued to this day.

In the hierarchy of self-abuse, Parsons was mixing with the richest and most reckless. After Phillips, Melcher and Davis, he re-established contact with Keith Richards, this time in the forlorn expectation that the Rolling Stone might produce his solo album from scratch. The group had recently founded Rolling Stones Records and Parsons hoped that he might be signed to the label. In the meantime, he and girlfriend Gretchen Burrell hung out in London and briefly visited his friend Ian Dunlop, who was now married and living in Tregidden, a village in Cornwall.

Thereafter, Parsons spent more time with Keith Richards. The most dissolute surviving member of the Stones was currently facing a twin threat from the Inland Revenue and high-grade heroin addiction. Outstanding tax liabilities were assaulting the very foundations of the Stones' empire, effectively forcing them into exile. Prince Rupert Lowenstein, the group's aristocratic accountant, confirmed that they would have to leave the country before the end of the tax year, which was less than two months away. Richards was a reluctant exile but agreed that this was the only solution. He also felt obliged to combat his drug habit in advance of their departure. Mick Jagger dutifully discussed the matter with William Burroughs, author of *The Naked Lunch* and *Junkie*. Burroughs explained to both Jagger and Richards that he had overcome his narcotic addiction under a treatment regime overseen by Dr John Dent whose use of apomorphine alleviated withdrawal symptoms during the torturous process colloquially known as 'cold turkey'. Dent was long dead but his nurse, known as 'Dr Smith' or 'Smitty', still used the method with some success.

Parsons, whose drug dependence rivalled that of Richards, elected to join him in the habit-breaking 'cure'. "I did a couple of clean-ups with Gram Parsons at this time," Richards recalled, "both unsuccessful." The redoubtable 'Smitty' had the demeanour of a no-nonsense hospital matron. Mollycoddling indulging rock stars was not part of her remit and she administered apomorphine with an air of clinical detachment and unsmiling efficiency. As Richards remembers: "We took this cure in Cheyne Walk, and it was Gram and me in my four-poster bed, the only guy I ever slept with. Except that we kept falling off the bed because we were twitching so much from the treatment. With a bucket to throw up in, if you could stop twitching for enough seconds to get near it. 'You got the bucket, Gram?' Our only outlet, if we could stand up, would be to go down and play the piano and sing for a bit, or as much as possible to kill time." The musicians survived their 72-hour ordeal, but kicking the heroin habit brought only temporary relief. "The problem is when you go back to your social circle – who are all drug pushers and junkies. In five minutes you can be back on the stuff again."

During this same period, Parsons also encountered Sam Hutt,

universally known as the rock 'n' roll doctor. Hutt had a home surgery in London's Exhibition Road in a flat that he shared with Family's lead singer Roger Chapman, and author Jenny Fabian. Hutt's patients included Keith Richards' young son Marlon, so when Gretchen said she was "feeling poorly" the Rolling Stone recommended a visit to Sam. When she and Gram arrived, Hutt was listening to an album by Fred Neil, which instantly attracted Parsons' attention. "Hey, that's Freddy Neil," he said, much to Hutt's amazement. The doctor asked, "How did you know it was Fred Neil?" He was floored when Parsons boasted that he not only knew who Neil was, but had actually played with him. "Who are you?" Hutt asked. The response "Gram Parsons" produced an unexpected smile of recognition.

It transpired that Hutt had been a Byrds' fan since 1965 and particularly enjoyed tripping on acid while listening to *Younger Than Yesterday*. He had not warmed to the country sound of *Sweetheart Of The Rodeo* but enjoyed the earthier delights of the Flying Burrito Brothers' *The Gilded Palace Of Sin*.

"I had an old copy of a Maccaferri guitar made by the famous Emile Grimshaw," Hutt recalls. "It was quite bassy. While I was talking to Gretchen, he picked it up and played 'You're Still On My Mind'. I pulled the curtain aside and said, 'Play it again!' I immediately saw the soul in it, which I hadn't noticed on the Byrds' version. After finishing the business with Gretchen, I subsequently became his chum and he took me into the dark heart of country and introduced me to George Jones, who was his big hero. For six months, I became Gram's doctor and his student of country. He did that with Keith Richards as well. He had the ability to get people who didn't otherwise acknowledge country as part of their roots to see how important it was."

Hutt correctly declines to say what he was treating Gretchen for, except that it was a minor complaint and certainly not drug-related. He would become increasingly aware of Parsons' predilection for hard drugs over the succeeding months, particularly after Gram joined the Rolling Stones' circus during their farewell English tour.

Before the close of the tax year on 5 April, the Stones relocated to France in order to stave off financial disaster. Jagger was about to marry Bianca Pérez Moreno de Macías in St Tropez, after which the Stones were scheduled to commence work on a new album. In July, Parsons joined the party at Nellcôte, a palatial Roman-style villa rented by Richards in the South of France. Debate still lingers whether Parsons actually appears on the sessions for the completed double album, *Exile On Main Street.* What is not contested is his frightening lapse into heroin addiction. Mick Jagger, at once protective and covetous of his songwriting partner, reacted coolly to Gram's swaggering presence. Unlike Richards, Parsons had no recording schedule to occupy his time or curb his excesses. Within a couple of weeks, he was unceremoniously exiled. Jo Bergman, the Stones PA, was instructed to tell him the bad news. "He was a physical wreck," she says. "Totally zonked out of his skull. Non-functioning."

Back in London, Parsons sought help from Dr Sam Hutt, who specialized in treating heroin addicts. "I wouldn't prescribe uppers and downers," he says. "They were very popular at that time in the rock family. I'd send them off to straight-looking doctors in Wimpole Street who'd give them bucket loads of amphetamines if that's what they wanted. I didn't want to be a grocer." Hutt preferred homeopathic medicine to Lomotil, which some claimed could get you off smack without the pain of withdrawal. Parsons was dicing with death at the time and Hutt was not convinced that he was trying to kick heroin. "He loved it. He didn't want to get off it. I always thought that the thing of taking massive amounts of heroin or getting close to overdose is so that people can pull you back from the edge. Maybe in some twisted way by them doing that, they show you how much they love you. I saw it more in terms of that than a cry for help. I think Gram was quite manipulative of the people around him, and I don't mean that in an accusative way. People are."

On more than one occasion, Hutt was called out on an emergency visit, only to find Parsons sitting on a lavatory seat or a chair with a needle in his arm, staring oblivion in the face. "He'd just had a fix and it blew him away and he forgot to take the needle out. I've seen junkies like that before. You're off. You're gone. You don't pull the needle out." Hutt's usual response when faced with a potential fatality was a heroin-antagonist followed by liberal amounts of black coffee. "When somebody is turning blue and beginning not to breathe properly . . . you use the opium as an antagonist and whack that straight into them and that brings them around. But it doesn't get them off heroin."

Gram's state was of special concern to his girlfriend Gretchen, who was cast in the role of ministering angel. "Gretchen was clean," Hutt points out, "and she was a strong woman. I don't want to get into too much amateur psychology. Who knows? She must have known what she was getting into – that he was a pretty man, very charming, very charismatic and, as we now say, 'what's not to love?' Women spend their lives trying to improve [us]. They're not being victims. It's a woman's role. I don't mean that in a sexist way. We often play up to that and get a bit boorish . . . and the woman will make us better. Gretchen might have thought: he's got all these positives, he's got the big negative where he likes getting too high, and maybe I can sort that out."

Parsons had other methods of coping. In the parlance of the time, he decided to "get it together in the country" as a temporary panacea. Once again, he visited Ian Dunlop and immersed himself in rural life, digging potatoes, hoeing weeds, sawing firewood, enjoying coastal walks and quaffing pints at the local pub. "It was the summertime in the English countryside," Dunlop reminisces. "When it's nice, it's great. Gram enjoyed it thoroughly and we had a wonderful time. He stayed for a fairly prolonged period." By all accounts, Parsons would have liked to have taken even more time out, but was distracted by a business call from the States and decided to return home. Before leaving, he announced that he and Gretchen were getting married.

The wedding provided another insight into Gram's family background. At this important juncture in his life, he once again turned to Bob Parsons, who organized the nuptials, which took place in New Orleans. The ceremony was officiated by Gram's spiritual mentor Jet Thomas who remembers a lavish reception. Colour photos of the ceremony reveal the golden-haired Gretchen looking radiant in her white wedding dress. Gram dresses less formally and appears weightier while sporting a bushier pencil moustache in the style of Michael Clarke. Tellingly, none of Parsons' rock star friends were invited to the wedding. This was a quiet, family affair and evidence of Gram's continued affection for his much maligned stepfather. The Snively family were well represented as expected. Gram's sister Avis was also happy to attend, despite claims that she was ostracized from Bob Parsons. The entire scenario underlines the point that the supposed 'evil stepfather' was a more ambivalent character than caricature allows.

Back in LA, it was not Parsons' marriage that was attracting gossip, but rather his weight. Writer Eve Babitz saw him upon his return and was shocked by the sudden loss of his Adonis looks. "The first thing everybody said when he came back from England was 'Gram is fat,'" she recalls. "It was like saying he was dead or had cancer. He looked terrible, like a Southern cop." Chris Hillman also noticed Parsons' weight gain and equated his physical change with a mental flabbiness which he described in gruesome detail. "He blew up, he became huge, yet he was wearing the same clothes he'd worn when he was 30 lbs lighter. It was a very sad sight." Comparing Parsons to Vegas period 'Fat Elvis', Hillman adds, "Gram had supposedly quit smack, and he was an alcoholic. He was this caricature . . . this good-looking kid who turned into this monster three years later, this overweight, loud, stupid person."

Despite this devastating appraisal, Hillman seemed happy to hang out with his former friend. The supposedly "loud, stupid person" was temporarily sober enough to be allowed to join the Burritos onstage at several shows in October 1971. Ironically, it was Rick Roberts, Parsons' replacement in the band, who unintentionally kickstarted the next stage of his career. Roberts, accompanied by Burrito banjoist Kenny Wertz, had dropped into a Washington club, Clyde's, and witnessed a sterling performance by a young, female singer. The following evening, Roberts persuaded a reluctant Hillman to check her out and he too saw enormous potential. They even fantasized about adding her to the Burritos in some capacity but, by then, it was too late. Hillman was about to join Stephen Stills in Manassas and the FBB was on its last legs. Playing the artistic matchmaker, Hillman instead recommended her to Parsons as a possible singing partner.

Emmylou Harris (born 2 April 1947, Birmingham, Alabama) had trodden an eventful road on her convoluted journey to Clyde's. The daughter of a Marines officer, she had a privileged upbringing, enhanced by her beauty queen looks and musical talent. An aspiring folk singer, Harris dropped out of university, where she'd studied drama, and moved to Greenwich Village in search of discovery. Subsequently, she married singer-songwriter Tom Slocum and moved to Nashville, where she added country music to her repertoire. Along the way, she recorded a solo album, *Gilded Bird*, for the small, independent label, Jubilee, but sales were negligible. After giving birth to a daughter, Hallie, the Slocums' marriage ended in divorce and Harris returned to her parents' farmhouse in Maryland, Washington.

Given her recent history, Harris was unsurprisingly rather jaded and out of touch with the music business. She hardly knew the Burritos or Parsons, so his call elicited polite interest rather than excitement. He agreed to take a train from Baltimore to Washington and sing with her onstage at Clyde's. One of the bar's waiters was impressed enough to place a sign in the window saying: 'Appearing Tonight: Gram Parsons'. It made no impression. "We went down to the cellar, sat among the beer crates and worked up 'I Fall To Pieces' and 'That's All It Took'," Harris recalls. "It was a rainy night and about five people were in the audience. We just did the two numbers . . ." After the show, Parsons pocketed her home phone number, promised great things, then departed. It would be many months before they met again.

Meanwhile, Eddie Tickner had commenced negotiations with Warners/Reprise in an attempt to revitalize Gram's recording career. Label head Mo Ostin, who had originally shown interest in the Flying Burrito Brothers, passed the decision on to A&R executive, Andy Wickham, an English expatriate with good instincts who had been instrumental in several key signings, among them Van Morrison. Wickham was aware of Parsons' past connection with the Stones, which Tickner believes may have helped close the deal. After hearing a selection of songs, Wickham immediately phoned Ostin confirming his interest.

On 15 June 1972, Parsons signed a 17-page agreement committing himself to Warner Bros. The deal erred on the side of caution and, typically for the time, allowed the record company maximum leverage for minimal commitment. Warners' obligations to Parsons did not extend beyond 14 June 1973, if they so chose, although he was shackled to them for the next five years. Following the initial one-year contract, Warners had the luxury of four separate, consecutive, irrevocable options of one year in which they could monitor Parsons' progress and continue with or drop him, depending on their whim and his relative success. During the first year of their association, he was obliged to complete sufficient master recordings for *two* complete albums, a hefty schedule for a performer not especially renowned for his work rate. This put Warners in an even more powerful position, safe in the knowledge that even if they chose not to renew his contract in 1973, they would still own two albums. There was, of course, a default clause confirming that if he failed to deliver the agreed number of albums in any year, the record company could duly terminate the agreement or, alternatively, extend the original option at their leisure to cover the period of any breach. In short, there was no way for Parsons to escape his obligations, bar death.

The advances and payments on offer were also carefully calculated. On signature of the contract, Parsons was due to receive a non-returnable advance of $5,000 to be recouped from future royalties. Following the delivery of the first album another $5,000 would be forthcoming. Within the same year, a second album would have to be completed for which Parsons would be paid $2,500 on commencement and a further $2,500 upon delivery.

By June 1973, Warners would be in a position to decide whether to renew Parsons' contract and, if so, a new album would be scheduled with a payment of $3,750 on commencement and a further $3,750 on delivery. This model was due to continue into 1974–75 with an increase to two payments of $5,000; then through 1975–76 with two payments of $6,250; and finally through 1976–77 with two payments of $7,500. This covered a total of six albums, always assuming Warners would persevere with the project.

The royalty rates offered were significantly higher than what he might have received in the early to mid-Sixties, but still very modest. For 45 rpm singles, he would receive 10.7 cents per copy sold. For albums sold in the US at $4.98, a royalty of 52.5 cents per copy was on offer, rising to 62 cents for albums retailing at $6.98, and 55.5 cents per copy for sales of 8-tracks and cassettes. There was an additional jackpot 'one million dollar' clause which allowed a retroactive royalty increase for any record certified gold by the Recording Industry Association of America. Since this required *net* sales in the US of one million dollars, Parsons' chances of achieving such an accolade were remote, to say the least.

On a more positive note, Parsons was allowed to veto the artwork and liner notes of any album and was provided the opportunity to submit a budget 14 days before commencement of the first album, detailing recording costs. This meant that he would be able to choose the musicians, arranger and producer. However, Warners insisted that recording costs could not exceed $25,000 and included a standard clause which might have been specially created for Parsons: "Costs of any session which is delayed or cancelled because of Artist's unavailability shall, at Company's option, be allocated to recording costs . . . or charged against any payments due Artist."

After calculating the likely recording costs, Parsons assigned Tickner the tough task of delivering his dream producer – Merle Haggard. A meeting was set up at Haggard's home near

Bakersfield during which they played with the country singer's train set and made vague plans about the album. Parsons was eager to employ Elvis Presley's band and encouraged Tickner to recruit legendary guitarist James Burton, pianist Glen D. Hardin and drummer Ron Tutt. They were happy to accept session work but, just before the recordings were scheduled to start, Haggard had a change of heart. "Gram was drinking heavily and wasn't in good shape," Tickner admits, "but he wanted to be sober for Merle. We put him up at the Roosevelt Hotel, while I went to bring Merle over. It didn't happen. I think Merle had some marital problems, or maybe had second thoughts about the deal. When I told Gram the bad news, he hit the bottle even harder. After that, there was a slump. I felt he needed to get back on track – fast." Instead, Parsons drowned his sorrows back at the Chateau Marmont. His wife Gretchen noticed a rapid deterioration in his health. "He was ill, and you can only beg someone so many times, 'Please don't bring these people over . . .' There would always be somebody going, 'Hey, Gram let me buy you a drink . . . look what I got for you.' I couldn't fight it."

There was certainly no shortage of visitors. Michael Clarke was invited over to indulge and listen to some material that Parsons was intending to include on his solo album. Clarke was accompanied by his buddy Joey Stec, who recalls an eventful evening. "As we're coming to the door, Gram says, 'Any blow?' I said, 'I got some, man.' Michael was sitting by the couch and for some reason I tried to jump over the couch into Michael's lap. I was loaded. I missed. There was this empty glass coffee table in front of the couch and it broke into millions of splinters. Everything went up in the air. Gretchen went crazy. She got so mad at me that she's never talked to me since. Still to this day. She was saying, 'Get him out of here, he's crazy, look what he did to our furniture.' Gram said: 'Be quiet, honey, go into the other room back there . . . He ain't going nowhere. These are my friends.' He put me into this chair in the corner, next to the stereo and tape recorder, placed these earphones on my head and said, 'Joey, don't move!'"

Parsons' recreational drug use brought him into contact with a new friend, Sid Kaiser. More than a decade older than Gram, he became something of a father figure, albeit one who provided him with cocaine and marijuana. "Everybody loved Sid, and it wasn't just because he had the best grass around," says Eddie Tickner. "He was generous and a true gentleman. He knew Lenny Bruce and Lord Buckley from way back, just like Jim Dickson. Sid was involved with Democrat fund-raising in the Kennedy era and he did some PR for actor Peter Lawford and dabbled in management – he was a Hollywood character. Gram enjoyed his company, as we all did."

"He was the connection," adds Tony Foutz. "But at the time it was a benign thing. Grow your own. Toke up. Drop out. It didn't have the stigma. This wasn't a calculating gangster world. Sid smoked good grass, did a little coke and liked to share it with his friends and that's about as far as it went. He wasn't manipulating guys for money, which is what happened with the cocaine business. He was a jazz aficionado and a loveable guy from the West Coast jazz era. He wasn't in it for anything or trying to get something from you. He was a sweetheart. Nobody mentions him, but everybody knew him."

Parsons' partying was not all fun and games. The aftermath was a comedown that left him bleary-eyed and slurring. Gretchen maintains that he was suffering blackouts and seizures, while other friends noticed worrying changes in his speech pattern. On many mornings he was shaking with the DTs. Eve Babitz recalls how he needed three tequilas to steady himself. Others remember he still had the junkie's sweet tooth and drank a cup filled with "two parts sugar to one part coffee, with a splash of cognac to liven things up". When ex-Shilo Paul Surratt visited the Chateau, he was shocked and saddened by the state of his old friend. "He was doing a lot of reds and it was so disappointing because he could hardly talk. He was so drugged. It was such a drag to see him like that because he'd always been so fresh. He was slurring his words. It was terrible. He was getting into all kinds of shit. It just really hurt because he'd always been like a brother to me."

* * *

As summer approached, Parsons attempted to cage his demons on a therapeutic spiritual retreat to Joshua Tree. He had good reason to feel sad. On 6 July 1972, his actor friend Brandon de Wilde was killed in a road accident. It was to be one of several tragedies that affected Parsons deeply over the next year. Perhaps he was thinking of de Wilde when he wrote a verse in his notebook about a young man intent on driving in the rain whose fate prompts the eulogy, "I loved him all the time like my brother."

Upon his return from the desert, Parsons was surprised to receive an invitation to work with two old friends in England. Since meeting Gram in his home surgery, the redoubtable Sam Hutt had experienced a musical odyssey. Quitting his London practice, he had moved to Saskatchewan, and ended up on the Canadian prairies. "I was right in the middle of nowhere in a little town of 700 people, with my Burrito Brothers albums and wall-to-wall country radio. The only band was a Norwegian and Ukrainian country & western outfit that I played with on Saturday nights." Hutt subsequently hitched from Canada to San Francisco and hung out with Commander Cody & His Lost Planet Airmen. "They were my kind of people, another bunch of hippies that loved country music and having a good time."

By the time Hutt returned to England in 1972, he had written a small catalogue of songs and was determined to form a band and record a country album. Seeking an established collaborator, he turned to Rik (Rick) Grech, a former member of Family, whose lead singer Roger Chapman had previously shared a flat with Hutt. It seemed an inspired choice, not least because Grech, although born in France, was of Ukrainian descent and familiar with the music that Hutt had been performing on the Prairies. Using Grech's contacts, Hutt secured the backing of the powerful Robert Stigwood Organization. They agreed to finance an album, assigning Grech as producer. After some preliminary discussion, they both hit on the idea of enlisting Parsons' support. Like Hutt, Grech had a passing friendship with the singer. They had first met when the Byrds played at the Piper Club in Rome in 1968, and hung out in London when Parsons played at Middle Earth and the Royal Albert Hall. When Grech toured the West Coast with the supergroup Blind Faith the following year, Parsons was again in attendance. Grech went on to join the ranks of Ginger Baker's Airforce and Traffic, and Parsons briefly saw him when visiting the UK in 1971. Gram was surprised to receive a call requesting his help, but was happy to spend some summer weeks in England.

In late July, Gram and Gretchen flew into the UK and were taken to the Grechs' Sussex farmhouse. "Rick and Gram went through this rebonding process," recalls his widow, Jenny Grech. "They were riding go-karts round the roads, drinking too much, but also starting to write songs." According to Hutt, everyone's secret intention was "not just to do my album, but to do an album with Gram". Unfortunately, darker forces were already threatening to sideline Hutt, who soon realized that the Grech/Parsons link was a match made in heroin hell rather than country heaven. "Rick and Gram were seriously into smack. That excluded me because it was the last thing I wanted to do. My album never got started. At one point, Rick went out, shot up and came back. He was very stoned and there was this wonderful moment when he was sitting on a high stool, playing the bass and, in slow motion, he fell on to the floor, didn't feel a thing, and kept on playing. I remember days and nights of hanging around, and Rick being completely off his face, fiddling with his new recording machine and not being able to work it. It all just fizzled out, as did my relationship with Gram. That was the end."

Conversely, for Parsons, reconnecting with Grech meant a new beginning. In a strange reversal of events, Grech suddenly became Gram's producer and the project that lay dormant since Haggard's volte face was now back underway. Relocating to California, they moved into the Bel Air Sands Hotel and began rehearsing with fiddler Byron Berline and banjoist Alan Munde. "That was what I called the picking and puking party," Jenny Grech wryly comments. "The combination of Gram and all the substances he was using, and these lovely but incredibly straight country musicians . . . Gram was genteel, polite, well-mannered, well-educated, sympathetic, spiritual – and totally mad as well. He and Rick were a lethal combination, as well as a creative one. They used to spur each other on in good ways and bad . . . Gram was really in bad shape. He'd changed so much since 1968; then, he was very uptight and together, but by 1972 he was suffering under some immense burden. His hands were shaking, he was tied up inside, and tired out." Selections from his various rehearsals with Grech, including bluesy jams like the intriguingly titled, fiddle-dominated 'Ain't No Beatle, Ain't No Rolling Stone', were briefly and belatedly issued on the 1995 archival oddity, *Cosmic American Music*.

No other sessions from the collaboration have been released but, studying Parsons' journals and notebooks from the period, it is interesting to see the ongoing struggle for creativity. Amid a scrawling mess of drunken doodlings, there are set lists, transcriptions of lyrics and further attempts to sort out his tax affairs. He details expenses covering several years, involving personal payments, touring/recording costs, doctors' bills, and even money spent on clothes from Nudie's, estimates of which are deemed 'Impossable' [sic]. Rather more interesting are references to several songs which were never recorded in the studio, but possibly attempted at home. Chief amongst them is 'Uncle Al', with its reflections on impending death ("I haven't very much time . . ."). Other obscure titles include 'Royal Jelly' (with the self-mythologizing opening line, "I love medicine" and chilling coda, "I can't find out in what hotel I'm dying"), 'Red Velvet', 'Beauty Is Eternal' and 'So Near To Being Right'. As with so many stages of Parsons' life, the art was buried beneath the excess.

Leaving Bel Air, the musicians moved to the Chateau Marmont, where Parsons made a long overdue telephone call. "It had almost become a routine," says Emmylou Harris, who had grown weary of Gram's fanciful promises. "He wanted me to make an album with him. Then the trail would go cold. A month later, he'd be on the phone again, spinning the same line." This time he was serious and sent her a plane ticket to prove his point. "I was amazed to say the least," she adds.

So was Barry Tashian, the next recruit. "It was a phone call out of the blue and, I must say, a welcome surprise. I was ready to do something. I'd been sitting around in my hometown not doing much, so I jumped at the chance. When I got to the Chateau, Emmylou was there. I was told I'd be playing rhythm guitar with Elvis' band." This was no idle boast. Having already approached those musicians earlier in the year, Parsons now took everyone on a trip to the Hilton International in Las Vegas to see them perform. "I got pretty drunk that night," Tashian says. "I don't remember anything much after Elvis' show. Rick Grech and Gram stayed up late and talked to James Burton, Ron Tutt and Glen D. Hardin about coming to record in LA. I was four sheets to the wind and in my room asleep by that time. I certainly didn't meet Elvis, and I don't think they did either."

With Eddie Tickner busily making calls, a formidable team of musicians were assembled for the album sessions which began at Wally Heider's Studio 4 in Hollywood during September 1972. Engineer Hugh Davies, who had worked with Merle Haggard, played a pivotal role in the recordings, especially after co-producer Rick Grech was briefly hospitalized having passed a kidney stone. In addition to the players already recruited, Parsons brought in current Byrds drummer John Guerin and Sam Goldstein (who had played on parts of *The Gilded Palace Of Sin*), bassist John Conrad and two steel guitar players, Buddy Emmons and Al Perkins. Glen D. Hardin, appointed musical director for the sessions, was heavily involved in the arrangements. The first night ended in humiliation for Parsons, who turned up drunk and was reduced to crawling across the floor searching for his guitar pick. Tickner feared that the sessions might end in similarly dissolute fashion to the previous ones with Terry Melcher. But Parsons was sufficiently contrite to ensure he was sober thereafter, at least during the actual recordings. Nevertheless, he was still shaky and his vocals seemed to have more of that tremulous quality than ever.

Warner Brothers must have been hopeful about the potential

of their new signing. Parsons was well respected among his contemporaries and his connections with Terry Melcher, Leon Russell, Delaney & Bonnie, and various Byrds, suggested that he was a talent waiting to blossom. This was, after all, the age of the singer-songwriter when troubled troubadours like James Taylor and Neil Young were suddenly shifting units in unbelievable amounts. Other musical changes seemed likely to work to Parsons' advantage. Recently, the Eagles had finally demonstrated that there was some sales potential in country rock after all. Their eponymous debut album spawned two US hits, the glorious 'Take It Easy', which sounded like a pastoral version of the Beach Boys, and 'Witchy Woman' a rockier number with a distinctive Native American beat. Around the corner lay Neil Young's Nashville-recorded *Harvest*, the most successful country rock-tinged album of the decade.

For once, Parsons' timing looked perfect, but market forecasts can prove deceptive. Neither Young nor the Eagles were especially interested in traditional country music. As their respective career trajectories demonstrated, it was only by phasing out country in favour of rock that they were able to sustain audience growth and maintain their multi-millionaire status. Parsons was actually on a very different path, closer to the honky tonk country that he had heard in Bakersfield and the old Louvin Brothers' recordings that he still loved with a passion. The only thing he had in common with James Taylor was heroin addiction, and there were no CS&N-style harmonies to ingratiate his vision to hip radio programmers or large audiences.

The modestly titled *GP* sounded like an album strangely out of time. In one sense, it was a distillation of everything Parsons had been working towards, although its conception may have been an accident of circumstance, rather than one of conscious design. As a showcase for his songwriting, it seemed only half-realized for an all-important first solo album with only five self-penned songs. Parsons was never prolific and, perhaps had he been so, a very different record would have emerged, more in keeping with the times. Instead, it was a stylistic pot-pourri. Indeed, it hardly seemed a solo album in anything other than name. There were many strange moments in which responsibility was not so much shared as given away. Parsons dutifully followed a demo of Rick Grech's 'Kiss The Children', a deceptively sentimental song that almost turned into a murder ballad. Far more bizarre and radical was the jarring inclusion of 'Cry One More Time', a song neither written nor sung by Parsons. What other contemporary *solo* artiste would dare delegate a song in such fashion? "I have no idea," says Barry Tashian, who was amazed when Parsons suggested he sing lead on the J. Geils Band cover. "We'd been sitting in Gram's living room in the Chateau and were just playing these songs that I'd brought along, none of which I'd written. I wish I had. Songs like 'Streets Of Baltimore, 'I Can't Dance' [held over till the next album] and 'Cry One More Time'. These were just songs that we sang and the fact that they ended up on the record was a complete surprise to me. When he asked me to sing 'Cry One More Time', it made me wonder about the whole situation. Was he going to form another Burritos group, or what? This was supposed to be a Gram Parsons solo album. I didn't understand it, myself."

For all his well-documented selfishness, Parsons was, at heart, a collaborative soul. The ultimate demonstration of this was his vocal work with Emmylou Harris, which displays a generosity and empathy that is at times magical. She dominates on the George Jones' standard 'That's All It Took' and achieves the perfect synthesis on the vibrant 'We'll Sweep Out The Ashes In The Morning'. "Sometimes I felt like we were Fred Astaire and Ginger Rogers," she says, "because I would just jump in, and he would never tell me which note to sing. I'd never done duet singing before. I didn't know the tenor from the baritone. I just followed his lead. He might go as far as to say, 'Why don't you go down and sing a low part rather than a high part,' but that was as close as we ever got to constructing the harmonies. We just sang together, constantly. After a while, I instinctively knew what he was going to do."

Parsons' compositions on *GP* varied from well meaning pastiche to something odder. 'Still Feeling Blue' and 'How Much I've Lied' were familiar country lamentations of lost love, spectacularly underwritten by a multiplicity of interlocking instrumentation, expertly played. "James Burton and I did twin parts like [those] heard on country records of the late Fifties and early Sixties," says Al Perkins. For engineer Hugh Davies the results were a "sort of funky country, not quite rock, but beyond traditional country." This description also applied to the closing 'Big Mouth Blues', a generic throwaway in the mould of 'Six Days On The Road', ideal for live performance.

While *GP* may have lacked the questing spirit of *The Gilded Palace Of Sin*, it retained much of its mystery. The oblique 'A Song For You' is as vocally alluring as it is lyrically baffling. Parsons has seldom sang so sensitively or featured a simile as oddly comic as "my land is like a wild goose". It is only in the third verse that the sorrow of abandonment is expressed in naturalistic terms. 'The New Soft Shoe' is similarly opaque. "The subject is that people use other people," Parsons told an interviewer, without elaborating on the conceit. In the opening verse, he travels back 50 years to tell the tale of automobile manufacturer Errett Lobban Cord, who is held in thrall by his financial backers. The action then switches to a Southern mall, where a man addresses a crowd and attempts to sell slippers. In the final verse, a television broadcaster lives only for public recognition. These fleeting, undeveloped episodes are punctuated by quirky homilies and the unifying image of the new soft shoe, a variant on the notion of the old con. "The song's basically about people getting ripped off," Parsons added. But there is nothing sarcastic or scathing in his vocal. He sings as if he is delivering an elegy.

The best self-penned composition on the album is 'She', in which Parsons succeeds in pulling off his favourite trick of creating lyrical ambiguity in the tradition of 'Hot Burrito # 1'and 'Hot Burrito # 2'. Indeed, the song serves as a companion piece to those earlier efforts, having been partly written with Chris Ethridge during the *Gilded Palace* period. The pair delivered the song to A&M for publishing purposes, then it was earmarked as a cover tune for an intended album by Priscilla Coolidge. According to Ethridge, they could no longer remember, or had not completed, the fourth verse. Priscilla's husband, Booker T, had no trouble filling in some key lines. "He helped with the verse beginning, 'They used to walk singing songs by the river'," Ethridge confirms, and although he is not featured in the writing credits, Booker received a share of the publishing income. Parsons also made some last-minute lyric changes during the session. "I had the part about 'She had faith, she had believing'," says Ethridge. "Gram sang, 'She prays every night to the Lord up above,' but those weren't the exact words. They should have been, 'She led all the people together singing praises of joy to the Lord up above.' The idea was that She led them in singing Hallelujah. I felt that was a clearer meaning, but Gram's words work too." Beyond such nuances lay the essence of mystery at the heart of the composition. The 'She' of the title is never actually named, nor is the corresponding 'He' who comes to her rescue. Like 'Hot Burrito # 1', in which eroticism and romance are inextricably linked, there is a tension within 'She' that is never resolved, but grows stronger with each new listening. Surprisingly, no commentator, critic or biographer has ever considered the racial aspect of the composition. We are told that She *slaved* in the cotton fields of the Delta, led a congregation in singing gospel and never knew what life was to give her. The details are slight, as they are in most of Parsons' compositions, but there is enough here to suggest that She may be a black cotton picker. When the unnamed 'He' deigns to take "a little pity" on her, the whole town comments on the matter, as if this was something extraordinary. Whether we are witnessing a master/slave relationship here is never spelt out, except in the latter's certainty that "she'd have to go away", again for reasons unexplained, but easily imagined. The ambiguities heighten with each passing line leaving an enduring image of the mysterious She, not as some universal abstract embodiment of womanhood, but a flesh and blood figure, who can also serve as a blank canvas for the listener's imagination. By preferring allusion and subtle suggestion to a straightforward narrative, Parsons maintains a racial tension without ever confirming its existence. It is no wonder that 'She' remains among his most enduring and impressive compositions.

Emmylou Harris was paid $500 for her contributions to *GP*, which she felt was a reasonably generous fee at the time. There was no sense of history in the making, nor even the prospect of ever hearing her contributions on record. She later admitted feeling a little sceptical that Warner/Reprise would issue the album because of Parsons' state, even though he had cut down his drinking in order to complete the work. After she returned to Washington, he slipped deeper into the quicksand grip of booze, cocaine and pills. His increasing alcoholism cost him at least one old friendship. On 4 December, he attended Chris Hillman's 28th birthday party at the Chateau Marmont, but the host was in no mood for his drunken antics. Once more taking the moral high ground, Hillman snapped and an ugly confrontation ensued. "Parsons was the kind of person who, when he did drink, was just horribly abusive to people around him. I had to literally throw him out of my party, like a man being thrown out of a bar. And I was really sad. It was really the last straw with him. He had stabbed me in the back too many times." Parsons was reduced to pounding on the door, like a dejected dog, but there was no way back into Hillman's life.

At the end of January 1973, *GP* was readied for release. Reprise provided a decent promotional campaign, including extensive advertising, but the sales were terrible. Once again, Parsons seemed lost in the wilderness between two disparate audiences. His dream of bridging a gap between the country and rock communities with a best-selling record increasingly resembled a doomed enterprise. Since joining the Byrds, it seemed that Parsons was selling fewer records with each successive release. *GP* did not even register in the US Top 200, an appalling statistic, made worse by the knowledge that 'country rock' was partly in vogue.

Parsons agreed to promote *GP* with a US tour, even though he knew that the top notch players from Elvis Presley's band would not be available. Nor would Rick Grech or Barry Tashian, leaving only Emmylou Harris from the original sessions. Parsons quickly assembled a pick-up band, the Fallen Angels, comprising Neil Flanz (pedal steel), N.D. Smart II (drums), Kyle Tullis (bass) and Gerry Mule (guitar). The players rehearsed at the home of Phil Kaufman, who was appointed tour manager. Smart was delayed in Nashville, so Jon Corneal sat in for a while and lent them his equipment. It all came together in two weeks and on the final night Kaufman organized a pre-tour party for which he cooked a lethal Mexican tripe stew, accompanied by copious amounts of beer and tequila. Entertainment was provided by a hired troupe, the peculiarly named Oily Scarf Wino Band. "They played Turkish Dixieland music," Corneal recalls. "They had a belly dancer with acne, a guy sitting on the floor tuning bedpans, a tuba player, a baritone horn player, and another person with a yellow cap and a fisherman's outfit playing a flugelhorn." It was quite an evening.

Evidently, the Fallen Angels were still recovering from the previous evening's shenanigans when they opened in Boulder, Colorado. It was a disastrous debut which testified to their lack of preparation and concentration. "We couldn't even play one song from beginning to end," Harris laments. Eddie Tickner flew in and threatened to cancel the tour if Parsons failed to deliver. Tickner also appointed N.D. Smart as band leader, thereby ensuring that rehearsals were tightened and a proper set list was established. Local guitarist Jock Bartley was added to the line-up, subsequently replacing Mule. Thereafter, the shows improved. "When Gram was together there was just nothing like his presence onstage," Harris recalls. "He had this extraordinary command, this amazing charisma and you just felt that all you had to do was get up and sing with him and you just knew that everything was going to be all right."

Nevertheless, it was still a ramshackle tour, punctuated by mini-dramas, comic interludes and memorable moments. At one stop, Parsons was arrested after a fracas with the police and spent a night in jail; he ritually humiliated a disc jockey in Austin for no apparent reason; he jammed with Linda Ronstadt and Neil Young in Houston, then bore the brunt of Jack Nitzsche's macabre humour. Jack told him he resembled Danny Whitten, the Crazy Horse guitarist who had recently died from a heroin overdose.

For Emmylou Harris, the Fallen Angels tour was an entrée into a closed community of macho tomfoolery, where she was known as the 'chick singer' who spent her leisure time knitting baby clothes and practising her vocals. As she recalled, with winningly wry humour: "I was put on a converted Greyhound bus with 'Gram Parsons' emblazoned across the side and surrounded by various musicians and fugitives from love and law and order. We set out to play country music and rock 'n' roll in the better hippie honky tonks of the nation. The rooms were small but the energy generated was of a special intensity. The crowds were there. They came to see this young man and to hear the voice that would break and crack but rise pure and beautiful and full with sweetness and pain. We didn't exactly break any box-office records, but there are people who will remember."

By the time the Fallen Angels reached the East Coast, they had achieved a modicum of musical tightness, unimaginable at the start of the tour. More importantly, Parsons was singing better than anyone remembered in months, if not years. Being on the road meant that he was forced to exercise his voice nightly, and the results confirmed the age old dictum, practice makes perfect. The long stretches on the road also meant that he had fewer distractions and was able to rehearse some new duets with Emmylou at the back of the bus. Concentrating on her own parts, Harris was still unaware of the full potential of this remarkable partnership. Her epiphany arrived when Parsons sat her down and played a cassette of them singing 'The Angels Rejoiced Last Night' and 'Love Hurts'. Opening her heart to his voice for the first time, she understood the depth of his emotion and its effect upon an audience. "Before then, I had been intrigued by what we were doing, but it was more about me. At that moment, it became about him and it became about the music and what we did together. I realized that I was part of something that was pretty extraordinary."

On 13 March 1973, the group recorded a show in front of a live audience at Radio WLIR-FM, Hempstead, New York. Belatedly issued in 1982 as *Live 1973,* it was later remixed and resequenced in the correct order and remains the only officially released document of the Fallen Angels. The recording quality is impressive and, apart from some leaden drumming caught too high in the mix, shows that the road band, despite their varying musical backgrounds, had found a common cause. But it is the Parsons/Harris duets that shine, most notably on 'We'll Sweep Out The Ashes In The Morning' and 'Love Hurts'. The derivative 'Bad Mouth Blues' works far better in a live setting than it ever did as part of *GP*. By contrast, 'The New Soft Shoe' is tentative, Gram's vocal is weak, and the backing lugubrious with none of the finesse previously provided by Elvis Presley's experienced musicians. There is a surprise rearrangement of 'Drug Store Truck Driving Man', possibly inspired by Joan Baez's Woodstock reading, which loses all the leavening irony and wry wit that characterized the Byrds' classic rendition. Parsons prefaces the song with a melodramatic introduction: "This is an old song that I did with the Byrds when I was in fear of getting my life taken away from me." What he is getting at here seems unclear at best. Tellingly, he deletes the wonderfully acerbic pay-off line, "This one's for you, Ralph", as if he has forgiven or forgotten the on-air criticisms of DJ Ralph Emery. That, in itself, is ironic as elsewhere on the live broadcast he tells the story of the Fallen Angels' visit to the superbly named Austin radio station KOKE, during which he vandalized their Emergency Broadcast System equipment and sabotaged an interview with the unfortunate DJ who is now unfairly named and shamed. "Rusty Bell got what he deserved," he says, with semi-humorous malice. There are two more surprises on *Live 1973*. 'Cry One More Time' allows us to hear Parsons' lead vocal on a radically different version of the song. Jock Bartley's scratchy lead guitar and Neil Flanz's steel offer a pleasing alternative to the standard R&B treatment familiar on *GP*. It merely adds to the mystery of why Parsons allowed Barry Tashian to perform a song seemingly so out of place, when Gram's own rendition fits perfectly well. Finally, there is a fine cover of Merle Haggard's 'California Cottonfields' a composition that could have graced either of Parsons' solo albums. It contains several lines that Gram would pay to have written. He enunciates these with due reverence, most notably the bitter allusion to the place "where labour camps are filled with worried men with broken dreams".

After returning home, Gram and Gretchen were invited on a trip to the Caribbean aboard Bob Parsons' boat. That Gram readily accepted spoke volumes about his relationship with his stepfather. As a trust fund kid, he could easily have chartered his own sailing adventure, but he clearly enjoyed the company of the ever sociable figure whom he had previously trusted to arrange his wedding reception, and much else. What happened on the voyage is still disputed, but everyone involved agrees that it ended badly. Gretchen claims Bob upset Gram by revealing that he had smuggled small bottles of vodka into his mother's hospital room, thereby hastening her demise. It's possible that Gram had previously been unaware of this tale, even though it had been broadcast by several members of the Snively clan, and even by Bob himself, who never saw anything sinister in his actions. Bob's wife Bonnie, who was also on the trip, has no recollection of any such conversation, and maintains that the real problem was Gram's casual drug use in foreign waters. Fearing the repercussions of a bust outside American territories, Bob played the paternal disciplinarian and Gram, predictably, rebelled. Considering his stepfather was suffering from liver disease after years of alcohol abuse, Gram's indignation was understandable. Another factor was the presence of the young Diane Parsons on the boat. Photos suggest that they were having an enjoyable trip, but Bob clearly did not approve of any drug taking in her remote presence, even if it was done discreetly. Gram curtailed the trip and headed back to Los Angeles. "After the break with Bob, Gram was never the same," Gretchen says. "His joy was gone." Parsons would never see his stepfather or sister Diane again.

Gram and Gretchen had recently moved out of the Chateau Marmont to a new home on Laurel Canyon Boulevard. Although this took him away from the constant flow of drug buddies and late-night visitors, his appetite for excess remained – and his marriage was now in trouble.

In June, Parsons was back on the road with Emmylou Harris as part of a short package tour with the Kentucky Colonels and Country Gazette, in anticipation of an autumn European jaunt which Tickner was currently negotiating. As detailed in the succeeding Clarence White obituary, it was not all peace and love on the road. A month later, White was killed. Parsons attended the funeral, drunk and distraught. At the graveside, he joined Bernie Leadon to sing an impromptu eulogy: 'Farther Along'. Later, he got more drunk in the company of his road manager, Phil Kaufman. Before the evening ended, they made an agreement that when either one of them died the other would ensure that the corpse was cremated in the desert. During this same period, Parsons was even more shaken by the news that his drug buddy Sid Kaiser had died of a heart attack while staying at actor Peter Lawford's home in Palm Springs. Kaiser had become one of Parsons' many father figures and the news of his demise hit hard. It may have contributed to an encroaching morbidity. "Death is a warm cloak," Parsons concluded. "An old friend. I regard death as something that comes up on the roulette wheel every once in a while . . . It's sad to lose a close friend. I've lost a lot of people close to me. It makes you a little bit stronger each time. They wouldn't want me to grieve. They would want me to go out and get drunk and have one on them. . . . I spend a lot of time up at Joshua Tree in the desert just looking at the San Andreas fault and I say to myself, 'I wish I was a bird drifting up above it . . .'" Parsons' prophecy almost came true that same month when a freak fire razed his Laurel Canyon home. Reportedly, he only survived by breaking through a plate glass window. Most of his possessions were lost in the blaze.

After the fire, Gram and Gretchen stayed at her father's house on nearby Mulholland Drive. Parsons was restless and soon moved out, taking up residence in a small property at the back of Phil Kaufman's house in Van Nuys. Friends claim he was considering divorce, but no legal documentation exists to confirm his intentions. Gram's drug taking continued apace, but the presence of Kaufman, who had worked in a similar capacity with the Rolling Stones, curbed his worst behaviour. Kaufman needed all his cajoling and confiscating skills to keep Parsons clean enough to begin work on a second solo album. Tickner once more recruited pianist Glen D. Hardin as musical director, along with guitarist James Burton, drummer Ron Tutt and bassist Emory Gordy. Additional players were brought in as needed, including fiddler Byron Berline, steel guitarist Al Perkins, guitarists Bernie Leadon and Herb Pedersen, and substitute drummer N.D. Smart. "There was a lot of energy going on in the studio for the whole of that album," says Emory Gordy. "Gram was bouncing around all over the place and Emmy was bouncing around him. They were great, very happy sessions . . . We laid down all the backing tracks in a week. Gram played us each of the songs he had got ready, and Glen would already have a basic chord chart written out prior to coming to the studio, and we all just took it from there. It was all very loose as far as formal arranging was concerned. We just played what we felt was right for the song, and it all seemed to fall together. If anything was wrong, we heard it on the playback and rectified it with a new take . . ."

"Gram's style was to start a number of songs and then delay finishing them until the last possible moment," adds Emmylou Harris. "Often, he'd work on an idea while it was fresh in his mind, and then set it aside until time demanded he complete it." The final song was 'In My Hour Of Darkness', the one new composition that Parsons had come up with while working on the album. "The song was done in maybe two takes, as were the rest of the tracks," says Harris, "and we cut it totally live. Everybody was playing together, and Gram and I were singing simultaneously, though they were only guide vocals, which we recorded with help from Linda Ronstadt." Harris received a unique co-writing credit for her contribution. "I was an energy source rather than composer on that one," she demurs. "All I really did was make a few odd suggestions in the wording of the lyric. It was really Gram's song, a song very personal to him, and I tend to feel that his giving me credit was just an example of his generosity, a token of friendship and an acknowledgement of my help."

After the sessions were completed, the album was mixed at Capitol Studios in Hollywood. Emmylou Harris departed, feeling upbeat about the future. Not only had she grown closer to Parsons, but he seemed to have found a new sense of responsibility. Noticing his declining drug and alcohol intake, she convinced herself that he had turned a corner. With a major tour only weeks away, he seemed healthier than at any time since their first meeting. Harris' prognosis may have been over-optimistic, but she had witnessed his improvement with her own eyes.

There is a general consensus that Parsons had either cut down or stopped taking heroin during the summer of 1973. Nevertheless, he was still drinking and taking cocaine behind the scenes. For reasons hedonistic or meditative, he decided to accompany some friends on a trip to Joshua Tree. The party included his old friend and new companion Margaret Fisher, his 'valet' from the Fallen Angels' tour, Michael Martin, and Martin's girlfriend, Dale McElroy. After downing several shots of whisky and Southern Comfort over lunch, plus some pills assumed to be downers, Parsons, along with Fisher, met a drug dealer back at the Joshua Tree Inn who injected morphine into their systems. Incautiously, Parsons insisted on repeating the dose in order to achieve a satisfactory high. Soon after, he was semi-comatose. Martin had already left Joshua, so Fisher called upon McElroy and both assisted Parsons to Room 8 at the Inn. With Parsons lapsing into near unconsciousness, Fisher told McElroy to get some ice cubes from an adjacent machine. An apocryphal story that later did the rounds suggests that someone was attempting to masturbate Parsons back to life or plunging ice cubes up his backside in an attempt to bring him around. The second part, featuring the ice cubes, was not fabricated, as both Fisher and McElroy testify. The cold cure succeeded in resuscitating Parsons who was evidently alert enough to joke about what the hell they were doing taking his trousers down. McElroy then returned to her room, leaving Fisher to watch over him. Some time passed – an hour or two by one reckoning – after which Fisher felt they should try and get some food and coffee for Parsons. She left McElroy in charge, then drove off. McElroy had no experience of dealing with drug abusers and later became alarmed when Parsons' breathing became laboured. She attempted CPR to the best of her ability, but Parsons then lapsed into unconsciousness. Fisher returned to this scene and, fearing the worst, someone called an ambulance. Details are sketchy at this point. Alan Barbary, the son of the motel's owners, claims he entered the room while McElroy was trying to revive Parsons and offered assistance, but to no avail. Neither McElroy nor Fisher mention his presence, but everyone was in shock at that stage anyway. One perplexing anomaly is the amount of time Fisher was absent from the motel. She now maintains it was approximately 20 minutes, a contention supported by McElroy who calculates it was certainly no longer than an hour. Yet, this is contradicted by Fisher's own statement to the investigating coroner of San Bernardino County in which she thinks she left around 8:00 pm to get food, at which point Parsons "did not look well". She then claimed to have called the motel around 11:00 pm to have "some friends" check on Parsons and, failing to locate them, rushed back to find him "not breathing at 11:45 pm". Apart from the mysterious time lapse – the contradictory details of which could be explained away for various reasons from shock to simple error – the rest is relatively clear. Parsons was taken by ambulance to the Hi-Desert Memorial Hospital in Yucca Valley and declared dead at 12.15 am on 19 September 1973. According to writer Ben Fong-Torres, who studied the subsequent blood tests: "A urinalysis showed traces of cocaine and amphetamines, and more than traces of morphine, at 166mg%. Liver and bile tests indicated morphine at 228mg% level." The autopsy report also noted needle punctures on the back of the left hand and left elbow indicating chronic and recent usage of drugs. Following an autopsy, the official cause of death was revealed as "Drug toxicity, days, due to multiple drug use, weeks."

All things considered, Parsons' death is relatively free of the crazier rumours usually surrounding rock 'n' roll fatalities. Compared to Brian Jones, Jim Morrison or Jimi Hendrix, Parsons' demise seems a relatively straightforward story. There are differing accounts from the participants about who was where when, and an unexplained time lapse, but overall a grim consensus about the main issue.

Stories later surfaced suggesting that Parsons may have had a heart condition. Jim Seiter claimed he heard about this in 1968 after taking Gram to a doctor and discussing the matter with manager Larry Spector. Sierra Records' founder John Delgatto also mentioned a possible heart problem, but now admits: "I have no other information other than what I heard from Eddie [Tickner]." Others claim Parsons was never the same since his motorcycle accident and suffered seizures requiring various prescription pills. How true any of these accounts are remains debatable. Ultimately, though, such conjecture is incidental. The coroner's report is emphatic enough in its conclusions.

On 20 September, the day after Gram's death, Gretchen L. Parsons opened probate proceedings at the Los Angeles Superior Court and was appointed the administrator of his estate. Among the personal property inventoried in the estate were writer's royalties for Gram Parsons' music.

While Gretchen was establishing her rights as Gram's widow, his stepfather Bob Parsons was arranging to have the body sent back to New Orleans for burial. As previously documented, Bob's every action, benign or otherwise, seems to have provoked more conspiracy theories than the Kennedy assassinations, and this was no exception. His motives were first questioned in print in the groundbreaking 1976 *Crawdaddy* article titled 'Gram Finale: The Profoundly Sick Life And Mysteriously Perverse Death Of The Prince Of Country-Rock'. Contained therein was a strange assertion: "The state of Louisiana's Napoleonic Law stipulates that male survivors are the sole inheritors of any estate. Apparently, Big Bob merely wanted a warm body to establish, in the eyes of a court, a New Orleans residency for Gram." The word "apparently" sounded like somebody had planted the story in the writers' minds. Moreover, unless he was a necromancer, how would Bob manage to conjure a 'warm body' from a corpse? Weirdly, nobody questioned the workings of the Napoleonic Code. Instead, the story was carried forward in successive commentaries and biographies and Bob Parsons was, as ever, vilified for supposedly seeking control of the estate.

While it was true that Louisiana had a legal system based on Napoleonic Code, completely different from other US states, this applied specifically to domiciled residents. Gram Parsons had never been domiciled or resident in Louisiana or spent much, if any, time there. Of course had he been domiciled in the state and died without leaving a will, his spouse would only inherit half of the 'community property' (assets accumulated by the couple while married). Any 'separate property' (that is assets owned before marriage or inherited property) could not be claimed by the spouse but would automatically go to any children of the couple or, if there was no such issue, to any brothers and sisters. In Gram's case, as a non-resident of Louisiana, all this was irrelevant. Gretchen L. Parsons, as Gram's widow, was always the legal benefactor.

While plans were underway for Parsons' funeral in New Orleans, there was a sinister twist to the tale. Police were informed that the body had been hijacked at Los International Airport. A burned casket containing a corpse was later discovered near Cap Rock in the Mojave Desert area not far from the Joshua Tree National Monument. The bizarre story momentarily brought Gram back into the media spotlight as a freak news item. One police official exclaimed, with B-movie precision: "It's like something out of Transylvania, out of the legend of Count Dracula."

With memories of the Tate/LaBianca murders still fresh in people's minds, there was briefly speculation about the possibility of a Manson-style cult involvement. It soon emerged that the bodysnatching saga was not as sinister as the press assumed. The ghouls were unmasked as Phil Kaufman and Michael Martin, who had cremated the body, believing that they had fulfilled the morbid pact that Parsons had entered into following Clarence White's funeral. Fortunately, nobody brought up Kaufman's colourful past, which had included a time in prison and a brief association with Charles Manson. Kaufman and Martin were subsequently each fined $300, plus $750 for destroying the coffin or, as one wry police official supposedly quipped, the crime of "Gram Theft Parsons". Parsons' charred corpse was flown to New Orleans for a funeral service, whose congregation included members of the Connor and Snively families, plus his widow Gretchen. Conspicuously absent were Gram's rock star friends, many of whom had firmly supported Kaufman's actions.

The remains of Gram Parsons' body were interred at the Garden of Memories Chapel of Peace Mausoleum and Memorial Park in Matairie, Louisiana. The grave was inscribed with the epitaph 'God's Own Singer', referring to a song from *Burrito Deluxe* actually written by Bernie Leadon rather than Gram. Given the wealth of compositions in Parsons' own songbook, it was a regrettable choice. Decades later, a bronze slab was placed at the graveside accompanied by a more appropriate verse from 'In My Hour Of Darkness'. Alas, even that tribute was marred by the careless carving which erroneously proclaimed Gram's birthdate as 'November 7' instead of 'November 5'.

A more raucous service took place at Kaufman's house where, in a supreme example of rock 'n' roll bad taste, he charged friends $5 to attend a wake featuring Bobby "Boris" Pickett And The Crypt-Kickers singing 'Monster Mash', while the assembled guzzled beer labelled 'Gram Pilsner'. DJ Dr Demento, who had previously penned one of the few insightful reviews of *The Gilded Palace Of Sin*, was on hand to spin some discs. The money raised helped pay Kaufman's fine.

There was a more sober gathering at the home of Barry Tashian in north west Connecticut. Several old friends were visiting, including John Nuese and Emmylou Harris. "We played some music together," Tashian remembers. "Emmylou brought a tape that she hadn't had a chance to play yet. It was a small reel-to-reel and we put it on that night after dinner. This was a mix of 'Brass Buttons' which she was hearing for the first time. It had a big effect on her and she pretty much broke down in tears. It was an emotional moment. The music was beautiful, of course."

Among Parsons' old friends, some were shocked by the dramatic news of his death, but many others sounded stoical, privately or publicly admitting that his lifestyle always seemed likely to end in premature death. There was no shortage of eulogies. Remarkably, for such a relatively unheralded figure, Parsons inspired a host of musical valedictions, including Poco's 'Crazy Eyes', the Eagles' 'My Man', supposedly Chris Hillman's 'Heavenly Fire', and Tom Russell's 'Joshua Tree'. John Phillips even wrote two: the respectful 'He Had That Sweet Country Sound' and the acerbic 'Gram's Song' which included some spiteful and incredibly vitriolic allusions to Jagger and Richards. The tribute and blame game continued in later years when Parsons became the poster boy of Americana roots music for a new generation of fans.

Grievous Angel was released in January 1974, four months after Parsons' death. The cover artwork was originally intended to feature both Gram and Emmylou, but the idea was scuppered in deference to his widow. Like *GP*, the new work was touted as a solo album, which was something of a misnomer. Those who judged the work in the context of the classic singer-songwriter albums of the period or knew the dating of the compositions could be forgiven for wondering if Parsons was running dry. The work included only one new original composition, the remainder consisting of older songs and a selection of well-chosen covers. In fairness, it should have been billed as Gram Parsons & Emmylou Harris, as her role was close to that of an artistic equal. Indeed, the album had more in common with George Jones & Tammy Wynette than with any of Parsons' singer-songwriter contemporaries in the country or rock fields. It was the firmest indicator yet of his desire to present himself and his work outside the limited confines of contemporary expectation.

Parsons wanted fame and success but, like all the great artistes, was not willing to subjugate his singular vision to the dictates of the marketplace. *Grievous Angel* would probably have been a superior *solo* record with more Parsons originals but, seen as a Gram & Emmylou album, it is arguably better served by the extensive range of material on offer. Its immersion in the past, through revivals of songs by the Everly Brothers and the Louvin Brothers, is matched by a striking modernity. There is a sure-footed artistry here that reveals Parsons at his most confident; the precision of his vocals and the harmonic blend he achieves with Harris enables the album to transcend its time. Nor does it sound like a one-off, but rather a springboard to a future that was tragically wiped clean.

Originally mislabelled solely as a Parsons' composition, the opening track, 'Return Of The Grievous Angel' displays none of the vocal frailty evident on parts of *GP*. It's an epic tale of romance realized after an on-road odyssey embracing 20,000 roads and a bewildering vista of prairies, saloons, billboards and truckstops. Parsons sings with the conviction and passion of the returning hero.

'Hearts On Fire' began as a comic parody by songwriter Walter Egan – a jocular play on words about 'heartburn'. In its original form, it would probably have sounded like a witty Shel Silverstein-style spoof of country mores, as executed by Dr Hook. Emmylou Harris' then boyfriend Tom Guidera saw its potential as a more serious song and revamped the lyrics. What ultimately emerges is a perfect vehicle for Gram and Emmylou's harmonic interplay. Parsons never wanders between the vocal lines, but captures the bittersweet sentiments that combine love, hatred, God and the Devil and culminate in the paradoxical image of a cold heart consumed by flame. The allusions to burning also recall Joyce Allsup's 'We'll Sweep Out The Ashes In The Morning', one of the best duets on *GP*.

Tom T. Hall's humorous 'I Can't Dance', which Barry Tashian introduced during rehearsals for the previous album, serves as light relief after the intensity of the opening two songs. Like 'Big Mouth Blues', it's a rousing audience pleaser that worked far better in live performance than on record.

The mid-section of the album features three songs from Parsons' back pages, newly presented without any significant differences to the lyrics or music. 'Brass Buttons', written as early as 1965 and attempted at various times on tape over the succeeding years, finally finds a home here. One of Parsons' most affecting melodies, it benefits greatly from the accomplished musicianship of the studio players and sounds surprisingly contemporary given its vintage. Although various commentators claim the song was written about Gram's mother, Parsons himself never confirmed this in any interview. Imposing such a reductive autobiographical interpretation limits the scope of the composition. It's certainly a song about loss ("she's gone"), but whether this is a result of death is never made explicit. What are we to make of ambiguous lines such as "My mind was young until she grew"? There is, of course, no specific reference to a mother in the lyric and the allusive sentiments could equally apply to a lover, lost friend or imagined icon.

'$1000 Wedding', the composition brutally rejected by the Flying Burrito Brothers, fits perfectly in the context of *Grievous Angel.* Its power lies in Parsons' narrative conviction and the emotion, barely held in check, as he relates a story of unbearable poignancy. Commentators and certain biographers have consistently overstated the assumed autobiographical elements in the song, excitedly connecting the lyrics with the story of Nancy Ross' proposed wedding to Gram and, specifically, the expensive wedding dress that was never collected from Nudie's. While that incident possibly inspired the composition, it is not alluded to in the song, which takes a completely different narrative direction. In the first verse, it is the groom who is left waiting at the altar by the young bride in what initially appears to be a familiar tale of abandonment. It may as well be a funeral, the narrator wryly notes. The jilted bridegroom spends the second verse drowning his sorrows with friends whose expressions and words of consolation are transparently unconvincing. Hearing these "old lies" makes him wish someone would spike his drink or "do him in". Again, the funeral imagery is presented as a refrain, the wedding celebration now resembling a drunken wake. In the final stanza, a clergyman offers a sermon, appears to refer to the baby Jesus and quotes Biblical scripture, including the parable of the lion lying down with the lamb. The lost bride is now referred to in the past tense and in the startling final few lines the metaphorical funeral is transformed into an actual memorial service. We are left with the consideration that the bride who "went away" didn't merely leave, but passed away. As with most of Parsons' best lyrics (from 'Hot Burrito # 1' through to 'She') the mystery is not entirely resolved to the listener's satisfaction, but the remaining ambiguities enhance our appreciation. As a songwriter, Parsons instinctively knew that inscrutability was preferable to cosy clarification.

The resurrection of the great 'Hickory Wind', peculiarly presented in medley form alongside the Louvin Brothers' 'Cash On The Barrelhead', may have been prompted by Joan Baez's cover version. If Parsons was keen to remind us of his most famous Byrds' song, its execution here seems oddly flippant. The fake applause, whistles, shouts and clinking bottles are a studio creation jokingly described as 'live from Northern Quebec', but there is nothing funny about this intrusive background noise which distracts and detracts from the sincerity of the original recording. Even Emmylou Harris was puzzled by Parsons' motives in reducing one of his most famous songs to an exercise in playful nostalgia. "Who knows what was going on in Gram's mind at that point? I think the medley had probably been for the fun of it to capture what a lot of those gigs were like. We didn't play big concert halls. We played wonderful clubs where people were standing and it was crowded and loud. People were into it, there was audience participation, so I don't think the medley was done as a complaint." A denuded version can be heard on the bonus tracks presented on *The Complete Reprise Sessions*. Harris' harmonies are well-executed, but the song is no match for the Byrds' original.

'Love Hurts' stands as a template for the Parsons/Harris harmonic partnership. It took considerable courage to tackle the Everly Brothers' seemingly unsurpassable version, but it is a perfect composition for a male/female duo. Their impeccable treatment makes a convincing case for an entire album of Felice and Boudleaux Bryant songs. Parsons might well have agreed, as two *Grievous Angel* outtakes featured fine versions of 'Brand New Heartache' and 'Sleepless Nights' from the same composers. These, along with a convincing cover of the Louvins' 'The Angels Rejoiced Last Night', appeared on the 1976 archival compilation, *Sleepless Nights*.

Parsons excursion into his recent past was completed with 'Ooh Las Vegas', a collaboration with Rick Grech from the *GP* era. It has the same exuberance as Elvis' 'Viva Las Vegas' but with a more sardonic edge. Written immediately after the band's visit to the Hotel International, when they got drunk and hit the casinos, it sums up an eventful evening. Once again, Emmylou Harris' soprano energizes the recording.

The concluding 'In My Hour Of Darkness' is both a hymn and an epitaph to three dead friends. In the first verse, Parsons eulogizes Brandon de Wilde, the actor who had played such an important role in his life and died tragically young at 30 on a "deadly Denver bend". The "country boy" of the second verse is Clarence White, whose funeral precipitated the pact that would posthumously project Parsons into cult celebrity. Finally, there is Sid Kaiser, the wise old man, whom Gram loved like a father and a friend. Bookending these tragic tales is a mournful chorus, featuring Emmylou Harris and Linda Ronstadt, which adds a ghostly dimension to the composition. Parsons' prayer in his hour of darkness effectively becomes the missing fourth verse in the song. In the end, he is singing his own epitaph, a mere four months before his untimely demise.

"Death sells" is a rock 'n' roll marketing cliché, but it did not apply to Gram Parsons. Even the publicity surrounding his bodysnatching and burned corpse was not enough to make *Grievous Angel* a hit record. It stalled at number 195 in the *Billboard* charts, 31 places lower than *The Gilded Palace Of Sin*, and 118 short of *Sweetheart Of The Rodeo*. Emmylou Harris must have been disappointed by the sales but was steely enough to continue his legacy. "It was both the beginning and the end," she says. "We had definite plans to continue to work together. This was what I wanted to do. When I hear the album there is a certain amount of sadness because Gram's career was cut so very short and he had so much to offer. His vision is inherent in the records he left behind and carried on by musicians who are influenced by those records. Certainly, I am the most obvious one . . ." In the years immediately after Parsons' death, she released covers of 'Ooh Las Vegas', 'Sin City', 'Wheels', 'Luxury Liner', 'She' and even wrote her own tribute, 'Boulder To Birmingham'. In 1985, she issued the 'concept album' *The Ballad Of Sally Rose*, partly inspired by her time working with Parsons. Inevitably, it focused attention on the nature of their relationship which Harris coyly avoided discussing for long periods of her career. In recent years, she has been more forthcoming and willing to scotch unfounded rumours. "There are people who had already decided that Gram and I had had this affair, which we didn't have, even though we were in love with each other and, if he had lived, we probably would have had an affair. But we *didn't*. All our energy was put into the music . . . He had an extraordinary effect on me and I will always love him and he will always be this dear, dear soul in my life that touched me so deeply."

* * *

While Emmylou Harris got on with the business of living, Bob Parsons went into alcoholic decline. On 11 November 1975, less than two years after Gram's demise, he died from cirrhosis of the liver, just like his late wife, Avis. He was 50 years old. There were other chilling comparisons with the fate of his stepson. Bob had always been concerned about Gram's drug use, only to find himself becoming a user during his final days. His old friend Gene Leedy visited him in New Orleans and was struck by his odd behaviour. "He acted real strange . . . I could tell he was on a little dope because he was hyper, talking and laughing. He had a big party and was an hour late with the dinner. He was cooking and everything, as before, but it wasn't up to par. He'd gotten in with some young kids, and they'd got him hooked on 'dope'. I think that was his demise. That's how he got on the wrong track. He was doing cocaine with this younger group." Perhaps the fact that Parsons realized he was dying from liver disease contributed to his recklessness. "He always used to say that the Snivelys died from cirrhosis of the liver and Bob's theory was that with all the food he ate, he'd never have to worry about that. He told me, 'Goddamn, I've got cirrhosis of the liver, I never thought I'd get that.'" Even with the Grim Reaper waiting in the wings, Bob never lost his licentious appetite. Like Gram, he had an extramarital encounter during the closing stages of his life. His ever patient wife Bonnie was amazed to discover that he was having an affair with one of her college friends. He could barely walk at the time. In a final macabre coincidence, there was a dispute over his bodily remains. His mother Lillian wanted Bob buried in the Christian tradition, but was overruled. The corpse was cremated.

Gram's sister Avis had her own problems, but seemed likely to survive the family curse of premature death. It was not to be. In 1991, she and her second daughter, 16-year-old Flora, perished in a freak boating accident. Avis was 40.

The attendant tragedies, reinforced by the macabre circumstances surrounding Parsons' death and 'cremation' have accentuated what Chris Hillman calls "this creepy thing surrounding Gram". He adds: "I've read where some people have claimed Death stalked Gram. That's garbage. Death didn't stalk Gram. Gram stalked death. He made his own choices."

"That's just the scar tissue," insists Tony Foutz. "Some go for the scars, not the soul. You have to ask, 'Why was this person abusing himself? Why did this happen?' It happened to a lot of people, as we know, and tragically. But Gram: you have to go beyond the tragedy in all of this. Listen to his music. He had his own voice that was eloquent and unique. You can also see it in his lyrics and hear it in his piano playing."

Writer Stanley Booth adds to that chorus. "All this darkness and this sinister quality, that was not Gram. Gram was the sweetest person you would ever meet. He was a very tender, loving person who had been hurt terribly and yet he was not imposing his pain on anybody. He was a great, great gentleman and a joy to be around."

Who could ever have imagined that Gram Parsons would inspire a cult following? Tribute concerts, festivals, fan gatherings and words of praise from younger musicians confirm his standing as a pioneer of alternative country and Americana. Parsons anticipated these movements most notably in his early work with the Flying Burrito Brothers, whose eclectic combination of country, R&B and soul established a lasting template. Parsons even provided a catchy, albeit misleading, generic title for this musical fusion: Cosmic American Music. The phrase, casually mentioned during an interview, has been widely repeated ever since, usually without explanation. It still reads as an oddly inappropriate summation. There is nothing remotely 'cosmic' about Parsons' music. On the contrary, he loved the earthiness of country and R&B and his own compositions eschewed the psychedelic trappings and spacy improvisations then in vogue. Cosmic American Music sounds closer in conception to something like the all-embracing 'history of twentieth-century music' double album that McGuinn envisaged for the Byrds after *Notorious.* Partly due to Parsons' influence and contributions, McGuinn's idea – a journey from Appalachian ballads through bluegrass and beyond into space rock – devolved into the more grounded *Sweetheart Of The Rodeo.* Listening to Parsons' entire oeuvre, 'cosmic' appears at best an alien adjective. His great contemporaries Mike Nesmith and Gene Clark arguably have a better claim to that title. Both earned a reputation as 'cosmic cowboys' for their quasi-philosophical meditations and employment of wordy, multi-syllabic lyrics. Nesmith wrote about 'unlimited time' and addressed "the beauty of infinite light" in 'Harmony Constant' on *And The Hits Just Keep On Coming* and spoke of "substance found in time and space" in 'Waking Mystery'. He even wrote a concept album, *The Prison,* released in a lavish box, containing a fancy booklet. Clark was even more subject to brilliant flights of fantasy. His masterpiece *No Other* combined heavenly gospel chorals with country instrumentation set against ornate lyrics that spoke of spiritual transcendence on the "cosmic range". This was never Parsons' terrain. To my certain knowledge he never used the word 'cosmic' in any song he ever wrote. Who knows what he meant, if anything, when throwing out the phrase Cosmic American Music to the media. Perhaps he was simply envisaging a music designed to unify the hippie longhairs and the country traditionalists at a time before the invention of the so-called Outlaw movement. In certain respects, Parsons prefigured the advent of 'progressive country'. Yet, all of this does not entirely explain why he became such a prominent symbol for purveyors of Americana and alternative country decades later. Somehow, his music became intertwined with the bizarre circumstances surrounding his death, creating an iconic image, far removed from the flesh and blood figure remembered by his friends, family and music associates.

Inevitably, Parsons' complicated life left behind many unanswered questions. There were rumoured illegitimate children, who may or may not have existed, and whose names have never been revealed. There were 'lost' recordings, most notably the nearly completed album with Terry Melcher, which disappeared, or was supposedly incinerated in a fire at his home. In fact, the entire album actually survives in perfect condition in a tape vault awaiting rediscovery. There were legal battles and court cases, fought decades after Parsons' death. There were even allegations of plagiarism, the details of which are perplexing enough to confound the imagination.

One of the first shocks in the immediate years after *Grievous Angel* was the realization that he didn't actually write what many saw as one of his last great songs, 'Return Of The Grievous Angel'. Oddly, it was not until 1976 that we learned of Thomas Brown, who had presented Parsons with a poem of the same title during the Fallen Angels' appearance at the club Oliver's in Boston back in February 1973. The song documented Brown's courtship of his later wife "Sweet Annie Rich" and the remainder was written in honour of Parsons, which was enough to convince listeners that he was the obvious composer, a belief reinforced by the writing credits on the album. Parsons was responsible for the music, but his lyrical additions were largely cosmetic. He had the lines about the "man on the radio", which he sang with great feeling, and he added the geographical reference "from Cheyenne to Tennessee" and replaced the phrase "roughnecks" with "kickers". Apart from these subtle changes, Brown's poem remained intact. So why wasn't Brown's name included in the credits from the outset? The common wisdom is that his identity was lost, along with most of Parsons' possessions, in the aforementioned Laurel Canyon fire. But the sheet containing the poem was saved. Either Brown neglected to sign his work, or Gram forgot to pass over the necessary information to his publishers. "It wasn't plagiarism," Eddie Tickner stresses. "Gram just wasn't well organized. He always admitted that the lyrics had been given to him by some guy in Boston, while he was on tour. I guess he couldn't remember his name. We expected him to come forward much earlier than he did. Then it was sorted out."

Of course, Parsons had a history of playful plagiarism going back years. During his school days, he had once submitted

Dylan's 'Mr Tambourine Man' for a poetry assignment. He informed various bandmates that he had written such well-known songs as 'It Was A Very Good Year', 'The Hills Of Shiloh' and 'You Know My Name', among others. Generally, the claims were so transparently preposterous that the only motive could have been mere mischief. Parsons had no need to show off and there are no indications of any insecurity about his songwriting or musical abilities. Perhaps he just liked spinning tales back then, the taller the better.

But the strangest story of all concerning Parsons' alleged plagiarism emerged in 2002. Bizarrely, it focused on what many regard as his greatest composition, 'Hickory Wind'. Chris Hillman concurs and has consistently called it "his signature song". However, according to singer-songwriter Sylvia Sammons, speaking in an online interview, she wrote 'Hickory Wind' around 1963. How it supposedly ended up in Parsons' hands she does not say, but she recalls singing the composition at various coffeehouses and clubs. Her account, which prompts far more questions than answers, really starts around May 1969 when she claims to have heard 'Hickory Wind' on the radio. "I was completely flabbergasted one day to hear a Joan Baez recording of my song. I had never been approached about publishing and yet, there it was. I remember phoning the radio show on which I heard the song and asking the host of the programme if the songwriter was given credit on the album, and if so, who it might be. I do not even recall now who he told me the credit went to." Her vagueness does not end there. Evidently, she was not aware of either the Byrds' original 1968 version or Parsons' later rendition on *Grievous Angel.* She reportedly claims to have surrendered the original tape recorded copy of her version, which she had mailed to herself as a means of establishing copyright, in return for a cash settlement. "I think, other than principle, I did better economically to have taken the money I did," she claims. "I am guessing, but I do not believe royalty payments would have amounted to the sum they imparted to me." If this were so, then we are talking about a lot of money here. But who paid this money, and what was the precise nature of the settlement? What exactly were the similarities between the songs? Was a back-up or work-in-progress copy of the tape ever recorded? Where is the documentation pertaining to any settlement? Sammons "with the help of a friend who was a music teacher" allegedly reached a settlement with "either Vanguard Records [Joan Baez's record label at the time] or a music publisher". The vagueness seems remarkable. Surely some record of the transaction, for business or tax purposes, would have been lodged somewhere. Who actually paid this money? In the circumstances, as described, Vanguard Records would surely have passed her over to the music publishers Tickson Music, which administered Parsons' catalogue under the title Wait And See. Neither Parsons nor Eddie Tickner ever mentioned any problem with 'Hickory Wind' during their lifetimes. Tickner's widow, Dolores, was unaware of any settlement. Jim Dickson, Tickner's former partner, has no recollection of ever hearing the name Sylvia Sammons in his life, nor of any claim, let alone payment, for the song. A spokesperson for Vanguard Records was quoted as saying, "We do not keep any correspondence dating back that far." Dickson found it hard to believe that Vanguard would pay money in such circumstances anyway. This was a publishing matter. There appears to have been no legal documentation mentioned by any of the parties involved, including the complainant, even though this would have been standard procedure in any copyright claim, no matter how serious or frivolous.

Complicating matters further, there are two witnesses who recall Parsons actually writing his part of the song. Jim Carlton remembers the composition coming together in early 1968, a handful of months before it was recorded for *Sweetheart Of The Rodeo*. "I was there when Bob Buchanan and Gram were working out 'Hickory Wind' as they'd just come from Coconut Grove where they'd visited Fred Neil and stopped in Winter Haven to retrieve Gram's stipend." In theory at least, Parsons could have heard the title 'Hickory Wind' in his coffee-house days and consciously or unconsciously revamped part of it but, as there is no tape available for comparison, who can say? If Parsons had known the song from several years before, how come it never featured in the repertoire of the Legends, the Village Vanguards or the Shilos? Given the song's obvious qualities, why were there no private recordings undertaken at Jim Carlton's house in 1965 and later? Since Parsons is no longer around to defend or explain the matter, we have only Sammons' general claim that the song was "stolen". When interviewed, she did not go into details about the nuances of melody or specific lines and words which might have thrown light on the matter. Co-composer Buchanan vividly remembers writing the second verse ("I started out younger . . .") which he recites line by line, complete with explication of the imagery and meaning he was intending to impart. Presumably, Sammons is not disputing this, but what, if anything, Parsons allegedly borrowed or plagiarized remains unclear and, regrettably, impossible to determine.

Another disputed legacy of Gram Parsons that provoked some bitterness was his songwriting catalogue. On the day after his death, his widow Gretchen had been appointed the administrator of his estate. Among the property inventoried in the estate were 11 songs, written or co-written by Parsons and published by Wait & See Music, later administered by Tickson Music. On 11 December 1985, over a decade after Parsons' death, Gretchen entered into a stipulation with Polly A. Parsons closing the estate and distributing its assets. It was agreed that Gretchen and Polly would each receive half of all *future* income from the inventoried royalty contracts, including those published by Wait & See. The stipulation also provided that any assets *not* shown on the inventory or discovered at a later date would be distributed to Polly in their entirety.

That might have been the end of the matter, but there was a further twist to the story at the end of 1990, following the release of the first Byrds' box set. Some time the following year, Saul Davis, who had briefly represented Gene Clark during the Eighties, contacted various subsidiary Byrds, including Gene

Parsons, John York and "possibly Skip Battin" asking about their remuneration from the package. None had been signed to CBS during their period in the Byrds so they were not due any money. Davis also contacted Polly A. Parsons, pointing out – if she didn't already know – that the box was being promoted with a sticker advertising the inclusion of several of Gram's long lost vocal performances from *Sweetheart Of The Rodeo*. Despite this, Sony Records were not paying her any money as Parsons was never signed directly to the label during his period in the Byrds. Subsequently, Davis told Polly Parsons that she should find a music business attorney who would represent her on a contingency basis. He suggested Neville Johnson, whom he knew socially. On 12 April 1991, Johnson and Parsons entered a fee agreement, the contents of which remain protected by attorney/client privilege and have never been revealed.

Sony Records were subsequently challenged about their use of Parsons' material on the box set and elected to settle the matter with a relatively modest payment rather than taking the matter to court. Or, as former Byrds' manager Jim Dickson caustically observed, "Sony had no balls at all . . . they settled and charged it to McGuinn." It was surely no coincidence that in subsequent years, McGuinn, backed by his wife Camilla, declined to appear in radio, television or magazine/book projects involving Parsons.

In June 1991, Johnson and Davis visited the offices of Len Freedman, who had recently purchased the Tickson music catalogue, part of which included the 11 songs written by Parsons. The meeting was short but, during their conversation, Freedman allegedly revealed that he had not received any documents or agreements confirming that Parsons' copyrighted compositions contained in the Wait & See catalogue had ever been transferred to Tickner.

Thereafter, a lawsuit was brought against Tickner to which Dickson and Freedman's names were appended. Judge Jerold A. Krieger of the Superior Court of Los Angeles dismissed the action without leave to amend, but that was not the end of the matter.

On 2 February 1995, Polly Parsons v. Edward Tickner *et al* was revisited at the Court of Appeal in an attempt to take the action to trial. The Appeal Court, by its nature, does not speculate on the ability of the plaintiff to support at a trial, allegations well pleaded, but merely makes its own independent judgement of the sufficiency of the complaint. Polly Parsons' suit had alleged fraud based on the notion that Gram had never signed over his copyrights for the 11 songs to Tickner in the first place. Tickner, who had an exemplary reputation in the music business, rightly pointed out that he had paid royalties on the songs for years. Of course, that could be turned on its head by the Machiavellian suggestion that by actually paying the royalties he was cleverly distracting attention from the fact that he didn't ever own the Wait & See catalogue.

Tickner continued to claim that there *were* written agreements but, two decades on, he could no longer locate all the paperwork. At first, it seemed that Polly Parsons' claims would be time barred under the statute of limitations. The Tickner respondents had demurred that under the Code of Civil Procedure there was a three-year limitation regarding fraud. The time for bringing a claim had therefore elapsed more than 16 years before on 19 September 1976 (three years after Gram Parsons' death). In addition, it was suggested that as the Wait & See catalogue had been included in the inventory of Parsons' estate, it could not be considered an 'after-discovered' asset. Relying on the *Probate Code section 573*, it was further suggested that since Polly was not the administrator of Parsons' estate she could not legally bring the action.

All of the above demurrers had been filed in December 1992 and heard on 7 January 1993, when the action had been dismissed. But there was a sting in the tail. A mere six days before, on 1 January, there had been a change in the law. The California Law Revision Committee's recommendation had succeeded in repealing and replacing the *Probate Code* with a new *Code of Civil Procedure*. The latter, which worked retroactively, provided that a decedent's successor was now entitled to pursue an action. The

Appeal Court recognized this, while also overturning the time-barred demurrer by determining that the three-year limitation actually began in June 1991 when Polly first discovered the alleged fraud and breach. Moreover, although the Wait & See catalogue had been included in the inventory of Parsons' estate, it had been scheduled as a "Writer's Royalty rights in . . . musical properties" which only provided for payment of royalty percentages, not the actual ownership of Wait & See.

For the foregoing reasons, the Appeal Court reversed the original dismissal, on 2 February 1995, allowing the action to proceed to trial. This was a major setback to Tickner *et al*, who had thought that the lawsuit was dead and buried. There were additional implications for Gretchen Parsons. If Polly won at trial and established ownership of Wait & See then the publishing would represent an after-discovered asset, which meant that she could claim 100 per cent of it and contest that Gretchen should no longer receive any monies from the catalogue. Moreover, she might also seek to recover all the royalty payments already paid by Tickner *et al* to Gretchen. In addition, if it was proven that Tickner *et al* had falsely masqueraded as owners of the catalogue their liability, going back years, could be scarily substantial. The stakes could hardly have been higher.

It would be another year before the matter was settled. Dickson had wanted Polly Parsons to submit to a blood test to determine whether she was the biological daughter of Gram Parsons but, according to Tickner, this motion was never entertained. What they did want was the presence of Polly at a deposition hearing. Instead, they subpoenaed Saul Davis, who was obliged to provide oral testimony under oath and submit various documents and "other tangible things". The deposition took place on 27 August 1996 at the Los Angeles offices of Tickner's lawyers Berry & Cahalan on Century Park East. In a 104-page deposition, some time was spent on attempting to discover whether Davis might receive any part of the settlement with Polly Parsons, a crucial issue. Davis maintained that he had worked as a researcher and investigator for lawyer Neville

Johnson's office, but testified, under oath, that there was no oral agreement of any kind between himself and Polly Parsons relating to the lawsuit, or any recoveries therefrom.

James Berry (for Cahahan & Berry): In any of these conversations was there any discussion as to what you would get out of this?
Saul Davis: No.

JB: Is your testimony that there was never any sort of agreement or contract or understanding between you and Miss Parsons?
SD: Correct.

JB: So if a third party said they had seen an agreement between the two of you, that person would not be telling the truth?
SD: Correct.

JB: And if that person testified that they had been asked to review the agreement between you and Miss Parsons, that person would be lying?
SD: Correct.

Davis proceeded to describe the genesis of the case and the various meetings, after which Berry produced one of the submitted documents.

JB: On the document that is headed Byrds CBS and McGuinn, third page the statement SD getting 37 and a half per cent. Do you know what that refers to?
SD: I believe that was related to a Gene Clark album.

One hour into the deposition, the parties agreed to take a five-minute recess. Upon their return, Polly Parsons' lawyer Neville Johnson announced that he was removing the three-page document. It was the most dramatic and amusing part of the deposition hearing, with some heated exchanges.

JB: You took it out of my possession while I was out of the room? I have seen it. I've been . . .
Neville Johnson: I'm taking it back. You'll have to go to court.

JB: I don't think it could have been privileged to begin with. For me to leave the room and have you take it back from me after I have seen it, after I have read it, after I asked a question about it.
NJ: Well, I did it and you have to go to court if you want to fight about it.

JB: So you are not going to give me the document. Is that correct?
NJ: Right.

JB: You're not going to return back to me what you took from me while I was out of the room?
NJ: It's privileged.

JB: Well that is a new one. I have never had that happen before. I guess I should have stayed in the room.

JB: [to SD]: You understand I'm going to bring a motion against you as well as against Johnson? Do you understand the motion to get that document?
SD: Yes, sir.

JB: And you are nonetheless declining to return the document that you and Mr Johnson gave to me about an hour ago?
SD: I just received it from Mr Johnson. Yes.

JB: Well, on that document there were a number of items of information, at least half a dozen former members of the Byrds, right?
SD: Correct.

JB: OK. Did Mr Johnson ever represent any of these people except Polly Parsons?
SD: I really don't know.

JB: To your knowledge did he?
SD: I don't know. . . .

JB: Were you employed by Mr Johnson for the purpose of contacting any of the people on that list other than Polly Parsons?
SD: I had conversations with a number of those people.

JB: That's not my question. Were you ever employed or retained by

Mr Johnson to contact any of the people on that list other than Polly Parsons?
SD: Yes . . .

JB: OK. Was your purpose in contacting those people to see if they could retain Mr Johnson as counsel?
SD: My job wasn't to solicit business for him. I talked to these people about the situation, asked them about the Byrds box set, for instance.

JB: Did you tell any of these people on that list the name Mr Johnson as an attorney they should consider retaining?
SD: I probably mentioned his name.

JB: To all of them, didn't you?
SD: I couldn't tell you.

The deposition continued with Mr Johnson interrupting to insist that there was no partnership between himself and Davis.

While these dramatic events were underway, Tickner made a crucial and unexpected breakthrough in unearthing his archives. "Eddie couldn't find the contracts," Dickson says, "but then he went back, looked again and did find them. He looked again after we were in the middle of it all and had spent a lot of money. He had to go up to Santa Barbara." It was typical of Gram Parsons that the 'missing' documents had partly resulted from his cavalier method of signing contracts. "He was the songwriter for a specific song and it had one song on the front and there were eight or nine on the back with Gram's signature . . . We found all but two, which was more than enough to show that it was still happening and operating at the time. When Eddie found them I thought it was pretty much over."

Dickson was correct. Within 48 hours of Saul Davis' deposition, James Berry Jr, on behalf of Berry & Cahalan despatched a letter by hand delivery to the offices of Neville L. Johnson, stating:

"In our conversation of this afternoon, you suggested that both sides bear their costs if the lawsuit were to be dismissed with prejudice. After our conversation, I spoke with Mr Tickner. Mr Tickner is prepared to bear his costs only if the lawsuit is dismissed forthwith in its entirety and with prejudice to Messrs. Tickner, Dickson, and Freedman, and if there is no reservation for future litigation of any issue or matter raised by this litigation.

I have enclosed a dismissal form for execution by your office. If I receive the executed form with a letter authorizing its immediate filing by 5:00 pm on Friday, August 30, then Mr Tickner will waive his costs in connection with this case. Otherwise we will be forced to file the OSCs [Order to Show Charge] re: contempt and multiple motions to compel and for sanctions on which we are currently working."

On 3 September 1996, a request for dismissal was submitted to the Superior Court of California, Los Angeles, by Neville L. Johnson & Associates, attorney for Polly Parsons, requesting dismissal of the action for breach of duty and fraud.

Two days later, James Berry wrote to Tickner, confirming:

Dear Eddie,

At long last, I hold in my hands a copy of the final dismissal with prejudice of this case against you, Jim Dickson and Len Freedman. It was a painful process for everybody concerned but we finally got the right result . . . I would be delighted to work with you in the future. Let's hope there's never a need.

James H. Berry, Jr

Dickson was not entirely pleased with the outcome. He had been keen for Tickner to continue the action in light of what had happened, but it was not to be. "Eddie was so exhausted and had spent so much money. He didn't want to go any further." Dickson estimates that "it cost us about $120,000 in legal fees", with the bulk of the money provided by Tickner. After it was all over, Dickson retained a lingering antipathy towards Saul Davis, evidenced in several intemperate eruptions that are largely unprintable. "If I wasn't here [in Hawaii]," he said, after the case was settled, "I'd probably be in jail for shooting Saul Davis." Tickner, himself, was predictably calmer about the entire affair, offering only a wry smile and a playfully caustic rejoinder.

The legal dispute was another unfortunate legacy of the Gram Parsons' story, although its conclusion before going to trial ensured that there was little or no publicity about the nature of the dispute. Since its completion, several books on Parsons have appeared, including one co-written by the plaintiff, Polly A. Parsons. She does not mention the legal dispute even once, and it is also absent from every other book. Instead, commentators and biographers have concentrated upon the family history as a means of understanding the flaws, foibles and triumphs of Gram Parsons.

The universal appeal of Gram Parsons' self-destructive family saga has often been seen in terms of some Gothic Southern tradition, along the lines of William Faulkner or Tennessee Williams. However, it transcends its geographical locale to take on something closer to elemental myth. The same sense of fatalism, hubris, catharsis and sudden death can be traced back to Greek tragedy and onwards through the Bible, Shakespeare and the Romantics and into the modern era. Eugene O'Neill should be placed alongside Faulkner and Williams as inheritors of the same tradition. For many fans and commentators, there is something irresistible about the notion of Parsons as some kind of multi-faceted romantic hero or rock 'n' roll martyr. It can and has been taken to ludicrous proportions. The mysterious removal of his body echoes the events following the Crucifixion; the cremation of his remains reminds us of Shelley's funeral pyre, and so on. Although Parsons did not commit suicide, most believe that he was half in love with tragic death. In 1973, the notion of leaving a good-looking corpse was still seen in some rock circles as the acme of cachet. Even the contemporaneous deaths of Brian Jones,

Jim Morrison, Jimi Hendrix and Janis Joplin were celebrated as much as mourned. Tellingly, the method of Parsons' cremation was initially greeted with approval by his musician friends, as shown by printed comments from Roger McGuinn, Bernie Leadon and even Emmylou Harris, who retained the services of 'bodysnatcher' Phil Kaufman for many years afterwards.

As the counterculture has grown older and more conservative, the romance of young death has been replaced by a certain grim preservation. Some, chiefly Chris Hillman, lament Parsons' elevation as sad evidence of the modern cult of celebrity, but it is surely something much older. Parsons, despite inspiring several books in his honour, never achieved the celebrity status of the aforementioned 'rock 'n' roll martyrs' nor their many successors such as Keith Moon, Sid Vicious, Kurt Cobain, or the rest of the ghostly cast. Gram remains a cult figure, whose record sales are steady, but unspectacular. There is considerable ambivalence about his character, even when speaking to the same interviewee. At times, he seems like a Janus figure – a Byrd who wasn't a Byrd; a son who we're told both loved and hated his stepfather; a songwriter who romanticized and sexualized his muse in the same song ('Hot Burrito # 1'); whose relationship with other characters in his orbit – whether they be Roger McGuinn, Chris Hillman, Keith Richards or even Emmylou Harris – are still subject to claim, counter claim and denial.

Early death guaranteed Parsons a place in the rock 'n' roll hall of morbidity, but the bodysnatching element transformed tragedy into myth. Alas, that sordid story has all too often eclipsed the music in terms of importance to some journalists. This is partly why the world of books prefers the story of Gram Parsons to that of Clarence White. White was a technically superior musician and his life story has a similar catalogue of family tragedies with an equally high body count. Yet, our psychological response to these two influential musicians is completely different. The White story deals with real life in all its tragic sadness, whereas the Parsons' saga offers the observer an escape through the prism of myth. Indeed, so overwhelming is the legend surrounding

Parsons that it has enabled him to challenge the powerful mythology of the Byrds. Gene Clark, Roger McGuinn, Michael Clarke and Chris Hillman, notwithstanding their other achievements, are engulfed and defined by their time in the Byrds. Only David Crosby and Gram Parsons have arguably transcended the group legacy by daring to create, or having thrust upon them, an equally enduring myth based on their own image.

GRAM PARSONS: NOTES

page 625: "You must remember something – he was never a member of the Byrds . . ." Chris Hillman, interviewed for the online website: *The Gram Parsons Project*. Hillman has repeated this assertion on various occasions. For example, during an interview with Sean Egan (*Goldmine*: 28 December 1981), he insisted: "Gram was not a member of the Byrds. That's a big misrepresentation because he really wasn't in the Byrds. He was a hired hand, so to speak."

page 627: "Her veil was held . . ." press cutting dated 24 March 1945.

page 628: "I'd have to say the biggest influence on my career . . ." *Los Angeles Free Press*: 25 October 1969. Reprinted from *Helix Seattle*. Interview uncredited in either publication, but I believe the journalist was Ed Leimbacher.

page 628: ". . . attended an Elvis Presley concert at the City Auditorium in Waycross . . ." When later recalling this epochal evening to interviewer Jan Donkers in 1972, Parsons recalled attending the show with female twins (later identified as Daphne and Diane Delano, the daughters of family friends). However, he wrongly suggested that Presley played second on the bill to Little Jimmy Dickens. "I just walked through Little Jimmy Dickens' dressing room and said, 'Hello, you're Elvis Presley . . .' He shook my hand and gave me an autograph." However, Little Jimmy Dickens was not even on the bill. Given the significance of the show, it was strange that Parsons' memory should be so vague.

page 629: "We are delighted . . ." Extract from letter, quoted in full in Ben Fong-Torres' *Hickory Wind: The Life And Times Of Gram Parsons* (London, Omnibus Press, 1991).

page 631: "You must be brave . . ." 'Little' Avis recalled her feelings about her father's death in her private memoirs later in life. "I was left to find comfort from somewhere inside myself," she wrote.

page 631: "I was scared to death of Waycross . . ." *Los Angeles Free Press*: 25 October 1969. Reprinted from *Helix Seattle*. Interview uncredited in either publication, but I believe the journalist was Ed Leimbacher.

page 632: "Bob Parsons was probably one of the most outstanding guys . . ." Gene Leedy, interviewed by the author. London/Winter Haven, Florida: 20 May 2009.

page 632: "Gram's stepfather was a disgusting, evil, manipulative person . . ." Chris Hillman, interviewed by Barney Hoskyns. *Mojo* 56: July 1998.

page 633: ". . . may smile, and smile . . ." William Shakespeare, *Hamle*t: I.v. 108.

page 633: "They were trying to sell . . ." Jim Carlton, interviewed by the author. London/Mount Dora, Florida: 5 March 2007. In 1954, Carlton's father had moved the family to Winter Haven from Chicago, where he had been on the staff of WGN when studios employed guitarists. The Chicago television show, *Ladies' Fair*, evolved into the popular radio show, *Florida Calling*.

page 633: "He never talked about it . . ." ibid.

page 634: ". . . an amateur rock 'n' roll group, the Pacers . . ." The Pacers featured Gram Parsons (guitar/piano/vocals), Jimmy Allen (guitar), Marvin Clevenger (bass) and Skip 'Flat Top' Rosser (drums).

page 634: ". . . nobody was any good then . . ." Carlton/Rogan. London/Mount Dora, Florida: 5 March 2007.

page 634: "He was grooming himself . . ." ibid.

page 634: ". . . Pamela Carnes . . ." Carnes is incorrectly referred to as 'Cairns' in other Parsons biographies.

page 635: "He was forever writing songs . . ." ibid.

page 635: "Stafford was taking lessons . . ." ibid.

page 635: "Don't become a professional musician . . ." ibid.

page 636: "We were all beginners . . ." ibid. This period is summed up by Carlton who adds, "Stafford was an evident talent and wanted to progress on guitar. He'd heard about my dad and Gram introduced Jim and me at the school talent show. My dad began giving Jim guitar lessons (at first free as he was so talented); because I was just beginning on bass, it was logical that I join the Legends. We'd all become good pals, the band needed a bass and logic prevailed . . . We played teen centres, proms and after-school dances in the gym. My first gig with a five-man edition of the Legends was playing an after-football dance that made us about $8 each. Except for Stafford, we were overpaid." Summing up the convoluted line-up changes at various gigs, Carlton concludes: "In short, a Legends' gig may or may not have had a horn or horn section, or even a real bassist in its early days. I remember the PA was a joke. It was a Premier brand about the size of a small carry-on bag. The head would accommodate one mike and the two speakers would extend to either side of the stage. Hilarious, in retrospect, but we didn't know any better. It must have been all of 15 watts."

page 636: "Carlton remembers Gram's mother . . ." David N. Meyer's biography credits Robert Parsons for the purchase, but either way it was probably Avis' money. The important point is that both parents supported the idea. Carlton has been quoted elsewhere suggesting that the uniform was topped off with a fancy 'L' emblazoned across the front, presumably the lapel pocket. He denies this curious detail. "They were [bought] off the rack from Belks, a ubiquitous Southern US department store."

page 636: "We'd hop off at the weekend . . ." ibid.

page 636: "Gram's family had so much money . . ." ibid.

page 637: "Gram became a great exponent . . ." ibid.

page 637: ". . . the playground of the stars . . ." ibid.

page 637: "He had a marvellous lifestyle . . ." ibid.

page 637: "That's the only work . . ." ibid.

page 638: "When my family went on vacation . . ." ibid.

page 639: "We had a job that evening . . ." Jon Corneal, interviewed by the author. London/Winter Haven, Florida: 24 June 2007. The fragmentation of the Legends began when Lamar Braxton moved away to college. Jim Carlton decided to switch to guitar ("It was a lot sexier than the stand-up bass"), and Gerald Chambers proved the perfect replacement. "It was clear that an electric bass was much better for the Legends," Carlton notes. "Gerald was a much better bass player and could sing harmony well."

page 639: "The best edition of the Legends . . ." Carlton/Rogan. London/Mount Dora, Florida: 5 March 2007.

page 640: ". . . was replaced by Bill Waldrop . . ." Stafford did not entirely sever his links with the Legends. He would often deputize for Bill Waldrop (aka Waldrup in some articles/books), depending on their mutual availability. "Bill and Jim were part of the 'Legends pool' and whoever was free got the gig," reveals Carlton. "Jim, of course, was first call but was making much more playing lounges. Our parents usually frowned on such gigs, so the rest of us stayed on the teen/prom circuit. Sometimes, Bill and Jim were *both* Legends, with Stafford playing lead and Waldrop playing bass lines on his Stratocaster's neck pick-up. As you rightly state, I was never in an edition of the Legends with Jon Corneal."

page 640: "Gerald Chambers changed his name . . ." The name change explains some of the confusion surrounding the Legends' convoluted membership. Incidentally, Kent LaVoie confirms that he never played onstage as a member of the Legends. This misconception probably stems from a photo caption in Sid Griffin's *Gram Parsons: A Music Biography*, where LaVoie is wrongly credited instead of Bill Waldrop (incorrectly referred to as Waldrup in other accounts). Similarly, Gerald Chambers' cousin Carl Chambers was never in the Legends, as is sometimes erroneously reported, but he too enjoyed success in later life. As Jim Carlton notes: "Carl and Gerald were first cousins. Carl later made a living playing with vintage bands. He was in a pretty important central Florida band called We The People at one time, even though it was a later conjugation. He also wrote a hit song for Alabama titled 'Close Enough To Perfect'. He must have lived off that royalty for quite a while."

page 641: "I sang at talent shows in high school . . ." Patricia 'Patti' Johnson, interviewed by the author. London/Sarasota, Florida: 25 February 2008.

page 641: "I didn't know him . . ." ibid.

page 641: "He said, 'I'm playing at this place . . .'" ibid.

page 642: "No, you can't do that . . ." ibid.

page 642: "I just did what I was told . . ." ibid.

page 642: "There was nothing . . ." ibid.

page 643: ". . . Bonnie Muma, a 19-year-old Winter Haven alumnus . . ." To clarify, Bonnie Muma was born in 1943. Biographer David Meyer rightly agrees that she was 19 years old when she was appointed as babysitter in 1962. However, on the next page, he mentions that she was "five years older than Gram" which presumably should read "three years older" as Gram was born in 1946.

page 643: "Avis became such a hopeless alcoholic . . ." Leedy/Rogan. London/Winter Haven, Florida: 20 May 2009.

page 644: "We're going to Tampa for dinner . . ." Patricia 'Patti' Johnson/Rogan. London/Sarasota, Florida: 25 February 2008.

page 644: "Tampa was over an hour away . . ." ibid.

page 644: "She was really supportive . . ." ibid.

page 644: "He didn't really talk about it . . ." ibid.

page 645: "A repertoire was soon established . . ." Woody Guthrie's 'This Land Is Your Land' found new popularity in the early Sixties and was covered by Bob Dylan, the Kingston Trio, the New Christy Minstrels and Peter, Paul & Mary. 'Don't Think Twice, It's All Right' was featured on *The Freewheelin' Bob Dylan,* released in spring 1963. The Civil Rights anthem 'If I Had A Hammer', originally written in 1949 by Pete Seeger and Lee Hayes, was popularized by the Weavers, then Peter, Paul & Mary. Trini Lopez also enjoyed an international hit with the song in 1963. 'Where Have All The Flowers Gone?' was a Ukrainian folk song, adapted by Seeger, with additional verses from Joe Hickerson. 'Puff, The Magic Dragon', written by Peter Yarrow and Leonard Lipton, had reached number 2 in the US charts in 1963. It seems pretty likely that Parsons owned Peter, Paul & Mary's album *Movin'*, which included 'This Land Is Your Land', 'The Hammer Song' (aka 'If I Had A Hammer'), 'Where Have All The Flowers Gone?' and 'Puff, The Magic Dragon'. The suggestion in another book that Parsons was performing Ian & Sylvia's 'You Were On My Mind' at this point is not possible as the song was not written until 1964.

page 645: "We sang some English ballads too . . ." Patricia 'Patti' Johnson/Rogan. London/Sarasota, Florida: 25 February 2008.

page 645: ". . . he had written the wistful 'It Was A Very Good Year' . . ."

Avis never lived long enough to hear the song transformed into a standard by Frank Sinatra. The track was issued as a single from his album, *September Of My Years,* at the end of 1965.

page 645: "I swear to you my knees were literally knocking . . ." Patricia 'Patti' Johnson/Rogan. London/Sarasota, Florida: 25 February 2008.

page 646: "We each had our artistic endeavours . . ." ibid.

page 647: "Gram said, 'Let's skip school . . .' " ibid.

page 647: "This was not a sloppy deal . . ." ibid.

page 647: "We drove through this little town . . ." ibid.

page 647: "We just wanted to go off . . ." ibid.

page 648: "There was no big announcement . . ." ibid.

page 649: "Gram never showed up for the rest of the school year . . ." ibid.

page 649: "There was speculation about the pregnancy . . ." ibid.

page 651: "I cried all night . . ." ibid.

page 652: "He was driven . . ." Luke Lewis, interviewed for the DVD documentary *Gram Parsons Fallen Angel,* directed by Gandulf Hennig, 2006.

page 652: ". . . Joe Kelly (upright bass) . . ." That evening, Kelly was forced to deputize on guitar for the absent George Wrigley. The Shilos had originally emerged from the Princeton Quartet, another Greenville band featuring Wrigley and Kelly. Wrigley and Kelly then teamed up with Surratt and Bryant Kendrick to form the Shiloh Singers, named after the battle of Shiloh. After Kendrick went to college, they abbreviated the group title to Shilos. "That was nothing more than a hang-on to the Kingston Trio, who were a big deal in 1959," says Kelly. "The four of us performed together for one summer before Kendrick went to college. The Princeton Quartet and the Shiloh Singers was when we were at junior high school. We dropped the 'h' [from Shilohs]. It was just some stylistic thing we wanted to do. We thought it looked better."

page 652: "What makes the stars go where they are? . . ." Paul Surratt, interviewed by the author. London/Los Angeles, California: 27–28 February 2007.

page 652: "We liked the Journeymen . . ." ibid. In every other interview he has done, including the first one with me, Surratt suggested that the song was 'Run Maggie Run' which he claimed was on the first Journeymen album. The song does not appear on that album and although the Journeymen did play the song on television, this occurred in the spring of 1964, several months after Parsons and the Shilos first encountered each other. Looking back, Surratt now says, "The song was 'Chase The Rising Sun'. I was wrong about the title. It *was* on the first Journeymen album." Joe Kelly agrees. "We always called it 'Run Maggie Run', but you have the correct title from the album. That Journeymen album is beautiful. Even today you can listen to it. Paul says we met Gram backstage but I don't think we did. He saw our name and he was going to sing 'The Hills Of Shiloh' that night. We met him jamming around, that's correct. I seem to remember it was out in the auditorium, walking around one of the aisles."

page 653: "I couldn't believe it . . ." ibid.

page 653: "We were a bunch of kids . . ." ibid.

page 653: "I have to credit him . . ." Joe Kelly, interviewed by the author. London/Alexandria, Virginia: 23 July 2009.

page 653: ". . . 'You Know My Name' . . ." As written on the New Christy Minstrels' album, *In Person*. The song was sometimes listed elsewhere as 'You Know My Voice (You Know My Name)'.

page 654: "RCA recording artist . . ." Undated article. *c.* late 1963, titled "Recording Artist Likes Greenville Music".

page 654: "I like Greenville's attitude . . ." ibid.

page 654: "It was a good crowd . . ." Kelly/Rogan. London/Alexandria, Virginia: 23 July 2009.

page 654: "I couldn't believe it . . ." Surratt/Rogan. London/Los Angeles, California: 27–28 February 2007.

page 655: "Well, Margaret Fisher . . ." The Parsons/Fisher dialogue has been repeated, virtually verbatim by Fisher, to biographers David Meyer and Jessica Hundley.

page 656: "I had mixed feelings . . ." Kelly/Rogan London/Alexandria, Virginia: 23 July 2009.

page 656: "Every night . . ." Gram Parsons' letter to Marilyn Garrett: 15 April 1964. Additional correspondence can be found in Bob Kealing's *Calling Me Home: Gram Parsons And The Roots Of Country Rock* (University Press Of Florida, 2012).

page 656: "I think George was jealous . . ." Surratt/Rogan. London/Los Angeles, California: 27–28 February 2007.

page 657: "It was pretty much democratic . . ." Kelly/Rogan. London/Alexandria, Virginia: 23 July 2009.

page 658: ". . . they weren't ready . . ." Surratt/Rogan. London/Los Angeles, California: 27–28 February 2007.

page 659: "I'm with you . . ." ibid.

page 659: "I don't believe . . ." ibid. Joe Kelly is also sceptical about Freeman's claims concerning the Sullivan show. "I never heard that. It was news to me. We had friends at school sending postcards to *The Andy Williams Show* trying to get the Shilos on there. But, of course, nothing ever happened. As for Sullivan, I think you hit the nail on the head there. I think Buddy was saying that to get some personal retribution. Just a little barb to say, 'I could have done something.'"

page 659: "We had three guys from Special Forces . . ." Kelly/Rogan. London/Alexandria, Virginia: 23 July 2009.

page 659: "He wasn't even coming to the beach . . ." ibid. Kelly adds: "That's when we parted ways. He still did get his equal cut, but that was the end of it."

page 660: "It was a drag . . ." Surratt/Rogan. London/Los Angeles, California: 27–28 February 2007.
page 660: "While I knew his idea was quixotic . . ." Jim Carlton email to author dated 28 March 2009.
page 660: "Carlton, that haircut . . ." ibid.
page 660: "Perhaps someday . . ." Parsons' contribution to Jim Carlton's yearbook.
page 661: "Norman was his name . . ." Kelly/Rogan. London/Alexandria, Virginia: 23 July 2009.
page 661: ". . . a cute, petite Jewish girl from the Village . . ." Surratt/Rogan. London/Los Angeles, California: 27–28 February 2007.
page 661: ". . . an olive complexion . . ." Kelly/Rogan. London/Alexandria, Virginia: 23 July 2009.
page 661: "The group survived on a poor diet . . ." Joe Kelly adds: "Between gigs, Paul and I walked around and there was a bar that we weren't supposed to be in because we weren't 21. They had good fried chicken, so we'd get that and a pizza from this bar and stand out on the sidewalk and eat it between sets. We'd get off work at one or two in the morning . . . We met this girl, Annie, who had a place several blocks away. She and her roommate had an artist's studio above a house and we stayed there, slept on the floor. Annie and I went to a baseball game one time and we'd get together occasionally in the daytime. Annie lived in Orchard Street. We had to walk through the lower East Side to get there and I remember this place where all the merchants would have their tables out. They'd bring stuff from the stores on to the sidewalk, like a bazaar. Parsons was back at Jack [Lewis'] place, so what he was doing at two or three in the morning, I've no recollection because I wasn't there to see it."
page 661: "We got up at one of those hootenannies . . ." Surratt/Rogan. London/Los Angeles, California: 27–28 February 2007.
page 661: ". . . found time to record a few songs . . ." The precise dates of the Dick Weissman studio recordings and apartment tapes are not known. The latter have since been released on *Gram Parsons The Early Years* box set with a suggested date of September 1965 although I believe Weissman's recordings took place the previous summer in New York. Two other contemporaneous recordings, unconnected with Weissman, are bundled in with these six recordings: 'The Great Silke' (aka 'Great Selchie Of Shule Skerry') and 'Race With The Wind'.
page 662: ". . . a convoluted and incoherent explanation . . ." Parsons' preamble to 'Hand Within The Glove' was puzzling rather than enlightening: "This is a song that takes place in a specific time and a specific place in which everyone has to decide for themselves when they hear it. It's a series of questions and answers between a person and another person or a group of people and questions and answers and statements and counter statements which build on these statements."

page 662: "We were a bunch of kids . . ." Surratt/Rogan. London/Los Angeles, California: 27–28 February 2007. Joe Kelly, incidentally, believes that they did meet Albert Grossman while in New York. However, when asked for a description of the man, he could remember nothing, beyond the name. Given Grossman's larger-than-life presence, this seems unlikely and inclines me to believe that they probably dealt with one of his assistants.

page 662: ". . . she moved to Canada . . ." According to Paul Surratt: "Zah went on to play in Canada and I later got a letter from her. She told me how much she missed us guys and hoped everything was well. But I was a kid. We'd all write for a little time and then your life moves on and unless you're really one of these people who intensely keeps in touch, away it goes."

page 663: "The letter said . . ." ibid.

page 664: "He was a gourmet cook . . ." Leedy/Rogan. London/Winter Haven, Florida: 20 May 2009. Bob Parsons' hosting skills even extended to the music selection. He paid Jim Carlton to compile a reel-to-reel tape of bossa nova numbers so that the country set in attendance could enjoy the background music.

page 664: "They got on well from what I saw . . ." Surratt/Rogan. London/Los Angeles, California: 27–28 February 2007.

page 664: "Bob Parsons was a decent guy . . ." Kelly/Rogan. London/Alexandria, Virginia: 23 July 2009.

page 664: "I didn't know where Gram had been . . ." Patricia 'Patti' Johnson/Rogan. London/Sarasota, Florida: 25 February 2008.

page 665: ". . . 'getting high' . . ." ibid.

page 665: "It was awful . . ." ibid.

page 665: "We got ready to leave . . ." Kelly/Rogan. London/Alexandria, Virginia: 23 July 2009.

page 666: ". . . issued 14 years later on Sierra Records as *The Early Years* . . ." Sierra Records seemed to have trouble co-ordinating the record's title. On the vinyl, it's printed as *The Early Years*, on the sleeve spine it reads, *The Early Years, Volume 1*, on the front cover it says *The Early Years 1963–1965* and on the back cover, *The Early Years, Vol. 1*. The vinyl, spine and front credits Gram Parsons alone, while the rear bills the work as Gram Parsons & The Shilos. There is no evidence of any likely *Volume 2* and the suggestion that there is material from 1963 and 1964 is equally mystifying.

According to the Sierra/Briar record company contract, the royalty payments on the album were divided as follows: 50 per cent to Gretchen Parsons; 40 per cent to Paul Surratt, and 10 per cent to George Wrigley III.

page 666: "I love that song . . ." Surratt/Rogan. London/Los Angeles, California: 27–28 February 2007.

page 666: 'Big Country' (erroneously credited to Jay Irwin) . . ." Jim

Carlton confirms: "Gram indeed wrote 'Big Country'. Jay Irwin was an old 'jazz guy' trombone player who owned a music store in Lakeland, Florida, and paid for the session for Gram to record the song. I have the original acetate. Jay is long gone, and missed, but truly had nothing whatsoever to do with the composition of 'Big Country'. I can assure you. I knew Jay very well and he thought Gram might have some talent and was ready with a few bucks if perhaps there was a chance the song would take off. In fact, Gram bought his first, and probably only, Stratocaster from Jay who had the Fender franchise at the time."

page 666: "The Shilos also feature a spirited reading of 'Bells Of Rhymney' . . ." Paul Surratt remembers: "We worked that out in a laundromat in Ponte Vedra, Florida. I used to love that one part where we'd sing because when we hit harmony it would sound like twice as many people. I used to live just for that."

page 667: "We had about 30 songs . . ." Surratt/Rogan. London/Los Angeles, California: 27–28 February 2007.

page 667: "I would give a thousand dollars . . ." ibid.

page 667: "He made a trip there . . ." Leedy/Rogan. London/Winter Haven, Florida: 20 May 2009.

page 668: "He told me he got into Harvard . . ." Carlton/Rogan. London/Mount Dora, Florida: 5 March 2007.

page 668: "I was trying to save the group . . ." Surratt/Rogan. London/Los Angeles, California: 27–28 February 2007.

page 668: "Before we went to Greenwich Village . . ." ibid.

page 668: "I'm sure my music . . ." Extract from Parsons' letter to Paul Surratt, reproduced on the sleeve of the archive album, *The Early Years Vol. I 1963–1965*.

page 669: "It all ended . . ." Surratt/Rogan. London/Los Angeles, California: 27–28 February 2007.

page 670: "What happened was . . ." Leedy/Rogan. London/Winter Haven, Florida: 20 May 2009.

page 670: "I remember that day very vividly . . ." Carlton/Rogan. London/Mount Dora, Florida: 5 March 2007.

page 670: "I pictured myself . . ." *Los Angeles Free Press*: 25 October 1969. Reprinted from *Helix Seattle*. Interview uncredited in either publication, but I believe the journalist was Ed Leimbacher.

page 672: "Nuese recommended his friend Ian Dunlop . . ." Dunlop sang and played saxophone and guitar with the Refugees from Providence, Rhode Island. He had also appeared in groups with Nuese including the preposterously named Happy Pantaloon & The Buckles and Desmond & The Lagondas. Dunlop's roots were in Cornwall, England, but he left there as a child. "I'm half-American and half-English," he says. "My father was Scottish and my mother Welsh. My father wanted to get out of Britain. It was a shambles then in the post-war period. They were still queuing [for food] up until the Fifties. It's funny how revisionists reshape the post-war history of Britain and seem to remember times that I wonder if they ever actually experienced." Dunlop is equally weary of rock critics mythologizing his meeting with Parsons as some kind of Road to Damascus experience. "The simple answer is that if you're golfers in the Algarve, you're likely to run into each other. If you're a musician, even in an immense city like New York or a smaller one like Cambridge, Massachusetts, where I was living, it's inevitable that you'll run into different musicians."

page 673: "He even received a telegram . . ." Larry Piro, interviewed by David W. Johnson. *Harvard Magazine*: July–August 1994.

page 673: "We had a very good relationship . . ." Ian Dunlop, interviewed by the author. London/Cornwall: 12 January 2009.

page 674: "A Harvard freshman . . ." *Harvard Crimson*: 21 October 1965. The article ends by quoting a verse from 'November Night' and mentions his backing group 'the Likes' [sic] noting: "They are flying to Nashville on Saturday September 30 to record their first single." The dating would appear to confirm that the interview was done a month before, but this is not the case. In 1965, 'September 30' fell on a Thursday not a Saturday. They actually meant 'Saturday October 30', nine days after the article was published.

page 674: "Gram himself . . ." ibid.

page 674: "Bobby asks questions . . ." Gram Parsons, interviewed by William Fripp. *Boston Sunday Globe*: 31 October 1965.

page 674: "It's not that Gram Parsons can't adjust . . ." ibid.

page 675: "The centre of attention . . ." David W. Johnson, 'Gram Parsons At Harvard . . .' *Harvard Magazine*: July–August 1994.

page 676: "His whole experience . . ." Piro/Johnson. *Harvard Magazine*: July–August 1994.

page 676: "I was turned off . . ." Warner Brothers promotional interview, December 1972.

page 677: ". . . intellectually capable . . ." Reverend James Ellison 'Jet' Thomas, interviewed by David W. Johnson. *Harvard Magazine*: July–August 1994.

page 677: ". . . who would later marry the family's teenage babysitter, Bonnie Muma . . ." Bonnie married Robert Parsons on 10 June 1967 by which time she was 24 years old.

page 677: "I wish there was some one thing I could . . ." Extract from letter, dated 8 November 1965.

page 678: "Harvard was very good . . ." Thomas/Johnson. *Harvard Magazine*: July–August 1994.

page 678: "They were complete songs . . ." Piro/Johnson. *Harvard Magazine*: July–August 1994.

page 679: "I had gotten away . . ." Patricia 'Patti' Johnson/Rogan. London/ Sarasota, Florida: 25 February 2008.

page 679: "I had the Ku Klux Klan chasing me . . ." ibid.

page 679: "It was unannounced . . ." ibid.

page 680: "It went from 'Let's go smoke pot' to . . ." ibid. Patti Johnson adds to her comments: "And I think I'm really glad that I knew him when I did. I think I knew him at probably one of the best stages of his life before the stardom. I wasn't a real tag along like a groupie . . . I love the time that we had together but I'm really glad that I didn't have the *bad* part. I had a part of his life that was probably one of the most fun and productive, even though there were problems with his family. I didn't have the star, druggy, groupie, crazy guy – whatever he became."

page 681: "We were working protracted engagements . . ." Dunlop/Rogan. London/Cornwall: 12 January 2009.

page 681: "Attempting to date Parsons' initial forays into country music . . ." During our interview, Paul Surratt recalled Parsons' country leanings while in the Shilos. "He wrote 'Big Country' and I was impressed with that. I didn't know much about his country writing at the time. I remember we were doing this show in South Carolina at an amusement park that's gone now. We did six shows a day, seven days a week and he always wanted to put in country stuff. He said, 'Let's do 'Salty Dog' – he always wanted to put one of those in. I kind of resented it at the time because I was a folk person." Jim Stafford's suggestion that Gram should sing country was mentioned in books by both Sid Griffin and Ben Fong-Torres. In the former, Stafford says: "He came back into town once and was talking real discouraged and he said he'd tried rock 'n' roll and he'd tried folk and he really didn't know what else to try and play. We had a talk and I said to him, 'You've got country roots, folk's a craze anyway, why don't you sing some C&W as a long-haired young guy?' Gram seemed to really like the idea. Now this is not to say he hadn't already thought of it. I'm telling you this not because I want it to be my idea to have Gram pioneer this form, but right after that he got involved in country-style rock . . ." Stafford's modest boast is fully supported by Jim Carlton, who says: "It was Jim Stafford who told Gram he should be doing country music. He said: 'Gram, that's where you ought to be!' He took his advice. When the folk thing petered out that's when Stafford suggested country music. Stafford was a pretty down home guy. His parents were from Tennessee and he cut his teeth on country music. Stafford's problem was that he's always been too LA for Nashville and too Nashville for LA." John Nuese's claims about teaching Parsons country guitar licks and turning him on to key singers have also appeared in several Parsons-related books, most recently in David N. Meyer's *Twenty Thousand Roads* in which he said: "I take credit for turning Gram on to this music . . . Gram did not know what was going on in country music. He knew no Buck Owens or Merle Haggard . . . When I turned them on to these singers, they all liked it . . ." Similar testimony can be heard on the DVD *Gram Parsons Fallen Angel.*

page 681: "On our local station . . ." Gram Parsons, interviewed by Jan Donkers, broadcast on Holland radio, 1972. My cassette tape claims August 1972, whereas Donkers in a recent reproduction of part of the tape in a music magazine feature suggests it was October/November 1972. Oddly, parts of the interview have sometimes been erroneously credited to Chuck Cassell, as part of an A&M promotional interview dated 3 March 1972.

page 682: "I was singing protest songs . . ." *Los Angeles Free Press*: 25 October 1969. Reprinted from *Helix Seattle*. Interview uncredited in either publication, but I believe the journalist was Ed Leimbacher.

page 682: "They reintroduced me . . ." Gram Parsons, interviewed by Judith Simms. *Rolling Stone*: 1 March 1973.

page 682: "It was a reaffirmation . . ." Dunlop/Rogan. London/Cornwall: 12 January 2009.

page 683: "We didn't go to the Bronx . . ." Barry Tashian, interviewed by the author. London/Nashville, Tennessee: 1 June 2008.

page 684: "Did I rate him as a songwriter? . . ." Dunlop/Rogan. London/ Cornwall: 12 January 2009.

page 684: "Technology was out of everybody's reach . . ." ibid.

page 684: "Every young American male had a problem . . ." ibid.

page 685: "That was the biggest gig we ever did . . ." ibid.

page 685: "We were always trying to do hard rock . . ." Parsons/Donkers, op cit.

page 686: "In an interview with author Ben Fong-Torres . . ." In his book *Hickory Wind*, Fong-Torres includes a lengthy interview with Ross in which she says, "I married Eleanor Roosevelt's grandson, Rex, at 16, 17. I was still married to Rex when I was with David." Unfortunately, I could find no further information about this person. Oddly, the listed offspring of Roosevelt's children, featured on the internet, does not appear to include anyone of this name – at least in the cursory search I undertook. Of course, there could be any number of reasons for this. Ross' daughter Polly who co-penned a memoir of Parsons, includes only a brief mention of 'Rex' who is said to have 'dated' her mother for a few years. Perplexingly, in her account, there is no mention of a marriage. Interestingly, Crosby does not mention Ross at all in his otherwise revealing first autobiography. The actual dating of Ross' romantic meeting with Parsons is claimed by her to have taken place around "Christmas time". She adds that "David . . . left for a Southern tour that night", which fits the chronology. The Byrds had only just finished recording *Younger Than Yesterday* and were booked to play a weekend package tour in the South, including three short sets at the Temple Theatre in Birmingham, Alabama on 10 December 1966.

page 688: "It was issued . . ." 'November Nights' was the fourth single released on Chisa following the Bwanas' 'Pretty Little Girl', Letta's 'Little Star' and Hugh Masekela's 'Chisa'. The label later issued albums by Monk Montgomery, Larry Carlton and the Jazz Crusaders, among others.

page 689: "He tried to get closer to God . . ." Tashian/Rogan. London/Nashville, Tennessee: 1 June 2008.

page 689: "Gram putting his fingers together . . ." ibid.

page 689: "We were very stoned . . ." Carlton/Rogan. London/Mount Dora, Florida: 5 March 2007.

page 689: "We had quite a few meetings . . ." Dunlop/Rogan. London/Cornwall: 12 January 2009. According to Dunlop, the International Submarine Band attempted a compromise of sorts by recording some heavier blues-based demos at Gold Star Studios, including Bobby Marchan's 'Hooked' and Little Milton's 'Feel So Bad'. Evidently, these have not been heard since and obviously failed to attract any major label interest at the time.

page 689: ". . . Dunlop playfully named the Flying Burrito Brothers . . ." Explaining the origin of the surreal name, Dunlop wearily notes: "I don't know. I'm renowned for my spontaneity and years at art school and for being an eccentric person." Some writers have stated that the group sometimes played under the name the Remains Of The International Main Street Flying Burrito Brothers Blues Band, but this was simply a joke that Parsons related to an interviewer many years later. "I never saw that [name] printed on a poster!" Dunlop adds laconically, while dismissing the rumour.

page 689: "We worked for weeks . . ." Dunlop/Rogan. London/Cornwall: 12 January 2009.

page 690: "That was absolutely deliberate . . ." ibid.

page 690: "He was with us at the first gig . . ." Tashian/Rogan. London/Nashville, Tennessee: 1 June 2008.

page 690: "It was all quite retro . . ." Dunlop/Rogan. London/Cornwall: 12 January 2009.

page 691: "We stayed with Denny Doherty . . ." Bob Simone, interviewed for an article on Fred Neil by Ben Edmonds. *Mojo* 75: February 2000. Buchanan, incidentally, took some photographs for the *Sessions* album.

page 692: "I had an offer that was more interesting . . ." Dunlop/Rogan. London/Cornwall: 12 January 2009.

page 693: "The way I looked at it . . ." ibid. Jay Ward was also an inspirational figure for the animator Matt Goering who famously named his *Simpsons*' lead character Homer Jay Simpson in his mentor's honour.

page 693: "Several things happened at once . . ." ibid.

page 694: "Finally, I got an album together . . ." Parsons/Donkers op cit.

page 694: "OK, just let me record an album . . ." ibid.

page 695: "The notion of a female producer . . ." This is no authorial exaggeration. In Bert Muirhead's book *The Producers' File*, published in 1984, there was a list of 1,019 record producers and their extensive album credits. Incredibly, the only female producers named were

Emmylou Harris (who produced an album for Delia Bell in 1983) and Suzi Jane Hokom for her work with the International Submarine Band. It's worth noting that the latter's production work with the Kitchen Cinq was credited to 'S.J. Hokom', as if to disguise or avoid any focus on her gender. The scarcity of female representation was not mentioned in Muirhead's book which was merely an A–Z listing rather than a commentary, but it is still an incredible, unnoticed statistic. Carefully counting the number of producers listed, it was salutary to witness the 1,017 to 2 ratio. The more so since this was published in the Eighties when the myth of female empowerment in the music business was accepted by many commentators too easily distracted by the chart success of 'New Wave Women' such as Madonna, Joan Armatrading, Chrissie Hynde, Debbie Harry, Kate Bush et al. Even in the various books and articles on Gram Parsons, Hokom's achievement of simply being allowed to produce a record is never mentioned, let alone appreciated. In passing, it is a strange coincidence that the only other female producer on the list, which covers several decades, should be Emmylou Harris.

page 695: "We also spent a few days . . ." Carlton/Rogan. London/Mount Dora, Florida: 5 March 2007.

page 696: "He played that song incessantly . . ." ibid.

page 696: ". . . a couple of honeys . . ." ibid.

page 697: "Gram came back to get his stipend . . ." ibid.

page 697: "Ah, forget it . . ." ibid.

page 697: "There was little light pollution . . ." Jim Carlton, email to the author: 29 March 2009.

page 697: "Thank you so much . . ." Carlton/Rogan. London/Mount Dora, Florida: 5 March 2007.

page 697: "He sang it pretty badly . . ." ibid.

page 697: "They looked at us like a dog . . ." Jim Carlton, email to the author: 29 March 2009.

page 698: "David Crosby was there . . ." Corneal/Rogan. London/Winter Haven, Florida: 24 June 2007.

page 699: "Larry Hagman was hanging out . . ." ibid.

page 699: "Sex was free . . ." ibid.

page 699: ". . . social events with Chris and Gram . . ." Dunlop/Rogan. London/Cornwall: 12 January 2009.

page 699: "Occasionally, we'd get a profile gig . . ." ibid.

page 699: "There was Ian Dunlop and Mickey Gauvin . . ." Tashian/Rogan. London/Nashville, Tennessee: 1 June 2008.

page 700: "They were into blues and R&B . . ." ibid. As a teenager, Bobby Keyes had played in bands with Buddy Holly and Bobby Vee. After his stint with the Burritos, he would be invited to appear on the Rolling Stones' *Let It Bleed, Sticky Fingers* (for which he provided the famous sax solo on 'Brown Sugar'), and *Exile On Main Street*, followed by an impressive list of session credits and concert appearances. Markham played in various Tulsa bands including a stint with Leon Russell (Russell Bridges) in the Fifties. Russell subsequently invited Markham to California where he secured a contract with Capitol and recorded *Chuck Meets Bo*. Markham was a frequent visitor to Russell's home studio during this period and became a crucial link between Gram Parsons and the Oklahoman musicians whose fusion of roots country and R&B so influenced his vaguely defined vision of a 'Cosmic American Music'.

page 700: "We hung out . . ." Dunlop/Rogan. London/Cornwall: 12 January 2009.

page 701: ". . . was in a band with some of the guys . . ." ibid.

page 701: ". . . showed me some cool stuff . . ." Tashian/Rogan. London/Nashville, Tennessee: 1 June 2008.

page 701: "Indian Ed'll lay more guitar on you . . ." *Los Angeles Free Press*: 25 October 1969. Reprinted from *Helix Seattle*. Interview uncredited in either publication, but I believe the journalist was Ed Leimbacher.

page 701: "Leon had a big thing . . ." Tashian/Rogan. London/Nashville, Tennessee: 1 June 2008.

page 701: "I was flown back from Nashville . . ." Corneal/Rogan. London/Winter Haven, Florida: 24 June 2007.

page 701: "She completely contradicted . . ." Over the years, the disagreements between the pair have centred on the recording process. Nuese told musician/writer Sid Griffin: "She and I disagreed on how to do things. She was into piecemeal recording, doing basic tracks then building stuff over them. I was into a thing, as Gram was, of recording the whole thing live." Hokom retorted to journalist/author Barney Hoskyns: "We pretty much cut the album live. It was, 'Let's go for that pure, raw sound that comes without too much fiddling around.' Only John insisted on doing his tracks separately."

page 702: "It was a Gram album . . ." Bob Buchanan, interviewed by David N. Meyer. *Twenty Thousand Roads – The Ballad Of Gram Parsons And His Cosmic American Music* (New York: Villard, 2007), p. 208.

page 703: "The choice of extraneous material . . ." One outtake from the sessions subsequently emerged – a rough version of Melvin Endsley's 'Knee Deep In The Blues', a track previously recorded by Guy Mitchell and Marty Robbins. It sounds like a rehearsal tape and probably was never in serious contention as an album track.

page 703: ". . . probably the best country album . . ." Parsons/Donkers. op cit.

page 704: "That was the heaviest emotional scene . . ." John Nuese, interviewed by Sid Griffin. *Gram Parsons: A Music Biography* (Pasadena, California: Sierra Records & Books, 1985), p. 52.

page 704: "According to Ross . . ." A frank account of the termination threat was provided by Ross in an interview included in Ben Fong-Torres'

Hickory Wind: The Life And Times Of Gram Parsons (London, Omnibus Press, 1991).

page 705: "Gram was always very influenced by Fred Neil . . ." Corneal/Rogan. London/Winter Haven, Florida: 24 June 2007.

page 705: "During their stay . . ." Previous biographies have tended to concertina Parsons' various trips to Winter Haven into one story. The various anecdotes provided by Jim Carlton, for instance, did not all occur in a single time frame. Over a period of three years' correspondence and interviews with him, I attempted to place his memories in correct chronological order using whatever secondary source material was available to provide some confirmation. The February 1968 *Playboy*, for example, was extremely useful here. The issue would have hit the stands some time in January and concert reports confirm that Parsons was gigging with the Byrds by the second or third week of February.

page 706: "Why don't you come with us now? . . ." Corneal/Rogan. London/Winter Haven, Florida: 24 June 2007.

page 706: "I can't, man . . ." ibid.

page 707: "It was a great album . . ." Gram Parsons, interviewed by Bud Scoppa, 1970. Original source unstated; the full interview was later featured in Sid Griffin's book.

page 707: "Gram's version of 'You Don't Miss Your Water' . . ." David N. Meyer. *Twenty Thousand Roads – The Ballad Of Gram Parsons And His Cosmic American Music* (New York: Villard, 2007), p. 258. A similar point was made by Spencer Leigh in an article on Parsons printed in *Country Music People* (September 2006), in which he said, "I prefer McGuinn's vocals, but then I have always loved his voice."

page 708: ". . . too much of that old Byrds' sound . . ." Parsons/Donkers, op cit.

page 708: ". . . this cat, the producer . . ." Parsons/Scoppa, op cit.

page 709: "I was left holding the bag . . ." Corneal/Rogan. London/Winter Haven, Florida: 24 June 2007.

page 710: "Suzi Jane Hokom said she . . ." ibid.

page 710: "It was timing . . ." ibid.

page 711: "The reason Gram and I were together . . ." Keith Richards, quoted in Victor Bockris. *Keith Richards: The Unauthorised* Biography (London: Omnibus Press, 2002), p. 120. Original source unidentified by author.

page 711: "Albert invited us . . ." Anthony Foutz, interviewed by the author. London/Westport, Mayo, Ireland: 16 September 2014.

page 711: ". . . the Andy Warhol . . ." ibid.

page 711: ". . . use of special effects . . ." "Why did they have to be 'special'?" Foutz asked himself. "Why not make them part of the visual narrative?"

page 712: "We were all interacting . . ." ibid.

page 712: "It wasn't about musicians . . ." ibid.
page 712: "It was like being in Marrakech . . ." ibid.
page 712: "I've found this beautiful boy! . . ." ibid.
page 713: "Michel had a big influence . . ." ibid.
page 713: "On 20 July . . ." Date documented in Bill Wyman (with Richard Havers) *Rolling With The Stones* (London: Dorling Kindersley, 2002), p. 307.
page 713: "We went up there . . ." Foutz/Rogan. London/Westport, Mayo, Ireland: 16 September 2014. The Stones' contingent returned to the UK and Parsons was probably fortunate to miss out on their autumn adventures, which were to have seismic ramifications on their story. In early September, Jagger and Anita Pallenberg started filming their parts in Donald Cammell's controversial film *Performance*, much to Keith Richards' affront. Brian Jones was back in court in the closing stages of his freefall and Marianne Faithfull had suffered a miscarriage. The intrigues are too convoluted even for an Endnote like this, but they have been discussed and dramatized in several Stones' biographies and rock star memoirs.
page 713: "Parsons . . . next move . . ." Prior to launching the Flying Burrito Brothers, Parsons contacted his old friend Richie Furay, then in the process of forming Poco. Parsons was eager to engage in some kind of collaboration, but the idea was never realized.
page 714: "Everything was really great . . ." Chris Hillman, interviewed by Pete Frame for 'The Grievous Angel' family tree, compiled in December 1981, printed in *The Complete Rock Family Trees* (London: Omnibus Press, 1993).
page 714: "To give you an example . . ." Hillman/Rogan. London: 28 April 1977.
page 714: "Gram wanted to show . . ." Foutz/Rogan. London/Westport, Mayo, Ireland: 16 September 2014.
page 715: ". . . funkier and older . . ." *Los Angeles Free Press*: 25 October 1969. Reprinted from *Helix Seattle*. Interview uncredited in either publication, but I believe the journalist was Ed Leimbacher.
page 716: "I had an alcohol problem . . ." Corneal/Rogan. London/Winter Haven, Florida: 24 June 2007.
page 716: "I never let drinking slow me down . . ." ibid.
page 716: "Here they were, both from Florida . . ." Chris Hillman, interviewed by Ben Fong-Torres. *Hickory Wind: The Life And Times Of Gram Parsons* (London, Omnibus Press, 1991), p. 107.
page 716: "I heard that . . ." Corneal/Rogan. London/Winter Haven, Florida: 24 June 2007.
page 717: "His dad was the town mayor . . ." Jim Carlton email to author dated 28 March 2009.
page 717: "Here [in Florida] when somebody said 'hillbilly' . . ." Corneal/Rogan. London/Winter Haven, Florida: 24 June 2007.

page 718: "I knew already that it was a big, awful joke . . ." Quoted in Pamela Des Barres. *I'm With The Band: Confessions Of A Groupie* (New York, Jove, 1987), p. 234.
page 718: "Do you remember the sacred sexuality . . ." ibid.
page 719: "There was a girl named Christine . . ." Hillman/Rogan. London: 28 April 1977.
page 719: "They were nice tunes . . ." Chris Ethridge, interviewed by the author. London/Meridian, Mississippi: 28 March 2009.
page 720: "I had that opening lick . . ." ibid.
page 721: "Larry Spector, the manager . . ." Chris Hillman, interviewed by Bruce Sylvester. *Goldmine*: 11 April 1997. The Christian mystic Edgar Cayce was known for predicting future events while in a trance.
page 721: "We predicted earthquakes . . ." Chris Hillman's notes, dated May 1988, featured on the CD, *The Best Of The Flying Burrito Brothers.*
page 723: "Gram Parsons is a good old boy . . ." Review by Stanley Booth. *Rolling Stone*: 17 May 1968. Parsons and Hillman were grateful for Stanley Booth's positive review in *Rolling Stone*, but carped at some of his lyric transcriptions. "It was a very comprehensive article," Parsons informed *Helix Seattle*, "except for the damn quotes from the songs, which were altogether wrong. '*Ventura* may be just my kind of town'. Really. 'I'm your *top*, I'm your old boy.' Jesus Christ, you cats. The words are '*Vancouver* . . .', 'I'm your *toy* . . .' Parsons wasn't misquoting the review; the mistakes were as stated, except that they were printed as "I'm you top", which Booth said was the "most effective" line on the album.
page 723: "If this were a time . . ." Reviewer Robert Christgau. *New York Times*: 8 June 1969.
page 724: ". . . never achieving a chart position . . ." *The Gilded Palace Of Sin* peaked at number 164 in *Billboard* whereas *Sweetheart Of The Rodeo* reached number 77.
page 724: "Even years later, the participants tended to reminisce about cards . . ." The best gambling tale is included in the preceding Michael Clarke chapter in this book. As Ethridge told me: "When we were on the train tour, we went through New Mexico and I think we stopped at Santa Fe. I found one of those coin purses with beads all around it. I was going to give it to my daughter. Anyhow we got back on the train and Michael was way down and losing about every hand [at poker]. I said, 'Here, Mike, I bought this a while ago, take it for good luck!' I threw it to him and he started winning and then he won every hand against Gram. I couldn't believe it. It was only when he got that little Indian purse with the beads on it. He said, 'It's magic!' Then he won another hand. Gram was so mad! He wanted to win badly. It wasn't about the money, he just wanted to win. It was so funny when Michael kept winning and winning. He had lost every hand before. Gram had been winning and really rubbing it in then, all of a sudden, Mike started

winning and he couldn't take it." Clarke, in his chapter, says the game took place at a hotel, but otherwise the accounts are similar. It's probable that the game took place in both places.

page 724: "In Philadelphia . . ." Chris Hillman, interviewed by Pete Frame for 'The Grievous Angel' family tree, compiled in December 1981, printed in *The Complete Rock Family Trees* (London: Omnibus Press, 1993).

page 725: "The Burritos seemed to have a really bright future . . ." ibid.

page 725: "*The Gilded Palace Of Sin* has won them . . ." Reviewer: Barrett Hansen. *Hit Parader* 64: November 1969. Hansen's argument was provocative, but well put. Although he assumed that they were photographed at an 'outhouse' on the front cover of *The Gilded Palace Of Sin* (it may well have been a shed of some kind), he understood the dilemmas they faced in 1969. "Instead of just doing their thing . . . they are trying so hard at being these two unlike things, rock and country . . . Like the combination of long, shaggy hair and custom-tailored C&W clothes; like having their album cover picture taken in front of an outhouse, and like inserting an obnoxious rock guitar, sounding like last year's Blue Cheer, into the gentle and fresh country sounds of 'Christine's Tune'. The words have their problems too . . . Dylan writes much better lyrics without being bothered by the culture gap as the Burrito Brothers obviously were. 'Hippie Boy', which closes the album, is a recitation in the manner of 'Deck Of Cards', and for the first three minutes or so it begins to look like the most effective and thoughtful statement anyone ever made about that culture gap. You want to have it played on every C&W station in the country, and have visions of it easing all the world's shorthair vs. longhair-type tension. And then they blow the whole thing at the climax, converting the whole thing into a cheap joke. The sing-along close of this tune ranks with the outhouse on the cover as a sophomore put-down of country ways."

page 725: "LiPuma played Gram some of the songs . . ." Steve Young, interviewed by the author. London/Nashville, Tennessee: 10 July 2007.

page 726: "A&M didn't know what to make of that album . . ." ibid.

page 726: "They've let us follow our concept . . ." *Fusion*: 26 March 1969.

page 727: ". . . strange women coming in and out . . ." Chris Hillman, interviewed by Judson Klinger and Greg Mitchell. *Crawdaddy*: October 1976.

page 727: "He wasn't a country bass player . . ." Gram Parsons, A&M promotional interview by Chuck Cassell: 3 March 1972.

page 727: "I suppose about the time he split . . ." ibid.

page 728: "Screaming pretensions . . ." Reviewer Ed Ochs. *Billboard*: 11 October 1969.

page 728: "Gram was playing 'Dark End Of The Street' . . ." Carlos Bernal, interviewed by the author. London/Los Angeles, California: 10 April 2008.

page 729: "Parsons shared a suite . . ." Foutz confirms that the suite number really was '4 F' – the same designation code that the draft board issued to those deemed unsuitable to serve in Vietnam.

page 729: "Go shoot something . . ." Foutz/Rogan. London/Westport, Mayo, Ireland: 16 September 2014. The original working title for the project was *Rutabaga Deluxe*, which Parsons partly borrowed for the FBB's second album, *Burrito Deluxe*. When the movie was mentioned in *Rolling Stone*, they titled it *Ecology 70*. Foutz had originally intended to make a documentary to test some of the special effects he had been working on with Douglas Trumbull.

page 729: ". . . photographer Andee Cohen . . ." As with so many of the people involved in the film, there was a long history between Foutz and Cohen. "I knew her since she was a teenager when she used to work in a boutique in Beverly Hills called Jax. Andee's sister was resident in Rome studying and Andee used to come and visit her. I would see her there. The next time I saw her was at director Roger Vadim's place. She was with James Fox and they were a couple." For a time, Cohen and Fox stayed at Cheyne Walk with Jagger and Faithfull, a period documented in various memoirs. Fox, of course, famously appeared alongside Jagger in *Performance*. Andee Cohen took some of the most powerful and expressive portrait shots of Parsons still in existence and she was a regular at Joshua Tree. "Andee was there all the time," Foutz recalls. "She took some really interesting photographs. It was like a tribal throwdown."

page 729: ". . . four cosmic kittens . . ." quoted in Ben Fong-Torres. *Hickory Wind: The Life And Times Of Gram Parsons* (London, Omnibus Press, 1991).

page 730: ". . . a *Wizard Of Oz* . . ." Leaflet for the *Saturation 70* Exhibition, The Horse Hospital, Bloomsbury, London: 6 September 2014.

page 730: "Gram liked the idea . . ." Foutz/Rogan. London/Westport, Mayo, Ireland: 16 September 2014.

page 730: "Everybody hung out . . ." ibid.

page 731: "McGuinn's complex . . ." ibid.

page 731: "He said, 'Take care of him . . .'" ibid.

page 731: "Only a few stills . . ." In a refreshingly groundbreaking article in *Mojo* 232 (March 2013), writer Chris Campion catalogued some of the lost scenes, accompanied by rare stills from photographers Tom Wilkes, Nancy Lee Andrews and Raeaane Rubenstein. In September 2014, an exhibition titled *Saturation 70* was presented at London's Horse Hospital with an introduction by Tony Foutz, Linda Leitch (née Lawrence) and her husband Donovan who played a set for those in attendance. The exhibition featured the remnants of the lost project: pages from Foutz's script, photos, production stills and, most unexpectedly, a five-minute showreel of selected scenes accompanied by the Flying Burrito Brothers' version of 'Wild Horses'.

page 732: "He was physically . . ." Stanley Booth, online interview with Jason Gross: July 2001.

page 733: "It was a great honour . . ." Jim Seiter, interviewed by the author. Redondo Beach, California: 28 July 1979. Seiter quoted almost the same Parsons quip to *Crawdaddy* (October 1976).

page 733: "Gram was over at Keith's house . . ." Bernie Leadon, interviewed by Judson Klinger and Greg Mitchell. *Crawdaddy*: October 1976.

page 733: "He was doing this mild cross-dressing . . ." Hillman/Hoskyns. *Mojo* 56: July 1998.

page 734: "He was almost like a lapdog . . ." Chris Hillman, interviewed by Bruce Sylvester. *Goldmine*: 11 April 1997.

page 734: "It's so weird . . ." Dolores Tickner (formerly McGuinn, née DeLeon), interviewed by the author. London/Tucson, Arizona: 13 January 2007.

page 734: "They pulled him over . . ." Roger McGuinn, interviewed by Judson Klinger and Greg Mitchell. *Crawdaddy*: October 1976.

page 734: ". . . love at first sight . . ." Gretchen Carpenter (formerly Parsons, née Burrell), interviewed for the DVD documentary *Gram Parsons Fallen Angel*, directed by Gandulf Hennig, 2006.

page 734: ". . . very charming . . ." ibid.

page 735: "a microcosm of society . . ." Mick Jagger, press conference for Rolling Stones' winter tour: 28 November 1969.

page 735: ". . . the only guy . . ." Keith Richards, interviewed for the DVD documentary *Gram Parsons Fallen Angel*, directed by Gandulf Hennig, 2006.

page 737: "The simple verities . . ." *Rolling Stone* review of the Flying Burrito Brothers at Altamont.

page 737: "Gram was kissing Michelle . . ." Stanley Booth. *The True Adventures Of The Rolling Stones* (London, William Heinemann, 1985).

page 738: "I had problems with Gram . . ." Jim Dickson, interviewed by the author. London/Costa Mesa, California: 24 May 2009.

page 738: "Gram and I just couldn't seem to hook up again . . ." Chris Hillman, interviewed by Pete Frame for 'The Grievous Angel' family tree, compiled in December 1981, printed in *The Complete Rock Family Trees* (London: Omnibus Press, 1993).

page 738: "The second album was a mistake . . ." Gram Parsons, A&M promotional interview by Chuck Cassell: 3 March 1972.

page 739: "Gram did a dynamite vocal . . ." Dickson/Rogan. London/Costa Mesa, California: 24 May 2009.

page 739: "All of a sudden . . ." ibid.

page 740: "At the last minute . . ." Jim Dickson, interviewed by the author. London/Costa Mesa, California: 10 January 2006.

page 741: "You're talking to the caustic one . . ." Chris Hillman, interviewed for the online website: *The Gram Parsons Project.*

page 741: "The thing Chris Hillman has never been able to face . . ." Jim Dickson, interviewed by the author. London/Maui, Hawaii: 3 August 1998. Dickson was basing this view largely on Hillman's onstage persona during the Byrds/Burritos period.
page 741: "By the time I got involved . . ." Jim Dickson, interviewed by the author. London/Costa Mesa, California: 30–31 July 2010.
page 743: "I can't really claim to have participated . . ." Gram Parsons, A&M promotional interview by Chuck Cassell: 3 March 1972.
page 743: "I wanted to see . . ." ibid.
page 744: "He hated to fly . . ." Chris Hillman, interviewed by Judson Klinger and Greg Mitchell. *Crawdaddy*: October 1976.
page 744: "I met Gram once . . ." Suzy Dick, interviewed by the author. London/Spokane, Washington: 11 May 1997.
page 744: "He wasn't strong enough . . ." Chris Hillman, interviewed by Sid Griffin. *Gram Parsons: A Music Biography* (Pasadena, California: Sierra Records & Books, 1985), p. 94.
page 745: "John, take me on that long white ride . . ." John Phillips with Jim Jerome. *Papa John* (London: Virgin, 1986)
page 745: "I love Chris . . ." Joey Stec, interviewed by the author. London/Los Angeles, California: 10/12 May 2009.
page 746: "Gram was so stoned . . ." Phil Kaufman, interviewed for the online website: *The Gram Parsons Project*.
page 746: "He was so out of it . . ." Hillman/Hoskyns. *Mojo* 56: July 1998.
page 746: "When our ways parted . . ." Chris Hillman, interviewed by Pete Frame for 'The Grievous Angel' family tree, compiled in December 1981, printed in *The Complete Rock Family Trees* (London: Omnibus Press, 1993).
page 746: "After *Burrito Deluxe* . . ." Dickson/Rogan. London/Costa Mesa, California: 10 January 2006.
page 747: "Gram was either drinking to forget . . ." Terry Melcher, interviewed by the author. London: 27 December 1977. Additional information: 28 December 1977.
page 747: "At the time we were living together . . ." Foutz/Rogan. London/Westport, Mayo, Ireland: 16 September 2014.
page 747–748: "I had been working with Terry . . ." Jim Dickson, interviewed by the author. London/Costa Mesa, California: 5 April 2009.
page 748: "They would think up great album titles . . ." Ginny Ganahl, interviewed by Judson Klinger and Greg Mitchell. *Crawdaddy*: October 1976.
page 748: "We were sitting around . . ." Tashian/Rogan. London/Nashville, Tennessee: 1 June 2008.
page 749: "I backed Gram . . ." Moon Martin, interviewed by the author. New York: February 1979. Part printed in *Dark Star* 20: May 1979.
page 750: "I did a couple . . ." *Life*, Keith Richards with James Fox (Weidenfeld & Nicolson, 2010), pp. 285–286.

page 750: "We took this cure . . ." ibid.
page 750: "The problem is . . ." Keith Richards, quoted in Philip Norman, *The Stones* (Elm Tree Books, 1984), p. 323.
page 751: ". . . feeling poorly . . ." Sam Hutt, interviewed by the author. London: 9 October 2007.
page 751: "Hey, that's Freddy Neil . . ." ibid.
page 751: "How did you know . . ." ibid.
page 751: "Who are you? . . ." ibid.
page 751: "I had an old copy . . ." ibid.
page 752: "In July, Parsons joined the party . . ." Parsons and Richards again bonded over their mutual love of country music, albeit with a diminishing collection of records at their fingertips. As Parsons recalled to Jan Donkers: "I got over to Europe and got together with Keith, but it was hard for us to find any contemporary country music records . . . I would bring as many as I could with me but they would get worn out or smashed or sat on or someone would pour champagne on them – after a while we got down to a pretty narrow collection."
page 752: "He was a physical wreck . . ." Jo Bergman, interviewed by Judson Klinger and Greg Mitchell. *Crawdaddy*: October 1976.
page 752: "I wouldn't prescribe . . ." Hutt/Rogan. London: 9 October 2007.
page 752: "Hutt preferred homeopathic medicine or Lomotil . . ." Hutt twice denied to me that he ever used Lomotil on Parsons. "We never used Lomotil for Gram!" he insists. Oddly, I have seen him quoted elsewhere saying the opposite.
page 752: "He loved it . . ." Hutt/Rogan. London: 9 October 2007.
page 752–753: "He'd just had a fix . . ." ibid.
page 753: "When somebody is turning blue . . ." ibid.
page 753: "Gretchen was clean . . ." ibid.
page 753: "It was the summertime . . ." Dunlop/Rogan. London/Cornwall: 12 January 2009.
page 754: "The first thing everybody said . . ." Eve Babitz, interviewed by Judson Klinger and Greg Mitchell. *Crawdaddy*: October 1976.
page 754: "He blew up . . ." Hillman/Hoskyns. *Mojo* 56: July 1998.
page 754: "Gram had supposedly quit smack . . ." Chris Hillman, interviewed by Ben Fong-Torres. *Hickory Wind: The Life And Times Of Gram Parsons* (London, Omnibus Press, 1991).
page 755: "Playing the artistic matchmaker . . ." This account of the introduction to Harris was related to the author by Chris Hillman. London: 28 April 1977. In several interviews, Harris also credits her babysitter for offering Gram her number. "The timing was amazing. You can be as cynical as you want in life but certain things happen that make you believe in synchronicity. The only reason Gram got my phone number was the gal who babysat for me happened to be at the show in Baltimore where he had come to see his old pals, the Burrito Brothers. She overheard them saying that they'd seen this girl who sang pretty good, but

they didn't know how to get in touch with her. And Tina just spoke up and said, 'Oh, I have her number.' Like they say, truth is stranger than fiction." (*Uncut* 124: August 2007).

page 755: "We went down to the cellar . . ." Emmylou Harris, interviewed by Peter Doggett. *Are You Ready For The Country* (London, Viking, 2000), p. 149.

page 756: "On 15 June 1972 . . ." Oddly the agreement appears to have been post-dated. The small print confirms that it supplanted a Letter of Agreement between Warners and Parsons dated 20 June 1972, five days after the date of the contract.

page 757: "Costs of any session . . ." ibid.

page 758: "Gram was drinking heavily . . ." Eddie Tickner, interviewed by the author. Redondo Beach, California: 20 July 1979. Additional interview: 22 July 1979. Although Haggard may have had reservations about Parsons' excessive drinking, he was not about to elevate him to outlaw status. Interviewed by Mark Rose in 1980 for San Francisco magazine *BAM*, Haggard bridled when it was suggested that Parsons might have been a little "too wild". "He was a pussy," Merle retorted. "Hell, he was just a long-haired kid. I thought he was a good writer. He was not wild, though. That's what was funny to me. All these guys running around in long hair talk about being wild and Rolling Stones. I don't think someone abusing themselves on drugs necessarily determines how *wild* they are. It might determine how *ignorant* they are." Parsons, who was reportedly shell-shocked by Haggard's rejection at the time, later looked back on the incident with a resigned air. "We were talking about the concept of him doing an album with me," he told Chuck Cassell. "He never really let on that he knew what it was, but he wanted to do it . . . then we both figured that we didn't have enough time. He's got his own way of doing things, and I've got my own way, and for the two of them to blend, it would take longer than I have the budget for, frankly. And I just don't want to stay up that much. I need my sleep."

page 758: "He was ill . . ." Gretchen Carpenter (formerly Parsons, née Burrell), interviewed by Barney Hoskyns. *Mojo* 56: July 1998.

page 758: "As we're coming to the door . . ." Stec/Rogan. London/Los Angeles, California: 10/12 May 2009.

page 759: "Everybody loved Sid . . ." Tickner/Rogan. Redondo Beach, California: 20 July 1979.

page 759: "He was the connection . . ." Foutz/Rogan. London/Westport, Mayo, Ireland: 16 September 2014.

page 759: ". . . two parts sugar . . ." Judson Klinger and Greg Mitchell. *Crawdaddy*: October 1976.

page 759: "He was doing a lot of reds . . ." Surratt/Rogan. London/Los Angeles, California: 27–28 February 2007.

page 760: "I was right in the middle of nowhere . . ." Hutt/Rogan. London: 9 October 2007.

page 760: "They were my kind of people . . ." ibid.

page 761: "Rick and Gram went through this rebonding . . ." Jenny Grech, interviewed by Peter Doggett. *Record Collector* 181: September 1994.

page 761: ". . . not just to do my album . . ." Hutt/Rogan. London: 9 October 2007.

page 761: "Rick and Gram were seriously into smack . . ." ibid.

page 761: "That was what I called . . ." Jenny Grech/Doggett. *Record Collector* 181: September 1994.

page 762: "Amid a scrawling mess of drunken doodlings . . ." Parsons' journals are a frustrating read, full of tantalizing pieces of information. At one point, he writes a 'Chart For Start' mentioning a dream team of musicians including Clarence White, Larry Knechtel, Sneeker (presumably Sneaky Pete Kleinow), Mac Dowell, Bobby Keyes, Junior Parker, Jimmy Karstein, Don Randi and 'Jesse' (bass/sax). Plus 'Keith's slide guitar'.

page 762: ". . . there are set lists . . ." The set lists, unpublished elsewhere, may be of interest to fans of the Flying Burrito Brothers. One typical set list (venue unstated) reads: 'Lazy Days', 'Cody, Cody', 'Image Of Me', 'High Fashion Queen', 'My Uncle', 'If You Gotta Go', 'Six Days On The Road', 'Honky Tonk Women', 'To Love Somebody', 'Hot Burrito # 1', 'Older Guys', 'Together Again', 'Down In The Churchyard', 'Bonie Moronie' and 'If You Want Me'. Another set follows this same pattern but includes the surprise addition of 'Heartbreak Hotel'. There's also a set from the Troubadour which includes a couple of oddities. It reads: 'Lazy Days', 'Wheels', 'Down In The Churchyard', 'Image Of Me', 'Man In The Fog', 'If You Gotta Go', 'Cody, Cody', 'Hot Burrito # 1', 'Break My Mind', 'Older Guys', 'Undo The Wrong', 'Common' (presumably 'Love Of The Common People'), 'Wild Horses', 'Hot Burrito # 2', 'Dream Baby', 'Honky Tonk Women', 'God's Own Singer', 'My Uncle', 'Atomic Power', 'Git Ourselves T', 'Older Guys', 'Man In The Fog', 'Down In The Churchyard'. In case anyone asks, 'Atomic Power' and 'Git Ourselves T' are a mystery to me too.

In a later section of the journals, Parsons lists four songs, presumably for performance: 'Lookin' For A New Mama', 'Washita Love Child', 'I Ain't No Beatle' (4/4+ Shuffle) and 'White Line Fever'. This is followed by a nine-song listing: 'I Fall To Pieces', 'White Line Fever', 'Yours, Love', 'Do Right Woman', 'Sleepless Nights', 'Family Bible', 'She Thinks I Still Care', 'It's All Wrong' and 'Sweet Dream Baby'. Finally, there is a further 11-song listing, featuring "I'm Still Feeling Blue', 'I Can't Keep My Heart', 'Zah's Blues', '$1,000 Wedding', 'Uncle Al', 'Echoes', 'Two Hearts', 'Lake Monster', 'Just As I Am', 'Okie Song', 'Widow Maker' and 'Act Naturally'.

page 762: "It had almost become a routine . . ." Emmylou Harris, interviewed by Peter Doggett. *Are You Ready For The Country* (London, Viking, 2000), p. 151.

page 762: "I was amazed to say the least . . ." ibid.
page 763: "It was a phone call out of the blue . . ." Tashian/Rogan. London/Nashville, Tennessee: 1 June 2008.
page 763: "I got pretty drunk that night . . ." ibid.
page 765: "I have no idea . . ." ibid.
page 765: "We'd been sitting in Gram's living room . . ." ibid.
page 765: "Sometimes I felt like we were . . ." Harris/Doggett. *Are You Ready For The Country* (London, Viking, 2000), p. 153.
page 766: "James Burton and I did twin parts . . ." Al Perkins, quoted in John M. Delgatto's liner notes for *GP/Grievous Angel* CD, 1990.
page 766: ". . . sort of funky country . . ." Hugh Davies, quoted in John M. Delgatto's liner notes for *GP/Grievous Angel* CD, 1990.
page 766: "The subject is that people . . ." Gram Parsons, quoted in Ben Fong-Torres' *Hickory Wind: The Life And Times Of Gram Parsons* (London, Omnibus Press, 1991). Original source uncertain and not stated.
page 766: "The song's basically about people getting ripped off . . ." Gram Parsons, interviewed by Maxine Sartori. WBCN Radio: *c.* February/March 1973.
page 767: "He helped with the verse . . ." Ethridge/Rogan. London/Meridian, Mississippi: 28 March 2009.
page 767: "I had the part about . . ." ibid.
page 768: "Parsons was the kind of person . . ." Hillman/Hoskyns. *Mojo* 56: July 1998.
page 769: "Nor would Rick Grech or Barry Tashian . . ." As Jenny Grech revealed to writer Peter Doggett: "After a few months away from Gram, Rick had come to see that it wasn't safe for him to follow Gram any further. He loved him, but it was too dangerous. So he turned down the chance to go on the road."
page 769: "They played Turkish Dixieland music . . ." Corneal/Rogan. London/Winter Haven, Florida: 24 June 2007.
page 769: "We couldn't even play one song . . ." Emmylou Harris, interviewed for *The Emmylou Harris Story*, BBC Radio 2: 29 April 2006.
page 769: "When Gram was together . . ." ibid.
page 770: "I was put on a converted Greyhound bus . . ." Emmylou Harris, quoted in the sleeve notes of Gram Parsons' CD *Sleepless Nights*.
page 770: "Before then, I had been intrigued . . ." Emmylou Harris, interviewed for *The Emmylou Harris Story*, BBC Radio 2: 29 April 2006.
page 772–773: "After the break . . ." Gretchen Carpenter (formerly Parsons, née Burrell), interviewed for the DVD documentary *Gram Parsons Fallen Angel*, directed by Gandulf Hennig, 2006.
page 773: ". . . Sid Kaiser had died of a heart attack . . ." Apologies to the reader for failing to provide the exact date of Kaiser's death. I was unable to unearth any published obituary or death certificate, and none of my interviewees was entirely sure which month he passed away, although several confirm it was around the time of Clarence White's

death. Unlike the UK where details of all birth, marriages and deaths are available at the Registrars' Office, there is no central office in the US which lists these. It is a very time consuming, frustrating and expensive process to track down some of these elusive dates, particularly when the subject is relatively obscure. According to Eddie Tickner, Kaiser died in Palm Springs from heart failure. If anyone has additional information confirming the precise date of death, please contact me via the publishers so that I can include the details in a future edition. Thanks.

page 773: "Death is a warm cloak . . ." Gram Parsons interview, dated July 1973. Selections from this interview were later used in the groundbreaking 1976 *Crawdaddy* article by Judson Klinger and Greg Mitchell. No biographer or commentator has since located the original tape or specific source of the quote.

page 774: "There was a lot of energy . . ." Emory Gordy, interviewed by Pete Frame, using his secret 'Mac Garry' pseudonym. *Zigzag* 59: April 1976.

page 774: "Gram's style was to start a number . . ." Emmylou Harris, interviewed by Pete Frame, using his secret 'Mac Garry' pseudonym. *Zigzag* 59: April 1976.

page 774: "The song was done in maybe two takes . . ." ibid.

page 775: "I was an energy source . . ." ibid.

page 775: "There is a general consensus . . ." One dissenting voice is Phil Kaufman's then girlfriend, Kathy Fenton, who is quoted in David N. Meyer's book (pp. 414–415) as witnessing Gram shooting up after the sessions were completed. Of course, this harrowing account might have been chronologically awry and happened earlier than Meyer assumes. Alternatively, it could have been a one-off fix. It may sound naïve to assume the latter, but reading Fenton's account, there is palpable sense of shock on her part and it ends with Parsons promising never to shoot up again. As described, the incident appears as exceptional rather than commonplace.

page 776: "Yet, this is contradicted by Fisher . . ." Ben Fong-Torres interviewed both Dale McElroy and Alan Barbary in *Hickory Wind*, but could not reach Margaret Fisher. David N. Meyer spoke to Fisher for *Twenty Thousand Roads*, but did not interview McElroy or Barbary. However, the accounts complement each other very well, with Fisher providing some frank and revealing details about Parsons shooting up and reiterating the presence of a drug dealer earlier in the day. Fong-Torres, unlike Meyer, quotes directly from Fisher's statement to the coroner, some details of which appear to contradict her more recent account, mainly concerning the length of time she was absent getting food and coffee. Was it 20 minutes as she told Meyer, or approximately 2 hours and 45 minutes as allegedly told to the coroner? Meyer chooses not to address or comment on these contradictions, although he favours her later testimony.

page 776–777: "A urinalysis showed . . ." Ben Fong-Torres consulted Dr Margaret Greenwald of the San Francisco Coroner's Office who after reviewing the blood tests and other details of the autopsy report agreed that the coroner of San Bernardino County "had come to a proper conclusion". Meyer cites no medical authority but, sensibly in my view, does not contest the coroner's report. Other commentators, clearly without access to the medical documentation and having spoken to none of Parsons' family or people involved in the death scene, have added some confusing conjecture. In the book *God's Own Singer*, Jason Walker claimed, "Gram had been prescribed an epilepsy medication called Phenobartibatal, for controlling the seizures that he had been experiencing as a result of his 1970 motorcycle accident." No source is given for this claim, which neither appears in the medical reports nor, to my knowledge, in any comment by anyone connected with Parsons. I can only imagine the author *assumed* that Parsons was using Phenobarbital because that's what he might have been prescribed for his alleged seizures. In which case, this assumes a lot without foundation. Interestingly, the only person ever to claim Parsons had seizures in the first place was his wife Gretchen. No one else has testified to this among his circle, although several have noted his shakes and slurred speech. Whether Parsons actually suffered seizures or something else remains conjectural. Gretchen has added that Parsons did not visit doctors and no known documentation survives to confirm whether or not he was taking any prescription medicine. To underline the dangers of lazy extrapolation, another more recent book, which includes some derivative chapters on Parsons, casually mentions he had epilepsy. This seems to have been a misreading of Walker, who mentioned the phrase 'epilepsy medication', without ever stating categorically that Parsons had epilepsy. Cutting through all this, I see no reason to add to what Fong-Torres wrote about the cause of death back in 1991, which still appears the most reliable and authoritative account on the medical aspects.

page 777: "On 20 September . . ." Cited in *Polly Parsons v. Edward Tickner et al*, Superior Court of Los Angeles County, No. BC055886, before Judge Jerold A. Krieger.

page 778: "The state of Louisiana's Napoleonic Law . . ." Judson Klinger and Greg Mitchell. *Crawdaddy*: October 1976.

page 778: "Instead the story was carried forward . . ." Even the normally diligent Ben Fong-Torres accepted this assertion without comment. In *Hickory Wind*, he repeats the *Crawdaddy* claim literally verbatim, copying their entire first sentence, then barely altering a word in the second sentence: "The state of Louisiana's Napoleonic Law stipulates that male survivors are the sole inheritors of any estate. Apparently, Bob wanted a body to help him establish a New Orleans residency for Gram." Given the forensic care with which Fong-Torres dealt with the circumstances of Gram's death and the medical details he pointed out so carefully, this lapse seems strange. He accepts the negative comments on Bob Parsons, as if they are fact, without bothering to comment upon their veracity or considering whether they make any legal sense. Amazingly, it was not until as late as 1997 that an alternate view was aired. David Meyer first challenged this claim in *Twenty Thousand Roads*. Like me, he was mystified by the constant references to a "Napoleonic Law" and "male survivors". As he confidently concluded: "Those assertions are mistaken. The location of Gram's body had no effect on any litigation Bob might pursue. Given that Gram was married, Bob Parsons had no standing . . . The facts indicate that Bob's only desire was to do right by his dead stepson." Indeed, it should be added that even if Parsons had been domiciled in Louisiana and there were grounds for contesting his 'separate property' under the Napoleonic Code, these assets would have gone to Avis (and probably Diane) Parsons, with Bob receiving nothing.

page 778: "Police were informed that the body had been stolen . . ." The police wasted no time investigating the matter. One person questioned was Parsons' old friend and former bandmate from the Shilos, Paul Surratt. "That was a strange thing," Surratt told me. "I think I heard about his death on the radio. I went over to the house where he was supposed to be, and that's when the coffin was stolen. He was gone. I didn't know what was going on. I heard that the body was going to be at the airport, so I drove down there to see his dad [Bob Parsons]. And they acted really weird at the airport. I didn't know what was going on. I didn't see his father. I couldn't find him, so I went back to my apartment. Then I got a call from the police saying, 'Are you Paul Surratt and are you wearing this and that?' I still had the same clothes on and I said, 'yeah'. They asked, 'Were you just down here at the airport asking questions about Gram Parsons?' I said, 'Yes I was. What's going on?' Then I was asked: 'Do you know anything about Mr Parsons' body being stolen?' I went, 'What?!' Then he said, 'Tell me about your relationship with him.' So I started from the beginning telling him we were in a group together – and he says, 'No, no, lately in the last couple of days or weeks!' I said, 'Well, I haven't seen Gram in six or eight months. I knew his father and I came down to see his dad before his body left.' He said, 'OK, never mind.' I asked, 'What's going on?' and he said, 'I can't get into that' or something. The next day it was all over the paper. It was really weird."

page 779: "It's like something out of Transylvania . . ." Klinger/Mitchell. *Crawdaddy*: October 1976.

page 780: "We played some music together . . ." Tashian/Rogan. London/Nashville, Tennessee: 1 June 2008.

page 783: "Who knows what was going on . . ." Emmylou Harris, quoted in Parke Puterbaugh's liner notes to Gram Parsons' *The Complete Reprise Sessions.*

page 785: "It was both the beginning and the end . . ." Emmylou Harris, interviewed by Spencer Leigh. 'Gram Parsons Behind the Legend 2'. *Country Music People*: October 2006.
page 785: "There are people who had already decided . . ." Emmylou Harris, interviewed for *The Emmylou Harris Story*, BBC Radio 2: 29 April 2006.
page 786: "He acted real strange . . ." Leedy/Rogan. London/Winter Haven, Florida: 20 May 2009.
page 786: "He always used to say . . ." ibid.
page 787: ". . . this creepy thing . . ." Chris Hillman, quoted in *Hot Burritos*, John Einarson with Chris Hillman (Jawbone, 2008), pp. 315–316.
page 787: "I've read . . ." ibid.
page 787: "That's just the scar tissue . . ." Foutz/Rogan. London/Westport, Mayo, Ireland: 16 September 2014.
page 787: "All this darkness . . ." Booth/Gross: July 2001.
page 789: "But the sheet containing the poem was saved . . ." It must have been since the album was not recorded until one month after the fire.
page 789: "It wasn't plagiarism . . ." Eddie Tickner, interviewed by the author. Tucson, Arizona: 28 October 2005.
page 790: ". . . his signature song . . ." Chris Hillman, quoted in the CD liner notes of Gram Parsons' *Sacred Hearts & Fallen Angels.*
page 790: "I was completely flabbergasted . . ." Sylvia Sammons, internet interview by David W. Johnson for "Crediting 'Hickory Wind'" on www.folklinks.com.
page 790: "I think, other than principle . . ." ibid.
page 791: ". . . with the help of a friend . . ." ibid.
page 791: "We do not keep . . ." ibid.
page 791: "I was there . . ." Carlton/Rogan. London/Mount Dora, Florida: 5 March 2007.
page 793: ". . . possibly Skip Battin . . ." Deposition of Saul Davis, taken at 2049 Century Park East, Suite 950, Los Angeles, California, before Lana L. Loper, commencing at 10 am: 27 August 1996.
page 793: "Sony had no balls . . ." Dickson/Rogan. London/Hawaii: 7 July 1997.
page 793: "Judge Jerold A. Krieger of the Superior Court of Los Angeles dismissed the action . . ." See Polly Parsons, Plaintiff and Appellant v. Edward Tickner *et al*, Defendants and Respondents, Superior Court of Los Angeles County, Case no. BC055886.
page 794: "On 2 February 1995, Polly Parsons v. Edward Tickner *et al* was revisited at the Court of Appeal . . ." One anomaly in the Appeal Court document is a reference to Polly Parsons' mother Nancy as being married to Gram. This is both surprising and confusing. In every written account of her relationship with Parsons (including the one co-written by her daughter Polly), we are told that they lived together, then split. Parsons evidently proposed marriage later on, although his motives in

doing so have been questioned. Supposedly a date was set, 31 January 1969, but no ceremony took place. The song '$1000 Wedding' is sometimes assumed to have been partly inspired by the incident, probably wrongly. Nancy Lee Ross allegedly took the name Parsons, which her daughter Polly also retained. Unsurprisingly, this has led to occasional confusion, although one would hardly expect a legal document to make such a serious slip. Then again, chroniclers of Parsons' life have not been immune to doublethink. In an extraordinary lapse of narrative logic, writer Jason Walker (see page 61 of his book *God's Own Singer*) refers to Parsons' treatment of his 'wife', adding "Nancy's faith in her *young husband* was shaken to the core". Bizarrely, six lines later, he contradicts himself by speaking of their "wedding plans" and now calls her his "pregnant *girlfriend*". Thereafter in the text, she remains a "girlfriend' and there is no further reference to Parsons as a "young husband".

page 796: "In any of these conversations . . ." and following examination. Deposition of Saul Davis, taken at 2049 Century Park East, Suite 950, Los Angeles, California, before Lana L. Loper, commencing at 10 am: 27 August 1996.

page 798: "Eddie couldn't find the contracts . . ." Dickson/Rogan. London/Hawaii: 7 July 1997.

page 798: "He was the songwriter . . ." Dickson/Rogan. London/Costa Mesa, California: 24 May 2009.

page 799: "In our conversation . . ." Hand delivered letter from James H. Berry, Jr of Berry & Cahalan, A Law Corporation, to Neville L. Johnson, Esq, dated 29 August 1996.

page 799: "Dear Eddie . . ." Letter from James H. Berry, Jr of Berry & Cahalan, A Law Corporation, to Edward Tickner, dated 5 September 1996.

page 799: "Eddie was so exhausted . . ." Dickson/Rogan. London/Costa Mesa, California: 10 January 2006.

page 799: ". . . it cost us about $120,000 . . ." Dickson/Rogan. London/Hawaii: 7 July 1997.

page 800: "If I wasn't here . . ." ibid.

5

CLARENCE WHITE

7 June 1944 – 15 July 1973

REVERENCE and respect are two words that spring instantly to mind when recalling the character and music of Clarence White. Understandably, his premature death at the age of 29 invites valedictions but, even taking these into account, the admiration expressed by critics, contemporaries and colleagues is remarkably consistent and heartfelt. Unlike his pioneering contemporary Gram Parsons, White's standing has been largely untouched by the cult of celebrity death. There are no books, television documentaries or films commemorating his life and work. The few articles acknowledging his importance tend to be found in specialist guitar or country magazines, and reissues of his work remain the provenance of small, independent labels.

Almost everyone who knew him argues that he is still underappreciated by a rock world more easily impressed by ego and grand gestures. White was always the master of understatement, a modest, behind-the-scenes player who came to prominence as a latter-day Byrd and entranced a generation with his guitar skills and breathtaking innovation. He helped introduce many, including myself, to a hitherto unknown musical terrain of authentic bluegrass and an intriguing parallel world of Bakersfield International country/pop. Equally importantly, he helped revitalize and virtually reinvent the Byrds at a time when they faced imminent extinction. It was largely his unflappable personality and inventive musicianship that stabilized the group at the end of the Sixties and unexpectedly transformed them into one of the best live acts of their time. Arguably the least ego-driven of all the Byrds, he remains the only member to have avoided offending somebody, somewhere along the line. In a band as volatile as the Byrds, this combination of diplomacy and musicianship was a unique trait.

Clarence's appreciation and understanding of group dynamics owed much to his upbringing in a talented musical family. Before they anglicized their name in 1939, the Whites were known under the more familiar French-Canadian monicker, LeBlanc. Originally from New Brunswick, Canada, Eric LeBlanc was one of 17 children, 14 of whom survived into adulthood. Music was second nature to the LeBlancs who regularly played music at home. Eric was adept at fiddle, banjo, guitar and harmonica and enjoyed collecting and trading instruments. Along with several of his siblings, he worked for his father in the construction trade, building houses in Maine. Just before the outbreak of World War II, he married Mildred Marie Cyr, who shared his love of country music. Their first son, Roland, was born in 1938, followed by a daughter, Joanne in 1939, then Eric (1942) and Clarence Joseph LeBlanc (1944). A second daughter, Rosemarie, the baby of the clan, arrived as late as 1955.

During the War, Eric served his time as a welder and pipe fitter on ships before returning to construction work and road building. His brother, Johnny, encouraged his interest in traditional music, as did their Uncle Willie (William), who lived in nearby Portland, Maine. "We used to go there on a Sunday afternoon and he'd take out his fiddle and play until you left," remembers Roland. "He knew a lot of tunes and my dad learned a lot of them from him. He played many Canadian tunes and there was a guy named Albert Sphere in Lewiston who played fiddle too. So we had Canadian and American tunes like 'Soldier's Joy', 'Ragtime Annie', 'Rubber Dolly', 'Born In Cabbagetown', 'Red Wing' and 'Golden Slippers'. My parents also had a collection of 78 rpm records so we used to hear music all the time. My dad would sit around, play the fiddle or strum the guitar and sing pitiful country songs. He'd play a couple of his favourite country tunes every morning before he went to work and I'd always listen to them."

Before long, the child Roland attempted to emulate his father by playing the fiddle but found he could not master the bow. He showed greater promise on flat-top guitar, but preferred a smaller instrument. Impressed by his efforts, Eric Senior bought him a mandolin and soon father and son were spending the mornings strumming together. Meanwhile, Joanne was displaying precocious talent as a singer, improving with each passing year. "I used to sing, just following [what was on] the radio," she recalls. "That was between the age of eight and ten." Clarence could barely talk while all this was happening, but recognized that his elders were having fun. Shortly after enrolling at school, he made his first tentative steps towards the music makers.

"It was 1949–50," Roland remembers. "Clarence was about five years old. I was sitting on the couch strumming the guitar and Joanne and I were singing. Now she really liked to sing. Clarence walked by and when we finished, he said, 'I want to do that!' So I then had him up next to me by my right side. I handed him a pick and he started strumming. I did the chords. I had the harmonica and played a simple tune. From then on, he wanted to play all the time."

Eric Snr had been at work when this epiphany occurred but laughed when Roland and Joanne enthusiastically related the story later that evening. The father was so pleased that he went straight out and purchased Clarence a ukulele. "Clarence started strumming along almost every time we played. When Eric [Jr] saw that Clarence was getting into the music with us, he decided that he wanted to do it. My dad fixed him up with a tenor banjo, and he started singing too." Before long, Clarence abandoned the ukulele in favour of the guitar.

Rural Maine offered few distractions from music and during snowbound days time was suspended as the family immersed themselves in singing and playing everything they knew. Roland listened to radio singers with covetous wonder, confiding to his mother his dream of following suit as a musician. Ever practical, she responded with a single watchword: "Practise". It was a message he dutifully passed on to Clarence and Eric whenever they were distracted by outdoor pursuits, which wasn't often. With Joanne adding string bass to her singing skills, the quartet suddenly found themselves with sufficient instrumentation and confidence to play in front of an audience. "It was Roland's idea for me to play bass," says Joanne. "I wasn't very good at it, but I tried. I don't even know where it came from. I imagine my father or Roland must have bought it."

The first known public performance by the White siblings took place at China Lake, Maine, sometime in 1952, in the unlikely setting of a 'grange hall'. Originally a pressure group for American farmers, the National Grange of the Order of Patrons of Husbandry, founded in 1867, encouraged rural communities to form cooperatives in order to protect themselves from economic and political injustices. Successful lobbying led to the passing of the Granger laws, which assisted farmers in various ways by establishing railroad commissions, regulating grain stores and mills and providing rural mail deliveries. Over the decades, the movement had gradually shed its militancy to become a largely social organization. Grange halls were the hub of the community, offering musical entertainment, charity concerts, Christmas pantomimes and private functions for its members. It was a pleasant enough environment for a group of youngsters to test their musical mettle. "These grange halls often had functions," Roland remembers. "My dad's brother-in-law had an uncle there who told them about us. We were brought there by my dad and we sat on chairs and played three or four tunes for them. That's all I remember. We went back again another time. Clarence had left his guitar against a wall and somebody leaned on it and broke the neck off. They got a collection going for us and somehow we replaced the guitar."

Clarence never got a chance to repay that favour with another show as the Whites were soon on the move. Eric Snr was experiencing difficulty finding work in Maine and sought the counsel of his extended family. Roland remembers his Aunt Alma and Uncle Armand, who'd moved to Burbank, California in 1952, reporting back with the encouraging entreaty: "There's plenty of work out here if you want to come."

In August 1954, the Whites loaded all their transportable effects into a Nash Rambler and headed for the Golden State. It was a five-day marathon trip. As promised, the father soon found gainful employment as a carpenter and ended up working at the Lockheed Aircraft Corporation where he would remain until his retirement over a decade later. The children adjusted to life in California very quickly, partly thanks to another lucky break. Within two weeks of their arrival, Aunt Alma happened to mention hearing about a talent show, sponsored by the radio station KXLA, Pasadena. They wasted no time checking it out and were amazed to be invited to perform on the Sunday afternoon show. Hosted by disc jockey Carl Deacon Moore, better known by his glorious nickname, the 'Squeaking Deacon', the show was broadcast from the premier Western swing music venue, the Riverside Rancho, situated on Riverside Drive on the fringes of Griffith Park. The White brothers played a spirited version of 'Ragtime Annie' and were thrilled to win first prize: a prestigious spot on country music DJ Bert 'Foreman' Phillips' television programme *County Barn Dance*, previously presented by Ralph T. Hicks, later executive director of the California Country Music Association. In preparation for this epoch, the show's producer gave the brothers a quaint make-over. Joanne recalls how "they dressed them up as little farmers and as they were little, they started calling them the Three Little Country Boys." The boys were thrilled to be in the company of such country stars as Lefty Frizzell, Bob Wills and the husband and wife duo Joe and Rose Lee Maphis.

With their new stage name, the group soon became regulars at the Riverside Rancho, and Joanne was invited to join them for their radio appearances. "I was like the guest sister," she says, "but I think they still called them the Country Boys whether there was a girl there or not. We used to go to the Riverside Rancho every

Sunday and it went out live over the radio. The place was full up and they used to yell out for more. I was pretty nervous, that's for certain." A photo taken during a performance on that show, captures this early zenith: Joanne, the featured vocalist, stands out front, centre stage, resplendent in a flared skirt and a sleeveless top, setting off her dark shoulder-length hair; behind her, dressed in farm overalls and white hats, are the three brothers; Eric is playing a large double bass, Roland smiles while strumming his mandolin, and on the far right stands the pint-sized Clarence, deadly serious as he stretches his small arms to accommodate a recently purchased acoustic guitar.

Soon, the boys settled at school and Roland supplemented his income packing groceries at Alexander's grocery market. The media contacts brought further performing opportunities, most notably the marathon *Rocket To Stardom*, the sole occasion that Joanne appeared with her brothers on television. Sponsored by a local car dealer, the show ran for six hours every Saturday on KHT, resuming at 11 pm for two more hours before switching to KTTV at 1 am, where it continued until 8.30 on Sunday morning. The congenial host, Bob Yeakel, enjoyed encouraging amateur talent and claimed that over 1,500 youngsters got their first break on his show, although few actually 'rocketed to stardom'. Joanne's rendition of the 1953 Hank Williams' hit 'Kaw-Liga' secured the group a first place finish. Away from the stage, the Whites attended regular get-togethers at friends' houses, where musical ideas were shared. Roland was surprised how quickly Clarence was assimilating new tunes. "He had an arch-topped Gretsch guitar and I could hear him playing 'Wildwood Flower' in his bedroom. I said, 'Can I join you? I want to play that too.' It was the first song we ever played melody on, although we didn't get to play it in public until as late as 1959." Clarence's inspiration was Mother Maybelle Carter whose solos on 'Wildwood Flower' influenced a legion of aspiring guitarists. It was an early indication of the direction he would take as a lead and rhythm player.

Back at the Rancho, Eric Snr ingratiated himself with Homer

Cleary, an Oklahoman fiddler, who generously taught the boys several key fiddle tunes for their repertoire, including 'Black Mountain Rag', 'Crazy Creek' and 'Home Sweet Home'. Clarence dutifully worked out the arrangements after endlessly listening to records loaned by Cleary. Meanwhile, the brothers discarded their hillbilly farm clothes and sought a more modern image courtesy of country tailor to the stars, Nudie Cohn.

Born in the Ukraine in 1902, Nuta Kotlyarenko had escaped the Jewish pogroms and emigrated to the USA, after which he established himself opening the New York store Nudie's, which specialized in erotic sequins and underwear for burlesque showgirls. In 1957, Cohn moved to California and set up Nudie's Rodeo Tailors on Lankershim Boulevard in North Hollywood which provided ostentatious western wear for such country stars as Roy Rogers, Hank Williams, Buck Owens and Porter Wagoner. Nudie's colourful rhinestone outfits became more ornate with each passing month and he famously designed Elvis Presley's iconic gold lamé suit. A year before the Presley commission, the White family invested in cowboy boots, belts and neckerchiefs. For Clarence and his brothers, this was cachet in excelsis – smart but subtle threads with no vulgar excesses, neatly complementing their music.

The early days in Burbank promised great things but this brief idyll was unexpectedly shattered by a major setback which threatened the future of the family group. Joanne, the main singer and focal centre of the quartet, suddenly found she had more pressing commitments which took her away from the music and prompted a premature retirement. As Roland explains: "Well, at a young age she met this man who was a few years older than her and got pregnant, so she didn't play anymore. It kind of broke that up which was really sad. And she ended up marrying at a very young age, 16 or 17, maybe younger." Joanne's first son, Richard, was born in July 1957, just two months before her eighteenth birthday. "My world pretty much turned upside down," she says. "But, no, I didn't have dreams of stardom. I really didn't have it in me, but they did."

The brothers continued performing as the quaintly titled Three Little Country Boys, but their musical horizons were expanding. Roland was still listening to country music until the day Uncle Armand enquired: "Have you heard of Bill Monroe? He's the mandolin player on the *Grand Ole Opry* and he plays fast." Roland was sufficiently intrigued to investigate and was amazed to find a bulging catalogue of Monroe's recordings at a Burbank record store. As an almost arbitrary choice he ordered a single, 'Pike County Breakdown'. He had no idea what a 'breakdown' was, but the sales assistant explained that it meant a fast instrumental. "We liked the record very much," Roland remembers of his first excursion into bluegrass. "It was like new music. So I ordered more records. I heard Earl Scruggs and we all loved his banjo playing. At that same Burbank store I ordered a brand new Gibson Mastertone banjo because somebody told me that's what he used. So, by about late 1955–1956, we were heading that way. I learned banjo and played on and off until we met Billy Ray in late 1957."

Billy Ray Lathum, originally from Arkansas, befriended the Whites and was invited to join the newly named Country Boys on five-string banjo. A few months later, Californian dobro player LeRoy Mack (McNees) was added to the line-up. Throughout this period, Clarence White was honing his skills as an acoustic guitarist and developing a distinctive rhythm style. "I spent almost every hour with my guitar," he recalled. "It was my whole life." Among his early cheerleaders were Joe and Rose Lee Maphis who encouraged his work on bluegrass guitar. Roland's expanding record collection also provided a welcome source of fresh material from Flatt & Scruggs, Mac Wiseman and Reno & Smiley. Clarence was intrigued by the prospect of playing lead like the Stanley Brothers' George Shuffler and had a hallelujah moment when Roland played him Don Reno's 'Country Boy Rock And Roll'.

Both Eric and Clarence were still at school when the Country Boys secured a week-long residency at Ed Pearl's prestigious folk haven, the Ash Grove. "Clarence played a few leads on the guitar while we were there," says Roland. "He played 'Wildwood Flower', which we didn't sing. Nobody ever sang 'Wildwood Flower', it was always done as an instrumental. We did 'Jimmy Brown The Newsboy' as we had a recording by Flatt & Scruggs which Clarence really liked. He couldn't do it with fingerpicks so he used flatpicks." The thrill of the Ash Grove was followed by the recording of a one-off single for Sundown Records, a cover of Lester Flatt's 'I'm Head Over Heels In Love With You' coupled with 'Kentucky Hills'. The single was sponsored by Tazwell Mitchell, a member of the Los Angeles Police Department, who happened to be a bluegrass fan with a home studio. According to Roland, the pressing run was no more than 500 copies. "We used to try and sell them at gigs and probably gave most of them away after a few years."

"We took our cues from the originals," recalls LeRoy Nees. "Flatt & Scruggs, the Stanley Brothers, Jim & Jesse. Clarence would go to church. His prayers were for us to succeed."

Although steeped in country and bluegrass, the Whites were not entirely immune to the effects of rock 'n' roll. There had been a subtle crossover between bluegrass and rockabilly, most tellingly on Elvis Presley's cover of Bill Monroe's 'Blue Moon Of Kentucky'. The leather-clad Virginian Gene Vincent also recorded Monroe's 'Rocky Road Blues'. Conversely, Flatt & Scruggs featured drums on several key recordings during the late Fifties, creating a rockabilly feel on 'Foggy Mountain Rock', 'Don't Let Your Deal Go Down' and 'Big Black Train' while Lester played guitar on 'Six White Horses'. Roland White was accepting of the newer styles, at least as a listener. "I'd bring home records that you could never bring home, the rockabilly stuff, and Fats Domino and Chuck Berry. But we stayed with the bluegrass. At one time we had a Les Paul electric guitar in my dad's box. It was lying around the house and I remember trying out a few Chuck Berry licks on it, but Clarence never gave it much attention. It was there for a few months, then it disappeared. My dad would come home with a different instrument every couple of months, then trade it."

Music dominated the lives of the children. "We always had a

houseful of musicians," Rosemarie remembers. "Billy Ray Lathum and LeRoy were living with us for a while. I remember playing poker with them for matchsticks. We had a den there and people came over at night. Bill Monroe brought his band and they would be there playing music till three or four in the morning. I would always interrupt them. I had to go to bed but when I woke up in the morning, they were still there. Mom was cooking them breakfast; they'd been up all night. This was the way it was all the time growing up."

In 1960, Clarence purchased a 1934 Martin D-28 at McCabe's guitar shop, inside the Ash Grove. Guitarist Tony Rice vividly recalls his first sight of the instrument. "I was nine and Clarence was 16. The Country Boys were playing on *Town Hall Party* and so was my father's band. Clarence was doing mostly rhythm work and hardly ever took a solo, but even then he had his own thing. Mostly, though, I was just fascinated with the guitar he was playing. It was the first Martin D-28 I'd ever seen. It was all beat up but I couldn't get over the white binding."

1961 was to prove an eventful but troubled year for the group. They achieved further fame via appearances on NBC-TV's *The Andy Griffith Show* (selections of which were included on a Capitol compilation, *Songs, Themes And Laughs From The Andy Griffith Show*), another one-shot single 'The Valley Below' b/w 'High On A Mountain' and a collaboration with Hal Poindexter. A tour of Missouri followed but was interrupted when Roland received his draft papers; he was inducted into the US Army for a two-year period of service. In order to bolster the line-up, Roger Bush was brought in on bass, followed briefly by Scott Hambly on mandolin and lead vocals. This was a tricky transitional period during which the recently married Eric White was sometimes absent touring with other musicians, including the Golden State Boys. Along the way, another single appeared – 'To Prove My Love For You' b/w 'Just Joshing' produced by Ralph and Carter Stanley. More importantly, there was an album underway: *The New Sound Of Bluegrass America*, recorded for the Nashville label Briar International on 18 September 1962.

The deal had been struck by Joe Maphis and his business partner and fellow country star, Johnny Bond. Joe had long championed the Country Boys who were regulars on his and Rosie Maphis' Sunday afternoon television show *Big W Roundup*, based in Bakersfield. Although the group had already recorded as singles artistes for Briar International, the label's A&R head Paul Cohen insisted that they must change their name for the forthcoming album. His reasoning was sound.

Bluegrass singer/guitarist Mac Wiseman had founded his own Country Boys as early as 1947 and they had toured extensively. It was left to Joe Maphis to come up with a new name – the Kentucky Colonels – presumably in part honour of their Kentuckian mentor, Bill Monroe. Maphis provided some effusive liner notes to *The New Sound Of Bluegrass America*, mentioning their television appearances with Andy Griffith and advertising his own *Big W Roundup*. Maphis also offered some erudite observations on the 'bluegrass' phenomenon: "Basically, it was a combination of stringed instruments unsullied by electrical amplification. But deep down it was a rousing and rhythmical means of expressing basic emotions, whether joyful or tearful. Because of its independence of electronics, it has a purely 'American Primitive' sound. A few critics who troubled to trek the Kentucky hills proclaimed it a true example of pure American music and placed it on a par with jazz. By and large their endorsement was ignored and 'Bluegrass' stayed in the bluegrass . . . Bluegrass music gained in local popularity throughout Dixieland – largely because a lot of it was programmed on WSM's *Grand Ole Opry*. A few Bluegrass units – such as that of pioneer Bill Monroe – began touring auditoriums and theatres. Abruptly, with that tide of popularity which can rise inexplicably in the musical world, Bluegrass was 'discovered' by all America. The endorsement of those early critics was given a belated stamp-of-approval by the public as it turned to 'the new sound of Bluegrass America.' "

The album was not released until 13 months after its completion, but it proved an important artefact. The song listing was dominated by LeRoy Mack compositions and featured some striking rhythmic patterns from Clarence, along with a handful of solos. "I got a copy of it while I was in the Army," Roland remembers. "I was impressed. All of a sudden Clarence was playing all these nice melodies on the guitar, filling in where the mandolin was missing. It was fast cross-picking that I hadn't heard him do in quite that way before."

Guitarist Bob Warford, later a Kentucky Colonel, saw them perform at a bluegrass festival at the Ice House, Pasadena. This provided a rare opportunity to hear Clarence play another instrument. "During the set he played mandolin on a couple of songs. He was actually a very good mandolin player and very different from a traditional player. It sounded much like playing a fiddle tune on guitar, but very good. I was impressed, obviously. His guitar playing was similar to Doc Watson's. It was not as off-the-wall a mixture of genres as it became a couple of years later, but he was already doing fiddle tunes." Clearly, Clarence was also maturing as a flatpick guitarist, evidence of which can be heard on Sierra Records' retrospective home-taped *33 Acoustic Guitar Instrumentals*. The label also compiled a selection of Country Boys/Kentucky Colonels material, covering the period 1961–65, on the archive album, *Livin' In The Past*. Clarence's influences take in the work of various players – Doc Watson, Don Reno, Merle Travis, Speedy Webb, Joe Maphis and Jimmy Bryant – but he deconstructs and stretches their original phrasing to create something fresh.

A clear signpost towards Clarence's development as a guitar player occurred the evening he first witnessed the blind guitarist Doc Watson perform at the Ash Grove. Watson was playing rhythm guitar with Tom 'Clarence' Ashley's old-time band. That night, Ashley was poorly, prompting Watson to take centre stage. Bluegrass lead guitar work usually featured two players on lead and rhythm, respectively. Watson did *both* on a single guitar and was adept at rearranging fiddle tunes like 'Black Mountain Rag'. The first thing White noticed was Watson employing a capo to play lead in the *C* chord, as if he was playing banjo. "This was another eye-opener for Clarence," says Roland. "Instead of playing in *A* and *D*, he just put a capo on his acoustic and played leads out of *G* and *C*. So this opened up a great big door for him, and he started doing more of the instrumental tunes like 'Soldier's Joy'. His technique developed like anybody else's would. After seeing Doc, his picking became an obsession, an everyday part of his life. To play music and practise every day. Whether we played gigs or not, he was always playing music."

Al Rosenberg, then a student of Anglo-American Folk Music at UCLA, was an Ash Grove regular, who later ran McCabe's guitar shop and was mentored by Doc Watson. Like many others, he was floored by White's technique. "As an acoustic guitar player there's never been anyone better. He was the best, the most far-out clear genius. So much so, that when Doc heard him playing at an Ash Grove rehearsal during the day, he grabbed my arm and said, 'Let's get out of here!' He was really pissed because Clarence had taken some stuff he'd played and done something and not given him credit. But Doc was a genius and he knew something. Clarence was beyond the pale, I promise you. He was a giant. The first time I saw Clarence was in the Three Little Country Boys and it was Clarence and Roland who were the talents. They could stand onstage with a single mike and thrill you to the marrow. They would shake you to your foundations if you were really interested in music and could appreciate it. Their instrumental music was incredible. When I saw them with Roger Bush, Billy Ray and LeRoy Mack they were the best bluegrass band in Los Angeles. These guys were the real deal. They were roots. Roger Bush was the MC, and he was articulate, as was LeRoy. Roland could write, but I know Clarence's wife-to-be wrote his letters. I don't know how literate the banjo player was. But these weren't guys from college like I was and most of the other people hanging around the Ash Grove. They were trying to make a living playing music, not recapturing American traditional vernacular music with delicate hands."

Clarence's first oblique connection to the future world of the Byrds occurred during this same period. He already had a passing acquaintance with Chris Hillman on the bluegrass circuit and next found himself working with Jim Dickson. At this point, Dickson was producing several folk and country acts, including the Dillards, and was keen to find an accomplished guitar player to work alongside banjoists Eric Weissberg and Marshall Brickman on the Elektra album *New Dimensions In Banjo And Bluegrass*. Rodney Dillard suggested White as the perfect candidate and Dickson was impressed, both by his brilliant crosspicking and his reserved manner.

In September 1963, Roland completed his two-year Army service and rejoined the Kentucky Colonels who swiftly set out on an extensive East Coast tour, appearing at key folk venues, including New York's Gerde's Folk City, the Unicorn in Boston, Club 47 in Cambridge and Washington's Ontario Place. David Grisman, then a mandolin player in the Garrett Mountain Boys, caught a set in Gerde's and was captivated. "I was mainly interested in checking out the mandolin, but the thing I remember about them most is that they were a really good bluegrass band. Their singing was a little different. They played the really good old stuff at a time when Flatt & Scruggs were playing Carnegie Hall . . . Clarence didn't move much and didn't make any expressions so the audience didn't really notice him. Of course, he stood out when he made a solo."

Accompanying the Colonels for part of the tour was their temporary new member, Kentuckian fiddle player Bobby Slone. It was through Slone that Clarence met his future bride, Julia Susan ('Susie') Hackney, who lived in the same county. Born 5 July 1944, Susie was barely a month younger than Clarence and their attraction was instant. "[Slone] knew Susie's sister and her husband," Roland explains. "Susie came out to visit one summer while she was still in school, and met Clarence, and she went back home and then came back and they fell in love . . . Susie ended up staying in California."

The Kentucky Colonels' prospects improved in 1964. Producer Richard 'Dick' Bock, owner of World-Pacific Records, attended one of their shows at the Ash Grove and agreed to a recording, evidently with financial assistance from the club's proprietor, Ed Pearl. There was one caveat: the small budget meant it had to be an instrumental album. The Colonels questioned this decision but were reassured by Pearl's glib rejoinder: "Well, jazz music doesn't have lyrics to it." Roland remembers Bock as easy to work with in the studio and the session was completed quickly. The resulting *Appalachian Swing!* achieved only moderate sales, as Bock predicted, but it remains a touchstone of the period. Musician Scott Nygaard described the modest 28-minute album as "the most complete and compact course in contemporary bluegrass guitar imaginable". Critic Jon Sievert rightly acknowledged the work as a showcase for Clarence White's technique as an interpretative player: "His masterful sense of timing and his soulful playing on that album had an immediate effect upon every guitarist who heard it. Using a combination of flatpicking, fingerpicking with his middle and ring fingers, and crosspicking, he introduced a brand new vocabulary to the flat-top steel-string guitar."

Among the album's seminal moments was the prototype of the later Byrds' arrangement of 'I Am A Pilgrim', which clearly had a marked effect on the young Chris Hillman, who had been following White's development since first seeing the Country Boys at the Ash Grove. "Clarence's acoustic guitar playing was learned from Joe Maphis and Doc Watson, and he got a lot of it probably from listening to Joseph Spence, the Bahamian guitarist who had this incredible sense of time. Listen to Clarence play, his timing was unbelievable, he would just barely make the downbeat of the next measure . . . Clarence was a really gifted player, he existed on another plane as far as his playing went. He could play fast, but it is the slow midtempo stuff he'd flatpick on which was just unbelievable. Clarence was in another dimension."

Three months before his 20th birthday, Clarence married his teen sweetheart Susie on 14 March in a ceremony at the Wee Kirk O' The Heather wedding chapel in Las Vegas. There was no time for a long honeymoon. Eleven days later, the Kentucky

Colonels were scheduled to appear at the second UCLA Folk Festival. That evening, guitarist Tut Taylor met the White brothers and persuaded them to appear on his own World-Pacific album. If we are to believe liner notes writer Louise Scruggs, the recordings took place three days after the UCLA gig. Tut Taylor reckons the session occurred at the same time the Colonels were playing a short residency at an LA club, the Cobblestone, which he taped for posterity. "I still have that tape," he says. "After listening to Clarence play, I finally got up enough nerve to ask him if he would play with me on my dobro tunes. I told him that I would give him $20." Clarence agreed to this modest fee and contributed to a taped session that was later issued as a private pressing titled *Tut & Clarence: Flatpicking*. "We got together at his apartment, I think," says Taylor. "I was so excited and so selfish that I wanted to take all the lead and not give Clarence any breaks. He had such rhythm going that I didn't want to break the spell. However, he did take a break on one of my tunes and I must say it was terrific. We each had a track so it turned out to be a good tape. It may well be one of the clearest tapes of his rhythm."

During April, a further series of recordings were made while the Colonels were playing a four-night residency at a Bay Area folk club, the Cabale Creamery. In attendance were two bluegrass buffs, Sandy Rothman and Brooks Adams Otis, who played guitar and banjo and rightly considered themselves custodians and connoisseurs of the Kentucky Colonels' music. "It was the most exciting week in my life at the time," Rothman remembers. "I spent almost every day and every night with them. Unfortunately, very few people knew who they were (or what bluegrass was) and so the audiences were always quite small. When I listen to the tapes from those nights I'm shocked to hear just a few of us clapping in the audience to such great music." It is a tribute to the enthusiasm and foresight of these aficionados that such rare recordings still exist. "Adams Otis recorded a lot of the shows that are now available on record and CD," Roland confirms, "plus performances at the Ash Grove. Rothman was a big fan and I remember him saying, 'I want to take you to this guy Campbell

Coe's house and listen to him play. He's got these Django Reinhardt records.' Well, we'd heard the name Django Reinhardt but I don't think any of us had heard him play. I'll tell you what, we were really surprised. It was great. Somehow Clarence got copies of the records and learned some of the licks, not the tunes, just the licks. Then he started incorporating them into his playing."

White became a great proselytizer of Reinhardt's work over the next few years, as musician Bob Warford testifies. "I first heard of Django Reinhardt from Clarence. He later called him 'Jangles' Reinhardt. I assume this was the time when 'Mr Bojangles' had come out. He told me about the collection of Reinhardt 78s he had heard. The person who'd played them for him put them on a reel-to-reel tape. They were excerpts that consisted largely of guitar solos. He gave me a copy of that tape which I still have. He listened to it a lot and incorporated, for example, a triplet lick in the middle of 'Julius Finkbine's Rag'. He'd taken other stuff from Django which he later put into 'Arkansas Traveller' and 'Alabama Jubilee'. It's funny when you listen to the tape you can hear where he got a number of those things."

Musicians have expressed both awe and wonder when listening to White's innovative styling. 'Julius Finkbine's Rag', a variation on the familiar 'Beaumont Rag', is frequently cited. As musician Scott Nygaard perceptively notes: "'Beaumont Rag' is often played with a stop of the rhythm section at the seventh measure of the seventh part allowing the player a little two-bar flourish with which to dazzle the audience, and White's contribution is nothing short of spectacular. It is another great, unexplainable phrase, the kind that elicits reflexive shouts or smiles in the audience and murmurs of awe from guitarists wondering how he ever thought of such a thing."

In July 1964, the Colonels played at the Newport Folk Festival on Rhode Island. Among their followers at the time was Jerry Garcia, who drove across country to see them play. He was fortunate enough to jam with Clarence when the musicians attended a party together. "Clarence was important in my life both as a friend and a player," he recalled. "He brought a kind of swing – a rhythmic openness – to bluegrass, and a unique syncopation. His feel has been incorporated by a lot of other players, but nobody has ever gotten the open quality of his rhythm. In the bluegrass world, the instruments characteristically are on top of or slightly in front of the beat. Bluegrass is forward-leaning music. Clarence's playing was way in [the] back of the beat, and that added an openness that was really breathtaking . . . He could play at any speed – bluegrass tempos – and even double them up. He's the first guy I heard who really knocked me out. He was totally accurate and he had wonderful economy."

While playing Newport, Clarence assisted at a guitar workshop hosted by his idol, Doc Watson. Garcia considered this a significant moment. "He was influenced a lot by Doc Watson, but as soon as he got the idea of what Doc was doing, he immediately expanded in a dozen different directions. He also added a bluesy quality – you can hear that best on 'I Am A Pilgrim'." The veteran guitar player later joined the Colonels onstage, an event captured on the retrospective Vanguard album, *Long Journey Home*.

Vanguard and Elektra were premier independent folk labels at the time and both expressed an interest in recording an instrumental album featuring Clarence's guitar work. While collecting material for this unrealized project, White reconnected with producer Jim Dickson, who was currently rehearsing the fledgling Byrds at World-Pacific Studios. At the time, the group had yet to be converted to the brilliant idea of recording Dylan's still unreleased 'Mr Tambourine Man' and, partly in frustration, Dickson gallantly passed on to Clarence his rough demo of the track featuring Dylan and Ramblin' Jack Elliott. "Doing the song at that point was more important to me than the Byrds," he admits. Although White's instrumental version would have had no significant effect on the pop marketplace, it would have proven an interesting historical curio as a precursor to the Byrds' famous folk-rock version.

Dylan was very keen to promote his material and, encouraged by Dickson, took time out to visit World-Pacific, an event that so charmed the Byrds that they made his song their new priority. Coincidentally, during his stay in LA, Dylan spent an evening at Clarence and Susie White's apartment. Earlier that day, he had presented Roland and Clarence with a folded paper, supposedly featuring the words and/or music to 'Mr Tambourine Man'. Despite the master's self-promotion, an electric bluegrass interpretation was never attempted. Clarence was eager for the Colonels to cover the composition, but met with a cool response. "They weren't at all keen on it, turned it down flat because they thought it was a stupid song and because they said electric folk was just unacceptable . . . you know that ethnic/purist squabbling that later because such a big issue."

Clarence's keenness to turn electric made perfect sense as the market for acoustic bluegrass was in severe decline. Despite talk of recording projects, the group had no firm offers to follow-up *Appalachian Swing!* Money was tight and performing opportunities were fewer. The decision to resist electric instrumentation did not mean that purists were necessarily more accepting of them. When Bill Monroe persuaded a Virginian promoter to host a bluegrass festival, the Colonels understandably expected to win a place on the bill. "The promoter was Carlton Haney," Roland recalls. "He turned us down because we didn't play the kind of music that his audience would like. That's the way he put it. We thought, 'but we're playing bluegrass'. I got to meet him later when I worked with Bill Monroe and I thought he was just a damned hillbilly!"

During that same period, Monroe visited the White family and was entertained by Eric Snr. It was a troubled time. The gregarious father had suffered a heart attack that year and thereafter his health was always a matter of concern. Undeterred, he determined to continue enjoying life to the full, even if he occasionally exasperated his more sober blooded advisers. "I was only nine when he had his first heart attack," his youngest daughter Rosemarie recalls. "After that he wasn't able to work. But he wouldn't listen to 'lifestyle advice'. He was eating stuff he knew he shouldn't have been eating. He had a partial blocking of the arteries in his legs and was supposed to have surgery done, but he never did."

Concert commitments for the Kentucky Colonels were sufficiently sparse to allow Roland to take a short break from the group while his wife Arline was having a baby. The remaining Colonels played a show or two as a trio and brought in David Grisman for their short residency at New York's Gaslight folk club. The mandolinist was thrilled to play in the group, particularly alongside Clarence. "I don't think any bluegrass guitarist had as precise a sense of timing. Nobody was syncopating like he was. Clarence had that unique way of twisting things around. When we used to do 'Bury Me Beneath The Willow' he would play the guitar a whole quarter of a measure off. He was into screwing with time, but in a very accurate way so that you knew what he meant. He had a very light, precise touch. There was very little motion. You couldn't believe what was coming out of him. Some guys look like they're really working and he was expressionless. They used to make fun of him because he always looked real serious."

Given the limited live performances, it is perhaps predictable that the extant tapes from this period are primarily private recordings. The archival album *Bush, Lathum & White* features a rehearsal recorded at the home of Leon and Wilma Houston, sans Roland. Clarence plays leads on every tune. "He even took some of my banjo licks, played them his way and they worked," Lathum remembers. Another tape, tentatively dated November 1964, was recorded by their faithful archivist, Brooks Adams Otis. "He had the Colonels at his house for a party," Sandy Rothman recalls. "Jerry Garcia and I were there, along with many other friends. Brooks made a tape of me and Clarence playing two guitars in his upstairs bedroom, sitting on the edge of his bed. Many years later, he gave those tapes to the owners of Rounder Records and they released one or two tunes from those sessions."

There was an unexpected upswing in the Kentucky Colonels' fortunes at the beginning of 1965. Improbably, they were invited to appear in a small movie, *The Farmer's Other Daughter*, backing country singer Ernest Ashworth, with assistance from guitarist Richard Greene and drummer Donavan Cotton. This was enough to persuade World-Pacific's Richard Bock to release a promotional single, 'Ballad Of Farmer Brown', but he was not willing to risk an album in an increasingly precarious marketplace. Undeterred, the Colonels expanded their ranks with the introduction of Scotty Stoneman whose anarchic fiddle-playing brought fresh animation to their work. One of 23 children, 13 of whom survived into adulthood and 12 of whom became members of his father's family group, the Stonemans, Scotty could boast a filial musical lineage stretching back to the nineteenth century. His father's epic 'The Titanic', recorded in 1925, had been an influential country hit. Scotty Stoneman's fiery playing style, which later prompted extravagant critical comparisons with Jimi Hendrix and Charlie Parker, rather than any contemporary fiddle exponent, was matched by a tempestuous, hard-drinking regime which would end his life prematurely during the same year as Clarence White's untimely demise.

Touring with Stoneman required the patience of an AA counsellor combined with the fortitude of a professional minder. "There were times in the Byrds where Clarence used to talk about people going crazy on the road," his later colleague Gene Parsons remembers. "He would always mention his time with Scotty Stoneman in the Kentucky Colonels. Scotty was an unbelievable fiddle player but he was also an alcoholic and he'd go crazy. At one point, they were trying to stop him from drinking. He managed to stay dry for two or three days but then he tried to jump out of a window. Clarence saved him from going out of that window. They then kept all alcohol away from him but he went and found some Aqua Velva [an alcohol-based aftershave] and drank a bottle of it. As a result, they had to take him to the hospital."

Stoneman's tenure in the Colonels lasted until September 1965 by which time the folk-rock boom was at its apotheosis with acts like the Byrds, Sonny & Cher and Barry McGuire selling millions of records. The public's fascination with Dylanesque electric folk left traditional bluegrass players even more culturally and commercially adrift. Clarence had already anticipated the trend and sold the worn Herringbone guitar seen on the cover of *Appalachian Swing!* in order to raise money for an electric instrument. His choice, a Fender Telecaster, came courtesy of the esteemed James Burton, session guitarist to the stars. The instrument had a pick-up configuration developed by the steel guitarist Red Rhodes which ensured its place as the premier country rock guitar. Nevertheless, adjusting to the new instrument took several months. "The transition was pretty strange," White admitted. "It was almost like starting all over again. You see, I was playing bluegrass, picking along to very fast fiddle tunes . . . I was achieving a fingerpicking sound, three-finger banjo style, but I was using one pick – flatpicking really fast . . . That way, I was able to get a loud ringing sound which was clear at the same time. Consequently, when I switched to electric I found I had too much strength and power in my right hand – I was making the strings jump and rattle, which led to distortion . . . I had to learn to use a more delicate touch in conjunction with the tone and volume controls. Similarly, I had to learn from scratch with my left hand; I'd done most of my playing in open tuning, using a capo – so as well as learning all the conventional chord structures and scales, I had to learn the whole neck. Because of this, I always maintain that I'm an electric guitarist working in rock, rather than a rock 'n' roll guitarist like Clapton or Beck, who came through blues, which was an area in which I'd had very little experience."

By late 1965, White was spending considerable time observing the Hollywood club scene, taking in acts from the Ash Grove to the Whisky. "It wasn't so much that I was getting bored with acoustic bluegrass; I could feel so many new things in the air and I wanted to get in the stream of what I thought was a new kind of music which combined what you could call a folk integrity and electric rock." He was particularly impressed by the Rising Sons, featuring Taj Mahal and Ry Cooder, whose drummer Kevin Kelley would later pre-empt him by joining the Byrds.

Other favourites included the Paul Butterfield Blues Band who befriended the White brothers and encouraged them by example. It was now clearer than ever to Clarence that the best way forward lay in attempting to combine roots-based music with a contemporary rock beat.

Reluctantly, but pragmatically, the other Colonels belatedly agreed to follow suit. "I had an electric mandolin," Roland says, "Billy Ray Lathum got an electric rhythm guitar, Roger Bush played electric bass and we had a drummer, Bert Haney." Unfortunately, the move to electric did not bring the new audiences Clarence had envisaged. Instead of breaking into hip Hollywood haunts, the Colonels were left floundering in nightclub hell. In a chilling echo of the Byrds' early experiences playing live, they were booked into a lounge situated in a bowling alley. Even their set was a little reminiscent of the Byrds' early folk-rock experiments, combining Beatles and Everly Brothers tunes, while searching for their own style. Roland and Clarence duetted on a handful of Buck Owens and Louvin Brothers songs, but the opportunity to employ their bluegrass pedigree was extremely limited. "We were doing some country standards for people to dance to but we could see there was no interest in bluegrass and it didn't seem feasible to carry it on." In a wonderfully incongruous moment, Roger Bush even attempted Chuck Berry's 'Memphis' with Roland plucking away on his electric mandolin accompanied by the distant sound of bowling skittles clattering in the background.

At the end of October 1965, the group decided to take an extended break, leaving Clarence free to seek session work or fraternize with other players. The following year, having moved to Bell, California, he struck up a friendship with his new neighbour Vern Gosdin and was invited to play some gigs with the Gosdin Brothers. "He said he was going be the best guitar player in the world one day, believe you me," Vern remembers. "Clarence and I used to go around club to club; the Palomino or the Foothill Club. I'd get onstage and he'd play guitar with me. If there was someone else, that was fine, but, if not, that was fine too. That's all we needed just the two of us."

On 12 May 1966, Clarence's first child Michelle was born while he and Susie were still living in a one-room apartment in Bell, situated on the west bank of the Los Angeles River. Seeking work to supplement his income, the guitarist and his brother Roland eagerly accepted a surprise invitation to record some demos with 'the Jewish Hillbilly' Zeke Manners. Born in 1911, Manners was a composer, multi-instrumentalist and radio DJ, who had led an orchestra named the Beverly Hillbillies during the 1930s. A prolific composer, he had written over a hundred songs, most famously 'The Pennsylvania Polka' (for the Andrews Sisters), 'Take My Wife Please' (recorded by comedian Henry 'Henny' Youngman), and 'Los Angeles' (co-written with the famous guitarist Les Paul). Coincidentally, Manners also wrote many songs with actor Buddy Ebsen, who starred as Jed Clampett in the Sixties television series, *The Beverly Hillbillies*. Manners enjoyed bluegrass and saw potential in employing the Whites in a duet formation, similar to the Louvin or Everly Brothers. With assistance from Roger Bush and a rhythm section, the Whites recorded Manners' song 'Everybody Has One But You' and Eric Weissberg and Dick Reicheg's 'Made Of Stone'. Clarence's and Roland's engaging two-part harmonies, redolent of the Everlys, showed great promise but the experiment was discontinued after the sudden death of Zeke's son. The demos remained in the vaults until as late as 2003 when they were exhumed for the fascinating retrospective, *Tuff & Stringy*.

It was during 1966 that White befriended a seasoned lounge band in search of rejuvenation. Louisiana-born Floyd 'Gib' Guilbeau, then aged 29, was already a veteran of the circuit. After leaving the Air Force in 1957, he worked in a trio as a guitarist cum drummer with ex-service buddies, singer Darrell Cotton and bassist Ernie Williams. Three years later, they added lead guitarist Wayne Moore and became the Four Young Men (aka Young Men Four), appearing regularly on the Southern California country circuit and recording for various independent labels. By

1963, they underwent a name change, relaunching themselves as the Castaways and appearing at lounges and casinos. When Williams grew weary of the Vegas circuit, he was replaced by Gene Parsons, whom Guilbeau had discovered playing banjo in a Hollywood music shop. Two more years passed before the group retired, disillusioned. Unable to settle back in Louisiana, Guilbeau returned to California to form a new group, the Reasons (aka the Fabulous Reasons). It was while playing the Jack Of Diamonds lounge in Palmdale that he struck up a friendship with Clarence White. "The minute I heard him play I knew he was a great player and that was even before he first played electric guitar," Guilbeau says.

Guilbeau's new band was suffering personnel changes and he urgently required a replacement rhythm section. Seeking solace in the familiar, he contacted two old friends: Gene Parsons and Wayne Moore. Having already switched from banjo to bass, Gene Parsons was informed that henceforth he would be the group's drummer, while Moore took on bass duties. Meanwhile, singer Darrell Cotton was busy working with his own band and had saved sufficient funds to finance a small label, Ion Records, situated on Hollywood's Crossroads Of The World. Guilbeau pitched his friend a couple of songs which Cotton agreed to release under his own name, with the newly-established Reasons as backing musicians. In order to enhance the two-track recordings, Guilbeau suggested they invite Clarence White to the session.

At this point, White was not that well known outside of bluegrass circles so his name made no impression on those present. "I loved bluegrass and was from a bluegrass background too, but I didn't know he'd done all this acoustic stuff until much later," admits Wayne Moore. "I'd never really heard of him. He never mentioned the Kentucky Colonels. Later, we went to his house a couple of times and met some of the old Kentucky Colonels, but I didn't know he'd played with them. I just thought he was a good guitarist." Gene Parsons was equally unaware of White's background when he attended that first session backing Darrell Cotton. "I was told to come down and do the session and someone said the guitar player was phenomenal. I thought, 'OK – a phenomenal guitar player!' He seemed a nice enough fellow, kind of shy and quiet. As it turned out, he *was* phenomenal. I'd never heard anything like it in my life. He'd just taken up the electric guitar and he was still using a capo on the neck because that was his experience in bluegrass." Some time after the session, Parsons discovered that White was the young guitarist who had played so wonderfully on the old Elektra album *New Dimensions In Banjo And Bluegrass*. "I was very impressed."

The Darrell Cotton single 'Don't Pity Me' was a decent composition with a strong, rousing vocal but fell victim to limited distribution and inadequate airplay. White's contribution was significant, not merely for the distorted lead guitar break, but as a first attempt to replicate the sound of a steel guitar, using a trick that would later inspire the invention of a new instrument. As writer Alex Palao carefully notes: "In the solo of 'Don't Pity Me', he throws in a 'nut pull', chiming a string at the 5th fret and then quickly pressing it down behind the nut, to produce a brief, high-pitched note akin to a steel guitar. It was a trick he had picked up from James Burton, who in turn had been inspired by steel player Harold Bradley 'Shot' Jackson, and was something only possible on the Telecaster."

White remained friendly with Guilbeau and company and occasionally joined them onstage at the Jack Of Diamonds, an arrangement that would become more binding the following year. For the remainder of 1966, White pursued session work and was gifted the chance of working on a couple of albums with Rick Nelson thanks to James Burton. This also allowed him the opportunity to promote the writing talents of his new friend, Gib Guilbeau. "Rick spread the word that he was looking for a Cajun song," Guilbeau explains, "and Clarence said, 'I know just the guy!' I went up to the studio, met Rick, played him a song ['Take A City Bride'] and recorded it right there. I was probably the only guy doing Cajun stuff with English lyrics then because I couldn't do a complete Cajun song. That would have sounded ridiculous, so it came out half and half." Capitol Records were so impressed that they released the song as a single early the following year. Nelson's attendant album, *Country Fever*, also displayed White's Telecaster technique to strong effect.

Inevitably, White gravitated towards the 'Byrds family' at the end of 1966, partly thanks to Jim Dickson who was still managing the group as well as overseeing the careers of the Gosdin Brothers and Gene Clark. That September, Dickson persuaded the Gosdins to attempt Clark's then unreleased Byrds' composition, 'The Reason Why'. Nothing came of that recording, but Dickson put the two acts together while preparing Clark's CBS solo album. Later in the sessions, White was asked to contribute some guitar parts. The Gosdins also took the opportunity to enlist him for a one-off single on Edict, 'One Hundred Years From Now'. Accompanying White for this historic recording were Chris Hillman and Michael Clarke. Always a fan of White's work, Hillman subsequently invited him to play on the Byrds' country-tinged 'Time Between' and 'The Girl With No Name' for *Younger Than Yesterday*. White's steel-guitar sounding Telecaster solos added a brighter tone to the tracks which neatly contrasted with Hillman's introspective, self-questioning lyrics.

Amid this flurry of studio activity, White unexpectedly reconnected with his brothers who had recently relaunched the Kentucky Colonels with banjoist Bob Warford, guitarist Dennis Morris and fiddler Jimmy Crane. Their relatively slight gigging schedule ensured that White was able to commit himself to the group for the next few months. "That incarnation lasted from late 1966 till the spring of 1967," Warford confirms. "Clarence joined the band full-time and played virtually all the shows, apart from a weekend at the Ash Grove in January. It was a great band. I enjoyed what Clarence was playing and the way we sounded. It's more impressive in retrospect than it was at the time, and I don't mean that negatively. Now you can say, 'Wow, that was legendary stuff' but nobody was thinking that at the time . . . What you hear now and what you heard then were two directions in bluegrass guitar. The questions were 'how many notes can I play per second?' and 'where do I put those notes?' Clarence had both of those abilities. He had the confidence to play quickly, but he also had the timing and taste to know *where* to play. I never heard him overplay anything."

Another aspect of White's playing, usually understated, is the subtle influence of blues guitar on his thinking. Even before he heard Jimi Hendrix, he was interested in incorporating aspects of the blues. "A couple of times at the Ash Grove, the other act on was Canned Heat," Warford says. "I remember Hank Vestine playing and Clarence listening to him. They talked afterwards. Obviously, Vestine wasn't a black blues player but there were a lot of blues influences in what he was doing. Certainly, Clarence was impressed with that music and he mentioned it to me, even then."

Warford was also in the perfect position to appreciate the different qualities and personalities of the brothers. "Boy, that's a question I've never been asked," he considers. "If you ask me what Clarence was like as a person, it's hard to define. Every time you'd see somebody who was a friend of yours in music, it was simply about music. You didn't hang out somewhere and play pool, you'd be playing an instrument or listening. Clarence wasn't outgoing, he was very quiet. But I thought the world of him. Eric was a great bass player but he was more boastful, although not without the ability to back it up. He would be more out-front than the others and willing to brag about things. Clarence was the furthest away from that, the dead opposite. Roland was in the middle, friendly and matter of fact. He never blew his horn and was always trying to keep everybody happy. I liked all three of the guys."

In February 1967, the Colonels recorded some demos which were subsequently harvested as backing tracks for a radio show *American Music Time,* hosted by Dave Spencer, complete with full applause to create the illusion of a live recording. Shiloh Records' owner Dale Davis, who later reissued these recordings, remembers the Colonels struggling to survive in an era when festivals were fewer and record companies were wary of roots music. "Clarence told me at the time, 'There ain't no money in bluegrass.' Underline that! That's what he said. Well, Mr Clarence believed that – and he had good reason to believe it. They got so they were sort of famous but they didn't make any damn money."

The Kentucky Colonels played their final Ash Grove show on 9 April 1967, after which Roland relocated to Nashville to work with his former bluegrass idol Bill Monroe. Clarence's future was by no means set in stone. His uncredited cameo appearances on the Byrds' recently released *Younger Than Yesterday* remained a trade secret outside the music industry and would not be revealed to the public until after he joined the group. White briefly had hopes of touring with ex-Byrd Gene Clark, having recently appeared alongside him for a couple of shows at the Whisky in a unique line-up including drummer 'Fast' Eddie Hoh and later Byrds bassist John York.

"I hadn't played with Clarence before," York says, "but I felt immediately that this guy was quite amazing. Anybody who encountered Clarence with any kind of musical sensibility would immediately react like that. He was phenomenal. He'd taken this bluegrass technique and was playing it on an electric guitar. No one played like that; no one else phrased like that; no one else had that kind of tone. I thought that it was a really special situation and I don't remember why we didn't continue." The main reason was Clark's famous reluctance to travel, which ruined all hopes of touring, prompting White to commit himself to more session work.

While White was seeking studio opportunities, his current playmates in the Reasons were busily employed with a new production company and label, Bakersfield International. The enterprise was run by the mercurial Gary Paxton, who had previously recorded both the Four Young Men and the Castaways. Paxton's emporium was merely an 8-track studio situated in a Hollywood garage, complete with wires connected to a tape machine in a bus conveniently parked outside. The first single on the label was 'Louisiana Rain' b/w 'Sweet Suzannah', credited to Guilbeau &

Parsons. It was the B-side that proved most appealing and might have become a hit with decent promotion. Having signed to the label in April, Gib & Gene were next promised a shot at an album which was largely completed, then postponed and finally sold on years later under the title *Cajun Country*. Financial constraints ensured that the label was restricted to singles releases thereafter, but there was plenty of work available and it would not be long before White would be recruited to the team. "We really didn't know what we were doing then," Guilbeau reflects. "We were just good friends, so we all pooled our talents and instruments and did whatever came to mind. We started doing records with a whole bunch of people and created that so-called Bakersfield sound."

With Rick Nelson's *Country Fever* selling reasonably, White was invited to appear at a veritable super session concert at Los Angeles' Shrine Auditorium. Among the backing musicians were White's great session mentor James Burton, bassist Joe Osborn, pianist Glen D. Hardin, drummer Junior Nichols and Bob Warford on banjo. "It was fascinating," Warford remembers. "We'd rehearsed at Universal Studios for a couple of weeks. Rick was really concentrating on his country stuff. At the time, James Burton was not a name that meant a lot to me. I'd heard a little bit about him, and that was it. Of course when we were rehearsing I was impressed with his playing. Then we went onstage and the first song of the set was 'My Bucket's Got A Hole In It'. When he got to the solo, James turned up the amp and just blew my socks off. The authority with which he played was absolutely stunning."

Playing onstage with Burton and White was enough to convince Warford where his future lay. "I went off into electric as well at that point," he says. Nevertheless, he and White still found time for some acoustic experimentation. "The weirdest part of it was when we got together in 1967 after the Colonels split. I was over at Clarence's house and we were playing one of the Reinhardt solos he had on tape. We sat up for two or three days playing this solo at half speed on his recorder and trying to learn the entire thing lick by lick. Ultimately, we got to where we could play it at one quarter of the speed that Reinhardt had done. It was the most difficult thing that I have ever done and Clarence said the same thing. It turned out to be a 45-second solo."

On 17 July, White signed a contract with Bakersfield International. Fittingly, his first contribution was the Gosdin Brothers' 'Hangin' On' b/w 'Multiple Heartaches', an excellent coupling on which the Reasons provided a strong backing, with White excelling on dobro. Later that year, it became a minor hit on the country charts. The third Bakersfield International single was billed exclusively under the name Clarence White. 'Tango For A Sad Mood' was a delightful classical piece while its B-side 'Tuff & Stringy', lasting a mere 85 seconds, was based around a simple country riff. Having already featured Gib & Gene and Clarence, the label added Wayne Moore to the roster as a soloist for the fourth release: 'Hey Juliana'. No longer merely a group, the Reasons had been transformed into a veritable four-man Brill Building – writing, performing and recording.

The Bakersfield International dream of creating a self-contained musical collective was inspired by its quixotic founder, Gary Paxton. Originally, a pop novelty merchant, as evidenced by his work with Skip & Flip, the Hollywood Argyles and, most famously, Boris Pickett & The Crypt Kickers ('Monster Mash'), Paxton retained a dual love of country music. There was something about the maudlin sentimentality, melodrama and self-effacing humour of the genre that appealed to his own impulsive, excitable character. As Bakersfield International historian Alec Palao rightly points out, the country/pop singles that Paxton was producing had an innocence and simplicity that contrasted with other artistes' more knowing attempts to bridge musical forms. "It was not the self-conscious synthesis of the Byrds or Burritos. Instead, steeped in the classic country tradition of old-fashioned, honest-to-goodness picking, singing and songwriting, the Bakersfield International label simply ploughed its own, unique and most fertile, country pop furrow."

Paxton later relocated his label and production company to its rightful home in Bakersfield. In a presumably unintended sardonic comment on his entire enterprise, the company was housed in the implausible setting of a former bank, whose flat-topped exterior resembled an architect's vision of an impregnable fortress. Alas, Paxton's secure building was not mirrored by fiscal thrift. On the few occasions when a financial windfall blew his way, Paxton reacted with the champagne-popping largesse of a lottery winner. After one sizeable publishing cheque arrived, he went on a bender, drove to Las Vegas and squandered every cent. The next morning he couldn't recall a thing. "He owed money and he came back broke," Guilbeau marvels. "Gary was very, very important in all our lives. We learned a hell of a lot from him. Being a songwriter, he pushed us heavily into writing songs. He wanted everybody to write and I guess I was one of the more prolific guys, so he pushed me harder. Gary Paxton did a lot of stuff and a lot of it he doesn't even remember because he was real drunk half the time!"

"I wrote a couple of songs with Gary's wife," Wayne Moore adds. "One was 'Guitar Picking Man', a comedy song about a guitar player. We just figured out a little story about somebody's wife running off with a guitar player or something. It was funny. Jan and I sat down and wrote that in half-an-hour. At the time Gib was the writer. I never liked writing but I helped write a few. We kind of all chipped in and decided upon everything. We were having a good time. Getting a hit wasn't real important to me, but it would have been fun if we did."

Clarence was an almost equally reluctant pupil but was badgered by Gary into collaborating with Jan on a handful of songs, the best of which was 'She's Gone', whose theme and execution was similar to Skeeter Davis' 'The End Of The World'. Gib and Jan sang a striking demo, which was subsequently passed on to the Gosdin Brothers for inclusion on their Columbia album, *Sounds Of Goodbye*, on which Clarence also played. Although well capable of composing a pop melody, White never mastered lyric writing. "He'd always give you some excuse," says Guilbeau. "'No, no, I'm not good at it. I can't do it' . . . He could never come up with a song, a title or an idea he liked. There was always something." If White was a reluctant composer, he could always be relied upon to transform a song with a startling solo. During the second half of 1967, the Byrds continued to invite him to their sessions and his outstanding work, again uncredited, helped transform *The Notorious Byrd Brothers* into one of the greatest albums of its time. His thrilling contributions to 'Wasn't Born To Follow' and 'Change Is Now' in particular were notable achievements.

While based in Palmdale, White was freer to commit himself to the Reasons and they played noticeably louder whenever he appeared onstage. The arduous sets at the Jack Of Diamonds were sometimes accompanied by unruly scenes that threatened to degenerate into a brawl. "These were wild cowboy people who lived in the desert," Moore recalls. "It was a wild nightclub and they used to get into fights. I remember one night they were fighting onstage and we just shoved them off and kept on playing. We were young then! We played 45-minute sets and there were five sets a night from 9 pm till two in the morning. We'd work a lot on Sunday afternoons too, take a break, have a meal and go back to work that night."

White's ubiquity was underlined by his presence in another studio/bar band: the Roustabouts. During the summer of 1967, Clarence had loaned Bob Warford his Fender Jazzmaster and invited him to tape some performances. "I had never played an electric guitar before," says Warford. "This was a chance to pick up some licks and start learning a new instrument." On 24 August, Warford lugged his reel-to-reel Tandberg stereo tape recorder to the appointed venue: the Arena Room, a bar attached to a bowling alley, the Jefferson Bowl, in Culver City. In addition to White, the Roustabouts included Arkansas steel guitarist Dennis Mathes, vocalist/bass/rhythm player Richard Arlen, drummer George Skinner (aka Stevens) and two guest country singers: Lee Ross and Jerry Inman. At first, Warford only taped White's electric guitar directly from his amplifier, but he returned for the following two nights to capture the whole band via the house system. The results were revealing. Kicking off with the Bob Morris instrumental 'Buckaroo', the sets included such diverse material as 'Release Me', 'There Goes My Everything' and 'Am I That Easy To Forget?' (all massive UK hits transposed from country to MOR by Engelbert Humperdinck!); Buck Owens' 'Act Naturally', 'Together Again', 'Sawmill' and 'Sam's Place'; Merle Haggard's 'Tonight The Bottle Let Me Down', 'The Fugitive', and 'I Threw Away The Rose'; George Jones' 'White Lightning'; Ray Charles' 'I Got A Woman' and 'I Can't Stop Loving You'; Chuck Berry's 'Johnny B. Goode' and 'Memphis'; Bill Monroe's 'Blue Moon Of Kentucky' and 'Kentucky Waltz'; 'Don Gibson's 'Oh Lonesome Me'; the evergreen American/Irish anthem 'Danny Boy', and two Dean Martin hits, 'You're Nobody Till Somebody Loves You' and 'Little Ole Wine Drinker Me'. The players seemed adept at turning their hands to crowd-pleasing country, rock and R&B standards.

By late autumn, the Roustabouts had secured a permanent residency working at the Nashville West, a club in the Azusa/El Monte area of Los Angeles. Vocalist Richard Arlen, whose single 'I'm Tied Down To You' featured Clarence, was still singing with the group most of the time. Dennis Mathes was retained, but there was a new rhythm section, featuring bassist Jim Alley who had a moderate country hit with 'Only Daddy That'll Walk The Line', and former big band/jazz drummer Bo Wagner.

Wagner's appointment provided White with another opportunity to expand his musical palate. Born in 1945, a year after the guitarist, Wagner was a child prodigy who had played with the post-war Glenn Miller Orchestra and the Lawrence Welk Band as well as heading a leading Las Vegas revue before moving into session work, appearing with the 5th Dimension and the Lewis & Clarke Expedition, among others. "I was asked to join the Roustabouts and Clarence and I hit it off and became close friends," Wagner recalls. "I didn't come from a country background, I'd been playing more jazz and big band. Although I was playing drums my favourite instrument was vibes and marimba. One of the reasons I took the job with the Roustabouts was to learn country music. Even though I'd played it, I hadn't *lived* it. I wanted to be in that environment, playing their clubs so that I could learn their approach, their dress, and so on. Country wasn't my main world but after I got with Clarence and the Roustabouts it became a major thing in my life. I loved it and got the feel for it by being around the people that came into the Nashville West. I immersed myself in it and Clarence loved the way I played and opened up that world and introduced me to everybody."

Given his interest in Django Reinhardt, it was hardly surprising that White would prove receptive to the jazz leanings of Wagner, who had much to impart. For a time, they became a two-man musical appreciation society, eagerly exchanging ideas. "Clarence didn't really read music and I did, so I started sitting down and teaching him a lot of things from a technical, schooled background. I wanted to show him jazz licks on my vibes, and jazz chords. I was able to help him and he taught me a lot of stuff that he naturally knew. Clarence realized his limitations. He didn't grow up in music school learning different styles. He came from another world. Sometimes he couldn't be part of a set that wasn't his style. But if he didn't know it, he wanted to learn it. He was aware and quickly attached himself to everybody. He came to me and said, 'Will you teach me these things? I want to learn them.' That's how you widen your scope. Not everybody is that open. They get into a niche and they stay there. Clarence was very aware of what he knew and what he didn't know and he wanted to get better and better so he did anything that came along. Clarence was very dedicated, very focused and wanted to be the best that he could be. He'd come from bluegrass but it was almost like he'd left his roots once he started branching out. Yet he could also incorporate his original bluegrass – it all merged together."

The new line-up of the Roustabouts did not stray beyond the Nashville West club. According to Wagner that was the *only* venue they ever played during his tenure. By his reckoning the line-up lasted at least a year which means that White was presumably playing in both the Roustabouts and the Reasons during the same time period. Complicating matters further, both bands seemed to take on the unofficial title of 'Nashville West'. "That was the common name," says Wagner. "That's what we all used. We didn't really say Roustabouts that much. We were the house band at the Nashville West. That's the way Clarence and I referred to it. Sometimes we'd have a night off where they would have somebody else play, but we were the main group. We were there almost every night of the week. After awhile the Roustabouts were referred to as the 'Nashville West Band'. The club and the band became synonymous because we stayed there so long."

On 27 November, Warford set up his tape recorder at the Nashville West to record an entire evening's entertainment. What was most extraordinary about the Roustabouts' repertoire was the number of tunes and lack of repetition between sets. Over several hours, they played almost 50 different songs, including White's readings of 'Last Date', 'Tango For A Sad Mood' and 'Tuff & Stringy'. Further selections from the song catalogues of Buck Owens ('Where Does The Good Times Gone') and Merle Haggard ('Sing Me Back Home') enhanced the set, along with borrowings from Jimmy Reed ('Big Boss Man'), the Kingston Trio ('Tom Dooley'), Les Paul & Mary Ford ('Vaya Con Dios'), Mel Tillis ('Mental Revenge') and Clydie King's 1962 hit 'Wolverton Mountain', among others. Wagner was the featured vocalist on unexpected covers of Robert Parker's 'Barefootin'', Sam The Sham & The Pharaohs' 'Wooly Bully', Tommy Roe's 'Sweet Pea', Jewel Akens' 'The Birds And The Bees' and the R&B standard, 'Hi-Heel Sneakers'. Guest vocalists Bobby Little and Johnny McKnight were also on hand to add a few numbers at the end of each set. Warford was there again the next evening for another set, bookended by 'Buckaroo'. Throughout the entire proceedings, White retained his customary implacable stage presence. "Onstage he was very serious," Wagner says. "He had those big eyebrows and looked stern but he was a real card. He loved to kid and play little pranks. He was kind, polite, light-hearted, funny, and a joy to be with. No ego, no attitude, a delight. But when he got down to playing he was serious. He was the best; he didn't have to shout it. All he had to do was play. Solo or special guitar work fell into Clarence's lap. There was nobody better. He did it all and was a genius at what he did. Clarence was a dedicated player who worked his ass off to learn as much as he could."

That learning experience was utilized by producer Gary Paxton, who soon added Bo Wagner to his roster of studio talent. "Gary used my vibes and marimba on sessions. I was involved in many capacities and Clarence and I were playing almost daily in the studio, and nightly with the Roustabouts. He expanded my entire recording career. Everybody took the recording groups more seriously and just looked at the Roustabouts as the gig band to make money. Dennis and Richard were trying to make the Roustabouts more of a real entity than it was, but Clarence and I had so much going on that it was a little hard to pull together." Although the Roustabouts continued playing into the New Year, Wagner had already committed himself to joining Paxton's operation in Bakersfield. "Gary gave me a great offer so I was the first to move up from LA on a permanent basis." From here on, White spent more time with the Reasons who were already retracing the steps of the Roustabouts.

Meanwhile, Bakersfield International continued to release singles featuring White, including Larry Scott's 'A Little Shoe Shine Boy's Christmas' and two songs that would later be covered by the Byrds: the Gosdin Brothers' 'There Must Be Someone' and Cajun Gib & Gene's 'Your Gentle Way(s) Of Lovin' Me'. Potentially there was so much product that it was impossible to release everything on Bakersfield International, so other obscure labels popped up from nowhere, partially financed by Paxton. As Paxton's contemporary and multi-label owner Dale Davis explains: "We were always looking for money to record somebody. We got financing in order to pay for studio time. Needless to say we were pretty poor most of the time. Many of these labels were part owned."

With Christmas 1967 approaching, Gene Parsons wrote to Gary Paxton about promoting 'Your Gentle Way(s) Of Lovin'

Me' while confirming his desire to move to Bakersfield early in the New Year. "Everyone is ready and anxious to make the move, I am especially anxious," he stressed. Parsons' sentiments were either premature or disingenuous, as both he and Guilbeau ultimately resisted the idea. "I never liked Bakersfield that much," recalls Guilbeau, "So I said, 'I'm not moving.' Then Gene said, 'Well, if you're not moving, I'm not moving.'" Paxton continued to woo them and eventually persuaded two of the Reasons to relocate. "Clarence and I moved up to Bakersfield, so did Vern and Rex Gosdin," Wayne Moore remembers. "I think we were all in the same apartment building on the edge of town. I know Vern was across the hall from me and I think Clarence was downstairs. We'd go over to Gary's and do a lot of sessions with different people, just about every day. We played a couple of clubs there maybe three or four nights a week. Gib and Gene would drive up from Palmdale for the shows and sessions."

Paxton took great satisfaction in securing the band a residency at the Hi-Life Supper Club, which specialized in sirloin steak and offered the added attraction of a teen-throb idol, Ricky Martino. The owner did his best to trumpet the arrival of the new band, complimenting the "very versatile Gib Guilbeau and Gene Parsons", singling out "the hilarious comedy antics of Wayne Moore" and introducing "the fantastic instrumental sound of Clarence White". Unfortunately, the proprietor's diligence did not extend as far as accurately naming the band. As Guilbeau says, "We were called the Gary Paxton Band because Gary had booked the place. People would come up and say, 'Who's Gary?' We'd say, 'He's not here. He's never been here!' They'd then ask, 'Then why are you called the Gary Paxton Band?' It was a long story, not worth telling."

Thereafter they were billed as 'Gib Guilbeau And The Reasons', but there was no happy ending. "We hated the place," says Guilbeau. "We tried to quit several times. But every time we tried, the owner would say, 'You guys can't quit, you've got to work another week, keep it going a bit longer.' It was a real dingy supper club with stuffed shirts in suits and ties. The first two hours it was like background music and we wanted to be loud. One time, a guy came up to Parsons and said, 'You're too loud, you've got to tone it down.' In the end he was playing drums with his fingers – and it was still too loud! Finally, we said, 'Look, it's not happening, nobody's having fun', so we quit." As a pungent comment on the entire fiasco, White took perverse pleasure in urinating over the club owner's car, then leading away his pack like a disgruntled dog.

"When that gig ended we were really glad we hadn't moved to Bakersfield," says Guilbeau. "There weren't that many country rock gigs to be had. They had the local yokels that had been playing the same bars for years. There was no way we could have ousted one of those. Clarence had an old Plymouth car. When Gene and I would leave to come back to Palmdale, he and Wayne would drive round local parks and knock over trash cans. Whatever was in front of them, they knocked it down! Needless to say, Clarence had been drinking. That's for sure."

"Well, we got bored in Bakersfield," Moore reiterates, "so we went out knocking down big orange barrels and those road signs. They were doing road construction and we were knocking them down on purpose which was not a very nice thing to do but at the time we thought it was pretty funny . . . Clarence was amusing and liked pulling little jokes on people."

White's love of playing the prankster contrasted markedly with his stage persona where his poker face encouraged audience members to wager on whether they could make him crack a smile. "He definitely had a quirky sense of humour," says Gene Parsons. "He played practical jokes on everybody. It was mostly Gib and I that helped him. Of course Gib would do things to him as well. I was lucky because I got to participate with both sides and for some reason they didn't bother with me very much, but I was allowed to take part. Gib would say, 'Let's put a banana peel in Clarence's guitar case?' Then Clarence would get madder than a hornet and say, 'Let's put this gigantic rock on Gib's '55 Ford hood.'"

For a short spell, the Reasons were fronted by singer Bruce E.

Oakes, with whom they cut a couple of singles. "He bought a little club in Palmdale called the King's Lounge just so all the musicians he knew would have a place to work," Wayne Moore recalls. "I guess he would be considered part of the band at that time. He sang with us every night. He worked as a lineman and got paid really well because it was a pretty dangerous job. We got a good crowd with him."

Archive tapes of the group's King's Lounge or Jack Of Diamonds performances have never appeared on either bootleg or official release, which surprises Wayne Moore. "We had a radio show for the Jack Of Diamonds. A DJ from Lancaster, California, would come out and record us live at the club in the afternoon. We might have tapes of it. That's something to think about. I'm surprised people haven't come up with more tapes and pictures. We worked together for at least two years, so you'd think there would be tapes out there. We didn't think much about recording live or taking pictures for some reason. I don't know why."

Remarkably, it was not a radio station, producer, recording engineer or record label owner that captured the live sound of this unheralded band, but their humble drummer, Gene Parsons. The setting was the Roustabouts' favourite, the Nashville West, a larger establishment than the Jack Of Diamonds, with a bigger audience. While playing there, the group informally adopted the club's name and it was under this title that their archival album of live recordings was first issued in autumn 1978. Parsons' two-track Sony 500 captures the act, circa early 1968, playing a varied set, featuring six lead vocals from Gib Guilbeau, including the familiar, retitled 'Sweet Susanna' and 'Louisiana Rain', two cameos from Wayne Moore and Gene Parsons, respectively, and White playing some impressive solos on an instrumental version of Bobbie Gentry's 'Ode To Billy Joe' and two break songs, 'Tuff & Stringy' and 'Nashville West'. White's weaving guitar interplay elevates the recording beyond the level of a mere curio, but the album also serves as an intriguing artefact of a jobbing band, serving their time on a punishing circuit. There is little attempt to establish any rapport with the audience and the lack of applause, deliberately deleted here, adds to the eerie sense of emotional detachment. The musicians sound tired in places, hardly surprising considering the long and late hours. Parsons' languid vocal on 'By The Time I Get To Phoenix' brilliantly captures this sense of ennui. What we are left with is a slice of audio-vérité that tells us more about the experience of hearing a late-night lounge band than it does about any impending musical revolution.

Nevertheless, Nashville West's fusion of country, pop and rock 'n' roll, marked by White's impressive guitar technique, was soon drawing some stellar guests including steel players Sneaky Pete Kleinow and Lloyd Green, pianist Glen D. Hardin and the newly appointed Byrd, Gram Parsons. "Sneaky worked in the band for a while," claims Wayne Moore. "Gram didn't, but he got up and sang with us. I think all the Byrds came up to the desert to sit in with the group at the Nashville West or the King's Lounge." What they witnessed was an often spontaneous mix of styles, including Guilbeau's Cajun-tinged compositions. "It was a pure bar band, but we refined that and took it in a different direction," says Guilbeau. "It became heavier with the rock beat and evolved. A lot of stuff we did out of boredom. For instance, I'd write a song that nobody had heard and I'd just start it and let everybody fall in. By the time we did the song two or three times it sounded pretty good, but it would be different every time. It wasn't polished and we didn't rehearse. We'd just show up and play. We got edgier and drew a lot of younger people as well as the local yokels, which was good."

Chris Ethridge, who would later join the Flying Burrito Brothers, remembers jamming with White at the Palomino one evening. Midway through a song, Ethridge leaned over to whisper something in his ear, nearly killing them both in the process. "A damn fire shot up from my lip to his ear and there was a great buzzing sound. My bass amp and his guitar amp weren't grounded. The shock burned my mouth and burned his ear. It nearly shocked us to death." Never one to lose his poise, Clarence casually turned to his colleague and deadpanned: "Hey, don't ever tell me that again!"

The indefatigable Gary Paxton did not know the meaning of hubris and continued to release product, as if intent on turning his bank vault into a hit factory, using the Nashville West/ Reasons band on numerous sessions. Their 'Nashville West' theme song was transformed into 'Hong Kong Hillbilly', a sprightly studio experiment with White's guitar drone used to remarkable effect. A rumour that he played sitar on the track is misleading. In common with the Byrds' Indian-influenced 'Why', this sounds more like a simulation. The instrument was most likely a Danelectro electric sitar designed to imitate the raga effects. "I certainly don't remember Clarence playing a sitar," Guilbeau agrees. "It could have been his guitar run through something else or he may have played an electric dobro through a Leslie speaker. We were always experimenting. Gary would come up with some weird stuff. What he had in mind was not so much sitar sounding. With 'Hong Kong Hillbilly' he was thinking oriental."

For Bakersfield International's eighth single, White received solo billing on 'Riff Raff' b/w 'Grandma Funderbunk's Music Box'. It was the latter, penned by White, that was most noteworthy, a multi-tracked variant on the famous 'Beaumont Rag', sweetened by a celeste. Other notable Paxton productions from the time included Dennis Payne's belatedly issued 'I'll Live Today', on which White adds a chiming riff straight out of the Byrds' 'Feel A Whole Lot Better', and the Spencers' delightfully irresistible 'Make Up Your Mind'. White was so impressed with Dave and Lou Spencer that he made time to appear in concert with them when they played locally. On one occasion, he was joined by two formidable players: his mentor James Burton and guitar disciple Bob Warford. "I was playing with the Spencers when they both sat in," Warford recalls. "We were going to trade off playing when James got up. He was playing pretty straightforward, not really impressive. Clarence leaned over and said, 'In about an hour from now he will blow us both out of this room.' And he was right. James got more and more assertive and played great."

Paxton's productions connected Clarence with so many acts that the numbers become bewildering. An appearance on Leon Copeland's 'Gotta Go See The World' was enough to encourage the song's composer, Merle Haggard, to check out the Reasons/ Nashville West in concert. Ex-boxer Jack Reeves, who helped set up the group's first residency at Nashville West, later used the group on his single 'Not Enough Of Me To Go Around'. Inevitably, the visiting Byrds, freshly intent on establishing themselves in the country market, invited White to play on their groundbreaking album, *Sweetheart Of The Rodeo*. His famous white Telecaster can be heard to strong effect on 'The Christian Life', 'Blue Canadian Rockies' and 'One Hundred Years From Now'. His approach is controlled yet casual, a legacy of countless studio sessions. "Clarence would always have that Viceroy cigarette in the peg-head of his guitar," Chris Hillman remembers. "He'd put it up there, wedge it into the low *E* string so that he could grab it and take a puff. He was a consummate professional – played great, knew what he was doing, and stretched out. He would always add something if we were going through multiple takes."

After completing the *Sweetheart* sessions, White traded his Telecaster for a Roy Noble acoustic guitar owned by Bob Warford. "It was Clarence's influence," Warford acknowledges. "I was in graduate school at the time and didn't have the money to be going out buying electric guitars. Clarence had this white Tele that I loved. Its sound was stunning. But he didn't quite know what to do with it. He didn't like the neck of it as much as his other one because the frets were very low, so he said he'd trade with me. It was an easy trade because although I liked the Noble I wasn't going to be spending my time as an acoustic player anymore."

This was another groundbreaking period in White's life. His work with Gary Paxton, Bakersfield International and the country-leaning Byrds enshrined his standing among the progenitors of what later became known as 'country rock'. Locating the origins of country rock requires another book but, suffice to say, the claimants are many. The Gram Parsons' lobby frequently cite the once obscure International Submarine Band's *Safe At Home*; Gene Clark enthusiasts point to his collaboration with the Gosdin Brothers; Chris Hillman trumpets his first composition 'Time Between' . . . and so on. Outside the competing Byrds, there are far earlier examples from Elvis Presley, Carl Perkins and the Everly Brothers to Rick Nelson, and beyond to the Beau Brummels, Buffalo Springfield, the Lovin' Spoonful and even the Monkees. Add to that the Band, the electrification of the Dillards, the emerging Dillard & Clark, the soon-to-be formed Flying Burrito Brothers and, of course, Bob Dylan's work from *John Wesley Harding* through *Nashville Skyline* and the canvas becomes more crowded. What impresses most is the way you can trace White's work in this area from the moment he first went electric in 1965 through many important and less well known sessions and the largely unheralded bar band exploits of the Reasons/Nashville West. "We were probably one of the first LA groups to do country rock," Guilbeau insists. "That's why those players came to watch and even sat in. After that came the Burritos, but we were first. Unfortunately, the record companies didn't want to hear it."

Not everyone was enamoured of White's switch to electric. "Clarence's life was playing and because he was raising a family he had to make that decision," says Gene Parsons. "He said, 'Am I going to be loyal to this wonderful traditional music that I love and probably starve to death, or am I going to get into a new area?' He'd already done sessions. I think his family really understood that he was doing what he had to do and they cheered him on. At one point Doc Watson said that he would disown him and they had been very close, but I think that [attitude] faded in time."

White ended his tenure with Gary Paxton with a contribution to the Sanland Brothers' 'Vaccination For The Blues'. Once more, White achieved that country twang with the 'nut pull' effect, employing Parsons as a 'third hand' to pull a string. "One of Clarence's innovative guitar techniques was to chime the high *E* or *B* string down above the nut," Parsons says. "This worked great in open position but on this particular tune he wanted to play the lick up the neck. He needed another hand to do it. I provided that third hand . . . I knew there had to be a way for Clarence to bend the string himself. I offered to install pedals and cables like those used on pedal steel guitars. Clarence refused because he wanted something that would fit inside his guitar case. After a couple of weeks, I came up with the idea of using the shoulder strap to actuate a string-pulling, note-bending mechanism. Not only would it fit into the guitar case, it would actually go inside the guitar. I drew up some plans that incorporated a steel guitar bridge that Sneaky Pete Kleinow procured for me. After a little convincing, Clarence bravely agreed to let me install this contraption in his beloved Telecaster."

While work continued on the Parsons/White Pull String device, a constellation of events culminated in Chris Hillman inviting his old friend to join the Byrds in July 1968. Having recently contributed to albums by Pat Boone (*Sanctuary*), Johnny Darrell (*California Stop-Over*), David Blue (*These 23 Days In September*) and Wynn Stewart (*Love's Gonna Happen To Me*; *Something Pretty; In Love*), White's income was increasing, but this was an offer he could not refuse. "I was into studio work making about $60,000 a year but it didn't take me long to realize that, since the age of six, I'd been used to entertaining people by playing music and what makes me most happy is the response from an audience. So I just couldn't do sessions anymore and I was real glad to join the Byrds. Honoured too." Although this spelt the end of his association with Paxton, who released him from his Bakersfield contract without a fuss, White would find far more prestigious sessions to play on over the next few years. His decision to leave came as no surprise to Gib Guilbeau. "For years, he'd said that if he ever had to play with another band it would be the Byrds.

He'd mentioned it long before. He really liked what they were doing and he knew Chris Hillman from the bluegrass days, so it was a natural step to take. One thing's for sure. Clarence was all music. His whole life was music. That's all he was interested in and that's all he ever wanted to be interested in, which was fine."

The possibility of the Reasons/Nashville West continuing without White was further undermined by his determination to enrol Gene Parsons as the next Byrds' drummer. "Clarence had been telling me they weren't happy with the drummer. I don't know why because I thought Kevin Kelley was good. But Clarence was saying, 'You're going to get in there because I'm going to see to it.' It all came about quite quickly." Hillman was also playing politics at this point and secretly hoped to wrest White away from the Byrds into a prototype Flying Burrito Brothers. White was never swayed. "When he mentioned Gram Parsons, I said, 'No', because I can't work with scatterbrain people. He would've drove me completely crazy!" Nevertheless, Eddie Tickner financed a recording with a line-up including Gram and Gene Parsons, White and Hillman, but the session has remained undetected ever since. As Gene notes: "The tapes disappeared into Eddie Tickner's vault and now that he's gone, they're gone too. I don't even know if they were any good. I don't remember much about it." Gib Guilbeau is also rumoured to have appeared on the recording which makes sense only when you consider that Tickner was playing the happy broker. Contrary to previous suggestions, Guilbeau stresses that Tickner did not discover Nashville West while attending one of their performances. "Eddie wasn't a clubber. He wouldn't show up at gigs – he hated them! But we knew Eddie for some reason. He took us under his wing and provided money for recording purposes and got things going."

Even with Gene Parsons safely installed in the Byrds, they continued to suffer internal dissension. Within weeks, Hillman quit in a violent rage only to re-emerge as Gram Parsons' leading partner in the Flying Burrito Brothers. With the Byrds' bass position vacant, Wayne Moore felt there was a chance that he might reunite with his former bandmates, but it was not to be. "They took Clarence and Gene and I thought maybe they'd hire me because they needed a bass player and I really liked the Byrds. They were one of my favourite groups back then." Forsaking Moore, the Byrds appointed John York, who had briefly worked with White in the Gene Clark Group. "They probably considered Wayne too hokey country," Guilbeau concludes.

The Reasons valiantly attempted to compensate for the loss of White and Parsons by revamping the line-up. Never afraid to challenge players to change instruments, Guilbeau persuaded Moore to switch to lead guitar, appointed a new drummer Stan Pratt, and brought in Eric White on bass. Clarence was amused to find his brother playing in his former band and took sardonic pleasure in advising Guilbeau of his quirkier ways. "Clarence said to me, 'I love my brother dearly but don't believe anything he tells you!' I said, 'OK' – and he was right on the money! He then added, 'And whatever you do, don't let him sing.' Eric and I then became friends. He wasn't at all like Clarence though. There's a whole different personality there. He was definitely more like the dad as a person. He was fun and a nice guy to have around. You could always count on Eric, no matter what. If you ever needed him, day or night, he'd be there. He always seemed willing to lend a hand."

Clarence remained on friendly terms with Guilbeau and they continued to socialize between touring dates. "When we were both at home, he and Susie would come over and my wife Ann and I would always do things, like go to Vegas. Often we'd get a call at nine in the evening and it'd be Clarence saying, 'We're bored and we're coming over!' Susie was a really nice lady and I liked her a lot." Despite his Byrds' commitments, White was there to help out when Guilbeau recorded a demo of 'Louisiana Woman' late in 1968. Tellingly, the other musicians included Gene Parsons and John York, effectively the new Byrds minus McGuinn. Guilbeau was equally thrilled when White turned up the following year to add some String Bender magic to his cover of Johnny Cash's 'Home Of The Blues'. "I was in the studio recording that song and 'Lodi' and Clarence was the lead player. We needed an intro and I had no idea what the hell to use. I said, 'Clarence could you come up with a four-bar intro on this thing?' He said, 'What do you want?' I told him, 'I've no idea, but something different.' In a split second he came up with an intro to 'Home Of The Blues' that was a classic. Listen to it. It's Clarence all over. I'd never have thought of it."

Guilbeau continued rehearsing with White following a session for Arlo Guthrie's *Running Down The Road.* They shared a room that evening, which Guilbeau soon regretted. "Clarence was snoring during the night and I couldn't get him to stop so I whacked him with a pillow a few times until he stopped." The next day, Guilbeau teased him about the incident, provoking another of their tit for tat practical jokes. "Everybody thought Clarence was quiet and shy, but they were totally wrong. He had a hidden character that a lot of people never knew. He was funny and loved to play jokes. When we went back to Arlo's place he said, 'Come in my car.' So I did. All of a sudden he's going 100 miles an hour down these curvy roads. He looks at me with that silly grin of his and says, 'You whacked me with a pillow last night, huh? Well, how do you like this?' I was yelling at him, 'Stop the damn car! I want out!' That was typical Clarence."

Eddie Tickner was still assisting the Reasons, pitching songs and promoting Guilbeau as a songwriter. "Eddie was like a second dad. He figured that after Gene and Clarence went to the Byrds, he wanted me to go solo, so he brought in people to produce records with me like Rodney Dillard and Herb Pedersen and people like that. He got me a deal with Happy Tiger Records which was the Flying Tiger Airline people. They had oodles of money and someone running the company who had no idea what the music business was all about, so I signed with them for about a year or so."

Arguably the most unlucky of White's former friends was the phlegmatic Wayne Moore whose easy-going nature and understated talents were never fully exploited. The sagacious Tickner felt he had the "youngest sounding voice" in the group and even made a rare visit to the Nashville West club to present him with the sheet music of the classic 'Early Morning Rain'. Characteristically, Moore squandered the opportunity to cover the song for a flimsy reason. "He didn't give me a tape and I couldn't read music, except really slowly. I got home and it took me so long to get a line that I never bothered to finish it. Eddie never got back to me about it and I never got back to him." When John York was later fired from the Byrds, Moore was not even in the running as a replacement. As Parsons says, "Wayne, God bless him, not to detract from what he could bring as a songwriter or guitarist, was not what I'd call a high-energy player which was what we were looking for. He'd probably gone back to Kentucky by then and wasn't really doing much music." Later, when Guilbeau and his band Swampwater were recruited by Linda Ronstadt, Moore, having switched to rhythm guitar, was deemed superfluous. "I told them, 'Go with her! Don't worry about me.' I don't regret anything that happened. I just take life as it comes."

Clarence White still offered assistance to old friends, including his heir apparent, Bob Warford. "He was quiet and shy and sometimes looked like he didn't really want people talking to him but he'd do anything to help somebody. He was very helpful to me. He loaned me lead guitars, encouraged me to go electric and made statements to people about me where he was stretching the envelope big time. Back in Nashville he'd recorded a couple of albums with Freddy Weller [*Games People Play* and *Listen To The Young Folks*] who was looking for somebody to play with him. Freddy told me that Clarence had said: 'The guy to get is Bob Warford; he can play anything I can play, and more.' Absolutely not true. But it was flattering and very kind, and I worked with Weller for a couple of years after that."

On 13 September 1969, Clarence's son Bradley was born and the family settled for a time in the Sherman Oaks area of Los Angeles. During his spell in the Byrds, White remained autonomous and free to do session work. Remarkably, given the Byrds' extensive recording and concert schedule, he contributed to a further series of albums, applying the Pull String (String Bender) to the work of Randy Newman (*12 Songs*), Joe Cocker (*Joe Cocker!),* Rusty Dean (*Wailing Time*), Delaney & Bonnie And Friends (*Motel Shot*), Linda Ronstadt (*Hand Sown, Home Grown*) and Maria Muldaur (*Maria Muldaur*), among others. As he noted of those sessions: "They'll wait till you're in town, work around your schedule to try and get everyone together. They get all these different people from different groups to play and that's a lot of fun. That's not like the sessions I had to do back in 1966 – they're having a lot more fun in the studios these days."

White's involvement with the Byrds has been documented extensively in *Volume 1* of this book but, taking an overview, it is interesting to observe how rapidly he made himself an indispensable asset. At first, McGuinn seemed in total control, establishing himself as the sole vocalist on *Dr Byrds & Mr Hyde* and limiting other's contributions. The Pull String (String Bender) was used sparingly on that album and White admitted feeling uncomfortable playing fuzz guitar on 'This Wheel's On Fire'. With *Ballad Of Easy Rider,* he sounds freer and the String Bender is employed to spectacular effect, most notably on the thrilling 'Tulsa County (Blue)'. Although modest about his vocal abilities, he was confident enough to sing the traditional 'Oil In My Lamp' alongside Gene Parsons. By the time of *(Untitled)*, White was universally acclaimed as a great rock guitarist and his interplay on the live side, from the uncoiling opening of 'Lover Of The Bayou' through the improvisation on the elongated 'Eight Miles High', catapulted the Byrds to fresh heights. "Clarence brought a new shining light to the live performances," says roadie Carlos Bernal. "It was tremendous. The Byrds always did good shows but when Clarence came with Gene Parsons, it opened up. Roger could stretch out a lot more and not be the only guitar player. He felt comfortable and confident that Clarence was never going to run him down whenever he stopped playing and went to do a solo of some sort. He'd always have a firm foundation with Clarence and a great rhythm section. Of course, Clarence's solos were spectacular."

McGuinn was so impressed that he often stepped aside, toning down his Rickenbacker to allow White a showcase. When McGuinn rose to the occasion on his best compositions – 'Chestnut Mare' and 'Just A Season' – the cross-playing between these greats displayed the Byrds at their finest. Ever generous, White also focused attention on his favourite singer-songwriters, encouraging the Byrds to feature the work of Lowell George ('Truck Stop Girl' and 'Willin'') and Jackson Browne ('Mae Jean Goes To Hollywood', 'Home Sweet Home' and 'Jamaica Say You Will'). Beyond these, his vocal cameos tended to be restricted to traditional country/gospel songs such as '(Is This) My Destiny' and 'Farther Along'. White promised to write his own lyrics but self-consciousness defeated this dream. Instead, he ended his stay with the Byrds with his finest and most moving performance: 'Bugler'. Fittingly, it was the last song recorded by the CBS version of the Byrds featuring the longest surviving line-up.

White's contribution to the group throws up the old conundrum: what is a Byrd? Accepting the Columbia contract as gospel, there were initially only three Byrds until the recording of 'Mr Tambourine Man' after which they became five. By early 1968, only two names remained: McGuinn and Hillman. Thereafter, the subsidiary members were effectively hired hands, an arrangement only partially sweetened by a vague profit-sharing agreement. Tellingly, no other member's name graced that treasured CBS contract. Nevertheless, only a pedantic curmudgeon would exclude White from beloved Byrd status. His contributions to *Younger Than Yesterday*, *The Notorious Byrd Brothers* and *Sweetheart Of The Rodeo*, followed by five more years as a full-time member in which his presence in the studio and on the road were crucial, testify to his importance. McGuinn has frequently acknowledged his value and, even at the final crucible, with the Byrds' dissolution severing all ties, he still wished to retain White in some capacity.

All this begs the question, why did White not attempt to improve his standing in the Byrds by insisting that McGuinn append his name to the CBS contract? Although this may seem a typical example of White's modesty and non-confrontational nature, Gene Parsons maintains that there were more practical reasons for not pressing this issue. "When Clarence and I first went with the Byrds, they were immersed in deep debt. They believed the manager, Larry Spector, had pretty much cleaned their clock. Later down the line, we were convinced by Roger's business manager at the time that our best way to go was a profit-sharing contract instead of going with Columbia. It's true that when Clarence decided about some issue and spoke, people did take notice, although Roger did whatever he felt would be best for Roger. One of the things that may have entered into it was that we were all looking down the line, realizing that the Byrds wasn't going to go on forever. Clarence, particularly, was most likely to be lusted after by record companies, so he was keeping his options open as a free agent. In other words, if he'd signed a five-year contract with Columbia, he would have been stuck with the Byrds [or, more accurately, the record label]. So, this might have been blind optimism, but was not complete naivety."

The invention of the Pull String (String Bender) ensured that White became a guitar hero of a unique sort. Nobody called him 'God' or played air guitar in their bedrooms listening to his solos. This was a man who enjoyed the anonymity of session work, preferred economy to exhibitionism and utilized the discipline of his bluegrass training. Onstage, he was expressionless and virtually immobile, just like Chris Hillman had been with the Byrds in 1965. In the early Seventies, when rock theatrics were all the rage, this was a powerful, almost subversive, comment on the times. It concentrated an audience's attention solely on his playing. As fellow Byrds traveller George Guttler once said: "He stood stock still, his fretting hand seemed to barely move, except to inexplicably pull down on the Telecaster neck with varying degrees of intensity. The notes he played literally came so fast that our minds couldn't process what he was doing."

White was a guitarist's guitarist and it was not only country or bluegrass players who extolled his brilliance. There was a memorable night backstage at the Whisky when an entourage of well-wishers passed through to offer thanks to the Byrds. Among them was a flamboyantly dressed musician, who headed straight for Clarence and said, with visible humility: "I just want to tell you how much I love your guitar playing." White accepted the praise with characteristic good grace and later enquired of his fellow Byrds, "Hey, who was that guy that came in to talk to me?"

"That was Jimi Hendrix," they told him.

What seems most endearing about this story is not just Hendrix's humility in acknowledging White's importance, but the fact that Clarence did not even recognize one of rock's most iconic figures. It underlines how detached he was from the world of celebrity. Up until the end of the Sixties, White's life appeared devoid of intense relationships, ego battles or hedonistic excess. Clarence was *the music* – everything else in the story seems at best an addendum or distraction. People still speak glowingly about him as a person, but there is a noticeable lack of complexity in these remembrances.

This sanitized version of White's life hints at hagiography but there are enough witnesses to confirm that it is sincere. What should not be ignored, however, are the changes that White underwent within two years of his arrival in the Byrds. A more worldly figure emerged who had to grapple with changing times, rock star expectations, pharmaceutical recreations and sexual temptations. At the time of joining the Byrds, White was clean-shaven and conservatively dressed – the antithesis of the cult of personality. Over time, he let his hair grow to his shoulders, sported a Van Dyck beard and invested in a cream/white Nudie suit and a purple cape. This wasn't exactly exotica on the scale of David Crosby's famous green suede cape or McGuinn's granny glasses, let alone the more garish Nudie suits modelled by Gram and company on *The Gilded Palace Of Sin*, but by White's standards it was an extreme fashion statement. His fellow Byrds soon found him a suitable nickname to accompany the uniform: Flash LeBlanc. The newly-invented Pull String (String Bender) was still an unsolved mystery, rather than a gimmick or topic of scholarly debate. Clarence apart, the only known Bender players at the end of the Sixties were Bob Warford, Bernie Leadon, and John Beland.

There is no doubt that White's extensive session work at this point brought him into contact with a wider musical circle than he had experienced during his time with Bakersfield International. Although often portrayed as the straight man, White was quite capable of over-indulging on the road. On a plane flight to Miami in October 1970, he met Jim Morrison who was heading to Florida to face the jury's verdict following an incident the previous year when the Doors' singer allegedly exposed his genitals onstage. White and Morrison appeared antithetical characters but evidently shared a sense of anarchic fun. Clarence's fellow Byrds were amused to find him indulging in a brandy drinking contest with Morrison in the upstairs lounge of the Boeing 707 on which they were travelling. The night ended with White challenging Morrison to a knife-throwing contest. Nobody remembers the victor.

Similar stories featuring White are not uncommon. Carlos Bernal recalls a visit to Nashville, where White introduced the latter-day Byrds to an old source of alcoholic delight. "We went to a place called the Exit Inn after the concert. It was a musicians' place and Clarence's brothers brought moonshine. It was the first time that we ever had it. We were out back and they had it wrapped in a white towel in the trunk of the car. I asked them, 'What do you do with this stuff?' They said, 'Basically, you have one shot and it's terrible, the second one you can sort of stand it, and the third shot should be it, especially if you like it. This was the obligatory clear glass swig over your shoulder. So we drank it. The next day we were staying at the King of the Road Hotel and the guys had to pay a cleaning bill. They'd fire-extinguished the hall under the influence of white lightning. Very harmless fun. They didn't care. Roger Miller's King of the Road Hotel was used to that from other country stars and thought it was pretty mild."

Moonshine was not the only vice that White enjoyed. Somewhere along the line, he acquired an appetite for cocaine. His comic reworking of Leadbelly's 'Take A Whiff' brought cheers from audiences immersed in the counterculture, but it was no joke. By late 1970, the Byrds were a fully-fledged coke band. The apogee of their live set was the elongated 'Eight Miles High' whose success depended, in Gene Parsons' words, "on which drugs we took". Playing the song also allowed McGuinn and White the opportunity to indulge themselves in a snorting interlude. "Clarence wasn't just singing 'Take A Whiff', he *was* taking a whiff!" says road manager Al Hersh. "You saw those shows and you remember that giant break in the middle with the bass and drum solos. That's when McGuinn and Clarence went offstage. They came over to the monitor mixer and we had their lines laid out for them. Sometimes they would leave those guys onstage for what seemed like hours. They would get so caught up in doing blow and hanging out with some chicks or drug dealers that they'd forget those other guys were still out there."

Of course, White still managed to play perfectly onstage, thrilling audiences with 'Soldier's Joy'/'Black Mountain Rag' and singing moving versions of Lowell George's 'Truck Stop Girl' and Jackson Browne's 'Home Sweet Home', a composition that was never released by the Byrds. Occasionally, there were opportunities to reconnect with past influences and associates. Famously, the Byrds were invited to appear on the television recording of *Earl Scruggs His Family & Friends*, which was later issued as an album and DVD. Appearing alongside Scruggs was a memorable moment for Clarence, who had always revered the banjo player.

Between the sessions for *(Untitled)* and *Byrdmaniax*, White was also asked to play guitar on a Gram Parsons solo project, produced by Terry Melcher. With Melcher in psychic freefall after the Manson trial and Parsons at his hedonistic worst, it was a chaotic and unproductive session. The legendary tapes later went missing, but they remain in safe hands at the time of writing. Although Parsons and White were in many ways antithetical in matters such as self-discipline and work ethic, they shared an intense love of roots music. Their upbringings could hardly have been more contrasting, but White was now flying closer to the rock 'n' roll excesses of his contemporaries than anyone might have assumed. "Clarence did coke and so did Gram," guitarist John Beland points out. "They did a lot together and were kindred spirits . . . But Clarence's life was not the train wreck that Gram's was. A session player like Clarence learns to adapt . . . Nobody would make a scene in front of Clarence or get on his case. He had this poker face that could be intimidating – he hardly said a word – but he was the opposite as a person. He was warm and funny. Clarence would sit down and be quiet and play his guitar part. And it would probably be brilliant. They got along together because Gram had a lot of respect, as everybody did, for Clarence's ability."

For White, cocaine was habitual but recreational, whereas for Gram Parsons it was becoming a full-time occupation. Beland had observed those crucial differences in their intake when he was invited to attend a Parsons' recording date. "One day Clarence asked if I would like to hang with him while he played on this guy's session at Sunset Sound . . . Later that night I'm cruising down the Strip with Clarence, who drove like a madman. We get to the studio and all the lights are low. Booze and drugs and groupies are everywhere. And in walks Gram Parsons, flanked by two tall, lean biker chicks . . . Anyway, I sat in the booth quietly and watched as the session proceeded well into the wee hours. After it was over and the musicians were packing up, Clarence brought me over to meet Gram, who was completely wiped out. 'Gram,' says Clarence, 'I want you to meet Linda [Ronstadt]'s guitar player, John Beland.' Gram gives me a long stare, smiles and throws his arms around me and says in that unforgettable Georgia drawl, 'Hey, John, you picked your goddamned ass off tonight.' As he's squeezing me I look behind him and see Clarence with his eyes rolled in the air, chuckling. I just said, 'Thanks, man' . . . even though I hadn't played a lick all night, but was only a spectator in the booth!"

Concomitant with White's introduction to the rock 'n' roll lifestyle was his renewed appreciation of the form. As road manager Al Hersh reminds us: "Clarence was just really starting to understand what it meant to play rock 'n' roll. It was so foreign to him that every night he was learning. At that time, it was amazing to watch the shows because he was coming up with stuff that was totally unique and nobody else even thought of doing. That came from his background. He had some incredible licks. Had he lived, I really think he would have been a major player. I think Clarence had a real future beyond anybody else [in the Byrds]."

Tellingly, during the final years of the Byrds, McGuinn allowed White a more prominent role in concert. According to roadie Jimmi Seiter, White was such a perfectionist that he would sometimes grab McGuinn's guitar before they went onstage and retune the instrument to his satisfaction. Hersh goes further, suggesting that McGuinn suffered a severe bout of insecurity and bowed to White's technical superiority. "The thing about Roger is he stopped playing. When I started mixing I said, 'Roger I didn't hear you really playing tonight?' He said, 'Well, I lay out a lot because Clarence is so good.' Finally, he broke down and told me that Clarence was so good that he intimidated him to the point where he didn't want to play. He thought that nobody was listening. He felt that the audience wasn't hearing the 12-string, that they were just listening to Clarence. I said, 'I'm telling you man, that's not the case. When your 12-string drops out it's huge. You guys are the Byrds and it's got to be there.' But he was very intimidated."

McGuinn's reaction was not entirely surprising. A dedicated player in his early days, McGuinn's work rate had eased off during the later period of the Byrds when personal, business and related professional commitments left little time for intense daily practice. By contrast, White never lost the iron discipline that he had displayed since his childhood. Touring with the Byrds also restricted his time but when it prevented him rehearsing, there was a physical reaction. Gene Parsons remembers one memorable occasion when they were flying across the country from city to city while their instruments were in transit. "The instruments were in one of the trucks travelling over land. We were flying to our destination where we'd pick up the instruments, so Clarence hadn't had a guitar in his hands for about three days. While we were flying I noticed that he had a tremor in his right arm. It was fairly pronounced. I said, 'Clarence what's wrong with your arm?' Then he told me, 'I haven't had a guitar to play and if I don't play a guitar once a day, my hand and my arm start trembling.' The muscles in his right arm were very prominent from flatpicking and the fingers of his left hand were flattened off at the end. This was a guy who had played guitar constantly since he was a little kid, so much so that it had actually deformed his body. That's how much the guitar meant to him."

Playing constantly with the Byrds brought its share of tensions, including some amusing moments on the road. When the group arrived in Portland on 9 March 1971, White seemed strangely out of sorts. He was sharing a motel room with Gene Parsons and while they were preparing for that evening's show, a bizarre conversation ensued. "Clarence looked really tired and kind of burned out. Suddenly, he rolled up his sleeves and said, 'Let's fight!' "

"What are you talking about?" Parsons replied.

"Let's fight. Go on, hit me!" Clarence responded.

Parsons insisted, "I don't want to hit you!" but White could not contain himself. "He hit me," the drummer continues. "I said, 'Whoa, buddy, cut it out!' but he said, 'You have to hit me or I'm going to go off here.' I told him I wouldn't hit him, then he said, 'Well, I'm going to have to hit you!' – and he hit me again. I grabbed him, subdued him and put him on the ground. I used to be a pretty good wrestler in high school and I was a lot bigger than him. I held him around the neck to protect myself because he was just flailing at me. I held him on the floor until finally he cried, 'Uncle! Uncle!' Then I let him go. He stood up, moved his head back and forth, freeing up his neck, and said, 'Thanks! That's just what I needed.' Then he sat down, turned on the television and quietly watched it. He'd just needed to burn off some nervous energy before the performance."

In the spring of 1971, the Byrds toured extensively occasionally supported by Rita Coolidge and the Dixie Flyers. Coolidge was still a relative unknown back then yet she already had a claim to be one of the greatest singer-songwriter muses of the age. Leon Russell had written the paean 'Delta Lady' in her honour and Joe Cocker took the song into the charts. Stephen Stills, an artiste who seemed to thrive on obsessive, tortured infatuations, turned from eulogizing Judy Collins towards an even more enticing figure. On 'Cherokee', from his début solo album, he dismissed the attractions of fortune and fame, but was clearly smitten by "the lady from Tennessee". By the time, he recorded his next album, he was pleading in 'Sugar Babe' – "come on, sweet Rita, you're my sugar babe" – sounding at once proprietorial and desperate. Meanwhile, Graham Nash had fallen for Coolidge and they briefly shared a home together while she provided the love and inspiration for his first solo album, *Songs For Beginners*. Stills' romantic defeat in the Rita Coolidge wars had a devastating effect on CSN&Y, brutally severing the ties between two of the participants. Some time would pass before the parties reconciled their differences sufficiently to perform together. It was left to David Crosby to document the debacle in his allegorical composition, 'Cowboy Movie' which, in classic western fashion, pointed the finger at the mysterious Indian girl as the instigator of chaos. "That was Rita Coolidge," he told me. Coolidge would later marry and record with Kris Kristofferson and, retiring from her role as chief rock muse, enjoyed a rewarding solo career.

Clarence White had been there from the beginning of Coolidge's career. He had recorded with her friends Leon Russell and Joe Cocker and contributed to her excellent début album. It was while promoting that record, supporting the Byrds, that their friendship blossomed. White was almost as smitten by Coolidge as the other men in her circle. Had he been a romantic singer-songwriter, he probably would have penned his own tribute to her charismatic womanhood. Touring intensifies relationships. At a time when the other Byrds were all involved in extra-marital affairs, White sought Coolidge's company. She was an extremely attractive confidante, with a wry sense of humour that matched his own. "It was an 'on the road' thing," says Carlos Bernal. "It happened to be that they were meeting in hotel rooms and stuff . . . We had these two-way radios that we were using to bug each other's rooms for fun. Sometimes a guy would want to broadcast from his room a girl that he met on the road. You could sit around and tune in your transistor radio to a band that the little bug microphone was tuned to . . . I put one in Clarence's room and Rita was there. For some reason, nothing was going on. It was boring, so we decided to get the microphone back. I was sent out to get it but Rita found out there was a microphone in the room and she went ballistic. She threw lamps and yelled and tried to catch me and I had to run for my life."

This pantomime confrontation inevitably provoked gossip which rapidly reached the ears of Susie White. By the time the Byrds' tour reached Rotterdam, Susie abruptly appeared, confronting Clarence before equally suddenly taking her leave. The guitarist pleaded innocent infatuation, but his dalliances with the rock 'n' roll lifestyle were increasingly placing a strain on his marriage.

It was during that same tour that Clarence encountered a woman who was to have a significant influence on his emotional life. London-born June Clark, blonde, model-thin and still only 21 years old, was a keen music fan. After leaving school in 1967, she had worked as a receptionist for the celebrated agent Harold Davison and was soon promoted as secretary to his colleague Barry Dickens and later headhunted by former Walker Brothers' manager, Maurice King. By the end of the decade she was employed as studio manager for photographer Jeremy King, but still attended gigs several times a week. She first encountered the Byrds on 1 May 1971 at the Speakeasy, where they were accompanied by publicist Allan McDougall. An introduction was provided by Carlos Bernal, their flirtatious party-loving assistant road manager. By the end of the evening, Bernal was enthusing about the Byrds' forthcoming date at the Royal Albert Hall and added June's name to the guest list. Twelve days later, she was backstage at the RAH post-show listening to excited talk about an impending appearance in Holland. Bernal, ever high-spirited and presumptuous, invited her to join the tour with full free board, on condition that she paid her own air fare.

In Rotterdam, June had her one and only encounter with Susie White, who was on the warpath over her suspicions about her husband and Rita Coolidge. After three days abroad, June Clark was felled by tonsillitis and forced to return to London mid-tour. Coincidentally, she flew back with Coolidge and her road manager Cleve Dupin, who kindly drove her home from the airport. "Rita was gorgeous," June recalls. "What man wouldn't fall in love with a gorgeous woman who could also sing?"

Ten days later, while the Byrds were still abroad, Clark was in her flat watching their pre-recorded appearance on *Disco 2*. They performed the 15-month old single 'Jesus Is Just Alright' and a surprise song from the quietest member of the group: 'Truck Stop Girl'. Seeing Clarence White on the BBC singing lead was an unexpected treat.

June Clark's diary underlines how speedily she became part of the Byrds' social circle. The same day they returned from the Continent, chief roadie Jimmi Seiter turned up at her flat to spend an evening watching British television. He probably welcomed the opportunity to enjoy some leisure time away from the Byrds who had undertaken an intense schedule, appearing at the Lincoln Festival and vowing to complete their next album, *Farther Along*, in little more than a week. June was invited to the CBS studios in New Bond Street on 28 July, the final day of the sessions, ostensibly to hang out with Gene Parsons and Clarence White. That evening she was pleasantly surprised when Clarence invited her to dinner at the Speakeasy. "It was just friendly. Clarence and I hadn't interacted other than talking. He was just one of the members of the band."

The dinner date brought the two together at crucial turning points in their lives. As had been evident on the tour, White's marriage was troubled. Clark was also in a vulnerable state. Since the age of 17 she had been dating Joey Molland who was currently enjoying success as lead guitarist with Badfinger. Less than two weeks before, he had ended their relationship with the crushing revelation that he intended to marry somebody else. It was small wonder that Clarence and June were attracted towards each other but the romance faced a number of obstacles. The first of these was provided by the unlikely figure of Rolling Stone Bill Wyman, who spotted White at the Speakeasy and, much to Clark's exasperation, bounded across the room like some fan paying tribute. "Bill was a very nice guy but I'll never forget that night. He came over to our table and sat next to Clarence because he wanted to talk to him. So I'm looking at Bill Wyman and he sat there for the whole bloody meal. I wasn't going to say, 'Excuse me, can you leave us?' and Clarence would never say, 'Can we have some private time?' – so we went along with it." The night ended on a platonic note, but a strong emotional connection had been made. The Byrds flew back to America the following day.

After the recent dramas with Susie, Clarence took stock of his life that autumn. Seeking a fresh start, the family moved from rented accommodation in Sherman Oaks to an idyllic home in Leona Valley. "This was out near Palmdale, in the Lancaster area," Bernal recalls. "Al Hersh and I used to visit him there all the time. He had a big ranch that he bought in the middle of nowhere. They had horses, a swimming pool, and a little dog they named Bugler. I remember Roger saying that might be weird karma for the dog. I'd sometimes spend the weekend there, play music, play pool and hang out in the pool. Clarence's mother and father lived there too, and the children, Michelle and Bradley, of course. The family was really easy-going and always playing music, which was a thrill for me because they were tremendous musicians."

The decision to move to Leona Valley in October 1971 had

proven of mutual benefit to everyone, but the remote setting demanded some readjustment. "It was unbelievable when we first got there," Clarence's sister Rosemarie recalls. "When we got out of the car, it was pitch dark and we were freaked out because there were no lights in the mountains. It was so dark I thought I was in outer space. The houses were few and far between because of the acreage. But it was a really cool house – two storeys, with a pool, a big old theme room, Clarence's music room and we each had our own bedroom. It was so big that we didn't have enough furniture for the house. The son Brad had a cat and I had a St Bernard which I had to get rid of because it was so big it was knocking the kids down. I know for a fact that Clarence didn't own horses . . . Maybe Carlos was on something when he thought he saw all that stuff. We had friends from across the street that would let us ride their horses, so perhaps he saw them and thought they were ours."

The dynamic in the White household was both formal and complex. Rosemarie recalls her own parents living separate lives as a couple, each occupying their own room and finding their own space. Temperamentally, they seemed worlds apart, although the marriage always remained solid. "My dad was outgoing but as far as them being happy living there, I'm not really sure. I think my mom was kind of shocked at first but after she got there she was OK . . . We were far away from town and my mother was in charge of cooking and cleaning and helping Susie. I'm not saying Susie never cooked but Mom helped a lot. After the first year, it started to affect her. She wasn't happy. But I'm not sure – it's just facial things I remember. She never told you how she was feeling, she always kept it inside . . . Part of the reason Clarence bought the big house and moved us up there was so Susie wouldn't be by herself. But every time Clarence went on the road there was friction and I don't remember why." Given the gossip about girls and drugs that Susie was already hearing, signs of tension were understandable. "If they had problems, they never showed anything," Rosemarie adds. "It was behind closed doors. If anybody knew, it would have been my mom. They might have talked to her, but I never knew anything. It was certainly stressful when Clarence was gone. And it seemed he was gone a lot."

Bridging the generations was Rosemarie herself, who bonded with her sister-in-law. "I spent a lot of time with Susie because Clarence was always gone. I tried to help with the kids and I think I caused her some hardship because Michelle and I were always fighting. She would do things and I would tell on her and Susie would get upset with me. I called her a brat all the time when she was little, and she remembers it to this day. But Susie was probably the most positive force in my life. She was a very sweet person and cared about her family and about being a good mom and doing the right thing. She was just the best. I just loved her to death. She even taught me how to drive and let me use her Grand Prix for my driving test and treated me like a daughter. When I look back, I appreciate that. My parents were older – my mother was 42 when she had me – and they didn't know how to deal with a teenager in those days. Susie brought me under her wing and was always there. I always looked up to her for that."

Having a brother who was an esteemed guitarist in one of the world's leading rock groups seldom impinged upon Rosemarie's teenage years. Clarence's quiet personality ensured that she never saw him as anything remotely resembling a rock god. Her youth precluded her from attending concerts, although she and her friends were invited to see the Byrds play the Hollywood Palladium on 24 November 1971. "If I'd been older I would have been more appreciative, but my friends were ecstatic when he said, 'I'll get you guys in'." For a brief period, her popularity soared among her small circle. "All of a sudden my school friends wanted to come over and play pool and hang out. That Christmas we were snowed in, but we were invited to go tobogganing. Clarence said, 'I'll come!' We were there so long that my boots were frozen to my feet and it took an hour to defrost them. But he had a blast and my friends all thought he was the greatest." Rosemarie also remembers a hunting expedition, where the family went out at night, armed to the teeth hunting rabbits, while she drove erratically in pursuit, causing her passengers, including Clarence, to fall into a crumpled heap. Such levity was welcomed as dark clouds gathered.

In January 1972, the Byrds returned to Europe for shows at London's Rainbow Theatre after which they attended the Midem conference in Cannes and ended their stay with a triumphant appearance at L'Olympia Theatre in Paris. During the tour, White reconnected with June Clark and their relationship blossomed. "We didn't sleep with each other for a while," she points out. "You see the gentleman there. Can you imagine another musician behaving in the same way? . . . He was completely the opposite of that. Clarence would come and spend evenings at my flat with me, just talking, watching television, having a cup of tea. That was Clarence . . . Even though I went out with musicians and I was into that world, I never smoked, I never drank and I never took drugs."

White was protective and admirably restrained in her company. Remarkably, throughout their time together, she never witnessed him taking cocaine or getting drunk. He was also circumspect about his home life. It was a taboo subject. "I never ever asked him about Susie," June emphasizes. "It wasn't my place to. If he'd wanted me to know he would have told me. I was just happy to be with him." Of course, Clark realized that the marriage had been in trouble before she became involved. While on tour, she heard accounts of tensions and differences that were difficult to ignore. "Susie didn't want him on the road at all, didn't want him to be in a band and wanted him to go to church. That's what I was told." Whether he succumbed to other temptations on the road was also something June never questioned. "I'd love to know any details about Susie and about anyone else he may have had an affair with. Why should I be his exclusive woman? As far as I was concerned, I was there and it was clear that he wanted me to be there. When he was in Europe I saw him every day and he phoned me from gigs. Clarence wasn't a womanizer. He wasn't like that. But if he met somebody he liked I'm sure he took advantage of it. He was young enough and in a position to."

The Byrds criss-crossed the USA during early 1972, a period in which White's vocal showcase 'Bugler' was elevated to second song in the set following the perennial opener, 'Lover Of The Bayou'. This was also the time when the rumoured reformation of the original Byrds was first mentioned in the rock press, a story that would weaken morale in the current line-up, ultimately precipitating their break-up. White tried to rise above the inevitable conflicts and was distracted by more serious worries about his father's health.

Eric White Snr suffered from a hereditary heart condition but his sprightly demeanour belied that worrying prognosis. Often he was frustrated by his body's unwillingness to obey his commands. "He tried to live life like he wanted to," says Rosemarie. "But when he tried to do anything around the house to help, he would become exerted. You could tell he was tired and wasn't able to do anything physical. He liked helping out the roadies, making speakers for the music room, but it was hard when he couldn't do anything. He couldn't even push a broom to sweep." The family advised him not to drink alcohol, but he could not resist a tipple. As part of his morning routine, he would visit Gib and Ann Guilbeau's home in El Camino, always greeting them with the refrain: "Hey, fix me some of that good coffee."

"That was his brandy and coffee," says Gib. "By the time he'd leave, he'd only have had one. He liked to hang out and was really into his bluegrass music. He knew all the players. He knew everybody. His wife [Mildred] was quiet – everybody thought she was just like Clarence. I don't know if she had her little ways but, if she did, she never showed it." Clarence was protective of his father, but brought him into the Byrds' circle and had allowed him to play a rousing harmonica part on the vibrant instrumental, 'Green Apple Quick Step'. His contributions were always welcome. "I remember he taught me to play 'Fugas' on the mandolin one summer," says Carlos Bernal. "That was a pretty obscure banjo/mandolin carnival kind of song, a tremendous ditty. After that, I played it in the dressing room while tuning up the guitars. Clarence cracked up. He said: 'Did my dad teach you that? Gee, only he would know 'Fugas'.'"

With his carpe diem attitude to life, the father gravitated to that saturnalia on Hesby Street known as Tweet Manor or the Byrdhouse. "It was a constant party and all the guys were having their affairs there," says Al Hersh. White Snr was both bemused and amused by the spectacle. As Bernal remembers: "He used to be the handyman down at Tweet Manor. He would be there two or three times a week helping out, doing carpentry or assisting with the amps or just relaxing by the swimming pool watching all the teenage girls that would be hanging out there." Improbably, Eric found that he was quite a hit with the girls who were transfixed by his sultry French/Canadian vocal inflexions and gentlemanly manner. "He was a charmer," Bernal says. "Adorable – and the women loved him to death of course." Al Hersh was amazed to see him flirting with some gorgeous "18-year-old twins". "He was a regular fixture at the house from then on because there was an endless supply of girls. He was just the happiest guy. It was really funny to see this older guy, who was sick at the time and wouldn't last much longer, having a really good time. It was funny for Clarence to see his dad chasing these teenage girls who were totally interested in him, and he just loved it." Sound engineer Dinky Dawson remembers Clarence trying to becalm his father, only to be told, "But this makes me feel young again, son!" As the old man rushed off to the swimming pool, Clarence relented, saying: "Oh, what the hell, just stop and catch your breath every once in a while."

Eric Snr's wilder side was let loose in the Byrdhouse in the most unexpected of ways. On one occasion, his wife Mildred turned up and was made the victim of an underhand trick. After requesting some tea, she was given a brew from the stove to which she reacted badly. "It was tea made from pot," her daughter Rosemarie recalls. "It affected her because she didn't drink or anything. For him to do that – and they were all laughing. I can remember them just standing by the stove laughing hysterically and her being really mad and then not talking to my father –

forever. She didn't party. She liked to have a good time but she would never do anything so out there." The long silence that followed this incident was colder than a Colorado winter.

Although fondly portrayed by its denizens, the Byrdhouse clearly wasn't all innocent fun. The participants recall the late-night parties, sexy girls and fine quality drugs, but these came at a cost. At that time, McGuinn and White had much in common, not least a lapsed Catholicism that nevertheless ensured that they were faithful husbands, at least until the start of the Seventies. In Hollywood, groupies were becoming more rapacious and confident in their approaches and ever more difficult to resist. The scene at Tweet Manor was symptomatic of the times. As Dinky Dawson wrote: "The Byrdhouse was usually a full house, with wives and mistresses arriving and departing with ever-increasing frequency, often just missing each other by minutes . . . it was like musical chairs, with couples bouncing from one mattress to another . . . It was madness, a non-stop love-fest." When Susie White heard rumours that her husband was being unfaithful with one of the local girls, she wasted no time in forcing a confrontation, ably assisted by McGuinn's wife.

"Ianthe [Dolores] and Susie came in and caught Roger and Clarence," says Carlos Bernal of the adulterous liaisons. "Clarence had already gotten in trouble for being with Rita Coolidge on the road and Susie found out about that. So there was a big horrible scene that happened, and it was a crying shame." While Dolores went off to remonstrate with her errant husband, Susie lambasted the Byrds' roadies in attendance. In a highly emotional outpouring, she exposed the shallowness of their cosy chauvinism, damned their libertarian excesses and lamented the way marriage and personal feelings had been tainted by the twin evils of cocaine and casual sex, made worse by deceit. What they saw as good old rock 'n' roll fun disguised a more sordid underbelly. Peer a little closer in a more cynical light and the scene became one of wrecked marriages, easily exploited girls, and drug-spiked tea. As Bernal recalls: "Susie attacked me and Al, of course, saying: 'You guys are supposed to be my friends and you don't let me know that my husband is cheating on me. You knew about this and yet you act like you're my friends. I feel embarrassed and insulted.' Of course she was right, you know . . . It was a horrible thing."

What had resembled a lustful paradise at the dawn of the Seventies was swiftly becoming an obstacle course in the art of divorce. Clarence would be the only latter-day Byrd whose marriage survived, although Dolores McGuinn already feared the worst and no one was surprised when he later separated from Susie. For the moment, they stayed together, but further dramas were already unfolding.

While still living in Leona Valley, the family suffered a bereavement. In the spring of 1972, the irrepressible Eric White Snr finally succumbed to heart failure. During the previous weeks, he had been sleeping longer than normal and his pallor was noticeable. "The blockage to the arteries of his leg brought on the massive heart attack that killed him," says Rosemarie. "That night I remember I woke up to somebody saying, 'Help me! Help me!' I went half-way down the stairs and it was pitch dark because the lights weren't on. But his light was on. He had the room downstairs at the other end of the music room and he was just sitting in a chair. I remember running back to get Mom and I think she got Susie and Clarence. Then the medics arrived and rushed him to Palmdale, which was about a half-hour or 45-minute drive from Leona Valley. So that probably didn't help matters."

The events of that day are also indelibly imprinted in the mind of Clarence's daughter, Michelle. "It was about 4 o clock in the morning. They tried to rush him to the hospital but he didn't make it. I didn't know about it until I woke up and was getting ready for school. I was putting my socks on and I had a sock half-way on when my father rushed into the doorway. [Through the door] I could see Rosemarie sitting on a bed crying but I didn't know what was going on. When he rushed in, he looked like he'd seen a ghost. He looked down at me, just grabbed me and started running through the hall with me. He rushed me to his room, sat down, took me on his lap and then he cried on my shoulder. I was just so hurt and was saying, 'Daddy, I didn't know grown-ups cried.' And he said, 'I'm just sad right now.' He was really trying to regain composure and he was hugging me. I asked 'What happened?' and he said, 'Grandpa went to heaven; Grandpa died.' That's when I chimed in, 'Well he's gone to heaven with the angels, Daddy. He's OK.' That was a big moment for me to hold on to."

Back in London, June Clark was growing restless. Several of her friends had emigrated to America and she was in search of a new challenge. She also missed Clarence whom she only saw when the Byrds appeared in Europe. At one point she considered relocating to Paris, but settled on California where several of her business contacts resided. "Clarence did not ask me to go," she stresses. "It was my decision."

On 13 May, she packed three suitcases and flew to LA where she was picked up by Seiter who drove her to Belmont Shore in Long Beach. There, she stayed with Kay High, a former secretary of Tito Burns, whom she had previously shared a flat with in London when working for Harold Davison. Kay soon became concerned about calls to her home from roadies and associates of the Byrds. All she knew was that the group had been produced by Terry Melcher who, in turn, had been connected with Charles Manson. Her alarm spoke volumes about the fears still lingering in the aftermath of the Tate/LaBianca mass murders.

June next moved into the Beverly Hills home of A&M producer Larry Marks and his wife, Marilyn. She had previously met Marks at a record company launch party in London, not realizing that he also had an oblique connection with the Byrds having partly produced Gene Clark's first album, plus the two Dillard & Clark LPs. Her cavalcade of visitations continued with Cleve Dupin, the road manager of Rita Coolidge. That, of course, brought back memories of her first meeting with Clarence back in the spring of 1971.

The excitement of staying with music business people in Los

Angeles wore thin after a few months. Clarence was "living out in the bloody desert" near Palmdale, so their time together was limited, but treasured. "Clarence was very quiet, very shy and very, very private. I adored him because he was not like other musicians. He was like the guy next door, really down to earth and enjoyed doing ordinary things. He'd take me to the Pancake House or we'd go and stay in a motel. He didn't need anything fancy or exceptional. He was kind, sweet and lovely to be with. He'd never make fun of or belittle you."

Maintaining their unspoken pact, June still resisted mentioning Susie. "He probably loved the fact that I respected that. Of course I wanted to know. It drove me crazy not knowing. I wanted to know *all* the details, even the details I didn't want to know! I was in love with the man. Imagine if you were going out with a woman and she was going back to her husband and children? It wasn't exactly what I wanted . . . but at the same time I thought, 'Well, you never know what's going to happen' . . . I know the man cared. If he'd have asked me to marry him, I would have done. I wanted to be with him. I knew he wouldn't live in England so I knew it would have to be me going out there . . . I question so much of this myself because I don't really know where our relationship was going." Of one thing, she was confident. "The man was in love with me. I have no doubt about that."

By the end of the summer, however, Clark concluded that she did not want to live in California. "I didn't like it and things just weren't settled enough." White was either unwilling or not yet ready to take the affair to a more advanced level. On 2 September 1972, June returned to London. Her four months of entangled romance on the West Coast left matters tantalizingly unresolved. Clarence's intentions remained uncertain, perhaps even to himself.

At the beginning of 1973, the Whites sought a fresh start, moving from their home in Leona Valley to a spacious house in Topanga, but it was an unhappy time. Susie had felt comfortable and secure when Clarence was in the Kentucky Colonels but the rock 'n' roll excesses of his final phase in the Byrds still cut deep. More than anything, she wanted the old Clarence back and concluded that this could only be achieved by a separation. Leaving behind the tinsel glamour of Hollywood, she returned to Kentucky, accompanied by their two children. For Clarence, this was a time to reassess his life and decide what he really wanted. Looking around him, all he could see were Byrds' divorces and break-ups. The group had been disintegrating before his eyes over recent months as McGuinn attempted to re-establish control and enforce some much needed musical changes. White agreed that the band was coasting, and felt they had somehow lost their way during the recording of *Byrdmaniax*, when their personal dalliances had proven fatally distracting. "The Byrds never achieved what they set out to do. Everything was right. We had positive thinking and knew we could become the biggest band in the world. Somewhere it got lost. If we went into a studio then Terry Melcher would come in and distract us. He used to drag Roger off on a solo trip. It was a shame. We'd get our heads together and someone would come and interfere. Anyone could walk up to Roger and turn his head. It was a great pity because he's such a beautiful guy. Roger would never speak up for himself. After the *Byrdmaniax* album we all just wanted to quit. It was bullshit . . . In the end we were lost on it." Although the Byrds had quickly completed a follow-up, *Farther Along*, the results were a little disappointing, although White's moving rendition of 'Bugler' was universally applauded.

White stood by McGuinn, even after the firing of his old friend, Gene Parsons. "I don't think we had too much comment on that," says Parsons. "Clarence apologized to me for not quitting and said, 'I've got to stay in here for a little longer but I'm going to get out.' He then said, '[John] Guerin's a good drummer, but he's not you.' I'm sure he was trying to be gentle with me."

For a time, Guerin's arrival brought a fresh impetus to the Byrds' live performances, but many fans were disappointed to see the group re-enacting the internal conflicts that had destroyed the previous line-ups. Once the original five reconvened to record their reunion album, McGuinn knew in his heart that the end was near. During their final few months together, the CBS version of the Byrds resembled an abandoned ship heading for the rocks. Once more, White had that strange sensation of being lost. "We had John Guerin and then Dennis Dragon. We were just doing concerts – the band was still good, we still had everything under control, and in fact when John Guerin was in the group that inspired us a lot and we were playing really excellently. But there really wasn't enough morale for us to rehearse new material and start thinking about a new album because there was that old Byrds [reunion] album coming out and all those head games and shit that was going on. I didn't particularly want to get involved with it too much longer. Then when Roger fired Skip, that was the end of it, as far as I was concerned. He wanted me to find a new bass player because I knew most of the musicians in LA but I really couldn't see us starting all over again."

McGuinn hoped that he could retain Clarence White in some capacity, even when the original Byrds were uppermost in everyone's mind. "I haven't thought specifically what Clarence's role would be in this," he said at the time, "but I know he's versatile enough to do it. I think he got into a rut, too, as good as he is. I think he could break out of that because he's playing the same licks he's been playing for three years. I guess I am too . . . Clarence and I haven't really been able to balance things out properly. We're great friends and I respect his work. But the thing is, frankly, he intimidates me! . . . In a way, I did let Clarence take over, but I plan to overcome that, little by little . . . I'm sort of insidious, I creep up on things . . . I think I'm going to get a six-string and play double six-string lines with Clarence. Cooperate with him a little more, get a little more elaborate without instrumentation." These optimistic words underestimated the extent of the disillusionment that had overtaken the group in their final stage. McGuinn was already thinking about a solo album and had faithfully promised David Crosby that the only group that would tour or record as the Byrds would be the original quintet.

* * *

The demise of the latter-day CBS Byrds was much mourned but, on a personal level, it was probably the best thing that could have happened to White. He promised Susie that he would try and get straight and save their marriage. Michelle treasures those rare moments when he visited Kentucky and she was transfixed whenever he phoned. "I was young but I do remember what was going on in my head. I knew something was wrong with him and Mom and she was really quiet and angry about it. But they were working things out over the phone. I remember he came out and spent some time with us. I was always trying to listen in on conversations. I didn't miss anything . . . I'm a big communicator with my kids, I tell them everything. They know everything about me. There's nothing that they don't know. But she wasn't like that. She was really strong and silent about things and always internalized her feelings. But I still knew they were working something out. When he visited us, he took a picture of me. I had a dress on that they'd bought in England. It was a cool picture. When he took it, he said: 'I want you to feel sad.' Isn't that ironic?"

The full extent of Clarence's reformation was demonstrated by his remarkable decision to resurrect the Kentucky Colonels. It was as if he was fulfilling Susie's dream of turning back the clock and reconnecting with his former self. High-rolling drug dealers and Hollywood groupies were not renowned for their love of bluegrass. This was an old yet still familiar world that promised Clarence a salvation of sorts, plus an opportunity to reconnect with his siblings. Roland had been playing mandolin and singing tenor with Lester Flatt's Nashville Grass when the call came from Clarence suggesting a reunion. Their musical lives had travelled different paths and seldom entwined in the previous six years. Remarkably, Roland had only seen the Byrds play live on one occasion and, even then, complained that it was too loud for his tastes. Their only notable get-together had been a family reunion at the Ash Grove two years before, featuring Eric Snr playing harmonica for possibly the last time onstage. Getting back together for rehearsals proved that everything was still in place.

"It was great," Roland recalls. "We just fell into it like we'd never quit. Clarence, Eric [Jr] and me always had this thing about timing. We'd been playing since we were kids, so we never had problems. It was like putting on a nice old pair of shoes."

Clarence's willingness to turn back the clock towards more innocent times was further manifested by his involvement in a bluegrass supergroup, specially formed to celebrate the work of the great Bill Monroe. The Los Angeles television station KCET had arranged for Monroe and his Bluegrass Boys to appear for a special on 13 February 1973, supported by a sextet that featured several of his bluegrass acolytes. The idea was that all the players would grace the stage for a grand finale, bringing together the father of bluegrass and his spiritual sons. Fate intervened when Monroe's bus broke down in Stockton, California, and he failed to show. Rather than rearranging the performance, the producers elected to complete a 30-minute concert of new bluegrass with the recently assembled musicians. Apart from Clarence, their ranks included singer/guitarist Peter Rowan and master fiddler Richard Greene from Seatrain; mandolinist David Grisman, late of Earth Opera; Bill Keith, former banjoist in Jim Kweskin's Jug Band, and guest bassist Stuart Schulman. The show was broadcast locally seven months later and was subsequently issued by Sierra in the video age, followed by an extended 42-minute CD. Although the group had limited rehearsal time, their performance was impressive, at once bowing to tradition and looking towards the future. White arranged and sang lead on 'I Am A Pilgrim', which he had first recorded as an instrumental on *Appalachian Swing!* in 1964. His vocal sounds rich and mature and stands well alongside the Byrds' version from *Sweetheart Of The Rodeo*. White's rendition is more traditional and there is no attempt to modernize the diction. Retaining archaisms and inversions, he sings lines such as "if I could touch but the hem of his garment" (not "just touch") while Grisman provides a prominent mandolin solo. Other highlights include the Rowan/White duet on Bill Browning's 'Dark Hollow', some fine picking on 'Red Rocking Chair' and the breathtaking finale, 'Orange Blossom Special', which Greene and Rowan had previously mastered in Seatrain.

Greene loved to play fast and stunned audiences with his versatility. Working with White, he recognized the subtleties in his playing and spoke of his musicianship with eloquence. "Clarence had an extreme dynamic range from soft to loud, but within mezzo-forte. It was sort of compressed, but very dynamic. He had these key notes – I call them major events – that would be 'medium loud', and the rest would be kind of quiet. And you didn't hear any pick noise. He kept the overall dynamic range in the lower levels, but within that there was great variation. I don't recall hearing too many people play that way, except classical guitarists like Julian Bream. Of course, Clarence knew nothing about that, but he intuitively understood the dynamics of classical music. So that right away sets him way off to the side of all the bluegrass players. His playing was so clean, and he was able to play very fast because he wasn't playing hard. If you play hard, it takes more energy per note. So he would save it. He was great at controlling his speed and not rushing."

The television recording proved so rewarding that the musicians regrouped, temporarily sans Bill Keith, for some shows at the Ash Grove the next month. With exceptional rapidity, Warner Brothers offered the group, now called Muleskinner, the chance to record an album. Produced by Richard Greene and the eminent Joe Boyd, *A Potpourri Of Bluegrass Jam* was another rushed affair which nevertheless captured the spontaneous rapport between the highly experienced participants. "We finished the entire recording in two weeks," Peter Rowan recalls. "We played it as we felt it, coming out of a bluegrass-rock tradition in those early days of the 1970s. Clarence's gentle soul was our unifying force, holding our music together; we had all the time in the world and no idea how quickly things would change."

For mandolinist David Grisman, Muleskinner was another example of White reclaiming his heritage. "He was greater than ever. Clarence was flawless in his rhythm playing and he'd do all sorts of things. He was doing something original that seemed to fit in totally with the traditional context. To me that was the whole thing. Here was a guy who was even better than Lester Flatt and Jimmy Martin. He had an artful way of injecting outrageous syncopations that always made sense. Nobody made a craft out of bluegrass rhythm until Clarence." The Muleskinner interlude was a saga lost in time, largely due to the sad delay in releasing the album which did not appear until 1974. By then, it sounded like a requiem, rather than a celebration.

In May 1973, the (New) Kentucky Colonels embarked on a short European tour, appearing in England, Holland and Sweden. Their performance at the London School of Economics was one of the cultural events of the year. For those of us whose appreciation of Clarence's acoustic guitar work had been limited to cameo spots in the Byrds' set, this was a long-awaited revelation. Hearing the Colonels transposed from the Ash Grove to the LSE was akin to witnessing a legendary historic appearance in current time. There was nothing nostalgic or retrospective about the performance as you sometimes find with revered blues or folk heroes connecting with younger audiences in their autumnal years. Even Roland, the oldest Colonel, was still in his mid-thirties and the music sounded fresh, vibrant and authentic. Close your eyes and you could imagine you were back in the Ash Grove a decade before. Their set, which included the much loved 'Soldier's Joy'/'Black Mountain Rag', was a unique treat and one of the most rewarding concerts of its time. Years later, an archive album *Live In Sweden, 1973,* credited to the White Brothers, presented their Stockholm show, but somehow failed to capture the ineffable majesty of the live experience.

Throughout the European tour, White was accompanied by June Clark. Given his recent attempts to reconcile with Susie, this seemed a strange decision but underlined how conflicted he felt. As ever, Clark accepted her role as mistress without making judgements or demands. "We enjoyed our relationship, as weird as it was. He didn't come back and say, 'Susie's found out about us, this isn't going to work and I can't see you any more.' That wasn't how it happened at all. He wanted to see me. In his heart it didn't end. It certainly didn't in mine. He introduced me to his two brothers who could have gone back and said anything to the family. They could have treated me like a groupie and completely ignored me, but they didn't. Eric was shy and quiet and Roland was warm and friendly."

The enduring memory of that tour for June Clark was Clarence's optimism and exuberance. "I'd never seen him so happy and content talking about his work. He was thrilled and excited, telling me everything he was doing and what he wanted on his album." These manic bursts of enthusiasm were followed by quieter moments during which he seemed unusually tired. "He was having these vitamin B 12 shots to keep him going. I thought that was a bit extreme. His eyes were bloodshot and he never looked rested. I said to him, 'You look absolutely exhausted!' He was putting everything into it. When we were staying in the hotel in Notting Hill I took a picture of him on the balcony. He went off that morning to see a doctor, but I don't think there was a health issue."

Following the European foray, the Colonels returned to the US and played one of their final dates at the Indian Springs Maryland Bluegrass Festival. White was enthusiastic about the group's future at this stage, seemingly happy to consider additional studio work. "The Colonels are carrying on where they left off. I want to see how far I can take them which will mean getting them to accept electric music . . . I'm really into bluegrass these days . . . Not being tied down anymore, like I was with the Byrds, makes me happy and free. I've made enough money to play the kind of music I want to. For a couple of years anyway. Bluegrass is really turning the kids on over in the States. Unlike never before you can actually make money out of it. I think the success of *Dueling Banjos* has a lot to do with it."

When White spoke of the Byrds, it was brutally evident that he had moved on. "I found that latest album, the one where the old Byrds got together, a little disappointing, like any other person would . . . I expected to hear that old jingle-jangle sound and it wasn't quite there." Revealingly, he saw himself detached from the insular rock 'n' roll lifestyle that had recently threatened to derail so much. "I'm not going to tie myself down to a group ever again. It keeps you from being able to experiment or do other things. I'm involved with probably four or five projects right now. Since the Byrds, it's all I've been wanting to do too. It's one of the reasons I'm not really sad the Byrds split up."

White was not exaggerating. In addition to the Colonels and Muleskinner, he had assisted Gene Parsons and Skip Battin on their début solo albums and had even done the same for Terry Melcher. Most importantly, he was at last preparing his own album and simultaneously working on a Skip Battin/Clarence White collaboration. This project had been gestating for several months, including a spell of pre-production rehearsals at Skip Battin's house in Topanga Canyon. Jazz guitarist Art Johnson, a good friend of Battin's, was briefly involved. "I was playing fiddle, mandolin and guitar on the road with Pat Boone. When I got back, Skip called and told me that Clarence was leaving the Byrds and they were auditioning guitar players . . . I said, 'Well, I'd love to meet Clarence anyway, I've always loved his playing.' So I went to Skip's house in Topanga and we jammed – Clarence, Skip, drummer John Guerin and myself." On first meeting White, Johnson found him a quiet, brooding character, but soon experienced his humorous side after committing a faux pas. "I'd worked with James Burton as a rhythm guitar player in studios and did a lot of string bending. Later I did a lot of pedal steel effects. The first time I picked up Clarence's String Bender I pulled the lever and broke the string. He just looked at me with that sombre face, then started laughing. I said, 'Goddamn it, I'm sorry' and he continued laughing, then pulled a string out of his case and we changed it together. He had a very dry, almost English sense of humour. It always used to crack me up. But, at the time, he was going through some marital and family problems and he was not a happy camper."

White was also drinking heavily, presumably in sorrow following his family's recent return to Kentucky. These rehearsals assuaged the pain and focused his attention on his music.

Johnson was thrilled when Battin phoned a couple of days later with good news. "He said quite a few guitar players had auditioned but Clarence chose me to be his backup guitarist on this project. We then started rehearsing a lot. Skip had his reel-to-reel TEAC going the whole time we were playing. Somewhere there are four-tracks of those rehearsals on tape . . . Clarence was going through a lot at that time – but what a musician and personality, and what a person to be around. He was the consummate bluegrass player but there was someone much deeper there. He'd spent a lot of time listening to Django Reinhardt and he had a rhythm that was not to be believed. He played a lot of syncopated licks. When you watched Clarence playing all he did was stare at his right hand. He never watched his left hand at all. This was his trademark, to stare at his right hand while he was picking."

The most intriguing aspects of these sessions were the range of styles covered. White seemed happy to allow the players to throw in ideas and, with two jazz musicians present (Guerin and Johnson) extended jamming was always likely. "At the first jam session, I had my new Fender 12-string electric with me," Johnson recalls. "Clarence picked up his Tele and I picked up the 12-string and, not even thinking about the Byrds, played a lot of stuff that sounded like fusion jazz. I was playing some different harmonies than Roger McGuinn would and we jammed on something for 20 or 25 minutes that Clarence was quite excited about. Maybe that's why I was chosen to do stuff with him at that point. Of course, there was a lot of acoustic stuff on which I played rhythm. Although bluegrass was not my metiér it worked for him. A lot of great guitarists had auditioned and there was no reason for me to be the guy who was called back to continue rehearsing. I think the reason was the possible influence of new harmonies for him. This guy was a fantastic picker."

Johnson insists that these rehearsals were spread "over four or five nights" and his personal highlight was witnessing White construct a brilliant mandolin part. "We were playing some bluegrass and Clarence had already played some great licks and had an overdubbed harmony with himself, just like his brother would. There was an open track for a solo and Skip – always the politician – said, 'Hey, Clarence it'd be great to have a mandolin solo there. What do you think?' "

To their bemusement, White abruptly stopped, picked up a bottle of Jim Beam bourbon and left the room. Nobody was sure whether he'd been offended by Battin's impromptu suggestion or simply needed a break. "We turned off the machine," Johnson continues, "and we had a cup of coffee, smoked a joint and talked. About 35 minutes later, Clarence came back and about a third of the bottle had gone. He'd got his mandolin. Then he sat down in front of the microphone and said, 'Roll the tape!' He then played the most ungodly beautiful mandolin solo. One take. And he never changed his expression. Skip, always enthusiastic, was saying, 'Man that was great.' Clarence, without changing expression, just put the mandolin down and went back to his bottle of Jim Beam. He then kind of saluted us and carried on drinking. That summed it up for me."

Neither Johnson nor Battin would be recalled when White finally started recording his own album with producer Jim Dickson. Battin was already working on a second solo album that would never be released in his lifetime, so White employed the more accomplished Lee Sklar, along with John Guerin and Ry Cooder. Other musicians invited included Herb Pedersen, Byron Berline, Roger Bush and Roland White. The recordings actually began as early as 24 March 1973 when Dickson supervised a preliminary session at what the tape box listed as 'Remote Recording Facilities'. Among the tracks completed were 'Don't Forget Me Little Darlin'', 'Sweet Mary', 'The World Needs A Melody', 'Lay Down Your Weary Tune', 'Lost Highway', 'The Fields Have Turned Brown', 'Do Right Woman', 'Man Of Constant Sorrow' and 'Heartache' (the Lowell George/Ivan Ulz composition, also listed as 'Truck Driver Song'). By the end of June, several more songs were completed, including Mickey Newbury's 'Why You Been Gone So Long', Tom Paxton's 'The Last Thing On My Mind', plus 'Never Ending Love', 'Alabama Jubilee' and two songs previously attempted with producer Lenny Waronker, 'Waterbed' and 'Lucky Me'. "Clarence and I did about a dozen songs that I taped," Dickson confirms. "Some were with his brother Roland when we were preparing the album. They were songs we ended up recording with the band because I said, 'Gee, Clarence, you listen to all these together and they have a "down" attitude.' We were going to go for a different kind of album after they came back from Europe and do an album that went from bluegrass to acid rock. But we only got a few songs done." Perhaps thinking back to these sessions, White hinted at the time of further experimentation. "I'll probably do something like a bluegrass instrumental, but I'm going to try experimenting with adding electric instruments – electric bass, drums, banjo, fiddle and electric guitar. Who knows, it might be bluegrass rock next – it's been about everything else."

Between sessions, White stayed busy and cut out the substance abuse that had threatened to destroy his marriage. He seemed happier and more optimistic than ever. According to McGuinn, he even started attending church services on Sunday. It was as if he had completely reconnected with the 'old Clarence' that Susie so treasured. They continued to speak regularly on the phone with White pushing for a reconciliation. Her hurt was still present but close friends confirm that she was ready to forgive her husband and save their marriage.

None of this was known to June Clark who was still sending cards and letters across the Atlantic. "It's a big mystery," she says, when confronted with details of White's plans. "Yes, I think he was conflicted because he had children. It would have been much easier for him to have chosen if it were just two women. Even then, he might have chosen Susie because he'd been with her for a long time. We'll never know. I have my fantasy. He never promised me anything, which was sweet of him. My philosophy was always, 'Don't promise me anything and I can never be disappointed. Don't tell me anything, please.' I just dream and like to think that Clarence might have ended up with me but I'm not surprised he was making an effort to go back to Susie. Why wouldn't he for the children, if not for anything else? He had two young children – it's not as if they were grown up. It's not as if he didn't care. He was a caring, loving, gentle man. He was very sweet and never said anything nasty. Of course to live with him might have been something else. I don't know because I never lived with him. But this is how I remember the man. Clarence was one of the loveliest people I have ever known. And I really mean that."

With his solo album currently underway, there was exciting news about a tour that sounded like a golden PR opportunity. Manager Eddie Tickner, in one of his brainstorming moments, came up with the idea of a revue, featuring the cream of the latter-day Byrds, their progenitors, and offspring, including the White Brothers, Gene Parsons, Skip Battin, Burritos Sneaky Pete Kleinow and Chris Ethridge, plus his current clients, Country Gazette and Gram Parsons & The Fallen Angels. It was an extraordinary line-up, guaranteed to cause a stir in Europe where the players were better known than in their homeland. Several of the acts, including Clarence, had albums scheduled for release later in the year and it was hoped that a combined push could maximize sales abroad where the marketplace was more sympathetic towards bluegrass and country rock. A skeletal US tour was organized for which everyone, bar Battin, was available. Clarence was in characteristically fine form playing with Roland, but soon faced an unexpected confrontation during one of the all-star finales. His attempt to detach himself from the drug culture was tested by the impertinent antics of Gram Parsons, who came close to sabotaging the entire evening. "We all came on as a backing band for Gram at the end," Gene Parsons recalls, "and he was drunk as a skunk. Either drunk, or he had taken some illicit drug but he was pretty out of it on that stage. We were doing some country tune and when it came time for Clarence to solo he played flawlessly with such taste, as he always did. But then Gram started waving at him to turn down. It became so blatant that it was embarrassing. But Clarence had experience doing comedy onstage with his family, so he started making a little comedy piece out of it. He hung his guitar up on the stand and was making facial expressions from behind Gram's back. That got the audience involved and they started to laugh. Gram, not realizing Clarence had hung up the guitar, was still telling him to turn down! The comedy routine saved us and we got through to the end of the night. Later, when I was packing up my drums on the raised stage, Clarence and Gram were on the ground below. Suddenly, Clarence grabbed Gram by the lapels, pulled him downwards and said: 'You son of a bitch. I know more about country music than you'll ever know in your life. Don't you ever do that to me again. Do you understand?' He read him the riot act. It was really funny to see short Clarence doing that to the tall and lanky Gram, who was kind of shaking in his boots. Gram just said, 'I do. I understand. I'm really sorry.' And they became fast friends again after that."

Those handful of dates filled with colleagues, familiar and new, were the last major shows White played. Chronicling the final month of his performing life throws up some minor mysteries since he was still happy to appear at small clubs at a minute's notice. Chris Darrow, a bluegrass contemporary from the Sixties and fiddle player for Kaleidoscope and the Nitty Gritty Dirt Band, maintains that he joined White onstage at the Ash Grove "a month before he died". Alas, he cannot confirm who else played. "It wasn't the Kentucky Colonels – we had a drummer and a bass player . . . in those days we were playing with everybody all the time. You'd just show up and play, and it was just another gig. It's weird when people like Clarence become these larger-than-life characters. Back then they were just people that you knew who were really good players."

Nashville West alumnus Wayne Moore had a similar experience, which he recalls more vividly. "I remember going to this club about two weeks before Clarence was killed. Gib, Gene and Clarence were playing at a place down in LA – I think it was in Montana, California. I sat in with them that night. Clarence was working on his album and he sang 'Never Ending Love', which I thought was really good. He said, 'This is a song off my new album.' When I left the stage they had a side door there. The audience couldn't see me but I was still there doing real funny walks and jumping across the door. I had Clarence in stitches. The whole band could see me and they were dying laughing. That was the last time I saw Clarence."

On Friday 13 July 1973, Roger McGuinn celebrated his 31st birthday at his home in Malibu. White was the sole Byrd from the penultimate line-up to attend. It was a cordial reunion during which McGuinn expressed his hopes that they would work together again. White, presumably, made a mental note to add McGuinn to his ever lengthening list of future projects. The following evening, Clarence joined his brothers and Gib Guilbeau for a jamming session, with some musicians of Eric's acquaintance, at the BJ Tavern in Palmdale. On the way there, Clarence stopped off at his widowed mother's home to have a meal and pick up a present that she had been minding for him since his birthday five weeks before. "He and Roland came to the house and wanted Mom to show them how she made her pot roast, which they always loved," Rosemarie recalls. "We had dinner and then they went and did the show with Eric. I hadn't seen very much of Clarence prior to that because they'd been on the road and he was living far away, so I didn't know what he was doing."

The evening show passed without incident, just another obscure date in Clarence's busy calendar. Across town at the Jack Of Diamonds, where the Reasons/Nashville West had played for many a season, a certain Yoko Ito was clubbing and drinking. Some allege that she was asked to leave the establishment after the resident group had completed their show. What is certain is that she had been drinking and was driving home just as the White brothers were loading equipment into their van at the end of the night. Her car hit Clarence full on, throwing him into the air. The impact was so strong that he reportedly ended up nearly 50 feet away. Roland suffered a dislocated arm while trying to pull his brother away from the speeding vehicle. Clarence was taken to hospital and medics confirmed that he was in a critical condition and had likely suffered extensive brain damage.

At 5 am, on Sunday morning, Gene Parsons received a phone call from Gib Guilbeau explaining the accident and confirming that a brain surgeon was being flown in to operate on Clarence. Approximately 20 minutes later, Guilbeau called again with the grim news that their friend was dead. It seemed scarcely believable.

Over the next 24 hours, reports of the tragedy reached Clarence's musician friends and loved ones. Poor Eric was cast in the role of grim messenger, relating the news to his sister Joanne, then waking Rosemarie and his mother. "There was a knock on the window and we were told there was an accident involving Roland and Clarence," says Rosemarie. "I remember sitting outside the emergency room in the hospital. There were chairs all lined up along the wall and I was close to the door of the room where Clarence was lying on the table. When that door opened, I remember him being completely bald and his beard was gone. They'd shaved all his hair off in case they had to do surgery. When they got the scans back, they realized no surgery would save him. He would have been a vegetable. Then the doctor came out, followed by a nurse and she had these paper cups and they all had a pill inside. She said, 'Take this, it will help with the stress.' The doctor told us that the blow to the back of the head had killed him instantly. When they revived him, it was only his heart that was going. He was already brain dead."

By now, Susie had heard the news and immediately flew back from Kentucky, clearly distraught. Back in Malibu, McGuinn's weekend party was evidently still going strong, well into its second night, when an early morning phone call shocked the revellers into cold sobriety. The fun-loving, acid-witted, former Dylan sidekick Bobby Neuwirth maintains that they were still hoping Clarence might make a belated reappearance at the party when they received the shock news. "We just started to cry. I was there with Roger and Kris Kristofferson, and we didn't know what we could do – except that in country music, there has always been this tradition that when something really bad happens, you sing. That's what June Carter Cash taught me when Janis Joplin died. So we wrote a song called 'Rock 'n' Roll Time'. We recorded it eventually . . . It was our way of saying goodbye to Clarence."

Chris Ethridge, who claims White had been scheduled to play alongside him at a session for Booker T at the Record Plant on the night of his death, heard the news in the early hours. "When I got home at five in the morning, the phone rang and it was Sneaky Pete. He told me what had happened. I couldn't believe it. It was just awful. I know some people who have never got over it. I never got over it, really. It hurt not to be able to hear him play any more. He was phenomenal – a fantastic guitar player and such a beautiful guy too. Clarence was probably the best guitar player that ever lived. He had so much God-given ability and it was just unbelievable what he could play. People who hadn't played with him didn't really understand that, and I got to play with him quite a bit."

The Byrds' former road manager Jimmi Seiter, who lived a few doors down from Clarence at the time, received the news from Spanky McFarlane. "It broke my heart, man. Later, I walked up the street to his house and just stood there. All the lights were on. But I didn't want to go in. I wouldn't have known what to say or what to do for Susie and the kids. But I could hear her crying and the kids crying. It was terrible. I just went home, then went up there a few days later and she was still crying. We had a nice talk. She said, 'Do you want any of this?' There was this guitar, and I would have loved to have had it, but I said, 'No'."

One person kept out of the information loop was June Clark. Despite being friends with various Byrds' members and associates, she was spared the awful news until nearly two days after the tragedy. Her friend Barbara Schiffmacher, a resident of Reseda, heard a bulletin on local radio and reacted immediately. On the morning of 16 July 1973 June was at her flat in Elm Park Gardens, Chelsea, when a cablegram arrived from Western Union. Her business colleagues often communicated via telegram so she did not assume this was bad news. She then opened the envelope and read the heart-stopping message: "June Bad News Clarence White Was Killed 7-14 I'm So Very Sorry Please Contact Me . . . Barbara."

The effect was numbing. "I fell apart," she remembers. "I couldn't stop crying for three days. I was crying uncontrollably and couldn't even talk. I couldn't go to work, I couldn't do anything. I had to stay at home. I couldn't function. I'd only seen him two months before and now, all of a sudden, he was dead. I didn't call anybody and nobody called me. I think everyone was in total shock."

That was certainly the case back in Los Angeles where relatives and loved ones gathered. For most of her visit, Susie stayed with her mother-in-law and Rosemarie, before all the parties reconvened at Eric's house in Palmdale, adjacent to the mortuary and church where the body was due to be interred.

On 19 July, five days after his death, White's funeral took place at St Mary's Catholic Church in Palmdale. It was intended to be a dignified service, in keeping with the family's wishes. An estimated one hundred musicians and friends attended, including former Byrds associates McGuinn and Hillman, Gene Parsons, Gram Parsons, Jim Dickson, Rita Coolidge, Gib Guilbeau, Byron Berline, Chris Ethridge – and many more. Some old friends were too distraught to pay their respects. "I couldn't go to Clarence's funeral," says Carlos Bernal. "I couldn't even stop crying for three days. I guess I wasn't prepared for the experience of having a best friend ripped out of my life."

Chris Ethridge remembers watching Clarence's mother seemingly falling apart in front of his eyes. "She couldn't help it, she was really hurt bad, crying and screaming and everything. It was awful. Terrible. Nobody expected that death to happen. I sure do miss him."

Rosemarie's memories of the day are captured in a fractured series of indiscriminate images: Roger and Linda McGuinn snapping countless photos of the crowd; some faceless people; a couple of musicians singing unprompted; red roses thrown into the casket as it was lowered into the ground.

As the body was being laid to rest, Gram Parsons and Bernie Leadon began singing 'Farther Along' and soon others joined in. The song was a fitting valediction on many levels. It was the only song to have been released as an album track in separate versions by both the Byrds and the Flying Burrito Brothers and testified to their shared heritage. More importantly, its humane sentiments were an uncannily appropriate comment on the senseless tragedy of White's death. A gospel/country song, it did not attempt to answer complex questions about life and death with instant, easy answers. The knowledge of God's ineffable plan was one of the sacred mysteries that could only be known on Judgement Day in the kingdom of eternity. "Farther along we'll understand why . . ." the song promised the mourners, while the lines "Cheer up my brothers . . ." sounded like the deceased offering soothing words of consolation for all those left behind.

Susie White badly needed such solace during the funeral and turned to Gene Parsons, as if willing him to make some sense of this terrible loss of life. "It was a sunny and sad day," he remembers. "We were all in shock and I was just numb. Susie took me to one side and she was tearful. You have to understand that Clarence and Susie had separated. She had gone back to Kentucky. Clarence had gotten into some drugs and she had said, 'You've got to get straightened out or just forget about me.' Well, it turned out that Clarence really did love Susie and he did get straight. He wasn't drinking or taking drugs. He got completely straightened out and he was going to get her back when he was taken. I guess they had reconciled over the phone and were looking forward to getting together. So it was really a heartbreaking situation. Susie said to me: 'Why did this have to happen?' I just had to tell her that sometimes there are no reasons, that things just happen. 'It's not your fault and it's not anything you caused to occur it's just the way things work sometimes.' She was devastated. Then, of course, as you know, it just got worse . . ."

* * *

Negotiations for the anticipated revue tour of Europe were compromised by White's death and finally curtailed following the demise of its headliner, Gram Parsons, on 19 September. A Kentucky Colonels compilation was postponed, for fear of cashing in; Clarence's solo album was never completed; Battin's second album *Topanga Skyline* was shelved, and Gram's Fallen Angels album *Grievous Angel* was delayed until early the following year. Only Gene Parsons' solo *Kindling* arrived on schedule, its contents featuring Clarence's guitar and harmonica on many of the tracks. Regrettably, Gene Parsons had no wish to exploit its potential and never again recorded for a major label. "Warners did not lose interest," he says. "When Clarence died, my desire to play music nearly died along with him. Warner Brothers were really pushing me to go on the road to promote the album and they wanted to do another album right away – and this was in the middle of a vinyl shortage. Well I did go on the road for a little bit, but it took everything I could do to do it and it wasn't really a successful tour, probably because of my lack of enthusiasm." Parsons eventually asked Eddie Tickner to negotiate the cancellation of his contract, effectively committing hara-kiri as a commercial recording artiste. "Clarence dying really cut my heart out. I still suffer from that. It's been 30 odd years but he was such an inspiration to me."

If Gene Parsons felt dejected by his friend's death, then Susie White's reaction was akin to despair. "She was never the same after my dad was killed," says her daughter Michelle. For a time, Susie attempted to adjust by returning to Kentucky, renting a house in Elkhorn City, and finding work as a secretary. But her pain seemed ever present. In a bizarre twist to this sad story, she seemed, unconsciously or otherwise, to be re-enacting the circumstances of her husband's tragedy. Less than two years after Clarence's death, she was involved in a near fatal automobile accident. "The first accident was in the middle of the night," Michelle recalls, "and she was by herself. I'm not sure if she was drinking but that's not what caused the accident. She was driving at a fast speed late at night and the car, a Capri, flipped. I didn't find out until later on that she may have been contemplating suicide. It was obvious that she was unhappy. Deliriously unhappy."

Susie replaced the Capri with the same model, and her life in Kentucky returned to some semblance of normality. A couple of years later, she had her second close encounter with the Grim Reaper while on the road. The emergency brake on her car evidently locked and the vehicle spiralled out of control, rolling across the road and throwing its sole occupant through the sun roof window. "A lady found her in the middle of a four-lane road, lying there bleeding," says Michelle. "She called the ambulance and they put a sheet over her body so that nobody could run her over. They thought she was dead. That's how bad it was. We're not sure if the emergency brake locked or she slammed it trying to commit suicide. We don't know . . . Later, I overheard some relatives talking about it but I guess if she was suicidal they tried to keep that from me. It was really terrible. They didn't think she was going to make it that night."

Gib Guilbeau and his wife Ann flew to Kentucky to visit her in hospital and were shocked by her condition. "She had some brain trauma," says Guilbeau. It was eerily reminiscent of the night of Clarence's death, where a brain surgeon had been contacted just before the guitarist passed away. "This night they also flew in a surgeon," Michelle recalls. "They took her to Kingsport, and they did emergency brain surgery. They literally opened up one part of her head. They found a blood clot and they had to do an operation. She had such severe injuries that they didn't know if she was going to make it that night, but she pulled through. Even then, they couldn't guarantee anything. We didn't know how she was going to do. When she woke up she was asking for my daddy again. She never did get her long-term memory back. It took some months for her to realize who we were. It was really hard. It took her almost a year to recuperate from that accident and to live on her own. She couldn't even take care of herself . . . They had to try and take care of her [and wait] for her wounds to heal and for her to be OK psychologically to be on her own. She was a lot like a child, and it angered her that she couldn't be a woman. She really had a hard time dealing with her emotions. They overtook her. She didn't really get to grieve over him and they loved each other so much. It was almost like a Romeo and Juliet story. When he was killed she didn't talk about it; she did nothing but mourn; she felt guilty and had a hard time communicating her feelings. Then she went into drinking – she was just a walking pain. It just took her over and she didn't want to go on any more without him. It was really sad."

While question marks hover over the previous two car crashes, there is no doubt that the final one, in July 1981, was a terrible accident, even more shocking, though obviously less public, than the collision which took the life of Clarence White. Although still troubled, Susie had reached "some level of contentment" and was keen for the family to move to Nashville. They spent a week and a half at Roland's home and, although nothing was confirmed, a relocation from Kentucky looked promising. It had been a pleasant vacation. On the ride home, the car was full of children, still excited by the adventure. As well as Susie's children – Michelle (aged 15) and Bradley (aged 11) – there was Roland's ten-year-old son, Lawrence. "We were on our way back from Nashville to Kentucky," Michelle recalls, "and we'd had a good time together. My mom had allergies real bad and we'd both taken some sinus medicine. She stopped and got herself an eight pack of Pony Millers. She may have had a beer or two, but they were tiny, baby Millers. They had nothing to do with the accident. It was about 5.30 in the afternoon and it was getting dark, the sky started to cloud up and it was going to storm. She went to pass a car. You know how there'll be a bright arrow telling you to stay in lane. Well, it wasn't on, but she didn't know that. She was going about 50–55 miles per hour in this bitty 1980 Volkswagen Rabbit. The car was fairly new, but real tiny. There was some state equipment that paints the road. It's a big steel piece that hangs out about three or four feet into the road. When she went past the car, she hit straight into it.

"I can barely remember being thrown against the dash, but I

didn't have one stitch. I was on the passenger side and my cousin Lawrence was behind me. We'd just stopped at a rest area and my brother Bradley and Lawrence had switched places. When we ran into the equipment, it snagged the whole left side of the car. All I can remember is Lawrence kind of squirming and I could hear him moaning behind me so I knew he was still alive. But I didn't feel any life where the others were sitting. I started to try and wake [Susie] up and I was crying for her because I knew one more accident was all it would take. I just knew this. That song 'Endless Love' was blaring on the radio. Then I could hear ambulances coming up behind us. I kept turning around and trying to reach for her, but there was no life. They were killed instantly. They didn't even know what went on and they didn't feel any pain. I was led out of the car and I can remember seeing her forearm laying on the ground beneath the back bumper. This man kept trying to pull me. He was doing his best but I was fighting him. I kept saying, 'Are they going to be brought in another ambulance?' But he wouldn't say anything to me. He couldn't answer yes or no. He couldn't tell me they'd died. He just said, 'Let's just check you out and look at this eye. You have a light concussion. We need to take you to the hospital.' So they put me and Lawrence side by side in the back of the ambulance and I kept listening for that other ambulance. I turned around and I clutched Lawrence's arm. He reached out to me and I reached out to him, and I told him: 'Lawrence don't ever leave me! Please don't ever leave me!'

"And here I am tearing up! I don't usually go into this story – it takes me back. But I kept repeating 'Just don't ever leave me' and he hasn't. And he was only ten and to this day Roland's son Lawrence is like a brother to me. They rushed us to the hospital and as they rode me down on the gurney, I kept trying to get up and look for them. I kept saying 'Where's this other ambulance? When is it coming?' A nurse looked down and said, 'Honey, just let it go.' And with those words – well, at least it gave me an answer that I didn't want to hear. I can remember it was devastating. I was angry. I almost felt betrayed that I was left behind. Phew!"

Thereafter, Michelle's life was, by her own admission "a screenplay". Orphaned at 15, she was taken in by her mother's sister and husband and remained in Pike County, Kentucky. "I didn't want to live in Pike County anymore. They said, 'Well, this is what Susie would have wanted.' So I resentfully lived with them. I know they were trying to help but I didn't want to live there. But I wasn't given a choice . . . there was so much I went through even after that accident. Nothing was ever really normal."

By the time Michelle was 18, she "got to drinking", then met a guy and married. "We started dating and I got pregnant. So I started staying with him and I really didn't want to marry him because I knew I didn't love him . . . We were just friends and I was trying to survive. I didn't feel like I had a place to live." In the background, there were money arguments with some relatives. "There was a lot of resentment going on and it fed my drinking." The marriage lasted five years, during which she gave birth to two boys. "We went to court over the kids and I moved to Nashville – he ended up with the eldest one and I ended up with the youngest one. The judge didn't prove me unfit . . . but they took my first born from me . . . They tried to talk about me like I was some kind of loser bum liar, some promiscuous nothing just walking the streets out here, that I was no good . . ." The saga continued . . . another marriage, another long-term but fraught relationship, the details of which are far too convoluted for this book. "I was in alcoholic relationships. I was trying to make something that could never be. I was trying to be a happy family somewhere . . . There was no grief counselling. Grief just took over . . . I kept cutting hair and getting by."

In 2007, Michelle ended an 11-year relationship and, five children on, she is presently single and sober having previously fallen into the grip of crack cocaine addiction. "I have much to reflect on and I'm gaining still. I've been clean and sober for five years this March [2008] and to this day, I'm in awe. It had to be God to carry me through some of the most desperate times. I guess I had the strength that I never knew I had, but I didn't have the confidence or self-esteem to go with it. And I have that now. I'm a totally different person."

As Clarence's executor, Michelle has frequently been called upon to sanction various reissue projects. Her father's musical legacy is significant and his acoustic work has inspired a generation of flatpickers. His electric string-bending exploits are echoed in the recordings of Marty Stuart, Steve Wariner and Vince Gill. Once an esoteric instrument, the String Bender can now be found in the guitar collections of some of rock's most famous players, including Pete Townshend, Jimmy Page and Keith Richards. White's former instruments have ended up in good hands. Tony Rice inherited his Martin D-28, while Bob Warford acquired the white 1953 Telecaster that featured on many classic recordings, including *Sweetheart Of The Rodeo*. Marty Stuart bought White's trademark 1956 Fender Telecaster on which the original Parsons/White Pull String was first installed. "The guitar really found me," says Stuart. "Roland White got me my gig with Lester Flatt and I was friends with the family. The guitar already had a following of its own by that time. I was always fascinated by it, lusted after it, and I'd even had a similar bender put in another guitar to try and duplicate the effect . . . I've never considered it my guitar, really. It's his and now it kind of has a life of its own. The sprig gets dry and squeaks so I spray WD-40 on it now and then, but I've never cleaned it. All the dirt inside and behind the strings is the original dirt. We call it 'Clarence'."

The instruments' new owners are well placed to sum up White's importance as a guitarist. Bob Warford says: "As a bluegrass player, I don't think I've ever heard anyone as good. It's harder for me to judge his electric playing simply because it was him encouraging me and loaning me a couple of guitars that meant I went electric myself. I started with the Bender shortly after he did and it became eerie after a while because we'd play almost identically. I then tried to play differently and ended up developing a somewhat different style but I was always impressed by his playing. He was certainly more influenced by rock players such as Hendrix, where I was more influenced by Clapton. He was much more adventurous in terms of playing 'bizarre' licks. You'd think, 'Hey, where did that come from?' I would be closer to the traditional player."

Marty Stuart adds: "Somebody once called his style 'quirky' and that's about the best description I ever heard. It was the way he placed his notes. As a country player, he was a monster. As a rock 'n' roller, he was so original. Had he lived I'd have to believe that Clarence would have eventually wound up in a country band, and I think that, hands down, he would have been the greatest guitar player there ever was."

These are bold claims, but hardly untypical of the praise heaped on White. He remains the quintessential guitarist's guitarist, an uncharacteristically old school figure. Sometimes, he appears like a character from another age, a purist who carried and maintained the weight of bluegrass tradition in the artificial arena of mainstream rock. That's how certain rock musicians and critics tend to view his contribution. However, when you speak to Roland White or some of his bluegrass contemporaries, the stress is less on authenticity than modernity. For them, Clarence was the great innovator, the risk taker, the quiet revolutionary: he defied the traditionalists, even his great mentor Doc Watson, by performing electric; he made a decent living playing sessions for stars: he joined a famous rock group. These were no small feats in the insular world of traditional bluegrass.

Traditionalist and innovator, White has been applauded by both camps. It is a tribute to his appeal that virtually everyone writes about him in hagiographical adjectives. It is hard to imagine a poor review of a White record nor can I recall any critic questioning his ascension to sainthood. Yet, he was not perfect. In truth, White's strengths and weaknesses were inextricably linked. One question that nobody asks is: could he have been even better? Probably not as a guitarist, but possibly as a more rounded writer/performer. White was always aware of his limitations. Lesser players than he blithely diversified into other areas without a care, but his strict bluegrass upbringing was accompanied by a natural reserve and self-consciousness that discouraged pretension. Chris Hillman shared many of the same characteristics but was still young enough when he joined the Byrds to take the leap into an alien pop environment, abandoning his prized mandolin for a cut price bass that initially he could not even play. It was that courage that made him a star in the Byrds and opened the door to new and unexpected highs and lows in Manassas, Souther, Hillman, Furay and McGuinn, Clark & Hillman. For a time in the mid-Seventies, he even emerged as an unlikely solo singer-songwriter with two major albums to his name.

White waited much longer before leaving bluegrass. Joining the Byrds brought him international renown and access to a mass market beyond session work. Although always looking ahead, White's reticence blocked certain opportunities. By his own admission, he was a singer of limited range, who never much liked his voice. Hillman had similar self-doubts, but he eventually led a band. There were far worse singers than White enjoying thriving careers at the end of the Sixties, but his perfectionism made him over-critical. Knowing that his vocal power could never equal his playing skill, he held back. Of course that never stopped Clapton or Hendrix – or Hillman for that matter. Clarence's compromise was to accrue lead vocal opportunities over time – roughly one per Byrds album – until he had sufficient experience to make an impact in live performance. The recording of 'Bugler' should have assuaged any lingering doubts about his abilities. It remains his most moving vocal performance.

While many critics, myself included, rave about White's musical contributions to 'Time Between', 'Change Is Now', 'Wasn't Born To Follow', 'Chestnut Mare' et al – it's crucial to note that none of these were his own compositions. All the publishing money on those songs went to other people. If White had co-written some of these he would have been a richer man. While it is true that he earned a healthy income playing sessions, sometimes at double rate, he would have made much more as a songwriter and this would have enhanced his legacy. Even his incomplete solo album shows a preference for covering other writers like Newbury or Paxton. Check White's BMI listing of registered songs and the number seems shockingly low for such an important musician.

This is not intended as a carping criticism. It may sound a bit like blaming great singers such as Frank Sinatra or Tony Bennett for failing to put pen to paper and relying on tunesmiths to conjure their emotional response. But White was not working in the Tin Pan Alley era and condescending counterculture rock critics of his period were not beyond impolitely dismissing the stars of previous generations as mere entertainers rather than creators. Such were the prejudices of the time, but White was part of that time. He knew the importance attached to composing and after working with Jackson Browne, he wanted to try lyric writing. Given his discipline and penchant for endless guitar practice, the rigours of songwriting should not have been so daunting. With his finely-tuned ear and melodic sense, he surely would have produced many memorable compositions with decent lyrics . . . but perhaps not. The Bakersfield songs credited solely to his name are pleasant, lightweight tunes, sometimes around 90 seconds' duration. His songwriting contributions to the Byrds, all instrumental collaborations with Gene Parsons, are enjoyable, but will never be ranked alongside the group's greatest work. We can only guess what might have been.

Musically, the missing era in White's life is the early Seventies, a time when record companies were still backing ex-Byrds and country players, as if they represented the future. This was an era when White's standing as a country/rock guitarist might have rivalled his legendary status as a bluegrass virtuoso. White had a three-album deal in boom time and there is every likelihood that Warner Brothers would have fulfilled the terms of that contract and allowed us to witness his blossoming as a solo artiste. It is fascinating, though ultimately fruitless, to imagine where Clarence White might have taken his music and his audience during those peak years of record company investment. Of course, cult legends were still subject to the marketplace, but it was only in the late

Seventies that the various ex-Byrds fell victim to corporate balance sheets.

By the early Eighties, all the Byrds had lost major label status and White would probably have gone the same way, along with McGuinn, Crosby, Clark, Hillman, Gene Parsons, and the rest. Of course, he could still have enjoyed success working with country stars, doing session work and belatedly finding fresh fame as an elder statesman in the age of alternative country and new bluegrass. His sister Rosemarie believes he would have moved to Nashville. "People speculate what he might be doing if he were still alive and I think he would have gone back to his roots. I think he was already planning to move to Nashville before he was killed. Roland and he would probably have done something together. Clarence would have done some electric recordings, but I think he would have gone back to bluegrass."

Nevertheless, his peak period, purely in commercial terms, would most likely have been the solo Warners years and those three lost solo albums, the contents of which we can only surmise. Would he have amazed us by writing some serious lyrics for the first time in his career? Or would he have retained a writer's block too frustrating to overcome? Were there yet more guitar-playing innovations from the man to astonish us all? We shall never know.

It hardly needs stating that it is better to consider what we have rather than speculate on what might have been. Perhaps White's innate modesty and unwillingness to be distracted from his main calling as a guitarist is what enabled him to create such great work. He certainly did not need to prove himself as a songwriter. That he achieved prominence working in both bluegrass and rock displays a remarkable versatility that cannot be overstated. As musician Scott Nygaard insists, without fear of contradiction: "Clarence White can rightly claim to be the only guitarist in history to have invented unique ways of playing both acoustic and electric guitar."

At the time of his death, White's discography was relatively sparse. Now, it is extensive. The archival/reissue campaign began in earnest during the second half of the Seventies thanks to specialist labels such as Sierra, Briar, Rounder and Shiloh. For a time, it seemed that the cupboard was bare, but Sierra's John Delgatto continued to unearth obscure tapes featuring rare 'lost' performances or home recordings. There have also been several tapes recorded on primitive equipment by dedicated bluegrass aficionados, lovingly restored for the CD/DVD age. More recently, Big Beat Records has mined the Bakersfield catalogue for all those ultra rare singles and outtakes that most of us believed we would never hear. The quality of the packaging, complete with informative essays and liner notes, has also been exemplary. Inevitably, the well must now be running dry but, just when you think it's all over, further rumours abound. A few years ago Shiloh's Dale Davis told me: "I've now had my label for 30 years. We're looking through my tape library and various things to put together a Kentucky Colonels album. We've got a lot of tapes and I've told my son: 'We don't want to use any tapes that do not contain the three brothers – Roland, Eric and Clarence.' I don't know if I can put together enough for a decent album, but I do have quite a bit of stuff."

It is not only White's pre-Byrds' bluegrass recordings that have attracted interest. Since the late Nineties, the Byrds' White-era catalogue has been reissued with bonus tracks, along with box sets and live recordings. All of these have reconfirmed how important Clarence White was in the history of this illustrious group. Listening to the 'new' recordings was not only an education and pleasure for fans but also an opportunity for McGuinn to revisit the past and appreciate the considerable contribution made by his former colleague. "It was very heart-warming to hear Clarence White that close . . . you could isolate him, and it was just Clarence playing. It was like he was alive again . . . My feeling about these reissues is it's a great way to get Clarence White's name more recognized because he's an unsung hero as guitar players go. You see these lists of Top 100 guitar players – he ought to be in the Top 10, man. And he isn't, and I think this stuff will help him out. Not that he physically benefits but I see Gram Parsons elevated to a level like Jim Morrison and I think, 'What about Clarence White?' "

CLARENCE WHITE: NOTES

page 834: "Before they anglicized their name . . ." Clarence's sister Joanne told me: "It was definitely 1939. The reason I know is because my mother told me they changed their name the year I was born."

page 834: "Their first son Roland . . ." Roland confirms that he was born in Madawaska, while the other children, including Clarence, were born in Lewiston, Maine.

page 834: "We used to go there on a Sunday afternoon . . ." Roland White, interviewed by the author. London/Nashville, Tennessee: 12–13 October 2007.

page 835: "I used to sing . . ." Joanne Bierbrauer (formerly Saxton, née White) interviewed by the author. London/Lancaster, California: 12 December 2008.

page 835: "It was 1949–50 . . ." Roland White/Rogan. London/Nashville, Tennessee: 12–13 October 2007.

page 835: "Clarence started strumming . . ." ibid.

page 836: "It was Roland's idea . . .' Joanne Bierbrauer (formerly Saxton, née White)/Rogan. London/Lancaster, California: 12 December 2008.

page 836: "The first known public performance by the White siblings . . ." Interestingly, Joanne White has no memory of performing at China Lake, so it may have been simply the three brothers at that particular show. Joanne concludes that she performed publicly with the group after they were working as the Country Boys.

page 836: "These grange halls . . ." Roland White/Rogan. London/Nashville, Tennessee: 12–13 October 2007.

page 837: "There's plenty of work out here . . ." ibid.

page 837: "The Riverside Rancho . . ." The spiritual home of Spade Cooley ('the king of Western Swing'), among others, the club was a landmark in Los Angeles' music history, but closed in 1959. Evidently ignoring its cultural significance, a concept that would have been unknown at the time, the Los Angeles Fire Department set fire to the building as part of a training exercise for its members. The musicians who played there moved on to the Palomino on Lavershim Boulevard, North Hollywood, which entertained most of the country players, legendary or otherwise, featured in this book.

page 837: ". . . they dressed them up as little farmers . . ." Joanne Bierbrauer (formerly Saxton, née White)/Rogan. London/Lancaster, California: 12 December 2008. According to Roland, the name was inspired by another act whom Hicks had discovered and named the Three Little Country Girls.

page 837: "I was like the guest sister . . ." Joanne Bierbrauer (formerly Saxton, née White)/Rogan. London/Lancaster, California: 12 December 2008.

page 838: "He had an arch-topped Gretsch guitar . . ." Roland White/Rogan. London/Nashville, Tennessee: 12–13 October 2007.
page 839: "Well, at a young age she met this man . . ." ibid.
page 839: "My world pretty much turned upside down . . ." Joanne Bierbrauer (formerly Saxton, née White)/Rogan. London/Lancaster, California: 12 December 2008.
page 839: "But, no . . ." Elaborating on Joanne's early life and first marriage, her younger sister Rosemarie adds: "She was working at a drive-in theatre at the time and that's when he came through the lines at the snack bar. That's when it all started. Soon after that, she was swept off her feet. She didn't realize what kind of person he was. We thought he was a very mean person. If she'd met somebody different, she probably could have continued with the music but he was too jealous and would not allow her. He was afraid that she might get tired of him or might meet somebody else and he'd lose her. That's just what his personality was. He would not let her go anywhere without him because of that reason. I think a lot of that was also why they didn't come over to the house . . . He was very jealous that the attention wasn't on him. He would get mad, so he pretty much kept her away from us."
page 840: "We liked the record very much . . ." Roland White/Rogan. London/Nashville, Tennessee: 12–13 October 2007.
page 840: "Billy Ray Lathum . . ." Oddly, Lathum is often called 'Latham' in various profiles, credits and record releases. Even his entry on Wikipedia at the time of writing is 'Billy Ray Latham'. Sierra's John Delgatto who issued the archival album *Bush, Lathum & White* confirms that it is Lathum. "I guess people don't care," Delgatto reflects. "I have seen his birth certificate, driver's license . . . I babysat his apartment back when he was with the Dillards . . . I am also his music publisher."
page 840: "I spent almost every hour . . ." Clarence White, interviewed by Pete Frame. London: 22 May 1973.
page 840: "Clarence played a few leads . . ." Roland White/Rogan. London/Nashville, Tennessee: 12–13 October 2007.
page 841: "We used to try and sell them . . ." ibid.
page 841: "We took our cues . . ." LeRoy McNees, interviewed by Alastair McKay. *Uncut*: November 2013.
page 841: "I'd bring home records . . ." Roland White/Rogan. London/Nashville, Tennessee: 12–13 October 2007.
page 841–842: "We always had a houseful of musicians . . ." Rosemarie Johnson (née White), interviewed by the author. London/Lancaster, California: 16 October 2008. Despite being raised in a musical family, Rosemarie did not play or sing. "I'm the only one," she says. "Even Joanne played bass and sang. But they were too busy to teach me. If my dad tried to teach me, I may not have been interested at the time. I was into my friends and had no time for music. When Roland came back

from Germany he tried to teach me the mandolin, but I was too little then. Of course, they had uncles and my dad to help and they didn't have to go to school and play music. They played music all day long, practised and practised. I was the only one that finished school."

page 842: "I was nine and Clarence was 16 . . ." Tony Rice, interviewed by Jon Sievert. *Frets*: September 1979.

page 842: ". . . via appearances on NBC-TV's *The Andy Griffith Show . . .*" Roland White also told me: "There was somebody from Desilu Productions called Steve Stebbins. He was a booking agent who brought a lot of the big stars to play in California. He knew who we were. They said, 'We want a string band for our show. Do you know anyone?' He told them, 'Well there's a family here, the White Family, they've got a little band, the banjo, guitar and mandolin.' They said, 'That's what we're looking for.' So he gave them our number, they called and we went down there and did the show . . . No, there wasn't any management interest in us. It was very difficult. We had many of these people who were a lot of help but no manager."

page 843: ". . . the label's A&R head Paul Cohen insisted . . ." Cohen had previously recorded Bill Monroe at Decca in 1951. The A&R man was known for his astuteness and sensitivity. During that same period he recorded Jim Eanes' cover of Fiddling Arthur Smith's 'I Took Her By Her Little Brown Hand'. The opening verse featured the lines, "The prettiest little coon gal you ever did see", prompting Cohen to remove the word 'coon' from the record. Eanes was puzzled as he had been performing the song in public frequently without attracting a single complaint or even comment. For additional information read Pete Kuykendall's 'Smilin' Jim Eanes', *Bluegrass Unlimited* 7 (February 1973, pp. 7–11) and Neil V. Rosenberg's *Bluegrass: A History* (University Of Illinois Press, 1985), p. 119.

page 843: "Basically, it was a combination . . ." Joe Maphis' liner notes from *The New Sound Of Bluegrass America.*

page 844: "I got a copy of it . . ." Roland White/Rogan. London/Nashville, Tennessee: 12–13 October 2007.

page 844: "During the set he played mandolin . . ." Bob Warford, interviewed by the author. London/Riverside, California: 13 July 2007.

page 844–845: "This was another eye-opener for Clarence . . ." Roland White, quoted in *Bluegrass Guitar* by Sid Griffin & Eric Thompson (Backbeat Books/Outline Press, 2006), p. 42.

page 845: "As an acoustic guitar player . . ." Al Rosenberg (now known as Al Ross), interviewed by the author. London/New York: 24 February 2008.

page 846: ". . . the Elektra album . . ." *New Dimensions In Banjo And Bluegrass* was reissued in 1973 as *Dueling Banjos* in order to cash in on the film, *Deliverance.* The new title track was recorded by Eric Weissberg and Steve Mandell but there was no reference to the album's earlier incarnation as *New Dimensions In Banjo And Bluegrass* and both Dickson's and White's names were conspicuously absent from the sleeve which featured no explanatory liner notes.

page 846: "In September 1963 . . ." That same month, the Kentucky Colonels appeared at the newly-built Bakersfield Civic Auditorium. In addition to their set, they also backed Johnny Bond. Two songs from the show, 'Green Corn' and 'Blue Ridge Mountain Blues', can be found on the Capitol Records compilation, *Country Music Hootenanny.*

page 846: "I was mainly interested . . ." David Grisman, quoted in *Frets*: March 1979, requoted in *Frets*: September 1979.

page 846: "[Slone] knew Susie's sister . . ." Roland White, quoted in Alec Palao's liner notes to *Tuff & Stringy: Sessions 1966–68.*

page 847: ". . . the most complete and compact course . . ." Scott Nygaard, *Acoustic Guitar*: October 1995.

page 847: "His masterful sense of timing . . ." Jon Sievert, *Frets*: September 1979.

page 847: "Clarence's acoustic guitar . . ." Chris Hillman, quoted in *Bluegrass Guitar* by Sid Griffin & Eric Thompson (Backbeat Books/Outline Press, 2006), p.41.

page 848: "I still have that tape . . ." Tut Taylor, quoted in Etsuo Eito's website *Clarence White Chronicles.*

page 848: "We got together at his apartment . . ." ibid.

page 848: "It was the most exciting week in my life . . ." Sandy Rothman, quoted in Etsuo Eito's website *Clarence White Chronicles.*

page 848: "Adams Otis recorded a lot of the shows . . ." Roland White/Rogan. London/Nashville, Tennessee: 12–13 October 2007. These 'Reinhardt sessions' were also taped for posterity. Sandy Rothman remembers: "Clarence and Roland came over to Campbell Coe's apartment near Telegraph Avenue and he made a tape of them playing together. I played back-up guitar. Campbell owned an original Selmer Macaferri guitar and played [with] some of Django Reinhardt's style so Clarence played 'Sheik Of Araby' and asked Campbell to play a guitar break. That was another great opportunity for me to see Clarence play lots of lead guitar very close-up." Campbell, himself, was a talented guitarist, an avid record collector, and owner of the Campus Music Shop.

page 849: "I first heard of Django Reinhardt from Clarence . . ." Warford/Rogan. London/Riverside, California: 13 July 2007.

page 849: "'Beaumont Rag' is often played . . ." Scott Nygaard, *Acoustic Guitar*: October 1995.

page 849: "Clarence was important in my life . . ." Jerry Garcia, interviewed by Rick Petreycik. *Ultimate Guitar*: 20 December 2000. Garcia went on to make the interesting observation: "He played almost like a bluegrass banjo player on the electric guitar. He also took advantage of the light set-up and the Telecaster snarl to get a kind of nasty, biting sound . . ." I put Garcia's observation about Clarence playing electric guitar like a bluegrass musician to Bob Warford, but he was not convinced. "I don't think so," he retorted. "I was a banjo player and ended up playing [guitar] more like banjo. In a sense he did some things similar to banjo – but he didn't use the banjo eight-note roll and things that are typical of banjo players, the basic stock in trade. Instead, he would play more around the beat. He would put flatpick runs, whether on acoustic or electric, and then use picking stuff as well. So I can see where somebody would say that [about the banjo influence] but I would disagree."

page 850: "He was influenced a lot by Doc Watson . . ." ibid.

page 850: "While collecting material . . ." There has always been some confusion regarding the proposed recording of 'Mr Tambourine Man'. Interviewed by Richard Williams in *Melody Maker* (15 May 1971), White revealed: "Vanguard and Elektra had been bidding for me to do a guitar album for them and I'd started getting material. The first demo I got was of 'Mr Tambourine Man' sung by Dylan and Ramblin' Jack Elliott. I've still got it." Later, in an interview with the same paper by Michael Benton, published in May 1973, he added: "At that time I wanted to get away from bluegrass. I tried to change the Kentucky Colonels with a demo I'd been sent by World-Pacific. It was 'Mr Tambourine Man' sung by Ramblin' Jack Elliott and Bob Dylan. I played it to them, but they couldn't understand what it was all about. I wanted to electrify folk but Eric and Roland didn't. I needed to try something different, so we broke up." Reconciling these two statements, along with the Frame interview, it seems that White considered the song both for a solo instrumental album and as a Kentucky Colonels track. In April 1989, I interviewed Jim Dickson and he was astounded by this story, admitting that he had no memory of offering White the song. "I brought the acetate down to World-Pacific and played it to them [the Byrds] but nobody was overwhelmed, but me. I kept insisting on it, met a lot of resistance, and they stopped doing it. The incident Clarence describes may have happened then due to their stopping it. I absolutely trust Clarence to tell the truth. If I tried to get him to do it, it would have been out of frustration. The reason I don't remember it is that it was probably based on an ill-tempered attitude on my part as a result of the Byrds refusing to do it." Over the years, Dickson has evidently reconstructed vague memories of what happened and now believes he may have been thinking in terms of working with White on an electric version and perhaps even forming a group around Clarence if the Byrds imploded.

page 850: "Doing the song . . ." Dickson/Rogan. Waldport, Oregon: 26–30 April 1989.

page 851: "Earlier that day . . ." The story of Dylan meeting the Whites was recounted in a letter by former Kentucky Colonels' friend and fan club president, Rosie Evans, printed on the internet site, *Clarence White Chronicles*. Her account adds to the rich mythology surrounding the history of the song, while her suspicious reaction to Dylan is equally priceless. Evans writes: "I recall one night the Colonels were leaving Clarence and Susie's apartment for an engagement at a club. The parking lot was full of fans that would be following the Kentucky Colonels to the club. A skinny drifter-looking person approached Roland. They talked for only a few minutes. Then Clarence spoke to the man. The man was going to stay at Clarence and Susie's apartment while the rest of us went to the club. There were kids there and I'd promised to babysit. Clarence trusted this man, and said I should go to the club with everyone. This man was Bob Dylan. The folded dirty paper he showed Roland & Clarence was the song 'Mr Tambourine Man'."

page 851: "They weren't at all keen . . ." White/Frame: London: 22 May 1973.

page 851: "The promoter was Carlton Haney . . ." Roland White/Rogan. London/Nashville, Tennessee: 12–13 October 2007.

page 851: "I was only nine . . ." Rosemarie Johnson (née White)/Rogan. London/Lancaster, California: 16 October 2008.

page 852: "I don't think any bluegrass guitarist had as precise a sense of timing . . ." David Grisman, interviewed by Rick Petreycik. *Ultimate Guitar*: 20 December 2000.

page 852: "He even took some of my banjo licks . . ." Billy Ray Lathum, extracted from liner notes to *Bush, Lathum & White From The Kentucky Colonels: Rare Performance*.

page 852: "He had the Colonels at his house for a party . . ." Sandy Rothman's contribution to Etsuo Eito's website *Clarence White Chronicles*. Presumably, Rothman is referring to the album *The Kentucky Colonels: On Stage* (Rounder 0199) which features him and Clarence playing 'Reno Ride' and 'Durham's Bull'. Rothman maintains this was from November 1964.

page 853: "There were times in the Byrds . . ." Gene Parsons, interviewed by the author. London/Mendocino, California: 19 May 2007.

page 854: "The transition was pretty strange . . ." White/Frame: London: 22 May 1973.

page 854: "It wasn't so much that I was getting bored . . ." ibid.

page 855: "I had an electric mandolin . . ." Roland White/Rogan. London/Nashville, Tennessee: 12–13 October 2007.

page 855: "We were doing some country standards . . ." ibid.

page 855: "He said he was going be the best guitar player . . ." Vern Gosdin, quoted in Alec Palao's liner notes to the Big Beat reissue of the Gosdin Brothers' *Sounds Of Goodbye*.

page 856: ". . . for the fascinating retrospective *Tuff & Stringy* . . ." One of the achievements of *Tuff & Stringy* is the erudition displayed by Alec

Palao in his engaging and revealing liner notes which add historical exactitude to this package of impossibly rare independent singles and previously unreleased curios.

page 857: "The minute I heard him play . . ." Gib Guilbeau, interviewed by the author. London/Palmdale, California: 18 September 2007.

page 857: "Seeking solace in the familiar . . ." The precise chronology of the genesis of the Reasons has been partially lost in time. While the order of events presented here is, by consensus, the most likely, Wayne Moore recalls it a little differently from the others. He suggests that Parsons and White were already in the group and working with Gary Paxton by the time he was brought back from Indiana to join them as bassist. "I'd moved back to Indiana and kind of dropped out of music when Gib called me," he told me in 2007. "They'd met Clarence while I was in Indiana. I only stayed back there for a year and, in the meantime, Gib and Gene had met Clarence and started doing recordings for Gary Paxton. Gib called me and said, 'Why don't you come back out? We're doing a lot of session work now and we have a new guitar player who's real good.' So I said, 'OK' and I went back out. I was ready to leave Indiana and was used to California by then. When I went back we were working with Clarence doing sessions and stuff. I went back to work with them under the name the Reasons at that time. We were playing clubs, the Jack Of Diamonds mostly." It should be stressed that Moore was recalling events from over 30 years ago, so the slight blips in the chronology are understandable.

page 857: "I loved bluegrass . . ." Wayne Moore, interviewed by the author. London/Rancho, New Mexico: 11 September 2007.

page 857: "I was told to come down and do the session . . ." Gene Parsons/ Rogan. London/Mendocino, California: 19 May 2007.

page 858: "I was very impressed . . ." ibid.

page 858: "The Darrell Cotton single . . ." The precise recording date of the Darrell Cotton session is not certain, although it was most likely late 1966. Assuming Gene Parsons is correct in his assertion that he first met Clarence White at this session, it is fascinating (from a Byrds' historical viewpoint) to consider that the guitarist began working with various Byrds during the same period or seemingly very soon after. Session listings confirm that White contributed to *Younger Than Yesterday* in November/December 1966 and presumably worked on the Gosdin Brothers' single 'One Hundred Years From Now' (also featuring Hillman and Clarke) around the same point. All this leaves the tantalizing, and not entirely remote, possibility that White may have actually recorded with Michael Clarke before Gene Parsons. Either way, it was a close run thing.

page 858: "In the solo . . ." Alec Palao, from the liner notes to *Tuff & Stringy: Sessions 1966–68.*

page 858: "Rick spread the word . . ." Guilbeau/Rogan. London/Palmdale,

California: 18 September 2007. 'Take A City Bride' later featured in the Byrds' live set and Gene Parsons recorded a memorable cover on his 1973 solo album, *Kindling*.

page 859: "The Gosdins also took the opportunity to enlist him for a one-off single on Edict, 'One Hundred Years From Now' . . ." This Gosdin Brothers' composition should not be confused with a song of the same title that appeared later on the Byrds' *Sweetheart Of The Rodeo* on which White also played.

page 859: "That incarnation lasted from late 1966 . . ." Warford/Rogan. London/Riverside, California: 13 July 2007. Oddly, the extremely impressive and authoritative websites administered by Etsuo Eito and Thomas Aubrunner, respectively, both state that this line-up played at the Ash Grove on 25 December 1966. It seems inconceivable that a folk club would open its doors on Christmas Day, particularly when most musicians and audience members would prefer to be at home with their families. Bob Warford's extensive tape collection features no such performance. "That's the first time I ever heard of a gig supposedly on Christmas Day," he says of the likely misprint. "I think I have tapes of all the shows we did at the Ash Grove. Looking at my tapes here, let's see, we played the Ash Grove on January 6th, 7th and 8th. I believe those were the days when Clarence wasn't there. We played March 12, then March 28th–31st. April 1st–2nd, April 7th and April 9th."

page 860: "A couple of times at the Ash Grove . . ." ibid.

page 860: "Boy, that's a question I've *never* been asked . . ." ibid.

page 860: "Clarence told me at the time . . ." Dale Davis, interviewed by the author. London/Orange County, California: 16 September 2007.

page 861: "I hadn't played with Clarence before . . ." John York, interviewed by the author. London/Claremont, Los Angeles, California: 11 June 2007.

page 862: "We really didn't know what we were doing then . . ." Guilbeau/Rogan. London/Palmdale, California: 18 September 2007.

page 862: "It was fascinating . . ." Warford/Rogan. London/Riverside, California: 13 July 2007.

page 862: "I went off into electric as well . . ." ibid.

page 862: "The weirdest part of it . . ." ibid.

page 863: "It was not the self-conscious synthesis . . ." Alec Palao, from the liner notes to Guilbeau & Parsons' *Louisiana Rain*.

page 864: "He owed money and he came back broke . . ." Guilbeau/Rogan. London/Palmdale, California: 18 September 2007.

page 864: "I wrote a couple of songs with Gary's wife . . ." Moore/Rogan. London/Rancho, New Mexico: 11 September 2007. Moore denies that 'Guitar Picking Man' was in any way inspired by Clarence White, despite its allusive title.

page 864: "Clarence was an almost equally reluctant pupil . . ." Gib Guilbeau concurs with this view: "He was pushed into it really. He co-wrote some songs with Jan Paxton who was Gary's wife and he came up with a melody idea, then Gary suggested he get Jan to help him write lyrics. The other stuff he did on his own were the instrumentals, but he was sort of pushed into writing them." The two other Jan Paxton/ Clarence White collaborations were 'Why Can't We Be' (released on Uni Records by the Great Love Trip) and a demo of 'Nature's Child' exclusively issued on the comprehensive *Tuff & Stringy*.

page 864: "He'd always give you some excuse . . ." Guilbeau/Rogan. London/Palmdale, California: 18 September 2007.

page 865: "These were wild cowboy people who lived in the desert . . ." Moore/Rogan. London/Rancho, New Mexico: 11 September 2007.

page 865: "I had never played an electric guitar . . ." Warford/Rogan. London/Riverside, California: 13 July 2007.

page 865: "On 24 August . . ." Never previously published, the set lists were as follows. First set: 25 songs recorded (electric guitar only) 10 of which are identified as 'The Fugitive', 'Release Me', 'Green, Green Grass Of Home', 'Kansas City', 'Apartment Number 9', 'Tuff & Stringy', 'Buckaroo', 'I'll Never Forget Old What's Her Name', 'Walk On By' and 'Buckaroo (Reprise)'. Second set: nine songs, five identified as 'Steel Guitar Rag', 'Memphis', 'Tennessee Waltz', 'Wooly Bully' and 'Buckaroo'. On 25 August, Warford recorded the entire band. First set captured on reel-to-reel features 21 songs: 'Buckaroo', 'It's Such A Pretty World Today', 'Maybe Today', 'Don't You Ever Get Tired Of Hurting Me', 'Release Me', 'Sam's Place', 'Am I That Easy To Forget?', 'The Fugitive', 'You're Nobody Till Somebody Loves You', 'Sawmill', 'The Last Word In Lonesome Is Me', 'Tom Dooley', 'Hula Hula Love', 'The Bottle Let Me Down', 'Act Naturally', 'I Can't Stop Loving You', 'Running Away From The Blues', 'Take Me As I Am Or Let Me Go', ''Cause I Have You', 'Faded Love' and 'Milk Cow Blues'. The second set for 25 August on reel-to-reel has 20 songs (or 24 if you count the medley as five): 'There Goes My Everything', 'White Lightning', 'Theme (Buckaroo?)', 'You Caught A Butterfly', 'Johnny B. Goode', 'I Threw Away The Rose', 'Blowin' In The Wind', 'Danny Boy', 'Together Again', 'Steel Guitar Rag', 'Kentucky Waltz', 'Theme (short)', 'Open Up Your Heart', 'Medley: 'My Arms Keep Reaching For You'/'These Lying Lips'/'It's All Over Now But The Crying'/'Oh Those Lonely Teardrops'/'Let's Have A Heart-To-Heart Talk', 'The Town Crier', 'Oh Lonesome Me', 'Caravan', 'Burning Bridges Behind Me', 'What Was Your Name Again?' and 'White Lightning'. The third set/reel-to-reel for 25 August features 'Faded Love', 'Blue Moon Of Kentucky', ''Cause I Have You', 'Pretty World Today', 'Honky Tonk', 'Kentucky Means Paradise', 'Vaya Con Dios', 'Think Of Me', 'Don't You Ever Get Tired Of Hurting Me', 'The Grizzly Bear', 'Last Letter', 'Roll In My Sweet Baby's Arms', 'I Got A Woman' and 'Theme (short)'. On 26 August, a third night of recording was attempted but cut short prematurely following an intervention from a representative of the Musicians' Union who objected to the taping. Nevertheless 11 more songs were captured on reel-to-reel: 'Buckaroo', 'The Shoe Goes On To The Other Foot', 'The Crystal Chandelier', 'Apartment Number 9', 'Walk Through This World With Me', 'Kansas City', 'Old What's Her Name', 'Together Again', 'Little Ole Wine Drinker Me', 'It's Such A Pretty World Today' and 'Buckaroo'.

page 866: ". . . who had a moderate country hit . . ." Warford/Rogan. London/Riverside, California: 13 July 2007.

page 866: "I was asked to join the Roustabouts . . ." Bo Wagner, interviewed by the author. London/Los Angeles, California: 18 May 2009.

page 867: "Clarence didn't really read music . . ." ibid.

page 868: "That was the common name . . ." ibid.

page 868: "On 27 November . . ." Warford recorded everything that evening over several reels of tape. "There were five sets, each about 45 minutes, a full evening starting at 9 pm and going through till 1.30 to 2.00 am." The first reel comprises 22 songs: 'Buckaroo', 'Act Naturally', 'Anita, It's Over', 'Wooly Bully', 'Sing Me Back Home', 'Tuff & Stringy', 'Barefootin'', 'Release Me', 'Mental Revenge', 'Together Again', 'Sweet Pea', 'Set Me Free', 'White Lightning', 'Tango For A Sad Mood', 'The Only Daddy That'll Walk The Line', 'Wolverton Mountain', 'Memphis (Intro)', 'It's Such A Pretty World Today', 'Old What's Her Name', 'I Washed My Hands In Muddy Water', 'My Elusive Dreams' and 'The Birds And The Bees'. The second reel features another 22 numbers: 'Letter From Home', 'Your Lily White Hands', 'Sing Me Back Home', 'Lonely Street', 'Big Boss Man', 'The Chokin' Kind', 'Going Home', 'I Think It's Best That You Forget Me', 'Memphis (Theme)', Hi-Heel Sneakers', 'Love's Gonna Happen To Me', 'Sing A Sad Song', 'Last Date', 'My Heart's Gonna Rise Again', 'Too Used To Being With You', 'Where Does The Good Times Go', 'If My Heart Had Windows', 'Theme', 'Mental Revenge', 'Danny Boy', 'Where Does The Good Times Go' [Bobby Little version] and 'White Lightning'. The final reel features the closing three songs of the evening: 'Send Me The Pillow That You Dream On', 'Memphis' and 'Night Train'. Warford returned the following evening (28 November), this time recording only seven songs: 'Buckaroo', 'Apartment Number Nine', 'Kansas City', 'Ever Since My Baby Went Away', 'Givin' In To You', 'I'm Tied Down To You' and 'Buckaroo (closing theme)'. Trivia students might be interested to learn that White's Vibrolux amplifier on the final night was set at volume (7), treble (7) and bass (7).

page 868: "Onstage he was very serious . . ." Wagner/Rogan. London/Los Angeles, California: 18 May 2009.

page 869: "Gary used my vibes . . ." ibid. Recalling his time working with

Gary Paxton, Wagner adds, "When Gary moved to Bakersfield and asked me to move there, I was one of the first to agree to that. We did a bit of commuting with the Roustabouts but then I had to leave in 1968. I was in the studio almost every single day recording 99 per cent of what Gary was doing during those years, playing drums, vibes, marimba and some keyboard stuff. Clarence was on the majority of things also. Occasionally, there'd be a band come in that had their rhythm section and Clarence would play with them. Most of the groups that came in weren't comfortable in the studio so Gary would replace everybody and have us learn their material and play. Then they would go out and perform it. I was doing drums there, Clarence was on guitar and Ben Benay played some guitar and bass. Gene Parsons was there some too, depending on the style of music we were playing. Besides country, we were doing rock and even what you might call hard rock. Luckily, I'd grown up knowing different styles of music, whereas some people were limited to a particular bag. The style didn't matter to me. That's why I worked so much. I did a lot of arranging for Gary. I'd write the horn and string arrangements and bring in local horn players from the college or symphony [orchestras] or whatever they had there. . . I hit it off with Dennis Mathes, the steel player, and we also worked together and became close friends. I got to meet all types of musicians but as far as being really close-knit and tight, the time with Clarence and Gary [was when] we became one. We just instantly knew what to do. We ended up having little names for chords and certain types of drum breaks or guitar parts. Gary would say, 'OK, guys, do this and that,' and we knew instantly with a whole repertoire of things to pool from . . . If we'd stayed in Bakersfield, Clarence and I would probably have had our own album together because we were developing this guitar/vibes/marimba thing that would have been different and unique."

page 869: "Gary gave me a great offer . . ." ibid. Wagner, coincidentally, later joined the group Eternity's Children, who deserve a brief discographical cameo in the Byrds' story as their album *Timeless* includes the rare Gene Parsons composition 'Christina In My Dreams' and the Clarence White/Jan Paxton collaboration, 'Nature's Child'. The saga is far too complicated to deal with here but Wagner, who saw the group as "a white 5th Dimension", was so impressed by their talents that he "left the Bakersfield/Hollywood music scene and moved to Louisiana just to play with Eternity's Children". Wagner later teamed up with several members to form the Paxton-produced offshoot Mississippi and later reconnected with Eternity Children's main writer Bruce Blackman in the Seventies hit group Starbuck.

page 869: "We were always looking for money . . ." Dale Davis/Rogan. London/Orange County, California: 16 September 2007.

page 870: "Everyone is ready and anxious . . ." Letter from Gene Parsons to Gary Paxton, dated 15 December 1967.

page 870: "I never liked Bakersfield that much . . ." Guilbeau/Rogan. London/Palmdale, California: 18 September 2007.

page 870: "Clarence and I moved up to Bakersfield . . ." Moore/Rogan. London/Rancho, New Mexico: 11 September 2007.

page 870: "We were called the Gary Paxton Band . . ." Guilbeau/Rogan. London/Palmdale, California: 18 September 2007.

page 870: "We hated the place . . ." ibid.

page 871: "When that gig ended . . ." ibid.

page 871: "Well, we got bored in Bakersfield . . ." Moore/Rogan. London/Rancho, New Mexico: 11 September 2007.

page 871: "He definitely had a quirky sense of humour . . ." Gene Parsons/Rogan. London/Mendocino, California: 19 May 2007.

page 872: "He bought a little club in Palmdale . . ." Moore/Rogan. London/Rancho, New Mexico: 11 September 2007.

page 872: "We had a radio show for the Jack Of Diamonds . . ." ibid.

page 872: "While playing there, the group informally adopted the club's name . . ." The mystery of Nashville West's name is another perplexing footnote in the Byrds story. Were the Reasons ever actually billed as Nashville West? Not so, according to the surviving members, although there is noticeable hesitation in their replies. "I don't think we ever played as Nashville West," says Wayne Moore, "but we worked at the Nashville West club." So they never actually performed as Nashville West? "No, I don't believe we did," adds Gene Parsons. "If we did, I certainly don't remember it." However, if this is the case, why did Gene Parsons, as producer and compiler, allow his tapes to be issued on Sierra under the group name Nashville West? And why, in interviews going back over 30 years, did he consistently refer to the band as Nashville West, while never once mentioning the Reasons? Equally perplexing is the case of Clarence White, who spoke of Nashville West as the group name in a number of interviews, again never mentioning the Reasons.

page 872: ". . . circa early 1968 . . ." The sleeve of *Nashville West* suggests that the tapes date from 1967 but judging from the material, which includes a cover of Glen Campbell's 'By The Time I Get To Phoenix' (a US chart hit in December 1967), it seems more likely that the show was taped a little later in early 1968.

page 873: "Sneaky worked in the band . . ." Moore/Rogan. London/Rancho, New Mexico: 11 September 2007.

page 873: "It was a pure bar band . . ." Guilbeau/Rogan. London/ Palmdale, California: 18 September 2007.

page 873: "A damn fire shot up . . ." Chris Ethridge, interviewed by the author. London/Meridian, Mississippi: 28 March 2009.

page 874: "I certainly don't remember Clarence playing a sitar . . ." Guilbeau/Rogan. London/Palmdale, California: 18 September 2007. Then again, an electric sitar does not resemble a sitar.

page 874: "I was playing with the Spencers . . ." Warford/Rogan. London/ Riverside, California: 13 July 2007.

page 875: "Clarence would always have that Viceroy cigarette . . ." Chris Hillman, interviewed by Alastair McKay. *Uncut*: November 2013.

page 875: "It was Clarence's influence . . ." Warford/Rogan. London/ Riverside, California: 13 July 2007. The Ray Noble guitar has provoked much comment. According to Warford: "It became the subject of internet chat and some of the history was interesting. It was built by Roy Noble and Clarence had been the one who first referred me to Noble. Some people on the *Clarence White Forum* website thought that Clarence had ordered a guitar that he thought Noble was going to make for him and then didn't get it. It may well be true because Noble's name was given to me by Clarence when I was looking for one. Noble had one that he had recently finished, which I loved, and so I bought it from him. Clarence really liked that Noble so he said he'd trade me the white Tele. He used that Noble for some period of time. I heard that the bridge was pulled out of it at one point and he had it repaired. Somebody posted photos of a guitar that was supposed to be that one on the *Clarence White Forum* and it was exactly the one I traded with him. It had very specific grain on the back. It had the three-piece back like a D-35 with some stunning grain on the Rosewood pieces and it was serial number 69. Roy Noble would keep the sound holes from all the guitars he made and he said to me, "Oh I just built this one – it's number 69.' In the photos that were posted on the web, that was the number inside the guitar."

page 876: "We were probably one of the first LA groups . . ." Guilbeau/ Rogan. London/Palmdale, California: 18 September 2007.

page 876: "Clarence's life was playing . . ." Gene Parsons/Rogan. London/ Mendocino, California: 19 May 2007.

page 877: "One of Clarence's innovative guitar techniques . . ." Gene Parsons on 'The History of The Third Hand' from his String Bender website.

page 877: "I was into studio work . . ." Clarence White, interviewed by Richard Williams. *Melody Maker*: c. June 1973.

page 877: "For years, he'd said that if he ever had to play with another band . . ." Guilbeau/Rogan. London/Palmdale, California: 18 September 2007.

page 878: "Clarence had been telling me . . ." Gene Parsons/Rogan. London/ Mendocino, California: 19 May 2007.

page 878: "When he mentioned Gram Parsons . . ." Clarence White, interviewed by John Byrne. *The State Beacon*: 26 October 1971.

page 878: "The tapes disappeared into Eddie Tickner's vault . . ." Gene Parsons/Rogan. London/Mendocino, California: 19 May 2007.

page 878: "Eddie wasn't a clubber . . ." Guilbeau/Rogan. London/ Palmdale, California: 18 September 2007.

page 879: "They took Clarence and Gene . . ." Moore/Rogan. London/Rancho, New Mexico: 11 September 2007.
page 879: "They probably considered Wayne . . ." Guilbeau/Rogan. London/Palmdale, California: 18 September 2007.
page 879: "Clarence said to me . . ." ibid.
page 879: "When we were both at home . . ." ibid.
page 879–880: "I was in the studio recording . . ." ibid.
page 880: "Clarence was snoring . . ." ibid.
page 880: "Everybody thought Clarence was quiet . . ." ibid.
page 880: "Eddie was like a second dad . . ." ibid.
page 881: "He didn't give me a tape . . ." Moore/Rogan. London/Rancho, New Mexico: 11 September 2007.
page 881: "Wayne, God bless him . . ." Gene Parsons/Rogan. London/Mendocino, California: 19 May 2007.
page 881: "I told them . . ." Moore/Rogan. London/Rancho, New Mexico: 11 September 2007.
page 881: "He was quiet and shy . . ." Warford/Rogan. London/Riverside, California: 13 July 2007.
page 882: "They'll wait till you're in town . . ." Clarence White, interviewed by Steve Peacock. *Sounds*: 29 January 1972.
page 882: "Clarence brought a new shining light . . ." Carlos Bernal, interviewed by the author. London/Los Angeles, California: 10 April 2008.
page 884: "When Clarence and I first went with the Byrds . . ." Gene Parsons/Rogan. London/Mendocino, California: 19 May 2007.
page 884: "He stood stock still . . ." George Guttler, letter to author, reproduced in *Full Circle* 18.
page 885: "I just want to tell you . . ." Gene Parsons/Rogan. London/Mendocino, California: 19 May 2007.
page 885: "Hey, who was that guy . . ." ibid.
page 885: "That was Jimi Hendrix . . ." ibid.
page 886: "Clarence apart, the only known Bender players at the end of the Sixties were Bob Warford . . ." Warford is able to date when his String Bender was built. "Gene was kind enough to give us the drawings for the Bender, with Clarence's OK. I do know within a three-month period when it was done. Mine was built between September and December 1968. The reason I know that is because some of the parts for it were done in the Physics department shop at the University of California, Riverside, where I was in graduate school. I took a course in metal shop that the Physics department was giving and that's how those parts got built. I know it was while that course was ongoing because I was also technically on the faculty of graduate students so I got somebody to build some of the parts that were in mine. It was completed right at the end of 1968."
page 886: "We went to a place called the Exit Inn . . ." Bernal/Rogan. London/Los Angeles, California: 10 April 2008.

page 887: ". . . on which drugs we took . . ." Gene Parsons/Rogan. London/Mendocino, California: 19 May 2007.
page 887: "Clarence wasn't just singing . . ." Hersh/Rogan. London/ Topanga Canyon, California: 12 April 2008.
page 888: "Clarence did coke . . ." John Beland, quoted in David N. Meyer. *Twenty Thousand Roads – The Ballad Of Gram Parsons And His Cosmic American Music* (New York: Villard, 2007) p. 341.
page 888: "One day Clarence asked . . ." John Beland, quoted in Etsuo Eito's website *Clarence White Chronicles.*
page 889: "Clarence was just really starting to understand . . ." Hersh/ Rogan. London/Topanga Canyon, California: 12 April 2008.
page 889: "The thing about Roger . . ." ibid.
page 890: "The instruments were in one of the trucks . . ." Gene Parsons/ Rogan. London/Mendocino, California: 19 May 2007.
page 890: "Clarence looked really tired . . ." ibid.
page 890: "What are you talking about? . . ." ibid.
page 890: "Let's fight . . ." ibid.
page 890: "I don't want to hit you . . ." ibid.
page 890: "He hit me . . ." ibid.
page 891: "That was Rita Coolidge . . ." David Crosby, interviewed by the author. London: 23 April 1980.
page 892: "It was an 'on the road' thing . . ." Bernal/Rogan. London/Los Angeles, California: 10 April 2008.
page 892: "London-born June Clark . . ." Born 6 September 1949, Clark was raised in Plumstead and was a regular clubber since the age of 14–15. She attended various shows by the Who (when they were still the High Numbers), ran a fan club for the Cat (whose line-up included Chris Thomas) and immersed herself in the Sixties' pop scene. "I loved the Who, the Action, the Creation and the Small Faces. Yes, you've got me – I was a little mod." Working for Harold Davison (soon to be husband of singer Marion Ryan, whose sons Paul & Barry Ryan enjoyed several hits) was the perfect entrée to the music business as his agency had represented an astonishing array of artistes embracing Frank Sinatra, Judy Garland, the Rolling Stones, the Dave Clark Five, the Kinks, the Small Faces, and countless more. Her later employer, Maurice King, was a formidable character whose roster included the Rockin' Berries, the Walker Brothers, Them and, of course, Scott Walker. King also owned the Starlite Club in Stratford Place, near New Oxford Street, a favourite hangout for pop stars and East End villains. Since the age of 17, June had been dating musician Joey Molland who would join Badfinger towards the end of 1969. The couple split on 14 May 1971, the day after June Clark attended the Byrds' performance at the Royal Albert Hall.
page 893: "Rita was gorgeous . . ." June Clark, interviewed by the author. London/New York: 12 February 2016.

page 893: "It was just friendly. . ." ibid.
page 894: "Bill was a very nice guy . . ." ibid.
page 894: "This was out near Palmdale . . ." Bernal/Rogan. London/Los Angeles, California: 10 April 2008.
page 895: "It was unbelievable . . ." Rosemarie Johnson (née White)/ Rogan. London/Lancaster, California: 16 October 2008. At the same time the White family were moving to Leona Valley, Eric Senior had invested in another property near the Fox Airfield, north of Lancaster.
page 895: "My dad was outgoing . . ." ibid.
page 895: "If they had problems, they never showed anything . . ." ibid.
page 896: "I spent a lot of time with Susie . . ." ibid.
page 896: "If I'd been older . . ." ibid.
page 896: "All of a sudden . . ." ibid.
page 897: "We didn't sleep with each other . . ." June Clark/Rogan. London/New York: 12 February 2016.
page 897: "I never ever asked . . ." ibid.
page 897: "Susie didn't want him . . ." ibid.
page 897: "I'd love to know any details . . ." ibid.
page 898: "He tried to live life . . ." Rosemarie Johnson (née White)/ Rogan. London/Lancaster, California: 16 October 2008.
page 898: "That was his brandy and coffee . . ." Guilbeau/Rogan. London/Palmdale, California: 18 September 2007.
page 898: "I remember he taught me . . ." Bernal/Rogan. London/Los Angeles, California: 10 April 2008.
page 899: "It was a constant party . . ." Hersh/Rogan. London/Topanga Canyon, California: 12 April 2008.
page 899: "He used to be the handyman . . ." Bernal/Rogan. London/Los Angeles, California: 10 April 2008.
page 899: "He was a charmer . . ." ibid.
page 899: "He was a regular fixture . . ." ibid.
page 899: "But this makes me feel young again . . ." Quoted in Dinky Dawson & Carter Alan. *Life On The Road* (New York: Billboard, 1998).
page 899: "Oh, what the hell . . ." ibid.
page 899: "It was tea made from pot . . ." Rosemarie Johnson (née White)/ Rogan. London/Lancaster, California: 16 October 2008.
page 900: "The Byrdhouse was usually a full house . . ." Quoted in Dinky Dawson & Carter Alan. *Life On The Road* (New York: Billboard, 1998).
page 900: "Ianthe [Dolores] and Susie came in . . ." Bernal/Rogan. London/ Los Angeles, California: 10 April 2008.
page 900: "Susie attacked me . . ." ibid.
page 901: "The blockage to the arteries . . ." Rosemarie Johnson (née White)/Rogan. London/Lancaster, California: 16 October 2008.
page 901: "It was about 4 o clock . . ." Michelle White, interviewed by the author. London/Nashville, Tennessee: 3 June 2008.

page 902: "Clarence did not ask me . . ." June Clark/Rogan. London/New York: 12 February 2016.
page 903: ". . . living out in the bloody desert . . ." ibid.
page 903: "Clarence was very quiet . . ." ibid.
page 903: "He probably loved the fact . . ." ibid.
page 903: "The man was in love . . ." ibid.
page 903: "I didn't like it . . ." ibid.
page 904: "The Byrds never achieved . . ." Clarence White, interviewed by Michael Benton. *Melody Maker*: 30 May 1973.
page 904: "I don't think we had too much comment on that . . ." Gene Parsons/Rogan. London/Mendocino, California: 19 May 2007.
page 905: "We had John Guerin . . ." White/Peacock. *Sounds*: 2 June 1973.
page 905: "I haven't thought specifically . . ." Roger McGuinn, interviewed by Eric Rudolph. *Crawdaddy*: October 1972.
page 906: "I was young but I do remember . . ." Michelle White/Rogan. London/Nashville, Tennessee: 3 June 2008.
page 906: "Their only notable get-together had been a family reunion . . ." The Ash Grove appearance was a five-day residency (13–17 January 1971). The White family were augmented by banjoist Pat McCloud and bassist George Dawson.
page 907: "It was great . . ." Roland White/Rogan. London/Nashville, Tennessee: 12–13 October 2007. Another factor in the reformation of the Kentucky Colonels was Clarence's desire to play more acoustic guitar. Surprisingly, he pointed out how he had lost his edge due to the pressures of touring with the Byrds. As he told *Sounds*' Steve Peacock: "It seemed like the first two years I was learning new things on the guitar all the time but in the last two years I was forgetting how to play the guitar. I didn't like that at all, and as far as the acoustic guitar was concerned I just felt so far from it. It's almost impossible to work it like that because if you just pick up your acoustic guitar for two songs at a show then that's usually the only time you see the thing. It's stored away with the equipment someplace, or when you're at home you've just been on the road every night for months and you don't feel like playing. But I'm doing a lot more playing now – even during the day with my brothers, we just sit around and play."
page 908: "Clarence had an extreme dynamic range . . ." Richard Greene, interviewed by Rick Petreycik. *Ultimate Guitar*: 20 December 2000.
page 908: "We finished the entire recording . . ." Peter Rowan, liner notes to Muleskinner's *A Potpourri Of Bluegrass Jam.*
page 908: "He was greater than ever . . ." David Grisman, interviewed by Jon Sievert. *Frets*: September 1979.
page 909: "In May 1973, the (New) Kentucky Colonels embarked on a short European tour . . ." Accompanying them was banjoist Herb Pedersen who was replaced by Alan Munde for the trip to Sweden. Roland White remembers that just before the European tour Clarence

purchased a Mark Whitebook handmade guitar with a large 'W' emblazoned on the peg head. "That was the last guitar he ever played."

page 909: "We enjoyed our relationship . . ." June Clark/Rogan. London/New York: 12 February 2016.

page 910: "I'd never seen him so happy . . ." ibid.

page 910: "He was having these vitamin B 12 shots . . ." ibid.

page 910: ". . . one of their final dates at the Indian Springs Maryland Bluegrass Festival . . ." At this date, the Colonels were accompanied onstage by guitarist John Kaparakis and banjoist Jack Hicks. Kaparakis shared his memories of the festival online in the *Clarence White Chronicles*: "Clarence had never played a bluegrass festival before Indian Springs, and he knew that many people in the audience would be listening for him to play lead guitar . . . For that reason, the New Kentucky Colonels asked me to join them onstage that weekend and play rhythm guitar. As you can imagine, that was absolutely the greatest honour and privilege that I ever had . . . The festival was three days long, Friday, Saturday and Sunday in the first weekend of June 1973 . . . On Saturday, Bill Monroe And His Blue Grass Boys were on the festival also, and we got Jack Hicks who was Bill Monroe's banjo player . . . That's how the band was made up. Clarence was very much impressed and touched by the crowd response and the reception given to him and the New Kentucky Colonels. It was a great first-ever bluegrass festival appearance for him – the audience just loved him and their music. Many musicians before and since Clarence White have been searching for that 'crossover' sound, a new type of music which will appeal equally to audiences in the bluegrass, folk and country markets. No one has yet found it. Clarence White would have been the first had he lived."

page 910: "The Colonels are carrying on . . ." White/Benton. *Melody Maker*: 30 May 1973.

page 910: "I found that latest album . . ." Clarence White, interviewed by David Renshaw. Press cutting: 1973.

page 911: "I'm not going to tie myself down . . ." ibid.

page 911: "I was playing fiddle, mandolin and guitar . . ." Art Johnson, interviewed by the author. London/Nice, France: 17 June 2007.

page 911: "I'd worked with James Burton . . ." ibid.

page 912: "He said quite a few guitar players . . ." Johnson/Rogan. London/Nice, France: 17 June 2007.

page 912: "At the first jam session . . ." ibid.

page 912: "We were playing some bluegrass . . ." ibid.

page 913: "We turned off the machine . . ." ibid.

page 914: "Clarence and I did about a dozen songs . . ." Dickson/Rogan. London/Costa Mesa, California: 10 January 2006. Dickson's business partner Eddie Tickner last saw White at a recording session only days before his death. According to Tickner, the guitarist said that he wasn't very busy and was keen to assist his client Gram Parsons who was currently working in another studio. Oddly, White said: "I don't want to play, I just want to be there as a friend in case he needs any help." Tickner was amazed to discover that White had also promised to help both Skip Battin and Gene Parsons on their solo projects. "He had helped on the Country Gazette album and he had his own album to do. And he had the guts to say to me he wasn't doing much and he'd like to help Gram . . . He never had any ulterior motives in doing things for people . . . That's the amazing man I knew. Everyone, once in a lifetime, should have the privilege of knowing a Clarence White."

page 914: ". . . an album that went from bluegrass to acid rock . . ." This may sound extraordinary, not least because it partly recalls McGuinn's doomed attempt to record a history of twentieth-century music, a project that devolved into *Sweetheart Of The Rodeo*. There is evidence that McGuinn and White were planning to work together and Jim Dickson's involvement as producer would have hastened that process. Dickson was always bringing ex-Byrds together on projects. Former publicist Jim Bickhart recalls attending a business meeting with Clarence, Eddie Tickner and a Warner Brothers executive just after the dissolution of the Byrds when the subject of White's solo album was mentioned. "We discussed the idea of having McGuinn produce some tracks for him to explore the 'space bluegrass' thing that the two of them seemed to have going. Clarence expressed some reservations, though he didn't go into why (in retrospect I gather he wanted a vacation from Roger after four years of Byrdcraziness). But he was open to talking to Roger about it."

page 914: "I'll probably do something like a bluegrass instrumental . . ." White/Peacock. *Sounds*: 2 June 1973.

page 914: "It's a big mystery . . ." June Clark/Rogan. London/New York: 12 February 2016.

page 914: "Yes, I think . . ." ibid.

page 915: "We all came on as a backing band for Gram . . ." Gene Parsons/Rogan. London/Mendocino, California: 19 May 2007.

page 916: ". . . a month before he died . . ." Chris Darrow, interviewed by the author. London/Riverside, California: 5 July 2007.

page 916: "It wasn't the Kentucky Colonels . . ." ibid.

page 916: "I remember going to the club . . ." Moore/Rogan. London/Rancho, New Mexico: 11 September 2007.

page 917: "He and Roland came to the house . . ." Rosemarie Johnson (née White)/Rogan. London/Lancaster, California: 16 October 2008.

page 918: "At 5 am . . ." The accounts of Clarence White's death and its immediate aftermath are generally consistent although the passage of time and traumatic nature of the events inevitably colours certain memories. The most reliable source, which I have utilized, is Gene Parsons' written account from the time. He sent a letter to Chrissie Oakes of the Byrds' Appreciation Society dated 17 July, less than two days after

Clarence's death, which stated: "I'm afraid I have some very sad news. You probably know by now anyway, but I thought I had better write to you. Clarence was hit by a car and killed last Sat. nite. Gib Guilbeau called us Sun. morning at 5:00 to tell us he was hit, but he was still alive then. He had extensive brain damage and they were flying in a brain surgeon. Twenty minutes later, Gib called back to tell us he was gone. The lady that was driving the car was drunk, and Clarence didn't have a chance. His brother Roland was with him and tried to pull him to safety, and he was injured also. Roland had a dislocated arm. There isn't much to say now, except that we loved him very much, and we'll miss him for the rest of our lives. For myself, personally, I'll never be able to play music again without thinking of my friend Clarence."

page 918: "There was a knock on the window . . ." Rosemarie Johnson (née White)/Rogan. London/Lancaster, California: 16 October 2008.

page 918: "We just started to cry . . ." Bobby Neuwirth, quoted in Peter Doggett. *Are You Ready For The Country* (London: Viking, 2000). Neuwirth's contention that White was intending to return to the party seems most unlikely. Judging from Neuwirth's other comments, he appears to have thought that Clarence was at the party on the Saturday evening, rather than the previous night. Of course, Neuwirth was remembering events from three decades before. McGuinn, in an early Seventies' interview, confirmed that Clarence had attended the party the night before the show at JB's which makes sense as this was also the date of Roger's birthday.

page 919: "When I got home . . ." Ethridge/Rogan. London/Meridian, Mississippi: 28 March 2009. Inevitably, there are conflicting accounts of what Clarence was intending to do on the evening of his death. Contradicting Neuwirth's account above, Ethridge says, "Clarence was coming to see me the night it happened. He'd sat in at a club called the Jack Of Diamonds [actually, it was BJ's] on Palmdale with his brothers and they'd played. He called the studio, the Record Plant in Los Angeles where I was recording with Booker T. He talked to Gary [Olazabal] who was the engineer. He was also Stevie Wonder's engineer, and later co-producer. Gary came in and said, 'Clarence just called and said to say sorry, he was running late, but he's leaving the club now.' He said he'd be there in a bit, but he never showed up."

page 919: "It broke my heart, man . . ." Jim Seiter, interviewed by the author. London/Hollywood, California: 18 October 1999. Seiter claims he had been intending to accompany Clarence to JB's that evening. "He called me the day before. He said, 'We're going out to Palmdale tomorrow night, we want you to come out.' I said, 'Give me a call tomorrow and let me know what time.' I was going to go with him, but I didn't get home in time, I got hung up in town. Then somebody called and I didn't go. It's 3 in the morning and Spanky McFarlane called me and said: 'Did you hear?' 'Hear what?' 'Clarence is dead.'"

Since Susie was still in Kentucky at the time of the tragedy and only a handful of people knew of his death at 5am on the Sunday morning, the likelihood is that McFarlane's phone call was the following night, by which time Susie would have flown in and returned to the house. Clarence's sister Rosemarie confirms that, upon arrival from Kentucky, Susie went directly to her mother's house and then on to Eric's Palmdale home.

page 920: "June Bad News . . ." Western Union International Inc Cablegram to June Clark, from Culver City, dated 16 July 1973. Although Barbara Schiffmacher says White died on '14/7' in the telegram, the actual time of death was after 5 am on Sunday 15 July.

page 920: "I fell apart . . ." June Clark/Rogan. London/New York: 12 February 2016.

page 920: "I couldn't go to Clarence's funeral . . ." Bernal/Rogan. London/Los Angeles, California: 10 April 2008.

page 920: "She couldn't help it . . ." Ethridge/Rogan. London/Meridian, Mississippi: 28 March 2009.

page 920: "Rosemarie's memories . . ." This snapshot account was a clear indication of her shock during the aftermath of Clarence's death. "I don't remember anything that happened in the church," she adds. "I remember a lot of people at the graveside, Roger being there with Linda. Taking pictures. Constantly taking pictures of the crowd. I remember the singing, but I didn't know who it was then. I didn't know it was Gram Parsons or anybody else partaking in it. Finally, I recall people putting single roses in the casket. But no specific faces. Then, I don't remember anything after that. Usually, you go to a house and you have a meal and share things. But if there was anything like that, I can't recall. It's all completely gone." That same summer, Rosemarie moved from home and married her teenage sweetheart, Bill Johnson. "We met when I was 16 and he was a year older than me. I was 17 when we got engaged and I'd just turned 18 when I graduated in 1973. We married in August, right after Clarence was killed. Bill was leaving to go to Australia. He was in the Navy and in order for me to go over there we had to be married before he left. It was 18 months before I was able to join him." Mildred White, incidentally, survived the tragic loss of her husband and son and lived for another 19 years, dying from cancer in 1992.

page 921: "It was a sunny and sad day . . ." Gene Parsons/Rogan. London/Mendocino, California: 19 May 2007.

page 922: "Warners did not lose interest . . ." ibid.

page 922: "Clarence dying really cut my heart out . . ." ibid.

page 922: "She was never the same after my dad was killed . . ." Michelle White/Rogan. London/Nashville, Tennessee: 3 June 2008.

page 922: "The first accident was in the middle of the night . . ." ibid.

page 923: "A lady found her in the middle of a four-lane road . . ." ibid.

page 923: "She had some brain trauma . . ." Guilbeau/Rogan. London/Palmdale, California: 18 September 2007.
page 923: "This night they also flew in a surgeon . . ." Michelle White/Rogan. London/Nashville, Tennessee: 3 June 2008.
page 924: ". . . some level of contentment . . ." ibid.
page 924: "We were on our way back from Nashville . . ." ibid.
page 924: "I can barely remember . . ." ibid.
page 925: "And here I am tearing up! . . ." ibid.
page 926: "I didn't want to live in Pike County . . ." ibid.
page 926: ". . . got to drinking . . ." ibid.
page 926: "We started dating and I got pregnant . . ." ibid.
page 926: "There was a lot of resentment . . ." ibid.
page 926: "We went to court over the kids . . ." ibid.
page 926: "I was in alcoholic relationships . . ." ibid.
page 926: "I have much to reflect on . . ." ibid.
page 927: "The guitar really found me . . ." Marty Stuart, quoted in *Vintage Guitar*: April 2003.
page 927: "As a bluegrass player . . ." Warford/Rogan. London/Riverside, California: 13 July 2007.
page 928: "Somebody once called his style 'quirky' . . ." Marty Stuart, interviewed by Rick Petreycik. *Ultimate Guitar*: 20 December 2000.
page 931: "People speculate what he might be doing . . ." Rosemarie Johnson (née White)/Rogan. London/Lancaster, California: 16 October 2008.
page 931: "Clarence White can rightly claim . . ." Scott Nygaard, writing in *Acoustic Guitar*: June 1998. Expanding his argument, Nygaard notes: "Most guitar icons/innovators have restricted their efforts to either the acoustic guitar or the electric guitar, and while some have tried their hand at both instruments, their usual approach has been to simply transfer one instrument's technique and style to the other, sometimes with less than satisfying results."
page 932: "I've now had my label for 30 years . . ." Dale Davis/Rogan. London/Orange County, California: 16 September 2007.
page 932: "It was very heart-warming . . ." Roger McGuinn, interviewed by Robert Wilonsky. *Dallas Texas Observer*: undated clipping.

6

SKIP BATTIN

18 February 1934 – 6 July 2003

SKIP Battin was technically the penultimate Byrd, although for most fans and commentators he is still seen as the eleventh and final member of the group. The oldest of the band by some distance, he was also unique in having had a chart career in the rock 'n' roll era. Always sociable and approachable, he displayed an uncommon immunity to boorish rock star egocentricity. Years of struggle in the aftermath of brief pop fame kept him grounded in later life. Battin was an irrepressible and positive character but beneath his upbeat, laid-back, exterior was a hard-working pragmatist. He might have enjoyed a thriving solo career but, following a promising debut album, there were limited opportunities to realize those ambitions. Like other of his contemporaries, he felt obliged by circumstance to play in second generation versions of bands such as New Riders Of The Purple Sage, the Flying Burrito Brothers and the latter-day Byrds' tribute outfits.

Battin's contribution to the Byrds has frequently been questioned by critics, including this author. His bass playing was an enormous asset and helped propel their live shows to great heights. The major problem lay in his songwriting, particularly in conjunction with lyricist Kim Fowley, some of whose novelty themes sat uneasily alongside the group's other work. Yet, the team was also capable of producing something genuinely strange and arresting, such as 'Absolute Happiness'. Even alone, Battin pulled off the eerily affective 'Well Come Back Home', the longest cut on the studio section of *(Untitled).* Battin's melodies proved equal parts memorable and derivative – notably on his Fats Domino-fixated 'Tunnel Of Love'. At first, he was a refreshing addition to the Byrds but, by the time of *Byrdmaniax* and *Farther Along*, many felt that his stylized contributions were compromising the quality of the albums. This was partly due to McGuinn's misplaced democracy or carelessness in not ferreting out the more outré selections and Battin's unwillingness to tailor his material to suit the Byrds. As he told me: "Well, you yourself often said that some of the songs didn't really fit in the Byrds."

Towards the end of his life, Battin was hoping to compile a box set of his life's work. This would have proven a fascinating document, detailing a myriad of musical styles spread over several decades. It would also have allowed us to see his Byrds' material in a wider artistic context and brought a greater resonance to a body of work that might otherwise have seemed perplexing.

Clyde Raybould Battin was born in Gallipolis, Ohio during the Hungry Thirties, a time when America had yet to recover from the Depression. His family were great believers in self-improvement. At the age of six, his grandmother taught him piano, inculcating a love of music that later led him to take up the guitar and fiddle. His father, a football coach at Middleport High, was haunted by unfulfilled ambitions. "The father's dream was to coach Ohio State," recalls one of Battin's old friends, Al Ross. "Aside from Notre Dame, Ohio State was probably the biggest college side in the country. The father wanted to coach there, but it didn't happen. It was a very sad thing. He ended up coaching a high school with a slowly declining population." A lot of hopes were invested in Clyde, who had a great aptitude for sport and a lifelong interest in American football and baseball. For a long time, field sports seemed his most likely career but a knee injury prevented him reaching the majors as a baseball player.

As the Second World War was nearing its end, Battin enrolled at the local East High School for a year, then relocated to

Worthington High where his sporting prowess and friendly personality ensured instant popularity. He excelled on the football field as a quarterback and enshrined himself in the school's sporting annals by coining their rousing 'Third Quarter Cheer'. "It was interactive," says Worthington alumna Maris Bennington Clary. "Clyde would get out in front of our crowd and everyone clapped in unison throughout the cheer. Clyde would say, 'What's the matter with our team?' and the crowd would reply, 'The team's all right!' I won't go through the whole cheer but I remember every word of it. I had a schoolgirl crush on Clyde as did many of the other girls in Worthington."

Like most youths of the period, Battin's major source of entertainment was listening to radio, often late into the night. "Radio was very conservative in the early Fifties," he told me. "There was no Elvis or rock 'n' roll back then and, even if there had been, we probably wouldn't have heard it in Ohio. But it wasn't all bad. I enjoyed a lot of country & western tunes and kept turning the dial on my radio like some safecracker trying to discover the right combination. I knew there was something out there in the ether. One night I found it."

Battin's epiphany occurred when he stumbled upon a Southern radio station near Texas whose broadcasts included a steady stream of high lonesome harmonies, hillbilly tunes, cowboy operas, frontier ballads and honky tonk songs. "They used to play country music all night long. I got very familiar with people like Hank Williams, Ernest Tubb, the Wilburn Brothers, Webb Pierce and Faron Young."

After graduating from Worthington on 5 June 1952, the 18-year-old moved to Tucson, enrolling at the University of Arizona, where he majored in Physical Education. His schooling was frequently interrupted by musical distractions and soon he was hanging around clubs and honky tonks, fraternizing with players and secretly hoping to appear onstage. One of the small groups he befriended was Earl Mock & The Mockingbirds, a middle-aged trio whose repertoire featured seasoned covers of country hits. Mock played lead guitar, backed by a steel player and a lead singer/rhythm guitarist. Traditionalists at heart, they frowned upon bass and drums, which at least meant that performance fees needed only to be split three ways. Mock secured them a regular gig at a Tucson honky tonk, where they played for five hours, six nights a week. A couple of months into their residency, the singer/rhythm player unexpectedly quit, leaving Mock in urgent need of a replacement. Seizing the opportunity, Battin pushed himself forward and secured the spot after impressing Mock with his knowledge of country hits. Clearly, all those hours spent listening to the radio had paid off.

Considering this was his first paid gig, Battin had done remarkably well to obtain the lead vocal position. He even encouraged Mock to add a temporary bass player, Chuck Lee. The group extended their itinerary, playing at various country bars, clubs and rodeos on the south Arizona circuit. Although Battin's studies were adversely affected, he welcomed the extra money and playing experience. Less than a year later, it was all over. Earl Mock, middle-aged with family commitments, felt he was not making enough money on the road and sought alternative employment.

Battin was disappointed by the band's dissolution, not least because he soon had domestic obligations that required additional income. Always popular with the girls, he married while still at college. His wife Patty Battin soon gave birth to a son, Dale, but this was no 'happy ever after' story. The marriage was brief and Dale surrendered Battin's surname in favour of a later stepfather named Rinkenberger.

This personal interlude interrupted Battin's academic and musical progress, but the latter was rapidly reactivated when he fell in with a whiz-kid polymath, whose erratic exploits over the next decade would embrace record production, songwriting, publishing, record label ownership and performing. Gary Sanford Paxton was a hyperactive excessive who shared Battin's love of country and rock 'n' roll and seemed constantly driven, even though the grand highways of his imagination had yet to be constructed. Born in Coffeyville, Kansas, in 1939, Paxton was brought up on a farm in a devoutly Christian household whose work ethic had a profound effect on his outlook. A troubled child, he suffered the trauma of sexual molestation at the age of seven but evidently never reported the occurrence to any of his family. Four years later, he contracted spinal meningitis. Debilitated physically and psychologically, he sought salvation in melody and discovered a perfect therapy in songwriting. In 1951, his family moved to Tucson and, over the next few years, Paxton became besotted by music. After leaving school at 16, he formed a young band, the Rockabillys, who won a local talent contest. Soon after, he met Battin and they clicked instantly as a partnership, sharing similar musical tastes and a penchant for attracting teenage girls. Like Battin, Paxton was a fresh-faced bridegroom and wasted no time marrying the teenage Betty Jean Brown, who would occasionally sing in his band as well as serving as his songwriting muse.

Using a new band name, the Pledges, the musicians cut a single at Audio Recorders, the Phoenix studio owned by Duane Eddy's producer, Floyd Ramsey. "We got a rhythm guitarist (Bobby Verbosh)," said Battin, "and I switched to bass because we didn't have anybody that could play it. I had to learn." Released on Rev Records, the Chuck Berry-influenced 'Betty Jean' was Paxton's paean to his young bride who is immortalized in a fictional universe that also namechecks 'Long Tall Sally', among others. The song's flip side, 'Bermuda Shorts', was Battin's first published song, co-written with Paxton. Inevitably, given its limited distribution, the single was little more than a collector's item, but it showed a talent for mimicry and an appreciation of familiar rock 'n' roll themes. In a prescient move, Paxton and Battin used the recording studio as a means to reinvent themselves under a variety of aliases. Like lottery ticket purchasers in search of a jackpot, they increased their chances by issuing multiple releases on different labels under such names as Gary & Clyde, Clyde Gary & His Orchestra, Clyde Battin and Chuck & Chuckles. Under the latter name, they recorded their least likely attempt at a hit, 'Bury The Hatchet', a comic macabre composition with the psychotic refrain: "I'll bury the hatchet right in your head."

1959 was to prove a watershed year for Battin and Paxton whose lives were turned upside down by a series of unforeseen events. Ever the amorist, Battin met a striking looking girl in Tempe, Arizona, named Jackie Stead and fell in love again. In what sounded like a re-run of his previous relationship, he soon married Jackie, who became pregnant which, in turn, caused a rethink about his career direction. For pragmatic reasons, he knuckled down to studying once more, fulfilling the credits required to obtain his much neglected degree. He was increasingly aware of Paxton's frustrations at their inability to achieve anything approaching a hit record. The initial euphoria of working in the studio was now wearing thin. Their final recording under the name Gary & Clyde was 'The Twister' whose B-side was the tellingly titled 'The Jackie Look'. Ostensibly inspired by Jackie Kennedy, the song also served as a tribute to Battin's new bride, echoing Paxton's previous paean to Betty Jean. In another nostalgic touch, Battin returned to Worthington High to recruit three young school sopranos to provide the choral backing: "We all wanna look like Jackie."

Gary Paxton's already chaotic life became ever more complicated during this same period of readjustment. Sitting in a restaurant one afternoon, he was accosted by an older woman who said: "I've been looking for you for a long time. I'm your mother." Paxton's initial reaction was disbelief but he agreed to pacify the strange woman by phoning his parents. He was at first greeted by silence, followed by the sound of sobbing. What unfolded was a saga akin to a soap opera. It transpired that the God-fearing guardians who had raised him were not his biological parents. His real name was Larry Wayne Stevens, the illegitimate offspring of a teenage couple who had given him up for adoption. This secret history had been kept from him, along with the knowledge that his two siblings were not blood relations. The shock news was difficult to digest. "I was suddenly confused to discover my whole existence was a lie." Bewildered and upset,

Paxton immediately left town, at first visiting his new mother's family in Washington, before moving to Oregon, where he found a suitably therapeutic occupation picking berries.

Paxton's abrupt departure was a blow to Battin, but marriage and college kept him occupied and he found additional employment as a disc jockey, playing his favourite country & western records for the Tucson radio station KMOP. Working around the clock, he kept the Pledges going by playing rock 'n' roll in local nightspots. "I must have had a lot of energy at the time. I was a disc jockey twice daily, four in the morning until seven, then another shift in the afternoon . . . I kept the name the Pledges. We were the first rock 'n' roll band in Tucson and were playing six nights a week. In the middle of all that, I got a surprise package in the mail."

As a disc jockey, Battin was used to receiving unsolicited discs, but this was different. Although he had never heard of the label – Brent Records – nor the artistes – Skip and Flip – the song titles 'It Was I' b/w 'Lunch Hour' were instantly familiar. Any doubts about their provenance were confirmed by a glance at the writing credits: Battin/Paxton. But how had they ended up on a record?

The previous year he and Paxton had recorded demos of those compositions at Floyd Ramsey's studio and assumed they were still gathering dust in some tape vault. Fortuitously, the recordings had reached the New York offices of Bob Shad, owner of Brent Records, a subsidiary of the larger Time Records. An accompanying letter revealed that Shad had purchased the masters and here was the result. As Battin recalled: "They said 'Hope you don't mind, but you're now Skip and Flip.' Bob Shad had decided to change our names. They did things like that in those days." Well used to pseudonymous titles by now, Battin was unfazed by such presumption, although he later chuckled upon learning that 'Skip & Flip' had been named after a couple of poodles owned by Shad's wife. Having already released several singles on similarly obscure labels, Battin had no reason to believe Brent Records could change his fortunes, but the connection with

Time provided some hope. They had recently enjoyed success with the Bell Notes' 'I've Had It' and boasted the resources and connections to infiltrate rock 'n' roll radio.

By the summer of 1959, Battin learned the barely believable news that the Skip & Flip single had entered the *Billboard* charts. It kept climbing, peaking at number 11. Seemingly overnight, Clyde Battin had lost his Christian name. Henceforth, he would be forever known as 'Skip' Battin. The record's success meant that Skip & Flip were needed for promotional work, including radio and television appearances and a concert tour. Battin had the Pledges at the ready for such an emergency, but nobody knew where to find 'Flip'.

Gary Paxton was picking berries from a tree on an Oregon farm when he heard a familiar song from a nearby car radio. He was so shocked that he nearly fell and injured himself. Rushing to the nearest radio station, he procured a copy of the single, then phoned Brent Records in New York confirming that he was a star. Immediately returning to Tucson, he reunited with Battin and they spent the summer on the road, as well as enjoying a prestigious television debut on *Dick Clark's American Bandstand.*

On 1 September 1959, Jackie gave birth to Skip's son, Brent, presumably named in tribute to the record label that had transformed their lives during the final months of her pregnancy. The hit duo rapidly recorded a follow-up, the raucously exuberant 'Fancy Nancy', which fared less well but gained decent radio play. A third single, a revival of Marvin & Johnny's R&B hit 'Cherry Pie', repeated the success of 'It Was I' peaking at number 11 in April 1960. Later, there was another attempt at 'Betty Jean' and a dance number, 'Hully Gully Cha Cha Cha', both of which flopped.

During their short hit run, Skip & Flip toured extensively, famously appearing at New York's Harlem Apollo, then switching to the West Coast for some dates in Hollywood. It was there that they first met the garrulous, larger-than-life Kim Fowley, a precocious Hollywood hustler, who played the PR game like

Tony Curtis in *The Sweet Smell Of Success*, while always knowing he was destined for far greater things. The ultimate pop Zelig, Fowley would become ubiquitous in the encyclopaedia of trash pop, playing major or bit parts in the lives of countless Hollywood moguls and musicians, both famous and obscure.

Born in the Philippines in 1939, Fowley had a family tree "covered in blood and bandages". The son of actor Douglas Fowley and Goldwyn Girl Shelby Payne, he was brought up in the golden age of Hollywood and witnessed its decadence first hand. "My father was an opium addict and my mother was a Valium freak," he casually recalls. Payne divorced her husband, who later spent time in a mental hospital before reactivating his career playing Doc Holliday in the television series *Wyatt Earp*. Subsequently, Payne married pianist William Friml, whose Prague-born father Rudolf had been a noted operetta composer in the 1920s and a co-founder of ASCAP (American Society of Composers, Authors and Publishers). Kim was amazed to discover that his step-grandfather's 30-year old compositions were suddenly popular again. The evergreens 'Indian Love Call' and 'Rose Marie' became massive hits for Slim Whitman in 1955, the latter establishing a long-standing record of 11 consecutive weeks at number 1 in the UK charts.

Kim's upbringing was a peculiar mixture of glamour and emotional impoverishment. The first few years of his life were spent in a foster home, an experience that left lasting scars and a sometimes ruthless independence. His late teens were marred by polio, which confined him to a wheelchair for the best part of a year. When he finally arose, the boy had become a gangly giant, 6 foot 5 inches tall, frighteningly thin and glowing with manic energy. He hung out with local gangs, got in trouble, then went on a brief army course to add mental and physical discipline to his character.

Determined to infiltrate the music industry, Fowley took a job at American International Records and was swiftly headhunted by the imperious Marty Melcher (husband of Doris Day) and placed on the payroll of Arwin Records, a division of the film company Arwin Productions. Fowley's job description was unspecified but involved talent spotting, song plugging and assisting with the company's publishing wing, Daywin Music. He swiftly recruited his friend Bruce Johnston as a songwriter for Daywin and they both teamed up with Marty's son Terry, who was also being groomed for the family business. The Melcher connection was the first of Fowley's several oblique links with future associates of the Byrds' family. His relationship with Terry, whom he would later work with on two Byrds' albums, was cordial but competitive. One afternoon, Marty lined up all three kids, complimenting Terry on his singing, Bruce on his playing and singing, then adding: "But I think Kim is smarter than you both as an A&R man." As Fowley says, "Terry never forgave me for that stepfatherly critique." The apprenticeship with Arwin lasted only a few months. "1959 was an interesting time. Elvis hadn't got out of the Army yet and Fabian and Frankie Avalon were the biggest thing in rock 'n' roll. I quit Arwin because Marty Melcher said I couldn't be vice president till I was 35. I was turning 20 and didn't want to wait another 15 years. I figured I was already good, so I went on the street with the knowledge I'd learned from him."

Fowley seemed in danger of overreaching himself, but he always had the luck or intuition to be hanging out in the right place. While frequenting the lobby of the American Recording Studios on the corner of Sunset and Vine, near the gas station where he was temporarily employed as a nightwatchman, he noticed a swanky white, big-finned Oldsmobile pulling a trailer. The occupants were Skip & Flip, enjoying their first promotional trip to Hollywood. They had booked a session at the studio, working with drummer Sandy Nelson, a former schoolfriend of Fowley's. That connection was enough to encourage Fowley to ingratiate himself with the duo. As Battin told me: "Gary Paxton and I were taking a break and in walked this guy who looked about 6 foot 7 inches, thin as a rail with an exquisitely tailored suit and a vest. I think he was 20 or 21 years old. He spoke to the engineer and said: 'My name is Kim Fowley and you *need* me.' He turned out to be everything that he said he was."

The weaver of a thousand stories and more, Fowley offered them his PR services, insisting that he could help them break into the West Coast market. He pointed out the limitations of Brent Records as a New York company and trumpeted his own achievements which largely consisted of some promotional work for the premier garage group, the Wailers, then enjoying underground success with the single 'Tall Cool One'. "In those days, it was all singles, hard work and shoe leather," says Fowley. "I had a list of the radio stations and knew how to work the phone, then go there in person. I was the tall cool guy passing out cigarettes to the disc jockeys. I looked like a giraffe and made everybody laugh. I was funny, a Benny Hill version of a giraffe. I'm a lethal thinker, but I play humour. Humour works when you're exaggerated in any physical way – tall, fat or tiny. All of a sudden their record was on the radio and things started happening . . . Gary Paxton was the white Ray Charles and Skip was the missing Everly Brother. He looked like Phil and Don Everly combined and could sing harmony like them. I thought he was one of the great harmony singers of rock 'n' roll."

Skip & Gary were so impressed by Fowley's rhetoric and chutzpah that they invited him to become their tour manager. "I was the road manager," Fowley notes. "Not personal manager. I was the Jimmi Seiter figure for Skip & Flip and their touring drummer. I would pick up the money and since I'd been in the Army and Air Force, I had learned how to fight. I knew how to hurt people in hand-to-hand combat and took no nonsense. I'd been in gangs before so I knew how to collect from bad guys who ran venues."

After completing the tour, Skip & Flip returned to Tucson, but nothing was ever quite the same. While Battin was happy performing onstage, Paxton became disenchanted with life on the road and saw his future in production, A&R and songwriting. It was a vision he shared with Fowley, and that meant returning to Hollywood. As is often the case in such break-ups, Paxton started to find fault with his partner, even claiming, without any concrete evidence beyond suspicion, that Skip had designs on his wife.

Perhaps Paxton was psychologically transferring his own transgressions onto another party for, by this point, his romantic life had become as convoluted as his labyrinthine discography. His once beloved Betty Ann was pregnant again, but Paxton was clearly somewhere else. "I was still married to her – I was engaged to a girl in Seattle and another in Tacoma. I was living in Seattle and driving back and forth to Tacoma and Oregon too. But I'd been on the road all the time, so eventually I left a guitar and a pair of boots at all three places and said, 'I'm going to go to Hollywood and make it big and then I'll send for you.' But I never saw any of them again. I just got in my car and drove to Hollywood."

Battin remained behind and continued promoting the new single 'Cherry Pie' on the road, utilizing a new 'Flip', Dave Marcell, whom he had met in Hollywood. After the thrills of the West Coast, Tucson seemed relatively drab and uneventful. By 1961, Battin grew tired of constantly commuting to Hollywood, so decided to move there permanently with the intention of pursuing an acting or musical career. The decision was no doubt hastened by the news that his former colleagues, Paxton and Fowley, had achieved the seemingly impossible by producing a song that had broken out of the local marketplace to become a national number 1 hit.

The Hollywood Argyles' 'Alley-Oop', an irresistible garage style novelty, kickstarted a cottage industry of small recordings. "In that first year, it seemed that we made a hundred singles," Fowley says. "There were record companies everywhere, little tiny ones, and it's $100 to make a record and $100 to press 500 copies, so with $200 you could change the world." Most of these conveyor belt recordings went nowhere, but the purveyors were always hoping for a lucky strike and, even if nothing happened, the cumulative small income from such a prolific output kept them going. It was always likely that such mercurial and self-consuming talents as Fowley and Paxton would eventually fall out. Their business model had been predicated on the twin myths of Paxton's wayward genius in the studio and Fowley's image as the fast-talking Hollywood hustler. Limited by this stereotype, Fowley lusted after greater fame as a writer and producer, so elected to branch out on his own, leaving Paxton to administer their company, Maverick Music.

By the beginning of 1962, Fowley had proven his point, courtesy of B. Bumble & The Stingers' 'Nut Rocker', a Top 30 US hit that stunned everyone by hitting number 1 in the UK charts. At this moment Skip Battin re-entered his life. "Right after 'Nut Rocker', I got their piano player Al Hazan together with Skip and myself for a record titled 'Daybreaker' by Skip & The Flippers [Kim & The Skippers]. It was the second record released on Russ Fi Records, which had given the world Vince Edwards, the television soap opera doctor Ben Casey. I did the A&R on the B-side of that single, 'Squealing Parrot Twist'. Vince had had a fight with the guys at Russ Fi, so we got to do the next release. We came close with 'Daybreaker' [serial number Russ Fi 2002] but it didn't get distributed properly. Skip then decided to do the duet thing again, working with Johnny 'Guitar' Leonard. I had previously produced the Innocents' 'Honest I Do' with Gary Paxton for the Indigo label. The Indigo guys then re-formed as Invicta and I introduced Skip to them. They liked him so much they made him head of A&R and he immediately signed himself and Johnny! I co-wrote the Battin/Fowley composition, 'The Marathon', a redneck, hillbilly, trailer park dance. It went nowhere, but the B-side 'More Marathon' became the theme tune of *Wink Martindale's Dance Party* broadcast every afternoon on Channel 9 KHJ TV from the Ocean Amusement Park. We got tons of airplay from that. The notoriety got them a gig as the houseband at the Interlude, which was situated upstairs at the Crescendo – the club owned by Gene Norman, later of GNP Crescendo Records."

Battin learned much from both Gary Paxton and Kim Fowley and followed their lead by recording for an array of different labels, often under thinly disguised pseudonyms such as Skip & The Hustlers, Teak Battyn & His Battmen, Sir Raybould & The

Blue Angels, Skip & The Flips and Bunky Battin. Even his wife got in on the act composing 1960's 'Make Believe Baby' (later released on Invicta by Don True) then co-writing (with Paxton) and recording 'The Morning After The Night Before' at the beginning of 1962.

Fowley continued to work with Skip on various projects, co-writing 'A Million Tears' for Ron Scudari (whom Kim nicknamed "the Italian Jerry Lee Lewis"), reviving Dean Martin's 'Return To Me' for the Values and, most famously, the Murmaids' US hit, 'Popsicles And Icicles'. "I produced the record, David Gates wrote the song and Skip did the vocal arrangements. They were doing barbershop and Skip was a great harmony guy. It was done at Gold Star but Skip wasn't in the studio. He worked with the girls pre-production. The song was number 1 in *Record World*, before the Beatles' 'I Want To Hold Your Hand' and reached number 3 in *Billboard*. So thank you, Skip."

Skip & Johnny also befriended and backed Troy Walker, memorably described by Fowley as "a Brigitte Bardot version of another Ray Charles white guy". "Anyone who could sing R&B was called the white Ray Charles. Troy had been in a duo with Timi Yuro. They were very popular as Troy & Timi back in 1959. They never had a hit, but Phil Spector and his sister Shirley used to go over to Mama Yuro's restaurant on Pico [Boulevard], where we all ate, including Skip. They gave us free food because we were all music industry types." For a time, Battin stayed at Fowley's palatial home. "Skip was saving his money then. This was a three-storey house with a swimming pool. A huge mansion which I had acquired. I was clever about finding property in those days because I had hit records. We had ten bedrooms and a pile of bathrooms and a million women. There were parties around the clock. People were rehearsing there too – it was a big rock 'n' roll house. Then Skip's wife and kid came out."

By this time, Battin had enrolled for a course in UCLA's post-graduate theatre programme in the hope of securing some acting parts. While there, he became interested in psychoanalysis and more esoteric subjects. "He learned hypnotism and how to do past life regression," says Terry Rogers, who later worked with Battin in the Eighties. "I was interested in what you could discover about yourself by doing that. Once, we found ourselves in Texas with three days off and he did that to me. It was quite an interesting experience. He was very good at hypnotism."

The hypnotist's family moved to Laurel Canyon at a time when Battin was reappraising his career strategy. He had issued a number of singles under his own name but all of them were for small labels and destined for obscurity. The Beatles were changing the world while he seemed locked in a time warp of old-school thinking dominated by novelty records and one-shot ideas. He enjoyed playing live with a small ensemble (the Group), but felt trapped by the persona he had created at the end of the previous decade. Locally, he was still known as the guy who'd enjoyed hits with 'It Was I' and 'Cherry Pie'. Promoters loved that tag line, but he knew that it was making him an anachronism, albeit one that could still command a reasonable fee.

If the Beatles prompted Battin to change, then Dylan and the Byrds caused a mind-altering transformation. "I remember the first night I saw the Byrds. There were two big events during that time that changed my life, seeing *A Hard Day's Night*, and the Byrds at Ciro's, which was really the clincher." A group meeting was called at Battin's home in the Hollywood Hills during which he told everyone that tailored suits, slicked-back hair and anaemic cover material were now passé. Henceforth, he wanted them to play original material or high class covers, preferably Dylan-inspired. "The Byrds just blew my mind completely and I freaked out. [Drummer] Billy Mundi was also into it, but the rest of the guys were a little sceptical about changing the image and getting out of the pattern of things. Although we had only achieved modest success, we were making a living from it."

Several of the players concluded that Battin was crazy and quit, but he remained committed to the dream of emulating Dylan. Over time, he released covers of 'I Don't Believe You' (retitled 'She Acts Like We Never Have Met') and 'Love Minus Zero' on single. His timing seemed perfect but without major label backing, the attempt to conjure a hit proved fruitless. As Battin lamented: "Right away our jobs became fewer because we could no longer be acceptable in the jukebox situation that we were in. Billy and I started getting through a lot of different musicians and we struggled through some pretty hard times."

Seeking sympathetic sidemen, Battin fell in with the gifted Van Dyke Parks, a Mississippi-born former child actor and classically trained musician, whose opaque lyrics would later find their perfect complement in the person of Beach Boy Brian Wilson. Parks offered a composition of his own, 'High Coin', previously recorded by Jackie De Shannon in 1964. It was issued as a single, backed by the promising Battin/Fowley composition, 'Mr Responsibility', but ultimately failed. In order to augment the sound, Parks suggested they recruit Steve Young as lead guitarist.

Young had moved to California from Alabama in 1963 after teaming with folk musicians Jim Connor and Richard Lockmiller. "They were real professionals," Young recalls, "and I was literally a wandering, drunken, guitar player like something out of a novel. I was just out there and didn't really care. I was in trouble with the Klan in Montgomery and there were threats going on. I didn't want to be there anyway, so I escaped to California." En route, Young stopped off to attend the wedding of Richard and Mimi Farina, who were close friends of Connor and Lockmiller. When the musicians finally reached Hollywood, Young accompanied them to an apartment on Melrose, where he was introduced to Van Dyke and his brother Carson Parks, then playing in the folk group, the Greenwood County Singers. "Van Dyke and his brother were like a tragi-comedy," Young remembers. "They were always at odds. Van Dyke was the crazy, creative one and his brother was the tried and true professional, almost like a Mitch Miller or something. It was funny. I was just hanging around at Van Dyke's on Melrose and I was really lost. He was the centre of things and everyone would come to that apartment, including Tim Hardin and Mama Cass, before she made it. Van Dyke was immediately fascinated by my playing and went on and on about it. I didn't understand most of what he said."

"Those were desperate days," Young continues. "I was invited over to Skip's house to talk about this group and he offered me the job as lead guitarist. I was starving and this was at least something that was tangible and entertaining. Skip Battin wasn't the hottest game in town. He was just a competent guy, a professional. I honestly never thought he was really that good or outstanding. But he had political connections and the desire to make things happen as he showed later by his ability to be part of the Byrds."

Young's sheltered upbringing in Alabama collided head-on with Hollywood's hedonism, a culture clash that Battin found amusing and liked to promote. "Skip did take me on a lot of adventures and it was entertaining. We were never really friends, it was just a professional relationship. He was fairly easy to deal with on the surface. A professional who'd get the job done. There were always a lot of people on the Sunset Strip and all that mad, cool stuff was happening. It was all exotic to me. Skip had a sense of humour. One time we went to Northern California and there were all these go-go dancers. There was a topless dancer next to me and Skip hadn't told me before we went on. On Halloween, we played at the Haunted House on Hollywood Boulevard and this elegant, blonde woman won a costume contest. I said 'What is this? She doesn't have a costume on.' Of course, it was a male and 'he' won. I was just a Southern boy, with that mindset, in the midst of all this. I remember another gig we played on the Sunset Strip with Van Dyke. I sang this heavy duty protest song I had written called 'Beverly Hills'. It was about revolution, the smug rich people and the banks . . . The actor Sal Mineo was in the audience that night. I saw the look of terror in his face and thought, 'What have I done?' "

There was a moment where Skip Battin & The Group might have achieved a coveted spot among the Hollywood club elite. According to Parks, they once supported the Byrds, although not at Ciro's as he assumed. "As we were exiting the stage, ever affable David Crosby mounted with the rest of the Byrds. He came up to me in his cape and pageboy. With a victorious taunt, he offered:

'I told you so.'" The sarcastic riposte emanated from an incident prior to the Byrds when Crosby was thinking of forming a group and sounded out Parks as a possible candidate, only to be rebuffed. "David didn't understand that performing in front of screaming fans would never really satisfy my aims. I don't regret my reticence as a team player in all of this." No doubt, there were several other players on the Strip who'd had such conversations with Crosby before he found the perfect candidates: McGuinn and Clark. Crosby's fleeting fraternization with Parks was no coincidence. The Mississippian's unusual classical/folk background, personal magnetism and Southern manners brought many talents to his door, not least a young, well-travelled Texan on a musical mission.

Stephen Stills arrived in Melrose like a tornado, eager to form a songwriting partnership with Parks. Soon, they completed the still unreleased 'Hello I've Returned' which was duly registered for copyright. If the cards had fallen a little differently, Stills might even have joined Battin's enterprise. "Skip and Van Dyke had met Stephen Stills in 1965 and he was in that group for a minute," says Kim Fowley. "A minute could have been a night or a week then. Stills was running around Hollywood doing everything. He'd just hit town and was showing up and playing guitar and singing harmony on people's records. They told me that when they were doing 'High Coin' he just walked in and said, 'I'm here to help you with this', and started playing. And he was really good."

Stills was ambitious and pushy enough to encourage his new contacts to allow him to perform with them. He befriended drummer Billy Mundi, who would later be invited to join the Buffalo Springfield, only to be replaced by Canadian Dewey Martin. Reminiscing about his time in Greenwich Village the previous year, Stills mentioned how he had met John Sebastian. He had dearly wanted to play bass in his band the Lovin' Spoonful but that spot went to Steve Boone. Now the Spoonful were in the charts with their debut single, 'Do You Believe In Magic?' In his determination to team up with Parks, Stills boasted that he could secure a support slot on one of the Spoonful's shows and suggested they form an offshoot group, dragging in Mundi and Young from Battin's band.

"It was called the Gas Company," Young recalls. "I know we did at least one gig, maybe two, opening for the Lovin' Spoonful in Arizona. I thought we played pretty good, but it was just a crazy moment with this rock audience waiting for the Lovin' Spoonful. We flew in and had all this room service and then I flew back to poverty. It was funny."

Van Dyke Parks was never likely to settle in a rock band and swiftly moved on. Battin brought in vocalist/guitarist Larry Smith to bolster the line-up, but it was downhill from there. As Battin concluded: "We were doing original material and some Dylan material but there wasn't a living to be made out of it. We were trying to copy the Byrds but do it a little more bluegrass . . . Steve Young was a real good picker . . . I was playing 12-string and we were doing a lot of Beatles tunes and Byrds things. It wasn't happening though, and it just petered out." Although Steve Young stayed on after Parks' departure, he never grew close to Battin who dutifully maintained his role as band leader.

"Most of the gigs I remember doing with Skip, Van Dyke Parks wasn't present," says Young. "Looking back, what pissed me off about Skip was that he would get me to turn down the guitar. When the playing was getting too much attention or the focus was on me, he didn't like that at all. That happened more than once . . . One night, at this Hollywood club, Stephen Stills brought somebody down. I don't remember who it was, except that he was tall and thin. I guess Stills thought this guy might want to hire me in some group. Skip was almost psychic about that kind of stuff. He was very perceptive. That night he really had me turn down. Stephen and the guy were digging my playing, that's why they were there. But they told me: 'Look, we just can't hear you.' Maybe it was understandable, but to have me turn down so low was a little out there . . . Skip was a decent guy, but it irritated me when I look back."

* * *

By the summer of 1967, with the flowering of the Monterey Pop Festival, Battin was acutely aware that rock fashions were changing once more. Sensing time passing, he was keener than ever to establish a credible band over which he could exercise control and fulfil his frustrated ambitions as a singer-songwriter. Like many other musicians, he gravitated to the Ash Grove in search of potential players. Battin first approached the talented guitarist David Cohen who was then working with Bobby Darin. Cohen suggested his friend and former roommate Al Rosenberg (aka 'Country Al') who was then managing McCabe's guitar shop inside the Ash Grove. "The owner, Ed Pearl, was a very bright, high energy Jewish radical, who did more for West Coast music than any person, including promoter Bill Graham," says Rosenberg, who was one of many players indebted to the proprietor. Battin soon learned that Rosenberg had been tutored by Doc Watson and was flexible enough to go along with his plans. "Skip just said, 'Let's get together and do something.' People were coming down to the Ash Grove – producers, managers, arrangers and writers – finding people who could do something on the guitar that no one else was doing. I was thrilled beyond words because Skip was a real rock 'n' roll guy. We started looking for other people to be in the band and he had some people in mind that he'd played with before, but I had Clarence White. I brought the two of them together. Clarence came over to my house and the three of us played, and Skip said 'I'd love to do something', although he wasn't certain. In his mind, Clarence wasn't part of folk rock. He was a country guitarist and a genius, but I don't know if Skip saw that . . . For Skip, Clarence was country music, which was something he more or less heard growing up in Ohio."

According to Battin, the trio "were going to sign a contract" but prevarication over White's involvement ended that idea. White returned to session work while Battin decided to nurture Rosenberg as a songwriter, using pick-up musicians from local bars as his backing band. After a systematic search, he brought in Kenny Kleist (keyboards), Lanny Mathyssen (aka Mathijssen) (guitar/vocals) and drummer Willie Pounds (later replaced by Chester McCracken) who had been working in a local R&B covers band, the Dawgs. As Rosenberg says: "These guys were a real black shoe, white cover band, playing beer parlours in the suburbs of Los Angeles. They had nowhere to go. Kenny was a farmer from Wisconsin, Lanny was a construction worker and there were so many drummers. Skip had to convert these guys who wanted to play any job that paid a dollar more than the last one. I was a decent guitarist who went into folk music because I was into traditional roots stuff. I was one of those self-conscious, middle-class college students trying to pretend that my parents were really sharecroppers, but really studying the music and caring about it. Skip then turned me into a songwriter. He kept me playing and embroidering the music. I wanted to play rock 'n' roll, to stand onstage and touch people with my mind, with my eyes, and play great licks and sleep with different women every night . . . He said, 'That's fine, but you're going to do *this*!' Chameleon that he was, Skip was a visionary. He had an idea, or at least a blueprint, of how he would take four disparate people and turn it into something. Skip was not a writer, but his driving and haunting force was to write. In lieu of being able to do that, he nurtured me. He made me discipline myself so that I became the main writer in the band. All the time, he was calling me up, having me come over, making me write, getting me high and sending me home."

Lanny Mathyssen was aware that the band was basically a duopoly. "It was Skip and Al doing lots of acid. They'd go on trips and plan to be gone for two or three days. Frankly, I was lightweight, chicken shit. I had one really bad acid trip once and smoked some dope that was probably laced. Since then, when a joint came around I would blow on it to light it up and make like I inhaled it. I would just drink beer and never really got into dope. A little pot, that was it. Pills? Forget it. But I liked the concept of being a rock 'n' roller. Al was basically a country picker and did all the bluegrass things whereas I made it retch and puke, that was my style of playing. I wanted to sound like Jimi Hendrix or Jimmy Page. I liked the guitar to scream and holler and maybe there wasn't much place for that."

While collating material, the new group earned an uncertain living performing at clubs and lounges. Battin was pragmatic enough to use his old contacts to maximum effect. "Skip had been worn out through years of playing 'Cherry Pie'," Rosenberg says. "You can be on a circuit and not necessarily be on the way up, but on the way down. That's what Skip was then. He played those clubs but that didn't do it for him. But he had this incredible number of markers out in the world. He could go to a club owner in Van Nuys, Reseda or Paramount and the guy would buy Skip a beer. I watched awe-inspired as he would talk the guy into giving us a job. We'd rehearse some Grateful Dead, Jefferson Airplane or Moby Grape stuff and play. The reason club owners agreed was that they made Skip promise to sing 'Cherry Pie'. That's a fact. He hated it, but we did it. As much as he could, he kept us away from those places and kept us heading towards the Corral and eventually the Whisky. The money wasn't important to him. He was trying to ride the Byrds or Dylan and wanted to make his own statement."

Battin's artistic aspirations were not always appreciated by the supporting cast in his band. The outspoken Lanny Mathyssen was a frequent thorn in his side, ever ready to question his musical direction and persona. "Skip was not really the person people got to know him as," Mathyssen contends. "He was preaching all the love and peace bullshit but, basically, like all of us in those days, he wanted to be a big star with a lot of money. When I first came over from Holland, I thought I was going to replace Elvis Presley. We all wanted that. What can you say? . . . I know I sound negative. I didn't think Skip was that good a bass player or a singer. He was more like a talker who wanted to be like Bob Dylan, I guess. As far as I was concerned, he'd got lucky with Skip & Flip because he was a cute looking guy with that All American face . . . We did get into some shocking arguments. In those days it was a hip thing to improvise and at some point I'd say, 'Skip, this is bullshit, we're just making noise and it sounds like shit. What happened to harmonies, lyrics and melodies?' He never liked it much when I said stuff like that."

Erratic payments frequently undermined morale, but Battin was psychologically astute enough to manipulate the band with money, promises and long-term plans. There were occasional distractions, including a tempting offer to join former Leaves' guitarist Bobby Arlin in a spin-off group. Rosenberg remembers seeing them perform in a local club. "They were a cover band in paisley shirts. Arlin was slick and competent and could play the Doors' 'Light My Fire' on guitar. That blew me away. But Skip took me aside and said, 'Don't go for this. He's copying somebody else, you've got original stuff.' It took me a long time to understand that he was right. These guys had gigs and we had nothing. Arlin wanted Skip and they thought he was silly [for turning them down], but he stayed with us." What Rosenberg did not know was that Battin had already played with Arlin, albeit briefly, in the grandly named Arlyn-Battyn Expedition, when a promoter friend had booked them for a short stint at Le Red Velour in Van Nuys back in April. Evidently, Skip was not keen to repeat that experience.

Realizing that he could no longer keep his own band together with cajoling assurances, Battin turned to ace scammer, Kim Fowley. He wrote and produced 'Silver Shadows' which they coupled with Mike Heron's 'Maybe Someday' and released as a single on the small label Living Legend Records. "This was about September/October 1967," Rosenberg confirms. "Kim was very bright and, in his own way, competent. He was part of the 'If you throw enough shit against the wall, it will stick' school." At this point, the group had still not settled on a permanent name, an encumbrance that Fowley greeted with characteristic impatience. "Kim said, 'Well, we've got to call you something, this is teenage dogshit.' That was one of his phrases at the time. Then he said, 'I don't care, call yourselves Evergreen Blueshoes or whatever you want!' Skip said, 'That's great!' I thought it was a dumb name, but that was fine. Kim was a guy who just ran his mouth. That's how the name came. He sent 500 promotional copies out and nothing happened, but we stayed the Evergreen Blueshoes. We worked for the next year, going as far as we could without the band breaking up, playing a lot, but making no money."

Battin insisted they perform at showcase gigs and formulated an ambitious repertoire combining folk, pop and psychedelia. Rosenberg was still writing and unearthing public domain songs from his folk days, such as the railroad song, 'Life's Railway To Heaven'. 'Cold Rain And Snow', from the Grateful Dead's eponymous debut album, was a crowd pleaser for the hippie set, and Battin threw in a couple of songs by the Incredible String Band's Mike Heron. After playing the Ash Grove and the Troubadour, the group secured a long-term residency at the Corral in Topanga. Some wag even referred to them as 'the Beatles of Topanga Canyon', though that too was part of the hype. "Those were the places where the record business people came to look for acts and plucked them out," Rosenberg stresses. "Topanga was where Canned Heat broke from. Skip knew all that. We could have played more places like the Cougar Lounge in the Valley which was paying two and a quarter a man per week, which was a lot of money then. I was independent, but the guys couldn't see why we didn't do that all the time. The reason we didn't was because the Cougar Lounge wanted Top 40, not the Grateful Dead. At the Ash Grove and the Corral you'd get seen and be appreciated. By this point we were getting to be very creative and had a following but we weren't making any money. I was a peacemaker between Skip and the other guys because I really liked them but he had no use for them and I can understand why. He knew they weren't going to have anything significant to say in the way of writing. They were players and good soldiers and I guess he was a good sergeant or captain. But I had a rebellion on my hands because they were going broke. They were moving in the middle of the night from one sleazy single room apartment to another."

Battin was still hoping to bag a big album deal that would enable him to fulfil his dream of reinvention as a credible artiste. "That's what Evergreen Blueshoes was about," says Rosenberg.

"It was a gigantic and heroic attempt to do something really significant. Skip wanted to achieve something that could compete with or be as important a statement as the Byrds." While Battin was playing the long game, fishing for a major record deal, Rosenberg was keen to get things moving. Guitarist David Cohen, who had first introduced Rosenberg to Battin, suggested they meet Mike Post, a talented 24-year-old musician/engineer with an impressive track record. Post claimed to have played guitar on Sonny & Cher's 'I Got You Babe' and appeared as a sessioner on recordings by Dean Martin and Sammy Davis Jr, as well as working with Kenny Rogers' group, the First Edition. He was about to win his first Grammy for Best Instrumental Arrangement on Mason Williams' 'Classical Gas'. Post had close connections with Jimmy Bowen, the former rockabilly singer and producer of the Rat Pack (Sinatra, Martin and Davis) who was keen to branch out and establish his own company, Amos Records.

Warners/Reprise had agreed to bankroll the project which reflected its founder's twin interests in country music and established stars from a previous age. Among Amos' signings were Bing Crosby and two country rock bands, Longbranch Pennywhistle and Shiloh, whose personnel would later merge to form the core of the mega-selling Eagles. Rosenberg was excited when Amos expressed an interest in signing Evergreen Blueshoes, but Battin was sceptical and still wanted to hold out for a better deal. He wasn't convinced that Amos could promote an act like Evergreen Blueshoes successfully, but the financial incentives were difficult to resist. With no other immediate takers and a band on the brink of revolt, Battin reluctantly lowered his sights and agreed to sign. Rosenberg believes that a combination of pressure from the band and his own personal circumstances, not least supporting his young son, Brent, dictated that decision.

"The acid test was that his wife Jackie was still working. In his mind that was the ultimate degradation. The barometer of whether you were successful or not was whether your wife had to work. He felt he was no longer able to support the family.

Remember he was older than us. Even though he may have wanted to be creative that was the minimum you had to do where he came from . . . Jackie was fairly tall and rapier thin with long, dyed blonde hair, very pretty like a Barbie doll. She was protective of Skip. I think she knew he screwed around but he was never flagrant about it and she may have let him get away with it. She really worked hard to keep the family together. They had an interesting place on the hillside in Laurel Canyon. She was quite careful in encouraging him not to take chances such as hiring a new drummer at the cost of losing the old one, or trying some new Owsley sunshine, royal purple paisley dragon . . ."

While preparing the album, Battin was still uncertain about the concept and even the type of music he wished to pursue. Drummer Chet McCracken was given firm directions, but Skip was never entirely happy with the sound. "We were all young then and hoping for the best," McCracken remembers. "My take at the time was that Skip and Al were the leaders and we did things their way. And that was fine with me because I was in a rock 'n' roll band playing the Whisky A Go-Go all summer. Skip was delightful to work with, but at times he was very difficult. As I look back now, it was one of the best drum lessons I ever had because they were definitive about what they wanted from a drummer. Skip seemed firmly rooted in folk music. I think he and Al had a subliminal problem with drummers to begin with. I don't think you'd classify either of them as rockers. They were more comfortable in the acoustic environment. But for some reason the music they were trying to pull off at the time required a drummer. They were never happy and I was trying to adhere to what they wanted. I had no idea what was going on. I was just playing my drums . . . The album was Skip's big statement, it was very eclectic. It wasn't just a collection of pop songs but more a short story."

With Mike Post producing, the group finally completed *The Ballad Of Evergreen Blueshoes.* Even in the context of those hippie times, it was a strange, eccentric, yet fascinating recording. It sounded like a concept album, although determining what the concept was proved baffling. The work commenced with a shaky recorder solo, played as though this was a school production of *Peter Pan*. Battin then launched into a melodramatic spoken-word narrative, full of archaisms, seemingly designed to set the scene. The song selection was beyond eclectic – two songs borrowed from the Incredible String Band, a ballad version of Chuck Berry's 'Johnny B Goode', an adaptation of Edgar Allan Poe's *The Raven*, a sped-up version of Dylan's 'Walking Down The Line', an obscure David Cohen instrumental, a handful of Rosenberg originals, a topical anti-draft protest 'Amsterdam In 1968' and the powerful climactic Battin/Fowley opus 'The Everblue Express' featuring an arrangement taken from the 'Mars' section of Holtz's *Planets Suite*. This was heady stuff. In imitation of the Beatles' *Sgt Pepper's*, there were no bands between the tracks, unless you count the portentous spoken-word introductions. At times, these bizarre interjections popped up in the middle of songs like discovered sounds from the speeches of a Pentecostal preacher or a television evangelist. The wild array of material and the self-conscious playfulness in its musical execution gave the album an unintended kitsch quality. At times, it sounded like a parody of a concept album, resembling the hippie lampoons then current on *Rowan & Martin's Laugh In* television show. It was the curse of Battin's career that even his more serious and ambitious endeavours could never quite escape the novelty tag. "Skip was trying to become imbued with the liberal spirit of the time," Rosenberg recalls, "but ultimately he was a guy from Ohio who had a hit record in 1959 and spent the rest of his life trying to get back there in a reasonable way, thinking about being current and staying with the music of today."

Looking back at the album, Battin was critical in his summation. "The Evergreen Blueshoes was a really good project but the shame of it was that the album we recorded did not really project what the group was into musically . . . The way we wanted those songs to go down was all in our heads and I was quite disappointed in the way the album turned out."

Rosenberg feels this was a severe understatement and remembers his colleague feeling bereft at the failure of his concept, even during the recording. "He was disenchanted when we went in the studio. Disenchanted because he couldn't write the way he wanted; disenchanted with the drummer and the other guys . . . Listening to the mix, he was bereft." Despite the pervasive sense of doom emanating from Battin, his more positive side encouraged hope. The group enjoyed playing the entire record live onstage, mischievously switching instruments to emphasize its visual possibilities. Their promising residency at the Corral ushered them into Hollywood for prestigious performances at the Whisky and the Kaleidoscope.

With the record readied for release, Battin met the art director to discuss a suitably arresting cover. During the same period, John Lennon and Yoko Ono were preparing to issue their avant-garde collection, *Two Virgins*, the first album ever to feature full-frontal nudity. The controversy surrounding the cover delayed that release by several months. Coincidentally, nudity was also a feature of the Jimi Hendrix Experience's double album, *Electric Ladyland*, which came out in the UK just before the Lennon/Ono record. Seizing the zeitgeist, Battin suggested that the band should also play the nudity card, albeit not so explicitly as to elicit a complete ban. Early one morning, the musicians assembled for a photo shoot at Griffith Park and were pictured dancing naked, as if they were part of some arcane pagan festival. "We gambolled around this area in Griffith Park and we all got naked except for the organ player," says Rosenberg. "I think he was playing a flute or recorder up a tree. His wife wouldn't let him appear nude so he wore red tights." Skip's wife Jackie was more daring and can be seen on the album sleeve joining in the frolics. In order not to offend public decency, the cover artwork was delicately disguised to remove anything explicit. Endearingly modest to modern eyes, it was nevertheless considered risqué and controversial at the time. "There was quite a stir about it in the record company," Rosenberg remembers. "Amos had Bing Crosby covering 'Hey Jude' at the time so they weren't delighted about a nude album cover. It may have delayed its release. Ultimately it was all a tempest in a teapot because nothing happened with the record."

Battin was totally disillusioned by the failure of *The Ballad Of Evergreen Blueshoes*, blaming the record company, management and seemingly almost everyone else associated with the project. "So much of this was coloured by Skip being frustrated at not being a decent writer," Rosenberg concludes. "It was his haunting and a grinding bugbear his whole life. He wanted very much to do what the Byrds and Dylan did – to create. He was a very good performer, a wonderful band leader, an inspirer, but a mediocre writer. His very heavy need to be creative was corrosive because it made him look to other places besides himself for problems. The album concept was Skip's and it was as close as he felt he could come to something creative. It was made, it sold about eight copies, and it died. I've never been able to listen to it since because it was too painful and I've never talked to anybody about it or heard from anyone who had an opinion on it . . . For maybe 20 minutes that band was quite an item in underground music in LA. It was almost all word of mouth, but we were headlining at the Whisky . . . I would have loved to see something happen to the album, just in terms of people saying, 'Wow, this was an interesting document of the period of the Vietnam War and the psychedelic music of Los Angeles.' We were playing love-ins and it was a really exciting time."

The group remained in a state of suspended animation in the months after the album's release, before drifting apart. According to Mathyssen, Battin was veering towards a more folkier, pastoral direction and suggested they dispense with the drummer. Predictably, Mathyssen baulked, then lost his temper. "A rock 'n' roll band without a drummer? Are you kidding me? He just wanted to go more country and that's when I said, 'I've had it, man. It's a bunch of bullshit.' The album came out but I never got much credit and they mixed my guitar out a hell of a lot. I said, 'I'm finished with this, it's a suck album, it's not going to go anywhere, it's all an ego trip for Skip.' His ego was as tall as the

Empire State Building then. I didn't get the concept. It was supposed to be like a big 45 that never stops and was supposed to tie all together. What was the concept? That we were the peace-makers, the fortune tellers? He wanted to be artsy fartsy and it was just bullshit."

Before long, the Evergreen Blueshoes had devolved into a fractious duo with an uncertain future. "Skip was still trying to write with me but I was becoming frustrated too," says Rosenberg. "We didn't have to sit there passively waiting for the album to happen or not. We could have done other things, but he seemed resigned. Skip had run his race with it. I always felt that, creatively, it was a high-water mark for him. He had never done anything as risky or wild. It was interesting, if nothing else."

Battin did not remain despondent for long. For a brief period, he attempted to find acting work, famously appearing under his semi-pseudonym Bunky Battin in the Don Siegel film, *Coogan's Bluff*. Always the trouper and self-improver, he decided to extend his musical skills by learning jazz guitar. On a visit to Wallach's Music City on the corner of Sunset and Vine, he saw a card offering guitar tuition. It had been placed by Art Johnson, a young session player who had already worked with Paul Horn, Tim Weisberg, Lynn Blessing and Richard Thompson. "My reputation was established in LA because I was the first rock/jazz guitarist," Johnson says. "They didn't use the word fusion then. There were very few guys integrating bebop and rock like me. I'd also played some country & western, and Skip was interested in that."

What separated Johnson from many of the elder jazz players in his circle was his keen appreciation of rock and willingness to work with unschooled musicians. "Players like Barney Kessell, who was my mentor, hated rock 'n' roll. But I was a generation younger than these guys. When Hendrix came on the scene I recall being in a room with a bunch of guitar players who were all shaking their heads. They knew producers would say, 'I want you to sound like *that*' – and they didn't have the slightest idea what he was up to. I heard him and thought, 'OK, I understand this.' I never tried to be Jimi Hendrix but I could cop that sound – the rotary speaker with the fuzz tone and a Stratocaster – and take it from there."

Battin was impressed by Johnson's musicianship and forward thinking and immediately invited him to his house off Kirkwood Drive, Laurel Canyon, for a practice session. "We started to form a fusion instrumental group based on long jams," says Johnson. "I was using a lot of jazz harmonies. I could write and arrange on the spot and none of these guys could. We did session work with singers and stuff and worked together for about a year." Among the players who collaborated with Battin at Kirkwood were drummers Eddie Hoh and Michael Botts (later of Bread), plus guitarist Mars Bonfire (aka Dennis Edmonton, composer of Steppenwolf's hit 'Born To Be Wild'). Battin regarded these jazz-inspired jams as enormously beneficial, but realized the music had limited commercial potential. "There isn't much of a market for that," he said. "During that dry spell I was starting to get into session work, maybe two or three sessions a week but I never really wanted it, was never fond of doing it." Most of the sessions came courtesy of Kim Fowley who, over the next year, employed Battin on his own album *Good Clean Fun*, Gene Vincent's *I'm Back And I'm Proud*, Warren Zevon's *Wanted Dead Or Alive* and Earth Island's *We Must Survive*.

Battin's resolve was tested by setbacks, but his positivism always won out. One evening, following a Fowley session, he came home late and parked his van in front of his garage on Kirkwood. During the night, thieves broke into the vehicle, stealing Battin's bass, Johnson's 1957 Telecaster and all their Fender amps. Driving up to Laurel Canyon, Johnson was shocked to see Battin's house surrounded by cops and was crestfallen by the robbery. "What do we do now?" he asked. Without missing a beat, Battin replied: "We're going down to Hollywood now to get new gear."

As Johnson remembers: "We picked the equipment up, came back and rehearsed that same day. Skip was Mr Positive. He didn't like negativity. He didn't have time for it. Even if something horrible happened, there had to be good coming out of it. That was Skip. He wouldn't settle for it otherwise. He became interested in Buddhism and tried to get me into the Nam Myoho Renge chant thing. I tried that for a while with him. It came in useful when we were playing together. Any type of mental discipline, if it is properly applied, has to expand the imagination. Skip was always ready to go, always ready to do it. He was never the world's greatest bass player but he was always inspired. This wasn't a guy who sat around practising all day long studying Berklee College of Music harmony books, but he had an intuitive quality. He would rise to your level whatever level that was. He would find a way."

"Of all the musicians I've known in my life," Johnson continues, "there's a guy who was always a sweetheart. Seriously. He was open for anything and always had a smile. He was a very smart businessman who didn't come across as a businessman. Skip was a great people person. You could have waltzed him into the president's office at Universal and he'd have been right at home, and he would have made the president feel right at home. You could take him to a bohemian coffee-house and he would light up the room while sitting there smiling and nodding his head. Even while listening to somebody strumming a guitar and singing some insipid lyric, he'd be all into it. I can picture him with his folded cowboy hat, boots and jeans and some kind of necklace that Jackie had woven or picked up some place. It was the same outfit all the time . . . He had a magic quality, an aura and a charisma which was totally based on not being pushy. He wasn't pretentious or an egotist but he was all show business – and I say that in a positive way. I think we played only one gig, but he knew how to appear onstage; he knew who was looking at him; he knew what facial expression he needed to fit the moment; he knew the importance of eye contact; he was very aware of the audience's potential to play you, which is half the battle. He was a camera person, and he understood that concept very well. Skip was a great guy and we shared a lot of happiness."

*   *   *

One of the stranger stories about Battin was his avid pursuit of the secret of youth. When Steve Young was on the road with him in 1965, he was intrigued to witness a ritual that sounded as though it had been taken from the imaginations of Robert Louis Stevenson or Edgar Allan Poe. "Skip and his manager used to take these shots. It was something like calf brain cells and it was supposed to give them energy and keep them young. I wanted to try this stuff and kept bugging them. They finally relented one day in a van on the way to Northern California. They were a little apprehensive about how it would affect me. It wasn't that big a deal but it seems I did get energy from it. The story they gave me was that it was some experimental thing. It was a shot with a needle, but it wasn't in the vein. It was a mystery I never understood."

That 'mystery' also fascinated Art Johnson who felt he was fraternizing with Dorian Gray. Even Jackie seemed exceptionally young to his eyes. "You could never tell how old either of them were. I couldn't tell. Skip didn't seem old at all but the way he talked I suspected that he must have been a bit older. If you're saying he was born in 1934, then he was 11 years older than me. I wouldn't have suspected it. The secret that Skip told me was that he was taking the same 'youth serum' as the actor Robert Cummings, whom he knew back then." Significantly, perhaps, Cummings was known for his preternatural young looks and had even authored a book in 1960 titled *Stay Young And Vital.*

Later, during the Byrds' period, road manager Al Hersh teased out some further information about this anti-ageing process. "I'm sure it came up in your investigations," he says. "There were so many people that you'd never associate with Skip that were hanging out with him at that time. I believe it was a 'drug' that John F. Kennedy was taking to resist ageing. There were a bunch of actors, not musicians, and JFK. It was a mixture of lamb urine or something with speed. They were taking this weird mixture to control ageing and a lot of very influential people were seeing this doctor. The only other person I heard about who was doing it was Kennedy. I was fascinated when Skip told me about it and it really cracked me up. It did have Dracula overtones. Skip did look very young for his age. I don't know whether he would have aged that way in any case, but something was going on! The age thing was really important to him because of the youthfulness of the guys he was playing with."

In September 1969, Battin received the biggest break of his career when he was offered the opportunity to replace John York in the Byrds. The invitation came via Gene Parsons and Clarence White, both of whom had worked with him in studios. "I liked his playing and we'd been doing sessions," Parsons recalls. "Skip had already lived in Hollywood and played with lots of people like Gene Vincent. The way he played was very tight and energetic, which was what we wanted." Although Battin's induction seemed a relative formality, he was determined to leave nothing to chance. "He told me that he learned every song the Byrds had ever recorded," says Kim Fowley. "Imagine that. All those Byrds songs. He memorized the bass and harmony parts and got the gig. They started playing and, without telling him what the song was, he'd play the bass part and come in with the third harmony. Skip had teaching credential and he was a smart guy."

McGuinn had no idea that the promising candidate was actually older than Elvis Presley. One of Battin's first assignments as a Byrd was to attend a photo session for an advertisement to promote their new album *Ballad Of Easy Rider*, on which he had not appeared. The recent loss of John York hardly inspired confidence among fans who had no reason to believe that Battin would last any longer than his predecessor. Although the group's association with the film *Easy Rider* brought them some much needed publicity, they were required to work harder than ever to re-establish credibility in the press and the marketplace. "The group wasn't a popular working group and the records weren't selling," according to Battin. "I'm not saying I had anything or much to do with their comeback, but we made a strong comeback . . ." Their success resulted from a combination of extensive touring and the acclaimed double album, *(Untitled)*. The work introduced Battin to the Byrds' world and the results were impressive. "*(Untitled)* wasn't a difficult album to record, but we did take our time over it and were careful. It was my first experience in the studio with unlimited time and we were able to do what we wanted without too much pressure."

The Battin compositions worked well in the context of a double album. 'You All Look Alike' (co-written by Gene Parsons) was a sardonic yet moving rumination on racial prejudice; 'Hungry Planet', with added lyrics and a stylish vocal from McGuinn, was a sound ecological lamentation; 'Well Come Back Home' combined an anti-Vietnam protest with a Buddhist chant to produce an epic finale that was pure Battin His importance was underlined on the live album where his bass playing could be heard to startling effect. Battin became known for his 'lead bass' and solidity as a rhythm player. His friend Chris Darrow, who took up the instrument himself with Kaleidoscope, had played with all three Byrds bassists over the years and provides a unique perspective. "Of the three, Chris Hillman was the most melodic, John York was the most classic player and Skip Battin was the most rhythmic. They were all great bass players and every one of them had their own approach. Skip had the same bass all of his life. There was an ethic that a lot of bass players had from the Fifties and the Sixties that they never changed their strings. Joe Osborn was the same way. I don't like to change strings – if one breaks I have to replace them all. It has to do with the temperature of the strings and they won't play in tune if they're not all the same. To my knowledge, Skip never changed his strings since the Fifties. He got a great tone that was really deep and thick, but it didn't have a long sustain to it. It was devised from the bass players that started in the Fifties. Skip was totally into that."

Of course, the improvisational work that Battin undertook with Art Johnson also allowed him to roam free on the jazzier material like 'Eight Miles High'. "Skip enjoyed jazz," says Parsons, "and one of the things that caused him to play that way was that he had become a Buddhist. He would sit down with his beads every day and chant. He learned all the chants in this book and they were fairly complicated and rhythmic. He incorporated some of those triplet rhythms and syncopations in his bass playing and you can hear it, particularly on 'Eight Miles High' when he just lets go. That jazz influence and the Buddhist rhythms created something unique."

Battin brought stability, grace and strength to the Byrds' live performances. For several years the band ran like a well-oiled machine but their morale was never the same after *Byrdmaniax*. Once Battin started writing almost exclusively with Kim Fowley their songs were singled out as unrepresentative of the Byrds. The lyrical themes became increasingly retro, from Fowley's tribute to golden age Hollywood ('Citizen Kane'), through early Sixties memories of Battersea Fun Fair ('Tunnel Of Love') to the final nadir of 'America's Great National Pastime', a novelty item that stylistically harked back to the Fifties. Fowley remained indignant at the way history fingered him as the villain of the partnership. "Ironically, I share David Crosby's resentment of the Skip Battin/Kim Fowley songs that don't sound like the Byrds. A lot of people think I forced Skip to write these weird things but I kept saying: 'You know Appalachian harmony, bluegrass harmony, country harmony. You're a hillbilly with a college education, goddamnit. Use your brain and be a member of a band.' I always fought him on it and said, 'Man, this is not the Byrds.' I knew because I was a Byrds dancer at Ciro's. I kept saying, 'Skip, why are we doing this when you should be writing Byrds songs? Write Byrd melodies and let me give you Dylanesque lyrics or at least Jacques Levy-type lyrics and then you'll fit in the group better.' But he didn't want to lose his identity. He wanted to be Tom Lehrer and play piano like Fats Domino . . . I told him, 'Don't! Tom Lehrer didn't make it singing political satire, and you're not going to make it either.' We fought and fought. Then I kept my mouth shut because I figured, 'Well, at least I got on the Byrds albums.' Man, I always got blamed for it and I always got mad. Goddamnit, I was trying to play the game."

Fowley's sophistry is partly persuasive until you remember that he was the sole lyricist. Had Battin collaborated on the lyrics then this argument would be convincing, but it was Fowley who presented those words to record and chose themes such as the semi-autobiographical 'Citizen Kane' and 'Precious Kate'. Moreover, it was Fowley's original idea to write the satirical 'America's Great National Pastime'. All these compositions betray his distinctive hand. When Battin wrote alone on 'Well Come Back Home' or with Gene Parsons on 'Yesterday's Train', the results were very different. Notwithstanding Fowley's alleged aesthetic misgivings, the cold facts are that he elected to submit these songs, wrote every word and evidently stood by them at the time. If he truly felt they were unrepresentative of the Byrds, why did he present them to Battin in the first place? "Because he was in the Byrds and they sold 200–300,000 albums every time. It was my pension plan. But I still say that Skip had that fatal flaw of secretly wanting to sing lead, even though he was a better sideman and a decent arranger. This all goes back to Skip and Flip, television, screaming girls and feckless youth. You never quite get over those memories of being the centre of attention. Skip fitted in with the Byrds up to a point, but he also had that psychological problem of knowing there could be more. He liked to have his own identity, even within the Byrds, and that may have affected his role as a team player, although he tried his best and was always easy to get along with. He certainly wasn't into conflict, which is probably why it worked for so long."

Arguably, the primary reason why several of the Battin-Fowley songs failed to fit into the Byrds' canon was their perceived lack of authenticity. The Byrds' image, like all images, was based on myth, but it provided a powerful identity, greater than its members ever understood. Bringing Fowley into the story was a dangerous ploy that threatened the very meaning of what constituted a Byrds song. It was as crazy as hearing one of his songs on a Beatles or Rolling Stones album. Nor was it solely about the songwriting. When he first appeared on a Byrds album, Fowley already had a reputation as a hustler and master of hype. He gleefully told *Rolling Stone* that he was 91 years old and had fornicated with over 7,000 women, then went on to relate breathtaking tales of countless notorious scams and music business adventures involving a cast worthy of a Cecil B. DeMille movie. Fowley was the embodiment of pop artifice, a champion of the trash aesthetic and a formidable self-publicist. In short, he was the total opposite of the Byrds, whose ethic was based on a notion of anti-artificiality which they shared with the majority of their counter-culture-loving audience. The Byrds established a brand name with a reputation for innovation and a disdain for the easy cash-in. They were the bastions of authenticity, the children of Dylan, originally inculcated by Jim Dickson to bring intelligence to pop and, in doing so, they rose above the murky environs inhabited by old school pranksters like Fowley. David Crosby would cringe if you dared mention his time in the Les Baxter Balladeers, whereas Fowley felt no embarrassment about his previous pop endeavours. Indeed, he spoke triumphantly of 'Alley-Oop' and 'Nut Rocker', as if they were cultural landmarks on a par with 'Mr Tambourine Man' or 'Eight Miles High'.

If Battin was still hoping to escape the stigma of being reminded of his pop past in Skip & Flip, then his choice of writing partner was decidedly odd. In the public's imagination, the Fowley connection spelt novelty and reconnected Battin with his earlier pop roots It was as if David Crosby was suddenly writing with Les Baxter or McGuinn co-composing with Bobby Darin, or Gene Clark rediscovering the sound of the New Christy Minstrels. Fowley may have been intelligent enough to appreciate the incongruity of the Battin-Fowley songs in a Byrds' context, but he never allowed aestheticism to get in the way of fiscal opportunity.

Fowley was Fowley and that meant a song written in 20 minutes, like the risible 'America's Great National Pastime', could become a Byrds song and even a single. It was only when Battin didn't understand a Fowley composition, such as 'Absolute Happiness', that he freed himself sufficiently to connect emotionally with the song. Battin always believed that 'Absolute Happiness' was his partner's empathetic attempt to celebrate Buddhism, not realizing that it was inspired by Fowley's lustful desire to infiltrate a religious cult and deflower its more attractive adherents. Battin's belief in the song's spurious sentiments resulted in his finest and most convincing vocal performance during his time in the Byrds. Elsewhere, he was unable to personalize lyrics or imbue the material with enough feeling to convince the listener that the words actually meant something. Fowley was a sardonic observer of the human condition, but his compositions betrayed an iciness that was, most likely, the legacy of his chaotic upbringing. He was always too detached emotionally to write a love song, let alone a love song of emotional conviction. Even 'Precious Kate', conceived as a eulogy to Kate Taylor, ended up centring attention on a California earthquake at the expense of its titular heroine.

Battin was aware that the material he sung in the Byrds was questionable. "We had that problem. Kim and I definitely had our own style which didn't mesh as well as we would have liked but, at the same time, that gave birth to a solo album." Comically, it was the novelty satire 'America's Great National Pastime', improbably issued as a Byrds single in the US, that won Battin a contract with Signpost Records. His strategy of recording material with the Byrds better suited to a soloist had actually paid dividends. Sessions began in April 1972 and were completed during the summer, but the album would not appear until the following January.

Skip utilizes the talents of various Byrds and associates, including Clarence White, McGuinn, John Guerin, former and current road managers Jimmi Seiter and Al Hersh, drummer Billy Mundi and singer Spanky McFarlane. The entire work is composed by Battin-Fowley and sounds like extensions of the material they had been producing for the Byrds. The crucial difference is that songs which would have appeared incongruous on a Byrds album work marvellously well in a solo setting. *Skip* is arguably Battin's career highlight, a thoroughly refreshing work that should have launched the singer as a successful solo recording artiste. The rollicking opener 'Undercover Man' is a plea to freaky rock 'n' rollers to stay together, laced with humorous and paranoid references to secret agents, whether they be from CBS or the FBI.

Fowley's influence is ever present, particularly on compositions based on memories or stories of the golden age of Hollywood, notably the cynical 'Valentino' and the stylistically odd 'Four Legs Are Better Than Two' with its references to Ginger Rogers and Fred Astaire. 'Central Park', a satiric putdown which contrasts the current reputation of the park with its grander state in 1922, was deemed strong enough to release as an A-side. The second single featured the impressive 'Ballad Of Dick Clark', a nostalgic romp chronicling Fowley and Battin's early memories of the rock 'n' roll era, with affectionate references to Fats Domino, Chuck Berry and Duane Eddy, along with the Penguins and Annette Funicello.

Battin's own world-view is more evident on the baseball anthem 'St Louis Browns', a poignant account of his fascination with the sport. The St Louis Browns were a team with a chequered history. Under various financial pressures and changes of fortune they lost their ground and ultimately their identity. After the 1953 season the team was uprooted, then transplanted eastwards to become the Baltimore Orioles. The migration severed all connections with their previous home, leaving former followers with tarnished or treasured memories. It could almost serve as an allegory of fame, found and lost. Battin, assisted by Fowley, provides an accurate account of the Browns' fall focusing on the arrival of owner Bill Veeck in 1951 and name-checking key players such as left-fielder Roy Seivers, pitcher 'Bullet' Bob Turley and the one-armed Pete Gray. Even for those unfamiliar with baseball history, Battin's valediction is both humorous and moving.

For many listeners the highlight of the album is the extraordinary 'Captain Video', a beautifully crafted and gently satirical sketch of Roger McGuinn, with references to 'Captain Soul' and '5 D (Fifth Dimension)' and subtle nods to his love of red wine and Albert Einstein (complete with speculations on the 'metaphysical mesh'). Inviting McGuinn to play on the record proved an inspired idea. Fowley would have preferred McGuinn to sing this self-referential anthem and his instincts appear sound.

Had this been written during the *Farther Along* sessions, it would have fitted perfectly on that album, especially if McGuinn had provided the laconic, world-weary lead vocal, as Fowley intended.

The closing track 'My Secret Life' celebrates Battin's love of music, travelling, dogs and Buddhism. It is also a powerful testament to the importance of friendship and once again demonstrates Battin's strengths when expressing emotional commitment and spirituality rather than merely embracing novelty. As he concludes: "My secret life is your love and it's sacred and together and we have it tonight."

Uniquely, Battin was the only member of the group to record and release a solo album while still a Byrd. Thanks to Fowley, he was also moonlighting on other projects including providing some music for *Ciao! Manhattan*, a fictionalized biography of Andy Warhol icon, Edie Sedgwick. Unfortunately, by the time *Skip* appeared, Battin's tenure as a Byrd was about to end. McGuinn had already dismissed Gene Parsons and belatedly decreed that Battin songs were no longer appropriate for the Byrds. Not long after, the bassist was fired, but there would be no replacement. Chris Hillman agreed to appear for a weekend date in February at the Capitol Theatre, Passaic, New Jersey, after which McGuinn dissolved the group.

Battin's adverse final days in the Byrds were parallelled by a turbulent period in his personal life. In common with the other members of the group, his marriage was under threat, partly as a result of dalliances on the road. Battin's sorrowful eyes, athletic physique and affable personality made him an easy target for groupies, not that he needed much encouragement. The womanizing Kim Fowley recalls how Skip's wife Jackie was growing tired of what she described as "puppies on the road". "Skip was always a ladies' man," he stresses, "but it was the Sixties and things were more liberal then. There were all these women on the road and – you know how that works."

At the time he joined the Byrds, Battin was still living happily in Laurel Canyon, next door to the group's former drummer

Kevin Kelley who, oddly enough, played no part in this unfolding saga. When Kelley vacated the premises, future Byrds' roadie Al Hersh moved in. He befriended the Battins and later began a relationship with Jackie that, remarkably enough, survived the era and remains intact at the time of writing. Amid this stormy phase, Battin and his family moved to Filo in Mendocino County. This rural retreat appealed to Battin's spiritual side and inspired him to write more, but there was no happy ending. Events reached a head following a dispute over some animals. "Skip had two beautiful Labrador retrievers," Gene Parsons recalls. "The local ranchers had told him: 'Keep your dogs inside at night because they'll pack with other dogs and go after our sheep.' Skip didn't believe them. He thought his dogs were passive and friendly. Well, one night those dogs went out with some others and killed 40 sheep and the ranchers pretty much ran him out of town, took the dogs and had them killed. That was such a difficult experience for those guys. They moved to Topanga after that. But that was the beginning of the end for Skip and Jackie."

"They were together for probably 13 years, then I got involved with Jackie in 1970," says Al Hersh. "I guess we consummated our relationship then. Skip had already moved on to other people. There were a lot of women on the road that Jackie found out about. It was just one of those things . . . Jackie and I and Skip all moved to Topanga together from Northern California. I decided to leave because Jackie and I were already happening, and it was kind of awkward. Skip and I were good friends, but they were on the outs anyway. It's not like I broke up the marriage, but there was a lot of underlying crap, so I moved to Malibu . . ."

Battin adjusted to the demise of the Byrds and the fragmentation of his marriage by keeping busy. Although *Skip* had failed to sell, record company interest in ex-Byrds was still strong. In what many regarded as an unlikely coupling, Battin announced that he was working on a joint album with Clarence White. The guitarist had already appeared on *Skip* playing a variety of instruments, including a wonderful mandolin break on 'Four Legs Are Better Than Two'. His presence alone meant that the new work would be taken seriously. Pre-production practice sessions (see the earlier Clarence White obituary for the full story) were undertaken at Battin's house with Art Johnson, among others. Then tragedy struck. Two days before the recordings were set to begin, White was killed. Kim Fowley, who had yet to hear of this terrible event, duly turned up at the studio to be greeted by a strange sight. "When I went to the session there was a Bible on a chair with Clarence's guitar and amp set up, as though he was going to play."

Like Gene Parsons, Battin seemed demoralized by White's death. Over the next few months he built a second house in Topanga and reluctantly completed the album, which reverted to a solo work. Surprisingly, Al Hersh was initially listed as producer on a tape purporting to be the finished album titled *Topanga Skyline*. Its contents, which include two versions of 'Roll In My Sweet Baby's Arms' and a couple of attempts at the Battin/Fowley number, 'Relax With Me', indicate that the running order or track selection was not quite finalized. *Topanga Skyline* was eventually issued in 2010 by Sierra Records, with Kim Fowley credited as producer and co-writer. Its contents indicate the exceptional quality of musicianship on offer, betraying a more country feel than its predecessor, *Skip*, with bluegrass familiars including a rousing 'Salty Dog Blues', 'Foggy Mountain Top' and the bonus track, 'Mountain Dew', the latter taken from the rehearsal sessions with Clarence White. Although the co-writes with Fowley are a mixed bag, they're salvaged by the belated presence of the evocative 'China Moon' and the moody strains of 'Wintergreen', two of their finer efforts. According to Battin, economic cutbacks prompted by a vinyl shortage scuppered the album's original release. He would never record another solo album for a major label.

Freed from touring and recording commitments, Battin spent the next eight months hanging out in Topanga, socializing and jamming with friends Spanky McFarlane and former Byrds' pick-up drummer, Jim Moon. This sojourn was interrupted by a call from McGuinn's agent, Ron Rainey, who was seeking a musician to replace Dave Torbert in New Riders Of The Purple Sage. Keen to get back to work, Battin accepted the offer. He was a strong presence on 1974's *Brujo*, which featured four Battin-Fowley compositions, of which the affecting 'Singing Cowboy' was a highlight. Thereafter, they toured busily, returning to the studio for the less impressive *Oh What A Mighty Time*, which featured Battin's cameo, 'Strangers On A Train'. "One of my least favourite albums," was Battin's curt assessment. "None of the Riders had that many tunes on the album because producer Bob Johnston came into the picture. He had his own ideas and brought most of the songs in."

After two years in the New Riders, Battin was seduced by an offer from Gene Parsons to join a reconstituted Flying Burrito Brothers. The timing could hardly have been worse for the Riders, who were in the process of signing a contract with MCA Records. Ever the pragmatist, Battin agreed to keep quiet about the Burritos' proposal and postpone his departure until the completion of the album *New Riders*. "At one time I was in both groups," he admitted, "but we did that album, and I think it's the best Riders album I've been associated with. We did the final tracks and mixes and then I drove down to Los Angeles and started on the Burritos album."

Manager Eddie Tickner had helped the Burritos win a contract with Columbia Records (CBS) at a time when country rock still seemed in the ascendant. In reality, the tide was turning and *Airborne*, released in the summer of 1976, would be their last studio album for a major record label. With Fowley unavailable, Battin had no new songs to proffer and seemed unwilling to delve into the archives by reviving material from the doomed *Topanga Skyline*. *Airborne* received tepid reviews and Battin subsequently admitted that the group should have unveiled the songs in live performance before entering the studio. Thereafter, they devolved into a quasi-tribute band, releasing live albums on small labels to undiscriminating fans. Chris Hillman, who surely never attended any of their concerts, could always be relied upon to argue the pointlessness of their existence in characteristically harsh terms. "Do I think those guys have a right to the name? Not at all! It would be the same as if I took my group and called it the Byrds and sang 'Mr Tambourine Man'. It makes me crazy that they did that . . . Maybe I wouldn't feel so bad if they had been really good, but they weren't. They were neither good vocally nor instrumentally. They took the Flying Burrito Brothers' name when they should have let it rest and they were even singing songs that Gram and I wrote."

With record companies clearing their rosters of country rock veterans, the live circuit provided the only opportunity to make a living. Battin elected to take a sabbatical during 1977 and hinted that he might retire permanently. His old friend Art Johnson remembers visiting him in his rural eyrie on what turned out to be an eventful afternoon. "That was the last time we saw each other. I'd lost track of him for awhile, but then we somehow hooked up again. He was living out in Agoura across some small creek in a cabin with some girl from Russia . . . This place was in the middle of nowhere. I had to take mountain trails and it was raining like hell. I drove my Mercedes across the creek bed and got on to this little path and saw Skip waving at me."

They spent a pleasant afternoon talking about the rehearsal tapes they'd made with Clarence White and some other projects, now forgotten. Eventually, Johnson headed off, only to discover that "the creek was a river" and the only option was to drive through the water. In midstream, the car stalled and Johnson had to ease his way through the side window to escape. Unfortunately, he neglected to remove a cash envelope containing session money of $4,000. "I went running back to Skip, screaming my head off in a huge panic. He came out and said, 'Oh my gosh!' which was one of his favourite expressions. But he had the patience to get inside the car, get it started and figure a way out of there to the other side of the creek. That was Skip!"

One year later, Battin returned to the Burritos, then almost rejoined the New Riders, before taking up an offer to tour Japan, a country not usually associated with country rock. The results were captured on another live album, *Close Encounters To The West Coast* (retitled *Live From Tokyo*), which underlined the Burritos' apparent devolution into a nostalgic covers band. In fairness, they did attempt further studio work following the recruitment of guitarist John Beland, but the results were not considered worthy of release and remained locked in the vaults for over a decade.

Touring with the Burritos was akin to playing the bar circuit for a basic wage, so it was hardly surprising that Battin was pleased to be offered the opportunity to release another solo album, albeit on the obscure Italian label, Appaloosa. *Navigator* was a desultory affair, dominated by Battin-Fowley songs including 'Skyscraper Sunset', 'Zig Zag' and 'North By Northwest' but, tellingly, these were eclipsed by surprise revivals of 'Citizen Kane' and 'Captain Video', even though the latter was patently inferior to the version on *Skip*. The Italian connection proved deeper than anyone could have expected. Battin fell in love with the country and invested time in learning the language. Linguistic differences actually worked to his advantage there, instantly negating all the prejudices associated with Fowley's persona and lyrical themes. In Italy, they seemed happy to accept Battin as a bona fide Byrd. He returned there in September 1981 as part of the American Country Rock All Stars, featuring Sneaky Pete Kleinow, Chris Darrow and Steve Duncan. After contributing to an album by local player Ricky Gianco, Battin persuaded Darrow to play a handful of gigs in a duet format.

Back in America, Skip continued playing in such unheralded aggregations as Battin, Kleinow & Friends, the New Dixie Flyers and the Older Brothers. He had been leading a peripatetic existence, but that soon changed when he met a young artist in unexpected circumstances. Patricia Cartabiano, born in 1955, was raised in Southern California before moving to Connecticut in the late Sixties. After completing an art degree, she worked as a painter in Mexico City, supplementing her income by teaching English. Her sister, Jeannie, a graphic designer, invited her to move to a rented house in Triunfo Canyon, Agoura Hills. It turned out that their fellow tenant Brian Polland was actually subletting the property from Battin, who arrived unexpectedly one evening. As Cartabiano recalls: "The funny thing is that instead of being upset that there were all these people living in his house, he politely asked if he could park his VW bus under the oak outside the cabin and camp there while he looked for another place to live." As the ultimate laid-back landlord, Battin soon ingratiated himself with his young house guests, frequently attending dinner parties and joining them on various musical outings. "He was a great dancer," says Patricia who, despite being 21 years his junior, soon formed a romantic attachment with the former Byrd.

Cartabiano accepted an invitation to accompany him on another Italian tour, prior to which he purchased a berry farm on the southern side of Mt Angel, Oregon. It was surely no coincidence that his former partner Gary Paxton had also been working on a berry farm in the area just before the release of the first Skip & Flip single. Inspired by this rural domestic idyll, Battin married Cartabiano in a ceremony at the farm. His eldest son Dale, who had recently re-entered his life, served as the best man. Local painter, mandolin player and singer, Connie Cohen, whom they had recently met at an organic food store, sang a wedding eulogy. It was not all cakes and ale for the Battins. Summer rains ruined their crop and Battin's limited mechanical skills initially proved an impediment. Nevertheless, he retained his characteristic optimism, befriended farm labourers, joined the local softball team and promised his new wife that all would be well.

"Skip was a gentleman and a gentle soul," she recalls. "He was a romantic. He would look over the boysenberry fields and be overcome with the beauty while I, standing next to him, would see two-thirds of the crop had been wiped out by root borer weevils. A financial disaster." They managed to sell the Mt Angel enterprise within a year and Skip soon found another more prosperous berry farm in nearby Woodburn, Oregon. Over the next couple of years, Patricia gave birth to two children, a son Jon-Clyde

(1984) and a daughter, Susanna (1986). In the interim, the Continental sojourns, during which Battin had duetted with singer/guitarist Ricky Mantoan, led to another album with the Italian label Appaloosa Records.

Don't Go Crazy, released in 1984, unexpectedly turned out to be Battin's best recording for years, with several songs equalling in merit his contributions to the Byrds. The haunting 'Santa Ana Wind', written by Fowley and Bob Rafkin (composer of 'Lazy Waters') was a spooky mood piece, with one of Battin's most expressive vocals and an inspired acoustic/electric guitar arrangement by engineer Irv Kramer. There were three Battin-Fowley numbers, originally written for *Topanga Skyline*: the piano-led 'Wintergreen' was another ambient piece in which Greg Harris' fiddle took on the sound of orchestral strings; 'Don't Go Down The Drain' was a witty, country romp that Fowley had written in Hawaii; 'Relax With Me' worked well, albeit with a synth keyboard accompaniment. Plus, there was a welcome revival of 'Do Not Disturb', previously covered by Gene Parsons on *Kindling*. Unfortunately for English-speaking listeners, the entire second side was largely given over to Battin's Italian composer friends. Ironically, this was bizarrely reminiscent of McGuinn allowing Battin-Fowley to include 'unrepresentative' material on Byrds albums. *Don't Go Crazy* had a schizoid quality, but it was never less than interesting. Even the 'Italian' side offered what sounded like a surreal political allegory ('Fango') and a bilingual philosophical reflection on life co-written by Battin ('Tonight'). As Battin's final solo album, it was a compromise of sorts, but nothing could detract from the power of its opening few songs. Given the budget and limited availability of the recording, this was a commendable feat.

That same year, Battin, Kleinow, Parsons and Harris toured Europe as the Peace Seekers on a memorable bill alongside Roger McGuinn. At the end of the evening, following two excellent sets, both artistes would take the stage for a grand finale of Byrds classics. All went well until their final show at Dingwalls in London. That evening, audience members were perplexed when

Gene Parsons announced from the stage that he was selling his guitar in order to scrounge enough money to pay for the flight back to America. It was no joke. Backstage, there was pandemonium. McGuinn had already vacated the venue, having collected his full fee, but a shortfall from the promoters had left the others stranded. The Peace Seekers felt McGuinn should have shared whatever money was available, but there was something deeper to their ire.

For Parsons, it must have brought back memories of his dispute with McGuinn over the profit-sharing agreement during the dying days of the CBS Byrds. Yet, Parsons was an oasis of calm compared to Battin. Everyone testifies to Battin's sanguine nature and ability to see the other person's point of view. Arguably the most stoical of the Byrds, he had even defended McGuinn's decision to fire him, pointing out to me that "sometimes it's necessary". Over the decades, I had interviewed and guardedly fraternized with Battin on a number of occasions, but never once had I witnessed the slightest hint of anger or bitterness. That night in Dingwalls, he was apoplectic and McGuinn's early exit probably averted an uglier incident. Years later, Battin started to write his autobiography, but only ever completed a handful of chapters. The first was a no-holds-barred account of that woeful evening. He seemed to regard the incident as symptomatic of all that had gone wrong with the Byrds. Battin would never play with McGuinn onstage again.

After the Peace Seekers, Battin joined yet another version of the Flying Burrito Brothers, releasing the desultory live album, *Cabin Fever*, in 1985. *Live From Europe*, was issued the following year. Sales, publicity and public interest were negligible.

Improbably, the next ex-Byrds collaboration featured two of its former bass players. With an almost wilful disregard of linear history, Battin formed a short-lived duo with the man he replaced in the Byrds: John York. They toured Italy during 1988, backed by Battin's Italian pals, Ricky Mantoan (pedal steel) and Beppe D'Angelo (drums). Much of their time was spent correcting promoters and audiences about who they actually were. "We used to laugh about it," York recalls. "Some of the promoters billed us as the Byrds and we'd say, 'No, you can't do that – it's not the Byrds'. There'd be posters that said 'formerly Byrds' and we said, 'Fine, you can call us 'formerly Byrds' but you can't call us *the* Byrds.' Sometimes Skip would have to stand up at the microphone before a gig and say in Italian: 'We are not the Byrds. We're guys that used to be in the Byrds.' Mostly nobody cared."

The only hostility they encountered on the tour was during a gig in Rome where the promoter took umbrage at their insistence he introduce them by explaining that they were *not* the Byrds. "After that, people just ignored us," says York. "They'd been trying to sell us as the Byrds. We asked for water, but nobody brought any. Finally, Skip put down his bass, walked to the bar and waited. They ignored him but finally he got a waitress to give him four glasses of water which we drank, then continued playing. Skip was a guy who had seen everything and was very centred. I don't think I ever saw him get upset. He just shrugged, stood in line, and waited for the water."

The tour ended in December with a two-night performance at a club in Vigliano that they attempted to record. Unfortunately, an irritating ground hum rendered the results unlistenable. After the show, they retired to an upstairs room and played some of the songs from the set. They did not think much more about it but York was amazed when, over 11 years later, an album containing the songs briefly appeared in Italy under the group name Family Tree. "It was a legitimate release," he admits, although he was never able to track down the obscure label Folkest Dische. The recording featured three Dylan compositions, including Battin's rendition of 'She Belongs To Me' in an arrangement that echoed the Dylan covers he had been playing live in 1965. Regrettably, there were no Battin songs on the album to balance York's two contributions ('Dandelion' and 'Christine'), but he opened with a competent cover of Bob Wills' 'My Shoes Keep Walking Back To You', followed by the Charles E. Calhoun barroom blues 'Smack Dab In The Middle', a revival of Donovan's 1965 hit 'Catch The Wind' and 'Witchi Tai To', written by the Native American composer Jim Pepper and inspired by a peyote healing mantra. The haunting, harmonic chanting with York testified to the potential of this unexpected collaboration.

For the remainder of his life, Battin seemed locked in the twilight dimension of the tribute band circuit. In January 1989, Michael Clarke launched his version of the 'Byrds', having recruited Battin, Terry Rogers, Jerry Sorn and Carlos Bernal for a three-month tour. As Rogers confirms: "Skip was playing keyboards on that first tour because he wanted to do something different and Carlos was on bass. I was basically the lead singer. Skip was very much into organic farming in Oregon. He'd been extremely busy with that up until the time he started working with Michael again in 1989. This was like his re-entry into playing a lot . . . Skip sang but he wasn't a great singer so when the harmonies came in I would switch to high harmony because I was the only one in the group that could sing them." Given Battin's past reputation as a harmony singer, this qualification seems strange, but Rogers was right to suggest that the musicians failed to achieve the clear harmonies characteristic of the McGuinn-era Byrds. That problem was partially solved in the spring when John York replaced Bernal on bass and added his distinctive high harmony to the mix. Commendably, York retained the same ambivalence about the authenticity of these 'Byrds' as he had done when first joining the post-Hillman line-up back in 1968. Conflicted about his role and the questionable merit of the entire enterprise, he became uncharacteristically insular. He also felt indignant that the group appeared to be a vehicle for Rogers and Sorn at the expense of himself and Battin. "These two guys from an Atlanta bar band were fronting the group. I really liked Terry, he was a great guy, but here's Michael, an original Byrd, and Skip and me who were in the Byrds and these two guys are up there singing 'Mr Tambourine Man' and 'Turn! Turn! Turn!' and all these Byrds songs. Never once did anybody turn around to me and Skip and say, 'Would you guys like to sing these songs?' There was no respect. It was all set up so that we were their back-up band. I respected Terry, but Jerry seemed to have no clue as to what the Byrds were supposed to sound like. They were so intent on it being a vehicle for them to get somewhere. They were riding on the back of this famous music and never looking at the guys in the band who'd actually been in the Byrds. And I'd been in Gene Clark's version of the Byrds too. I said this to Skip. He was 12 years older than me, so his attitude was far more mature. It didn't matter to him. He just said, 'Ah, I don't care, I'm just happy to be out on the road playing, I go out for a while, I get this experience of playing in front of audiences, then I go back to my berry farm and I have my weekend gig there.' He was content with it all. In that sense his Buddhism panned out. He wasn't expecting anything beyond what was happening and he was a very calming presence in the midst of this other situation that made no sense. For me, it was a low point in my life. I was drinking a bottle of wine just to get through the gig, then going back to the hotel and falling asleep. I reached the point where I couldn't do it anymore, no matter how much they needed my support."

When York's wife reached the latter stages of her pregnancy, he felt free to bail out, after which the quintet reverted to a foursome with Battin back on bass. "It was so much stronger and so good that we decided to keep it that way," Rogers says. "Skip was a very good bassist. He laid down a very strong groove. He wasn't a schooled musician, but a natural one. Rather than talking a lot, the way to get things going with him was just to play and say, 'Try this!' He had a little studio on his farm in Oregon and we used to go there and write and record stuff. Skip was definitely a team player. There was never any star trip going on with him at all."

In October 1989, the 'Byrds' travelled to the UK where they played a series of low-key gigs on the nostalgia circuit. Battin seemed happy to play third string in the band and was largely unfazed by Clarke's excessive drinking and Sorn's displays of 'rock star ego'. Whereas, you'd once have found Battin indulging in cocaine after a show, here he seemed more interested in catching up on American football results. His Zen-like coolness was a much needed asset on a tour fuelled by alcohol and uncertainty.

Sorn seemed to have delusions of grandeur about the prospects of the group, despite the fact that they neither had a record contract nor any interest from the media. One of my enduring memories of the tour was witnessing Battin taking Sorn aside like a wise old uncle, pointing at Michael Clarke downing tumblers of vodka, and whispering: "Look, this whole thing could be over next week." In the past, both in Evergreen Blueshoes and the Byrds, Battin knew it was important to push himself forward and promote his work. Here, he concluded that it did not matter, so he was content to lay back, play a gig, and look forward to returning home to Oregon.

John York also belatedly realized that Battin had organized his life in such a way that his subsidiary role with the Rogers-era 'Byrds' was a relative inconsequence. "Skip was a wonderful, sweet man. He took a lot of shit from Byrds people who criticize him and say he didn't fit in the band. I've been talking a lot to Kim Fowley about that. Musically Skip was mining a certain area, almost like vaudeville. This was early American music, nothing slick, and people didn't like it; they didn't get it. He was always up against that. But now when he went home from the road, he had a berry farm and a weekend gig at the local Holiday Inn. He loved it. He told me he could play whatever the hell he wanted and the people in town loved him. There was a piano there that he liked and he became the song man. That's really where he was always coming from. It's a shame more people didn't get that or that he didn't have more encouragement to do that outside of the Byrds."

Battin's low-key musical exploits back in Oregon remain the most obscure and undocumented part of his career. His friend Connie Cohen was a community folk singer who became a name on the local 'women's coffee-house circuit'. She grew frustrated singing folk standards, telling friends: "Everyone knows these songs and they're a joy, but we need new words, we need something to say." Battin was quick to encourage her songwriting ambitions. "He said, 'Wow, this is important stuff, I've got a studio in the barn. Why don't you come and just record something?' That was the beginning of my taking it seriously. I started writing more songs during that time. We would get together with a circle of people in a living room once a week and play. Skip was really my mentor and taught me everything about singing into a microphone and working in a studio. He was so positive and supportive and had such faith in my writing. We got inspired working together putting these ideas down on tape and it really made a huge difference to my life. The first two projects we did in the early Nineties were on cassette tape only and the final one, later in the decade, was on CD."

Another local player whom Battin assisted was Brian Cutean. "Skip had this nice little studio where he'd recorded Connie's first two albums. It was all analogue. When I visited the berry farm he was working, doing the berries. It was hard work. He made no bones about the fact that it was hard work, but I never heard him complain. I never heard him complain about anything. He was a peaceful cat. I'd given him a demo of a song to listen to ['9-0 Decadedance'] and when he came to the studio he was more than amply prepared. He told me the song reminded him of New Riders Of The Purple Sage, which I took as a real compliment. He appreciated its ecological message. The bass playing was very melodic and he had a lot of fun with it. Afterwards, he thanked me for the session and I was so jazzed that he played on it. The other song we did was 'Song From Afar' which took some digs politically." Unfortunately, financial constraints prevented Cutean from releasing the songs at the time, although '9-0 Decadedance' did appear many years later on his 1999 album, *Parkeetfishhead.*

In addition to these studio get-togethers, Battin played some sporadic dates in Portland, most memorably a performance or two at a British-themed pub, the Fox & Hounds. This line-up, including Cohen, Cutean and folk singer/pianist Nancy Tannler, were sometimes joined by other old friends. "He brought several different people together and had different groups," Connie Cohen confirms. "He had a band that played at some outdoor festivals around the Valley and one time I sat in with them for a song." The unnamed ensemble may well have included Terry

Rogers, who recalls visiting Oregon during this period. "He played with a little group of local musicians and I did a couple of those with him. He had a nice thing going there."

These serene shows contrasted with the more robust performances required by the imitation Byrds, but Battin's fitness both amused and amazed his bandmates. "He seemed to have more energy than the younger guys around him," Rogers notes. At one time, the group played at a baseball stadium in North Carolina and Battin befriended the maintenance officer. "He and Skip started telling stories about the old days and how both of them played." The intense discussion culminated in a challenge race. "They got down at one end of the field and raced to the other end, both going as hard out as they could. They basically tied, but it was so funny. Afterwards, they were completely out of breath and laughed about being too old to be out there doing such foolishness."

Michael Clarke's decline into alcoholism meant that he was a loose cannon on the road and subject to mood swings and macho japes. At one show on the European tour he threw a drumstick at Battin, hitting him in the back. Skip indignantly returned the missile but was still upset after they'd done their encore. A confrontation seemed inevitable. "I knew Skip was pissed off," Rogers recalls, "and I was trying to intercept him but he just took me by the shoulders, looked me in the eye, pushed me to the side and said, 'Just stand right there.' Then he got down in a football position and as soon as Michael came walking out of the wings he ran right up to him, grabbed him by the neck and said, 'Don't ever do that to me again!' That was the only time I ever saw Skip act like that." On another occasion, Battin saved Rogers from a rampaging Michael Clarke during a tempestuous tour of Italy.

These confrontations on the road gradually infiltrated Battin's home life, with devastating consequences. In the past, he had been able to juggle domestic and band commitments comfortably but, during the early Nineties, his wife Patricia noticed changes in his personality. He spent more time alone in his studio, smoking dope. More alarmingly, there were intense mood swings whenever he returned home from a tour. "The farm was supposed to be income to get Skip off the road," she says. "He was tired of that life and wanted to do something different. Eventually, he went back on the road to support the farm and would be gone for weeks at a time. I was raising two kids and running the farm as best I could . . . Skip would come off the road and be exhausted. After sleeping for 24 hours, he would generally have a mental meltdown. There would be a huge fight over – [it] could be anything. The fact that I put the jelly jars in the canning cupboard when he liked to drink out of them. One time he had arranged to sell a piano, which I did for him while he was on the road. When I told him it was done, he became violent. He never actually hit me, but it was scary nonetheless to see him break things. These tantrums became regular every time he returned. This was the end of things for us. I had two kids I needed to take care of and began to find a way out of an increasingly bad situation."

After touring with Michael Clarke's Byrds for a few years, Battin finally fell victim to a cost-cutting exercise. Under pressure to raise money, Clarke uncharacteristically became Chancellor of the Exchequer and decided that flying Battin out from Oregon was no longer economical. Without informing Rogers, Clarke recruited Manny Yanes, a talented jazz-style bassist and friend of Firefall's David Muse, who was based near Michael in St Petersburg, Florida. Much younger than the others, and old enough to be Battin's son, Yanes subsequently moved to Nashville and was replaced by Michael 'Supe' Granda from the Ozark Mountain Daredevils. By this point, Clarke was suffering from liver disease and another bass player, Ed Kane, joined the revolving line-up.

After Michael's death in December 1993, Rogers was asked by manager Steve Green to continue the group under the slightly less provocative name, the Byrds Celebration. Battin was brought back, alongside new members, Scott Nienhaus and Ron Gremp. Nienhaus initially shared many of John York's ambivalent feelings about the group. "When Terry asked me to join, I wrestled with it for quite a while because I knew about the lawsuit with Michael, so I wasn't sure if it was a good thing for me to do or not.

But I listened to the live recordings they'd done and I thought, 'This is right up my alley.' My first guitar was a 12-string, I'd always been a harmony singer and I was a big Crosby fan. I knew I'd be able to play the electric 12-string and play acoustic . . . I'm not bad-mouthing Jerry Sorn, but I didn't think he'd been right for the band. I didn't like the way he treated the music. He just overplayed."

Nienhaus was excited by the prospect of playing with a former Byrd, not least because he originally hailed from St Louis where Battin's song 'St Louis Browns' was a local anthem. During their first rehearsals, his ardour cooled when he discovered that Battin had his own way of working. "When Skip came in everything changed. He pretty well had all of his parts burned in his head. Terry and I had to rearrange everything we'd been working on to make it work. But after a couple of gigs, I realized it was great. Skip was an old school bass player and the nicest guy. He really brought this great spirit to the band and was a gentle soul. Although soft-spoken, he was very witty and had a great rapport with the audience. By the end of the show, he'd have them in the palm of his hand because he was so funny. He made them laugh and made us all laugh." As the touring progressed, Battin became more animated and developed a dancing routine involving uncoordinated jumps and frantic dashes across the stage at unexpected moments. "It was hilarious," says Nienhaus. "Even if it was a small stage in a nightclub, he'd jump on the floor into the audience, then run back and forth at the front with them. He was in better shape than we were. We had to grab the guitar cord attached to the amplifier to make sure he didn't yank the amp off the stage with him." On a couple of occasions, Battin re-enacted an old trick he had once performed with the Byrds. During the climax of 'Eight Miles High' he threw his guitar high into the air and attempted to catch it like a football player receiving a pass. "It went right through his arms and slammed on to the stage making this horrible noise but everybody cheered because it was so funny. He then went up to the microphone and yelled, 'I'm a hundred years old!' That's the guy he was."

Nienhaus also witnessed Battin's more serious side away from the stage. After rehearsals, they would sometimes sit in the dark watching the stars and discussing nothing in particular. "We'd just lay in these recliners and have the quietest conversations. He would spot satellites crossing the sky. It was actually moving and those are the times I really cherished." Battin had good reason to feel reflective and wistful. His decade-long marriage to Patricia Cartabiano was about to end. The break-up seemed a precursor to darker news over the next few years.

There was a surprise for fans of the early Seventies Byrds' rhythm section when Gene Parsons briefly joined the Celebration enterprise for a European tour, but after returning to America he went back to his String Bender business in Caspar. According to Rogers, there were serious talks with Sneaky Pete Kleinow about using members of the Byrds' Celebration, including Parsons and Battin, to form a touring version of the Flying Burrito Brothers, but the project remained unrealized. Instead, the Byrds Celebration soldiered on, with Nienhaus' pal Vincenzo Barrenco drafted in as the new drummer. Inevitably, they faced the perennial problem of misrepresentation by promoters, who conveniently ignored the word 'Celebration'. Nienhaus was naïve enough to be shocked whenever he encountered a poster presumptuously proclaiming the arrival of 'the original Byrds' or the more subtle, but still misleading, 'Byrds celebration tour . . .' For commentators such as myself, not to mention the three surviving original Byrds, it was self-evident that any title including the word 'Byrds' would always be subject to misuse.

Battin stayed out of the controversy as much as possible, but he was now facing more serious problems. The dissolution of his marriage meant that he had to sell their beloved farm on Bonney Road, Woodburn, Oregon. For a short time, he rented a place in nearby Silverton, then moved into a seniors' mobile home park in the same area. His appearance in the trailer park caused an instant and unexpected reaction. The residents recently had problems with a long-haired, bicycle-riding hippie who was eventually removed from the park by police. Suddenly, Battin appeared on a bicycle, sporting long hair and a bohemian demeanour. Ever flirtatious, he had eyes on a woman in an adjacent mobile home named Peggy Taylor. "He was riding by my house one day and saw me and my sister," she recalls. "He didn't say anything but every time I turned around I'd see him outside." Having completed his reconnaissance mission, he approached Taylor with the provocative line: "I've been meaning to talk to you. Are you single?" After confirming her non-marital status, he asked "Do you like music?" Then, he invited her to attend a concert. She politely declined, but Battin was undeterred. The next thing she knew, he was appearing at a morning coffee group she attended and had also joined the same exercise class. "He kept showing up everywhere I was. Finally, I stopped and talked to him and said, 'Maybe I owe you an apology, you wanted to talk before and I cut you off.' That day we talked for hours on end and we were together ever since. He wasn't one to brag and I had no idea about the Byrds. He said he was a musician and brought some photo albums to show me as a good way of getting acquainted. There were these pictures of tours he'd done all over the world. It was overwhelming at first."

The loss of his berry farm was a bitter blow to Battin, but he adapted to changing circumstances with that familiar phlegmatic air. Over the years, he had grown a lot closer to his eldest son, Dale Rinkenberger, who was a serious collector of bass guitars. Terry Rogers was so impressed by his knowledge of music and organizational skills that he offered him a job. "We talked to Dale several times about coming on tour with us as a road manager. He was obviously a smart guy and we would have liked to have him around, working with us." Rinkenberger seriously considered the proposal and asked for a little time to make arrangements. Tragically, time was not on his side. "He had a brain aneurysm and suddenly dropped dead," Rogers confirms. The shock of losing a son, still in his mid-thirties, was another terrible blow for Battin to bear. Nor was it the last piece of distressing news.

* * *

Terry Rogers began to notice that his bandmate's short-term memory seemed a trifle scattered. During conversations, Skip would often ask the same question more than once, as if he had not been concentrating. Peggy Taylor also noticed that he seemed rather more forgetful than other people, but thought nothing more about it. "He just told me he had a bad memory." On tour one evening, the band were playing their finale of Byrds hits, segueing from 'So You Want To Be A Rock 'n' Roll Star' into 'Eight Miles High'. This was the cue for Battin to lead into that familiar opening bass line but, inexplicably, he fluffed his part. When Nienhaus looked around, he saw that Skip had a blank look, as if he had suddenly been transported somewhere else. Rogers responded by playing the bass line on his guitar and Battin immediately picked up the riff and completed the show with his usual aplomb. Nobody thought too much about those missing couple of seconds, which they laughed off as a concentration lapse. Given recent events, it was hardly surprising that Battin might have had other things on his mind.

Despite his cavalier response, Battin believed that these lapses of memory were symptomatic of something more serious. Few knew that his father had suffered from Alzheimer's disease in later life and Skip could not rid himself of a nagging suspicion that he might have the same condition. A doctor's appointment confirmed the worst. Scott Nienhaus recalls first hearing the news when they were in their mini-van heading for a gig in Anderson, North Carolina. Battin remarked, almost in passing, that he'd seen his doctor and was in the early stages of Alzheimer's. "Oddly, it wasn't that big a surprise to us, at least not to me. I said, 'Skip, look on the bright side, you'll get to meet new 'old' friends every day.' He laughed, and we all laughed. That was how we were with each other. We were just trying to make light of it at the time."

On a more serious note, Battin announced that he was giving up smoking marijuana. "He thought that might have had something to do with it," says Rogers.

The Byrds Celebration shows continued, but thankfully the participants showed some integrity by completing a decent album without using the legendary name. Recorded in the spring of 1995, the privately released *Empty Room* was credited to 'The Rogers/Nienhaus Band with Skip Battin'. Battin's minor billing was entirely justified as he appeared on only five of the album's ten songs. His sole lead vocal was on a revival of 'Citizen Kane' in an arrangement similar to that featured on *Navigator*, albeit with the simulated sound of a wind-up gramophone playing a scratchy 78 as an added attraction. *Empty Room* was a welcome release, but it was not widely available and although it promised a more legitimate parallel career, the tribute game still provided greater financial security.

Battin continued to honour his commitments to the Byrds Celebration and once onstage he played as well as ever. His relationship with Peggy had deepened and he relied increasingly upon her support and love. The last time I spoke to Battin was on 3 June 1997. Listening back to the tape with the benefit of hindsight, there are signs of hesitation and a certain lack of animation and articulation, but at the time none of that seemed unusual. I assumed he was just a little tired. His memories of his early career seemed intact and he was still reasonably strong on dates and reminiscences. He was planning to record another solo album for a local label and, encouraged by my positive comments on 'Absolute Happiness', agreed that he might consider re-recording that song. He confirmed that he was definitely redoing 'Precious Kate'. At the time, I had heard of his grand plans to compile a box set chronicling his career, but this had already been put on the long finger, presumably for financial reasons. It would obviously have been an administrative nightmare clearing permissions, especially if he was trying to issue the material on a privately funded or small label with limited resources. We spoke of his many rare recordings from the early Sixties and he was particularly informative about these obscure releases and provided some much needed details about rare labels and B-sides. He still had a cache of old Skip & Flip 45s stashed in a box, along with many of his studio collaborations with Kim Fowley. Naturally, we spoke about the Byrds, although, having covered their career with him in previous decades, I restricted our conversation to selected songs. Nevertheless, he still provided a revealing overview of his time with the group that testified to his positive outlook.

"Changes started right away," he reflected. "You only ride that high for a little bit. There was such strength, vitality and energy and everybody was so positive. It was kind of a 'religious' period and that showed in the work and in their songs and rap sessions. A lot of people wanted to hear what the Byrds had to say, both in music and one on one. We were extremely covered by the media then. They had to sort us out just to allow us to eat breakfast sometimes. It got to be heavy. We were definitely high profile. There were a huge number of things to do and people to talk to. We just didn't stop. We all discovered that we weren't happy working as four people. After four years, we wanted our own niche because we'd learned so much, and we'd all changed too. Everybody was really tight up until just before the end." And how did he get on with McGuinn? "Absolutely great. Of course things don't last and stay good forever, especially with high tension musicians of which I am one. That's life." Thereafter, we spoke of future plans and he indicated that Steve Green was organizing a tour of the UK in February 1998. "I'm looking forward to England," he concluded, with evident relish. "I really like to travel and do Europe and fly over France and Germany if I can and see my favourite place, Italy."

The tentative UK tour never happened, of course, and by 1998, Battin's recording and performing life were reaching an end. "Terry took on the responsibility of looking after Skip on the road and making sure he got to the hotel," Scott Nienhaus recalls, "but the Alzheimer's got worse. There were times when Skip became really confused and it was hard to watch. We'd finish a show and on the way back to the hotel he'd say, 'What time's the show?' I said, 'Well, Skip, we just finished the show an hour ago and we're going back to the hotel to eat, but we've got another one tomorrow.' Then, he'd be OK with that."

By then, Battin had ceased travelling across country with the group but would fly direct to selected dates. "Very often, he had to change flights," says Rogers, "and he had enough wherewithal to find someone to take him to the airline desk he was flying from, hand them the ticket and say, 'Can you tell me where I need to go?' "

Clearly, travelling had become a demanding adventure. Even getting home to Silverton afterwards was a tortuous and torturous experience. "One time he landed in Portland and took a taxi," Peggy Taylor remembers. "The driver didn't know how to get to Silverton and Skip couldn't tell him. He was giving him different directions. By the time they got to Silverton the driver grabbed his money, took off and ran. At that point I moved in with him because he really needed help."

Battin was still determined to record a solo album and enlisted Taylor as an amateur sound engineer. "He had a music studio set up and did a bit of work in the house, but he couldn't really function as a musician. He was going to do this album in Portland for Burnside Records. We started doing it in the studio and suddenly he stopped, called me over and said, 'The piano just turned upside down on me!' He had to walk out and leave it. We just stopped right in the middle of the project. He couldn't finish it."

The insidious onslaught of Alzheimer's inevitably put paid to touring. "It wasn't really serious until 1998," says Peggy. "By then he was scared to travel by himself." Playing live had proven therapeutic, but the emotional strain was systemically draining his energies and spirit. Rogers realized this when trying to organize a plane trip. "Peggy really did look after him and she was great," says Rogers, "but I couldn't take it anymore. The last straw was when we had these dates planned. I'd bought the plane tickets ahead of time and sent them on to him. Peggy had to go out of town for several days and while she was away he phoned me up every day during the week before we were set to leave on this trip. He'd say, 'I'm looking at this ticket – am I supposed to go to the airport now?' I'd tell him, 'No, Skip, get your calendar off the wall, put it in front of you, it's five days from now. Mark what today is and when you're leaving and if you forget, mark it again . . .' He seemed to take comfort from that but, the next day, it would be the same thing again. He was so stressed out over that particular incident that I just couldn't do it to him anymore. I can only imagine the amount of stress that he was going through just trying to remember what he was supposed to be doing."

Scott Nienhaus was resigned to the news of Battin's retirement from the stage. "The last time I saw Skip was at the airport, the day after our show with the Little River Band at the County Fairgrounds in Scottsbluff, North Dakota, on August 22, 1998. I kept the stage pass from that gig as a memento, although I didn't know at the time that it was to be Skip's last show." Nevertheless, a permanent replacement was already waiting in the wings. Michael Curtis, an alumnus of the Gene Clark 'Byrds' and Buffalo Springfield Revisited, had already played a couple of dates and toured Brazil with the Celebration, so his appointment came as no surprise.

The final days of Skip Battin are sad to relate. Only a few years before, he seemed to have carved out an idyllic life for himself. Unlike many of the rock 'n' roll casualties in this two-volume book, he had been living happily on his berry farm, touring extensively with the Byrds Celebration, then returning home to play weekends at local clubs. Now, even those memories were starting to fade as confusion overwhelmed him. On his better days, he still enjoyed playing the bass and made one final studio appearance, guesting on the title track of Connie Cohen's CD *Heading Out.*

"I didn't know he was as challenged as much as he was with his memory," she says. "We had a rehearsal out in Silverton and he was a little wary. I decided that it was really important for me to get him on there, if he wanted to, even though I wasn't sure how it would work out. We went into the studio and it was a bit of a struggle, but really special." Local drummer Carlton Jackson, who had recently assisted Battin in the studio, ensured that the rhythm section worked well. "When we did that project Carlton was a total champ. He was a super guy and his understanding of what was going on with Skip helped us pull it off in a beautiful way. It felt really special and I'm still proud of that project." Battin would have loved to have done more but with each passing month the Alzheimer's siphoned his memory until even his Fender bass became an alien object.

With a new century underway, the Alzheimer's had worsened to such an extent that Battin was admitted to the Alterra Clare Bridge care facility in Salem, Oregon. There, he clung desperately to music as a lingering connection to a fading past. Sometimes, he attempted to play piano in one of the rooms, ever eager to entertain the other patients. "I've often thought if you stripped everything away from Skip he would remain a musician," Patricia Battin considers. "*That* was his core."

As a mark of respect, as much as therapy, the staff would play him Byrds' songs to ease his soul. Peggy Taylor witnessed his deterioration and those treasured moments when music brought a sudden animation. "Even after he reached the point where he couldn't play an instrument, he would hear his music in the care facility and his right hand would go up and down automatically as though he were strumming a guitar."

Witnessing the advanced stages of Alzheimer's was difficult for everybody, especially his younger son. "Jon couldn't handle it," Peggy remembers. "He never came around anymore. He wouldn't go see his dad. He never came to visit. Skip's daughter Susanna was a sweetheart. She would go see him quite a bit." Patricia Battin has bittersweet memories of those visits. "Jon was nervous about his dad being ill and was reluctant to see him that way. Susanna, on the other hand, went every Wednesday to play piano with him all through his illness. Peggy helped him through a lot . . . These are sad memories, my daughter with tears streaming down her cheeks but smiling into her dad's eyes."

With Dale dead, Skip's second son, Brent, re-established regular contact and grew closer to his father in his final years. They had been out of touch for long periods, but when Peggy Taylor called with the grim news of Skip's condition, Brent, now entering his thirties, reacted positively. "They had kind of a strange relationship," says Al Hersh. "I encouraged him to patch things up before Skip got too far gone with the Alzheimer's." Brent visited his father on several occasions and evidently enjoyed learning more about those missing years. "He collected a lot of Skip's material and was putting it all together," Taylor recalls. Along with the memorabilia was a suitcase full of Battin's rare 45s, which Brent had transferred on to CD-R. It might yet form the basis of a serious archival retrospective.

Despite a lifetime in music, Battin had little or no friends left in the business who were willing or able to offer solace. There were few visitors from the old days and no benefits or tribute concerts to highlight his plight. "I wanted to visit him really badly," says Scott Nienhaus, "but at the time we were all still broke. We couldn't afford to drive down the street, but I really wanted to go and visit him. Somebody said that he had our picture with him and he would talk about the band. When Terry talked to him on the phone he'd ask when the next gig was. It was really sad."

Battin continued to receive some morale-boosting visits from his Oregon friends. Brian Cutean remembers attending the nursing facility on several occasions, accompanied by Patricia and Susanna Battin, Connie Cohen and her husband Kenny, and visiting folk singer Anne Feeney. "We took our guitars," Cutean remembers. "The first time Skip was on top of things. When we started singing certain songs he could remember the words pretty well, but you could tell he was forgetful. I don't think he recognized anybody by that time. We'd play Bob Dylan or Byrds songs that we felt he would know and it was beautiful. Sometimes he could remember the words and it made him happy that we were playing. He became animate."

The one person from the Byrds' era who took time to travel to Oregon was Gene Parsons. "The last time I saw Skip was at the Alzheimer's care facility that was his final home on this Earth. It was so good to see him. I recounted some of our escapades on the road and this brought a smile to his lips and laughter. At times he would try to form sentences but the words would not come. I could see the frustration on his face, this man who learned to speak fluent Italian in his late fifties. He did manage to form one short sentence though as I said goodbye that day: 'Take me with you.'"

On 6 July 2003, Skip Battin was on his deathbed at Alterra Clare Bridge. Patricia and Susanna were shocked by his condition. "He was catatonic and unable to move or respond. It was bad." Later, Peggy urgently put through a message to his son, Brent, asking him to call. "I was finally able to reach Brent. Even though Skip was just semi-conscious and barely able to speak at that point, Brent did get to talk to him on the phone that afternoon." By the evening, Skip had passed away. He was 69 years old.

A memorial was held at Silver Falls State Park. "[It was] under a canopy of firs," Patricia Battin remembers. "We played music, sang and shared all the funny stories. Both my children came (my son was very reluctant), letters from abroad were read. It made for a wonderful send-off that really became our last memory of Skip Battin." As a touching final tribute, the two Oregon musicians, Connie Cohen and Brian Cutean, offered a moving rendition of the reincarnation ode from *(Untitled)*: 'Yesterday's Train'. "That song has always moved me deeply," Cutean reflects. "Of course given the context of where we were singing it, it was an amazing experience. I had been in touch recently with Gene Parsons, whom I hadn't met before, and he sent the eulogy which was read there. It was a beautiful piece."

SKIP BATTIN: NOTES

page 956: "Well, you yourself said . . ." Skip Battin, interviewed by the author. New York: 3 July 1979.

page 956: "The father's dream . . ." Al Rosenberg (now known as Al Ross), interviewed by the author. London/New York: 24 February 2008.

page 957: "It was interactive . . ." Maris Bennington Clary, quoted in the *Worthington High School Newsletter*: 2008.

page 957: "Radio was very conservative . . ." Battin/Rogan. New York: 3 July 1979.

page 957: "They used to play country music . . ." Skip Battin, interviewed by Barry Ballard. London: 22 September 1976. Part published in *Omaha Rainbow* 11: December 1976.

page 959: "Using a new band name, the Pledges . . ." The Pledges included Battin and Paxton, backed by Bobby Verbosh (guitar), Dick Gabriel (saxophone) and Reed Clemens (drums). Battin recalls that they retained Clemens for some of their recordings under different names.

page 959: "We got a rhythm guitarist . . ." Battin/Ballard: 22 September 1976. Part published in *Omaha Rainbow* 11: December 1976.

page 960: "In another nostalgic touch . . ." The girl sopranos used on 'The Jackie Look' were Molly Inscho, Betsey Potter and Erica Frazier.

page 960: "I was suddenly confused . . ." Gary Paxton, quoted in Alec Palao's CD liner notes to *Hollywood Maverick The Gary S. Paxton Story.*

page 961: "I must have had a lot of energy at the time . . ." Battin/Ballard: 22 September 1976. Part published in *Omaha Rainbow* 11: December 1976.

page 961: "They said 'Hope you don't mind . . .' " ibid.

page 963: ". . . covered in blood and bandages . . ." Kim Fowley, interviewed by the author. London/Redlands, California: 27–28 June 2007.

page 963: "My father was an opium addict . . ." ibid.

page 964: "But I think Kim is smarter . . ." ibid.

page 964: "Terry never forgave me . . ." ibid.

page 964: "1959 was an interesting time . . ." ibid.

page 964: "Gary Paxton and I . . ." Skip Battin, interviewed by the author. London/Silverton, Oregon: 3–4 June 1997.

page 965: "In those days, it was all singles . . ." Fowley/Rogan. London/Redlands. California: 27–28 June 2007.

page 965: "I was the road manager . . ." ibid.

page 966: "I was still married to her . . ." Paxton/Palao, CD liner notes to *Hollywood Maverick The Gary S. Paxton Story.*

page 966: "In that first year . . ." Kim Fowley, quoted in Alec Palao's CD liner notes to *Hollywood Maverick The Gary S. Paxton Story.*

page 967: "Right after 'Nut Rocker' . . ." Fowley/Rogan. London/Redlands, California: 27–28 June 2007.

page 967: "Battin learned much . . ." Correctly dating Battin's singles releases during the early to mid-Sixties has taxed the powers of even the most specialist discographers. It is not just the many different labels and group names that have proven perplexing but the lack of publishing dates. American singles releases, unlike those in the UK, do not include the year the song was published or recorded. Determining a release date, particularly for an obscure small label recording, has often been at best guesswork. The order and even the purported year of release of many Battin singles should be greeted with caution, even when perusing seemingly authoritative websites. For example, 'Daybreaker' has been listed as late as 1965 in some discographies, whereas Fowley is insistent it was done approximately three years earlier. One site assumes, incorrectly, that 'Rod Scuderi' [sic] was not a real person, but a Fowley/Battin *nom de plume.* There are similar, though smaller, inconsistencies with releases by Gary & Clyde and some of Battin's many other pseudonymous recordings. It's been suggested to me that his perplexing name change from Battin to Battyn was due to his involvement in different unions or twin affiliations with ASCAP and BMI. Another minor mystery. It is a shame that Battin's complete catalogue of recordings from this period, a Herculean task, admittedly, has not been captured on a definitive archival release. Battin had begun such a project independently during his final years, but no one has since revived the idea.

page 968: "I produced the record . . ." Fowley/Rogan. London/Redlands, California: 27–28 June 2007.

page 968: ". . . a Brigitte Bardot . . ." ibid.

page 968: "Anyone who could sing R&B . . ." ibid.

page 968: "Skip was saving his money then . . ." ibid.

page 968: "He learned hypnotism . . ." Terry Rogers, interviewed by the author. London/East Alton, Illinois: 14–15 July 2007.

page 969: "I remember the first night I saw the Byrds . . ." Battin/Ballard: 22 September 1976. Part published in *Omaha Rainbow* 11: December 1976.

page 969: "The Byrds just blew my mind completely . . ." ibid.

page 970: "Right away our jobs became fewer . . ." ibid.

page 970: "They were real professionals . . ." Steve Young, interviewed by the author. London/Nashville, Tennessee: 10 July 2007.

page 970: "Van Dyke and his brother were like a tragi-comedy . . ." ibid.

page 971: "Those were desperate days . . ." ibid.

page 971: "Skip did take me on a lot of adventures . . ." ibid.

page 971: "As we were exiting the stage . . ." Van Dyke Parks, email reply to the author: 3 July 2007.

page 972: "David didn't understand that performing . . ." ibid.

page 972: "Skip and Van Dyke had met Stephen Stills . . ." Fowley/Rogan. London/Redlands, California: 27–28 June 2007.

page 973: "It was called the Gas Company . . ." Young/Rogan. London/Nashville, Tennessee: 10 July 2007.

page 973: "We were doing original material . . ." Battin/Ballard: 22 September 1976. Part published in *Omaha Rainbow* 11: December 1976.

page 973: "Most of the gigs I remember doing . . ." Young/Rogan. London/Nashville, Tennessee: 10 July 2007.

page 974: "The owner, Ed Pearl . . ." Al Rosenberg (aka Al Ross)/Rogan. London/New York: 24 February 2008.

page 974: "Skip just said, 'Let's get together and do something . . .'" ibid.

page 974: ". . . Lanny Mathyssen (aka Mathijssen) (guitar/vocals) . . ." Lanny had been the bass player in the Dawgs but agreed to switch to bass in deference to Battin. He had already anglicized his surname to Mathyssen by this point, but Battin suggested he revert to the Dutch spelling in the later album credits for *The Ballad Of Evergreen Blueshoes.* "I wanted to save the American tongue," says Lanny, "so I substituted 'y' for 'j'. It's the same [sound] in Holland. They thought it looked more exotic as 'Mathijssen' and told me to use the original."

page 975: "These guys were a real black shoe, white cover band . . ." Al Rosenberg (aka Al Ross)/Rogan. London/New York: 24 February 2008.

page 975: "It was Skip and Al basically . . ." Lanny Mathyssen, interviewed by the author. London/Lakewood, Colorado: 5 July 2010.

page 976: "Skip had been worn out . . ." Al Rosenberg (aka Al Ross)/ Rogan. London/New York: 24 February 2008.

page 976: "Skip was not really the person . . ." Mathyssen/Rogan. Lakewood, Colorado: 5 July 2010.

page 977: "They were a cover band in paisley shirts . . ." Al Rosenberg (aka Al Ross)/Rogan. London/New York: 24 February 2008. Battin's initial interest in Arlin's invitation was understandable. The Leaves had scored a hit with a version of 'Hey Joe' which former Byrds' roadie Bryan MacLean had learned from David Crosby and played with Love. MacLean had presented the song to the Leaves who released two versions with original guitarist Bill Rhinehart (aka Rinehart). Both failed to chart. They recut the song with Bobby Arlin who added a distinctive fuzztone instrumental break. It was this version of 'Hey Joe' that became a US hit, peaking at number 31 on *Billboard* in May 1966 and topping the local charts in Los Angeles. The Byrds' version was issued two months later as an album track on *Fifth Dimension.* Always interested in any oblique connection to the Byrds, Battin felt obliged to hear the Leaves play.

page 977: "This was about September/October 1967 . . ." ibid. Lanny Mathyssen has different memories of how the name Evergreen Blueshoes was coined. "We were just kicking around names. We wanted something that meant forever and all of a sudden and was quirky. How about Evergreen Blueshoes? Like 'Blue Suede Shoes' . . . evergreen shoes."

page 977: "Kim said, 'Well, we've got to call you something . . .'" Al Rosenberg (aka Al Ross)/Rogan. London/New York: 24 February 2008.

page 978: "Those were the places where the record business people came . . ." ibid.

page 978: "That's what Evergreen Blueshoes was about . . ." ibid.

page 979: "The acid test was that his wife Jackie was still working . . ." ibid.

page 980: "We were all young then . . ." Chester 'Chet' McCracken, interviewed by the author. London/Los Angeles, California: 9 July 2010.

page 981: "Skip was trying to become imbued with the liberal spirit . . ." Al Rosenberg (aka Al Ross)/Rogan. London/New York: 24 February 2008.

page 981: "The Evergreen Blueshoes was a really good project . . ." Battin/

Ballard: 22 September 1976. Part published in *Omaha Rainbow* 11: December 1976.

page 982: "He was disenchanted . . ." Al Rosenberg (aka Al Ross)/Rogan. London/New York: 24 February 2008.

page 982: ". . . prestigious performances at the Whisky . . ." The Evergreen Blueshoes appeared at the Whisky A Go-Go on the same bill as Spirit from 14–17 March 1968. On another occasion, they were support for Albert King.

page 982: "We gambolled around this area in Griffith Park . . ." Al Rosenberg (aka Al Ross)/Rogan. London/New York: 24 February 2008.

page 982: "There was quite a stir about it . . ." ibid.

page 983: "So much of this was coloured by Skip being frustrated . . ." ibid.

page 983: "A rock 'n' roll band without a drummer? . . ." Mathyssen/Rogan. London/Lakeland, Colorado: 5 July 2010. Mathyssen believes they may have played a gig without a drummer, but nobody else can confirm this. Chet McCracken does not even remember being fired and assumed the band simply split up. "At one point the band disbanded and I went on my merry way, not really looking back. I just went on to other things. Honestly, I don't remember what happened. It had run its course and I was on to the next band. Breaking up the group was the big signal to me that Skip was disappointed. Nobody was taking him seriously and that's why the group broke up. That's probably why I had no problem moving on because I didn't want to be around that type of atmosphere anymore." McCracken and Mathyssen soon reunited in a showband, playing the Las Vegas circuit.

page 984: "Skip was still trying to write . . ." Al Rosenberg (aka Al Ross)/Rogan. London/New York: 24 February 2008.

page 984: "My reputation was established in LA . . ." Art Johnson, interviewed by the author. London/Nice, France: 17 June 2007.

page 984: "Players like Barney Kessell . . ." ibid.

page 985: "We started to form a fusion instrumental group . . ." ibid.

page 985: "There isn't much of a market . . ." Battin/Ballard: 22 September 1976. Part published in *Omaha Rainbow* 11: December 1976.

page 985: "What do we do now? . . ." Johnson/Rogan. London/Nice, France: 17 June 2007.

page 985: "We're going down to Hollywood now . . ." ibid.

page 985: "We picked the equipment up . . ." ibid.

page 986: "Of all the musicians I've known in my life . . ." ibid.

page 987: "Skip and his manager used to take these shots . . ." Young/Rogan. London/Nashville, Tennessee: 10 July 2007.

page 987: "You could never tell how old . . ." Johnson/Rogan. London/Nice, France: 17 June 2007.

page 987: "I'm sure it came up in your investigations . . ." Al Hersh, interviewed by the author. London/Topanga Canyon, California: 12 April 2008.

page 988: "I liked his playing . . ." Gene Parsons, interviewed by the author. London/Fort Bragg, Mendocino, California: 19 May 2007.

page 988: "He told me that he learned every song . . ." Fowley/Rogan. London/Redlands, California: 27–28 June 2007.

page 988: "The group wasn't . . ." Battin/Ballard: 22 September 1976. Part published in *Omaha Rainbow* 11: December 1976.

page 989: "*(Untitled)* wasn't a difficult album . . ." ibid.

page 989: "Of the three, Chris Hillman . . ." Chris Darrow, interviewed by the author. London/Riverside, California: 5 July 2007.

page 989: "Skip enjoyed jazz . . ." Gene Parsons/Rogan. London/Fort Bragg, Mendocino, California: 19 May 2007.

page 990: "Ironically, I share David Crosby's resentment . . ." Fowley/Rogan. London/Redlands, California: 27–28 June 2007. Fowley went on to argue his point, revealing: "I did all the lyrics and he did the music. I would come in with lyrics already typed and I'd sing them to him in Roger McGuinn's voice, trying to get him to get the message. Then he'd get mad and rewrite it as Skip Battin. The songs were more Roger than Skip ever was. I would sing 'Citizen Kane' like that but he said, 'No!' I have demos of me singing 'Citizen Kane' and 'Precious Kate' and you can hear me imitating Roger's singing. Then Skip would get in on it and it never came out like that." Fowley's argument is not entirely convincing. Listening to the original demos, his voice is obviously different from Battin's. Maybe he was attempting to imitate Dylan or McGuinn, but mostly the songs sound like Fowley. Obviously, when Battin sings the lyrics, he sounds like Battin. The suggestion that Battin 'rewrote' these songs does not stand up to scrutiny. Lyrically, Battin made no changes at all and the melodies are almost unaltered. The demo of 'Citizen Kane' includes a homely harmonica, providing a slightly folkier air and is closer to the way Battin played the song in concert and on the later albums, *Navigator* and *Empty Room*. Any changes to 'Citizen Kane' on *Byrdmaniax* had nothing to do with Battin and everything to do with Terry Melcher's ornate production.

page 991: "Because he was in the Byrds . . ." ibid.

page 993: "We had that problem . . ." Battin/Ballard: 22 September 1976. Part published in *Omaha Rainbow* 11: December 1976.

page 993: "Sessions began in April 1972 . . ." Although the album credits for *Skip* claim rather vaguely that the work was recorded in the 'summer of 1972', the diaries of Al Rosenberg (whose name does not appear on the record) indicate that sessions began on 21 April 1972. That evening, he attended a double session from 5–8 pm and 9–12 pm. The diary confirms that the producer was Eric Malamud and the studio was Paramount Recording Studios at Santa Monica and Vine. The diary also reveals that Battin had called Rosenberg several times in the preceding weeks about the proposed album.

page 994: 'St Louis Browns' . . . Even the song's more outlandish details are based on fact, not invention. Battin eulogizes one player who was supposedly only 4 foot 11 inches. This was the famous Eddie Gaedel, who was actually 3 foot 7 inches and made a single plate appearance for the Browns in one of the great publicity stunts in the history of the game.

page 994: "Inviting McGuinn to play on the record . . ." Battin once let slip in an interview that McGuinn's guitar part was re-recorded before the album was released, but that comment may have been mischievous, particularly considering his later fall-out with Roger following the infamous incident at Dingwalls in 1984.

page 995: ". . . puppies on the road . . ." Fowley/Rogan. London/Redlands, California: 27–28 June 2007.

page 995: "Skip was always a ladies' man . . ." ibid.

page 996: "Skip had two beautiful Labrador retrievers . . ." Gene Parsons/Rogan. London/Fort Bragg, Mendocino, California: 19 May 2007.

page 996: "They were together for probably 13 years . . ." Hersh/Rogan. London/Topanga Canyon, California: 12 April 2008.

page 997: "When I went to the session . . ." Fowley/Rogan. London/Redlands, California: 27–28 June 2007.

page 997: ". . . Its contents . . ." The *Topanga Skyline* tape lists Al Hersh as producer, with contributions from Al Perkins (pedal steel guitar, dobro, guitar); Roland White (mandolin, guitar), Michael Botts (drums), Roger Bush (bass), Chris Ethridge (bass), Byron Berline (fiddle), Alan Munde (banjo), Herb Pedersen (vocals) and Bob Beeman (guitar). The track listing reads: 'Salty Dog Blues'; 'Bolts Of Blue'; 'Stoned Sober'; 'Relax With Me'; 'Relax With Me' (second version); 'Don't Go Down The Drain'; 'Roll In My Sweet Baby's Arms'; 'Roll In My Sweet Baby's Arms' (second version); 'Hully Gully'; 'Foggy Mountain Top'; 'Wintergreen'. The 2010 Sierra album credits the drummer as Mike Bowden, not Botts, while Kim Fowley gets the producer credit, not Al Hersh. The track listing differs slightly with the inclusion of 'Willow In The Wind', the removal of one of the versions of 'Relax Your Mind' and the addition of a later version of 'China Moon'.

page 998: "One of my least favourite albums . . ." Battin/Ballard: 22 September 1976. Part published in *Omaha Rainbow* 11: December 1976.

page 998: "At one time I was in both groups . . ." ibid.

page 999: "Do I think . . ." Chris Hillman, interviewed by the author. London: 28 April 1977. Part published in *Dark Star* 10: August 1977.

page 999: "That was the last time we saw each other . . ." Johnson/Rogan. London/Nice, France: 17 June 2007.

page 999: "I went running back to Skip . . ." ibid.

page 1000: ". . . Battin persuaded Darrow to play a handful of gigs in a duet format . . ." Darrow later transferred a cassette of one of their rehearsals on to CD for distribution among his friends. Titled *The Milano Sessions*, the CD-R features: 'Everglades'; 'Santa Ana Wind'; 'Hard On The Trail'; 'Tell Him No'; 'Zig Zag'; 'Time Will Tell'; 'On The Road

Again'; 'Tell Me How'; 'Take A Chance'; 'Slippin' And Slidin''; 'Austin, Texas'; 'Nite Owl'.

page 1000: "Back in America . . ." Battin and Kleinow's 'Friends' included Greg Harris (guitar), John Serena (bass) and Ed Ponder (drums); the New Dixie Flyers added Michael Ripley (keyboards) and Johnny Meeks (lead guitar) formerly of Gene Vincent's Blue Caps; the Older Brothers included Kleinow, Ponder and vocalist Larry Dale.

page 1001: "The funny thing is . . ." Patricia Battin (née Cartabiano), email interview with the author. Silverton, Oregon: 14 October 2008.

page 1001: "He was a great dancer . . ." ibid.

page 1001: "Local painter . . ." Connie Cohen elaborates: "The Community Food Store was a food co-op where we pooled together and created a place to get organic food. That's how I met them. I was working at the store and they came in. We started chatting and I invited them over to have supper with us just because I liked them. They hadn't been on the farm very long then . . . I had no idea about Skip's history in the Byrds or that he was a pretty cool musician."

page 1001: "Skip was a gentleman . . ." Rogan/Patricia Battin (née Cartabiano), email interview with the author. Silverton, Oregon: 14 October 2008.

page 1003: ". . . sometimes it's necessary . . ." Battin/Rogan. New York: 3 July 1979.

page 1003–1004: "We used to laugh about it . . ." John York, interviewed by the author. London/Claremont, Los Angeles, California: 11 June 2007.

page 1004: "After that people just ignored us . . ." ibid.

page 1004: "It was a legitimate release . . ." ibid.

page 1005: "Skip was playing keyboards on that first tour . . ." Rogers/Rogan. London/East Alton, Illinois: 14–15 July 2007.

page 1005: "These two guys from an Atlanta bar band . . ." York/Rogan. London/Claremont, Los Angeles, California: 11 June 2007.

page 1006: "It was so much stronger . . ." Rogers/Rogan. London/East Alton, Illinois: 14–15 July 2007.

page 1007: "Look, this whole thing could be over next week . . ." Quote overheard by the author. London: 12 October 1989.

page 1007: "Skip was a wonderful, sweet man . . ." York/Rogan. London/Claremont, Los Angeles, California: 11 June 2007.

page 1007: "Everyone knows these songs . . ." Connie Cohen, interviewed by the author. London/Portland, Oregon: 9 October 2008.

page 1007: "He said, 'Wow, this is important stuff . . .'" ibid.

page 1008: "Skip had this nice little studio . . ." Brian Cutean, interviewed by the author. London/Portland, Oregon: 23–24 September 2008.

page 1008: "He brought several different people . . ." Cohen/Rogan. London/Portland, Oregon: 9 October 2008.

page 1009: "He played with a little group . . ." Rogers/Rogan. London/East Alton, Illinois: 14–15 July 2007.

page 1009: "He seemed to have more energy . . ." ibid.

page 1009: "He and Skip started telling stories . . ." ibid.
page 1009: "They got down at one end of the field . . ." ibid.
page 1009: "I knew Skip was pissed off . . ." Rogers/Rogan. London/East Alton, Illinois: 14–15 July 2007.
page 1010: "The farm was supposed to be income . . ." Rogan/Patricia Battin (née Cartabiano), email interview with the author. Silverton, Oregon: 14 October 2008. Although Battin was yet to be diagnosed with Alzheimer's, Patricia wonders whether his post tour mood swings might have been symptomatic of the condition. She assumed that his erratic behaviour and lapses in concentration were caused by excessive smoking of marijuana, exacerbated by tensions on the road, but it seems likely that the Alzheimer's was already evident. "What a terrible thing to happen . . . I often wonder how things might have gone if Skip had not gotten ill. Every once in a while I have a dream of him well and alive. I sense that he is happy and I am happy to see him."
page 1010: "When Terry asked me to join . . ." Scott Nienhaus, interviewed by the author. London/East St Louis, Illinois: 26 June 2007. Nienhaus had joined the group a little earlier than Battin when they were on the road playing without Michael Clarke, who was terminally ill.
page 1011: "When Skip came in everything changed . . ." ibid.
page 1011: "It was hilarious . . ." ibid.
page 1011: "It went right through his arms . . ." ibid.
page 1012: "We'd just lay in these recliners . . ." ibid.
page 1013: "He was riding by my house one day . . ." Peggy Taylor, interviewed by the author. London/Silverton, Oregon: 29 July 2007.
page 1013: "I've been meaning to talk to you . . ." ibid.
page 1013: "Do you like music? . . ." ibid.
page 1013: "He kept showing up everywhere . . ." ibid.
page 1013: "We talked to Dale several times . . ." Rogers/Rogan. London/East Alton, Illinois: 14–15 July 2007.
page 1013: "He had a brain aneurysm . . ." ibid.
page 1014: "He just told me he had a bad memory . . ." Peggy Taylor/Rogan. London/Silverton, Oregon: 29 July 2007.
page 1014: "Oddly, it wasn't that big a surprise . . ." Nienhaus/Rogan. London/East St Louis, Illinois: 26 June 2007.
page 1014: "He thought that might have had something to do with it . . ." Rogers/Rogan. London/East Alton, Illinois: 14–15 July 2007.
page 1016: "Changes started right away . . ." Skip Battin, interviewed by the author. London/Silverton, Oregon: 3–4 June 1997.
page 1016: "Absolutely great . . ." ibid.
page 1016: "I'm looking forward to England . . ." ibid.
page 1016: "Terry took on the responsibility . . ." Nienhaus/Rogan. London/East St Louis, Illinois: 26 June 2007.
page 1016–1017: "Very often, he had to change flights . . ." Rogers/Rogan. London/East Alton, Illinois: 14–15 July 2007.

page 1017: "One time he landed in Portland . . ." Peggy Taylor/Rogan. London/Silverton, Oregon: 29 July 2007.

page 1017: "He had a music studio set up . . ." ibid.

page 1017: "It wasn't really serious until 1998 . . ." ibid.

page 1017: "Peggy really did look after him . . ." Rogers/Rogan. London/East Alton, Illinois: 14–15 July 2007.

page 1018: "The last time I saw Skip was at the airport . . ." Nienhaus/Rogan. London/East St Louis, Illinois: 26 June 2007.

page 1018: "I didn't know he was as challenged . . ." Cohen/Rogan. London/Portland, Oregon: 9 October 2008.

page 1018: "When we did that project . . ." ibid.

page 1019: "I've often thought . . ." Rogan/Patricia Battin (née Cartabiano), email interview with the author. Silverton, Oregon: 14 October 2008.

page 1019: "Even after he reached the point . . ." Peggy Taylor/Rogan. London/Silverton, Oregon: 29 July 2007.

page 1019: "Jon couldn't handle it . . ." ibid.

page 1019: "Jon was nervous . . ." Rogan/Patricia Battin (née Cartabiano), email interview with the author. Silverton, Oregon: 14 October 2008.

page 1019: "They had kind of a strange relationship . . ." Hersh/Rogan. London/Topanga Canyon, California: 12 April 2008.

page 1020: "He collected a lot of Skip's material . . ." Peggy Taylor/Rogan. London/Silverton, Oregon: 29 July 2007.

page 1020: "I wanted to visit him really badly . . ." Nienhaus/Rogan. London/East St Louis, Illinois: 26 June 2007.

page 1020: "We took our guitars . . ." Rogan/Cutean. London/Portland, Oregon: 23–24 September 2008. According to Brian Cutean, Anne Feeney was a folk and labour singer. "She had a song called 'Have You Been To Jail For Justice?' that Peter, Paul & Mary recorded."

page 1020: "The last time I saw Skip . . ." Gene Parsons' undated round robin tribute, written shortly after Skip Battin's death.

page 1021: "He was catatonic . . ." Rogan/Patricia Battin (née Cartabiano), email interview with the author. Silverton, Oregon: 14 October 2008.

page 1021: "I was finally able to reach Brent . . ." Peggy Taylor/Rogan. London/Silverton, Oregon: 29 July 2007.

page 1021: "[It was] under a canopy . . ." Rogan/Patricia Battin (née Cartabiano), email interview with the author. Silverton, Oregon: 14 October 2008.

page 1021: "That song has always moved me . . ." Rogan/Cutean. London/Portland, Oregon: 23–24 September 2008. Cutean adds: "At the memorial celebration they made backstage passes with Skip's picture on them. They were handed out to everyone and we wrote our relationship to him on the back and wore them. I still have mine in my truck. I look at it every time I drive anywhere, so he's right there with me. He was an exemplary cat."

DISCOGRAPHY

VOLUME 2

The extensive discography in *Requiem For The Timeless, Volume 1* concentrated exclusively on Byrds' releases, bootlegs, sessionography, television appearances and other group related activity. Readers requiring further information on specific releases by the Byrds should consult the lengthy discography therein. This volume focuses on the individual Byrds' work on albums *before* and *after* the group.

As previously, this discography concentrates on US and UK releases, unless indicated otherwise. Serial numbers refer to the original release on LP or CD. Selective re-releases that include additional material are also included. DVDs, video collections, samplers, promotional releases intended purely for radio broadcast and other non-retailable items are all excluded. Special vinyl re-releases, multi-disc packages and compilations with no fresh material or specific interest are generally not featured. Unauthorized or semi-legitimate live recordings, many taken from bootleg tapes or similar, are also excluded. The cut off date for this discography is December 2016.

In addition to the basic discography, this volume features detailed copyright registrations of *all* the Byrds, a lengthy section on unreleased songs and a final alphabetical listing of all their known compositions.

ALBUM CONTRIBUTIONS

The following is a complete list of US/UK albums on which each of the Byrds has played as a permanent group member. If a US or UK number is not listed then the record was not issued in that territory.

JAMES ROGER McGUINN

Albums with the Limeliters:

Tonight In Person RCA LPM/LSP 2272 (US)/RCA RD-27237/SF 5114 (UK).
'There's A Meeting Here Tonight'; 'Molly Malone'; 'The Monks Of St Bernard'; 'Seven Daffodils'; 'Hey Li Lee'; 'Headin' For The Hills'; 'The Far Side Of The Hill'; 'Rumania'; 'Madeira, M'Dear'; 'Proshchal'.
Released January 1961 (US)/November 1961 (UK).

Albums with the Chad Mitchell Trio:

Mighty Day On Campus Kapp KL 1262/KS 3262 (US).
'Mighty Day'; 'Rum By Gum'; 'The Whistling Gypsy'; 'Super Skier'; 'Dona Dona Dona'; 'Whup Jamboree'; 'Lizzie Borden'; 'Tail Toddle'; 'Johnnie'; 'Puttin' On The Style'; 'Hang On The Bell, Nellie'; 'On My Journey'.
Released February 1962 (US).

The Chad Mitchell Trio At The Bitter End Kapp KL 1281/KS 3281 (US).
'The John Birch Society'; 'Hello Susan Brown'; 'The Unfortunate Man'; 'Blues Around My Head'; 'James James Morrison Morrison; 'The Great Historical Bum (The Bragging Song)'; 'Alberta'; 'Golden Vanity'; 'Moscow Nights'; 'Come Along Home (Tom's Song)'; 'You Can Tell The World'; 'Last Night I Had The Strangest Dream'.
Released July 1962 (US).

Albums with the Byrds:

See Discography *Volume 1* under the following sections: *Byrds Singles, Albums, Compilations* and *Archival Albums* for fuller details of release dates, complete track listings, alternate serial numbers, special issues/editions, and more.

Mr Tambourine Man Columbia CL 2372 (mono)/Columbia CS 9172 (stereo) (US). CBS BPG 62571 (mono)/CBS SBPG 62571 (stereo) (UK). Remastered CD edition with bonus tracks: Columbia Legacy CK 64845 (US)/Columbia Legacy 483705 2 (UK).

Turn! Turn! Turn! Columbia CL 2454 (mono)/Columbia CS 9254 (stereo) (US). CBS BPG 62652 (mono)/CBS SBPG 62652 (stereo) (UK). Remastered CD edition with bonus tracks: Columbia Legacy CK 64846 (US)/Columbia Legacy 483706 2 (UK).

Fifth Dimension Columbia CL 2549 (mono)/Columbia CS 9349 (stereo) (US). CBS BPG 62783 (mono)/CBS SBPG 62783 (stereo) (UK). Remastered CD edition with bonus tracks: Columbia Legacy CK 64847(US)/Columbia Legacy 483707 2 (UK).

Younger Than Yesterday Columbia CL 2642 (mono)/Columbia CS 9442 (stereo) (US). CBS BPG 62988 (mono)/CBS SBPG 62988 (stereo) (UK). Remastered CD edition with bonus tracks: Columbia Legacy CK 64848 (US)/Columbia Legacy 483708 2 (UK).

The Notorious Byrd Brothers Columbia CL 2775 (mono)/Columbia CS 9575 (stereo) (US). CBS 63169 (mono)/CBS S 63169 (stereo) (UK). Remastered CD edition with bonus tracks: Columbia Legacy CK 65151 (US)/Columbia Legacy 486751 2 (UK).

Sweetheart Of The Rodeo Columbia CL 9670 (mono)/Columbia CS 9670 (stereo) (US). CBS 63353 (mono)/CBS S 63353 (stereo) (UK). Remastered CD edition with bonus tracks: Columbia Legacy CK 65150 (US)/Columbia

Legacy 486752 2 (UK). Special issue *Sweetheart Of The Rodeo* [*Legacy Edition*]: Columbia Legacy COL 510921 2 (US).

Dr Byrds & Mr Hyde Columbia CL 9755 (mono)/Columbia CS 9755 (stereo) (US). CBS 63545 (mono)/CBS S 63545 (stereo) (UK). Remastered CD edition with bonus tracks: Columbia Legacy CK 65113 (US)/Columbia Legacy 486753 2 (UK).

Ballad Of Easy Rider Columbia CS 9942 (stereo) (US). CBS S 63795 (stereo) (UK). Remastered CD edition with bonus tracks: Columbia Legacy CK 65114 (US)/Columbia Legacy 486754 2 (UK).

(Untitled) Columbia G 30127 (stereo) (US). CBS S 64095 (stereo) (UK). Remastered CD edition with bonus tracks: *(Untitled)/(Unissued)* Columbia Legacy C2K 65847 (US)/Columbia Legacy 495077 2 (UK).

Byrdmaniax Columbia KC 30640 (stereo) (US). CBS S 64389 (stereo) (UK). Remastered CD edition with bonus tracks: Columbia Legacy CK 65848 (US)/Columbia Legacy 495079 2 (UK).

Farther Along Columbia KC 31050 (stereo) (US). CBS S 64676 (stereo) (UK). Remastered CD edition with bonus tracks: Columbia Legacy CK 65849 (US)/Columbia Legacy 495078 2 (UK).

Byrds Asylum SD 5058 (US)/Asylum SYLA 8754 (UK).

Archival albums with the Byrds:

Preflyte Together ST-T-1001 (US)/Bumble GEXP 8001 (UK).
The Original Singles Volume 1 1965–1967 CBS 31851 (UK)/Columbia FC 37335 (US).
The Original Singles Volume 2 1967–1969 CBS 32103 (UK).
Never Before Re-Flyte MH 70318 (US).
In The Beginning Rhino R2 70244 (US).
Sanctuary Sundazed LP 5061 (US).
Sanctuary II Sundazed LP 5065 (US).
Sanctuary III Sundazed LP 5066 (US).
The Preflyte Sessions Sundazed SC 11116 (US).
Sanctuary IV Sundazed LP 5090 (US).
The Columbia Singles '65–'67 Sundazed LP 5130/P2 55624 (US).
Live At The Fillmore – February 1969 Columbia/Legacy CK 65910 (US)/Columbia/Legacy 495080 2 (UK).
Another Dimension Sundazed SEP 2 10-168 (US).
Live At The Royal Albert Hall 1971 Sundazed LP 5189/Sundazed SC 11177 (US).
Preflyte [extended version] Floating World FLOATD6122 (UK).

Box Sets with the Byrds:

The Byrds Columbia Legacy 46773 (US)/Columbia Legacy 4676112 (UK).
12 Dimensions The Columbia Recordings 1965–1972 (13-CD box set) Columbia 497610 2/4976102000 (UK).

There Is A Season (4-CD box set and DVD) Columbia/Legacy 82876877002 (US/UK).
The Complete Columbia Albums Collection Columbia Legacy 886978738028 (US).

Isolated appearances with the Byrds:

See *Volume 1*: *Byrds Albums, Guest Slots/Rarities, Compilations* and *Archival Albums* for fuller details of release dates and alternate territory serial numbers.

Early LA Together ST-T-1014 (US).
Don't Make Waves MGM 4483 ST (US).
Candy ABC ABCS OC-9 (US)/Stateside SSL 10276 (UK).
Roadmaster A&M 87584 (Holland).
Earl Scruggs, His Family And Friends Columbia 30584 (US)/CBS 64777 (UK).
Banjoman Sire SA 7527(US)/Sire SRK 6026 (UK).
Monterey International Pop Festival Rhino R2 70506 (US)/Castle Communications ROK CD 102 (UK).
3 Byrds Land In London 1977 Strange Fruit SFRSCD 001 (UK).
3 Byrds In London 1977 – Live At The BBC Mastertone 8228 (US).
Byrd Parts Raven RVCD 77 (Australia).
Byrd Parts 2 Raven RVCD 165 (Australia).
Sixties Transition Sierra SXCD 6027 (US)/Floating World FLOATM6125 (UK).
Previously issued material also appears on the soundtracks to *Easy Rider, Homer, Forrest Gump* and *The Limey.*

Compilations/Hits Collections with the Byrds:

See *Volume 1* for additional details.

The Byrds Greatest Hits Columbia CL 2716 (US)/CBS SBPG 63107 (UK).
The Byrds Greatest Hits Volume 2 CBS S 64650 (UK).
Best Of Volume 2 Columbia C31795 (US).
History Of The Byrds CBS 68242 (UK).
Return Of The Byrds Columbia Realm 2V 8006-7 (US).
The Byrds CBS 88320 (UK).
The Byrds Play Dylan Columbia PC 36293 (US)/CBS 31795 (UK).
The Very Best Of The Byrds Columbia CS P-P2 17596 (US).
The Byrds Collection Castle Communications CCSLP 151 (UK).
The Very Best Of The Byrds Columbia CBS 4634189 2 (Holland/UK).
Full Flyte Raven RVCD 10 (Australia).
Free Flyte Sony Music Special Products A 17733 (US).
Greatest Hits Remastered Columbia 467843 2 (UK).
20 Essential Tracks From The Boxed Set: 1965–1970 Columbia/Legacy CK 47884/471665-2 (US/UK).
Definitive Collection Columbia 480548 9 (UK).
Nashville West Sony Music Special Products A 28123 (US).

The Very Best Of The Byrds Columbia 487995 2 (UK).
The Best Of The Byrds Columbia 488146 2 (UK).
Super Hits Columbia Legacy 504725 2 (UK)/Columbia Legacy CK 65637 (US).
The Byrds Greatest Hits Columbia/Legacy CK 66230 (US).
The Byrds Sony Music Special Products A 30827 (US).
The Byrds Play The Songs Of Bob Dylan Columbia 501946 2 (UK).
The Byrds Play Dylan Columbia/Legacy CK 85430 (US).
The Essential Byrds Columbia Legacy 512249 2 (UK)/Columbia Legacy C2K 89110 (US).
Mojo Presents . . . An Introduction To The Byrds – 24 Classic Songs Columbia 512778 2 (UK).
Mr Tambourine Man – The Best Of The Byrds Sony Music Media SMM 516489-2 (Germany/UK).
America's Great National Treasure Sony/BMG A 96086 (US).
The Very Best Of The Byrds Sony/BMG 82876 85514 2 (UK).
Byrds: A Collection Sony BMG 88697 12448 2 (UK).
The Byrds Play Dylan Sony BMG 88697 25267 2 (UK).
Playlist: The Very Best Of The Byrds Columbia Legacy 88697 39219 2 (US).
Steel Box Sony BMG 88697 459812 (UK).
Eight Miles High – The Best Of The Byrds Sony/Camden 88697 63627 2 (UK).
Setlist: The Very Best Of The Byrds Live Columbia/Legacy 88697 97753 2 (US).
Turn! Turn! Turn!: The Ultimate Collection Sony/Columbia Music 88875 151652 (UK).
The 60s – The Byrds Sony Music 8888377667 2 (US).

Solo and post-Byrds recordings:

Easy Rider Dunhill DSX-50063 (US)/Stateside SSL 5018 (UK).
Includes solo 'Ballad Of Easy Rider' and 'It's Alright Ma (I'm Only Bleeding)'.
Released October 1969 (US)/January 1970 (UK).

Roger McGuinn Columbia KC 31946 (US)/CBS 62574 (UK).
'I'm So Restless'; 'My New Woman; 'Lost My Drivin' Wheel'; 'Draggin' '; 'Time Cube'; 'Bag Full Of Money'; 'Hanoi Hannah'; 'Stone'; 'Heave Away'; 'M'Linda'; 'The Water Is Wide'. See details of 2004 reissue later in this section.
Released June 1973 (US)/August 1973 (UK).

Peace On You Columbia KC 32956 (US)/CBS 80171 (UK).
'Peace On You'; 'Without You'; 'Going To The Country'; '(Please Not) One More Time'; 'Same Old Sound'; 'Do What You Want To'; 'Together'; 'Better Change'; 'Gate Of Horn'; 'The Lady'. See details of 2004 reissue later in this section.
Released August 1974 (US)/August 1974 (UK).

Roger McGuinn And Band Columbia PC 33541 (US)/CBS 80877 (UK).
'Lisa'; 'So Long'; 'Lover Of The Bayou'; 'Circle Song'; 'Born To Rock 'n' Roll'; 'Bull Dog'; 'Knockin' On Heaven's Door'; 'Painted Lady'; 'Easy Does It'; 'Somebody Loves You'. See details of 2004 reissue later in this section.
Released June 1975 (US)/August 1975 (UK).

Cardiff Rose Columbia PC 35154 (US)/CBS 81369 (UK).
'Take Me Away'; 'Jolly Roger'; 'Rock And Roll Time'; 'Friend'; 'Partners In Crime'; 'Up To Me'; 'Round Table'; 'Pretty Polly'; 'Dreamland'. See details of 2004 reissue later in this section.
Released May 1976 (US)/June 1976 (UK).

Thunderbyrd Columbia PC 34656 (US)/CBS 81883 (UK).
'All Night Long'; 'It's Gone'; 'Dixie Highway'; 'American Girl'; 'We Can Do It All Over Again'; 'Why Baby Why'; 'I'm Not Lonely Anymore'; 'Golden Loom'; 'Russian Hill'.
Released March 1977 (US)/May 1977 (UK).

Back From Rio Arista ARCD 8648 (US)/Arista 261 348 (UK).
'Someone To Love'; 'Car Phone'; 'You Bowed Down'; 'Suddenly Blue'; 'The Trees Are All Gone'; 'King Of The Hill'; 'Without Your Love'; 'The Time Has Come'; 'Your Love Is A Gold Mine'; 'Back From Rio Interlude'; 'If We Never Meet Again'.
Released January 1991 (US)/February 1991 (UK).

Born To Rock And Roll Columbia CK 47494 (US)/Columbia 471269-2/ Columbia/Legacy COL 488223 2 (UK).
Compilation. 'I'm So Restless'; 'My New Woman'; 'Draggin''; 'The Water Is Wide'; 'Same Old Sound'; 'Bag Full Of Money'; 'Gate Of Horn'; 'Peace On You'; 'Lover Of The Bayou'; 'Stone (The Lord Loves A Rolling Stone)'; 'Lisa'; 'Take Me Away'; 'Jolly Roger'; 'Friend'; 'Dreamland'; 'Dixie Highway'; 'American Girl'; 'Up To Me'; 'Russian Hill'; 'Born To Rock And Roll'.
Includes an alternate take of 'Bag Full Of Money'.
Released August 1991 (US)/March 1992 (UK).

Live From Mars Hollywood HR 620 090-2 (US)/Hollywood 162-090-2 (UK).
'Heartbreak Hotel'; 'Daddy Roll 'Em'; 'Gate Of Horn'; 'Chestnut Mare'; 'The Bells Of Rhymney'; 'Turn! Turn! Turn!'; 'Beach Ball'; 'Wild Mountain Thyme'; 'You Showed Me'; 'Mr Tambourine Man (acoustic)'; 'Mr Tambourine Man (electric)'; 'Mr Spaceman'; 'Eight Miles High'; 'So You Want To Be A Rock 'n' Roll Star'; 'King Of The Hill'; 'May The Road Rise'; 'Fireworks'; 'May The Road Rise'.
Released November 1996 (US)/January 1997 (UK).

McGuinn's Folk Den Vol. 1 CD via mp3 release: 2720-0000020790-1999022 (US).
'Mighty Day'; 'Pushboat'; 'John The Revelator'; 'The Bonny Ship The Diamond'; 'John Henry'; 'The Handsome Cabin Boy'; 'Wayfaring Stranger';

'Finnegan's Wake'; 'James Alley Blues'; 'Home On The Range'; 'Mary Had A Baby'.
Released February 1999 (US).

McGuinn's Folk Den Vol. 2 CD via mp3 release: 25147932316026-12919 (US).
'John Riley'; 'Virgin Mary'; '900 Miles'; 'Old Paint'; 'Easter Morn'; 'Old Texas'; 'Springfield Mountain'; 'In The Evenin''; 'Buffalo Skinners'; 'The Argonaut'; 'Liverpool Girls'.
Released July 1999 (US).

McGuinn's Folk Den Vol. 3 CD via mp3 release: 14945985545-31893 (US).
'In Fair Nottamun Town'; 'I'm Alabama Bound'; 'Sail Away Lady'; 'Get Along Little Dogies'; 'Brisbane Ladies'; 'Ain' No Mo' Cane On De Brazis' ['Cane Blues']; 'Blood Red Roses'; 'Oh You New York Girls'; 'The Cold Coast Of Greenland'; 'Trouble In Mind'; 'I Saw 3 Ships'; 'Greenland Whale Fisheries'. The final track only appeared on the second edition of the CD.
Released December 1999 (US).

McGuinn's Folk Den Vol. 4 CD via mp3 release: 3858965845720-63938 (US).
'Willie Moore'; 'Star Spangled Banner'; 'Alberta'; 'If I Had Wings'; 'East Virginia'; 'Faithless Flora'; 'South Australia'; 'Boatman'; 'Whiskey In The Jar'; 'The Cruel War'; 'Auld Lang Syne'.
Released August 2000 (US).

Treasures From The Folk Den Appleseed Recordings APR CD 1046 (US).
'Wagoner's Lad' (with Joan Baez and Eliza Carthy); 'Dink's Song' (with Pete Seeger and Josh White Jr); 'Bonnie Ship The Diamond' (with Judy Collins); 'Cane Blues'; 'Reel' (with Eliza Carthy); 'Fair Nottamun Town' (with Jean Ritchie); 'John The Revelator' (with Jean Ritchie and Odetta); 'Alabama Bound' (with Pete Seeger); 'Finnegan's Wake' (with Tommy Makem); 'In The Evenin'' (with Pete Seeger); 'Willie Moore' (with Joan Baez and Eliza Carthy); 'The Brazos River' (with Frank & Mary Hamilton); 'Sail Away Lady' (with Odetta); 'John Riley' (with Judy Collins); 'Trouble In Mind' (with Josh White Jr); 'Whiskey In The Jar' (with Tommy Makem); 'The Virgin Mary' (with Odetta); 'Pete's Song' (with Pete Seeger). Plus hidden bonus track: 'In The Evenin''.
Released August 2001 (US).

In The Spirit Of Love CD via mp3 release: 61027968649-212045 (US).
'Trials Blues'; 'Easter Morn'; 'Wayfaring Stranger'; 'Battle Hymn Of The Republic'; 'John The Revelator'; 'I Saw 3 Ships'; 'I Heard The Bells On Christmas Day'; 'Virgin Mary'; 'The 12 Days Of Christmas'; 'Mary Had A Baby'.
Released August 2002 (US).

The Sea: Songs By Roger McGuinn CD via mp3 release: 5731046287982-260566 (US).
'The Sea'; 'South Australia'; 'Liverpool Girls'; 'The Argonaut'; 'Oh You New

York Girls'; 'The Cold Coast Of Greenland'; 'The Handsome Cabin Boy'; 'The Greenland Whale'; 'The Bonny Ship The Diamond'; 'The Whale Catchers'; 'Blood Red Roses'.
Released August 2003.

Roger McGuinn Sundazed SC 6201/Sony Music A 53397 (US).
Original album reissued, with bonus tracks 'Jamaica Say You Will' and 'John, John'.
Released January 2004 (US).

Peace On You Sundazed SC 6202/Sony A53403 (US).
Original album reissued with bonus track, 'Rock & Roll Time'. Released January 2004 (US).

Limited Edition April First Productions AFP 0401 (US).
'If I Needed Someone'; 'Parade Of Lost Dreams'; 'Shady Grove'; 'James Alley Blues'; 'On And On'; 'Southbound 95'; 'Castanet Dance'; 'Shenandoah'; 'When The Saints Go Marching In'; 'Saint James Infirmary'; 'May The Road Rise To Meet You'; 'Echoes Live'; 'Made In China'.
Released April 2004 (US).

Live At The XM Studio 05/27/2004 Re: Live iTunes download.
'My Back Pages'; 'Gate Of Horn'; 'He Was A Friend Of Mine'; 'She Don't Care About Time'; 'The Bells Of Rhymney'; 'Mr. Spaceman'; 'You Ain't Going Nowhere'; 'Pretty Boy Floyd'; 'I Want To Grow Up To Be A Politician'; 'Lover Of The Bayou'; 'Chestnut Mare'; 'Goin' Back'; 'Ballad Of Easy Rider'; 'Wasn't Born To Follow'; 'Lost My Driving Wheel'; 'Don't You Write Her Off'; 'American Girl'; 'King Of The Hill'; 'Mr Tambourine Man'; 'Turn! Turn! Turn!'; 'Eight Miles High'.
Released May 2004 (US).

Roger McGuinn And Band Sundazed SC 6203/Sony A53483 (US).
Released: October 2004 (US). Original album reissued with bonus tracks 'Wasn't Born To Follow (live)' and 'Chestnut Mare (live)'.

Cardiff Rose Sundazed SC 6204 (US)/Sony 52484 (UK).
Original album reissued with bonus tracks 'Soul Love' (demo recording) and 'Dreamland' (live).
Released: October 2004 (US).

The Folk Den Project 1995–2005 April First Productions AFP 402 (US).
CD 1: 'Follow The Drinking Gourd'; 'Mighty Day'; 'Gypsy Rover'; 'On Top Of Old Smokey'; 'Easter Morn'; 'Dink's Song'; 'Boatman'; 'Brandy Leave Me Alone'; 'Banks Of [The]Ohio'; '12 Gates To The City'; 'Ain't No Mo Cane On De Brasis'; 'We Wish You A Merry Christmas'; 'All My Trials'; 'Cindy'; 'The Colorado Trail'; 'Cumberland Mountain Bear Chase'; 'Alabama Bound'; 'Bring Me A Little Water, Sylvie'; 'Go Tell Aunt Rhodie'; 'Makes A Long Time Man Feel Bad'; 'Spanish Is The Loving Tongue'; 'Erie Canal'; 'Springfield Mountain'; 'Old Paint'; 'Rubin Ranzo'.

CD 2: 'Silver Dagger'; 'Oh Freedom'; 'Railroad Bill'; 'East Virginia'; 'Coffee Grows On White Oak Trees'; 'So Early In The Spring'; 'Golden Vanity'; 'Down By The Riverside'; 'Buffalo Skinners'; 'Waltzing Matilda'; 'The Riddle Song'; 'Virgin Mary'; 'The Handsome Cabin Boy'; 'Ezekiel Saw A Wheel'; 'Heave Away'; 'Oh Mary Don't You Weep'; 'Red River Valley'; 'Brisbane Ladies'; 'Battle Hymn Of The Republic'; 'Old Texas'; 'Rock Island Line'; 'Wagoner's Lad'; 'There's A Hole In The Bucket'; 'Wild Goose'; 'To Morrow'.
CD 3: 'James Alley Blues'; 'The Cruel War'; 'Wayfaring Stranger'; 'Pushboat'; 'America For Me'; 'Old Riley'; 'Finnegan's Wake'; 'Pretty Saro'; 'Catch The Greenland Whale'; 'Drunken Sailor'; 'Lost Jimmy Whelan'; 'The First Noël'; 'Get Along Little Doggies'; 'Roddy McCorley'; 'He's Got The Whole World In His Hands'; 'Haul Away Joe'; 'John The Revelator'; 'Sail Away Lady'; 'Delia's Gone'; 'Spanish Ladies'; 'Trouble In Mind'; 'Wildwood Flower'; 'Away In A Manger'; 'The Cold Cold Coast Of Greenland'; 'Salty Dog Blues'.
CD 4: 'Wanderin''; 'The Argonaut'; 'Lilly Of The West'; 'Michael Row The Boat Ashore'; 'Stewball'; 'Let The Bullgine Run'; 'The Gallows Pole'; 'The John B's Sails'; 'Willie Moore'; 'St James Infirmary'; 'Kilgary Mountain'; 'The Twelve Days Of Christmas'; 'Wild Mountain Thyme'; 'New York Girls'; 'Streets Of Laredo'; 'Mary Had A Baby'; 'The House Of The Rising Sun'; 'Greenland Whale Fisheries'; 'Shenandoah'; 'The Bonny Ship The Diamond'; 'Sailor Lad'; 'This Train'; 'Liverpool Gals'; 'Home On The Range'; 'When The Saints Go Marching In'.
The spelling of certain songs alters slightly on the many Folk Den-related releases.
Released November 2005 (US).

Live From Spain April First Productions CD AFP 403 (US).
'My Back Pages'; 'Ballad Of Easy Rider'; 'Wasn't Born To Follow'; 'On Easter Morn He Rose'; 'Mr Spaceman'; 'Pretty Boy Floyd'; 'You Ain't Going Nowhere'; 'Drugstore Truck Drivin' Man'; 'Chimes Of Freedom'; 'On And On'; 'Lover Of The Bayou'; 'Chestnut Mare'; 'Jolly Roger'; 'Bells Of Rhymney'; '5 D (Fifth Dimension)'; 'Mr Tambourine Man'; 'Turn! Turn! Turn!'; 'Eight Miles High'; 'So You Want To Be A Rock 'N' Roll Star'; 'May The Road Rise To Meet You'; 'Knockin' On Heaven's Door'.
Released March 2007 (US).

22 Timeless Tracks From The Folk Den Project April First Productions AFP 0404 (US).
'Wanderin''; 'Follow The Drinking Gourd'; 'Oh Freedom'; 'Railroad Bill'; 'Cane Blues'; 'Coffee Grows On Wild Oak Trees'; 'Waltzing Matilda'; 'Ezekiel Saw A Wheel'; 'Mighty Day'; 'Down By The Riverside'; 'The Colorado Trail'; 'So Early In The Spring'; 'Lily Of The West'; 'Stewball'; 'St James Infirmary'; 'Drunken Sailor'; 'Silver Dagger'; 'Wild Mountain Thyme'; 'James Alley Blues'; 'The Cruel War'; 'The John B's Sails'; 'The Boll Weevil'.
Released May 2008 (US).

Roger McGuinn's Thunderbyrd – West Coast Legends Vol. 4 (Rockpalast Festival 1977) MIG 90317 (Germany).
'Lover Of The Bayou'; 'American Girl'; 'Mr Spaceman'; 'Why Baby Why'/'Tiffany Queen'; 'Golden Loom'; 'Juice Head'; 'Chestnut Mare'; 'Midnight Dew'; 'Dixie Highway'; 'We Can Do It All Over Again'; 'Shoot 'Em' (aka 'Victor's Theme: Shoot Him'); 'I'll Feel A Whole Lot Better'; 'Turn! Turn! Turn!'; 'Mr Tambourine Man'; 'Eight Miles High'.
Released May 2010 (Germany). Issued on CD and DVD.

CCD April First Productions AFP 040 (US).
'Running Down To Old Maui'; 'Randy Dandy Oh'; 'So Early In The Spring'; 'Catch The Greenland Whale'; 'Go To Sea Once More'; 'South Australia'; 'Let The Bullgine Run'; 'Back To Sea'; 'Golden Vanity'; 'Heave Away Me Johnnies'; 'The Argonaut'; 'Spanish Ladies'; 'The Bonny Ship The Diamond'; 'Sailor Lad'; 'A Roving'; 'The Cold Cold Coast Of Greenland'; 'Away Rio'; 'Haul Away Joe'; 'Drunken Sailor'; 'The Handsome Cabin Boy'; 'Greenland Whale Fisheries'; 'Liverpool Gals'; 'Ruben Ranzo'.
Released: June 2011 (US).

Stories, Songs & Friends AFP CD 0406 (US).
Box set. CD 1: 'My Back Pages'; 'Ballad Of Easy Rider'; 'Mr Spaceman'; 'Pretty Boy Floyd'; 'You Ain't Going Nowhere'; 'Drug Store Truck Drivin' Man'; 'Old Blue'; 'Pretty Saro'; 'Gambler's Blues'; 'Rock Island Line'; '5 D (Fifth Dimension)'; 'Russian Hill'; 'Parade Of Lost Dreams'; 'Living In The Country'.
CD 2: 'Lover Of The Bayou'; 'Chestnut Mare'; 'I Want To Grow Up To Be A Politician'; 'Just A Season'; 'Jolly Roger'; 'The Bells Of Rhymney'; 'Randy Dandy Oh'; 'Soldier's Joy'; 'The Water Is Wide'; 'You Showed Me'; 'The Byrds' Story' [spoken word]; 'Mr Tambourine Man'; 'Eight Miles High'; 'Turn! Turn! Turn!'; 'So You Want To Be A Rock 'n' Roll Star'; 'Feel A Whole Lot Better'; 'Leave Her Johnny, Leave Her'; 'May The Road Rise To Meet You'.
Plus bonus DVD.
Released February 2014 (US).

The Folk Den Project – Twentieth Anniversary Edition CD Baby (US/UK).
CD 1: 'Drill Ye Tarriers'; 'The Blackest Crow'; 'This Little Light Of Mine'; 'Rolling Down To Old Maui'; 'King Kong Kitchie Kitchie Ke Me O'; 'I Know Where I'm Going'; 'Peg And Awl'; 'This Month Of January'; 'Old Plank Road'; 'Come And Go With Me To That Land'; 'Paddy And The Whale'; 'Jimmy Brown'; 'The Squirrel'; 'Banks Of Newfoundland'; 'Isn't It Grand?'; 'Swing Low Sweet Chariot'; 'The Boll Weevil'; 'Polly Vaughn'; 'Whup Jamboree'; 'There's A Meeting Here Tonight'; 'St Clair's Defeat'; 'Wade In The Water'; 'No Payday In Detroit'; 'Christmas Is Coming'; 'I Saw Three Ships'.
CD 2: 'Hard Times Of Old England'; '900 Miles'; 'Let My People Go!'; 'John Riley'; 'Cripple Creek'; 'In The Evenin''; 'Old Joe Clark'; 'She Will Never

Marry'; 'Paddy West'; 'Old Blue'; 'Away With Rum'; 'Take A Drink On Me'; 'Tell Ole Gil'; 'She'll Be Coming Round The Mountain'; 'The Great Silkie Of Sule Skerry'; 'Yellow Rose Of Texas'; 'Winter's Almost Gone'; 'A Roving'; 'Engine 143'; 'Dry Bones'; 'Darlin' Corey'; 'I've Got The Joy, Joy, Joy'; 'Down In The Valley'; 'Angels We Have Heard On High'; 'What Child Is This?'
CD 3: 'Black Mountain Rag'; 'Fair And Tender Ladies'; 'The Crawdad Song'; 'Blow The Man Down'; 'Children Go Where I Send Thee'; 'Tarrytown'; 'All The Pretty Little Horses'; 'Pay Me My Money Down'; 'Old Chisholm Trail'; 'Give Me Oil In My Lamp'; 'Housewife's Lament'; 'Away Rio'; 'Sugar Baby'; 'The Bears Went Over The Mountain'; 'Bury Me On The Lone Prairie'; 'Cold Rain And Snow'; 'John Hardy'; 'The Cobbler'; 'John Henry'; 'Go To Sea Once More'; 'The Coo Coo'; 'I Heard The Voice Of Jesus'; 'Nine Pound Hammer'; 'Glory Glory'; 'I Heard The Bells On Christmas Day'.
CD 4: 'Katie Morey'; 'Every Time I Feel The Spirit'; 'Back To Sea'; 'When Jones's Ale Was New'; 'Pretty Polly'; 'I'm On My Way'; 'Risselty Rosselty Now Now Now'; 'When I First Came To This Land'; 'South Australia'; 'Jacob's Dream'; 'February Song'; 'I'll Fly Away'; 'To Welcome Poor Paddy Home'; 'My Home's Across The Smokey Mountains'; 'This Old Man'; 'Alberta'; 'We Are Crossing The Jordan River'; 'The Fatal Flower Garden'; 'Randy Dandy Oh'; 'Whoa Back Buck'; 'Joshua Fit The Battle Of Jericho'; 'The Coast Of Peru'; 'God Rest Ye Merry Gentlemen'; 'Leave Her Johnny Leave Her (Live)'.
Released July 2016 (US/UK).

As McGuinn, Clark & Hillman:
McGuinn, Clark & Hillman Capitol SW 11910 (US)/Capitol EST 11910 (UK).
'Long Long Time'; 'Little Mama'; 'Don't You Write Her Off'; 'Surrender To Me'; 'Backstage Pass'; 'Stopping Traffic'; 'Feelin' Higher'; 'Sad Boy'; 'Release Me Girl'; 'Bye Bye Baby'.
Released January 1979 (US)/March 1979 (UK). The 2001 CD reissue features bonus demo versions of 'Surrender To Me' and the previously unreleased compositions, 'Little Girl' and 'I Love Her'.

City Capitol ST 12043(US)/Capitol EST 12043 (UK).
'Who Taught The Night'; 'One More Chance'; 'Won't Let You Down'; 'Street Talk'; 'City'; 'Skate Date'; 'Givin' Herself Away'; 'Deeper In'; 'Painted Fire'; 'Let Me Down Easy'.
Released January 1980 (US)/February 1980 (UK).

Return Flight Edsel EDCD 358 (UK).
Compilation. 'Long Long Time'; 'Don't You Write Her Off'; 'Surrender To Me'; 'Backstage Pass'; 'Sad Boy'; 'Who Taught The Night'; 'City'; 'Givin' Herself Away'; 'Let Me Down Easy'; 'Between You And Me'; 'Angel'; 'King For A Night'; 'Turn Your Radio On'; 'Skate Date'.
Released December 1992 (UK).

Return Flight II Edsel EDCD 373 (UK).
Compilation. 'Little Mama'; 'Stopping Traffic'; 'Feelin' Higher'; 'Release Me Girl'; 'Bye Bye Baby'; 'One More Chance'; 'Won't Let You Down'; 'Street Talk'; 'Deeper In'; 'Painted Fire'; 'Mean Streets'; 'Entertainment'; 'Soul Shoes'; 'Love Me Tonight'; 'A Secret Side Of You'; 'Ain't No Money'; 'Making Movies'. The final track, 'Making Movies', was previously only available as the B-side of their US single, 'Turn Your Radio On'.
Released June 1993 (UK).

The Capitol Collection Acadia/Evangeline 805772818620 (UK).
Compilation. 'Long Long Time'; 'Little Mama'; 'Don't You Write Her Off'; 'Surrender To Me'; 'Backstage Pass'; 'Stopping Traffic'; 'Feelin' Higher'; 'Sad Boy'; 'Release Me Girl'; 'Bye Bye Baby'; 'Who Taught The Night'; 'One More Chance'; 'Won't Let You Down'; 'Street Talk'; 'City'; 'Skate Date'; 'Givin' Herself Away'; 'Deeper In'; 'Painted Fire'; 'Let Me Down Easy'; 'Mean Streets'; 'Entertainment'; 'Soul Shoes'; 'Between You And Me'; 'Angel'; 'Love Me Tonight'; 'King For A Night'; 'A Secret Side Of You'; 'Ain't No Money'; 'Turn Your Radio On'; 'Making Movies'; 'Surrender To Me'; 'Little Girl'; 'I Love Her'.
This 2 CD compilation contains all previously released McGuinn, Clark & Hillman recordings.
Released January 2008 (UK).

In September 2007, the song 'Fair And Tender Ladies' from a McGuinn/Clark concert at New York's Bottom Line in 1977 was premiered on McGuinn's website, the Folk Den.

As McGuinn/Hillman:
McGuinn/Hillman Capitol SOO 12108 (US)/Capitol EA ST 12108 (UK).
'Mean Streets'; 'Entertainment'; 'Soul Shoes'; 'Between You And Me'; 'Angel'; 'Love Me Tonight'; 'King For A Night'; 'A Secret Side Of You'; 'Ain't No Money'; 'Turn Your Radio On'.
Released September 1980 (US)/October 1980 (UK).

In addition to the above, McGuinn has also appeared on the City Surfers' single 'Beach Ball' b/w 'Sun Tan Baby' and played on several guitar and banjo albums: *The 5-String Story* (Delyse Envoy VOY 9158), *The 12-String Story* (Delyse Envoy VOY 9159), *The 12-String Story* (London SH-F 8285), *The Twelve String Story Volume 1* (Horizon WP 1626), *The Twelve String Story Volume 2* (Horizon WP 1635), *Feuding Banjos* (Olympic 7105), *Anthology Of The Banjo* (Bellaphon BJS 4036), *Anthology Of The 12-String Guitar* (Bellaphon BJS 4044), *Anthology Of The Blues Guitar* (Everest TR 2071) and *5-String Banjo Greats* (Liberty LRP 3357). These were subsequently repackaged and reissued on countless labels during the CD age.

He has also appeared on the Various Artistes' album *Acoustic Aid* (Oxymoron 9851), the tribute album to Arthur Alexander, *Adios Amigo* (Demon FIEND 754), *30th Anniversary Tribute To Bob Dylan* (Columbia

47400), the collections *2 Up Presents Country* and *Radiomafia Guests*, the compilation *The Harry Smith Connection: A Live Tribute To The Anthology Of American Folk Music* (Smithsonian Folkways Recordings 88247) on which he collaborates with Wilco's Jeff Tweedy and Jay Bennett on 'East Virginia Blues', the Various Artistes 3 CD box set *107.1 KGSR Broadcasts Vol. 8* (KGSR 8) which features a live version of 'James Alley Blues', *Live At The World Café Volume 14 – The Next Decade* (World Café Records XP1014) on which he performs 'Eight Miles High' live, plus the tribute album *Beautiful Dreamer – The Songs Of Stephen Foster* (American Roots Publishing/Emergent 519692-2) featuring 'Jeannie With The Light Brown Hair'. A version of 'East Virginia' is also performed on 2005's *True Folk* (Folk Alliance FAT FCC001). A new version of 'Up To Me' was included on the giveaway album *Dylan Covered*, available with the September 2005 issue of the UK's *Mojo* music magazine. There is a rare collaboration with Calexico performing 'One More Cup Of Coffee' on the soundtrack to the film *I'm Not There* (Columbia 8869712038) and an appearance on the tribute *My Favorite Martin – Legendary Guitarists Playing Legendary Guitars*. McGuinn also appears on Barry McGuire's new version of 'Eve Of Destruction' on the download collection, *Peace Through Music*. McGuinn has also re-recorded 'Turn! Turn! Turn! for inclusion in the film *The Song* and its accompanying soundtrack, *The Song Album*. Readers keen to see the cover artwork and track listings for most of these rarities are advised to view the website Byrdsflyte run by Raoul Verolleman.

McGuinn has also appeared as a contributor on records by the following artistes: Hoyt Axton (*The Balladeer; Greenback Dollar; Saturday's Child*), Judy Collins (*Judy Collins 3*), Bobby Darin (*Earthy!; 18 Yellow Roses; The Capitol Years; As Long As I'm Singing – The Bobby Darin Collection*), the Irish Ramblers (*The Patriot Game*), Theodore Bikel (*A Folksinger's Choice*), David Hemmings (*Happens*), Bob Gibson (*Bob Gibson*), Charles Lloyd (*Waves*), Skip Battin (*Skip*), Earl Scruggs (*Earl Scruggs Revue; Anniversary Special Volume; Super Jammin'*), Gene Clark (*Roadmaster; Flying High*), Bob Dylan (*Pat Garrett & Billy The Kid; Bob Dylan Live 1975 – The Rolling Thunder Revue – The Bootleg Series Volume 5*), Kinky Friedman (*Lasso From El Paso*), Bo Diddley (*The 20th Anniversary Of Rock 'n' Roll*), the Beach Boys (*The Beach Boys Love You; Made In The USA; Still Crusin'; Summer In Paradise*), Susan Lynch (*Big Reward*), Vern Gosdin (*There Is A Season*), Peter Case (*Peter Case*), Crowded House (*I Feel Possessed*, EP; *Weather With You*, EP), Elvis Costello (*Spike*), the Nitty Gritty Dirt Band (*Will The Circle Be Unbroken, Vol 2; Nitty Gritty Dirt Band & Roger McGuinn Live),* the Headlights (*Earthbound*), Crosby, Stills & Nash (*Live It Up*), the Simpsons (*The Simpsons Sing The Blues*), Willie Nile (*Places I Have Never Been*), Tom Petty & The Heartbreakers (*Into The Great Wide Open*), Aimee Mann (*Whatever*), Leon Redbone (*Whistling In The Wind*), the Kennedys (*Life Is Large*), Randy Scruggs (*Crown Of Jewels*), Mary Lou Lord (*Got No Shadow*), Al Perkins (*Snapshots*), Bruce Kula (*Ars Gratia Whatever*), Dolly Parton (*Those Were The Days*), Bruce Springsteen And The E Street Band (*Magic Tour Highlights*, EP),

Edward Rogers (*You Haven't Been Where I've Been*) and Will Dailey (*Fashion Of Distraction*, EP). The 2015 archival album, *Bottom Line Archive Series, In Their Own Words,* credited to Pete Seeger and Roger McGuinn with Vin Scelsa, features a recording from New York's Bottom Line on 18 May 1994 with Scelsa introducing Seeger and McGuinn, talking and playing songs from their back pages.

Folk Den Recordings

McGuinn's discography is complicated by the existence of the Folk Den, an online site that enables downloads. Below is a chronological list of all the songs available since its inception in November 1995 to the cut off point of this discography in December 2016. The songs were invariably premiered on the first day of the month, with the exception of 'Engine 143' which was made available on 28 February 2014. A number of these songs were released in the marketplace (see under 'Solo And Post-Byrds Recordings' earlier in this discography).

11/95 'Old Paint'
12/95 'Virgin Mary'
1/96 'The Argonaut'
2/96 'John Riley'
3/96 'To Morrow'
4/96 'Easter'
5/96 'Springfield Mountain'
6/96 'Buffalo Skinners'
7/96 'New York Girls'
8/96 'Cold Coast Of Greenland'
9/96 'Tribute To Bob Gibson'
10/96 'Lost Jimmy Whelan'
11/96 'Golden Vanity'
12/96 'What Child Is This'
1/97 'In The Evenin''
2/97 'Alberta'
3/97 'Sailor Lad'
4/97 'Brisbane Ladies'
5/97 'Wayfaring Stranger'
6/97 'East Virginia'
7/97 'This Train'
8/97 'South Australia'
9/97 'Go To Sea Once More'
10/97 'Wild Goose'
11/97 'Wagoner's Lad'
12/97 'Mary Had A Baby'
1/98 'The Cold Cold Coast Of Greenland'
2/98 'Brandy Leave Me Alone'
3/98 'Finnegan's Wake'
4/98 'Bound To Australia'
5/98 'The Handsome Cabin Boy'
6/98 'The James Alley Blues'
7/98 'Pushboat'
8/98 'John Henry'
9/98 'Home On The Range'
10/98 'Mighty Day'
11/98 'John The Revelator'
12/98 'The Bonny Ship The Diamond'
1/99 'The Brazos River'
2/99 '900 Miles'
3/99 'Old Texas'
4/99 'Blood Red Roses'
5/99 'Alabama Bound'
6/99 'Liverpool Gals'
7/99 'Get Along Little Doggies'
8/99 'Trouble In Mind'
9/99 'Sail Away Lady'
10/99 'Fair Nottamun Town'
11/99 'Ain't No Mo' Cane On De Brasis'
12/99 'I Saw Three Ships'
1/00 'Auld Lang Syne'
2/00 'Greenland Whale Fisheries'
3/00 'Dink's Song'

4/00 'Lilly Of The West'
5/00 'Kilgary Mountain'
6/00 'Willie Moore'
7/00 'Star Spangled Banner'
8/00 'The Cruel War'
9/00 'Cumberland Mountain Bear Chase'
10/00 'Coffee Grows On White Oak Trees'
11/00 'Makes A Long Time Man Feel Bad'
12/00 'The Twelve Days Of Christmas'
1/01 'Stewball'
2/01 'The Riddle Song'
3/01 'Catch The Greenland Whale'
4/01 'The Colorado Trail'
5/01 'The House Of The Rising Sun'
6/01 'The Water Is Wide'
7/01 'Nancy Whiskey'
8/01 'Bring Me A Little Water, Sylvie'
9/01 'Streets Of Laredo'
10/01 'America For Me'
11/01 'Battle Hymn Of The Republic'
12/01 'I Heard The Bells On Christmas Day'
1/02 'Waltzing Matilda'
2/02 'Spanish Is The Loving Tongue'
3/02 'Roddy McCorley'
4/02 'Rock Island Line'
5/02 'Michael Row The Boat Ashore'
6/02 'Tarrytown'
7/02 'All My Trials'
8/02 'Delia's Gone'
9/02 'Railroad Bill'
10/02 'Wildwood Flower'
11/02 'I Am A Pilgrim'
12/02 'Away In A Manger'
1/03 'When The Saints Go Marching In'
2/03 'St James Infirmary'
3/03 'Pretty Saro'
4/03 'Wild Mountain Thyme'
5/03 '12 Gates To The City'
6/03 'Squid-Jigging Ground'
7/03 'He's Got The Whole World In His Hands'
8/03 'Go Tell Aunt Rhodie'
9/03 'Shenandoah'
10/03 'Banks Of Ohio'
11/03 'Heave Away'
12/03 'We Wish You A Merry Christmas'
1/04 'The Gallows Pole'
2/04 'Silver Dagger'
3/04 'Drunken Sailor'
4/04 'Ezekiel Saw A Wheel'
5/04 'Gypsy Rover'
6/04 'Salty Dog Blues'
7/04 'Down By The Riverside'
8/04 'Haul Away Joe'
9/04 'Oh Freedom'
10/04 'Spanish Ladies'
11/04 'The John B's Sails'
12/04 'The First Noël'
1/05 'Cindy'
2/05 'Let The Bullgine Run'
3/05 'Follow The Drinking Gourd'
4/05 'Wanderin''
5/05 'So Early In The Spring'
6/05 'Old Riley'
7/05 'On Top Of Old Smokey'
8/05 'Erie Canal'
9/05 'Red River Valley'
10/05 'There's A Hole In The Bucket'
10/05 'Ruben Ranzo'
11/05 'Oh Mary Don't You Weep'
12/05 'Children Go Where I Send Thee'
1/06 'St Clair's Defeat'
2/06 'Mary Had A Little Lamb'
3/06 'Wade In The Water'
4/06 'Greensleeves'
5/06 'Molly Malone'
6/06 'Pretty Polly'
7/06 'Katie Morey'
8/06 'Every Time I Feel The Spirit'
9/06 'Perry's Victory'
10/06 'Whup Jamboree'

11/06 'Housewife's Lament'
12/06 'Joy To The World'
1/07 'This Little Light Of Mine'
2/07 'The House Carpenter'
3/07 'The Great Silkie Of Sule Skerry'
4/07 'Glory, Glory'
5/07 'The Butcher's Boy'
6/07 'King Kong Kitchie Kitchie Ki Me O'
7/07 'The Coo Coo'
8/07 'Sugar Baby'
9/07 'Fair And Tender Ladies'
10/07 'The Ballad Of The Boll Weevil'
11/07 'Old Blue'
12/07 'O Come All Ye Faithful'
1/08 'Away Rio'
2/08 'Old Joe Clark'
3/08 'Blow The Man Down'
4/08 'Cripple Creek'
5/08 'Come And Go With Me To That Land'
6/08 'I Know Where I'm Going'
7/08 'Going Down The Road Feeling Bad'
8/08 'Skip To My Lou'
9/08 'Darlin' Corey'
10/08 'Joshua Fit The Battle Of Jericho'
11/08 '500 Miles'
12/08 'Go Tell It To The Mountain'
1/09 'No Payday In Detroit'
2/09 'Nobody Knows You When You're Down And Out'
3/09 'My Home's Across The Smokey Mountains'
4/09 'Old Plank Road'
5/09 'Dry Bones'
6/09 'A Roving'
7/09 'Old Chisholm Trail'
8/09 'When I First Came To This Land'
9/09 'Drill Ye Tarriers'
10/09 'I'll Fly Away'
11/09 'Frozen Logger'
12/09 'Christmas Is Coming'
1/10 'Take This Hammer'
2/10 'Randy Dandy Oh'
3/10 'She Never Will Marry'
4/10 'Black Mountain Rag'/'Soldier's Joy'
5/10 'Big Rock Candy Mountain'
6/10 'All The Pretty Little Horses'
7/10 'I'm On My Way'
8/10 'Whoa Back Buck'
9/10 'Rolling Down To Old Maui'
10/10 'Pay Me My Money Down'
11/10 'The Bears Went Over The Mountain'
12/10 'Back To Sea'
1/11 'Barbara Allen'
2/11 'Henry Martin'
3/11 'Polly Vaughn'
4/11 'The Squirrel'
5/11 'To Welcome Poor Paddy Home'
6/11 'Leave Her Johnny Leave Her'
7/11 'Paul & Silas'
8/11 'The Coast Of Peru'
9/11 'Bury Me Not On The Lone Prairie'
10/11 'Black Is The Color Of My True Love's Hair'
11/11 'The Cobbler'
12/11 'God Rest Ye Merry Gentlemen'
1/12 'Eddystone Light'
2/12 'Titanic'
3/12 'Paddy West'
4/12 'Let My People Go!'
5/12 'Down In The Valley'
6/12 'When Jones's Ale Was New'
7/12 'Jacob's Dream'
8/12 'Isn't She Grand'
9/12 'Give Me Oil In My Lamp'
10/12 'Darling Clementine'
11/12 'Away With Rum'
12/12 'We Three Kings'
1/13 'John Hardy'
2/13 'Banks Of Newfoundland'
3/13 'The Moonshiner'
4/13 'Swing Low Sweet Chariot'

5/13 'Early One Morning'
6/13 'We Are Crossing The Jordan River'
7/13 'I've Been Working On The Railroad'
8/13 'I Heard The Voice Of Jesus'
9/13 'Jimmy Brown'
10/13 'Swannanoa Tunnel'
11/13 'She'll Be Coming Round The Mountain'
12/13 'It Came Upon A Midnight Clear'
1/14 'The Month Of January'
2/14 'Winter's Almost Gone'
2/14 'Engine 143'
4/14 'The Lazy Farmer Boy'
5/14 'Take A Drink On Me'
6/14 'Peg & Awl'
7/14 'Hard Times Of Old England'
8/14 'Tell Old Gil'
9/14 'Risselty Rosselty Now Now Now'
10/14 'Henry Lee'
11/14 'Little Moses'
12/14 'The Cherry Tree Carol'
1/15 'The Ash Grove'
2/15 'Paddy And The Whale'
3/15 'The Crawdad Song'
4/15 'The Rainbow'
5/15 'Acres Of Clams'
6/15 'Yellow Rose Of Texas' [new version]
7/15 'The Eclipse'
8/15 'Cold Rain And Snow'
9/15 'The Blackest Crow'
10/15 'Nine Pound Hammer'
11/15 'There's A Meetin' Here Tonight'
12/15 'Angels We Have Heard On High'
1/16 'The Fatal Flower Garden'
2/16 'February Song'
3/16 'This Old Man'
4/16 'Joy, Joy, Joy, Joy, Down In My Heart'
5/16 'My Bonnie Lies Over The Ocean'
6/16 'The Dodger Song'
7/16 'The Belle Of Belfast City'
8/16 'Deep Blue Sea'
9/16 'Lonesome Valley'
10/16 'Blue Tail Fly'
11/16 'The Farmer In The Dell'
12/16 'One Horse Open Sleigh'

Several of the above titles are spelt or punctuated slightly differently on the many Folk Den record/CD/MP3 releases. Note that two songs were featured in October 2005.

GENE CLARK

Albums with the New Christy Minstrels:
Today Columbia CL 2159/CS 8959 (US).
'Company Of Cowards'; 'This Ol' Riverboat'; 'Love Theme'; 'Whistlin' Dixie'; 'Anything Love Can Buy'; 'Ladies'; 'Charleston Town'; 'Company Q Whistle March'; 'Way Down In Arkansas'; 'Brackenby's Music Box'; 'Riverboat Theme'; 'Today'.
Released: March 1964 (US).

Land Of Giants Columbia CL 2187/CS 8987 (US).
'Land Of Giants'; 'Joe Magarac'; 'John Henry And The Steam Drill'; 'Paul Bunyan'; 'Casey Jones'; 'Stormy'; 'Mighty Big Ways'; 'Mount Rushmore';

'Blacksmith Of Brandywine'; 'Natural Man'; 'Appleseed John'; 'El Camino Real'; 'My Name Is Liberty'.
Released July 1964 (US)

Although he is pictured on the sleeve of the New Christy Minstrels' *Merry Christmas!* (Columbia CL 2096/CS 8896 US/CBS (S)BPG 62287 UK) the recording was completed immediately before his induction. *Land Of Giants* was recorded at the beginning of December 1963 but was not issued until the following summer, long after Clark had left. Confusingly, *Today* was recorded from 21–24 January 1964, well after *Land Of Giants*, but was issued four months before its successor. There is still some doubt whether Clark managed to attend the three-day *Today* sessions, so quickly were they executed. He left the New Christy Minstrels approximately six weeks after the *Today* recordings. He does contribute to the soundtrack of the film, *Advance To The Rear*.

Albums with the Byrds:
See Discography *Volume 1* under the following sections: *Byrds Singles, Albums, Compilations* and *Archival Albums* for fuller details of release dates, complete track listings, alternate serial numbers, special issues/editions, and more.

Mr Tambourine Man Columbia CL 2372 (mono)/Columbia CS 9172 (stereo) (US). CBS BPG 62571 (mono)/CBS SBPG 62571 (stereo) (UK). Remastered CD edition with bonus tracks: Columbia Legacy CK 64845 (US)/Columbia Legacy 483705 2 (UK).

Turn! Turn! Turn! Columbia CL 2454 (mono)/Columbia CS 9254 (stereo) (US). CBS BPG 62652 (mono)/CBS SBPG 62652 (stereo) (UK). Remastered CD edition with bonus tracks: Columbia Legacy CK 64846 (US)/Columbia Legacy 483706 2 (UK).

Fifth Dimension Columbia CL 2549 (mono)/Columbia CS 9349 (stereo) (US). CBS BPG 62783 (mono)/CBS SBPG 62783 (stereo) (UK). Remastered CD edition with bonus tracks: Columbia Legacy CK 64847(US)/Columbia Legacy 483707 2 (UK).

Byrds Asylum SD 5058 (US)/Asylum SYLA 8754 (UK).

Archival albums with the Byrds:
Preflyte Together ST-T-1001 (US)/Bumble GEXP 8001 (UK).
The Original Singles Volume 1 1965–1967 CBS 31851 (UK)/Columbia FC 37335 (US).
Never Before Re-Flyte MH 70318 (US).
In The Beginning Rhino R2 70244 (US).
Sanctuary Sundazed LP 5061 (US).
The Preflyte Sessions Sundazed SC 11116 (US).
The Columbia Singles '65–'67 Sundazed LP 5130/P2 55624 (US).
Another Dimension Sundazed SEP 2 10-168 (US)
Preflyte [extended version] Floating World FLOATD6122 (UK).

Box Sets with the Byrds:

The Byrds Columbia Legacy 46773 (US)/Columbia Legacy 4676112 (UK).
12 Dimensions The Columbia Recordings 1965–1972 (13-CD box set) Columbia 497610 2/4976102000 (UK).
There Is A Season (4-CD box set and DVD) Columbia/Legacy 82876877002 (US/UK).
The Complete Columbia Albums Collection Columbia Legacy 886978738028 (US).

Isolated appearances with the Byrds:

See *Volume 1* under *Archival Albums* and *Guest Slots/Rarities* for fuller details of release dates and alternate serial numbers.

Early LA Together ST-T-1014 (US).
Roadmaster A&M 87584 (Holland).
3 Byrds Land In London 1977 Strange Fruit SFRSCD 001 (UK).
3 Byrds In London 1977 – Live At The BBC Mastertone 8228 (US).
Byrd Parts Raven RVCD 77 (Australia).
Byrd Parts 2 Raven RVCD 165 (Australia).
Sixties Transition Sierra SXCD 6027 (US)/Floating World FLOATM6125 (UK).

The original Byrds line-up, albeit not together at the same session, performed two songs on *Roadmaster*: 'She's The Kind Of Girl' and 'One In A Hundred'. This album was for many years only available as a Dutch import (A&M 87584 IT). Previously issued material also appears on the soundtracks to *Homer* and *Forrest Gump* and the Elektra compilations mentioned earlier.

Compilations/Hits Collections with the Byrds:

See *Volume 1* for additional details.
The Byrds Greatest Hits Columbia CL 2716 (US)/CBS SBPG 63107 (UK).
The Byrds Greatest Hits Volume 2 CBS S 64650 (UK).
Best Of Volume 2 Columbia C31795 (US).
History Of The Byrds CBS 68242 (UK).
Return Of The Byrds Columbia Realm 2V 8006-7 (US).
The Byrds CBS 88320 (UK).
The Byrds Play Dylan Columbia PC 36293 (US)/CBS 31795 (UK).
The Very Best Of The Byrds Columbia CS P-P2 17596 (US).
The Byrds Collection Castle Communications CCSLP 151 (UK).
The Very Best Of The Byrds Columbia CBS 4634189 2 (Holland/UK).
Full Flyte Raven RVCD 10 (Australia).
Free Flyte Sony Music Special Products A 17733 (US).
Greatest Hits Remastered Columbia 467843 2 (UK).
20 Essential Tracks From The Boxed Set: 1965–1970 Columbia/Legacy CK 47884/471665-2 (US/UK).
Definitive Collection Columbia 480548 9 (UK).

Nashville West Sony Music Special Products A 28123 (US).
The Very Best Of The Byrds Columbia 487995 2 (UK).
The Best Of The Byrds Columbia 488146 2 (UK).
Super Hits Columbia Legacy 504725 2 (UK)/Columbia Legacy CK 65637 (US).
The Byrds Greatest Hits Columbia/Legacy CK 66230 (US).
The Byrds Sony Music Special Products A 30827 (US).
The Byrds Play The Songs Of Bob Dylan Columbia 501946 2 (UK).
The Byrds Play Dylan Columbia/Legacy CK 85430 (US).
The Essential Byrds Columbia Legacy 512249 2 (UK)/Columbia Legacy C2K 89110 (US).
Mojo Presents . . . An Introduction To The Byrds – 24 Classic Songs Columbia 512778 2 (UK).
Mr Tambourine Man – The Best Of The Byrds Sony Music Media SMM 516489-2 (Germany/UK).
America's Great National Treasure Sony/BMG A 96086 (US).
The Very Best Of The Byrds Sony/BMG 82876 855142 (UK).
Byrds: A Collection Sony BMG 88697 12448 2 (UK).
The Byrds Play Dylan Sony BMG 88697 25267 2 (UK).
Playlist: The Very Best Of The Byrds Columbia Legacy 88697 39219 2 (US).
Steel Box Sony BMG 88697 459812 (UK).
Eight Miles High – The Best Of The Byrds Sony/Camden 88697 63627 2 (UK).
Turn! Turn! Turn!: The Ultimate Collection Sony/Columbia Music 88875 151652 (UK).
The 60s – The Byrds Sony Music 8888377667 2 (US).

Solo and post-Byrd recordings:

Gene Clark With The Gosdin Brothers Columbia CL 2618/CS 9418 (US)/CBS 62934 (UK).
'Echoes'; 'Think I'm Gonna Feel Better'; 'Tried So Hard'; 'Is Yours Is Mine'; 'Keep On Pushin''; 'I Found You'; 'So You Say You Lost Your Baby'; 'Elevator Operator'; 'The Same One'; 'Couldn't Believe Her'; 'Needing Someone'.
Released February 1967 (US)/April 1967 (UK). Reissued on Edsel Records on CD in June 1997. See later in this section for the Sundazed extended reissue.

White Light A&M SD 4292 (US)/AMLS 64292 (UK).
'The Virgin'; 'With Tomorrow'; 'White Light'; 'Because Of You'; 'One In A Hundred'; 'For A Spanish Guitar'; 'Where My Love Lies Asleep'; 'Tears Of Rage'; '1975'.
Released August 1971 (US)/November 1971 (UK).

Early LA Sessions Columbia KC 31123 (US).
'Tried So Hard'; 'Keep On Pushin''; 'Think I'm Gonna Feel Better'; 'Is Yours Is Mine'; 'Echoes'; 'The Same One'; 'Needing Someone'; 'So You Say You Lost Your Baby'; 'Couldn't Believe Her'; 'I Found You'.

This was a completely re-produced version of Clark's first solo album, with additional vocals, tracks resequenced and 'Elevator Operator' deleted. Released July 1972 (US).

Roadmaster A&M 87584 IT (Holland)/Edsel ED 198 (UK).
'She's The Kind Of Girl'; 'One In A Hundred'; 'Here Tonight'; 'Full Circle Song'; 'In A Misty Morning'; 'Rough And Rocky'; 'Roadmaster'; 'I Really Don't Want To Know'; 'I Remember The Railroad'; 'She Don't Care About Time'; 'Shooting Star'.
Archival compilation of unissued studio material.
Released January 1973 (Holland)/October 1986 (UK).

American Dreamer Soundtrack Mediarts 41-12 (US).
Clark contributed two tracks to the soundtrack: 'Outlaw Song' and 'American Dreamer'.
Released 1971.

No Other Asylum 7E-1016 (US)/Asylum SYL 9020 (UK).
'Life's Greatest Fool'; 'Silver Raven'; 'No Other'; 'Strength Of Strings'; 'From A Silver Phial'; 'Some Understanding'; 'The True One'; 'Lady Of The North'.
Released September 1974 (US)/January 1975 (UK). See later in this section for details of Warners' extended reissue.

Two Sides To Every Story RSO RS-1-3011 (US)/RSO 2394 176 (UK).
'Home Run King'; 'Lonely Saturday'; 'In The Pines'; 'Kansas City Southern'; 'Give My Love To Marie'; 'Sister Moon'; 'Marylou'; 'Hear The Wind'; 'Past Addresses'; 'Silent Crusade'.
Released February 1977 (US)/March 1977 (UK). See later in this section for details of High Moon's extended reissue.

The Farmer HM 1001 (US).
Film soundtrack. Includes two Clark contributions 'American Dreamer' and 'Outside The Law' ['Outlaw Song'], both different takes.
Released *c.* 1977.

Firebyrd Takoma 7112 (US)/Making Waves SPIN 122 (UK).
'Tambourine Man'; 'Something About You Baby'; 'Rodeo Rider'; 'Rain Song'; 'Vanessa'; 'If You Could Read My Mind'; 'Feel A Whole Lot Better'; 'Made For Love'; 'Blue Raven'.
Released March 1984 (US)/1987 (UK). The UK edition was originally scheduled for August 1986, but the release was delayed when Making Waves went into receivership.

Echoes Columbia/Legacy CK 48523 (US).
Compilation. 'Boston'; 'For Me Again'; 'I Knew I'd Want You'; 'Here Without You'; 'Set You Free This Time'; 'If You're Gone'; ' Is Yours Is Mine'; 'So You Say You Lost Your Baby'; 'Tried So Hard'; 'Needing Someone'; 'Echoes'; 'The Same One'; 'Couldn't Believe Her'; 'Keep On Pushin''; 'I Found You'; 'Elevator Operator'; 'Think I'm Gonna Feel Better'; 'The French

Girl'; 'Only Colombe'; 'So You Say You Lost Your Baby'. Includes the previously unreleased 'The French Girl' and 'Only Colombe', plus a fascinating demo outtake of 'So You Say You Lost Your Baby'.
Released September 1991 (US).

American Dreamer 1964–1974 Raven RVCD 21 (Australia).
Compilation. Includes a previously unreleased mix of 'Full Circle' and the rare 'American Dreamer' and 'Outlaw Song'.
Released February 1993 (Australia).

This Byrd Has Flown Edsel EDCD 436 (UK).
Compilation. 'Tambourine Man'; 'Vanessa'; 'Rain Song'; 'C'est La Bonne Rue'; 'If You Could Read My Mind'; 'Dixie Flyer'; 'Feel A Whole Lot Better'; 'Rodeo Rider'; 'All I Want'; 'Something About You'; 'Made For Love'; 'Blue Raven'.
Essentially a revamped version of Firebyrd with tracks resequenced and three previously unavailable tracks: 'C'est La Bonne Rue', 'Dixie Flyer' and 'All I Want'.
Released July 1995 (UK).

Flying High A&M 540 725-2 (UK).
2 CD set. Disc 1: 'You Showed Me'; 'Feel A Whole Lot Better'; 'Set You Free This Time'; 'She Don't Care About Time'; 'Tried So Hard'; 'So You Say You Lost Your Baby'; 'The French Girl'; 'Los Angeles'; 'I Pity The Poor Immigrant'; 'That's Alright By Me'; 'Train Leaves Here This Morning'; 'Why Not Your Baby'; 'The Radio Song'; 'Git It On Brother'; 'Something's Wrong'; 'Wall Around Your Heart'; 'No Longer A Sweetheart Of Mine'; 'Through The Morning, Through The Night'; 'Kansas City Southern'; 'Polly'; 'Dark Hollow'; 'One In A Hundred'; 'She's The Kind Of Girl'.
Disc 2: 'With Tomorrow'; 'For A Spanish Guitar'; 'The Virgin'; 'Opening Day'; 'Winter In'; 'The American Dreamer'; 'Full Circle Song'; 'In A Misty Morning'; 'I Remember The Railroad'; 'Silver Raven'; 'The True One'; 'Lady Of The North'; 'Hear The Wind'; 'Silent Crusade'; 'Past Addresses'; 'Fair And Tender Ladies'; 'Changes'; 'Mr Tambourine Man'.
This compilation featured seven previously unreleased songs: 'Los Angeles', 'I Pity The Poor Immigrant', 'That's Alright By Me', 'Wall Around Your Heart', 'Dark Hollow', 'Opening Day' and 'Winter In'.
Released September 1998 (UK).

Gene Clark With The Gosdin Brothers Sundazed LP 5062 (US).
Reissue of the original album on 180 gram vinyl, complete with bonus tracks: 'Only Colombe' (at the end of side 1) and 'The French Girl' and 'So You Say You Lost Your Baby' (demo) appended to side 2.
Released July 2000 (US). The later CD version included the following bonus tracks: 'Tried So Hard', 'Elevator Operator' (both previously unissued alternate versions), 'Only Colombe' and 'The French Girl' (previously unissued mono versions, the former with more prominent backing vocals), 'So You Say You Lost Your Baby' and 'Is Yours Is Mine' (both acoustic demos).

Gypsy Angel Evangeline GEL 4030 (UK).
'Pledge To You'; 'Mississippi Detention Camp'; 'Kathleen'; 'Rock Of Ages'; 'The Last Thing On My Mind'; 'Dark Of My Moon'; 'Your Fire Burning'; 'Freedom Walk'; 'Love Wins Again'; 'Back In My Life Again'; 'Day For Night'; 'Gypsy Rider'.
Released July 2001 (UK).

Under The Silvery Moon Delta Deluxe 47 06768 (UK).
'Mary Sue'; 'Carry On'; 'Don't You Know'; 'You Just Love Cocaine'; 'Dancing On The Moon'; 'Nothing But An Angel'; 'More Than That Now'; 'Liona'; 'Washington Square'; 'My Marie'; 'With You I Can't Lose'; 'Fair And Tender Ladies'; 'Sleep Will Return'; 'Immigrant Girl'; 'Dangerous Games'; 'Rest Of Your Life'; 'You Better Move On'; 'Deportee'; 'Almost Saturday Night'; 'When Jokers Are Wild'; 'The Panther'; 'Gypsy Rider'; 'Del Gato'; 'You Better Move On'; 'The Hurting Game'; 'That Part Of You'; 'Dragon's Eye'; 'Can't Say No'; 'Will You Still Love Me Tomorrow?'.
Released scheduled 3 September 2001 (UK). 2 CD set withdrawn prior to release.

White Light Universal/A&M 493 209-2 (UK).
Original album, plus CD bonus tracks: 'Because Of You' (alternate mix); 'Stand By Me'; 'Ship Of The Lord'; 'Opening Day'; 'Winter In'.
Released July 2002 (UK).

Under The Silvery Moon Delta Deluxe 47 23839 (UK).
'Mary Sue'; 'Carry On'; 'Don't You Know'; 'Nothing But An Angel'; 'More Than That Now'; 'Sleep Will Return'; 'Will You Still Love Me Tomorrow'; 'Immigrant Girl'; 'Rest Of Your Life'; 'My Marie'; 'Fair And Tender Ladies'; 'Can't Say No'; 'Dangerous Games'; 'You Just Love Cocaine'.
Released December 2003 (UK).

No Other Warner Strategic Marketing 8122 73701-2 (UK).
Original album, plus CD bonus tracks: 'Train Leaves Here This Morning'; 'Life's Greatest Fool' (alternate take); 'Silver Raven' (alternate take); 'No Other' (alternate take); 'From A Silver Phial' (alternate take); ' Some Misunderstanding' (alternate take); 'Lady Of The North' (alternate take).
Released August 2003 (UK).

Silverado '75 Collectors' Choice CCC-924 (US).
'Long Black Veil'; 'Kansas City Southern'; 'For A Spanish Guitar'; 'Home Run King'; 'Here Without You'; 'No Other'; 'Daylight Line'; 'Set You Free This Time'; 'She Darked The Sun'; 'In The Pines'; 'Train Leaves Here This Morning'; 'Silver Raven'. (Subtitled *Live & Unreleased* on the front sleeve only).
Released April 2008 (US).

Here Tonight – The White Light Demos Omnivore OVLP/OVCD 60 (US).
'White Light'; 'Here Tonight'; 'For No One'; 'For A Spanish Guitar'; 'Please Mr Freud'; 'Jimmy Christ'; 'Where My Love Lies Asleep'; 'The Virgin';

'Opening Day'; 'Winter In'; 'Because Of You'; 'With Tomorrow'.
Released March 2013 (US).

Two Sides To Every Story High Moon HMRCD-02 (US).
Original album, plus download cards for the following:
'Life's Greatest Fool'; 'The True One'; 'Radio Song'; 'Silver Raven'; 'No Other'; 'In The Pines'; 'Hear The Wind'; '(I'll) Feel A Whole Lot Better'; 'I'll Be Back'; 'She Darked The Sun'; 'Kansas City Southern'; 'From A Silver Phial'; 'Home Run King'; 'Sister Moon'; 'Daylight Line'. All of the above were from Ebbet's Field, Denver, Colorado, October 1975. (The track listing erroneously places 'No Other' before 'Silver Raven'. It is corrected here above).
'What Is Meant Will Be'; 'Wheel Of Time'; 'Some Misunderstanding'; 'She Don't Care About Time'. The above are from Mother Blues, Dallas, Texas, 24 May 1975. 'I Saw A Dream Come True', live at the Tango, 1984, plus a 1974 interview with Gene Clark by DJ B. Mitchel Reed.
Released April 2013 (US). Deluxe Edition: November 2014 (US).

The Lost Studio Sessions 1964–1982 Sierra SACD 2201/SHF 2101 (vinyl) (US).
1964 Solo Sessions: 'The Way I Am'; 'I'd Feel Better'; 'That Girl'; 'A Worried Heart'; 'If There's No Love'.
Hugh Masekela Sessions 1967: 'Back Street Mirror'; 'Don't Let It Fall Through'.
1969–1970 Solo Sessions: 'Back To The Earth Again'; 'The Lighthouse'; 'The Awakening Within'; 'Sweet Adrienne'; 'Walking Through This Lifetime'; 'The Sparrow'; 'Only Yesterday's Gone'.
Gene Clark With The Flying Burrito Brothers: 'She Darked The Sun'.
1972 Sessions: 'Roll In My Sweet Baby's Arms'; 'She Don't Care About Time'; 'Don't This Road Look (Rough And Rocky)'; 'Bars Have Made A Prisoner Out Of Me'.
1982 Nyteflyte Sessions: 'One Hundred Years From Now'; 'The Letter'; 'Still Feeling Blue'; 'No Memories Hangin' Round'; '(I'll) Feel A Whole Lot Better'.
Bonus CD: 'The Virgin'; 'She's The Kind Of Girl'; '1975'; 'One In A Hundred'. Plus extra bonus CD for subscribers: 'All For Him' and 'Why Can't I Have Her Back Again'.
The 'Ultimate Limited Edition Complete Set' features a 180-gram, 2-LP vinyl set; 24 -track hybrid CD/SACD; 1985 Gene Clark DVD interview; holographic numbered vinyl double album and hybrid CD/SACD; booklet; digital download card to MP 3 files of all 24 songs, four additional songs on the bonus CD, plus an extra CD of two songs.
Released November 2016 (US). Vinyl edition: delayed (US).

As Dillard & Clark:

The Fantastic Expedition Of Dillard & Clark A&M SD 4158 (US)/A&M AMLS 939 (UK).
'Out On The Side'; 'She Darked The Sun'; 'Don't Come Rollin''; 'Train Leaves Here This Morning'; 'With Care From Someone'; 'The Radio Song'; 'Git It On Brother (Git In Line Brother)'; 'In The Plan'; 'Something's Wrong'.
The CD version issued on Edsel (EDCD 192), added three tracks previously released on single, 'Why Not Your Baby', 'Lyin' Down The Middle' and 'Don't Be Cruel'.
Released November 1968 (US)/July 1969 (UK).

Through The Morning Through The Night A&M SD 4203 (US)/A&M AMLS 966 (UK).
'No Longer A Sweetheart Of Mine'; 'Through The Morning, Through The Night'; 'Rocky Top'; 'So Sad'; 'Corner Street Bar'; 'I Bowed My Head And Cried Holy'; 'Kansas City Southern'; 'Four Walls'; 'Polly'; 'Roll In My Sweet Baby's Arms'; 'Don't Let Me Down'. The album title does not include a comma, although the song does.
Released September 1969 (US)/February 1970 (UK).

Grass Roots A&M AMLB 51038 (UK).
This A&M UK sampler features one side each of previously released material from Dillard & Clark and the Flying Burrito Brothers.
Released October 1972 (UK).

Kansas City Southern A&M 86436 ZT (Holland).
'Lyin' Down The Middle'; 'Out On The Side'; 'Why Not Your Baby'; 'Train Leaves Here This Morning'; 'Don't Be Cruel'; 'Something's Wrong'; 'Kansas City Southern'; 'Polly'; 'Rocky Top'; 'So Sad'; 'In The Plan'; 'For A Spanish Guitar'.
This Dutch release is included here because it was the first compilation to include those three rare tracks previously only available on single: 'Why Not Your Baby', 'Lyin' Down The Middle' and 'Don't Be Cruel'.
Released 1975 (Holland).

The Fantastic Expedition Of Dillard & Clark/ Through The Morning Through The Night Mobile Fidelity Sound Lab MFCD-1-791 (US).
The two albums combined on the Mobile Fidelity CD series.
Released May 1989 (US).

As McGuinn, Clark & Hillman:

McGuinn, Clark & Hillman Capitol SW 11910 (US)/Capitol EST 11910 (UK).
'Long Long Time'; 'Little Mama'; 'Don't You Write Her Off'; 'Surrender To Me'; 'Backstage Pass'; 'Stopping Traffic'; 'Feelin' Higher'; 'Sad Boy'; 'Release Me Girl'; 'Bye Bye Baby'.
Released January 1979 (US)/March 1979 (UK). The 2001 CD reissue

features bonus demo versions of 'Surrender To Me' and the previously unreleased compositions 'Little Girl' and 'I Love Her'.

City Capitol ST 12043 (US)/Capitol EST 12043 (US).
'Who Taught The Night'; 'One More Chance'; 'Won't Let You Down'; 'Street Talk'; 'City'; 'Skate Date'; 'Givin' Herself Away'; 'Deeper In'; 'Painted Fire'; 'Let Me Down Easy'.
Released January 1980 (US)/February 1980 (UK).

Return Flight Edsel EDCD 358 (UK).
Compilation. See McGuinn section for full track listing.
Released December 1992 (UK).

Return Flight II Edsel EDCD 373 (UK).
Compilation. See McGuinn section for full track listing.
Released June 1993 (UK).

The Capitol Collection Acadia/Evangeline 805772818620 (UK).
Compilation. See McGuinn section for full track listing.
Released January 2008 (UK).

In September 2007, the song 'Fair And Tender Ladies' from a McGuinn/Clark concert at New York's Bottom Line in 1977 was premiered on McGuinn's website, the Folk Den.

As Gene Clark and Carla Olson:
So Rebellious A Lover Rhino RNLP 7083 (US)/Demon FIEND 89 (UK).
'The Drifter'; 'Gypsy Rider'; 'Every Angel In Heaven'; 'Del Gato'; 'Deportee (Plane Wreck At Los Gatos)'; 'Fair And Tender Ladies'; 'Almost Saturday Night'; 'I'm Your Toy (Hot Burrito No. 1)'; 'Are We Still Making Love'; 'Why Did You Leave Me Today'; 'Don't It Make You Wanta Go Home'. The CD version (Fiend CD 89) contains one extra track: 'Lovers Turnaround'. On the 1992 issue on Razor And Tie (RE 1992), 'Lovers Turnaround' was replaced by three recordings from late 1989: 'Number One Is To Survive', 'Mary Sue' and a live version of 'Del Gato'. In 2003, the album was reissued (Fuel 2000: 302061 354 2) with the following bonus tracks: 'Changes', 'Day For Night', 'Jokers Are Wild', 'Winning Hand', 'Lovers Turnaround' and 'Broken Hearts And Broken Dreams'.
Released April 1987 (US/UK).

Silhouetted In Light (In Concert) Demon FIEND CD 710 (UK).
'Your Fire Burning'; 'Number One Is To Survive'; 'Love Wins Again'; 'Fair And Tender Ladies'; 'Photograph'; 'Set You Free This Time'; 'Last Thing On My Mind'; 'Gypsy Rider'; 'Train Leaves Here This Morning'; 'Almost Saturday Night'; 'Del Gato'; '(I'll) Feel A Whole Lot Better'; 'She Don't Care About Time'; 'Speed Of The Sound Of Loneliness'; 'Will The Circle Be Unbroken?' The Japanese version of this CD features an additional version of 'Here Without You'.
Released February 1992 (UK).

Gene Clark With Cara Olson In Concert Collectors' Choice CCM-839 (US). 'Silver Raven'; 'Tried So Hard'; 'My Marie'; 'Rodeo Rider'; 'Gypsy Rider'; 'Train Leaves Here This Morning'; 'Hear The Wind'; 'Number One Is To Survive'; 'Mary Sue'; 'Del Gato'; 'Your Fire Burning'; 'Number One Is To Survive'; 'Love Wins Again'; 'Fair And Tender Ladies'; 'Photograph'; 'Set You Free This Time'; 'Last Thing On My Mind'; 'Gypsy Rider'; 'Train Leaves Here This Morning'; 'Almost Saturday Night'; 'Del Gato'; '(I'll) Feel A Whole Lot Better'; 'She Don't Care About Time'; 'Speed Of The Sound Of Loneliness'; 'Will The Circle Be Unbroken'; 'Here Without You'.
Released August 2008 (US).

In addition to the above Clark allegedly recorded a rare single, 'Blue Ribbons' b/w 'Artesian' with Joe Meyers & the Sharks. An extract from a tape of 'Blue Ribbons' was included in the DVD documentary *The Byrd Who Flew Alone.* Clark was once rumoured to have appeared on the Flying Burrito Brothers' single 'Tried So Hard' though this was unconfirmed by any documentation. Clark also wrote several songs never released in his lifetime but picked up by other artistes. Important early releases include 'Back Street Mirror' (originally titled 'How Hard It Would Be') which appeared on David Hemmings' *Happens* (MGM E-4490) in 1966. Clark's original was recently exhumed for the archival album, *The Lost Studio Sessions 1964–1982.*

No Clark recordings are available of 'Till Today' and 'Long Time', which ended up on the eponymous album by the Rose Garden (Atco SD 33-225) in 1968. That same year a single bearing his co-writing credit was issued by Mac McClanahan & The Rhythm Busters: 'That Nonsense Stuff' b/w 'No Sweeter Love'. Both sides were in rockabilly mode, not dissimilar stylistically to Clark's contemporaneous recording of 'Don't Be Cruel'. No further details of Clark's alleged collaboration are known. They may well be the work of a different 'Gene Clark'. BMI suggest a certain Roy Eugene Clark.

Clark also guested on records by Merry Go Round (*Merry-Go-Round*), Doug Dillard (*The Banjo Album*), Bob Lind (*Since There Were Circles*), Steve Young (*Rock, Salt And Nails*), Roger McGuinn (*Roger McGuinn*), the Flying Burrito Brothers (*Close Up The Honky Tonks; Honky Tonk Heaven*), Cooker (*Bout Time*), Primitive Future ('The Game' single), Three O'Clock (*Baroque Hoedown*), the Textones ('Midnight Mission' single; *Through The Canyon*; *Back In Time*), the Long Ryders (*Native Sons*) and Carla Olson (*Carla Olson*). Various Artiste compilations featuring Gene Clark include *Time Will Be The Wiser* (Triad TRCD 001), *True Voices* (Demon FIEND CD 165) and *Tombstone After Dark* (Demon FIEND CD 713). The Sundazed label sporadically issues previously released Clark material on single, sometimes for record store day. Among these releases are reissues of 'Echoes'/'I Found You'; the intended but never released single version of 'One In A Hundred'/'She's The Kind Of Girl'; and Dillard & Clark's 'Why Not Your Baby'/'Lyin' Down The Middle'. Finally, the archival Australian releases *Byrd Parts* Raven RVCD 77 (1998) and *Byrd Parts 2* Raven RVCD 165 (2003) are of especial interest. The first features mainly 'Byrds' family' tracks, including Clark's rare composition 'Back Street Mirror' recorded by David Hemmings. Dillard & Clark and McGuinn, Clark & Hillman are also featured. The second collection is crucial to any serious collector of Clark's work as it features the previously unavailable 'Why Can't I Have Her Back Again?' and 'If I Hang Around'.

DAVID CROSBY

Albums with Cate School Drama Society:

Cuttin' Capers Private pressing (US).
'Dear Mr Lonelyhearts'. Crosby's earliest known recording was this stage appearance in the production of *Cuttin' Capers* performed at Santa Barbara's Cate School in Carpenteria. Subtitled 'A Musical Comedy In Two Parts', it featured Crosby in the role of 'plotting student' Link Day. This was a private pressing with Crosby enjoying a distinctive lead on the aforementioned track. A selection was subsequently broadcast on TV's Biography Channel when Crosby was the subject.
Released 1958 (US).

Albums with Les Baxter Balladeers:

Jack Linkletter Presents A Folk Festival Crescendo GNP 95 (US).
This live album features the Les Baxter Balladeers on the following: 'Medley: Ride Up/Lonesome Traveler'; 'Midnight Special'; 'Baiion'; 'Linin Track'; 'Banks Of The Ohio'.
Released November 1963 (US).

Albums with the Byrds:

See Discography *Volume 1* under the following sections: *Byrds Singles, Albums, Compilations* and *Archival Albums* for fuller details of release dates, complete track listings, alternate serial numbers, special issues/editions, and more.

Mr Tambourine Man Columbia CL 2372 (mono)/Columbia CS 9172 (stereo) (US). CBS BPG 62571 (mono)/CBS SBPG 62571 (stereo) (UK). Remastered CD edition with bonus tracks: Columbia Legacy CK 64845 (US)/Columbia Legacy 483705 2 (UK).

Turn! Turn! Turn! Columbia CL 2454 (mono)/Columbia CS 9254 (stereo) (US). CBS BPG 62652 (mono)/CBS SBPG 62652 (stereo) (UK). Remastered CD edition with bonus tracks: Columbia Legacy CK 64846 (US)/Columbia Legacy 483706 2 (UK).

Fifth Dimension Columbia CL 2549 (mono)/Columbia CS 9349 (stereo) (US). CBS BPG 62783 (mono)/CBS SBPG 62783 (stereo) (UK). Remastered CD edition with bonus tracks: Columbia Legacy CK 64847(US)/Columbia Legacy 483707 2 (UK).

Younger Than Yesterday Columbia CL 2642 (mono)/Columbia CS 9442 (stereo) (US). CBS BPG 62988 (mono)/CBS SBPG 62988 (stereo) (UK).

Remastered CD edition with bonus tracks: Columbia Legacy CK 64848 (US)/Columbia Legacy 483708 2 (UK).

The Notorious Byrd Brothers Columbia CL 2775 (mono)/Columbia CS 9575 (stereo) (US). CBS 63169 (mono)/CBS S 63169 (stereo) (UK). Remastered CD edition with bonus tracks: Columbia Legacy CK 65151 (US)/Columbia Legacy 486751 2 (UK).

Byrds Asylum SD 5058 (US)/Asylum SYLA 8754 (UK).

Archival albums with the Byrds:

Preflyte Together ST-T-1001 (US)/Bumble GEXP 8001 (UK).
The Original Singles Volume 1 1965–1967 CBS 31851 (UK)/Columbia FC 37335 (US).
The Original Singles Volume 2 1967–1969 CBS 32103 (UK).
Never Before Re-Flyte MH 70318 (US).
In The Beginning Rhino R2 70244 (US).
Sanctuary Sundazed LP 5061 (US).
Sanctuary II Sundazed LP 5065 (US).
The Preflyte Sessions Sundazed SC 11116 (US).
The Columbia Singles '65–'67 Sundazed LP 5130/P2 55624 (US).
Another Dimension Sundazed SEP 2 10-168 (US).
Preflyte [extended version] Floating World FLOATD6122 (UK).

Box Sets with the Byrds:

The Byrds Columbia Legacy 46773 (US)/Columbia Legacy 4676112 (UK).
12 Dimensions The Columbia Recordings 1965–1972 (13-CD box set) Columbia 497610 2/4976102000 (UK).
There Is A Season (4-CD box set and DVD) Columbia/Legacy 82876877002 (US/UK).
The Complete Columbia Albums Collection Columbia Legacy 886978738028 (US).

Isolated appearances with the Byrds:

See *Volume 1*: *Archival Albums* and *Archival CDs* for fuller details of release dates and alternate territory serial numbers.

Early LA Together ST-T-1014 (US).
Includes Crosby solo on 'Willie Jean' and 'Come Back Baby'.
Don't Make Waves MGM SE 4483 ST (US).
Roadmaster A&M 87584 IT (Holland).
Monterey International Pop Festival Rhino R2 70506 (US)/Castle Communications ROK CD 102 (UK).
Byrd Parts Raven RVCD 77 (Australia).
Includes Crosby solo on 'Willie Jean' and 'Come Back Baby'.
The Preflyte Sessions Sundazed LP 5114 (US).
Includes Crosby solo on 'Willie Jean', 'Come Back Baby', 'Jack Of Diamonds' and 'Get Together'.

Byrd Parts 2 Raven RVCD 168 (Australia)
Includes 'Baiion' (Les Baxter Balladeers), Crosby's 'Jack Of Diamonds', 'Get Together' and the otherwise unavailable 'Brotherhood Of The Blues'.
Sixties Transition Sierra SXCD 6027 (US)/Floating World FLOATM6125 (UK).
Features Crosby on 'Willie Jean' and 'Come Back Baby', plus the rare Bud Shank/Crosby collaboration, 'Charisma'.

Previously issued material also appears on the soundtracks to *Homer* and *Forrest Gump*, *The Limey* and the Elektra compilations mentioned in *Volume 1*.

Compilations/Hits Collections with the Byrds:
See *Volume 1* for additional details.
The Byrds Greatest Hits Columbia CL 2716 (US)/CBS SBPG 63107 (UK).
The Byrds Greatest Hits Volume 2 CBS S 64650 (UK).
Best Of Volume 2 Columbia C31795 (US).
History Of The Byrds CBS 68242 (UK).
Return Of The Byrds Columbia Realm 2V 8006-7 (US).
The Byrds CBS 88320 (UK).
The Byrds Play Dylan Columbia PC 36293 (US)/CBS 31795 (UK).
The Very Best Of The Byrds Columbia CS P-P2 17596 (US).
The Byrds Collection Castle Communications CCSLP 151 (UK).
The Very Best Of The Byrds Columbia CBS 4634189 2 (Holland/UK).
Full Flyte Raven RVCD 10 (Australia).
Free Flyte Sony Music Special Products A 17733 (US).
Greatest Hits Remastered Columbia 467843 2 (UK).
20 Essential Tracks From The Boxed Set: 1965–1970 Columbia/Legacy CK 47884/471665-2 (US/UK).
Definitive Collection Columbia 480548 9 (UK).
Nashville West Sony Music Special Products A 28123 (US).
The Very Best Of The Byrds Columbia 487995 2 (UK).
The Best Of The Byrds Columbia 488146 2 (UK).
Super Hits Columbia Legacy 504725 2 (UK)/Columbia Legacy CK 65637 (US).
The Byrds Greatest Hits Columbia/Legacy CK 66230 (US).
The Byrds Sony Music Special Products A 30827 (US).
The Byrds Play The Songs Of Bob Dylan Columbia 501946 2 (UK).
The Byrds Play Dylan Columbia/Legacy CK 85430 (US).
The Essential Byrds Columbia Legacy 512249 2 (UK)/Columbia Legacy C2K 89110 (US).
Mojo Presents . . . An Introduction To The Byrds – 24 Classic Songs Columbia 512778 2 (UK).
Mr Tambourine Man – The Best Of The Byrds Sony Music Media SMM 516489-2 (Germany/UK).
America's Great National Treasure Sony/BMG A 96086 (US).
The Very Best Of The Byrds Sony/BMG 82876 855142 (UK).

Byrds: A Collection Sony BMG 88697 12448 2 (UK).
The Byrds Play Dylan Sony BMG 88697 25267 2 (UK).
Playlist: The Very Best Of The Byrds Columbia Legacy 88697 39219 2 (US).
Steel Box Sony BMG 88697 45981 2 (UK).
Eight Miles High – The Best Of The Byrds Sony/Camden 88697 63627 2 (UK).
Setlist: The Very Best Of The Byrds Live Columbia/Legacy 88697 97753 2 (US).
Turn! Turn! Turn!: The Ultimate Collection Sony/Columbia Music 88875 151652 (UK).
The 60s – The Byrds Sony Music 888837766 2 (US).

As Crosby, Stills & Nash:

Crosby, Stills & Nash Atlantic SD 8229 (US)/Atlantic 588 189 (UK).
'Suite: Judy Blue Eyes'; 'Marrakesh Express'; 'Guinnevere'; 'You Don't Have To Cry'; 'Pre-Road Downs'; 'Wooden Ships'; 'Lady Of The Island'; 'Helplessly Hoping'; 'Long Time Gone'; '49 Bye-Byes'.
Released June 1969 (US)/August 1969 (UK).

CSN Atlantic SD 19104 (US)/Atlantic K50369 (UK).
'Shadow Captain'; 'See The Changes'; 'Carried Away'; 'Fair Game'; 'Anything At All'; 'Cathedral'; 'Dark Star'; 'Just A Song Before I Go'; 'Run From Tears'; 'Cold Rain'; 'In My Dreams'; 'I Give You Give Blind'.
Released June 1977 (US)/June 1977 (UK).

Replay Atlantic 16026 (US)/Atlantic K 50766 (UK).
Compilation. 'Carry On' (edited); 'Marrakesh Express'; 'Just A Song Before I Go'; 'First Things First'; 'Shadow Captain'; 'To The Last Whale: A. Critical Mass B. Wind On The Water'; 'Love The One You're With'; 'Pre-Road Downs'; 'Change Partners'; 'I Give You Give Blind' (remix); 'Cathedral'.
Released December 1980 (US)/March 1981 (UK).

Daylight Again Atlantic 19360 (US)/Atlantic K 50896 (UK).
'Turn Your Back On Love'; 'Wasted On The Way'; 'Southern Cross'; 'Into The Darkness'; 'Delta'; 'Since I Met You'; 'Too Much Love To Hide'; 'Song For Susan'; 'You Are Alive'; 'Might As Well Have A Good Time'.
Released June 1982 (US)/August 1982 (UK).

Allies Atlantic 80075 (US)/Atlantic 78-0075-1 (UK).
'War Games'; 'Raise A Voice'; 'Turn Your Back On Love'; 'Barrel Of Pain (Half-Life)'; 'Shadow Captain'; 'Dark Star'; 'Blackbird'; 'For Free'; 'Wasted On The Way'; 'For What It's Worth'.
Released June 1983 (US)/July 1983 (UK).

Live It Up Atlantic 782107 (US)/Atlantic 7567-82107-1 (UK).
'Live It Up'; 'If Anybody Had A Heart'; 'Tomboy'; 'Haven't We Lost Enough?'; 'Yours And Mine'; '(Got To Keep) Open'; 'Straight Line'; 'House Of Broken Dreams'; 'Arrows'; 'After The Dolphin'.
Released June 1990 (US)/June 1990 (UK).

Crosby, Stills & Nash 4 Compact Disc Set Atlantic 782319-2 (US)/7567-82319-2 (UK).
4 CD box set.
Disc 1: 'Suite: Judy Blue Eyes' (previously unreleased electric alternate mix); 'Helplessly Hoping' (previously unreleased CSN&Y live studio version); 'You Don't Have To Cry' (previously unreleased first recording); 'Wooden Ships'; 'Guinnevere' (previously unreleased early demo); 'Marrakesh Express'; 'Long Time Gone'; 'Blackbird' (previously unreleased live studio version); 'Lady Of The Island'; 'Song With No Words (Tree With No Leaves)' (previously unreleased live studio version); 'Almost Cut My Hair' (previously unreleased unedited original version); 'Teach Your Children'; 'Horses Through A Rainstorm' (previously unreleased); 'Déjà Vu'; 'Helpless'; '4+20' (previously unreleased alternate mix); 'Laughing'; 'Carry On'/'Questions' (*Déjà Vu* version, retitled).
Disc 2: 'Woodstock' (previously unreleased 1969 alternate mix); 'Ohio'; 'Love The One You're With'; 'Our House'; 'Old Times Good Times'; 'The Lee Shore' (previously unreleased version); 'Music Is Love'; 'I'd Swear There Was Somebody Here'; 'Man In The Mirror' (previously unreleased live version); 'Black Queen' (previously unreleased live version); 'Military Madness'; 'Urge For Going' (previously unreleased version); 'I Used To Be A King'; 'Simple Man' (previously unreleased alternate mix); 'Southbound Train'; 'Change Partners'; 'My Love Is A Gentle Thing' (previously unreleased); 'Word Game'; 'Johnny's Garden'; 'So Begins The Task'; 'Turn Back The Pages'.
Disc 3: 'See The Changes' (previously unreleased version); 'It Doesn't Matter'; 'Immigration Man'; 'Chicago/We Can Change The World'; 'Homeward Through The Haze' (previously unreleased version); 'Where Will I Be?'; 'Page 43'; 'Carry Me'; 'Cowboy Of Dreams'; 'Bittersweet'; 'To The Last Whale: A. Critical Mass B. Wind On The Water'; 'Prison Song'; 'Another Sleep Song'; 'Taken At All' (previously unreleased CSN&Y version); 'In My Dreams'; 'Just A Song Before I Go'; 'Shadow Captain'; 'Dark Star' (*Allies* version); 'Cathedral'.
Disc 4: 'Wasted On The Way'; 'Barrel Of Pain (Half-Life)'; 'Southern Cross'; 'Daylight Again'; 'Thoroughfare Gap'; 'Wild Tales' (previously unreleased live version); 'Dear Mr Fantasy' (previously unreleased version); 'Cold Rain'; 'Got It Made' (previously unreleased version); 'Tracks In The Dust'; 'As I Come Of Age' (previously unreleased CS&N version); '50/50'; 'Drive My Car' (previously unreleased version); 'Delta'; 'Soldiers Of Peace' (previously unreleased version); 'Yours And Mine'; 'Haven't We Lost Enough?'; 'After The Dolphin'; 'Find The Cost Of Freedom'.
Released October 1991 (US)/December 1991 (UK).

After The Storm Atlantic 782654 (US)/Atlantic 7567-82654-2 (UK).
'Only Waiting For You'; 'Find A Dream'; 'Camera'; 'Unequal Love'; 'Till It Shines On You'; 'It Won't Go Away'; 'These Empty Days'; 'In My Life'; 'Street To Lean On'; 'Bad Boys'; 'After The Storm'; 'Panama'.
Released August 1994 (US)/September 1994 (UK).

Woodstock '94 A&M 540 289 (US).
Features CS&N performing 'Déjà Vu'.
Released 1994 (US).

Greatest Hits Atlantic/Rhino R2 76537 (US)/Atlantic/Rhino 08122 76537 2 (UK).
'Suite: Judy Blue Eyes'; 'Long Time Gone'; 'Just A Song Before I Go'; 'Southern Cross'; 'Marrakesh Express'; 'Helplessly Hoping'; 'Shadow Captain'; 'Our House'; 'Guinnevere'; 'See The Changes'; 'Teach Your Children'; 'Wooden Ships'; 'Delta'; '49 Bye Byes'; 'Wasted On The Way'; 'Carry On'/'Questions'; 'In My Dreams'; 'Cathedral'; 'Daylight Again'.
Released March 2005 (US/UK).

Demos Atlantic/Rhino 8122-79864-3 (US).
'Marrakesh Express'; 'Almost Cut My Hair'; 'You Don't Have To Cry'; 'Déjà Vu'; 'Sleep Song'; 'My Love Is A Gentle Thing'; 'Be Yourself'; 'Music Is Love'; 'Singing Call'; 'Long Time Gone'; 'Chicago'; 'Love The One You're With'.
Released May 2009 (US). Front cover title: *CSN Demos.*

Crosby, Stills & Nash 2012 CSN Records 409-5 (US).
2 CDs and DVD.
CD 1: 'Carry On'/'Questions'; 'Marrakesh Express'; 'Long Time Gone'; 'Military Madness'; 'Southern Cross'; 'Lay Me Down'; 'Almost Gone'; 'Wasted On The Way'; 'Radio'; 'Bluebird'; 'Déjà Vu'; 'Wooden Ships'.
CD 2: 'Helplessly Hoping'; 'In Your Name'; 'Girl From The North Country'; 'As I Come Of Age'; 'Guinnevere'; 'Johnny's Garden'; 'So Begins The Task'; 'Cathedral'; 'Our House'; 'Love The One You're With'; 'For What It's Worth'; 'Teach Your Children'; 'Suite: Judy Blue Eyes'.
DVD: 'Carry On'/'Questions'; 'Marrakesh Express'; 'Long Time Gone'; 'Military Madness'; 'Southern Cross'; 'Lay Me Down'; 'Almost Gone'; 'Wasted On The Way'; 'Radio'; 'Bluebird'; 'Déjà Vu'; 'Wooden Ships'; 'Helplessly Hoping'; 'In Your Name'; 'Girl From The North Country'; 'As I Come Of Age'; 'Guinnevere'; 'Johnny's Garden'; 'So Begins The Task'; 'Cathedral'; 'Our House'; 'Love The One You're With'; 'For What It's Worth'; 'Teach Your Children'; 'Suite: Judy Blue Eyes'.
DVD Bonus Footage: A Conversation with David Crosby, Stephen Stills and Graham Nash. On the road interviews with band and crew.
Released July 2012 (US).

CS&N also appear on the Various Artistes' recording *Nintendo: White Knuckle Scorin'* performing 'How Have You Been', the Various Artistes' *Red Hot & Country* performing 'Teach Your Children', *Woodstock Diary* singing 'Blackbird' and *Woodstock 94* (US edition) playing 'Déjà Vu'. The single 'Chippin' Away' is available on a CD single, but not on an album. 'Chuck's Lament (A Child's Dream)' is available solely as a B-side. The soundtrack of *Flipper* features CS&N singing on the film's theme song. The album *No*

Nukes contains live versions of 'You Don't Have To Cry', 'Long Time Gone' and 'Teach Your Children'.

In October 2010, *Time Life* (25806-D) issued The 25th Anniversary Rock & Roll Hall Of Fame Concerts. The 2 CD-set of 'Night 1' featured Crosby, Stills & Nash's 'Woodstock' and 'Almost Cut My Hair'; the trio also performed alongside Bonnie Raitt on 'Love Has No Pride'; with Jackson Browne on 'The Pretender'; with James Taylor on 'Mexico'; and with James Taylor on 'Love The One You're With'. Paul Simon joined Crosby & Nash on 'Here Comes The Sun'.

As Crosby, Stills, Nash & Young:

Déjà Vu Atlantic SD 7200 (US)/Atlantic 2401 001 (UK).
'Carry On'; 'Teach Your Children'; 'Almost Cut My Hair'; 'Helpless'; 'Woodstock'; 'Déjà Vu'; 'Our House'; '4+20'; 'Country Girl'; 'Everybody I Love You'.
Released March 1970 (US)/May 1970 (UK).

Woodstock Cotillion SD3-500 (US)/Atlantic 2657 001 (UK).
Includes 'Suite: Judy Blue Eyes', 'Wooden Ships' and 'Sea Of Madness'.
Released May 1970 (US)/July 1970 (UK).

Four Way Street Atlantic SD-2-902 (US)/Atlantic 2657 007 (UK).
'Suite: Judy Blue Eyes'; 'On The Way Home'; 'Teach Your Children'; 'Triad'; 'The Lee Shore'; 'Chicago'; 'Right Between The Eyes'; 'Cowgirl In The Sand'; 'Don't Let It Bring You Down'; '49 Bye-Byes/America's Children'; 'Love The One You're With'; 'Pre-Road Downs'; 'Long Time Gone'; 'Southern Man'; 'Ohio'; 'Carry On'; 'Find The Cost Of Freedom'.
Released April 1971 (US)/May 1971 (UK). The CD version (Atlantic 7567-82408-2; July 1992) includes the bonus tracks: 'King Midas In Reverse'; 'Laughing'; 'Black Queen'; 'Medley: The Loner/Cinnamon Girl/Down By The River'.

Woodstock II Cotillion SD2-400 (US)/Atlantic 2657 003 (UK).
Includes '4+20', 'Marrakesh Express' and 'Guinnevere'.
Released March 1971 (US)/May 1971 (UK).

So Far Atlantic 18100 (US)/Atlantic K 50023 (UK).
Compilation. 'Déjà Vu'; 'Helplessly Hoping'; 'Wooden Ships'; 'Teach Your Children'; 'Ohio'; 'Find The Cost Of Freedom'; 'Woodstock'; 'Our House'; 'Helpless'; 'Guinnevere'; 'Suite: Judy Blue Eyes'.
Released August 1974 (US)/August 1974 (UK).

American Dream Atlantic 781888 (US)/Atlantic WX 233 781888-1 (UK).
'American Dream'; 'Got It Made'; 'Name Of Love'; 'Don't Say Good-bye'; 'This Old House'; 'Nighttime For The Generals'; 'Shadowland'; 'Drivin' Thunder'; 'Clear Blue Skies'; 'That Girl'; 'Compass'; 'Soldiers Of Peace'; 'Feel Your Love'; 'Night Song'.
Released November 1988 (US)/November 1988 (UK).

Woodstock: 25th Anniversary Box Set Atlantic 782636 (US)/Atlantic 7567-82636 (UK).
Includes 'Suite: Judy Blue Eyes', 'Find The Cost Of Freedom', 'Guinnevere', 'Marrakesh Express', '4+20' and 'Sea Of Madness'.
Released August 1994 (US)/September 1994 (UK).

Looking Forward Reprise 47436-2 (US)/Reprise 9362474362 (UK).
'Faith In Me'; 'Looking Forward'; 'Stand And Be Counted'; 'Heartland'; 'Seen Enough'; 'Slowpoke'; 'Dream For Him'; 'No Tears Left'; 'Out Of Control'; 'Someday Soon'; 'Queen Of Them All'; 'Sanibel'.
Released October 1999 (US)/November 1999 (UK). Also available as double LP in the UK (Reprise 47436-1).

Déjà Vu Live Reprise 512606-2 (US)/Reprise 9362-48939-1 (UK).
'What Are Their Names?'; 'Living With War' – Theme; 'After The Garden'; 'Military Madness'; 'Let's Impeach The President'; 'Déjà Vu'; 'Shock And Awe'; 'Families'; 'Wooden Ships'; 'Looking For A Leader'; 'For What It's Worth'; 'Living With War'; 'Roger And Out'; 'Find The Cost Of Freedom'; 'Teach Your Children'; 'Living With War' – Theme (Reprise)'. Bonus track at iTunes, 'The Restless Consumer'.
Released July 2008 (US)/August 2008 (UK).

Woodstock 40 Years On: Back To Yasgur's Farm Rhino R2 519761 (US)/Rhino 812279313 (UK).
Includes 'Suite: Judy Blue Eyes', 'Guinnevere', 'Marrakesh Express', '4+20', 'Sea Of Madness', and 'Wooden Ships'.
Released August 2009 (US/UK).

CSNY 1974 Rhino R1-541729 (US)/Rhino 8122796035 (UK).
3 CD box set, with DVD. Also available as single CD: Rhino R2-547132 (US)/Rhino 603497899920 (UK). Plus 6 LP/DVD, limited edition box.
CD 1: 'Love The One You're With'; 'Wooden Ships'; 'Immigration Man'; 'Helpless'; 'Carry Me'; 'Johnny's Garden'; 'Traces'; 'Grave Concern'; 'On The Beach'; 'Black Queen'; 'Almost Cut My Hair'.
CD 2: 'Change Partners'; 'The Lee Shore'; 'Only Love Can Break Your Heart'; 'Our House'; 'Fieldworker'; 'Guinnevere'; 'Time After Time'; 'Prison Song'; 'Long May You Run'; 'Goodbye Dick'; 'Mellow My Mind'; 'Old Man'; 'Word Game'; 'Myth Of Sisyphus'; 'Blackbird'; 'Love Art Blues'; 'Hawaiian Sunrise'; 'Teach Your Children'; 'Suite: Judy Blue Eyes'.
CD 3: 'Déjà Vu'; 'My Angel'; 'Pre-Road Downs'; 'Don't Be Denied'; 'Revolution Blues'; 'Military Madness'; 'Long Time Gone'; 'Pushed It Over The End'; 'Chicago'; 'Ohio'.
DVD: 'Only Love Can Break Your Heart'; 'Almost Cut My Hair'; 'Grave Concern'; 'Old Man'; 'Johnny's Garden'; 'Our House'; 'Déjà Vu'; 'Pushed It Over The End'.
Released July 2014 (US/UK).

CSN&Y also appear on the film soundtracks *The Strawberry Statement* and *SWALK*, albeit with previously released material. A live version of 'Pushed It

Over The End' was released in Italy in 1982 on a 12-inch single (Warner Bros W24040) accompanying the box set, *The Neil Young Heritage – 12 Albums*.

As David Crosby:
If I Could Only Remember My Name Atlantic SD 7203 (US)/Atlantic 2401 005 (UK).
'Music Is Love'; 'Cowboy Movie'; 'Tamalpais High (At About 3)'; 'Laughing'; 'What Are Their Names'; 'Traction In The Rain'; 'Song With No Words (Tree With No Leaves)'; 'Orleans'; 'I'd Swear There Was Somebody Here'.
Released March 1971 (US)/April 1971 (UK).

Oh Yes I Can A&M 5232 (US)/A&M AMA 5232 (UK).
'Drive My Car'; 'Melody'; 'Monkey And The Underdog'; 'In The Wide Ruin'; 'Tracks In The Dust'; 'Drop Down Mama'; 'Lady Of The Harbor'; 'Distances'; 'Flying Man'; 'Oh Yes I Can'; 'My Country 'Tis Of Thee'.
Released February 1989 (US)/February 1989 (UK).

Thousand Roads Atlantic 782484-2 (US)/Atlantic 7567-82484-2 (UK).
'Hero'; 'Too Young To Die'; 'Old Soldier'; 'Through Your Hands'; 'Yvette In English'; 'Thousand Roads'; 'Columbus'; 'Helpless Heart'; 'Coverage'; 'Natalie'.
Released April 1993 (US)/May 1993 (UK).

It's All Coming Back To Me Now... Atlantic 7-82620-2 (US)/Atlantic 7567-82620-2 (UK).
'In My Dreams'; 'Rusty And Blue'; 'Hero'; 'Till It Shines On You'; 'Thousand Roads'; 'Cowboy Movie'; 'Almost Cut My Hair'; 'Déjà Vu'; 'Long Time Gone'; 'Wooden Ships'.
Released January 1995 (US)/March 1995 (UK).

David Crosby King Biscuit Flower Hour 70710-88007-2 (US).
'Tracks In The Dust'; 'Guinnevere'; 'Compass'; 'In My Dreams'; 'Drive My Car'; 'Lady Of The Harbor'; 'Oh Yes I Can'; 'Monkey And The Underdog'; 'Delta'; 'Déjà Vu'; 'Nighttime For The Generals'; 'Wooden Ships'; 'Almost Cut My Hair'; 'Long Time Gone'.
Unlike other King Biscuit radio show recordings, this 1989 concert received a commercial release.
Released August 1996 (US).

Voyage Atlantic/Rhino R2 77628 (US).
3 CD box set. Disc 1: 'Eight Miles High' (Byrds); 'Renaissance Fair' (Byrds); 'Everybody's Been Burned' (Byrds); 'Wooden Ships' (CS&N); 'Guinnevere' (CS&N); 'Long Time Gone' (CS&N); 'Déjà Vu' (CSN&Y); 'Almost Cut My Hair' (CSN&Y); 'Tamalpais High (At About 3)'; 'Song With No Words (Tree With No Leaves)'; 'What Are Their Names?'; 'I'd Swear There Was Somebody Here'; 'Where Will I Be?' (C&N); 'Page 43' (C&N); 'Critical Mass' (C&N); 'Carry Me' (C&N); 'Bittersweet' (C&N); 'Naked In The Rain' (C&N); 'Dancer' (C&N).

Disc 2: 'Shadow Captain' (CS&N); 'In My Dreams' (CS&N); 'Delta' (CS&N); 'Compass' (CSN&Y); 'Tracks In The Dust'; 'Arrows' (CS&N); 'Hero'; 'Yvette In English'; 'Rusty And Blue' (CPR); 'Somehow She Knew' (CPR); 'Breathless' (CPR); 'Map To Buried Treasure' (CPR); 'At The Edge' (CPR); 'Through Here Quite Often' (C&N); 'My Country 'Tis Of Thee'.
Disc 3: 'Long Time Gone' (Demo) (C&S); 'Guinnevere' (Alternate Mix); 'Almost Cut My Hair' (Demo); 'Games' (Demo); 'Déjà Vu' (Demo) (C&N); 'Triad' (Demo); 'Cowboy Movie' (Studio Version); 'Kids And Dogs' (previously unreleased); 'Have You Seen The Stars Tonite?' (Alternate Mix) (Paul Kantner/Jefferson Starship); 'The Lee Shore' (Live) (C&N); 'Traction In The Rain' (Live) (C&N); 'King Of The Mountain' (Unreleased Demo); 'Homeward Through The Haze' (Alternate Mix) (CSN&Y); 'Samurai' (Studio Version); 'Climber' (Studio Version) (CSN&Y); 'Dream For Him' (Live) (CSN&Y).
Released October 2006 (US).

If I Could Only Remember My Name Atlantic/Rhino R2 73204 (US).
Reissue. Bonus track: 'Kids And Dogs', plus DVD with surround sound, lyrics and video.
Released October 2006 (US). Also released as 180 gram vinyl LP on Rhino 8122798666 in April 2010.

Croz Blue Castle BCR 1142-1 (US/UK).
'What's Broken'; 'Time I Have'; 'Holding On To Nothing'; 'The Clearing'; 'Radio'; 'Slice Of Time'; 'Set That Baggage Down'; 'If She Called'; 'Dangerous Night'; 'Morning Falling'; 'Find A Heart'. Deluxe edition includes digital download videos of the above, plus 'Déjà Vu'; 'Turn! Turn! Turn!' (with Chris Hillman). Also released as 180 gram vinyl LP Blue Castle BCR 1143-8.
Released: January 2014 (US/UK).

Lighthouse GroundUp Music/Verve Records B0025264-02 (US)/ GroundUp Music/Verve 060255723868 (UK).
'Things We Do For Love'; 'The Us Below'; 'Drive Out To The Desert'; 'Look In Their Eyes'; 'Somebody Other Than You'; 'The City'; 'Paint You A Picture'; 'What Makes It So'; 'By The Light Of Common Day'. Also issued on 180 gram vinyl LP GroundUp Music/Verve Records B0025319-01.
Released: October 2016 (US/UK).

As Crosby & Nash:

Graham Nash/David Crosby Atlantic 19117 (US)/Atlantic K 50011 (UK).
'Southbound Train'; 'Whole Cloth'; 'Blacknotes'; 'Strangers Room'; 'Where Will I Be?'; 'Page 43'; 'Frozen Smiles'; 'Games'; 'Girl To Be On My Mind'; 'The Wall Song'; 'Immigration Man'.
Released April 1972 (US)/May 1972 (UK).

Wind On The Water ABC ABCS 902 (US)/Polydor 2310 428 (UK).
'Carry Me'; 'Mama Lion'; 'Bittersweet'; 'Take The Money And Run'; 'Naked

In The Rain'; 'Love Work Out'; 'Low Down Payment'; 'Cowboy Of Dreams'; 'Homeward Through The Haze'; 'Fieldworker'; 'To The Last Whale: A. Critical Mass B. Wind On The Water'.
Released September 1975 (US)/December 1975 (UK).

Whistling Down The Wire ABC ABCS 956 (US)/Polydor 2310 468 (UK).
'Spotlight'; 'Broken Bird'; 'Time After Time'; 'Dancer'; 'Mutiny'; 'J.B.'s Blues'; 'Marguerita'; 'Taken At All'; 'Foolish Man'; 'Out Of The Darkness'.
Released July 1976 (US/UK).

Crosby – Nash Live ABC ABCS 1042 (US)/Polydor 2310 165 (UK).
'Immigration Man'; 'The Lee Shore'; 'I Used To Be A King'; 'Page 43'; 'Fieldworker'; 'Simple Man'; 'Foolish Man'; 'Mama Lion'; 'Déjà Vu'.
Released November 1977 (US/UK). Reissued in 2000 with bonus tracks 'King Of The Mountain' and 'Bittersweet'.

The Best Of David Crosby And Graham Nash ABC ABCS 1102 (US)/Polydor 2310 626 (UK).
Compilation. 'Love Work Out'; 'The Wall Song'; 'Wild Tales'; 'Carry Me'; 'Out Of The Darkness'; 'Southbound Train'; 'Laughing'; 'Chicago'; 'Bittersweet'; 'To The Last Whale: A. Critical Mass B. Wind On The Water'.
Released September 1978 (US)/January 1979 (UK).

The Bread And Roses Festival Of Music Fantasy 79011 (US).
Various artistes, includes David Crosby ('The Lee Shore') and Crosby, Bernstein, Nash ('Power').
Released December 1979 (US).

Another Stoney Evening Grateful Dead Records GDCD 4057 (US).
Anticipatory Crowd; 'Déjà Vu'; 'Wooden Ships'; 'Man In The Mirror'; 'Orleans'; '[I] Used To Be A King'; 'Traction In The Rain'; '[The] Lee Shore'; 'Southbound Train'; 'Laughing'; 'Triad'; 'Where Will I Be'; 'Stranger's Room'; 'Immigration Man'; 'Guinnevere'; 'Teach Your Children'; Exit Sounds.
Released January 1998 (US).

The Best Of Crosby & Nash The ABC Years MCA 088 112 575-2 (US).
Compilation. 'Carry Me'; 'Mama Lion'; 'Bittersweet'; 'Take The Money And Run'; 'Naked In The Rain'; 'Love Work Out'; 'Homeward Through The Haze'; 'To The Last Whale: A. Critical Mass B. Wind On The Water'; 'Spotlight'; 'Broken Bird'; 'Time After Time'; 'Mutiny'; 'Taken At All'; 'Foolish Man'; 'Out Of The Darkness'; 'Immigration Man' (Live); 'The Lee Shore' (Live); 'I Used To Be A King' (Live); 'Déjà Vu' (Live).
Released October 2002 (US).

Crosby Nash Sanctuary SANDD 293 (US).
2 CD set. Disc 1: 'Lay Me Down'; 'Puppeteer'; 'Through Here Quite Often'; 'Grace'; 'Jesus Of Rio'; 'I Surrender'; 'Luck Dragon'; 'On The Other Side Of Town'; 'Half Your Angels'; 'They Want It All'; 'How Does It Shine?'

Disc 2: 'Don't Dig Here'; 'Milky Way Tonight'; 'Charlie'; 'Penguin In A Palm Tree'; 'Michael (Hedges Here)'; 'Samurai'; 'Shining On Your Dreams'; 'Live On (The Wall)'; 'My Country 'Tis Of Thee'.
Released August 2004 (US).

Crosby Nash: Highlights Sanctuary 86427 (US).
'Lay Me Down'; 'Milky Way Tonight'; 'Don't Dig Here'; 'Penguin In A Palm Tree'; 'I Surrender'; 'Through Here Quite Often'; 'They Want It All'; 'Puppeteer'; 'Live On (The Wall)'; 'Grace'; 'Jesus Of Rio'; 'How Does It Shine?'; 'My Country 'Tis Of Thee'.
Released July 2006 (US). Edited version of *Crosby Nash.*

As CPR (Crosby Pevar Raymond):
CPR Samson Music GC 0145 (US).
'Morrison'; 'That House'; 'One For Every Moment'; 'At The Edge'; 'Somebody Else's Town'; 'Rusty And Blue'; 'Somehow She Knew'; 'Little Blind Fish'; 'Yesterday's Child'; 'It's All Coming Back To Me Now'; 'Time Is The Final Currency'.
Released June 1998 (US).

Live At Cuesta College [Self-released. No label or serial number] (US).
2 CD set. Disc 1: 'In My Dreams'; 'Tracks In The Dust'; 'Homeward Through The Haze'; 'Rusty And Blue'; 'Thousand Roads'; 'For Free'; 'Morrison'; 'Somehow She Knew'; 'Till It Shines On You'.
Disc 2: 'Time Is The Final Currency'; 'Where Will I Be?'; 'Page 43'; 'Delta'; 'Déjà Vu'; 'One For Every Moment'; 'Guinnevere'; 'Wooden Ships'.
Released December 1998 (US).

Live At The Wiltern Samson Music GC 0148 (US).
2 CD set. Disc 1: 'Morrison'; 'Little Blind Fish'; 'One For Every Moment'; 'That House'; 'Homeward Through The Haze'; 'At The Edge'; 'It's All Coming Back'; 'Rusty And Blue'; 'Delta'.
Disc 2: 'Dream For Him'; 'Old Soldier'; 'Hero'; 'Long Time Gone'; 'Déjà Vu'; 'Eight Miles High'; 'Ohio'; 'Almost Cut My Hair'.
Released September 1999 (US).

Just Like Gravity Gold Circle Entertainment GI 20002-2 (US)/GI 20002-2 (UK).
'Map To Buried Treasure'; 'Breathless'; 'Darkness'; 'Gone Forever'; 'Eyes Too Blue'; 'Jerusalem'; 'Kings Get Broken'; 'Angel Dream'; 'Katie Did'; 'Climber'; 'Coyote King'; 'Just Like Gravity'.
Released June 2001 (US/UK).

A live CPR version of 'Déjà vu' can be found on *On The Mountain 3* recorded at KMTT-FM studios. A live version of 'At The Edge' is featured on *2 Meter Sessies Vol. 8.*

In addition to the above, David Crosby has guested on recordings by Buffalo Springfield (*Buffalo Springfield Again*); Joni Mitchell (*Song To A Seagull;*

Ladies Of The Canyon; Court And Spark; The Hissing Of Summer Lawns), Jefferson Airplane (*Crown Of Creation; Volunteers*), Morning Glory (*Two Suns Worth*), the Flying Burrito Brothers (*The Gilded Palace Of Sin*), John Sebastian (*John B. Sebastian*), Bob Gibson (*Bob Gibson*), Stephen Stills (*Stephen Stills; Stephen Stills 2; Stills;* 4 CD box set *Carry On*), Paul Kantner/Jefferson Starship (*Blows Against The Empire*), Paul Kantner/Grace Slick (*Sunfighter*), Cyrus Faryar (*Cyrus*), Hot Tuna (*Burgers*).

Jackson Browne (*Jackson Browne; For Everyman; The Pretender; World In Motion; I'm Alive; Looking East*), Graham Nash (*Songs For Beginners; Wild Tales; Earth And Sky; Songs For Survivors;* 3 CD box set *Reflections*), Everly Brothers (*Stories We Could Tell*), Rick Roberts (*Windmills*), Neil Young (*Harvest; Journey Through The Past; Time Fades Away; On The Beach; Zuma; Decade; Archives Vol 1)*, Gene Clark (*Roadmaster*), Paul Kantner, Grace Slick & David Freiberg (*Baron Von Tollbooth And The Chrome Nun).*

Roger McGuinn (*Roger McGuinn; Back From Rio*), Grace Slick (*Manhole*), Art Garfunkel (*Breakaway; Watermark*), James Taylor (*Gorilla*; *In The Pocket*), Phil Lesh & Ned Lagin (*Seastones*), Dave Mason (*Split Coconut*), Carole King (*Thoroughbred; Carole King: In Concert*), John David Souther (*Black Rose*), Elton John (*Blue Moves*), the Section (*Fork It Over*), Jimmy Webb (*El Mirage; Suspending Disbelief; Still Within The Sound Of My Voice*), Gary Wright (*Headin' Home*), Sally Rogers (*The Unclaimed Pint*), Kenny Rankin (*Hiding In Myself*), Bonnie Raitt (*Nick Of Time; Longing In Their Hearts*), Phil Collins (*. . . But Seriously)*.

Bob Dylan (*Under The Red Sky*), Michael Hedges (*Taproot; Torched*), Marc Cohn (on Various Artistes' *Barcelona Gold; The Rainy Season*), Eddy Clearwater (*A Real Good Time Live!*); Indigo Girls (*Rites Of Passage*), Willie Nelson (*Across The Borderline*), Jack Tempchin & the Seclusions (*After The Rain*), Kenny Loggins (*Return To Pooh Corner; December*), Nicolette Larson (*Sleep, Baby, Sleep*), Stevie Nicks (*Street Angel*), Hootie & the Blowfish (*Cracked Rear View*), Stephen Bishop (*Blue Guitars*), Robert Drew Fezzey And Friends (Various Artistes *Overture Records Presents Take A Bite Outta This, Vol. 1*), Anastasia & John (*That's You And Me; Little Man*).

Chris Hillman (*Like A Hurricane*), Dana Pomfret (*Soul Collage*), Doug Ingoldsby (*Can't Do This Alone*), Venice (*2 Meter Sessies*), Jeff Bridges (*Be Here Soon*), David Gilmour (*On An Island; Remember That Night – Live At The Albert Hall*), Nils Lofgren (*Sacred Weapon*), Karen Dalton (*Cotton Eyed Joe Live In Boulder 1962*), Joel Rafael (*Thirteen Stories High*), Steve Postell (*Time Still Knocking*), Al Jardine (*A Postcard From California*), John Mayer (*Born And Raised*), Don Felder (*Road To Forever*), Jonathan Wilson (*Fanfare*), Joe Walsh (*Analog Man*), Joan Baez (*75th Birthday Celebration*) and Kenny White (*Long List Of Priors*).

Crosby produced and wrote Blackburn & Snow's 1966 single 'Stranger In A Strange Land' using the pseudonym Samuel F. Omar. Crosby also guested on *The Astrology Album* (1967) and receives a production credit on the 1968 single 'Hello' b/w 'Good Day' by Things To Come. In 1969, Crosby produced

Leonard Cohen's 'Like A Bird' (a prototype of 'Bird On A Wire') and 'Nothing To One' (later known as 'You Know Who I Am') both of which appeared as bonus tracks on the 2007 CD reissue of *Songs From A Room*. He also provided the music for Dan Peterson's lyric 'Dirt Poor' in 1973. Crosby is credited with backing vocals on the 1988 Various Artistes' collection, *Stay Awake*. The 1993 Phil Collins extended single/EP *Hero*, features Crosby on all three tracks, including the rare 'Fare Thee Well'. The title track of the tribute album *Return Of The Grievous Angel* features a duet between Crosby and Lucinda Williams. Crosby (as part of C&N) also appears on the 1999 charity album *Sing Out For Seva* in support of the Seva Foundation performing 'Wooden Ships'. He appears with Chris Hillman & Herb Pedersen singing 'Turn! Turn! Turn!' on the 2006 Various Artistes' collection, *Tales From The Tavern, Vol. 1*. Of all the guest appearances mentioned herein, perhaps the most obscure is 'Cross The Plains', his contribution to Travis Edmonson's 1962 live album *Travis On Cue* (Horizon WP 1606) and 1962's *Travis On His Own* (Reprise R9 6035).

MICHAEL CLARKE

Albums with the Byrds:
See Discography *Volume 1* under the following sections: *Byrds Singles, Albums, Compilations* and *Archival Albums* for fuller details of release dates, complete track listings, alternate serial numbers, special issues/editions, and more.

Mr Tambourine Man Columbia CL 2372 (mono)/Columbia CS 9172 (stereo) (US). CBS BPG 62571 (mono)/CBS SBPG 62571 (stereo) (UK). Remastered CD edition with bonus tracks: Columbia Legacy CK 64845 (US)/Columbia Legacy 483705 2 (UK).

Turn! Turn! Turn! Columbia CL 2454 (mono)/Columbia CS 9254 (stereo) (US). CBS BPG 62652 (mono)/CBS SBPG 62652 (stereo) (UK). Remastered CD edition with bonus tracks: Columbia Legacy CK 64846 (US)/Columbia Legacy 483706 2 (UK).

Fifth Dimension Columbia CL 2549 (mono)/Columbia CS 9349 (stereo) (US). CBS BPG 62783 (mono)/CBS SBPG 62783 (stereo) (UK). Remastered CD edition with bonus tracks: Columbia Legacy CK 64847(US)/Columbia Legacy 483707 2 (UK).

Younger Than Yesterday Columbia CL 2642 (mono)/Columbia CS 9442 (stereo) (US). CBS BPG 62988 (mono)/CBS SBPG 62988 (stereo) (UK). Remastered CD edition with bonus tracks: Columbia Legacy CK 64848 (US)/Columbia Legacy 483708 2 (UK).

The Notorious Byrd Brothers Columbia CL 2775 (mono)/Columbia CS 9575 (stereo) (US). CBS 63169 (mono)/CBS S 63169 (stereo) (UK). Remastered CD edition with bonus tracks: Columbia Legacy CK 65151 (US)/Columbia Legacy 486751 2 (UK).

Byrds Asylum SD 5058 (US)/Asylum SYLA 8754 (UK).

Archival albums with the Byrds:

Preflyte Together ST-T-1001 (US)/Bumble GEXP 8001 (UK).
The Original Singles Volume 1 1965–1967 CBS 31851 (UK)/Columbia FC 37335 (US).
The Original Singles Volume 2 1967–1969 CBS 32103 (UK).
Never Before Re-Flyte MH 70318 (US).
In The Beginning Rhino R2 70244 (US).
Sanctuary Sundazed LP 5061 (US).
Sanctuary II Sundazed LP 5065 (US).
The Preflyte Sessions Sundazed SC 11116 (US).
The Columbia Singles '65–'67 Sundazed LP 5130/P2 55624 (US).
Another Dimension Sundazed SEP 2 10-168 (US)
Preflyte [extended version] Floating World FLOATD6122 (UK).

Box Sets with the Byrds:

The Byrds Columbia Legacy 46773 (US)/Columbia Legacy 4676112 (UK).
12 Dimensions The Columbia Recordings 1965–1972 (13-CD box set) Columbia 497610 2/4976102000 (UK).
There Is A Season (4-CD box set and DVD) Columbia/Legacy 82876877002 (US/UK).
The Complete Columbia Albums Collection Columbia Legacy 886978738028 (US).

Isolated appearances with the Byrds:

See *Volume 1*: *Byrds Albums, Guest Slots/Rarities, Compilations and Archival Albums* for fuller details of release dates and alternate territory serial numbers.

Early LA Together ST-T-1014 (US).
Don't Make Waves MGM 4483 ST (US).
Roadmaster A&M 87584 (Holland).
Monterey International Pop Festival Rhino R2 70506 (US)/Castle Communications ROK CD 102 (UK).
Byrd Parts Raven RVCD 77 (Australia).
Byrd Parts 2 Raven RVCD 165 (Australia).
Sixties Transition Sierra SXCD 6027 (US)/Floating World FLOATM6125 (UK).

Previously issued material also appears on the soundtracks to *Homer* and *Forrest Gump* and *The Limey*.

Compilations/Hits Collections with the Byrds:

See *Volume 1* for additional details.

The Byrds Greatest Hits Columbia CL 2716 (US)/CBS SBPG 63107 (UK).
The Byrds Greatest Hits Volume 2 CBS S 64650 (UK).
Best Of Volume 2 Columbia C31795 (US).
History Of The Byrds CBS 68242 (UK).
Return Of The Byrds Columbia Realm 2V 8006-7 (US).

The Byrds CBS 88320 (UK).
The Byrds Play Dylan Columbia PC 36293 (US)/CBS 31795 (UK).
The Very Best Of The Byrds Columbia CS P-P2 17596 (US).
The Byrds Collection Castle Communications CCSLP 151 (UK).
The Very Best Of The Byrds Columbia CBS 4634189 2 (Holland/UK).
Full Flyte Raven RVCD 10 (Australia).
Free Flyte Sony Music Special Products A 17733 (US).
Greatest Hits Remastered Columbia 467843 2 (UK).
20 Essential Tracks From The Boxed Set: 1965–1970, Columbia/Legacy CK 47884/471665-2 (US/UK).
Definitive Collection Columbia 480548 9 (UK).
Nashville West Sony Music Special Products A 28123 (US).
The Very Best Of The Byrds Columbia 487995 2 (UK).
The Best Of The Byrds Columbia 488146 2 (UK).
The Very Best Of Columbia 487995 2 (UK).
Super Hits Columbia Legacy 504725 2 (UK)/Columbia Legacy CK 65637 (US).
The Byrds Greatest Hits Columbia/Legacy CK 66230 (US).
The Byrds Sony Music Special Products A 30827 (US).
The Byrds Play The Songs Of Bob Dylan Columbia 501946 2 (UK).
The Byrds Play Dylan Columbia/Legacy CK 85430 (US).
The Essential Byrds Columbia Legacy 512249 2 (UK)/Columbia Legacy C2K 89110 (US).
Mojo Presents . . . An Introduction To The Byrds – 24 Classic Songs Columbia 512778 2 (UK).
Mr Tambourine Man – The Best Of The Byrds Sony Music Media SMM 516489-2 (Germany/UK).
America's Great National Treasure Sony/BMG A 96086 (US).
The Very Best Of The Byrds Sony/BMG 82876 855142 (UK).
Byrds: A Collection Sony BMG 88697 12448 2 (UK).
The Byrds Play Dylan Sony BMG 88697 25267 2 (UK).
Playlist: The Very Best Of The Byrds Columbia Legacy 88697 39219 2 (US).
Steel Box Sony BMG 88697 459812 (UK).
Eight Miles High – The Best Of The Byrds Sony/Camden 88697 63627 2 (UK).
Setlist: The Very Best Of The Byrds Live Columbia/Legacy 88697 97753 2 (US).
Turn! Turn! Turn!: The Ultimate Collection Sony/Columbia Music 88875 151652 (UK).
The 60s – The Byrds Sony Music 8888377667 2 (US).

With the Flying Burrito Brothers:

Burrito Deluxe A&M SD 4258 (US)/A&M AMLS 983 (UK).
'Lazy Days'; 'Image Of Me'; 'High Fashion Queen'; 'If You Gotta Go'; 'Man In The Fog'; 'Farther Along'; 'Older Guys'; 'Cody, Cody'; 'God's Own Singer'; 'Down In The Churchyard'; 'Wild Horses'.
Released May 1970 (US/UK).

The Flying Burrito Brothers A&M SD 424295 (US)/A&M AMLS 64295 (UK). 'White Line Fever'; 'Colorado'; 'Hand To Mouth'; 'Tried So Hard'; 'Just Can't Be'; 'To Ramona'; 'Four Days Of Rain'; 'Can't You Hear Me Calling'; 'All Alone'; 'Why Are You Crying'.
Released June 1971 (US/UK).

Last Of The Red Hot Burritos A&M SD 4343 (US)/A&M AMLS 64343 (UK). 'Devil In Disguise'; 'Six Days On The Road'; 'My Uncle'; 'Dixie Breakdown'; 'Don't Let Your Deal Go Down'; 'Orange Blossom Special'; 'Ain't That A Lot Of Love'; 'High Fashion Queen'; 'Don't Fight It'; 'Hot Burrito # 2'; 'Losing Game'.
Released February 1972 (US/UK). Three additional tracks, 'Money Honey', 'Wake Up Little Susie' and 'One Hundred Years From Now', were included on the Australian CD reissue in 2008.

Grass Roots A&M AMLB 51038 (UK).
This A&M UK sampler features one side each of previously released material from Dillard & Clark and the Flying Burrito Brothers.
Released October 1972 (UK).

Honky Tonk Heaven A&M 87585 XDT (Holland).
Compilation. 2 record set. 'Tonight The Bottle Let Me Down'; 'Angel'; 'Close Up The Honky Tonks'; 'Green, Green Grass Of Home'; 'Break My Mind'; 'Just Because'; 'Dim Lights'; 'Crazy Arms'; 'Boney Moroney'; 'Sing Me Back Home'; 'Six Days On The Road'; 'To Love Somebody'; 'Honky Tonk Women'; 'Lodi'; 'Together Again'; 'Did You See'; 'Beat The Heat'; 'Pick Me Up On Your Way Down'; 'Payday'; 'In My Own Small Way'; 'Feel Good Music'; 'Here Tonight'.
This Dutch release includes rare outtakes, thus its inclusion here.
Released January 1974 (Holland).

Close Up The Honky Tonks A&M SD 3631 (US)/A&M AMLH 63631(UK). Compilation. 'Hot Burrito #2'; 'Do Right Woman'; 'Wheels'; 'Sin City'; 'Christine's Tune (Devil in Disguise)'; 'Hot Burrito #1'; 'God's Own Singer'; 'If You Gotta Go, Go Now'; 'High Fashion Queen'; 'Cody, Cody'; 'Wild Horses'; 'The Train Song'; 'Close Up The Honky Tonks'; 'Sing Me Back Home'; 'Bony Moronies' [sic]; 'To Love Somebody'; 'Break My Mind'; 'Beat The Heat'; 'Did You See'; 'Here Tonight'; 'Money Honey'; 'Roll Over Beethoven'; 'Wake Up Little Susie'.
Includes outtakes. Effectively a response to the Dutch compilation *Honky Tonk Heaven.*
Released July 1974 (US/UK).

Sleepless Nights A&M SD 4578 (US)/A&M AMLH 64578 (UK).
Compilation. 'Brand New Heartache'; 'Tonight The Bottle Let Me Down'; 'Sing Me Back Home'; 'Your Angel Steps Out Of Heaven'; 'Crazy Arms'; 'Sleepless Nights'; 'Close Up The Honky Tonks'; 'Together Again'; 'Honky Tonk Women'; 'Green, Green Grass Of Home'; 'Dim Lights'; 'The Angels Rejoiced Last Night'.

Includes earlier outtakes, this one focusing on Gram Parsons.
Released May 1976 (US)/June 1976 (UK).

Dim Lights, Thick Smoke And Loud, Loud Music Edsel ED CD 197 (UK).
Compilation. 'The Train Song'; 'Close Up The Honky Tonks'; 'Sing Me Back Home'; 'Tonight The Bottle Let Me Down'; 'Your Angel Steps Out Of Heaven'; 'Crazy Arms'; 'Together Again'; 'Honky Tonk Women'; 'Green, Green Grass Of Home'; 'Dim Lights'; 'Bony Moronie'; 'To Love Somebody'; 'Break My Mind'.
Includes outtakes see *Honky Tonk Heaven* for similar.
Released March 1987 (UK).

Farther Along: The Best Of The Flying Burrito Brothers. A&M CD 5216 (US).
Compilation. 'Christine's Tune (Devil In Disguise)'; 'Sin City'; 'Do Right Woman'; 'Dark End Of The Street'; 'Wheels'; 'Juanita'; 'Hot Burrito # 1'; 'Hot Burrito # 2'; 'Do You Know How It Feels'; 'Break My Mind'; 'Farther Along'; 'Cody, Cody'; 'God's Own Singer'; 'Wild Horses'; 'Dim Lights'; 'Just Because'; 'Six Days On The Road'; 'To Love Somebody'; 'Close Up The Honky Tonks'; 'Sing Me Back Home'; 'I Shall Be Released'.
Includes outtakes, most notably an alternate take of 'Sing Me Back Home' and the previously unissued 'I Shall Be Released'.
Released October 1988 (US).

Out Of The Blue A&M 540408-2 (US/UK).
Compilation. 2 CD set. 'Sing Me Back Home'; 'Hot Burrito #2'; 'Break My Mind'; 'Dark End Of The Street'; 'Cody Cody'; 'Wheels'; 'Hot Burrito #1'; 'Sin City'; 'Do Right Woman'; 'God's Own Singer'; 'Older Guys'; 'Train Song'; 'Lazy Days'; 'Christine's Tune'; 'Close Up The Honky Tonks'; 'Do You Know How It Feels'; 'High Fashion Queen'; 'Man In The Fog'; 'To Love Somebody'; 'My Uncle'; 'Hippie Boy'; 'Juanita'; 'Image Of Me'; 'Farther Along'; 'If You Gotta Go'; 'Bony Moronie'; 'Six Days On The Road'; 'Wild Horses'; 'Down In The Churchyard'; 'Wake Up Little Susie' (live); 'Pick Me Up On Your Way Down'; 'Just Because'; 'Lodi'; 'Money Honey' (live); 'I Shall Be Released'; 'White Line Fever'; 'Ain't That A Lot Of Love' (live); 'Don't Fight It' (live); 'Losing Game' (live); 'Tried So Hard'; 'All Alone'; 'One Hundred Years From Now' (live).
Over familiar material, but includes rare live versions of several songs.
Released April 1996 (US/UK).

Hot Burritos! The Flying Burrito Brothers Anthology 1969–1972 A&M 490610 (US)/A&M 54074 (UK).
Compilation. 2 CD set. Disc 1: 'Christine's Tune (Devil In Disguise)'; 'Do Right Woman'; 'Dark End Of The Street'; 'My Uncle'; 'Wheels'; 'Juanita'; 'Hot Burrito # 1'; 'Hot Burrito # 2'; 'Do You Know How It Feels'; 'Hippie Boy'; 'The Train Song'; 'Lazy Days'; 'Image Of Me'; 'High Fashion Queen'; 'If You Gotta Go'; 'Man In The Fog'; 'Farther Along'; 'Older Guys'; 'Cody Cody'; 'God's Own Singer'; 'Down In The Churchyard'; 'Wild Horses'.

Disc 2: 'Six Days On The Road'; 'Close Up The Honky Tonks'; 'Break My Mind'; 'Dim Lights'; 'Sing Me Back Home'; 'Tonight The Bottle Let Me Down'; 'To Love Somebody'; 'White Line Fever'; 'Colorado'; 'Hand To Mouth'; 'Tried So Hard'; 'Just Can't Be'; 'To Ramona'; 'Four Days Of Rain'; 'Can't You Hear Me Calling'; 'All Alone'; 'Why Are You Crying'; 'Here Tonight'; 'Ain't That A Lot Of Love' (live); 'Losing Game' (live).
Released April 2000 (US/UK).

The Best Of The Flying Burrito Brothers – The Millennium Collection A&M 493056 (US).
Compilation. 'Christine's Tune'; 'Sin City'; 'Do Right Woman'; 'Dark End Of The Street'; 'Wheels'; 'Hot Burrito # 2'; 'Train Song'; 'Lazy Days'; 'Cody, Cody'; 'Break My Mind'; 'Together Again'; 'Wild Horses'.
Released: June 2001 (US).

Sin City – The Very Best Of The Flying Burrito Brothers A&M 069 4932642 (US).
Compilation. 'Christine's Tune'; 'Sin City'; 'Do Right Woman'; 'Dark End Of The Street'; 'My Uncle'; 'Wheels'; 'Juanita'; 'Hot Burrito # 1'; 'Hot Burrito # 2'; 'Do You Know How It Feels'; 'Hippie Boy'; 'The Train Song'; 'Lazy Days'; 'Image Of Me'; 'High Fashion Queen'; 'If You Gotta Go'; 'Man In The Fog'; 'Farther Along'; 'Older Guys'; 'Cody, Cody'; 'God's Own Singer'; 'Down In The Churchyard'; 'Wild Horses'; 'Six Days On The Road'; 'Close Up The Honky Tonks'.
Released April 2002 (US).

The Collection Spectrum 9820305 (UK).
Compilation. 'Break My Mind'; 'Sing Me Back Home'; 'Close Up The Honky Tonks'; 'Image Of Me'; 'White Line Fever'; 'Six Days On The Road'; 'Dim Lights'; 'Tonight The Bottle Let Me Down'; 'Sin City'; 'Dark End Of The Street'; 'Pick Me Up On Your Way Down'; 'God's Own Singer'; 'Green Green Grass Of Home'; 'Crazy Arms'; 'Together Again'; 'Wake Up Little Susie'; 'Here Tonight'; 'Your Angel Steps Out Of Heaven'.
Released January 2005 (UK).

The Definitive Collection Hip-O-Select 80008781-02 (US).
Compilation. 'Christine's Tune'; 'Sin City'; 'Do Right Woman'; 'Dark End Of The Street'; 'My Uncle'; 'Wheels'; 'Juanita'; 'Hot Burrito # 1'; 'Hot Burrito # 2'; 'Do You Know How It Feels'; 'Hippie Boy'; 'The Train Song'; 'Lazy Days'; 'Image Of Me'; 'High Fashion Queen'; 'If You Gotta Go'; 'Man In The Fog'; 'Farther Along'; 'Older Guys'; 'Cody, Cody'; 'God's Own Singer'; 'Down In The Churchyard'; 'Wild Horses'; 'Six Days On The Road'; 'Close Up The Honky Tonks'.
Released April 2007 (US).

Live At The Avalon Ballroom 1969 Amoeba Records AM0002 (US).
2 CD set. Disc 1 (4 April): 'Close Up The Honky Tonks'; 'Dark End Of The Street'; 'Medley: Undo The Right/Somebody's Back In Town'; 'She Once Lived Here'; 'We've Got To Get Ourselves Together'; 'Lucille'; 'Hot Burrito # 1';

'Hot Burrito # 2'; 'Long Black Limousine'; 'Mental Revenge'; 'Sin City'. Special bonus tracks: '$1000 Wedding'; 'When Will I Be Loved'.
Disc 2 (6 April): 'Medley: Undo The Right/Somebody's Back In Town'; 'She Once Lived Here'; 'Mental Revenge'; 'We've Got To Get Ourselves Together'; 'Lucille'; 'Sin City'; 'You Win Again'; 'Hot Burrito # 1'; 'Hot Burrito # 2'; 'You're Still On My Mind'; 'The Train Song'; 'Long Black Limousine'; 'Dream Baby (How Long Must I Dream)'; 'Do Right Woman'.
Released: October 2007 (US). The front cover credits this as *'Gram Parsons With The Flying Burrito Brothers'*. The spine says it is *'Gram Parsons Archives Vol. 1'*.

Authorized Bootleg: Fillmore East, New York., N.Y., Late Show, Nov. 7 1970 Hip-O-Select 001520702 (US).
'Lazy Days'; 'One Hundred Years From Now'; 'My Uncle'; 'Cody, Cody'; 'Christine's Tune (Devil In Disguise)'; 'I Am A Pilgrim'; 'Dixie Breakdown'; 'Willie And The Hand Jive'; 'Wild Horses'; 'Feel Good Music'; 'Hot Burrito # 2'; 'Six Days On The Road'.
Released February 2011 (US).

With Firefall:

Firefall Atlantic SD 18174 (US)/Atlantic K 50260 (UK).
'It Doesn't Matter'; 'Love Isn't All'; 'Livin' Ain't Livin'; 'No Way Out'; 'Dolphin's Lullaby'; 'Cinderella'; 'Sad Ol' Love Song'; 'You Are The Woman'; 'Mexico'; 'Do What You Want'.
Released April 1976 (US/UK).

Luna Sea Atlantic SD 19101 (US)/Atlantic K 50355 (UK).
'So Long'; 'Just Remember I Love You'; 'Sold On You'; 'Someday Soon'; 'Just Think'; 'Getaway'; 'Only A Fool'; 'Head On Home'; 'Piece Of Paper'; 'Even Steven'.
Released August 1977 (US/UK). Reissued on CD by Rhino with bonus tracks: 'Tropical Night', 'Rainforest', 'Ya Never Know' and 'Over You'.

Elan Atlantic SD 19183 (US)/Atlantic K 50494 (UK).
'Strange Way'; 'Sweet And Sour'; 'Wrong Side Of Town'; 'Count Your Blessings'; 'Get You Back'; 'Anymore'; 'Baby'; 'Goodbye, I Love You'; 'Sweet Ann'; 'Winds Of Change'.
Released October 1978 (US)/January 1979 (UK). Reissued on CD by Rhino with bonus tracks: 'New Man', 'Headed For A Fall' and 'Sharpshootin' At The Senator'.

Undertow Atlantic SD 16006 (US).
'Love That Got Away'; 'Headed For A Fall; 'Only Time Will Tell'; 'Laugh Or Cry'; 'Stardust'; 'If You Only Knew'; 'Some Things Never Change'; 'Business Is Business'; 'Leave It Alone'; 'Undertow'.
Released March 1980 (US). Reissued on CD by Rhino with bonus tracks: 'Just What You Need', 'Crying In The Night' and 'Lips'.

The Best Of Firefall Atlantic SD 19316 (US)/Atlantic K 50839 (UK).
Compilation. 'You Are The Woman'; 'Just Remember I Love You'; 'Strange Way'; 'Cinderella'; 'Staying With It'; 'Goodbye, I Love You'; 'Headed For A Fall'; 'So Long'; 'Love That Got Away'; 'Mexico'.
Released November 1981 (US)/December 1981 (UK).

Greatest Hits Atlantic/Rhino R2 71055 (US).
Compilation. 'Livin' Ain't Livin''; 'Cinderella'; 'You Are The Woman'; 'Mexico'; 'It Doesn't Matter'; 'Just Remember I Love You'; 'So Long'; 'Someday Soon'; 'Strange Way'; 'Goodbye, I Love You'; 'Sweet And Sour'; 'Love That Got Away'; 'Headed For A Fall'; 'Staying With It'; 'Break Of Dawn'; 'Always'; 'Runaway Love'; 'Run Run Away'.
Released September 1992 (US). Includes abbreviated mix of 'Strange Way'.

The Essentials Atlantic/Rhino 76047 (US).
Compilation. 'Livin' Ain't Livin'' (single version); 'You Are The Woman' (album version); 'Cinderella' (single version); 'Just Remember I Love You' (album version); 'So Long' (album version); 'Strange Way' (single version); 'Goodbye, I Love You' (single version); 'Headed For A Fall' (single version); 'Love That Got Away' (album version); 'Staying With It' (album version); 'Always' (album version); 'Mexico' (album version).
Released June 2002 (US).

Alive In America Renaissance RMED 00702 (US).
'Cinderella'; 'Mexico'; 'Goodbye, I Love You'; 'Get You Back'; 'Just Remember I Love You'; 'Sweet And Sour'; 'No Way Out'; 'It Doesn't Matter Anymore'; 'Lips!'; 'Anymore'; 'Strange Way'; 'Livin' Ain't Livin''; 'Just What You Need'; 'Colorado'.
Released January 2006 (US).

With Jerry Jeff Walker:

Cow Jazz South Coast/MCA 5355 (US).
'Dealing With The Devil'; 'Don't Think Twice, It's Alright'; 'Old '59'; 'Green Back Dollar'; 'Loving Of The Game'; 'Laying My Life On The Line'; 'Still Around'; 'Promise'; 'Tangee'; 'Wind'.
Released September 1982 (US).

Clarke has also guested on albums by Gene Clark (*Gene Clark With The Gosdin Brothers; Roadmaster; Early LA Sessions*), the Gosdin Brothers ('One Hundred Years From Now' single), Dillard & Clark (*The Fantastic Expedition Of Dillard & Clark*), Barry McGuire (*Barry McGuire & The Doctor*), Roger McGuinn (*Roger McGuinn*), Terry Melcher (*Terry Melcher*), the Dependables (*Klatu Berrada Niktu*), Twin Engine (*Twin Engine*) and Country Funk (*Zuma*). He is also featured on the 1991 cassette recording *The Legacy Album* featuring his own version of the 'Byrds' on the track 'The Flame'. The album is credited to the South Florida Musicians Unite For AIDS Relief.

CHRIS HILLMAN

Albums with the Scottsville Squirrel Barkers:
Blue Grass Favorites Crown CLP 5346/CST 346 (US).
'Shady Grove'; 'Home Sweet Home'; 'Katy Klyne'; 'Swamp Coot'; 'The Willow Tree'; 'Walking Cane'; 'Three Finger Breakdown'; 'Cripple Creek'; 'Crown Junction Breakdown'; 'Ruebin's Train'.
The label copy, in contrast to the sleeve, simply titles the album, *Blue Grass.*
Released 1962 (US).

Albums with the Hillmen:

The Hillmen Together ST-T-1012 (US).
'Fair And Tender Ladies'; 'Winsborough Cotton Mill Blues'; 'Wheel Hoss'; 'Farethewell' [*sic*]; 'Go'in Up' [sic]; 'With These Chains'; 'When The Ship Comes In'; 'Roll On Muddy River'; 'Blue Grass Chopper'; 'Ranger's Command'; 'Prisoner's Plea'.
Although never released at the time of its recording in 1964, tapes of the Hillmen were compiled for this retrospectively released album on Together in 1969. The album was later reissued on the Dutch label Negram and included the previously unheard 'Copper Kettle'. In 1981, the work was remixed and reissued on Sugar Hill Records (SH-3719) complete with four unissued tracks, 'Brown Mountain Light', 'Sangeree', 'Barbara Allen' and 'Back Road Fever'. Finally, in July 2007, Sierra Records reissued the original album on CD, complete with original and new liner notes and reverting to the mix recording engineer Dave Hassinger used on the Together release. Sierra's CD also included six additional tracks: 'Brown Mountain Light', 'Sangaree', 'Barbara Allen', 'Back Road Fever', 'Copper Kettle' and 'Salt Creek'.
Released 1969 (US).

Albums with the Byrds:
See Discography *Volume 1* under the following sections: *Byrds Singles, Albums, Compilations* and *Archival Albums* for fuller details of release dates, complete track listings, alternate serial numbers, special issues/editions, and more.

Mr Tambourine Man Columbia CL 2372 (mono)/Columbia CS 9172 (stereo) (US). CBS BPG 62571 (mono)/CBS SBPG 62571 (stereo) (UK). Remastered CD edition with bonus tracks: Columbia Legacy CK 64845 (US)/Columbia Legacy 483705 2 (UK).

Turn! Turn! Turn! Columbia CL 2454 (mono)/Columbia CS 9254 (stereo) (US). CBS BPG 62652 (mono)/CBS SBPG 62652 (stereo) (UK). Remastered CD edition with bonus tracks: Columbia Legacy CK 64846 (US)/Columbia Legacy 483706 2 (UK).

Fifth Dimension Columbia CL 2549 (mono)/Columbia CS 9349 (stereo) (US). CBS BPG 62783 (mono)/CBS SBPG 62783 (stereo) (UK). Remastered

CD edition with bonus tracks: Columbia Legacy CK 64847(US)/Columbia Legacy 483707 2 (UK).

Younger Than Yesterday Columbia CL 2642 (mono)/Columbia CS 9442 (stereo) (US). CBS BPG 62988 (mono)/CBS SBPG 62988 (stereo) (UK). Remastered CD edition with bonus tracks: Columbia Legacy CK 64848 (US)/Columbia Legacy 483708 2 (UK).

The Notorious Byrd Brothers Columbia CL 2775 (mono)/Columbia CS 9575 (stereo) (US). CBS 63169 (mono)/CBS S 63169 (stereo) (UK). Remastered CD edition with bonus tracks: Columbia Legacy CK 65151 (US)/Columbia Legacy 486751 2 (UK).

Sweetheart Of The Rodeo Columbia CL 9670 (mono)/CS 9670 (stereo) (US). CBS 63353 (mono)/CBS S 63353 (stereo) (UK). Remastered CD edition with bonus tracks: Columbia Legacy CK 65150 (US)/Columbia Legacy 486752 2 (UK). Special issue *Sweetheart Of The Rodeo* [*Legacy Edition*]: Columbia Legacy COL 510921 2 (US).

Byrds Asylum SD 5058 (US)/Asylum SYLA 8754 (UK).

Archival albums with the Byrds:

Preflyte Together ST-T-1001 (US)/Bumble GEXP 8001 (UK).
The Original Singles Volume 1 1965–1967 CBS 31851 (UK)/Columbia FC 37335 (US).
The Original Singles Volume 2 1967–1969 CBS 32103 (UK).
Never Before Re-Flyte MH 70318 (US).
In The Beginning Rhino R2 70244 (US).
Sanctuary Sundazed LP 5061 (US).
Sanctuary II Sundazed LP 5065 (US).
The Preflyte Sessions Sundazed SC 11116 (US).
Sanctuary IV Sundazed LP 5090 (US).
The Columbia Singles '65–'67 Sundazed LP 5130/P2 55624 (US).
Another Dimension Sundazed SEP 2 10-168 (US).
Preflyte [extended version] Floating World FLOATD6122 (UK).

Box Sets with the Byrds:

The Byrds Columbia Legacy 46773 (US)/Columbia Legacy 4676112 (UK).
12 Dimensions The Columbia Recordings 1965–1972 (13-CD box set) Columbia 497610 2/4976102000 (UK).
There Is A Season (4-CD box set and DVD) Columbia/Legacy 82876877002 (US/UK).
The Complete Columbia Albums Collection Columbia Legacy 886978738028 (US).

Isolated appearances with the Byrds:

See *Volume 1*: *Byrds Albums, Guest Slots/Rarities, Compilations* and *Archival Albums* for fuller details of release dates and alternate territory serial numbers.

Early LA Together ST-T-1014 (US).

Don't Make Waves MGM 4483 ST (US).
Roadmaster A&M 87584 (Holland).
Monterey International Pop Festival Rhino R2 70506 (US)/Castle Communications ROK CD 102 (UK).
3 Byrds Land In London 1977 Strange Fruit SFRSCD 001 (UK).
3 Byrds In London 1977 – Live At The BBC Mastertone 8228 (US).
Byrd Parts Raven RVCD 77 (Australia).
Byrd Parts 2 Raven RVCD 165 (Australia).
Sixties Transition Sierra SXCD 6027 (US)/Floating World FLOATM6125 (UK).
Previously issued material also appears on the soundtracks to *Easy Rider*, *Homer*, *Forrest Gump* and *The Limey*.

Compilations/Hits Collections with the Byrds:
See *Volume 1* for additional details.
The Byrds Greatest Hits Columbia CL 2716 (US)/CBS SBPG 63107 (UK).
The Byrds Greatest Hits Volume 2 CBS S 64650 (UK).
Best Of Volume 2 Columbia C31795 (US).
History Of The Byrds CBS 68242 (UK).
Return Of The Byrds Columbia Realm 2V 8006-7 (US).
The Byrds CBS 88320 (UK).
The Byrds Play Dylan Columbia PC 36293 (US)/CBS 31795 (UK).
The Very Best Of The Byrds Columbia CS P-P2 17596 (US).
The Byrds Collection Castle Communications CCSLP 151 (UK).
The Very Best Of The Byrds Columbia CBS 4634189 2 (Holland/UK).
Full Flyte Raven RVCD 10 (Australia).
Free Flyte Sony Music Special Products A 17733 (US).
Greatest Hits Remastered Columbia 467843 2 (UK).
20 Essential Tracks From The Boxed Set: 1965–1970 Columbia/Legacy CK 47884/471665-2 (US/UK).
Definitive Collection Columbia 480548 9 (UK).
Nashville West Sony Music Special Products A 28123 (US).
The Very Best Of The Byrds Columbia 487995 2 (UK).
The Best Of The Byrds Columbia 488146 2 (UK).
Super Hits Columbia Legacy 504725 2 (UK)/Columbia Legacy CK 65637 (US).
The Byrds Greatest Hits Columbia/Legacy CK 66230 (US).
The Byrds Sony Music Special Products A 30827 (US).
The Byrds Play The Songs Of Bob Dylan Columbia 501946 2 (UK).
The Byrds Play Dylan Columbia/Legacy CK 85430 (US).
The Essential Byrds Columbia Legacy 512249 2 (UK)/Columbia Legacy C2K 89110 (US).
Mojo Presents . . . An Introduction To The Byrds – 24 Classic Songs Columbia 512778 2 (UK).
Mr Tambourine Man – The Best Of The Byrds Sony Music Media SMM 516489-2 (Germany/UK).

America's Great National Treasure Sony/BMG A 96086 (US).
The Very Best Of The Byrds Sony/BMG 82876 855142 (UK).
Byrds: A Collection Sony BMG 88697 12448 2 (UK).
The Byrds Play Dylan Sony BMG 88697 25267 2 (UK).
Playlist: The Very Best Of The Byrds Columbia Legacy 88697 39219 2 (US).
Steel Box Sony BMG 88697 45981 2 (UK).
Eight Miles High – The Best Of The Byrds Sony/Camden 88697 63627 2 (UK).
Setlist: The Very Best Of The Byrds Live Columbia/Legacy 88697 97753 2 (US).
Turn! Turn! Turn!: The Ultimate Collection Sony/Columbia Music 88875 151652 (UK).
The 60s – The Byrds Sony Music 8888377667 2 (US).

With the Flying Burrito Brothers:
The Gilded Palace Of Sin A&M SD 4175 (US)/A&M AMLS 931 (UK).
'Christine's Tune'; 'Sin City'; 'Do Right Woman'; 'Dark End Of The Street'; 'My Uncle'; 'Wheels'; 'Juanita'; 'Hot Burrito # 1'; 'Hot Burrito # 2'; 'Do You Know How It Feels'; 'Hippie Boy'.
Released March 1969 (US)/April 1969 (UK).

Burrito Deluxe A&M SD 4258 (US)/A&M AMLS 983 (UK).
'Lazy Days'; 'Image Of Me'; 'High Fashion Queen'; 'If You Gotta Go'; 'Man In The Fog'; 'Farther Along'; 'Older Guys'; 'Cody, Cody'; 'God's Own Singer'; 'Down In The Churchyard'; 'Wild Horses'.
Released May 1970 (US/UK).

The Flying Burrito Brothers A&M SD 4295 (US)/A&M AMLS 64295 (UK).
'White Line Fever'; 'Colorado'; 'Hand To Mouth'; 'Tried So Hard'; 'Just Can't Be'; 'To Ramona'; 'Four Days Of Rain'; 'Can't You Hear Me Calling'; 'All Alone'; 'Why Are You Crying'.
Released June 1971 (US/UK).

Last Of The Red Hot Burritos A&M SD 4343 (US)/A&M AMLS 64343 (UK).
'Devil In Disguise'; 'Six Days On The Road'; 'My Uncle'; 'Dixie Breakdown'; 'Don't Let Your Deal Go Down'; 'Orange Blossom Special'; 'Ain't That A Lot Of Love'; 'High Fashion Queen'; 'Don't Fight It'; 'Hot Burrito # 2'; 'Losing Game'.
Released February 1972 (US/UK). Three additional tracks, 'Money Honey', 'Wake Up Little Susie' and 'One Hundred Years From Now', were included on the Australian CD reissue in 2008.

Grass Roots A&M AMLB 51038 (UK).
This A&M UK sampler features one side each of previously released material from Dillard & Clark and the Flying Burrito Brothers.
Released October 1972 (UK).

Honky Tonk Heaven A&M 87585 XDT (Holland).
Compilation. See Michael Clarke section for track listing.
Released January 1974 (Holland).

Close Up The Honky Tonks A&M SD 3631 (US)/A&M AMLH 63631 (UK).
Compilation. See Michael Clarke section for track listing.
Released July 1974 (US/UK).

Sleepless Nights A&M SD 4578 (US)/A&M AMLH 64578 (UK).
Compilation. See Michael Clarke section for track listing.
Released May 1976 (US)/June 1976 (UK).

Dim Lights, Thick Smoke And Loud, Loud Music Edsel ED CD 197 (UK).
Compilation. See Michael Clarke section for track listing.
Released March 1987 (UK).

Farther Along: The Best Of The Flying Burrito Brothers A&M CD 5216 (US).
Compilation. See Michael Clarke section for track listing.
Released October 1988 (US).

Out Of The Blue A&M 540408-2 (US/UK).
Compilation. See Michael Clarke section for track listing.
Released April 1996 (US/UK).

Hot Burritos! The Flying Burrito Brothers Anthology 1969–1972 A&M 490610 (US)/A&M 54074 (UK).
Compilation. See Michael Clarke section for track listing.
Released April 2000 (US/UK).

The Best Of The Flying Burrito Brothers – The Millennium Collection A&M 493056 (US).
Compilation. See Michael Clarke section for track listing.
Released: June 2001 (US).

Sin City – The Very Best Of The Flying Burrito Brothers A&M 069 4932642 (US).
Compilation. See Michael Clarke section for track listing.
Released April 2002 (US).

The Collection Spectrum 9820305 (UK).
Compilation. See Michael Clarke section for track listing.
Released January 2005 (UK).

The Definitive Collection Hip-O-Select 80008781-02 (US).
Compilation. See Michael Clarke section for track listing.
Released April 2007 (US).

Live At The Avalon Ballroom 1969 Amoeba Records AM0002 (US).
See Michael Clarke section for track listing. The front cover credits this as *'Gram Parsons With The Flying Burrito Brothers'*. The spine says it is *'Gram Parsons Archives Vol. 1'*.
Released: October 2007 (US).

Authorized Bootleg: Fillmore East, N.Y., N.Y., Late Show, Nov. 7 1970 Hip-O-Select 001520702 (US).
See Michael Clarke section for track listing.
Released February 2011 (US).

With Manassas:

Stephen Stills/Manassas Atlantic SD 903 (US)/Atlantic K 60021 (UK).
'Song Of Love'; 'Rock & Roll Crazies'; 'Cuban Bluegrass'; 'Jet Set (Sigh)'; 'Anyway'; 'Both Of Us (Bound To Lose)'; 'Fallen Eagle'; 'Jesus Gave Love Away For Free'; 'Colorado'; 'So Begins The Task'; 'Hide It So Deep'; 'Don't Look At My Shadow'; 'It Doesn't Matter'; 'Johnny's Garden'; 'Bound To Fall'; 'How Far'; 'Move Around'; 'The Love Gangster'; 'What To Do'; 'Right Now'; 'The Treasure'; 'Blues Man'.
Released April 1972 (US)/May 1972 (UK).

Down The Road Atlantic SD 7250 (US)/Atlantic K 40440 (UK).
'Isn't It About Time'; 'Lies'; 'Pensamiento'; 'So Many Times'; 'Business On The Street'; 'Do You Remember The Americans'; 'Down The Road'; 'City Junkies'; 'Guaguancó De Veró'; 'Rollin' My Stone'.
Released April 1973 (US)/May 1973 (UK).

Still Stills: The Best Of Stephen Stills Atlantic SD 18201 (US)/Atlantic K 50327 (UK).
Compilation. Includes some Manassas material, all previously released.
Released December 1976 (US/UK).

Pieces Eyewall/Rhino 8122-79850-0 (US).
'Witching Hour'; 'Sugar Babe'; 'Lies'; 'My Love Is A Gentle Thing'; 'Like A Fox'; 'Word Game'; 'Tan Sola Y Triste'; 'Fit To Be Tied'; 'Love And Satisfy'; 'High And Dry'; 'Panhandle Rag'; 'Uncle Pen'; 'Do You Remember The Americans'; 'Dim Lights, Thick Smoke (And Loud, Loud Music)'; 'I Am My Brother'.
Released September 2009 (US).

As Souther, Hillman, Furay Band:

The Souther, Hillman, Furay Band Asylum 7E-1006 (US)/Asylum SYLA 8758 (UK).
'Fallin' In Love'; 'Heavenly Fire'; 'The Heartbreaker'; 'Believe Me'; 'Border Town'; 'Safe At Home'; 'Pretty Goodbyes'; 'Rise And Fall'; 'The Flight Of The Dove'; 'Deep, Dark And Dreamless'.
Released July 1974 (US)/August 1974 (UK).

Trouble In Paradise Asylum 7E-1036 (US)/Asylum SYLA 8760 (UK).
'Trouble In Paradise'; 'Move Me Real Slow'; 'For Someone I Love'; 'Mexico'; 'Love And Satisfy'; 'On The Line'; 'Prisoner In Disguise'; 'Follow Me Through'; 'Somebody Must Be Wrong'.
Released June 1975 (US)/September 1975 (UK).

As Chris Hillman:

Slippin' Away Asylum 7E-1062 (US)/Asylum K 53041(UK).
'Step On Out'; 'Slippin' Away'; 'Falling Again'; 'Take It On The Run'; 'Blue Morning'; 'Witching Hour'; 'Down In The Churchyard'; 'Love Is The Sweetest Amnesty'; 'Midnight Again'; '(Take Me In Your) Lifeboat'.
Released June 1976 (US/UK).

Clear Sailin' Asylum 7E 1104 (US)/Asylum K 53060 (UK).
'Nothing Gets Through'; 'Fallen Favorite'; 'Quits'; 'Hot Dusty Roads'; 'Heartbreaker'; 'Played The Fool'; 'Lucky In Love'; 'Rollin' And Tumblin''; 'Ain't That Peculiar'; 'Clear Sailin''. [The track 'Played The Fool' is titled 'Playing The Fool' on the album sleeve].
Released September 1977 (US)/August 1977 (UK).

Morning Sky Sugar Hill 3729 (US)/Sundown SDLP 053 (UK).
'Tomorrow Is A Long Time'; 'The Taker'; 'Here Today & Gone Tomorrow'; 'Morning Sky'; 'Ripple'; 'Good Time Charlie's Got The Blues'; 'Don't Let Your Sweet Love Die'; 'Mexico'; 'It's Happening To You'; 'Hickory Wind'.
Released November 1982 (US)/November 1987 (UK).

Desert Rose Sugar Hill 3743 (US)/Spindrift SPIN 113 (UK).
'Why You Been Gone So Long'; 'Somebody's Back In Town'; 'Wall Around Your Heart'; 'Rough & Rowdy Ways'; 'Desert Rose'; 'Running The Roadblocks'; 'I Can't Keep You In Love With Me'; 'Treasure Of Love'; 'Ashes Of Love'; 'Turn Your Radio On'.
Released August 1984 (US)/November 1984 (UK).

Like A Hurricane Sugar Hill SHCD 3878 (US).
'Back's Against The Wall'; 'Angels' Cry'; 'Sooner Or Later'; 'Carry Me Home'; 'Run Again'; 'Second Wind'; 'When You Walk In The Room'; 'Like A Hurricane'; 'Living On The Edge'; 'Forgiveness'; 'I'm Still Alive'; 'Heaven's Lullaby'.
Released June 1998 (US).

The Other Side Sovereign/Cooking Vinyl COOK CD 340 (US/UK).
'Eight Miles High'; 'True Love'; 'Drifting'; 'The Other Side'; 'Heaven Is My Home'; 'Touch Me'; 'The Wheel'; 'True He's Gone'; 'Heavenly Grace'; 'It Doesn't Matter'; 'Missing You'; 'The Water Is Wide'; 'I Know I Need You'; 'Our Savior's Hands'. The download version of the album featured an extra song, 'Old Rockin' Chair', which was also issued as a CD single.
Released June 2005 (US/UK).

As McGuinn, Clark & Hillman:

McGuinn, Clark & Hillman Capitol SW 11910 (US)/Capitol EST 11910 (UK).
'Long Long Time'; 'Little Mama'; 'Don't You Write Her Off'; 'Surrender To Me'; 'Backstage Pass'; 'Stopping Traffic'; 'Feelin' Higher'; 'Sad Boy'; 'Release Me Girl'; 'Bye Bye Baby'.

Released January 1979 (US)/March 1979 (UK). The 2001 CD reissue features bonus demo versions of 'Surrender To Me' and the previously unreleased compositions 'Little Girl' and 'I Love Her'.

City Capitol ST 12043 (US)/Capitol EST 12043 (UK).
'Who Taught The Night'; 'One More Chance'; 'Won't Let You Down'; 'Street Talk'; 'City'; 'Skate Date'; 'Givin' Herself Away'; 'Deeper In'; 'Painted Fire'; 'Let Me Down Easy'.
Released January 1980 (US)/February 1980 (UK).

Return Flight Edsel EDCD 358 (UK).
Compilation. See McGuinn section for track listing.
Released November 1992 (UK).

Return Flight II Edsel EDCD 373 (UK).
Compilation. See McGuinn section for track listing.
Released June 1993 (UK).

The Capitol Collection Acadia/Evangeline 805772818620 (UK).
See McGuinn section for track listing.
Released January 2008 (UK).

As McGuinn/Hillman:
McGuinn/Hillman Capitol SOO 12108 (US)/Capitol EA ST 12108 (UK).
'Mean Streets'; 'Entertainment'; 'Soul Shoes'; 'Between You And Me'; 'Angel'; 'Love Me Tonight'; 'King For A Night'; 'A Secret Side Of You'; 'Ain't No Money'; 'Turn Your Radio On'.
Released September 1980 (US)/October 1980 (UK).

With the Desert Rose Band:
The Desert Rose Band MCA Curb 5991 (US)/Curb/RCA ZL 90202 (UK).
'One Step Forward'; 'Love Reunited'; 'He's Back And I'm Blue'; 'Leave This Town'; 'Time Between'; 'Ashes Of Love'; 'One That Got Away'; 'Once More'; 'Glass Hearts'; 'Hard Times'.
Released April 1987 (US)/March 1988 (UK).

Running Curb/MCA 42169 (US).
'She Don't Love Nobody'; 'Running'; 'Hello Trouble'; 'I Still Believe In You'; 'Summer Wind'; 'For The Rich Man'; 'Step On Out'; 'Homeless'; 'Livin' In The House'; 'Our Songs'.
Released September 1988.

Pages Of Life MCA/Curb 42233-2 (US).
'Story Of Love'; 'Start All Over Again'; 'Missing You'; 'Just A Memory'; 'God's Plan'; 'Darkness On The Playground'; 'Our Baby's Gone'; 'Time Passes Me By'; 'Everybody's Hero'; 'In Another Lifetime'; 'Desert Rose'.
Released January 1990 (US).

True Love MCA MCAD 10407 (US).
'You Can Go Home'; 'It Takes A Believer'; 'Twilight Is Gone'; 'No-One Else'; 'A Matter Of Time'; 'Undying Love'; 'Behind These Walls'; 'True Love'; 'Glory And Power'; 'Shades Of Blue'.
Released July 1991 (US).

Life Goes On Curb 474969-2 (UK)
'What About Love'; 'Night After Night'; 'Walk On By'; 'Love's Refugees'; 'Life Goes On'; 'That's Not The Way'; 'Till It's Over'; 'Hold On'; 'A Little Rain'; 'Throw Me A Lifeline'.
Released September 1993 (UK).

A Dozen Roses: Greatest Hits MCA 10018 (US).
Compilation. 'Love Reunited'; 'One Step Forward'; 'He's Back And I'm Blue'; 'She Don't Love Nobody'; 'Summer Wind'; 'I Still Believe In You'; 'Hello Trouble'; 'Start All Over Again'; 'Story Of Love'; 'Will This Be The Day'; 'Come A Little Closer'; 'The Price I Pay'.
This compilation includes the otherwise unavailable singles 'Will This Be The Day' and 'Come A Little Closer', plus 'The Price I Pay' from Emmylou Harris' *Duets*.
Released January 1991 (US).

Traditional Curb Pinnacle 77602 (US).
Compilation. 'Undying Love'; 'Once More'; 'Price I Pay'; 'True Love'; 'Step On Out'; 'Time Between'; 'Our Songs'; 'Missing You'; 'Desert Rose'; 'Hard Times'.
Released January 1993 (US).

Sixteen Roses: *Greatest Hits* Curb 012/The Hit Label CURCD 012 (US/UK).
Compilation. 'Love Reunited'; 'One Step Forward'; 'He's Back And I'm Blue'; 'She Don't Love Nobody'; 'Summer Wind'; 'I Still Believe In You'; 'Hello Trouble'; 'Start All Over Again'; 'Story Of Love'; 'What About Love'; 'Life Goes On'; 'True Love'; 'Undying Love'; 'Price I Pay'; 'That's Not The Way'; 'Desert Rose'.
Released April 1994 (US/UK).

Best Of Desert Rose Band Curb 793790 (US).
'Love Reunited'; 'One Step Forward'; 'He's Back And I'm Blue'; 'Summer Wind'; 'I Still Believe In You'; 'She Don't Love Nobody'; 'Hello Trouble'; 'Start All Over Again'; 'In Another Lifetime'; 'Story Of Love';
Released February 2014 (US).

As Chris Hillman & Herb Pedersen:

Bakersfield Bound Sugar Hill SH CD 3852 (US).
'Playboy'; 'Which One Is To Blame'; 'Close Up The Honky Tonks'; 'Brand New Heartache'; 'Congratulations, Anyway'; 'It's Not Love (But It's Not Bad)'; 'He Don't Deserve You Anymore'; 'There Goes My Love'; 'My Baby's

Gone'; 'The Lost Highway'; 'Time Goes So Slow'; 'Just Tell Me Darlin''; 'Bakersfield Bound'.
Released May 1996 (US).

Way Out West Back Porch 72438 11978-2-0 (US).
'Backporch Boy'; 'There You Go'; 'Invitation To The Blues'; 'No Longer A Sweetheart Of Mine'; 'Problems'; 'Better Man Than That'; 'The Old Cross Road'; 'Sugar Cane'; 'After All Is Said And Done'; 'You Done Me Wrong'; 'Save The Last Dance For Me'; 'Are You Missing Me?'; 'That's The Way It Was'; 'You're Learning'; 'Our Love It Don't Come Easy'; 'Good Year'; 'Backporch Boy (Outro)'.
Released June 2002 (US).

At Edwards Barn Rounder 0652 (US).
'Going Up Home'; 'Love Reunited'; 'Turn! Turn! Turn! (To Everything There Is A Season)'; 'If I Could Only Win Your Love'; 'Tu Cancion'; 'Our Savior's Hands'; 'Wheels'; 'Have You Seen Her Face'; 'Eight Miles High'; 'Together Again'; 'Desert Rose'; 'Sin City'; 'The Cowboy Way'; 'Wait A Minute'; 'Heaven's Lullaby'. Bonus track 'It Doesn't Matter' available exclusively as a download from iTunes USA.
Released September 2010 (US).

As Rice, Rice, Hillman & Pedersen:
Out Of The Woodwork Rounder CD 0390 (US).
'Hard Times'; 'Lord Won't You Help Me'; 'Somewhere On The Road Tonight'; 'No One Else'; 'Streetcorner Stranger'; 'So Begins The Task'; 'Dimming Of The Day'; 'Just Me And You'; 'Do Right Woman'; 'Change Coming Down'; 'Story Of Love'; 'Only Passing Through'.
Released January 1997 (US).

Rice, Rice, Hillman & Pedersen Rounder 0450 (US).
'Doesn't Mean That Much Anymore'; 'Side Effects Of Love'; 'One Of These Days'; 'Never Ending Song Of Love'; 'Friend Of The Devil'; 'Out Among The Stars'; 'Moonshine'; 'Moment Of Glory'; 'The Year Of El Nino'; 'Hearts Overflowing'; 'I Will'; 'The Walkin' Blues'; 'I'll Be On That Good Road Someday'.
Released October 1999 (US).

Running Wild Rounder 11661-0483-2 (US).
'San Antone'; 'You're Running Wild'; 'Things We Said Today'; '4 + 20'; 'Two Of A Kind'; 'Passin' Through'; 'The Mystery That Won't Go Away'; 'Take Me Back Again'; 'Maybe She'll Get Lucky'; 'Hard Hearted'; 'It's A Long Way To The Top Of The World'; 'About Love'.
Released October 2001 (US).

Hillman has also guested on numerous records including those of Tut Taylor (*12-String Dobro*), Don Parmley (*5-String Banjo! With 12-String Guitar!*), Gene Clark (*Gene Clark With The Gosdin Brothers; Early LA Sessions; Roadmaster; No*

Other; Firebyrd), David Hemmings (*Happens*), Dillard & Clark (*The Fantastic Expedition Of Dillard & Clark; Through The Morning Through The Night*), Bob Gibson (*Bob Gibson*), Marc Ellington (*Marc Ellington*), Cherokee (*Cherokee*), Barry McGuire (*Barry McGuire & The Doctor*).

Rick Roberts (*Windmills; She Is A Song),* Roger McGuinn (*Roger McGuinn*), Poco (*Crazy Eyes*), Rusty Wier (*Stoned, Slow, Rugged*), Terry Melcher (*Terry Melcher*), Bob Neuwirth (*Bob Neuwirth),* Dirk Hamilton (*You Can Sing On The Left Or Bark On The Right*), Richie Furay (*Dance A Little Light; I Am Sure*), Dan Fogelberg (*The Innocent Age; High Country Snows; The Wild Places*), Stephen Stills (*Right By You*), Daniel (*Winning The West*), Herb Pedersen (*Lonesome Feeling*), Gene Clark & Carla Olson (*So Rebellious A Lover*), the 77s (*The 77s; Sticks And Stones*), the Lonesome Strangers (*Lonesome Pine*), the Nitty Gritty Dirt Band (*Will The Circle Be Unbroken, Volume Two*).

David West (*Arcane; Pickin' On Southern Rock; Broken Down Believers*), Pamela Polland (*Heart Of The World*), Electric Range (*Electric Range*), Lyle Lovett (*Road To Ensenada*), Steve Hill (*Gold Highway; Feathers And Stone; House For Sale*), the Rincon Ramblers (*The Green Rolling Hills Of La Conchita*), J. Peter Boles (*J. Peter Boles*), Bill And Bonnie Hearne (*Watching Life Through A Windshield*), Dwight Yoakam (*Tomorrow's Sounds Today*), Byron Berline Band (*Clark/Parsons Tribute Album*), the Gosdin Brothers (*Sounds Of Goodbye* reissue bonus tracks), Al Perkins (*Snapshots*), Leroy Mack (*Smiles And Tears*), Twin Engine (*Twin Engine*).

Johnny Rivers (*Reinvention Highway*), Steve Spurgin (*Tumbleweed Town*), the Woodys (*Telluride To Tennessee*), the Bellamy Brothers (*Angels & Outlaws Volume 1*), Sheri Lee (*When The Blue Sky Ends*), I See Hawks In LA (*California Country*), Brad Colerick (*Cottonwood*), Chris Jones (*Too Far Down The Road*), Michael Weston King (*A New Kind Of Loneliness*), Sherri Lee (*Where The Blue Skies End*), the Coal Porters (*Turn The Water On, Boy!*), and Donna Loren (*Magic*).

Hillman featured heavily on the Christian bluegrass albums *Down Home Praise* (Maranatha! Music MM 0104), *Ever Call Ready* (Maranatha! Music MM 0139/A&M WR 8310) and *Country Gospel* (Maranatha! Music CD 8764). He also contributes to the Various Artistes' recording *God Loves Country*. Hillman also appeared on the 1994 Sugar Hill compilation *Daddies Sing Goodnight* to which he contributed a song he wrote with his daughter Catherine, 'Lullaby Time In The Desert', while Hillman & Pedersen contributed to the Christmas CD *Tinsel Tunes* (Sugar Hill SH 3855). The CD *Country Music For Kids* (Disney Spotlight 60837-2) also features Hillman performing 'Little Birdie'. An alternate take of the Desert Rose Band's 'She Don't Love Nobody' was available on their promotional sampler (MCA/Curb CD 33-3304). The Hillman/Roberts composition 'Did You See' was featured on various Flying Burrito Brothers' compilations, while 'Fooled Again' was issued as a B-side of the Desert Rose Band's single 'Start All Over Again'. Hillman also duetted with Jennifer Warnes on the Lowell George tribute *Rock 'n' Roll Doctor*. More recently, he has featured on the fund-raising 2005 album, *Songs For Sophie: A Collings Collective* and alongside Herb Pedersen (and David Crosby) on 2006's *Tales From The Tavern Vol. 1*. He also has a cameo appearance on 2007's *The Gift: A Tribute To Ian Tyson*. In 2013, he appeared on the Various Artistes' compilation, *Divided & United: The Songs Of The Civil War*.

Hillman has also done production work on records by the Gosdin Brothers ('One Hundred Years From Now' single), Rick Roberts (*She Is A Song*), Dan McCorison (*Dan McCorison*), Street Talk ('Leaving The Country' b/w 'Falling To Pieces' single) and Steve Hill (*We'll Always Have Texas*).

KEVIN KELLEY

With The Rising Sons:

Rising Sons Featuring Taj Mahal And Ry Cooder Columbia/Legacy CK 52828 (US)/ 472865 2 (UK).
'Statesboro Blues'; 'If The River Was Whiskey (Divin' Duck Blues)'; 'By And By (Poor Me)'; 'Candy Man'; 'Train'; 'Let The Good Times Roll'; '.44 Blues'; '11th Street Overcrossing'; 'Corrin, Corrina', 'Tulsa County'; 'Walkin' Down The Line'; 'The Girl With Green Eyes'; 'Sunny's Dream'; 'Spanish Lace Blues'; 'The Devil's Got My Woman'; 'Take A Giant Step'; 'Flyin' So High'; 'Dust My Broom'; 'Last Fair Deal Gone Down'; 'Baby, What You Want Me To Do?'; 'Statesboro Blues'; 'I Got A Little'.
Released September 1992 (US)/May 1993 (UK). Archive recording.

With Fever Tree:

For Sale Ampex 10113 (US).
'I Put A Spell On You'; 'Come On In'; 'She Comes In Colors'; 'Girl Oh Girl Don't Push Me'; 'You're Not The Same'; 'Hey Mister'; 'Hey Joe (Where You Gonna Go)'. This is the correct running order. On the outer sleeve the track listing is incorrect and some songs have slightly different titles such as 'Girl Don't Push Me' and 'You're Not The Same Baby'.
Released 1971 (US).
Kelley does not appear on later Fever Tree releases.

Albums with the Byrds:

See Discography *Volume 1* under the following sections: *Byrds Singles, Albums, Compilations* and *Archival Albums* for fuller details of release dates, complete track listings, alternate serial numbers, special issues/editions, and more.

Sweetheart Of The Rodeo Columbia CL 9670 (mono)/CS 9670 (stereo) (US). CBS 63353 (mono)/CBS S 63353 (stereo) (UK). Remastered CD edition with bonus tracks: Columbia Legacy CK 65150 (US)/Columbia Legacy 486752 2 (UK). Special issue *Sweetheart Of The Rodeo* [*Legacy Edition*]: Columbia Legacy COL 510921 2 (US).

Archival albums with the Byrds:

The Original Singles Volume 2 1967–1969 CBS 32103 (UK).
Sanctuary IV Sundazed LP 5090 (US).

Box Sets with the Byrds:

The Byrds Columbia Legacy 46773 (US)/Columbia Legacy 4676112 (UK).
12 Dimensions The Columbia Recordings 1965–1972 (13-CD box set) Columbia 497610 2/4976102000 (UK).
There Is A Season (4-CD box set and DVD) Columbia/Legacy 82876877002 (US/UK).
The Complete Columbia Albums Collection Columbia Legacy 886978738028 (US).

Compilations/Hits Collections with the Byrds:

See *Volume 1* for additional details.
The Byrds Greatest Hits Volume 2 CBS S 64650 (UK).
Best Of Volume 2 Columbia C31795 (US).
History Of The Byrds CBS 68242 (UK).
Return Of The Byrds Columbia Realm 2V 8006-7 (US).
The Byrds CBS 88320 (UK).
The Byrds Play Dylan Columbia PC 36293 (US)/CBS 31795 (UK).
The Byrds Collection Castle Communications CCSLP 151 (UK).
The Very Best Of The Byrds Columbia CBS 4634189 2 (Holland/UK).
Full Flyte Raven RVCD 10 (Australia).
Free Flyte Sony Music Special Products A 17733 (US).
Greatest Hits Remastered Columbia 467843 2 (UK).
Definitive Collection Columbia 480548 9 (UK).
Nashville West Sony Music Special Products A 28123 (US).
The Very Best Of The Byrds Columbia 487995 2 (UK).
The Best Of The Byrds Columbia 488146 2 (UK).
The Byrds Play The Songs Of Bob Dylan Columbia 501946 2 (UK).
The Byrds Play Dylan Columbia/Legacy CK 85430 (US).
The Essential Byrds Columbia Legacy 512249 2 (UK)/Columbia Legacy C2K 89110 (US).
Mojo Presents . . . An Introduction To The Byrds – 24 Classic Songs Columbia 512778 2 (UK).
Mr Tambourine Man – The Best Of The Byrds Sony Music Media SMM 516489-2 (Germany/UK).
America's Great National Treasure Sony/BMG A 96086 (US).
The Very Best Of The Byrds Sony/BMG 82876 855142 (UK).
Byrds: A Collection Sony BMG 88697 12448 2 (UK).
The Byrds Play Dylan Sony BMG 88697 25267 2 (UK).
Playlist: The Very Best Of The Byrds Columbia Legacy 88697 39219 2 (US).
Steel Box Sony BMG 88697 45981 2 (UK).
Eight Miles High – The Best Of The Byrds Sony/Camden 88697 63627 2 (UK).
Turn! Turn! Turn!: The Ultimate Collection Sony/Columbia Music 88875 151652 (UK).

With Jesse Wolff & Whings:

Jesse Wolff & Whings Shelter SW 8907 (US).
'Shut The Door'; 'Life In The Country'; 'Don't Cry Your Life Away'; 'Another Song For You'; 'In The Morning'; 'Some Other Time'; 'Inspiration On The Highway'; 'Hard To Win'; 'Take My Pain Away'; 'Set Me Free'; 'Lookin' Back'.
Released April 1972 (US).

After leaving the Byrds, Kelley undertook session work, guesting on albums by Phil Ochs (*Gunfight At Carnegie Hall*), John Fahey (*The Yellow Princess*), Frank Kinsel (*At Home*), Michael Cohen (*What Did You Expect?*) and Judee Sill (*Dreams Come True*). To confuse us all, there is another Kevin Kelly [not Kelley] who played piano backing Joan Baez during the Rolling Thunder Revue. This may well be the guest player on albums by Tim Buckley, James Taylor, Bryn Haworth, Eric Andersen and the Babys. Either way, it was not the Byrds' Kevin Kelley whose keyboards skills were not proficient enough to secure session work in this area. A possible third Kevin Kelly can be heard singing on a 1980 album by Arlen Roth.

GRAM PARSONS

With the Shilos:

The Early Years Vol. I 1963–1965 Sierra SRS 8702 (US)/Sundown SDLP 101 (UK).
'I May Be Right'; 'Big Country'; 'Zah's Blues'; 'Mary Don't You Weep'; 'Bells Of Rhymney'; 'Goin' Away, Don't You Wanta Go'; 'They Still Go Down'; 'On My Journey Home'; 'Surfinanny'; 'Oh Didn't They Crucify My Lord'.
Released February 1979 (US)/May 1984 (UK).

With the International Submarine Band:

Safe At Home LHI 12001 (US).
'Blue Eyes'; 'I Must Be Somebody Else You've Known'; 'A Satisfied Mind'; 'Folsom Prison Blues'/'That's Alright'; 'Miller's Cave'; 'I Still Miss Someone'; 'Luxury Liner'; 'Strong Boy'; 'Do You Know How It Feels To Be Lonesome?'
Released April 1968 (US). This album was remixed, resequenced and reissued on Shiloh (SLP 4088) in February 1979 as *Gram Parsons* and finally received a UK release in 1985 under its original title on Statik Records (STATLP 26). The International Submarine Band also issued the otherwise unavailable US singles 'The Russians Are Coming! The Russians Are Coming!'/'Truck Driving Man' (Ascot 2218) and 'Sum Up Broke'/'One Day Week' (Columbia 4-43935).

Albums with the Byrds:

See Discography *Volume 1* under the following sections: *Byrds Singles, Albums, Compilations* and *Archival Albums* for fuller details of release dates, complete track listings, alternate serial numbers, special issues/editions, and more.

Sweetheart Of The Rodeo Columbia CL 9670 (mono)/CS 9670 (stereo) (US). CBS 63353 (mono)/CBS S 63353 (stereo) (UK). Remastered CD edition with bonus tracks: Columbia Legacy CK 65150 (US)/Columbia Legacy 486752 2 (UK). Special issue *Sweetheart Of The Rodeo* [*Legacy Edition*]: Columbia Legacy COL 510921 2 (US).

(Untitled) Columbia G 30127 (stereo) (US)/CBS S 64095 (stereo) (UK). Remastered CD edition with bonus tracks: *(Untitled)/(Unissued)* Columbia Legacy C2K 65847 (US)/Columbia Legacy 495077 2 (UK). Although not a member of the Byrds, Parsons appears as a backing vocalist on 'All The Things'.

Archival albums with the Byrds:

The Original Singles Volume 2 1967–1969 CBS 32103 (UK).
Sanctuary IV Sundazed LP 5090 (US).

Box Sets with the Byrds:

The Byrds Columbia Legacy 46773 (US)/Columbia Legacy 4676112 (UK).
12 Dimensions The Columbia Recordings 1965–1972 (13-CD box set) Columbia 497610 2/4976102000 (UK).
There Is A Season (4-CD box set and DVD) Columbia/Legacy 82876877002 (US/UK).
The Complete Columbia Albums Collection Columbia Legacy 886978738028 (US).

Compilations/Hits Collections with the Byrds:

See *Volume 1* for additional details.
The Byrds Greatest Hits Volume 2 CBS S 64650 (UK).
Best Of Volume 2 Columbia C31795 (US).
History Of The Byrds CBS 68242 (UK).
Return Of The Byrds Columbia Realm 2V 8006-7 (US).
The Byrds CBS 88320 (UK).
The Byrds Play Dylan Columbia PC 36293 (US)/CBS 31795 (UK).
The Byrds Collection Castle Communications CCSLP 151 (UK).
The Very Best Of The Byrds Columbia CBS 4634189 2 (Holland/UK).
Full Flyte Raven RVCD 10 (Australia).
Free Flyte Sony Music Special Products A 17733 (US).
Greatest Hits Remastered Columbia 467843 2 (UK).
Definitive Collection Columbia 480548 9 (UK).
Nashville West Sony Music Special Products A 28123 (US).
The Very Best Of The Byrds Columbia 487995 2 (UK).
The Best Of The Byrds Columbia 488146 2 (UK).
The Byrds Play The Songs Of Bob Dylan Columbia 501946 2 (UK).
The Byrds Play Dylan Columbia/Legacy CK 85430 (US).
The Essential Byrds Columbia Legacy 512249 2 (UK)/Columbia Legacy C2K 89110 (US).

Mojo Presents . . . An Introduction To The Byrds – 24 Classic Songs Columbia 512778 2 (UK).
Mr Tambourine Man – The Best Of The Byrds Sony Music Media SMM 516489-2 (Germany/UK).
America's Great National Treasure Sony/BMG A 96086 (US).
The Very Best Of The Byrds Sony/BMG 82876 855142 (UK).
Byrds: A Collection Sony BMG 88697 12448 2 (UK).
The Byrds Play Dylan Sony BMG 88697 25267 2 (UK).
Playlist: The Very Best Of The Byrds Columbia Legacy 88697 39219 2 (US).
Steel Box Sony BMG 88697 45981 2 (UK).
Eight Miles High – The Best Of The Byrds Sony/Camden 88697 63627 2 (UK).
Turn! Turn! Turn!: The Ultimate Collection Sony/Columbia Music 88875 151652 (UK).

With the Flying Burrito Brothers:
The Gilded Palace Of Sin A&M SD 4175 (US)/A&M AMLS 931 (UK).
See Chris Hillman section for release dates and full track listing.

Burrito Deluxe A&M SD 4258 (US)/A&M AMLS 983 (UK).
See Michael Clarke section for release dates and full track listing.

Grass Roots A&M AMLB 51038 (UK).
This A&M UK sampler features one side each of previously released material from Dillard & Clark and the Flying Burrito Brothers.
Released October 1972 (UK).

Honky Tonk Heaven A&M 87585 XDT (Holland).
Compilation. See Michael Clarke section for track listing.
Released January 1974 (Holland).

Close Up The Honky Tonks A&M SD 3631 (US)/A&M AMLH 63631 (UK).
Compilation. See Michael Clarke section for track listing.
Released July 1974 (US/UK).

Sleepless Nights A&M SD 4578 (US)/A&M AMLH 64578 (UK).
Compilation. See Michael Clarke section for track listing.
Released May 1976 (US)/June 1976 (UK).

Dim Lights, Thick Smoke And Loud, Loud Music Edsel ED CD 197 (UK).
Compilation. See Michael Clarke section for track listing.
Released March 1987 (UK).

Farther Along: The Best Of The Flying Burrito Brothers A&M CD 5216 (US).
Compilation. See Michael Clarke section for track listing.
Released October 1988 (US).

Out Of The Blue A&M 540408-2 (US/UK).
Compilation. See Michael Clarke section for track listing.
Released April 1996 (US/UK).

Hot Burritos! The Flying Burrito Brothers Anthology 1969–1972 A&M 490610 (US)/A&M 54074 (UK).
Compilation. See Michael Clarke section for track listing.
Released April 2000 (US/UK).

The Best Of The Flying Burrito Brothers – The Millennium Collection A&M 493056 (US).
Compilation. See Michael Clarke section for track listing.
Released: June 2001 (US).

Sin City – The Very Best Of The Flying Burrito Brothers A&M 4932642 (US).
Compilation. See Michael Clarke section for track listing.
Released April 2002 (US).

The Collection Spectrum 9820305 (UK).
Compilation. See Michael Clarke section for track listing.
Released January 2005 (UK).

The Definitive Collection Hip-O-Select 80008781-02 (US).
Compilation. See Michael Clarke section for track listing.
Released April 2007 (US).

Live At The Avalon Ballroom 1969 Amoeba Records AM0002 (US).
See Michael Clarke section for track listing.

Released: October 2007 (US). The front cover credits this as *'Gram Parsons With The Flying Burrito Brothers'*. The spine says it is *'Gram Parsons Archives Vol. 1'*.

Authorized Bootleg: Fillmore East, N.Y., N.Y., Late Show, Nov. 7 1970
Hip-O-Select 001520702 (US).
See Michael Clarke section for track listing.
Released February 2011 (US).

As Gram Parsons:
GP Warners/Reprise WB MS 2123 (US)/Warners/Reprise K44228 (UK).
'Still Feeling Blue'; 'We'll Sweep Out The Ashes In The Morning'; 'A Song For You'; 'Streets Of Baltimore'; 'She'; 'That's All It Took'; 'The New Soft Shoe'; 'Kiss The Children'; 'Cry One More Time'; 'How Much I've Lied'; 'Big Mouth Blues'.
Released January 1973 (US)/March 1973 (UK).

Grievous Angel Warners/Reprise MS 2171 (US)/Warners/Reprise K 54018 (UK).
'Return Of The Grievous Angel'; 'Hearts On Fire'; 'I Can't Dance'; 'Brass Buttons'; '$1000 Wedding'; 'Medley Live From Northern Quebec (A) Cash On The Barrelhead, (B) Hickory Wind'; 'Love Hurts'; 'Ooh Las Vegas'; 'In My Hour Of Darkness'.
Released January 1974 (US)/June 1974 (UK).

Gram Parsons And The Fallen Angels – Live 1973 Sierra GP 1973 (US)/Sundown SDLP 003 (UK).
'We'll Sweep Out The Ashes'; 'Big Mouth Blues'; 'The New Soft Shoe'; 'Streets Of Baltimore'; 'Cry One More Time'; 'California Cottonfields'; 'Love Hurts'; 'Country Baptizing'; 'Drug Store Truck Drivin' Man'; 'That's All It Took'; 'Six Days On The Road'.
Released April 1982 (US)/November 1983 (UK).

Gram Parsons WEA K 57008 (UK).
Compilation. 'We'll Sweep Out The Ashes In The Morning'; 'Hearts On Fire'; 'Kiss The Children'; 'That's All It Took'; 'Love Hurts'; 'In My Hour Of Darkness'; 'Return Of The Grievous Angel'; 'Still Feeling Blue'; '$1000 Wedding'; 'Ooh Las Vegas'; 'The New Soft Shoe'; 'How Much I've Lied'; 'Medley Live From Northern Quebec (A) Cash On The Barrelhead, (B) Hickory Wind'.
Released April 1982 (UK).

Warm Evenings, Pale Mornings, Bottled Blues Raven RVCD 24 (Australia).
Compilation. Includes the International Submarine Band's 'Truck Driving Man'.
Released June 1992 (Australia).

Cosmic American Music Sundown CDSD 077 (UK).
'Song For You'; 'Kentucky Blues'; 'Streets Of Baltimore'; 'Folsom Prison Blues'; 'Lovesick Blues'; 'The New Soft Shoe'; 'How Much I've Lied'; 'Still Feeling Blue'; 'Still Feeling Blue'; 'Ain't No Beatle, Ain't No Rolling Stone'; 'Medley: How Can I Forget You/Cry One More Time'; 'A Song For You'; 'Streets Of Baltimore'; 'That's All It Took'; 'Somebody's Back In Town'; 'More And More'; 'Teaching Emmy To Sweep Out The Ashes'; 'Daddy's Fiddle'; 'We'll Sweep Out The Ashes In The Morning'; 'Cold Cold Heart'; 'That's All It Took'; 'A Song For You'.
The tapes for this album were originally auctioned at Christie's on 8 September 1994. After briefly appearing, the album was withdrawn and subsequently reissued under the same number with additional credit to Rick Grech.
Released August 1996 (UK).

Another Side Of This Life Sundazed SC11092 (US).
'Codine'; 'Wheel Of Fortune'; 'Another Side Of This Life'; 'High Flyin' Bird'; 'November Nights'; 'Zah's Blues'; 'Reputation'; 'That's The Bag I'm In'; 'Willie Jean'; 'They Still Go Down'; 'Pride Of Man'; 'The Last Thing On My Mind'; 'Hey Nellie Nellie'; 'She's The Woman I Love'/'Good Time Music'; 'Brass Buttons'; 'I Just Can't Take It Anymore'; 'Searchin''; 'Candy Man'.
Released December 2000 (US).

Sacred Hearts And Fallen Angels: The Gram Parsons Anthology WSM/Rhino 8122-76780-2 (US)/(UK).
2 CD Compilation. Disc 1: The International Submarine Band: 'Blue Eyes';

'Luxury Liner'; 'Do You Know How It Feels To Be Lonesome?'; 'I Must Be Somebody Else You've Known'; 'Miller's Cave'; 'Knee Deep In The Blues'. The Byrds: 'Hickory Wind'; 'You're Still On My Mind'; 'The Christian Life'; 'You Don't Miss Your Water'; 'One Hundred Years From Now'. The Flying Burrito Brothers: 'Christine's Tune (Devil In Disguise)'; 'Sin City'; 'Do Right Woman'; 'Dark End Of The Street'; 'Wheels'; 'Juanita'; 'Hot Burrito # 1'; 'Hot Burrito # 2'; 'High Fashion Queen'; 'Older Guys'; 'Cody Cody'; 'Wild Horses'; 'Sing Me Back Home'.
Disc 2: The Flying Burrito Brothers: 'To Love Somebody'. Gram Parsons: 'Still Feeling Blue'; 'We'll Sweep Out The Ashes In The Morning'; 'A Song For You'; 'Streets Of Baltimore'; 'She'; 'The New Soft Shoe'; 'Kiss The Children'; 'How Much I've Lied'. Gram Parsons & The Fallen Angels: 'Drug Store Truck Drivin' Man'; 'That's All It Took'; 'California Cotton Fields'. Gram Parsons: 'Return Of The Grievous Angel' (remix); 'Hearts On Fire'; 'Brass Buttons'; '$1000 Wedding'; 'Love Hurts'; 'Ooh Las Vegas'; 'In My Hour Of Darkness'; 'Brand New Heartache'; 'Sleepless Nights'; 'The Angels Rejoiced Last Night'.
Released May 2001 (US)/(UK).

The Complete Reprise Sessions Reprise/Rhino R2 74669 (US)/(UK).
3 CD Compilation. Disc 1. 'Still Feeling Blue'; 'We'll Sweep Out The Ashes In The Morning'; 'A Song For You'; 'Streets Of Baltimore'; 'She'; 'That's All It Took'; 'The New Soft Shoe'; 'Kiss The Children'; 'Cry One More Time'; 'How Much I've Lied'; 'Big Mouth Blues'. Bonus tracks: *GP* radio promo; Gram Parsons interview; WBCN interview with Maxine Sartori; 'Love Hurts' (Gram Parsons & Emmylou Harris); 'Sin City' (Gram Parsons, Emmylou Harris and N.D. Smart).
Disc 2. 'Return Of The Grievous Angel'; 'Hearts On Fire'; 'I Can't Dance'; 'Brass Buttons'; '$1000 Wedding'; 'Medley Live From Northern Quebec (A) Cash On The Barrelhead, (B) Hickory Wind'; 'Love Hurts'; 'Ooh Las Vegas'; 'In My Hour Of Darkness'. Bonus tracks: 'Return Of The Grievous Angel' (instrumental); Gram Parsons interview.
Disc 3. 'She' (alternate version); 'That's All It Took' (alternate version); 'Still Feeling Blue' (alternate version); 'Kiss The Children' (alternate version); 'Streets Of Baltimore' (alternate version); 'We'll Sweep Out The Ashes In The Morning' (alternate version); 'The New Soft Shoe' (alternate version); 'Return Of The Grievous Angel # 1' (alternate version); 'In My Hour Of Darkness' (alternate version); 'Ooh Las Vegas' (alternate version); 'I Can't Dance' (alternate version); 'Sleepless Nights' (alternate version); 'Love Hurts' (alternate version); 'Brass Buttons' (alternate version); 'Hickory Wind' (alternate version); 'Brand New Heartache'; 'Sleepless Nights'; 'The Angels Rejoiced Last Night'.
Released June 2006 (US)/(UK).

Gram Parsons – The Early Years Box Set Sierra SBXGP 2100 (US).
CD 1: *Gram Parsons & The Shilos – The Early Years, Volume 1.*
'I May Be Right'; 'Big Country'; 'Zah's Blues'; 'Mary Don't You Weep'; 'Bells

Of Rhymney'; 'Goin' Away, Don't Wanta Go'; 'They Still Go Down'; 'On My Journey Home'; 'Surfinanny'; 'Oh Didn't They Crucify My Lord'.
CD 2: *Gram Parsons – The Early Years, Volume 2.*
'The Great Silke'; 'Race With The Wind'; 'The Rains Come Down'; 'Hand Within The Glove'; 'Rolling Stone'; 'Darkest Years'; 'That Kind Of Livin''; 'A River Is Made Out Of Raindrops'; 'Just Can't Take It Any More' (Gram Parsons & The Like); 'November Nights' (Gram Parsons & The Like); 'Together Again' (Brandon DeWilde with Gram Parsons & The Like); 'Do Right Woman' (Brandon DeWilde & Gram Parsons); 'Hickory Wind' (Brandon DeWilde & Gram Parsons); 'Apple Tree' (take one; snippet, 'hidden' bonus track).
CD 3*: Big Mouth Blues: A Conversation With Gram Parsons.*
Audio tape interview with Chuck Cassell.
DVD: *Gram Parsons & The Fallen Angels Live.*
'Big Mouth Blues'; 'The New Soft Shoe'; 'Streets Of Baltimore'; 'Six Days On The Road'; 'Hot Burrito #1' (bonus clip).
LP: *Gram Parsons & The Shilos – The Early Years Volume 1* (180 gram pure virgin vinyl LP picture disc): 'I May Be Right'; 'Big Country'; 'Zah's Blues'; 'Mary Don't You Weep'; 'Bells Of Rhymney'; 'Goin' Away, Don't Wanta Go'; 'They Still Go Down'; 'On My Journey Home'; 'Surfinanny'; 'Oh Didn't They Crucify My Lord'.
Also includes posters and booklets.
Released November 2010 (US).

The Early Years Mini CD (Limited Edition) Sierra SBXGP 9000 (US).
'Another Side Of Life'; 'Maco Light'; 'Run Little Boy, Run'; 'Big Country' (solo – alternate take); '$1000 Wedding'; 'Hot Burrito # 1'.
Tracks 1-4 are solo vocal performances recorded by Dick Weissman in New York: September 1965. Tracks 5–6 are solo vocal performances recorded *c.* 1970–71 by Cal Frisk.
Released November 2010 (US).

Gram Parsons has also made guest appearances on records by Jack Wilce ('Apple Pie, Mother And The Flag' single), Christmas Spirit ('Christmas Is My Time Of Year'/'Will You Still Believe In Me' single), Steve Young (*Rock Salt And Nails*), the Byrds (*(Untitled)),* Fred Neil (*Other Side Of This Life*), Delaney and Bonnie (*Motel Shot*), the Rolling Stones (*Exile On Main Street*), Jesse Ed Davis (*Jesse Davis!*), Rick Grech (*The Last Five Years*) and the archival compilation *Byrd Parts* (Raven).

CLARENCE WHITE

With the Kentucky Colonels:

The New Sound Of Bluegrass America Briar M 109 (US).
'Three Finger Blues'; 'I'll Be Coming Home Tomorrow'; 'If You're Ever Gonna Love Me'; 'Banjo Picking Fever'; 'I Might Take You Back Again';

'Memphis Special'; 'Cabin In The Sky'; 'Leroy's Ramble'; 'Howdy Hoss'; 'Won't You Call Me Darling'; 'Rainbow Shining Somewhere'; '420 Special'; 'Just Joshing'; 'To Prove My Love For You'.
Released October 1963 (US).

Appalachian Swing! World-Pacific 1821 (US).
'Clinch Mountain Back-Step'; 'Nine Pound Hammer'; 'Listen To The Mocking Bird'; 'Wild Bill Jones'; 'Billy In The Low Ground'; 'Lee Highway'; 'I Am A Pilgrim'; 'Prisoner's Song'; 'Sally Goodin'; 'Faded Love'; 'John Henry'; 'Flat Fork'.
Released April 1964 (US).

The Kentucky Colonels Featuring Roland And Clarence White United Artists UAS 29514 (UK).
'Clinch Mountain Back-Step'; 'Nine Pound Hammer'; 'Listen To The Mocking Bird'; 'Wild Bill Jones'; 'Billy In The Low Ground'; 'Lee Highway'; 'That's What You Get For Loving Me'; 'I Am A Pilgrim'; 'Prisoner's Song'; 'Sally Goodin'; 'The Ballad Of Farmer Brown'; 'Faded Love'; 'John Henry'; 'Flat Fork'.
This was a re-release of *Appalachian Swing!*, with the addition of two songs previously available on single only: 'That's What You Get For Loving Me' and 'The Ballad Of Farmer Brown'.
Released May 1974 (UK).

Livin' In The Past Takoma Briar BT 7202 (US).
Intro: Jerry Garcia; 'Fire On The Mountain'; 'If You're Ever Gonna Love Me'; 'Julius Finkbine's Rag'; 'Dark Hollow'; 'He Said If I Be Lifted Up'; 'Memphis Special'; 'Shuckin' The Corn'; 'Angel Of Death'; 'Barefoot Nellie'; 'Train '45'; 'Hard Hearted'; 'Chug-A-Lug'; 'Journey's End (A Life Of Sorrow)'; 'Sheik Of Araby'; 'A Good Woman's Love'; 'Listen To The Mocking Bird'; 'Old Joe Clark'; 'Jordan'; 'Shady Grove'.
Released April 1976 (US). Reissued in October 1978 on Briar SBR 4202. Reissued in April 1997 on Sierra (6018) with bonus tracks 'Get Down On Your Knees And Pray', 'Lee Highway Blues', 'Ocean Of Diamonds', 'Alabama Jubilee', 'Sunny Side Of The Mountain' and 'I Am A Pilgrim'.

Kentucky Colonels 1965–67 Rounder 0070 (US).
'New River Train'; 'Blue Moon Of Kentucky'; 'Lee Highway'; 'Don't Let Your Deal Go Down'; 'Soldier's Joy'; 'Wicked Path Of Sin'; 'Rawhide'; 'Bucking Mule'; 'How Mountain Girls Can Love'; 'Black Mountain Rag'; 'Sunny Side Of The Mountain'; 'Jimmy's Barnyard Shuffle'; 'You Won't Be Satisfied That Way'; 'Clinch Mountain Backstep'; 'Let Me Fall'.
Released April 1976 (US).

Scotty Stoneman, Live In LA With The Kentucky Colonels Briar SBR 4206 (US).
'Oklahoma Stomp'; 'Once A Day'; 'Eighth Of January'; 'Any Damn Thing'; 'Down Yonder'; 'Sally Goodin'; 'A Wound Time Can't Erase'; 'Cherokee Waltz'; 'Cacklin' Hen'; 'Goodnight Irene'.

Taken from two live recordings: the Cobblestone Club, North Hollywood (August 1965) and the Ash Grove, Hollywood (27 March 1965). CD issues include the bonus tracks 'Lee Highway Blues', 'Shuckin' The Corn', 'Listen To The Mockingbird' and 'Orange Blossom Special'.
Released September 1978 (US).

Kentucky Colonels 1966 Shiloh SLP 4084 (US).
'Soldier's Joy'; 'The Fugitive'; 'Ruben's Train'; 'One Tear'; 'I Might Take You Back Again'; 'Take Off Your Cheaters' [alternate]; 'Take Off Your Cheaters'; 'Old Country Church'; 'Earl's Breakdown'; 'Give This Message To Your Heart'; 'Ruben's Train'; 'Cotton Eyed Joe'; 'Soldier's Joy'.
Released August 1978 (US).

Clarence White And The Kentucky Colonels Rounder 0098 (US).
'Prisoner's Song'; 'Good Woman's Love'; 'Whitewash Chimney'; 'Listen To The Mocking Bird'; 'Teardrops In My Eyes'; 'Working On A Building'; 'Alabama Jubilee'; 'I Am A Pilgrim'; 'Billy And The Low Ground'; 'Bury Me Beneath The Willow'; 'Footprints In The Snow'; 'Wildwood Flower'; 'Farewell Blues'; 'When You're Smiling'.
Released October 1980 (US).

The Kentucky Colonels On Stage Rounder ROU 0199 (US)/Sundown SDLP 050 (UK).
'John Hardy'; 'Used To Be'; 'Shackles And Chains'; 'Durham's Bull'; 'Mountain Dew'; 'I Might Take You Back Again'; 'Bluegrass Breakdown'; 'Flop Eared Mule'; 'I Wonder How The Old Folks Are At Home'; 'Over In The Glory Land'; 'Reno Ride'; 'Ocean Of Diamonds'; 'Bending The Strings'.
Released May 1984 (US)/July 1984 (UK).

Long Journey Home Vanguard VCD 77004 (US).
'Roll On Buddy'; 'Bill Cheatham'; 'There Ain't Nobody Gonna Miss Me When I'm Gone'; 'Shuckin' The Corn'; 'A Beautiful Life'; 'Get Down On Your Knees And Pray'; 'Over In The Glory Land'; 'Sally Ann'; 'Brakeman's Blues'; 'Soldier's Joy'; 'Listen To The Mocking Bird'; 'Farewell Blues'; 'Lonesome Road Blues'; 'Beaumont Rag'; 'Footprints In The Snow'; 'Long Journey Home'; 'In The Pines'; 'Chicken Reel'; 'Old Hickory'; 'Auld Lang Syne'; 'Nola'; 'Flat Fork'; 'Shady Grove'.
Released October 1991 (US).

Live In Stereo Double Barrel DBR 1001 (US).
Intro; 'Train 45'; 'Green Corn'; 'Shuckin' The Corn'; 'Dark Hollow'; 'Salt Creek'; 'All The Good Times (Are Past And Gone)'; 'Soldier's Joy'; 'You Won't Be Satisfied'; 'Alabama Jubilee'; 'Columbus Stockade'; 'Mockin' Banjo'; 'Workin' On A Building'; 'Prisoner's Song'; 'It Ain't Gonna Rain No More'; 'Johnson's Old Gray Mule'; 'Fair And Tender Ladies'; 'Bluegrass Breakdown'; 'Long Journey Home'; 'Howdy Hoss'; 'Shady Grove'.
Released 1999 (US). Reissued: July 2003 (US).

The New Sound Of Bluegrass America Music Scene Inc M-109 (Japan).
CD reissue on the original 1963 album, including bonus tracks: 'Just Like Old Times', 'Buck's Run' and 'I Hear Him Calling'.
Released July 2007 (Japan).

As Tut Taylor, Roland & Clarence White:

Dobro Country World-Pacific 1829 (US).
'Freight Train'; 'Dobro Country'; 'Pickin' Flat'; 'Lonesome Dobro'; 'Hang Your Head In Shame'; 'Steel Guitar Rag'; 'Just Because'; 'A Fool Such As I'; 'The Sinking Of The Ruben James'; 'Frankie And Johnny'; 'Nobody's Darling But Mine'; 'Black Ridge Ramble'.
Released May 1964 (US).

With Nashville West:

Nashville West Sierra SRS 8701 (US)/Sundown SDLP 1011 (UK).
'Nashville West'; 'Mental Revenge'; 'I Wanna Live'; 'Sweet Susanna'; 'Green, Green Grass Of Home'; 'Love Of The Common People'; 'Tuff & Stringy'; 'Washed My Hands In Muddy Water'; 'Ode To Billy Joe'; 'Louisiana Rain'; 'Send Me Back Home'; 'Memphis'; 'By The Time I Get To Phoenix'; 'Nashville West'.
Released August 1978 (US)/1984 (UK). A reference on the spine of the Sierra album to 0798 is not part of the serial number but an indicator to distributors that the retail price was $7.98.

Nashville West Sierra SXCD 6016/Rev-Ola CR REV 23 (UK).
Reissue of the above on CD with four bonus tracks: 'Greensleeves'; 'C.C. Rider'; 'Columbus Stockade Blues'; 'Mom And Dad's Waltz'.
Released April 1997 (US)/March 2003 (UK).

Albums with the Byrds:

See Discography *Volume 1* under the following sections: *Byrds Singles, Albums, Compilations* and *Archival Albums* for fuller details of release dates, complete track listings, alternate serial numbers, special issues/editions, and more.

Younger Than Yesterday Columbia CL 2642 (mono)/Columbia CS 9442 (stereo) (US). CBS BPG 62988 (mono)/CBS SBPG 62988 (stereo) (UK). Remastered CD edition with bonus tracks: Columbia Legacy CK 64848 (US)/Columbia Legacy 483708 2 (UK).
Although not a member of the Byrds at this point, White appeared on 'Time Between' and 'The Girl With No Name'.

The Notorious Byrd Brothers Columbia CL 2775 (mono)/Columbia CS 9575 (stereo) (US). CBS 63169 (mono)/CBS S 63169 (stereo) (UK). Remastered CD edition with bonus tracks: Columbia Legacy CK 65151 (US)/Columbia Legacy 486751 2 (UK).
Although not a member of the Byrds at this point, White appeared on 'Change Is Now' and 'Wasn't Born To Follow'.

Sweetheart Of The Rodeo Columbia CL 9670 (mono)/CS 9670 (stereo) (US). CBS 63353 (mono)/CBS S 63353 (stereo) (UK). Remastered CD edition with bonus tracks: Columbia Legacy CK 65150 (US)/Columbia Legacy 486752 2 (UK). Special issue *Sweetheart Of The Rodeo* [*Legacy Edition*]: Columbia Legacy COL 510921 2 (US).
White guested on this album and was a full-time, salaried member by the time it was released.

Dr Byrds & Mr Hyde Columbia CL 9755 (mono)/CS 9755 (stereo) (US). CBS 63545 (mono)/CBS S 63545 (stereo) (UK). Remastered CD edition with bonus tracks: Columbia Legacy CK 65113 (US)/Columbia Legacy 486753 2 (UK).

Ballad Of Easy Rider Columbia CS 9942 (stereo) (US)/CBS S 63795 (stereo) (UK). Remastered CD edition with bonus tracks: Columbia Legacy CK 65114 (US)/Columbia Legacy 486754 2 (UK).

(Untitled) Columbia G 30127 (stereo) (US)/CBS S 64095 (stereo) (UK). Remastered CD edition with bonus tracks: *(Untitled)/(Unissued)* Columbia Legacy C2K 65847 (US)/Columbia Legacy 495077 2 (UK).

Byrdmaniax Columbia KC 30640 (stereo) (US)/CBS S 64389 (stereo) (UK). Remastered CD edition with bonus tracks: Columbia Legacy CK 65848 (US)/Columbia Legacy 495079 2 (UK).

Farther Along Columbia KC 31050 (stereo) (US)/CBS S 64676 (stereo) (UK). Remastered CD edition with bonus tracks: Columbia Legacy CK 65849 (US)/Columbia Legacy 495078 2 (UK).

Archival albums with the Byrds:

The Original Singles Volume 2 1967–1969 CBS 32103 (UK).
Sanctuary II Sundazed LP 5065 (US).
Sanctuary III Sundazed LP 5066 (US).
Sanctuary IV Sundazed LP 5090 (US).
The Columbia Singles '65–'67 Sundazed LP 5130/P2 55624 (US).
Live At The Fillmore – February 1969 Columbia/Legacy CK 65910 (US)/Columbia/Legacy 495080 2 (UK).
Live At The Royal Albert Hall 1971 Sundazed LP 5189/Sundazed SC 11177 (US).

Box Sets with the Byrds:

The Byrds Columbia Legacy 46773 (US)/Columbia Legacy 4676112 (UK).
12 Dimensions The Columbia Recordings 1965–1972 (13-CD box set) Columbia 497610 2/4976102000 (UK).
There Is A Season (4-CD box set and DVD) Columbia/Legacy 82876877002 (US/UK).
The Complete Columbia Albums Collection Columbia Legacy 886978738028 (US).

Isolated appearances with the Byrds:

See *Volume 1*: *Byrds Albums, Guest Slots/Rarities, Compilations* and *Archival Albums* for fuller details of release dates and alternate territory serial numbers.

Earl Scruggs, His Family And Friends Columbia 30584 (US)/CBS 64777 (UK).
Banjoman Sire SA 7527(US)/Sire SRK 6026 (UK).

White's work, along with the other Byrds' instruments, is not evident on 'Child Of The Universe' from the *Candy* soundtrack, which featured McGuinn backed by an orchestra. White is on *Easy Rider*, however, guesting on the Byrds' 'Wasn't Born To Follow' from *The Notorious Byrd Brothers*.

Compilations/Hits Collections with the Byrds:

See *Volume 1* for additional details.

The Byrds Greatest Hits Volume 2 CBS S 64650 (UK).
Best Of Volume 2 Columbia C31795 (US).
History Of The Byrds CBS 68242 (UK).
Return Of The Byrds Columbia Realm 2V 8006-7 (US).
The Byrds CBS 88320 (UK).
The Byrds Play Dylan Columbia PC 36293 (US)/CBS 31795 (UK).
The Very Best Of The Byrds Columbia CS P-P2 17596 (US).
The Byrds Collection Castle Communications CCSLP 151 (UK).
The Very Best Of The Byrds Columbia CBS 4634189 2 (Holland/UK).
Full Flyte Raven RVCD 10 (Australia).
20 Essential Tracks From The Boxed Set: 1965–1970 Columbia/Legacy CK 47884/471665-2 (US/UK).
Definitive Collection Columbia 480548 9 (UK).
Nashville West Sony Music Special Products A 28123 (US).
The Very Best Of The Byrds Columbia 487995 2 (UK).
The Best Of The Byrds Columbia 488146 2 (UK).
Super Hits Columbia Legacy 504725 2 (UK)/Columbia Legacy CK 65637 (US).
The Byrds Sony Music Special Products A 30827 (US).
The Byrds Play The Songs Of Bob Dylan Columbia 501946 2 (UK).
The Byrds Play Dylan Columbia/Legacy CK 85430 (US).
The Essential Byrds Columbia Legacy 512249 2 (UK)/Columbia Legacy C2K 89110 (US).
Mojo Presents . . . An Introduction To The Byrds – 24 Classic Songs Columbia 512778 2 (UK).
Mr Tambourine Man – The Best Of The Byrds Sony Music Media SMM 516489-2 (Germany/UK).
America's Great National Treasure Sony/BMG A 96086 (US).
The Very Best Of The Byrds Sony/BMG 82876 855142 (UK).
Byrds: A Collection Sony BMG 88697 12448 2 (UK).
The Byrds Play Dylan Sony BMG 88697 25267 2 (UK).

Playlist: The Very Best Of The Byrds Columbia Legacy 88697 39219 2 (US).
Steel Box Sony BMG 88697 459812 (UK).
Eight Miles High – The Best Of The Byrds Sony/Camden 88697 63627 2 (UK).
Setlist: The Very Best Of The Byrds Live Columbia/Legacy 88697 97753 2 (US).
Turn! Turn! Turn!: The Ultimate Collection Sony/Columbia Music 88875 151652 (UK).
The 60s – The Byrds Sony Music 88883 77667 2 (US).

With the White Brothers (aka New Kentucky Colonels):
The White Brothers, The New Kentucky Colonels, Live In Sweden (1973) Rounder 0073 (US).
'Why You Been Gone So Long'; 'Banjo Boy Chimes'; 'Last Thing On My Mind'; 'Sally Goodin'; 'Take A Whiff On Me'; 'Rawhide'; 'If You're Ever Gonna Love Me'; 'I'm Blue And I'm Lonesome'; 'Alabama Jubilee'; 'You Won't Be Satisfied That Way'; 'Soldier's Joy'/'Black Mountain Rag'; 'I Know What It Means To Be Lonesome'; 'Blackberry Blossom'; 'New River Train'.
Released May 1976 (US).

The New Kentucky Colonels Live In Holland 1973 Roland White Music RW 0001 (US).
'Fire On The Mountain'; 'Never Ending Song Of Love'; 'Dixie Breakdown'; 'The Fields Have Turned Brown'; 'Take A Whiff (On Me)'; 'Is This My Destiny'; 'Mocking Banjo'; 'If You're Ever Gonna Love Me'; 'Last Thing On My Mind'; 'Dark Hollow'; 'Soldier's Joy'/'Black Mountain Rag'; 'Why You Been Gone So Long?'; 'Roll In My Sweet Baby's Arms'/'Will You Be Lovin' Another Man?'; 'I Know What It Means To Be Lonesome'; 'Working On A Building'; 'Rawhide'.
Released June 2013 (US). Credited to the New Kentucky Colonels.

Other albums:
Muleskinner Warner Brothers BS 2787 (US)/Edsel ED 219 (UK).
'Muleskinner Blues'; 'Blue And Lonesome'; 'Footprints In The Snow'; 'Dark Hollow'; 'Whitehouse Blues'; 'Opus 57 In G Minor'; 'Runways Of The Moon'; 'Roanoke'; 'Rain And Snow'; 'Soldier's Joy'; 'Blue Mule'.
Released May 1974 (US)/March 1987 (UK).

Muleskinner Live Sierra OXCD 6001 (US).
'New Camptown Races'; 'Dark Hollow'; 'Land Of The Navajo'; 'Blackberry Blossom'; 'Knockin' On Your Door'; 'Opus 57 In G Minor'; 'Red Rocking Chair'; 'Going To The Races'; 'Eighth Of January'; 'I Am A Pilgrim'; 'The Dead March'; 'Sitting Alone In The Moonlight'; 'Orange Blossom Special'.
Released January 1992 (US).

Silver Meteor Sierra SRS 8706 (US).
'Never Ending Love'; 'Last Thing On My Mind'; 'Alabama Jubilee'; 'Why You Been Gone So Long'; 'Silver Meteor'; 'A Good Love Is Like A Good

Song'; 'I'm On My Way Home Again'; 'Cuckoo Bird'; 'The Bramble And The Rose'; 'Living In The Country'; 'The Knight Upon The Road'; 'Hitch-Hiker'.
This compilation contains four tracks that White recorded for the solo album he was working on immediately prior to his death: 'Never Ending Love', 'Last Thing On My Mind', 'Alabama Jubilee' and 'Why You Been Gone So Long'. Two further tracks, 'Waterbed' and 'Lucky Me', have yet to obtain an official release.
Released April 1980 (US).

33 Acoustic Guitar Instrumentals Sierra 26023-2 (US).
'Wildwood Flower'; 'Master's Bouquet'; 'Bury Me Beneath The Willow'; 'Black Mountain Rag'; 'Billy In The Low Ground'; 'I'm So Happy'; 'He Will Set Your Fields On Fire'; 'Sugarfoot Rag'; 'Nine Pound Hammer'; 'Cripple Creek'; 'Under The Double Eagle'; 'Farewell Blues'; 'I Am A Pilgrim'; 'Country Boy Rock & Roll'; 'Forsaken Love'; ' False Hearted Lover'; 'Black Jack Davy'; 'Banks Of The Ohio'; 'Jimmy Brown The Newsboy'; 'Sally Goodin'; 'Buckin' Mule'; 'Shady Grove'; 'Pike County Breakdown'; 'Old Joe Clark'; 'Arkansas Traveller'; 'Footprints In The Snow'; 'In The Pines'; 'Journey's End'; 'Pretty Polly'; 'Cotton Eyed Joe'; 'Clinch Mountain Backstep'; 'Randy Lynn Rag'; 'Mandolin Medley'.
Released August 2000 (US). Reissued by Rural Rhythm (RHY 1019) in August 2003.

Louisiana Rain Big Beat CDWIKD 219 (US).
'Your Gentle Ways Of Loving Me'; 'Louisiana Cottonfields'; 'Workin' On A Tugboat'; 'Into The Darkness Of Your Mind'; 'Louisiana Rain'; 'Sweet Sugar Blues'; 'Walk With Sam'; 'Sweet Suzannah'; 'Miles & Cities'; 'Young Country Girl'; 'Multiple Heartaches'; 'Two People'; 'Desperation's Back Again'; 'Happy Cajun Man'; 'Mr Somebody'; 'Sweet Rosie'; 'I Get A Hurt On Inside'; 'Woman's Disgrace'; 'There's Still A Little Something In Your Mind'; 'Louisiana Woman'; 'Home Of The Blues'; 'Lodi'; 'World Of Dreams'; 'If It's Me I'm A Fool'; 'On Pins & Needles'. Credited to Guilbeau & Parsons, this archival retrospective details their collaboration.
Released: November 2002 (US).

Tuff & Stringy (Sessions 1966–68) Big Beat CDIKD 227 (US).
'Hong Kong Hillbilly' [aka 'Nashville West'] (Clarence White); 'Mother-In-Law' (Gary Paxton); 'Make Up Your Mind' (Spencers); 'Grandma Funderbunk's Music Box' (Clarence White); 'Guitar Pickin' Man' (Wayne Moore); 'Vaccination For The Blues' (Sanland Brothers); 'Don't Pity Me' (Darrell Cotton); 'Gotta Go See The World' (Leon Copeland); 'Everybody Has One But You' (Kentucky Colonels); 'She's Gone' (Gib & Jan); 'Tuff & Stringy' (Clarence White); 'I'm Tied Down To You' (Richard Arlen); 'Hey Juliana' (Wayne Moore); 'Last Date' (Clarence White); 'I'll Live Today' (Dennis Payne); 'Not Enough Of Me To Go Round' (Jack Reeves); 'Riff-Raff' (Clarence White); 'If We Could Read' (Darrell Cotton); 'Rocks In

My Head' (Wayne Moore); 'Made Of Stone' (Kentucky Colonels); 'Buckaroo' (Clarence White); 'Adam & Eve' (Clarence White); 'Why Can't We Be' (Great Love Trip); 'Nature's Child' (Jan & Clarence); 'Tango For A Sad Mood' (Clarence White); 'If We Could Read' backing track (Darrell Cotton). Credited to Clarence White, this sumptuous set, complete with excellent liner notes and an extended essay, documents much of his pre-Byrds session work. Released April 2003 (US).

Rare Performance Shikata 1005 (US).
'Shucking The Corn'; 'Chug-A-Lug'; 'She's No Angel'; 'Salty Dog'; 'Just Stay Around'; 'Dixie Breakdown'; 'Mocking Banjo'; 'Once More'; 'Green Corn'; 'Rubin's [sic] Train'; 'Don't Let Your Deal Go Down'; 'Soldier's Joy' ['Flop Eared Mule]'; 'Black Eyed Susie'; 'Sally Ann'; 'Cumberland Gap'; 'Shady Grove'; 'Chicken Real'; 'Little Darlin' Pal Of Mine'; 'The Crawdad Song'; 'Pike County Breakdown'; 'Soldier's Joy'; 'Arkansas Traveler'.
Released 2003 (US). Credited to Bush, Lathum & White. The final six tracks on the disc feature Roland White and Bobby Slone.

Tut And Clarence Flatpicking Tutlee TL 1003 (US).
'Picking Peanuts'; 'False Hearted Lover'; 'Happy Dobro'; 'Sweet Georgia Brown'; 'Panhandle Rag'; 'What A Friend'; 'All Smiles Tonight'; 'Dobro Twist'; 'Playing Around'; 'Lonesome Dobro'; 'Tennessee Dulcimer Works'; 'Sleepy Head'; 'Maggie'; 'Wabash Cannonball'; 'Dobro Country'; 'Little Green Pill'; 'Steel Guitar Blues'; 'Faded Love'; 'Careless Love'; 'Hawaiian Sunset'; 'Happy Pickers'; 'Sweet Picking Time In Toomsboro, GA'; 'Picking Flat'; 'Turn Around'.
Released 2003. Archive recording from 1965 credited to Tut And Clarence.

Flatpick Sierra/Rural Rhythm RHY 1024 (US).
'John Henry Blues'; 'Reno Ride'; 'Salt Creek'; 'Kickin' Mule'; 'Big Sandy River'; 'Sheik Of Araby'; 'Black Mountain Blues'/'Soldier's Joy'; 'Durham's Reel'; 'Barefoot Nellie'; 'Weeping Willow'; 'Ragtime Annie'; 'When You're Smiling'; 'Columbus Stockade Blues'; 'Texas Gales/Blackberry Rag'; 'Silver Bells'; 'San Antonio Rose'; 'Listen To The Mocking Bird'; 'Laughing Guitar'; 'Alabama Jubilee 1973'.
Released: October 2006 (US).

Flatpick (Extended Edition) Sierra SZCD 6026 (US).
Original album. Extra CD includes 'Kickin' Mule'; 'Sheik Of Araby'; 'Soldier's Joy'/'Black Mountain Rag'; 'Way Downtown'; 'Crawdad Song'; 'New River Train'; 'Julius Finkbine's Rag'; 'Billy In The Lowground'; 'Fire On The Mountain'. Guitar Instruction Tape: 'Sally Goodin''; 'Black Mountain Rag'; 'Farewell Blues'. Live Spring 1973: 'Moonlight Waltz'; 'Old Joe Clark'. Album Recording Session, 1973: 'Lost Highway'.
Released December 2006 (US).

White Lightnin' Sierra SXCD 6030 (US).
'No Title Yet Blues' [*New Dimensions In Banjo & Bluegrass* version]; 'Tuff &

Stringy' [Nashville West studio version]; 'Tango For A Sad Mood' [Roustabouts live]; 'Buckaroo' [Roustabouts live at Nashville West]; 'Tuff & Stringy' [Roustabouts live at Nashville West]; 'Yesterday's Train' [Byrds rehearsals]; 'Sally Goodin Meets The Byrds' [Byrds rehearsals]; 'Oakridge Tennessee' [Freddy Weller – *Games People Play*]; 'Louisiana Redbone' [Freddy Weller – *Games People Play*]; 'Birmingham' [Freddy Weller – *Games People Play*]; 'Freeborn Man' [Freddy Weller – *Games People Play*]; 'Dear Landlord' [Joe Cocker – *Joe Cocker!*]; 'Cuckoo Bird' [Everly Brothers sessions]; 'From Eden To Canaan' [Everly Brothers sessions, take 2]; 'I'm On My Way Home Again' [Everly Brothers sessions, take 1], 'I'm On My Way Home Again', 'White's Lightning' [Byrds]; 'Around The Barn' [Clarence White/Gene Parsons jam session]. A special version was also issued on DVD featuring 'Truck Stop Girl' and 'Take A Whiff On Me'.
Released December 2008 (US). Although released in December 2008 (and confirmed as such by Sierra) the copyright on the record actually states 2009.

Bush, Lathum & White Sierra SXCD 6033 (US).
This compilation features the first 16 songs included on the previously listed Shikata release, *Rare Performance*, credited to Bush, Lathum & White.
Released: April 2011 (US).

White also appeared on several singles as a member of the Country Boys, including 'I'm Head Over Heels In Love With You'/'Kentucky Hills' (Sundown), 'The Valley Below'/'High On A Mountain' (Republic) and 'To Prove My Love For You'/'Just Joshing' (Briar). As a soloist, White appeared on a couple of singles on Bakersfield: 'Tango For A Sad Mood'/'Tuff And Stringy' and 'Grandma Funderbunk's Music Box'/'Riff-Raff'. He can also be heard on a number of Various Artistes' compilations, including *Themes & Laughs From The Andy Griffith Show* (Capitol), *Country Music Hootenanny* (Capitol), *Bluegrass Special* (World-Pacific), *Suite Steel: The Pedal Steel Guitar Album* (Elektra), *Bakersfield Rebels* (Big Beat), *Son Of Rounder Banjo* (Rounder), *Guitar Player Presents Legends Of Country Guitar, Volumes 1 and 2* (Rhino) and *Byrd Parts* and *Byrd Parts 2* (Raven).

As a session player White also guested on numerous recordings, including those of Eric Weissberg, Marshall Brickman & Company (*New Dimensions In Banjo & Bluegrass*), Rick Nelson (*Bright Lights & Country Music; Country Fever*; *Country*; *String Along With Rick; Rick's Rarities 1964–1974*), the Gosdin Brothers (singles: 'Hangin' On'/'Multiple Heartaches'; 'Sounds Of Goodbye'/'The Victim', 'There Must Be Someone'/'She Still Wishes I Were You'; 'One Hundred Years From Now'/'No Matter Where You Go'; 'Louisiana Man'/'Till The End'; *Sounds Of Goodbye* CD issue), Gary Paxton (singles 'It's My Way Of Loving You'/'My Heart Won't Let My Lips Say Goodbye'; 'You Do The Best You Can'/'Goin' Thru The Motions'; 'Mother-In-Law'/'Miles And Cities'; plus see *Tuff & Stringy*), Leon Copeland (see *Tuff & Stringy*), Richard Arlen ('I'm Tied Down To You'/'I Keep Givin' In To You'; plus see *Tuff & Stringy*), Wayne Moore (see *Tuff & Stringy*), Larry

Scott ('A Little Shoe Shine Boy's Christmas'/'The Teacher' single), Cajun Gib And Gene ('Sweet Rosie'/'Your Gentle Ways Of Loving Me' single), the Monkees (*Pisces, Aquarius, Capricorn & Jones Ltd*; *Listen To The Band* box set), the Sanland Brothers ('Red Roses (For My Baby)'/'Vaccination For The Blues', plus see *Tuff & Stringy*), Bruce E. Oaks/Bruce Oakes (singles: 'The Lineman Song'/'I Don't Play Love'; 'I'll Live Today'/'On Pins And Needles'; *Picking With Friends*), Floyd 'Gib' Guilbeau (singles: 'Baby Lock The Door'/'Don't Ask Me Why'; 'Cry Cry Darlin''/'Red Water'; 'What Kind Of Flower'/'Bon Soir Blues'.

Gib Guilbeau; *Cajun Country*; *Toe Tappin' Music*; *Classic Guilbeau*), the Spencers ('King And Queen Of Fools'/'Make Up Your Mind' single, plus see *Tuff & Stringy*), Leon Copeland ('Gotta Go See The World'/'I'm Looking For My Mind' single), Eldon Fault ('Livin' In The Lap Of Luxury'/'Welcome Home Pow' single), Dennis Payne ('I'll Live Today'/'Guitar Pickers Blues' single; plus see *Tuff & Stringy*), Jack Reeves ('Not Enough Of Me To Go Around'/'Six Million Teardrops' single; plus see *Tuff & Stringy*), Darrell Cotton (singles 'Don't Pity Me'/'If We Could Read'; 'Come Free My Mind'/'If We Could Read'; plus see *Tuff & Stringy*).

Gene Clark (*Gene Clark With The Gosdin Brothers*; *Early LA Sessions*; *Roadmaster*), Great Love Trip ('Why Can't We Be'/'Noah' single; plus see *Tuff & Stringy*), Wynn Stewart (*Love's Gonna Happen To Me; Something Pretty; In Love; Let The Whole World Sing With Me; Yours Forever; You Don't Care What Happens To Me*), David Blue (*These 23 Days In September*), Sal Valentino ('Silkie'/'Song For Rochelle' single), Lewis & Clarke ('Gypsy Song Man'/'Daddy's Plastic Child' single), Kenny Vernon ('That'll Be The Day'/ 'I'd Go Right Back' single), Pat Boone (*Departure*).

Eternity's Children (*Timeless; From Us Unto You: The Original Singles*), Mistress Mary (*Housewife*), Rusty Dean (*Wailin' Time; Country Hits Of Today, A Country Bouquet Of Hits*), Jimmie Lee Morris ('Talk About Lonesome'/'Fill It Up' single), the Bakersfield Five (*Buckaroo Featuring Tiger By The Tail*), the Country Ladies (*The Hit Songs Of The Country Ladies*), the Modern Country Friends (*Country-Politan*), Everly Brothers ('I'm On My Way Back Home Again'/'Cuckoo Bird' single; *Stories We Could Tell*; *Roots*; *Chained To A Memory* box set).

Freddy Weller (*Games People Play; Listen To The Young Folks*), Arlo Guthrie (*Running Down The Road; Washington County*; *Hobo's Lullaby*; *Last Of The Brooklyn Cowboys*), Linda Ronstadt (*Hand Sown . . . Home Grown*), Joe Cocker (*Joe Cocker!*), Johnny Darrell (*California Stop-Over*), Phil Ochs (*Greatest Hits*), Randy Newman (*12 Songs*), Rita Coolidge (*Rita Coolidge; Nice Feelin'*), Marc Benno (*Minnows*), Delaney & Bonnie And Friends (*Motel Shot*), Paul Siebel (*Jack-Knife Gypsy*), Mother Hen (*Mother Hen*), Jackson Browne (*Jackson Browne; Late For The Sky*), Joel Scott Hill/Chris Ethridge/Johnny Barbata (*L.A. Getaway*), Earl Scruggs (*Earl Scruggs, His Family And Friends*), Skip Battin (*Skip; Topanga Skyline*), Country Gazette (*Don't Give Up Your Day Job*), Maria Muldaur (*Maria Muldaur*), Gene Parsons (*Kindling*), Terry Melcher (*Terry Melcher*), Flying Burrito Brothers (*Flying High*), Doc Watson & Family (*Treasures Untold*) and Twin Engine (*Twin Engine*).

GENE PARSONS

As Cajun Gib and Gene:

Cajun Country Alshire S5121 (US).
'Louisiana Rain'; 'Sweet Susanna'; 'Happy Cajun Man'; 'Sweet Rosie'; 'Sweet Sugar Blues'; 'Walk With Sam'; 'Louisiana Cottonfields'; 'I Get A Hurt On Inside'; 'Multiple Heartaches'; 'Young Country Girl'.
This was released as a solo Gib Guilbeau album but was, in fact, the previously unreleased album which Cajun Gib and Gene had recorded for Bakersfield International.
Released 1969 (US).

As Guilbeau & Parsons:

Louisiana Rain Big Beat CDWIKD 219 (US).
'Your Gentle Ways Of Loving Me'; 'Louisiana Cottonfields'; 'Workin' On A Tugboat'; 'Into The Darkness Of Your Mind'; 'Louisiana Rain'; 'Sweet Sugar Blues'; 'Walk With Sam'; 'Sweet Suzannah'; 'Miles & Cities'; 'Young Country Girl'; 'Multiple Heartaches'; 'Two People'; 'Desperation's Back Again'; 'Happy Cajun Man'; 'Mr Somebody'; 'Sweet Rosie'; 'I Get A Hurt On Inside'; 'Woman's Disgrace'; 'There's Still A Little Something In Your Mind'; 'Louisiana Woman'; 'Home Of The Blues'; 'Lodi'; 'World Of Dreams'; 'If It's Me I'm A Fool'; 'On Pins & Needles'. Credited to Guilbeau & Parsons, this archival retrospective details their collaboration.
Released November 2002 (US).

With Nashville West:

Nashville West Sierra SRS 8701 (US).
See Clarence White section for track listing.

Albums with the Byrds:

See Discography *Volume 1* under the following sections: *Byrds Singles, Albums, Compilations* and *Archival Albums* for fuller details of release dates, complete track listings, alternate serial numbers, special issues/editions, and more.

Dr Byrds & Mr Hyde Columbia CL 9755 (mono)/CS 9755 (stereo) (US). CBS 63545 (mono)/CBS S 63545 (stereo) (UK). Remastered CD edition with bonus tracks: Columbia Legacy CK 65113 (US)/Columbia Legacy 486753 2 (UK).

Ballad Of Easy Rider Columbia CS 9942 (stereo) (US)/CBS S 63795 (stereo) (UK). Remastered CD edition with bonus tracks: Columbia Legacy CK 65114 (US)/Columbia Legacy 486754 2 (UK).

(Untitled) Columbia G 30127 (stereo) (US)/CBS S 64095 (stereo) (UK). Remastered CD edition with bonus tracks: *(Untitled)/(Unissued)* Columbia Legacy C2K 65847 (US)/Columbia Legacy 495077 2 (UK).

Byrdmaniax Columbia KC 30640 (stereo) (US)/CBS S 64389 (stereo) (UK). Remastered CD edition with bonus tracks: Columbia Legacy CK 65848 (US)/Columbia Legacy 495079 2 (UK).

Farther Along Columbia KC 31050 (stereo) (US)/CBS S 64676 (stereo) (UK). Remastered CD edition with bonus tracks: Columbia Legacy CK 65849 (US)/Columbia Legacy 495078 2 (UK).

Archival albums with the Byrds:

The Original Singles Volume 2 1967–1969 CBS 32103 (UK).
Sanctuary III Sundazed LP 5066 (US).
Live At The Fillmore – February 1969 Columbia/Legacy CK 65910 (US)/Columbia/Legacy 495080 2 (UK).
Live At The Royal Albert Hall 1971 Sundazed LP 5189/Sundazed SC 11177 (US).

Box Sets with the Byrds:

The Byrds Columbia Legacy 46773 (US)/Columbia Legacy 4676112 (UK).
12 Dimensions The Columbia Recordings 1965–1972 (13-CD box set) Columbia 497610 2/4976102000 (UK).
There Is A Season (4-CD box set and DVD) Columbia/Legacy 82876877002 (US/UK).
The Complete Columbia Albums Collection Columbia Legacy 886978738028 (US).

Isolated appearances with the Byrds:

See *Volume 1*: *Byrds Albums, Guest Slots/Rarities, Compilations* and *Archival Albums* for fuller details of release dates and alternate territory serial numbers.

Earl Scruggs, His Family And Friends Columbia 30584 (US)/CBS 64777 (UK).

Parsons' work, along with the other Byrds' instruments, is not evident on 'Child Of The Universe' from the *Candy* soundtrack, which featured McGuinn backed by an orchestra. Parsons appears on the soundtrack of *Easy Rider*, backing McGuinn on harmonica.

Compilations/Hits Collections with the Byrds:

See *Volume 1* for additional details.
The Byrds Greatest Hits Volume 2 CBS S 64650 (UK).
Best Of Volume 2 Columbia C31795 (US).
History Of The Byrds CBS 68242 (UK).
Return Of The Byrds Columbia Realm 2V 8006-7 (US).
The Byrds CBS 88320 (UK).
The Byrds Play Dylan Columbia PC 36293 (US)/CBS 31795 (UK).
The Very Best Of The Byrds Columbia CS P-P2 17596 (US).
The Byrds Collection Castle Communications CCSLP 151 (UK).

Full Flyte Raven RVCD 10 (Australia).
20 Essential Tracks From The Boxed Set: 1965–1970 Columbia/Legacy CK 47884/471665-2 (US/UK).
Definitive Collection Columbia 480548 9 (UK).
Nashville West Sony Music Special Products A 28123 (US).
The Very Best Of The Byrds Columbia 487995 2 (UK).
The Best Of The Byrds Columbia 488146 2 (UK).
Super Hits Columbia Legacy 504725 2 (UK)/Columbia Legacy CK 65637 (US).
The Byrds Sony Music Special Products A 30827 (US).
The Byrds Play The Songs Of Bob Dylan Columbia 501946 2 (UK).
The Byrds Play Dylan Columbia/Legacy CK 85430 (US).
The Essential Byrds Columbia Legacy 512249 2 (UK)/Columbia Legacy C2K 89110 (US).
Mojo Presents . . . An Introduction To The Byrds – 24 Classic Songs Columbia 512778 2 (UK).
Mr Tambourine Man – The Best Of The Byrds Sony Music Media SMM 516489-2 (Germany/UK).
America's Great National Treasure Sony/BMG A 96086 (US).
The Very Best Of The Byrds Sony/BMG 82876 85514 2 (UK).
Byrds: A Collection Sony BMG 88697 12448 2 (UK).
The Byrds Play Dylan Sony BMG 88697 25267 2 (UK).
Playlist: The Very Best Of The Byrds Columbia Legacy 88697 39219 2 (US).
Steel Box Sony BMG 88697 45981 2 (UK).
Eight Miles High – The Best Of The Byrds Sony/Camden 88697 63627 2 (UK).
Setlist: The Very Best Of The Byrds Live Columbia/Legacy 88697 97753 2 (US).
Turn! Turn! Turn!: The Ultimate Collection Sony/Columbia Music 88875 151652 (UK).
The 60s – The Byrds Sony Music 8888377667 2 (US).

As Gene Parsons:

Kindling Warner Brothers BS 2687 (US)/Warner Brothers K 46257 (UK).
'Monument'; 'Long Way Back'; 'Do Not Disturb'; 'Willin''; 'On The Spot'; 'Take A City Bride'; 'Sonic Bummer'; 'I Must Be A Tree'; 'Drunkard's Dream'; 'Banjo Dog'; '(And)Back Again'.
Released September 1973 (US)/May 1974 (UK).

Melodies Sierra SRS 8703 (US)/Sundown SDLP 008 (UK).
'My Kingdom For A Car'; 'Melodies From A Bird In Flyght'; 'Mama Papa'; 'Won't Last Long'; 'Way Out There'; 'Hot Burrito # 1'; 'No Fire Here Tonight'; 'Pastime'; 'Little Jewels'; 'Why You Been Gone So Long'.
Released February 1979 (US)/May 1984 (UK).

The Kindling Collection Sierra SXCD 6007 (US).
Compilation, includes the unissued Flying Burritos Brothers' track, 'Wind And Rain'.
Released July 1994 (US).

Gene Parsons In Concert – I Hope They Let Us In Stringbender Music SBR 002 (US).
'Swing Down'; 'Sweet Suzannah'; 'Rhumba Man'; 'Gunga Din'; 'Abilene'; 'Bugler'; 'Do Not Disturb'; 'Dark Moon'; 'Willin''; 'Take A City Bride'; 'Sweet Desert Childhood'; 'Studebaker Story'; 'Banjo Dog'; 'Way Out There'; 'I Must Be A Tree'; 'Old Blue'; 'You Ain't Going Nowhere'.
Released May 2001 (US).

With the Flying Burrito Brothers:

Flying Again Columbia 33817 (US)/CBS 69184 (UK).
'Easy To Get On'; 'Wind And Rain'; 'Why Baby Why'; 'Dim Lights, Thick Smoke'; 'You Left The Water Running'; 'Building Fires'; 'Sweet Desert Childhood'; 'Bon Soir Blues'; 'River Road'; 'Hot Burrito # 3'.
Released October 1975 (US)/December 1975 (UK).

Airborne Columbia 34222 (US)/CBS 81433 (UK).
'Out Of Control'; 'Waiting For Love To Begin'; 'Toe Tapping Music'; 'Quiet Man'; 'Northbound Bus'; 'Big Bayou'; 'Walk On The Water'; 'Linda Lu'; 'Border Town'; 'She's A Sailor'; 'Jesus Broke The Wild Horse'.
Released July 1976 (US/UK).

From Another Time Shiloh SCD 4094 (US).
'Diggi Diggi Li'; 'Wheels'; 'Dim Lights, Thick Smoke'; 'Faded Love'; 'Devil In Disguise'; 'Building Fires'; 'Bon Soir Blues'; 'White Line Fever'; 'Sin City'; 'She Thinks I Still Care'; 'Why Baby Why'; 'Close Up The Honky Tonks'.
Released May 1991 (US).

Sin City Relix RRCD 2052 (US).
'White Line Fever'; 'Faded Love'; 'Wheels'; 'Do Right Woman'; 'If You Got The Money'; 'Take A City Bride'; 'Waiting For Love To Begin'; 'Why Baby Why'; 'Hot Burrito # 2'; 'Sin City'; 'Orange Blossom Special'; 'Close Up The Honky Tonks'; 'Beat The Heat'; 'Will The Circle Be Unbroken'.
Released 1992 (US).

As Parsons Green:

Birds Of A Feather Sierra SE 4223 (US).
'Don't Miss Your Water'; 'Birds Of A Feather'; 'Lookin' For Trouble'; 'California Blues'; 'Lily's Hotbread'; 'No, You're Not Broken'; 'Swing Down'; 'Spoon River'; 'Wind & Rain'; 'Catch The Wind'; 'Quiet Joys Of Brotherhood'.
Released May 1988. The limited edition pre-release cassette version includes the otherwise unavailable 'Love Was Lord Of All'.

Live From Caspar Stringbender SBR 003 (US).
'Coast Hotel'; 'Sin City'; 'Just Away'; 'California Blues'; 'Cowboy Girl'; 'Chief Seattle'; 'Sweet Desert Childhood'; 'Banjo Dog'; 'Drunkard's Dream'; 'Lookin' For Trouble'; 'Life Carries On'; 'Get Up Blues'.
Released February 2002 (US).

As Haywire:
Nature Quest – Bluegrass Music North Sound Music 18236 6011 2 (US).
'O Come All Ye Faithful'; 'Angels We Have Heard On High'; 'Joy To The World'; 'Go Rest Ye Merry Gentlemen'; 'Jingle Bells'; 'O Little Town Of Bethlehem'; 'We Three Kings'; 'I'll Fly Away'; 'Hark! The Herald Angels Sing'; 'Deck The Halls'; 'Away In A Manger'; 'The First Noel'; 'O Christmas Tree'; 'Silent Night – O Holy Night'; 'Bluegrass Christmas Medley'.
Released December 1998 (US).

As Gene Parsons, Joe Craven, Bill Douglass:
Bluegrass Season's Greetings Stringbender SBR 103 (US).
'The First Noel'; 'Hark! The Herald Angels Sing'; 'I'll Fly Away'; 'O Come All Ye Faithful'; 'God Rest Ye Merry Gentlemen'; 'Angels We Have Heard On High'; 'Joy To The World'; 'We Three Kings'; 'Jingle Bells'; 'O Little Town Of Bethlehem'; 'Deck The Halls'; 'Away In A Manger'; 'O Tannenbaum (O Christmas Tree)'; 'Silent Night'; 'De Bass Be De Bottom'; 'I'll Fly Away (weird)'.
Released December 2002 (US).

Parsons has also guested on recordings by 'Floyd' Gib Guilbeau (singles: 'Home Of The Blues'/'Lodi'; 'Empty Words Of Love'/'In The Morning'; 'Baby Lock The Door'/'Don't Ask Me Why'; 'Cry Cry Darlin''/'Red Water'; 'What Kind Of Flower'/'Bon Soir Blues'; *Gib Guilbeau*; *Cajun Country; Toe Tappin' Music*; *Classic Guilbeau*), the Gosdin Brothers (singles: 'Hangin' On'/'Multiple Heartaches'; 'There Must Be Someone'/'She Still Wishes I Were You'; 'Louisiana Man'/'Till The End'; *Sounds Of Goodbye* CD reissue), Gary Paxton (singles: 'It's My Way Of Loving You'/'My Heart Won't Let My Lips Say Goodbye'; 'You Do The Best You Can'/'Goin' Thru The Motions'; 'Mother-In-Law'/'Miles And Cities'; plus see *Tuff & Stringy*), Clarence White (singles: 'Tango For A Sad Mood'/'Tuff And Stringy'; 'Grandma Funderbunk's Music Box'/'Riff-Raff'; *Tuff & Stringy; White Lightnin'*).

Wayne Moore (see *Tuff & Stringy*), Larry Scott (single: 'A Little Shoe Shine Boy's Christmas'/'The Teacher' single), Cajun Gib And Gene (single: 'Sweet Rosie'/'Your Gentle Ways Of Loving Me'), Kenny Vernon (single: 'Ain't That A Shame'/'Miles And Miles And Miles'), Bruce E. Oaks/Bruce E. Oakes (singles: 'The Lineman Song'/'I Don't Play Love'; 'I'll Live Today'/'On Pins And Needles'; *Picking With Friends*), the Sanland Brothers (single: 'Red Roses (For My Baby)'/'Vaccination For The Blues', plus see *Tuff & Stringy*), Eldon Fault (single: 'Livin' In The Lap Of Luxury'/'Welcome Home Pow'), Christmas Spirit ('Christmas Is My Time Of Year'/'Will You Still Believe In Me' single), Rusty Dean (*Country Hits Of Today; A Country Bouquet Of Hits*).

Everly Brothers (single: 'I'm On My Way Back Home Again'/'Cuckoo Bird'; *Chained To A Memory* box set), Arlo Guthrie (*Running Down The Road; Last Of The Brooklyn Cowboys*), Eternity's Children (*Timeless; From Us Unto You: The Original Singles*), Randy Newman (*12 Songs; Sail Away*), Phil Ochs (*Greatest Hits*), Malvina Reynolds (single: 'Little Boxes'/'Cement Octopus';

Malvina Reynolds), Dion (*Suite For Late Summer*), Earl Scruggs (*Earl Scruggs, His Family And Friends*), Pacific Steel Company (*Pacific Steel Company*); Elliott Murphy (*Aquashow*), Sneaky Pete Kleinow (*Sneaky Pete; The Legend & The Legacy*), Delta Sisters (*Music From The Old Timey Hotel*), Philo Hayward (*Rounder*), David & Jude (*Living In Sin*), Tom O'Neill (*Road Of Life*).

Paolo Bonfanti (*On My Backdoor Someday*), Dan Paul (*World Without Walls*), Beppe Gambetta (*Good News From Home; Blu Di Genova; Slade Stomp*), Antonia Lamb (*Amazing Tracks*), Karen Almquist (*Tracking Of Time*), Tex Beaumont (*One-Eyed Jack; Restless Heart*), Meridian Green (*In The Heart Of This Town*), Peter Oliva (*The Eye Of The Storm; Postcard From The Promised Land*), Holly Tannen (*Rime Of The Ancient Matriarch*), Hoffi Hofstetter (*Docker Hill Road*), Totte Bergström (*In His Own Way*).

Patrice Ka'ohi (*Island Of The Sun*), Peter & Valerie Oliva (*History*), the Court & Spark (*Bless You*), John Hinshelwood (*Holler Til Dawn*), Chuck McCabe (*Bad Gravity Day*), Julian Dawson (*Hillbilly Zen*), Pat Johnson (*Famous Butterflies*), Steel Train (*Twilight Tales From The Prairies Of The Sun*), Sally Spring (*Mockingbird*), the Human Revolution (*Love Revolution*), Steven Bates Band (*Killer Rock And Roll*), the Court And Spark (*Bless You*), Marco Zanzi (*Time To Start Again*), the Piedmont Brothers Band (*Back To The Country*) and Jeff Slate (*Birds Of Paradox*).

Previously issued solo material is featured on the archival compilation *Byrd Parts* (Raven). Parsons also appears on the original soundtrack of the film, *Performance* and on the Various Artistes compilations, *Boys & Girls Club Vol. 1, Country Greats – Timeless Country Classic, Local Licks Live* and *Bakersfield Rebel.*

JOHN YORK

Albums with the Byrds:

See Discography *Volume 1* under the following sections: *Byrds Singles, Albums, Compilations* and *Archival Albums* for fuller details of release dates, complete track listings, alternate serial numbers, special issues/editions, and more.

Dr Byrds & Mr Hyde Columbia CL 9755 (mono)/CS 9755 (stereo) (US). CBS 63545 (mono)/CBS S 63545 (stereo) (UK). Remastered CD edition with bonus tracks: Columbia Legacy CK 65113 (US)/Columbia Legacy 486753 2 (UK).

Ballad Of Easy Rider Columbia CS 9942 (stereo) (US)/CBS S 63795 (stereo) (UK). Remastered CD edition with bonus tracks: Columbia Legacy CK 65114 (US)/Columbia Legacy 486754 2 (UK).

Archival albums with the Byrds:

The Original Singles Volume 2 1967–1969 CBS 32103 (UK).
Sanctuary III Sundazed LP 5066 (US).
Live At The Fillmore – February 1969 Columbia/Legacy CK 65910 (US)/Columbia/Legacy 495080 2 (UK).

Box Sets with the Byrds:

The Byrds Columbia Legacy 46773 (US)/Columbia Legacy 4676112 (UK).
12 Dimensions The Columbia Recordings 1965–1972 (13-CD box set) Columbia 497610 2/4976102000 (UK).
There Is A Season (4-CD box set and DVD) Columbia/Legacy 82876877002 (US/UK).
The Complete Columbia Albums Collection Columbia Legacy 886978738028 (US).

Compilations/Hits Collections with the Byrds:

See *Volume 1* for additional details.
The Byrds Greatest Hits Volume 2 CBS S 64650 (UK).
Best Of Volume 2 Columbia C31795 (US).
History Of The Byrds CBS 68242 (UK).
Return Of The Byrds Columbia Realm 2V 8006-7 (US).
The Byrds CBS 88320 (UK).
The Byrds Play Dylan Columbia PC 36293 (US)/CBS 31795 (UK).
Full Flyte Raven RVCD 10 (Australia).
20 Essential Tracks From The Boxed Set: 1965–1970 Columbia/Legacy CK 47884/471665-2 (US/UK).
Definitive Collection Columbia 480548 9 (UK).
Nashville West Sony Music Special Products A 28123 (US).
The Very Best Of The Byrds Columbia 487995 2 (UK).
The Best Of The Byrds Columbia 488146 2 (UK).
The Byrds Sony Music Special Products A 30827 (US).
The Byrds Play The Songs Of Bob Dylan Columbia 501946 2 (UK).
The Byrds Play Dylan Columbia/Legacy CK 85430 (US).
The Essential Byrds Columbia Legacy 512249 2 (UK)/Columbia Legacy C2K 89110 (US).
Mojo Presents . . . An Introduction To The Byrds – 24 Classic Songs Columbia 512778 2 (UK).
Mr Tambourine Man – The Best Of The Byrds Sony Music Media SMM 516489-2 (Germany/UK).
The Very Best Of The Byrds Sony/BMG 82876 855142 (UK).
The Byrds Play Dylan Sony BMG 8869 725267 2 (UK).
Playlist: The Very Best Of The Byrds Columbia Legacy 88697 39219 2 (US).
Steel Box Sony BMG 88697 459812 (UK).
Eight Miles High – The Best Of The Byrds Sony/Camden 88697 63627 2 (UK).
Setlist: The Very Best Of The Byrds Live Columbia/Legacy 88697 97753 2 (US).
Turn! Turn! Turn!: The Ultimate Collection Sony/Columbia Music 88875 151652 (UK).
The 60s – The Byrds Sony Music 88883 77667 2 (US).

As John York:

Sacred Path Songs [no label] 34657-2828-9 (bar code) (US)/CD No Guru/Taxim NG 2001-2 (Germany).
'Drum/Invocation: Iroquois'; 'Earth Mother Flute'; 'Omaha Tribal Prayer'; 'Pomo Clapperstick Blues'; 'Winged Ones'; 'Ancestors'; 'Cherokee Cradleboard Song'; 'Thunderbeings'; 'Sky Daughter Flute/Eagles Quest'; 'Shaman's Death'; 'Lovers Duet (Kokopelli & Ice Flower)'; 'Just One Arrow'.
This cassette-only release was given away as companion music to the book *Sacred Path Cards* by Jamie Sams. In 2002, it was reissued on CD by No Guru/Taxim Records.
Released 1991 (cassette) (US)/2002 (CD) (Germany).

Claremont Dragon Taxim TX 2038-2 TA (Germany).
'On Whose Door'; 'Rubiah'; 'Another Life'; 'No More War'; 'Heartache Suzanne'; 'Jennifer Tsai'; 'Target Of A Thousand Arrows'; 'Money Like Rain'; 'Daddy's Gonna Pick Her Man'; 'Oh My Children'; 'Half-Breeds Are The Hope Of The World'; 'My Lai'; 'Spirit Is Stronger Than Anything'.
Released August 1999 (Germany).

Arigatou Baby [original release, no label or serial number on CD disc] (US).
'Jealous Gun'; 'Roadside Cross'; 'I Can't Find The Moon'; 'She Likes To Shine My Shoes'; 'One Step From Homeless'; 'Angel Dance'; 'Tuesday's Train'; 'We Came For Love'; 'I Know I Will See You'; 'Lady On The Highway'; 'I Want To Go Now'; 'Never Doubt My Love'; 'Down In That Hole'; 'Dandelion'; 'Gypsy Life'.
Released December 2006 (US).

West Coast Revelation [CDR release only, no serial number] (US).
'Angels And Trucks'; 'The Earth Is Getting Warmer'; 'East Coast Confidential'; 'Flower Girls'; 'West Coast Revelation # 1'; 'Psychedelic'; 'West Coast Revelation # 2'; 'Movin' Out For Years'; 'West Coast Revelation # 3'; 'Picnic In Eternity'; 'Silver '60s # 1'; 'Halfway House'; 'Silver '60s # 2'; 'Laurel Canyon And Topanga'; 'Silver '60s # 3'; 'Rock 'n' Roll Is Another Name For Freedom'; 'Hangin' Out'; 'Queen Of The Blues'; '21st Century'; 'Memories Of Days Gone By'; 'Japan And Europe'; 'Sayonara'.
Released September 2007 (US). Extended issue above, released July 2008.

Cameos [mp3 download only]
'Come Back And Take Me'; 'Rainbow'; 'Some Days Even The Birds Sing A Sad Song'; 'Achilles' Heel'; 'Ghost Flowers'.
Released October 2010.

Fanfare For 2 Global Recording Artists GRA 13062 (US).
'Half Moon Bay'; 'Lone Wolf, No Club'; 'Together At The Time'; 'Red, White & Blue'; 'Coyote'; 'I Feel It Now'; 'Sea Of Wine'; 'Wasn't That You'; 'You Just Love Cocaine'; 'Power Of Now'; 'Reach Out (I'll Be There)'; 'Behind The Scenes'; 'Lucky & The Trash Angel'; 'Set Up For Heartbreak (For Ruby)'.
Released February 2012 (US).

As Jamie Sams & John York:

Clan Mother Songs Rain Records [no serial number on CD disc] (US).
'Invocation'; 'Tionee – The Pathfinder'; 'The Final Beginning'; 'All My Relations'; 'Rue-mai-ya, The Remembering'; 'The Clan Mother's Song'; 'Wata-Jis, Evening Star'; 'Celebrate The Earth'; 'Midnight's Song'; 'Crack In The Universe'; 'Welcoming 5th World'.
Released 1992 (cassette)/2004 (CD) (US).

As CRY:

CRY Coyote 0000056 (US).
'My Marie'; 'On The Run'; 'After The Storm'; 'The Hurting Game'; 'A Rose Is A Rose'; 'Once In A Lifetime'; 'I Need To Fly'; 'Mary Sue'; 'Immigrant Girl'; 'Sleep Will Return'; 'Somewhere After Midnight'; Washington Square'.
Released: October 2000 (US). Evidently, 'reissued' the following month with the number 0000056 with a copyright notice confirming the date of creation as 1999.

As Family Tree:

Family Tree Folkest Dische DPO4 2001 (Italy).
'My Shoes Keep Walking Back To You'; 'Dandelion'; 'Smack Dab In The Middle'; 'She Belongs To Me'; 'Blowin' In The Wind'; 'Catch The Wind'; 'Why You Been Gone So Long'; 'Christine'; 'It Takes A Lot To Laugh, It Takes A Train To Cry'; 'Witchi Tai To'.
Released: 2000 (Italy).

As John York & Yukiko Matsuyama:

Koto [no label or serial number on CD disc]
'Furusato'; 'Tengu'; 'Koto'; 'Murasaki'; 'Tomorrow Never Knows'; 'Yoake'; 'This Is The Day'; 'Katen no Odori'; 'Amanogawa'.
Released September 2003 (US).

As Barry McGuire With John York:

Barry McGuire's Trippin' The 60's – The Show Songs Live Bearmark Records BMR 001 (US).
'Green Green'; 'The Times They Are A-Changin''/'Blowin' In The Wind'; 'Mr Tambourine Man'/'Turn! Turn! Turn!'; 'Eve Of Destruction'; 'California Dreamin''/'Monday, Monday'/'Creeque Alley'; 'San Francisco'; 'Dolphins'; 'Everybody's Talkin''; 'Daydream'; 'Hair'; 'Do You Believe In Magic?'; 'Green Back Dollar'; 'Joy To The World'; 'Reason To Believe'; 'If I Were A Carpenter'; 'City Of New Orleans'; 'Woodstock'; 'Dancin' In The Street'; 'In My Life'.
Recorded live at the Coffee Gallery Backstage – Altadena, California on 19 December, 2008, this includes a 20-page booklet with stories about the songs.
Released June 2009 (US).

As John York And Kim Fowley:

West Coast Revelation Global Recording Artists
CD issue, co-credited to Kim Fowley. See under John York for full track listing. Released June 2011 (US).

John York also appeared on various singles prior to joining the Byrds, including the Bees ('Forget Me Girl'/'Baby Let Me Follow You Down'; 'Leave Me Be'/'She's An Artist') and Sir Douglas Quintet ('She Digs My Love'/'When I Sing The Blues'). During the mid-Seventies, he appeared on the Museums' single 'Train In The Desert'/'Sweet Names Of Spanish Ladies'. He also guested on recordings by Guilbeau & Parsons (*Louisiana Rain*), the Mamas & The Papas (*The Papas & The Mamas*), Jack Street Band (*Jack Street Band*), Chris Darrow (*Coyote/Straight From The Heart*; *Various Artistes: Everybody Slides Vol. 2; Coyote*), Katie Trickett (*The Next Time*), Don Sanders (*Sourdough Cowboy*), Mojave (*Tumbleweed Circuit*), Jamie Sams & Meatball Fulton (*The Land Of Enchantment*), Peter Lewis (*Peter Lewis*), Nick Binkley (*Pin Stripe Brain*), World Nation (*Songs Of The Colorado River*), Chris Darrow & Max Buda (*Harem Girl: An Original Narrative Suite By The Sheiks Of Love Orchestra*), Anita Kruse (*Creation Flight*), Gene Clark (*Under The Silvery Moon*), Steven T. (*Damage*), Toulouse Engelhardt Meets Remi Kabaka (*A Child's Guide To Einstein*), Michael Foley (*Fear And Forgiveness*) and Carla Olson (*Have Harmony, Will Travel*).

SKIP BATTIN

With the Evergreen Blueshoes:

The Ballad Of Evergreen Blueshoes Amos 7002 (US)/London SHU 8399 (UK). 'Life's Railway To Heaven'; 'Walking Down The Line'; 'Line Out'; 'Amsterdam In 1968'; 'Everything's Fine Right Now'; 'Johnny B Goode'; 'The Hedgehog's Song'; 'The Raven'; 'Mrs Cohen's Little Boy'; 'Moon Over Mount Olympus'; 'Jewish Teahouse'; 'The Everblue Express'.
Released 1969 (US)/September 1969 (UK).

Albums with the Byrds:

See Discography *Volume 1* under the following sections: *Byrds Singles, Albums, Compilations* and *Archival Albums* for fuller details of release dates, complete track listings, alternate serial numbers, special issues/editions, and more.

(Untitled) Columbia G 30127 (stereo) (US)/CBS S 64095 (stereo) (UK). Remastered CD edition with bonus tracks: *(Untitled)/(Unissued)* Columbia Legacy C2K 65847 (US)/Columbia Legacy 495077 2 (UK).

Byrdmaniax Columbia KC 30640 (stereo) (US)/CBS S 64389 (stereo) (UK). Remastered CD edition with bonus tracks: Columbia Legacy CK 65848 (US)/Columbia Legacy 495079 2 (UK).

Farther Along Columbia KC 31050 (stereo) (US)/CBS S 64676 (stereo) (UK).

Remastered CD edition with bonus tracks: Columbia Legacy CK 65849 (US)/Columbia Legacy 495078 2 (UK).

Archival albums with the Byrds:

Sanctuary III Sundazed LP 5066 (US).
Live At The Royal Albert Hall 1971 Sundazed LP 5189/Sundazed SC 11177 (US).

Box Sets with the Byrds:

The Byrds Columbia Legacy 46773 (US)/Columbia Legacy 4676112 (UK).
12 Dimensions The Columbia Recordings 1965–1972 (13-CD box set) Columbia 497610 2/4976102000 (UK).
There Is A Season (4-CD box set and DVD) Columbia/Legacy 82876877002 (US/UK).
The Complete Columbia Albums Collection Columbia Legacy 886978738028 (US).

Isolated appearances with the Byrds:

See *Volume 1*: *Byrds Albums, Guest Slots/Rarities, Compilations* and *Archival Albums* for fuller details of release dates and alternate territory serial numbers.

Earl Scruggs, His Family And Friends Columbia 30584 (US)/CBS 64777 (UK).
Banjoman Sire SA 7527(US)/Sire SRK 6026 (UK).

Compilations/Hits Collections with the Byrds:

See *Volume 1* for additional details.

The Byrds Greatest Hits Volume 2 CBS S 64650 (UK).
Best Of Volume 2 Columbia C31795 (US).
History Of The Byrds CBS 68242 (UK).
The Byrds CBS 88320 (UK).
The Byrds Play Dylan Columbia PC 36293 (US)/CBS 31795 (UK).
The Very Best Of The Byrds Columbia CS P-P2 17596 (US).
The Byrds Collection Castle Communications CCSLP 151 (UK).
Full Flyte Raven RVCD 10 (Australia).
20 Essential Tracks From The Boxed Set: 1965–1970 Columbia/Legacy CK 47884/471665-2 (US/UK).
Definitive Collection Columbia 480548 9 (UK).
Nashville West Sony Music Special Products A 28123 (US).
The Very Best Of The Byrds Columbia 487995 2 (UK).
Super Hits Columbia Legacy 504725 2 (UK)/Columbia Legacy CK 65637 (US).
The Byrds Play The Songs Of Bob Dylan Columbia 501946 2 (UK).
The Byrds Play Dylan Columbia/Legacy CK 85430 (US).
The Essential Byrds Columbia Legacy 512249 2 (UK)/Columbia Legacy C2K 89110 (US).
Mojo Presents . . . An Introduction To The Byrds – 24 Classic Songs Columbia 512778 2 (UK).

Mr Tambourine Man – The Best Of The Byrds Sony Music Media SMM 516489-2 (Germany/UK).
America's Great National Treasure Sony/BMG A 96086 (US).
The Very Best Of The Byrds Sony/BMG 82876 855142 (UK).
Byrds: A Collection Sony BMG 88697 12448 2 (UK).
The Byrds Play Dylan Sony BMG 88697 25267 2 (UK).
Playlist: The Very Best Of The Byrds Columbia Legacy 88697 39219 2 (US).
Steel Box Sony BMG 88697 45981 2 (UK).
Eight Miles High – The Best Of The Byrds Sony/Camden 88697 63627 2 (UK).
Setlist: The Very Best Of The Byrds Live Columbia/Legacy 88697 97753 2 (US).
Turn! Turn! Turn!: The Ultimate Collection Sony/Columbia Music 88875 151652 (UK).

As Skip Battin:

Skip Signpost SP 8408 (US)/Signpost SG 4255 (UK).
'Undercover Man'; 'The Ballad Of Dick Clark'; 'Captain Video'; 'Central Park'; 'Four Legs Are Better Than Two'; 'Valentino'; 'Human Being Blues'; 'The St Louis Browns'; 'Cobras'; 'My Secret Life'.
Released January 1973 (US/UK).

Navigator Appaloosa AP 014 (Italy).
'Skyscraper Sunset'; 'Willow In The Wind'; 'China Moon'; 'Here Comes Love'; 'Lonely Weekends'; 'Captain Video'; 'Zig Zag'; 'North By Northwest'; 'American East'; 'Citizen Kane'.
Released 1982 (Italy).

Don't Go Crazy Appaloosa AP 034 (Italy).
'Santa Ana Wind'; 'Wintergreen'; 'Don't Go Down The Drain'; 'Do Not Disturb'; 'Relax With Me'; 'Non E Francesca'; 'La Gatta'; 'Speranza'; 'Fango'; 'Tonight'.
Released 1984 (Italy).

Topanga Skyline Sierra SXCD 6031 (US).
'Salty Dog Blues'; 'Bolts Of Blue'; 'Stoned Sober'; 'Relax With Me'; 'Willow In The Wind'; 'Don't Go Down The Drain'; 'Roll In My Sweet Baby's Arms 1&2'; 'Hully Gully'; 'Foggy Mountain Top'; 'Wintergreen'; 'China Moon'. Enhanced CD includes MPEG video clip of Battin performing 'Searchin'' and 'She Acts Like We Never Have Met' (aka 'I Don't Believe You') from a local television dance show dated January 1965.
Released March 2010 (US).

With New Riders Of The Purple Sage:

Brujo Columbia PC 334145 (US)/CBS 80405 (UK).
'Old Man Noll'; 'Ashes Of Love'; 'You Angel You'; 'Instant Armadillo Blues'; 'Workingman's Woman'; 'On The Amazon'; 'Big Wheels'; 'Singing Cowboy'; 'Crooked Judge'; 'Parson Brown'; 'Neon Rose'.
Released October 1975 (US)/December 1975 (UK).

Oh What A Mighty Time Columbia PC 33688 (US)/CBS 69182 (UK).
'Mighty Time'; 'I Heard You Been Layin' My Old Lady'; 'Strangers On A Train'; 'Up Against The Wall, Redneck'; 'Take A Letter, Maria'; 'Little Old Lady'; 'On Top Of Old Smoky'; 'Over & Over'; 'La Bamba'; 'Going Round The Horn'; 'Farewell Angelina'.
Released October 1975 (US)/December 1975 (UK).

New Riders MCA 2196 (US)/MCA MCF 2758 (UK).
'Fifteen Days Under The Hood'; 'Annie May'; 'You Never Can Tell'; 'Hard To Handle'; 'Dead Flowers'; 'Don't Put Her Down'; 'Honky Tonkin' (I Guess I Done Me Some)'; 'She's Looking Better Every Beer'; 'Can't Get Over You'; 'The Swimming Song'.
Released May 1976 (US)/July 1976 (UK).

Live On Stage Relix RRCD 2059 (US).
'Panama Red'; 'Little Old Lady'; 'Instant Armadillo Blues'; 'Henry'; 'Glendale Train'; 'Nadine'; 'Singin' Cowboy'; 'Take A Letter, Maria'; 'I Will Never Make You Blue'; 'La Bamba'.
Released 1993 (US).

Armadillo World HQ Austin TX, 6/13/1975 Kufala 125 (US).
'I Don't Know You'; 'Panama Red'; 'Lonesome L.A. Cowboy'; 'Austin, Texas'; 'Instant Armadillo Blues'; 'Teardrops In My Eyes'; 'Dirty Business'; 'Henry'; 'Sutter's Mill'; 'Dim Lights, Thick Smoke'; 'Louisiana Lady'; 'Strangers On A Train'; 'Portland Woman'; 'I'm Bringing Home Good News'; 'You Angel You'; 'She's No Angel'; 'My Dog Peaches'; 'On The Amazon'; 'Before The Next Teardrop Falls'; 'Over And Over'; 'Whiskey'; 'Crooked Judge'; 'I Will Never Make You Blue'; 'New Orleans'; 'La Bamba'; 'Glendale Train'; 'Dead Flowers'; 'Nadine'.
Released January 2005 (US).

Cactus Juice Arcadia ACAD 8122 (UK).
Compilation 2-CD set including the albums *Brujo* and *Oh What A Mighty Time* on which Battin appears.
Released September 2006 (UK).

With the Flying Burrito Brothers:
Airborne Columbia 34222 (US)/CBS 81433 (UK).
See track listing in Gene Parsons section.

Cabin Fever Relix RRLP 2008 (US).
'Wheels'; 'Hot Burrito # 2'; 'Hickory Wind'; 'Do Right Woman'; 'Uncle Pen'; 'Louisiana Man'; 'She Belongs To Me'; 'Six Days On The Road'; 'Mr Spaceman'; 'Bugler'.
Released October 1985 (US).

Live From Tokyo Regency Records REG 79001 (US)/Sundown SDLP 025 (UK).
'Big Bayou'; 'White Line Fever'; 'Dim Lights, Thick Smoke'; 'There'll Be No

Teardrops Tonight'; 'Roll In My Sweet Baby's Arms'; 'Hot Burrito # 2'; 'Colorado'; 'Rocky Top'; 'Six Days On The Road'; 'Truck Drivin' Man'. This album was originally recorded at Kudan-Kaikan, Tokyo, and released in Japan under the title *Close Encounters To The West Coast* (Columbia YX 7218 N).
Released June 1979 (US)/January 1986 (UK).

Live From Europe Relix RRLP 2022 (US).
'Streets Of Baltimore'; 'Cash On The Barrelhead'; 'Mystery Train'; 'Christine's Tune (Devil In Disguise)'; 'Take A City Bride'; 'Come A Little Closer'; 'Blue Eyes'; 'Citizen Kane'; 'Don't Go Down The Drain'; 'Help Is On Its Way'.
Released 1986 (US).

Live Marlstone TLP 1986 (Holland).
'Streets Of Baltimore'; 'Cash On The Barrelhead'; 'Help Is On Its Way'; 'Roll On Brother'; 'Come A Little Closer'; 'Star Of The Show'; 'Spittin' Image'; 'Sin City'; 'Christine's Tune'; 'Foggy Mountain Breakdown'; 'Sitting In A 747'; 'Mystery Train'.
Released 1986 (Holland).

Hollywood Nights 1979–82 Sundown CDSD 079 (UK).
'She Belongs To Everyone But Me'; 'Somewhere Tonight'; 'Baby, How'd We Ever Get This Way'; 'Too Much Honky Tonkin''; 'Midnight Magic Woman'; 'My Abandoned Heart'; 'She's A Friend Of A Friend'; 'Louisiana'; 'Cheating Kind Of Love'; 'Why Must The Ending Always Be So Sad'; 'That's When You Know It's Over'; 'You'; 'I Swear I Don't Miss You Anymore'; 'She's A Hell Of A Deal'; 'Another Shade Of Grey'; 'Damned If I'll Be Lonely Tonight'; 'If Something Should Come Between Us'; 'When You're Giving Yourself To A Stranger'; 'Run To The Night'; 'Coast To Coast'; 'Closer To You'; 'True Love Never Runs Dry'; 'Tell Me It Ain't So'. Later reissued under the titles *Flying Burrito Brothers In Concert featuring Sneaky Pete Kleinow*, *Too Much Honky Tonkin 1979–1982* and *The Masters*.
Released May 1990 (UK).

Sin City Relix RRCD 2052 (US).
See Gene Parsons for track listing.
Released 1992 (US).

As the Burrito Brothers:
Hearts On The Line Curb JZ 7464-37004-1 (US).
'That's When You Know It's Over'; 'She's A Friend Of A Friend'; 'Isn't That Just Like Love'; 'She Belongs To Everyone But Me'; 'Why Must The Ending Always Be So Sad'; 'Family Tree'; 'Damned If I'll Be Lonely Tonight'; 'Does She Wish She Was Single Again'; 'Too Much Honky Tonkin''; 'Oh Lonesome Me'.
Released January 1981 (US).

As Sneaky Pete, Skip Battin, Ricky Mantoan:
Live In Italy Moondance MR 8002 (Italy).
'My Back Pages'; 'Christine's Tune (Devil In Disguise)'; 'Sneaky Attack'; 'Sing Me Back Home'; 'Cannonball Rag'; 'Walk On The Water'; 'You Ain't Going Nowhere'; 'Spanish Harlem'; 'Santa Ana Wind'; 'Speedin' West'; 'Knockin' On Heaven's Door'; 'So You Want To Be A Rock 'n' Roll Star'.
Recorded: November 1985. Released 1986 (Italy).

As Rogers/Nienhaus Band With Skip Battin:
Empty Room TriEngel Records TRI2RN1 (US).
'This Disguise'; 'I'm The One'; 'That's Not What I Had In Mind'; 'Tricou House'; 'Empty Room'; 'The Flame'; 'On The Water'; 'Arevederci Rome'; 'Citizen Kane'; 'Amsterdam'.
Recorded March-April 1995. TriEngel Records is listed specifically as the distributor. Battin appears on only five songs: 'I'm The One', 'Tricou House', 'The Flame', 'Citizen Kane', and 'Amsterdam'.
Released: 1995 (US). Reissued in 2010 with hidden bonus track, 'China Moon'.

As Family Tree:
Family Tree Folkest Dische DPO4 2001 (Italy).
'My Shoes Keep Walking Back To You'; 'Dandelion'; 'Smack Dab In The Middle'; 'She Belongs To Me'; 'Blowin' In The Wind'; 'Catch The Wind'; 'Why You Been Gone So Long'; 'Christine'; 'It Takes A Lot To Laugh, It Takes A Train To Cry'; 'Witchi Tai To'.
Released: 2000 (Italy).

During his pre-Byrd career, Battin appeared on countless singles for small labels, sometimes along with other artistes, under a bewildering number of group names and pseudonyms. The following is a necessarily selective listing:

As the Pledges: 'Betty Jean' b/w 'Bermuda Shorts' (Rev Records).
As Gary & Clyde: 'Why Not Confess' b/w 'Johnny Risk' (Rev Records); 'The Twister' b/w 'The Jackie Look' (May Records).
As Clyde Battin: 'Twister' b/w 'Daybreak' (May Records).
As Skip & Flip: 'It Was I' b/w 'Lunch Hour' (Brent Records US/Top Rank UK); 'Fancy Nancy' b/w 'It Could Be' (Brent Record US/Top Rank UK); 'Cherry Pie' b/w '(I'll Quit) Crying Over You' (Brent Records US/Top Rank UK); 'Teenage Honeymoon' b/w 'Hully Gully Cha Cha Cha' (Brent Records); 'Betty Jean' b/w 'Doubt' (Time Records); 'Green Door' b/w 'Willow Tree' (Brent Records) and 'Over The Mountain' b/w 'One More Drink For Julie' (Brent Records).
As Skip And Johnny: 'The Marathon, Pts 1 & 2 (Invicta Records); 'The Marathon' b/w 'More Marathon' (Invicta Records).
As Skip And The Flips: 'Tossin' And Turnin'' b/w 'Everyday I Have To Cry' (California Records).
As Kim And The Skippers: 'Daybreaker' b/w 'Beat' (Russ Fi Records).

As Sir Raybould And The Blue Angels: 'Big Top' b/w 'Daybreaker' (Cenco Records).
As Clyde Gary & His Orchestra: 'Tami's Dance' b/w 'Chestnut Drive' (Shad Records).
As Teak Battyn & The Battmen: 'Something's Got A Hold Of Me' b/w 'Please Forgive Me' (Invicta Records).
As Skip & The Hustlers: 'Dance Of The Sand Fleas' b/w 'In The Soup' (Invicta Records).
As the Skip Battin Combo: 'Can't Stop Twistin'' b/w 'Quarter To Three In Moscow' (Indigo Records).
As Skip Battin: 'Searchin'' b/w 'Mr Responsibility' (Groove Records); 'She Acts Like We Never Have Met' b/w 'Searchin'' (Groove Records).
As Skip Battyn: 'What's Mine Is Mine' b/w 'Ten Feet Tall' (Groove Records); 'Love Minus Zero' b/w 'Mr Responsibility' (Egan Records).
As Skip Battyn And The Group: 'The Dating Game Theme' b/w 'Night Time Girl' (Aurora Records); 'High Coin' b/w 'Mr Responsibility (Record Records).
As Bunky Battin: 'Motor Psycho Nitemare Pt 1' b/w 'Motor Psycho Nitemare Pt II (Plymouth Records).

Battin has also guested on recordings by artistes including Rick Nelson (*Love And Kisses; Rick's Rarities 1964–1974*), Kim Fowley ('Astrology' b/w 'Other Side' single; *Good Clean Fun*), Gene Vincent (*I'm Back And I'm Proud*), Chuck And Chuckles ('Bury The Hatchet' b/w 'One Hundred Baby' single), the Prehistorics ('Alley Oop-Cha-Cha-Cha' b/w 'Oh Blues' single), Ron Scuderi ('A Million Tears' b/w 'Night And Day' single), Doyle Madden With The Madmen ('Love Is A Game' b/w 'We're Through' single), Armageddon (*Armageddon*), Earth Island (*We Must Survive*), Warren Zevon (*Wanted Dead Or Alive*), Earl Scruggs (*Earl Scruggs, His Family & Friends; Anniversary Special*), Pacific Steel Company (*Pacific Steel Company*), Sneaky Pete Kleinow (*Sneaky Pete Kleinow; The Legend & The Legacy*), Thomas & Richard Frost (*Visualize*), Jim Ringer (*Endangered Species*), Ricky Gianco (*Non Si Puo Smettere Di Fumare*), Max Meazza (*Personal Exile*), Gary Paxton (*Hollywood Maverick – The Gary S. Paxton Story*), Clarence White (*White Lightnin'*), Brian Cutean (*Parakeetfishhead*) and Connie Cohen (*Heading Out*).

In addition, Battin has been a producer or co-producer on Lette And Junior's single 'Coming Back Home To You' b/w 'Blues In The Night' (Cub Records), Jack Bartley With The Jackies' single 'The Jackie Look' b/w 'My Heart Stood Still' (Kenco Records), the Values' single 'Return To Me' b/w 'That's The Way' (Invicta Records), Don True's single 'Make Believe Baby' b/w 'What Does A Dream Mean' (Invicta Records), Bab Cooper's single 'Honest I Do' b/w 'Just Couldn't Please Me' (Indigo Records), Bobby James' single '5000 Years Ago' b/w 'Memories Linger' (Indigo Records), the Calendars' single 'September Song' b/w 'You Don't Fall In Love' (Chattahoochee Records), part of the Innocents' *Classic Innocents* (Ace Records) and Connie Cohen's *Heading Out.*

COMPOSITIONS

A-Z CHECKLIST

This section features an A-Z list of copyrighted compositions, works in progress, arrangement credits and unreleased songs by the individual Byrds. For details of co-writing credits for any of these songs please consult the later sections 'Original Byrds Copyright Registrations' and 'Unreleased Compositions', respectively.

JAMES ROGER McGUINN

Since starting the Folk Den, McGuinn has copyrighted many of his adaptations and arrangements of traditional songs.

'A Roving'
'Acres Of Clams'
'Ain No Mo' Cane On De Brasis'
'Airport Hotel'
'Airport Song, The'
'Alabama Bound'
'Alberta'
'All About You'
'All My Trials'
'All The Pretty Little Horses'
'All The Things'
'America For Me'
'Angels We Have Heard On High'
'Antique Sandy'
'Argonaut, The'
'Artificial Energy'
'Ash Grove, The'
'Auld Lang Syne'
'Away In A Manger'
'Away Rio'
'Away With Rum'
'B. J. Blues'
'Back From Rio Interlude'
'Back To Sea'
'Bad Night At The Whiskey'
'Bag Full Of Money'
'Ballad Of Easy Rider'
'Ballad Of The Boll Weevil, The'
'Banjo Bach'
'Banks Of Newfoundland'
'Banks Of Ohio'
'Barbara Allen'
'Battle Hymn Of The Republic'
'Beach Ball'
'Bears Went Over The Mountain, The'
'Belle Of Belfast City, The'
'Big Rock Candy Mountain'
'Black Is The Color Of My True Love's Hair'
'Black Mountain Rag'/'Soldier's Joy'
'Blackest Crow, The'
'Blood Red Roses'
'Blow The Man Down'
'Blue Tail Fly'
'Bonny Ship Diamond, The'
'Born To Rock 'n' Roll'
'Bound To Australia'
'Brandy Leave Me Alone'
'Brazos River, The'
'Break Song'
'Bring Me A Little Water, Sylvie'
'Brisbane Ladies'
'Buffalo Skinners'
'Bury Me Not On The Lone Prairie'
'Butcher's Boy, The'
'Bye Bye Baby'
'Byrds Story, The'
'C.T.A. – 102'
'Candy'
'Cane Blues' (aka 'Ain No Mo Cane On De Brasis')

'Captain Soul'
'Car Phone'
'Castanet Dance'
'Catch The Greenland Whale'
'Catching Rainbows'
'Change Is Now'
'Cherry Tree Carol, The'
'Chestnut Mare'
'Child Of The Universe'
'Children Go Where I Send Thee'
'Christmas Is Coming'
'Cindy'
'City'
'Coast Of Peru, The'
'Cobbler, The'
'Coffee Grows On White Oak Trees'
'Cold Coast Of Greenland'
'Cold Rain And Snow'
'Colorado Trail, The'
'Come And Go With Me To That Land'
'Come On Now'
'Coo Coo, The'
'Crawdad Song, The'
'Cripple Creek'
'Cruel War, The'
'Cumberland Mountain Bear Chase'
'Darlin' Corey'
'Darling Clementine'
'Deep Blue Sea'
'Delia's Gone'
'Ding Dang'
'Dink's Song'
'Dixie Highway'
'Dodger Song, The'
'Dolphin's Smile'
'Don't Be Long'
'Don't Make Waves'
'Don't You Write Her Off'
'Down By The Riverside'
'Down In The Valley'
'Draft Morning'
'Draggin''
'Drifting In The Galaxy'
'Drill Ye Tarriers'
'Drug Store Truck Drivin' Man'
'Drunken Sailor'
'Dry Bones'
'Dubbio'
'Early One Morning'
'East Virginia'
'Easter'
'Easy Does It'
'Echoes Live'
'Eclipse, The'
'Eddystone Light'
'Eight Miles High'
'Engine 143'
'Entertainment'
'Erie Canal'
'Every Time I Feel The Spirit'
'Ezekiel Saw A Wheel'
'Fair And Tender Ladies'
'Fair Nottamun Town'
'Farmer In The Dell, The'
'Fatal Flower Garden, The'
'February Song'
'Fiddler A Dram (Moog Experiment)'
'Finnegan's Wake'
'Fireworks'
'First Noël, The'
'5 D (Fifth Dimension)'
'500 Miles'
'518'
'Follow The Drinking Gourd'
'Friend'
'Frozen Logger'
'Gallows Pole, The'
'Gate Of Horn'
'Get Along Little Doggies'
'Get To You'
'Give Me Oil In My Lamp'
'Glory, Glory'
'Go Tell Aunt Rhodie'
'Go Tell It To The Mountain'
'Go To Sea Once More'
'God Rest Ye Merry Gentlemen'
'Going Down The Road Feeling Bad'
'Golden Vanity'
'Good King James'
'Gorgeous'

'Grapes Of Wrath'
'Great Silkie Of Sule Skerry, The'
'Greenland Whale'
'Greenland Whale Fisheries'
'Greensleeves'
'Gypsy Rover'
'Handsome Cabin Boy, The'
'Hanoi Hannah'
'Hard Times Of Old England'
'Haul Away Joe'
'He Was A Friend Of Mine'
'He's Got The Whole World In His Hands'
'Heave Away'
'Henry Lee'
'Henry Martin'
'Here She Comes Again'
'Home On The Range'
'House Carpenter, The'
'House Of The Rising Son, The'
'Housewife's Lament'
'Hungry Planet'
'I Am A Pilgrim'
'I Heard The Bells On Christmas Day'
'I Heard The Voice Of Jesus'
'I Know My Rider (aka 'I Know You Rider')
'I Know Where I'm Going'
'I Love Her'
'I Saw Three Ships'
'I See You'
'I Wanna Grow Up To Be A Politician'
'I'll Fly Away'
'I'm Not Lonely Anymore'
'I'm On My Way'
'I've Been Working On The Railroad'
'In The Evenin''
'Isn't She Grand'
'It Came Upon A Midnight Clear'
'It Won't Be Wrong'
'It's Gone'
'It's No Use'
'Jacob's Dream'
'James Alley Blues'
'Jimmy Brown'
'John B's Sails, The'
'John Henry'
'John Riley'
'John The Revelator'
'Jolly Roger'
'Joshua Fit The Battle Of Jericho'
'Joy, Joy, Joy, Joy, Down In My Heart'
'Joy To The World'
'Just A Season'
'Kathleen's Song'
'Katie Morey'
'Kilgary Mountain'
'King Apathy III'
'King For A Night'
'King Kong Kitchie Kitchie Ki Me O'
'King Of The Hill'
'La Ballata Della Liberata'
'Lady, The'
'Lazy Farmer Boy, The'
'Leave Her Johnny Leave Her'
'Let My People Go!'
'Let The Bullgine Run'
'Light Up The Darkness'
'Lilly Of The West'
'Lisa'
'Little Bear'
'Little Girl'
'Little Moses'
'Liverpool Gals'
'Living Legend'
'Lonesome Valley'
'Long Jam'
'Lost Jimmy Whelan'
'Love Beyond Compare'
'Love That Never Dies'
'Lover Of The Bayou'
'M 'Linda'
'Made In China'
'Makes A Long Time Man Feel Bad'
'Making Movies'
'Mary Had A Baby'
'Mary Had A Little Lamb'
'May The Road Rise'
'Michael Row The Boat Ashore'
'Mighty Day'
'Molly Malone'

'Month Of January, The'
'Moog Raga'
'Moonshiner, The'
'Mr Spaceman'
'My Bonnie Lies Over The Ocean'
'My Home's Across The Smokey Mountains'
'My New Woman'
'Nancy Whiskey'
'New York Girls'
'900 Miles'
'Nine Pound Hammer'
'No Payday In Detroit'
'Nobody Knows You When You're Down And Out'
'NPR Interlude Music'
'O Come All Ye Faithful'
'Oh Freedom'
'Oh Mary Don't You Weep'
'Oh! Susannah'
'Old Blue'
'Old Chisholm Trail'
'Old Joe Clark'
'Old John Robertson'
'Old Paint'
'Old Plank Road'
'Old Riley'
'Old Texas'
'On And On'
'On Easter Morn He Rose'
'On Top Of Old Smokey'
'One Horse Open Sleigh'
'One More Chance'
'Only Girl (I Adore), The'
'Paddy And The Whale'
'Paddy West'
'Pale Blue'
'Parade Of Lost Dreams'
'Partners In Crime'
'Paul & Silas'
'Pay Me My Money Down'
'Peg & Awl'
'Perry's Victory'
'Please Let Me Love You'
'Polly Vaughn'
'Pretty Polly'
'Pretty Saro'
'Price, The'
'Pushboat'
'Railroad Bill'
'Rainbow, The'
'Ramblin' Banjo'
'Ramblin' On'
'Randy Dandy Oh'
'Rebellious Eyes'
'Red River Valley'
'Renaissance Fair'
'Rescue Mission'
'Riddle Song, The'
'Risselty Rissolty Now Now Now'
'Rock Island Line'
'Rock 'n' Roll Time'
'Rocket To Stardom'
'Roddy McCorley'
'Rolling Down To Old Maui'
'Round Table'
'Ruben Ranzo'
'Rumblin' On'
'Russian Hill'
'Sail Away Lady'
'Sailor Lad'
'Salty Dog Blues'
'Same Old Sound'
'Severe Mercy'
'Shady Grove'
'She Never Will Marry'
'She'll Be Coming Round The Mountain'
'Shenandoah'
'Shoot 'Em' (aka 'Victor's Theme: Shoot Him')
'Silver Dagger'
'Skate Date'
'Skip To My Lou'
'So Early In The Spring'
'So You Want To Be A Rock 'n' Roll Star'
'Someone To Love'
'South Australia'
'Southbound 95'
'Space Odyssey'
'Spanish Is The Loving Tongue'

'Spanish Ladies'
'Springfield Mountain'
'Squid-Jigging Ground'
'Squirrel, The'
'St Clair's Defeat'
'St James Infirmary'
'Stanley's Song'
'Star Spangled Banner'
'Stewball'
'Streets Of Laredo'
'Suddenly Blue'
'Sugar Baby'
'Sunshine Love'
'Swannanoa Tunnel'
'Sweet Mary'
'Sweet Memories'
'Swing Low Sweet Chariot'
'Take A Drink On Me'
'Take Me Away'
'Take This Hammer'
'Talkin' L.A.'
'Tarrytown'
'Tears, The'
'Tell Old Gil'
'There's A Hole In The Bucket'
'There's A Meetin' Here Tonight'
'These Days'
'This Little Light Of Mine'
'This Old Man'
'This Train'
'Thursday (Jim's Day)'
'Tiffany Queen'
'Tiffany Queen II'
'Time Cube'
'Time Has Come'
'Titanic'
'To Morrow'
'To Welcome Poor Paddy Home'
'Together'
'Trees Are All Gone, The'
'Tribute To Bob Gibson'
'Trouble In Mind'
'Turn Your Radio On'
'Turtle Soup'
'Twelve Days Of Christmas, The'
'12 Gates To The City'
'2-4-2 Fox Trot (The Lear Jet Song)'
'Universal Mind Decoder'
'Virgin Mary'
'Wade In The Water'
'Wagoner's Lad'
'Wait And See'
'Waltzing Matilda'
'Wanderin''
'War's Mystery'
'Water Is Wide, The'
'Wayfaring Stranger'
'We Are Crossing The Jordan River'
'We Three Kings'
'We Wish You A Merry Christmas'
'What Child Is This'
'When I First Came To This Land'
'When Jones's Ale Was New'
'When The Saints Go Marching In'
'White's Lightning'
'Whoa Back Buck'
'Whup Jamboree'
'Why'
'Wild Goose'
'Wild Mountain Thyme'
'Wildwood Flower'
'Willie Moore'
'Wings Of Love'
'Winter's Almost Gone'
'Without You'
'Without Your Love'
'Woman'
'Yellow Rose Of Texas'
'Yellow Rose Of Texas' [new version]
'You And Me'
'You Are The One'
'You Showed Me'
'You Won't Have To Cry'
'Your Love Is A Goldmine'

GENE CLARK

'Adios Terri'
'After The Storm'
'All For Him'
'All I Want'
'Along The Way'

'America'
'American Dreamer'
'American Song, The'
'Awakening Within, The'
'Back In My Life Again'
'Back Street Mirror'
'Back To The Earth Again'
'Backstage Pass'
'Bakersfield Train'
'Battle Of The Sexes'
'Because Of You'
'Belfast Song'
'Big Bad Mama'
'Big City Girl'
'Blue Raven'
'Boston'
'Boyfriend Girlfriend'
'Can't Get You Off My Mind'
'Can't Get You Out Of My Life'
'Can't Say Yes, Can't Say No'
'Carry On'
'Changing Heart'
'Christine'
'Colors'
'Communications'
'Corner Street Bar'
'Couldn't Believe Her'
'Crazy Ladies'
'Dancing On The Moon'
'Dangerous Games'
'Dark Of My Moon'
'Day For Night'
'Daylight Line, The'
'Del Gato'
'Denver Or Wherever'
'Doctor, Doctor'
'Don't Come Rollin''
'Don't Let It Fall Through'
'Don't You Know What You Want'
'Down On The Pier'
'Dragon's Eye'
'Echoes'
'Eight Miles High'
'Elevator Operator'
'Emptiness, The'
'Fair And Tender Ladies'
'Fair Game'
'Falling For You'
'Feel A Whole Lot Better'
'Feelin' Higher'
'For A Spanish Guitar'
'For Me Again'
'For No One'
'Forgive Me Girl'
'Freedom Walk'
'From A Silver Phial'
'From Darkness'
'Full Circle'
'Gorgeous'
'Got To Get You Off My Mind'
'Gypsy Rider'
'Hang Tough'
'Have You Seen The Faces (Of The Dreamers In The Rain?)'
'Hear The Wind'
'Heart In The Right Place'
'Here Tonight'
'Here Without You'
'Hillbilly Child'
'Home Run King'
'Hula Bula Man' (see 'Seventh Avenue Train')
'Hurting Game, The'
'I Am Without You'
'I Bowed My Head And Cried Holy'
'I Found You'
'I Get Along'
'I Just Like You'
'I Knew I'd Want You'
'I Need To Fly'
'I Remember The Railroad'
'I Saw A Dream Come True'
'I Want You To Stay With Me'
'I Wondered Why'
'I'd Feel Better'
'I'll Change Your Life'
'If I Hang Around'
'If There's No Love'
'If You Knew'
'If You're Gone'
'Immigrant Girl'
'In A Misty Morning'

'In The Pines'
'In The Plan'
'Is Yours Is Mine'
'It's Easy Now'
'It's No Use'
'Jimmy Christ'
'Kansas City Southern'
'Kathleen'
'Keep On Pushin''
'Lady Of The North'
'Last Of The Blue Diamond Miners'
'Life And Times'
'Life's Greatest Fool'
'Lighthouse, The'
'Line Down The Middle' (see 'Lyin' Down The Middle')
'Liona'
'Little Mama'
'Little Sister'
'Little Village'
'Lonely Saturday'
'Long Time, A'
'Look Who's Missing Who'
'Looking For Reasons'
'Los Angeles'
'Love Deluxe'
'Love Holds On'
'Love Opus In Time'
'Love Wins Again'
'Love's A Loaded Word'
'Lovers Turnaround'
'Lyin' Down The Middle' (aka 'Line Down The Middle')
'Made For Love'
'Marie' (aka 'My Marie')
'Mary Sue'
'Maybe You Think'
'Mile Away Murphy'
'Mississippi Detention Camp'
'More Than That Now'
'My Favorite Things'
'My Love Don't Care About Time' (see 'She Don't Care About Time')
'Needing Someone'
'Never Before' (aka 'The Day Walk')
'1975'
'No Other'
'No Sweeter Love'
'No Wonder'
'Nothing But An Angel'
'Old Mountain God, The'
'On Her Own'
'On Tenth Street'
'On The Bright Side'
'On The Run With A Loaded Gun'
'Once In A Lifetime'
'Once In A Lifetime' [different song]
'One In A Hundred'
'One Way Road'
'Only Colombe'
'Only Chance You Take, The'
'Only Girl (I Adore), The'
'Only Yesterday's Gone'
'Opening Day'
'Out On The Side'
'Outlaw Song'
'Over The Mountain'
'Painted Fire'
'Panther, The'
'Past Addresses'
'Past My Door'
'Past Tense'
'Please Let Me Love You'
'Please Mr Freud'
'Pledge To You'
'Polly (Come Home)'
'Quicksand'
'Radio Song, The'
'Rain Song, The'
'Reason Why (I Cry), The'
'Release Me Girl'
'Rest Of Your Life'
'Rock Of Ages'
'Rodeo Rider'
'Rose Is A Rose, A
'Same One, The'
'San Francisco'
'Set You Free This Time'
'7.30 Mode'
'Seventh Avenue Train'
'She Ain't My Woman No More'

'She Darked The Sun'
'She Don't Care About Time' (aka 'My Love Don't Care About Time')
'She Has A Way'
'She Told Me'
'She's Made Up Her Mind'
'She's The Kind Of Girl'
'Ship Of The Lord'
'Shooting Star'
'Show No Mercy'
'Silent Crusade'
'Silver Raven'
'Sister Moon'
'Sleep Will Return'
'Slip Away'
'So Much More'
'So You Say You Lost Your Baby'
'Some Misunderstanding'
'Something About You Baby'
'Something's Wrong'
'Sometime And Again'
'Somewhere After Midnight'
'Sparrow, The'
'Straight From The Heart'
'Strange And Different Way'
'Strength Of Strings'
'Surrender'
'Sweet Adrienne'
'Testing 159'
'That Girl'
'That Nonsense Stuff'
'That Part Of You'
'That's Alright By Me'
'That's What You Want'
'That's Why'
'These Days'
'Think I'm Gonna Feel Better'
'Through The Morning, Through The Night'
'Till Today'
'Too Many Days'
'Train Leaves Here This Morning'
'Trail Of Tears'
'Translations'
'Tried So Hard'
'True One, The'
'Turtle Soup'
'Understand Me Too'
'Virgin, The'
'Walking Through This Lifetime'
'Washington Square'
'Way I Am, The'
'Way That I Feel, The'
'We Came For Love'
'What Happens Then'
'What Is Meant Will Be'
'Whatever'
'Wheel Of Time, The'
'Where Does The Love Go'
'Where My Love Lies Asleep'
'While You're Here'
'White Light'
'Why Can't I Have Her Back Again?'
'Why Did You Leave Me Today'
'Why Not Your Baby'
'Will The Circle Be Unbroken'
'Winning Hand'
'Winter In'
'With Care From Someone'
'With Tomorrow'
'With You I Can't Lose'
'Won't Let You Down'
'World Turns All Around Her, The'
'Worried Heart, A'
'Yesterday, Am I Right?'
'You And I'
'You And Me'
'You Movin''
'You Showed Me'
'You Won't Have To Cry'
'Your Fire Burning'

DAVID CROSBY

'Airport Song, The'
'Alexander Graham Bell'
'Almost Cut My Hair'
'Angel Dream'
'Anything At All'
'Arrows'
'At The Edge'

'Bittersweet'
'Both Sides Of The Road'
'Breathless'
'Broken Bird'
'Brotherhood Of The Blues'
'By The Light Of Common Day'
'Camera'
'Captain Soul'
'Carry Me'
'Charisma'
'Charlie'
'Child Is Coming, A'
'Chuck's Lament (A Child's Dream)'
'City, The'
'Clearing, The'
'Climber'
'Compass'
'Cowboy Movie'
'Critical Mass'
'Cross The Plains'
'Dancer'
'Dangerous Night'
'Darkness'
'Déjà Vu'
'Delta'
'Distances'
'Dolphin's Smile'
'Draft Morning'
'Dream For Him'
'Drive My Car'
'Drive Out To The Desert'
'Drop Down Mama'
'Eight Miles High'
'Everybody's Been Burned'
'Eyes Too Blue'
'Find A Heart'
'Flying Man'
'Foolish Man'
'Games'
'Gone Forever'
'Guinnevere'
'Have You Seen The Stars Tonite'
'Hero'
'Holding On To Nothing'
'Homeward Through The Haze'
'How Does It Shine'
'I Know My Rider' (aka 'I Know You Rider')
'I'd Swear There Was Somebody Here'
'I'm Just A Young Man'
'I See You'
'If She Called'
'In My Dreams'
'Is It Really Monday'
'It Happens Each Day'
'It's All Coming Back To Me Now'
'It's Been Raining'
'Just Like Gravity'
'Kids And Dogs'
'King Of The Mountain' (aka 'Winning')
'Kings Get Broken'
'Lady Friend'
'Lady Of The Harbor'
'Last 100 Yards Of Freedom'
'Laughing'
'Lee Shore, The'
'Little Blind Fish'
'Long Live The King'
'Long Time Gone'
'Look In Their Eyes'
'Low Down Payment'
'Luck Dragon'
'Melody'
'Mind Gardens'
'Monkey And The Underdog'
'Morning Falling'
'Morrison'
'Music Is Love'
'My Country 'Tis Of Thee'
'Naked In The Rain'
'Nighttime For The Generals'
'Northern Border'
'Oh Yes I Can'
'Orleans'
'Out Of The Darkness'
'Page 43'
'Paint You A Picture'
'Psychodrama City'
'Radio'
'Renaissance Fair'

'Right Girl, Wrong Time'
'Rusty And Blue'
'Samurai'
'Set The Baggage Down'
'Shadow Captain'
'Slice Of Time'
'Somebody Else's Town'
'Somebody Home'
'Somebody Other Than You'
'Somehow She Knew'
'Song With No Words (Tree With No Leaves)'
'Stand And Be Counted'
'Stranger In A Strange Land'
'Street To Lean On'
'Taken At All'
'Taking It All'
'Tamalpais High (At About 3)'
'That House'
'These Empty Days'
'They Want It All'
'Things We Do For Love'
'Thousand Roads'
'Through Here Quite Often'
'Time I Have'
'Til It Shines On You'
'Time After Time'
'Time Is The Final Currency'
'To Have And To Hold-BG Cues'
'Tracks In The Dust'
'Traction In The Rain'
'Triad'
'Tribal Gathering'
'Truth About You'
'Us Below, The'
'Wait And See'
'Wall Song, The'
'What Are Their Names'
'What Makes It So'
'What Time I Have'
'What's Broken'
'What's Happening?!?!'
'Where Will I Be?'
'Whole Cloth'
'Why'
'Wild Mountain Thyme'
'Winning' (aka 'King Of The Mountain')
'Wooden Ships'
'Yesterday's Child'
'You And Me'
'Yours And Mine'
'Yvette In English'

MICHAEL JAMES CLARKE

'Artificial Energy'
'Captain Soul'
'Just Think'
'Wild Mountain Thyme'

CHRIS HILLMAN

'After All Is Said And Done'
'All Alone'
'All Dressed Up'
'All I Ever Need Is You'
'Angel'
'Angels' Cry'
'Artificial Energy'
'Back's Against The Wall'
'Backporch Boy'
'Bakersfield Bound'
'Beautiful Sound'
'Behind These Walls'
'Better Man Than That'
'Bidin' My Time'
'Blue Moon Rising'
'Blue Morning'
'Bluegrass Chopper'
'Bodies Rest And Motion-BG Cues'
'Borrowing Time'
'Both Of Us (Bound To Lose)'
'Bytt Ar Bytt'
'Can't You Hear Me Calling'
'Captain Soul'
'Carry Me Home'
'Change Coming Down'
'Change Is Now'
'Christine's Tune' (aka 'Devil In Disguise')

'Clear Sailin''
'Cody Cody'
'Come A Little Closer'
'Cowboy Way, The'
'Darkness On The Playground'
'Deeper In'
'Desert Rose'
'Devil In Disguise' (aka 'Christine's Tune')
'Did You See'
'Different Rivers Run'
'Doesn't Mean That Much Anymore'
'Dolphin's Smile'
'Don't Make Waves'
'Down In The Churchyard'
'Draft Morning'
'Drifting'
'Entertainment'
'Ek Skridt Frem'
'Everybody's Hero'
'Fall By The Roadside'
'Fallen Favorite'
'Falling Again'
'Feeling Inside'
'Follow Me Through'
'Fooled Again'
'For The Rich Man'
'Forgiveness'
'Get To You'
'Girl With No Name, The'
'Glass Hearts'
'Glory And Power'
'God's Plan' (aka 'God's Own Plan')
'Good Year'
'Hand To Mouth'
'Hard Times'
'Have You Seen Her Face'
'Heaven Is My Home'
'Heaven's Lullaby'
'Heavenly Fire'
'Heavenly Grace'
'High Fashion Queen'
'Hippie Boy'
'Homeless'
'Hot Dusty Roads'
'I Am A Pilgrim'
'I Don't Want To Leave This Town'
'I Hear Singing'
'I Know I Need You'
'I Know My Rider' (aka 'I Know You Rider')
'I'm Still Alive'
'I Still Believe In You'
'I Will'
'If You Leave Me Now'
'In Another Lifetime'
'It Doesn't Matter'
'It Doesn't Matter' (alternate version)
'It's About Love'
'It's Only Love'
'It Takes A Believer'
'Juanita'
'Just A Memory'
'Just Can't Be'
'Just Me And You'
'Just Passin' Through'
'(Just) Tell Me Darlin''
'Just Walk On By'
'King For A Night'
'Leave This Town'
'Let Me Down Easy'
'Let Me Get Out'
'Lies'
'Life Goes On'
'Like A Hurricane'
'Little Birdie'
'Little Rain, A'
'Livin' In The House' (aka 'House She Grew Up In')
'Living On The Edge'
'Long Gone'
'Long Long Time'
'Love And Satisfy'
'Love Reunited'
'Love's Refugees'
'Love's Worth More Than Gold'
'Lucky In Love'
'Lullaby Time In The Desert'
'Make Yourself Believe'

'Making The Change'
'Matter Of Time, A'
'Maybe She'll Get Lucky'
'Mean Streets'
'Midnight Again'
'Midnight Heart'
'Midnight Maker'
'Missing You'
'Moment Of Glory'
'Move Me Real Slow'
'My Uncle'
'Natural Harmony'
'Night After Night'
'No One Else'
'Nothing Gets Through'
'Old John Robertson'
'Old Rocking Chair'
'Older Guys'
'One Step Forward'
'One That Got Away'
'Other Side, The'
'Our Savior's Hands'
'Our Songs'
'Playing The Fool' [aka 'Played The Fool']
'Pretty Polly'
'Price I Pay'
'Prisoner Of Love'
'Relax Your Mind'
'Remember Love'
'Rise And Fall'
'Rollin' And Tumblin''
'Run Again'
'Running'
'Running The Roadblocks'
'Sad Boy'
'Safe At Home'
'San Antone'
'Second Wind'
'Shades Of Blue'
'Sin City'
'Skate Date'
'Slippin' Away'
'So Many Times'
'So You Want To Be A Rock 'n' Roll Star'
'Somewhere On The Road Tonight'
'Sooner Or Later'
'Start All Over Again'
'Step On Out'
'Stopping Traffic'
'Story Of Love'
'Street Talk'
'Summer Wind'
'Take It On The Run'
'Take Me In Your Lifeboat'
'Taking Her Time'
'Talkin' L.A.'
'That's Not The Way'
'That's The Way It Was'
'There You Go'
'Things Will Be Better'
'Thoughts And Words'
'Throw Me A Lifeline'
'Till It's Over'
'Time Between'
'Time For Love'
'Time Passes Me By'
'Touch Me'
'Train Song, The'
'Tribal Gathering'
'True Love'
'Tu Cancion'
'Turn Your Radio On'
'Twilight Is Gone'
'Universal Mind Decoder'
'Vitr Ve Skalach'
'Walkin' Blues, The'
'War's Mystery'
'Water Is Wide, The'
'What About Love'
'Wheel, The'
'Wheels'
'When Love's Gone Bad'
'Who Taught The Night'
'Wild Mountain Thyme'
'Will This Be The Day'
'Wind Did Blow'
'With You In Mind'
'Words She Writes Tonite'
'You Can Go Home'

KEVIN KELLEY

'All I Have Are Memories'
'Baby's Coming Back Today'
'Candy Man'
'Devil's Got My Woman'
'Divin' Duck Blues'
'Dreaming My Life Away'
'Drifter, The'
'Dust My Broom'
'Dusty Road'
'.44 Blues'
'Home Again'
'I Found Paradise'
'If The River Was Whiskey'
'Last Fair Deal Goin' Down'
'Let Yourself Go'
'Look At Me'
'Looking For Freedom'
'Rat Race'
'Sail Away'
'Sugar Pie'
'Summertime Romance'
'Travelin' Mood'
'Wind Has Been My Friend, The'
'You Got To Be Free'

GRAM PARSONS

'Apple Pie'
'Big Country'
'Big Mouth Blues'
'Blessing For Being'
'Blue Eyes'
'Blurry Slurry Night'
'Bodies Rest And Motion-BG Cues'
'Brass Buttons'
'Button, The'
'Bytt Ar Bytt'
'Christine's Tune'
'Cody, Cody'
'Darkest Years'
'Devil In Disguise' (aka 'Christine's Tune')
'Do You Know How It Feels To Be Lonesome?'
'Down In The Churchyard'
'Drug Store Truck Drivin' Man'
'Farther Along'
'Hand Within The Glove'
'Hickory Wind'
'High Fashion Queen'
'Hippie Boy'
'Hometown Boogie'
'Hot Burrito # 1'
'Hot Burrito # 2'
'How Much I've Lied'
'In My Hour Of Darkness'
'Jesus Is More Than A Name'
'Juanita'
'Just Can't Take It Any More'
'L.A. Custom Blues'
'Last Date'
'Lazy Days'
'Luxury Liner'
'Man In The Fog'
'My Uncle'
'New Soft Shoe, The'
'No One Knows I'm Lonesome'
'November Night(s)'
'Oh Didn't They Crucify My Lord'
'Older Guys'
'On My Journey Home'
'One Day Week'
'One Hundred Years From Now'
'Ooh Las Vegas'
'Pretty Polly'
'Race With The Wind'
'Rains Come Down, The'
'Real Sunday Driving'
'Return Of The Grievous Angel'
'River Is Made Out Of Raindrops, A'
'Rolling Stone'
'She'
'Sin City'
'Song For You, A'
'Still Feeling Blue'
'Strong Boy'
'Sum Up Broke'
'Surfinanny'
'That Kind Of Livin''
'$1,000 Wedding'
'Two Hearts'

'Train Song, The'
'Vitr Ve Skalach'
'Wheels'
'Zah's Blues'

CLARENCE J. WHITE

'Antique Sandy'
'B.J. Blues'
'Black Mountain Rag'
'Bristol Steam Convention Blues'
'Build It Up'
'Byrdgrass'
'Don't Let Your Deal Go Down'
'Farther Along'
'Grandma Funderbunk's Music Box'
'Green Apple Quick Step'
'Hong Kong Hillbilly'
'Listen To The Mockingbird'
'Long Jam'
'Lucky Me'
'Nashville West'
'Nature's Child'
'Oil In My Lamp'
'On The Spot'
'She's Gone'
'Soldier's Joy'
'Waterbed'
'White's Lightning'
'Why Can't We Be'

GENE PARSONS

'And Back Again'
'Antique Sandy'
'B. B. Class Road'
'B. J. Blues'
'Banjo Dog'
'Birds Fly South'
'Birds Of A Feather'
'Break Song'
'Bristol Steam Convention Blues'
'Build It Up'
'California Subduction Blues'
'Chief Seattle'
'Christina In My Dreams'
'Coast Hotel'
'Come On Wind'
'Dark Moon'
'Get Down Your Line'
'Get Up Blues'
'Green Apple Quick Step'
'Gunga Din'
'Hong Kong Hillbilly'
'Hot Burrito # 3'
'I'll Live Today'
'I Must Be A Tree'
'Just Away'
'Lily's Hotbread'
'Little Jewels'
'Long Jam'
'Long Way Back'
'Lorax In Laytonville'
'Mama Papa'
'Melodies From A Bird In Flyght'
'Monument'
'Nashville West'
'No Fire Here Tonight'
'No You're Not Broken'
'Nuclear Days'
'Oil In My Lamp'
'On The Spot'
'Out Of Control'
'Pale Blue'
'Pastime'
'Riff-Raff'
'Sarah Lou'
'Sonic Bummer'
'Sweet Desert Childhood'
'Talk To Me'
'Wind And Rain'
'Won't Last Long'
'Yesterday's Train'

JOHN YORK

'Abandoned Fabric'
'Absolutely Free'
'All At The Party'
'All My Relations'
'American Blues'
'Ancestors'

'Angel Turned Into A Whore'
'Angels Of The Penitentiary'
'Another Life'
'B.J. Blues'
'Beautiful Changes'
'Behind The Scenes'
'Beirut'
'Best Is Yet To Come, The'
'Bridget's Bardo'
'Candy'
'Caravan'
'Celebrate The Earth'
'Change My Eyes'
'Cherokee Cradleboard Song'
'Christine'
'Clad Mother's Song'
'Classic Way Of Saying Goodbye'
'Coyote'
'Crack In The Universe'
'Daddy's Gonna Pick Her Man'
'Dance Of The Orchard Ghosts'
'Day After Day'
'Distant Call'
'Dog My Cats'
'Don't Jump Baby'
'Dream Of Peace'
'Driving In The Sun'
'Eagle's Quest'
'Earth Mother Flute'
'Echo Of Love'
'8th Face Opus'
'Engine # 853'
'Fantasy'
'Feather Ache'
'Fido'
'Final Beginning'
'Get Ready To Cry'
'Give Yourself A Gift (The Underwear Song)'
'Goodbye On The Runway'
'Half Breeds Are The Hope Of The World'
'Half Moon Bay'
'Heartache Suzanne'
'I Can't Sleep'
'I Feel It Now'
'I Heard Your Name Upon The Wind'
'I Want To Be Forgiven'
'I Want You To Stay With Me'
'I Wish It Was All Up To Me'
'I'm In Love With You'
'I'm Never Comin' Back'
'If By Chance'
'Iroquois Drum Invocation'
'Johnnie Walker'
'Jolly Molly'
'Just One Arrow'
'Kakoro Ire'
'Kind Of Man I Used To Be, The'
'Life'
'Listenin' To The Radio'
'Lone Wolf, No Club'
'Lone Yucca'
'Look In Your Eyes, The'
'Love's Misfortunes'
'Lover's Duet (Kokopelli And Ice Flower)'
'Lucky & The Trash Angel'
'Mary Sue'
'Matane'
'Midnight's Song'
'Miracle'
'Money Like Rain'
'More Money'
'Never Give Up'
'Nice To See You Mohammed'
'No More War'
'Nothin' Left For Me To Do'
'O Precious Child'
'Oh My Children'
'Old World Parents'
'Omaha Tribal Prayer'
'On Whose Door'
'Once You Have Lost It'
'One Track Mind'
'Other Side Of Love, The'
'Place Where I Am Dreaming, The'
'Pomo Clapperstick Blues'
'Power Of Now'
'Q's Song'
'Question Of Love'

'Quiet River'
'Red, White & Blue'
'Rose Is A Rose, A'
'Round World'
'Rubiah'
'Rui Mai Ya The Remembering'
'Sail Down: Hawk Song'
'Santa Ana Winds'
'Save It For A Rainy Day'
'Sea Of Wine'
'Selfish Lover Blues'
'Set Up For A Heartbreak'
'Shaman's Death'
'Sky Daughter Flute'
'Snake Sheds Its Skin'
'Snow Rose'
'Soft Shoulder Blues'
'Spirit Is Stronger'
'Straight From The Heart'
'Sun Always Shines For The Cool, The'
'Target Of A Thousand Arrows'
'Texas Preacher Man'
'This Is Your World'
'Thunderbeings'
'Tionee The Pathfinder'
'Today Will Not Be Missed'
'Together At The Time'
'Trouble With My Car'
'Underture'
'UR TV (You Are TV)
'Valentine On A Railroad Track'
'Valerie'
'Walkin' The Lonely Beach'
'Wasn't That You'
'Wata Jis Evening Star'
'Waves Of Jealousy'
'Way You Love A Fool, The'
'We Are Horticultural'
'We Came For Love'
'We've Been Evicted'
'We've Had A Beautiful Time'
'Weave O Woman'
'Welcoming The 5th World'
'White Lies'
'Whoever Noticed Me'
'Why Can't We Be Lovers'
'Winged Ones'
'Won't Somebody Touch Me'
'You Can Never Go Back'
'You Just Love Cocaine'
'You Nurture Everything'
'You Wish'
'You Won't See Me Runnin'
'Your Love Has Freed Me'

SKIP BATTIN

'Absolute Happiness'
'America's Great National Pastime'
'American East'
'Antique Sandy'
'Austin, Texas'
'Ballad Of Dick Clark, The'
'Bermuda Shorts'
'Big Wheels'
'Black Cat Blues'
'Bolts Of Blue'
'Born Dancer'
'Break Song'
'Bury The Hatchet'
'California Swamp Dance'
'Captain Video'
'Central Park'
'China Moon'
'Citizen Kane'
'Cobras'
'Coming Back Home To You'
'Dance Of The Sand Fleas'
'Devil Doll'
'Do Not Disturb'
'Don't Go Down The Drain'
'E.S.P. Reader'
'Everblue Express, The'
'Faded Blue'
'Fancy Nancy'
'Four Legs Are Better Than Two'
'Frail Ocean, The'
'Gulf Of Mexico'
'Here Comes Love'
'Hully Gully Cha Cha Cha'

'Human Being Blues'
'Hungry Planet'
'In The Funky Mountain Woods'
'It Was I'
'Jackie Look, The' (aka 'We Wanna Look Like Jackie')
'Jail House Blues'
'Life's Railway To Heaven'
'Line Out'
'Long Jam'
'Lunch Hour'
'Meanie'
'Morning Dew'
'Mr Jukebox'
'Mr Responsibility'
'My Secret Life'
'Neon Rose'
'North By Northwest'
'On The Amazon'
'Other Side Of The Moon, The'
'Precious Kate'
'Question Of Temperature, Version 1'
'Question Of Temperature, Version 2'
'Raven, The'
'Red China'
'Relax With Me'
'Romance Of The Western Hills'
'Santa Ana Wind'
'Save Our World We Must Survive'
'Singing Cowboy'
'Singin' River'
'Skyscraper Sunset'
'Speranza'
'St Louis Browns'
'Stoned Sober'
'Strangers On A Train'
'Sunrise On Sunset' (see 'Skyscraper Sunset')
'Tami's Dance'
'Tom Eagelton'
'Tonight'
'Top Of The Tree'
'Tunnel Of Love'
'Twister, The' (aka 'When The Twister Came To Town', 'The Day The Twister Came To Town')
'Undercover Man'
'United States Of Love'
'Valentino'
'Well Come Back Home'
'What Does A Dream Mean'
'What's Mine Is Mine'
'Willow In The Wind'
'Wintergreen'
'Yesterday's Train'
'You All Look Alike'
'Zig Zag'

Battin has been credited erroneously on BMI submissions with the songs 'Fango' (Gianco-Manfred), 'La Gatta' (Mogol-Bacal) and 'Non E Francesca' (Mogol-Battisti), which have been amended here.

ORIGINAL BYRDS COPYRIGHT REGISTRATIONS

The list below details the original copyright registrations of the individual Byrds, followed by a song's first known appearance on record, usually as an album track (sometimes as a single) depending upon the time frame. All compositions by the individual Byrds that appeared on Byrds' single, even after the release of a parent album, are featured. Rather reluctantly, I have added a preceding note to known A- and B-side singles appearances by the various solo and Byrds off-shoot projects, but these do not profess to be definitive, not least because of the exclusion of various promotional, radio-only and non-US/UK foreign releases. If in doubt, just refer to the original album source as printed.

The nature of copyright registrations, significantly those at the Library of Congress, is far from straightforward. Usually they are registered shortly after the release of a recording ('date of publication'), but sometimes they appear in advance of a release date closer to the time of the 'date of creation'. However, quite a large number also appear considerably later than date of publication. Some officially released recordings are missed or simply not registered at all (indicated here by 'n/a' if they could not be found). This is particularly evident in the case of John York, for example, whose albums were issued on smaller or private labels. But the copyright datings below are significant and may be cross-checked with the detailed recording and release dates in the main discography. Readers are also advised to consult the exhaustive sessionography, complete with *recording dates* featured in *Requiem For The Timeless, Volume 1.* Additionally, the reader is directed to the subsequent 'Unreleased Compositions' section and the preceding A-Z listing for a speedy cross-reference of all known songs.

JAMES ROGER McGUINN

(aka James Joseph McGuinn)

1963

24 June 'Beach Ball' (with Frank Gari) City Surfers' single, A-side. *Live From Mars.*

2 July 'Come On Now' (with Jane Schorr) Unreleased.

2 July 'Love Beyond Compare' (with Jane Schorr) Unreleased.

2 July 'You Are The One' (with Jane Schorr) Unreleased.

26 November 'Ramblin' On' *The Twelve String Story* (London); *The Twelve String Story Volume II* (Horizon).

n/a 'Banjo Bach' *Feuding Banjos – Bluegrass Banjo Of The Southern Mountains.*

1964

7 May 'Rumblin' On' *Anthology Of The Banjo.*

7 October 'Don't Be Long' (with Harvey Gerst) Beefeaters' single, B-side.

7 October 'Please Let Me Love You' (with Gene Clark aka Harold Eugene Clark, and Harvey Gerst) Beefeaters' single, A-side. *Garden Of Earthly Delights* (US compilation).

1965

8 February 'I Knew I'd Want You' (with Gene Clark) single, B-side. *Mr Tambourine Man.*

13 April 'It's No Use' (with Gene Clark aka Harold Eugene Clark) *Mr Tambourine Man.*

13 April 'You Won't Have To Cry' (with Gene Clark aka Harold Eugene Clark) *Mr Tambourine Man.*

1 November 'You Showed Me' (with Gene Clark aka Harold Eugene Clark) *Preflyte.*

17 December 'The Airport Song' (with David Crosby) *Preflyte*.
30 December 'He Was A Friend Of Mine' (new words and arrangement) *Turn! Turn! Turn!*.
30 December 'Wait And See' (with David Crosby) *Turn! Turn! Turn!*.

1966
21 March 'Eight Miles High' (with Gene Clark and David Crosby) single, A-side. *Fifth Dimension.*
21 March 'Why' (with David Crosby) single, B-side. Re-recorded *Younger Than Yesterday*.
13 July '5 D (Fifth Dimension)' single, A-side. *Fifth Dimension.*
5 August 'I See You' (with David Crosby) *Fifth Dimension.*
5 August 'Mr Spaceman' single, A-side. *Fifth Dimension.*
24 August 'Oh! Susannah' (arranged and adapted) *Turn! Turn! Turn!*.
24 August 'Wild Mountain Thyme' (arranged and adapted with David Crosby, Chris Hillman and Michael Clarke) *Fifth Dimension.*
7 December 'So You Want To Be A Rock 'n' Roll Star' (with Chris Hillman) single, A-side. *Younger Than Yesterday.*
n/a 'I Know My Rider (aka 'I Know You Rider') (arrangement with David Crosby and Chris Hillman) *Never Before* CD.
n/a '2-4-2 Fox Trot (The Lear Jet Song) *Fifth Dimension.*
n/a 'When The Saints Go Marching In (Saints Soul Song)' *The Twelve String Story* (Delyse Envoy).

1967
17 February 'CTA – 102' (with Robert J. Hippard) *Younger Than Yesterday.*
17 February 'Renaissance Fair' (with David Crosby) single, B-side. *Younger Than Yesterday.*
13 March 'Don't Make Waves' (with Chris Hillman) single, B-side. Alternate version on film soundtrack of *Don't Make Waves.*
13 March 'Thursday (Jim's Day)' Unreleased.
21 November 'Talkin' LA' (with Chris Hillman and David Hemmings) David Hemmings' *Happens.*
21 November 'War's Mystery' (with Chris Hillman and David Hemmings) David Hemmings' *Happens.*
18 December 'Good King James' (with David Hemmings and Bill Martin) David Hemmings' *Happens.*

1968
22 November 'Child Of The Universe' (with Dave Grusin) single, B-side. *Dr Byrds & Mr Hyde*. Alternate version on film soundtrack of *Candy.*
n/a 'I Am A Pilgrim' (arrangement and adaptation with Chris Hillman) single, A-side. *Sweetheart Of The Rodeo.*

1969
31 January 'Bad Night At The Whiskey' (with Joey Richards) single, A-side. *Dr Byrds & Mr Hyde.*

31 January 'Drug Store Truck Drivin' Man' (with Gram Parsons) single, B-side. *Dr Byrds & Mr Hyde.*

10 March 'B. J. Blues' (with John York, Gene Parsons* and Clarence White) *Dr Byrds & Mr Hyde.* *Incorrectly assigned to 'Graham 'Gram' Parsons'.

7 April 'Candy' (with John York) *Dr Byrds & Mr Hyde.*

7 April 'King Apathy III' *Dr Byrds & Mr Hyde.*

17 June 'The Only Girl (I Adore)' (with Gene Clark) *Early LA.*

18 August 'Ballad Of Easy Rider' single, A-side. *Ballad Of Easy Rider*, alternate version by McGuinn on *Easy Rider.*

n/a 'Fiddler A Dram (Moog Experiment) (aka 'Jenny Comes Along') *Ballad Of Easy Rider* CD, expanded edition.

n/a 'Old Blue' (arrangement and adaptation) single, B-side. *Dr Byrds & Mr Hyde.*

1970

13 November 'Artificial Energy' (with Chris Hillman and Michael Clarke) single, B-side. *The Notorious Byrd Brothers.*

13 November 'Draft Morning' (with David Crosby and Chris Hillman) *The Notorious Byrd Brothers.*

13 November 'Get To You' (with Chris Hillman) *The Notorious Byrd Brothers.*

30 November 'Change Is Now' (with Chris Hillman) single, B-side. *The Notorious Byrd Brothers.*

30 November 'Dolphin's Smile' (with David Crosby and Chris Hillman) *The Notorious Byrd Brothers.*

30 November 'Space Odyssey' (with Robert Hippard) *The Notorious Byrd Brothers.*

30 December 'All The Things' (with Jacques Levy) *(Untitled).*

n/a 'Break Song' (with Clyde R. Battin, Gene Victor Parsons and William Isaac Travis) Unreleased.

n/a 'Long Jam' (with Clarence J. White, Gene Victor Parsons and 'writer unknown') Unreleased.

1971

27 January 'Chestnut Mare' (with Jacques Levy) single, A-side edit. *(Untitled).*

27 January 'Just A Season' (with Jacques Levy) single, B-side. *(Untitled).*

27 January 'Lover Of The Bayou' (with Jacques Levy) *(Untitled).*

21 June 'Hungry Planet' (with Skip Battin and Kim Fowley) *(Untitled).*

9 November 'I Trust' single, A-side. *Byrdmaniax.*

9 November 'I Wanna Grow Up To Be A Politician' (with Jacques Levy) *Byrdmaniax.*

9 November 'Kathleen's Song' (with Jacques Levy) *Byrdmaniax.*

9 November 'Pale Blue' (with Gene Parsons) *Byrdmaniax.*

1972

4 February 'Antique Sandy' (with Skip Battin, Gene Parsons, Clarence White and Jimmi Seiter) *Farther Along.*

8 February 'Tiffany Queen' *Farther Along.*

1973

16 April 'Born To Rock 'n' Roll' *Byrds.*
16 April 'Sweet Mary' (with Jacques Levy) *Byrds.*
19 July 'Bag Full Of Money' (with Jacques Levy) *Roger McGuinn.*
19 July 'Draggin'' (with Jacques Levy) single, A-side. *Roger McGuinn.*
19 July 'Hanoi Hannah' (with Jacques Levy) *Roger McGuinn.*
19 July 'I'm So Restless' (with Jacques Levy) *Roger McGuinn.*
19 July 'M' Linda' (with Jacques Levy) *Roger McGuinn.*
19 July 'My New Woman' (with Jacques Levy) single, B-side. *Roger McGuinn.*
19 July 'Time Cube' (with Robert Hippard) *Roger McGuinn.*

1974

22 April 'Rescue Mission' (with Kris Kristofferson, Seymour Cassel and Bobby Neuwirth) Kris Kristofferson's *Spooky Lady's Slide Show.*
22 April 'Rock 'n' Roll Time' (with Kris Kristofferson and Bobby Neuwirth) *Cardiff Rose.*
19 August 'Gate Of Horn' (with Jacques Levy) *Peace On You.*
19 August 'Same Old Sound' (with Jacques Levy) *Peace On You.*
19 August 'The Lady' (with Jacques Levy) *Peace On You.*
19 August 'Together' (with Jacques Levy) *Peace On You.*
19 August 'Without You' (with Jacques Levy) *Peace On You.*
29 November 'The Water Is Wide' (trad. arranged by McGuinn) *Roger McGuinn.*

1975

6 June 'Easy Does It' *Roger McGuinn And Band.*
6 June 'Lisa' *Roger McGuinn And Band.*
22 July 'Rocket To Stardom' (with Kris Kristofferson and Bobby Neuwirth) Kris Kristofferson's *Who's To Bless And Who's To Blame.*

1976

13 July 'Jolly Roger' (with Jacques Levy) *Cardiff Rose.*
13 July 'Partners In Crime' (with Jacques Levy) *Cardiff Rose.*
13 July 'Round Table' (with Jacques Levy) *Cardiff Rose.*
13 July 'Take Me Away' (with Jacques Levy) *Cardiff Rose.*

1977

19 January 'Ding Dang' (with Brian Wilson) *The Beach Boys Love You.*
11 March 'Dixie Highway' (with Jacques Levy) *Thunderbyrd.*
11 March 'I'm Not Lonely Anymore' (with Jacques Levy) *Thunderbyrd.*
11 March 'It's Gone' (with Jacques Levy) *Thunderbyrd.*
11 March 'Russian Hill' (with Jacques Levy) single, B-side. *Thunderbyrd.*
n/a 'Shoot 'Em' (aka 'Victor's Theme: Shoot Him') (with Patrick S. Ferrell) *3 Byrds Land In London.* Registered at BMI as 'Shoot Him' and on the film soundtrack as 'Victor's Theme: Shoot Him'.

1978

11 December 'Bye Bye Baby' (with Robert Hippard) single, B-side. *McGuinn, Clark & Hillman.*

11 December 'Don't You Write Her Off' (with Robert Hippard) single, A-side. *McGuinn, Clark & Hillman.*

11 December 'I Love Her' (with Robert Hippard) *McGuinn, Clark & Hillman* CD, expanded edition.

11 December 'Little Bear' (aka 'Little Girl') *McGuinn, Clark & Hillman* CD, expanded edition.

1980

1 February 'City' (with Camilla McGuinn) *City.*

1 February 'One More Chance' (with Jacques Levy) single, A-side. *City.*

1 February 'Skate Date' (with Camilla McGuinn and Chris Hillman) *City.*

8 July 'Entertainment' (with Chris Hillman) *McGuinn/Hillman.*

8 July 'King For A Night' (with Chris Hillman) single, A-side. *McGuinn/Hillman.*

8 July 'Turn Your Radio On' (with Chris Hillman) single, A-side. *McGuinn/Hillman.*

4 August 'Making Movies' (with Camilla McGuinn) single, B-side. *Return Flight II.*

1981

20 April 'Severe Mercy' (with Camilla McGuinn) Unreleased.

20 April 'Wedding Song' (with Camilla McGuinn) Unreleased.

20 April 'Woman' (with Camilla McGuinn) Unreleased.

14 September 'America For Me' (music; original words by Henry Van Dyke) *The Folk Den Project 1995–2005.*

1982

27 September 'Light Up The Darkness' (with Camilla McGuinn) Unreleased.

27 September 'Sweet Memories' (with Camilla McGuinn) Unreleased.

27 September 'Take Good Care' (with Camilla McGuinn) Unreleased.

27 September 'Wings Of Love' (with Camilla McGuinn) Unreleased.

1983

6 September '518' Unreleased.

6 September 'Personal Computer' Unreleased.

1984

11 June 'The Tears' (with Camilla McGuinn) Unreleased.

1 October 'The Price' (with Camilla McGuinn) Unreleased.

1987

24 September 'Sunshine Love' (with Camilla McGuinn) Unreleased.

28 September 'Living Legend' (with Camilla McGuinn) Unreleased.

28 September 'Tiffany Queen II' Unreleased.

1989

27 February 'Someone To Love' (with Camilla McGuinn) single A-side. *Back From Rio.*

17 November 'Flight 713' (with Chris Hillman) *Never Before* CD.

17 November 'Moog Raga' *Never Before* CD.

1990

10 September 'Love That Never Dies' (with Stan Lynch). *The Byrds* box set.

10 September 'White's Lightning' (with Clarence White) [recorded 2 June 1970] *The Byrds* box set.

1991

8 February 'Car Phone' (with Mike Campbell) single, B-side. *Back From Rio.*

8 February 'King Of The Hill' (with Tom Petty) single, A-side. *Back From Rio.*

8 February 'Someone To Love' (with Camilla McGuinn) *Back From Rio.*

8 February 'Suddenly Blue' (with Scott Cutler and Dennis Morgan) *Back From Rio.*

8 February 'The Time Has Come' (with Scott Cutler) single, B-side. *Back From Rio.*

8 February 'The Trees Are All Gone' (with Camilla McGuinn) *Back From Rio.*

8 February 'Without Your Love' (with Camilla McGuinn) *Back From Rio.*

8 February 'Your Love Is A Gold Mine' (with David A. Stewart) single, A-side. *Back From Rio.*

14 November 'You Bowed Down' (with Declan MacManus aka Elvis Costello) *Back From Rio.*

n/a 'Back From Rio Interlude' (with Tom Petty and Jeff Lynne). *Back From Rio.*

1992

3 June 'May The Road Rise' (with Camilla McGuinn) *Live From Mars.*

3 June 'On And On We Go' (with Camilla McGuinn) *Limited Edition.*

1994

n/a 'Turtle Soup' (with Gene Clark). DJ Food's *Jazz Breaks Volume 5.*

1996

25 March 'Castanet Dance' (with Camilla McGuinn) *Limited Edition.*

25 March 'Made In China' (with Camilla McGuinn) *Limited Edition.*

25 March 'Parade Of Lost Dreams' (with Camilla McGuinn) *Limited Edition.*

25 March 'Rebellious Eyes' (with Camilla McGuinn) *Live From Mars.*

20 April 'You And Me' (with Gene Clark and David Van Cortlandt Crosby) *Mr Tambourine Man* CD, expanded edition.

19 July 'Mr Spaceman' *Live From Mars.*

19 August 'Southbound 95' (with Camilla McGuinn) *Limited Edition.*

1997

21 January 'Fireworks' (retitled version of 'Rebellious Eyes') (with Camilla McGuinn) *Live From Mars.*

28 July 'Airport Hotel' (with Dennis Morgan and Scott Cutler) Dennis Morgan's *Attic Chronicles, Vol. 1.*

1999

14 July 'Buffalo Skinners' (arrangement and additional lyrics) *The Folk Den Project 1995–2005.*
23 December 'Blood Red Roses' (arrangement) *McGuinn's Folk Den Vol. 3.*
23 December 'Brisbane Ladies' (arrangement) *McGuinn's Folk Den Vol. 3.*
23 December 'Cane Blues' (arrangement) *Treasures From The Folk Den.*
23 December 'Cold Cold Coast Of Greenland' (arrangement and additional lyrics) *McGuinn's Folk Den Vol. 3.*
n/a 'I Saw Three Ships' (arrangement) *McGuinn's Folk Den Vol. 3*
n/a 'Mary Had A Baby' (arrangement) *McGuinn's Folk Den Vol. 3*

2000

1 May 'The Argonaut' (arrangement and additional lyrics) *McGuinn's Folk Den Vol. 2.*
1 May 'Easter Morn' (arrangement) *McGuinn's Folk Den Vol. 2.*
1 May 'Get Along Little Doggies' (arrangement) *McGuinn's Folk Den Vol. 3.*
1 May 'Greenland Whale' (arrangement) *The Sea: Songs By Roger McGuinn.*
1 May 'I'm Alabama Bound' (arrangement and additional lyrics) *McGuinn's Folk Den Vol. 3.*
1 May 'In The Evenin' (arrangement) *McGuinn's Folk Den Vol. 2.*
1 May 'John Riley' (arrangement) *McGuinn's Folk Den Vol. 2.*
1 May 'John The Revelator (arrangement) (words: Camilla McGuinn) *McGuinn's Folk Den Vol. 1.*
1 May 'Liverpool Girls' (arrangement) *McGuinn's Folk Den Vol. 2.*
1 May '900 Miles' (arrangement) *McGuinn's Folk Den Vol. 2.*
1 May 'Oh, You New York Girls' (arrangement) *McGuinn's Folk Den Vol. 3.*
1 May 'Old Paint' (arrangement) *McGuinn's Folk Den Vol. 2.*
1 May 'Old Texas' (arrangement) *McGuinn's Folk Den Vol. 2.*
1 May 'Sail Away Lady' (arrangement) *McGuinn's Folk Den Vol. 3.*
1 May 'Springfield Mountain' (arrangement) *McGuinn's Folk Den Vol. 2.*
1 May 'Trouble In Mind' (arrangement) *McGuinn's Folk Den Vol. 3.*
1 May 'Virgin Mary' (arrangement) *McGuinn's Folk Den Vol. 2.*

2001

n/a 'Dink's Song' *Treasures From The Folk Den.*

2002

n/a 'All My Trials' (arrangement) *In The Spirit Of Love.*
n/a 'Battle Hymn Of The Republic' (arrangement) *In The Spirit Of Love.*

2003

19 March 'Pete's Song' (new words and adapted music to Pete Seeger composition) *Treasures From The Folk Den.*
1 August 'I Am A Pilgrim' (arrangement with Chris Hillman) *Sweetheart Of The Rodeo.*

11 August 'Pretty Polly' (arrangement with Chris Hillman) *The Byrds* box set. *Sweetheart Of The Rodeo* CD, expanded edition.
11 August 'Stanley's Song' (with Robert J. Hippard) *The Byrds* box set.

2004
2 April 'Echoes Live' *Limited Edition.*
2 April 'James Alley Blues' (arrangement with Camilla McGuinn) *Limited Edition.*
2 April 'Shady Grove' (arrangement with Camilla McGuinn) *Limited Edition.*
2 April 'Shenandoah' (arrangement with Camilla McGuinn) *Limited Edition.*

2005
n/a 'Bring Me A Little Water, Sylvie' *The Folk Den Project 1995–2005.*
n/a 'Cindy' *The Folk Den Project 1995–2005.*
n/a 'Colorado Trail' (with Camilla McGuinn) *The Folk Den Project 1995–2005.*
n/a 'Delia's Gone' *The Folk Den Project 1995–2005.*
n/a 'Ezekiel Saw A Wheel' *The Folk Den Project 1995–2005.*
n/a 'Follow The Drinking Gourd' *The Folk Den Project 1995–2005.*
n/a 'The Gallows Pole' *The Folk Den Project 1995–2005.*
n/a 'Go Tell Aunt Rhodie' *The Folk Den Project 1995–2005.*
n/a 'Lilly Of The West' *The Folk Den Project 1995–2005.*
n/a 'Makes A Long Time Man Feel Bad' *The Folk Den Project 1995–2005.*
n/a 'Michael Row The Boat Ashore' *The Folk Den Project 1995–2005.*
n/a 'Oh Freedom' *The Folk Den Project 1995–2005.*
n/a 'Railroad Bill' *The Folk Den Project 1995–2005.*
n/a 'Sailor Lad' *The Folk Den Project 1995–2005.*
n/a 'Silver Dagger' *The Folk Den Project 1995–2005.*
n/a 'So Early In The Spring' *The Folk Den Project 1995–2005.*
n/a 'St James Infirmary' (aka 'Saint James Infirmary') *Limited Edition. The Folk Den Project 1995–2005.*
n/a '12 Gates To The City' *The Folk Den Project 1995–2005.*
n/a 'Waltzing Matilda' *The Folk Den Project 1995–2005.*
n/a 'Wanderin'' *The Folk Den Project 1995–2005.*
n/a 'When The Saints Go Marching In' *Limited Edition. The Folk Den Project 1995–2005.*

2010
n/a 'Gorgeous' (with Harold Eugene Clark, Mike Dean, Malik Yusef El Shabazz, Scott Ramon Seguro Mescudi, Kanye West, Ernest Dion Wilson and Corey Todd Woods) sampled contribution to Kanye West's *My Beautiful Dark Twisted Fantasy.*

2011
n/a 'Back To Sea' *CCD.*
n/a 'Go To Sea Once More' *CCD.*
n/a 'Randy Dandy Oh' *CCD.*
n/a 'Running Down To Old Maui' *CCD.*

2012

n/a 'These Days' (with Harold Eugene Clark, Matthew Alan Prime and Michael James Stafford) sampled contribution to Maverick Sabre's *Lonely Are The Brave.*

2014

n/a 'The Byrds' Story' [spoken word] *Stories, Songs & Friends.*
n/a 'Leave Her Johnny, Leave Her' *Stories, Songs & Friends.*
n/a 'Grapes Of Wrath' (with Camilla McGuinn). Unreleased.

2016

n/a 'One Horse Open Sleigh' (with Camilla McGuinn) Unreleased.

GENE CLARK

1964

7 October 'Please Let Me Love You' (with Jim McGuinn and Harvey Gerst). Beefeaters' single, A-side. *Garden Of Earthly Delights* (US compilation).
n/a 'Why Can't I Have Her Back Again' *Byrd Parts 2.*

1965

8 February 'I Knew I'd Want You' single, B-side. *Mr Tambourine Man.*
13 April 'You Won't Have To Cry' (with Jim McGuinn) *Mr Tambourine Man.*
13 April 'It's No Use' (with Jim McGuinn) *Mr Tambourine Man.*
10 May 'Feel A Whole Lot Better' single, B-side. *Mr Tambourine Man.*
10 May 'Here Without You' *Mr Tambourine Man.*
10 September 'She Has A Way' *Preflyte.*
10 September 'You Movin'' *Preflyte.*
1 November 'If You're Gone' *Turn! Turn! Turn!.*
1 November 'My Love Don't Care About Time' (retitled 'She Don't Care About Time') single, B-side.
1 November 'Set You Free This Time' *Turn! Turn! Turn!.*
1 November 'That's What You Want' Unreleased.
1 November 'The Emptiness' Unreleased. Possibly original and correct title of 'The Day Walk' (aka 'Never Before').
1 November 'The Reason Why (I Cry)' *Preflyte.*
1 November 'The World Turns All Around Her' *Turn! Turn! Turn!.*
1 November 'You Showed Me' (with Jim McGuinn) *Preflyte.*

1966

21 March 'Eight Miles High' (with Jim McGuinn and David Crosby) single, A-side. *Fifth Dimension.*
21 September 'Elevator Operator' (with Joe Larson and Bill Rinehart) *Gene Clark With The Gosdin Brothers.*
21 September 'I Found You' single, B-side. *Gene Clark With The Gosdin Brothers.*
21 September 'Keep On Pushin'' (with William B. Rinehart) *Gene Clark With The Gosdin Brothers.*

21 September 'Needing Someone' *Gene Clark With The Gosdin Brothers.*
21 September 'That's Why' Unreleased.
21 September 'The Same One' *Gene Clark With The Gosdin Brothers.*
21 September 'The Way (That) I Feel' Unreleased.
21 September 'Too Many Days' Unreleased.
21 September 'Tried So Hard' *Gene Clark With The Gosdin Brothers.*
21 September 'She's Made Up Her Mind'. Unreleased.
10 October 'Couldn't Believe Her' *Gene Clark With The Gosdin Brothers.*
10 October 'Is Yours, Is Mine' *Gene Clark With The Gosdin Brothers.*
10 October 'On The Bright Side' Unreleased.
10 October 'Think I'm Gonna Feel Better' *Gene Clark With The Gosdin Brothers.*
31 October 'A Long Time' Rose Garden's *The Rose Garden.*
31 October 'Big City Girl' Unreleased.
31 October 'Doctor, Doctor' Unreleased.
31 October 'Echoes' single, A-side. *Gene Clark With The Gosdin Brothers.*
31 October 'If I Hang Around' *Byrd Parts 2.*
31 October 'Maybe You Think' Unreleased.
31 October 'On Tenth Street' Unreleased.
31 October 'She Told Me' Unreleased.
31 October 'Sometime And Again' Unreleased.
31 October 'While You're Here' Unreleased.
31 October 'Understand Me Too' Unreleased.
5 December 'So You Say You Lost Your Baby' single, A-side. *Gene Clark With The Gosdin Brothers.*

1967

24 February 'Don't Let It Fall Through' *The Lost Studio Sessions 1964–1982.*
21 April 'Back Street Mirror' David Hemmings' *Happens. The Lost Studio Sessions 1964–1982.*
21 April 'Bakersfield Train' Unreleased.
21 April 'Can't Get You Off My Mind' Unreleased.
21 April 'Down On The Pier' Unreleased.
21 April 'One Way Road' Unreleased.
21 April 'Only Colombe' Sundazed archival single, A-side. *Echoes*
21 April 'Whatever' Unreleased.
15 May 'I'd Feel Better' *The Lost Studio Sessions 1964–1982.*
15 May 'If There's No Love' *The Lost Studio Sessions 1964–1982.*
15 May 'The Way I Am' *The Lost Studio Sessions 1964–1982.*
29 May 'A Worried Heart' *The Lost Studio Sessions 1964–1982.*
29 May 'All For Him' bonus track for subscribers *The Lost Studio Sessions 1964–1982.*
29 May 'Along The Way' Unreleased.
29 May 'Don't You Know What You Want' Unreleased.
29 May 'I Am Without You' Unreleased.
29 May 'It's Easy Now' Unreleased.

29 May 'So Much More' Unreleased.
29 May 'That Girl' *The Lost Studio Sessions 1964–1982.*
29 May 'Translations' Unreleased.

1968

n/a 'Los Angeles' *Flying High.*
n/a 'That's Alright By Me' *Flying High.*
4 April 'Till Today' Rose Garden's *The Rose Garden.*
1 July 'No Sweeter Love' (with Mac McClanahan) single, B-side.
(see comments in 'Unreleased Compositions' page 1188)
1 July 'That Nonsense Stuff' (with Mac McClanahan) single, A-side.
(see comments in 'Unreleased Compositions' page 1188)
28 October 'Don't Come Rollin'' (with Doug Dillard and Bernard Mathew Leadon III) *The Fantastic Expedition Of Dillard & Clark.*
28 October 'In The Plan' (with Doug Dillard and Bernard Mathew Leadon III) *The Fantastic Expedition Of Dillard & Clark.*
28 October 'Out On The Side' single, B-side. *The Fantastic Expedition Of Dillard & Clark.*
28 October 'She Darked The Sun' (with Bernard Mathew Leadon III) *The Fantastic Expedition Of Dillard & Clark.*
28 October 'Something's Wrong' (with Doug Dillard) *The Fantastic Expedition Of Dillard & Clark.*
28 October 'The Radio Song' (with Bernard Mathew Leadon III) single, B-side. *The Fantastic Expedition Of Dillard & Clark.*
28 October 'Train Leaves Here This Morning' (with Bernard Mathew Leadon III) single, A-side. *The Fantastic Expedition Of Dillard & Clark.*
28 October 'With Care From Someone' (with Doug Dillard and Bernard Mathew Leadon III) *The Fantastic Expedition Of Dillard & Clark.*

1969

13 March 'Lyin' Down The Middle' (with Laramie Edward Smith) single, A-side. *Kansas City Southern.*
17 June 'Boston' *Preflyte.*
17 June 'For Me Again' *Preflyte.*
17 June 'The Only Girl (I Adore)' (with Jim McGuinn) *Early LA.*
17 June 'Tomorrow Is A Long Ways Away' (with Jim McGuinn) *In The Beginning.*
16 July 'Why Not Your Baby' single, A-side. *Kansas City Southern.*
9 October 'Corner Street Bar' *Through The Morning Through The Night.*
9 October 'Kansas City Southern' *Through The Morning Through The Night.*
9 October 'Polly (Come Home)' *Through The Morning Through The Night.*
9 October 'Through The Morning, Through The Night' *Through The Morning Through The Night.*
26 November 'One In A Hundred' *White Light.*
n/a 'Back To The Earth Again' *The Lost Studio Sessions 1964–1982.*
n/a 'Only Yesterday's Gone' *The Lost Studio Sessions 1964–1982.*

n/a 'The Awakening Within' *The Lost Studio Sessions 1964–1982.*
n/a 'The Lighthouse' *The Lost Studio Sessions 1964–1982.*
n/a 'The Sparrow' *The Lost Studio Sessions 1964–1982.*
n/a 'Walking Through This Lifetime' *The Lost Studio Sessions 1964–1982.*

1971
3 March 'For A Spanish Guitar' *White Light.*
3 March 'For No One' *Here Tonight – The White Light Demos.*
3 March 'Here Tonight' *Roadmaster.*
3 March 'Where My Love Lies Asleep' *White Light.*
3 March 'White Light' *White Light.*
24 March 'Because Of You' *White Light.*
24 March 'Opening Day' *Flying High.*
24 March 'Please Mr Freud' *Here Tonight – The White Light Demos.*
24 March 'The Virgin' *White Light.*
24 March 'Winter In' *Flying High.*
14 April 'Jimmy Christ' *Here Tonight – The White Light Demos.*
15 April 'American Dreamer' *American Dreamer Soundtrack.*
15 April 'Outlaw Song' *American Dreamer Soundtrack.*
26 April 'With Tomorrow' *White Light.*
4 October '1975' *White Light.*

1972
2 August 'Jesus Love' (with Al G. Teoli). Unreleased.
(Different Gene Clark: see comments in 'Unreleased Compositions' page 1188)

1973
14 May 'Changing Heart' *Byrds.*
14 May 'Full Circle' single, A-Side. *Byrds. Roadmaster.*
25 September '(Theme For) Kay Seventy'. Unreleased.
(see comments in 'Unreleased Compositions' page 1188)

1974
21 October 'From A Silver Phial' single, B-side. *No Other.*
21 October 'Lady Of The North' (with Doug Dillard) *No Other.*
21 October 'Life's Greatest Fool' single, A-side. *No Other.*
21 October 'No Other' single, A-side. *No Other.*
21 October 'Silver Raven' *No Other.*
21 October 'Some Misunderstanding' *No Other.*
21 October 'Strength Of Strings' *No Other.*
21 October 'The True One' single, B-side. *No Other.*

1975
8 December 'Forgive Me, Girl' (with Thomas Jefferson Kaye) Thomas Jefferson Kaye's *Not Alone* (Clark credit omitted).
n/a 'I Saw A Dream Come True' *Two Sides To Every Story* reissue: download card.
n/a 'The Daylight Line' *Silverado '75.*
n/a 'What Is Meant Will Be' *Two Sides To Every Story* reissue: download card.
n/a 'Wheel Of Time' *Two Sides To Every Story* reissue: download card.

1976

29 June 'A Thousand Doors' (with Albert Teoli). Unreleased.
(Different Gene Clark: see comments in 'Unreleased Compositions' page 1188)

1977

4 April 'Hear The Wind' *Two Sides To Every Story.*
4 April 'Home Run King' single, A-side. *Two Sides To Every Story.*
4 April 'I Remember The Railroad' *Roadmaster.*
4 April 'In A Misty Morning' *Roadmaster.*
4 April 'Lonely Saturday' single, B-side. *Two Sides To Every Story.*
4 April 'Past Addresses' *Two Sides To Every Story.*
4 April 'Roadmaster' *Roadmaster.*
(erroneously credited to Gene Clark, see page 1189)
4 April 'She's The Kind Of Girl' *Roadmaster.*
4 April 'Shooting Star' *Roadmaster.*
4 April 'Silent Crusade' *Two Sides To Every Story.*
4 April 'Sister Moon' *Two Sides To Every Story.*
6 April 'Can't Get You Out Of My Life' Unreleased.
9 May 'In The Pines' (traditional, adapted and arranged). *Two Sides To Every Story.*
17 June 'Jealousy' (with Skip Scarborough) Bobbie Humphrey's *Tailor Made.*
(see comments in 'Unreleased Compositions' page 1188)
n/a 'Denver Or Wherever' (with Bobby Neuwirth and Thomas Jefferson Kaye) *3 Byrds Land In London.*

1978

30 October 'Backstage Pass' single, A-side. *McGuinn, Clark & Hillman.*
30 October 'Feelin' Higher' (with Terri Jean Messina) *McGuinn, Clark & Hillman.*
6 December 'Little Mama' single, B-side. *McGuinn, Clark & Hillman.*
28 December 'Release Me, Girl' (with Thomas Jefferson Kaye). Previously registered as 'Forgive Me, Girl' – altered melody and additional lyrics. *McGuinn, Clark & Hillman.*

1979

21 February 'Crazy Ladies' (with Thomas Jefferson Kaye and Willy Kontos). Thomas Jefferson Kaye's *Not Alone.*
20 November 'Let There Be Happiness' Unreleased.
(Different Gene Clark: see comments in 'Unreleased Compositions' page 1188)

1980

26 February 'Kentucky Town Waltz' (with Robert Harsh). Unreleased.
(see comments in 'Unreleased Compositions' page 1188)

1985

4 January 'Blue Raven' *Firebyrd.*
4 January 'Made For Love' *Firebyrd.*
4 January 'Rain Song' (with Andrew Kandanes) *Firebyrd.*

4 January 'Rodeo Rider' (with Andrew Kandanes) *Firebyrd.*
4 January 'Something About You Baby' (with Andrew Kandanes) *Firebyrd.*
(All of the above include the additional information: date of pub. 5 March 1984).

1987
13 April 'Fair And Tender Ladies' (adaptation and arrangement) *So Rebellious A Lover.*
13 April 'Gypsy Rider' (with Rick Clark) *So Rebellious A Lover.*
n/a 'Lovers Turnaround' (with Thomas Jefferson Kaye) *So Rebellious A Lover.*

1988
5 April 'Never Before' [sound cassette: date of creation, listed as '1964', actually 1965] *Never Before.*

1989
1 January 'Mary Sue' (with John York and Patrick Gerald Robinson) *So Rebellious A Lover.*
n/a 'Winning Hand' *So Rebellious A Lover* expanded edition.

1991
14 January 'Rock Of Ages' (with Michael Nold and Carla Olson) Carla Olson's *Reap The Whirlwind.*
23 December 'Day For Night' [pub. 1 September 1989] Textones' *Through The Canyon.*

1992
1 February 'Love Wins Again' *Silhouetted In Light.*
1 February 'Your Fire Burning' *Silhouetted In Light.*

1993
14 April 'Gene Clark and Pat Robinson Collection'. Individual songs not listed. Below are a selection of the songs issued from the collection.
'A Rose Is A Rose' (with Patrick Gerald Robinson and John York) *CRY.*
'After The Storm' (with Patrick Gerald Robinson) *CRY.*
'Can't Say No' (with Patrick Gerald Robinson) *Under The Silvery Moon.*
'Carry On' (with Patrick Gerald Robinson) *Under The Silvery Moon.*
'Dancing On The Moon' (with Patrick Gerald Robinson and R. Marinell) *Under The Silvery Moon* 2 CD-set. *Withdrawn Before Release.*
'Dangerous Games' (with Patrick Gerald Robinson) *Under The Silvery Moon.*
'Dragon's Eye' (with Patrick Gerald Robinson) *Under The Silvery Moon.* 2 CD-set. *Withdrawn Before Release.*
'Can't Say Yes, Can't Say No' (aka 'Can't Say No)' (with Patrick Gerald Robinson) *Under The Silvery Moon* 2 CD-set. *Withdrawn Before Release.*
'Fair And Tender Ladies' (traditional arrangement) *Under The Silvery Moon.*
'I Need To Fly' (with Patrick Gerald Robinson and John York) *CRY.*
'Immigrant Girl' (with Patrick Gerald Robinson) *Under The Silvery Moon.*
'Immigrant Girl' (with Patrick Gerald Robinson and John York) *CRY.*
'Mary Sue' (with Patrick Gerald Robinson and John York) *CRY.*

'More Than That Now' (with Patrick Gerald Robinson) *Under The Silvery Moon.*
'My Marie' (with Patrick Gerald Robinson) *Under The Silvery Moon.*
'Nothing But An Angel' (with Patrick Gerald Robinson) *Under The Silvery Moon.*
'On The Run (With A Loaded Gun)' (with Patrick Gerald Robinson) *CRY.*
'Once In A Lifetime' (with Patrick Gerald Robinson) *CRY.*
'Rest Of Your Life' (with Patrick Gerald Robinson) *Under The Silvery Moon.*
'Sleep Will Return' (with Patrick Gerald Robinson) *Under The Silvery Moon.*
'Sleep Will Return' (with Patrick Gerald Robinson and John York) *CRY.*
'Somewhere After Midnight' (with Patrick Gerald Robinson) *CRY.*
'That Part Of You' (with Patrick Gerald Robinson) *Under The Silvery Moon* 2 CD-set. *Withdrawn.*
'The Hurting Game' (with Patrick Gerald Robinson) *CRY.*
'The Panther' (with Patrick Gerald Robinson) *Under The Silvery Moon* 2 CD-set. *Withdrawn Before Release.*
'Washington Square' (with Patrick Gerald Robinson) *CRY.*
'With You I Can't Lose' *Under The Silvery Moon* 2 CD-set. *Withdrawn Before Release.*
(for additional details on 'Gene Clark and Pat Robinson Collection' see pages 402–405 in 'Gene Clark Notes' and pages 1189–1190 in the 'Unreleased Compositions' section.
20 September 'Will The Circle Be Unbroken?' (arrangement with Carla Olson) *Silhouetted In Light.*

1994

n/a 'Turtle Soup' (with Roger McGuinn). *Jazz Breaks Volume 5.*

1996

5 April 'We Came For Love' (with John York and Billy Darnell). Electric Range's *Electric Range.*
20 April 'You And Me' (with Roger McGuinn and David Crosby) *Mr Tambourine Man* CD, expanded edition.

2001

n/a 'Back In My Life Again' *Gypsy Angel.*
n/a 'Dark Of My Moon' *Gypsy Angel.*
n/a 'Freedom Walk' *Gypsy Angel.*
n/a 'Kathleen' *Gypsy Angel.*
n/a 'Mississippi Detention Camp' *Gypsy Angel.*
n/a 'Pledge To You' *Gypsy Angel.*

2010

n/a 'Gorgeous' (with James Joseph McGuinn, Mike Dean, Malik Yusef El Shabazz, Scott Ramon Seguro Mescudi, Kanye West, Ernest Dion Wilson and Corey Todd Woods) sampled contribution to Kanye West's *My Beautiful Dark Twisted Fantasy.*

2012

n/a 'These Days' (with James Joseph McGuinn, Matthew Alan Prime and Michael James Stafford) sampled contribution to Maverick Sabre's *Lonely Are The Brave.*

DAVID CROSBY

1962

27 December 'Cross The Plains'. Travis Edmonson's live *Travis On Cue* and *Travis On His Own.*

1962–63

n/a 'Another Town' Unreleased.
n/a 'Hey Lady' Unreleased.
n/a 'I'm A Drifter' Unreleased.
n/a 'It Ain't Gonna Be That Way' Unreleased.
n/a 'It's Been Raining' Unreleased.
n/a 'Right Girl, Wrong Time' Unreleased.
n/a 'Something Gotta Happen Pretty Soon' Unreleased.
n/a 'Time Of A Man' Unreleased.

1964

18 June 'Jack Of Diamonds' (adaptation of Civil War song with new words). *The Preflyte Sessions.*
n/a 'Brotherhood Of The Blues' *Byrd Parts 2.*
n/a 'Charisma' (with Bud Shank) *Sixties Transition.*
n/a 'I'm Just A Young Man' (see 1995) *Preflyte* [2012 CD, expanded edition].

1965

17 December 'The Airport Song' (with Jim McGuinn) *Preflyte.*
30 December 'Wait And See' (with Jim McGuinn) *Turn! Turn! Turn!*

1966

28 February 'Stranger In A Strange Land' Blackburn & Snow single, A-side. Instrumental backing track, *Turn! Turn! Turn!* CD, expanded edition.
21 March 'Eight Miles High' (with Gene Clark and Jim McGuinn) single, A-side. *Fifth Dimension.*
21 March 'Why' (with Jim McGuinn) single, B-side. Re-recording *Younger Than Yesterday.*
28 July 'Captain Soul' (with Michael Clarke, Jim McGuinn and Chris Hillman) single, A-side. *Fifth Dimension.*
5 August 'I See You' (with Jim McGuinn) *Fifth Dimension.*
5 August 'What's Happening?!?!' single, B-side. *Fifth Dimension.*
24 August 'Wild Mountain Thyme' (arranged and adapted, with Jim McGuinn, Michael Clarke and Chris Hillman) *Fifth Dimension.*
n/a 'I Know My Rider' (aka 'I Know You Rider') (arrangement with James Roger McGuinn and Chris Hillman) *Never Before* CD.
n/a 'Psychodrama City' *Never Before* CD.

1967
17 February 'Mind Gardens' *Younger Than Yesterday.*
17 February 'Renaissance Fair' (with Jim McGuinn) single, B-side. *Younger Than Yesterday.*
20 February 'Everybody's Been Burned' single, B-side. *Younger Than Yesterday.*
7 August 'Lady Friend' single, A-side. *The Original Singles Volume 2, 1967–1969.*

1968
10 April 'Games' *Graham Nash/David Crosby.*
10 April 'Laughing' single, B-side. *If I Could Only Remember My Name.*
10 April 'Triad' Jefferson Airplane's *Crown Of Creation.*
10 June 'You Sit There' Unreleased.
12 June 'Wooden Ships' (with Stephen Stills and Paul Kantner) *Crosby, Stills & Nash.*
17 June 'Tomorrow Is A Long Ways Away' (with Jim McGuinn and Gene Clark) *In The Beginning.*
5 September 'Long Time Gone' single, B-side. *Crosby, Stills & Nash.*
5 September 'Is It Really Monday?' Unreleased.
5 December 'Guinnevere' [registered as 'Guenevere Green'] *Crosby, Stills & Nash.*

1970
29 January 'Almost Cut My Hair' *Déjà Vu.*
29 January 'Déjà Vu' single, B-side. *Déjà Vu.*
29 January 'The Lee Shore' *Four Way Street.*
13 August 'Have You Seen The Stars Tonite' (with Paul Kantner) Paul Kantner Jefferson Starship's *Blows Against The Empire.*
n/a 'A Child Is Coming' (with Paul Kantner and Grace Slick) Paul Kantner Jefferson Starship's *Blows Against The Empire.*
n/a 'Taking It All' (with Paul L. Kantner) Unreleased.
13 November 'Draft Morning' (with R. McGuinn and Chris Hillman) *The Notorious Byrd Brothers.*
30 November 'Dolphin's Smile' (with R. McGuinn and Chris Hillman) *The Notorious Byrd Brothers.*
30 November 'Tribal Gathering' (with Chris Hillman) *The Notorious Byrd Brothers.*

1971
3 March 'Cowboy Movie' *If I Could Only Remember My Name.*
3 March 'Music Is Love' (with Graham Nash and Neil Young) single, A-side. *If I Could Only Remember My Name.*
3 March 'Traction In The Rain' single, B-side. *If I Could Only Remember My Name.*
3 March 'What Are Their Names' (with Neil Young, Jerry Garcia, Phil Lesh and Michael Shrieve) *If I Could Only Remember My Name.*
19 April 'I'd Swear There Was Somebody Here' *If I Could Only Remember My Name.*

19 April 'Orleans' single, A-side. *If I Could Only Remember My Name.*
19 April 'Song With No Words (Tree With No Leaves)' *If I Could Only Remember My Name.*
19 April 'Tamalpais High (At About 3)' *If I Could Only Remember My Name.*

1972
5 May 'Page 43' *Graham Nash/David Crosby.*
5 May 'The Wall Song' single, B-side. *Graham Nash/David Crosby.*
5 May 'Where Will I Be?' *Graham Nash/David Crosby.*
5 May 'Whole Cloth' single, B-side. *Graham Nash/David Crosby.*

1973
18 April 'Long Live The King' single, B-side. *Byrds.*
24 July 'Dirt Poor' (with Dan Peterson). Unreleased.

1974
8 October 'Carry Me' single, A-side. *Wind On The Water.*
8 October 'Time After Time' *Whistling Down The Wire.*

1975
27 January 'Homeward Through The Haze' *Wind On The Water.*
10 March 'Low Down Payment' *Wind On The Water.*
28 August 'Bittersweet' single, B-side. *Wind On The Water.*
28 August 'Critical Mass' *Wind On The Water.*
28 August 'Naked In The Rain' (with Graham Nash) *Wind On The Water.*
28 August 'Winning' (later retitled 'King Of The Mountain') *Crosby – Nash Live* CD, expanded edition.
8 October 'Broken Bird' (with Graham Nash) *Whistling Down The Wire.*

1976
14 May 'Foolish Man' *Whistling Down The Wire.*
14 May 'Last 100 Yards Of Freedom' (with Graham Nash) Unreleased.
14 May 'Taken At All' (with Graham Nash) *Whistling Down The Wire.*
21 May 'Out Of The Darkness' (with Graham Nash and Craig Doerge) single, A-side. *Whistling Down The Wire.*
12 August 'Dancer' *Whistling Down The Wire.*

1977
14 April 'Anything At All' single, B-side. *CSN.*
14 April 'In My Dreams' *CSN.*
9 May 'Shadow Captain' (with Craig Doerge) single, B-side. *CSN.*

1979
14 March 'Distances' *Oh Yes I Can.*
14 March 'Drive My Car' single, A-side. *Oh Yes I Can.*

1982
18 June 'Delta' *Daylight Again.*

1984

5 April 'Rondelet' (with Helen Bingham, David Crosby listed as 'author of anon. contribution')

1986

14 February 'Melody' (with Craig Doerge) *Oh Yes I Can.*
17 June 'Compass' single, 12-inch, B-side. *American Dream.*
27 October 'Alexander Graham Bell' Unreleased.

1987

30 March 'Chuck's Lament (A Child's Dream)' (with Stephen Stills, Graham Nash and Joe Vitale) single, B-side.
14 December 'Lady Of The Harbor' (with Craig Doerge) single, A-side. *Oh Yes I Can.*
14 December 'Monkey And The Underdog' (with Craig Doerge) *Oh Yes I Can.*
14 December 'Nighttime For The Generals' *American Dream.*

1988

3 January 'It Happens Each Day' *Never Before.*
5 August 'Drop Down Mama' single, B-side. *Oh Yes I Can.*
5 August 'Tracks In The Dust' (with Craig Doerge) single, B-side. *Oh Yes I Can.*
5 August 'Oh Yes I Can' *Oh Yes I Can.*
20 December 'Flying Man' (with Craig Doerge) *Oh Yes I Can.*

1989

14 July 'Compass' [re-registered] *American Dream.*

1990

2 July 'Yours And Mine' (with Graham Nash and Craig Doerge) *Live It Up.*
23 July 'Arrows' (with Michael Hedges) *Live It Up.*

1991

7 June 'These Empty Days' (with Graham Nash) *After The Storm.*
16 September 'Thousand Roads' *Thousand Roads.*

1992

21 April 'Yvette In English' (with Joni Mitchell) *Thousand Roads.*

1993

30 November 'Hero' (with Phil Collins) single, A-side. *Thousand Roads.*

1994

28 February 'Rusty And Blue' *It's All Coming Back To Me Now....*
28 February 'Till It Shines On You' *It's All Coming Back To Me Now...*
15 April 'The Fisher King Song' [later retitled 'Somehow She Knew'] *CPR.*
4 November 'Camera' (with Stephen Stills) *After The Storm.*
4 November 'Street To Lean On' (with Michael Hedges) *After The Storm.*

1995

26 June 'I'm Just A Young Man' (date of creation cited: 1964). *Preflyte* [2012 CD, expanded edition].

1996

20 April 'You And Me' (with Gene Clark and Roger McGuinn) *Mr Tambourine Man* CD, expanded edition.

1998

30 March 'At The Edge' (with Jeff Pevar and James Raymond) *CPR*.
30 March 'It's All Coming Back To Me Now' (with Jeff Pevar) *CPR*.
30 March 'Little Blind Fish' (with Jeff Pevar) *CPR*.
30 March 'Morrison' *CPR*.
30 March 'Somebody Else's Town' (with Jeff Pevar and James Raymond) *CPR*.
30 March 'Somehow She Knew' (with Craig Doerge) *CPR*.
30 March 'That House' (with Jeff Pevar and James John Raymond) *CPR*.
30 March 'Time Is The Final Currency' *CPR*.
30 March 'Yesterday's Child' (with James Raymond) *CPR*.

2000

19 June 'Dream For Him' [date of pub. 26 October 1999] *Looking Forward*.
19 June 'Stand And Be Counted' (with James Raymond) [date of pub. 26 October 1999] *Looking Forward*.
n/a 'King Of The Mountain' *Crosby – Nash Live* CD, expanded edition. See 'Winning' on 28 August 1975.

2004

24 May 'My Country 'Tis Of Thee' (arrangement with Graham Nash) *Crosby Nash*.
12 October 'Luck Dragon' (with James Raymond) *Crosby Nash*.
n/a 'Charlie' (with Dean Parks) *Crosby Nash*.
n/a 'How Does It Shine?' *Crosby Nash*.
n/a 'Samurai' *Crosby Nash*.
n/a 'They Want It All' *Crosby Nash*.
n/a 'Through Here Quite Often' (with Dean Parks) *Crosby Nash*.

2005

4 April 'Angel Dream' (with James Raymond and Graham Nash) [date of pub. 19 June 2001] *Just Like Gravity*.
4 April 'Breathless' (with Jeff Pevar and James Raymond) [date of pub. 19 June 2001] *Just Like Gravity*.
4 April 'Coyote King' (with James Raymond, Jeff Pevar, Steve DiStanislao & Andrew Ford) *Just Like Gravity*.
4 April 'Darkness' (with Jeff Pevar and James Raymond) [date of pub. 19 June 2001] *Just Like Gravity*.
4 April 'Eyes Too Blue' (with James Raymond) [date of pub. 19 June 2001] *Just Like Gravity*.

4 April 'Gone Forever' (with Jeff Pevar and James Raymond) [date of pub. 19 June 2001] *Just Like Gravity*.
4 April 'Map To Buried Treasure' (with James Raymond, Jeff Pevar, Steve DiStanislao & Andrew Ford) *Just Like Gravity*.
n/a 'Climber' *Just Like Gravity*.
n/a 'Just Like Gravity' *Just Like Gravity*.
n/a 'Katie Did' (with Jeff Pevar) *Just Like Gravity*.
n/a 'Kings Get Broken' *Just Like Gravity*.

2006
n/a 'Kids And Dogs' *Voyage*.

2012
2 August 'Cause I'm Missing Him Tonight' [poem].

2014–2015
n/a 'Dangerous Night' (with James John Raymond) single, A-side. *Croz*.
n/a 'Find A Heart' (with James John Raymond and Marcus Quinn Eaton) *Croz*.
n/a 'Holding On To Nothing' (with Sterling Price) *Croz*.
n/a 'Morning Falling' (with James John Raymond) *Croz*.
n/a 'If She Called' *Croz*.
n/a 'Radio' (with James John Raymond) single, A-side. *Croz*.
n/a 'Slice Of Time' (with Marcus Quinn Eaton and James John Raymond) *Croz*.
n /a 'Set The Baggage Down' (with Shane Fontayne) *Croz*.
n/a 'Time I Have' *Croz*.

2016
n/a 'By The Light Of Common Day' (with Becca Stevens) *Lighthouse*.
n/a 'Drive Out To The Desert' *Lighthouse*.
n/a 'Look In Their Eyes' (with Michael League) *Lighthouse*.
n/a 'Paint You A Picture' *Lighthouse*.
n/a 'Somebody Home' Snarky Puppy's *Family Dinner Volume 2*.
n/a 'Somebody Other Than You' (with Michael League) *Lighthouse*.
n/a 'The City' (with Michael League) *Lighthouse*.
n/a 'The Us Below' (with Michael League) *Lighthouse*.
n/a 'Things We Do For Love' (with Michael League) *Lighthouse*.
n/a 'What Makes It So' *Lighthouse*.

MICHAEL CLARKE

1966
28 July 'Captain Soul' (with Jim McGuinn, David Crosby and Chris Hillman) single, B-side. *Fifth Dimension*.
24 August 'Wild Mountain Thyme' (arranged and adapted with Jim McGuinn, Chris Hillman and David Crosby) *Fifth Dimension*.

1970

13 February 'Artificial Energy' (with R. McGuinn and Chris Hillman) single, B-side. *The Notorious Byrd Brothers.*

1977

n/a 'Just Think' (with Mark C. Andes, Jock Bartley, Larry Burnett, David R. Muse and Richard James Roberts) *Luna Sea.*

CHRIS HILLMAN

1966

28 July 'Captain Soul' (with Michael Clarke, Jim McGuinn and David Crosby) single, B-side. *Fifth Dimension.*
24 August 'Wild Mountain Thyme' (with Jim McGuinn, David Crosby and Michael Clarke) *Fifth Dimension.*
7 December 'Girl With No Name' *Younger Than Yesterday.*
7 December 'Have You Seen Her Face' *Younger Than Yesterday.*
7 December 'Relax Your Mind' Unreleased.
7 December 'Remember Love' Unreleased.
7 December 'So You Want To Be A Rock 'n' Roll Star' (with Jim McGuinn) single, A-side. *Younger Than Yesterday.*
7 December 'Thoughts And Words' *Younger Than Yesterday.*
7 December 'Time Between' *Younger Than Yesterday.*
7 December 'Time For Love' Unreleased.
7 December 'When Love's Gone Bad' Unreleased.
n/a 'I Know My Rider' (aka 'I Know You Rider') (arrangement with James Roger McGuinn and David Crosby) *Never Before* CD.

1967

21 April 'Don't Make Waves' (with Jim McGuinn) single, B-side. Alternate version film soundtrack of *Don't Make Waves.*
21 April 'I Hear Singing' Unreleased.
7 August 'Old John Robertson' (with Jim McGuinn) single, B-side. *The Notorious Byrd Brothers.*
21 November 'Talkin'' LA' (with R. McGuinn and David Hemmings) David Hemmings' *Happens.*
21 November 'War's Mystery' (with R. McGuinn and David Hemmings) David Hemmings' *Happens.*

1968

n/a 'I Am A Pilgrim' (arrangement and adaptation with Roger McGuinn) single, A-side. *Sweetheart Of The Rodeo.*

1969

19 February 'Christine's Tune' (with Gram Parsons) *The Gilded Palace Of Sin.*
19 February 'Hippie Boy' (with Gram Parsons) *The Gilded Palace Of Sin.*
19 February 'Juanita' (with Gram Parsons) *The Gilded Palace Of Sin.*
19 February 'My Uncle' (with Gram Parsons) *The Gilded Palace Of Sin.*

19 February 'Sin City' (with Gram Parsons) *The Gilded Palace Of Sin.*
19 February 'Wheels' (with Gram Parsons) single, B-side. *The Gilded Palace Of Sin.*
26 May 'The Train Song' (with Gram Parsons) single, A-side. *Close Up The Honky Tonks.*
22 December 'Bluegrass Chopper' (with Vern Gosdin, Rex Gosdin and Don Parmley) *The Hillmen.*

1970

2 February 'Cody, Cody' (with Gram Parsons) single, B-side. *Burrito Deluxe.*
21 May 'Down In The Churchyard' (with Gram Parsons) single, B-side. *Burrito Deluxe.*
21 May 'High Fashion Queen' (with Gram Parsons) *Burrito Deluxe.*
21 May 'Older Guys' (with Gram Parsons and Bernie Leadon) single, A-side. *Burrito Deluxe.*
13 November 'Artificial Energy' (with R. McGuinn and Michael Clarke) single, B-side. *The Notorious Byrd Brothers.*
13 November 'Draft Morning' (with David Crosby and R. McGuinn) *The Notorious Byrd Brothers.*
13 November 'Get To You' (with R. McGuinn) *The Notorious Byrd Brothers.*
13 November 'Natural Harmony' *The Notorious Byrd Brothers.*
30 November 'Change Is Now' (with R. McGuinn) single, B-side. *The Notorious Byrd Brothers.*
30 November 'Dolphin's Smile' (with David Crosby and R. McGuinn) *The Notorious Byrd Brothers.*
30 November 'Tribal Gathering' (with David Crosby) *The Notorious Byrd Brothers.*

1971

7 June 'All Alone' (with Rick Roberts) *The Flying Burrito Brothers.*
7 June 'Can't You Hear Me Calling' (with Rick Roberts) *The Flying Burrito Brothers.*
7 June 'Hand To Mouth' (with Rick Roberts) *The Flying Burrito Brothers.*
7 June 'Just Can't Be' (with Rick Roberts) *The Flying Burrito Brothers.*

1972

6 March 'Both Of Us (Bound To Lose)' (with Stephen Stills) *Stephen Stills/Manassas.*
6 March 'It Doesn't Matter' (with Stephen Stills) single, A-side. *Stephen Stills/Manassas.*
2 October 'So Many Times' (with Stephen Stills) single, B-side. *Down The Road.*
18 December 'Isn't It About Time' (with Stephen Stills) single, A-side. *Down The Road.*
18 December 'Lies' *Down The Road.*
18 December 'Love And Satisfy' *Trouble In Paradise.*

1973

20 February 'Borrowing Time' (with Joe Lala) *Byrds.*
20 February 'Fall By The Roadside' Unreleased.
20 February 'Feeling Inside' Unreleased.
20 February 'Things Will Be Better' (with Dallas Taylor) single, A-side. *Byrds.*
24 September 'Follow Me Through' *Trouble In Paradise.*
24 September 'Make Yourself Believe' Unreleased.
24 September 'Safe At Home' (with Richie Furay) *The Souther, Hillman, Furay Band.*

1974

24 May 'Heavenly Fire' (with Len Fagan) single, B-side. *The Souther, Hillman, Furay Band.*
24 May 'Midnight Maker' (with Len Fagan) Unreleased.
24 May 'Rise 'n' Fall' (with Len Fagan) *The Souther, Hillman, Furay Band.*
24 May 'With You In Mind' (with Len Fagan) Unreleased.

1975

19 May 'Blue Morning' *Slippin' Away.*
19 May 'Falling Again' *Trouble In Paradise.*
19 May 'Move Me Real Slow' single, B-side. *Trouble In Paradise.*
19 May 'Slippin' Away' *Slippin' Away.*
19 May 'Take It On The Run' *Trouble In Paradise.*

1976

21 January 'Midnight Again' *Slippin' Away.*
21 January 'Step On Out' (with Peter Knobler) *Slippin' Away.*
3 August 'It Doesn't Matter' (with Stephen Stills and Richard J. Roberts) *Firefall.*

1977

8 April 'Clear Sailin'' (with Richard Marx and Rick Roberts) *Clear Sailin'.*
8 April 'Fallen Favorite' (with Peter Knobler) *Clear Sailin'.*
8 April 'Hot Dusty Roads' (with Peter Knobler) *Clear Sailin'.*
8 April 'Lucky In Love' (with Peter Knobler) *Clear Sailin'.*
8 April 'Nothing Gets Through' (with Peter Knobler) *Clear Sailin'.*
8 April 'Played The Fool' (with Dan McCorison) *Clear Sailin'.*
8 April 'Prisoner Of Love' Unreleased.
8 April 'Rollin' And Tumblin'' *Clear Sailin'.*
15 December 'Did You See' (with Rick Roberts) *Honky Tonk Heaven.*

1978

8 December 'Long Long Time' (with Rick Roberts) *McGuinn, Clark & Hillman.*
8 December 'Sad Boy' single, B-side. *McGuinn, Clark & Hillman.*
8 December 'Stopping Traffic' (with Peter Knobler) *McGuinn, Clark & Hillman.*

1980

22 January 'Deeper In (Is All You Get)' (with Douglas L.A. Foxworthy) single, B-side. *City.*
1 February 'Skate Date' (with R. McGuinn and Camilla McGuinn) *City.*
11 March 'Let Me Down Easy' (with Peter Knobler) *City.*
11 March 'Street Talk' (with Peter Knobler and John Sambataro) single, B-side. *City.*
11 March 'Who Taught The Night?' (with Peter Knobler) *City.*
8 July 'Entertainment' (with R. McGuinn) *McGuinn/Hillman.*
8 July 'King For A Night' (with R. McGuinn) *McGuinn/Hillman.*
8 July 'Turn Your Radio On' (with R. McGuinn) single, A-side. *McGuinn/Hillman.*
11 July 'Angel' (with Douglas L.A. Foxworthy) *McGuinn/Hillman.*
11 July 'Mean Streets' (with Douglas L.A. Foxworthy) *McGuinn/Hillman.*

1984

29 February 'Any Day Now' (arranged with Al Perkins) [pub. 17 May 1983] *Down Home Praise.*
29 February 'On The Sea Of Life' (arranged with Al Perkins) [pub. 17 May 1983] *Down Home Praise.*
29 February 'The Church In The Wildwood' (arranged with Al Perkins) [pub. 17 May 1983] *Down Home Praise.*
11 September 'Desert Rose' (with Bill Wildes) *Desert Rose.*
11 September 'Running The Roadblocks' (with Peter Knobler) *Desert Rose.*

1986

11 March 'I'll Be No Stranger There' (arranged and adapted: words with Bernie Leadon and David Mansfield) *Ever Call Ready.*

1987

17 March 'Leave This Town' (with Bill Wildes) single, B-side. *The Desert Rose Band.*
4 May 'Hard Times' (with Bill Wildes and Jon Bradford) single, B-side. *The Desert Rose Band.*
4 May 'One That Got Away' (with Peter Knobler) single, B-side. *The Desert Rose Band.*
13 November 'Love Reunited' (with Steve Hill) *The Desert Rose Band.*
13 November 'One Step Forward' (with Bill Wildes) single, A-side. *The Desert Rose Band.*
1 December 'Glass Hearts' (with Steve Hill) single, B-side. *The Desert Rose Band.*

1988

16 August 'Our Songs' (with Steve Hill) [pub. 11 July] *Running.*
16 August 'Summer Wind' (with Steve Hill) [pub. 21 March] single, A-side. *Running.*
7 October 'For The Rich Man' (with Steve Hill) *Running.*
25 October 'Homeless' (with Steve Hill) *Running.*

25 October 'I Still Believe In You' (with Steve Hill) [pub. 21 March] single, A-side. *Running.*
25 October 'Livin' In The House' (with Steve Hill) single, B-side. *Running.*
25 October 'Running' (with Steve Hill) [pub. 21 March] *Running.*

1989
8 September 'Fooled Again' (with Steve Hill and Michael Woody) single, B-side.
17 November 'Flight 713 (Song Number 2)' (with R. McGuinn) [pub. 1 May]. *Never Before* CD.

1991
6 February 'The Price I Pay' (with Bill Wildes) [pub. 15 May 1990] Emmylou Harris' *Duets.*
20 March 'Come A Little Closer' (with Steve Hill) [pub. 1 January] single, A-side. *A Dozen Roses.*
20 March 'Will This Be The Day' (with Steve Hill) [pub. 1 January] single, A-side. *A Dozen Roses.*
26 August 'Darkness On The Playground' (with Steve Hill) single, B-side. *Pages Of Life.*
26 August 'Everybody's Hero' (with Michael Woody) [pub. 1 January 1990] single, B-side. *Pages Of Life.*
26 August 'God's Plan' (with Steve Hill) *Pages Of Life.*
26 August 'In Another Lifetime' (with Steve Hill) single, A-side. *Pages Of Life.*
26 August 'Just A Memory' (with John Jorgenson) [pub. 1 January 1990] single, B-side. *Pages Of Life.*
26 August 'Missing You' (with Tom Russell and Richard Sellars) [pub. 1 January 1990] *Pages Of Life.*
26 August 'Start All Over Again' (with Steve Hill) *Pages Of Life.*
26 August 'Story Of Love' (with Steve Hill) [pub. 1 January 1990] single, A-side. *Pages Of Life.*
26 August 'Time Passes Me By' (with Steve Hill) *Pages Of Life.*
11 December 'Behind These Walls' (with Michael Woody) *True Love.*
11 December 'Glory And Power' (with Steve Hill) single, B-side. *True Love.*
11 December 'It Takes A Believer' (with Michael Woody) *True Love.*
11 December 'No One Else' (with Herb Pedersen) *True Love.*
11 December 'Shades Of Blue' (with Steve Hill) single, B-side. *True Love.*
11 December 'You Can Go Home' (with Jack Tempchin) single, B-side. *True Love.*

1992
22 May Chris Hillman Songs. Chris Hillman and Catherine Rose Hillman. Specific titles not listed.
n/a 'Little Birdie' *Country Music For Kids.*

1993
29 March 'All Dressed Up' (with Steve Hill) Unreleased.
29 March 'Bidin' My Time' (with Steve Hill) Steve Hill's *House For Sale.*

29 March 'Blue Moon Rising' (with Steve Hill) Steve Hill's *Gold Highway.*
29 March 'Different Rivers Run' (with Steve Hill) Steve Hill's *Gold Highway.*
29 March 'It's About Love' (with Steve Hill) Steve Hill's *Decisions.*
29 March 'Let Me Feel Love' (with Steve Hill) Unreleased.
29 March 'Long Gone' (with Steve Hill) Steve Hill's *Gold Highway.*

1994

5 January 'What About Love?' (with Steve Hill) [pub. 1 July 1993] single, A-side. *Life Goes On.*
n/a 'Lullaby Time In The Desert' compilation *Daddies Sing Goodnight.*

1996

22 November 'Just Tell Me Darlin'' (with Bill Wildes) *Bakersfield Bound.*
n/a 'If You Leave Me Now' (with Steve Hill) Steve Hill's *Gold Highway.*
n/a 'The Words She Writes Tonight' (with Herb Pedersen) Laurel Canyon Ramblers' *Blue Rambler 2.*

1997

27 February 'Universal Mind Decoder' (with Roger McGuinn). *The Notorious Byrd Brothers* CD, expanded edition.
3 March 'Change Coming Down' (with Steve Hill) *Out Of The Woodwork.*
3 March 'Somewhere On The Road Tonight' (with Alan Thornhill) *Out Of The Woodwork*
29 December 'Taking Her Time' (with Alan Thornhill and Jim Monahan) Rincon Ramblers' *The Green Rolling Hills Of La Conchita.*

1998

29 June 'Angels' Cry' (with Steve Hill) *Like A Hurricane.*
29 June 'Back's Against The Wall' (with Steve Hill) *Like A Hurricane.*
29 June 'Carry Me Home' (with Steve Hill) *Like A Hurricane.*
29 June 'Forgiveness' (with Steve Hill) *Like A Hurricane.*
29 June 'Heaven's Lullaby' (with Steve Hill) *Like A Hurricane.*
29 June 'I'm Still Alive' (with Steve Hill) *Like A Hurricane.*
29 June 'Like A Hurricane' (with Steve Hill) *Like A Hurricane.*
29 June 'Living On The Edge' (with Steve Hill) *Like A Hurricane.*
29 June 'Run Again' (with Steve Hill) *Like A Hurricane.*
29 June 'Second Wind' (with Michael L. Woody) *Like A Hurricane.*
29 June 'Sooner Or Later' (with Steve Hill) *Like A Hurricane.*

1999

5 August 'Love's Worth More Than Gold' (with Bill Wildes) Rose Maddox and John Jorgenson's *The Moon Is Rising.*
n/a 'Comin' Back To Me' (with Steve Hill) Steve Hill's *Decisions.*
n/a 'Even Time Won't Pass Us By' (with Steve Hill) Steve Hill's *Decisions.*

2000

n/a 'Maybe Lucky' (with Steve Hill) Steve Hill's *House For Sale.*

2002

26 March 'Backporch Boy' *Way Out West.*
9 April '[Just] Passin' Through' (with Stephen Hill) *Running Wild.*
9 April 'Maybe She'll Get Lucky' (with Stephen Hill) *Running Wild.*
9 April 'San Antone' (with Stephen Hill) *Running Wild.*
19 August 'After All Is Said And Done' (with Stephen Hill) *Way Out West.*
19 August 'Better Man Than That' (with Stephen Hill) *Way Out West.*
19 August 'Good Year' (with Stephen Hill) *Way Out West.*
19 August 'That's The Way It Was' (with Stephen Hill) *Way Out West.*
19 August 'There You Go' (with Stephen Hill) *Way Out West.*

2003

11 August 'I Am A Pilgrim' (with Roger McGuinn) arrangement and adaptation *Sweetheart Of The Rodeo.*
11 August 'Pretty Polly' (with Roger McGuinn) musical arrangement. *The Byrds* box set. *Sweetheart Of The Rodeo* CD, expanded edition.

2005

13 July 'Drifting' (with Steve Hill) *The Other Side.*
13 July 'Heaven Is My Home' (with Steve Hill) *The Other Side.*
13 July 'Heavenly Grace' (with Steve Hill) *The Other Side.*
13 July 'I Know I Need You' (with Steve Hill) *The Other Side.*
13 July 'Our Savior's Hands' (with Steve Hill) *The Other Side.*
13 July 'The Other Side' (with Steve Hill) *The Other Side.*
13 July 'The Wheel' (with Steve Hill) *The Other Side.*
13 July 'The Water Is Wide' (arrangement with Herb Pedersen) *The Other Side.*
13 July 'Touch Me' (with Steve Hill) *The Other Side.*
13 July 'True Love' (with Steve Hill) *The Other Side.*
n/a 'Old Rocking Chair' single, download for *The Other Side.*

2007

n/a 'Let Me Get Out' (with Steve Hill) Steve Hill's *We'll Always Have Texas.*
n/a 'Me And You' (with Steve Hill) Steve Hill's *We'll Always Have Texas.*
n/a 'No One' (with Steve Hill) Steve Hill's *We'll Always Have Texas.*

2009

13 March 'Doesn't Mean That Much Anymore' (with Steve Hill) [date of pub. 5 October 1999] *Rice, Rice, Hillman & Pedersen.*
13 March 'I Will' (with Steve Hill) [date of pub. 5 October 1999] *Rice, Rice, Hillman & Pedersen.*
13 March 'The Walkin' Blues' (with Steve Hill) [date of pub. 5 October 1999] *Rice, Rice, Hillman & Pedersen.*

2015

n/a 'Beautiful Sound (with John L. Jorgenson) John Jorgenson's *Divertuoso*, 3-CD box set.

n/a 'Let Me Get Out Of This World Alive' (with Steve Hill) John Jorgenson's 3-CD box set, *Divertuoso*.

KEVIN KELLEY

1982

24 August 'All I Have Are Memories' [date of creation: 1968]. *Sweetheart Of The Rodeo* Legacy Edition. Plus 31 additional Kelley compositions, titles unlisted. Although this information is sealed, it is likely that this document contains the following 15 songs: 'Baby's Coming Back Today', 'Dreaming My Life Away', 'The Drifter', 'Dusty Road', 'Home Again', 'I Found Paradise', 'Let Yourself Go', 'Look At Me', 'Looking For Freedom', 'Rat Race', 'Sail Away', 'Summertime Romance', 'Travelin' Mood', 'The Wind Has Been My Friend' and 'You Got To Be Free'. The rest remain unknown.

1993

7 April 'Candy Man' (arrangement with Ryland Peter Cooder, Henry St Claire Fredericks (aka Taj Mahal), Stephen Nicolas Gerlach (aka Jesse Lee Kincaid) and Gary Alfred Marker) [date of creation: 1965; pub. 15 September 1992] single, B-side. *Rising Sons Featuring Taj Mahal And Ry Cooder.*

7 April 'The Devil's Got My Woman' (arrangement with Ryland Peter Cooder, Henry St Claire Fredericks (aka Taj Mahal), Stephen Nicolas Gerlach (aka Jesse Lee Kincaid) and Gary Alfred Marker) [date of creation: 1965; pub. 15 September 1992] single, A-side. *Rising Sons Featuring Taj Mahal And Ry Cooder.*

7 April 'Divin' Duck Blues' (arrangement with Ryland Peter Cooder, Henry St Claire Fredericks (aka Taj Mahal), Stephen Nicolas Gerlach (aka Jesse Lee Kincaid) and Gary Alfred Marker) [date of creation: 1965; pub. 15 September 1992]. *Rising Sons Featuring Taj Mahal And Ry Cooder.*

7 April 'Dust My Broom' (arrangement with Ryland Peter Cooder, Henry St Claire Fredericks (aka Taj Mahal), Stephen Nicolas Gerlach (aka Jesse Lee Kincaid) and Gary Alfred Marker) [date of creation: 1965; pub. 15 September 1992]. *Rising Sons Featuring Taj Mahal And Ry Cooder.*

7 April '.44 Blues' (arrangement with Ryland Peter Cooder, Henry St Claire Fredericks (aka Taj Mahal), Stephen Nicolas Gerlach (aka Jesse Lee Kincaid) and Gary Alfred Marker) [date of creation: 1965; pub. 15 September 1992]. *Rising Sons Featuring Taj Mahal And Ry Cooder.*

7 April 'If The River Was Whiskey' (arrangement with Ryland Peter Cooder, Henry St Claire Fredericks (aka Taj Mahal), Stephen Nicolas Gerlach (aka Jesse Lee Kincaid) and Gary Alfred Marker) [date of creation: 1965; pub. 15 September 1992]. *Rising Sons Featuring Taj Mahal And Ry Cooder.*

7 April 'Last Fair Deal Goin' Down' (aka 'Last Fair Deal Gone Down' (arrangement with Ryland Peter Cooder, Henry St Claire Fredericks (aka Taj Mahal), Stephen Nicolas Gerlach (aka Jesse Lee Kincaid) and Gary

Alfred Marker) [date of creation: 1965; pub. 15 September 1992]. *Rising Sons Featuring Taj Mahal And Ry Cooder.*

7 April 'Look At Me' (arrangement with Ryland Peter Cooder, Henry St Claire Fredericks (aka Taj Mahal), Stephen Nicolas Gerlach (aka Jesse Lee Kincaid) and Gary Alfred Marker) [date of creation: 1965; pub. 15 September 1992]. *Rising Sons Featuring Taj Mahal And Ry Cooder.*

7 April 'Sugar Pie' (arrangement with Ryland Peter Cooder, Henry St Claire Fredericks (aka Taj Mahal), Stephen Nicolas Gerlach (aka Jesse Lee Kincaid) and Gary Alfred Marker) [date of creation: 1965; pub. 15 September 1992]. Unreleased.

GRAM PARSONS

1963

13 May 'Big Country' *Gram Parsons – The Early Years Vol. I 1963–1965.*

13 May 'Race With The Wind' *Gram Parsons – The Early Years* box set.

1967

24 February 'November Night' (aka 'November Nights') Peter Fonda single, A-side. *Another Side Of This Life.*

24 February 'Sum Up Broke' (with John Nuese) International Submarine Band single, A-side.

15 November 'Do You Know How It Feels To Be Lonesome' (with Barry Goldberg). Songwriters' document. International Submarine Band's *Safe At Home.*

1968

9 February 'Blue Eyes' single, A-side. International Submarine Band's *Safe At Home.*

9 February 'Do You Know How It Feels To Be Lonesome' International Submarine Band's *Safe At Home.*

9 February 'Strong Boy' International Submarine Band's *Safe At Home.*

1969

31 January 'Drug Store Truck Drivin' Man' (with Roger McGuinn) single, B-side. *Dr Byrds & Mr Hyde.*

9 February 'Luxury Liner' single, B-side. International Submarine Band's *Safe At Home.*

19 February 'Christine's Tune' (with Chris Hillman) *The Gilded Palace Of Sin.*

19 February 'Hippie Boy' (with Chris Hillman) *The Gilded Palace Of Sin.*

19 February 'Hot Burrito # 1' (with Chris Ethridge) single, B-side. *The Gilded Palace Of Sin.*

19 February 'Hot Burrito # 2' (with Chris Ethridge) *The Gilded Palace Of Sin.*

19 February 'Juanita' (with Chris Hillman) *The Gilded Palace Of Sin.*

19 February 'My Uncle' (with Chris Hillman) *The Gilded Palace Of Sin.*

19 February 'Sin City' (with Chris Hillman) *The Gilded Palace Of Sin.*

19 February 'Wheels' (with Chris Hillman) single, B-side. *The Gilded Palace Of Sin.*
9 April 'Brass Buttons' *Grievous Angel.*
26 May 'The Train Song' (with Chris Hillman) single, A-side. *Close Up The Honky Tonks.*
20 October 'Hickory Wind' (with Bob Buchanan) *Sweetheart Of The Rodeo.*
20 October 'One Hundred Years From Now' *Sweetheart Of The Rodeo.*

1970
2 February 'Cody, Cody' (with Chris Hillman) single, B-side. *Burrito Deluxe.*
21 May 'Down In The Churchyard' (with Chris Hillman) single, A-side. *Burrito Deluxe.*
21 May 'High Fashion Queen' (with Chris Hillman) *Burrito Deluxe.*
21 May 'Lazy Days' single, B-side. *Burrito Deluxe.*
21 May 'Older Guys' (with Chris Hillman and Bernie Leadon) single, A-side. *Burrito Deluxe.*
n/a 'Apple Tree' Johnny Rivers' *Slim Slo Slider.*

1971
28 June 'She' (with Chris Ethridge) single, B-side. *GP.*

1973
12 January 'Big Mouth Blues' *GP.*
12 January 'The New Soft Shoe' single, A-side *GP.*
29 January 'A Song For You' *GP.*
29 January 'How Much I've Lied' (with David Rifkin) *GP.*
29 January 'Still Feeling Blue' *GP.*

1974
21 January 'Return Of The Grievous Angel' (with Thomas Brown) single, A-side. *Grievous Angel.*
21 January '$1000 Wedding' *Grievous Angel.*
n/a 'In My Hour Of Darkness' (with Emmylou Harris) single, B-side. *Grievous Angel.*
n/a 'Ooh Las Vegas' (with Rick 'Rik' Grech) *Grievous Angel.*

1975
24 April 'Real Sunday Driving' (words: Gram Parsons and John J. Soter; words and music: Edward H. Porter) Unreleased.

2000
21 August 'Blessing For Being (words: Gram Parsons; music: Jim Lauderdale). Various Artistes' *The Gram Parsons Notebook: The Last Whippoorwill.*
n/a 'Blurry Slurry Night' (with Mike A. Ward) Various Artistes' *The Gram Parsons Notebook: The Last Whippoorwill.*
n/a 'Jesus Is More Than A Name' (with Ed Berghoff, Eddie Leroy Cunningham Jr and Mike A. Ward) Various Artistes' *The Gram Parsons Notebook: The Last Whippoorwill.* Eddie Cunningham's *I Can't Wait.*

n/a 'No One Knows I'm Lonesome' (with Mike A. Ward) Various Artistes' *The Gram Parsons Notebook: The Last Whippoorwill.*

n/a 'The Button' (with Eddie Leroy Cunningham Jr, Eddie Dunbar and Mike A. Ward) Various Artistes' *The Gram Parsons Notebook: The Last Whippoorwill.*

2007

25 June 'L.A. Custom Blues' (with Carl Jackson) [pub. date: 27 June 2000] Various Artistes' *The Gram Parsons Notebook: The Last Whippoorwill.*

CLARENCE WHITE

1966–68

n/a 'Grandma Funderbunk's Music Box' Clarence White single. *Tuff & Stringy (Sessions 1966–68).*

n/a 'Hong Kong Hillbilly' (with Gene Victor Parsons) Clarence White single. *Tuff & Stringy (Sessions 1966-68).*

n/a 'Listen To The Mockingbird' (traditional arrangement) *Scotty Stoneman, Live In LA With The Kentucky Colonels.*

n/a 'Nashville West' (with Gene Victor Parsons) *Dr Byrds & Mr Hyde.*

n/a 'Nature's Child' (with Janice Louise Paxton) Jan & Clarence single. *Tuff & Stringy (Sessions 1966–68).*

n/a 'She's Gone' (with Janice Louise Parsons) Gib & Jan single. *Tuff & Stringy (Sessions 1966–68).*

n/a 'Why Can't We Be' (with Janice Louise Parsons) Great Love Trip single. *Tuff & Stringy (Sessions 1966–68).*

1969

10 March 'B. J. Blues' (with Roger McGuinn, John York, Gene Parsons*) *Dr Byrds & Mr Hyde.*

*incorrectly registered to 'Graham Parsons'

17 November 'Oil In My Lamp' (with Gene Victor Parsons) single, B-side. *Ballad Of Easy Rider.*

n/a 'Build It Up' (with Gene Victor Parsons) [recorded 23 June 1969] *Ballad Of Easy Rider* CD, expanded edition.

1970

n/a 'Long Jam' (with James Roger McGuinn, Gene Victor Parsons and 'writer unknown') Unreleased.

n/a 'Soldier' Joy'/'Black Mountain Rag' *The Byrds* box set.

1971

14 February 'Green Apple Quick Step' (with Gene Victor Parsons) *Byrdmaniax.*

n/a 'Byrdgrass' (with Gene Victor Parsons) [recorded 24 February 1971] *Byrdmaniax* CD, expanded edition.

1972

4 February 'Antique Sandy' (with Roger McGuinn, Skip Battin, Gene Parsons and Jimmi Seiter) *Farther Along*.

14 February 'Bristol Steam Convention Blues (with Gene Parsons) *Farther Along*.

14 February 'Green Apple Quick Step' (with Gene Parsons) *Byrdmaniax*.

n/a 'Farther Along' (arrangement) *Farther Along*.

1973

15 August 'On The Spot' (with Gene Parsons and Floyd August Guilbeau) *Kindling*.

1977

n/a 'Don't Let Your Deal Go Down' (arrangement with Alan Munde and Roland Joseph White) Country Gazette's *What A Way To Make A Living*.

Clarence is not included on the album's writing credits, but his name is registered alongside his brother and Alan Munde at BMI.

1990

10 September 'White's Lightning' (with Roger McGuinn) [recorded 2 June 1970] *The Byrds* box set.

GENE PARSONS

1966–68

n/a 'Hong Kong Hillbilly' (with Clarence White) Clarence White single. *Tuff & Stringy (Sessions 1966–68).*

n/a 'Nashville West' (with Clarence White) *Dr Byrds & Mr Hyde*.

n/a 'Riff-Raff' (with Gary S. Paxton) Clarence White single. *Tuff & Stringy (Sessions 1966–68).*

1968

n/a 'Christina In My Dreams' (with Janice Louise Paxton) Eternity Children's *Timeless*.

1969

10 March 'B. J. Blues' (with Roger McGuinn, John York, Clarence White) *Dr Byrds & Mr Hyde*. Incorrectly registered to 'Graham Parsons' (Gram Parsons) in the Library Of Congress.

19 March 'I'll Live Today' (with Floyd August Guilbeau) Dennis Payne single. *Tuff & Stringy (Sessions 1966–68).*

17 November 'Gunga Din' *Ballad Of Easy Rider*.

17 November 'Oil In My Lamp (arrangement with Clarence White) single, B-side. *Ballad Of Easy Rider*.

n/a 'Build It Up' (with Clarence White) [recorded 23 June 1969] *Ballad Of Easy Rider* CD, expanded edition.

1970

25 November 'Yesterday's Train' (with Skip Battin aka Clyde R. Battin Jr) *(Untitled)*.

n/a 'Break Song' (with Clyde R. Battin Jr, Roger McGuinn and William Isaac Travis) Unreleased.
n/a 'Long Jam' (with James Roger McGuinn, Clarence White and 'writer unknown') Unreleased.

1971
9 November 'Pale Blue' (with Roger McGuinn) *Byrdmaniax.*
n/a 'Byrdgrass' (with Clarence White) [recorded 24 February] *Byrdmaniax* CD, expanded edition.

1972
4 February 'Antique Sandy' (with Roger McGuinn, Skip Battin, Clarence White and Jimmi Seiter) *Farther Along.*
14 February 'B.B. Class Road' (with Stuart Dawson) *Farther Along.*
14 February 'Bristol Steam Convention Blues' (with Clarence White) *Farther Along.*
14 February 'Get Down Your Line' *Farther Along.*
14 February 'Green Apple Quick Step' (with Clarence White) *Byrdmaniax.*

1973
11 July 'And Back Again' *Kindling.*
11 July 'Banjo Dog' *Kindling.*
11 July 'Long Way Back' *Kindling.*
11 July 'Monument' *Kindling.*
11 July 'Sonic Bummer' *Kindling.*
15 August 'I Must Be A Tree' (with Floyd August Guilbeau) *Kindling.*
15 August 'On The Spot' (with Floyd August Guilbeau and Clarence J. White) *Kindling.*

1975
n/a 'Hot Burrito No. 3' (with Chris Ethridge, Floyd August Guilbeau, Truman Scott Hill and Peter E. Kleinow) Flying Burrito Brothers' *Flying Again.*
n/a 'Sweet Desert Childhood' Flying Burrito Brothers' *Flying Again.*

1976
n/a 'Out Of Control' (with Floyd August Guilbeau) Flying Burrito Brothers' *Airborne.*

1979
5 December 'Little Jewels (For Lilybet)' (with Camille J. Parsons) *Melodies.*
5 December 'Mama, Papa' *Melodies.*
5 December 'Melodies From A Bird In Flyght' (with Camille J. Parsons) *Melodies.*
5 December 'No Fire Here Tonight' *Melodies.*
5 December 'Pastime' *Melodies.*
5 December 'Won't Last Long' (with Camille J. Parsons and Steve Zaretsky) *Melodies.*

1982

23 August 'Dark Moon' (with Peter Oliva) *Gene Parsons In Concert – I Hope They Let Us In.*

23 August 'Nuclear Days' (with Peter Oliva) Unreleased.

18 October 'The Singer' (arrangement credit, words and music Barbara L. Willborn, with additional arrangement credits to Gene Parsons, Kevin Fraser and Jon Robbins).

1991

13 November 'Birds Of A Feather' (with Meridian Green) *Birds Of A Feather.*

13 November 'Lily's Hotbread' *Birds Of A Feather.*

13 November 'No, You're Not Broken' (with Meridian Green) *Birds Of A Feather.*

n/a 'California Subduction Blues' (with Meridian Green) Unreleased.

n/a 'Wind And Rain' (with Floyd August Guilbeau) *Birds Of A Feather.*

1998

1 September 'Just Away' (with Meridian Green and Lenny Laks) Meridian Green's *In The Heart Of This Town.*

1 September Three StringBender Songs [no additional titles]

n/a 'Birds Fly South' (with Meridian Green) Meridian Green's *In The Heart Of This Town.*

n/a 'Come On Wind' (with Meridian Green) Meridian Green's *In The Heart Of This Town.*

n/a 'Lorax In Laytonville' (with Meridian Green) Meridian Green's *In The Heart Of This Town.*

n/a 'Sarah Lou' (with Meridian Green) Meridian Green's *In The Heart Of This Town.*

2002

3 May 'Chief Seattle' (with Meridian Green and Lenny Laks) *Live From Caspar.*

3 May 'Coast Hotel' (with Meridian Green and Lenny Laks) *Live From Caspar.*

n/a 'Get Up Blues' (with Meridian Green) *Live From Caspar.*

2004

23 February 'We Really Tried To Love' (with Robert Wessell) Unreleased.

3 June 'Talk To Me' (with Meridian Green) Unreleased.

JOHN YORK

1966

10 March 'Round World' Unreleased.

1969

10 March 'B. J. Blues' (with Roger McGuinn, Gene Parsons* and Clarence White). *Dr Byrds & Mr Hyde.* *Incorrectly registered to 'Graham Parsons'.

7 April 'Candy' (with Roger McGuinn) *Dr Byrds & Mr Hyde.*

1970
26 January 'Fido' *Ballad Of Easy Rider.*

1986
14 March 'Love's Misfortunes' Unreleased.

1987–88
n/a 'I'm Never Comin' Back' (with Shawn Jones) Unreleased.
n/a 'Question Of Love' (with Shawn Jones) Unreleased.

1988
26 September 'The Taking Of Flight 847 – The Uli Derrickson Story' Unreleased.
26 September 'Beirut' (with Joseph Nasser) Unreleased.

1991
n/a 'Ancestors' *Sacred Path Songs.*
n/a 'Cherokee Cradleboard Song' *Sacred Path Songs.*
n/a 'Earth Mother Flute' *Sacred Path Songs.*
n/a 'Iroquois Drum Invocation' (with Jamie Sue Sams) *Sacred Path Songs.*
n/a 'Just One Arrow' *Sacred Path Songs.*
n/a 'Lovers Duet (Kokopelli & Ice Flower)' *Sacred Path Songs.*
n/a 'Omaha Tribal Prayer' *Sacred Path Songs.*
n/a 'Pomo Clapperstick Blues' *Sacred Path Songs.*
n/a 'Shaman's Death' *Sacred Path Songs.*
n/a 'Sky Daughter Flute'/'Eagle's Quest' *Sacred Path Songs.*
n/a 'Thunderbeings' *Sacred Path Songs.*
n/a 'Winged Ones' *Sacred Path Songs.*

1992
26 October 'Mary Sue' (with Gene Clark and Pat Robinson) *So Rebellious A Lover.*
n/a 'All My Relations' (with Jamie Sue Sams) *Clan Mother Songs.*
n/a 'Celebrate The Earth' (with Jamie Sue Sams) *Clan Mother Songs.*
n/a 'Crack In The Universe' (with Jamie Sue Sams) *Clan Mother Songs.*
n/a 'Midnight's Song' (with Jamie Sue Sams) *Clan Mother Songs.*
n/a 'Rue-mai-ya, The Remembering' (aka 'Rui Mai Ya The Remembering') (with Jamie Sue Sams) *Clan Mother Songs.*
n/a 'The Clan Mother's Song' (with Jamie Sue Sams) *Clan Mother Songs.*
n/a 'The Final Beginning' (with Jamie Sue Sams) *Clan Mother Songs.*
n/a 'Tionee The Pathfinder' (with Jamie Sue Sams) *Clan Mother Songs.*
n/a 'Wata Jis Evening Star' (with Jamie Sue Sams) *Clan Mother Songs.*
n/a 'Welcoming The Fifth World (with Jamie Sue Sams) *Clan Mother Songs.*

1993
n/a 'I Want To Be Forgiven' (with Shawn Jones and Roy E. Swedeen) Shawn Jones' *Shawn Jones*, limited edition cassette.

1996

5 April 'We Came For Love' (with Gene Clark and Billy Darnell) Electric Range's *Electric Range.*

1997

n/a 'A Distant Call' (with Chris Darrow) Chris Darrow's *Coyote/Straight From The Heart.*

n/a 'Lone Yucca'(with Chris Darrow and Ian Beardsley) Chris Darrow's *Coyote/Straight From The Heart.*

n/a 'The Snake Sheds Its Skin' (with Chris Darrow and Ian Beardsley) Chris Darrow's *Coyote/Straight From The Heart.*

1999

n/a 'Another Life' *Claremont Dragon.*
n/a 'Daddy's Gonna Pick Her Man' *Claremont Dragon.*
n/a 'Half-Breeds Are The Hope Of The World' *Claremont Dragon.*
n/a 'Heartache Suzanne' (with Nicky Hopkins) *Claremont Dragon.*
n/a 'Jennifer Tsai' *Claremont Dragon.*
n/a 'Money Like Rain' *Claremont Dragon.*
n/a 'No More War' *Claremont Dragon.*
n/a 'Oh My Children' *Claremont Dragon.*
n/a 'On Whose Door' *Claremont Dragon.*
n/a 'Rubiah' *Claremont Dragon.*
n/a 'Spirit Is Stronger Than Anything' *Claremont Dragon.*
n/a 'Target Of A Thousand Arrows' *Claremont Dragon.*

2000

n/a 'A Rose Is A Rose' (with Pat Robinson) *CRY.*
n/a 'Christine' (with Gene Clark and Pat Robinson) *Family Tree.*

2003

n/a 'Amanogawa' (with Yukiko Matsuyama) *Koto.*
n/a 'Furusato' (with Yukiko Matsuyama) *Koto.*
n/a 'Katen no Odori' (with Yukiko Matsuyama) *Koto.*
n/a 'Koto' (with Yukiko Matsuyama) *Koto.*
n/a 'Murasaki' (with Yukiko Matsuyama) *Koto.*
n/a 'Tengu' (with Yukiko Matsuyama) *Koto.*
n/a 'This Is The Day' (with Yukiko Matsuyama) *Koto.*
n/a 'Yoake' (with Yukiko Matsuyama) *Koto.*
10 November 'You Just Love Cocaine' *Under The Silvery Moon. Fanfare For 2.*

2006

n/a 'Angel Dance' *Arigatou Baby.*
n/a 'Dandelion' *Arigatou Baby.*
n/a 'Down In That Hole' *Arigatou Baby.*
n/a 'Gypsy Life' *Arigatou Baby.*
n/a 'I Can't Find The Moon' *Arigatou Baby.*
n/a 'I Know I Will See You' *Arigatou Baby.*
n/a 'I Want To Go Now' *Arigatou Baby.*

n/a 'Jealous Gun' *Arigatou Baby.*
n/a 'Lady Of The Highway' *Arigatou Baby.*
n/a 'Never Doubt My Love' *Arigatou Baby.*
n/a 'One Step From Homeless' *Arigatou Baby.*
n/a 'Roadside Cross' *Arigatou Baby.*
n/a 'She Likes To Shine My Shoes' *Arigatou Baby.*
n/a 'Tuesday's Train' *Arigatou Baby.*

2007
n/a 'Angels And Trucks' (with Kim Fowley) *West Coast Revelation.*
n/a 'East Coast Confidential' (with Kim Fowley) *West Coast Revelation.*
n/a 'Flower Girls' (with Kim Fowley) *West Coast Revelation.*
n/a 'Halfway House' (with Kim Fowley) *West Coast Revelation.*
n/a 'Hangin' Out' (with Kim Fowley) *West Coast Revelation.*
n/a 'Japan And Europe' (with Kim Fowley) *West Coast Revelation.*
n/a 'Laurel Canyon And Topanga' (with Kim Fowley) *West Coast Revelation.*
n/a 'Memories Of Days Gone By' (with Kim Fowley) *West Coast Revelation.*
n/a 'Movin' Out For Years' (with Kim Fowley) *West Coast Revelation.*
n/a 'Picnic In Eternity' (with Kim Fowley) *West Coast Revelation.*
n/a 'Psychedelic' (with Kim Fowley) *West Coast Revelation.*
n/a 'Queen Of The Blues' (with Kim Fowley) *West Coast Revelation.*
n/a 'Rock 'n' Roll Is Another Name For Freedom' (with Kim Fowley) *West Coast Revelation.*
n/a 'Sayonara' (with Kim Fowley) *West Coast Revelation.*
n/a 'Silver '60s # 1' (with Kim Fowley) *West Coast Revelation.*
n/a 'Silver '60s # 2' (with Kim Fowley) *West Coast Revelation.*
n/a 'Silver '60s # 3'(with Kim Fowley) *West Coast Revelation.*
n/a 'The Earth Is Getting Warmer' (with Kim Fowley) *West Coast Revelation.*
n/a '21st Century' (with Kim Fowley) *West Coast Revelation.*
n/a 'West Coast Revelation # 1' (with Kim Fowley) *West Coast Revelation.*
n/a 'West Coast Revelation # 2' (with Kim Fowley) *West Coast Revelation.*
n/a 'West Coast Revelation # 3' (with Kim Fowley) *West Coast Revelation.*

2010
n/a 'Achilles' Heel' *Cameo.*
n/a 'Come Back And Take Me' *Cameo.*
n/a 'Ghost Flowers' *Cameo.*
n/a 'Rainbow' (with Roy E. Swedeen) *Cameo.*
n/a 'Some Days Even The Birds Sing A Sad Song' *Cameo.*

2012
n/a 'Behind The Scenes' *Fanfare For 2.*
n/a 'I Feel It Now' *Fanfare For 2.*
n/a 'Lone Wolf, No Club' *Fanfare For 2.*
n/a 'Lucky & The Trash Angel' *Fanfare For 2.*
n/a 'Power Of Now' *Fanfare For 2.*
n/a 'Red, White & Blue' *Fanfare For 2.*

n/a 'Sea Of Wine' *Fanfare For 2.*
n/a 'Set Up For Heartbreak (For Ruby)' *Fanfare For 2.*
n/a 'Together At The Time' (with Kim Fowley) *Fanfare For 2.*

SKIP BATTIN

1958

24 July 'Her Bermuda Shorts' (with Gary Paxton) Pledges' single, B-side.

1959

6 May 'Lunch Hour' (with Gary Paxton) Skip & Flip single, B-side.
16 September 'Fancy Nancy' (with Gary Paxton) Skip & Flip single, A-side.
2 November 'Bury The Hatchet' (with Gary Paxton) Chuck & Chuckles single, A-side.
n/a 'The Jackie Look (We Wanna Look Like Jackie)'. Gary & Clyde single, B-side. Later issued as an A-side in 1961 by Jack Bartley With The Jackies.

1960

8 February 'Tami's Dance' (with Gary Paxton) Clyde Gary & His Orchestra single, A-side.
29 June 'Hully Gully Cha Cha Cha' (with Gary Paxton) Skip & Flip single, A-side.

1961

28 August 'When The Twister Came To Town'. Issued as 'The Twister' as an A-side single by Clyde Battin.
n/a 'A Million Tears' Ron Scuderi single, A-side.

1962

6 March 'Coming Back Home To You' Lette And Junior single, A-side.
n/a 'The Marathon' (with Kim Fowley) Skip & Johnny single, A-side.
n/a 'What Does A Dream Mean' Don True single, B-side. The A-side, 'Make Believe Baby', was written by Skip's wife, Jackie Battin.

1964

n/a 'Mr Responsibility' (with Kim Fowley) Skip Battyn single, B-side. Also issued as a B-side by Skip Battin & The Group.
n/a 'What's Mine Is Mine' (with Mary Dean) Skip Battyn single, A-side.

1965

n/a 'Daybreaker' (with Kim Fowley) Kim & The Skippers single, A-side. Also issued as a B-side by Sir Raybould & The Blue Angels.

1968

10 September 'The Everblue Express' (with Kim Fowley) *The Ballad Of Evergreen Blueshoes.*
10 September 'Life's Mountain Railroad' retitled 'Life's Railway To Heaven' (with A.P. Rosenberg, K. Kleist, L. Mathijssen and C. McCracken) *The Ballad Of Evergreen Blueshoes.*

10 September 'The Raven' (with A.P. Rosenberg) *The Ballad Of Evergreen Blueshoes.*
8 October 'Line Out' (with A.P. Rosenberg) *The Ballad Of Evergreen Blueshoes.*

1970

1 April 'Save Our World, We Must Survive' (with Kim Vincent Fowley) Earth Island's *We Must Survive.*
1 October 'You All Look Alike' (with Kim Fowley) *(Untitled).*
23 November 'Well Come Back Home' (aka 'Welcome Back Home') *(Untitled).*
25 November 'Yesterday's Train' (with Gene Parsons) *(Untitled).*
n/a 'Break Song' (with, Roger McGuinn, Gene Parsons and William Isaac Travis) Unreleased.
n/a 'Long Jam' (with James Roger McGuinn, Clarence White and Gene Parsons. Battin referred to as 'writer unknown') Unreleased.

1971

1 June 'Absolute Happiness' (with Kim Fowley) *Byrdmaniax.*
1 June 'Citizen Kane' (with Kim Fowley) single, B-side. *Byrdmaniax.*
1 June 'Tunnel Of Love' (with Kim Fowley) *Byrdmaniax.*
21 June 'Hungry Planet' (with Kim Fowley and Roger McGuinn) *(Untitled).*
2 July 'America's Great National Pastime' (with Kim Fowley) single, A-side. *Farther Along.*
2 July 'Precious Kate' (with Kim Fowley) *Farther Along.*

1972

4 February 'Antique Sandy' (with Roger McGuinn, Gene Parsons, Clarence White and Jimmi Seiter) *Farther Along.*
1 September 'The Ballad Of Dick Clark' (with Kim Fowley) single, A-side. *Skip.*
1 September 'Captain Video' (with Kim Fowley) *Skip.*
1 September 'Central Park' (with Kim Fowley) single, A-side. *Skip.*
1 September 'China Moon' (with Kim Fowley and Brian Elliot) *Navigator.*
1 September 'Cobras' (with Kim Fowley) *Skip.*
1 September 'Four Legs Are Better Than Two' (with Kim Fowley) *Skip.*
1 September 'Human Being Blues' (with Kim Fowley) *Skip.*
1 September 'My Secret Life' (with Kim Fowley) *Skip.*
1 September 'Red China' (with Kim Fowley) Kim Fowley's *International Heroes.*
1 September 'The St Louis Browns' (with Kim Fowley) single, B-side. *Skip.*
1 September 'Undercover Man' (with Kim Fowley) *Skip.*
1 September 'Valentino' (with Kim Fowley) *Skip.*

1973

9 March 'Born Dancer' (with Kim Vincent Fowley) Kim Fowley's *International Heroes.*

9 March 'Do Not Disturb' (with Kim Fowley) *Kindling.*
9 March 'E.S.P Reader' (with Kim Fowley) Kim Fowley's *International Heroes.*
n/a 'Bolts Of Blue' (with Kim Fowley) *Topanga Skyline.*
n/a 'Don't Go Down The Drain' (with Kim Fowley) *Don't Go Crazy. Topanga Skyline.*
n/a 'Relax With Me' (with Kim Fowley) *Don't Go Crazy. Topanga Skyline.*
n/a 'Skyscraper Sunset' (with Kim Fowley) *Navigator. Topanga Skyline.*
n/a 'Stoned Sober' (with Kim Fowley) *Topanga Skyline.*
n/a 'Wintergreen' (with Kim Fowley) *Don't Go Crazy. Topanga Skyline.*

1974
3 October 'Big Wheels' (with Kim Vincent Fowley) *Brujo.*
3 October 'Neon Rose' (with Kim Vincent Fowley) *Brujo.*
3 October 'On The Amazon' (with Kim Vincent Fowley) *Brujo.*
3 October 'Singing Cowboy' (with Kim Vincent Fowley) *Brujo.*
n/a 'California Swamp Dance' (with Kim Fowley) Kim Fowley's *Animal God Of The Street.*

1975
n/a 'Austin, Texas' (with Kim Vincent Fowley) *Armadillo World HQ Austin TX, 6/13/1975.*
n/a 'Strangers On A Train' (with Kim Fowley) *Oh What A Mighty Time.*

1977
19 May 'Sunrise On Sunset' (with Kim Fowley and Mark Anthony) Hollywood Stars' *The Hollywood Stars.*

1982
n/a 'Willow In The Wind' (with Kim Fowley) *Navigator.*

1983
18 April 'Jail House Blues' Unreleased.
n/a 'Zig Zag' (with Kim Fowley) *Navigator.*

1984
13 December 'Here Comes Love' (with Kim Fowley) *Navigator.*
13 December 'North By Northwest' (with Kim Fowley) *Navigator.*
13 December 'Wrong Kind Of Guy' (with Kim Fowley) Unreleased.
n/a 'Fango' (with Gianfranco Manfredi) *Don't Go Crazy.*
n/a 'Speranza' (with Gianfranco Manfredi) *Don't Go Crazy.*
n/a 'Tonight' (with Gianfranco Manfredi) *Don't Go Crazy.*

2002
9 April Skip Battin/Kim Fowley, 14 songs, no individual titles. Date of creation: 1969.

2014
n/a 'Black Cat Blues' Eliot Eidelman's *The California Sun.*

UNRELEASED COMPOSITIONS

The list below features songs composed but never released by a member of the Byrds. In cases where the compositions were specifically written for or recorded by another artiste, an explanation follows the listing.

JAMES ROGER McGUINN

'All About You' (with Stanley Lynch and Benmont M. Tench III)
'Break Song' (with Clyde R. Battin, Gene Victor Parsons and William Isaac Travis)
'Catching Rainbows'
'Come On Now' (with Jane Schorr)
'Ding Dang' (with Brian Wilson)
'Drifting In The Galaxy' (with Robert J. Hippard)
'Dubbio' (with Carrera Ettore, Robert James Hippard and Antonio Mennillo)
'518'
'Good King James' (with David Hemmings and Bill Martin)
'Grapes Of Wrath' (with Camilla McGuinn)
'Here She Comes Again' (with Chris Hillman)
'I Love Her' (with Robert J. Hippard)
'La Ballata Della Liberata' (with U. Bertini)
'Light Up The Darkness' (with Camilla McGuinn)
'Little Bear'
'Living Legend' (with Camilla McGuinn)
'Long Jam' (with Clarence White, Gene Victor Parsons and 'writer unknown')
'Love Beyond Compare' (with Jane Schorr)
'NPR Interlude Music'
'Price, The' (with Camilla McGuinn)
'Rebellious Eyes' (with Camilla McGuinn)
'Rescue Mission' (with Cassel Seymour, Kris Kristofferson and Robert Neuwirth)
'Rocket To Stardom' (with Kris Kristofferson and Bob Neuwirth)
'Severe Mercy' (with Camilla McGuinn)
'Sunshine Love' (with Camilla McGuinn)
'Sweet Memories' (with Camilla McGuinn)
'Talkin' LA' (with Chris Hillman and David Hemmings)
'Tears, The' (with Camilla McGuinn)
'These Days' (with Harold Eugene Clark, Matthew Alan Prime and Michael James Stafford)
'Thursday (Jim's Day)'
'War's Mystery' (with Chris Hillman and David Hemmings)
'Wings Of Love' (with Camilla McGuinn)
'Woman' (with Camilla McGuinn)
'You Are The One' (with Jane Schorr)

There are a number of obscure songs listed above. As can be seen in the copyright listings section, the Jane Schorr collaborations, 'Come On Now', 'Love Beyond Compare' and 'You Are The One', all pre-date the Byrds. When I interviewed McGuinn about these compositions he admitted (rather like a living computer) that they had been erased from his memory banks. "I couldn't even hum them for you now," he said.

The McGuinn-credited composition 'La Ballata Della Liberata' was registered by Patian Music (that's an amalgamation of 'Patrick' and 'Ianthe', Roger's eldest son and then wife, Dolores, respectively). The Italian translation is 'Paint Your Wagon, Liberata'. The equally unknown 'Dubbio', which has been registered for decades as a McGuinn/Hippard collaboration, with Carrera Ettore and Antonio Mennillo, is another Italian word, meaning 'Doubt'. The date of the composition is not known, although Hippard's involvement suggests it was around the end of the Sixties or early Seventies.

'Break Song' was never recorded as a specific song by the Byrds, but it was used in live performance and Clarence White often called it 'Hold It!'. Given Clyde 'Skip' Battin's writing credit on the publishing it was clearly registered some time in 1970. However, the John York period Byrds frequently used the 'Break Song' and indeed you can hear the words "let's do the 'Break Song'" during the closing medley on *Dr Byrds & Mr Hyde*, although it is not credited on that record.

'Long Jam' would appear to be a workout with the latter day Byrds, which would strongly indicate that the person listed as 'writer unknown' was Skip Battin.

'Stone (The Lord Loves A Rolling Stone)', written by Dan Penn and Lindon Dewey (aka 'Spooner') Oldham Jr, was erroneously assigned to Roger McGuinn on the BMI website, but correctly credited on the McGuinn album, *Peace On You.*

Cover versions or songs for other artistes listed above include 'Good King James' (with David Hemmings and Bill Martin), 'War's Mystery' and 'Talkin' LA' (co-written with Chris Hillman and David Hemmings) all of which appeared on David Hemmings' 1967 album, *Happens.*

McGuinn co-wrote 'Ding Dang' with Brian Wilson, which appeared on the Beach Boys' album, *The Beach Boys Love You.*

Although unreleased by McGuinn, 'Rescue Mission' (co-composed with Seymour Cassel, Kris Kristofferson and Robert Neuwirth) appeared on Kristofferson's album, *Spooky Lady's Slide Show*. That album's follow up *Who's To Bless And Who's To Blame* included 'Rocket To Stardom' (co-composed with Kris Kristofferson and Robert Neuwirth).

The song 'Turtle Soup', which appears on DJ Food's 1994 album *Jazz Breaks Volume 5,* borrows from the McGuinn/Clark composition, 'You Showed Me'. DJ Food is erroneously referred to as 'DJ Flood' in the copyright listing. 'Gorgeous' is a track by Kanye West on his 2010 album *My Beautiful Dark Twisted Fantasy* which also samples the Turtles' cover of the McGuinn/Clark composition, 'You Showed Me'. It appears yet again on 'These Days' from Maverick Sabre's 2012 album, *Lonely Are The Brave.*

GENE CLARK

'Adios Terri'
'After The Storm' (with John York and Patrick Gerald Robinson)
'Along The Way'
'America' (with Rick Danko)
'American Song, The'
'Bakersfield Train'
'Battle Of The Sexes'
'Belfast Song'
'Big Bad Mama'
'Big City Girl'
'Boyfriend Girlfriend' (with Patrick Gerald Robinson)
'Can't Get You Off My Mind'
'Can't Get You Out Of My Life'
'Can't Say Yes, Can't Say No' (with Patrick Gerald Robinson)
'Chicken Bones' (with Jim McDonald) (see page 1188)*
'Colors' (with Patrick Gerald Robinson and Robby Romero)
'Communications'
'Crazy Ladies' (with Thomas Jefferson Kaye and Willy Kontos)
'Dancing On The Moon' (with Patrick G. Robinson and R. Marinell)
'Doctor, Doctor'
'Don't You Know What You Want'
'Down On The Pier'
'Dragon's Eye' (with Patrick Gerald Robinson)
'Emptiness, The'
'Fair Game' (with Patrick Gerald Robinson and Nicky Hopkins)
'Falling For You' (with Patrick Gerald Robinson)
'Father, Forgive Them' (see page 1188)*
'Forgive Me, Girl' (with Thomas Jefferson Kaye)
'From Darkness'
'Gorgeous' (with James Joseph McGuinn, Mike Dean, Malik Yusef El Shabazz, Scott Ramon Seguro Mescudi, Kanye West, Ernest Dion Wilson and Corey Todd Woods)
'Got To Get You Off My Mind'
'Hang Tough' (with Patrick Gerald Robinson and Nicky Hopkins)
'Have You Seen The Faces (Of The Dreamers In The Rain?)'
'Heart In The Right Place'
'Hillbilly Child'
'Hurting Game, The' (with Patrick Gerald Robinson)
'I Am Without You'
'I Get Along'
'I Just Like You'
'I Need To Fly' (with John York and Patrick Gerald Robinson)
'I Want You To Stay With Me' (with John York)

'I Was Alone' (with Kent Barker) (see page 1188)*
'I Wondered Why'
'I'll Change Your Life'
'I'll Miss You For A While' (with Jim McDonald) (see page 1188)*
'If You Knew' (with Thomas Paul Slocum)
'It's Easy Now'
'Jesus Love' (with Albert G. Teoli) (see page 1188)*
'Jealousy' (with Skip Scarborough) (see page 1188)*
'Just One More Kiss And Then Go' (with James MacBenoit and Larry Dorn) (see page 1188)*
'Kentucky Town Waltz' (with Robert Harsh) (see page 1188)
'Last Of The Blue Diamond Miners' (with Thomas Jefferson Kaye)
'Let There Be Happiness' (see page 1188)*
'Liona' (with Patrick Gerald Robinson)
'Long Time, A'
'Little Sister'
'Little Village' (with Garth L. Beckington)
'Look Who's Missing Who' (with Patrick Gerald Robinson and John Arrias)
'Looking For Reasons' (with Patrick G. Robinson and Nicky Hopkins)
'Love Opus In Time'
'Love Deluxe' (with Patrick Gerald Robinson and Nicky Hopkins)
'Love Holds On' (with Patrick Gerald Robinson)
'Love's A Loaded Word' (with Patrick G. Robinson and Nicky Hopkins)
'Maybe You Think'
'Mile Away Murphy'
'My Favorite Things'
'No Sweeter Love' (with Mac McClanahan) (see page 1188)
'No Wonder' (with Thomas Jefferson Kaye and Willy Kontos)
'Old Mountain God, The'
'On Her Own'
'On Tenth Street'
'On The Bright Side'
'On The Run With A Loaded Gun' (with Thomas Paul Slocum and Patrick Gerald Robinson)
'Once In A Lifetime' (with Patrick Gerald Robinson)
'Once In A Lifetime' (with Tom Slocum)
'Only Chance You Take, The' (with Patrick Gerald Robinson and Nicky Hopkins)
'One Way Road'
'Over The Mountain'
'Page Douze Septieme' (see page 1188)*
'Panther, The' (with Patrick Gerald Robinson)
'Past My Door'
'Past Tense'
'Past Tonight'

'Please Help Me Sweet Jesus' (with William Alden Skold aka Bill Alden) (see page 1188)*
'Quicksand' (with Bonnie Karlyle and Patrick Gerald Robinson)
'Rose Is A Rose, A' (with John York and Patrick Gerald Robinson)
'San Francisco'
'7.30 Mode'
'Seventh Avenue Train' (with Thomas Jefferson Kaye)
'She Ain't My Woman No More' (with Thomas Jefferson Kaye and Ben Schaeufele, aka Ben Keith)
'She Told Me'
'She's Made Up Her Mind'
'Show No Mercy' (with Bonnie Karlyle and Patrick Gerald Robinson)
'So Much More'
'Sometime And Again'
'Somewhere After Midnight' (with Patrick Gerald Robinson)
'Straight From The Heart'
'Strange And Different Way'
'Surrender' (with Bonnie Karlyle and Patrick Gerald Robinson)
'Testing 159'
'That Nonsense Stuff' (with Mac McClanahan) (see page 1188)
'That Part Of You' (with Patrick Gerald Robinson)
'That's What You Want'
'That's Why'
'(Theme For) Kay Seventy' (see page 1188)*
'These Days' (with James Joseph McGuinn, Matthew Alan Prime and Michael James Stafford)
'Till Today'
'Too Many Days'
'Trail Of Tears'
'Translations'
'Turtle Soup' (with Roger McGuinn)
'Understand Me Too'
'Washington Square' (with Patrick Gerald Robinson)
'Way (That) I Feel, The'
'We Came For Love' (with John Foley York and Billy Darnell)
'What Happens Then' (with Patrick Gerald Robinson)
'Whatever'
'Where Does The Love Go' (with Patrick Gerald Robinson and Nicky Hopkins)
'While You're Here'
'With You I Can't Lose'
'Yesterday, Am I Right?'
'You And I' (with Patrick Gerald Robinson)

Those songs above followed by an asterisk were credited to Clark at either BMI or the Library of Congress, but the publishing details confirm that they were almost certainly a 'different' Gene Clark. For the record, the publishers on the following underline this: 'Chicken Bones' (Rover Music), 'I'll Miss You For A While' (Rover Music), 'I Was Alone' (Eagle Music) and 'Just One More Kiss And Then Goodbye' (EMI Longitude Music).

'Let There Be Happiness' (registered 2 November 1979) cites Clark's birth year as 1942, not an unusual error, but evidence enough that this too was not our Gene Clark.

Before the age of sampling, Clark received a music only additional credit to the song 'Jealousy' (see 17 June 1977), which was initially claimed by the Clark estate but since rescinded. There is no evidence that Clark ever worked in any way with Skip Scarborough, suggesting that this is merely a coincidence of name. Robert Harsh's co-write on 'Kentucky Town Waltz' was registered as a 'sound cassette' with Gene Clark contributing music, but nothing more. 'Page Douze Septieme' and '(Theme For) Kay Seventy' are no longer listed as Clark copyrights. The latter was originally submitted without any publishing details. No further details are known of these compositions.

Two other writers named 'Gene Clark' have been incorrectly caught up in the listings: Albert G. Teoli co-wrote the songs 'Jesus Love' (registered 2 August 1972) and 'A Thousand Doors' (29 June 1976) with a certain 'Gene Clark'. Given Teoli's age and history this was never a credible collaboration with the former Byrd, except to say that the latter song was registered in the same section as 'Crazy Ladies', thereby causing momentary doubt. Two other songs credited to 'Gene Clark' – 'Father, Forgive Them' (registered 16 January 1977) and 'Please Help Me Sweet Jesus' (with William Alden Skold aka Bill Alden, registered 27 October 1986) – were at one time claimed by Kelly Clark at the Library of Congress, but are again a different Gene Clark. All of the above compositions can confidently be excluded from the canon.

A rare instance of Clark apparently surrendering his song to another publisher occurred with 'Don't Let It Fall Through' which was listed (see 24 February 1967) as Skyhill Music, the publishing outlet of Leon Russell who was involved in the sessions as arranger. All other Clark compositions from this period were registered with Tickson Music.

Mac McClanahan & The Rhythm Busters' rare rockabilly-styled 1968 single 'That Nonsense Stuff' b/w 'No Sweeter Love' features a co-credit for 'Gene Clark' on both sides, but the original publishing details appear tantalizingly blank on the Library of Congress submission, which may have been deliberate. Perplexingly, the BMI submission identifies the co-writer as a certain 'Roy Eugene Clark' which surely indicates that this was not our 'Gene Clark'. However, both songs were successfully claimed as Gene Clark copyrights by his sons Kelly and Kai Clark on 11 January 1996. They are currently registered under the name 'Gene Clark (Harold Eugene Clark)' and, significantly or not, remain so to this day.

Two songs not included in my listing above were incorrectly credited to Gene Clark, even though they actually featured on his own discs. Amazingly, Ian Tyson's 'The French Girl' is still listed at the Library of Congress and BMI as a Clark composition, a mistake carried forward after its appearance on the Gene Clark album, *Echoes*. Another common error is the track 'Roadmaster' which was credited to Clark on the album of the same name and later reissues. It still appears on BMI as a Clark composition (with publishers listed as Universal Music Careers) but before Gene released his version it had already appeared on Freddy Weller's 1972 album *The Roadmaster* (complete with the definite article) in a more upbeat country arrangement. Its composing credit *should* read: Frederick Wilton Weller and Lindon Dewey (aka 'Spooner') Oldham Jr.

The song 'Seventh Avenue Train' was issued under the alternate title 'Hula Bula Man' on *3 Byrds Land In London*. 'Denver Or Wherever' from the same album is credited to Clark, Neuwirth and Kaye on the CD, but does not appear to have been registered for claim by Gene Clark or his estate.

All other compositions mentioned here are Clark copyrights or have appeared on tapes, either live or in the studio. There are still, as the list reveals, many Clark songs registered and recorded during 1966–67 that have yet to be released. In addition, of course – as discussed in the main text – Clark made countless home tapes and demos. Many, if not most, of these remain extant, and there is still hope that they might be released in the fullness of time.

There are various other artefacts. Clark contributed the song 'Don't You Know What You Want' (aka 'Don't Know What You Want') to a projected single by the Cookie Fairies, which was never issued. The acetate titled *Gene Clark Sings For You* includes two previously unpublished songs recorded in 1967: 'Past Tense' and '7:30 Mode'. Its remaining contents feature songs listed at the Library of Congress and elsewhere.

Pat Robinson and John York (without Gene Clark) issued a dozen songs, copyrighted in 2000, all of which were co-written by Clark and had been originally conceived during the Eighties. Apart from 'Mary Sue', previously premiered on *So Rebellious A Lover*, the list did not include any songs later featured on the single disc archival album, *Over The Silvery Moon*. The compositions featured included: 'My Marie', 'On The Run (With A Loaded Gun)', 'After The Storm', 'The Hurting Game', 'A Rose Is A Rose', 'Once In A Lifetime', 'I Need To Fly', 'Immigrant Girl', 'Sleep Will Return', 'Somewhere After Midnight' and 'Washington Square'.

Eight more songs featuring Clark singing and playing, although not *officially* released, appear on the withdrawn double CD version of Delta Records' *Under The Silvery Moon*: 'Dancing On The Moon', 'Dragon's Eye', 'Liona', 'That Part Of You', 'The Hurting Game', 'The Panther', 'Washington Square' and 'With You I Can't Lose'.

Several of the Clark/Robinson collaborations reveal odd anomalies when comparing writing credits with publishing sources. John Arrias, who received a co-writing credit on 'Nothing But An Angel' and 'More Than That Now' on the withdrawn *Under The Silvery Moon*, loses his credit on both songs on the revised version and in the BMI listing. John York also loses his co-writing credit for 'Sleep Will Return' from *CRY*. Patrick Robinson suffers the same with 'Rest Of Your Life' at BMI even though he does receive a co-writing credit on *both* versions of the record. Oddly, 'Dancing On The Moon' is not registered at BMI at all under Clark's name.

Of course, a considerable number of songs recorded when Clark and Robinson were working together failed to appear on either the released version of *Under The Silvery Moon*, the withdrawn double edition or even the *CRY* album of covers by Robinson and York.

Listed in the Unreleased section herein, they include 'Boyfriend Girlfriend' (Robinson/Clark), 'Fair Game' (Clark/Robinson/Hopkins), 'Falling For You' (Clark/Robinson), 'Hang Tough' (Clark/Robinson/Hopkins), 'Look Who's Missing Who' (Clark/Robinson/Arrias), 'Looking For Reasons' (Clark/Robinson/Hopkins), 'Love Deluxe (Clark/Robinson/Hopkins), 'Love Holds On' (Robinson/Clark), 'Love's A Loaded Word' (Clark/Robinson/Hopkins), 'Quicksand' (Clark/Robinson/Karlyle), 'Show No Mercy' (Clark/Robinson/Karlyle), 'Surrender' (Clark/Robinson/Carlyle), 'The Only Chance You Take' (Clark/Robinson/Hopkins), 'What Happens Then' (Clark/Robinson), 'When You Love Someone' (Clark/Robinson/Hopkins), 'Where Does The Love Go' (Clark/Robinson/Hopkins) and 'You And I' (Clark/Robinson). Robinson, himself, provided these documents with full annotations and credits. He added: " 'Colors' might not be on this list but we did that with actor Robby Romero. We did that for the movie *Colors*, featuring Dennis Hopper." Despite Clark's past association with Hopper none of his work was featured in the film.

In order to avoid confusion, Robinson also lists a number of songs that are solely *his* compositions: 'Bulletproof Heart', 'I Need A Love', 'It's All In Your Eyes', 'Muscle And Bone', 'One Time Two Time', 'Prisoners Of Time', 'Slip Away' and 'True Blue'. Several Clark/Robinson compositions listed herein have appeared on dubious foreign releases credited to 'the Byrds'. See pages 404–406 in the 'Gene Clark Notes' section for a full account of the fiasco.

Numerous songs, although unreleased by Clark, were issued by other artistes. Going back through the years, these include: 'Till Today' and 'Long Time' (both on the Rose Garden's *The Rose Garden*), 'Day For Night' (the Textones' *Through The Canyon*), 'Rock Of Ages' (Carla Olson's *Reap The Whirlwind*), 'Forgive Me Girl' and 'Crazy Ladies' (both on Thomas Jefferson Kaye's *Not Alone*), 'We Came For Love' (Electric Range's *Electric Range*) and 'Straight From The Heart' (Western Electric's *Western Electric*).

The song 'Turtle Soup', which appears on DJ Food's 1994 album *Jazz Breaks Volume 5,* samples the McGuinn/Clark composition, 'You Showed Me'. DJ Food is erroneously referred to as 'DJ Flood' in the copyright listing. 'Gorgeous' is a track by Kanye West on his 2010 album *My Beautiful Dark Twisted Fantasy* which also samples the Turtles' cover of McGuinn/Clark's composition, 'You Showed Me'. It appears yet again on 'These Days' from Maverick Sabre's 2012 album, *Lonely Are The Brave*. Clark therefore ends up sharing songwriter credits *after* his death with people he never met.

DAVID CROSBY

'Alexander Graham Bell'
'Another Town'
'Coast Road'
'Cross The Plains' (demo version)
'Dirt Poor' (with Dan Peterson)
'Doing My Best'
'Draft Morning' (solo version with alternate lyrics)
'Flower Bomb Song'
'Gothic Blues'
'He's An American'
'Hey Lady'
'I'm A Drifter'
'I'm Flying' (with Michael Hedges)
'Is It Really Monday?'
'It Ain't Gonna Be That Way'
'It's Been Raining'
'Jigsaw'
'Last 100 Yards Of Freedom' (with Graham Nash)
'Little Blind Fish' (with Stephen Stills, Graham Nash and Neil Young)
'Naomi' (with Terry O. Callier)
'Paper Glider'
'Right Girl, Wrong Time'
'Somebody Home'
'Something Gotta Happen Pretty Soon'
'Stranger In A Strange Land' (vocal version)
'Taking It All' (with Paul L. Kantner)
'To Have And To Hold-BG Cues' (with James J. Raymond and Stacia A. Raymond)
'Time Of A Man'
'What Makes It So'
'You Sit There'
'You're Worth Waiting For'
'Your Life Is What You Fill Your Day With'
'Your Own Ride'

Although 'Cross The Plains' was released by Travis Edmonson, Crosby's own solo version remains unissued. The song 'It's Been Raining' (mentioned in first chapter of *Requiem For The Timeless, Volume 1*) was featured on a live recording by Judy Roderick, released unofficially as *Hootenanny At The Attic 1961–1962*. He provides backing on 10 songs, then performs lead vocal on what sounds like one of his earliest compositions, although it has never been registered for copyright.

'Right Girl, Wrong Time' is an unregistered pre-Byrds' composition extant as a home recording, along with 'Cross The Plains' in 1962. 'It Ain't Gonna Be That Way', 'Another Town', 'Something Gotta Happen Pretty Soon', 'Hey Lady', 'Time Of A Man' and 'I'm A Drifter' are from the same era.

'Gothic Blues' was listed in the Atlantic Records' session book but no song of that title appears as a copyright registration at BMI or the Library of Congress, although that is nothing unusual.

Crosby's co-write on 'Naomi' was belatedly issued in 1998 on Terry Callier's *First Light: Chicago 1969–1971* (Premonition Records). It is not known whether a demo version still exists.

As noted in the copyright registrations section, Crosby co-wrote two songs for the Paul Kantner Jefferson Starship's *Blows Against The Empire*: 'A Child Is Coming' and 'Have You Seen The Stars Tonite'. There is additionally a registration for 'Taking It All', which remains unreleased.

Crosby also recorded a number of songs with Jerry Garcia/Paul Kantner in 1971 which may yet deserve classification as co-writing collaborations: 'Leather Bat', 'Electric Bat', 'Under Anaesthesia', 'Dope Rap', 'Walking In The Mountains', 'Over Jordan' and 'Planet Earth/Rock 'n' Roll Orchestra'. Indeed, one of these 'Under Anaesthesia' is a mischievous retitling of the unreleased 'You Sit There'.

'Little Blind Fish' (rewritten and credited to Crosby/Jeff Pevar) and 'Somehow She Knew' (a retitled version of 'Fisher King Song' with the additional credit – Craig Doerge) were included on CPR's eponymous debut album.

'Doing My Best' was recorded in the spring of 1983 but has never been registered so it may be a cover rather than a Crosby composition.

'Your Own Ride' was premiered, as a lyric at least, on his website in 2001. As confirmed in the main discography, the previously unissued 'Brotherhood Of The Blues' was included on *Byrd Parts,* while the once rare 'Kids And Dogs' and 'King Of The Mountain' belatedly appeared on Crosby's 2006 box set, *Voyage*. 'To Have And To Hold-BG Cues' is published by Beverly Fax Music and Fox Film Music Corporation.

Lastly, 'Somebody Home' emerged from Crosby's collaboration with the ensemble Snarky Puppy. It was recently included on Snarky Puppy's *Family Dinner Volume 2*, issued in February 2016.

MICHAEL CLARKE

No unreleased compositions have been registered in Clarke's name or are known to exist in any recorded form.

CHRIS HILLMAN

'All Dressed Up' (with Steve Edward Hill)
'All I Ever Need Is You' (with Steve Edward Hill)
'Beautiful Sound' (with John R. Jorgenson)
'Biding My Time' (with Steve Edward Hill)
'Blue Moon Rising' (with Steve Edward Hill)

'Different Rivers Run' (with Stephen Edward Hill)
'Et Skridt Frem' (with Bill Parker Wildes)
'Fall By The Roadside'
'Feeling Inside'
'Here She Comes Again' (with Roger McGuinn)
'I Hear Singing'
'If You Leave Me Now' (with Steve Edward Hill)
'It's About Love' (with Stephen Edward Hill)
'It's Only Love' (with Peter Knobler)
'(Just) Walk On By' (with Alan R. Thornhill)
'Last Date' (with Gram Parsons)
'Let Me Get Out Of This World Alive' (with Steve Hill)
'Little Birdie'
'Long Gone' (with Stephen Edward Hill)
'Love's Worth More Than Gold' (with Bill Wildes)
'Making The Change'(with Steve Hill)
'Make Yourself Believe'
'Midnight Heart'
'Midnight Maker' (with Len Fagan)
'Prisoner Of Love'
'Relax Your Mind'
'Remember Love'
'Taking Her Time' (with Alan Thornhill and Jim Monahan)
'Time For Love'
'Two Hearts' (with Gram Parsons)
'Vitr Ve Skalach' (with Gram Parsons)
'War's Mystery' (with Roger McGuinn and David Hemmings)
'When Love's Gone Bad'
'Wind Did Blow' (with Stephen Edward Hill)
'With You In Mind' (with Len Fagan)
'Words She Writes Tonight, The' (with Herb Pedersen)

Cover versions of the above include 'Talkin' LA' and 'War's Mystery' on David Hemmings' *Happens*, 'Love's Worth More Than Gold' on Rose Maddox & John Jorgenson's 1996 album, *The Moon Is Rising*.

Steve Hill's *Gold Highway* features five songs co-written with Hillman: 'Different Rivers Run', 'Long Gone', 'If You Leave Me Now', 'Blue Moon Rising' and 'God's Plan'. *Feathers And Stone* features three more: 'Living On The Edge', 'I'm Still Alive' and 'Hurricane'. Hill's 1999 album *Decisions* offers half a dozen additional writing collaborations: 'Comin' Back To Me', 'Come A Little Closer', 'I Will', 'It's About Love', 'For The Rich Man' and 'Even Time Won't Pass Us By'. The follow-up, *House For Sale*, offers two more: 'Bidin' My Time' and 'Maybe Lucky'. *We'll Always Have Texas* offers five: 'No One', 'Better Man', 'Let Me Get Out', 'Me And You ' and 'Wheel'.

The Rincon Ramblers' eponymous album also feature two Hillman co-credits: '(Just) Walk On By' and 'Taking Her Time'. The 1992 Disney compilation *Country Music For Kids* features Hillman's adaptation of the traditional song, 'Little Birdie'. 'The Words She Writes Tonight' can be found on the Laurel Canyon Ramblers' 1996 album, *Blue Rambler 2*. Finally, John Jorgenson's 2015 *Divertuoso*, a 3-CD box set, includes 'Beautiful Sound' and 'Let Me Get Out Of This World Alive'.

The remaining unreleased compositions listed in this section are all of interest but several are mouthwateringly elusive. Pride of place goes to 'Relax Your Mind', 'Remember Love', 'Time For Love' and 'When Love's Gone Bad', all of which were registered for copyright on 7 December 1966 on the same day as 'Time Between', 'The Girl With No Name' and 'Thoughts And Words'. Incredible to think that Hillman had so much in reserve for *Younger Than Yesterday*. Shortly afterwards there was another lost contribution: 'I Hear Singing'. This was one of his great songwriting sprees.

Almost equally intriguing are a couple of lost collaborations with Gram Parsons: 'Last Date' and 'Two Hearts'. Studio recordings of these have yet to appear. As for 'Vitr Ve Skalach'. Who knows? It resembles a Polish translation, but has been registered at BMI for decades as a Hillman/Parsons composition via Irving Music, the publishing arm of A&M. There's a sprinkling of Souther, Hillman, Furay period obscurities ('Fall By The Wayside', 'Feeling Inside', 'Midnight Maker' and 'With You In Mind') while 'Et Skridt Frem' (recently removed from the listings) is simply a Danish translation of the Desert Rose Band's 'One Step Forward'.

KEVIN KELLEY

'Baby's Coming Back Today'
'Dreaming My Life Away'
'Drifter, The'
'Dusty Road'
'Home Again'
'I Found Paradise'
'Let Yourself Go'
'Look At Me'
'Looking For Freedom'
'Rat Race'
'Sail Away'
'Sugar Pie' (with Ryland Peter Cooder, Henry Fredericks, Stephen Gerlach and Gary Alfred Marker)
'Summertime Romance'
'Travelin' Mood'
'Wind Has Been My Friend, The'
'You Got To Be Free'

A number of additional unlisted/unreleased Kelley compositions were posthumously registered at the Library of Congress on 24 August 1982. Many of the Rising Sons' arrangements were adapted from blues classics including

'.44 Blues' (Willie Dixon), 'Devil's Got My Woman' (Skip James), 'If The River Was Whiskey (Divin' Duck Blues)' (Sleepy John Estes), 'Dust My Broom' (Robert Johnson), 'Candy Man' (Reverend Gary Davis) and 'Last Fair Deal Gone Down' (Robert Johnson). The above were credited as arrangements to Kelley with Ryland Peter Cooder, Henry Fredericks, Stephen Gerlach and Gary Alfred Marker.

GRAM PARSONS

'Apple Tree'
'Beauty Is Eternal'
'Between Your Hands And Mine'
'Blurry Slurry Night' (with Mike A. Ward)
'Blessing For Being (with Jim Lauderdale)
'Button, The' (with Eddie Leroy Cunningham Jr, Eddie Dunbar and Mike A. Ward)
'Hometown Boogie'
'Honda Rides'
'Jesus Is More Than A Name' (with Ed Berghoff, Eddie Leroy Cunningham Jr and Mike A. Ward)
'L.A. Custom Blues' (with Carl Jackson)
'Last Date' (with Chris Hillman)
'Night Walk'
'No One Knows I'm Lonesome' (with Mike A. Ward)
'Pam'
'Place To Be Going, A'
'Real Sunday Driving'(words: Gram Parsons and John J. Soter; words and music: Edward H. Porter)
'Red Velvet' (with Rick Grech)
'Royal Jelly'
'Silence Of The Soul'
'Small Boy's World'
'So Near To Being Right'
'Some Blues Thing'
'Two Hearts' (with Chris Hillman)
'Uncle Al'
'Vitr Ve Skalach' (with Chris Hillman)
'Won't Ask Me'

Gram Parsons' song catalogue has been well mined over the years and archival releases have included many of his more obscure compositions but a number remain elusive. While at Harvard, he wrote a batch of songs several of which were never heard again: 'A Place To Be Going', 'Between Your Hands And Mine', 'Honda Rides', 'Night Walk', 'Pam', 'Small Boy's World', 'Some Blues Thing' and 'Won't Ask Me'. Like most of his compositions from this period they were not registered with BMI or the Library of Congress.

'Apple Tree', never released by Parsons, was covered by Johnny Rivers. A very short snippet of Parsons' recording of the song appears as a 'hidden track' on *Gram Parsons – The Early Years Box Set.*

There were also two seemingly lost songs co-written with Chris Hillman during their Flying Burrito Brothers' years: 'Last Date' and 'Two Hearts'.

'Vitr Ve Skalach' is registered solely at BMI as a Parsons/Hillman composition. 'Hometown Boogie' is confirmed as a Gram Parsons composition at BMI with the publishing registered as GPJ Music which administers his post-A&M titles covering his solo work. I'm unsure if this is the tune often referred to as 'Gram Boogie' which Gram supposedly wrote when he was 11 years old.

'Beauty Is Eternal', 'Red Velvet', 'Royal Jelly', 'So Near To Being Right', 'Silence Of The Soul' and 'Uncle Al' were lyrics included in two of his later unpublished notebooks and no audio recordings are known to exist. Parsons pays particular attention to 'Uncle Al', which is written more than once. He also provides handwritten lyrics for Merle Haggard's 'Mother Queen Of My Heart' and Jimmie Rodgers' 'Lookin' For A New Mama'. 'Red Velvet' betrays the hand of Rick Grech – literally when observing its use of capital letters and calligraphy, but also in its lyrical references to England. Alas, precise dates of composition of all these songs are not provided. Nor have they been registered with BMI or the Library of Congress. Judging from other material mentioned in the same context, these would appear to be from 1970–1972. Additionally, one of the Notebooks, later given to Rick Grech, includes an untitled composition whose opening lines are "I jimmied the lock . . . but it was wrong from the start".

'Real Sunday Driving', copyrighted in 1975, features only lyrics from Parsons, plus John J. Soter, with music provided by Edward H. Porter. 'Blessing For Being', 'Blurry Slurry Night', 'The Button', 'Jesus Is More Than A Name', 'L.A. Custom Blues' and 'No One Knows I'm Lonesome' are tribute songs adapted from lyrics in another of the Gram Parsons' Notebooks owned by former International Submarine Band member John Nuese. The material was included on *The Gram Parsons Notebook: The Last Whippoorwill* (Shell Point 1223).

Lastly, several previously unreleased Parsons compositions were issued on *Gram Parsons – The Early Years Box Set* (Sierra SBXGP 2100) in November 2010: 'The Rains Come Down', 'The Hand Within The Glove', 'Rolling Stone', 'The Darkest Years', 'That Kind Of Livin'', 'A River Is Made Out Of Raindrops' and 'Just Can't Take It Any More'. None of these have yet appeared in the Library of Congress list of copyrighted songs nor in the BMI listings.

CLARENCE WHITE

'Lucky Me'
'Waterbed'

Both 'Lucky Me' and 'Waterbed' were intended for inclusion on Clarence White's uncompleted 1973 solo album. Jim Dickson passed his cassette tapes of these songs to me in 1989. Although neither song is registered at the Library of Congress or BMI, Sierra Records' John Delgatto insists that they are both Clarence White compositions. No unreleased compositions have been registered by Clarence White. The 2003 archival album *Tuff & Stringy (Sessions 1966–68)* includes his more obscure pre-Byrds songwriting credits: 'Grandma Funderbunk's Music Box' (White), 'Hong Kong Hillbilly' (White/Gene Parsons) and the White/Jan Paxton co-writes: 'She's Gone', 'Why Can't We Be' and 'Nature's Child'.

GENE PARSONS

'Birds Fly South' (with Meridian Green)
'California Subduction Blues' (with Meridian Green)
'Christina In My Dreams' (with Janice Louise Paxton)
'Come On Wind' (with Meridian Green)
'I'll Live Today' (with Floyd 'Gib' Guilbeau)
'Just Away' (with Meridian Green and Lenny Laks)
'Lorax In Laytonville' (with Meridian Green)
'Nuclear Days' (with Peter Oliva)
'Sarah Lou' (with Meridian Green)
'Talk To Me' (with Meridian Green)

Most of the above have been released by another artistes. 'Birds Fly South', 'Come On Wind', 'Just Away', 'Lorax In Laytonville' and 'Sarah Lou' all appeared on Meridian Green's solo album, *In The Heart Of This Town.*

'I'll Live Today' was recorded as a single by Dennis Payne and it also appears on the archive album *Tuff & Stringy (Sessions 1966–68)*. 'Christina In My Dreams' was covered by Eternity's Children on their album, *Timeless.*

The unreleased 'California Subduction Blues' (with Meridian Green) might easily be confused with 'California Blues' on *Birds Of A Feather* but the latter was written by Jimmie Rodgers. Both 'Nuclear Days' and 'Talk To Me' have never been released by anybody, as far as I know. The former was written with Peter Oliva while they were working together in the short-lived Gene Parsons Band in 1982. They completed several other demos including 'You Don't Miss Your Water', 'Real Life Problems', 'Dark Moon', 'California Blues' and 'TV's Gonna Save The World', but only 'Dark Moon' (see *Gene Parsons In Concert – I Hope They'll Let Us In*) is registered as a Parsons composition.

One track submitted on a CD and including Gene Parsons' name was 'The Singer' (18 October 1982) with words and music written by Barbara L.

'Bobbi' Willborn, with additional arrangement credits to Gene Parsons, Kevin Fraser and Jon Robbins. Parsons is also credited with playing steel guitar, which provides cause for doubt about his involvement unless it is a reference to his B-Bender guitar.

Parsons' registrations have been prone to mistakes and confusion. At both the Library of Congress and BMI, his contribution to 'B.J. Blues' from *Dr Byrds & Mr Hyde* has been wrongly credited to Gram Parsons. 'Nuclear Days' (with Peter Oliva) was registered for copyright at the Library of Congress on 23 August 1982 but does not appear in the BMI catalogue. Conversely, there are a number of songs credited to Parsons on the BMI listing that are incorrectly assigned, including 'Cactus Kid's Talkin' Blues', 'The Beautiful Texas Waltz', 'Toy Guitar' (aka 'The Mad Bassoon', written with Maxine Johnson) and 'Man She's Nice'. All these were composed by Gene Parson (without the 's'), a rockabilly/country performer whose major work was released in the late Fifties. All were issued on single during the 1957–58 period and, although interesting artefacts in themselves, have nothing to do with Gene Parsons, who was only a teenager at the time of their release. It is one thing to be mistaken for Gram Parsons but to be misidentified as Gene Parson is even stranger.

JOHN YORK

'Abandoned Fabric'
'Absolutely Free'
'All At The Party'
'American Blues'
'Angel Turned Into A Whore'
'Angels Of The Penitentiary' (with Mic Takamatsu)
'Beautiful Changes' (with Spooner Oldham and Nadia York)
'Beirut' (with Joseph F. Nasser)
'Best Is Yet To Come, The' (with NadiaYork, Johnny Perez and Phil Seymour)
'Bridget's Bardo'
'Caravan'
'Change My Eyes'
'Classic Way Of Saying Goodbye' (with Nadia York)
'Dance Of The Orchard Ghosts'
'Day After Day'
'Distant Call, A' (with Chris Darrow)
'Dog My Cats'
'Don't Jump Baby'
'Dream Of Peace'
'Driving Into The Sun'
'Echo Of Love'
'8th Face Opus'
'Engine # 853'

'Fantasy'
'Feather Ache'
'Get Ready To Cry' (with Sumi Nakano)
'Give Yourself A Gift (The Underwear Song)' (with Kim Fowley)
'Goodbye On The Runway'
'I Can't Sleep'
'I Heard Your Name Upon The Wind'
'I Want To Be Forgiven' (with Shawn Jones and Roy E. Swedeen)
'I Want You To Stay With Me' (with Gene Clark)
'I Wish It Was All Up To Me'
'I'm In Love With You'
'I'm Never Comin' Back' (with Shawn Jones)
'If By Chance'
'Johnnie Walker' (with Nadia York)
'Jolly Molly'
'Kakoro Ire'
'Kind Of Man I Used To Be, The'
'Life'
'Listenin' To The Radio'
'Lone Yucca'(with Chris Darrow and Ian Beardsley)
'Look In Your Eyes, The'
'Love's Misfortunes'
'Matane'
'Miracle'
'More Money' (with Nadia York)
'Never Give Up'
'Nice To See You Mohammed'
'Nothin' Left For Me To Do' (with Roy E. Swedeen)
'O Precious Child' (with Annie Thompson, Edward Schouse and Buzz Bellmont)
'Old World Parents'
'Once You Have Lost It'
'One Track Mind'
'Other Side Of Love, The' (with Nadia York)
'Place Where I Am Dreaming, The'
'Q's Song'
'Question Of Love' (with Shawn Jones)
'Quiet River' (with David Behrman)
'Round World'
'Sail Down: Hawk Song' (with Annie Thompson)
'Santa Ana Winds'
'Save It For A Rainy Day'
'Selfish Lover Blues'
'Snake Sheds Its Skin, The' (with Chris Darrow and Ian Beardsley)
'Snow Rose'
'Soft Shoulder Blues'
'Straight From The Heart' (with Annie Thompson and Buzz Bellmont)

'Sun Always Shines For The Cool, The' (with Miguel Pinero)
'Taking Of Flight 847 – The Uli Derrickson Story, The'
'Texas Preacher Man' (with Jamie Sams)
'This Is Your World' (with Kim Fowley)
'Today Will Not Be Missed'
'Trouble With My Car'
'Underture'
'UR TV (You Are TV) (with Johnny Perez, Nadia York and Phil Seymour)
'Valentine On A Railroad Track'
'Valerie' (with Nadia York)
'Walkin' The Lonely Beach'
'Waves Of Jealousy'
'Way You Love A Fool, The'
'We Are Horticultural'
'We Came For Love'(with Gene Clark and Billy Darnell)
'We've Been Evicted' (with Marc B. Ray)
'We've Had A Beautiful Time' (with Nadia York)
'Weave O Woman' (with Annie Thompson)
'White Lies'
'Whoever Noticed Me'
'Why Can't We Be Lovers'
'Won't Somebody Touch Me' (with Marc B. Ray)
'You Can Never Go Back' (with Irving Jones)
'You Nurture Everything'
'You Wish'
'You Won't See Me Runnin''
'Your Love Has Freed Me'

Of the above, 'We Can For Love' was recorded by Electric Range. 'A Distant Call', 'Lone Yucca' and 'The Snake Sheds Its Skin' appeared on Chris Darrow's album, *Coyote/Straight From The Heart.* 'I Want To Be Forgiven' was included on a limited edition cassette: Shawn Jones' *Shawn Jones.*

Amazingly, the remaining compositions have not been released by anybody. John York confirms that nine of these songs are either instrumentals or works in progress, minus lyrics: 'Abandoned Fabric', 'Bridget's Bardo' [sic], 'Dance Of The Orchard Ghosts', 'Dog My Cats', 'Dream Of Peace', 'Kakoro Ire', 'Matane', 'Q's Song' and 'Underture'.

SKIP BATTIN

'Born Dancer' (with Kim Vincent Fowley)
'Bury The Hatchet' (with Gary Sanford Paxton)
'California Swamp Dance' (with Kim Fowley)
'Devil Doll' (with Kim Vincent Fowley)
'Coming Back Home To You'
'Dance Of The Sand Fleas' (with Cockrum and Gaorgano)

'ESP Reader' (with Kim Vincent Fowley)
'Faded Blue' (with Kim Vincent Fowley)
'Frail Ocean, The' (with Kim Vincent Fowley)
'In The Funky Mountain Woods' (with Kim Vincent Fowley)
'Jail House Blues'
'Meanie'
'Morning Dew'
'Mr Jukebox' (with Kim Vincent Fowley)
'Question Of Temperature, Version 1' (with Kim Vincent Fowley)
'Question Of Temperature, Version 2' (with Kim Vincent Fowley)
'Other Side Of The Moon, The' (with Kim Vincent Fowley)
'Red China' (with Kim Vincent Fowley)
'Romance Of The Western Hills' (with Kim Vincent Fowley)
'Save Our World We Must Survive' (with Kim Vincent Fowley)
'Singin' River' (with Kim Vincent Fowley)
'Tom Eagelton' (with Kim Vincent Fowley)
'Top Of The Tree' (with Kim Vincent Fowley)
'United States Of Love' (with Kim Vincent Fowley)
'What Does A Dream Mean'
'Wrong Kind Of Guy'

A selection of the above have been recorded by other artistes. Chuck & Chuckles covered 'Bury The Hatchet' which appeared on the 1998 compilation, *It Was I: The Very Best Of Skip & Flip*; it can also be found on the 2006 compilation *Hollywood Maverick – The Gary S. Paxton Story*.

'Coming Back Home To You' appeared in 1961 as a single by Lette And Junior on Cub Records (Cub K 9101), which Battin also produced. 'What Does A Dream Mean' appeared as a single by Don True on Invicta in 1962; 'Meanie' appeared as the B-side of Johnny Leonard's 'Sea Of Love' on Invicta Records.

Skip & The Hustlers released 'Dance Of The Sand Fleas' as a single on Invicta. Earth Island released 'Save Our World We Must Survive' on their 1969 album, *We Must Survive*. 'The Frail Ocean' appeared on Kim Fowley's 1970 album, *The Day The Earth Stood Still*.

Kim Fowley issued 'Born Dancer', 'ESP Reader' and 'Red China' on his 1973 album, *International Heroes*. 'California Swamp Dance' appeared on Fowley's 1975 album, *Animal God Of The Street*.

Two songs credited to 'Battin' on singles, turn out to be composed not by Skip, but by his wife, Jackie Battin: 'Make Believe Baby' (1960) and 'The Morning After The Night Before' (composed by Jackie Battin & Gary Paxton, copyright registered on 23 February 1962).

Battin and Fowley have been credited erroneously on BMI submissions with the songs 'Fango' (Gianco-Manfred), 'La Gatta' (Mogol-Bacal) and 'Non E Francesca' (Mogol-Battisti) from the 1984 Italian release, *Don't Go Crazy*. Tellingly, these songs do not appear under Battin or Fowley's submissions to the Library of Congress.

On a few occasions, Battin's name has not been included in the small print of the actual disc. Rocky & The Border Kings' 1972 B-side, 'Gulf Of Mexico', credits Kim Fowley, G. Butcher and Michael Checik as composers, but the submission to the Library of Congress dated 9 March 1973 (pertaining to 18 July 1972) adds Battin as co-writer. 'Austin Texas' (included on the New Riders Of The Purple Sage's *Armadillo World HQ Austin TX, 6/13/1975* omits Battin but his co-writing credit with Kim Fowley is clearly logged at BMI.

As noted earlier, the Byrds' 'Long Jam' studio session credits McGuinn, White, Parsons and 'writer unknown'. This sounds like part of the extended jam included on 'Eight Miles High', or something similar, in which case it is clearly Battin, who played a prominent part in the 'long jam'.

Two of the unreleased songs listed above have deceptively familiar titles. 'Morning Dew' is credited as a Battin composition so presumably it is not the Bonnie Dobson standard made famous by Fred Neil, Tim Rose and the Grateful Dead. Although a song titled 'Question Of Temperature' was a minor US hit for the Balloon Farm in 1967 (later appearing on the acclaimed psychedelic compilation *Nuggets*), the mysterious 'A Question Of Temperance, Versions 1 & 2' is evidently a similarly titled song composed and copyright registered at BMI by Battin and Fowley.

Index

Singles releases are in roman type and albums are in italics. Persons listed in parentheses refer to the name of the recording or performing artistes of the particular song. Composers, where cited, are listed separately under their own names.